# NEW WORLDS
## OF
# LITERATURE

W.W. NORTON & COMPANY, INC.
also publishes

THE NORTON ANTHOLOGY OF AMERICAN LITERATURE
*edited by Nina Baym et al.*

THE NORTON ANTHOLOGY OF ENGLISH LITERATURE
*edited by M. H. Abrams et al.*

THE NORTON ANTHOLOGY OF LITERATURE BY WOMEN
*edited by Sandra M. Gilbert and Susan Gubar*

THE NORTON ANTHOLOGY OF MODERN POETRY
*edited by Richard Ellmann and Robert O'Clair*

THE NORTON ANTHOLOGY OF POETRY
*edited by Alexander W. Allison et al.*

THE NORTON ANTHOLOGY OF SHORT FICTION
*edited by R. V. Cassill*

THE NORTON ANTHOLOGY OF
CONTEMPORARY FICTION
*edited by R. V. Cassill*

THE NORTON ANTHOLOGY OF WORLD MASTERPIECES
*edited by Maynard Mack et al.*

THE NORTON FACSIMILE OF
THE FIRST FOLIO OF SHAKESPEARE
*prepared by Charlton Hinman*

THE NORTON INTRODUCTION TO LITERATURE
*edited by Carl E. Bain, Jerome Beaty, and J. Paul Hunter*

THE NORTON INTRODUCTION TO THE SHORT NOVEL
*edited by Jerome Beaty*

THE NORTON READER
*edited by Arthur M. Eastman et al.*

THE NORTON SAMPLER
*edited by Thomas Cooley*

and
THE NORTON CRITICAL EDITIONS

# NEW WORLDS
# OF
# LITERATURE

## Jerome Beaty
*Emory University*

## J. Paul Hunter
*The University of Chicago*

W · W · NORTON & COMPANY

New York • London

Printed in the United States of America.

The text of this book is composed in Janson,
with display type set in Centaur.
Composition by Vail-Ballou. Manufacturing by R. R. Donnelley.
Book design by Suzanne Bennet.

First Edition

Library of Congress Cataloging-in-Publication Data
New worlds of literature / edited by Jerome Beaty and J. Paul Hunter.
—1st ed.
p.    cm.
Bibliography: p.
1. America—Literatures.    2. American literature—Minority
authors.    I. Beaty, Jerome, 1924–    .    II. Hunter, J. Paul, 1934–    .
PN846.N4    1989
810'.8'0054—dc19          88-19483

ISBN 0-393-95759-4

W. W. Norton & Company, Inc., 500 Fifth Avenue, New York, N. Y. 10110
W. W. Norton & Company Ltd., 37 Great Russell Street, London WC1B 3NU

2 3 4 5 6 7 8 9 0

# CONTENTS

# 2            FAMILY DEVOTIONS     115

# 3            HERITAGE     239

# 6    THE MAN FROM MARS

# 7    FENCES

# 8           CROSSING     785

# 9         IN THE AMERICAN SOCIETY     905

## IO  DOMINION  1049

# INTRODUCTION

This book is intended as an anthology for an introductory course in the study of literature or as a reader for a course in composition. A glance at the table of contents, however, may prove puzzling, because this does not look like the familiar college reader or anthology. Where are Shakespeare and Hawthorne, Dickinson and Dickens, Jonathan Swift and E. B. White? Not only are almost all the traditional Big Names missing, but many of the names and titles you do find are likely to be unfamiliar. To be sure, all but a few of the works here are contemporary: all but one of the selections were written since World War I, most since World War II, and many since Vietnam. Even so, where are Hemingway and Faulkner, Lawrence and Woolf and Joyce? At a time when so many, from the White House to the little red schoolhouse, are lamenting the ignorance of America's youth about the Great Books or the Great Tradition, why produce a college textbook that, on the surface, would seem to do so little to close the "culture gap"?

Though all the selections in this text were chosen because of their high quality—their beauty, profundity, incisiveness, power, or a combination of such qualities—they are not meant to *replace* the reading of Sophocles, Virgil, Dante, Cervantes, Shakespeare, Goethe, George Eliot, Whitman. Although an hour spent reading recent Native American poetry cannot at the same time be spent reading Montaigne, there is no conflict of interest between the classical and new. And while a generous portion of the classics should be read by every college student, by every citizen, to read them archeologically and out of context—cramming culture as if for a multiple-choice test—is probably not the best way to be introduced to the best that has been felt, thought, and written by the men and women of past centuries.

Each new generation looks at its past from a different position, and that position is in part defined by the works of the present. In order to be able to read the great works of the past and to make them a meaningful part of our own lives and experience, most of us need first to be enthralled and informed by the works of our own time and tradition. The time you spend reading is not fixed: an hour of Maya Angelou does not mean you have no time for Aristophanes. If you read Angelou with pleasure and excitement, you are likely to find time to read more—and sometime perhaps read Aristophanes. And when you come to him, you will come better prepared to understand and enjoy.

Three of the functions of this text, therefore, are to present you with some poems, stories, plays, and prose pieces of our own time and place for their own sake; to give you a perspective through which you can see and appreciate the great works of the past; and to arouse your interest in reading literature and whet your appetite for more.

The selections here were first written in English, which would seem appropriate in a text intended at least in part as a reader for student writers. All the pieces are by writers of the United States, Canada, and the Caribbean (although many were born elsewhere). This, too, seems appropriate if one of the purposes is to define our own place as well as time. So, it must be confessed, the selections are "provincial," narrow in space and time.

It cannot have escaped your notice, however, as you glanced at the table of contents, that there are not only a number of unfamiliar names among the authors but strange names as well—strange, that is, as in "foreign-sounding." The name Edward Young, the author of the eighteenth-century poem "Night Thoughts," might have been unfamiliar to many had it appeared here, but Li-Young Lee is both unfamiliar and strange: not Anglo-Saxon, not even Euro-American. Peter Blue Cloud and Marcela Christine Lucero-Trujillo and Bharati Mukherjee are all American names—that is, names of Americans—but they do not sound much like the British names of "our" forefathers, names like Washington, Jefferson, Madison. When Gloria Steinem reached her fortieth birthday, someone wanted to compliment her by telling her that she didn't look forty; she replied that this is what forty looks like nowadays. Well, Durango Mendoza and Agha Shahid Ali as well as Toni Morrison and Flannery O'Connor and Michael Blumenthal and John Fante and Noel Perrin are what American names sound like toward the end of the twentieth century. American people, as well as American names, look different now from the stereotype many of us may still have in mind. Mitsuye Yamada insists on the new reality of what Americans look like:

## MIRROR MIRROR

People keep asking where I come from
says my son
Trouble is      I'm american on the inside
                and oriental on the outside
      No Doug
Turn that outside in
THIS is what American looks like.

Because the stereotypes, never entirely true and now more misleading than ever, are still prevalent, we have deliberately sought to redress the balance somewhat and have deliberately selected excellent, exciting works that emphasize the fact that America is now more than ever not only a multinational but multicontinental culture. To hear the sound of African or Asian rhythms come through traditional Anglo-American forms, as in a poem, say, by Audre Lorde or Cathy Song, is to hear the new, to hear the future. And thereafter T. S. Eliot, Whitman, Keats, and Donne will never sound exactly the same as they did before such new poems were written. We will read the poetry of the past with new eyes and ears—*our* eyes and ears.

That the reader shares in the creation of the meaning of a work is a premise of much recent criticism, especially of the "reader-response" and receptionalist schools. That what is new changes the tradition, gives a new perspective on the works of the past, is neither so new nor so radical a proposition (traditionalist-conservative-modernist T. S. Eliot enunciated it more than seventy years ago in an essay called "Tradition and the Individual Talent"). The aim of this anthology is to educate your individual reading talent so that you know where you are and so that you can therefore better see the particularity and the permanence of the works of the past.

The cultural diversity of the selections is not just a rich *literary* experience and a way of enriching your reading experience of the great works of the tradition, however; it is also intended to enrich or to prepare you for the cross-cultural experiences that are inevitable in modern American life. For the stereotypes exist and persist in life as well as in literature, and they influence us even when we know better, even it seems when we are the people being stereotyped. Barbara Cameron, in an essay entitled "Gee, You Don't Seem like an Indian from the Reservation," tells of her feelings when she was three years old: "My family took me to my first pow-wow. I kept asking my grandmother, 'Where are the Indians? Where are the Indians? Are they going to have bows and arrows?' I was very curious and strangely excited about the prospect of seeing real live Indians even though I myself was one."

The reality of cultural diversity in a culture that mythically considers itself homogeneous—more or less Anglo-Saxon—raises the question of who are the "we" referred to in textbooks like this. The editorial assumption seems always to have been "white European-Americans" (sometimes even white Euro-American males), but the two white Euro-American male editors of *New Worlds of Literature* know this is not true now. *You* are more than likely to be female, and there is at least a one-in-four chance that you will not be of European, much less Anglo-Saxon, origin. What does it feel like to be included in a "we" that doesn't quite fit us? (Richard Olivas describes just such a feeling in his poem in chapter 4, p. 350.)

One of the rhetorical difficulties in editing this volume arises from our awareness of the diversity of our audience. Who *are* you? Do you need the word "chalupa" explained? Would you be insulted if we did annotate it? puzzled if we did not? What do we mean when we say "we" or "you"? We struggled with such questions and probably did not always come up with the right answer or expression; we apologize for places where we may have failed. But these are questions our whole society is struggling with; this anthology, we believe, is one step toward an answer.

When the experience of recent Americans or "other Americans," including those who were here when Columbus "discovered" America, is incorporated in literature, it gives a sense of legitimacy, of acceptance, and of pride. Maxine Hong Kingston cried when she saw Chinese-American characters onstage in a play by David Henry Hwang:

> There—on the stage, in public—were our gestures, our voices, our accents, our own faces. It isn't sad scenes that bring the tears, but a realization of how isolated we've been, and a wonder that our private Chinese lives and secret language can be communally understood. To see even one person

indicate "myself" by pointing to his nose makes me know I am not alone; there are two of us. But to be among an audience at a play—here are many of us. Here is a community. We become proud to the bones.

Many of the pieces testify to the sense of community—not only the cultural or ethnic community, but also to the larger community of the national, multiethnic culture that is now the real America and the real experience of all of us. Not all of the works are written by "minority" Americans. Some, like Sharon Olds's "On the Subway," are about cross-cultural experiences from the "majority" viewpoint; some, like Barbara Thompson's "Crossing," are about American experiences of other cultures. Given the almost infinite variety of the ethnic tapestry of the United States, Canada, and the Caribbean, it would be impossible to represent all of us specifically. The emphasis is on major groups now emerging or entering American society in significant numbers and ways—Afro-Americans, Asian-Americans, Hispanic-Americans, and Native Americans—though, alas, not every tribe or national culture is adequately, appropriately, or proportionately represented, and some may not be represented at all. Our aim is not primarily sociological or demographic but merely to give a generous sampling of the kinds of experiences making their way into literature and the consciousness of us all in the last decades of the twentieth century.

We have not, however, organized chapters according to ethnic ghettos, nor have we tried for "one of each" in each chapter. We have included some groups whose entry into America took place or began to take place fifty or a hundred years ago—the Irish and Jews, Eastern Europeans and Italians, Armenians and Greeks—in part to suggest the continuity of the ethnic and cultural enrichment of American society, in part also to acknowledge the continuity of the resistance of "old settlers" to new; for many of those still somewhat beyond the pale, such as black Americans and Native Americans, have been at it a very long time indeed. We have no particular sociological axe to grind—this is a literature text. We do not necessarily assume that the single reasonable aim of all cultures is somehow to "melt" into America. A significant number of the pieces here insist on the maintenance of the old ethnic traditions, customs, and beliefs. That America is multiracial, multicultural, is undeniable; just what form that multifaceted America will take is still a question, and an important and exciting one.

*New Worlds of Literature* generally moves outward in space, time, and community. The first two chapters include works that chiefly deal with home and family, the next two with the cultural community and its forebears and traditions. The fifth chapter focuses on language as an aspect of the individual's sense of identity, as a bond for the ethnic culture, and as a barrier in the larger society. Chapter 6 centers on aliens, strangers, or our own experience of being the stranger. The next chapter deals with ethnic or racial conflicts or barriers, and chapter 8 with the crossing of those barriers, for better or worse, chiefly through male-female relationships. In chapter 9, "new" or minority Americans seek to understand or search for a role in the larger society. The works in the final chapter suggest varieties of ways in which Americans relate to whatever is beyond self and society.

The headnotes to each chapter seek to lead you into experiencing the works that follow and at the same time relating the experiences in the works to those of your own life. The headnotes to the individual pieces, on the other hand, offer thumbnail biographies of the author, occasionally with a statement of the author's about his or her own work, and a sentence or two about the specific work. These individual headnotes, like the chapter head-notes, do not seek to limit your response but to lead or entice you into the work.

Each piece is followed by one or more study questions. We have tried to avoid asking "What am I holding in my hand?" questions as well as "Don't you think so, too?" ones. The aim is to stimulate your perceptions and thought as well as, in some instances, to urge you to relate the experience within the work to your own experiences. As is the practice in Norton anthologies, there are informational—not interpretive—footnotes; we have not footnoted words that can be quickly found in a college dictionary, and we have chosen not to footnote certain words where context and careful reading make the sense clear.

Though the organization of the text is primarily thematic, the after-word to each chapter takes up one of the elements of literature, so that you will have, by the end, the major tools for analyzing and appreciating the formal aspects of literature. These elements are taken up in an order that both makes literary sense and also suits the thematic structure; thus it seems appropriate in the chapter entitled "Home" to discuss setting, in "Family Devotions" to treat character, in "Dominion," symbol and myth. For quick reference, a glossary summarizes the literary terms used in the text.

The thematic and experiential organization of the text seems particu-larly appropriate to a course in which frequent student writing is a central element. The poems, stories, plays, and nonfiction prose pieces, given their subject matter and their relevance to contemporary American experience, should inevitably stimulate student themes: personal essays related to the experiences of the literary works, comparisons and contrasts of pieces with similar content, argument, research papers (particularly, but not only, on the cross-cultural conditions and issues in our society), imitations or parodies, as well as literary analysis. At the end of each chapter are suggestions for paper topics and writing projects.

You may be using this book as a reader for writing, as an anthology inviting you into the serious and enjoyable study of literature, or even as a rich but unsystematic exploration of contemporary American society through literature. Whatever your aim, may the journey be intellectually, psychologically, sociologically, and emotionally stimulating and profitable. And fun.

Jerome Beaty
J. Paul Hunter

The editors wish to thank Paula Gunn Allen, Andrew Beaty, Shawn Beaty, John Benedict, Suzanne Bennett, Clark Blaise, Jay Douglas Canfield, Peter Dowell, Pam Durban, Marianne Eismann, Susan Gaustad, Ellen Harris, Debra Hunter, Kathryn Hunter, Irwin Hyatt, Roger Kaplan, Ruth Looper, Ricardo Gutierrez Mouat, Bharati Mukherjee, Diane O'Connor, Nancy Palmquist, Walter Reed, Carter Revard, Laura Reyes, Lawrence Rothfield, Harry Rusche, Ronald Schuchard, Barbara Thompson, Helena Maria Viramontes, and Melissa Walker.

Special thanks to Eric Iversen for extraordinary assistance in everything from biography to photography, and to Barry Wade, without whose guidance and support this work would not have been begun, much less completed.

# NEW WORLDS
## OF
# LITERATURE

# HOME

"Home" is many things to many people. Quite beyond a particular place with specific memories and associations, home is a feeling, a state of mind. To be "at home" means to feel comfortable, at ease, secure in familiar surroundings. "At home" usually suggests satisfaction more than it indicates an address. Still, home is a specific place (or sometimes more than one place) for every one of us: it may be the place we live now, or the place where we were born, or the place our parents or ancestors came from, or the place where the presence of relatives and friends makes us feel most as if we belong.

Home is usually a certain house, apartment, or room, but it also often means a block or neighborhood, town or city, region or country. We are from Elm Street, East Harlem, the North End, or Los Angeles; we identify ourselves as Chicagoans, Floridians, Chicanas, Barbadians; or we may say we are Mexican, Greek, Welsh, or Korean—not necessarily meaning that we ourselves ever lived in another country but that "our people" came from there at some time in the past. When we say we feel at home in Maine, or San Antonio, or Jamaica, or Japan, we mean that something about it feels "right" to us, that the people and their ways seem familiar, or that the landscape, vegetation, or buildings prompt our memories. Home can, of course, mean lots of unpleasant things as well, especially for those who had difficult childhoods or who felt too restricted or hurt by their families, playmates, or communities. Home does not always feel good, but it always feels familiar.

Every experience of home—whether positive and based on feelings of pleasure and belonging, or negative and based on feelings of pressure and disappointment—is highly personal and based on very particular, often very private, feelings. Sometimes it is difficult to communicate just how one feels about a place to someone who has never been there, especially if that person is from a different family background and grew up with different habits and experiences, or if that person is from another region or another country with different customs. Still, feelings about home—both good and bad—are widely shared across places and cultures, and the particular details of growing up in one place often generate the same feelings as similar experiences in a home halfway across the world or in a different kind of family or culture.

Trying to understand what home is like for someone else can be difficult, but it may give us, for a moment, a sense of what it might be like to be someone different with different expectations from life. It can also give us a richer and more exact sense of ourselves, how we live, and what we value. What place we call home—where it is, what it looks like, who is there, and how it makes us feel—tells us a lot about us as people. In literature, as in life, home often becomes a fabric of emotions and an index of values as well as a specific place.

# Michael Anthony

One of the best-known Caribbean writers, Michael Anthony was born in Trinidad in 1932, and, except for four years in England and two years in Brazil, he has continued to live there. He is the author of many stories about growing up in Trinidad, but considers himself "essentially a novelist"; his most familiar books include *The Games Were Coming* (1963), *Green Days by the River* (1967), *Streets of Conflict* (1976), and *All That Glitters* (1981).

"Sandra Street" describes how a young schoolboy who is a little ashamed of his own unfashionable section of town learns to appreciate, through the eyes of others, the special features of a neighborhood he knows so well that he has come to take its beauties and benefits for granted.

## SANDRA STREET

Mr Blades, the new teacher, was delighted with the compositions we wrote about Sandra Street. He read some aloud to the class. He seemed particularly pleased when he read what was written by one of the boys from the other side of the town.

"Sandra Street is dull and uninteresting," the boy wrote. "For one half of its length there are a few houses and a private school (which we go to) but the other half is nothing but a wilderness of big trees." Mr Blades smiled from the corners of his mouth and looked at those of us who belonged to Sandra Street. "In fact," the boy wrote, "*it* is the only street in our town that has big trees, and I do not think it is a part of our town at all because it is so far and so different from our other streets."

The boy went on to speak of the gay attractions on the other side of the town, some of which, he said, Sandra Street could never dream to have. In his street, for instance, there was the savannah where they played football and cricket, but the boys of Sandra Street had to play their cricket in the road. And to the amusement of Mr Blades, who also came from the other side of the town, he described Sandra Street as a silly little girl who ran away to the bushes to hide herself.

Everyone laughed except the few of us from Sandra Street, and I knew what was going to happen when school was dismissed, although Mr Blades said it was all a joke and in fact Sandra Street was very fine. I did not know whether he meant this or not, for he seemed very much amused and I felt this was because he came from the other side of the town.

He read out a few more of the compositions. Some of them said very nice things about Sandra Street, but those were the ones written by ourselves. Mr Blades seemed delighted about these, too, and I felt he was trying to appease us when he said that they showed up new aspects of the beauty of Sandra Street. There were only a few of us who were appeased, though, and he noticed this and said all right, next Tuesday we'll write about the other side of the town. This brought fiendish laughter from some of us from Sandra Street, and judging from the looks on the faces of those from the other side of the town, I knew what would happen next Tuesday, too, when school was dismissed. And I felt that whatever happened it wasn't going to make any difference to our side or to the other side of the town.

Yet the boy's composition was very truthful. Sandra Street was so different from the other streets beyond. Indeed, it came from the very quiet fringes and ran straight up to the forests. As it left the town there were a few houses and shops along it, and then the school, and after that there were not many more houses, and the big trees started from there until the road trailed off to the river that bordered the forests. During the day all would be very quiet except perhaps for the voice of one neighbour calling to another, and if some evenings brought excitement to the schoolyard, these did very little to disturb the calmness of Sandra Street.

Nor did the steel band gently humming from the other side of the town. I had to remember the steel band because although I liked to hear it I had to put into my composition that it was very bad. We had no steel bands in Sandra Street, and I thought I could say that this was because we were decent, cultured folk, and did not like the horrible noises of steel bands.

I sat in class recalling the boy's composition again. Outside the window I could see the women coming out of the shops. They hardly passed each other without stopping to talk, and this made me laugh. For that was exactly what the boy had written—that they could not pass without stopping to talk, as if they had something to talk about.

I wondered what they talked about. I did not know. What I did know was that they never seemed to leave Sandra Street to go into the town. Maybe they were independent of the town! I chuckled a triumphant little chuckle because this, too, would be good to put into my composition next Tuesday.

Dreamingly I gazed out of the window. I noticed how Sandra Street stood away from the profusion of houses. Indeed, it did not seem to belong to the town at all. It stood off, not proudly, but sadly, as if it wanted peace and rest. I felt all filled up inside. Not because of the town in the distance but because of this strange little road. It was funny, the things the boy had written; he had written in anger what I thought of now in joy. He had spoken of the pleasures and palaces on the other side of the town. He had said why they were his home sweet home. As I looked at Sandra Street, I, too, knew why it was my home sweet home. It was dull and uninteresting to him but it meant so much to me. It was . . .

"Oh!" I started, as the hand rested on my shoulder. 11

"It's recess," said Mr Blades. 12

"Oh! . . . yes, sir." The class was surging out to the playground. I didn't seem to have heard a sound before. 13

Mr Blades looked at me and smiled. "What are you thinking of?" he said. 14

He seemed to be looking inside me. Inside my very mind. I stammered out a few words which, even if they were clear, would not have meant anything. I stopped. He was still smiling quietly at me. "You are the boy from Sandra Street?" he said. 15

"Yes, sir." 16

"I thought so," he said. 17

What happened on the following Tuesday after school was a lot worse than what had ever happened before, and it was a mystery how the neighbours did not complain or Mr Blades did not get to hear of it. We turned out to school the next morning as if all had been peaceful, and truly, there was no sign of the battle, save the little bruises which were easy to explain away. 18

We kept getting compositions to write. Mr Blades was always anxious to judge what we wrote but none gave him as much delight as those we had written about Sandra Street. He had said that he knew the other side of the town very well and no one could fool him about that, but if any boy wrote anything about Sandra Street he would have to prove it. And when he had said that, he had looked at me and I was very embarrassed. I had turned my eyes away, and he had said that when the mango season came he would see the boy who didn't speak the truth about Sandra Street. 19

Since that day I was very shy of Mr Blades, and whenever I saw him walking towards me I turned in another direction. At such times there would always be a faint smile at the corners of his mouth. 20

I stood looking out of the school window one day thinking about this and about the compositions when again I felt a light touch and jumped. 21

"Looking out?" Mr Blades said. 22

"Yes, sir." 23

He stood there over me and I did not know if he was looking down at me or looking outside, and presently he spoke; "Hot, eh?" 24

"Yes," I said. 25

He moved in beside me and we both stood there looking out of the window. It was just about noon and the sun was blazing down on Sandra Street. The houses stood there tall and rather sombre-looking, and there seemed to be no movement about save for the fowls lying in the shadows of the houses. As I watched this a certain sadness came over me and I looked over the houses across to the hills. Suddenly my heart leapt and I turned to 26

Mr Blades, but I changed my mind and did not speak. He had hardly noticed that I looked up at him. I saw his face looking sad as his eyes wandered about the houses. I felt self-conscious as he looked at the houses for they no longer were new and the paint had been washed off them by the rains and they had not been repainted. Then, too, there were no gates and no fences around them as there were in the towns, and sometimes, with a great flurry, a hen would scamper from under one house to another leaving dust behind in the hot sun.

I looked at Mr Blades. He was smiling faintly. He saw me looking at him. "Fowls," he said. 27

"There are no gates," I apologized. 28

"No, there are no gates." And he laughed softly to himself. 29

"Because . . ." I had to stop. I did not know why there were no gates. 30

"Because you did not notice that before." 31

"I noticed that before," I said. 32

Looking sharply at me he raised his brows and said slowly: "You noticed that before. Did you put that in your composition? You are the boy from Sandra Street, are you not?" 33

"There are more from Sandra Street." 34

"Did you notice the cedar grove at the top?" he went on. "You spoke of the steel band at the other side of the town. Did you speak of the river? Did you notice the hills?" 35

"Yes," 36

"Yes?" His voice was now stern and acid. His eyes seemed to be burning up from within. 37

"You noticed all this and you wrote about Sandra Street without mentioning it, eh? How many marks did I give you?" 38

"Forty-five." 39

He looked surprised. "I gave you forty-five for writing about the noises and about the dirty trams of the town? Look!" he pointed, "do you see?" 40

"Mango blossoms," I said, and I felt like crying out: "*I wanted to show it to you!*" 41

"Did you write about it?" 42

"No." I just wanted to break out and run away from him. He bent down to me. His face looked harder now, though kind, but I could see there was fury inside him. 43

"There is something like observation, Steve," he said. "*Observation*. You live in Sandra Street, yet Kenneth writes a composition on your own place better than you." 44

"He said Sandra Street was soppy," I cried. 45

"Of course he said it was soppy. It was to his purpose. He comes from the other side of the town. What's he got to write on—gaudy houses with gates like prisons around them? High walls cramping the imagination? The milling crowd with faces impersonal as stone, hurrying on buses, hurrying off trams? Could he write about that? He said Sandra Street was soppy. 46

Okay, did you prove it wasn't so? Where is your school and his, for instance?"

I was a little alarmed. Funny how I did not think of that point before. 47 "Here," I said. "In Sandra Street."

"Did you mention that?" 48

Mercifully, as he was talking, the school bell sounded. The fowls, star- 49 tled, ran out into the hot sun across the road. The dust rose, and above the dust, above the houses, the yellow of mango blossom caught my eye.

"The bell, sir." 50

"Yes, the bell's gone. What's it now—Geography?" 51

"Yes, sir," I said. And as I turned away he was still standing there, 52 looking out into the road.

It was long before any such thing happened again. Though often when 53 it was dry and hot I stood at the window looking out. I watched the freedom of the fowls among the tall houses, and sometimes the women talked to each other through the windows and smiled. I noticed, too, the hills, which were now streaked with the blossoms of the poui, and exultantly I wondered how many people observed this and knew it was a sign of the rains. None of the mango blossoms could be seen now, for they had already turned into fruit, and I knew how profuse they were because I had been to the hills.

I chuckled to myself. *There is something like observation, Steve.* And how I 54 wished Mr Blades would come to the window again so I could tell him what lay among the mango trees in the hills.

I knew that he was not angry with me. I realized that he was never angry 55 with any boy because of the parts the boy came from. We grew to like him, for he was very cheerful, though mostly he seemed dreamy and thoughtful. That is, except at composition time.

He really came to life then. His eyes would gleam as he read our com- 56 positions and whenever he came to a word he did not like he would frown and say any boy was a sissy to use such a word. And if a composition pleased him he would praise the boy and be especially cheerful with him and the boy would be proud and the rest of us would be jealous and hate him.

I was often jealous. Mr Blades had a passion for compositions, and I was 57 anxious to please him to make up for that day at the window. I was anxious to show him how much I observed and often I noted new things and put them into my compositions. And whenever I said something wonderful I knew it because of the way Mr Blades would look at me, and sometimes he would take me aside and talk to me. But many weeks ran out before we spoke at the window again.

I did not start this time because I had been expecting him. I had been 58 watching him from the corners of my eyes.

"The sun's coming out again," he said. 59

"It's cloudy," I said. 60

The rains had ceased but there were still great patches of dark cloud in 61 the sky. When the wind blew they moved slowly and cumbersomely, but if the sun was free of one cloud there would soon be another. The sun was shining brightly now, although there was still a slight drizzle of rain, and I could smell the steam rising from the hot pitch and from the galvanized roofs.

"Rain falling sun shining," Mr Blades said. And I remembered that they 62 said at such times the Devil fought his wife, but when Mr Blades pressed me to tell what I was laughing at I laughed still more and would not say. Then thoughtfully he said, "You think they're all right?"

"What, sir?" 63

"In the 'mortelle root." 64

I was astonished. I put my hands to my mouth. How did he know? 65

He smiled down at me: "You won't be able to jump over now." And the 66 whole thing came back. I could not help laughing. I had put into my composition how I had gone into the hills on a Sunday evening, and how the mango trees were laden with small mangoes, some full, and how there were banana trees among the immortelle and poui. I had written, too, about the bunch of green bananas I had placed to ripen in the immortelle roots and how afterwards I had jumped across the river to the other bank.

"They're all right," I said, and I pretended to be watching the steam 67 rising from the hot pitch.

"I like bananas," said Mr Blades. I was sure that he licked his lips as he 68 looked towards the hills.

I was touched. I felt as one with him. I liked bananas, too, and they 69 always made me lick my lips. I thought now of the whole bunch which must be yellow by now inside the immortelle roots.

"Sir . . ." I said to him, hesitating. Then I took the wild chance. And 70 when he answered, a feeling of extreme happiness swept over me.

I remember that evening as turning out bright, almost blinding. The winds had pushed away the heavy clouds, and the only evidence of the rains was the little puddles along Sandra Street. I remember the hills as being strange in an enchanted sort of way, and I felt that part of the enchantment came from Mr Blades being with me. We watched the leaves of the cocoa gleaming with the moisture of the rains, and Mr Blades confessed he never thought there was so much cocoa in the hills. We watched the cyp, too, profuse among the laden mango trees, and the redness of their rain-picked flowers was the redness of blood.

We came to the immortelle tree where I had hidden the bananas. I watched 72 to see if Mr Blades licked his lips but he did not. He wasn't even watching.

"Sir," I said in happy surprise, after removing the covering of trash from 73 the bunch. Mr Blades was gazing across the trees. I raised my eyes. Not far below, Sandra Street swept by, bathed in light.

"The bananas, sir," I said. 74

"*Bananas!*" he cried, despairingly. "Bananas are all you see around you, 75 Steve?"

I was puzzled. I thought it was for bananas that we had come to the hills. 76

"Good heavens!" he said with bitterness. "To think that you instead of Kenneth should belong to Sandra Street." 77

# STUDY QUESTIONS

1. List all the things we learn about Steve. In what ways does he change as the story develops? How old is he at the time of the episode? Is he the same age when he tells the story? What indications are there in the story for your answer?

2. What functions does Mr. Blades perform for Steve? for the story? In what ways do his attitudes affect your evaluation of what is attractive about Sandra Street? Why is it significant that he lives on the other side of town? How do Steve's perceptions of his teacher change? What does Mr. Blades's memory for the details in Steve's composition suggest about him?

3. According to Kenneth, what are the virtues of his own "home sweet home"? What features of Steve's home, in Sandra Street, are implied in the opening three paragraphs of the story? What do we later learn about the neighborhood that extends our sense of what life is like in Sandra Street?

4. How does the fight after school relate to Steve's feelings about Sandra Street? to the main THEMES* of the story?

5. What details make it clear that the story takes place on a Caribbean island? Besides the fruit and vegetation, what features of the place are important to the story? What customs of the people seem distinctive to the culture on the island? Which customs are crucial to the effects of the story?

6. How do the differences in people's habits—conversations, street customs, the ways their houses are built and their lawns are kept—express the values of the two different cultures in the town? Which side of town do you like better? Which details in the story are most important to making you feel that way?

7. What skills of observation does Steve learn by writing about his street? What does he fail to notice until the end? What does his preoccupation with bananas in the final scene reveal about his limits as an observer?

8. The changing relationship between Steve and Mr. Blades is important to our understanding of Steve, and much of the action involves conversation and interaction between the two. Does the story keep our central attention on Steve and his perceptions of himself or on the teacher? on the relationship between the two or on the boy's understanding of where he came from? What values implicit in Sandra Street are still mysteries to the boy at the end of the story? Do you think the NARRATOR of the story would be as kind to Mr. Blades if the episode described in the story had not happened long ago?

*Words in small capitals are defined in the glossary.

9. What kind of person does the story suggest that Steve turned out to be? What evidence is there in the story itself?

# Ellen Gilchrist

Ellen Gilchrist's reputation as a writer has grown rapidly since 1979 when, at the age of forty-four, she published her first book, a collection of poems called *The Land Surveyor's Daughter*. Since then she has published a novel (*The Annunciation* [1983]) and three highly acclaimed collections of short stories, *In the Land of Dreamy Dreams* (1981), from which the following story is taken; *Victory over Japan* (1984); and *Drunk with Love* (1986). She has held a grant from the National Endowment for the Arts and has won the American Book Award for fiction. She now lives in Jackson, Mississippi, and is often heard as a storyteller and essayist on National Public Radio.

In the following story, a teenage girl from a small Indiana town goes on a visit to Mississippi and temporarily constructs a new romantic identity for herself.

# TRAVELER

It was June in southern Indiana. I was locked in the upstairs bathroom studying the directions on a box of Tampax when the invitation came.  1

"LeLe," my father called, coming up the stairs with the letter in his hand. "Come out of there. Come hear the news. You're going to the Delta."[1]  2

It seems my cousin Baby Gwen Barksdale's mother had died of a weak liver, and rather than leave the poor girl alone in a house with a grieving widower the family had invited me to Mississippi to spend the summer as her companion. There was even a suggestion that I might stay and go to school there in the fall.  3

What luck that the invitation came just as my own mother, giving in to a fit of jealous rage, left my father and fled to New Orleans to have a nervous breakdown.  4

"You'll love it in Clarksville," my father assured me. "Baby Gwen is just your age and just your speed. She'll be so glad to see you." And he pressed several more twenty-dollar bills into my hand and helped me pack my summer clothes.  5

---

1. Flat, fertile farmland in Mississippi along the Mississippi River.

"You try it for the summer, LeLe," he said. "We'll decide about school later on."

He might need to decide later on, but my mind was made up. I couldn't wait to leave Franklin, Indiana, where the students at Franklin Junior High had made the mistake of failing to elect me cheerleader. I wasn't unpopular or anything like that, just a little on the plump side.

Baby Gwen Barksdale, I whispered to myself as I arranged my things on the Pullman seat. I was sweating heavily in a pink linen suit, and my straw hat was making my head itch, but I sat up straight, trying to look like a lady. I had the latest edition of *Hit Parade Magazine* on my lap, and I was determined to learn every word of the Top Ten on the train ride.

Baby Gwen Barksdale, I said to myself, remembering the stories my father had told me. Baby Gwen, queen of the Delta subdeb dances, daughter of the famous Gwendolyn Montgomery Paine of Shaw, granddaughter of my grandmother's sainted sister, Frances Paine of Natchez. Baby Gwen Barksdale, daughter of Britain Barksdale who played halfback on the Ole Miss Sugar Bowl team.

It was all too good to be true. I marched myself down to the diner and ate several desserts to calm myself down.

By the time the Illinois Central made it all the way to Clarksville, Mississippi, my linen dress was helplessly wrinkled, my third pair of white gloves was damp and stained from the dye of the magazine, and my teeth were worn out from being brushed.

But there on the platform she waited, Baby Gwen Barksdale herself, five feet two inches of sultry dark-skinned, dark-eyed beauty. (The Barksdales have French blood.) She looked exactly like Ida Lupino.[2] She was wearing a navy blue dotted Swiss sun dress and high-heeled shoes and her slip was showing, a thin line of ecru lace. Her dark pink lipstick exactly matched her fingernail polish, and she smelled divinely of Aprodisia perfume.

She was accompanied by a strong boy who smiled a lot and turned out to be the sheriff's son. He had come along to carry the luggage.

"I'm so glad you could come," she said, hugging me for the fourth time. "I can't believe you came all the way on the train by yourself."

"No one in Franklin believed I'd do it either," I said. "I just got elected cheerleader and practically the whole football team came to the station to tell me goodbye. They didn't believe I was leaving. Of course, they all know about Bob Aaron. That's the college boy I love. He's got cancer of the thyroid gland. My parents won't let me go out with him because he's Jewish. He's already had about five operations. He's having one right now in St. Louis. So I might as well be down here."

"Oh, LeLe, that's terrible. It's like my mother. I know just how you feel."

2. London-born actress (1918– ) famous for playing romantic film roles.

"Well, anyway, I'm here now and we can stick together," I said, taking    17
a deep breath of the Aprodisia. "I love your perfume. It's wonderful."

"It's my signature," she said. "I wear Aprodisia in the summer and Tigress    18
in the winter. There's a bottle in my purse. You can put some on if you want
to."

We walked over to the Oldsmobile and Baby Gwen got behind the wheel.    19
She was so short she had to sit on straw pillows to see over the dash, but she
turned out to be a superb driver. The sheriff's son climbed into the back seat
with my bags, and the three of us drove off down the streets of the town,
past the gin and the post office and the Pontiac place, and on down the river
road to a white frame house at the end of a street that dead-ended at the
levee.

So I arrived in Clarksville, chattering away to a spellbound audience,    20
spraying my neck and arms with Aprodisia perfume, happier than I had ever
been in my life.

After her mother's funeral Baby Gwen had moved into the master bed-    21
room as her father was too brokenhearted to ever enter that part of the house
again.

I was led up the stairs and into a large sunny room with bay windows    22
and a pale blue chaise lounge. There was a dressing room with a private bath
and walk-in closets. Everything was just as Big Gwen had left it.

The closets were filled with unbelievable clothes. Navy blue and green    23
and black silk dresses, gray and beige and brown gabardine suits, pastel evening dresses, house dresses, sun dresses, wool coats, skirts, jackets. There
were twenty or thirty pairs of high-heeled shoes and a dozen hatboxes. There
were drawers full of handmade underwear. There was a fur stole and several
negligees and a real Japanese kimono.

It was all ours.    24

"You can wear anything you want to," Baby Gwen said. "Most of them    25
are too long for me."

Best of all was the dressing table. It was three feet long with a padded    26
stool and a large mirror surrounded by light bulbs.

On its surface, in a sea of spilled powder, were dozens of bottles and    27
jars. Every product ever manufactured by Charles of the Ritz must have been
there. There was foundation cream, astringent, eye shadow, rouge, clarifier,
moisturizer, cleanser, refining oil, facial mask, night cream, hand cream,
wrinkle cream, eye cream, all pervaded by the unforgettable smell of Reve-
nescence, Charles of the Ritz's secret formula moisturizer.

There were hairpins, hand mirrors, tweezers, eyelash curlers, combs,    28
hair rollers, mascara wands, cuticle sticks, nail polish, emery boards. There
were numerous bottles of perfume and cologne and a cut-glass bowl filled
with lipsticks.

I had never seen anything like it. I could hardly wait to sit down on the    29
little padded stool and get started.

"You want a Coca-Cola?" Baby Gwen asked, growing bored with my   30
inspection of her riches. "Some boys I know are coming over later this afternoon to meet you."

"Can we smoke?" I asked, pulling my Pall Malls out of my purse.   31

"We can do anything we want to do," she said, picking a Ronson lighter   32
off the dressing table and handing it to me. She was smiling the famous
Barksdale slow smile.

That night we lay awake until two or three in the morning telling each   33
other our life stories. I told her about Bob Aaron's lymph node cancer, and
she told me about her cousin Maurice, who taught French and hated Clarksville and was married to an unpleasant woman who sang in the choir. Maurice was secretly in love with Baby Gwen. He couldn't help himself. He had
confessed his love at a spring wedding reception. Now they were waiting for
Baby Gwen to grow up so they could run away together. In the meantime
Baby Gwen was playing the field so no one would suspect.

Finally, exhausted by our passions, we fell asleep in each other's arms,   34
with the night breezes blowing in the windows off the river, in our ironed
sheets and our silk pajamas and our night cream, with the radio playing an
all-night station from New Orleans. Oh, Bob, Bob, I whispered into Baby
Gwen's soft black hair. Oh, Maurice, Maurice, she sighed into my hair rollers.

In the morning I woke early and wandered downstairs. I went into the   35
kitchen, opened the freezer, found a carton of vanilla ice cream, and began
to eat it with my fingers, standing with the freezer door open, letting the cool
air blow on my face.

After a while I heard the back door slam and Sirena came in. She was   36
the middle-aged black woman who turned out to be the only person in charge
of us in any way. Baby Gwen's father disappeared before dawn to carry the
mail and came home in the evenings and sank into his chair with his bourbon
and his memories. Occasionally he would put in an appearance at the noon
meal and ask us if we wanted anything.

I barely managed to close the freezer door before Sirena caught me.   37
"You want me to make you some breakfast?" she said.

"No, thank you," I said. "I don't eat in the daytime. I'm on a diet."   38

I have always believed Sirena found my fingerprints in that ice cream.   39
One way or the other I wasn't fooling her, she knew a Yankee when she saw
one, even if I was Mr. Leland's daughter.

I wandered into the living room and read a *Coronet* for a while. Then I   40
decided to go back upstairs and see if Baby Gwen was awake.

I found her in the bathroom sitting upright in a tub of soapy water while   41
Sirena knelt beside it slowly and intently bathing her. I had never seen a
grown person being bathed before.

Sirena was running her great black hand up and down Baby Gwen's   42
white leg, soaping her with a terry-cloth washrag. The artesian well water
was the color of urine and smelled of sulphur and sandalwood soap, and

Sirena's dark hand was thick and strong moving along Baby Gwen's flawless skin. I sat down on the toilet and began to make conversation.

"You want to take a sunbath after a while," I said. "I'm afraid I'll lose my tan."   43

"Sure," she said. "We can do whatever you want to. Someone called a while ago and asked us to play bridge this afternoon. Do you like to play bridge?"   44

"I love it," I said. "That's practically all we do in Indiana. We play all the time. My mother plays duplicate. She's got about fifty silver ashtrays she won at tournaments."   45

"I bet you're really good," she said. She was squirming around while Sirena took her time finishing the other leg.   46

I lit a cigarette, trying not to look at Baby Gwen's black pubic hair. I had never seen anyone's pubic hair but my own, which was red. It had not occurred to me that there were different colors. "Want a drag?" I asked, handing her the cigarette. She nodded, wiped her hand on her terry-cloth turban, took a long luxurious drag, and French inhaled.   47

The smoke left her mouth in two little rivers, curled deliciously up over the dark hairs above her lips, and into her nostrils. She held it for a long moment, then exhaled slowly through her lips. The smoke mingled with the sunlight, and the steam coming from the bathwater rose in ragged circles and moved toward the open window.   48

Baby Gwen rose from the water, her flat body festooned with blossoms of sandalwood soap, and Sirena began to dry her with a towel.   49

So our life together took shape. In the mornings we sunbathed from 11:00 to 12:00. Thirty minutes on one side and thirty minutes on the other. There were two schools of thought concerning sunbathing. One, that it gave you wrinkles. The other, that it was worth it to look good while you were young.   50

Baby Gwen and I subscribed to the second theory. Still, we were careful to keep our faces oiled so we wouldn't ruin our complexions. There is no way you could believe how serious we were about such matters. The impenetrable mystery of physical beauty held us like a spell.   51

In the morning we spread our blankets in the backyard where a patch of sunlight shone in through the high branches of the elm trees. We covered the blankets with white sheets and set out our supplies, bottles of baby oil, bottles of iodine, alarm clock, eye pads, sunglasses, magazines. We carefully mixed seven drops of iodine with seven ounces of baby oil, shook it for three minutes, then rubbed it on the uncovered parts of each other's bodies. How I loved the feel of Baby Gwen's rib cage under my fingers, the smoothness of her shaved legs. How I dreaded it when her fingers touched the baby fat on my own ribs.   52

When we were covered with oil we would lie back and continue our   53 discussion of our romances. I talked of nothing but the ill-fated Bob Aaron, of the songs I would write and dedicate to his memory, of the trip I would take to his deathbed, of the night he drove me home from a football game and let me wear his gloves, of the child I would have by another man and name for him, Robert or Roberta, Bob or Bobbie.

The other thing that fascinated me was the development of my "reputation." I was intensely interested in what people thought of me, in what was being said about me. I set about to develop a reputation in Clarksville as a "madcap," a "wild child," a girl who would do anything. A summer visitor from Washington, D.C., said in my hearing that I reminded him of a young Zelda Fitzgerald and, although I didn't know exactly who Zelda Fitzgerald was, I knew that she had married a writer and drank like a fish and once danced naked in a fountain in Rome. It sounded like a wonderful thing to have said about myself, and I resolved to try to live up to it.   54

How wonderful it was to be "home," where people knew "who I was," where people thought I was "hilarious" and "crazy" and "just like Leland." I did everything I could think of to feed my new image, becoming very outspoken, saying *damn* and *hell* at every opportunity, wearing dark glasses all the time, even to church. I must have been the first person of normal vision ever to attend the Clarksville Episcopal Church wearing dark glasses.   55

Baby Gwen's grandmother called every few days to see how we were getting along and once, in a burst of responsibility, came over bringing a dozen pairs of new cotton underpants she had bought for us at the Chinaman's store.   56

We never could figure out where she got the idea that we were in need of cotton underpants, unless Sirena had mentioned it to her. Perhaps Sirena had tired of hand washing the French lingerie we had taken to wearing every day.   57

The grandmother had outlived both her daughters and existed in a sort of dreamy half-world with her servants and her religion.   58

Mostly we kept her satisfied by glowing telephone reports of our popularity and by stopping by occasionally to sit on her porch and have a Coca-Cola.   59

I fell in love nearly every day with one or the other of the seemingly endless supply of boys who came over to call from Drew and Cleveland and Itta Bena and Tutweiler and Rosedale and Leland. Baby Gwen drew boys like honey, and there were always plenty left over to sit around the living room listening to my nonstop conversation.   60

Boys came by in the evenings, boys called on the telephone, boys invaded our daily bridge games, boys showed up after church, boys took us swimming at the Clarksville Country Club, boys drove us around the cotton fields and down to the river and out to the bootlegger's shack.   61

The boy I liked best was a good-natured football player named Fielding Reid. Fielding had eyes so blue and hair so blonde and shoulders so wide   62 and teased me so unmercifully about my accent that I completely forgot he was the steady boyfriend of Clarice Fitzhugh, who was off on a trip to Mexico with her family. Fielding had taken to hanging around Baby Gwen and me while he waited for Clarice's return.

He loved to kibitz on our bridge games, eating all the mints and pecans   63
from the little dishes and leaning over my shoulder cheering me on. In the afternoons we played endless polite bridge games, so different from the bitter hard-fought bridge I had played in the forgotten state of Indiana.

Although I was an erratic and unpredictable bidder, I was a sought-after   64
partner for I held good cards and nearly always won.

There was a girl from Drew named Sarah who came over several after-   65
noons a week to play with us. She was Fielding's cousin and she had a wooden arm painted the color of her skin. It was not a particularly well made arm, and the paint was peeling in several places on the hand. She was pleasant enough looking otherwise and had nice clothes with loose sleeves that hid the place where the false arm joined the real one.

I made a great show of being nice to Sarah, lighting her cigarettes, ask-   66
ing her opinion about things, letting her be my bridge partner. She was delighted with the attention I gave her and was always telling someone how "wonderful" I was and how much it meant to her to have me in Clarksville.

The wrist and fingers of Sarah's false arm were hinged and she could   67
move the joints with her good hand and lock them in place. She was in the habit of holding the wooden arm in front of her when she was seated at the bridge table. Then she would place her bridge hand in the wooden fingers and play out of it with her good hand.

Of course, anyone sitting on either side of her could see her cards by   68
the slightest movement of their eyes. It took a lot of pressure off me when she was my partner.

Fielding thought I was "wonderful" too. He went around saying I was   69
his "partner" and took me into his confidence, even telling me his fears that the absent Clarice Fitzhugh was being unfaithful to him in Mexico. That she might be "using" him.

Don't worry, I assured him. Clarice was a great girl. She wouldn't use   70
anyone. He must trust her and not listen to idle gossip. Everything would be fine when she got home, and so forth. Part of my new reputation was that "LeLe never says a bad word about anyone," "LeLe always looks on the bright side," "everyone feels like they've known LeLe all their lives," "you can tell LeLe *anything*."

I was beginning to believe my own publicity, that I was someone very   71
special, that there might be some special destiny in store for me.

Several times that summer I was filled with an elation so powerful and   72
overwhelming that it felt as though my body were leaving the earth. This always happened at night, when I was alone in the yard, caught in the shadow of the Nandina bushes which covered the side of the house like bright dark

clouds. I remember standing in the starlight filled with som
joy. It would become very intense, like music. I was terribly
feelings and could not bring myself to speak of them, even t

Often that summer I was given to seizures of abrupt excit....
was dressing. I would catch a glimpse of myself in a mirror and burst into
laughter, or, deciding for a moment that I was pretty, begin to tremble and
jump up and go dancing around the room.

I had a recurrent dream that summer. I dreamed that I was walking
through our old house in Indiana and I would notice that the dining room
opened up into rooms and rooms I had not known existed, strange and oddly
shaped rooms full of heavy furniture, expensive dusty dressers with drawers
full of treasures, old gowns and sweaters and capes, jewels and letters and
old documents, wills and deeds and diaries. These rooms opened onto patios
and sun porches and solariums, and I saw that we were wealthy people. I
wanted to run back and find my parents and tell them what I had found, but
my curiosity drove me forward. I had to keep opening doors until I knew the
extent of our riches, so I kept on moving through the strange rooms until I
woke.

One morning Fielding came by unexpectedly and asked me to go with
him to see about some repairs for his car. We left it with a mechanic at the
filling station and walked to the Mayflower Café, a place on the square where
farmers and merchants gathered in the mornings for coffee and gossip. I had
never been alone in a restaurant with a boy, and I was excited and began
talking very fast to cover my excitement. I ordered doughnuts and began
turning my turquoise ring around on my finger so the waitress would think
it was a wedding band.

"I've been wanting to talk to you alone," Fielding said.

"Sure," I said, choking on a powdered doughnut. It was all too wonderful, sitting in a booth so early in the morning with a really good-looking boy.

"LeLe," he said, smiling at me and reaching across the table to hold my
hand. There was his garnet class ring, blazing at me from the tabletop. At
any moment it might be mine. I could scarcely breathe. "LeLe," he repeated,
"I don't want you to get me wrong when I say this. I don't want to hurt your
feelings or anything, but, well, I really want to tell you something." He
squeezed my hand tighter. "LeLe, you would be a really beautiful girl if you
lost ten pounds, do you know that? Because you have a beautiful face. I'm
only saying this because we've gotten to be such good friends and I thought
I ought . . ."

I was stunned. But I recovered. "I'm not really this fat," I said. "At
home I'm a cheerleader and I'm on the swimming team and I'm very thin.
But last year the boy I love got cancer and I've been having a lot of trouble
with my thyroid since then. The doctors think there may something wrong
with my thyroid or my metabolism. I may have to have an operation pretty
soon."

"Oh, LeLe," he said. "I didn't know it was anything like that. I thought maybe you ate too much or something." He reached out and took my other hand. I was still holding part of a doughnut.

"Don't worry about it, Fielding. How could you know. You didn't hurt my feelings. Besides, I don't mind. The operation may not be so bad. It isn't like having polio or something they can't fix. At least I have something they can fix." 81

"Oh, LeLe." 82

"Don't worry about it. And don't tell anyone about it, even Baby Gwen. I don't want people feeling sorry for me. So it's a secret." 83

"Don't worry, LeLe. I'll never tell anyone. Are you sure it'll be all right? About the operation I mean?" 84

"Oh, sure. I might not even have to have it. My thyroid might get better all by itself." 85

After that Fielding and I were closer than ever. I began to halfway believe the part about the thyroid trouble. My mother was always talking about her thyroid and taking some sort of little white pill for it. 86

Late one afternoon Baby Gwen and I were sitting on the porch swing talking to Fielding. It was one of those days in August when you can smell autumn in the air, a feeling of change coming over the world. I had won at bridge that afternoon. I had made seven hearts doubled and redoubled with Fielding looking over my shoulder, and I was filled with a sense of power. 87

"Let's all go swimming tomorrow," I said. "They'll be closing the pool soon and I need to practice my strokes." 88

"Let's go to the lake," Fielding said. "I haven't made my summer swim across the lake. I was waiting for Russell to get home, but I don't guess he'll be back in time so I might as well go on and swim it myself." 89

"I'll swim it with you," I heard myself saying. "I'm a Junior Red Cross Lifesaver. I can swim forever. 90

"You couldn't swim this," he said. "It's five miles." 91

"I can swim a lot further than that," I said. "I practically taught swimming at camp. I never got tired." 92

"What about your . . . you know . . . your condition?" 93

"That's all right," I said. "Exercise is good for me. I'm supposed to go swimming all I can. The doctors said it was the best thing I could do." 94

Baby Gwen looked puzzled. "You can't swim all the way across the lake without a boat," she said. "Girls don't ever swim across the lake." 95

"I can swim it," I said, "I've been further than that at camp lots of times. What time you want to go, Fielding?" 96

By the time he came to pick us up the next morning I had calmed Baby Gwen down and convinced her there was nothing to worry about. I really was a good swimmer. Swimming was of no importance to me one way or the other. What mattered to me was that a boy of my own choosing, a first-rate boy, was coming to take me somewhere. Not coming for Baby Gwen and taking me along to be nice, but *coming for me*. 97

I had been awake since dawn deciding what to wear. I finally settled on    98
my old green Jantzen and a white blouse from Big Gwen's wardrobe. The
blouse had little shoulder pads and big chunky buttons and fell across my
shoulders and arms in soft pleats. I wasn't worried at all about swimming the
lake. The only thing that worried me was whether the blouse was long enough
to cover my stomach.

Baby Gwen went with us. As soon as we left the shore she was supposed    99
to drive around to the other side and watch for us. All the way out to the
lake she sat beside me looking worried.

"You ought to have a boat going along beside you," she said.    100

"We don't need a boat," I said. "I'm a Junior Red Cross Lifesaver. I can    101
swim all day if I want."

"It's O.K.," Fielding said. "Russell and I do it every summer."    102

By the time we got to the lake I felt like I could swim the Atlantic    103
Ocean. The sun was brilliant on the blue water, and as soon as Fielding
stopped the car I jumped out and ran down to the shore and looked out across
the water to the pine trees on the far shore. It didn't look so far away, only
very blue and deep and mysterious. I took off my blouse and shoes and
waded out into the water. How clean it felt, how cool. I put my face down
and touched my cheek to the water. I felt the water across my legs and
stomach. My body felt wonderful and light in the water. I rose up on my
toes and my legs felt strong and tall. I pulled in my stomach until my ribs
stuck out. I was beautiful. I was perfect. I began to throw handfuls of water
up into the air. The water caught in the sunlight and fell back all around me.
I threw more into the air and it fell all around me, falling in pieces of steel
and glass and diamonds, diamonds falling all around me. I called out, "Come
on, Fielding. Either we're swimming across this lake or we aren't."

"Wait," he called back. "Wait up." Then he was beside me in the water    104
and I felt his hands around my waist and the pressure of his knee against my
thigh. "Let's go then," he said in a low sweet voice. "Let's do this together."

Then we began to swim out, headed for the stand of pine and oak and    105
cypress on the far shore.

The time passed as if in a dream. My arms moved easily, taking turns    106
pulling the soft yielding water alongside my body. I was counting out the
strokes, one, two, three, four, five, six, seven, eight, one, two, three, four,
five, six, seven, eight . . . over and over in the good old-fashioned Australian
crawl. Every now and then Fielding would touch my arm and we would roll
over on our backs and rest for a few minutes, checking our position. Then
we would swim for a while on our sides, resting. There were long banks of
clouds on the horizon and far overhead a great hawk circling like a black
planet. Everytime I looked up he was there.

We swam for what seemed to be a long, long time, but whenever I    107
looked ahead the trees on the shore never seemed to come any closer.

"Are you sure we're going in a straight line," I said, when we turned    108
over to rest for a moment.

"I think so," Fielding said. "The current might be pulling us a little to the left. There's nothing we can do about it now anyway." [109]

"Why," I said. "Why can't we do anything about it?" [110]

"Well, we can't go back," he said. "We're past the point of no return." [111]

The point of no return, I said to myself. Maybe we would die out here and they would change the name of the lake in honor of us. Lake LeLe, Lake Leland Louise Arnold, Lover's Lake. "Don't worry about it then," I said. "Just keep on swimming." [112]

Perhaps an hour went by, perhaps two. The sun was hot on the water, and every now and then a breeze blew up. Once a barge carrying logs to the sawmill passed us without noticing us. We treaded water while it passed and then rocked in the wake for several minutes. They had passed us as though we didn't exist. After the barge went by we began to swim with more determination. I was beginning to feel cold, but it didn't seem to really matter. Nothing mattered but this boy and the sun and the clouds and the great hawk circling and the water touching me everywhere. I put down my head and began to count with renewed vigor, one, two, three, four, five, six, seven, eight, one, two, three, four, . . . [113]

"LeLe," Fielding called out. "LeLe, put your feet down. Put your feet down, LeLe." I looked up and he was standing a few feet away holding his hands up in the air. I let my feet drop and my toes touched the cool flat sand. We were on the sandbar. Then we were laughing and hugging and holding on to each other and moving toward the shore where Baby Gwen stood calling and calling to us. It was wonderful, wonderful, wonderful, wonderful. I was wonderful. I was dazzling. I was LeLe Arnold, the wildest girl in the Mississippi Delta, the girl who swam Lake Jefferson without a boat or a life vest. I was LeLe, the girl who would do anything. [114]

All the way home in the car Fielding kept his arm around me while he drove and Baby Gwen fed me little pieces of the picnic lunch and I was happier than I had ever been in my life and I might have stayed that way forever but when we got home there was a message saying that my parents were on their way to Clarksville to take me home. [115]

My parents. I had forgotten they existed. My father had gotten lonely and driven to New Orleans and talked my mother into coming home. [116]

Later that afternoon they arrived. It seemed strange to see our Buick pulling up in Baby Gwen's driveway. My father got out looking very young and my mother was holding on to his arm. She looked like a stranger, thin and beautiful in a black cotton peasant dress with rows of colored rickrack around the hem and sleeves. Her hair was cut short and curled around her face in ringlets. I was almost afraid to touch her. Then she ran from my father's side and grabbed me in her arms and whirled me around and around and I smelled the delicate perfume on her skin and it made me feel like crying. [117]

When she put me down I turned to my father. "I'm not going home," I said, putting my hands on my hips. [118]

"Oh, yes you are," he said, so I went upstairs and began to pack my clothes.    119

Baby Gwen followed me up the stairs. "You can have the kimono," she said. "I want you to have it." She folded it carefully and packed it with tissue paper in a box from Nell's and Blum's and put it beside my suitcase.    120

"Come sit by me, Baby Gwen, and tell me the news," my mother said, and Baby Gwen went over and sat by her on the chaise. My mother put her arms around her and began to talk in a bright voice inviting her to spend Christmas with us in Indiana.    121

"It will snow for sure," my mother said. "And LeLe can show you the snow."    122

We left Clarksville early the next morning. Baby Gwen stood in the doorway waving goodbye. She was wearing a pink satin robe stained in places from where she had sweated in it during the hot nights of July, and her little nipples stuck out beneath the soft material.    123

I kept hoping maybe Fielding had gotten up early to come and tell me goodbye, but he didn't make it.    124

"I'll fix those hems when she comes to visit," my mother said, "and do something about that perfume."    125

I was too tired to argue. All the way to Indiana I slumped in the back seat eating potato chips and sneaking smokes in filling-station restrooms when we stopped for gas.    126

Then it was another morning and I woke up in my old room and put on my shorts and rode my bicycle over to Cynthia Carver's house. She was in the basement doing her Saturday morning ironing. Cynthia hated to iron. How many mornings had I sat on those basement steps watching the forlorn look on her face while she finished her seven blouses.    127

"So I might as well be dead," I said, taking a bite of a cookie. "So, anyway, I wish I was dead," I repeated, as Cynthia hung a blouse on a hanger and started on a dirndl skirt. "Here I am, practically engaged to this rich plantation owner's son . . . Fielding. Fielding Reid, LeLe Reid . . . so, anyway, my mother and father come and drag me home practically the same day we fell in love. I don't know how they got wind of it unless that damn Sirena called and told them. She was always watching everything I did. Anyway, they drag me home and I bet they won't even let him write to me."    128

"What's that perfume?" Cynthia said, lifting her eyes from the waistband of the skirt.    129

"That's my signature," I said. "That's what I wear now. Tigress in the winter and Aprodisia in the summer. That what this writer's wife always wore. She got pneumonia or something from swimming in the winter and died when she was real young. Everyone in Clarksville thinks I'm just like her. She was from Mississippi or something. I think she's sort of my father's cousin."    130

Cynthia pulled the dirndl off the ironing board and began on a pair of pedal pushers. I leaned back on the stairs, watching the steam from the pedal    131 pushers light up the space over Cynthia Carver's disgruntled Yankee head. I was dreaming of the lake, trying to remember how the water turned into diamonds in my hands.

## STUDY QUESTIONS

1. How much does LeLe tell us about her life in Franklin, Indiana? What aspects of her home and school life is she unhappy with? What indications are there that she is unhappy with herself? What does she want to get away from? How old is LeLe? What clues are there early in the story about her age? How important to the story is her age?

2. List all of the changes LeLe makes in herself or her history when she gets to Mississippi. What patterns do you see in her lies and imaginings? What kind of reputation does she want to have? What kind of person does she want to be? What differences are there between her real and imagined selves? Why does she feel more at home in Mississippi than in Indiana?

3. Can you tell when LeLe is not telling the truth? What clues are there? Does she have any characteristic ways of expressing herself when she lies or exaggerates? What do you make of her tendency to construct sad and tragic stories about her friends? Given the unreliability of her accounts of herself to her friends, what makes you think she is telling us the truth in the story?

4. How important is LeLe's mother to the story? What do you make of the flippant way she describes her mother's going away? How important to the story is LeLe's father? Describe LeLe's conception of her family. What aspects of family life are important to her?

5. Where is LeLe's "home"? Does her definition of home change in the course of the story?

6. What do you imagine LeLe's life will be like when she goes back to school in Indiana? In what ways will her Mississippi experiences have changed her? How do you know?

7. Why does LeLe believe that going away from home and the place in which she is known gives her the freedom of a new identity?

# Luis Cabalquinto

Born in the Philippines (at Magarao, Camarines), Luis Cabalquinto was educated at the University of the Philippines and at Cornell and now lives and works in New York City. He has also attended several writers' workshops, including Bread

Loaf, and studied with the poet Galway Kinnell at New York University. His poems have appeared in a variety of poetry journals, including the *American Poetry Review*. He has received the Dylan Thomas Poetry Award from the New School for Social Research, an Academy of American Poets poetry prize from NYU, and a Fellowship Award in poetry from the New York Foundation for the Arts.

The following poem captures a powerful sense of belonging, peace, and satisfaction: its speaker finds, in familiar habits and sights, a sense of needs fulfilled and time that has been stopped.

# HOMETOWN

After a supper of mountain rice
And wood-roasted river crab
I sit on a long bench outside
The old house, looking at a river

Alone, myself, again away                                    5
From that other self in the city
On this piece of ancestor land
My pulses slowed, I am at peace

I have no wish but this place
To remain here in a stopped time                           10
With stars moving on that water
And in the sky a brightness

Answering: I want nothing else
But this stillness filling me
From a pure darkness over the land                         15
That smells ever freshly of trees

The night and I are quiet now
But for small laughter from a neighbor
The quick sweep of a winged creature
And a warm dog, snuggled by my feet                        20

## STUDY QUESTIONS

1. The poem is full of details and images of things in motion, and yet it emphasizes a stillness in which nothing, including time, moves at all. How do you explain the contradiction? How do the several sights, smells, and sounds contribute to the

poem's quiescence? to its tranquillity? How does the punctuation—or lack of it—contribute?

2. Why are the specific details of supper presented? Why the detail about how the crab is roasted? What does the supper imply about the person who speaks the poem? What other details help to characterize the SPEAKER?

3. Why is an "other self" (line 6) mentioned? What kind of contrast does the mention of the city imply? What other absences help to set the mood of the poem?

4. How long has the speaker been attached to this place? In the absence of specific facts about years, how is the impression of permanence created? What different IMAGES of satisfaction does the poem present?

5. Are you surprised that the poet now lives in the United States rather than the Philippines? Does the fact affect your reading of the poem in any way? your appreciation of it? What does the fact of his exile or immigration suggest about his sense of roots? Do you think that a person's sense of "home" is likely to be weakened or strengthened by living in a "foreign" place?

# Edward Hirsch

E dward Hirsch teaches at the University of Houston. His poems have appeared in many journals and magazines and have been collected in *For the Sleepwalkers* (1981) and *Wild Gratitude* (1986). He has held fellowships from the John Simon Guggenheim Foundation, the American Council of Learned Societies, and the National Endowment for the Arts, and he has won a number of prestigious awards for his poetry, including several from the American Academy of Poets. Born in Chicago in 1950, he comes from a family with roots in Eastern Europe.

This poem presents the memories and reveries of someone who now lives in a home for the aged but who also has vivid recollections of a home far away and long ago.

## IN A POLISH HOME FOR THE AGED (CHICAGO, 1983)

It's sweet to lie awake in the early morning
Remembering the sound of five huge bells
Ringing in the village at dawn, the iron
Notes turning to music in the pink clouds.

It's nice to remember the flavor of groats                          5
Mixed with horse's blood, the sour tang
Of unripe peppers, the smell of garlic
Growing wildly in Aunt Stefania's garden.

I can remember my grandmother's odd claim
That her younger brother was a mule                                 10
Pulling an ox-cart across a lapsed meadow
In the first thin light of a summer morning;

Her cousin, Irka, was a poorly-planted tree
Wrapping itself in a dress of white blossoms.
I could imagine an ox-cart covered with flowers,                    15
The sound of laughter rising from damp branches.

Some nights I dream that I'm a child again
Flying through the barnyard at six a.m.:
My mother milks the cows in the warm barn
And thinks about her father, who died long ago,                     20

And daydreams about my future in a large city.
I want to throw my arms around her neck
And touch the sweating blue pails of milk
And talk about my strange, childish nightmares.

God, you've got to see us to know how happy                         25
We were then, two dark caresses of sunlight.
Now I wake up to the same four walls staring
At me blankly, and the same bare ceiling.

Somehow the morning starts over in the home:
Someone coughs in the hall; someone calls out                      30
An unfamiliar name, a name I don't remember;
Someone slams a car door in the distance.

I touch my feet to the cold tile floor
And listen to my neighbor stirring in his room
And think about my mother's peculiar words                          35
After my grandmother died during the war:

"One day the light will be as thick as a pail
Of fresh milk, but the pail will seem heavy.
You won't know if you can lift it anymore,
But lift it anyway. Drink the day slowly."                          40

## STUDY QUESTIONS

1. What "facts" are we given about the SPEAKER? What memories of childhood are presented? How much do we know about family? about places of origin?

2. How much are we told about the "village" (line 3) of long ago? What clues are there about where the village was? What customs help define the village and the family? How far away does the village seem to be in time? in place?

3. How much do we know about the speaker's present life? What seem to be the speaker's primary emotions now? How much do we know about the place where the speaker lies awake?

4. What is accomplished by having the poem set in the speaker's waking moment?

5. What does the advice in the final STANZA of the poem mean? How does it relate to the speaker's present state of mind and situation? to the opening lines of the poem?

# Cathy Song

Born in 1955 in Hawaii, Cathy Song attended the University of Hawaii, Wellesley College (B.A., 1977), and Boston University (M.A., 1981). She is the author of *Picture Bride* (winner of the Yale Younger Poets Award in 1982), in which the title poem tells the story of her Korean grandmother, who was sent for as a mail-order bride in Hawaii on the basis of her photograph.

The poem that follows is taken from her latest book, *Frameless Windows, Squares of Light* (1988). The poem is at least in part autobiographical: Song lived in Denver for several years and is the mother of a young boy and girl. The speaker here has never been to China but is highly conscious of a powerful heritage and sense of the past, so much so that her son imagines that heaven is really in China.

# HEAVEN

He thinks when we die we'll go to China.
Think of it—a Chinese heaven
where, except for his blond hair,
the part that belongs to his father,
everyone will look like him.                                    5

China, that blue flower on the map,
bluer than the sea
his hand must span like a bridge
to reach it.
An octave away.                                          10

I've never seen it.
It's as if I can't sing that far.
But look—
on the map, this black dot.
Here is where we live,                                   15
on the pancake plains
just east of the Rockies,
on the other side of the clouds.
A mile above the sea,
the air is so thin, you can starve on it.                20
No bamboo trees
But the alpine equivalent,
reedy aspen with light, fluttering leaves.
Did a boy in Guangzhou[1] dream of this
as his last stop?                                        25

I've heard the trains at night
whistling past our yards,
what we've come to own,
the broken fences, the whiny dog, the rattletrap cars.
It's still the wild west,                                30
mean and grubby,
the shootouts and fistfights in the back alley.
With my son the dreamer
and my daughter, who is too young to walk,
I've sat in this spot                                    35
and wondered why here?
Why in this short life,
this town, this creek they call a river?

He had never planned to stay,
the boy who helped to build                              40
the railroads for a dollar a day.[2]
He had always meant to go back.
When did he finally know
that each mile of track led him further away,
that he would die in his sleep,                          45

---

1. Usually called Canton, a seaport city in southeastern China.

2. The railroads used immigrant day labor (most of it Chinese) to lay the tracks in the nineteenth century.

dispossessed,
having seen Gold Mountain,
the icy wind tunneling through it,
these landlocked, makeshift ghost towns?

It must be in the blood,                                    50
this notion of returning.
It skipped two generations, lay fallow,
the garden an unmarked grave.
On a spring sweater day
it's as if we remember him.                                 55
I call to the children.
We can see the mountains
shimmering blue above the air.
If you look really hard
says my son the dreamer,                                    60
leaning out from the laundry's rigging,
the work shirts fluttering like sails,
you can see all the way to heaven.

## STUDY QUESTIONS

1. Explain the "notion of returning" (line 51) that seems so powerful in the boy. How does the SPEAKER herself feel about China as homeland?

2. How much do we find out about the grandfather who first came to the U.S. mainland? How much do we know about what became of him?

3. Why are we given so many details of the speaker's present location "just east of the Rockies" (l. 17)? What is the meaning of "dispossessed" (l. 46)?

4. Describe the sense of the past that the poem creates. Describe the mood of the poem. What kind of picture does the speaker present of herself? of her children? What else do we know about the immediate family?

# Lee Ki Chuck

Born in Seoul, Korea, "Lee Ki Chuck" (a pseudonym) came to the United States with his family in 1973. They first settled in a Los Angeles suburb but later moved to the New York metropolitan area.

The following "autobiography," taken from an oral interview in 1975, recounts the difficulties of growing up in a culture that seemed exotic in prospect but that became a nightmare. Anxious to settle into his new "home" and become thoroughly American, Lee Ki Chuck found instead that his moorings in Korean culture were gone and that, as yet, there were no new useful habits or values to replace them.

# FROM KOREA TO HEAVEN COUNTRY

Before, I was Oriental guy, right? But different society—everything is different—like girl friend and study and spending money and riding car. 1

I came here and I bought Pinto car. I was driving very crazy. One day my friend was driving crazy, Mustang, make follow me. I thought, "Americans are very lucky, they are always having good time." I was kind of hating inside. I never want to lose *anything*—even studies, sports, anything—I didn't want to lose to American. So I just beat him. After that time people know I am driving crazy. People just come to me, racing, so I raced every time. Then during last year, I wrecked up one car, first car, and I was *crazy*. I was racing with friend. I hit a tree. I have so many tickets from the police. [Laughs.] In a twenty-five-mile [zone], sixty miles I drove. I had so many warning tickets. I know that is very bad. You can't go to Harvard with these kind of tickets. I don't drive now anymore. 2

I have matured a lot since I got to this country. I smoke a lot, too. I used to smoke because I was curious—now one day, one pack. Every time I get up in the morning is so pain. And drinking. I found I like rock concert. So interesting, different. Like I go in the morning, 4:00. Those are nice guys I get drunk with, whiskey, go down to the beach and go swimming. Found a lot of crazy. 3

Actually my immigration was very hard. I had so many times crying. That was really a terrible time. I guess is all right now, really. I am so happy. And then, after my mother came here, my father was getting all right. They found I skip school so many times, getting bad, but they didn't tell anything to me. "Do whatever you want, but just don't be bad about it." They gave me another chance. 4

I'm still Korean. I was really trying to make good friend with American. I have a friend but I never think he is my best friend. American friend I can never make best friend. They just like "hi" friends. "Hi." "Hi." 5

*What was your reaction to girls in this country?* 6

Oh yeh, girls. When I was in Korea—like if I have girl friend—very innocent, talking about philosophy, society, politics, every time. It is hard to even touch hand there. You understand? Very innocent. This is Korea. 7

I met these few girls in this country, but I don't like them. They are 8 more strong on the physical than I am. [Laughs.] Every time, is physical. Every time I try to talk to them about life, they say, "I think you are too smart. I don't think I can follow you." That's what everybody says.

I tried suicide. When I hit the tree, I was almost dead—fifty miles, I hit. But I didn't die. I was lucky—just a scratch and sore on the face. That was my fault. My friend, he couldn't stop his car, and he hit my car and the breaking window and spread out the glass. Insurance paid for car. Was total. And then after that, when I was getting really bad in the school—skipping school, drinking, doing marijuana outside—I come by home about 1:00. During school days, too. Sometimes I work. I make a lot of money. Like moonlight can make thirty, forty dollars, busboy, tips and they pay check, too, at the hotel. Make a lot of money, and then I can get whatever I want. 9

I can't face my principal. He's very nice but I couldn't face him so I just took twenty pills. Slept, but I didn't die. My mother didn't tell it to my father. Twenty, that's what I only regret, and my mother said, "You can die with twenty pills." But in the America, if you take sleeping pills a lot, you never die, but just the body inside is changed. 10

All of my friends in the Korea they still think I am having very good time. I don't tell them what happened to me. I have a car, and they think I am very rich. 11

If I come to America, I thought that America was really heaven country. I saw so many movie. I saw cars, everyone drives car. If I go to America, I can drive. I can watch TV, everything. I thought I was really heading to heaven. But that's wrong. You have to try to make heaven. Everybody still, everybody think all immigration come to this country. Before they come here they think of this country as heaven. This country, if you try, if you walk out, you can make money, you can be rich here. It's a really nice country, actually. 12

I used to be with a lot of friends, but now I am alone always. I didn't know what I am searching. I used a lot of philosophy book, but I can't find any answers. That's all American way. Everyone says I try too hard. Really, I want to make a lot of experience; I thought experience was good. If there is bad, don't even try. That's all I wanted to say to young people. I didn't expect I would smoke a lot like this. If there is a bad, don't even try, like racing cars, don't even try. You are going to have an accident. Is very bad. 13

You say I look like a quiet boy—but outside. Inside is very different. 14

## STUDY QUESTIONS

1. What does the first sentence of the interview suggest about Lee Ki Chuck's sense of identity? Are there signs by the end of the piece that he has begun to develop a new identity? What evidence is there that he has begun to grow up after the suicide attempts?

2. In what different ways do the opinions—or presumed opinions—of those left behind in Korea affect Lee's attitudes? his behavior? What evidence is there that Lee cares deeply about the opinions of others?

3. What is Lee's attitude toward his principal? toward his father? (The mother he mentions in paragraph 4 is really his stepmother; his mother remained in Korea.) toward authority figures more generally?

4. For Lee when he arrives, what does "America" represent? What are the values of "home"?

# Agha Shahid Ali

Originally from Kashmir (and a graduate of the University of Kashmir), Agha moved to New Delhi and then to the United States to receive his advanced degrees (M.A., University of Delhi, 1970; M.F.A., University of Arizona, 1985; Ph.D., Penn State, 1984). He has written poetry exclusively in English since the age of ten, and he now lives in Tucson, Arizona. A scholar as well as a poet, Agha is the author of *T. S. Eliot as Editor;* his first volume of poetry, *The Half-Inch Himalayas,* was published in 1987.

In the following poem from that volume, a postcard from home becomes a reminder not only of a place and its appearance but also of a range of emotions associated with a past life in a homeland that now seems very remote.

## POSTCARD FROM KASHMIR

*(for Pavan Sahgal)*

Kashmir shrinks into my mailbox,
my home a neat four by six inches.

I always loved neatness. Now I hold
the half-inch Himalayas in my hand.

This is home. And this the closest                    5
I'll ever be to home. When I return,
the colors won't be so brilliant,

the Jhelum's waters[1] so clean,
so ultramarine. My love
so overexposed.                                                    10

And my memory will be a little
out of focus, in it
a giant negative, black
and white, still undeveloped.


## STUDY QUESTIONS

1. The present in the poem quickly fades into the past and then leaps into the future. What aspects of the past seem now to be lost forever? Why, if there is to be a "return" to Kashmir later (line 6), is the postcard "the closest I'll ever be to home" (ll. 5–6)? Why is it important to the poem that the Himalayan scene is miniaturized? that it is idealized?

2. How much do we know about the SPEAKER? How does the miniaturization of his homeland lead him to think about old feelings? Why will the colors be lessened and the water not be so clean when the speaker actually does return?

3. Explain how the language of photography works in the poem. What does it mean that love, in future times, will not be "so overexposed" (l. 10)? that memory will be "out of focus" (l. 12)? "undeveloped" (l. 14)? that in it will be "a giant negative" (l. 13)?

4. What, besides a particular place, does home mean to the speaker?


# Michael Blumenthal

Born of Jewish refugee parents in 1949, Michael Blumenthal grew up in a German-speaking home in the Washington Heights section of Manhattan. He was trained as a lawyer, but since the late 1970s he has been primarily a poet, supporting himself by teaching, writing speeches, editing, and working as an arts administrator, psychotherapist, and television producer. He now teaches at Harvard. He is the author of three books of poetry, including *Laps* (1984), which won the Juniper Prize.

The following poem recalls childhood in Washington Heights through the eyes of a ten-year-old boy.

---

1. The river Jhelum runs through Kashmir and Pakistan.

# WASHINGTON HEIGHTS, 1959

Even the bad news came slowly and was afraid.
Grandmothers tapped their way up the steep hill
to Bennett Park, gradual as mealybugs along
the stem of a coleus. A pink rubber ball, some
small boy's humble playground, would roll by,                            5
and some gray girl would lift to where the mind
said step but the old legs wouldn't answer.

Trees danced their lonely dance in fields of concrete.
Each one we came to, we called: country. What grass
we knew lived by the river, a place our mothers called:          10
don't play there, it isn't safe anymore. Safety
was the day's dull wisdom, their past a net we swam
against, a high tide. Risk was small and fragile, tied
to a wave called future, sinking every laugh it came upon.

Fishing, our bait was bubble gum and daydreams,                 15
our creels filled with old beer cans wished to bass,
prophylactics weaving like white eels in a Hudson
we dreamt clean as a mountain river. Five old bottles
meant a chance to find your hero and a piece of bubble
gum besides, snow a chance to claim your arms again.            20

Childhood reading was obituaries in *Aufbau:*[1] name,
maiden name, place of birth, surviving relatives,
death the one occasion we were sure of. Black ties
meant another neighbor wouldn't be there anymore,
candles that memory would find us. Scarred bricks              25
held auditions for home plate, lines on pavement
drew a floor for dancing.

Saturday was Sabbath and the slow turned slower.
Those who couldn't carry with their arms grew heavy
with their faith. Each year, we set the table                        30
for a man who never came, ate bitter herbs,
read aloud some dreams that never quite rang true.[2]

---

1. A New York German-language newspaper.

2. Traditionally, Jews celebrate Passover each year with a *seder*, a dinner at which a place is set for the prophet Elijah, bitter herbs are eaten as a reminder of the exile in Egypt, and dreams of meeting "next year in Jerusalem" are repeated.

Constancy was Mario, tapping his Cats Paw heels to walk
on old cloth shoes stretched wide with aching. His
deep black hair turned grey with years, but the sound                    35
of hammer to rubber to steel stayed firm with a sense
of praying. Friends died and aging backs bent towards
the earth, slow and predictable as corn husks in November.
As long as the mail kept coming, we smiled, waited
for the ice truck, buried the dead, called it home.                      40

# STUDY QUESTIONS

1. The first line of the poem implies that childhood in Washington Heights was both slow and fearful. What makes it seem so slow, in retrospect, to the person remembering childhood? How does the way the poem is constructed emphasize the slowness? What aspects of childhood are especially fearful? How much of the fear involves mysterious events or unknown persons?

2. Explain in detail the image of slowness and infirmity in the description of grandmothers in the first STANZA.

3. In stanza 2, what does the "miscalling" of the two places imply about the differences between generations? What does it imply about the actual landscape? about the way fear was communicated? What does "their" in line 8 refer to? What does "their" in line 12 refer to? In what sense is the past a "net" (l. 12)? a "tide" (l. 13)?

4. Which details dramatize most fully the urban quality of "home" in the poem? What instances are there of rural images, dreams, or activities transformed into artificial substitutes? Why does it seem to the SPEAKER that the dreams mentioned in the *seder* ritual "never quite rang true" (l. 32)?

5. What images of reliability and continuity does the poem contain? What images of temporariness or loss? How secure does the speaker seem to have felt when he was a child? How is his understanding of "home" different now that he is grown? How can you tell that the poem represents an adult remembering childhood through earlier eyes? What indications are there in the poem of adult perspective?

6. How much are we told in the poem about the Washington Heights neighborhood? List all the details we are given. What were the other people who lived there like? How much a part of the neighborhood does the boy feel? What details establish his place in the neighborhood?

# Vanessa Howard

V anessa Howard wrote this poem in the sixties, when she was a teenager growing up in New York. The poem describes a sense of "home" that is stifling,
enslaved, and inescapable.

## ESCAPE THE GHETTOS OF NEW YORK

escaping the ghettos of New York
they trip
off they go into a paradise of
LSD, heroin, pot and speed
fantasy                                                    5
the ecstasy of drugs

escaping the ghettos of New York
they drink
off they go into a paradise of
wine, beer, scotch, and gin                               10
fantasy
the ecstasy of alcohol

to break through
only to return
yes, only to return to the                                15
hell of an empty wine bottle
crushed beside the wall
in anger
no little drop left
to free a straining soul                                  20
to the hell of
an empty needle or a smoked down
red all dreams gone up
in smoke

> escaping the ghettos of New York                              25
> they leave for a while
> but they always always
> return

## STUDY QUESTIONS

1. Is the poem's title advice, command, or simply statement? How can you tell?

2. The poem pictures life in "the ghettos of New York" as alternating between "paradise" (lines 3, 9) and "hell" (ll. 16, 21). Explain how the IMAGERY of the poem connects the two in order to suggest that they involve the same things. Explain fully the implications of "fantasy" (ll. 5, 11), "ecstasy" (ll. 6, 12), and "dreams" (l. 23).

3. What do the last two lines of the poem mean?

# Lance Henson

Lance Henson, a Cheyenne Indian who lives on the farm where he was reared in Oklahoma, has published ten books, the latest of which is *Another Song for America* (1987). He was raised by his grandparents in traditional culture and studied creative writing at the University of Tulsa. Many of his poems explore the inner feelings of Native Americans and suggest the mythic quality of Native American life.

In the following poem, the feelings generated by a particular transient place lead to specific memories and thoughts of a place quite different—home.

## poem near midway truck stop

> along the turner turnpike at a rest stop between
> oklahoma city and tulsa
> i feel the morning sun inch over the leaves of a small elm
> rising to the scent of sage and wildflowers i lean on one
> elbow                                                           5
>
> beyond the field the sound of cars and a lone water tower
> mark a small town

i remove the knife from under the sleeping bag
and place it in the sheath on my hip.

ho hatama hestoz na no me[1]                                    10
it is july
i imagine coffee in a pale cup on a wooden table
far from here
and look west toward home

## STUDY QUESTIONS

1. How much do we know about the SPEAKER? Why are we not told what the speaker is doing at the truck stop in Oklahoma? Why are we given so much detail about the feel, smell, and sounds of the moment?

2. What is accomplished by the sudden shift into the Cheyenne language? What contrasts are there between the actual observations and the imagined cup of coffee? What similarities exist between the experience and imagination?

# Carter Revard

Born into an Osage and white family in Oklahoma in 1931, Carter Revard—whose Indian name, Nompewathe, means "fear-inspiring"—won a Rhodes Scholarship to Oxford, earned a doctorate at Yale, and now teaches at Washington University in St. Louis. His poetry is widely published in a variety of magazines and in almost every anthology of Native American writing. His volume *Ponca War Dances* was published in 1980.

The following poem describes two very different but closely related sensuous experiences that define a wonderful feeling of richness in the universe, "between home and away."

---

1. There is a powerful trembling around me (Cheyenne). [Author's note]

# DRIVING IN OKLAHOMA

On humming rubber along this white concrete
    lighthearted between the gravities
of source and destination like a man
     halfway to the moon
    in this bubble of tuneless whistling           5
at seventy miles an hour from the windvents,
      over prairie swells rising
and falling, over the quick offramp
that drops to its underpass and the truck
     thundering beneath as I cross          10
with the country music twanging out my windows,
    I'm grooving down this highway feeling
technology is freedom's other name when
                    —a meadowlark
    comes sailing across my windshield       15
      with breast shining yellow
    and five notes pierce
       the windroar like a flash
      of nectar on mind
gone as the country music swells up and      20
     drops me wheeling down
    my notch of cement-bottomed sky
     between home and away
              and wanting
to move again through country that a bird      25
    has defined wholly with song
       and maybe next time see how
he flies so easy, when he sings.

## STUDY QUESTIONS

1. What does it mean to be "between the gravities / of source and destination" (lines 2–3)? How does this expression relate to line 23?

2. How, exactly, does the second half of the poem contradict the conclusion that "technology is freedom's other name" (l. 13)?

3. What formal features in the poem contribute to the sense of speed: line divisions? lack of punctuation? word choices? Which word choices seem to you particularly

important to the rapid pace of the first part of the poem? Explain how the pacing of the poem is controlled.

4. How many different sounds does the poem describe? Which visual IMAGES are most important to the effects of the poem?

5. Which sounds in the poem are the sounds of "home"? Which are the sounds of "away"?

6. Explain how the last two lines sum up the poem's ACTION and connect its THEMES.

# Neil Bissoondath

Neil Bissoondath was born in Trinidad in 1955 into a family who originally came to the West Indies from India. His is a famous literary family: he is the nephew of V. S. and Shiva Naipaul, both well-known writers. A volume of Bissoondath's stories, *Digging Up the Mountains*, was published in 1986; he now lives in Toronto, having moved there in 1973 to study French at York University.

In the story below, an idealistic young businessman returns triumphantly to the Caribbean island of his birth but discovers that his return is interpreted by his old friends as stupidity and failure.

## THERE ARE A LOT OF WAYS TO DIE

It was still drizzling when Joseph clicked the final padlocks on the door. The name-plate, home-painted with squared gold letters on a black background and glazed all over with transparent varnish to lend a professional tint, was flecked with water and dirt. He took a crumpled handkerchief from his back pocket and carefully wiped the lettering clean: JOSEPH HEAVEN: CARPET AND RUG INSTALLATIONS. The colon had been his idea and he had put it in over his wife's objections. He felt that it provided a natural flow from his name, that it showed a certain reliability. His wife, in the scornful voice she reserved for piercing his pretensions, had said, "That's all very well and good for Toronto, but you think people here care about that kind of thing?" But she was the one people accused of having airs, not him. As far as he was concerned, the colon was merely good business; and as the main beneficiary of the profits, she should learn to keep her mouth shut.

He had forgotten to pick up his umbrella from just inside the door where he had put it that morning. Gingerly, he extended his upturned palm, feeling the droplets, warm and wet, like newly spilled blood. He decided they were too light to justify reopening the shop, always something of an event because of the many locks and chains. This was another thing she didn't like, his obsession, as she called it, with security. She wanted a more open storefront, with windows and showcases and well-dressed mannequins smiling blankly at the street. She said, "It look just like every other store around here, just a wall and a door. It have nothing to catch the eye." He replied, "You want windows and showcases? What we going to show? My tools? The tacks? The cutter?" Besides, the locks were good for business, not a week went by without a robbery in the area. Displaying the tools would be a blatant invitation, and a recurrent nightmare had developed in which one of his cutters was stolen and used in a murder.

Across the glistening street, so narrow after the generosity of those he had known for six years, the clothes merchants were standing disconsolately in front of their darkened stores, hands in pockets, whistling and occasionally examining the grey skies for the brightening that would signal the end of the rain and the appearance of shoppers. They stared blankly at him. One half-heartedly jabbed his finger at a stalactitic line of umbrellas and dusty rain-coats, inviting a purchase. Joseph showed no interest. The merchant shrugged and resumed his tuneless whistling, a plaintive sound from between clenched front teeth.

Joseph had forgotten how sticky the island could be when it rained. The heat, it seemed, never really disappeared during the night. Instead, it retreated just a few inches underground, only to emerge with the morning rain, condensing, filling the atmosphere with steam. It put the lie to so much he had told his Canadian friends about the island. The morning rain wasn't as refreshing as he'd recalled it and the steam had left his memory altogether. How could he have sworn that the island experienced no humidity? Why had he, in all honesty, recalled tender tropical breezes when the truth, as it now enveloped him, was the exact, stifling opposite? Climate was not so drastically altered, only memory.

He walked to the end of the street, his shirt now clinging to his shoulders. The sidewalk, dark and pitted, seemed to glide by under his feet, as if it were itself moving. He squinted, feeling the folds of flesh bunching up at the corner of his eyes, and found he could fuzzily picture himself on Bloor Street, walking past the stores and the bakeries and the delicatessens pungent with Eastern European flavors, the hazy tops of buildings at Bloor and Yonge far away in the distance. He could even conjure up the sounds of a Toronto summer: the cars, the voices, the rumble of the subway under the feet as it swiftly glided towards downtown.

Joseph shook himself and opened his eyes, not without disappointment. He was having this hallucination too often, for too long. He was ashamed of it and couldn't confess it even to his wife. And he mistrusted it, too: might not even this more recent memory also be fooling him, as the other had done?

Was it really possible to see the tops of buildings at Yonge from Bathurst? He wanted to ask his wife, pretending it was merely a matter of memory, but she would see through this to his longing and puncture him once more with that voice. She would call him a fool and not be far wrong. Were not two dislocations enough in one man's lifetime? Would not yet a third prove him a fool?

Their return had been jubilant. Friends and relatives treated it as a victory, seeking affirmation of the correctness of their cloistered life on the island, the return a defeat for life abroad. The first weeks were hectic, parties, dinners, get-togethers. Joseph felt like a curiosity, an object not of reverence but of silent ridicule, his the defeat, theirs the victory. The island seemed to close in around him.

They bought a house in the island's capital. The town was not large. Located at the extreme north-western edge of the island, having hardly expanded from the settlement originally established by Spanish adventurers as a depot in their quest for mythic gold, the town looked forever to the sea, preserving its aura of a way-station, a point at which to pause in brief respite from the larger search.

At first, Joseph had tried to deny this aspect of the town, for the town was the island and, if the island were no more than a way-station, a stopover from which nothing important ever emerged, then to accept this life was to accept second place. A man who had tasted of first could accept second only with delusion: his wife had taken on airs, he had painted his black-and-gold sign.

Then the hallucination started, recreating Bloor Street, vividly recalling the minute details of daily life. He caught himself reliving the simple things: buying milk, removing a newspaper from the box, slipping a subway token into the slot, sitting in a park. A chill would run through him when he realized they were remembrances of things past, possibly lost forever. The recollected civility of life in Toronto disturbed him, it seemed so distant. He remembered what a curious feeling of well-being had surged through him whenever he'd given directions to a stranger. Each time was like an affirmation of stability. Here, in an island so small that two leisurely hours in a car would reveal all, no one asked for directions, no one was a stranger. You couldn't claim the island: it claimed you.

The street on which their house stood used to be known all over the island. It was viewed with a twinge of admired notoriety and was thought of with the same fondness with which the islanders regarded the government ministers and civil servants who had fled the island with pilfered cash: an awed admiration, a flawed love. The cause of this attention was a house, a mansion in those days, erected, in the popular lore, by a Venezuelan general who, for reasons unknown, had exiled himself to a life of darkly rumored obscurity on the island. As far as Joseph knew, no one had ever actually seen the general: even his name, Pacheco, had been assumed. Or so it was claimed; no one had ever bothered to check.

Eventually the house became known as Pacheco House, and the street as Pacheco Street. It was said that the house, deserted for as long as anyone could remember and now falling into neglect, had been mentioned passingly in a book by an Englishman who had been looking into famous houses of the region. It was the island's first mention in a book other than a history text, the island's first mention outside the context of slavery.

The house had become the butt of schoolboys' frustration. On their way home after school, Joseph and his friends would detour to throw stones at the windows. In his memory, the spitting clank of shattering glass sounded distant and opaque. They had named each window for a teacher, thus adding thrust and enthusiasm to their aim. The largest window, high on the third floor—the attic, he now knew, in an island which had no attics—they named LeNoir, after the priest who was the terror of all students unblessed by fair skin or athletic ability. They were more disturbed by the fact that the priest himself was black; this seemed a greater sin than his choice of vocation. They had never succeeded in breaking the LeNoir window. Joseph might have put this down to divine protection had he not lost his sense of religion early on. It was a simple event: the priest at his last try at communion had showered him with sour breath the moment the flesh of Christ slipped onto Joseph's tongue. Joseph, from then on, equated the wafer with decaying flesh.

The LeNoir window went unscathed for many years and was still intact when, after the final exams, Joseph left the island for what he believed to be forever.

The raindrops grew larger, making a plopping sound on the sidewalk. A drop landed on his temple and cascaded down his cheek. He rubbed at it, feeling the prickly stubble he hadn't bothered to shave that morning.

Pacheco House was just up ahead, the lower floors obscured by a jungle of trees and bush, the garden overgrown and thickening to impenetrability. Above the treeline, the walls—a faded pink, pockmarked by the assault of stones and mangoes—had begun disintegrating, the thin plaster falling away in massive chunks to reveal ordinary grey brick underneath. The remaining plaster was criss-crossed by cracks and fissures created by age and humidity.

During his schooldays, the grounds had been maintained by the government. The house had been considered a tourist attraction and was displayed in brochures and on posters. An island-wide essay competition had been held, "The Mystery of Pacheco House," and the winning essay, of breathless prose linked by words like *tropical* and *verdant* and *lush* and *exotic*, was used as the text of a special brochure. But no tourists came. The mystery withered away to embarrassment. The government quietly gave the house up. The Jaycees, young businessmen who bustled about in the heat with the added burden of jackets and ties, offered to provide funds for the upkeep. The offer was refused with a shrug by the Ministry of Tourism, with inexplicable murmurings of "colonial horrors" by the Ministry of Culture. The house was left to its ghosts.

From the street Joseph could see the LeNoir window, still intact and dirt-streaked. He was surprised that it still seemed to mock him. 18

Joseph had asked his nephew, a precocious boy who enjoyed exhibiting his scattered knowledge of French and Spanish and who laughed at Joseph's clumsy attempts to resurrect the bits of language he had learnt in the same classes, often from the same teachers, if the boys still threw stones at Pacheco House. No, his nephew had informed him, after school they went to the sex movies or, in the case of the older boys, to the whorehouses. Joseph, stunned, had asked no more questions. 19

The rain turned perceptibly to a deluge, the thick, warm drops penetrating his clothes and running in rivulets down his back and face. The wild trees and plants of the Pacheco garden nodded and drooped, leaves glistening dully in the half-light. The pink walls darkened as the water socked into them, eating at the plaster. The LeNoir window was black; he remembered some claimed to have seen a white-faced figure in army uniform standing there at night. The story had provided mystery back then, a real haunted house, and on a rainy afternoon schoolboys could feel their spines tingle as they aimed their stones. 20

On impulse Joseph searched the ground for a stone. He saw only pebbles; the gravel verge had long been paved over. Already the sidewalk had cracked in spots and little shoots of grass had fought their way out, like wedges splitting a boulder. 21

He continued walking, oblivious of the rain. 22

Several cars were parked in the driveway of his house. His wife's friends were visiting. They were probably in the living room drinking coffee and eating pastries from Marcel's and looking through *Vogue* pattern books. Joseph made for the garage so he could enter, unnoticed, through the kitchen door. Then he thought, "Why the hell?" He put his hands into his pockets—his money was soaked and the movement of his fingers ripped the edge off a bill—and calmly walked in through the open front door. 23

His wife was standing in front of the fake fireplace she had insisted on bringing from Toronto. The dancing lights cast multicolored hues on her caftan. She almost dropped her coffee cup when she saw him. Her friends, perturbed, stared at him from their chairs which they had had grouped around the fireplace. 24

His wife said impatiently, "Joseph, what are you doing here?" 25

He said, "I live here." 26

She said, "And work?" 27

He said, "None of the boys show up this morning." 28

"So you just drop everything?" 29

"I postponed today's jobs. I couldn't do all the work by myself." 30

She put her cup down on the mantelpiece. "Go dry yourself off. You wetting the floor." 31

Her friend Arlene said, "Better than the bed."                          32

They all laughed. His wife said, "He used to do that when he was a       33
little boy, not so, Joseph?"

She looked at her friends and said, "You know, we having so much         34
trouble finding good workers. Joseph already fire three men. Looks like we're
going to have to fire all these now."

Arlene said, "Good help so hard to find these days."                     35

His wife said, "These people like that, you know, girl. Work is the last  36
thing they want to do."

Arlene said, "They 'fraid they going to melt if rain touch their skin."   37

His wife turned to him. "You mean not one out of twelve turned up this    38
morning?"

"Not one."                                                               39

Arlene, dark and plump, sucked her teeth and moved her tongue around,    40
pushing at her cheeks and making a plopping sound.

Joseph said, "Stop that. You look like a monkey."                        41

His wife and Arlene stared at him in amazement. The others sipped        42
their coffee or gazed blankly at the fireplace.

Arlene said witheringly, "I don't suffer fools gladly, Joseph."          43

He said, "Too bad. You must hate being alone."                           44

His wife said, "Joseph!"                                                 45

He said, "I better go dry off." Still dripping, he headed for the bed-   46
room. At the door he paused and added, "People should be careful when
they talking about other people. You know, glass houses . . ." He was suddenly exhausted: what was the point? They all knew Arlene's story. She had
once been a maid whose career was rendered transient by rain and imagined
illness; she had been no different from his employees. Her fortune had
improved only because her husband—who was referred to behind his back
as a "sometimes worker" because sometimes he worked and sometimes he
didn't—had been appointed a minister without portfolio in the government.
He had lost the nickname because now he never worked, but he had gained
a regular cheque, a car and a chauffeur, and the tainted respectability of
political appointment.

Joseph slammed the bedroom door and put his ear to the keyhole: there    47
was a lot of throat-clearing; pages of a *Vogue* pattern book rustled. Finally his
wife said, "Come look at this pattern." Voices oohed and ahhed and cooed.
Arlene said, "Look at this one." He kicked the door and threw his wet shirt
on the bed.

The rain had stopped and the sky had cleared a little. His wife and her  48
friends were still in the living room. It was not yet midday. His clothes had
left a damp patch on the bed, on his side, and he knew it would still be wet
at bedtime. He put on a clean set of clothes and sat on the bed, rubbing the
dampness, as if this would make it disappear. He reached up and drew the
curtains open; grey, drifting sky, vegetation drooping and wet, like wash on

a line; the very top of Pacheco House, galvanized iron rusted through, so thin in parts that a single drop of rain might cause a great chunk to go crashing into the silence of the house. Except maybe for the bats, disintegration was probably the only sound now to be heard in Pacheco House. The house was like a dying man who could hear his heart ticking to a stop.

Joseph sensed that something was missing. The rainflies, delicate ant-like creatures with brown wings but no sting. Defenceless, wings attached to their bodies by the most fragile of links, they fell apart at the merest touch. After a particularly heavy rainfall, detached wings, almost transparent, would litter the ground and cling to moist feet like lint to wool. As a child, he used to pull the wings off and place the crippled insect on a table, where he could observe it crawling desperately around, trying to gain the air. Sometimes he would gingerly tie the insect to one end of a length of thread, release it, and control its flight. In all this he saw no cruelty. His friends enjoyed crushing them, or setting them on fire, or sizzling them with the burning end of a cigarette. Joseph had only toyed with the insects; he could never bring himself to kill one.

There was not a rainfly in sight. The only movement was that of the clouds and dripping water. In the town, the insects had long, and casually, been eradicated. He felt the loss.

He heard his wife call her friends to lunch. He half expected to hear his name but she ignored him: he might have not been there. He waited a few more minutes until he was sure they had all gone into the dining room, then slipped out the front door.

Water was gurgling in the drains, rushing furiously through the iron gratings into the sewers. In the street, belly up, fur wet and clinging, lay a dead dog, a common sight. Drivers no longer even bothered to squeal their tires.

Joseph walked without direction, across streets and through different neighborhoods, passing people and being passed by cars. He took in none of it. His thoughts were thousands of miles away, on Bloor Street, on Yonge Street, among the stalls of Kensington Market.

He was at National Square when the rain once more began to pound down. He found a dry spot under the eaves of a store and stood, arms folded, watching the rain and the umbrellas and the raincoats. A man hurried past him, a handkerchief tied securely to his head the only protection from the rain. It was a useless gesture, and reminded Joseph of his grandmother's warnings to him never to go out at night without a hat to cover his head, "because of the dew."

National Square was the busiest part of town. Cars constantly sped by, horns blaring, water splashing. After a few minutes a donkey cart loaded with fresh coconuts trundled by on its way to the Savannah, a wide, flat park just north of the town where the horse races were held at Christmas. A line of impatient cars crept along behind the donkey cart, the leaders bobbing in and out of line in search of an opportunity to pass.

Joseph glanced at his watch. It was almost twelve-thirty. He decided to [56] have something to eat. Just around the corner was a cheap restaurant frequented by office workers from the government buildings and foreign banks which enclosed the square. Holding his hands over his head, Joseph dashed through the rain to the restaurant.

Inside was shadowed, despite the cobwebby fluorescent lighting. The [57] walls were lined with soft-drink advertisements and travel posters. One of the posters showed an interminable stretch of bleached beach overhung with languid coconut-tree branches. Large, cursive letters read: Welcome To The Sunny Caribbean. The words were like a blow to the nerves. Joseph felt like ripping the poster up.

A row of green metal tables stretched along one wall of the rectangular [58] room. A few customers sat in loosened ties and shirt-sleeves, sipping beer and smoking and conversing in low tones. At the far end, at a table crowded with empty bottles and an overflowing ashtray, Joseph noticed a familiar face. It was lined and more drawn than when he'd known it, and the eyes had lost their sparkle of intelligence; but he was certain he was not mistaken. He went up to the man. He said, "Frankie?"

Frankie looked up slowly, unwillingly, emerging from a daydream. He [59] said, "Yes?" Then he brightened. "Joseph? Joseph!" He sprang to his feet, knocking his chair back. He grasped Joseph's hand. "How you doing, man? It's been years and years. How you doing?" He pushed Joseph into a chair and loudly ordered two beers. He lit a cigarette. His hand shook.

Joseph said, "You smoking now, Frankie?" [60]

"For years, man. You?" [61]

Joseph shook his head. [62]

Frankie said, "But you didn't go to Canada? I thought somebody tell [63] me . . ."

"Went and came back. One of those things. How about you? How the [64] years treat you?"

"I work in a bank. Loan officer." [65]

"Good job?" [66]

"Not bad." [67]

Joseph sipped his beer. The situation wasn't right. There should have [68] been so much to say, so much to hear. Frankie used to be his best friend. He was the most intelligent person Joseph had ever known. This was the last place he would have expected to find him. Frankie had dreamt of university and professorship, and it had seemed, back then, that university and professorship awaited him.

Frankie took a long pull on his cigarette, causing the tube to crinkle and [69] flatten. He said, "What was Canada like?" Before Joseph could answer, he added, "You shouldn't have come back. Why did you come back? A big mistake." He considered the cigarette.

The lack of emotion in Frankie's voice distressed Joseph. It was the voice [70] of a depleted man. He said, "It was time."

Frankie leaned back in his chair and slowly blew smoke rings at Joseph. 71
He seemed to be contemplating the answer. He said, "What were you doing
up there?"

"I had a business. Installing carpets and rugs. Is a good little business. 72
My partner looking after it now."

Frankie looked away, towards the door. He said nothing. 73

Joseph said, "You ever see anybody from school?" 74

Frankie waved his cigarette. "Here and there. You know, Raffique dead. 75
And Jonesy and Dell."

Joseph recalled the faces: boys, in school uniform. Death was not an 76
event he could associate with them. "How?"

"Raffique in a car accident. Jonesy slit his wrists over a woman. Dell 77
. . . who knows? There are a lot of ways to die. They found him dead in the
washroom of a cinema. A girl was with him. Naked. She wasn't dead. She's
in the madhouse now."

"And the others?" Joseph couldn't contemplate the death roll. It seemed 78
to snuff out a little bit of his own life.

"The others? Some doing something, some doing nothing. It don't mat- 79
ter."

Joseph said, "You didn't go to university." 80

Frankie laughed. "No, I didn't." 81

Joseph waited for an explanation. Frankie offered none. 82

Frankie said, "Why the hell you come back from Canada? And none of 83
this 'It was time' crap."

Joseph rubbed his face, feeling the stubble, tracing the fullness of his 84
chin. "I had some kind of crazy idea about starting a business, creating jobs,
helping my people."

Frankie laughed mockingly. 85

Joseph said, "I should have known better. We had a party before we 86
left. A friend asked me the same question, why go back. I told him the same
thing. He said it was bullshit and that I just wanted to make a lot of money
and live life like a holiday. We quarreled and I threw him out. The next
morning he called to apologize. He was crying. He said he was just jealous."
Joseph sipped the beer, lukewarm and sweating. "Damn fool."

Frankie laughed again. "I don't believe this. You mean to tell me you 87
had the courage to leave *and* the stupidity to come back?" He slapped the
table, rocking it and causing an empty beer bottle to fall over. "You always
used to be the idealist, Joseph. I was more realistic. And less courageous.
That's why I never left."

"Nobody's called me an idealist for years." The word seemed more 88
mocking than Frankie's laugh.

Frankie said, "And now you're stuck back here for good." He shook his 89
head vigorously, drunkenly. "A big, idealistic mistake, Joseph."

"I'm not stuck here." He was surprised at how much relief the thought 90
brought him. "I can go back any time I want."

"Well, go then." Frankie's voice was slurred, and it held more than a hint of aggressiveness.

Joseph shook his head. He glanced at his watch. He said, "It's almost one. Don't you have to get back to work?"

Frankie called for another beer. "The bank won't fall down if I'm not there."

"We used to think the world would fall down if not for us."

"That was a long time ago. We were stupid." Frankie lit another cigarette. His hand shook badly. "In this place, is nonsense to think the world, the world out there, have room for you."

Joseph said, "You could have been a historian. History was your best subject, not so?"

"Yeah."

"You still interested in history?"

"Off and on. I tried to write a book. Nobody wanted to publish it."

"Why not?"

"Because our history doesn't lead anywhere. It's just a big, black hole. Nobody's interested in a book about a hole."

"You know anything about Pacheco House?"

"Pacheco House? A little."

"What?"

"The man wasn't a Venezuelan general. He was just a crazy old man from Argentina. He was rich. I don't know why he came here. He lived in the house for a short time and then he died there, alone. They found his body about two weeks later, rottening and stinking. They say he covered himself with old cocoa bags, even his head. I think he knew he was going to die and after all that time alone he couldn't stand the thought of anyone seeing him. Crazy, probably. They buried him in the garden and put up a little sign. And his name wasn't really Pacheco either, people just called him that. They got it from a cowboy film. I've forgot what his real name was but it don't matter. Pacheco's as good as any other."

"That's all? What about the house itself?"

"That's all. The house is just a house. Nothing special." Frankie popped the half-finished cigarette into his beer bottle, it sizzled briefly. He added, "R.I.P. Pacheco, his house and every damn thing else." He put another cigarette between his lips, allowing it to droop to his chin, pushing his upper lip up and out, as if his teeth were deformed. His hands shook so badly he couldn't strike the match. His eyes met Joseph's.

Joseph couldn't hold the gaze. He was chilled. He said, "I have to go."

Frankie waved him away.

Joseph pushed back his chair. Frankie looked past him with bloodshot eyes, already lost in the confusion of his mind.

Joseph, indicating the travel poster, offered the barman five dollars for it. The man, fat, with an unhealthy greasiness, said, "No way."

Joseph offered ten dollars.

The barman refused. 113
Joseph understood: it was part of the necessary lie. 114

Grey clouds hung low and heavy in the sky. The hills to the north, their 115
lower half crowded with the multicolored roofs of shacks, poverty plain from
even so great a distance, were shrouded in mist, as if an inferno had recently
burned out and the smoke not yet cleared away.

Some of his workers lived there, in tiny, crowded one-room shacks, 116
with water sometimes a quarter-mile away at a mossy stand-pipe. There was
a time when the sight of these shacks could move Joseph to pity. They were,
he believed, his main reason for returning to the island. He really had said,
"I want to help my people." Now the sentence, with its pomposity, its naive-
ty, was just an embarrassing memory, like the early life of the minister's
wife.

But he knew that wasn't all. He had expected a kind of fame, a continual 117
welcome, the prodigal son having made good, having acquired skills, returning home to share the wealth, to spread the knowledge. He had anticipated
a certain uniqueness but this had been thwarted. Everyone knew someone
else who had returned from abroad—from England, from Canada, from the
States. He grew to hate the stock phrases people dragged out: "No place like
home, this island is a true Paradise, life's best here." The little lies of self-
doubt and fear.

The gate to Pacheco House was chained but there was no lock: a casual 118
locking-up, an abandonment. The chain, thick and rusted, slipped easily to
the ground, leaving a trace of gritty oxide on his fingertips. He couldn't push
the gate far; clumps of grass, stems long and tapering to a lancet point, blocked
it at the base. He squeezed through the narrow opening, the concrete pillar
rough and tight on his back, the iron gate leaving a slash of rust on his shirt.
Inside, wild grass, wet and glistening, enveloped his legs up to his knees.
The trees were further back, thick and ponderous, unmoving, lending the
garden the heavy stillness of jungle.

Walking, pushing through the grass, took a little effort. The vegetation 119
sought not so much to prevent intrusion as to hinder it, to encumber it with
a kind of tropical lassitude. Joseph raised his legs high, free of the tangle of
vines and roots and thorns, and brought his boots crashing down with each
step, crushing leaves into juicy blobs of green and brown, startling underground colonies of ants into frenzied scrambling. Ahead of him, butterflies,
looking like edges of an artist's canvas, fluttered away, and crickets, their
wings beating like pieces of stiff silk one against the other, buzzed from tall
stalk to tall stalk, narrowly avoiding the grasshoppers which also sought escape.
A locust, as long as his hand and as fat, sank its claws into his shirt, just
grazing the surface of his skin. He flicked a finger powerfully at it, knocking
off its head; the rest of the body simply relaxed and fell off.

Once past the trees, Joseph found himself at the house. The stone foun- 120
dation, he noticed, was covered in green slime and the wall, the monotony

of which was broken only by a large cavity which must once have been a window, stripped of all color. He made his way to the cavity and peered through it into the half-darkness of a large room. He carefully put one leg through, feeling for the floor. The boards creaked badly but held.

The room was a disappointment. He didn't know what he had expected— he hadn't really thought about it—but its emptiness engendered an atmosphere of uncommon despair. He felt it was a room that had always been empty, a room that had never been peopled with emotion or sound, like a dried-up old spinster abandoned at the edge of life. He could smell the pungency of recently disturbed vegetation but he didn't know whether it came from him or through the gaping window. 121

He made his way to another room, the floorboards creaking under the wary tread of his feet; just another empty space, characterless, almost shapeless in its desertion. A flight of stairs led upwards, to the second floor and yet another empty room, massive, dusty, cobwebs tracing crazy geometric patterns on the walls and the ceiling. In the corners the floorboards had begun to warp. He wondered why all the doors had been removed and by whom. Or had the house ever had doors? Might it not have been always a big, open, empty house, with rooms destined to no purpose, with a façade that promised mystery but an interior that took away all hope? 122

He had hoped to find something of Pacheco's, the merest testament to his having existed, a bed maybe, or a portrait, or even one line of graffiti. But were it not for the structure itself, a vacuous shell falling steadily to ruin, and the smudges of erroneous public fantasy fading like the outer edges of a dream, Pacheco might never have existed. Whatever relics might have been preserved by the government had long been carted away, probably by the last workmen, those who had so cavalierly slipped the chain around the gate, putting a period to a life. 123

Joseph walked around the room, his footsteps echoing like drumbeats. Each wall had a window of shattered glass and he examined the view from each. Jumbled vegetation, the jungle taking hold in this one plot of earth in the middle of the town: it was the kind of view that would have been described in the travel brochures as *lush* and *tropical*, two words he had grown to hate. Looking through the windows, recalling the manicured grounds of his youth, he felt confined, isolated, a man in an island on an island. He wondered why anyone would pay a lot of money to visit such a place. The answer came to him: for the tourist, a life was not to be constructed here. The tourist sought no more than an approximation of adventure; there was safety in a return ticket and foreign passport. 124

There was no way to get to the attic, where the LeNoir window was. Another disappointment: the object of all that youthful energy was nothing more than an aperture to a boxed-in room, airless and musty with age and probably dank with bat mess. 125

He made his way back down the stairs and out the gaping front door. The air was hot and sticky and the smell of vegetation, acrid in the humidity, was almost overpowering. 126

Frankie had said that Pacheco was buried in the garden and that a marker   127
had been erected. Joseph knew there was no hope of finding it. Everything
was overgrown: the garden, the flowers, the driveway that had once existed,
Pacheco's grave, Pacheco himself, the mysterious South American whose last
act was to lose his name and his life in sterile isolation.

Joseph began making his way back to the gate. Over to the left he could   128
see the path he had made when going in, the grass flat and twisted, twigs
broken and limp, still dripping from the morning rain. He felt clammy, and
steamy perspiration broke out on his skin.

At the gate, he stopped and turned around for a last look at the house:   129
he saw it for what it was, a deceptive shell that played on the mind. He
looked around for something to throw. The base of the gate-pillars was cracked
and broken and moss had begun eating its way to the centre. He broke off a
piece of the concrete and flung it at the LeNoir window. The glass shattered,
scattering thousands of slivers into the attic and onto the ground below.

His wife wasn't home when he returned. The house was dark and silent.   130
Coffee cups and plates with half-eaten pastries lay on the side-tables. The
false fireplace had been switched off. On the mantelpiece, propped against
his wife's lipstick-stained cup, was a notepad with a message: "Have gone
out for the evening with Arlene. We have the chauffeur and the limo coz
Brian's busy in a cabinet meeting. Don't know what time I'll be back." She
hadn't bothered to sign it.

He ripped the page from the notepad: he hated the word "coz" and the   131
word "limo" and he felt a special revulsion for "Arlene" and "Brian," ficti-
tious names assumed with the mantle of social status. As a transient domestic, Arlene had been called Thelma, the name scribbled on her birth certificate,
and Brian's real name was Balthazar. Joseph avoided the entire issue by simply referring to them as the Minister and the Minister's Wife. The sarcasm
was never noticed.

He took the notepad and a pencil and sat down. He wrote *Dear* then   132
crossed it out. He threw the page away and started again. He drew a circle,
then a triangle, then a square: the last disappointment, it was the most difficult act. Finally, in big square letters, he wrote, *I am going back.* He put the
pad back on the mantelpiece, switched on the fireplace lights, and sat staring
into their synchronized dance.

## STUDY QUESTIONS

1. What reasons does the NARRATOR give for having returned to the island? What do
   others assume about his reasons for returning? What other "reasons" are implied
   by the story?

2. Describe Joseph's CHARACTER. Which memories of his childhood mean most to
   him? What does he care about most in his present life? What memories of Toronto

does he cherish most? What characteristics in his friends does he care most about? How does he feel about his wife's life-style? What bothers him most about the habits of her friends? What bothers him most about their values?

3. What does the episode in which he returns to his house unannounced demonstrate about Joseph's values? about his degree of success? about his attitudes toward the people on the island? Why does he dislike Arlene so intensely?

4. How much do we know about Joseph's marriage? What strategies does the story use to undermine Joseph's wife? Which of her characteristics are particularly objectionable? On what sorts of values does the marriage seem to be based?

5. Explain Joseph's "hallucinations" about the fashionable areas of Toronto. How do his memories of his childhood relate to his feelings about Toronto? How does his sense of Pacheco House relate to his idea of Toronto? How does his discovery of the "real" history of Pacheco House relate to the main THEME of the story? to Joseph's other discoveries about his beliefs and illusions? How would you state the theme of the story?

6. What do the fates of Joseph's boyhood friends have to do with his sense of himself now? What does Joseph's "memory," when he lived in Toronto, of Caribbean weather have to do with his character? with his ideas of "home"? with his values? with his ability to handle the implied criticisms of his friends?

7. What does the chance encounter with Frankie "prove" to Joseph about his memories? about his values? about his self-perceptions?

8. Where is "home" to Joseph? What characteristics of home are most important in his scheme of values? Does his idea of home change during the story? Does his sense of values change?

9. What does the apparent permanence of "LeNoir" mean to Joseph when he first mentions his childhood adventures at Pacheco House? What does the breaking of the window seem to mean to Joseph once his illusions begin to break? How do the various details that Joseph observes during his invasion of Pacheco House help him to define his changing notion of himself?

10. How critical is the story of island habits and practices? What kinds of behavior are criticized most heavily? Does the story sympathize with Joseph's idealism? make fun of it? regard it as unrealistic? How do you feel about Joseph by the end of the story? What strategies does the author use to make you feel that way? What word best describes the attitude of the author toward Joseph? What word best describes the TONE of the story?

11. How important to the story's effects is the rain during Joseph's return home? How important is the heat? Describe the effect upon the story's MEANING of its time SETTING. In what ways is the remembered time in Toronto different in quality?

12. What values does Canada come to stand for in the story? What values does the island stand for? What values does each of the characters stand for? How important to the story is Joseph's profession?

13. What does the title of the story mean?

# Elena Padilla

E ducated at the Universities of Puerto Rico and Chicago and at Columbia University, Elena Padilla is professor of public administration at New York University.

The following selection, the final chapter from Padilla's 1958 study *Up from Puerto Rico*, describes how Puerto Ricans who come to the U.S. mainland sometimes look back to the island as "home" and sometimes come to think of it as totally foreign, having altogether adopted their new place and its habits and values.

## MIGRANTS: TRANSIENTS OR SETTLERS?

Many Hispanos see their lives and those of their children as unfolding in this country. To them, Puerto Rico is something of the past, and for many of the children who are growing up or have grown up in the United States, Puerto Rico is less than an echo; it is a land they have never visited, a "foreign country." Some migrants consciously decide at some point or other to make their homes here, to stay in this country permanently, never again turning back to look at Puerto Rico. These are to be found even among recent migrants. They are the people who view their future as being tied up with whatever life in New York may offer. We can call these Hispanos settlers, and can distinguish them from transients or those who regard their future life as gravitating toward Puerto Rico and who hope to return to live there later on, after their children have grown up or when they have enough savings to buy a house or start a business.

Settlers who have migrated to New York as adults are those who have lost or who give little importance to their relationships with their home towns, their friends and relatives who are still in Puerto Rico or are recent migrants to New York. They have cut off their emotional ties with the homeland, but they may still have significant interpersonal relationships with their kin and within cliques that may consist largely of persons from their own home town who are residents of New York. The settler fulfills or expects to fulfill his social needs in relation to living in New York.

One sort of settler has in his formative years moved away from his home    3
town, rural or urban, in Puerto Rico to another town or city in the island
itself. He started to break away from the primary relations and bonds of his
home town then. By the time he comes to New York, he has already experienced life situations in which primary groups derived from his home town
contexts have no longer operated for him, in which he has developed new
social bonds, wherever he may have been. The primary group relationships
of this kind of settler lack the continuity and history of those of the settler
who, throughout his life, whether in Puerto Rico or New York, has been
able to continue depending and relying on persons known to him for many
years.

The consequent social adjustments that the settlers here have made are    4
the outcome of a gradual process of adaptation to living in New York, and of
recognizing that home, friends, and other interests are here and not in Puerto
Rico. The settler may be oriented within the ethnic group of Puerto Ricans
in New York, partially by his participation in the cliques and other small
groups of people from his home town and in those of his New York neighbors. But the one who has lost his primary ties with a home town and has
been exposed to a greater variety of group experiences in Puerto Rico through
moving about there is likely to become involved in New York in groups and
cliques that are not derived from any particular home town context. The
kinds of adjustments he can make to these changing group situations is related
to his own background experiences as a migrant in Puerto Rico itself. There
he may have reacted to and resolved the social stresses of the uprooting he
underwent as a migrant, acquiring as a result the social techniques for making it easier to establish satisfactory social relationships outside of home town
and family settings.

The migrant who is essentially a transient, on the other hand, still main-    5
tains ties with the homeland: he has a strong feeling of having a country in
Puerto Rico, a national identity there, and there he has friends and relatives
whom he writes, visits, and can rely upon. "If things get bad" (si las cosas se
ponen malas), he can go back to Puerto Rico and get sympathy and help from
those he grew up with. The transient migrants can be expected to feel obli-
gated to their Puerto Rican friends and relatives, should these come to New
York. The settler, on the other hand, is likely to say that he will "not return
to Puerto Rico even if I have to eat stones in New York," and he will feel
less bound to friends and relatives left in the island.

But becoming a settler does not necessarily involve a conscious decision.    6
Transients may change into settlers as life orientations and social relations
that are satisfactory and meaningful to them become part of their life in New
York. The fundamental difference between settlers and transients is that the
settler's life is organized in New York, while that of the transient is both in
New York and in Puerto Rico.

In New York the lives of Puerto Ricans must, obviously, undergo pro-    7
found changes. For those who learn American life in a slum like Eastville,

the experience is one thing. For Puerto Ricans who were in better circumstances and had better life-chances in the island, it is another: they can begin life in New York as members of the middle class and avoid the particular cultural and social difficulties that beset the residents of Eastville. Yet all have their difficulties. Many overcome them. Many Eastvillers have made their way out of the slum into satisfactory fulfillment of their aspirations for themselves and their children. Others have returned to Puerto Rico.

One of the matters that concern Eastville Puerto Ricans is what has happened and is happening to Puerto Ricans in New York. Among migrants, social and cultural changes among Hispanos are a conscious preoccupation. They see the results of change in their own lives and in those of their friends. It is on this basis that they evaluate social behavior. Their awareness also reflects the conflicting values, orientations, and ambivalence of New York Hispanos. **8**

True, old migrants and Hispanos who have grown up in New York regard recent migrants as representing a departure from their culture and as being socially inferior; on the other hand, recent migrants, in turn, express discontent with the ways Hispanos "are"—behave—in this country. George Espino, a New York–born man of Puerto Rican parents, voiced a sentiment frequently heard from others who like himself have grown up in New York: "The Puerto Ricans that are coming over today, well, they're the most hated people . . . the most hated people." Migrants, particularly those who have come as adults, contrast and evaluate the changes they experienced in their lives in Puerto Rico with those they are experiencing in New York. To them, changes here in family life, in the expectancies of what family members can demand of each other, in the ways children are brought up, in marital behavior, and in the behavior of men, women, and children—all these factors that govern daily life—are of concern. Migrants are conscious of these changes and speak of how they have something to do both with modern life and with living in New York. Some of these changes are acceptable and "good," while others are disapproved of and considered "bad." **9**

Migrants write of their experiences in New York, tell of them on visits to Puerto Rico, or show in their behavior the new ways they have adopted. In Puerto Rico some of these types of behavior are considered to be for the best, others for the worst. Potential migrants in the island know their future life in New York is going to be different from their life in Puerto Rico. How, and to what extent, however, is part of the adventure and "changing environment" they will find in New York. **10**

The impact of New York life on Puerto Rican migrants is described in fact and popular fancy, but whether it is described glowingly, soberly, or depressingly depends on the aspirations, frustrations, hopes, and anxieties of the one who is speaking. Men, women, and children change in New York, it is said. How? **11**

Clara Fredes, now a mother of three, who migrated after the Second World War when she was a teen-ager, replied to a member of the field team **12** when asked if there were any differences between "the way people act here and in Puerto Rico," that "when women get here they act too free. They go out and stand in the street and don't cook dinner or anything. Puerto Rican women in New York City are bad. They talk to other men beside their husband, and just aren't nice. They boss the men. In Puerto Rico a wife obeys her husband, and keeps house, and takes care of her children. But here they run wild. [They are] all day long in the candy store talking and forgetting about their houses. Men here don't always support their wives and children. They are too free too. They think they can get away with everything, but I think it's the women's fault. They are so bad. They don't take care of the children right. The children [are] out on the streets at all hours of the night."

Another informant, Gina Ortiz, said that Puerto Rican women in New York like to go dancing the mambo and drinking and that "they don't do it in Puerto Rico. In Puerto Rico the woman who smokes and drinks is a bad woman."  13

Rose Burgos also explained changes in the behavior of women migrants. "[It is] because they work and they have too much freedom. In Puerto Rico the wife is always in the house. Here they go out, they go to work, get together with another girl, drink beer, and so on. In Puerto Rico they don't do that."  14

Women who want to be rated as "good" do not admit to having changed in these directions. They would claim that they do not drink, smoke, or work outside the home, though they may acknowledge having changed in such areas as child-rearing, including giving greater freedom to their children.  15

Among changes that men undergo in New York, Dolores Miro mentioned that "some of them take friends. The friends like to drink and has women in the street. They change. They like to do same thing the friends do. . . . In Puerto Rico they have the same friends always, but here they have friends from other places, other towns. Some of them are good friends, some bad."  16

Good men are expected not to change in New York, but to continue recognizing their obligations to their wives and children. They may say they do not have friends in New York because friends get a man in trouble.  17

A couple that consider themselves good and as having a satisfactory relationship with each other and their children may deny changes in their lives in New York. Manuel and Sophia Tres, in telling a fieldworker about themselves, said, "We don't have any change. We still the same." Manuel continued, "Some of them [Hispanos] when they come here they want to go to the bar and drink, are drunk people and have plenty girl friends," to which Sophia added, "because they make more money to spend. We are not changed, we have the same customs."  18

In New York children also change, in a variety of ways. It is more difficult to make them respect their parents and elders, and one must keep  19 them upstairs in order to prevent their becoming too uncontrollable and bad. For Juana Roman: "In Puerto Rico the fathers don't want the children to do what they want. They are strict; is better there. In Puerto Rico if your kids do anything wrong, the father punishes. Here you can't punish a big boy. . . . One day my boy went with another boy and they took a train and got lost, and when I got to the Children's Shelter, the lady said, 'Don't punish the boy,' and I said, 'Oh yes [I will punish him], I don't want him to do it again.' I see many kids that they do what they want."

Antonia Velez, now in her mid-thirties, finds that in this country people 20 are nice to old people, but says that in Puerto Rico old people are more respected. Her children do not respect in the same way she respected her father and mother in Puerto Rico when she was a child. Yet she is acceptant to some of the changes in patterns of respect she finds among her children. Says she, "Everybody is nice with the old people here in this country. They take care better of the old people and the children. I didn't pay too much attention to it in Puerto Rico. They are nice too. Everybody respects old people. The children are more respectful to old people in Puerto Rico than here . . . I know. I never used to argue with my mother in Puerto Rico. If she had a reason or no, I keep quiet. And with my father too. The word that he said was the only word to me. If he said not to go to a movie, I didn't discute [argue] that with him. I didn't go. No here. The children are more free here. Tommy, when I say, do that, and he don't want to and he explains me why, I don't mind that. I think it is better for him. You know, we didn't do that but it was not good inside. I think so, because they are human beings too. I love my father and mother because they are so good to me. If I didn't go to movies they may have the reason to say no, but I don't know it. Maybe that way, if I know it, I would have been better."

Children who have migrated recently at ages when they had friends and 21 were allowed to play in the yards and streets in their home towns and now are being reared "upstairs in the home" speak of their past life in Puerto Rico with nostalgia. Lydia Rios, age twelve, says that "here one cannot do anything," referring to having to remain at home, sitting and watching from a window the play of other children, except when she goes to church or school.

Advantages listed of living in New York are the higher wages and income, 22 better opportunities to educate the children, better medical care, more and better food, more and better clothes, furniture, and material things here than in Puerto Rico. In New York one can even save money to go back to Puerto Rico and purchase a house. Which place is better to live in is contingent on whether the migrant has realized or is on his way to realizing the aspirations and hopes connected with his coming to New York.

For Emilio Cruz it is better to live in New York than in Puerto Rico. "I 23 think life in New York is better. We have better living in New York and can give the children the food they want and need. When we work we have more money. We spend more here but we earn more so we can live better. In

Puerto Rico we rent a house [for] $10.00 or $12.00 a month, and here we [pay] so much [more] money and [must have] a lease too, [of] two or three years in New York."

Migrants speak of the future with reference to a good life, and a good life can be realized either in New York or in Puerto Rico, though one must search for it. As Rafael Dorcas put it, "A good life is when we work and we has the things we need for all the family. I think that's a good life." 24

## STUDY QUESTIONS

1. What kinds of evidence does Padilla use to demonstrate the various points she makes? What kind of research has apparently gone into the study?

2. What kind of person, according to Padilla, is most likely to return to Puerto Rico? to look back upon earlier years in Puerto Rico with nostalgia or regret? What kind of person adapts most readily to mainland ways?

3. What are the characteristic ways in which Puerto Ricans find life different, according to Padilla, in New York? In what ways are those who move to New York most likely to change?

4. Choose one of the people quoted by Padilla, and analyze the words that person uses to express the fears and hopes of the migration experience. In what ways are that person's values expressed? How can you tell, from the words the person uses, what he or she cares most about?

5. How can you tell, for the people quoted in this essay, where "home" really is?

# Louise Erdrich

Although primarily known as a novelist and writer of prose sketches, Louise Erdrich is also a poet of distinction. She is of Chippewa and German-American descent; she grew up in North Dakota and now lives in New Hampshire with her husband and five children. Her best-known novel, *Love Medicine* (1984), won the National Book Critics Circle Award and was a national best-seller. It was followed by *The Beet Queen* (1986) and *Tracks* (1988). Philip Roth called her "the most interesting new American novelist to have appeared in years."

In the following poem, "home" suggests a place of refuge from present and past oppression, and its values are not so much specified as represented by the freedom it offers from pain.

# INDIAN BOARDING SCHOOL: THE RUNAWAYS

Home's the place we head for in our sleep.
Boxcars stumbling north in dreams
don't wait for us. We catch them on the run.
The rails, old lacerations that we love,
shoot parallel across the face and break                                    5
just under Turtle Mountains. Riding scars
you can't get lost. Home is the place they cross.

The lame guard strikes a match and makes the dark
less tolerant. We watch through cracks in boards
as the land starts rolling, rolling till it hurts                          10
to be here, cold in regulation clothes.
We know the sheriff's waiting at midrun
to take us back. His car is dumb and warm.
The highway doesn't rock, it only hums
like a wing of long insults. The worn-down welts                           15
of ancient punishment lead back and forth.

All runaways wear dresses, long green ones,
the color you would think shame was. We scrub
the sidewalks down because it's shameful work.
Our brushes cut the stone in watered arcs                                  20
and in the soak frail outlines shiver clear
a moment, things us kids pressed on the dark
face before it hardened, pale, remembering
delicate old injuries, the spines of names and leaves.

## STUDY QUESTIONS

1. Who are the "we" that the poem is about? How much do we learn about them?
   What do they look like? In what ways has their school stamped its identity on
   them? In what ways have they tried to stamp their identity on the school? What
   do they dislike or fear? In what ways is the power of their feelings indicated?

2. Even though age is not mentioned and we are given no exact number of people,
   how is a sense communicated of the size and character of the group? How does the
   poem suggest their single-mindedness?

3. Where, exactly, is "home" for the runaways? How much do we know about it? Describe as fully as you can what it looks like. What values or feelings does it seem to represent to the SPEAKER? Do the specific locations in the poem restrict or enhance the power of the feeling the poem addresses? Why?

4. How is the dream quality of the experience maintained even when the details are vividly presented?

5. What do the runaways want to escape from? In what different ways is "the enemy" represented? Why is no visual description given of the sheriff? What do we know about him?

6. The language of hurt and injury pervades the poem; it is even used to describe the landscape. Find all the words you can that suggest pain in the present or in the past. In each separate case, who or what is it that seems to have been injured? What do the "old lacerations" (line 4), "scars" (l. 6), and "worn-down welts" (l. 15) imply about the relationship between past and present, history and contemporary life? How do the injuries to the land relate to the injuries the runaways themselves feel?

# Maurice Kenny

Maurice Kenny, of Mohawk ancestry, was born and reared in northern New York State near the St. Lawrence River and now teaches at North Country Community College. His first book of poetry, *Dead Letters Sent,* was published in 1959, and (one of the most prolific Native American poets) he has now published ten volumes, including *The Mama Poems* (1984). Kenny travels extensively, often by Greyhound bus.

"Going Home" describes a bus ride back to the poet's origins in the countryside of upstate New York and confronts the frustrated feeling that a long life in the city has cut off the old ties to home.

## GOING HOME

The book lay unread in my lap
snow gathered at the window
from Brooklyn it was a long ride
the Greyhound followed the plow
from Syracuse to Watertown                                    5

to country cheese and maples
tired rivers and closed paper mills
home to gossipy aunts . . .
their dandelions and pregnant cats . . .
home to cedars and fields of boulders                    10
cold graves under willow and pine
home from Brooklyn to the reservation
that was not home
to songs I could not sing
to dances I could not dance                              15
from Brooklyn bars and ghetto rats
to steaming horses stomping frozen earth
barns and privies lost in blizzards
home to a Nation, Mohawk
to faces, I did not know                                 20
and hands which did not recognize me
to names and doors
my father shut

# STUDY QUESTIONS

1. Why does the description of the journey "home" mix sights along the road with personal memories? Which lines describe which?

2. Why does "the book [lie] unread in my lap" (line 1)? With what aspects of the SPEAKER's life is the book connected? What substitutes for the book on the trip?

3. Why is the reservation said to be "not home" (l. 13)? List all of the things mentioned in the poem that cut the speaker off from the reservation. What things tie him to it? How is Brooklyn characterized? Explain the emotional effects of the contrast between rats and horses (ll. 16, 17); between bars and "barns and privies lost in blizzards" (ll. 16, 18).

4. How much do we know about the father? What seems to have been involved in his shutting of doors?

5. Describe the attitudes of the speaker toward his upstate "home." What contradictions do you find in his attitude? Do the contradictions mean that he is insincere? confused? that his feelings are complicated? that he is torn between deep loyalties from the past and feelings from his own limited personal experience?

6. Do you think the speaker is likely to leave Brooklyn and move to upstate New York? What evidence does the poem provide?

7. In speaking of this poem, Kenny has written:

    So I travel home/north to the re-birth of chicory, burdock, tadpoles, otters and the strawberry. I fly with geese who, like myself, have wintered in a more southern clime, or salmon who have matured in the ocean. I travel home to those natal waters. "Home" is with your people who stand on that earth and partake of its nourishment, spiritual and corporeal. And though some, like yourself, have wandered they too cannot refrain from returning picking time. Once fingers have been lowered to the earth they cannot be retracted.

How do you explain the strong attraction to land and the earth in someone who has spent most of his life in a city of concrete and busy populous streets?

# Lorna Dee Cervantes

Born in San Francisco in 1954, Lorna Dee Cervantes is of Mexican descent. She published her first book of poems, *Emplumada*, in 1981. She was educated at San Jose City College and San Jose State University and is the founder of Mango Publications, a small press that publishes books and a literary magazine.

"Freeway 280" describes the "burying" of nature by modern progress, but suggests the resilience of nature, including human nature, in the face of attempts to suppress or kill vitality and wildness.

## FREEWAY 280

Las casitas[1] near the gray cannery,
nestled amid wild abrazos[2] of climbing roses
and man-high red geraniums
are gone now. The freeway conceals it
all beneath a raised scar.                                                5

But under the fake windsounds of the open lanes,
in the abandoned lots below, new grasses sprout,
wild mustard remembers, old gardens
come back stronger than they were,
trees have been left standing in their yards.                            10
Albaricoqueros, cerezos, nogales . . .[3]

1. Little houses. [Author's note]
2. Bear hugs.
3. Apricot trees, cherry trees, walnut trees. [Author's note]

Viejitas come here with paper bags to gather greens.
Espinaca, verdolagas, yerbabuena . . .[4]

I scramble over the wire fence
that would have kept me out.                                    15
Once, I wanted out, wanted the rigid lanes
to take me to a place without sun,
without the smell of tomatoes burning
on swing shift in the greasy summer air.

Maybe it's here                                                20
en los campos extraños de esta ciudad[5]
where I'll find it, that part of me
mown under
like a corpse
or a loose seed.                                               25

# STUDY QUESTIONS

1. How much do we know about the places the poem describes? How much do we know about the SPEAKER? Make a list of all the facts we are given about people and places. What relationships between people and land are implied?

2. Find all the places in the poem where nature is contrasted with artificial or man-made things; where wildness is contrasted with restraint; where growth is contrasted with death.

3. What "facts" are we given about the freeway? What words used to describe the freeway tend to color our emotional responses to it? What effect does it seem to have on the landscape? on people? How are these effects dramatized? How did the speaker formerly feel about the freeway (lines 16–19)? What seems to have changed her mind? How is her attitude toward "home" different now from what it was when she "wanted out" (l. 16)?

4. How do the human characteristics described in the last half of the poem relate to the characteristics of nature in the first part? What is the common enemy?

5. What does each of the four STANZAS accomplish? Although there are four stanzas, the poem breaks into two main parts. Where, exactly, does the break occur? How is the break indicated? Describe the relationship between the two parts.

6. What terms and IMAGES earlier in the poem are summarized in the contrast between "corpse" and "loose seed" (ll. 24–25)?

---

4. Spinach, purslane, mint. [Author's note] *Viejitas:* old women.
5. In the strange fields of this city. [Author's note]

# Wakako Yamauchi

B orn in 1924 in California (where she still lives), Wakako Yamauchi is best known
as a writer of short stories, which have been widely anthologized.

In the following play, a series of related conflicts are dramatized: between husband and wife, between families, between men and women, between generations,
between cultures. The play, which Yamauchi adapted from one of her short stories,
was first performed in Los Angeles in 1977; it has also been adapted for television.

## AND THE SOUL SHALL DANCE

### Characters

MURATA, 40, Issei[1] farmer.
HANA, Issei wife of Murata.
MASAKO, 11, Nisei daughter of the Muratas.
OKA, 45, Issei farmer.
EMIKO, 30, wife of Oka.
KIYOKO, 14, Oka's daughter.

### Place and Time

The action of the play takes place on and between two small farms in Southern California's Imperial Valley in the early 1930s.

## ACT I

### Scene 1

*Summer 1935, afternoon. Interior of the Murata house. The set is spare. There is a
kitchen table, four chairs, a bed, and on the wall, a calendar indicating the year and
month: June, 1935. There is a doorway leading to the other room. Props are: a bottle*

---

1. First-generation Japanese-American. *Nisei:* second-generation.

*of sake, two cups, a dish of chiles, a phonograph, and two towels hanging on pegs on
the wall. A wide wooden bench sits outside.*

*The bathhouse has just burned to the ground due to the carelessness of* MASAKO,
*Nisei daughter, 11. Off stage there are sounds of* MURATA, *40, Issei farmer, putting
out the fire.*

*Inside the house* HANA MURATA, *Issei wife, in a drab house dress, confronts*
MASAKO *(wearing summer dress of the era).* MASAKO *is sullen and somewhat defiant.*
HANA *breaks the silence.*

HANA: How could you be so careless, Masako? You know you should be extra
careful with fire. How often have I told you? Now the whole bathhouse
is gone. I told you time and again, when you stoke a fire, you should
see that everything is swept into the fireplace.

[MURATA *enters. He's dressed in old work clothes. He suffers from heat and
exhaustion.*]

MURATA: [*Coughing.*] Shack went up like a match box . . . This kind of weather
dries everything . . . just takes a spark to make a bonfire out of dry
timber.

HANA: Did you save any of it?

MURATA: No. Couldn't . . .

HANA: [*To* MASAKO.] How many times have I told you . . .

[MASAKO *moves nervously.*]

MURATA: No use crying about it now. *Shikata ga nai.* It's gone now. No more
bathhouse. That's all there is to it.

HANA: But you've got to tell her. Otherwise she'll make the same mistake.
You'll be building a bathhouse every year.

[MURATA *removes his shirt and wipes off his face. He throws his shirt on a chair
and sits at the table.*]

MURATA: *Baka!* Ridiculous!

MASAKO: I didn't do it on purpose.

[*She goes to the bed, opens a book.* HANA *follows her.*]

HANA: I know that but you know what this means? It means we bathe in a
bucket . . . inside the house. Carry water in from the pond, heat it on
the stove . . . We'll use more kerosene.

MURATA: Tub's still there. And the fireplace. We can still build a fire under
the tub.

HANA: [*Shocked.*] But no walls! Everyone in the country can see us!

MURATA: Wait 'til dark then. Wait 'til dark.

HANA: We'll be using a lantern. They'll still see us.

MURATA: Angh! Who? Who'll see us? You think everyone in the country

waits to watch us take a bath? Hunh? You know how stupid you sound?
Ridiculous!

HANA: [*Defensively.*] It'll be inconvenient.

[HANA *is saved by a rap on the door.* OKA, *Issei neighbor, 45, enters. He is short and stout, dressed in faded work clothes.*]

OKA: Hello! Hello! Oi! What's going on here? Hey! Was there some kind of fire?

[HANA *rushes to the door to let* OKA *in. He stamps the dust from his shoes and enters.*]

HANA: Oka-san![2] You just wouldn't believe . . . We had a terrible thing happen.

OKA: Yeah. Saw the smoke from down the road. Thought it was your house. Came rushing over. Is the fire out?

[MURATA *half rises and sits back again. He's exhausted.*]

MURATA: [*Gesturing.*] Oi, oi. Come in . . . sit down. No big problem. It was just our bathhouse.

OKA: Just the *furoba*, eh?

MURATA: Just the bath.

HANA: Our Masako was careless and the *furoba* caught fire. There's nothing left of it but the tub.

[MASAKO *looks up from her book, pained. She makes a very small sound.*]

OKA: Long as the tub's there, no problem. I'll help you with it. [*He starts to roll up his sleeves.* MURATA *looks at him.*]

MURATA: What . . . now? Now?

OKA: Long as I'm here.

HANA: Oh, Papa. Aren't we lucky to have such friends?

MURATA: [*To* HANA.] Hell, we can't work on it now. The ashes are still hot. I just now put the damned fire out. Let me rest a while. [*To* OKA.] Oi, how about a little *sake*? [*Gesturing to* HANA.] Make *sake* for Oka-san. [OKA *sits at the table.* HANA *goes to prepare the* sake. *She heats it, gets out the cups and pours it for the men.*] I'm tired . . . I am *tired*.

HANA: Oka-san has so generously offered his help . . .

[OKA *is uncomfortable. He looks around and sees* MASAKO *sitting on the bed.*]

OKA: Hello, there, Masako-chan. You studying?

MASAKO: No, it's summer vacation.

MURATA: [*Sucking in his breath.*] Kids nowadays . . . no manners . . .

HANA: She's sulking because I had to scold her.

---

2. A suffix indicating polite address, roughly equivalent to Mr., Mrs., Ms. The suffixes *-chan* and *-kun* (below) are affectionate or diminutive.

[MASAKO *makes a small moan.*]

MURATA: Drink, Oka-san.

OKA: [*Swallowing.*] Ahhh, that's good.

MURATA: Eh, you not working today?

OKA: No . . . no . . . I took the afternoon off today. I was driving over to Nagatas' when I saw this big black cloud of smoke coming from your yard.

HANA: It went up so fast . . .

MURATA: What's up at Nagatas'? [*To* HANA]. Get the chiles out. Oka-san loves chiles.

[HANA *opens a jar of chiles and puts them on a plate. She serves the men and gets her mending basket and walks to* MASAKO. MASAKO *makes room for her on the bed.*]

OKA: [*Helping himself.*] Ah, chiles. [MURATA *looks at* OKA, *the question unanswered.*] Well, I want to see him about my horse. I'm thinking of selling my horse.

MURATA: Sell your horse!

OKA: [*He scratches his head.*] The fact is, I need some money. Nagata-san's the only one around made money this year, and I'm thinking he might want another horse.

MURATA: Yeah, he made a little this year. And he's talking big . . . big! Says he's leasing twenty more acres this fall.

OKA: Twenty acres?

MURATA: Yeah. He might want another horse.

OKA: Twenty acres, eh?

MURATA: That's what he says. But you know his old woman makes all the decisions. [OKA *scratches his head.*]

HANA: They're doing all right.

MURATA: Henh. Nagata-kun's so hen-pecked, it's pathetic. Peko-peko. [*He makes motions of a hen pecking.*]

OKA: [*Feeling the strain.*] I better get over there.

MURATA: Why the hell you selling your horse?

OKA: I need cash.

MURATA: Oh, yeah. I could use some too. Seems like everyone's getting out of the depression but the poor farmers. Nothing changes for us. We go on and on planting our tomatoes and summer squash and eating them . . . Well, at least it's healthy.

HANA: Papa, do you have lumber?

MURATA: Lumber? For what?

HANA: The bath.

MURATA: [*Impatiently.*] Don't worry about that. We need more *sake* now.

[HANA *rises to serve him.*]

OKA: You sure Nagata-kun's working twenty more acres?

MURATA: Last I heard. What the hell; if you need a few bucks, I can loan you . . .

OKA: A few hundred. I need a few hundred dollars.

MURATA: Oh, a few hundred. But what the hell you going to do without a horse? Out here a man's horse is as important as his wife.

OKA: [*Seriously.*] I don't think Nagata will buy my wife. [*The men laugh, but* HANA *doesn't find it so funny.* MURATA *glances at her. She fills the cups again.* OKA *makes a half-hearted gesture to stop her.* MASAKO *watches the pantomine carefully.* OKA *swallows his drink in one gulp.*] I better get moving.

MURATA: What's the big hurry?

OKA: Like to get the horse business done.

MURATA: Ehhhh . . . relax. Do it tomorrow. He's not going to die, is he?

OKA: [*Laughing.*] Hey he's a good horse. I want to get it settled today. If Nagata-kun won't buy, I got to find someone else. You think maybe Kawaguchi . . .?

MURATA: Not Kawaguchi . . . Maybe Yamamoto.

HANA: What is all the money for, Oka-san? Does Emiko-san need an operation?

OKA: Nothing like that . . .

HANA: Sounds very mysterious.

OKA: No mystery, Mrs. No mystery. No sale, no money, no story.

MURATA: [*Laughing.*] That's a good one. "No sale, no money, no . . ." Eh, Mama. [*He points to the empty cups.* HANA *fills the cups and goes back to* MASAKO.]

HANA: [*Muttering.*] I see we won't be getting any work done today. [*To* MASAKO.] Are you reading again? Maybe we'd still have a bath if you . . .

MASAKO: I didn't do it on purpose.

MURATA: [*Loudly.*] I sure hope you know what you're doing. Oka-kun. What'd you do without a horse?

OKA: I was hoping you'd lend me yours now and then . . . [*He looks at* HANA.] I'll pay for some of the feed.

MURATA: [*Emphatically waving his hand.*] Sure! Sure!

OKA: The fact is, I need that money. I got a daughter in Japan and I just got to send for her this year.

[HANA *comes to life. She puts down her mending and sits at the table.*]

HANA: A daughter? You have a daughter in Japan? Why, I didn't know you had children. Emiko-san and you . . . I thought you were childless.

OKA: [*Scratching his head.*] We are. I was married before.

MURATA: You son-of-a-gun!

HANA: Is that so? How old is your daughter?

OKA: Kiyoko must be . . . fifteen now. Yeah, fifteen.

HANA: Fifteen! Oh, that *would* be too old for Emiko-san's child. Is Kiyoko-san living with relatives in Japan?

OKA: [*Reluctantly.*] Yeah, with grandparents. With Shizue's parents. Well, the fact is, Shizue, that's my first wife, and Emiko were sisters. They come from a family with no sons. I was a boy when I went to work for the family . . . as an apprentice . . . they're blacksmiths. Later I married Shizue and took on the family name—you know, *yoshi*—because they had no sons.[3] My real name is Sakakihara.

MURATA: Sakakihara! That's a great name!

HANA: A magnificent name!

OKA: No one knows me by that here.

MURATA: Should have kept that . . . Sakakihara.

OKA: [*Muttering.*] I don't even know myself by that name.

HANA: And Shizue-san passed away and you married Emiko-san?

OKA: Oh, yeah. Shizue and I lived with the family for a while and we had the baby . . . that's, you know, Kiyoko . . . [*The liquor has affected him and he's become less inhibited.*] Well, while I was serving apprentice with the family, they always looked down their noses at me. After I married, it got worse . . . That old man . . . Angh! He was terrible! Always pushing me around, making me look bad in front of my wife and kid. That old man was mean . . . ugly!

MURATA: Yeah, I heard about that apprentice work—*detchi-boko* . . . Heard it was damned humiliating.

OKA: That's the God's truth!

MURATA: Never had to do it myself. I came to America instead. They say *detchi-boko* is bloody hard work.

OKA: The work's all right. I'm not afraid of work. It's the humiliation! I hated them! Pushing me around like I was still a boy . . . Me, a grown man! And married to their daughter! [MURATA *groans in sympathy.*] Well, Shizue and I talked it over and we decided the best thing was to get away. We thought if I came to America and made some money . . . you know, send her money until we had enough, I'd go back and we'd leave the family . . . you know, move to another province . . . start a small business, maybe in the city, a noodle shop or something.

MURATA: That's everyone's dream. Make money, go home and live like a king.

OKA: I worked like a dog. Sent every penny to Shizue. And then she died. She died on me!

[HANA *and* MURATA *observe a moment of silence in respect for* OKA's *anguish.*]

HANA: And you married Emiko-san.

OKA: I didn't marry her. They married her to me! Right after Shizue died.

HANA: But Oka-san, you were lucky . . .

OKA: Before the body was cold! No respect! By proxy. The old man wrote me they were arranging a marriage by proxy for me and Emiko. They

3. Yoshi is a procedure wherein a man is married into a family that has no sons and is obliged to carry the wife's family name and continue the lineage. [Author's note]

said she'd grown to be a beautiful woman and would serve me well.

HANA: Emiko-san *is* a beautiful woman.

OKA: And they sent her to me. Took care of everything! Immigration, fare, everything.

HANA: But she's your sister-in-law—Kiyoko's aunt. It's good to keep the family together.

OKA: That's what I thought. But hear this: Emiko was the favored one. Shizue was not so pretty, not so smart. They were grooming Emiko for a rich man—his name was Yamoto—lived in a grand house in the village. They sent her to schools; you know, the culture thing: tea ceremony, you know, all that. They didn't even like me, and suddenly they married her to me.

MURATA: Yeah. You don't need all that formal training to make it over here. Just a strong back.

HANA: And a strong will.

OKA: It was all arranged. I couldn't do anything about it.

HANA: It'll be all right. With Kiyoko coming . . .

OKA: [*Dubiously.*] I hope so . . . I never knew human beings could be so cruel. You know how they mistreated my daughter? You know after Emiko came over, things got from bad to worse and I *never* had enough money to send to Kiyoko.

MURATA: They don't know what it's like here. They think money's picked off the ground here.

OKA: And they treated Kiyoko so bad. They told her I forgot about her. They told her I didn't care—they said I abandoned her. Well, she knew better. She wrote to me all the time and I always told her I'd send for her . . . soon as I got the money. [*He shakes his head.*] I just got to do something this year.

HANA: She'll be happier here. She'll know her father cares.

OKA: Kids tormented her for not having parents.

MURATA: Kids are cruel.

HANA: Masako will help her. She'll help her get started at school. She'll make friends . . . she'll be all right.

OKA: I hope so. She'll need friends. [*He considers he might be making a mistake after all.*] What could I say to her? Stay there? It's not what you think over here? I can't help her? I just have to do this thing. I just have to do this one thing for her.

MURATA: Sure . . .

HANA: Don't worry. It'll work out fine.

[MURATA *gestures to* HANA. *She fills the cup.*]

MURATA: You talk about selling your horse, I thought you were pulling out.

OKA: I wish I could. But there's nothing else I can do.

MURATA: Without money, yeah . . .

OKA: You can go into some kind of business with money, but a man like me

. . . no education . . . there's no kind of job I can do. I'd starve in the city.

MURATA: Dishwashing, maybe. Janitor . . .

OKA: At least here we can eat. Carrots, maybe, but we can eat.

MURATA: All the carrots we been eating 'bout to turn me into a rabbit.

[*They laugh.* HANA *starts to pour more wine for* OKA *but he stops her.*]

OKA: I better not drink any more. Got to drive to Nagata-san's yet. [*He rises and walks over to* MASAKO.] You study hard, don't you? You'll teach Kiyoko English, eh? When she gets here . . .

HANA: Oh, yes. She will.

MURATA: Kiyoko-san could probably teach her a thing or two.

OKA: She won't know about American ways . . .

MASAKO: I'll help her.

HANA: Don't worry, Oka-san. She'll have a good friend in our Masako. [*They move toward the door.*]

OKA: Well, thanks for the *sake*. I guess I talk too much when I drink. [*He scratches his head and laughs.*] Oh. I'm sorry about the fire. By the way, come to my house for your bath . . . until you build yours again.

HANA: [*Hesitantly.*] Oh, uh . . . thank you. I don't know if . . .

MURATA: Good! Good! Thanks a lot. I need a good hot bath tonight.

OKA: Tonight, then.

MURATA: We'll be there.

HANA: [*Bowing.*] Thank you very much. *Sayonara.*

OKA: [*Nodding.*] See you tonight.

[OKA *leaves.* HANA *faces her husband as soon as the door closes.*]

HANA: Papa, I don't know about going over there.

MURATA: [*Surprised.*] Why?

HANA: Well, Emiko-san . . .

MURATA: [*Irritated.*] What's the matter with you? We need a bath and Oka's invited us over.

HANA: [*To* MASAKO.] Help me clear the table. [MASAKO *reluctantly leaves her book and begins to clear the table.*] Papa, you know we've been neighbors already three, four years and Emiko-san's never been very hospitable.

MURATA: She's shy, that's all.

HANA: Not just shy . . . she's strange. I feel like she's pushing me off . . . she makes me feel like—I don't know—like I'm prying or something.

MURATA: Maybe you are.

HANA: And never put out a cup of tea . . . If she had all that training in the graces . . . why, a cup of tea . . .

MURATA: So if you want tea, ask for it.

HANA: I can't do that, Papa. She's strange . . . I don't know . . . [*To* MASAKO.] When we go there, be very careful not to say anything wrong.

MASAKO: I never say anything anyway.

HANA: [*Thoughtfully.*] Would you believe the story Oka-san just told? Why, I never knew . . .

MURATA: There're lot of things you don't know. Just because a man don't . . . talk about them, don't mean he don't feel . . . don't think about . . .

HANA: [*Looking around.*] We'll have to take something . . . There's nothing to take . . . Papa, maybe you can dig up some carrots.

MURATA: God, Mama, be sensible. They got carrots. Everybody's got carrots.

HANA: Something . . . maybe I should make something.

MURATA: Hell, they're not expecting anything.

HANA: It's not good manners to go empty-handed.

MURATA: We'll take the *sake*.

[HANA *grimaces.* MASAKO *sees the record player.*]

MASAKO: I know, Mama. We can take the Victrola! We can play records for Mrs. Oka. Then nobody has to talk.

[MURATA *laughs.*]

*Fade out.*

## Scene 2

*That evening. We see the exterior wall of the Okas' weathered house. There is a work-able screen door and a large screened window. Outside there is a wide wooden bench that can accommodate three or four people. There is one separate chair and a lantern stands against the house.*

*The last rays of the sun light the area in a soft golden glow. This light grows gray as the scene progresses and it is quite dark at the end of the scene.*

*Through the screened window,* EMIKO OKA, *Issei woman, 30, can be seen walking erratically back and forth. She wears a drab cotton dress but her grace and femininity come through. Her hair is bunned back in the style of Issei women of the era.*

OKA *sits cross-legged on the bench. He wears a Japanese summer robe* (yukata) *and fans himself with a round Japanese fan.*

*The Muratas enter.* MURATA *carries towels and a bottle of* sake. HANA *carries the Victrola, and* MASAKO *a package containing their* yukatas.

OKA: [*Standing to receive the Muratas.*] Oh, you've come. Welcome!

MURATA: Yah . . . Good of you to ask us.

HANA: [*Bowing.*] Yes, thank you very much. [*To* MASAKO.] Say "hello," Masako.

MASAKO: Hello.

HANA: And "thank you."

MASAKO: Thank you.

[OKA *makes motion of protest.* EMIKO *stops her pacing and watches from the window.*]

HANA: [*Glancing briefly at the window.*] And how is Emiko-san this evening?

OKA: [*Turning toward the house.*] Emi! Emiko!

HANA: That's all right. Don't call her out. She must be busy.

OKA: [*Half rising.*] Emiko!

[EMIKO *comes to the door.* HANA *starts a deep bow toward the door.*]

MURATA: *Konbanwa!* ("*Good evening!*")

HANA: *Konbanwa*, Emiko-san. I feel so bad about this intrusion. Your husband has told you, our bathhouse was destroyed by fire and he graciously invited us to come use yours.

[EMIKO *shakes her head.*]

OKA: I didn't have a chance to . . .

[HANA *recovers and nudges* MASAKO.]

HANA: Say hello to Mrs. Oka.

MASAKO: Hello, Mrs. Oka.

[HANA *lowers the Victrola on the bench.*]

OKA: What's this? You brought a phonograph?

MASAKO: It's a Victrola.

HANA: [*Laughing indulgently.*] Yes. Masako wanted to bring this over and play some records.

MURATA: [*Extending the wine.*] Brought a little *sake* too.

OKA: [*Taking the bottle*] Ah, now that I like. Emiko, bring out the cups.

[*He waves at his wife, but she doesn't move. He starts to ask again, but decides to get them himself. He enters the house and returns with two cups.* EMIKO *seats herself on the single chair. The Muratas unload their paraphernalia;* OKA *pours the wine, the men drink,* HANA *chatters and sorts the records.* MASAKO *stands by, helping her.*]

HANA: Yes, our Masako loves to play records. I like records too . . . and Papa, he . . .

MURATA: [*Watching* EMIKO.] They take me back home. The only way I can get there . . . in my mind.

HANA: Do you like music, Emiko-san? [EMIKO *looks vague but smiles faintly.*] Oka-san, you like them, don't you?

OKA: Yeah. But I don't have a player. No chance to hear them.

MURATA: I had to get this for them. They wouldn't leave me alone until I got it. Well . . . a phonograph . . . what the hell, they got to have *some* fun.

HANA: We don't have to play them, if you'd rather not . . .

OKA: Play. Play them.

HANA: I thought we could listen to them and relax [*She extends some records to* EMIKO.] Would you like to look through these, Emiko-san? [EMIKO *doesn't respond. She pulls out a sack of Bull Durham and starts to roll a cigarette.* HANA *pushes* MASAKO *to her.*] Take these to her. [MASAKO *moves toward* EMIKO *with the records.* MASAKO *stands watching her as she lights her cigarette.*] Some of these are very old. You might know them, Emiko-san. [*She sees* MASAKO *watching* EMIKO.] Masako, bring those over here. [*She laughs uncomfortably.*] You might like this one, Emiko-san . . . [*She starts the player.*] Do you know it?

[*The record whines out "Kago No Tori."*[4] EMIKO *listens with her head cocked. She smokes her cigarette. She becomes wrapped in nostalgia and memories of the past.* MASAKO *watches her carefully.*]

MASAKO: [*Whispering.*] Mama, she's crying.

[*Startled,* HANA *and* MURATA *look toward* EMIKO.]

HANA: [*Pinching* MASAKO.] Shhh. The smoke is in her eyes.
MURATA: Did you bring the record I like, Mama?

[EMIKO *rises abruptly and enters the house.*]

MASAKO: There were tears, Mama.
HANA: From yawning, Masako. [*Regretfully, to* OKA.] I'm afraid we've offended her.
OKA: [*Unaware.*] Hunh? Aw . . . no . . . pay no attention . . . no offense . . .

[MASAKO *looks toward the window.* EMIKO *stands forlornly and slowly drifts into a dance.*]

HANA: I'm very sorry. Children, you know . . . they'll say anything, anything that's on their minds.

[MURATA *notices* MASAKO *watching* EMIKO *through the window and tries to divert her attention.*]

MURATA: The needles. Masako, where're the needles?
MASAKO: [*Still watching.*] I forgot them.

[HANA *sees what's going on.* OKA *is unaware.*]

HANA: Masako, go take your bath now. Masako . . .

[MASAKO *reluctantly picks up her towel and leaves.*]

OKA: Yeah, yeah . . . take your bath.
MURATA: [*Sees* EMIKO *still dancing.*] Change the record, Mama.
OKA: [*Still unaware.*] That's kind of sad.
MURATA: No use to get sick over a record. We're supposed to enjoy.

[HANA *stops the record.* EMIKO *disappears from the window.* HANA *selects a lively ondo—"Tokyo Ondo."*]

HANA: We'll find something more fun. [*The three begin to tap to the music.*] Can't

4. See lyrics, p. 105.

you just see the festival? The dancers, the bright *kimonos*, the paper lanterns bobbing in the wind, the fireflies . . . How nostalgic . . . Oh, how nostalgic . . .

[*From the side of the house* EMIKO *appears. Her hair is down, she wears an old straw hat. She dances in front of the Muratas. They're startled. After the first shock, they watch with frozen smiles. They try to join* EMIKO'S *mood but something is missing.* OKA *is grieved. He finally stands as though he's had enough.* EMIKO, *now close to the door, ducks into the house.*]

HANA: That was pretty . . . very nice . . .

[OKA *settles down and grunts.* MURATA *clears his throat and* MASAKO *returns from her bath.*]

MURATA: You're done already? [*He's glad to see her.*]
MASAKO: I wasn't very dirty. The water was too hot.
MURATA: Good! Just the way I like it.
HANA: Not dirty?
MURATA: [*Picking up his towel.*] Come on, Mama . . . scrub my back.
HANA: [*Laughing embarrassedly.*] Oh, oh . . . well . . . [*She stops the player.*] Masako, now don't forget . . . crank the machine and change the needle now and then.
MASAKO: I didn't bring them.
HANA: Oh. Oh . . . all right. I'll be back soon . . . don't forget . . . crank.

[*She leaves with her husband.* OKA *and* MASAKO *are alone.* OKA *is awkward and falsely hearty.*]

OKA: So! So you don't like hot baths, eh?
MASAKO: Not too hot.
OKA: [*Laughing.*] I thought you like it real hot. Hot enough to burn the house down. That's a little joke. [MASAKO *busies herself with the records to conceal her annoyance.*] I hear you're real good in school. Always top of the class.
MASAKO: It's a small class. Only two of us.
OKA: When Kiyoko comes, you'll help her in school, yeah? You'll take care of her . . . a favor for me, eh?
MASAKO: Okay.
OKA: You'll be her friend, eh?
MASAKO: Okay.
OKA: That's good. That's good. You'll like her. She's a nice girl too. [OKA *stands, yawns, and stretches.*] I'll go for a little walk now.

[*He touches his crotch to indicate his purpose.* MASAKO *turns her attention to the records and selects one, "The Soul Shall Dance,"*[5] *and begins to sway to the music. The song draws* EMIKO *from the house. She looks out the window, sees* MASAKO *is alone and begins to slip into a dance.*]

5. Full lyrics are given on p. 105.

EMIKO: Do you like that song, Masa-chan? [MASAKO *is startled and draws back. She remembers her mother's warning. She doesn't know what to do. She nods.*] That's one of my favorite songs. I remember in Japan I used to sing it so often . . . my favorite song . . . [*She sings along with the record.*]

> Akai kuchibiru
> Kappu ni yosete
> Aoi sake nomya
> Kokoro ga odoru . . .

Do you know what that means, Masa-chan?

MASAKO: I think so . . . The soul will dance?

EMIKO: Yes, yes, that's right.

> The soul shall dance. Red lips against a glass
> Drink the green . . .

MASAKO: Wine?

EMIKO: [*Nodding*] Drink the green wine.

MASAKO: Green? I thought wine is purple.

EMIKO: [*Nodding.*] Wine is purple . . . but this is a green liqueur. [EMIKO *holds up one of the china cups as though it were crystal, and looks at it as though the light were shining through it and she sees the green liquid.*] It's good . . . it warms your heart.

MASAKO: And the soul dances.

EMIKO: Yes.

MASAKO: What does it taste like? The green wine . . .

EMIKO: Oh, it's like . . . it's like . . .

[*The second verse starts. "Kurai yoru yume, Setsunasa yo, Aoi sake nomya, Yume mo odoru . . ."*]

MASAKO: In the dark night . . .

EMIKO: Dreams are unbearable . . . insufferable . . . [*She turns sad.*]

MASAKO: Drink the . . .

EMIKO: [*Nodding.*] Drink the green wine . . .

MASAKO: And the dreams will dance.

EMIKO: [*Softly.*] I'll be going back one day . . .

MASAKO: To where?

EMIKO: My home . . . Japan . . . my real home. I'm planning to go back.

MASAKO: By yourself?

EMIKO: [*Nodding.*] Oh, yes. It's a secret. You can keep a secret?

MASAKO: Unhn. I have lots of secrets . . . all my own . . . [*The music stops.* EMIKO *sees* OKA *approaching and disappears into the house.* MASAKO *attends to the record and does not know* EMIKO *is gone.*] Secrets I never tell anyone.

OKA: Secrets? What kind of secrets? What did she say?

MASAKO: Oh. Nothing.

OKA: What did you talk about?

MASAKO: Nothing . . . Mrs. Oka was talking about the song. She was telling me what it meant . . . about the soul.

OKA: [*Scoffing.*] Heh! What does she know about soul? [*Calming down.*] Ehhh . . . some people don't have them . . . souls.

MASAKO: [*Timidly.*] I thought . . . I think everyone has a soul. I read in a book . . .

OKA: [*Laughing.*] Maybe . . . maybe you're right. I'm not an educated man, you know . . . I don't know too much about books. When Kiyoko comes you can talk to her about it. Kiyoko is very . . . [*From inside the house, we hear* EMIKO *begin to sing loudly at the name* KIYOKO *as though trying to drown it out.* OKA *stops talking. Then resumes.*] Kiyoko is very smart. You'll have a good time with her. She'll learn your language fast. How old did you say you are?

MASAKO: Almost twelve.

[*By this time* OKA *and* MASAKO *are shouting, trying to be heard above* EMIKO's *singing.*]

OKA: Kiyoko is fifteen . . . Kiyoko . . . [OKA *is exasperated. He rushes into the house seething.* MASAKO *hears* OKA's *muffled rage. "Behave yourself" and "kit-chigai" come through.* MASAKO *slinks to the window and looks in.* OKA *slaps* EMIKO *around.* MASAKO *reacts to the violence.* OKA *comes out.* MASAKO *returns to the bench in time. He pulls his fingers through his hair and sits next to* MASAKO. *She very slightly draws away.*] Want me to light a lantern?

MASAKO: [*Shaken.*] No . . . ye- . . . okay . . .

OKA: We'll get a little light here . . .

[*He lights the lantern as the Muratas return from their bath. They are in good spirits.*]

MURATA: Ahhhh . . . Nothing like a good hot bath.

HANA: So refreshing . . .

MURATA: A bath should be taken hot and slow. Don't know how Masako gets through so fast.

HANA: She probably doesn't get in the tub.

MASAKO: I do. [*Everyone laughs.*] Well I do.

[EMIKO *comes out. She has a large purple welt on her face. She sits on the separate chair, hands folded, quietly watching the Muratas. They look at her with alarm.* OKA *engages himself with his fan.*]

HANA: Oh! Emiko-san . . . what . . . ah-ah . . . whaa . . . [*She draws a deep breath.*] What a nice bath we had . . . such a lovely bath. We do appreciate your hos . . . pitality. Thank you so much.

EMIKO: Lovely evening, isn't it?

HANA: Very lovely. Very. Ah, a little warm, but nice . . . Did you get a chance to hear the records? [*Turning to* MASAKO.] Did you play the records for Mrs. Oka?

MASAKO: Ye- . . . no . . . The needle was . . .

EMIKO: Yes, she did. We played the records together.

MURATA: Oh, you played the songs together?

EMIKO: Yes . . . yes . . .

MURATA: That's nice . . . Masako can understand pretty good, eh?

EMIKO: She understand everything . . . everything I say.

MURATA: [*Withdrawing.*] Oh, yeah? Eh, Mama, we ought to be going . . . [*He closes the player.*] Hate to bathe and run but . . .

HANA: Yes, yes. Tomorrow is a busy day. Come, Masako.

EMIKO: Please . . . stay a little longer.

MURATA: Eh, well, we got to be going.

HANA: Why, thank you, but . . .

EMIKO: It's still quite early.

OKA: [*Indicating he's ready to say goodbye.*] Enjoyed the music. And the *sake*.

EMIKO: The records are very nice. Makes me remember Japan. I sang those songs . . . those very songs . . . Did you know I used to sing?

HANA: [*Politely.*] Why, no . . . no. I didn't know that. You must have a very lovely voice.

EMIKO: Yes.

HANA: No, I didn't know that. That's very nice.

EMIKO: Yes, I sang. My parents were very strict . . . they didn't like it. They said it was frivolous. Imagine?

HANA: Yes, I can imagine. Things were like that . . . in those days singing was not considered proper for nice . . . I mean, only for women in the profess- . . .

MURATA: We better get home, Mama.

HANA: Yes, yes. What a shame you couldn't continue with it.

EMIKO: In the city I did do some classics: the dance, and the *koto*, and the flower, and, of course, the tea . . . [*She makes the proper gesture for the different disciplines.*] All those. Even some singing . . . classics, of course.

HANA: [*Politely.*] Of course.

EMIKO: All of it is so disciplined . . . so disciplined. I was almost a *natori*.[6]

HANA: Oh! How nice.

EMIKO: But everything changed.

HANA: Oh!

EMIKO: I was sent here to America. [*She glares at* OKA.]

HANA: Oh, too bad . . . I mean, too bad about your *natori*.

MURATA: [*Loudly to* OKA.] So did you see Nagata today?

OKA: Oh, yeah. Yeah.

MURATA: What did he say? Is he interested?

OKA: Yeah. Yeah. He's interested.

---

6. Certified artiste.

MURATA: He likes the horse, eh?

OKA: Ah . . . yeah.

MURATA: I knew he'd like him. I'd buy him myself if I had the money.

OKA: Well, I have to take him over tomorrow. He'll decide then.

MURATA: He'll buy . . . he'll buy. You'd better go straight over to the ticket office and get that ticket. Before you—ha-ha—spend the money.

OKA: Ha-ha. Yeah.

HANA: It'll be so nice when Kiyoko-san comes to join you. I know you're looking forward to it.

EMIKO: [*Confused.*] Oh . . . oh . . .

HANA: Masako is so happy. It'll be good for her too.

EMIKO: I had more freedom in the city . . . I lived with an aunt and she let me . . . She wasn't so strict.

[MURATA *and* MASAKO *have their gear together and stand ready to leave.*]

MURATA: Good luck on the horse tomorrow.

OKA: Yeah, thanks.

HANA: [*Bowing.*] Many, many thanks.

OKA: [*Nodding toward the* sake.] Thanks for the *sake.*

HANA: [*Bowing again.*] Goodnight, Emiko-san. We'll see you again soon. We'll bring the records too.

EMIKO: [*Softly.*] Those songs . . . those very songs . . .

MURATA: Let's go, Mama.

[*The Muratas pull away. Light follows them and grows dark on the Okas. The Muratas begin walking home.*]

HANA: That was uncomfortable.

MASAKO: What's the matter with . . .

HANA: Shhhh!

MURATA: I guess Oka has his problems.

MASAKO: Is she really *kitchigai?*

HANA: Of course not. She's not crazy. Don't say that word, Masako.

MASAKO: I heard Mr. Oka call her that.

HANA: He called her that?

MASAKO: I . . . I think so.

HANA: You heard wrong, Masako. Emiko-san isn't crazy. She just likes her drinks. She had too much to drink tonight.

MASAKO: Oh.

HANA: She can't adjust to this life. She can't get over the good times she had in Japan. Well, it's not easy . . . but one has to know when to bend . . . like the bamboo. When the winds blow, bamboo bends. You bend or crack. Remember that, Masako.

MURATA: [*Laughing wryly.*] Bend, eh? Remember that, Mama.

HANA: [*Softly.*] You don't know . . . it isn't ever easy.

MASAKO: Do you want to go back to Japan, Mama?

HANA: Everyone does.

MASAKO: Do you, Papa?

MURATA: I'll have to make some money first.

MASAKO: I don't. Not me. Not Kiyoko . . .

HANA: After Kiyoko-san comes, Emiko will have company and things will straighten out. She has nothing to live on but her memories. She doesn't have any friends. At least I have my friends at church . . . at least I have that. She must get awful lonely.

MASAKO: I know that. She tried to make friends with me.

HANA: She did? What did she say?

MASAKO: Well, sort of . . .

HANA: What did she say?

MASAKO: She didn't say anything. I just felt it. Maybe you should be her friend, Mama.

MURATA: Poor woman. We could have stayed longer.

HANA: But you wanted to leave. I tried to be friendly. You saw that. It's not easy to talk to Emiko. She either closes up, you can't pry a word from her, or else she goes on and on . . . all that . . . that . . . about the *koto* and tea and the flower . . . I mean, what am I supposed to say? She's so unpredictable. And the drinking . . .

MURATA: All right, all right, Mama.

MASAKO: Did you see her black eye?

HANA: [*Calming down.*] She probably hurt herself. She wasn't very steady.

MASAKO: Oh, no. Mr. Oka hit her.

HANA: I don't think so.

MASAKO: He hit her. I saw him.

HANA: You saw that? Papa, do you hear that? She saw them. That does it. We're not going there again.

MURATA: Aww . . . Oka wouldn't do that. Not in front of a kid.

MASAKO: Well, they didn't do it in front of me. They were in the house.

MURATA: You see . . .

HANA: That's all right. You just have to fix the bathhouse. Either that or we're going to bathe at home . . . in a bucket. We're not going . . . we'll bathe at home. [MURATA *mutters to himself.*] What?

MURATA: I said all right, it's the bucket then. I'll get to it when I can.

[HANA *passes* MURATA *and walks ahead.*]

*Fade out.*

## Scene 3

*Same evening. Lights crossfade to the exterior of the Oka house. The Muratas have just left.* EMIKO *sits on the bench. Her back is to* OKA. OKA, *still standing, looks at her contemptuously as she takes the bottle and one of the cups to pour herself a drink.*

OKA: Nothing more disgusting than a drunk woman. [EMIKO *ignores him.*] You made a fool of yourself. *Washi baka ni shite!* You made a fool of me! [EMIKO *doesn't move.*]

EMIKO: One can only make a fool of one's self.

OKA: You learn that in the fancy schools, eh? [EMIKO *examines the pattern on her cup.*] Eh? Eh? Answer me! [EMIKO *ignores.*] I'm talking to you. Answer me! [*Menacing.*] You don't get away with that. You think you're so fine . . . [EMIKO *looks off into the horizon.* OKA *turns her roughly around.*] When I talk, you listen! [EMIKO *turns away again.* OKA *pulls the cup from her hand.*] Goddamnit! What'd you think my friends think of you? What kind of ass they think I am? [*He grabs her shoulders.*]

EMIKO: Don't touch me . . . don't touch me.

OKA: Who the hell you think you are? "Don't touch me, don't touch me." Who the hell! High and mighty, eh? Too good for me, eh? Don't put on the act for me . . . I know who you are.

EMIKO: Tell me who I am, Mister Smart Peasant.

OKA: Shut your fool mouth, goddamnit! Sure! I'll tell you. I know all about you . . . Shizue told me. The whole village knows.

EMIKO: Shizue!

OKA: Yeah! Shizue. Embarrassed the hell out of her, your own sister.

EMIKO: Embarrassed? I have nothing to be ashamed of. I don't know what you're talking about.

OKA: [*Derisively.*] You don't know what I'm talking about. I know. The whole village knows. They're all laughing at you. At me! Stupid Oka got stuck with a second-hand woman. I didn't say anything because . . .

EMIKO: I'm not second-hand!

OKA: Who you trying to fool? I know. Knew long time ago . . . Shizue wrote me all about your affairs in Tokyo. The men you were mess- . . .

EMIKO: Affairs? Men?

OKA: That man you were messing with . . . I knew all along. I didn't say anything because you . . . I . . .

EMIKO: I'm not ashamed of it.

OKA: You're not ashamed! What the hell! Your father thought he was pulling a fast one on me . . . thought I didn't know nothing . . . thought I was some kind of dumb ass . . . I didn't say nothing because Shizue's dead . . . Shizue's dead. I was willing to give you a chance.

EMIKO: [*Laughing.*] A chance?

OKA: Yeah! A chance! Laugh! Give a *joro* another chance. Sure, I'm stupid . . . dumb.

EMIKO: I'm not a whore. I'm true . . . he knows I'm true.

OKA: True! Ha!

EMIKO: You think I'm untrue just because I let . . . let you . . . There's only one man for me.

OKA: Let me [*Obscene gesture.*] you? I can do what I want with you. Your father palmed you off on me—like a dog or cat—an animal . . . couldn't do nothing with you. Even that rich dumb Yamoto wouldn't have you. Your father—greedy father—so proud . . . making big plans for you . . . for himself. Ha! The whole village laughing at him . . . [EMIKO *hangs her head.*] Shizue told me. And she was working like a dog . . . trying to keep your goddamn father happy . . . doing my work and yours.

EMIKO: My work?

OKA: Yeah, your work too! She killed herself working! She killed herself . . . [*He has tender memories of his dull, uncomplaining wife.*] Up in the morning getting the fires started, working the bellows, cleaning the furnace, cooking, and late at night working with the sewing . . . tending the baby . . . [*He mutters.*] The goddamn family killed her. And you . . . you out there in Tokyo with the fancy clothes, doing the [*He sneers.*] dance, the tea, the flower, the *koto*, and the . . . [*Obscene gesture.*]

EMIKO: [*Hurting.*] Achhhh . . .

OKA: Did you have fun? Did you have fun on your sister's blood? [EMIKO *doesn't answer.*] Did you? He must have been a son-of-a-bitch . . . What would make that goddamn greedy old man send his prize mare to a plow horse like me? What kind of bum was he that your father . . .

EMIKO: He's not a bum . . . he's not a bum.

OKA: Was he Korean? Was he *Etta?* That's the only thing I could figure.

EMIKO: I'm true to him. Only him.

OKA: True? You think he's true to you? You think he waits for you? Remembers you? *Aho!* Think he cares?

EMIKO: [*Nodding quietly.*] He does.

OKA: And waits ten years? *Baka!* Go back to Japan and see. You'll find out. Go back to Japan. *Kaire!*

EMIKO: In time.

OKA: In time? How about now?

EMIKO: I can't now.

OKA: Ha! Now! Go now! Who needs you? Who needs you? You think a man waits ten years for a woman? You think you're some kind of . . . of . . . diamond . . . treasure . . . he's going to wait his life for you? Go to him. He's probably married with ten kids. Go to him. Get out! Goddamn *joro* . . . Go! Go!

[OKA *sweeps* EMIKO *off the bench.*]

EMIKO: [*Hurting.*] Ahhhh! I . . . I don't have the money. Give me money to . . .

OKA: If I had money I would give it to you ten years ago. You think I been eating this *kuso* for ten years because I like it?

EMIKO: You're selling the horse . . . Give me the . . .

OKA: [*Scoffing.*] That's for Kiyoko. I owe you nothing.

EMIKO: Ten years, you owe me.

OKA: Ten years of what? Misery? You gave me nothing. I give you nothing.

You want to go, pack your bag and start walking. Try cross the desert. When you get dry and hungry, think about me.

EMIKO: I'd die out there.

OKA: Die? You think I didn't die here?

EMIKO: I didn't do anything to you.

OKA: No, no you didn't. All I wanted was a little comfort and . . . you . . . no, you didn't. No. So you die. We all die. Shizue died. If she was here, she wouldn't treat me like this . . . [*He thinks of his poor dead wife.*] Ah, I should have brought her with me. She'd be alive now. We'd be poor but happy . . . like . . . like Murata and his wife . . . and the kid . . .

EMIKO: I wish she were alive too. I'm not to blame for her dying. I didn't know . . . I was away. I loved her. I didn't want her to die . . . I . . .

OKA: [*Softening.*] I know that. I'm not blaming you for that . . . And it's not my fault what happened to you either . . . [EMIKO *is silent and* OKA *mistakes that for a change in attitude. He is encouraged.*] You understand that, eh? I didn't ask for you. It's not my fault you're here in this desert . . . with . . . with me . . . [EMIKO *weeps.* OKA *reaches out.*] I know I'm too old for you. It's hard for me too . . . but this is the way it is. I just ask you be kinder . . . understand it wasn't my fault. Try make it easier for me . . . for yourself too.

[OKA *touches her and she shrinks from his touch.*]

EMIKO: Ach!

OKA: [*Humiliated again.*] Goddamn it! I didn't ask for you! *Aho!* If you was smart you'd done as your father said . . . cut out that *saru shibai* with the *Etta* . . . married the rich Yamoto. Then you'd still be in Japan. Not here to make my life so miserable. [EMIKO *is silent.*] And you can have your *Etta* . . . and anyone else you want. Take them all on . . . [OKA *is worn out. It's hopeless.*] God, why do we do this all the time? Fighting, fighting all the time. There must be a better way to live . . . there must be another way.

[OKA *waits for a response, gives up, and enters the house.* EMIKO *watches him leave and pours herself another drink. The storm has passed, the alcohol takes over. She turns to the door* OKA *disappeared into.*]

EMIKO: Because I must keep the dream alive . . . the dream is all I live for. I am only in exile now. Because if I give in, all I've lived before . . . will mean nothing . . . will be for nothing . . . Because if I let you make me believe this is all there is to my life, the dream would die . . . I would die . . . [*She pours another drink and feels warm and good.*]

*Fade out.*

# ACT II

## Scene 1

*Mid-September, afternoon. Muratas' kitchen. The calendar reads September.* MASAKO *is at the kitchen table with several books. She thumbs through a Japanese magazine.* HANA *is with her sewing.*

MASAKO: Do they always wear kimonos in Japan, Mama?

HANA: Most of the time.

MASAKO: I wonder if Kiyoko will be wearing a kimono like this?

HANA: [*Peering into* MASAKO's *magazine.*] They don't dress like that . . . not for every day.

MASAKO: I wonder what she's like.

HANA: Probably a lot like you. What do you think she's like?

MASAKO: She's probably taller.

HANA: Mr. Oka isn't tall.

MASAKO: And pretty . . .

HANA: [*Laughing.*] Mr. Oka . . . Well, I don't suppose she'll look like her father.

MASAKO: Mrs. Oka is pretty.

HANA: She isn't Kiyoko-san's real mother, remember.

MASAKO: Oh. That's right.

HANA: But they are related. Well, we'll soon see.

MASAKO: I thought she was coming in September. It's already September.

HANA: Papa said Oka-san went to San Pedro a few days ago. He should be back soon with Kiyoko-san.

MASAKO: Didn't Mrs. Oka go too?

HANA: [*Glancing toward the Oka house.*] I don't think so. I see lights in their house at night.

MASAKO: Will they bring Kiyoko over to see us?

HANA: Of course. First thing, probably. You'll be very nice to her, won't you?

[MASAKO *leaves the table and finds another book.*]

MASAKO: Sure. I'm glad I'm going to have a friend. I hope she likes me.

HANA: She'll like you. Japanese girls are very polite, you know.

MASAKO: We have to be or our Mamas get mad at us.

HANA: Then I should be getting mad at you more often.

MASAKO: It's often enough already, Mama. [*She opens a hardback book.*] Look at this, Mama . . . I'm going to show her this book.

HANA: She won't be able to read at first.

MASAKO: I love this story. Mama, this is about people like us—settlers—it's about the prairie. We live in a prairie, don't we?

HANA: Prairie? Does that mean desert?

MASAKO: I think so.

HANA: [*Nodding and looking bleak.*] We live in a prairie.

MASAKO: It's about the hardships and the floods and droughts and how they have nothing but each other.

HANA: [*Nodding.*] We have nothing but each other. But these people—they're white people.

MASAKO: [*Nodding.*] Sure, Mama. They come from the east. Just like you and Papa came from Japan.

HANA: We come from the far far east. That's different. White people are different from us.

MASAKO: I know that.

HANA: White people among white people . . . that's different from Japanese among white people. You know what I'm saying?

MASAKO: I know that. How come they don't write books about us . . . about Japanese people?

HANA: Because we're nobodies here.

MASAKO: If I didn't read these, there'd be nothing for me . . .

HANA: Some of the things you read, you're never going to know.

MASAKO: I can dream, though.

HANA: [*Sighing.*] Sometimes the dreaming makes the living harder. Better to keep your head out of the clouds.

MASAKO: That's not much fun.

HANA: You'll have fun when Kiyoko-san comes. You can study together, you can sew, and sometime you can try some of those fancy American recipes.

MASAKO: Mama, you have to have chocolate and cream and things like that.

HANA: We'll get them.

[*We hear the putt-putt of* OKA's *old car.* MASAKO *and* HANA *pause and listen.* MASAKO *runs to the window.*]

MASAKO: I think it's them!

HANA: The Okas?

MASAKO: It's them! It's them!

[HANA *stands and looks out. She removes her apron and puts away her sewing.*]

HANA: Two of them. Emiko-san isn't with them. Let's go outside.

[OKA *and* KIYOKO, *14, enter.* OKA *is wearing his going-out clothes: a sweater, white shirt, dark pants, but no tie.* KIYOKO *walks behind him. She is short, chunky, broadchested and very self-conscious. Her hair is straight and banded into two shucks. She wears a conservative cotton dress, white socks and two-inch heels.* OKA *is proud. He struts in, his chest puffed out.*]

OKA: Hello, hello . . . We're here. We made it! [*He pushes* KIYOKO *forward.*] This is my daughter, Kiyoko. [*To* KIYOKO.] Murata-san . . . remember I was talking about? My friends . . .

KIYOKO: [*Barely audible, bowing deeply.*] Hajime mashite yoroshiku onegai shimasu . . .

HANA: [*Also bowing formally.*] I hope your journey was pleasant.

OKA: [*While the women are still bowing, he pushes* KIYOKO *toward* MASAKO.] This is Masako-chan; I told you about her . . .

[MASAKO *is shocked at* KIYOKO's *appearance. The girl she expected is already a woman. She stands with her mouth agape and withdraws noticeably.* HANA *rushes in to fill the awkwardness.*]

HANA: Say hello, Masako. My goodness, where are your manners? [*She laughs apologetically.*] In this country they don't make much to-do about manners. [*She stands back to examine* KIYOKO.] My, my, I didn't picture you so grown up. My, my . . . Tell me, how was your trip?

OKA: [*Proudly.*] We just drove in from Los Angeles just this morning. We spent the night in San Pedro and the next two days we spent in Los Angeles . . . you know, Japanese town.

HANA: How nice!

OKA: Kiyoko was so excited. Twisting her head this way and that—couldn't see enough with her big eyes. [*He imitates her fondly.*] She's from the country, you know . . . just a big country girl. Got all excited about the Chinese dinner—we had a Chinese dinner. She never ate it before.

[KIYOKO *covers her mouth and giggles.*]

HANA: Chinese dinner!

OKA: Oh, yeah. Duck, pakkai, chow mein, seaweed soup . . . the works!

HANA: A feast!

OKA: Oh, yeah. Like a holiday. Two holidays. Two holidays in one.

HANA: [*Pushes* MASAKO *forward.*] Two holidays in one! Kiyoko-san, our Masako has been looking forward to meeting you.

KIYOKO: [*Bowing again.*] Hajime mashite . . .

HANA: She's been thinking of all sorts of things she can do with you: sewing, cooking . . .

MASAKO: Oh, Mama.

[KIYOKO *covers her mouth and giggles.*]

HANA: It's true, Kiyoko-san. She's been looking forward to having a best friend.

[KIYOKO *giggles again and* MASAKO *pulls away.*]

OKA: Kiyoko, you shouldn't be so shy. The Muratas are my good friends and you should feel free with them. Ask anything, say anything . . . right?

HANA: Of course, of course. [*She is slightly annoyed with* MASAKO.] Masako, go in and start the tea. [MASAKO *enters the house.*] I'll call Papa. He's in the yard. Papa! Oka-san is here! [*To* KIYOKO.] Now tell me, how was your trip? Did you get seasick?

KIYOKO: [*Bowing and nodding.*] Eh ("yes"). A little . . .

OKA: Tell her. Tell her how sick you got.

[KIYOKO *covers her mouth and giggles.*]

HANA: Oh, I know, I know. I was too. That was a long time ago. I'm sure things are improved now. Tell me about Japan . . . what is it like now? They say it's so changed . . . modern . . .

OKA: Kiyoko comes from the country . . . backwoods. Nothing changes much there from century to century.

HANA: Ah! That's true. That's why I love Japan. And you wanted to leave. It's unbelievable. To come here!

OKA: She always dreamed about it.

HANA: Well, it's not really that bad.

OKA: No, it's not that bad. Depends on what you make of it.

HANA: That's right. What you make of it. I was just telling Masako today . . .

[MURATA *enters. He rubs his hands to take off the soil and comes in grinning. He shakes* OKA's *hand.*]

MURATA: Oi, oi . . .

OKA: Yah . . . I'm back. This is my daughter.

MURATA: No! She's beautiful!

OKA: Finally made it. Finally got her here.

MURATA: [*To* KIYOKO.] Your father hasn't stopped talking about you all summer.

HANA: And Masako too.

KIYOKO: [*Bowing.*] Hajime mashite . . .

MURATA: [*Acknowledging with a short bow.*] Yah. How'd you like the trip?

OKA: I was just telling your wife—had a good time in Los Angeles. Had a couple of great dinners, took in the cinema—Japanese pictures, bought her some American clothes.

HANA: Oh, you bought that in Los Angeles.

MURATA: Got a good price for your horse, eh? Lots of money, eh?

OKA: Nagata's a shrewd bargainer. Heh. It don't take much money to make her happy. She's a country girl.

MURATA: That's all right. Country's all right. Country girl's the best.

OKA: Had trouble on the way back.

MURATA: Yeah?

OKA: Fan belt broke.

MURATA: That'll happen.

OKA: Lucky I was near a gasoline station. We were in the mountains. Waited in a restaurant while it was getting fixed.

HANA: Oh, that was good.

OKA: Guess they don't see Japanese much. Stare? Terrible! Took them a long time to wait on us. Dumb waitress practically threw the food at us. Kiyoko felt bad.

HANA: Ah! That's too bad . . . too bad. That's why I always pack a lunch when we take trips.

MURATA: They'll spoil the day for you . . . those barbarians!

OKA: Terrible food too. Kiyoko couldn't swallow the dry bread and bologna.

HANA: That's the food they eat!

MURATA: Let's go in . . . have a little wine. Mama, we got wine? This is a celebration.

HANA: I think so . . . a little . . . [*They enter the house talking.* MASAKO *has made the tea, and* HANA *begins to serve the wine.*] How is your mother? Was she happy to see you?

KIYOKO: Oh, she . . . yes . . .

HANA: I just know she was surprised to see you so grown up. Of course, you remember her from Japan, don't you?

KIYOKO: [*Nodding.*] *Eh* ("yes"). I can barely remember. I was very young . . .

HANA: Of course. But you do, don't you?

KIYOKO: She was gone most of the time . . . at school in Tokyo. She was very pretty, I remember that.

HANA: She's still very pretty.

KIYOKO: *Eh.* She was always laughing. She was much younger then.

HANA: Oh now, it hasn't been that long ago.

[MASAKO *leaves the room to go outside. The following dialogue continues muted as light goes dim in the house and focuses on* MASAKO. EMIKO *enters, is drawn to the* MURATA *window and listens.*]

OKA: We stayed at an inn on East First Street. *Shizuokaya.* Whole inn filled with Shizuoka people . . . talking the old dialect. Thought I was in Japan again.

MURATA: That right?

OKA: Felt good. Like I was in Japan again.

HANA: [*To* KIYOKO.] Did you enjoy Los Angeles?

KIYOKO: [*Nodding.*] *Eh.*

OKA: That's as close as I'll get to Japan.

MURATA: *Mattakuna!* That's for sure.

[*Outside* MASAKO *becomes aware of* EMIKO.]

MASAKO: Why don't you go in?

EMIKO: Oh. Oh. Why don't you?

MASAKO: They're all grown-ups in there. I'm not grown up.

EMIKO: [*Softly.*] All grown-ups . . . Maybe I'm not either. [*Her mood changes.*] Masa-chan, do you have a boy friend?

MASAKO: I don't like boys. They don't like me.

EMIKO: Oh, that will change. You will change. I was like that too.

MASAKO: Besides, there're none around here . . . Japanese boys . . . There are some at school, but they don't like girls.

HANA: [*Calling from the kitchen.*] Masako . . .

[MASAKO *doesn't answer.*]

EMIKO: Your mother is calling you.

MASAKO: [*Answering her mother.*] Nani? ("What?")

HANA: [*From the kitchen.*] Come inside now.

EMIKO: You'll have a boy friend one day.

MASAKO: Not me.

EMIKO: You'll fall in love one day. Someone will make the inside of you light up, and you'll know you're in love. [*She relives her own experience.*] Your life will change . . . grow beautiful. It's good, Masa-chan. And this feeling you'll remember the rest of your life . . . will come back to you . . . haunt you . . . keep you alive . . . five, ten years . . . no matter what happens . . . keep you alive.

HANA: [*From the kitchen.*] Masako . . . come inside now.

[MASAKO *turns aside to answer and* EMIKO *slips away.*]

MASAKO: What, Mama?

[HANA *comes out.*]

HANA: Come inside. Don't be so unsociable. Kiyoko wants to talk to you.

MASAKO: [*Watching* EMIKO *leave.*] She doesn't want to talk to me. You're only saying that.

HANA: What's the matter with you? Don't you want to make friends with her?

MASAKO: She's not my friend. She's your friend.

HANA: Don't be so silly. She's only fourteen.

MASAKO: Fifteen. They said fifteen. She's your friend. She's an old lady.

HANA: Don't say that.

MASAKO: I don't like her.

HANA: Shhh! Don't say that.

MASAKO: She doesn't like me either.

HANA: Ma-chan. Remember your promise to Mr. Oka? You're going to take her to school, teach her the language, teach her the ways of Americans.

MASAKO: She can do it herself. You did.

HANA: That's not nice, Ma-chan.

MASAKO: I don't like the way she laughs.

[*She imitates* KIYOKO *holding her hand to her mouth and giggling and bowing.*]

HANA: Oh, how awful! Stop that. That's the way the girls do in Japan. Maybe she doesn't like your ways either. That's only a difference in manners. What you're doing now is considered very bad manners. [*She changes tone.*] Ma-chan . . . just wait—when she learns to read and speak, you'll have so much to say to each other. Come on, be a good girl and come inside.

MASAKO: It's just old people in there, Mama. I don't want to go in.

[HANA *calls* KIYOKO *away from the table and speaks confidentially to her.*]

HANA: Kiyoko-san, please come here a minute. Maybe it's better for you to talk to Masako alone. [KIYOKO *leaves the table and walks to* HANA *outside.*] Masako has a lot of things to tell you about . . . what to expect in school and things . . .

MURATA: [*Calling from the table.*] Mama, put out something . . . chiles . . . for Oka-san.

[HANA *leaves the two girls and enters the house.* KIYOKO *and* MASAKO *stand awkwardly,* KIYOKO *glancing shyly at* MASAKO.]

MASAKO: Do you like it here?
KIYOKO: [*Nodding.*] *Eh.*

[*There's an uncomfortable pause.*]

MASAKO: School will be starting next week . . .
KIYOKO: [*Nodding.*] *Eh.*
MASAKO: Do you want to walk to school with me?
KIYOKO: [*Nodding.*] Ah.

[MASAKO *rolls her eyes and tries again.*]

MASAKO: I leave at 7:30.
KIYOKO: Ah.

[*There's a long pause.* MASAKO *finally gives up and moves off stage.*]

MASAKO: I have to do something

[KIYOKO *watches her leave and uncertainly moves back to the house.* HANA *looks up at* KIYOKO *coming in alone, sighs, and quietly pulls out a chair for her.*]

*Fade out.*

## Scene 2

*November night. Interior of the Murata house. Lamps are lit. The family is at the kitchen table.* HANA *sews,* MASAKO *does her homework,* MURATA *reads the paper. They're dressed in warm robes and having tea. Outside thunder rolls in the distance and lightning flashes.*

HANA: It'll be *ohigan* ("an autumn festival") soon.
MURATA: Something to look forward to.

HANA: We will need sweet rice for *omochi* ("rice cakes").

MURATA: I'll order it next time I go to town.

HANA: [*To* MASAKO.] How is school? Getting a little harder?

MASAKO: Not that much. Sometimes the arithmetic is hard.

HANA: How is Kiyoko-san doing? Is she getting along all right?

MASAKO: She's good in arithmetic. She skipped a grade already.

HANA: Already? That's good news. Only November and she skipped a grade! At this rate she'll be through before you.

MASAKO: Well, she's older.

MURATA: Sure, she's older, Mama.

HANA: Has she made any friends?

MASAKO: No. She follows me around all day. She understands okay, but she doesn't talk. She talks like, you know . . . she says "ranchi" for lunch and "ranchi" for ranch too, and like that. Kids laugh and copy behind her back. It's hard to understand her.

HANA: You understand her, don't you?

MASAKO: I'm used to it. [MURATA *smiles secretly.*]

HANA: You should tell the kids not to laugh; after all, she's trying. Maybe you should help her practice those words . . . show her what she's doing wrong.

MASAKO: I already do. Our teacher told me to do that.

MURATA: [*Looking up from his paper.*] You ought to help her all you can.

HANA: And remember when you started school you couldn't speak English either.

MASAKO: I help her.

[MURATA *rises and goes to the window. The night is cold. Lightning flashes and the wind whistles.*]

MURATA: Looks like a storm coming up. Hope we don't have a freeze.

HANA: If it freezes, we'll have another bad year. Maybe we ought to start the smudge pots.

MURATA: [*Listening.*] It's starting to rain. Nothing to do now but pray.

HANA: If praying is the answer, we'd be in Japan now . . . rich.

MURATA: [*Wryly.*] We're not dead yet. We still have a chance. [HANA *glares at this small joke.*] Guess I'll turn in.

HANA: Go to bed . . . go to bed. I'll sit up and worry.

MURATA: If worrying was the answer, we'd be around the world twice and in Japan. Come on, Mama. Let's go to bed. It's too cold tonight to be mad. [*There's an urgent knock on the door. The family react to it.*] Dareh da! ("Who is it!") [MURATA *goes to the door and pauses.*] Who is it!

KIYOKO: [*Weakly.*] It's me . . . help me . . .

[MURATA *opens the door and* KIYOKO *enters. She's dressed in a kimono with a shawl thrown over. Her legs are bare except for a pair of straw* zori. *Her hair is stringy from the rain and she trembles from the cold.*]

MURATA: My God! Kiyoko-san! What's the matter?

HANA: Kiyoko-san! What is it?

MURATA: What happened?

KIYOKO: [*Gasping.*] They're fighting . . . they're fighting.

MURATA: Ah . . . don't worry . . . those things happen. No cause to worry. Mama, make tea for her. Sit down and catch your breath. I'll take you home when you're ready.

HANA: Papa, I'll take care of it.

MURATA: Let me know when you're ready to go home.

HANA: It must be freezing out there. Try to get warm. Try to calm yourself.

MURATA: Kiyoko-san . . . don't worry.

[HANA *waves* MASAKO *and* MURATA *off.* MURATA *leaves.* MASAKO *goes to her bed in the kitchen.*]

HANA: Papa, I'll take care of it.

KIYOKO: [*Looking at* MURATA's *retreating form.*] I came to ask your help.

HANA: You ran down here without a lantern? You could have fallen and hurt yourself.

KIYOKO: I don't care . . . I don't care.

HANA: You don't know, Kiyoko-san. It's treacherous out there . . . snakes, spiders . . .

KIYOKO: I must go back . . . I . . . I . . . you . . . please come with me.

HANA: First, first, we must get you warm . . . Drink your tea.

KIYOKO: But they might kill each other. They're fighting like animals. Help me stop them!

[HANA *goes to the stove to warm a pot of soup.*]

HANA: I cannot interfere in a family quarrel.

KIYOKO: It's not a quarrel . . . it's a . . .

HANA: That's all it is. A family squabble. You'll see. Tomorrow . . .

[KIYOKO *rises and puts her hand on* HANA's *arm.*]

KIYOKO: Not just a squabble . . . please! [*She starts toward the door but* HANA *restrains her.*]

HANA: Now listen. Listen to me, Kiyoko-san. I've known your father and mother a little while now. I suspect it's been like this for years. Every family has some kind of trouble.

KIYOKO: Not like this . . . not like this.

HANA: Some have it better—some worse. When you get married, you'll understand. Don't worry. Nothing will happen. [*She takes a towel from the wall and dries* KIYOKO's *hair.*] You're chilled to the bone. You'll catch your death . . .

KIYOKO: I don't care . . . I want to die.

HANA: Don't be silly. It's not that bad.

KIYOKO: They started drinking early in the afternoon. They make some kind of brew and hide it somewhere in the desert.

HANA: It's illegal to make it. That's why they hide it. That home brew is poison to the body . . . and the mind too.

KIYOKO: It makes them crazy. They drink it all the time and quarrel constantly. I was in the other room studying. I try so hard to keep up with school.

HANA: We were talking about you just this evening. Masako says you're doing so well . . . you skipped a grade?

KIYOKO: It's hard . . . hard . . . I'm too old for the class and the children . . . [*She remembers all her problems and starts to cry again.*]

HANA: It's always hard in a new country.

KIYOKO: They were bickering and quarreling all afternoon. Then something happened. All of a sudden I saw them on the floor . . . hitting and . . . and . . . He was hitting her in the stomach, the face . . . I tried to stop them, but they were so . . . drunk.

HANA: There, there . . . It's probably all over now.

KIYOKO: Why does it happen like this? Nothing is right. Everywhere I go . . . Masa-chan is so lucky. I wish my life was like hers. I can hardly remember my real mother.

HANA: Emiko-san is almost a real mother to you. She's blood kin.

KIYOKO: She hates me. She never speaks to me. She's so cold. I want to love her but she won't let me. She hates me.

HANA: I don't think that's true, Kiyoko-san.

KIYOKO: I know it's true.

HANA: No. I don't think you have anything to do with it. It's this place. She hates it. This place is so lonely and alien.

KIYOKO: Then why didn't she go back? Why did they stay here?

HANA: You don't know. It's not so simple. Sometimes I think . . .

KIYOKO: Then why don't they make the best of it here? Like you?

HANA: That isn't easy either. Believe me. [*She goes to the stove to stir the soup.*] Sometimes . . . sometimes the longing for homeland fills me with despair. Will I never return again? Will I never see my mother, my father, my sisters again? But what can one do? There are responsibilities here . . . children . . . [*She draws a sharp breath.*] And another day passes . . . another month . . . another year. Eventually everything passes. [*She takes the soup to* KIYOKO.] Did you have supper tonight?

KIYOKO: [*Bowing gratefully.*] Ah. When my . . . my aunt gets like this, she doesn't cook. No one eats. I don't get hungry anymore.

HANA: Cook for yourself. It's important to keep your health.

KIYOKO: I left Japan for a better life here . . .

HANA: It isn't easy for you, is it? But you must remember your filial duty.

KIYOKO: It's so hard.

HANA: But you can make the best of it here, Kiyoko-san. And take care of

yourself. You owe that to yourself. Eat. Keep well. It'll be better, you'll
see. And sometimes it'll seem worse. But you'll survive. We do, you
know . . . we do . . . [*She looks around.*] It's getting late.

KIYOKO: [*Apprehensively.*] I don't want to go back.

HANA: You can sleep with Masako tonight. Tomorrow you'll go back. And
you'll remember what I told you. [*She puts her arms around* KIYOKO, *who is
overcome with self-pity and begins to weep quietly.*] Life is never easy, Kiyoko-
san. Endure. Endure. Soon you'll be marrying and going away. Things
will not always be this way. And you'll look back on this . . . this night
and you'll . . .

[*There is a rap on the door.* HANA *exchanges glances with* KIYOKO *and goes to
answer it. She opens it a crack.* OKA *has come looking for* KIYOKO. *He's dressed
in an overcoat and holds a wet newspaper over his head.*]

OKA: Ah! I'm sorry to bother you so late at night . . . the fact is . . .

HANA: Oka-san . . .

OKA: [*Jovially.*] Good evening, good evening . . . [*He sees* KIYOKO.] Ah . . .
there you are . . . Did you have a nice visit?

HANA: [*Irritated.*] Yes, she's here.

OKA: [*Still cheerful.*] Thought she might be. Ready to come home now?

HANA: She came in the rain.

OKA: [*Ignoring* HANA'*s tone.*] That's foolish of you, Kiyoko. You might catch
cold.

HANA: She was frightened by your quarreling. She came for help.

OKA: [*Laughing with embarrassment.*] Oh! Kiyoko, that's nothing to worry about.
It's just we had some disagreement . . .

HANA: That's what I told her, but she was frightened all the same.

OKA: Children are . . .

HANA: Not children, Oka-san. Kiyoko. Kiyoko was terrified. I think that was
a terrible thing to do to her.

OKA: [*Rubbing his head.*] Oh, I . . . I . . .

HANA: If you had seen her a few minutes ago . . . hysterical . . . shaking . . .
crying . . . wet and cold to the bone . . . out of her mind with worry.

OKA: [*Rubbing his head.*] Oh . . . I . . . don't know what she was so worried
about.

HANA: You. You and Emiko fighting like you were going to kill each other.

OKA: [*There's nothing more to hide. He lowers his head in penitence.*]
Aaaaaachhhhhhh . . .

HANA: I know I shouldn't tell you this, but there're one or two things I have
to say: You sent for Kiyoko-san and now she's here. You said yourself
she had a bad time in Japan, and now she's having a worse time. It isn't
easy for her in a strange new country; the least you can do is try to keep
her from worrying . . . especially about yourselves. I think it's terrible
what you're doing to her . . . terrible!

OKA: [*Bowing in deep humility.*] I am ashamed . . .

HANA: I think she deserves better. I think you should think about that.

OKA: [*Still in his bow.*] I thank you for this reminder. It will never happen again. I promise.

HANA: I don't need that promise. Make it to Kiyoko-san.

OKA: [*To* KIYOKO.] Come with Papa now. He did a bad thing. He'll be a good Papa from now. He won't worry his little girl again. All right? All right? [*They move to the door.*]

KIYOKO: Thank you so much. [*She takes* MURATA's *robe and tries to return it.*]

OKA: Madam. I thank you again.

HANA: [*To* KIYOKO.] That's all right. You can bring it back tomorrow. [*Aside to* KIYOKO.] Remember . . . remember what we talked about. [*Loudly.*] Goodnight, Oka-san.

[*They leave.* HANA *goes to* MASAKO, *who lies on the bed. She covers her.* MURATA *appears from the bedroom. He's heard it all. He and* HANA *exchange a glance and together they retire to their room.*]

*Fade out.*

### Scene 3

*The next morning. The Murata house and yard.* HANA *and* MURATA *have already left the house to examine the rain damage in the fields.* MASAKO *prepares to go to school. She puts on a coat and picks up her books and lunch bag. Meanwhile,* KIYOKO *slips quietly into the yard. She wears a coat and carries* MURATA's *robe and sets it on the outside bench.* MASAKO *walks out and is surprised to see* KIYOKO.

MASAKO: Hi. I thought you'd be . . . sick today.

KIYOKO: Oh. I woke up late.

MASAKO: [*Scrutinizing* KIYOKO's *face.*] Your eyes are red.

KIYOKO: [*Averting her eyes.*] Oh. I . . . got . . . sand in it. Yes.

MASAKO: Do you want to use eye drops? We have eye drops in the house.

KIYOKO: Oh . . . no. That's all right.

MASAKO: That's what you call bloodshot.

KIYOKO: Oh.

MASAKO: My father gets it a lot. When he drinks too much.

KIYOKO: Oh . . .

[MASAKO *notices* KIYOKO *doesn't have her lunch.*]

MASAKO: Where's your lunch bag?

KIYOKO: I . . . forgot it.

MASAKO: Did you make your lunch today?

KIYOKO: Yes. Yes, I did. But I forgot it.

MASAKO: Do you want to go back and get it?

KIYOKO: No, that's all right. [*They are silent for a while.*] We'll be late.

MASAKO: Do you want to practice your words?

KIYOKO: [*Thoughtfully.*] Oh . . .

MASAKO: Say, "My."

KIYOKO: My?

MASAKO: Eyes . . .

KIYOKO: Eyes.

MASAKO: Are . . .

KIYOKO: Are.

MASAKO: Red.

KIYOKO: Red.

MASAKO: Your eyes are red. [KIYOKO *doesn't repeat it.*] I . . . [KIYOKO *doesn't cooperate.*] Say, "I."

KIYOKO: I.

MASAKO: Got . . .

KIYOKO: Got.

MASAKO: Sand . . . [KIYOKO *balks.*] Say, "I."

KIYOKO: [*Sighing.*] I.

MASAKO: Reft . . .

KIYOKO: Reft.

MASAKO: My . . .

KIYOKO: My.

MASAKO: Runch . . .

KIYOKO: Run . . . Lunch. [*She stops.*] Masako-san, you are mean. You are hurting me.

MASAKO: It's a joke! I was just trying to make you laugh!

KIYOKO: I cannot laugh today.

MASAKO: Sure you can. You can laugh. Laugh! Like this! [*She makes a hearty laugh.*]

KIYOKO: I cannot laugh when you make fun of me.

MASAKO: Okay, I'm sorry. We'll practice some other words then, okay? [KIYOKO *doesn't answer.*] Say, "Okay."

KIYOKO: [*Reluctantly.*] Okay . . .

MASAKO: Okay, then . . . um . . . um . . . [*She still teases and talks rapidly.*] Say . . . um . . . "She sells sea shells on the sea shore." [KIYOKO *turns away indignantly.*] Aw, come on, Kiyoko! It's just a joke. Laugh!

KIYOKO: [*Imitating sarcastically.*] Ha-ha-ha! Now you say, "*Kono kyaku wa yoku kaki ku kyaku da!*"

MASAKO: Sure! I can say it! Kono kyaku waki ku kyoku kaku . . .

KIYOKO: That's not right.

MASAKO: Koki kuki kya . . .

KIYOKO: No.

MASAKO: Okay, then. You say, "Sea sells she shells . . . shu . . . sss . . ."

[*They both laugh,* KIYOKO *with her hands over her mouth.*]

MASAKO: [*Taking* KIYOKO's *hands from her mouth.*] Not like that! Like this! [*She gives a big belly laugh.*]

KIYOKO: Like this? [*She imitates* MASAKO.]

MASAKO: Yeah, that's right! You're not mad anymore?

KIYOKO: I'm not mad anymore.

MASAKO: Okay. You can share my lunch today because we're . . .

KIYOKO: "Flends?"

> [MASAKO *looks at* KIYOKO, *they giggle and move on.* HANA AND MURATA *come in from assessing the storm's damage. They are dressed warmly.* HANA *is depressed.* MURATA *tries hard to be cheerful.*]

MURATA: It's not so bad, Mama.

HANA: Half the ranch is flooded . . . at least half.

MURATA: No-no. A quarter, maybe. It's sunny today . . . it'll dry.

HANA: The seedlings will rot.

MURATA: No, no. It'll dry. It's all right—better than I expected.

HANA: If we have another bad year, no one will lend us money for the next crop.

MURATA: Don't worry. If it doesn't drain by tomorrow, I'll replant the worst places. We still have some seed left. Yeah, I'll replant . . .

HANA: More work.

MURATA: Don't worry, Mama. It'll be all right.

HANA: [*Quietly.*] Papa, where will it end? Will we always be like this—always at the mercy of the weather—prices—always at the mercy of the Gods?

MURATA: [*Patting* HANA's *back.*] Things will change. Wait and see. We'll be back in Japan by . . . in two years . . . guarantee . . . Maybe sooner.

HANA: [*Dubiously.*] Two years . . .

MURATA: [*Finds the robe on the bench.*] Ah, look, Mama. Kiyoko-san brought back my robe.

HANA: [*Sighing.*] Kiyoko-san . . . poor Kiyoko-san . . . and Emiko-san.

MURATA: Ah, Mama. We're lucky. We're lucky, Mama.

> [HANA *smiles sadly at* MURATA.]

*Fade out.*

## Scene 4

*The following spring, afternoon. Exterior of the Oka house. Oka is dressed to go out. He wears a sweater, long-sleeved white shirt, dark pants, no tie. He puts his foot on the bench to wipe off his shoe with the palm of his hand. He straightens his sleeve, removes a bit of lint and runs his fingers through his hair. He hums under his breath.* KIYOKO *comes from the house. Her hair is frizzled with a permanent wave, she wears a gaudy new dress and a pair of new shoes. She carries a movie magazine—*Photoplay *or* Modern Screen.

OKA: [*Appreciatively.*] Pretty. Pretty.

KIYOKO: [*Turning for him.*] It's not too *hadeh?*[7] I feel strange in colors.

---

7. Gaudy.

OKA: Oh no. Young girls should wear bright colors. There's time enough to wear gray when you get old. Old lady colors. [KIYOKO *giggles.*] Sure you want to go to the picture show? It's such a nice day . . . shame to waste in a dark hall.

KIYOKO: Where else can we go?

OKA: We can go to the Muratas.

KIYOKO: All dressed up?

OKA: Or Nagatas. I'll show him what I got for my horse.

KIYOKO: [*Laughing.*] Oh, I love the pictures.

OKA: We don't have many nice spring days like this. Here the season is short. Summer comes in like a dragon . . . right behind . . . breathing fire . . . like a dragon. You don't know the summers here. They'll scare you. [*He tousles* KIYOKO's *hair and pulls a lock of it. It springs back. He shakes his head in wonder.*] Goddamn. Curly hair. Never thought curly hair could make you so happy.

KIYOKO: [*Giggling.*] All the American girls have curly hair.

OKA: Your friend Masako like it?

KIYOKO: [*Nodding.*] She says her mother will never let her get a permanent wave.

OKA: She said that, eh? Bet she's wanting one.

KIYOKO: I don't know about that.

OKA: Bet she's wanting some of your pretty dresses too.

KIYOKO: Her mother makes all her clothes.

OKA: Buying is just as good. Buying is better. No trouble that way.

KIYOKO: Masako's not so interested in clothes. She loves the pictures, but her mother won't let her go. Some day, can we take Masako with us?

OKA: If her mother lets her come. Her mother's got a mind of her own . . . a stiff back.

KIYOKO: But she's nice.

OKA: [*Dubiously.*] Oh, yeah. Can't be perfect, I guess. Kiyoko, after the harvest I'll have money and I'll buy you the prettiest dress in town. I'm going to be lucky this year. I feel it.

KIYOKO: You're already too good to me . . . dresses, shoes, permanent wave . . . movies . . .

OKA: That's nothing. After the harvest, just wait . . .

KIYOKO: Magazines . . . You do enough. I'm happy already.

OKA: You make me happy too, Kiyoko. You make me feel good . . . like a man again . . . [*That statement bothers him.*] One day you're going to make a young man happy. [KIYOKO *giggles.*] Someday we going to move from here.

KIYOKO: But we have good friends here, Papa.

OKA: Next year our lease will be up and we got to move.

KIYOKO: The ranch is not ours?

OKA: No. In America, Japanese cannot own land. We lease and move every two, three years. Next year we going to go someplace where there's young fellows. There's none good enough for you here. [*He watches* KIYOKO *giggle.*] Yeah. You going to make a good wife. Already a good cook. I like your cooking.

KIYOKO: [*A little embarrassed.*] Shall we go now?

OKA: Yeah. Put the magazine away.

KIYOKO: I want to take it with me.

OKA: Take it with you?

KIYOKO: Last time, after we came back, I found all my magazines torn in half.

OKA: [*Looking toward the house.*] Torn?

KIYOKO: This is the only one I have left.

OKA: [*Not wanting to deal with it.*] All right. All right.

[*The two prepare to leave when the door opens.* EMIKO *stands there, her hair is unkempt and she looks wild. She holds an empty can in one hand, the lid in the other.*]

EMIKO: Where is it?

[OKA *tries to make a hasty departure.*]

KIYOKO: Where is what?

[OKA *pushes* KIYOKO *ahead of him, still trying to make a getaway.*]

EMIKO: Where is it? Where is it? What did you do with it? [EMIKO *moves toward* OKA. *He can't ignore her and he stops.*]

OKA: [*With false unconcern to* KIYOKO.] Why don't you walk on ahead to the Muratas?

KIYOKO: We're not going to the pictures?

OKA: We'll go. First you walk to the Muratas. Show them your new dress. I'll meet you there.

[KIYOKO *picks up a small package and exits.* OKA *sighs and shakes his head.*]

EMIKO: [*Shaking the can.*] Where is it? What did you do with it?

OKA: [*Feigning surprise.*] With what?

EMIKO: You know what. You stole it. You stole my money.

OKA: *Your* money?

EMIKO: I've been saving that money.

OKA: Yeah? Well, where'd you get it? Where'd you get it, eh? You stole it from me! Dollar by dollar . . . You stole it from me! Out of my pocket!

EMIKO: I saved it!

OKA: From my pocket!

EMIKO: It's mine! I saved for a long time . . . Some of it I brought from Japan.

OKA: *Bakayuna!*[8] What'd you bring from Japan? Nothing but some useless kimonos. [OKA *starts to leave but* EMIKO *hangs on to him.*]

EMIKO: Give back my money! Thief!

8. Stupid woman.

OKA: [*Swings around and balls his fists but doesn't strike.*] Goddamn! Get off me!

EMIKO: [*Now pleading.*] Please give it back . . . please . . . please . . . [*She starts to stroke him.* OKA *pulls her hands away and pushes her from him.*] Oni!

OKA: [*Seething.*] *Oni?* What does that make you? *Oni baba?* Yeah, that's what you are . . . a devil!

EMIKO: It's mine! Give it back . . .

OKA: The hell! You think you can live off me and steal my money too? How stupid you think I am?

EMIKO: [*Tearfully.*] But I've paid . . . I've paid . . .

OKA: With what?

EMIKO: You know I've paid.

OKA: [*Scoffing.*] You call that paying?

EMIKO: What did you do with it?

OKA: I don't have it.

EMIKO: It's gone? It's gone?

OKA: Yeah! It's gone. I spent it. The hell! Every last cent.

EMIKO: The new clothes . . . the curls . . . restaurants . . . pictures . . . shoes . . . My money . . . my going-home money . . .

OKA: You through?

EMIKO: What will I do? What will . . .

OKA: I don't care what you do. Walk. Use your feet. Swim to Japan. I don't care. I give you no more than you gave me. Now I don't want anything. I don't care what you do. [*He walks away.*]

[EMIKO *still holds the empty can. Off stage we hear* OKA's *car door slam and the sound of his old car starting off. Accustomed to crying alone, she doesn't utter a sound. Her shoulders begin to shake, her dry soundless sobs turn to a silent laugh. She wipes the dust gently from the can as though comforting a friend. Her movements become sensuous, her hands move on to her own body, around her throat, over her breasts, to her hips, caressing, soothing, reminding her of her lover's hands.*]

*Fade out.*

## Scene 5

*Same day, late afternoon. Exterior of the Murata house. The light is soft.* HANA *is sweeping the yard;* MASAKO *hangs a glass wind chime on the exposed wall.*

HANA: [*Directing* MASAKO.] There . . . there. That's a good place.

MASAKO: Here?

HANA: [*Nodding.*] It must catch the slightest breeze. [*Sighing and listening.*] It brings back so much . . . That's the reason I never hung one before. I guess it doesn't matter much any more . . .

MASAKO: I thought you liked to think about Japan.

HANA: [*Laughing sadly.*] I didn't want to hear that sound so often . . . get too used to it. Sometimes you hear something too often, after a while you don't hear it anymore . . . I didn't want that to happen. The same thing happens to feelings too, I guess. After a while you don't feel any more. You're too young to understand that yet.

MASAKO: I understand, Mama.

HANA: Wasn't it nice of Kiyoko-san to give us the *furin?*

MASAKO: I love it. I don't know anything about Japan, but it makes me feel something too.

HANA: Maybe someday when you're grown up, gone away, you'll hear it and remember yourself as this little girl . . . remember this old house, the ranch, and . . . your old mama . . .

MASAKO: That's kind of scary.

[EMIKO *enters unsteadily. She carries a bundle wrapped in a colorful scarf "furoshiki." In the packages are two beautiful kimonos.*]

HANA: Emiko-san! What a pleasant surprise! Please sit down. We were just hanging the *furin.* It was so sweet of Kiyoko-san to give it to Masako. She loves it.

[EMIKO *looks mildly interested. She acts as normal as she can throughout the scene, but at times drops her facade, revealing her desperation.*]

EMIKO: Thank you. [*She sets her bundle on the bench but keeps her hand on it.*]

HANA: Your family was here earlier. [EMIKO *smiles vaguely.*] On their way to the pictures, I think. [*To* MASAKO.] Make tea for us, Ma-chan.

EMIKO: Please don't . . .

HANA: Kiyoko-san was looking so nice—her hair all curly . . . Of course, in our day, straight black hair was desirable. Of course, times change.

EMIKO: Yes.

HANA: But she did look fine. My, my, a colorful new dress, new shoes, a permanent wave—looked like a regular American girl. Did you choose her dress?

EMIKO: No . . . I didn't go.

HANA: You know, I didn't think so. Very pretty, though. I liked it very much. Of course, I sew all Masako's clothes. It saves money. It'll be nice for you to make things for Kiyoko-san too. She'd be so pleased. I know she'd be pleased . . . [*While* HANA *talks,* EMIKO *plucks nervously at her package. She waits for* HANA *to stop talking.*] Emiko-san, is everything all right?

EMIKO: [*Smiling nervously.*] Yes.

HANA: Masako, please go make tea for us. See if there aren't any more of those crackers left. Or did you finish them? [*To* EMIKO.] We can't keep anything in this house. She eats everything as soon as Papa brings it home. You'd never know it, she's so skinny. We never have anything left for company.

MASAKO: We hardly ever have company anyway.

[HANA *gives her daughter a strong look, and* MASAKO *goes into the house.* EMIKO *is lost in her own thoughts. She strokes her package.*]

HANA: Is there something you . . . I can help you with? [*Very gently.*] Emiko-san?

EMIKO: [*Suddenly frightened.*] Oh no. I was thinking . . . Now that . . . now that . . . Masa-chan is growing up . . . older . . .

HANA: [*Relieved.*] Oh, yes. She's growing fast.

EMIKO: I was thinking . . . [*She stops, puts the package on her lap and is lost again.*]

HANA: Yes, she *is* growing. Time goes so fast. I think she'll be taller than me soon. [*She laughs weakly, stops and looks puzzled.*]

EMIKO: Yes.

[EMIKO'*s depression pervades the atmosphere.* HANA *is affected by it. The two women sit in silence. A small breeze moves the wind chimes. At the moment light grows dim on the two lonely figures.* MASAKO *comes from the house with a tray of tea. The light returns to normal again.*]

HANA: [*Gently.*] You're a good girl.

[MASAKO *looks first to* EMIKO *then to her mother. She sets the tray on the bench and stands near* EMIKO, *who seems to notice her for the first time.*]

EMIKO: How are you?

[HANA *pours the tea and serves her.*]

HANA: Emiko-san, is there something I can do for you?

EMIKO: There's . . . I was . . . I . . . Masa-chan will be a young lady soon . . .

HANA: Oh, well, now I don't know about "lady."

EMIKO: Maybe she would like a nice . . . nice . . . [*She unwraps her package.*] I have kimonos . . . I wore in Japan for dancing . . . maybe she can . . . if you like, I mean. They'll be nice on her . . . she's so slim . . .

[EMIKO *shakes out a robe.* HANA *and* MASAKO *are impressed.*]

HANA: Ohhhh! Beautiful!

MASAKO: Oh, Mama! Pretty! [HANA *and* MASAKO *finger the material.*] Gold threads, Mama.

HANA: Brocade!

EMIKO: Maybe Masa-chan would like them. I mean for her school programs . . . Japanese school . . .

HANA: Oh, no! Too good for country. People will be envious of us . . . wonder where we got them.

EMIKO: I mean for festivals . . . *Obon, Hana Matsuri* . . .

HANA: Oh, but you have Kiyoko-san now. You should give them to her. Has she seen them?

EMIKO: Oh . . . no . . .

HANA: She'll love them. You should give them to her . . . not our Masako.

EMIKO: I thought . . . I mean I was thinking of . . . if you could give me a little . . . if you could pay . . . manage to give me something for . . .

HANA: But these gowns, Emiko-san—they're worth hundreds.

EMIKO: I know, but I'm not asking for that. Whatever you can give . . . only as much as you can give.

MASAKO: Mama?

HANA: Masako, Papa doesn't have that kind of money.

EMIKO: Anything you can give . . . anything . . .

MASAKO: Ask Papa.

HANA: There's no use asking. I know he can't afford it.

EMIKO: [*Looking at* MASAKO.] A little at a time.

MASAKO: Mama?

HANA: [*Firmly.*] No, Masako. This is a luxury. [HANA *folds the gowns and puts them away.* MASAKO *is disappointed.* EMIKO *is devastated.* HANA *sees this and tries to find some way to help.*] Emiko-san, I hope you understand . . . [EMIKO *is silent trying to gather her resources.*] I know you can sell them and get the full price somewhere. Let's see . . . a family with a lot of growing daughters . . . someone who did well last year . . . Nagatas have no girls . . . Umedas have girls but no money . . . Well, let's see . . . Maybe not here in this country town. Ah . . . You can take them to the city, Los Angeles, and sell them to a store . . . or Terminal Island . . . lots of wealthy fishermen there. Yes, that would be the place. Why, it's no problem, Emiko-san. Have your husband take them there. I know you'll get your money. He'll find a buyer. I know he will.

EMIKO: Yes.

[EMIKO *finishes folding and ties the scarf. She sits quietly.*]

HANA: Please have your tea. I'm sorry . . . I really would like to take them for Masako but it just isn't possible. You understand, don't you? [EMIKO *nods.*] Please don't feel so . . . so bad. It's not really a matter of life or death, is it? Emiko-san?

[EMIKO *nods again.* HANA *sips her tea.*]

MASAKO: Mama? If you could ask Papa . . .

HANA: Oh, the tea is cold. Masako could you heat the kettle?

EMIKO: No more. I must be going. [*She picks up her package and rises slowly.*]

HANA: [*Looking helpless.*] So soon? Emiko-san, please stay. [EMIKO *starts to go.*] Masako will walk with you. [*She pushes* MASAKO *forward.*]

EMIKO: It's not far.

HANA: Emiko-san? You'll be all right?

EMIKO: Yes . . . yes . . . yes . . .

HANA: [*Calling as* EMIKO *exits.*] I'm sorry, Emiko-san.

EMIKO: Yes . . .

[MASAKO *and* HANA *watch as* EMIKO *leaves. The light grows dim as though a cloud passed over.* EMIKO *exits.* HANA *strokes* MASAKO's *hair.*]

HANA: Your hair is so black and straight . . . nice . . .

[*They stand close. The wind chimes tinkle; light grows dim. Light returns to normal.* MURATA *enters. He sees this tableau of mother and child and is puzzled.*]

MURATA: What's going on here?

[*The two women part.*]

HANA: Oh . . . nothing . . . nothing . . .
MASAKO: Mrs. Oka was here. She had two kimo- . . .
HANA: [*Putting her hand on* MASAKO's *shoulder.*] It was nothing . . .
MURATA: Eh? What'd she want?
HANA: Later, Papa. Right now, I'd better fix supper.
MURATA: [*Looking at the sky.*] Strange how that sun comes and goes. Maybe I didn't need to irrigate—looks like rain. [*He remembers and is exasperated.*] Ach! I forgot to shut the water.
MASAKO: I'll do it, Papa.
HANA: Masako, that gate's too heavy for you.
MURATA: She can handle it. Take out the pin and let the gate fall all the way down. All the way. And put the pin back. Don't forget to put the pin back.
HANA: And be careful. Don't fall in the canal.

[MASAKO *leaves.*]

MURATA: What's the matter with that girl?
HANA: Nothing. Why?
MURATA: Usually have to beg her to do . . .
HANA: She's growing up.
MURATA: Must be that time of the month.
HANA: Oh, Papa, she's too young for that yet.
MURATA: [*Genially as they enter the house.*] Got to start some time. Looks like I'll be out-numbered soon. I'm out-numbered already.

[HANA *glances at him and quietly sets about preparations for supper.* MURATA *removes his shirt and sits at the table with a paper. Light fades slowly.*]

*Fade out.*

## Scene 6

*Same evening. Exterior, desert. There is at least one shrub.* MASAKO *appears, walking slowly. From a distance we hear* EMIKO *singing the song "And the Soul Shall Dance."* MASAKO *looks around, sees the shrub and crouches under it.* EMIKO *appears. She's dressed in her beautiful kimono tied loosely at her waist. She carries a branch of sage. Her hair is loose.*

EMIKO: *Akai kuchibiru / Kappu ni yosete / Aoi sake nomya / Kokoro ga odoru . . . Kurai yoru no yume / Setsu nasa yo . . .*

[*She breaks into a dance, laughs mysteriously, turns round and round, acting out a fantasy.* MASAKO *stirs uncomfortably.* EMIKO *senses a presence. She stops, drops her branch and walks off stage singing as she goes.*]

EMIKO: *Aoi sake nomya / Yume mo odoru . . .*

[MASAKO *watches as* EMIKO *leaves. She rises slowly and picks up the branch* EMIKO *has left. She looks at the branch, moves forward a step and looks off to the point where* EMIKO *disappeared. Light slowly fades until only the image of* MASAKO's *face remains etched in the mind.*]

*Fade out.*

## KOKORO GA ODORU

Akai kuchibiru
Kappu ni yosete
Aoi sake nomya
Kokoro ga odoru

Kurai yoru no yume
Setsu nasa yo
Aoi sake nomya
Yume mo odoru

Asa no munashisa
Yume wo chirasu
Sora to kokoro wa
Sake shidai

Futari wakare no
Samishisa yo
Hitori sake nomya
Kokoro ga odoru

## AND THE SOUL SHALL DANCE

Red lips
Press against a glass
Drink the green wine
And the soul shall dance

Dark night dreams
Are unbearable
Drink the green wine
And the dreams will dance

Morning's reality
Scatter the dreams
Sky and soul
Depend on the wine

The loneliness of
The two apart
Drink the wine alone
And the soul shall dance

LYRICS BY WAKAKO YAMAUCHI

## KAGO NO TORI

Aitasa, mita sa ni
Kowa sa wo wasure
Kurai yomichi wo
Tada hitori

## THE CAGED BIRD
(She)

In the desire to meet her
And the wish to see her
He forgets his fear and
Walks the dark streets alone.

|                          | (He)                          |
|--------------------------|-------------------------------|
| Aini kita no ni          | Though I've come to tryst     |
| Naze dete awanu?         | Why do you not come out?      |
| Boku no yobu koye        | My voice calling you—         |
| Wasure taka?             | Have you forgotten it?        |

|                          | (She)                             |
|--------------------------|-----------------------------------|
| Anata no yobu koye       | Your voice calling me             |
| Wasure ma senu ga        | I have not forgotten, but         |
| Deru ni derareru         | To leave, to be able to leave—    |
| Kago no tori             | No choice for the caged bird.     |

POPULAR SONG

# STUDY QUESTIONS

1. How does the play establish on the stage the sense of importance that the home has to each family? How personal to each family is the sense of place in the family house? What indications are there that the invitation to share the bathhouse is a very personal, almost intimate act?

2. How does each of the CHARACTERS feel about Japan? In each case, how are his or her feelings revealed? Which characters show the most interest in American ways and in adapting to life in America? Who resists most?

3. What facts about the life of Japanese farmers in America in the 1930s emphasize the rootlessness felt by the two families? In what ways does the action of the play emphasize the lack of a sense of permanence? In what ways does the SETTING emphasize the transience of things? of a sense of place? of loyalties?

4. What do the two families have in common? How are they different? How are the differences dramatized?

5. In what specific ways are the two young girls alike? How does the scene in which Masako makes fun of Kiyoko's language and giggling emphasize their similarity? What tonal function does the scene perform?

6. How important to the mood of the play is the kind of set provided for the performance? What specific directions in the text seem crucial to creating the possibilities of mood? If you were staging the play, how would you light the stage for the final scene? What other scenes would pose the biggest staging challenges? How would you stage the scene differently if you were adapting the play for television? for a film?

7. What props, beyond those absolutely necessary to the plot and action, would you use onstage to remind the audience that the main characters are constantly thinking of life in Japan?

8. How does the setting concretely indicate the passage of time? If you were turning the play into a film, what alternatives might you use to indicate changing seasons

and passing time? How important to the THEME of the play is the audience's sense that time has passed and seasons have changed?

9. The accidental burning of the bathhouse serves, early in the play, as a reason for the two families to interact and for scenes to take place in the Okas' house. Does the destruction of the bathhouse perform other dramatic functions as well?

# Audre Lorde

Author of nine books (mostly collections of poetry, such as *Coal* [1976] and *The Black Unicorn* [1978], but also including a fictionalized memoir she calls a "bio-mythography," *Zami: A New Spelling of My Name* [1982]), Audre Lorde lives on Staten Island in New York City. She has taught at the John Jay College of Criminal Justice and, since 1981, at Hunter College. She was born in New York in 1934, but her family comes from the West Indies.

"Home" describes a trip back to the island of ancestral origins, Carriacou, a small island in the Grenadines and part of the nation of Grenada. The poem explores the power of half-forgotten customs and phrases to influence later behavior and relationships.

# HOME

We arrived at my mother's island
to find your mother's name in the stone
we did not need    to go to the graveyard
for affirmation
our own genealogies                                              5
the language of childhood wars.

Two old dark women
in the back of the Belmont lorry
bound for L'Esterre
blessed us   greeting                                          10
Eh Dou-Dou you look *too* familiar
to you   to me
it no longer mattered.

# STUDY QUESTIONS

1. How much do we know about the "we" in the poem? about the SPEAKER herself? about her companion? What clues does the poem give about the occasion for the visit to the island?

2. What details in the poem make it possible to determine which island is involved in the episode? What does the poem imply about the distinctiveness of language on the island? How does the recording of dialogue in the second STANZA relate to THEMES introduced in the first stanza?

3. What does the fact that the strangers look familiar to the two old women have to do with facts introduced in the poem's opening lines?

4. Is it significant that the poem is cast in the past tense? Why does the visual recognition of the two old women "no longer" matter? What does the title of the poem mean?

# SETTING

Place and time are both crucially important in narratives and in most other writings. In most of the selections in this chapter, some particular place that is (or was) home seems to represent the single most important influence on a person's identity, and the feelings associated with that place are powerful and crucial to a sense of self. In Audre Lorde's poem "Home," for example, the power of place helps to define the SPEAKER even though she seems never to have been to that place before and is at least a generation removed from it. She is returning to her roots, to a place that has influenced her because her mother was born there, not because she herself remembers personal experiences there. But the details of that place are important to her and important to the effects the poem has on us as readers.

In other selections, a specific memory of a specific place sets the mood or creates a certain set of emotions and values associated with home. In "Sandra Street," for example, the main CHARACTER comes to understand what his street and his neighborhood mean to him only when he feels it under attack, and suddenly its features, which had seemed ordinary before, take on significance and personal value.

Sometimes more than one place is important. In "There Are a Lot of Ways to Die," for example, both the town in the Caribbean and the now-distant Toronto are home (in different ways) to Joseph. Sometimes details about a particular place—windows, a room, a street, stores, a mountain, or a view across a river—trigger strong emotions in the mind of the person seeing or remembering them, and often the vividness of detail in a description of place is heavily responsible for the effect a story or poem has on the reader.

Time is equally important in most of the selections here, especially in the narratives. Poems, because they are short and may not tell a story, are often more concerned just to establish a mood or set of attitudes, and time may sometimes be less important to them; but they still need to be "placed" both temporally and spatially. In the accounts of "home" here, two different—and contrasting—versions of time are often important. One time frame involves the period remembered—usually a period in childhood or youth in which sense impressions were powerful and some sort of personal expectations were set. When people reminisce about "home," they may travel far back in time, and it is usually important to have some sense of how old they were at the time so that we know how to interpret their interpretation, as in "Washington Heights, 1959." The other time frame is that of the present—that is, the time from which the person looks back, as in "Postcard from Kashmir." Sometimes, as in "Freeway 280" or "In a Polish Home for the Aged," the selection is clear about the double time setting—present adulthood and remembered past, separated by at least several decades—and at other times the contrast is implicit.

Both time and place are matters of SETTING—that is, the context where the ACTION takes place. Setting locates the action in a particular room or in a certain city and gives us a certain year or season or time of day. Setting is almost always important to the way a piece of literature affects us and thus is an important element to consider in reading—or in your own writing. At the least, setting establishes mood or gives particularity to the action, but often setting makes the action possible, believable, or meaningful. In plays, the setting is usually described explicitly in the beginning; we are told what the stage looks like and what the audience is to imagine as the time and place of action. In narratives, the setting may be less obvious but often is just as important. In "Sandra Street," for example, place becomes very much the subject of the narrative itself, and in "Traveler," particular features of the location in which the story takes place are crucial to the attitudes of characters who live or visit there.

And so is time. For both of these stories, the impressionable age of the person having the experience is crucial to the discovery—each must be young and be quite unsure of his or her own values for the story to work—

and the time of year has in each case something quite specific to do with the feelings of "indoors" and "outdoors." In "Traveler," the sense of vacation from reality and identity depends heavily on the story's setting in a sprawling hot summer in which time seems to stretch out endlessly.

Even in poems, where action is often less explicit and where location sometimes may seem arbitrary, it is a good idea to try to be clear about setting. It is, in fact, a good rule of thumb, when beginning to read any piece of literature, to ask basic questions about where and when, as well as who and why. The particular location of the speaker who is reading the postcard is not specified in "Postcard from Kashmir," but Kashmir, the place from which the card comes, is all important. And in "Washington Heights, 1959," both the place and time of action are, as the title implies, absolutely crucial to our understanding and shared feeling of what a particular time-bound boyhood in an immigrant neighborhood was like.

Setting is, however, not necessarily simple. In "Washington Heights, 1959," for example, the events in the poem are remembered from a much later perspective, and the temporal setting is really a double one—that of events experienced as a young boy and remembered as a man. Place and time may have complex emotional associations, too, as in "There Are a Lot of Ways to Die," where returning to the island carries political and moral, as well as personal and private, meanings to the main character. Memory, in literature as in life, is not always accurate, nor perspective reliable. Sometimes there is a tension between events and events remembered, sometimes between the ways things seem to different people.

Setting is a part of the complex perspective on people and action that is offered to a reader; it helps set TONE and MOOD and it helps to realize both CHARACTER and PLOT. It is one of the basic *elements* of literature (some of which are discussed briefly at the end of individual chapters in this book). Interacting with one another, elements often bring about a complexity that goes beyond the identifiable effect of any single element alone.

# WRITING
# ABOUT THE READING

## PERSONAL ESSAYS AND NARRATIVES

1. Think about the place you consider home: the room, the house or apartment building, the street, the neighborhood, the city or town. Write an essay in which you describe, for someone of your own age and background, your home and what it means to you. Be sure to include physical details that help to demonstrate the things you value most. Be sure, too, to provide a sense of yourself in the way you describe your surroundings. Before beginning to write, consider carefully what aspects of your home are most important to you, what means the most to you emotionally; think carefully about how you are going to convey a sense of your feelings about home. Try to provide this sense without commenting directly on how much you like or dislike particular things.

2. Write a letter to a friend describing the place you live while you are at college. Choose one object in your room to concentrate on as an example of what is important to you in your present life. Provide enough detail about how you use that object to suggest some revealing things about yourself as a person. Be sure to fit the description to your assumed "audience"—that is, describe your room and the details of your life in ways that would be interesting to the particular person you have chosen as the receiver of your letter.

3. Write a letter (as in #2 above) to an uncle or grandmother (or some other relative you don't live with) or to some adult friend of your family's. Pretend that you have received a present, something that will be useful to you in school, and that you are writing to say thank you and at the same time to provide a picture of what your daily life is like at your college. Give a detailed picture of some SETTING that is important to you nearly every day at college—a place where you study, or go to class, or talk with friends, or take time to play and relax.

4. Think of some important event in your childhood that took place in the house you were then living in. Write a story about that event, paying particular attention to show the role that your home had in the story. Try to capture a sense of what you felt like at the time, how you saw things (did objects, for example, seem to you much larger then than they do now?), and how much you then understood of the "meaning" of the event. Try to figure out a way to convey a contrast between your present evaluation of the event and the value you put upon it at the time.

# IMITATIONS AND PARODIES

1. Write an imitation of "Sandra Street." You will want to see your neighborhood (or a neighborhood you invent) with the eyes of an outsider, but tell the story in your own voice.

2. Write an imitation (or parody) of "Traveler," in which you travel away from your own home to a place where you can depart from the truth about yourself. Be sure to clue your readers in (as Ellen Gilchrist does) to the truth even when you are departing from it—make yourself as wonderful as you wish yourself to be, but let us also see the real you.

# ARGUMENTATIVE PAPERS

1. Write a brief speech of the kind you would like to deliver at the school assembly of a town near yours, proving that your hometown is superior to the one in which you are delivering the speech.

2. Write a reply to a friend who has written to ask you what kind of neighborhood you like best. In no more than 200 or 300 words, describe the kind of ideal community you would like to live in, suggesting both what kind of mix of people you would want to have living there and what kinds of buildings, open spaces, and businesses you would want there.

# RESEARCH PAPERS

1. In the library, look up at least three books or other sources of information on a place where you used to live. (If you have always lived in the same place, choose a city or country that you have always wanted to live in.) Find out the population, details of climate, ethnic and racial mix, basis of its economy, employment statistics, tax rates, transportation systems. Then look up the same information for the city you live in. Write a paragraph of no more than 100 words comparing the features of the two places in *one* category.

2. On the basis of the information you have discovered, write a brief historical account of your hometown from its founding to the present time. Limit yourself to 500 words, and choose the details carefully to try to suggest the "character" of the town as you know it.

# 2

# FAMILY DEVOTIONS

W e are all part of a family of one kind or another. Even the most solitary person in the world is apt to be defined—in literature or in life—in relation to a family. That family may be absent or unknown; it may not fit the old stereotype of television families—a bread-winning father, 2.8 children, a dog named Spot, and a house in the suburbs—or even Bill Cosby's new version. Still, we have all had to deal with emotions involving mother and father—whether biological or adoptive, absent or present—sisters and brothers, daughters and sons. We often resemble our relatives physically and mentally, for better or worse. We look like Dad. We have Mother's sense of humor. We have a way of turning our head that is just like Aunt Maria.

Sometimes our physical, social, and emotional bonds to our family cause embarrassment, resentment, and anger, but almost always a very special love as well. We are tied to family, yet we are different: we are ourselves. Belonging to another generation from that of our parents, we have different tastes in music; different preferences in clothes and forms of entertainment; different experiences, ideas, and beliefs. There often develops, then, a division, sometimes a failure of understanding, a generation gap, even in the most close-knit of families. And between even the closest of siblings there usually arises some sort of rivalry or competition for attention, affirmation, and love. Emotions in a family setting tend to be intense. Perhaps that is why so many writers, trying to portray feelings and make them come to life, situate the people they describe within a family.

These family emotions are especially strong when we live in times of great social change. In twentieth-century North America, where change has been rapid and great and the population mobile, the generation gap sometimes seems very wide indeed. Few of us live in the same town from birth to marriage(s), even fewer in the house or town or on the farm that has been in the family for generations. Our parents may have been part of a totally different culture—rural, perhaps, while we are urban; inhabiting a racially segregated society while we are in transition toward some form of integration. The gap is dramatic when we are the children of migrants or immigrants, citizens of a different national or ethnic culture, perhaps with different beliefs and values as well as different food, clothing, language. Even sisters and brothers may differ as to whether they should retain some of the old language and customs of their parents or become wholly "American," as defined by their friends at school and other people their own age or those they see in films or on television.

The selections in this chapter deal with mothers and fathers and children; they are expressions of love and pride, of debt and regret. They explore the search to accommodate the self, the family, and the larger society. Like those in the first chapter, they are concerned with "home," but here the focus is not on a place but on the people who make that place home.

# Tony Ardizzone

C hicagoan Tony Ardizzone has published two novels, *In the Name of the Father* and *Heart of the Order* (winner of the Virginia Prize for fiction), and a volume of short stories, *The Evening News*, which won the Flannery O'Connor Award and from which "My Mother's Stories" is taken.

Through her stories and his, a son lovingly reconstructs the high points of his mother's life and character.

## MY MOTHER'S STORIES

They were going to throw her away when she was a baby. The doctors said she was too tiny, too frail, that she wouldn't live. They performed the baptism right there in the sink between their pots of boiling water and their rows of shining instruments, chose who would be her godparents, used water straight from the tap. Her father, however, wouldn't hear one word of it. He didn't listen to their *she'll only die anyway* and *please give her to us* and *maybe we can experiment.* No, the child's father stood silently in the corner of the room, the back of one hand wiping his mouth and thick mustache, his blue eyes fixed on the black mud which caked his pants and boots.

*Nein,*[1] he said, finally. *Nein, die anyvay.*

With this, my mother smiles. She enjoys imitating the man's thick accent. She enjoys the sounds, the images, the memory. Her brown eyes look past me into the past. She draws a quick breath, then continues.

You can well imagine the rest. How the farmer took his wife and poor sickly child back to his farm. How the child was nursed, coddled, fed cow's milk, straight from the tops of the buckets—the rich, frothy cream. How the child lived. If she hadn't, I wouldn't be here now in the corner of this room, my eyes fixed on her, my mother and her stories. For now the sounds and pictures are *my* sounds and pictures. Her memory, my memory.

I stand here, remembering. The family moved. To Chicago, the city by the Great Lake, the city of jobs, money, opportunity. Away from northwestern Ohio's flat fields. The child grew. She is a young girl now, enrolled in school, Saint Teresa's, virgin. Chicago's Near North Side. The 1930s.

1. No (German).

And she is out walking with her girlfriend, a dark Sicilian. Spring, late afternoon. My mother wears a small pink bow in her brown hair.

Then from across the black pavement of the school playground comes a      6
lilting stream of foreign sound, language melodic, of the kind sung solemnly at High Mass. The Sicilian girl turns quickly, smiling. The voice is her older brother's, and he too is smiling as he stands inside the playground fence. My mother turns but does not smile. She is modest. Has been properly, strictly raised. Is the last of seven children and, therefore, the object of many scolding eyes and tongues. Her name is Mary.

Perhaps our Mary, being young, is somewhat frightened. The boy behind      7
the high fence is older than she, is in high school, is finely muscled, dark, deeply tanned. Around his neck hang golden things glistening on a thin chain. He wears a sleeveless shirt—his undershirt. Mary doesn't know whether to stay with her young friend or to continue walking. She stays, but she looks away from the boy's dark eyes and gazes instead at the worn belt around his thin waist.

That was my parents' first meeting. His name is Tony, as is mine. This      8
is not a story she tells willingly, for she sees nothing special in it. All of the embellishments are mine. I've had to drag the story out of her, nag her from room to room. Ma? Ask your father, she tells me. I ask my father. He looks up from his newspaper, then starts to smile. He's in a playful mood. He laughs, then says: I met your mother in Heaven.

She, in the hallway, overhears. Bull, she says, looking again past me.      9
He didn't even know I was alive. My father laughs behind his newspaper. I was Eva's friend, she says, and we were walking home from school— I watch him, listening as he lowers the paper to look at her. She tells the story.

She knows how to tell a pretty good story, I think. She's a natural. She      10
knows how to use her voice, when to pause, how to pace, what expressions to mask her face with. Her hand slices out the high fence. She's not in the same room with you when she really gets at it; her stories take her elsewhere, somewhere back. She's there again, back on a 1937 North Side sidestreet. My father and I are only witnesses.

Picture her, then. A young girl, frightened, though of course for no      11
good reason—my father wouldn't have harmed her. I'll vouch for him. I'm his first son. But she didn't know that as the afternoon light turned low and golden from between distant buildings. Later she'd think him strange and rather arrogant, flexing his tanned muscles before her inside the fence, like a bull before a heifer. And for years (wasted ones, I think) she didn't give him a second thought, or so she claims—the years that she dated boys who were closer to her kind. These are her words.

Imagine those years, years of *ja Fräulein, ja, bitte, entschuldigen Sie,*[2] years      12
of pale Johnnys and freckled Fritzes and hairy Hermans, towheads all, who take pretty Mary dancing and roller-skating and sometimes downtown on

2. Yes miss, yes, please, excuse me.

the El to the movie theaters on State Street to see Clark Gable, and who buy popcorn and ice cream for her and, later, cups of coffee which she then drank with cream, and who hold her small hand and look up at the Chicago sky as they walk with her along the dark city streets to her father's flat on Fremont. Not *one* second thought? I cannot believe it. And whenever I interrupt to ask, she waves me away like I'm an insect flying between her eyes and what she really sees. I fold my arms, but I listen.

She was sweeping. This story always begins with that detail. With broom      13
in hand. Nineteen years old and employed as a milliner and home one Saturday and she was sweeping. By now both her parents were old. Her mother had grown round, ripe like a fruit, like she would. Her father now fashioned wood. A mound of fluff and sawdust grows in the center of the room and she is humming, perhaps something from Glenn Miller, or she might have sung, as I've heard her do while ironing on the back porch, when from behind the locked back screen door there was suddenly a knock and it was my father, smiling.

She never tells the rest of the details. But this was the afternoon he      14
proposed. Why he chose that afternoon, or even afternoon at all, are secrets not known to me. I ask her and she evades me. *Ask your father.* I ask him and he says he doesn't know. Then he looks at her and laughs, his eyes smiling, and I can see that he is making up some lie to tell me. I watch her. Because I loved her so much I couldn't wait until that night, he says. My mother laughs and shakes her head. No, he says, I'll tell you the truth this time. Now you really know he's lying. I was just walking down the street and the idea came to me. See, it was awful hot. His hand on his forehead, he pretends he had sunstroke. My mother laughs less.

There were problems. Another of her stories. They follow one after the      15
next like cars out on the street—memories, there is just no stopping them. Their marriage would be mixed. Not in the religious sense—that would have been unthinkable—but in terms of language, origin, tradition. Like mixing your clubs with your hearts, mixing this girl from Liechtenstein with this boy from Sicily. Her family thought she was, perhaps, lowering herself. An Italian? Why not your kind? And his family, likewise, felt that he would be less than happy with a non-Sicilian girl. She's so skinny, they told him. *Misca!*[3] Mary's skin and bones. When she has the first baby she'll bleed to death. And what will she feed you? Cabbages? *Marry your own kind.*

At their Mass someone failed to play "Ave Maria." Since that was the      16
cue for my mother to stand and then to place a bouquet of flowers on Mary's side altar, she remained at the center altar, still kneeling, waiting patiently for the organist to begin. He was playing some other song, not "Ave Maria." The priest gestured to her. My mother shook her head.

She was a beautiful bride, and she wore a velvet dress. You should see      17
the wedding photograph that hangs in the hallway of their house in Chicago.

3. Gracious!

Imagine a slender brown-haired bride in white velvet shaking her head at the priest who's just married her. No, the time is not yet for the young woman to stand, for her to kneel in prayer before the altar of the Virgin. This is her wedding day, remember. She is waiting for "Ave Maria."

She is waiting to this day, for the organist never did play the song, and the priest again motioned to her, then bent and whispered in her ear, and then, indignant, crushed, the young bride finally stood and angrily, solemnly, sadly waited for her maid of honor to gather the long train of her flowing velvet dress, and together the two marched to the Virgin's side altar. 18

She tells this story frequently, whenever there is a wedding. I think that each time she begins the story she is tempted to change the outcome, to make the stupid organist suddenly stop and slap his head. To make the organist begin the chords of "Ave Maria." That kind of power isn't possible in life. The organist didn't stop or slap his head. 19

I wonder if the best man tipped him. If my father was angry enough to complain. If the muscles in his jaws tightened, if his hands turned to fists, if anyone waited for the organist out in the parking lot. I am carried away. 20

Details *are* significant. Literally they can be matters of life and death. An organist makes an innocent mistake in 1946 and for the rest of her life a woman is compelled to repeat a story, as if for her the moment has not yet been fixed, as if by remembering and then speaking she could still influence the pattern of events since passed. 21

Life and death— 22

I was hoping the counterpart wouldn't be able to work its way into this story. But it's difficult to keep death out. The final detail. Always coming along unexpectedly, the uninvited guest at the banquet, acting like you were supposed to have known all along that he'd get there, expecting to be seated and for you to offer him a drink. 23

My father called yesterday. He said he was just leaving work to take my mother again to the hospital. Tests. I shouldn't call her yet. No need to alarm her, my father said. Just tests. We'll keep you posted. My mother is in the hospital. I am not Meursault.[4] 24

I must describe the counterpart, return, begin again. With 1947, with my mother, delirious, in labor. Brought to the hospital by my father early on a Saturday, and on Monday laboring still. The doctors didn't believe in using drugs. She lay three days, terrified, sweating. On Monday morning they brought my father into the room, clad in an antiseptic gown, his face covered by a mask. She mistook him for one of the doctors. When he bent to kiss her cheek she grabbed his arm and begged him. Doctor, doctor, can you give me something for the pain? 25

That Monday was Labor Day. Ironies exist. Each September now, on my older sister Diana's birthday, my mother smiles and tells that story. 26

4. Narrator of Albert Camus's *The Stranger* (1942).

Each of us was a difficult birth. Did my father's family know something after all? The fourth, my brother Bob, nearly killed her. He was big, over ten pounds. The doctors boasted, proudly, that Bob set their personal record. The fifth child, Jim, weighed almost ten-and-a-half pounds, and after Jim the doctors fixed my mother so that there wouldn't be a sixth child. I dislike the word *fixed*, but it's an appropriate word, I think. 27

When I was a child my mother once took Diana and me shopping, to one of those mom-and-pop stores in the middle of the block. I remember a blind man who always sat on a wooden milk crate outside the store with his large dog. I was afraid of the dog. Inside the store we shopped, and my mother told us stories, and the three of us were laughing. She lifted a carton of soda as she spoke. Then the rotted cardboard bottom of the carton gave way and the soda bottles fell. The bottles burst. The sharp glass bounced. She shouted and we screamed, and as she tells this story she makes a point of remembering how worried she was that the glass had reached our eyes. But then some woman in the store told her she was bleeding. My mother looked down. Her foot was cut so badly that blood gushed from her shoe. I remember the picture, but then the face of the blind man's dog covers up the image and I see the wooden milk crate, the scratched white cane. 28

The middle child, Linda, is the special one. It was on a Christmas morning when they first feared she was deaf. Either Diana or I knocked over a pile of toy pans and dishes—a pretend kitchen—directly behind the one-year-old child playing on the floor, and Linda, bright and beautiful, did not move. She played innocently, unaffected, removed from the sound that had come to life behind her. Frantic, my mother then banged two of the metal dinner plates behind Linda's head. Linda continued playing, in a world by herself, softly cooing. 29

What I can imagine now from my mother's stories is a long procession of doctors, specialists, long trips on the bus. Snow-covered streets. Waiting in sterile waiting rooms. Questions. Answers. More questions. Tests. Hope. Then, no hope. Then guilt came. Tony and Mary blamed themselves. 30

Forgive the generalities. She is a friendly woman; she likes to make others laugh. Big-hearted, perhaps to a fault, my mother has a compulsion to please. I suspect she learned that trait as a child, being the youngest of so many children. Her parents were quite old, and as I piece her life together I imagine them strict, resolute, humorless. My mother would disagree were she to hear me. But I suspect that she's been bullied and made to feel inferior, by whom or what I don't exactly know, and, to compensate, she works very hard at pleasing. 31

She tells a story about how she would wash and wax her oldest brother's car and how he'd pay her one penny. How each day, regardless of the weather, she'd walk to a distant newsstand and buy for her father the *Abendpost*.[5] How she'd be sent on especially scorching summer days by another of her brothers 32

5. Evening Post, a German-language newspaper.

for an ice cream cone, and how as she would gingerly carry it home she'd take not one lick. How could she resist? In my mother's stories she's always the one who's pleasing.

Her brown eyes light up, and like a young girl she laughs. She says she 33 used to cheat sometimes and take a lick. Then, if her brother complained, she'd claim the ice cream had been melted by the sun. Delighted with herself, she smiles. Her eyes again twinkle with light.

I am carried away again. If it were me in that story I'd throw the cone 34 to the ground and tell my brother to get his own damn ice cream.

You've seen her. You're familiar with the kind of house she lives in, the 35 red brick two-flat. You've walked the tree-lined city street. She hangs the family's wash up in the small backyard, the next clothespin in her mouth. She picks up the squashed paper cups and the mustard-stained foot-long hot dog wrappers out in the front that the kids from the public school leave behind as they walk back from the Tastee-Freeze on the corner. During the winter she sweeps the snow. Wearing a discarded pair of my father's earmuffs. During the fall she sweeps leaves. She gets angry when the kids cut through the backyard, leaving the chain-link gates open, for the dog barks then and the barking bothers her. The dog, a female schnauzer mutt, is called Alfie. No ferocious beast—the plastic BEWARE OF DOG signs on the gates have the harsher bite. My mother doesn't like it when the kids leave the alley gate open. She talks to both her neighbors across both her fences. Wearing one of Bob's old sweaters, green and torn at one elbow, she bends to pick up a fallen autumn twig. She stretches to hang the wash up—the rows of whites, then the coloreds. She lets Alfie out and checks the alley gate.

Summer visit. Over a mug of morning coffee I sit in the kitchen reading 36 the *Sun-Times*. Alfie in the backyard barks and barks. My mother goes outside to quiet her. I turn the page, reading of rape or robbery, something distant. Then I hear the dog growl, then again bark. I go outside.

My mother is returning to the house, her face red, angry. Son of a B, 37 she says. I just caught some punk standing outside the alley gate teasing Alfie. She points. He was daring her to jump at him, and the damn kid was holding one of the garbage can lids over his head, just waiting to hit her. My mother demonstrates with her hands.

I run to the alley, ready to fight, to defend. But there is no one in the 38 alley.

My mother stands there on the narrow strip of sidewalk, her hands now 39 at her sides. She looks tired. Behind her in the yard is an old table covered with potted plants. Coleus, philodendron, wandering Jew. One of the planters, a statue of the Sacred Heart of Jesus. Another, Mary with her white ceramic hands folded in prayer. Mother's Day presents of years ago. Standing in the bright morning sun.

And when I came out, my mother continues, the punk just looked at 40 me, real snotty-like, like he was *daring* me, and then he said come on and hit me, lady, you just come right on and hit me. I'll show you, lady, come on.

And then he used the *F* word. She shakes her head and looks at me.

Later, inside, as she irons one of my father's shirts, she tells me another 41
story. It happened last week, at night. The ten o'clock news was on. Time
to walk Alfie. She'd been feeling lousy all day so Jim took the dog out front
instead.

So he was standing out there waiting for Alfie to finish up her business 42
when all of a sudden he hears this engine and he looks up, and you know
what it was, Tony? Can you guess, of all things? It was this car, this *car*,
driving right down along the sidewalk with its lights out. Jim said he dove
straight for the curb, pulling poor Alfie in the middle of number two right
with him. And when they went past him they swore at him and threw an
empty beer can at him. She laughs and looks at me, then stops ironing and
sips her coffee. Her laughter is from fear. Well, you should have heard your
little brother when he came back in. Boy was he steaming! They could have
killed him they were driving so fast. The cops caught the kids up at Tastee-
Freeze corner. We saw the squad car lights from the front windows. It was
a good thing Jim took the dog out that night instead of me. She sprinkles the
shirt with water from a Pepsi bottle. Can you picture your old mother diving
then for the curb?

She makes a tugging gesture with her hands. Pulling the leash. Saving 43
herself and Alfie. Again she laughs. She tells the story again when Jim comes
home.

At first the doctors thought she had disseminated lupus erythematosus. 44
Lupus means wolf. It is primarily a disease of the skin. As lupus advances,
the victim's face becomes ulcerated by what are called butterfly eruptions.
The face comes to resemble a wolf's. Disseminated lupus attacks the joints
as well as the internal organs. There isn't a known cure.

And at first they made her hang. My mother. They made her buy a 45
sling into which she placed her head, five times each day. Pulling her head
from the other side was a heavy water bag. My father put the equipment up
on the door of my bedroom. For years when I went to sleep I stared at that
water bag. She had to hang for two-and-a-half hours each day. Those were
the years that she read every book she could get her hands on.

And those were the years that she received the weekly shots, the corti- 46
sone, the steroids, that made her puff up, made her put on the weight the
doctors are now telling her to get rid of.

Then one of the doctors died, and then she had to find new doctors, and 47
then again she had to undergo their battery of tests. These new doctors told
her that she probably didn't have lupus, that instead they thought she had
severe rheumatoid arthritis, that the ten years of traction and corticosteroids
had been a mistake. They gave her a drugstore full of pills then. They told
her to lose weight, to exercise each night.

A small blackboard hangs over the kitchen sink. The markings put there 48
each day appear to be Chinese. Long lines for these pills, dots for those, the
letter *A* for yet another. A squiggly line for something else.

The new doctors taught her the system. When you take over thirty pills 49
a day you can't rely on memory.

My father called again. He said there was nothing new. Mary is in the 50
hospital again, and she'd been joking that she's somewhat of a celebrity. So
many doctors come in each day to see her. Interns. Residents. They hold
conferences around her bed. They smile and read her chart. They question
her. They thump her abdomen. They move her joints. They point. One
intern asked her when she had her last menstrual cycle. My mother looked
at the young man, then at the other doctors around her bed, then smiled and
said twenty-some years ago but I couldn't for the life of me tell you which
month. The intern's face quickly reddened. My mother's hysterectomy is
written there in plain view on her chart.

They ask her questions and she recites her history like a litany. 51

Were the Ohio doctors right? Were they prophets? *Please give her to us.* 52
*Maybe we can experiment.*

My father and I walk along the street. We've just eaten, then gone to 53
Osco for the evening paper—an excuse, really, just to take a walk. And he is
next to me suddenly bringing up the subject of my mother's health, just as
suddenly as the wind from the lake shakes the thin branches of the trees. The
moment is serious, I realize. My father is not a man given to unnecessary
talk.

I don't know what I'd do without her, he says. I say nothing, for I can 54
think of nothing to say. We've been together for over thirty years, he says.
He pauses. For nearly thirty-four years. Thirty-four years this October. And,
you know, you wouldn't think it, but I love her so much more now. He
hesitates, and I look at him. He shakes his head and smiles. You know what
I mean? he says. I say yes and we walk for a while in silence, and I think of
what it must be like to live with someone for thirty-four years, but I cannot
imagine it, and then I hear my father begin to talk about that afternoon's ball
game—he describes at length and in comic detail a misjudged fly ball lost in
apathy or ineptitude or simply in the sun—and for the rest of our walk home
we discuss what's right and wrong with our favorite baseball team, our thorn-
in-the-side Chicago Cubs.

I stand here, not used to speaking about things that are so close to me. I 55
am used to veiling things in my stories, to making things wear masks, to
telling my stories through masks. But my mother tells her stories openly, as
she has done so all of her life—since she lived on her father's farm in Ohio,
as she walked along the crowded 1930 Chicago streets, to my father overseas
in her letters, to the five of us children, as we sat on her lap, as we played in
the next room while she tended to our supper in the kitchen. She tells them
to everyone, to anyone who will listen. She taught Linda to read her lips.

I learn now to read her lips. 56

And I imagine one last story. 57

Diana and I are children. Our mother is still young. Diana and I are 58 outside on the sidewalk playing and it's summer. And we are young and full of play and happy, and we see a dog, and it comes toward us on the street. My sister takes my hand. She senses something, I think. The dog weaves from side to side. It's sick, I think. Some kind of lather is on its mouth. The dog growls. I feel Diana's hand shake.

Now we are inside the house, safe, telling our mother. Linda, Bob, and 59 Jim are there. We are all the same age, all children. Our mother looks outside, then walks to the telephone. She returns to the front windows. We try to look out the windows too, but she pushes the five of us away.

No, she says. I don't want any of you to see this. 60

We watch her watching. Then we hear the siren of a police car. We 61 watch our mother make the sign of the Cross. Then we hear a shot. Another. I look at my sisters and brothers. They are crying. Worried, frightened, I begin to cry too.

Did it come near you? our mother asks us. Did it touch you? Any of 62 you? Linda reads her lips. She means the funny dog. Or does she mean the speeding automobile with its lights off? The Ohio doctors? The boy behind the alley gate? The shards of broken glass? The wolf surrounded by butterflies? The ten-and-a-half-pound baby?

Diana, the oldest, speaks for us. She says that it did not. 63

Our mother smiles. She sits with us. Then our father is with us. Bob 64 cracks a smile, and everybody laughs. Alfie gives a bark. The seven of us sit closely on the sofa. Safe.

That actually happened, but not exactly in the way that I described it. 65 I've heard my mother tell that story from time to time, at times when she's most uneasy, but she has never said what it was that she saw from the front windows. A good storyteller, she leaves what she has all too clearly seen to our imaginations.

I stand in the corner of this room, thinking of her lying now in the 66 hospital.

I pray none of us looks at that animal's face. 67

## STUDY QUESTIONS

1. What is the occasion of the NARRATOR* retelling his mother's stories? The mother's stories are presented more or less chronologically according to when in her life they occurred. What other reason is there for beginning, as the narrator does, with "They were going to throw her away when she was a baby" (paragraph 1)? Why does the mother enjoy this story?

*Words in small capitals are defined in the glossary.

2. The narrator says his mother is good at telling stories, and that he and his father "are only witnesses" (par. 10) to her stories. Why are they only witnesses? Why does that make her a good storyteller?

3. In what sense is the marriage of the mother and father "mixed" (par. 15)?

4. Why does the narrator wonder if the best man at his mother and father's wedding tipped the organist who forgot to play "Ave Maria," and how his father reacted (par. 20)? Why does he think his mother is compelled to repeat that story so often?

5. What phrase in paragraph 21 makes the narrator shift from speaking of the wedding that took place thirty-four years earlier to the present?

6. Why is the story of the narrator's birth the "counterpart" (par. 25) to his mother's situation at present?

7. What does the narrator mean when he says, in paragraph 35, "You've seen her [my mother]"?

8. How does the narrator describe the difference between his stories and his mother's stories (par. 55)? Why is this story, "My Mother's Stories," more like his mother's stories than his own?

9. In the story of the mad dog that the narrator tells—not exactly as it happened— his mother asks, "Did it touch you? Any of you?" Linda—or the narrator—says, "She means the funny dog," but he then goes on to ask if she meant a number of other things (par. 62). What do these things have in common? What, then, does the question "Did it touch . . . [a]ny of you?" mean?

10. The narrator says his mother is a good storyteller, and a good storyteller leaves some things she knows and has seen to the imagination. Is the narrator a good storyteller? If so, what does he seem to know but not tell, to leave to your imagination?

11. What do you understand the last sentence of the story to mean?

# Irving Layton

Born in Rumania in 1912 as Israel Lazarovitch, Irving Layton has lived in Canada, chiefly Montreal, since his family emigrated when he was an infant. He has taught in a Montreal secondary school and many universities, and edited a journal, but primarily he has been and is a poet, a very prolific one.

This short, personal, unconventional, and tough lyric poem is typical of several of his modes. He does not blink at his mother's faults, but his love for her and his grief at her death come through wrenchingly.

# KEINE LAZAROVITCH
## 1870–1959

When I saw my mother's head on the cold pillow,
Her white waterfalling hair in the cheeks' hollows,
I thought, quietly circling my grief, of how
She had loved God but cursed extravagantly his creatures.

For her final mouth was not water but a curse,          5
A small black hole, a black rent in the universe,
Which damned the green earth, stars and trees in its stillness
And the inescapable lousiness of growing old.

And I record she was comfortless, vituperative,
Ignorant, glad, and much else besides; I believe          10
She endlessly praised her black eyebrows, their thick weave,
Till plagiarizing Death leaned down and took them for his mould.

And spoiled a dignity I shall not again find,
And the fury of her stubborn limited mind;
Now none will shake her amber beads and call God blind,          15
Or wear them upon a breast so radiantly.

O fierce she was, mean and unaccommodating;
But I think now of the toss of her gold earrings,
Their proud carnal assertion, and her youngest sings
While all the rivers of her red veins move into the sea.          20

## STUDY QUESTIONS

1. How does the end of the first STANZA surprise you? Is there a word in the second stanza that surprises you? If so, why? How does the last word in the fourth stanza surprise you?

2. Why does the speaker call Death "plagiarizing" (line 12)? What does the last line of the poem mean?

3. What does the speaker admire in his mother?

# Merle Woo

A writer of both fiction and drama, Merle Woo has lectured in Asian-American studies at the University of California, Berkeley. Her work has been published in *Bridge, Hanai,* and *This Bridge Called My Back.*

In the following selection, Woo speaks directly to her mother, detailing generational as well as personal differences among Asian-American women and expressing her own powerful feelings about racism, sexism, and the traditions that work against change even in the face of discrimination and humiliation.

## LETTER TO MA

January, 1980

Dear Ma,

I was depressed over Christmas, and when New Year's rolled around, do you know what one of my resolves was? Not to come by and see you as much anymore. I had to ask myself why I get so down when I'm with you, my mother, who has focused so much of her life on me, who has endured so much; one who I am proud of and respect so deeply for simply surviving.

I suppose that one of the main reasons is that when I leave your house, your pretty little round white table in the dinette where we sit while you drink tea (with only three specks of Jasmine) and I smoke and drink coffee, I am down because I believe there are chasms between us. When you say, "I support you, honey, in everything you do except . . . except . . ." I know you mean except my speaking out and writing of my anger at all those things that have caused those chasms. When you say I shouldn't be so ashamed of Daddy, former gambler, retired clerk of a "gook suey" store, because of the time when I was six and saw him humiliated on Grant Avenue by two white cops, I know you haven't even been listening to me when I have repeatedly said that I am not ashamed of him, not you, not who we are. When you ask, "Are you so angry because you are unhappy?" I know that we are not talking to each other. Not with understanding, although many words have passed between us, many hours, many afternoons at that round table with Daddy out in the front room watching television, and drifting out every once in a while to say "Still talking?" and getting more peanuts that are so bad for his health.

We talk and talk and I feel frustrated by your censorship. I know it is     3
unintentional and unconscious. But whatever I have told you about the classes
I was teaching, or the stories I was working on, you've always forgotten
within a month. Maybe you can't listen—because maybe when you look in
my eyes, you will, as you've always done, sense more than what we're actually
saying, and that makes you fearful. Do you see your repressed anger mani-
fested in me? What doors would groan wide open if you heard my words
with complete understanding? Are you afraid that your daughter is breaking
out of our shackles, and into total anarchy? That your daughter has turned
into a crazy woman who advocates not only equality for Third World people,
for women, but for gays as well? Please don't shudder, Ma, when I speak of
homosexuality. Until we can all present ourselves to the world in our com-
pleteness, as fully and beautifully as we see ourselves naked in our bedrooms,
we are not free.

After what seems like hours of talking, I realize it is not talking at all,     4
but the filling up of time with sounds that say, "I am your daughter, you are
my mother, and we are keeping each other company, and that is enough."
But it is not enough because my life has been formed by your life. Together
we have lived one hundred and eleven years in this country as yellow women,
and it is not enough to enunciate words and words and words and then to
have them only mean that we have been keeping each other company. I
desperately want you to understand me and my work, Ma, to know what I
am doing! When you distort what I say, like thinking I am against all "cau-
casians" or that I am ashamed of Dad, then I feel anger and more frustration
and want to slash out, not at you, but at those external forces which keep us
apart. What deepens the chasms between us are our different reactions to
those forces. Yours has been one of silence, self-denial, self-effacement; you
believing it is your fault that you never fully experienced self-pride and freedom of choice. But listen, Ma, only with a deliberate consciousness is my
reaction different from yours.

When I look at you, there are images: images of you as a little ten-year-     5
old Korean girl, being sent alone from Shanghai to the United States, in
steerage with only one skimpy little dress, being sick and lonely on Angel
Island[1] for three months; then growing up in a "Home" run by white missionary women. Scrubbing floors on your hands and knees, hauling coal in
heavy metal buckets up three flights of stairs, tending to the younger children, putting hot bricks on your cheeks to deaden the pain from the terrible
toothaches you always had. Working all your life as maid, waitress, sales-
clerk, office worker, mother. But throughout there is an image of you as
strong and courageous, and persevering: climbing out of windows to escape
from the Home, then later, from an abusive first husband. There is so much
more to these images than I can say, but I think you know what I mean.

1. The largest island in San Francisco Bay, formerly used, like Ellis Island in New York, as an entry point
   for immigrants.

Escaping out of windows offered only temporary respites; surviving is an everyday chore. You gave me, physically, what you never had, but there was a spiritual, emotional legacy you passed down which was reinforced by society: self-contempt because of our race, our sex, our sexuality. For deeply ingrained in me, Ma, there has been that strong, compulsive force to sink into self-contempt, passivity, and despair. I am sure that my fifteen years of alcohol abuse have not been forgotten by either of us, nor my suicidal depressions.

Now, I know you are going to think that I hate and despise you for your self-hatred, for your isolation. But I don't. Because in spite of your withdrawal, in spite of your loneliness, you have not only survived, but been beside me in the worst of times when your company meant everything in the world to me. I just need more than that now, Ma. I have taken and taken from you in terms of needing you to mother me, to be by my side, and I need, now, to take from you two more things: understanding and support for who I am now and my work.

We are Asian American women and the reaction to our identity is what causes the chasms instead of connections. But do you realize, Ma, that I could never have reacted the way I have if you had not provided for me the opportunity to be free of the binds that have held you down, and to be in the process of self-affirmation? Because of your life, because of the physical security you have given me: my education, my full stomach, my clothed and starched back, my piano and dancing lessons—all those gifts you never received—I saw myself as having worth; now I begin to love myself more, see our potential, and fight for just that kind of social change that will affirm me, my race, my sex, my heritage. And while I affirm myself, Ma, I affirm you.

Today, I am satisfied to call myself either an Asian American Feminist or Yellow Feminist. The two terms are inseparable because race and sex are an integral part of me. This means that I am working with others to realize pride in culture and women and heritage (the heritage that is the exploited yellow immigrant: Daddy and you). Being a Yellow Feminist means being a community activist and a humanist. It does not mean "separatism," either by cutting myself off from non-Asians or men. It does not mean retaining the same power structure and substituting women in positions of control held by men. It does mean fighting the whites and the men who abuse us, straightjacket us and tape our mouths; it means changing the economic class system and psychological forces (sexism, racism, and homophobia) that really hurt all of us. And I do this, not in isolation, but in the community.

We no longer can afford to stand back and watch while an insatiable elite ravages and devours resources which are enough for all of us. The obstacles are so huge and overwhelming that often I do become cynical and want to give up. And if I were struggling alone, I know I would never even attempt to put into action what I believe in my heart, that (and this is primarily because of you, Ma) Yellow Women are strong and have the potential to be powerful and effective leaders.

I can hear you asking now, "Well, what do you mean by 'social change and leadership'? And how are you going to go about it?" To begin with we must wipe out the circumstances that keep us down in silence and self-efface-ment. Right now, my techniques are education and writing. Yellow Feminist means being a core for change, and that core means having the belief in our potential as human beings. I will work with anyone, support anyone, who shares my sensibility, my objectives. But there are barriers to unity: white women who are racist, and Asian American men who are sexist. My very being declares that those two groups do not share my complete sensibility. I would be fragmented, mutilated, if I did not fight against racism and sexism together.

And this is when the pain of the struggle hits home. How many white women have taken on the responsibility to educate themselves about Third World people, their history, their culture? How many white women really think about the stereotypes they retain as truth about women of color? But the perpetuation of dehumanizing stereotypes is really very helpful for whites; they use them to justify their giving us the lowest wages and all the work they don't want to perform. Ma, how can we believe things are changing when as a nurse's aide during World War II, you were given only the tasks of changing the bed linen, removing bed pans, taking urine samples, and then only three years ago as a retired volunteer worker in a local hospital, white women gave themselves desk jobs and gave you, at sixty-nine, the same work you did in 1943? Today you speak more fondly of being a nurse's aide during World War II and how proud you are of the fact that the Red Cross showed its appreciation for your service by giving you a diploma. Still in 1980, the injustices continue. I can give you so many examples of groups which are "feminist" in which women of color were given the usual least important tasks, the shitwork, and given no say in how that group is to be run. Needless to say, those Third World women, like you, dropped out, quit.

Working in writing and teaching, I have seen how white women con-descend to Third World women because they reason that because of our oppression, which they know nothing about, we are behind them and their "progressive ideas" in the struggle for freedom. They don't even look at his-tory! At the facts! How we as Asian American women have always been fighting for more than mere survival, but were never acknowledged because we were in our communities, invisible, but not inaccessible.

And I get so tired of being the instant resource for information on Asian American women. Being the token representative, going from class to class, group to group, bleeding for white women so they can have an easy answer— and then, and this is what really gets to me—they usually leave to never continue their education about us on their own.

To the racist white female professor who says, "If I have to watch every-   14
thing I say I wouldn't say anything," I want to say, "Then get out of teaching."

To the white female poet who says, "Well, frankly, I believe that poli-   15
tics and poetry don't necessarily have to go together," I say, "Your little taste
of white privilege has deluded you into thinking that you don't have to fight
against sexism in this society. You are talking to me from your own isolation
and your own racism. If you feel that you don't have to fight for me, that
you don't have to speak out against capitalism, the exploitation of human and
natural resources, then you in your silence, your inability to make connections, are siding with a system that will eventually get you, after it has gotten
me. And if you think that's not a political stance, you're more than simply
deluded, you're crazy!"

This is the same white voice that says, "I am writing about and looking   16
for themes that are 'universal.' " Well, most of the time when "universal" is
used, it is just a euphemism for "white": white themes, white significance,
white culture. And denying minority groups their rightful place and time in
U.S. history is simply racist.

Yes, Ma, I am mad. I carry the anger from my own experience and the   17
anger you couldn't afford to express, and even that is often misinterpreted
no matter how hard I try to be clear about my position. A white woman in
my class said to me a couple of months ago, "I feel that Third World women
hate me and that *they* are being racist; I'm being stereotyped, and I've never
been part of the ruling class." I replied, "Please try to understand. Know our
history. Know the racism of whites, how deep it goes. Know that we are
becoming ever more intolerant of those people who let their ignorance be
their excuse for their complacency, their liberalism, when this country (this
world!) is going to hell in a handbasket. Try to understand that our distrust
is from experience, and that our distrust is power*less*. Racism is an essential
part of the status quo, power*ful*, and continues to keep us down. It is a rule
taught to all of us from birth. Is it no wonder that we fear there are no
exceptions?"

And as if the grief we go through working with white women weren't   18
enough; so close to home, in our community, and so very painful, is the lack
of support we get from some of our Asian American brothers. Here is a quote
from a rather prominent male writer ranting on about a Yellow "sister":

> . . . I can only believe that such blatant sucking off of the identity is the
> work of a Chinese American woman, another Jade Snow Wong Pochahon-
> tas yellow. Pussywhipped again. Oh, damn, pussywhipped again.

Chinese American woman: "another Jade Snow Wong Pochahontas yel-   19
low." According to him, Chinese American women sold out—are contemp-
tuous of their culture, pathetically strain all their lives to be white, hate Asian
American men, and so marry white men (the John Smiths)—or just like

Pochahontas: we rescue white men while betraying our fathers; then marry white men, get baptized, and go to dear old England to become curiosities of the civilized world. Whew! Now, that's an indictment! (Of all women of color.) Some of the male writers in the Asian American community seem never to support us. They always expect us to support them, and you know what? We almost always do. Anti-Yellow men? Are they kidding? We go to their readings, buy and read and comment on their books, and try to keep up a dialogue. And they accuse us of betrayal, are resentful because we do readings together as Women, and so often do not come to our performances. And all the while we hurt because we are rejected by our brothers. The Pochahontas image used by a Chinese American man points out a tragic truth: the white man and his ideology are still over us and between us. These men of color, with clear vision, fight the racism in white society, but have bought the white male definition of "masculinity": men only should take on the leadership in the community because the qualities of "originality, daring, physical courage, and creativity" are "traditionally masculine."[2]

Some Asian men don't seem to understand that by supporting Third [20] World women and fighting sexism, they are helping themselves as well. I understand all too clearly how dehumanized Dad was in this country. To be a Chinese man in America is to be a victim of both racism and sexism. He was made to feel he was without strength, identity, and purpose. He was made to feel soft and weak, whose only job was to serve whites. Yes, Ma, at one time I was ashamed of him because I thought he was "womanly." When those two white cops said, "Hey, fat boy, where's our meat?" he left me standing there on Grant Avenue while he hurried over to his store to get it; they kept complaining, never satisfied, "That piece isn't good enough. What's the matter with you, fat boy? Don't you have respect? Don't wrap that meat in newspapers, either; use the good stuff over there." I didn't know that he spent a year and a half on Angel Island; that we could never have our right names; that he lived in constant fear of being deported; that, like you, he worked two full-time jobs most of his life; that he was mocked and ridiculed because he speaks "broken English." And Ma, I was so ashamed after that experience when I was only six years old that I never held his hand again.

Today, as I write to you of all these memories, I feel even more deeply [21] hurt when I realize how many people, how so many people, because of racism and sexism, fail to see what power we sacrifice by not joining hands.

But not all white women are racist, and not all Asian American men are [22] sexist. And we choose to trust them, love and work with them. And there are visible changes. Real tangible, positive changes. The changes I love to see are those changes within ourselves.

Your grandchildren, my children, Emily and Paul. That makes three [23] generations. Emily loves herself. Always has. There are shades of self-doubt

2. *AIIEEEEE! An Anthology of Asian American Writers*, editors Frank Chin, Jeffery Paul Chan, Lawson Fusao Inada, Shawn Wong (Washington, D.C.: Howard University Press, 1974). [Author's note]

but much less than in you or me. She says exactly what she thinks, most of the time, either in praise or in criticism of herself or others. And at sixteen she goes after whatever she wants, usually center stage. She trusts and loves people, regardless of race or sex (but, of course, she's cautious), loves her community and works in it, speaks up against racism and sexism at school. Did you know that she got Zora Neale Hurston and Alice Walker on her reading list for a Southern Writers class when there were only white authors? That she insisted on changing a script done by an Asian American man when she saw that the depiction of the character she was playing was sexist? That she went to a California State House Conference to speak out for Third World students' needs?

And what about her little brother, Paul? Twelve years old. And remember, Ma? At one of our Saturday Night Family Dinners, how he lectured Ronnie (his uncle, yet!) about how he was a male chauvinist? Paul told me once how he knew he had to fight to be Asian American, and later he added that if it weren't for Emily and me, he wouldn't have to think about feminist stuff too. He says he can hardly enjoy a movie or TV program anymore because of the sexism. Or comic books. And he is very much aware of the different treatment he gets from adults: "You have to do everything right," he said to Emily, "and I can get away with almost anything." 24

Emily and Paul give us hope, Ma. Because they are proud of who they are, and they care so much about our culture and history. Emily was the first to write your biography because she knows how crucial it is to get our stories in writing. 25

Ma, I wish I knew the histories of the women in our family before you. I bet that would be quite a story. But that may be just as well, because I can say that *you* started something. Maybe you feel ambivalent or doubtful about it, but you did. Actually, you should be proud of what you've begun. I am. If my reaction to being a Yellow Woman is different than yours was, please know that that is not a judgment on you, a criticism or a denial of you, your worth. I have always supported you, and as the years pass, I think I begin to understand you more and more. 26

In the last few years, I have realized the value of Homework: I have studied the history of our people in this country. I cannot tell you how proud I am to be a Chinese/Korean American Woman. We have such a proud heritage, such a courageous tradition. I want to tell everyone about that, all the particulars that are left out in the schools. And the full awareness of being a woman makes me want to sing. And I do sing with other Asian Americans and women, Ma, anyone who will sing with me. 27

I feel now that I can begin to put our lives in a larger framework. Ma, a larger framework! The outlines for us are time and blood, but today there is breadth possible through making connections with others involved in community struggle. In loving ourselves for who we are—American women of color—we can make a vision for the future where we are free to fulfill our human potential. This new framework will not support repression, hatred, 28 exploitation and isolation, but will be a human and beautiful framework, created in a community, bonded not by color, sex or class, but by love and the common goal for the liberation of mind, heart, and spirit.

Ma, today, you are as beautiful and pure to me as the picture I have of    29
you, as a little girl, under my dresser-glass.

I love you,
Merle

## STUDY QUESTIONS

1. What facts are we given about the circumstances Woo's mother and father faced? How did each of them respond to discrimination or abuse? What responses and attitudes does Woo's mother seem to be sensitive about? Which anecdote seems to you most powerful in suggesting the problems faced by the older generation?

2. State as precisely as you can the differences between generations of Asian-Americans, as Woo presents them. What differences of attitude between men and women in the Asian-American community does Woo emphasize?

3. Against whom is the anger directed? What subjects seem to generate the most powerful emotions? What attitudes in others upset her most?

4. Note the variations in TONE from paragraph to paragraph. Describe how the letter moves from personal to political concerns; from frustration to anger to compassion. What devices and principles of organization does Woo use to structure the letter?

5. What strategies does Woo to make her mother feel loved and appreciated even in the face of strong criticism? List all of the places in which she expresses love; in which she expresses respect; in which she expresses concern about being misunderstood; in which she expresses common cause with her mother's concerns.

   Do you ever feel that the mother is being patronized? Are there places where Woo seems too hard on her mother? too easy? Do you think she establishes an appropriate balance in her attitudes toward her mother? Does her rhetoric seem effective?

   How do you think you would feel if you were to receive such a letter from a child of yours when you are old? Do you feel like sending such a letter to one of your parents?

6. Are there parts of the letter with which you disagree? If so, state clearly your reasons for disagreeing. Which parts do you agree with most strongly?

# Yvonne Sapia

Yvonne Sapia's family came from Puerto Rico to New York, where, in 1946, she was born. She moved to Florida in 1956 and has lived there since, attending the University of Florida and Florida State University, where she is now resident poet and editor of a humanities publication, *Woodrider*. *Valentino's Hair*, from which "Defining the Grateful Gesture" is taken, won the Samuel French Morse Poetry Prize in 1987.

When you were a child, you'd eat whatever your mother put before you, wouldn't you? Isn't that what you will tell your children?

## DEFINING THE GRATEFUL GESTURE

According to our mother,
when she was a child
what was placed before her
for dinner was not a feast,
but she would eat it                                    5
to gain back the strength
taken from her by long hot days
of working in her mother's house
and helping her father make
candy in the family kitchen.                            10
No idle passenger
travelling through life was she.

And that's why she resolved
to tell stories about
the appreciation for satisfied hunger.                  15
When we would sit down
for our evening meal
of arroz con pollo
or frijoles negros con plátanos[1]
she would expect us                                     20
to be reverent to the sources

1. Rice with chicken, black beans with plantains. [Author's note]

of our undeserved nourishment,
and to strike a thankful pose
before each lift of the fork
or swirl of the spoon.                                    25

For the dishes she prepared
we were ungrateful,
she would say, and repeat
her archetypal tale about the Perez
brothers from her girlhood town of Ponce,                 30
who looked like ripe mangoes,
their cheeks rosed despite poverty.

My mother would then tell us about the day
she saw Mrs. Perez searching
the neighborhood garbage,                                 35
picking out with a missionary's care
the edible potato peels, the plantain skins,
the shafts of old celery to take
home to her muchachos[2]
who required more food                                    40
than she could afford.

Although my brothers and I never
quite mastered the ritual
of obedience our mother craved,
and as supplicants failed                                 45
to feed her with our worthiness,
we'd sit like solemn loaves of bread,
sighing over the white plates
with a sense of realization, or relief,
guilty about possessing appetite.                         50

# STUDY QUESTIONS

1. What is the effect of the SPEAKER not claiming authority for what her mother tells her, but opening "According to our mother" (line 1)? What effect or emphasis is achieved by putting the verb and subject at the end of the last sentence in the first verse paragraph ("No idle passenger / traveling through life was she" [ll. 11–12])?

2. What are the "sources" of the children's nourishment (l. 21)? Why is that nourishment "undeserved"?

2. Boys. [Author's note]

3. How did Mrs. Perez manage to feed her children with their large appetites? What is supposed to be the lesson for the speaker and her brothers or sisters in the story about the Perez family?

4. Does the mother want them to eat or not? In what way do the mother's stories put the children in a double bind, so that they are somehow wrong if they eat and if they do not?

5. In what sense does the poem suggest that the mother expects to be fed as well as to feed?

# Rhoda Schwartz

Rhoda Schwartz, daughter of a Russian-Jewish father and Midwestern mother, was born in Atlantic City and grew up in Elmira, New York. She has been co-editor of *The American Poetry Review*.

Each of the numbered verse paragraphs seems to deal with a photograph (though the second may deal with two) and takes off in memory or projection from the photograph, on occasion jumping backward and forward in time and from America to Russia or vice versa.

## OLD PHOTOGRAPHS

*1.*

We are returning together. The train is late at every
stop on the way, detained by the banging of switchmen and
flares. It's the dead of winter. Snow has made bones
out of the trees. The huts are covered by drifts so
white our eyes hurt in the morning. Our conversation is                 5
disjointed. We won't be able to stand it when the
train gets in. Candles burn in the aisles. We are
lurching towards the next day and the next. You keep
telling me I should go back to Russia. The train is
a black holocaust going through the mountains. Tomorrow,            10
we will be there. It is never the same. Someday, tell
me how beautiful it was when we went back together.
Say my name.

*2.*

My Russian great-grandmother: I would not be surprised to see
a crow sitting on her shoulder. Black silk dress—pleats heavy          15
and twisted like the rills of the Caucasus, she stands erect in
her garden—the long, slender hands touching the knob of the
summer chair. Is she brown with age or is it the old sepia
photograph? She is frowning. She says, to no one in particular,
what can I do with the 15-year-old upstart, my grandson,               20
in Bialystok prison for six months because he hates the Tsar, loves
Chekhov and marched in a parade before the revolution?

My father's friends are throwing rolls to him over the prison
walls with messages. He laughs. I love him.

He told me his grandmother hit him with Russian birch twigs to         25
subdue him. When he tried to row across the Dnieper
in a boat smaller than a toy, they laughed.
Father, when you hid your books in the hayloft, and argued with
Gogol late at night, I was there in your sperm waiting to hear your story.

The ship that brought you to America had no library. You cursed its    30
keel—the hunger—the gold slipped through your fingers when you
disembarked. The shore was lonely. I want you to know I would have
loved you if I could have loved you, still hidden in your sperm
with Gogol and Pushkin. What a foursome. I would have
lost to you on purpose. I wish I could tear                            35
down every Russian birch tree that hurt you before I could say I was sorry.

*3.*

The walls were taller than the prison
at Bialystok. You were shorter than the guards. Did you ever spit
at them—kick the dirt and yell down with the Tsar, or did you eat
your black bread quietly, pee in a trench, dig holes                   40
for posts and think about the time you would leave for America?

*4.*

I am dreaming of you sitting in a buggy with your uncle,
holding the reins of an old horse. The reins look like
dried tobacco leaves. I think of your wallet, the same
color and texture, whenever I reach into a drawer of silk             45
scarves and suddenly touch it. I am old
and wrinkled as the tobacco leaf. I swim into daydreams about you.
You are smiling because you are young and your hair is black
and curly and Pushkin is waiting for you back in the hayloft.

You were a romantic; a sensualist even then. Sometimes,     50
I wake up crying because I've seen you in a pine box, eyes
closed against living. You told me to always
be full of love and gentle with men. I try to remember.


5.

When you came to America, why did you think
the St. Lawrence river was like the Dnieper and try to row     55
across it in a rowboat? You were too slight
to do it, but you did it
while the steamships blew their horns in anger.
You told me the fog was rolling in like puffs of black cotton
and you were scared.     60
They let you off with a warning—
You sold expensive things to millionaires
and became a capitalist.
I used to pretend your name was Marco Polo
when you opened the packing crates     65
and showed me Italian linens, Spanish shawls and Chinese
vases. We put them all in a row and talked about them.
I was your best audience. It was hard for either
one of us to spell Czechoslovakia.

## STUDY QUESTIONS

1. How many photographs are there? Describe them.

2. How much of the SPEAKER's father's life story can you reconstruct from the poem?

3. What seem to be the qualities in her father that the speaker loves?

# Cynthia Kadohata

Charlie-O, it seems, just happens to be Japanese (-American). Does ethnic or cultural background have anything to do with the behavior of the characters? with the way the story develops?

# CHARLIE-O

When I was fifteen, I was almost as tall as the man I have always thought of as my father. He was five feet three, and his name was Charles Osaka—Charlie-O to everyone except my mother, who called him Charles when she didn't like him and Chuck when she did, just as she called me Olivia or Livvie, depending on my behavior. Charlie-O was almost always cheerful, and he had a childlike joie de vivre that would not quite have fit a larger man. My mother's mother forced my mother to marry him, though I didn't know that until I'd grown up. I don't know how exactly my grandmother found him, but I later heard she'd first brought him to Fresno to meet my mother when my mother was seven months pregnant with me. Charlie-O came from a small town in Oregon called Florence. When I was older, he used to keep a picture on his bureau of my mother on prom night, when she was seventeen, and sometimes I wonder whether that was the picture my grandmother first sent him to get him to Fresno. He married my mother when she was eight months pregnant, and in time they had three sons, making me the only girl. But I think that I was always Charlie-O's favorite, and that if he'd loved me less he would have spoiled me the way I sometimes felt he wanted to. My real father had visited me several times, but he was married and had other children, and we never became close. So I was devoted to Charlie-O and followed him everywhere when I was quite young—he even took me to his poker games—and sometimes I brought him to Parents' Day at my school, where, starting in the fifth grade, he was shorter than some of my classmates. As I grew older, though, I no longer cared about poker games or Parents' Days, and Charlie-O and I began to grow apart. That hurt him. By the time I was fifteen, my allegiances had shifted to my mother. At thirty-three, she was graceful and pensive and sincere—things I wanted to be when I grew up. Charlie-O was loud, undignified. 1

I was born in Fresno, but shortly after my birth Charlie-O took my mother and me to his home in Florence. I loved it there, but when I was fifteen we moved, suddenly and very much against my will. I was furious with Charlie-O for taking us from Oregon. I had friends, babysitting jobs, and my first boyfriend, and during the summer, when the windows were always open, the ocean air would drift through our house, so that I could feel its touch when I woke in the mornings. I would go for walks not long after first light, but sometimes Charlie-O, an amateur painter, would already be outside painting on the beach. I would look back at our house and see tendrils of fog moving into the windows, and it seemed as if we lived in a house in the clouds. I knew that after I left Florence my friends would still build fires on the beaches at night, my boyfriend would soon find a new 2 girlfriend, and by the following week my employers would have found new babysitters—maybe better ones than I. I resented not just that I would lose my old life in Oregon but that I was replaceable. I wanted to grow up to be like my mother, who struck me as a woman who couldn't be replaced.

We were moving to, of all places, the Ozarks. Charlie-O said he wanted    3
to move to Arkansas because he had a chance to buy into a garage a friend of his owned. In Oregon he worked in a garage for somebody else.

We put our furniture in a trailer and drove to Arkansas. Our arrival was    4
inauspicious. It was almost midnight when Charlie-O announced that, first, he believed we were in Arkansas; second, he believed we were lost; and, third, we had run out of gas. I was the only one awake.

"How do you know we're in Arkansas if we're lost?" I said. I put on my    5
longest face.

"Don't worry, honey-dog," he said. He smiled, but his eyes didn't look    6
happy. His eyes looked uncertain, and they seemed to be asking me some-thing—nothing specific, just asking.

I got out a map. "Where's the highway?" I said.    7

He didn't know. It was raining hard, and the rain formed rivers down    8
the windshield. The raindrops made the windows look like textured glass. Charlie-O got out, and I pressed my nose against the back-seat window and watched him squint into the darkness as the rain splashed on his face. He was looking down the road, but I didn't see why he couldn't look from inside the dry car. It was as if he were under a spell. I lowered the window. The air was warmer than I'd expected.

"What are you doing?"    9

"Just seeing what's what," he said. "I'm gonna walk down a ways and    10
try to get us some gas." As he set off, he appeared as sturdy as always but even smaller than usual. In the car my three brothers and my mother slept on. I rolled up the window and ran after Charlie-O, almost slipping in the mud as I hurried. He walked on surefootedly.

"If I were me, I wouldn't be doing this," I said. "I would just wait in    11
the car."

We went a long way, but we never thought of turning back. We were    12
both very stubborn. We'd always been alike that way. There was nothing but bush around us, and sometimes—maybe it was the play of sky light off the rain—I would think I saw lights in the leaves. Charlie-O didn't look either right or left as he walked, and I thought how much more scared I would be without him.

We got gas at a gas station and returned to the car. My youngest brother    13
had awoken. He cringed from me. "You're all wet," he said, as if my wetness were a contagious disease.

"Just a little water," boomed Charlie-O. "Ain't nothing to have a cow    14
about."

In front of my friends, his way of talking had lately embarrassed me,    15 but it didn't now. He was wet and tired, and though it had been he who'd decided we would leave Oregon, he'd lived there a long time and I suddenly realized that he was losing a lot, too.

We found a highway after a while, and then a motel. I'd heard my parents say the day before that they would take two rooms tonight—one for me and my brothers, Ben, Walker, and Peter, and one for themselves. I knew it was so that they could make love. Only a couple of years earlier, I wouldn't have understood completely why it was so important for them to get their own room, as they sometimes did on vacations. 16

A tired-looking man with rollers in his hair registered us at the motel. Lightning lit the sky like a flash of sunlight. When I watched my parents at the counter, they seemed to be the same person. Maybe it was just that they lived in the same world, bought their clothes at the same stores, ate the same foods. In any case, they matched. Yet I knew that sometimes my mother felt lonely and my father felt alone. And though my mother was barely taller than Charlie-O, she always struck me as womanly, whereas my father was boyish. 17

"One room?" said the man. 18

"Yes, plus cots, if you have any," said my mother. 19

The man got a cot. "Only have one. I won't charge you. We usually charge a dollar, but I understand. I've got seven of my own." A cry came from a back room. "There's one now," the man said with a sigh. He yawned and shook his head, and a loose roller jiggled. 20

Charlie-O turned and winked at me, and when we got outside he said, "Remember—you can always trust a man with seven children and the nerve to wear rollers in his hair." Charlie-O carried the cot to the room. Then he and I went to a coffee shop, where he got coffee and stole packets of sugar and containers of ersatz cream to give to my brothers, because they couldn't come. They were too young to be out so late. Ben was ten, Walker nine, and Peter four. 21

Back in the room, the lights were off, and everyone was already asleep— my mother in the bed and the boys on the floor. I wondered why my mother had decided to take just one room. Did it mean that my parents weren't getting along in ways I couldn't see? Everything changed so quickly, and without my noticing. 22

I thought I remembered a time when my parents had been unable to keep their hands off one another, always walking arm in arm, or stopping to kiss lightly. But the memory was there and then not there. On the way down from Oregon, we'd taken only one motel room whenever we stopped, but somewhere in Utah my parents had made love anyway—quietly—probably after they thought that we were all asleep. I thought they'd *had* to make love or they wouldn't have—not with me and my brothers in the room. They'd never made love on vacations when we'd taken only one room. Something about their lovemaking that night, about the sound of it, seemed to me some- how hopeless. I had to go to the bathroom badly, and by the time they finally 23 fell asleep and I could get up, I had decided that if it came to that I would wet my bed before I would let them know I was awake. It was not the sex that I thought I ought not to have heard but the hopelessness.

I was on the cot, and my eyes were closed. I heard my mother and Charlie-O begin speaking, though I couldn't hear what they were saying. Finally she said something, and my father didn't answer. I heard the sheets rustle. I thought they were going to make love, but they didn't. Then they did. I opened my eyes and saw their bodies moving beneath the sheets. I felt guilty for watching, so I closed my eyes again and averted my face. But I couldn't help listening closely; they were almost as silent as if they were asleep. 24

Afterward, my mother said, "It doesn't make any sense." I had no idea what she was talking about, but she sounded fearful, disappointed—a way she rarely sounded, or allowed herself to sound. Yet sometimes I thought she was disappointed with her life, and I wondered how much of that might be due to me and my brothers—maybe we weren't the kind of children she would have hoped for. For a moment I began to drift off, and as I drifted I thought that I would rather have her be unhappy with me than with Charlie-O. Then I woke up again, and wondered why I had thought that. 25

My parents fell asleep. The cot squeaked softly as I shook my feet up and down, back and forth. I lay still then and realized that Walker, on the floor in the corner near the cot, wasn't breathing evenly—he was awake. The others were asleep. Walker had probably heard our parents making love. I wished he hadn't. It seemed to me a burden to have heard, and I didn't want him to have that burden. 26

"Walk?" I said. 27

"Huh." 28

"Good night." 29

He didn't answer, but I knew that he felt comforted not to be alone, and soon he fell asleep. So did I. Maybe I felt comforted, too. 30

Arkansas was humid, and the clouds at night were unnaturally white, as if someone had spilled bleach on the black sky. I liked to sit late in the back yard, and in bed each night my arms and legs would be covered with mosquito bites, some of them as big and round as quarters, others longer, thinner, like welts. We lived near the outside of our town in one of a cluster of old houses close to some apple orchards. My father was a big believer in organizations, and he joined a bowling team, a golf club, and a group of small-business owners, which was really sort of a poker club. After he'd bought a half interest in his garage, he subscribed to a business newsletter, and whenever he was reading it we would all have to be very quiet around the house. I tried to make friends with some of the children of my parents' new friends, but it was hard, and whenever I didn't fit in I would hate Charlie-O, because I thought it meant that I was more like him than like my mother. There was a boy I liked in our town. I didn't think he liked me, but 31 just his being there made me hopeful for a future that was as lush as I lately imagined my mother's past—I knew she'd loved my real father a great deal, and I thought she loved Charlie-O. My mother was amused by my crush. "You forget everything so easily when you're fifteen," she said, referring to my forgotten Oregon boyfriend. She was right about him but wrong about my memory. There were many things that I remembered. For instance, I remembered that my grandmother, before she died, had frequently told me that if I hoped to get what I wanted in the future I would always have to take great care with what meagre looks I had. At night I would take off my clothes and stand on the rim of the bathtub so that I could see my body in the medicine-cabinet mirror. But I knew that if I didn't get what I wanted in life it wouldn't be because my skin was not the smoothest, or my hair not the blackest and straightest—not because I didn't look the best. I knew that much about my future.

The first time I spent more than a few minutes with a boy I liked was about half a year after we'd arrived, when Charlie-O and my mother were driving him, his parents, and me to a party—children were always invited to the parties of my parents' new friends. I sat next to the boy in the car, and I was nervous and chewing my fingernails. Charlie-O laughed and said. "I remember when you were little you used to chew your toenails." 32

I felt mortified, but the boy didn't seem to have heard. I slunk down in my seat. 33

Charlie-O continued, "And then after you'd bit them off you used to swallow them." 34

I considered flinging myself out of the car to my death, but we were going only thirty miles an hour, and I probably would have just got a concussion. I looked at the boy and he smiled, and for the first time I thought he might like me. 35

Charlie-O had just resumed his art interest, and on Saturdays he would take me when he went painting landscapes. In Oregon I would never go painting with him, though he asked all of us to. Since I didn't really feel close to him any longer, perhaps it was two-faced of me to make such a turn-around, here where I had no friends and needed company—any company. 36

He was not a good painter. He painted pictures of forests, with solid yellow sunbeams plunging through the trees like missiles from heaven, and his clouds were applied in thick globs, "for texture." But it was fun to go painting with him. At the time, I wanted to be a biologist, and I would take along my microscope and examine insects, blades of grass, whatever I came upon. Other times, I would paint. Charlie-O showed me how to hold a brush—not like a pencil but the way you would hold a brush to paint a house. That, he said, is how the Impressionists held brushes. 37

Though his paintings were dreadful, he hung them up in the garage and offered them for sale. Sometimes he painted me and my brothers, and hung up those pictures as well. Once, when I stopped by the garage, he told a customer that he'd painted pictures of all his children. 38

The customer pointed to a picture of four-year-old Peter. "Is that you?" she said to me.                                                                                                          39

"That's my brother," I said. "But my brother and I look a *lot* alike. People *always* get us mixed up."                                                                                          40

The woman said. "How nice."                                                                                                                                                                       41

"Have you ever sold a painting?" I asked Charlie-O after she'd left.                                                                                                                              42

"Oh, sure," he said. He winked and pointed to his head with his forefinger. "I've sold lots of paintings." In his imagination, he meant.                                                        43

My mother had had an affair in Oregon, but I didn't find that out until almost a year after we'd come to Arkansas. I walked into the living room one day and came upon Charlie-O and my mother standing in the center of the room, doing nothing, saying nothing. I hadn't heard any shouting, but something in the room felt the way it did when there'd just been a big fight in the house. Peter had been peeking out the window, but he turned when he heard me walk in. He appeared pleased to see me.                                               44

"What's going on?" I said.                                                                                                                                                                        45

"There's a man out there waiting for Mom."                                                                                                                                                        46

My parents still didn't move, and I went to the window. On the walkway stood a man I'd seen around in Florence—a friend of my mother's. At first I didn't know why he was out there—why he didn't come in. Understanding came to me physically before it came mentally; my whole body flushed and grew tense, and then I understood who the man was: my mother's lover.                                                                                                     47

"Who is it?" whispered Peter. Though young, he had an instinctive ability to detect when something had gone wrong.                                                                              48

"The enemy," I whispered back. I suddenly hated that man. "Remember, Peter," I whispered fiercely, "if you ever see that man, he's the *enemy*." Peter looked scared, and I wished I hadn't spoken.                                                       49

First Charlie-O went outside to talk to the man, then my mother went, and then the man left. The house was extra quiet. My parents went into the bedroom to talk. We were supposed to go to a party later—it was a local novelist's birthday—but I figured now we wouldn't go. But after a while my mother went into the bathroom to get ready. I worked with my microscope. I studied dust, hair, tap water, spit. I studied dirt, fly wings, a seashell from Oregon. As I worked I kept thinking of a fight I'd overheard a few weeks before we left Oregon. My mother had been crying, and she said, "I tell you I *am* grateful. But now—Do you still want me?" Charlie-O said he didn't know. "I don't know if you *should* still want me," she said. "And I don't know if I want you to."                                                                                                      50

Charlie-O had a few beers, and when we got in the car he took a wrong turn almost immediately. It was easy to do. The town we lived in was green. There was the wild green of sprawling oaks and maples, the honeysuckle vines in untended fields. Each street looked like the one before: green everywhere.                                                                                                              51

At one corner Charlie-O said, "Should I make a right here?" 52
"No," I said. 53
He turned anyway, too sharply, and we ended up in a ditch. 54
"Whoops, sweetie-dog," he said, "I thought you said yes. I thought she 55
said yes."
We sat there for several minutes, as if we'd simply come to a very long 56
traffic light. Eventually, Charlie-O said, "All right," and got out of the car,
slipping almost immediately and falling to the ground. My mother and I got
out to help him. He lay on the ground with his eyes open, blinking. We
lifted him into the car, then patted down the dirt around the wheels. We
weren't sure whether that was what we were supposed to do, but it made us
feel better. I pushed in back with my brothers while our mother accelerated,
the wheels whipping dirt into the air. The car didn't budge. Despite protests
from my mother, my father got out of the car. "Aw, I can help," he said. He
pushed with my brothers and me. I found myself pushing harder than before.
My legs stretched out as I tried to get into a good position, and my cheek
rested against the cool metal of the trunk. The effort took me over, and I
realized how badly I wanted my father to be able to say later that he had
helped to get us out of the ditch. I thought that that would help the marriage
somehow. But it was no good. The car remained stuck. Finally, my mother
and I found a house and a man came to help us, and my mother took over
the driving.

The novelist, whom Charlie-O played golf with sometimes, owned a 57
small farm. The boy I liked was at the party, and he stood out back and
talked with me while the grown-ups, mostly the fathers, got drunk. Some of
the drunk men took off their blazers and dress shirts and got into a field and
started chasing some animals—a few sheep and pigs and a goat. There was a
dog, too. After a while a couple of the women and some of the kids joined
in. In fact, the man who owned the farm was running around with his wife
and two kids. Everybody was chasing without actually trying to catch anything—they just felt like whooping and having fun. Some of the drunker
men actually seemed to have taken on the running style of the animals; for
instance, one man began taking little steps, like the short-legged sheep.
A couple of women were talking next to where the boy and I stood. 58
They watched serenely, as if their husbands and friends were playing cro-
quet or badminton.
"I adore that dress Marie is wearing," said one of them. Marie was the 59
daughter of the novelist. She was having a great time running around.
"Isn't she getting married soon?" said the other woman. 60
"Yes." 61
"When is she getting married?" 62
"Oh," said the first woman, watching Marie fall on her face. "Some 63
Saturday, I guess."
The boy frowned and bit his lip, as if he didn't understand something, 64

and then his face lit up with discovery. "Life is funny," he said.

I really liked that boy. 65

Charlie-O tackled the dog. "Got me a pig!" He looked at the animal in 66 his arms. "Got me a dog," he said.

There was a tussle with the dog, and then everyone was up and chasing 67 the animals again. Over the field, fleets of bleached clouds raced through the sky, and above the sounds of shouting rose the ubiquitous chirp of crickets.

Charlie-O, tired, walked over to me. His mouth was bleeding a bit—I 68 guess from the struggle with the dog—but he was sweaty and happy, not happy with his life or with himself but happy with his exertion. He wiped his mouth. "Did you see that?" he said. "Thought I had me a pig."

The animals suddenly all spread out, running every which way, and 69 there was general confusion in the field.

My father wasn't watching anymore. He had turned the other way, and 70 was gazing past me. I turned, too, and saw my mother coming forward. Charlie-O didn't move, but she walked over. They stood for an instant facing each other, and he gave her that look—the one with the question in it. He seemed confused, and then he said, "Thought I had me a pig."

My mother was lovely and radiant, and suddenly she reached out to 71 touch his face. The touch was sad, and also loving—sad because loving but not in love. "The boys are asleep," she said gently. "I think we'd better get going." She tugged at my hair affectionately and walked inside.

Charlie-O wiped his mouth again and turned to the field. 72

"Aren't we leaving?" I said. 73

He put his arm around the boy's shoulders. "So you like my daughter?" 74 he said.

The boy's jaw dropped, almost imperceptibly, and then he sort of hunched 75 up one shoulder and averted his eyes.

"She's a honey-dog, ain't she?" said Charlie-O. 76

"She is," the boy mumbled. He smiled with embarrassment, and he 77 looked cute and silly.

Then Charlie-O put his arm around me, too, and we stood and watched 78 the end of the chase. A couple of people hoisted a pig into the air.

"Poor thing," said the boy. "I'm glad I ain't a pig." 79

Someone fell down, and the boy looked at me. "My dad," he said. He 80 went off to help.

"Are you O.K., Dad?" I heard him say. 81

"Never felt better," said his father as he got up. 82

Charlie-O watched, not seeing. I looked down and saw a cricket hop 83 onto his foot. "I never saw a cricket do that before," I said.

Charlie-O nodded abstractedly, and his face looked old in the same light 84 that had made my mother so radiant. He still had his arm around me. "Promise me something," he said.

"O.K." 85

"Promise me you'll never break anyone's heart." 86

## STUDY QUESTIONS

1. What do you think Charlie-O's motivation was in marrying the NARRATOR's mother when she was already eight months pregnant with someone else's baby? Why do you think he favors the narrator over his own three sons? How do you feel about his favoring her?

2. What is it that makes the narrator and Charlie-O grow apart?

3. Why do they suddenly move away from Florence, Oregon?

4. What does the episode with the car in the ditch contribute to your understanding of the story? of Charlie-O?

5. What does the last sentence of the story imply? How do you feel about the narrator's mother?

# Simon J. Ortiz

Simon J. Ortiz, of the Acoma Pueblo in New Mexico, earned his master's degree at the University of Iowa, has taught at several universities, and edits the Navajo publication *Rough Rock News*. Among his published books are *A Good Journey*, *Going for the Rain*, *Fight Back: For the Sake of the People, for the Sake of the Land*, *Howbah Indians*, and *From Sand Creek* (which won the Pushcart Prize in 1982).

Like several of the selections that follow in this chapter, this is a lament for and a tribute to a dead father. Here it is the gentleness and the wisdom—"saying things"—that are remembered.

## MY FATHER'S SONG

Wanting to say things,
I miss my father tonight.
His voice, the slight catch,
the depth from his thin chest,
the tremble of emotion                                        5
in something he has just said
to his son, his song:

We planted corn one Spring at Acu—
we planted several times
but this one particular time                                    10
I remember the soft damp sand
in my hand.

My father had stopped at one point
to show me an overturned furrow;
the plowshare had unearthed                                     15
the burrow nest of a mouse
in the soft moist sand.

Very gently, he scooped tiny pink animals
into the palm of his hand
and told me to touch them.                                      20
We took them to the edge
of the field and put them in the shade
of a sand moist clod.

I remember the very softness
of cool and warm sand and tiny alive mice                       25
and my father saying things.

## STUDY QUESTIONS

1. Who is the SPEAKER of the final four verse paragraphs? Who is the father in those paragraphs?

2. What are the significance and effect of the repetition of the word "sand"?

# Li-Young Lee

Li-Young Lee was born in 1957 in Jakarta, Indonesia, to Chinese parents "who were classically educated and in the habit of reciting literally hundreds of ancient Chinese poems." His father was jailed by then-dictator Sukarno for nineteen months, seventeen of them in a leper colony. After his escape, the family fled from country to country, and then settled in western Pennsylvania, where his father became a Presbyterian minister. Lee has published a volume of poems called *Rose* (1986). "I . . . believe the King James Bible to contain some of the greatest poetry in the world," he says, "and I hope to own some of its simplicity, glory, and mystery in my own writing one day."

Just as the Ortiz poem above pays tribute to the father's gentleness and knowledge, so this one lovingly remembers the father's gentleness and skill, and how it has made the son a gentler and more skillful man.

# THE GIFT

To pull the metal splinter from my palm
my father recited a story in a low voice.
I watched his lovely face and not the blade.
Before the story ended he'd removed
the iron sliver I thought I'd die from.     5

I can't remember the tale
but hear his voice still, a well
of dark water, a prayer.
And I recall his hands,
two measures of tenderness     10
he laid against my face,
the flames of discipline
he raised above my head.

Had you entered that afternoon
you would have thought you saw a man     15
planting something in a boy's palm,
a silver tear, a tiny flame.
Had you followed that boy
you would have arrived here,
where I bend over my wife's right hand.     20

Look how I shave her thumbnail down
so carefully she feels no pain.
Watch as I lift the splinter out.
I was seven when my father
took my hand like this,     25
and I did not hold that shard
between my fingers and think,
*Metal that will bury me,*
christen it Little Assassin,
Ore Going Deep for My Heart.     30
And I did not lift up my wound and cry,

*Death visited here!*
I did what a child does
when he's given something to keep.
I kissed my father.                                                          35

## STUDY QUESTIONS

1. What is the SPEAKER doing in the present tense of the poem?

2. Of what from the past does his action remind him?

3. What is "the gift"?

# Li-Young Lee

The loss of the father is new here, the mother replaces him at the family meal, and his recent, quiet death is remembered.

## EATING TOGETHER

In the steamer is the trout
seasoned with slivers of ginger,
two sprigs of green onion, and sesame oil.
We shall eat it with rice for lunch,
brothers, sister, my mother who will                                         5
taste the sweetest meat of the head,
holding it between her fingers
deftly, the way my father did
weeks ago. Then he lay down
to sleep like a snow-covered road                                            10
winding through pines older than him,
without any travelers, and lonely for no one.

## STUDY QUESTIONS

1. What is the effect of setting the poem at the ritual of mealtime?

2. Explore and explain the comparison of the father's lying down to a snow-covered road (lines 9–12).

# Saul Bellow

Author of eleven works of fiction, winner of three National Book Awards, a Pulitzer Prize, and the crown of them all, the Nobel Prize, Saul Bellow ("simply the best writer we have," according to the *New York Times Book Review*) was born in Lachine, Quebec, in 1915, but is more often identified with Chicago, where he attended school and now teaches (at the University of Chicago).

"A Silver Dish," like the poems by Ortiz and Lee, is a loving tribute to a dead father, but the narrator here reveals his father's sly, awesome amorality as well.

# A SILVER DISH

What do you do about death—in this case, the death of an old father? If you're a modern person, sixty years of age, and a man who's been around, like Woody Selbst, what do you do? Take this matter of mourning, and take it against a contemporary background. How, against a contemporary background, do you mourn an octogenarian father, nearly blind, his heart enlarged, his lungs filling with fluid, who creeps, stumbles, gives off the odors, the moldiness or gassiness, of old men. I *mean!* As Woody put it, be realistic. Think what times these are. The papers daily give it to you—the Lufthansa pilot in Aden is described by the hostages on his knees, begging the Palestinian terrorists not to execute him, but they shoot him through the head. Later they themselves are killed. And still others shoot others, or shoot themselves. That's what you read in the press, see on the tube, mention at dinner. We know now what goes daily through the whole of the human community, like a global death-peristalsis.

Woody, a businessman in South Chicago, was not an ignorant person.

He knew more such phrases than you would expect a tile contractor (offices, lobbies, lavatories) to know. The kind of knowledge he had was not the kind for which you get academic degrees. Although Woody had studied for two years in a seminary, preparing to be a minister. Two years of college during the Depression was more than most high-school graduates could afford. After that, in his own vital, picturesque, original way (Morris, his old man, was also, in his days of nature, vital and picturesque), Woody had read up on many subjects, subscribed to *Science* and other magazines that gave real information, and had taken night courses at De Paul and Northwestern in ecology, criminology, existentialism. Also he had traveled extensively in Japan, Mexico, and Africa, and there was an African experience that was especially relevant to mourning. It was this: on a launch near the Murchison Falls in Uganda, he had seen a buffalo calf seized by a crocodile from the bank of the White Nile. There were giraffes along the tropical river, and hippopotamuses, and baboons, and flamingos and other brilliant birds crossing the bright air in the heat of the morning, when the calf, stepping into the river to drink, was grabbed by the hoof and dragged down. The parent buffaloes couldn't figure it out. Under the water the calf still threshed, fought, churned the mud. Woody, the robust traveler, took this in as he sailed by, and to him it looked as if the parent cattle were asking each other dumbly what had happened. He chose to assume that there was pain in this, he read brute grief into it. On the White Nile, Woody had the impression that he had gone back to the pre-Adamite past, and he brought reflections on this impression home to South Chicago. He brought also a bundle of hashish from Kampala. In this he took a chance with the customs inspectors, banking perhaps on his broad build, frank face, high color. He didn't look like a wrongdoer, a bad guy; he looked like a good guy. But he liked taking chances. Risk was a wonderful stimulus. He threw down his trenchcoat on the customs counter. If the inspectors searched the pockets, he was prepared to say that the coat wasn't his. But he got away with it, and the Thanksgiving turkey was stuffed with hashish. This was much enjoyed. That was practically the last feast at which Pop, who also relished risk or defiance, was present. The hashish Woody had tried to raise in his backyard from the Africa seeds didn't take. But behind his warehouse, where the Lincoln Continental was parked, he kept a patch of marijuana. There was no harm at all in Woody, but he didn't like being entirely within the law. It was simply a question of self-respect.

After that Thanksgiving, Pop gradually sank as if he had a slow leak. 3 This went on for some years. In and out of the hospital, he dwindled, his mind wandered, he couldn't even concentrate enough to complain, except in exceptional moments on the Sundays Woody regularly devoted to him. Morris, an amateur who once was taken seriously by Willie Hoppe, the great pro himself, couldn't execute the simplest billiard shots anymore. He could only conceive shots; he began to theorize about impossible three-cushion combinations. Halina, the Polish woman with whom Morris had lived for over forty years as man and wife, was too old herself now to run to the hospital.

So Woody had to do it. There was Woody's mother, too—a Christian convert—needing care; she was over eighty and frequently hospitalized. Everybody had diabetes and pleurisy and arthritis and cataracts and cardiac pacemakers. And everybody had lived by the body, but the body was giving out.

There were Woody's two sisters as well, unmarried, in their fifties, very  4
Christian, very straight, still living with Mama in an entirely Christian bungalow. Woody, who took full responsibility for them all, occasionally had to put one of the girls (they had become sick girls) in a mental institution. Nothing severe. The sisters were wonderful women, both of them gorgeous once, but neither of the poor things was playing with a full deck. And all the factions had to be kept separate—Mama, the Christian convert; the fundamentalist sisters; Pop, who read the Yiddish paper as long as he could still see print; Halina, a good Catholic. Woody, the seminary forty years behind him, described himself as an agnostic. Pop had no more religion than you could find in the Yiddish paper, but he made Woody promise to bury him among Jews, and that was where he lay now, in the Hawaiian shirt Woody had bought for him at the tilers' convention in Honolulu. Woody would allow no undertaker's assistant to dress him, but came to the parlor and buttoned the stiff into the shirt himself, and the old man went down looking like Ben-Gurion in a simple wooden coffin, sure to rot fast. That was how Woody wanted it all. At the graveside, he had taken off and folded his jacket, rolled up his sleeves on thick freckled biceps, waved back the little tractor standing by, and shoveled the dirt himself. His big face, broad at the bottom, narrowed upward like a Dutch house. And, his small good lower teeth taking hold of the upper lip in his exertion, he performed the final duty of a son. He was very fit, so it must have been emotion, not the shoveling, that made him redden so. After the funeral, he went home with Halina and her son, a decent Polack like his mother, and talented, too—Mitosh played the organ at hockey and basketball games in the Stadium, which took a smart man because it was a rabble-rousing kind of occupation—and they had some drinks and comforted the old girl. Halina was true blue, always one hundred percent for Morris.

Then for the rest of the week Woody was busy, had jobs to run, office  5
responsibilities, family responsibilities. He lived alone; as did his wife; as did his mistress: everybody in a separate establishment. Since his wife, after fifteen years of separation, had not learned to take care of herself, Woody did her shopping on Fridays, filled her freezer. He had to take her this week to buy shoes. Also, Friday night he always spent with Helen—Helen was his wife de facto. Saturday he did his big weekly shopping. Saturday night he devoted to Mom and his sisters. So he was too busy to attend to his own feelings except, intermittently, to note to himself, "First Thursday in the grave." "First Friday, and fine weather." "First Saturday; he's got to be getting used to it." Under his breath he occasionally said, "Oh, Pop."

But it was Sunday that hit him, when the bells rang all over South  6

Chicago—the Ukrainian, Roman Catholic, Greek, Russian, African Methodist churches, sounding off one after another. Woody had his offices in his warehouse, and there had built an apartment for himself, very spacious and convenient, in the top story. Because he left every Sunday morning at seven to spend the day with Pop, he had forgotten by how many churches Selbst Tile Company was surrounded. He was still in bed when he heard the bells, and all at once he knew how heartbroken he was. This sudden big heartache in a man of sixty, a practical, physical, healthy-minded, and experienced man, was deeply unpleasant. When he had an unpleasant condition, he believed in taking something for it. So he thought: What shall I take? There were plenty of remedies available. His cellar was stocked with cases of Scotch whisky, Polish vodka, Armagnac, Moselle, Burgundy. There were also freezers with steaks and with game and with Alaskan king crab. He bought with a broad hand—by the crate and by the dozen. But in the end, when he got out of bed, he took nothing but a cup of coffee. While the kettle was heating, he put on his Japanese judo-style suit and sat down to reflect.

Woody was moved when things were *honest*. Bearing beams were honest, undisguised concrete pillars inside high-rise apartments were honest. It was bad to cover up anything. He hated faking. Stone was honest. Metal was honest. These Sunday bells were very straight. They broke loose, they wagged and rocked, and the vibrations and the banging did something for him—cleansed his insides, purified his blood. A bell was a one-way throat, had only one thing to tell you and simply told it. He listened. 7

He had had some connections with bells and churches. He was after all something of a Christian. Born a Jew, he was a Jew facially, with a hint of Iroquois or Cherokee, but his mother had been converted more than fifty years ago by her brother-in-law, the Reverend Doctor Kovner. Kovner, a rabbinical student who had left the Hebrew Union College in Cincinnati to become a minister and establish a mission, had given Woody a partly Christian upbringing. Now, Pop was on the outs with these fundamentalists. He said that the Jews came to the mission to get coffee, bacon, canned pineapple, day-old bread, and dairy products. And if they had to listen to sermons, that was okay—this was the Depression and you couldn't be too particular—but he knew they sold the bacon. 8

The Gospels said it plainly: "Salvation is from the Jews." 9

Backing the Reverend Doctor were wealthy fundamentalists, mainly Swedes, eager to speed up the Second Coming by converting all Jews. The foremost of Kovner's backers was Mrs. Skoglund, who had inherited a large dairy business from her late husband. Woody was under her special protection. 10

Woody was fourteen years of age when Pop took off with Halina, who worked in his shop, leaving his difficult Christian wife and his converted son and his small daughters. He came to Woody in the backyard one spring day and said, "From now on you're the man of the house." Woody was practicing with a golf club, knocking off the heads of dandelions. Pop came into the 11 yard in his good suit, which was too hot for the weather, and when he took off his fedora the skin of his head was marked with a deep ring and the sweat was sprinkled over his scalp—more drops than hairs. He said, "I'm going to move out." Pop was anxious, but he was set to go—determined. "It's no use. I can't live a life like this." Envisioning the life Pop simply *had* to live, his free life, Woody was able to picture him in the billiard parlor, under the El tracks in a crap game, or playing poker at Brown and Koppel's upstairs. "You're going to be the man of the house," said Pop. "It's okay. I put you all on welfare. I just got back from Wabansia Avenue, from the relief station." Hence the suit and the hat. "They're sending out a caseworker." Then he said, "You got to lend me money to buy gasoline—the caddie money you saved."

Understanding that Pop couldn't get away without his help, Woody     12
turned over to him all he had earned at the Sunset Ridge Country Club in Winnetka. Pop felt that the valuable life lesson he was transmitting was worth far more than these dollars, and whenever he was conning his boy a sort of high-priest expression came down over his bent nose, his ruddy face. The children, who got their finest ideas at the movies, called him Richard Dix. Later, when the comic strip came out, they said he was Dick Tracy.

As Woody now saw it, under the tumbling bells, he had bankrolled his     13
own desertion. Ha ha! He found this delightful; and especially Pop's attitude of "That'll teach you to trust your father." For this was a demonstration on behalf of real life and free instincts, against religion and hypocrisy. But mainly it was aimed against being a fool, the disgrace of foolishness. Pop had it in for the Reverend Doctor Kovner, not because he was an apostate (Pop couldn't have cared less), not because the mission was a racket (he admitted that the Reverend Doctor was personally honest), but because Doctor Kovner behaved foolishly, spoke like a fool, and acted like a fiddler. He tossed his hair like a Paganini (this was Woody's addition; Pop had never even heard of Paganini). Proof that he was not a spiritual leader was that he converted Jewish women by stealing their hearts. "He works up all those broads," said Pop. "He doesn't even know it himself, I swear he doesn't know how he gets them."

From the other side, Kovner often warned Woody, "Your father is a     14
dangerous person. Of course, you love him; you should love him and forgive him, Voodrow, but you are old enough to understand he is leading a life of wice."

It was all petty stuff: Pop's sinning was on a boy level and therefore     15
made a big impression on a boy. And on Mother. Are wives children, or what? Mother often said, "I hope you put that brute in your prayers. Look what he has done to us. But only pray for him, don't see him." But he saw him all the time. Woodrow was leading a double life, sacred and profane. He accepted Jesus Christ as his personal redeemer. Aunt Rebecca took advantage of this. She made him work. He had to work under Aunt Rebecca. He filled in for the janitor at the mission and settlement house. In winter, he had to feed the coal furnace, and on some nights he slept near the furnace room, on

the pool table. He also picked the lock of the storeroom. He took canned pineapple and cut bacon from the flitch with his pocketknife. He crammed himself with uncooked bacon. He had a big frame to fill out.

Only now, sipping Melitta coffee, he asked himself: Had he been so hungry? No, he loved being reckless. He was fighting Aunt Rebecca Kovner when he took out his knife and got on a box to reach the bacon. She didn't know, she couldn't prove that Woody, such a frank, strong, positive boy, who looked you in the eye, so direct, was a thief also. But he was also a thief. Whenever she looked at him, he knew that she was seeing his father. In the curve of his nose, the movements of his eyes, the thickness of his body, in his healthy face, she saw that wicked savage Morris. 16

Morris, you see, had been a street boy in Liverpool—Woody's mother and her sister were British by birth. Morris's Polish family, on their way to America, abandoned him in Liverpool because he had an eye infection and they would all have been sent back from Ellis Island. They stopped awhile in England, but his eyes kept running and they ditched him. They slipped away, and he had to make out alone in Liverpool at the age of twelve. Mother came of better people. Pop, who slept in the cellar of her house, fell in love with her. At sixteen, scabbing during a seamen's strike, he shoveled his way across the Atlantic and jumped ship in Brooklyn. He became an American, and America never knew it. He voted without papers, he drove without a license, he paid no taxes, he cut every corner. Horses, cards, billiards, and women were his lifelong interests, in ascending order. Did he love anyone (he was so busy)? Yes, he loved Halina. He loved his son. To this day, Mother believed that he had loved her most and always wanted to come back. This gave her a chance to act the queen, with her plump wrists and faded Queen Victoria face. "The girls are instructed never to admit him," she said. The Empress of India speaking. 17

Bell-battered Woodrow's soul was whirling this Sunday morning, indoors and out, to the past, back to his upper corner of the warehouse, laid out with such originality—the bells coming and going, metal on naked metal, until the bell circle expanded over the whole of steel-making, oil-refining, power-producing mid-autumn South Chicago, and all its Croatians, Ukrainians, Greeks, Poles, and respectable blacks heading for their churches to hear Mass or to sing hymns. 18

Woody himself had been a good hymn singer. He still knew the hymns. He had testified, too. He was often sent by Aunt Rebecca to get up and tell a churchful of Scandihoovians that he, a Jewish lad, accepted Jesus Christ. For this she paid him fifty cents. She made the disbursement. She was the bookkeeper, fiscal chief, general manager of the mission. The Reverend Doctor didn't know a thing about the operation. What the Doctor supplied was the fervor. He was genuine, a wonderful preacher. And what about Woody himself? He also had fervor. He was drawn to the Reverend Doctor. The Reverend Doctor taught him to lift up his eyes, gave him his higher life. Apart from this higher life, the rest was Chicago—the ways of Chicago, 19 which came so natural that nobody thought to question them. So, for instance, in 1933 (what ancient, ancient times!), at the Century of Progress World's Fair, when Woody was a coolie and pulled a rickshaw, wearing a peaked straw hat and trotting with powerful, thick legs, while the brawny red farmers—his boozing passengers—were laughing their heads off and pestered him for whores, he, although a freshman at the seminary, saw nothing wrong, when girls asked him to steer a little business their way, in making dates and accepting tips from both sides. He necked in Grant Park with a powerful girl who had to go home quickly to nurse her baby. Smelling of milk, she rode beside him on the streetcar to the West Side, squeezing his rickshaw puller's thigh and wetting her blouse. This was the Roosevelt Road car. Then, in the apartment where she lived with her mother, he couldn't remember that there were any husbands around. What he did remember was the strong milk odor. Without inconsistency, next morning he did New Testament Greek: The light shineth in darkness—*to fos en te skotia fainei*—and the darkness comprehended it not.

And all the while he trotted between the shafts on the fairgrounds he had one idea, nothing to do with these horny giants having a big time in the city: that the goal, the project, the purpose was (and he couldn't explain why he thought so; all evidence was against it)—God's idea was that this world should be a love world, that it should eventually recover and be entirely a world of love. He wouldn't have said this to a soul, for he could see himself how stupid it was—personal and stupid. Nevertheless, there it was at the center of his feelings. And at the same time, Aunt Rebecca was right when she said to him, strictly private, close to his ear even, "You're a little crook, like your father." 20

There was some evidence for this, or what stood for evidence to an impatient person like Rebecca. Woody matured quickly—he had to—but how could you expect a boy of seventeen, he wondered, to interpret the viewpoint, the feelings, of a middle-aged woman, and one whose breast had been removed? Morris told him that this happened only to neglected women, and was a sign. Morris said that if titties were not fondled and kissed, they got cancer in protest. It was a cry of the flesh. And this had seemed true to Woody. When his imagination tried the theory on the Reverend Doctor, it worked out—he couldn't see the Reverend Doctor behaving in that way to Aunt Rebecca's breasts! Morris's theory kept Woody looking from bosoms to husbands and from husbands to bosoms. He still did that. It's an exceptionally smart man who isn't marked forever by the sexual theories he hears from his father, and Woody wasn't all that smart. He knew this himself. Personally, he had gone far out of his way to do right by women in this regard. What nature demanded. He and Pop were common, thick men, but there's nobody too gross to have ideas of delicacy. 21

The Reverend Doctor preached, Rebecca preached, rich Mrs. Skoglund preached from Evanston, Mother preached. Pop also was on a soapbox. Everyone was doing it. Up and down Division Street, under every lamp, 22 almost, speakers were giving out: anarchists, Socialists, Stalinists, single-tax-ers, Zionists, Tolstoyans, vegetarians, and fundamentalist Christian preach-ers—you name it. A beef, a hope, a way of life or salvation, a protest. How was it that the accumulated gripes of all the ages took off so when trans-planted to America?

And that fine Swedish immigrant Aase (Osie, they pronounced it), who had been the Skoglunds' cook and married the eldest son, to become his rich, religious widow—she supported the Reverend Doctor. In her time she must have been built like a chorus girl. And women seem to have lost the secret of putting up their hair in the high basketry fence of braid she wore. Aase took Woody under her special protection and paid his tuition at the seminary. And Pop said . . . But on this Sunday, at peace as soon as the bells stopped banging, this velvet autumn day when the grass was finest and thickest, silky green: before the first frost, and the blood in your lungs is redder than sum-mer air can make it and smarts with oxygen, as if the iron in your system was hungry for it, and the chill was sticking it to you in every breath . . . Pop, six feet under, would never feel this blissful sting again. The last of the bells still had the bright air streaming with vibrations.

On weekends, the institutional vacancy of decades came back to the warehouse and crept under the door of Woody's apartment. It felt as empty on Sundays as churches were during the week. Before each business day, before the trucks and the crews got started, Woody jogged five miles in his Adidas suit. Not on this day still reserved for Pop, however. Although it was tempting to go out and run off the grief. Being alone hit Woody hard this morning. He thought: Me and the world; the world and me. Meaning that there always was some activity to interpose, an errand or a visit, a picture to paint (he was a creative amateur), a massage, a meal—a shield between him-self and that troublesome solitude which used the world as its reservoir. But Pop! Last Tuesday, Woody had gotten into the hospital bed with Pop because he kept pulling out the intravenous needles. Nurses stuck them back, and then Woody astonished them all by climbing into bed to hold the struggling old guy in his arms. "Easy, Morris, Morris, go easy." But Pop still groped feebly for the pipes.

When the tolling stopped, Woody didn't notice that a great lake of quiet had come over his kingdom, the Selbst Tile warehouse. What he heard and saw was an old red Chicago streetcar, one of those trams the color of the stockyard steer. Cars of this type went out before Pearl Harbor—clumsy, big-bellied, with tough rattan seats and brass grips for the standing passen-gers. Those cars used to make four stops to the mile, and ran with a wallow-ing motion. They stank of carbolic or ozone and throbbed when the air compressors were being charged. The conductor had his knotted signal cord to pull, and the motorman beat the foot gong with his mad heel.

Woody recognized himself on the Western Avenue line and riding through a blizzard with his father, both in sheepskins and with hands and faces raw, the snow blowing in from the rear platform when the doors opened and getting into the longitudinal cleats of the floor. There wasn't warmth enough inside to melt it. And Western Avenue was the longest car line in the world, the boosters said, as if it was a thing to brag about. Twenty-three miles long, made by a draftsman with a T square, lined with factories, storage buildings, machine shops, used-car lots, trolley barns, gas stations, funeral parlors, six-flats, utility buildings, and junkyards, on and on from the prairies on the south to Evanston on the north. Woodrow and his father were going north to Evanston, to Howard Street, and then some, to see Mrs. Skoglund. At the end of the line they would still have about five blocks to hike. The purpose of the trip? To raise money for Pop. Pop had talked him into this. When they found out, Mother and Aunt Rebecca would be furious, and Woody was afraid, but he couldn't help it.

Morris had come and said, "Son, I'm in trouble. It's bad."

"What's bad, Pop?"

"Halina took money from her husband for me and has to put it back before old Bujak misses it. He could kill her."

"What did she do it for?"

"Son, you know how the bookies collect? They send a goon. They'll break my head open."

"Pop! You know I can't take you to Mrs. Skoglund."

"Why not? You're my kid, aren't you? The old broad wants to adopt you, doesn't she? Shouldn't I get something out of it for my trouble? What am I—outside? And what about Halina? She puts her life on the line, but my own kid says no."

"Oh, Bujak wouldn't hurt her."

"Woody, he'd beat her to death."

Bujak? Uniform in color with his dark-gray work clothes, short in the legs, his whole strength in his tool-and-die-maker's forearms and black fingers; and beat-looking—there was Bujak for you. But, according to Pop, there was big, big violence in Bujak, a regular boiling Bessemer inside his narrow chest. Woody could never see the violence in him. Bujak wanted no trouble. If anything, maybe he was afraid that Morris and Halina would gang up on him and kill him, screaming. But Pop was no desperado murderer. And Halina was a calm, serious woman. Bujak kept his savings in the cellar (banks were going out of business). The worst they did was to take some of his money, intending to put it back. As Woody saw him, Bujak was trying to be sensible. He accepted his sorrow. He set minimum requirements for Halina: cook the meals, clean the house, show respect. But at stealing Bujak might have drawn the line, for money was different, money was vital substance. If they stole his savings he might have had to take action, out of respect for the substance, for himself—self-respect. But you couldn't be sure that Pop hadn't invented the bookie, the goon, the theft—the whole thing. He was capable of it, and you'd be a fool not to suspect him. Morris knew that Mother and Aunt Rebecca had told Mrs. Skoglund how wicked he was.

l him for her in poster colors—purple for vice, black for his
l flames: a gambler, smoker, drinker, deserter, screwer of
ist. So Pop was determined to reach her. It was risky for
Reverend Doctor's operating costs were met by Skoglund
ow paid Woody's seminary tuition; she bought dresses for
the little sisters.

Woody, now sixty, fleshy and big, like a figure for the victory of Amer- 37
ican materialism, sunk in his lounge chair, the leather of its armrests softer
to his fingertips than a woman's skin, was puzzled and, in his depths, disturbed by certain blots within him, blots of light in his brain, a blot combining pain and amusement in his breast (how did *that* get there?). Intense thought
puckered the skin between his eyes with a strain bordering on headache.
Why had he let Pop have his way? Why did he agree to meet him that day,
in the dim rear of the poolroom?

"But what will you tell Mrs. Skoglund?" 38

"The old broad? Don't worry, there's plenty to tell her, and it's all true. 39
Ain't I trying to save my little laundry-and-cleaning shop? Isn't the bailiff
coming for the fixtures next week?" And Pop rehearsed his pitch on the
Western Avenue car. He counted on Woody's health and his freshness. Such
a straightforward-looking body was perfect for a con.

Did they still have such winter storms in Chicago as they used to have? 40
Now they somehow seemed less fierce. Blizzards used to come straight down
from Ontario, from the Arctic, and drop five feet of snow in an afternoon.
Then the rusty green platform cars, with revolving brushes at both ends,
came out of the barns to sweep the tracks. Ten or twelve streetcars followed
in slow processions, or waited, block after block.

There was a long delay at the gates of Riverview Park, all the amuse- 41
ments covered for the winter, boarded up—the dragon's-back high-rides, the
Bobs, the Chute, the Tilt-a-Whirl, all the fun machinery put together by
mechanics and electricians, men like Bujak the tool-and-die-maker, good with
engines. The blizzard was having it all its own way behind the gates, and
you couldn't see far inside; only a few bulbs burned behind the palings.
When Woody wiped the vapor from the glass, the wire mesh of the window
guards was stuffed solid at eye level with snow. Looking higher, you saw
mostly the streaked wind horizontally driving from the north. In the seat
ahead, two black coal heavers, both in leather Lindbergh flying helmets, sat
with shovels between their legs, returning from a job. They smelled of sweat,
burlap sacking, and coal. Mostly dull with black dust, they also sparkled here
and there.

There weren't many riders. People weren't leaving the house. This was 42
a day to sit legs stuck out beside the stove, mummified by both the outdoor
and the indoor forces. Only a fellow with an angle, like Pop, would go and
buck such weather. A storm like this was out of the compass, and you kept
the human scale by having a scheme to raise fifty bucks. Fifty soldiers! Real
money in 1933.

"That woman is crazy for you," said Pop.

"She's just a good woman, sweet to all of us."

"Who knows what she's got in mind. You're a husky kid. Not such a kid, either."

"She's a religious woman. She really has religion."

"Well, your mother isn't your only parent. She and Rebecca and Kovner aren't going to fill you up with their ideas. I know your mother wants to wipe me out of your life. Unless I take a hand, you won't even understand what life is. Because they don't know—those silly Christers."

"Yes, Pop."

"The girls I can't help. They're too young. I'm sorry about them, but I can't do anything. With you it's different."

He wanted me like himself, an American.

They were stalled in the storm, while the cattle-colored car waited to have the trolley reset in the crazy wind, which boomed, tingled, blasted. At Howard Street they would have to walk straight into it, due north.

"You'll do the talking at first," said Pop.

Woody had the makings of a salesman, a pitchman. He was aware of this when he got to his feet in church to testify before fifty or sixty people. Even though Aunt Rebecca made it worth his while, he moved his own heart when he spoke up about his faith. But occasionally, without notice, his heart went away as he spoke religion and he couldn't find it anywhere. In its absence, sincere behavior got him through. He had to rely for delivery on his face, his voice—on behavior. Then his eyes came closer and closer together. And in this approach of eye to eye he felt the strain of hypocrisy. The twisting of his face threatened to betray him. It took everything he had to keep looking honest. So, since he couldn't bear the cynicism of it, he fell back on mischievousness. Mischief was where Pop came in. Pop passed straight through all those divided fields, gap after gap, and arrived at his side, bent-nosed and broad-faced. In regard to Pop, you thought of neither sincerity nor insincerity. Pop was like the man in the song: he wanted what he wanted when he wanted it. Pop was physical; Pop was digestive, circulatory, sexual. If Pop got serious, he talked to you about washing under the arms or in the crotch or of drying between your toes or of cooking supper, of baked beans and fried onions, of draw poker or of a certain horse in the fifth race at Arlington. Pop was elemental. That was why he gave such relief from religion and paradoxes, and things like that. Now, Mother *thought* she was spiritual, but Woody knew that she was kidding herself. Oh, yes, in the British accent she never gave up she was always talking to God or about Him—please God, God willing, praise God. But she was a big substantial bread-and-butter down-to-earth woman, with down-to-earth duties like feeding the girls, protecting, refining, keeping pure the girls. And those two protected doves grew up so overweight, heavy in the hips and thighs, that their poor heads looked long and slim. And mad. Sweet but cuckoo—Paula cheerfully cuckoo, Joanna depressed and having episodes.

"I'll do my best by you, but you have to promise, Pop, not to get me in Dutch with Mrs. Skoglund." 54

"You worried because I speak bad English? Embarrassed? I have a mockie[1] accent?" 55

"It's not that. Kovner has a heavy accent, and she doesn't mind." 56

"Who the hell are those freaks to look down on me? You're practically a man and your dad has a right to expect help from you. He's in a fix. And you bring him to her house because she's bighearted, and you haven't got anybody else to go to." 57

"I got you, Pop." 58

The two coal trimmers stood up at Devon Avenue. One of them wore a woman's coat. Men wore women's clothing in those years, and women men's, when there was no choice. The fur collar was spiky with the wet, and sprinkled with soot. Heavy, they dragged their shovels and got off at the front. The slow car ground on, very slow. It was after four when they reached the end of the line, and somewhere between gray and black, with snow spouting and whirling under the street lamps. In Howard Street, autos were stalled at all angles and abandoned. The sidewalks were blocked. Woody led the way into Evanston, and Pop followed him up the middle of the street in the furrows made earlier by trucks. For four blocks they bucked the wind and then Woody broke through the drifts to the snowbound mansion, where they both had to push the wrought-iron gate because of the drift behind it. Twenty rooms or more in this dignified house and nobody in them but Mrs. Skoglund and her servant Hjordis, also religious. 59

As Woody and Pop waited, brushing the slush from their sheepskin collars and Pop wiping his big eyebrows with the ends of his scarf, sweating and freezing, the chains began to rattle and Hjordis uncovered the air holes of the glass storm door by turning a wooden bar. Woody called her "monk-faced." You no longer see women like that, who put no female touch on the face. She came plain, as God made her. She said, "Who is it and what do you want?" 60

"It's Woodrow Selbst. Hjordis? It's Woody." 61

"You're not expected." 62

"No, but we're here." 63

"What do you want?" 64

"We came to see Mrs. Skoglund." 65

"What for do you want to see her?" 66

"Just tell her we're here." 67

"I have to tell her what you came for, without calling up first." 68

"Why don't you say it's Woody with his father, and we wouldn't come in a snowstorm like this if it wasn't important." 69

The understandable caution of women who live alone. Respectable old-time women, too. There was no such respectability now in those Evanston 70

---

1. Jewish, a pejorative term.

houses, with their big verandas and deep yards and with a servant like Hjordis, who carried at her belt keys to the pantry and to every closet and every dresser drawer and every padlocked bin in the cellar. And in High Episcopal Christian Science Women's Temperance Evanston, no tradespeople rang at the front door. Only invited guests. And here, after a ten-mile grind through the blizzard, came two tramps from the West Side. To this mansion where a Swedish immigrant lady, herself once a cook and now a philanthropic widow, dreamed, snowbound, while frozen lilac twigs clapped at her storm windows, of a new Jerusalem and a Second Coming and a Resurrection and a Last Judgment. To hasten the Second Coming, and all the rest, you had to reach the hearts of these scheming bums arriving in a snowstorm.

Sure, they let us in. 71

Then in the heat that swam suddenly up to their mufflered chins Pop 72
and Woody felt the blizzard for what it was; their cheeks were frozen slabs. They stood beat, itching, trickling in the front hall that *was* a hall, with a carved newel post staircase and a big stained-glass window at the top. Picturing Jesus with the Samaritan woman. There was a kind of Gentile closeness to the air. Perhaps when he was with Pop, Woody made more Jewish observations than he would otherwise. Although Pop's most Jewish characteristic was that Yiddish was the only language he could read a paper in. Pop was with Polish Halina, and Mother was with Jesus Christ, and Woody ate uncooked bacon from the flitch. Still, now and then he had a Jewish impression.

Mrs. Skoglund was the cleanest of women—her fingernails, her white 73
neck, her ears—and Pop's sexual hints to Woody all went wrong because she was so intensely clean, and made Woody think of a waterfall, large as she was, and grandly built. Her bust was big. Woody's imagination had investigated this. He thought she kept things tied down tight, very tight. But she lifted both arms once to raise a window and there it was, her bust, beside him, the whole unbindable thing. Her hair was like the raffia you had to soak before you could weave with it in a basket class—pale, pale. Pop, as he took his sheepskin off, was in sweaters, no jacket. His darting looks made him seem crooked. Hardest of all for these Selbsts with their bent noses and big, apparently straightforward faces was to look honest. All the signs of dishonesty played over them. Woody had often puzzled about it. Did it go back to the muscles, was it fundamentally a jaw problem—the projecting angles of the jaws? Or was it the angling that went on in the heart? The girls called Pop Dick Tracy, but Dick Tracy was a good guy. Whom could Pop convince? Here Woody caught a possibility as it flitted by. Precisely because of the way Pop looked, a sensitive person might feel remorse for condemning unfairly or judging unkindly. Just because of a face? Some must have bent over backward. Then he had them. Not Hjordis. She would have put Pop into the street then and there, storm or no storm. Hjordis was religious, but she was wised up, too. She hadn't come over in steerage and worked forty years in Chicago for nothing.

Mrs. Skoglund, Aase (Osie), led the visitors into the front room. This, the biggest room in the house, needed supplementary heating. Because of fifteen-foot ceilings and high windows, Hjordis had kept the parlor stove burning. It was one of those elegant parlor stoves that wore a nickel crown, or miter, and this miter, when you moved it aside, automatically raised the hinge of an iron stove lid. That stove lid underneath the crown was all soot and rust, the same as any other stove lid. Into this hole you tipped the scuttle and the anthracite chestnut rattled down. It made a cake or dome of fire visible through the small isinglass frames. It was a pretty room, three-quarters paneled in wood. The stove was plugged into the flue of the marble fireplace, and there were parquet floors and Axminster carpets and cranberry-colored tufted Victorian upholstery, and a kind of Chinese étagère, inside a cabinet, lined with mirrors and containing silver pitchers, trophies won by Skoglund cows, fancy sugar tongs and cut-glass pitchers and goblets. There were Bibles and pictures of Jesus and the Holy Land and that faint Gentile odor, as if things had been rinsed in a weak vinegar solution.

"Mrs. Skoglund, I brought my dad to you. I don't think you ever met him," said Woody.

"Yes, Missus, that's me, Selbst."

Pop stood short but masterful in the sweaters, and his belly sticking out, not soft but hard. He was a man of the hard-bellied type. Nobody intimidated Pop. He never presented himself as a beggar. There wasn't a cringe in him anywhere. He let her see at once by the way he said "Missus" that he was independent and that he knew his way around. He communicated that he was able to handle himself with women. Handsome Mrs. Skoglund, carrying a basket woven out of her own hair, was in her fifties—eight, maybe ten years his senior.

"I asked my son to bring me because I know you do the kid a lot of good. It's natural you should know both of his parents."

"Mrs. Skoglund, my dad is in a tight corner and I don't know anybody else to ask for help."

This was all the preliminary Pop wanted. He took over and told the widow his story about the laundry-and-cleaning business and payments overdue, and explained about the fixtures and the attachment notice, and the bailiff's office and what they were going to do to him; and he said, "I'm a small man trying to make a living."

"You don't support your children," said Mrs. Skoglund.

"That's right," said Hjordis.

"I haven't got it. If I had it, wouldn't I give it? There's bread lines and soup lines all over town. Is it just me? What I have I divvy with. I give the kids. A bad father? You think my son would bring me if I was a bad father into your house? He loves his dad, he trusts his dad, he knows his dad is a good dad. Every time I start a little business going I get wiped out. This one is a good little business, if I could hold on to that little business. Three people work for me, I meet a payroll, and three people will be on the street, too, if

I close down. Missus, I can sign a note and pay you in two months. I'm a common man, but I'm a hard worker and a fellow you can trust."

Woody was startled when Pop used the word "trust." It was as if from all four corners a Sousa band blew a blast to warn the entire world: "Crook! This is a crook!" But Mrs. Skoglund, on account of her religious preoccupations, was remote. She heard nothing. Although everybody in this part of the world, unless he was crazy, led a practical life, and you'd have nothing to say to anyone, your neighbors would have nothing to say to you, if communications were not of a practical sort, Mrs. Skoglund, with all her money, was unworldly—two-thirds out of this world. 84

"Give me a chance to show what's in me," said Pop, "and you'll see what I do for my kids." 85

So Mrs. Skoglund hesitated, and then she said she'd have to go upstairs, she'd have to go to her room and pray on it and ask for guidance—would they sit down and wait. There were two rocking chairs by the stove. Hjordis gave Pop a grim look (a dangerous person) and Woody a blaming one (he brought a dangerous stranger and disrupter to injure two kind Christian ladies). Then she went out with Mrs. Skoglund. 86

As soon as they left, Pop jumped up from the rocker and said in anger, "What's this with the praying? She has to ask God to lend me fifty bucks?" 87

Woody said, "It's not you, Pop, it's the way these religious people do." 88

"No," said Pop. "She'll come back and say that God wouldn't let her." 89

Woody didn't like that; he thought Pop was being gross and he said, "No, she's sincere. Pop, try to understand: she's emotional, nervous, and sincere, and tries to do right by everybody." 90

And Pop said, "That servant will talk her out of it. She's a toughie. It's all over her face that we're a couple of chiselers." 91

"What's the use of us arguing," said Woody. He drew the rocker closer to the stove. His shoes were wet through and would never dry. The blue flames fluttered like a school of fishes in the coal fire. But Pop went over to the Chinese-style cabinet or étagère and tried the handle, and then opened the blade of his penknife and in a second had forced the lock of the curved glass door. He took out a silver dish. 92

"Pop, what is this?" said Woody. 93

Pop, cool and level, knew exactly what this was. He relocked the étagère, crossed the carpet, listened. He stuffed the dish under his belt and pushed it down into his trousers. He put the side of his short thick finger to his mouth. 94

So Woody kept his voice down, but he was all shook up. He went to Pop and took him by the edge of his hand. As he looked into Pop's face, he felt his eyes growing smaller and smaller, as if something were contracting all the skin on his head. They call it hyperventilation when everything feels tight and light and close and dizzy. Hardly breathing, he said, "Put it back, Pop." 95

Pop said, "It's solid silver; it's worth dough." 96

"Pop, you said you wouldn't get me in Dutch."                                    97

"It's only insurance in case she comes back from praying and tells me    98
no. If she says yes, I'll put it back."

"How?"                                                                                         99

"It'll get back. If I don't put it back, you will."                                    100

"You picked the lock. I couldn't. I don't know how."                            101

"There's nothing to it."                                                                   102

"We're going to put it back now. Give it here."                                   103

"Woody, it's under my fly, inside my underpants. Don't make such a    104
noise about nothing."

"Pop, I can't believe this."                                                              105

"For cry-ninety-nine, shut your mouth. If I didn't trust you I wouldn't   106
have let you watch me do it. You don't understand a thing. What's with
you?"

"Before they come down, Pop, will you dig that dish out of your long   107
johns."

Pop turned stiff on him. He became absolutely military. He said, "Look,   108
I order you!"

Before he knew it, Woody had jumped his father and begun to wrestle   109
with him. It was outrageous to clutch your own father, to put a heel behind
him, to force him to the wall. Pop was taken by surprise and said loudly,
"You want Halina killed? Kill her! Go on, you be responsible." He began to
resist, angry, and they turned about several times, when Woody, with a trick
he had learned in a Western movie and used once on the playground, tripped
him and they fell to the ground. Woody, who already outweighed the old
man by twenty pounds, was on top. They landed on the floor beside the
stove, which stood on a tray of decorated tin to protect the carpet. In this
position, pressing Pop's hard belly, Woody recognized that to have wrestled
him to the floor counted for nothing. It was impossible to thrust his hand
under Pop's belt to recover the dish. And now Pop had turned furious, as a
father has every right to be when his son is violent with him, and he freed
his hand and hit Woody in the face. He hit him three or four times in mid-
face. Then Woody dug his head into Pop's shoulder and held tight only to
keep from being struck and began to say in his ear, "Jesus, Pop, for Christ
sake remember where you are. Those women will be back!" But Pop brought
up his short knee and fought and butted him with his chin and rattled Woody's
teeth. Woody thought the old man was about to bite him. And because he
was a seminarian, he thought: Like an unclean spirit. And held tight. Gradually Pop stopped threshing and struggling. His eyes stuck out and his mouth
was open, sullen. Like a stout fish. Woody released him and gave him a hand
up. He was then overcome with many many bad feelings of a sort he knew
the old man never suffered. Never, never. Pop never had these groveling
emotions. There was his whole superiority. Pop had no such feelings. He
was like a horseman from Central Asia, a bandit from China. It was Mother,
from Liverpool, who had the refinement, the English manners. It was the

preaching Reverend Doctor in his black suit. You have refinements, and all they do is oppress you? The hell with that.

The long door opened and Mrs. Skoglund stepped in, saying, "Did I imagine, or did something shake the house?" 110

"I was lifting the scuttle to put coal on the fire and it fell out of my hand. I'm sorry I was so clumsy," said Woody. 111

Pop was too huffy to speak. With his eyes big and sore and the thin hair down over his forehead, you could see by the tightness of his belly how angrily he was fetching his breath, though his mouth was shut. 112

"I prayed," said Mrs. Skoglund. 113

"I hope it came out well," said Woody. 114

"Well, I don't do anything without guidance, but the answer was yes, and I feel right about it now. So if you'll wait, I'll go to my office and write a check. I asked Hjordis to bring you a cup of coffee. Coming in such a storm." 115

And Pop, consistently a terrible little man, as soon as she shut the door, said, "A check? Hell with a check. Get me the greenbacks." 116

"They don't keep money in the house. You can cash it in her bank tomorrow. But if they miss that dish, Pop, they'll stop the check, and then where are you?" 117

As Pop was reaching below the belt, Hjordis brought in the tray. She was very sharp with him. She said, "Is this a place to adjust clothing, Mister? A men's washroom?" 118

"Well, which way is the toilet, then?" says Pop. 119

She had served the coffee in the seamiest mugs in the pantry, and she bumped down the tray and led Pop down the corridor, standing guard at the bathroom door so that he shouldn't wander about the house. 120

Mrs. Skoglund called Woody to her office and after she had given him the folded check said that they should pray together for Morris. So once more he was on his knees, under rows and rows of musty marbled-cardboard files, by the glass lamp by the edge of the desk, the shade with flounced edges, like the candy dish. Mrs. Skoglund, in her Scandinavian accent—an emotional contralto—raising her voice to Jesus-uh Christ-uh, as the wind lashed the trees, kicked the side of the house, and drove the snow seething on the windowpanes, to send light-uh, give guidance-uh, put a new heart-uh in Pop's bosom. Woody asked God only to make Pop put the dish back. He kept Mrs. Skoglund on her knees as long as possible. Then he thanked her, shining with candor (as much as he knew how), for her Christian generosity and he said, "I know that Hjordis has a cousin who works at the Evanston YMCA. Could she please phone him and try to get us a room tonight so that we don't have to fight the blizzard all the way back? We're almost as close to the Y as to the car line. Maybe the cars have even stopped running." 121

Suspicious Hjordis, coming when Mrs. Skoglund called to her, was burning now. First they barged in, made themselves at home, asked for money, had to have coffee, probably left gonorrhea on the toilet seat. Hjordis, Woody 122 remembered, was a woman who wiped the doorknobs with rubbing alcohol after guests had left. Nevertheless, she telephoned the Y and got them a room with two cots for six bits.

Pop had plenty of time, therefore, to reopen the étagère, lined with 123 reflecting glass or German silver (something exquisitely delicate and tricky), and as soon as the two Selbsts had said thank you and goodbye and were in midstreet again up to the knees in snow, Woody said, "Well, I covered for you. Is that thing back?"

"Of course it is," said Pop. 124

They fought their way to the small Y building, shut up in wire grille 125 and resembling a police station—about the same dimensions. It was locked, but they made a racket on the grille, and a small black man let them in and shuffled them upstairs to a cement corridor with low doors. It was like the small-mammal house in Lincoln Park. He said there was nothing to eat, so they took off their wet pants, wrapped themselves tightly in the khaki army blankets, and passed out on their cots.

First thing in the morning, they went to the Evanston National Bank 126 and got the fifty dollars. Not without difficulties. The teller went to call Mrs. Skoglund and was absent a long time from the wicket. "Where the hell has he gone?" said Pop.

But when the fellow came back, he said, "How do you want it?" 127

Pop said, "Singles." He told Woody, "Bujak stashes it in one-dollar bills." 128

But by now Woody no longer believed Halina had stolen the old man's 129 money.

Then they went into the street, where the snow-removal crews were at 130 work. The sun shone broad, broad, out of the morning blue, and all Chicago would be releasing itself from the temporary beauty of those vast drifts.

"You shouldn't have jumped me last night, Sonny." 131

"I know, Pop, but you promised you wouldn't get me in Dutch." 132

"Well, it's okay. We can forget it, seeing you stood by me." 133

Only, Pop had taken the silver dish. Of course he had, and in a few days 134 Mrs. Skoglund and Hjordis knew it, and later in the week they were all waiting for Woody in Kovner's office at the settlement house. The group included the Reverend Doctor Crabbie, head of the seminary, and Woody, who had been flying along, level and smooth, was shot down in flames. He told them he was innocent. Even as he was falling, he warned that they were wronging him. He denied that he or Pop had touched Mrs. Skoglund's property. The missing object—he didn't even know what it was—had probably been misplaced, and they would be very sorry on the day it turned up. After the others were done with him, Dr. Crabbie said that until he was able to tell the truth he would be suspended from the seminary, where his work had been unsatisfactory anyway. Aunt Rebecca took him aside and said to him, "You are a little crook, like your father. The door is closed to you here."

To this Pop's comment was "So what, kid?" 135

"Pop, you shouldn't have done it." 136

"No? Well, I don't give a care, if you want to know. You can have the    137
dish if you want to go back and square yourself with all those hypocrites."

"I didn't like doing Mrs. Skoglund in the eye, she was so kind to us."    138
"Kind?"    139
"Kind."    140
"Kind has a price tag."    141

Well, there was no winning such arguments with Pop. But they debated    142
it in various moods and from various elevations and perspectives for forty
years and more, as their intimacy changed, developed, matured.

"Why did you do it, Pop? For the money? What did you do with the    143
fifty bucks?" Woody, decades later, asked him that.

"I settled with the bookie, and the rest I put in the business."    144
"You tried a few more horses."    145
"I maybe did. But it was a double, Woody. I didn't hurt myself, and at    146
the same time did you a favor."

"It was for me?"    147
"It was too strange of a life. That life wasn't *you*, Woody. All those    148
women . . . Kovner was no man, he was an in-between. Suppose they made
you a minister? Some Christian minister! First of all, you wouldn't have been
able to stand it, and second, they would throw you out sooner or later."

"Maybe so."    149
"And you wouldn't have converted the Jews, which was the main thing    150
they wanted."

"And what a time to bother the Jews," Woody said. "At least *I* didn't    151
bug them."

Pop had carried him back to his side of the line, blood of his blood, the    152
same thick body walls, the same coarse grain. Not cut out for a spiritual life.
Simply not up to it.

Pop was no worse than Woody, and Woody was no better than Pop.    153
Pop wanted no relation to theory, and yet he was always pointing Woody
toward a position—a jolly, hearty, natural, likable, unprincipled position. If
Woody had a weakness, it was to be unselfish. This worked to Pop's advantage, but he criticized Woody for it, nevertheless. "You take too much on
yourself," Pop was always saying. And it's true that Woody gave Pop his
heart because Pop was so selfish. It's usually the selfish people who are loved
the most. They do what you deny yourself, and you love them for it. You
give them your heart.

Remembering the pawn ticket for the silver dish, Woody startled him-    154
self with a laugh so sudden that it made him cough. Pop said to him after his
expulsion from the seminary and banishment from the settlement house, "You
want in again? Here's the ticket. I hocked that thing. It wasn't so valuable as
I thought."

"What did they give?"    155
"Twelve-fifty was all I could get. But if you want it you'll have to raise    156
the dough yourself, because I haven't got it anymore."

"You must have been sweating in the bank when the teller went to call 157
Mrs. Skoglund about the check."

"I was a little nervous," said Pop. "But I didn't think they could miss 158
the thing so soon."

That theft was part of Pop's war with Mother. With Mother, and Aunt 159
Rebecca, and the Reverend Doctor. Pop took his stand on realism. Mother
represented the forces of religion and hypochondria. In four decades, the
fighting never stopped. In the course of time, Mother and the girls turned
into welfare personalities and lost their individual outlines. Ah, the poor
things, they became dependents and cranks. In the meantime, Woody, the
sinful man, was their dutiful and loving son and brother. He maintained the
bungalow—this took in roofing, pointing, wiring, insulation, air-condition-
ing—and he paid for heat and light and food, and dressed them all out of
Sears, Roebuck and Wieboldt's, and bought them a TV, which they watched
as devoutly as they prayed. Paula took courses to learn skills like macramé-
making and needlepoint, and sometimes got a little job as recreational worker
in a nursing home. But she wasn't steady enough to keep it. Wicked Pop
spent most of his life removing stains from people's clothing. He and Halina
in the last years ran a Cleanomat in West Rogers Park—a so-so business
resembling a laundromat—which gave him leisure for billiards, the horses,
rummy and pinochle. Every morning he went behind the partition to check
out the filters of the cleaning equipment. He found amusing things that had
been thrown into the vats with the clothing—sometimes, when he got lucky,
a locket chain or a brooch. And when he had fortified the cleaning fluid,
pouring all that blue and pink stuff in from plastic jugs, he read the *Forward*[2]
over a second cup of coffee, and went out, leaving Halina in charge. When
they needed help with the rent, Woody gave it.

After the new Disney World was opened in Florida, Woody treated all 160
his dependents to a holiday. He sent them down in separate batches, of course.
Halina enjoyed this more than anybody else. She couldn't stop talking about
the address given by an Abraham Lincoln automaton. "Wonderful, how he
stood up and moved his hands, and his mouth. So real! And how beautiful
he talked." Of them all, Halina was the soundest, the most human, the most
honest. Now that Pop was gone, Woody and Halina's son, Mitosh, the organist
at the Stadium, took care of her needs over and above Social Security, splitting expenses. In Pop's opinion, insurance was a racket. He left Halina nothing but some out-of-date equipment.

Woody treated himself, too. Once a year, and sometimes oftener, he left 161
his business to run itself, arranged with the trust department at the bank to
take care of his gang, and went off. He did that in style, imaginatively,
expensively. In Japan, he wasted little time on Tokyo. He spent three weeks
in Kyoto and stayed at the Tawaraya Inn, dating from the seventeenth cen-

2. Yiddish daily newspaper.

tury or so. There he slept on the floor, the Japanese way, and bathed in scalding water. He saw the dirtiest strip show on earth, as well as the holy places and the temple gardens. He visited also Istanbul, Jerusalem, Delphi, and went to Burma and Uganda and Kenya on safari, on democratic terms with drivers, Bedouins, bazaar merchants. Open, lavish, familiar, fleshier and fleshier but (he jogged, he lifted weights) still muscular—in his naked person beginning to resemble a Renaissance courtier in full costume—becoming ruddier every year, an outdoor type with freckles on his back and spots across the flaming forehead and the honest nose. In Addis Ababa he took an Ethiopian beauty to his room from the street and washed her, getting into the shower with her to soap her with his broad, kindly hands. In Kenya he taught certain American obscenities to a black woman so that she could shout them out during the act. On the Nile, below Murchison Falls, those fever trees rose huge from the mud, and hippos on the sandbars belched at the passing launch, hostile. One of them danced on his spit of sand, springing from the ground and coming down heavy, on all fours. There, Woody saw the buffalo calf disappear, snatched by the crocodile.

Mother, soon to follow Pop, was being lightheaded these days. In company, she spoke of Woody as her boy—"What do you think of my Sonny?"— as though he was ten years old. She was silly with him, her behavior was frivolous, almost flirtatious. She just didn't seem to know the facts. And behind her all the others, like kids at the playground, were waiting their turn to go down the slide: one on each step, and moving toward the top.

Over Woody's residence and place of business there had gathered a pool of silence of the same perimeter as the church bells while they were ringing, and he mourned under it, this melancholy morning of sun and autumn. Doing a life survey, taking a deliberate look at the gross side of his case—of the other side as well, what there was of it. But if this heartache continued, he'd go out and run it off. A three-mile jog—five, if necessary. And you'd think that this jogging was an entirely physical activity, wouldn't you? But there was something else in it. Because, when he was a seminarian, between the shafts of his World's Fair rickshaw, he used to receive, pulling along (capable and stable), his religious experiences while he trotted. Maybe it was all a single experience repeated. He felt truth coming to him from the sun. He received a communication that was also light and warmth. It made him very remote from his horny Wisconsin passengers, those farmers whose whoops and whore cries he could hardly hear when he was in one of his states. And again out of the flaming of the sun would come to him a secret certainty that the goal set for this earth was that it should be filled with good, saturated with it. After everything preposterous, after dog had eaten dog, after the crocodile death had pulled everyone into his mud. It wouldn't conclude as Mrs. Skoglund, bribing him to round up the Jews and hasten the Second Coming, imagined it, but in another way. This was his clumsy intuition. It went no further. Subsequently, he proceeded through life as life seemed to want him to do it.

There remained one thing more this morning, which was explicitly 164 physical, occurring first as a sensation in his arms and against his breast, and, from the pressure, passing into him and going into his breast.

It was like this: When he came into the hospital room and saw Pop with 165 the sides of his bed raised, like a crib, and Pop, so very feeble, and writhing, and toothless, like a baby, and the dirt already cast into his face, into the wrinkles—Pop wanted to pluck out the intravenous needles and he was piping his weak death noise. The gauze patches taped over the needles were soiled with dark blood. Then Woody took off his shoes, lowered the side of the bed, and climbed in and held him in his arms to soothe and still him. As if he were Pop's father, he said to him, "Now, Pop. Pop." Then it was like the wrestle in Mrs. Skoglund's parlor, when Pop turned angry like an unclean spirit and Woody tried to appease him, and warn him, saying, "Those women will be back!" Beside the coal stove, when Pop hit Woody in the teeth with his head and then became sullen, like a stout fish. But this struggle in the hospital was weak—so weak! In his great pity, Woody held Pop, who was fluttering and shivering. From those people, Pop had told him, you'll never find out what life is, because they don't know what it is. Yes, Pop—well, what is it, Pop? Hard to comprehend that Pop, who was dug in for eighty-three years and had done all he could to stay, should now want nothing but to free himself. How could Woody allow the old man to pull the intravenous needles out? Willful Pop, he wanted what he wanted when he wanted it. But what he wanted at the very last Woody failed to follow, it was such a switch.

After a time, Pop's resistance ended. He subsided and subsided. He 166 rested against his son, his small body curled there. Nurses came and looked. They disapproved, but Woody, who couldn't spare a hand to wave them out, motioned with his head toward the door. Pop, whom Woody thought he had stilled, only had found a better way to get around him. Loss of heat was the way he did it. His heat was leaving him. As can happen with small animals while you hold them in your hand, Woody presently felt him cooling. Then, as Woody did his best to restrain him, and thought he was succeeding, Pop divided himself. And when he was separated from his warmth, he slipped into death. And there was his elderly, large, muscular son, still holding and pressing him when there was nothing anymore to press. You could never pin down that self-willed man. When he was ready to make his move, he made it—always on his own terms. And always, always, something up his sleeve. That was how he was.

## STUDY QUESTIONS

1. Woody asks himself, in the first sentence of the story, "What do you do about death—in this case, the death of an old father?" His answer is, "be realistic." Is Woody realistic? What does he do about the death of his old father?

2. Woody's "African experience" is said to be "especially relevant to mourning" (paragraph 2). At this point in the story, what does that seem to mean? The episode is referred to again near the end of the story (par. 161) and then again two paragraphs later (par. 163). In what ways does it seem "relevant to mourning" now?

3. Woody and his father both lie, cheat, steal, commit adultery, and otherwise violate moral norms. How do you feel about these characters? Are they hateful? despicable? Are there any things about them you like? Is there anything that makes you forgive them or exonerate them? anything that makes you admire them? If the last, how can you explain your responses?

4. "Pop took his stand on realism. Mother represented the forces of religion and hypochondria" (par. 159). Where does Woody stand? Is there any sense in which he is religious?

5. "Pop was no worse than Woody, and Woody was no better than Pop. . . . If Woody had a weakness, it was to be unselfish. . . . And it's true that Woody gave Pop his heart because Pop was so selfish. It's usually the selfish people who are loved the most. They do what you deny yourself, and you love them for it" (par. 153).
    What does "selfish" mean in this context? Is there any sense in which you think this rather cynical observation is true? Find out what Selbst means in German. How is that meaning relevant?

6. How does Woody feel about his father's trickery? What is Pop's final trick? The story is not just about Woody's father but about his father's death; why, then, is it called "A Silver Dish"? Why is that episode dwelled on at such length? How is the episode of the dish related to Pop's death?

# Jimmy Santiago Baca

Born in New Mexico in 1952, Jimmy Santiago Baca wrote the poems in his collection *Immigrants in Our Own Land* (1979), from which "Ancestor" is taken, while he was in prison. His most recent volume, *Martin & Meditations on the South Valley* (1987), consists of two long narrative poems. He now lives on a small farm outside Albuquerque.

"Ancestor" is an unconventional tribute to the unconventional love of an unconventional father, in praise of a freedom that would make some people uneasy because it might look so much like irresponsibility.

# ANCESTOR

It was a time when they were afraid of him.
My father, a bare man, a gypsy, a horse
with broken knees no one would shoot.
Then again, he was like the orange tree,
and young women plucked from him sweet fruit.                    5
To meet him, you must be in the right place,
even his sons and daughter, we wondered
where was papa now and what was he doing.
He held the mystique of travelers
that pass your backyard and disappear into the trees.          10
Then, when you follow, you find nothing,
not a stir, not a twig displaced from its bough.
And then he would appear one night.
Half covered in shadows and half in light,
his voice quiet, absorbing our unspoken thoughts.              15
When his hands lay on the table at breakfast,
they were hands that had not fixed our crumbling home,
hands that had not taken us into them
and the fingers did not gently rub along our lips.
They were hands of a gypsy that filled our home                20
with love and safety, for a moment;
with all the shambles of boards and empty stomachs,
they filled us because of the love in them.
Beyond the ordinary love, beyond the coordinated life,
beyond the sponging of broken hearts,                          25
came the untimely word, the fallen smile, the quiet tear,
that made us grow up quick and romantic.
Papa gave us something: when we paused from work,
my sister fourteen years old working the cotton fields,
my brother and I running like deer,                            30
we would pause, because we had a papa no one could catch,
who spoke when he spoke and bragged and drank,
he bragged about us: he did not say we were smart,
nor did he say we were strong and were going to be rich someday.
He said we were good. He held us up to the world for it to see,  35
three children that were good, who understood love in a quiet way,
who owned nothing but calloused hands and true freedom,
and that is how he made us: he offered us to the wind,
to the mountains, to the skies of autumn and spring.

He said, "Here are my children! Care for them!"          40
And he left again, going somewhere like a child
with a warrior's heart, nothing could stop him.
My grandmother would look at him for a long time,
and then she would say nothing.
She chose to remain silent, praying each night,          45
guiding down like a root in the heart of earth,
clutching sunlight and rains to her ancient breast.
And I am the blossom of many nights.
A threefold blossom: my sister is as she is,
my brother is as he is, and I am as I am.                50
Through sacred ceremony of living, daily living,
arose three distinct hopes, three loves,
out of the long felt nights and days of yesterday.

# STUDY QUESTIONS

1. The first five lines offer a series of contradictions: the SPEAKER's father is a mere ("bare") man, and rather worthless ("a horse / with broken knees"), but he is loved by young women, and feared by "them." Can you reconcile these contradictions? put them together to make a composite picture? What is the portrait that emerges? the effect?

2. In lines 6–19, it is chiefly the father's long absences that are described, and what he did not give or do for his family. How do you feel about him at this point in the poem? If your response is not entirely negative, even here, try to explain in terms of the words of the text just how the speaker manages to make you accept this "unfatherly" behavior.

3. To what does the speaker attribute the fact that he and his brother and sister grew up "quick and romantic" (l. 27)?

4. Why does the father think his children, whom he sees rather rarely, are "good" (l. 35)?

5. Are you convinced by this poem that the father was a good and loving father and that his "child rearing" was successful?

# Stephen Shu Ning Liu

B orn in Fu-Ling, China, in 1930, Stephen Shu Ning was in an expeditionary
army in World War II, emigrated to America in 1952, and, while working his
way toward a doctorate in English (from the University of North Dakota), was a
dishwasher, hamburger cook, white mice caretaker, and janitor. Dr. Liu won the
National Endowment for the Arts Award in 1981–82 and the PEN fiction contest in
1983. He has contributed poetry to over 200 literary magazines and published a bilingual volume of poems (written in English and translated by himself into Chinese)
called *Dream Journeys to China* (1982). He teaches at Clark County Community College
in Las Vegas.

The father's control and power that are celebrated here make his death and pow-
erlessness to return all the more poignant, though there is a sense in which the speaker
seems almost to believe and almost to make the reader believe that this powerful,
"magic" being might indeed come sweeping back from the dead.

## MY FATHER'S MARTIAL ART

When he came home Mother said he looked
like a monk and stank of green fungus.
At the fireside he told us about life
at the monastery: his rock pillow,
his cold bath, his steel-bar lifting                                          5
and his wood-chopping. He didn't see
a woman for three winters, on Mountain O Mei.

"My Master was both light and heavy.
He skipped over treetops like a squirrel.
Once he stood on a chair, one foot tied                                       10
to a rope. We four pulled; we couldn't
move him a bit. His kicks could split
a cedar's trunk."

I saw Father break into a pumpkin
with his fingers. I saw him drop a hawk                                       15
with bamboo arrows. He rose before dawn, filled

our backyard with a harsh sound *hah, hah, hah:*
there was his Black Dragon Sweep, his Crane Stand,
his Mantis Walk, his Tiger Leap, his Cobra Coil. . . .
Infrequently he taught me tricks and made me                    20
fight the best of all the village boys.

From a busy street I brood over high cliffs
on O Mei, where my father and his Master sit:
shadows spread across their faces as the smog
between us deepens into a funeral pyre.                          25

But don't retreat into night, my father.
Come down from the cliffs. Come
with a single Black Dragon Sweep and hush
this oncoming traffic with your *hah, hah, hah.*

## STUDY QUESTIONS

1. Where is the SPEAKER's father now?

2. Was the speaker close to his father? What evidence is there about how he feels about his father?

# Sherley Williams

B orn in Bakersfield, California, in 1944, Sherley Williams was educated at California State University at Fresno, Howard University, and Brown University. She has taught at Federal City College, California State University at Fresno, and the University of California, San Diego, where she is now professor of literature and chair of the department. A highly regarded poet, she is author of *Give Birth to Brightness* (1972), *The Peacock Poems* (1975), and the novel *Dessa Rose* (1986).

This amusing, tender, and triumphant poem, like Toni Cade Bambara's stories, uses Black English. It also uses a conventional rhyme scheme—in which the second and fourth lines of the four-line stanzas rhyme—which can hardly contain the loose, colloquial, conversational lines.

# SAY HELLO TO JOHN

I swear I ain't done what Richard
told me bout jumpin round and stuff.
And he knew I wouldn't do nothin to make the baby
come, just joke, say I'mo cough

this child up one day.                                            5
So in the night when I felt the water tween
my legs, I thought it was pee and I laid
there wonderin if maybe I was in a dream.

Then it come to me that my water broke and I went
in to tell Ru-ise. *You been havin pains?*                        10
she ask. I hear her fumblin for the light.
Naw, I say. Don't think so. The veins

stand out along her temples. *What time
is it?* Goin on toward four o'clock.
*Nigga, I told you:*                                              15
*You ain't havin no babies, not*

*in the middle of the night.*
*Get yo ass back to bed.*
*That ain't nothin but pee.* And what
I know bout havin kids cept what she said?                        20

Second time it happen, even she
got to admit this mo'n pee.
And the pain when it come, wa'n't bad
least no mo'n I eva expect to see

again. I remember the doctor smilin,                              25
sayin, Shel, you got a son.
His bright black face above me
sayin, Say hello to John.

## STUDY QUESTIONS

1. Who is Richard? Why does he recommend that the SPEAKER "[jump] round" (line 2)?

2. What can you infer about Ru-ise and her relationship to the speaker? From that conversation, what do you learn about the speaker?

3. What are all the implications and emotions that surround "hello" in the final line?

# Simon J. Ortiz

Simon J. Ortiz, of the Acoma Pueblo in New Mexico, earned his master's degree at the University of Iowa, has taught at several universities, and edits the Navajo publication *Rough Rock News*. Among his published books are *A Good Journey*, *Going for the Rain*, *Fight Back: For the Sake of the People, for the Sake of the Land*, *Howbah Indians*, and *From Sand Creek* (which won the Pushcart Prize in 1982).

Stop reading after the first verse paragraph and try to imagine how you would complete this poem. Then read how Ortiz finishes it.

## SPEAKING

I take him outside
under the trees,
have him stand on the ground.
We listen to the crickets,
cicadas, million years old sound.                    5
Ants come by us.
I tell them,
"This is he, my son.
This boy is looking at you.
I am speaking for him."                               10

The crickets, cicadas,
the ants, the millions of years
are watching us,

hearing us.
My son murmurs infant words,
speaking, small laughter
bubbles from him.
Tree leaves tremble.
They listen to this boy
speaking for me.                                                              20

## STUDY QUESTIONS

1. Each STANZA of this brief poem contains ten lines. The first three lines of the first
   stanza and the final three lines of the second make up a "frame." Inside that frame
   are two seven-line sections, each made up of two or three sentences. Compare the
   first sentences of each (lines 4–7 and 11–14). What is the function of the opening
   frame (ll. 1–3)? What is the function of the closing frame (ll. 18–20)?

2. The insects and the years listen and respond to the boy's babble but not to the
   father's language. What does this suggest about the relationship of man to nature?

# Naomi Long Madgett

Author of more than a half-dozen volumes of poetry, including *Songs to a Phantom Nightingale* (1941), *One and the Many* (1956), *Star by Star* (1965), *Pink Ladies in the Afternoon* (1972), and *Exits and Entrances* (1978), Naomi Long Madgett is professor emeritus of English at Eastern Michigan University.

Madgett's poem treats growing up from the parent's point of view.

# OFFSPRING

I tried to tell her:
    This way the twig is bent.
    Born of my trunk and strengthened by my roots,
    You must stretch newgrown branches
    Closer to the sun                                                    5
    Than I can reach.

I wanted to say:
    Extend my self to that for atmosphere
    Only my dreams allow.

But the twig broke,                                          10
And yesterday I saw her
Walking down an unfamiliar street,
    Feet confident,
    Face slanted upward toward a threatening sky,
And                                                          15
    She was smiling
    And she was
    Her very free,
    Her very individual,
    Unpliable                                                20
    Own.

## STUDY QUESTIONS

1. What is it that the SPEAKER tried to tell her daughter? Does the speaker now think that she was right or wrong?

2. What does it mean that the twig "broke" (line 10)? What is implied by "threatening sky" (l. 14)? What earlier words in the poem refer to the sky or something in or like the sky?

3. What is the TONE of the poem? How does the speaker seem to feel about her daughter's present, grown-up self? What is the force or significance of the last word in the poem?

# Maya Angelou

Maya Angelou's ongoing autobiography has now reached five volumes, and she is still a relatively young woman. But no wonder. Besides writing the autobiography, three volumes of poetry, and a ten-part television series (which she also produced), Angelou has toured Europe and Africa as an actress (in *Porgy and Bess*), studied and taught dance, served as the Northern coordinator for the Southern Christian Leadership Conference, and served on the Commission of International Women's Year and on the Board of Trustees of the American Film Institute. She was understandably named "Woman of the Year" by the *Ladies Home Journal* in 1975.

"My Brother Bailey and Kay Francis" (editors' title) is from the first volume of the autobiography, *I Know Why the Caged Bird Sings*. It is set in Stamps, Arkansas, where her mother had sent her and her older brother, Bailey, to live with their grandmother (whom she calls Momma), who, with (Great-) Uncle Willie, kept a store. It has that bittersweet humor, warmth, and inclusive but not uncritical humanity that mark Angelou's work.

# MY BROTHER BAILEY
# AND KAY FRANCIS

Weekdays revolved on a sameness wheel. They turned into themselves so steadily and inevitably that each seemed to be the original of yesterday's rough draft. Saturdays, however, always broke the mold and dared to be different.

Farmers trekked into town with their children and wives streaming around them. Their board-stiff khaki pants and shirts revealed the painstaking care of a dutiful daughter or wife. They often stopped at the Store to get change for bills so they could give out jangling coins to their children, who shook with their eagerness to get to town. The young kids openly resented their parents' dawdling in the Store and Uncle Willie would call them in and spread among them bits of sweet peanut patties that had been broken in shipping. They gobbled down the candies and were out again, kicking up the powdery dust in the road and worrying if there was going to be time to get to town after all.

Bailey played mumbledypeg with the older boys around the chinaberry tree, and Momma and Uncle Willie listened to the farmers' latest news of the country. I thought of myself as hanging in the Store, a mote imprisoned on a shaft of sunlight. Pushed and pulled by the slightest shift of air, but never falling free into the tempting darkness.

In the warm months, morning began with a quick wash in unheated well water. The suds were dashed on a plot of ground beside the kitchen door. It was called the bait garden (Bailey raised worms). After prayers, breakfast in summer was usually dry cereal and fresh milk. Then to our chores (which on Saturday included weekday jobs)—scrubbing the floors, raking the yards, polishing our shoes for Sunday (Uncle Willie's had to be shined with a biscuit) and attending to the customers who came breathlessly, also in their Saturday hurry.

Looking through the years, I marvel that Saturday was my favorite day in the week. What pleasures could have been squeezed between the fan folds of unending tasks? Children's talent to endure stems from their ignorance of alternatives.

After our retreat from St. Louis, Momma gave us a weekly allowance.    6
Since she seldom dealt with money, other than to take it in and to tithe to
the church, I supposed that the weekly ten cents was to tell us that even she
realized that a change had come over us, and that our new unfamiliarity
caused her to treat us with a strangeness.

I usually gave my money to Bailey, who went to the movies nearly every    7
Saturday. He brought back Street and Smith cowboy books for me.

One Saturday Bailey was late coming back from the Rye-al-toh. Momma    8
had begun heating water for the Saturday-night baths, and all the evening
chores were done. Uncle Willie sat in the twilight on the front porch mum-
bling or maybe singing, and smoking a ready-made. It was quite late. Mothers had called in their children from the group games, and fading sounds of
"Yah . . . Yah . . . you didn't catch me" still hung and floated into the Store.

Uncle Willie said, "Sister, better light the light." On Saturdays we used    9
the electric lights so that last-minute Sunday shoppers could look down the
hill and see if the Store was open. Momma hadn't told me to turn them on
because she didn't want to believe that night had fallen hard and Bailey was
still out in the ungodly dark.

Her apprehension was evident in the hurried movements around the    10
kitchen and in her lonely fearing eyes. The Black woman in the South who
raises sons, grandsons and nephews had her heartstrings tied to a hanging
noose. Any break from routine may herald for them unbearable news. For
this reason, Southern Blacks until the present generation could be counted
among America's arch conservatives.

Like most self-pitying people, I had very little pity for my relatives'    11
anxiety. If something indeed had happened to Bailey, Uncle Willie would
always have Momma, and Momma had the Store. Then, after all, we weren't
their children. But I would be the major loser if Bailey turned up dead. For
he was all I claimed, if not all I had.

The bath water was steaming on the cooking stove, but Momma was    12
scrubbing the kitchen table for the umpteenth time.

"Momma," Uncle Willie called and she jumped. "Momma." I waited in    13
the bright lights of the Store, jealous that someone had come along and told
these strangers something about my brother and I would be the last to know.

"Momma, why don't you and Sister walk down to meet him?"    14

To my knowledge Bailey's name hadn't been mentioned for hours, but    15
we all knew whom he meant.

Of course. Why didn't that occur to me? I wanted to be gone. Momma    16
said, "Wait a minute, little lady. Go get your sweater, and bring me my
shawl."

It was darker in the road than I'd thought it would be. Momma swung    17
the flashlight's arc over the path and weeds and scary tree trunks. The night
suddenly became enemy territory, and I knew that if my brother was lost in
this land he was forever lost. He was eleven and very smart, that I granted,

but after all he was so small. The Bluebeards and tigers and Rippers could eat him up before he could scream for help.

Momma told me to take the light and she reached for my hand. Her voice came from a high hill above me and in the dark my hand was enclosed in hers. I loved her with a rush. She said nothing—no "Don't worry" or "Don't get tender-hearted." Just the gentle pressure of her rough hand conveyed her own concern and assurance to me. 18

We passed houses which I knew well by daylight but couldn't recollect in the swarthy gloom. 19

"Evening, Miz Jenkins." Walking and pulling me along. 20

"Sister Henderson? Anything wrong?" That was from an outline blacker than the night. 21

"No ma'am. Not a thing. Bless the Lord." By the time she finished speaking we had left the worried neighbors far behind. 22

Mr. Willie Williams' Do Drop Inn was bright with furry red lights in the distance and the pond's fishy smell enveloped us. Momma's hand tightened and let go, and I saw the small figure plodding along, tired and old-mannish. Hands in his pockets and head bent, he walked like a man trudging up the hill behind a coffin. 23

"Bailey." It jumped out as Momma said, "Ju," and I started to run, but her hand caught mine again and became a vise. I pulled, but she yanked me back to her side. "We'll walk, just like we been walking, young lady." There was no chance to warn Bailey that he was dangerously late, that everybody had been worried and that he should create a good lie or, better, a great one. 24

Momma said, "Bailey, Junior," and he looked up without surprise. "You know it's night and you just now getting home?" 25

"Yes, ma'am." He was empty. Where was his alibi? 26

"What you been doing?" 27

"Nothing." 28

"That's all you got to say?" 29

"Yes, ma'am." 30

"All right, young man. We'll see when you get home." 31

She had turned me loose, so I made a grab for Bailey's hand, but he snatched it away. I said, "Hey, Bail," hoping to remind him that I was his sister and his only friend, but he grumbled something like "Leave me alone." 32

Momma didn't turn on the flashlight on the way back, nor did she answer the questioning Good evenings that floated around us as we passed the darkened houses. 33

I was confused and frightened. He was going to get a whipping and maybe he had done something terrible. If he couldn't talk to me it must have been serious. But there was no air of spent revelry about him. He just seemed sad. I didn't know what to think. 34

Uncle Willie said, "Getting too big for your britches, huh? You can't come home. You want to worry your grandmother to death?" Bailey was so far away he was beyond fear. Uncle Willie had a leather belt in his good 35 hand but Bailey didn't notice or didn't care. "I'm going to whip you this time." Our uncle had only whipped us once before and then only with a peach-tree switch, so maybe now he was going to kill my brother. I screamed and grabbed for the belt, but Momma caught me. "Now, don't get uppity, miss, 'less you want some of the same thing. He got a lesson coming to him. You come on and get your bath."

From the kitchen I heard the belt fall down, dry and raspy on naked skin. Uncle Willie was gasping for breath, but Bailey made no sound. I was too afraid to splash water or even to cry and take a chance of drowning out Bailey's pleas for help, but the pleas never came and the whipping was finally over. 36

I lay awake an eternity, waiting for a sign, a whimper or a whisper, from the next room that he was still alive. Just before I fell exhausted into sleep, I heard Bailey: "Now I lay me down to sleep, I pray the Lord my soul to keep, if I should die before I wake, I pray the Lord my soul to take." 37

My last memory of that night was the question, Why is he saying the baby prayer? We had been saying the "Our Father, which art in heaven" for years. 38

For days the Store was a strange country, and we were all newly arrived immigrants. Bailey didn't talk, smile or apologize. His eyes were so vacant, it seemed his soul had flown away, and at meals I tried to give him the best pieces of meat and the largest portion of dessert, but he turned them down. 39

Then one evening at the pig pen he said without warning, "I saw Mother Dear." 40

If he said it, it was bound to be the truth. He wouldn't lie to me. I don't think I asked him where or when. 41

"In the movies." He laid his head on the wooden railing. "It wasn't really her. It was a woman named Kay Francis. She's a white movie star who looks just like Mother Dear." 42

There was no difficulty believing that a white movie star looked like our mother and that Bailey had seen her. He told me that the movies were changed each week, but when another picture came to Stamps starring Kay Francis he would tell me and we'd go together. He even promised to sit with me. 43

He had stayed late on the previous Saturday to see the film over again. I understood, and understood too why he couldn't tell Momma or Uncle Willie. She was our mother and belonged to us. She was never mentioned to anyone because we simply didn't have enough of her to share. 44

We had to wait nearly two months before Kay Francis returned to Stamps. Bailey's mood had lightened considerably, but he lived in a state of expectation and it made him more nervous than he was usually. When he told me that the movie would be shown, we went into our best behavior and were the exemplary children that Grandmother deserved and wished to think us. 45

It was a gay light comedy, and Kay Francis wore long-sleeved white silk shirts with big cuff links. Her bedroom was all satin and flowers in vases, and her maid, who was Black, went around saying "Lawsy, missy" all the 46 time. There was a Negro chauffeur too, who rolled his eyes and scratched his head, and I wondered how on earth an idiot like that could be trusted with her beautiful cars.

The whitefolks downstairs laughed every few minutes, throwing the discarded snicker up to the Negroes in the buzzards' roost. The sound would jag around in our air for an indecisive second before the balcony's occupants accepted it and sent their own guffaws to riot with it against the walls of the theater. 47

I laughed, too, but not at the hateful jokes made on my people. I laughed because, except that she was white, the big movie star looked just like my mother. Except that she lived in a big mansion with a thousand servants, she lived just like my mother. And it was funny to think of the whitefolks' not knowing that the woman they were adoring could be my mother's twin, except that she was white and my mother was prettier. Much prettier. 48

The movie star made me happy. It was extraordinary good fortune to be able to save up one's money and go see one's mother whenever one wanted to. I bounced out of the theater as if I'd been given an unexpected present. But Bailey was cast down again. (I had to beg him not to stay for the next show.) On the way home he stopped at the railroad track and waited for the night freight train. Just before it reached the crossing, he tore out and ran across the tracks. 49

I was left on the other side in hysteria. Maybe the giant wheels were grinding his bones into a bloody mush. Maybe he tried to catch a boxcar and got flung into the pond and drowned. Or even worse, maybe he caught the train and was forever gone. 50

When the train passed he pushed himself away from the pole where he had been leaning, berated me for making all that noise and said, "Let's go home." 51

One year later he did catch a freight, but because of his youth and the inscrutable way of fate, he didn't find California and his Mother Dear—he got stranded in Baton Rouge, Louisiana, for two weeks.

## STUDY QUESTIONS

1. Why is Bailey late coming home? Why doesn't he tell his grandmother or Uncle Willie the reason? Why is his grandmother, given the time and place, particularly worried? Why, according to Angelou, have Southern blacks, until the present generation, been "among America's arch conservatives" (paragraph 10)? What does it mean that Angelou says Bailey "was all I claimed, if not all I had" (par. 11)? Why is Momma "scrubbing the kitchen table for the umpteenth time" (par. 12)? Why does Angelou suddenly love Momma?

2. Why does Bailey say a "baby prayer" that night instead of the "Our Father" (par. 38)? Why was the Store for several days "a strange country, and we were all newly

arrived immigrants" (par. 39)? Why, two months later, are the children on their best behavior?

3. What is the response of the blacks in the balcony to the laughter of the whites below at the idiotic antics of the blacks on the screen? (Why are all the blacks sitting upstairs?) Why does Angelou laugh? What is her response to Kay Francis, the white actress? What is Bailey's response? Why does Bailey rush across the tracks in front of the oncoming train? What happens to him?

# David Henry Hwang

S on of immigrant Chinese-American parents, David Henry Hwang (born 1957) is one of the most exciting young playwrights in America. *FOB* won the 1981 Obie Award for best play as well as several other awards, and both *The Dance and the Railroad* and *Family Devotions* won a 1982 Drama Desk nomination. His plays have been produced across the United States, as well as in Singapore and Hong Kong. *The Dance and the Railroad* appeared on national television, and his plays have appeared in *Best Short Plays of 1982*, *Best Plays of 1981–82*, and *New Plays USA 1*. His play *M. Butterfly* opened on Broadway in 1988 and won the Tony Award as best play of the year.

In *Family Devotions,* the interplay—often the clash—between the young American-born, Americanized Chinese and the older Chinese-Americans who came to this country, and even those who stayed in China, goes beyond the personal and familial to the political and religious in a play that is humorous, satirical, fantastic, and serious all at once.

## FAMILY DEVOTIONS

### CHARACTERS

JOANNE, late thirties, Chinese American raised in the Philippines.
WILBUR, her husband, Japanese American, nisei (second generation).
JENNY, their daughter, seventeen.
AMA, Joanne's mother, born in China, emigrated to the Philippines, then to America.
POPO, Ama's younger sister.
HANNAH, Popo's daughter and Joanne's cousin, slightly older than Joanne.
ROBERT, Hannah's husband, Chinese American, first generation.

DI-GOU, Ama and Popo's younger brother, born and raised in China, still a
resident of the People's Republic of China (P.R.C.).
CHESTER, Hannah and Robert's son, early twenties.

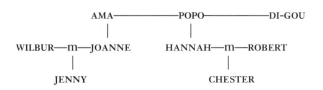

# ACT I

*The sunroom and backyard of a home in Bel Air. Everywhere is glass—glass roof,
glass walls. Upstage of the lanai/sunroom is a patio with a barbecue and a tennis
court. The tennis court leads offstage. As the curtain rises, we see a single spotlight on
an old Chinese face and hear Chinese music or chanting. Suddenly, the music becomes
modern-day funk or rock 'n' roll, and the lights come up to reveal the set.*

*The face is that of* DI-GOU, *an older Chinese man wearing a blue suit and carrying an old suitcase. He is peering into the sunroom from the tennis court, through
the glass walls. Behind him, a stream of black smoke is coming from the barbecue.*

JOANNE: [*Offstage*] Wilbur! Wilbur!

> [DI-GOU *exits off the tennis court. Enter* JOANNE, *from the house. She is a Chinese
> American woman, attractive, in her mid-thirties. She sees the smoke coming from
> the barbecue.*]

JOANNE: Aiii-ya! [*She heads for the barbecue, and on her way notices that the sunroom
is a mess.*] Jenny! [*She runs out to the barbecue, opens it up. Billows of black
smoke continue to pour out.*] Oh, gosh. Oh, golly. [*To offstage*] Wilbur! [*She
begins pulling burnt objects out of the barbecue.*] Sheee! [*She pulls out a chicken,
dumps it onto the ground.*] Wilbur! [*She pulls out another chicken, does the
same.*] Wilbur, the heat was too high on the barbecue! [*She begins pulling
out burnt objects and tossing them all over the tennis court.*] You should have
been watching it! It could have exploded! We could all have been blown
up! [*She picks up another chicken, examines it.*] You think we can have some
of this? [*She pauses, tosses it onto the court.*] We'll get some more chickens.
We'll put barbecue sauce on them and stick them into the microwave.

[*She exits into the house holding a chicken on the end of her fork.*] Is this okay, do you think?

[WILBUR *appears on the tennis court. He is a Japanese American man, nisei, in his late thirties. His hair is permed. He wears tennis clothes.*]

WILBUR: Hon? [*He looks around.*] What's up? [*He picks a burnt chicken off the tennis court.*] Hon? [*He walks over to the barbecue.*] Who—? Why's the heat off? [*He walks around the tennis court picking up chickens.*] Jesus! [*He smears grease on his white tennis shirt, notices it.*] Aw, shit! [*He dumps all the chickens except one, which he has forgotten to pick up, back into the barbecue. He walks into the sunroom, gets some ice, and tries to dab at the stain.*] Hon? Will you come here a sec? [*He exits into the house.*]

[JENNY *appears on the tennis court. She is seventeen,* WILBUR *and* JOANNE's *daughter. She carries a large wire-mesh box.*]

JENNY: Chickie! [*Looking around*] Chickie? Chickie, where the hell did you go? You know, it's embarrassing. It's embarrassing being this old and still having to chase a chicken all over the house. [*She sees the lone burnt chicken on the court. She creeps over slowly, then picks it up.*] Blaagh! Who cooked this? See, Chickie, this is what happens—what happens when you're a bad chickie.

[CHESTER, *a young Chinese American male in his early twenties, appears on the tennis court. He tries to sneak up on* JENNY.]

JENNY: [*To chicken*] Look, if you bother Popo and Ama, I'm gonna catch shit, and you know what that means for you—chicken soccer. You'll be sorry. [CHESTER *is right behind* JENNY.] You'll be sorry if you mess with me. [*She turns around, catching* CHESTER.] Oh, good. You have to be here, too.
CHESTER: No, I don't. I've gotta pack.
JENNY: They'll expect you to be here when that Chinese guy gets here. What's name? Dar-gwo?
CHESTER: I dunno. Dah-gim?
JENNY: Doo-goo? Something.
CHESTER: Yeah. I'm not staying.
JENNY: So what else is new?
CHESTER: I don't have time.
JENNY: You luck out 'cause you don't live here. Me—there's no way I can get away. When you leaving?
CHESTER: Tomorrow.
JENNY: Tomorrow? And you're not packed?
CHESTER: Don't rub it in. Listen, you still have my green suitcase?
JENNY: Yeah. I wish *I* had an excuse not to be here. All I need is to meet another old relative. Another goon.
CHESTER: Yeah. Where's my suitcase?
JENNY: First you have to help me find Chickie.

CHESTER: Jesus!

AMA: [*Offstage*] Joanne!

CHESTER: [*To* JENNY] All right. I don't want them to know I'm here.

[CHESTER *and* JENNY *exit.* POPO *and* AMA *enter. They are* JOANNE's *aunt and mother, respectively.*]

AMA: Joanne! Joanne! Jenny! Where is Joanne?

POPO: Probably busy.

AMA: Where is Jenny? Joanne?

POPO: Perhaps you can find, ah, Wilbur.

AMA: Joanne!

POPO: Ah, you never wish to see Wilbur.

AMA: I see him at wedding. That is enough. He was not at church again today.

POPO: Ah?

AMA: He will be bad influence when Di-gou arrive. Wilbur—holy spirit is not in him.

POPO: Not matter. He can perhaps eat in kitchen.

AMA: Outside!

POPO: This is his house.

AMA: All heart must join as one—

POPO: He may eat inside!

AMA: —only then, miracles can take place.

POPO: But in kitchen.

AMA: Wilbur—he never like family devotions.

POPO: Wilbur does not come from Christian family.

AMA: He come from Japanese family.

POPO: I mean to say, we—ah—very fortunate. Mama teach us all Christianity. Not like Wilbur family.

AMA: When Di-gou arrive, we will remind him. What Mama tells us.

POPO: Di-gou can remember himself.

AMA: No.

POPO: But we remember.

AMA: You forget—Di-gou, he lives in China.

POPO: So?

AMA: Torture, Communists. Make him work in rice fields.

POPO: I no longer think so.

AMA: In rice field, all the people wear wires in their heads—yes! Wires force them work all day and sing Communist song. Like this! [*She mimes harvesting rice and singing.*]

POPO: No such thing!

AMA: Yes! You remember Twa-Ling? Before we leave China, before Communist come, she say, "I will send you a picture. If Communists are good, I will stand—if bad, I will sit."

POPO: That does not mean anything!

AMA: In picture she sent, she was lying down!

POPO: Picture was not sent for ten years. Probably she forget.

AMA: You wait till Di-gou arrive. You will see.

POPO: See what?

AMA: Brainwash! You watch for little bit of wires in his hair.

[POPO *notices the lone burnt chicken on the tennis court.*]

POPO: What's there?

AMA: Where?

POPO: There—on cement.

AMA: Cannot see well.

POPO: There. Black.

AMA: Oh. I see.

POPO: Looks like *gao sai.*

AMA: They sometimes have problem with the dog.

POPO: Ha!

AMA: Very bad dog.

POPO: At home, dog do that?—we shoot him.

AMA: Should be punish.

POPO: Shot! [*Pause*] That no *gao sai.*

AMA: No? What then?

POPO: I don't know.

AMA: Oh, I know.

POPO: What?

AMA: That is Chickie.

POPO: No. That no Chickie.

AMA: They have a chicken—"Chickie."

[*They get up, head toward the chicken.*]

POPO: No. That one, does not move.

AMA: Maybe sick. [*They reach the chicken.*] Aiii-ya! What happen to Chickie!

POPO: [*Picking it up*] This chicken very sick! [*She laughs.*]

AMA: Wilbur.

POPO: Huh?

AMA: Wilbur—his temper is very bad.

POPO: No!

AMA: Yes. Perhaps Chickie bother him too much.

POPO: No—this is only a chicken.

AMA: "Chickie" *is* chicken.

POPO: No—this—another chicken.

AMA: How you know?

POPO: No matter now. Like this, all chicken look same. Here. Throw away. No good.

AMA: Very bad temper. Japanese man. [AMA *sees* POPO *looking for a trash can.*] Wait.

POPO: Huh?

AMA: Jenny—might want to keep it.

POPO: This?

AMA: Leave here until we know. [*She takes the chicken from* POPO.]

POPO: No, throw away. [*She takes it back.*] Stink up whole place soon.

AMA: Don't want to anger Wilbur!

POPO: You pig-head!

AMA: He do this to Chickie—think what he will do to us?

POPO: *Zin gao tza!* [Always so much trouble!]

AMA: You don't know Japanese man!

> [AMA *knocks the chicken from* POPO's *hands; they circle around it like boxers sparring.*]

POPO: *Pah-di!* [Spank you!]

AMA: Remember? During war? Pictures they show us? Always—Japanese man kill Chinese!

POPO: Go away, pig-head!

AMA: In picture—Japanese always kill and laugh, kill and laugh.

POPO: If dirty, should throw away!

AMA: Sometimes—torture and laugh, too.

POPO: Wilbur not like that! Hardly even laugh!

AMA: When he kill Chickie, then he laugh!

> [*They both grab the chicken;* JOANNE *enters, sees them.*]

JOANNE: Hi, Mom, Auntie. Who cleaned up the chicken?

AMA: Huh? This is not Chickie?

POPO: [*To* AMA] Tell you things, you never listen. *Gong-gong-ah!* [Idiot!]

JOANNE: When's Hannah getting here?

POPO: Hannah—she is at airport.

JOANNE: We had a little accident and I need help programming the micro-wave. Last time, I put a roast inside and it disintegrated. She should be here already.

AMA: Joanne, you prepare for family devotions?

JOANNE: Of course, Mom. I had the maid set up everything just like you said. [*She exits.*]

AMA: Good. Praise to God will bring Di-gou back to family. Make him rid of Communist demon.

POPO: He will speak in tongue of fire. Like he does when he is a little boy with See-goh-poh.

> [WILBUR *enters the tennis court with an empty laundry basket. He heads for the barbecue.* JOANNE *follows him.*]

JOANNE: [*To* WILBUR] Hon, what are you going to do with those?

WILBUR: [*Referring to the burnt chicken*] I'm just going to give them to Grizzly. [*He piles the chickens into the basket.*]

JOANNE: All right. [*She notices that the mess in the lanai has not been touched.*] Jenny! [*To* WILBUR] But be careful not to give Grizzly any bones! [JOANNE *exits.*]

WILBUR: [*To* AMA *and* POPO] How you doin', Mom, Auntie?

AMA: [*To* POPO, *sotto voce*] Kill and laugh.

WILBUR: Joanne tells me you're pretty excited about your brother's arrival— pretty understandable, after all these years—what's his name again? Di- ger, Di-gow, something . . .

AMA: Di-gou!

WILBUR: Yeah, right. Gotta remember that. Be pretty embarrassing if I said the wrong name. Di-gou.

POPO: Di-gou is not his name.

WILBUR: What? Not his—? What is it again? Di-gow? De—?

AMA: Di-gou!

WILBUR: Di-gou.

POPO: That is not his name.

WILBUR: Oh. It's the tones in Chinese, isn't it? I'm saying the wrong tone: Di-gou? or Di-gou? Or—

POPO: Di-gou meaning is "second brother."

WILBUR: Oh, I see. It's not his name. Boy, do I feel ignorant in these situa- tions. If only there were some way I could make sure I don't embarrass myself tonight.

AMA: Eat outside.

WILBUR: Outside?

POPO: Or in kitchen.

WILBUR: In the kitchen? That's great! You two are real jokers, you know?

AMA: No. We are not.

WILBUR: C'mon. I should bring you down to the club someday. The guys never believe it when I tell them how much I love you two.

AMA: [*To* POPO] *Gao sai.*

[JENNY *enters the sunroom.*]

WILBUR: Right. *"Gao sai"* to you, too. [*He starts to leave, sees* JENNY.] Wash your hands before you play with your grandmother.

JENNY: [*To* WILBUR] Okay, Dad. [*To* AMA] Do I have to, Ama?

AMA: No. Of course not.

JENNY: Can I ask you something personal?

AMA: Of course.

JENNY: Did Daddy just call you "dog shit"?

AMA: Jenny!

POPO: Yes. Very good!

JENNY: Doesn't that bother you?

POPO: [*To* AMA] Her Chinese is improving!

JENNY: We learned it in Chinese school.

AMA: Jenny, you should not use this American word.

JENNY: Sorry. It just slipped out.

AMA: You do not use such word at school, no?

JENNY: Oh, no. Of course not.

AMA: You should not use anyplace.

JENNY: Right.

POPO: Otherwise—no good man wants marry you.

JENNY: You mean, no rich man.

AMA: No—money is not important.

POPO: As long as he is good man.

[*Pause*]

AMA: Christian.

POPO: Chinese.

AMA: Good education.

POPO: Good school.

AMA: Princeton.

POPO: Harvard.

AMA: Doctor.

POPO: Surgeon.

AMA: Brain surgeon.

POPO: Surgeon general.

AMA: Otherwise—you marry anyone that you like.

JENNY: Ama, Popo—look, I'm only seventeen.

POPO: True. But you can develop the good habits now.

JENNY: I don't want to get married till I'm at least thirty or something.

POPO: Thirty! By that time we are dead!

AMA: Gone to see God!

POPO: Lie in ground, arms cross!

JENNY: Look at it this way: how can I be a good mother if I have to follow my career around?

AMA: Your career will not require this.

JENNY: Yeah, it will. What if I have to go on tour?

AMA: Dental technicians do not tour.

JENNY: Ama!

POPO: Only tour—one mouth to next mouth: "Hello. Clean your teeth?"

JENNY: Look, I'm telling you, I'm going to be a dancer.

AMA: We say—you can do both. Combine skills.

JENNY: That's ridiculous.

POPO: Be first dancing dental technician.

JENNY: I don't wanna be a dental technician!

POPO: Dancing dental technician very rare. You will be very popular.

JENNY: Why can't I be like Chester?

AMA: You cannot be like Chester.

JENNY: Why not!

POPO: You do not play violin. Chester does not dance. No hope.

JENNY: I know, but, I mean, he's a musician. Why can't I be a dancer?

AMA: Chester—his work very dangerous.

JENNY: Dangerous?

AMA: He just receive new job—play with Boston Symphony.

JENNY: Yeah. I know. He's leaving tomorrow. So? What's so bad about Boston?

AMA: Conductor—Ozawa—he is Japanese.

JENNY: Oh, no. Not this again.

AMA: Very strict. If musicians miss one note, they must kill themself!

JENNY: Don't be ridiculous. That's no reason why I can't be like Chester.

POPO: But Chester—he makes plenty money.

JENNY: Yeah. Right. Now. But he has to leave home to do it, see? I want a career, too. So what if I never get married?

AMA: Jenny! You must remember—you come from family of See-goh-poh. She was a great evangelist.

JENNY: I know about See-goh-poh. She was your aunt.

AMA: First in family to become Christian.

POPO: She make this family chosen by God.

JENNY: To do what? Clean teeth?

AMA: Jenny!

JENNY: Look, See-goh-poh never got married because of her work, right?

AMA: See-goh-poh was marry to God.

POPO: When Di-gou arrive, he will tell you his testimony. How See-goh-poh change his life.

AMA: Before, he is like you. [To POPO] You remember?

POPO: Yes. He is always so fussy.

JENNY: I'm not fussy.

AMA: Stubborn.

POPO: Complain this, complain that.

JENNY: I'm not complaining!

AMA: He will be very happy to meet you. Someone to complain with.

JENNY: I'm just telling you, there's no such thing as a dancing dental technician.

AMA: Good. You will be new discovery.

POPO: When Di-gou is a little boy, he never play with other children. He only read the books. Read books—and play tricks.

AMA: He is very naughty.

POPO: He tell other children there are ghosts hide inside the tree, behind the bush, in the bathroom at night.

AMA: One day, he feed snail poison to gardener.

POPO: Then, when he turns eight year old, See-goh-poh decide she will bring him on her evangelism tour. When he return, he has the tongue of fire.

JENNY: Oh, c'mon—those kind of things only happened in China.

AMA: No—they can happen here as well.

POPO: Di-gou at eight, he goes with See-goh-poh on her first evangelism tour—

they travel all around Fukien—thirty day and night, preach to all villages. Five hundred people accept Christ on these thirty day, and See-
goh-poh heal many sick, restore ear to deaf, put tongue in mouth of
dumb, all these thing and cast out the demon. Perhaps even one dead
man—dead and wither—he rise up from his sleep. Di-gou see all this
while carry See-goh-poh's bag and bring her food, ah? After thirty day,
they return home. We have large banquet—perhaps twelve different
dish that night—outside—underneath—ah—cloth. After we eat, See-
goh-poh say, "Now is time for Family Devotions, and this time, he will
lead." See-goh-poh point to Di-gou, who is still a boy, but he walk up
in front of table and begin to talk and flame begin to come from his
mouth, over his head. Fire. Fire, all around. His voice—so loud—praise
and testify the miracle of God. Louder and louder, more and more fire,
till entire sky fill with light, does not seem to be night, like middle of
day, like twelve noon. When he finish talk, sun has already rise, and
cloth over our head, it is all burn, gone, ashes blow away.

[JOANNE enters, pulling CHESTER behind. He carries a suitcase.]

JOANNE: Look who's here!
POPO: Chester—good you decide to come.
JOANNE: He looked lost. This house isn't that big, you know. [Exits.]
AMA: [To CHESTER] You come for reunion with Di-gou. Very good.
CHESTER: Uh—look, I really can't stay. I have to finish packing.
AMA: You must stay—see Di-gou!
CHESTER: But I'm leaving tomorrow.

[Doorbell]

CHESTER: Oh, no.
JOANNE: Can someone get that?
JENNY: Too late!            [Simultaneously]
POPO: Di-gou!
AMA: [To CHESTER] You must! This will be Di-gou!

[WILBUR crosses with basket, now full of chicken bones.]

WILBUR: I'll get it. Chester, good to see you made it. [Exits.]
JENNY: He almost didn't.
CHESTER: I'm really short on time. I gotta go. I'll see you tomorrow at the
    airport.
POPO: Chester! When Di-gou arrive, he must see whole family! You stay!

[CHESTER pauses, decides to stay.]

CHESTER: [To JENNY] This is ridiculous. I can't stay.
JENNY: I always have to. Just grin a lot when you meet this guy. Then every-
    one will be happy.
CHESTER: I don't wanna meet this guy!

[WILBUR *enters with* HANNAH *and* ROBERT, *who are* CHESTER'S *parents.* HANNAH *is* POPO'S *daughter. They are five to ten years older than* JOANNE *and* WILBUR.]

WILBUR: [*To* ROBERT] What? What do you mean?

AMA: [*Stands up on a chair; a speech*] Di-gou, thirty year have pass since we last see you—

WILBUR: [*To* AMA] Not now, Ma.

AMA: Do you still love God?

ROBERT: What do you mean, "What do you mean?" That's what I mean.

HANNAH: He wasn't there, Wilbur. [*To* AMA] Auntie! Di-gou isn't with us.

AMA: What? How can this be?

ROBERT: Those Chinese airliners—all junk stuffs—so inefficient.

AMA: Where is he?

POPO: [*To* ROBERT] You sure you look close?

ROBERT: What "look close"? We just waited for everyone to get off the plane.

AMA: Where is he?

HANNAH: [*To* AMA] We don't know, Auntie! [*To* CHESTER] Chester, are you packed?

AMA: Don't know?

CHESTER: [*To* HANNAH] No, I'm not. And I'm really in a hurry.

HANNAH: You're leaving tomorrow! Why aren't you packed?

CHESTER: I'm trying to, Mom.

[ROBERT *pulls out a newspaper clipping, shows it to* CHESTER.]

ROBERT: Look, son, I called the Chinese paper, used a little of my influence— they did a story on you—here.

CHESTER: [*Looks at clipping*] I can't read this, Dad! It's in Chinese!

ROBERT: [*Takes back clipping*] Little joke, there.

AMA: [*To anyone who will listen*] Where is he?

HANNAH: [*To* AMA] Auntie, ask Wilbur. [*To* CHESTER] Get packed!

CHESTER: All right!

WILBUR: [*Trying to explain to* AMA] Well, Mom, they said he wasn't at—

AMA: [*Ignoring* WILBUR *totally*] Where is he?!

[ROBERT *continues to study the newspaper clipping, points a section out to* CHESTER.]

ROBERT: Here—this is where it talks about my bank.

CHESTER: I'm going to pack.

HANNAH: [*To* CHESTER] Going?

CHESTER: [*To* HANNAH] You said I should—

HANNAH: [*To* CHESTER] You have to stay and see Di-gou!

[WILBUR *makes another attempt to explain the situation to* AMA.]

WILBUR: [*To* AMA] See, Mom, I guess—

AMA: [*Ignoring him again*] Where is he?

[ROBERT *continues studying his clipping, oblivious.*]

ROBERT: [*Translating, to* CHESTER] It says, "Great Chinese violinist will conduct and solo with New York Philharmonic."
CHESTER: What? It says what?
HANNAH: [*To* CHESTER] You came without being packed?

[AMA *decides to look for* DI-GOU *on her own, and starts searching the house.*]

AMA: Di-gou! Di-gou!
WILBUR: [*Following* AMA] Ma, listen. I'll explain.
HANNAH: [*To* CHESTER] How can you be so inefficient?
CHESTER: [*To* ROBERT] Dad, I just got a job playing in the violin section in Boston.
AMA: Di-gou! Di-gou!
CHESTER: [*To* ROBERT] I'm not conducting, and—
ROBERT: [*To* CHESTER] Ssssh! I know. But good publicity—for the bank.
HANNAH: [*To* CHESTER] Well, I'll help you pack later. But you have to stay till Di-gou arrives. Sheesh!
CHESTER: I can't believe this!
AMA: [*Continuing her search*] Di-gou! Are you already in bathroom? [*Exits.*]
HANNAH: [*To* AMA] Auntie, he wasn't at the airport! [*To* WILBUR] Why didn't you tell her?
WILBUR: [*Following* AMA] I'm trying! I'm trying! [*Exits.*]
ROBERT: It's those Communist airlines, I'm telling you. Inefficient.
HANNAH: We asked at the desk. They didn't have a flight list.
AMA: [*Entering*] Then where is he?
WILBUR: [*Entering, in despair*] Joanne, will you come here?
ROBERT: They probably left him in Guam.
POPO: [*To* ROBERT] We give you that photograph. You remember to bring it?
ROBERT: Of course I remembered.
HANNAH: [*To* POPO] Mom, it's not Robert's fault.
POPO: [*To* HANNAH] Should leave him [*Refers to* ROBERT] in car.
HANNAH: I tried.
ROBERT: In the car?
HANNAH: He wanted to come in.
ROBERT: It's hot in the car!
AMA: [*To* ROBERT] Suffer, good for you.
POPO: [*To* HANNAH] You cannot control your husband.
ROBERT: I suffer enough.
HANNAH: He said he could help.
POPO: He is wrong again.
AMA: What to do now?

[JENNY *exits in the confusion;* JOANNE *enters.*]

JOANNE: What's wrong now?

WILBUR: They lost your uncle.

JOANNE: Who lost him?

HANNAH: We didn't lose him.

AMA: [*To* ROBERT] You ask at airport desk?

ROBERT: I'm telling you, he's in Guam.

JOANNE: [*To* HANNAH] How could you lose a whole uncle?

HANNAH: We never had him to begin with!

JOANNE: So where is he?

ROBERT: Guam, I'm telling—!

POPO: [*To* ROBERT] Guam, Guam! Shut mouth or go there yourself!

HANNAH: [*A general announcement*] We don't know where he is!

JOANNE: Should I call the police?

WILBUR: You might have looked longer at the airport.

HANNAH: That's what I said, but he [*Refers to* ROBERT] said, "Aaah, too much trouble!"

POPO: [*To* ROBERT] See? You do not care about people from other province besides Shanghai.

ROBERT: [*To* POPO] Mom, I care. It's just that—

POPO: [*To* ROBERT] Your father trade with Japanese during war.

WILBUR: Huh?

ROBERT: Mom, let's not start that—

POPO: Not like our family. We die first!

WILBUR: What's all this about?

ROBERT: Hey, let's not bring up all this other junk, right?

POPO: [*To* ROBERT] You are ashamed.

ROBERT: The airport is a big place.

WILBUR: [*To* ROBERT] Still, you should've been able to spot an old Chinese man!

ROBERT: Everyone on that plane was an old Chinese man.

AMA: True. All Communist look alike.

HANNAH: Hold it, everybody! [*Pause*] Listen, Di-gou has this address, right?

AMA: No.

HANNAH: No? [*To* POPO] Mom, you said he did.

POPO: Yes. He does.

AMA: [*To* POPO] Yes? But I did not write to him.

POPO: I did.

AMA: Now, Communist—they will know this address.

POPO: Never mind.

AMA: No safety. Bomb us.

HANNAH: Okay, he has this address, and he can speak English—after all, he went to medical school here, right? So he shouldn't have any problem.

JOANNE: What an introduction to America.

HANNAH: All we can do is wait.

ROBERT: We went up to all these old Chinese men at the airport, asked them,

"Are you our Di-gou?" They all said yes. What could we do? They all looked drunk, bums.

JOANNE: Maybe they're all still wandering through the metal detectors, looking for their families, and will continue till they die.

[CHESTER *wanders onto the tennis court, observes the following section from far upstage.*]

JOANNE: I must have been only about seven the last time Di-gou visited us in the Philippines.

AMA: Less.

JOANNE: Maybe less.

WILBUR: Honey, I'm sure everyone here has a memory, too. You don't see them babbling about it, do you?

JOANNE: The last thing I remember about Di-gou, he was trying to convince you grown-ups to leave the Philippines and return to China. There was a terrible fight—one of the worst that ever took place in our complex. I guess he wanted you to join the Revolution. The fight was so loud that all our servants gathered around the windows to watch.

AMA: They did this?

POPO: Shoot them.

JOANNE: I guess this was just around 1949. Finally, Di-gou left, calling you all sorts of terrible names. On his way out, he set fire to one of our warehouses. All us kids sat around while the servants tried to put it out.

POPO: No. That was not a warehouse.

HANNAH: Yeah, Joanne—the warehouses were concrete, remember?

JOANNE: [*To* HANNAH] But don't you remember a fire?

HANNAH: Yes.

POPO: I think he burn a pile of trash.

ROBERT: [*To* WILBUR] I know how you feel. They're always yap-yap-yapping about their family stories—you'd think they were the only family in China. [*To* HANNAH] I have memories, too.

HANNAH: You don't remember anything. You have a terrible memory.

ROBERT: Look, when I was kidnapped, I didn't know—

HANNAH: Sssssh!

JOANNE: Quiet, Robert!

POPO: Like broken record—ghang, ghang, ghang.

WILBUR: [*To* ROBERT] I tell you what: you wanna take a look at my collection of tax shelters?

ROBERT: Same old stuff?

WILBUR: No. Some new ones.

[*They exit.* DI-GOU *appears on the tennis court; only* CHESTER *sees him, but* CHESTER *says nothing.* CHESTER *watches* DI-GOU *watching the women.*]

JOANNE: Anyway, he set fire to something and the flames burned long into the night. One servant was even killed in it, if I remember correctly. I think Matthew's nursemaid was trying to put it out when her dress caught fire and, like a fool, she ran screaming all over the complex. All the adults were too busy to hear her, I guess, and all the kids just sat there and watched this second fire, moving in circles and screaming. By morning, both fires were out, and our tutors came as usual. But that day, nothing functioned just right—I think the water pipes broke in Sah-Zip's room, the cars wouldn't start—something—all I remember is servants running around all day with one tool or another. And that was how Di-gou left Manila for the last time. Left Manila and returned to China—in two fires—one which moved—and a great rush of handymen.

[DI-GOU *is now sitting in their midst in the sunroom. He puts down his suitcase. They turn and see him. He sticks his thumb out, as if for hitchhiking, but it is pointed in the wrong direction.*]

DI-GOU: "Going my way?"

AMA: Di-gou!

DI-GOU: "Hey, baby, got a lift?"

POPO: You see? Our family members will always return.

JOANNE: [*To* DI-GOU] Are you—? Oh, you're—? Well, nice—How did you get here?

DI-GOU: [*Pulls a book out of his jacket*] Our diplomacy handbook. Very useful.

POPO: Welcome to America!

DI-GOU: [*Referring to the handbook*] It says, "When transportation is needed, put your thumb as if to plug a hole."

AMA: [*On chair*] Di-gou, thirty year have passed—

DI-GOU: [*Still reading*] "And say, 'Going my way?' "

AMA: Do you still believe in God?

DI-GOU: "Or, 'Hey, baby, got a lift?' "

AMA: Do you?

HANNAH: [*To* AMA] Auntie, he's explaining something.

DI-GOU: It worked! I am here!

AMA: [*Getting down off chair*] Still as stubborn as before.

DI-GOU: Hello, my sisters.

POPO: Hello, Di-gou. This is my daughter, Hannah.

HANNAH: [*To* DI-GOU] Were you at the airport? We were waiting for you.

DI-GOU: Hannah. Oh, last time, you were just a baby.

AMA: [*Introducing* JOANNE] And Joanne, remember?

JOANNE: Hello, Di-gou. How was your flight?

DI-GOU: Wonderful, wonderful.

POPO: Where is Chester? Chester! [CHESTER *enters the lanai.*] Him—this is number one grandson.

DI-GOU: Oh, you are Chester. You are the violinist, yes?

CHESTER: You're Di-gou?

DI-GOU: Your parents are so proud of you.

HANNAH: We are not. He's just a kid who needs to pack.

AMA: Where is Jenny? Jenny!

HANNAH: [*To* DI-GOU] We figured you'd be able to get here by yourself.

DI-GOU: Oh, yes. [*He sticks out his thumb.* JENNY *enters.*]

JOANNE: Jenny! Say, "Hi, Di-gou."

JENNY: Hi, Di-gou.

DI-GOU: [*To* JOANNE] This is your daughter?

JOANNE: Yes. Jenny. [*Pause*] Jenny, say, "Hi, Di-gou."

JENNY: Mom, I just did!

JOANNE: Oh. Right.

JENNY: Will you cool out?

DI-GOU: Jenny, the last time I saw your mother, she was younger than you are now.

JENNY: He's kinda cute.

JOANNE: Jenny, your granduncle is not cute.

DI-GOU: Thank you.

JENNY: [*To* JOANNE] Can I go now?

AMA: Why you always want to go?

JENNY: Sorry, Ama. Busy.

JOANNE: [*Allowing* JENNY *to leave*] All right.

DI-GOU: [*To* JENNY] What are you doing?

JENNY: Huh? Reading.

DI-GOU: Oh. Schoolwork.

JENNY: Nah. *Vogue.* [*Exits.*]

JOANNE: I've got to see about dinner. [*To* HANNAH] Can you give me a hand? I want to use my new Cuisinart.

HANNAH: All right. What do you want to make?

JOANNE: I don't know. What does a Cuisinart do?

[HANNAH *and* JOANNE *exit;* DI-GOU, AMA, POPO, *and* CHESTER *are left in the sunroom.*]

AMA: Di-gou, thirty year have pass. Do you still love God?

DI-GOU: Thirty-three.

AMA: Ah?

POPO: 1949 to 1982. Thirty-three. He is correct.

AMA: Oh. But you do still love God? Like before?

DI-GOU: You know, sisters, after you left China, I learned that I never did believe in God. [*Pause*]

AMA: What!

POPO: How can you say this?

CHESTER: Ama, Popo, don't start in on that—he just got here.

POPO: You defend him?

AMA: [*Chasing* CHESTER *out to tennis court*] You both are influence by bad people.

POPO: Spend time with bums! Communist bum, musician bum, both same.

DI-GOU: Just to hear my sisters after all these years—you may speak whatever you like.

AMA: Do you still love God?

DI-GOU: I have much love.

AMA: For God?

DI-GOU: For my sisters. [*Pause*]

POPO: You are being very difficult.

AMA: You remember when you first become Christian?

POPO: You travel with See-goh-poh on her first evangelism tour? Before we move to Philippines and you stay in China? Remember? You speak in tongues of fire.

DI-GOU: I was only eight years old. That evening is a blur to me.

AMA: Tonight—we have family devotions. You can speak again. Miracles. You still believe in miracles?

DI-GOU: It is a miracle that I am here again with you!

POPO: Why you always change subject? You remember Ah Hong? Your servant? How See-goh-poh cast out his opium demon?

DI-GOU: I don't think that happened.

AMA: Yes! Remember? After evangelism tour—she cast out his demon.

POPO: Ah Hong tell stories how he eats opium, then he can see everything so clear, like—uh—glass. He can see even through wall, he say, and can see—ah—all the way through floor. Yes! He say he can see through ground, all the way to hell. And he talk with Satan and demon who pretend to be Ah Hong's dead uncles. You should remember.

DI-GOU: I vaguely recall some such stories.

[DI-GOU *opens up his suitcase during* POPO's *following speech and takes out two small Chinese toys and a small Chinese flag. He shows them to* POPO, *but she tries to ignore them.*]

POPO: Demon pretend to be ghost, then show himself everyplace to Ah Hong— in kitchen, in well, in barn, in street of village. Always just sit there, never talk, never move, just sit. So See-goh-poh come, call on God, say only, "Demon begone."

AMA: And from then on, no more ghost, no more opium.

POPO: You—you so happy, then. You say, you will also cast out the demon.

DI-GOU: We were all just children. [*He lines the toys up on the floor.*]

AMA: But you have faith of a child.

DI-GOU: Ah Hong didn't stop eating opium, though. He just needed money. That's why two years later, he was fired.

AMA: Ah Hong never fired!

POPO: I do not think so.

DI-GOU: Yes, my tenth, eleventh birthday, he was fired.

AMA: No—remember? Ah Hong die many year later—just before you come to America for college.

DI-GOU: No, he was fired before then.

POPO: No. Before you leave, go to college, you must prepare your own suitcase. [*To* AMA] Bad memory.

AMA: Brainwash.

[ROBERT *and* WILBUR *enter;* CHESTER *exits off the tennis court.* ROBERT *and* WILBUR *surround* DI-GOU.]

ROBERT *and* WILBUR: Welcome!

WILBUR: How you doing, Di-gow?

ROBERT: [*Correcting* WILBUR] Di-gou!

WILBUR: Oh, right. "Di-gou."

ROBERT: [*To* DI-GOU] We tried to find you at the airport.

WILBUR: [*To* DI-GOU] That means "second brother."

ROBERT: So, you escaped the Communists, huh?

WILBUR: Robert and I were just—

ROBERT: Little joke, there.

WILBUR: —looking at my collection of tax shelters.

ROBERT: China's pretty different now, huh?

WILBUR: You care to take a look?

ROBERT: I guess there's never a dull moment—

WILBUR: Probably no tax shelters, either.

ROBERT: —waiting for the next cultural revolution.

WILBUR: Oh, Robert!

ROBERT: Little joke, there.

WILBUR: [*To* DI-GOU] That's how he [*Refers to* ROBERT] does business.

ROBERT: Of course, I respect China.

WILBUR: He says these totally outrageous things.

ROBERT: But your airlines—so inefficient.

WILBUR: And people remember him.

ROBERT: How long were you in Guam?

WILBUR: [*To* ROBERT] He wasn't in Guam!

ROBERT: No?

WILBUR: [*To* DI-GOU] Well, we're going to finish up the tour.

ROBERT: My shelters are all at my house.

WILBUR: Feel welcome to come along.

ROBERT: His [*Refers to* WILBUR] are kid stuff. Who wants land in Montana?

WILBUR [*To* ROBERT] Hey—I told you. I need the loss.

[WILBUR *and* ROBERT *exit, leaving* DI-GOU *with* AMA *and* POPO. *There is a long silence.*]

DI-GOU: Who are they?

POPO: Servants.

AMA: Don't worry. They will eat outside. In America, servants do not take over their masters' house.

DI-GOU: What are you talking about?

AMA: We know. In China now, servants beat their masters.

DI-GOU: Don't be ridiculous. I have a servant. A chauffeur.

[ROBERT *reenters.*]

ROBERT: Hey, Di-gou—we didn't even introduce ourselves.

DI-GOU: Oh, my sisters explained it to me.

ROBERT: I'm Robert. Hannah's my wife. [ROBERT *puts his arm around* DI-GOU.] When we married, I had nothing. I was working in grocery stores, fired from one job after another. But she could tell—I had a good heart.

DI-GOU: It is good to see servants marrying into the moneyed ranks. We are not aware of such progress by even the lowest classes.

[*Pause*]

ROBERT: Huh?

DI-GOU: To come to this—from the absolute bottom of society.

ROBERT: Wait, wait, I mean, sure, I made progress, but "the bottom of society"? That's stretching it some, wouldn't you say?

DI-GOU: Did you meet Hannah while preparing her food?

ROBERT: Huh? No, we met at a foreign students' dance at UCLA.

DI-GOU: Oh. You attended university?

ROBERT: Look, I'm not a country kid. It's not like I was that poor. I'm from Shanghai, you know.

POPO: [*To* ROBERT] Ssssh! Neighbors will hear!

ROBERT: I'm cosmopolitan. So when I went to college, I just played around at first. That's the beauty of the free-enterprise system, Di-gou. If you wanna be a bum, it lets you be a bum. I wasted my time, went out with all those American girls.

POPO: One girl.

ROBERT: Well, one was more serious, a longer commitment . . .

POPO: Minor.

DI-GOU: What?

POPO: He go out with girl—only fifteen year old.

ROBERT: I didn't know!

POPO: [*To* ROBERT] How come you cannot ask?

ROBERT: I was just an FOB.[1] This American girl—she talked to me—asked me out—kissed me on first date—and I thought, "Land of opportunity!" Anyway, I decided to turn my back on China.

POPO: [*To* DI-GOU] He cannot even ask girl how old.

ROBERT: This is my home. When I wanted to stop being a bum, make money, it let me. That's America!

DI-GOU: I also attended American university. Columbia Medical School.

ROBERT: Right. My wife told me.

POPO: [*To* ROBERT] But he does not date the minor!

---

1. "Fresh off the boat": new immigrant.

ROBERT: [*To* POPO] How was I supposed to know? She looked fully developed!

[AMA *and* POPO *leave in disgust, leaving* ROBERT *alone with* DI-GOU.]

ROBERT: [*To* DI-GOU] Well, then, you must understand American ways.

DI-GOU: It has been some time since I was in America.

ROBERT: Well, it's important to let me tell you. Look, I have a friend who's an immigration lawyer. If you want to stay here, he can arrange it—present visitor. I'm thinking of your family—

ROBERT: I know, but listen. I did it. Never had any regrets. We might be able to get your family over, too.

DI-GOU: Robert, I cannot leave China.

ROBERT: Huh? Look, Di-gou, people risk their lives to come to America. If only you could talk to—to the boat people.

DI-GOU: Uh—the food here looks very nice.

ROBERT: Huh? Oh, help yourself. Go ahead.

DI-GOU: Thank you. I will wait.

ROBERT: No, go on!

DI-GOU: Thank you, but—

ROBERT: Look, in America, there's so much, we don't have to be polite at all!

DI-GOU: Please—I'm not yet hungry.

ROBERT: Us Chinese, we love to eat, right? Well, here in America, we can be pigs!

DI-GOU: I'm not hungry.

ROBERT: I don't see why you can't—? Look. [*He picks up a piece of food, a* bao.[2]] See? [*He stuffs the whole thing into his mouth.*] Pigs!

DI-GOU: Do you mind? I told you, I'm not—

ROBERT: I know. You're not hungry. Think I'm hungry? No, sir! What do I have to do to convince you? Here. [*He drops a tray of* guo-tieh *on the ground, begins stomping them.*] This is the land of plenty!

DI-GOU: Ai! Robert!

[ROBERT *continues stomping them like roaches.*]

ROBERT: There's one next to your foot! [*He stomps it.*] Gotcha!

DI-GOU: Please! It is not right to step on food!

ROBERT: "Right"? Now, see, that's your problem in the P.R.C.—lots of justice, but you don't produce.

[WILBUR *enters, catching* ROBERT *in the act.*]

WILBUR: Robert? What are you—? What's all this?

ROBERT: [*Stops stomping*] What's the big deal? You got a cleaning woman, don't you?

[JENNY *enters.*]

2. Steamed bun, frequently filled with pork. *Guo-tieh* (below): fried dumplings, or "pot stickers."

JENNY: Time to eat yet? [*She sees the mess.*] Blaagh.

[HANNAH *enters.*]

HANNAH: What's all this?

JENNY: Never mind.

[JENNY *exits;* WILBUR *points to* ROBERT, *indicating to* HANNAH *that* ROBERT *is responsible for the mess.* AMA *and* POPO *also enter at this moment, and see* WILBUR*'s indication.*]

DI-GOU: In China, the psychological problems of wealth are a great concern.

POPO: Ai! Who can clean up after man like this!

WILBUR: Robert, I just don't think this is proper.

AMA: Wilbur—not clean himself.

ROBERT: Quiet! You all make a big deal out of nothing!

DI-GOU: I am a doctor. I understand.

POPO: But Robert—he also has the fungus feet.

ROBERT: Shut up, everybody! Will you all just shut up? I was showing Di-gou American ways!

[WILBUR *takes* DI-GOU*'s arm.*]

WILBUR: [*To* DI-GOU] Uh—come out here. I'll show you some American ways.

[WILBUR *and* DI-GOU *go out to the tennis court.*]

ROBERT: [*To* WILBUR] What do you know about American ways? You were born here!

POPO: [*To* AMA] Exercise—good for him.

ROBERT: Only us immigrants really know American ways!

POPO: [*To* AMA, *pinching her belly*] Good for here.

HANNAH: [*To* ROBERT] Shut up, dear. You've done enough damage today.

[WILBUR *gets* DI-GOU *a racket.*]

AMA: [*To* POPO] In China, he [*Refers to* DI-GOU] receives plenty exercise. Whenever Communists, they come torture him.

WILBUR: [*On tennis court, to* DI-GOU] I'll set up the machine. [*He goes* OFF.]

ROBERT: [*In sunroom, looking at tennis court*] What's so American about tennis?

HANNAH: [*To* ROBERT] Yes, dear.

ROBERT: You all ruined it!

HANNAH: You ruined the *guo-tieh*, dear.

ROBERT: What's a few *guo-tieh* in defense of America?

DI-GOU: [*To* WILBUR] I have not played tennis since my college days at Columbia.

ROBERT: [*To* HANNAH] He [*refers to* DI-GOU] was being so cheap! Like this was a poor country!

HANNAH: He's lived in America before, dear.

ROBERT: That was years ago. When we couldn't even buy a house in a place like this.

HANNAH: Yes, dear. Now let's go in and watch the Betamax.

ROBERT: No!

HANNAH: C'mon!

[ROBERT *and* HANNAH *exit. On the tennis court,* DI-GOU *and* WILBUR *stand next to each other, facing offstage. A machine offstage begins to shoot tennis balls at them, each ball accompanied by a small explosive sound. A ball goes by;* DI-GOU *tries to hit it, but it is too high for him. Two more balls go by, but they are also out of* DI-GOU's *reach. A fourth ball is shot out, which hits* WILBUR.]

WILBUR: Aaaah!

[*Balls are being shot out much faster now, pummeling* WILBUR *and* DI-GOU. AMA *and* POPO *continue to sit in the sunroom, staring away from the tennis court, peaceful and oblivious.*]

DI-GOU: Aaah!

WILBUR: I don't—! This never happened—!

DI-GOU: Watch out!

WILBUR: I'll turn off the machine.

DI-GOU: Good luck! Persevere! Overcome! Oh! Watch—!

[*A volley of balls drives* WILBUR *back.* AMA *and* POPO *hear the commotion, look over to the tennis court. The balls stop shooting out.*]

ROBERT: Tennis.

AMA: A fancy machine.

[*They return to looking downstage. The balls begin again.*]

WILBUR: Oh no!

AMA: Wilbur—he is such a bad loser.

POPO: Good exercise, huh? His age—good for here. [*She pinches her belly.*]

DI-GOU: I will persevere! [DI-GOU *tries to get to the machine, is driven back.*]

WILBUR: No! Di-gow!

DI-GOU: I am overcome!

WILBUR: Joanne! [*He begins crawling like a guerrilla toward the machine and finally makes it offstage. The balls stop, presumably because* WILBUR *reached the machine.* DI-GOU *runs off the court.*]

DI-GOU: [*Breathless*] Is it time yet . . . that we may cease to have . . . such enjoyment?

[WILBUR *crosses back onto the tennis court and into the lanai.*]

WILBUR: [*To offstage*] Joanne! This machine's too fast. I don't pay good money to be attacked by my possessions! [*Exits.*]

[AMA *and* POPO *get up, exit into the house, applauding* DI-GOU *as they go, for his exercise.*]

AMA *and* POPO: [*Clapping*] Good, good, very good!

[DI-GOU *is left alone on the tennis court. He is hit by a lone tennis ball.* CHESTER *enters, with a violin case. It is obvious that he has thrown that ball.*]

CHESTER: Quite a workout, there.

DI-GOU: America is full of surprises—why do all these products function so poorly?

CHESTER: Looks like "Made in U.S." is gonna become synonymous with defective workmanship. [*Pause*] You wanna see my violin?

DI-GOU: I would love to.

CHESTER: I thought you might. Here. [*He removes the violin from its case.*] See? No "Made in U.S." label.

DI-GOU: It is beautiful.

CHESTER: Careful! The back has a lacquer which never dries—so don't touch it, or you'll leave your fingerprints in it forever.

DI-GOU: Imagine that. After I die, someone could be playing a violin with my fingerprint.

CHESTER: Funny, isn't it?

DI-GOU: You know, I used to play violin.

CHESTER: Really?

DI-GOU: Though I never had as fine an instrument as this.

CHESTER: Try it. Go ahead.

DI-GOU: No. Please. I get more pleasure looking at it than I would playing it. But I would get the most pleasure hearing you play.

CHESTER: No.

DI-GOU: Please?

CHESTER: All right. Later. How long did you play?

DI-GOU: Some years. During the Cultural Revolution, I put it down.

CHESTER: Must've been tough, huh? [CHESTER *directs* DI-GOU's *attention to the back of his violin.*] Look—the back's my favorite part.

DI-GOU: China is my home, my work. I had to stay there. [DI-GOU *looks at the back of the violin.*] Oh—the way the light reflects—look. And I can see myself in it.

CHESTER: Yeah. Nice, huh?

DI-GOU: So you will take this violin and make music around the world.

CHESTER: Around the world? Oh, you probably got a misleading press clipping. See, my dad . . .

DI-GOU: Very funny.

CH[...] *[...ling]* Yeah. See, I'm just playing in the Boston Symphony. I'm
      [...]morrow.

[...]rtunate, then, to come today, or perhaps I would never meet

[...], I wasn't even planning to come here.

[...]ld be terrible. You know, in China, my wife and I had no
_.ildren—for the good of the state. [DI-GOU *moves to where he left the Chinese
toys earlier in the act. He picks them up and studies them.*] All these years, I
try to imagine—what does Hannah look like? What does her baby look
like? Now, I finally visit and what do I find? A young man. A violinist.
The baby has long since disappeared. And I learn I'll never know the
answer to my question.

*[Silence]*

CHESTER: Di-gou, why did you come here?

DI-GOU: My wife has died, I'm old. I've come for my sisters.

CHESTER: Well, I hope you're not disappointed to come here and see your
    sisters, your family, carry on like this.

DI-GOU: They are still my sisters.

CHESTER: I'm leaving here. Like you did.

DI-GOU: But, Chester, I've found that I cannot leave the family. Today—
    look!—I follow them across an ocean.

CHESTER: You know, they're gonna start bringing you to church.

DI-GOU: No. My sisters and their religion are two different things.

CHESTER: No, they're not. You've been away. You've forgotten. This family
    breathes for God. Ever since your aunt, See-goh-poh.

DI-GOU: See-goh-poh is not the first member of this family.

CHESTER: She's the first Christian.

DI-GOU: There are faces back further than you can see. Faces long before the
    white missionaries arrived in China. Here. [*He holds* CHESTER's *violin so
    that its back is facing* CHESTER, *and uses it like a mirror.*] Look here. At your
    face. Study your face and you will see—the shape of your face is the
    shape of faces back many generations—across an ocean, in another soil.
    You must become one with your family before you can hope to live
    away from it.

CHESTER: Oh, sure, there're faces. But they don't matter here. See-goh-poh's
    face is the only one that has any meaning here.

DI-GOU: No. The stories written on your face are the ones you must believe.

CHESTER: Stories? I see stories, Di-gou. All around me. This house tells a
    story. The days of the week tell a story—Sunday is service, Wednesday
    and Friday are fellowship, Thursday is visitation. Even the furniture
    tells stories. Look around. See-goh-poh is sitting in every chair. There's
    nothing for me here.

DI-GOU: I am here.

CHESTER: You? All right. Here. [CHESTER *turns the back of the violin toward* DI-

GOU, *again using it like a mirror.*] You look. You wanna know what I see? I see the shape of your face changing. And with it, a mind, a will, as different as the face. If you stay with them, your old self will go, and in its place will come a new man, an old man, a man who'll pray.

DI-GOU: Chester, you are in America. If you deny those who share your blood, what do you have in this country?

AMA: [*From offstage*] All right? Ready?

CHESTER: Your face is changing, Di-gou. Before you know it, you'll be praying and speaking in tongues.

AMA: [*Still offstage*] One, two, three, four!

[*The "Hallelujah Chorus" begins. The choir enters, consisting of* WILBUR, JOANNE, ROBERT, HANNAH, *and* POPO. *They are led by* AMA, *who stands at a movable podium which is being pushed into the room by* ROBERT *and* WILBUR *as they sing. (The choir heads for the center of the room, where the podium comes to rest, with* AMA *still on it, and the "Hallelujah Chorus" ends.)* ROBERT *begins singing the tenor aria "Every Valley Shall Be Exalted," from Handel's* Messiah.]

ROBERT: "Every valley, every valley . . ."

HANNAH: Quiet, Robert!

ROBERT: But I want my solo!

JOANNE: [*To* ROBERT] Ssssh! We already decided this.

ROBERT: [*Continuing to sing*] ". . . shall be exalted . . ."

JOANNE: [*Yelling offstage*] Jenny!

AMA: [*To* ROBERT] Time for Family Devotions! Set up room!

[*They begin to arrange the room like a congregation hall, with the pulpit up front.*]

ROBERT: But it's a chance to hear my beautiful voice.

JENNY: [*From offstage*] Yeah! What?

POPO: [*To* ROBERT] Hear at home, hear in car. Now set up room.

JOANNE: [*Yelling offstage*] Jenny! Devotions!

JENNY: [*From offstage*] Aw, Mom.

JOANNE: [*Yelling offstage*] Devotions!

JENNY: [*Entering*] All right.

ROBERT: [*To* HANNAH] You know what this is? This is the breakdown of family authority.

HANNAH: [*To* ROBERT] You have all the authority, dear. Now shut up.

[JENNY *goes over to* CHESTER.]

JENNY: Hey, you still here? I thought for sure you'd have split by now.

CHESTER: I will.

JENNY: You gotta take it easier. Do like me. I act all lotus blossom for them. I say, "Hi, uncle this and auntie that." It's easy.

ROBERT: Look—all this free time. [*Sings*] "Every valley . . ."

POPO: Shoot him!

[*The room is set up.*]

AMA: We begin! Family Devotions! [AMA *flips a switch. A neon cross is lit up.*]
JENNY: [*To* CHESTER] Looks like a disco.

[*Everyone is seated except* DI-GOU. *The rest of the family waits for him. He walks over and sits down.* AMA *bows down to pray. Everyone bows except* CHESTER *and* DI-GOU, *but since all other eyes are closed, no one notices their noncompliance.* AMA *begins to pray.*]

AMA: Dear Father, when we think of your great mercy to this family, we can only feel so grateful, privilege to be family chose for your work. You claim us to be yours, put your mark on our heart.

[CHESTER *gets up, picks up his violin, gets* DI-GOU's *attention.*]

AMA: Your blessing begin many year ago in China.

[CHESTER *begins playing; his music serves as underscoring to* AMA's *prayer.*]

AMA: When See-goh-poh, she hear your word—from missionary. Your spirit, it touch her heart, she accept you, she speak in tongue of fire.

[CHESTER *begins to move out of the room as he plays.*]

AMA: You continue, bless See-goh-poh. She become agent of God, bring light to whole family, until we are convert, we become shining light for you all through Amoy.

[CHESTER *stops playing, looks at* DI-GOU, *waves good-bye, and exits.* DI-GOU *gets up, walks to where* CHESTER *was standing before he left, and waves good-bye.*]

AMA: Let us praise your victory over Satan. Praise your power over demon. Praise miracle over our own sinful will. Praise your victory over even our very hearts. Amen.

[AMA *conducts the choir in the ending of the "Hallelujah Chorus." As they sing, she notices* DI-GOU's *chair is empty. She turns and sees him waving. They look at each other as the "Hallelujah Chorus" continues.* CURTAIN.]

# ACT II

*A moment later. As the curtain rises, all are in the same positions they occupied at the end of Act I.* AMA *and* DI-GOU *are looking at each other. The choir ends the "Hallelujah Chorus."* DI-GOU *walks back toward his chair, and sits.* AMA *notices that* CHESTER's *seat is empty.*

AMA: Where is Chester?
HANNAH: I heard his violin.

AMA: This is family devotions.

ROBERT: The kid's got a mind of his own.

HANNAH: He probably went home to pack, Auntie. He's really in a hurry.

JENNY: Can I go look?

AMA: Why everyone want to go?

JENNY: But he forgot his suitcase. [*She points to the green suitcase, which* CHESTER *has left behind.*]

POPO: [*To* JENNY] Di-gou, he will want to hear you give testimony.

[JENNY *sits back down.*]

AMA: Now—Special Testimony. Let us tell of God's blessing! Who will have privilege? Special Testimony! Who will be first to praise? [*Silence*] He is in our presence! Open His arms to us! [*Silence*] He is not going to wait forever—you know this! He is very busy!

[ROBERT *stands up, starts to head for podium.* POPO *notices that* ROBERT *has risen, points to him.*]

POPO: No! Not him!

AMA: [*To* ROBERT] He is very bored with certain people who say same thing over and over again.

WILBUR: Why don't we sit down, Robert?

JENNY: C'mon, Uncle Robert.

HANNAH: Dear, forget it, all right?

ROBERT: But she needed someone to start. I just—

POPO: [*To* ROBERT] She did not include you.

WILBUR: Can't you see how bored they are with that, Robert?

ROBERT: Bored.

WILBUR: Everybody else has forgotten it.

ROBERT: Forgotten it? They can't.

JOANNE: We could if you'd stop talking about it.

ROBERT: But there's something new!

WILBUR: Of course. There always is.

ROBERT: There is!

JOANNE: [*To* WILBUR] Don't pay attention, dear. It just encourages him.

WILBUR: [*To* JOANNE] Honey, are you trying to advise *me* on how to be diplomatic?

JOANNE: I'm only saying, if you let Hannah—

WILBUR: You're a real stitch, you know that? You really are.

JOANNE: Hannah's good at keeping him quiet.

ROBERT: Quiet?

WILBUR: [*To* JOANNE] Look, who was voted "Mr. Congeniality" at the club last week—you or me?

ROBERT: Hannah, who are you telling to be quiet?

HANNAH: Quiet, Robert.

WILBUR: [*To* JOANNE] Afraid to answer? Huh? Who? Who was "Mr. Congeniality"? Tell me—were you "Mr. Congeniality"?

JENNY: [*To* WILBUR] I don't think she stood a chance, Dad.

WILBUR: [*To* JENNY] Who asked you, huh?

JENNY: "Mr. Congeniality," I think.

WILBUR: Don't be disrespectful.

AMA: We must begin Special Testimony! Who is first?

POPO: I talk.

JOANNE: Good.

POPO: Talk from here. [*She stands.*] Long time since we all come here like this. I remember long ago, family leave China—the boat storm, storm, storm, storm, all around, Hannah cry. I think, "Aaah, why we have to leave China, go to Philippines?" But I remember Jonah, when he did not obey God, only then seas become—ah—dangerous. And even after, after Jonah eaten by whale, God provide for him. So if God has plan for us, we live; if not [*She looks at* DI-GOU.] we die. [*She sits.*] Okay. That's all.

[*Everyone applauds.*]

AMA: Very good! Who is next?

ROBERT: I said, I'd be happy to—

HANNAH: How about Jenny?

JENNY: Me?

JOANNE: Sure, dear, c'mon.

JENNY: Oh . . . well . . .

POPO: [*To* DI-GOU] You see—she is so young, but her faith is old.

JENNY: After I do this, can I go see what's happened to Chester?

POPO: [*To* JENNY] First, serve God.

ROBERT: Let her go.

POPO: Then, you may see about Chester.

JENNY: All right. [*She walks to the podium.*]

POPO: [*To* DI-GOU] I will tell you what each sentence meaning.

DI-GOU: I can understand quite well.

POPO: No. You are not Christian. You need someone—like announcer at baseball game—except announce for God.

JENNY: [*At podium, she begins testimony.*] First, I want to say that I love you all very much. I really do.

POPO: [*To* DI-GOU] That meaning is, she love God.

JENNY: And I appreciate what you've done for me.

POPO: [*To* DI-GOU] She loves us because we show her God.

JENNY: But I guess there are certain times when even love isn't enough.

POPO: [*To* DI-GOU] She does not have enough love for you. You are not Christian.

JENNY: Sometimes, even love has its dark side.

POPO: [*To* DI-GOU] That is you.

JENNY: And when you find that side, sometimes you have to leave in order to come back in a better way.

POPO: [*To* DI-GOU] She cannot stand to be around you.

JENNY: Please. Remember what I said, and think about it later.

POPO: [*To* DI-GOU] You hear? Think!

JENNY: Thank you.

[*Everyone applauds.*]

AMA: Good, good.

JENNY: Can I go now?

ROBERT: [*To* HANNAH] What was she talking about?

AMA: [*To* JENNY] Soon, you can be best testifier—do testimony on TV.

JENNY: Can I go now?

JOANNE: All right, Jenny.

JENNY: Thanks. [*Exits.*]

ROBERT: [*To* POPO] Why don't you interpret for *me?* I didn't understand what she was talking about. Not a bit.

POPO: Good.

ROBERT: Good? Don't you want me to be a better Christian?

POPO: No. Not too good. Do not want to live in same part of Heaven as you.

ROBERT: Why not? It'll be great, Popo. We can tell stories, sing—

POPO: In Heaven, hope you live in basement.

ROBERT: Basement? C'mon, Popo, I'm a celebrity. They wouldn't give me the basement. They'll probably recognize my diplomacy ability, make me ambassador.

JOANNE: To Hell?

ROBERT: Well, if that's the place they send ambassadors.

POPO: Good. You be ambassador.

AMA: Special Testimony! Who is next?

ROBERT: [*Asking to be recognized*] Ama?

AMA: [*Ignoring him*] Who is next?

ROBERT: Not me. I think Wilbur should speak.

AMA: [*Disgusted*] Wilbur?

WILBUR: Me?

ROBERT: Yeah.

WILBUR: Well, I don't really . . .

ROBERT: Tell them, Wilbur. Tell them what kind of big stuffs happen to you. Tell them how important you are.

WILBUR: Well, I . . .

AMA: Would you . . . like to speak . . . Wilbur?

WILBUR: Well, I'd be honored, but if anyone else would rather . . .

ROBERT: We want to hear what you have to be proud of.

WILBUR: All right. [WILBUR *takes the podium;* AMA *scurries away.*] Uh—well, it's certainly nice to see this family reunion. Uh—last week, I was voted "Mr. Congeniality" at the club.

ROBERT: What papers was it in?

WILBUR: Huh?

ROBERT: Was it in the L.A. *Times?* Front page? Otis Chandler's paper?

HANNAH: [*A rebuff*] Robert!

POPO: [*To* ROBERT] Devotions is not question-and-answer for anyone except God.

ROBERT: God sometimes speaks through people, doesn't He?

POPO: He has good taste. Would not speak through you.

ROBERT: [*Undaunted, to* WILBUR] Show me one newspaper clipping. Just one!

WILBUR: Well, besides the *Valley Green Sheet* . . .

ROBERT: The *Valley Green Sheet?* Who pays for that? Junk. People line their birdcages with it.

WILBUR: Well, I suppose from a media standpoint, it's not that big a deal.

AMA: [*To* JOANNE] What means "congeniality"?

JOANNE: It means "friendly," sort of.

ROBERT: [*To* WILBUR] So why are you talking about it? Waste our time?

WILBUR: Look, Robert, it's obviously a token of their esteem.

ROBERT: Junk stuffs. Little thing. Who cares?

AMA: [*To herself*] "Mr. Friendly"?

ROBERT: It's embarrassing. What if clients say to me, "You're a bank president but your relative can only get into the *Valley Green Sheet?*" Makes me lose face. They think my relatives are bums.

AMA: [*To* JOANNE] He is "Mr. Friendly"?

WILBUR: Look, Robert, the business is doing real well. It's not like that's my greatest accomplishment.

AMA: [*To* JOANNE] How can he be "Mr. Friendly"? He always kill and laugh.

JOANNE: Mom!

ROBERT: [*To* WILBUR] Does your business get in the paper?

WILBUR: Computer software happens to be one of the nation's fastest-grow-ing—

ROBERT: So what? Lucky guess. Big deal.

WILBUR: It was an educated choice, not luck!

[ROBERT *gets up, starts to head for the podium.*]

ROBERT: Anyone can make money in America. What's hard is to become . . . a celebrity.

WILBUR: You're not a celebrity!

ROBERT: Yes, I am. That's the new thing. See, I just wanted to say that—[*He nudges* WILBUR *off the podium, takes his place.*]—when I was kidnapped, I didn't know if I would live or die.

POPO: [*Turns and sees* ROBERT *at the podium*] Huh?

JOANNE: Robert, forget it!

POPO: How did he get up there?

WILBUR: [*To* JOANNE] I'm perfectly capable of handling this myself.

POPO: He sneak up there while we are bored!

WILBUR: [*To* POPO] I'm sorry you found my testimony boring.

ROBERT: [*To* WILBUR] It was. [*To the assemblage*] Now hear mine.

JOANNE: We've all heard it before.

HANNAH: [*To* ROBERT] They're tired, dear. Get down.

ROBERT: Why? They listened to Wilbur's stuff. Boring. Junk.

JOANNE: "I didn't know if I would live or die." "I didn't know if I would live or die."

ROBERT: Di-gou, he hasn't heard. Have you, Di-gou?

DI-GOU: Is this when you didn't know if you would live or die?

ROBERT: How did—? Who told him?

POPO: I cannot think of enough ways to shoot him! Rifle! Arrows!

HANNAH: [*To* ROBERT] Sit down!

ROBERT: But there's something new!

HANNAH: I think we better let him speak, or he'll never shut up.

ROBERT: She's right. I won't.

JOANNE: All right. Make it quick, Robert.

ROBERT: All right. As I was saying, I didn't know if I would live or die.

JOANNE: You lived.

ROBERT: But the resulting publicity has made me a celebrity. Every place I go, people come up to me—"Aren't you the one that got kidnapped?" When I tell them how much the ransom was, they can hardly believe it. They ask for my autograph. Now—here's the new thing. I met these clients last week, told them my story. Now these guys are big shots and they say it would make a great movie. Yeah. No kidding. They made movies before. Not just regular movie, that's junk stuffs. We want to go where the big money is—we want to make a miniseries for TV. Like "Shogun." I told them, they should take the story, spice it up a little, you know? Add some sex scenes—we were thinking that I could have some hanky-panky with one of my kidnappers—woman, of course—just for audience sake—like Patty Hearst. I told them I should be played by Marlon Brando. And I have the greatest title: "Not a Chinaman's Chance." Isn't that a great title? "Not a Chinaman's Chance." Beautiful. I can see the beginning already: I'm walking out of my office. I stop to help a man fixing a flat tire.

HANNAH: All right, dear. That's enough.

ROBERT: Meanwhile, my secretary is having sex with my kidnapper.

HANNAH: Kidnap! Kidnap! That's all I ever hear about!

ROBERT: But, Hannah, I didn't know if I would live or die.

HANNAH: I wish you'd never even been kidnapped.

JOANNE: Well, what about Wilbur?

WILBUR: Leave me out of this.

JOANNE: Wilbur, you could be kidnapped.

WILBUR: I know, I know. It just hasn't happened yet, that's all.

HANNAH: Listen, Joanne. Count your blessings. It's not that great a thing. If they live, they never stop talking about it.

ROBERT: But the publicity!—I sign newspapers all the time!

JOANNE: I'm just saying that Robert's not the only one worth kidnapping.

HANNAH: Joanne, no one's saying that.

AMA: Yes. We all desire Wilbur to be kidnapped also.

POPO: And Robert. Again. This time, longer.

JOANNE: I mean, Wilbur has a lot of assets.

ROBERT: Wilbur, maybe next time you can get kidnapped.

WILBUR: Never mind, honey.

JOANNE: You do.

WILBUR: I can defend myself.

ROBERT: But it takes more than assets to be kidnapped. You have to be cosmopolitan.

HANNAH: Hey, wait. What kind of example are we setting for Di-gou?

ROBERT: See? That's why I'm talking about it. To show Di-gou the greatness of America. I'm just an immigrant, Di-gou, an FOB—but in America, I get kidnapped.

HANNAH: I mean, a Christian example.

DI-GOU: Oh, do not worry about me. This is all very fascinating.

JOANNE: [To ROBERT] So, you think you're cosmopolitan, huh?

ROBERT: I am. Before they let me loose, those kidnappers—they respected me.

JOANNE: They probably let you go because they couldn't stand to have you in their car.

POPO: Probably you sing to them.

ROBERT: No. They said, "We've been kidnapping a long time, but—"

JOANNE: Because we can't stand to have you in our house! [Pause]

ROBERT: [To JOANNE] Now what kind of example are you setting for Di-gou?

WILBUR: Joanne, just shut up, okay?

HANNAH: [To DI-GOU] It's not always like this.

JOANNE: [To WILBUR] You never let me talk! You even let him [Refers to ROBERT] talk, but you never let me talk!

AMA: [To JOANNE] He [Refers to WILBUR] cannot deprive you of right to speak. Look. No gun.

ROBERT: Joanne, I have to tell this because Di-gou is here.

DI-GOU: Me?

JOANNE: [To ROBERT] You tell it to waiters!

ROBERT: Joanne, I want him [Refers to DI-GOU] to understand America. The American Dream. From rags to kidnap victim.

JOANNE: [To ROBERT] Well, I don't like you making Di-gou think that Wilbur's a bum.

WILBUR: [To JOANNE] Dear, he doesn't think that.

JOANNE: [To DI-GOU] You see, don't you, Di-gou? This house. Wilbur bought this.

DI-GOU: It is a palace.

JOANNE: It's larger than Robert's.

HANNAH: Joanne, how can you sink to my husband's level?

ROBERT: My house would be larger, but we had to pay the ransom.

POPO: Waste of money.

JOANNE: Look, all of you always put down Wilbur. Well, look at what he's done.

WILBUR: [*To* JOANNE] Just shut up, all right?

JOANNE: [*To* WILBUR] Well, if you're not going to say it.

WILBUR: I don't need you to be my PR firm.

ROBERT: [*To anybody*] He doesn't have a PR firm. We do. Tops firm.

JOANNE: [*To* WILBUR] Let me say my mind!

WILBUR: There's nothing in your mind worth saying.

JOANNE: What?

WILBUR: Face it, honey, you're boring.

AMA: [*To* WILBUR] At least she does not torture!

WILBUR: Please! No more talking about torture, all right?

AMA: All right. I will be quiet. No need to torture me.

POPO: [*To* DI-GOU] This small family disagreement.

JOANNE: So I'm boring, huh?

WILBUR: [*To* JOANNE] Look, let's not do this here.

POPO: [*To* DI-GOU] But power of God will overcome this.

JOANNE: I'm boring—that's what you're saying?

HANNAH: Joanne! Not in front of Di-gou!

JOANNE: [*To* DI-GOU] All right. You're objective. Who do you think is more boring?

DI-GOU: Well, I can hardly—

WILBUR: Please, Joanne.

POPO: [*To* DI-GOU] Do you understand how power of God will overcome this?

JOANNE: He [*Refers to* WILBUR] spends all his time with machines, and he calls me boring!

AMA: Di-gou, see the trials of this world?

WILBUR: [*To* JOANNE] Honey, I'm sorry, all right?

JOANNE: Sure, you're sorry.

AMA: [*To* DI-GOU] Argument, fight, no-good husbands.

WILBUR: "No-good husbands"?

[ROBERT, *in disgust exits into the house.*]

AMA: [*To* DI-GOU] Turn your eyes from this. [POPO *and* AMA *turn* DI-GOU's *eyes from the fight.*]

JOANNE: [*To* WILBUR] She's [*Refers to* AMA] right, you know.

WILBUR: All right, honey, let's discuss this later.

JOANNE: Later! Oh, right.

[WILBUR *runs off into the house;* JOANNE *yells after him.*]

JOANNE: When we're with *your* family, that's when you want to talk about my denting the Ferrari.

HANNAH: Joanne! Don't be so boring!

JOANNE: [*To* HANNAH] With *our* family, it's "later."

AMA: [*To* DI-GOU] Look up to God!

[POPO *and* AMA *force* DI-GOU *to look up.*]

DI-GOU: Please! [DI-GOU *breaks away from the sisters' grip, but they knock him down.*]

POPO: Now—is time to join family in Heaven.

AMA: Time for you to return to God.

HANNAH: [*To* JOANNE] Look—they're converting Di-gou.

POPO: Return. Join us for eternity.

AMA: Pray now.

[POPO *and* AMA *try to guide* DI-GOU *to the neon cross.*]

DI-GOU: Where are we going?

AMA: He will wash you in blood of the lamb.

POPO: Like when you are a child. Now! You bow down!

HANNAH: Ask God for His forgiveness.

JOANNE: You won't regret it, Di-gou.

DI-GOU: Do you mind? [*He breaks away.*]

POPO: Why will you not accept Him?

AMA: There is no good reason.

DI-GOU: I want to take responsibility for my own life.

POPO: You cannot!

AMA: Satan is rule your life now.

DI-GOU: I am serving the people.

AMA: You are not.

POPO: You serve them, they all die, go to Hell. So what?

DI-GOU: How can you abandon China for this Western religion?

AMA: It is not.

POPO: God is God of all people.

DI-GOU: There is no God!

[*Pause*]

AMA: There is too much Communist demon in him. We must cast out demon.

POPO: Now, tie him on table.

DI-GOU: This is ridiculous. Stop this.

[*The women grab* DI-GOU, *tie him on the table.*]

POPO: We have too much love to allow demon to live.

DI-GOU: What?

POPO: [*To* JOANNE *and* HANNAH, *who are hesitating*] Now!

DI-GOU: You can't—!

POPO: Now! Or demon will escape!

AMA: We must kill demon.

POPO: Shoot him!

AMA: Kill for good.

POPO: Make demon into *jok!*[3]

DI-GOU: This is barbaric! You live with the barbarians, you become one yourself!

POPO: Di-gou, if we do not punish your body, demon will never leave.

AMA: Then you will return to China.

POPO: And you will die.

AMA: Go to Hell.

POPO: And it will be too late.

DI-GOU: I never expected Chinese children to tie down their elders. [DI-GOU *is now securely tied to the table.*]

HANNAH: All right. We're ready.

POPO: Now—you give your testimony.

DI-GOU: I'll just lie here and listen, thank you.

AMA: You tell of God's mercies to you.

JOANNE: How He let you out of China.

AMA: Where you are torture.

JOANNE: Whipped.

POPO: After thirty year, He let you out. Praise Him!

DI-GOU: I will never do such a thing!

HANNAH: If you wait too long, He'll lose patience.

POPO: Now—tell of your trip with See-goh-poh.

POPO: The trip which begin your faith.

DI-GOU: I was only eight years old. I don't remember.

POPO: Tell how many were convert on her tour.

HANNAH: Tell them, Di-gou.

DI-GOU: I cannot.

JOANNE: Why? Just tell the truth.

POPO: Tell how you saw the miracle of a great evangelist, great servant of God.

HANNAH: Tell them before they lose their patience.

DI-GOU: I'm sorry. I will not speak.

POPO: Then we are sorry, Di-gou, but we must punish your body. Punish to drive out the demon and make you speak.

HANNAH: Don't make them do this, Di-gou.

AMA: If you will not speak See-goh-poh's stories in language you know, we will punish you until you speak in tongue of fire. [AMA *hits* DI-GOU *with an electrical cord, using it like a whip.*]

JOANNE: Please, Di-gou!

HANNAH: Tell them!

AMA: Our Lord was beat, nails drive through His body, for our sin. Your body must suffer until you speak the truth. [AMA *hits him.*]

HANNAH: Tell them, See-goh-poh was a great evangelist.

3. A Chinese rice porridge. [Author's note]

AMA: You were on her evangelism tour—we were not—you must remember her converts, her miracle. [*Hit*]

JOANNE: Just tell them and they'll let you go!

AMA: Think of See-goh-poh! She is sit! [*Hit*] Sit beside God. He is praising her! Praise her for her work in China.

[CHESTER *enters the tennis court; he looks into the sunroom and sees* AMA *hit* DI-GOU.]

AMA: She is watching you!

[*Hit.* CHESTER *tries to get into the sunroom, but the glass door is locked. He bangs on it, but everyone inside stands shocked at* AMA's *ritual, and no one notices him. He exits off the tennis court, running.*]

AMA: Praying for you! Want you to tell her story! [*Hit*]

AMA: We will keep you in float. Float for one second between life and death. Float until you lose will to hold to either—hold to anything at all.

[AMA *quickly slips the cord around* DI-GOU's *neck, begins pulling on it.* JOANNE *and* HANNAH *run to get* AMA *off of* DI-GOU. CHESTER *enters from the house, with* JENNY *close behind him. He pulls* AMA *off of* DI-GOU.]

CHESTER: Ama! Stop it!

[DI-GOU *suddenly breaks out of his bonds and rises up on the table. He grabs* CHESTER. *The barbecue bursts into flames.* DI-GOU, *holding on to* CHESTER, *begins speaking in tongues.*]

AMA: [*Looking up from the ground*] He is speaking in tongues! He has returned!

[*Everyone falls to their knees.*]

[*As* DI-GOU's *tongues continue,* CHESTER *is suddenly filled with words, and begins interpreting* DI-GOU's *babbling.*]

CHESTER: Di-gou at eight goes with See-goh-poh on her first evangelism tour. Di-gou and See-goh-poh traveling through the summer heat to a small village in Fukien. Sleeping in the straw next to See-goh-poh. Hearing a sound. A human sound. A cry in my sleep. Looking up and seeing a fire. A fire and See-goh-poh. See-goh-poh is naked. Naked and screaming. Screaming with legs spread so far apart. So far that a mouth opens up. A mouth between her legs. A mouth that is throwing up blood, spitting out blood. More and more blood. See-goh-poh's hands making a baby out of the blood. See-goh-poh hits the blood baby. Hits the baby and the baby cries. Watching the baby at See-goh-poh's breast. Hearing the sucking.

[AMA *and* POPO *spring up.*]

POPO: Such a thing never happened!

AMA: See-goh-poh never did this!

POPO: This is not tongues. This is not God. This is demon!

CHESTER: Sucking. Praying. Sucking. Squeezing. Crying.

AMA: He is possess by demon!

CHESTER: Biting. Blood. Milk.

POPO: Both have the demon!

CHESTER: Blood and milk. Blood and milk running down.

AMA: [*To the other women*] You pray.

CHESTER: Running down, further and further down.

POPO: We must cast out the demon!

[DI-GOU's *tongues slowly become English, first overlapping, then overtaking* CHESTER's *translation.* CHESTER *becomes silent and exhausted, drops to the ground.*]

CHESTER *and* DI-GOU: Down. Down and into the fire. The fire down there. The fire down there.

[DI-GOU *breaks the last of his bonds, gets off the table.*]

DI-GOU: [*To the sisters*] Your stories are dead now that you know the truth.

AMA: We have faith. We know our true family stories.

DI-GOU: You do not know your past.

AMA: Are you willing to match your stories against ours?

[DI-GOU *indicates his willingness to face* AMA, *and the two begin a ritualistic battle.* POPO *supports* AMA *by speaking in tongues.* AMA *and* DI-GOU *square off in seated positions, facing one another.*]

AMA: We will begin. How many rooms in our house in Amoy?

DI-GOU: Eighteen. How many bedrooms?

AMA: Ten. What year was it built?

DI-GOU: 1893. What year was the nineteenth room added?

AMA: 1923.

DI-GOU: On whose instructions?

AMA: See-goh-poh.

DI-GOU: What year did See-goh-poh die?

AMA: 1945. What disease?

DI-GOU: Malaria. How many teeth was she missing?

AMA: Three.

DI-GOU: What villages were on See-goh-poh's evangelism tour? [*Silence*] Do you know?

AMA: She preached to all villages in Fukien.

DI-GOU: Name one. [*Silence*] Do you know? Your stories don't know. It never happened.

AMA: It did! What year was she baptized? [*Silence*] What year was she baptized?

DI-GOU: She was never baptized.

AMA: You see? You don't remember.

DI-GOU: Never baptized.

AMA: It was 1921. Your stories do not remember.

DI-GOU: Who was converted on her evangelism tour?

AMA: Perhaps five hundred or more.

DI-GOU: Who? Name one. [*Silence*]

AMA: It is not important.

DI-GOU: You see? It never happened.

AMA: It did.

DI-GOU: You do not remember. You do not know the past. See-goh-poh never
preached.

AMA: How can you say this?

DI-GOU: She traveled.

AMA: To preach.

DI-GOU: To travel.

AMA: She visited many—

DI-GOU: I was there! She was thrown out—thrown out on her evangelism
tour when she tried to preach. [*Silence*]

AMA: It does not matter.

DI-GOU: You forced her to invent the stories.

AMA: We demand nothing!

DI-GOU: You expected! Expected her to convert all Amoy!

AMA: She did!

DI-GOU: Expected many miracles.

AMA: She did! She was a great—

DI-GOU: Expected her not to have a baby.

AMA: She had no husband. She had no baby. This is demon talk. Demon
talk and lie.

DI-GOU: She turned away from God.

AMA: We will never believe this!

DI-GOU: On her tours she could both please you and see China.

[POPO's *tongues become weaker; she starts to falter.*]

AMA: See-goh-poh was a great—

DI-GOU: Only on her tours could she see both China and her baby.

AMA: She was a great . . . a great evangelist . . . many . . .

DI-GOU: Where is she buried?

AMA: . . . many miracle . . .

DI-GOU: She is not buried within the walls of the church in Amoy.

AMA: . . . many miracle a great evangelist . . .

[POPO *collapses.*]

DI-GOU: In her last moment, See-goh-poh wanted to be buried in Chinese
soil, not Christian soil. You don't know. You were in the Philippines.

[*Pause*] I come to bring you back to China. Come, sisters. To the soil you've forsaken with ways born of memories, of stories that never happened. Come, sisters. The stories written on your face are the ones you must believe.

[AMA *rises from her chair.*]

AMA: We will never believe this! [*She collapses back into her chair, closes her eyes.*]

[*Silence*]

DI-GOU: Sisters? [*Silence*] Sisters!

[JENNY, CHESTER, JOANNE, HANNAH, *and* DI-GOU *stare at the two inert forms.*]

CHESTER: Jenny! Jenny!

[JENNY *goes to* CHESTER'*s side.*]

JOANNE: Hannah? Hannah—come here.

[HANNAH *does not move.*]

HANNAH: I see.
JOANNE: No! Come here!
HANNAH: I know, Joanne. I see.
DI-GOU: Once again. Once again my pleas are useless. But now—this is the last time. I have given all I own.

[POPO *and* AMA *have died.* DI-GOU *picks up his suitcase and the Chinese toys, heads for the door.*]

JOANNE: [*To* DI-GOU] Are you leaving?
DI-GOU: Now that my sisters have gone, I learn. No one leaves America. And I desire only to drive an American car—very fast—down an American freeway. [DI-GOU *exits.*]
JOANNE: [*Yelling after him*] This is our home, not yours! Why didn't you stay in China! This is not your family!

[JENNY *starts to break away from* CHESTER, *but he hangs on to her.* JOANNE *turns, sees the figures of* AMA *and* POPO.]

JOANNE: Wilbur! Wilbur, come here!
JENNY: [*To* CHESTER] Let go of me! Get away! [*She breaks away from* CHESTER.] I don't understand this, but whatever it is, it's ugly and it's awful and it causes people to die. It causes people to die and I don't want to have anything to do with it.

[JENNY *runs out onto the tennis court and away. On her way, she passes* ROBERT, *who has entered onto the court.* ROBERT *walks into the sunroom. Silence.*]

ROBERT: What's wrong with her? She acts like someone just died. [*Silence. He pulls up a chair next to* CHESTER.] Let's chit-chat, okay?

CHESTER: Sure, Dad.

ROBERT: So, how's Dorrie? [*Silence*] How much they paying you in Boston? [*Silence*] Got any new newspaper clippings?

[*Silence*]

[CHESTER *gets up, picks up his suitcase, walks onto the tennis court, and shuts the glass doors.*]

[AMA *and* POPO *lie in the center of the room.* JOANNE *and* HANNAH *stare at them.* ROBERT *sits, staring off into space.*]

[CHESTER *turns around, looks through the glass door onto the scene.*]

[*The* LIGHTS BEGIN TO DIM *until there is a single spotlight on* CHESTER's *face, standing where* DI-GOU *stood at the beginning of the play.*]

[*The shape of* CHESTER's *face begins to change.*]

*Curtain*

# STUDY QUESTIONS

## ACT I

1. How do the stage directions, suggesting that as the curtain rises we hear first Chinese music or chanting and then funk or rock 'n' roll, literally "set the stage" for the play that is to follow? How is the music related to Wilbur's appearance and dress when we first see him?

2. What is revealed by Jenny's and Chester's not being able to remember Di-gou's name? How would you speak these lines if you were Jenny or Chester? Would you subtly make it clear that you really know the name but are pretending not to, or would you play it straight? What would each suggest to the audience?

3. Why does Ama want Wilbur to eat outside? Why does she assume that Wilbur has done Chickie in?

4. What is Ama's version of life in Communist China?

5. What does Di-gou's name mean?

6. How would you read Wilbur's lines when he tells Ama and Popo (who have just suggested he eat outside or in the kitchen): "C'mon. I should bring you down to the club someday. The guys never believe it when I tell them how much I love you two"?

7. What kind of man does Ama want Jenny to marry? Is she happy with her daughter Joanne's marriage? What career does Ama want her to follow? What does Jenny want to do?

8. Why does Ama think that Chester, who is going to play the violin in the Boston Symphony Orchestra, has a dangerous job?

9. How does Popo describe Di-gou's evangelical preaching?

10. Why does Popo think her son-in-law Robert did not try very hard to find Di-gou at the airport? What does she accuse his father of?

11. When Di-gou is found and Ama gets a chance to speak with him, what does she want to find out about him?

12. How does Robert try to convince Di-gou that he should defect to America and that this is the land of plenty?

13. Why has Di-gou come to America?

14. What does Di-gou mean when he tells Chester, near the end of Act I, that Chester must "become one with your family before you can hope to live away from it"? What does Chester tell Di-gou will happen to him if he stays here too long with his sisters?

15. How does the music at the end of the act relate to that at the beginning?

16. How does Act I end? What do you expect will happen in Act II?

## ACT II

1. What is Jenny's "testimony"? How does Popo "translate" it for Di-gou?

2. What is "Not a Chinaman's Chance"?

3. Why is Di-gou tied to the table? Who ties him? What happens when he breaks his bonds? Who interprets what he says? What story does Di-gou tell of his evangelical trip with See-goh-poh? What is the response of Ama and Popo to the story?

4. What is the nature of the ritualistic battle between Di-gou and Ama? What does Di-gou say See-goh-poh did on her tour? Why did she tell Ama and Popo it was an evangelical tour?

5. Why has Di-gou come to his sisters? What happens to Ama and Popo when he tells them that See-goh-poh lost her religion and that they must not believe in a Western religion like Christianity? What does he decide to do?

6. What does the final stage direction—"[*The shape of Chester's face begins to change*]"— mean in terms of the rest of the play?

## GENERAL QUESTIONS

1. What is the religious aspect of this play? Is it anti-Christian? anti-religious?

2. How does this play treat Communism? America?

3. Describe each of these CHARACTERS—Di-gou, Ama, Robert, Wilbur. Use specific lines and details to support your descriptions. Who would you say is (are) the central or most sympathetic character(s) in the play?

4. Explain the title.

5. If you were directing this play, how would you deal with the fantastic scene at the climax (Di-gou speaking in tongues of fire)? Would you prepare in the early scenes for what seems to be a change in tone (making Ama almost as sinister as she is funny, for example), or would you play it for the shock effect? Defend your choice.

6. Describe the generation gap in the play. Is the play evenhanded or does it take sides? If it takes sides, which side does it take?

<br>

# AFTERWORD

# CHARACTERIZATION

Most literature is about people, but works that center on families focus on the similarities and differences between individuals with special intensity. The particular traits (or *characteristics*) of a person suggest that person's CHARACTER—what it is that makes him or her distinctive. Individuals portrayed in literature are often referred to as *characters*. The way in which the author describes them and the process of defining them is usually called CHARACTERIZATION. Among the means of characterization, in addition to direct analysis, is describing the way characters look (their physical appearance and their clothing, bearing, makeup, and so on); the way they speak; the way they think, or what they think; what they do; and what other people say about them.

Cynthia Kadohata tells us that Charlie-O is always cheerful and has a "childlike joie de vivre." Tony Ardizzone's mother, we are told, by a Tony who seems to be the author, is friendly, with a compulsion to please; she's big-hearted and makes others laugh. Irving Layton's mother, he tells us, was fierce, mean, unaccommodating, comfortless, vituperative, ignorant, glad, dignified, and with a stubborn, limited mind.

Sometimes such analysis or description is filtered through the mind of another character, most often that of the NARRATOR, as Bellow describes Pop through Woody: "In regard to Pop, you thought of neither sincerity nor insincerity. . . . he wanted what he wanted when he wanted it. Pop

<br>

231

was physical; Pop was digestive, circulatory, sexual. . . . Pop was elemental" (paragraph 53).

But characterization is not always that direct. In life, we often conclude something about a person's character from the way he or she looks. In literature, the author is responsible for the character's appearance, or at least for how that appearance is conveyed to us. Probably more often than in life, the physical characteristics are fairly good indications of the inner person. That Charlie-O is only five-foot-three seems consistent with, maybe even a contributing factor to, his role as victim. Keine Lazarovitch's "small black hole" of a mouth, and her thickly woven black eyebrows, help reveal her negative but vital nature. To a profound and ironical writer like Saul Bellow, character written in the face can, paradoxically, mislead the "sensitive." Woody Selbst and his father have big faces, bent noses; they look dishonest. And they are dishonest, especially Pop. But "sensitive" people, anxious not to judge by appearances, give Pop the benefit of the doubt, and are therefore more easily manipulated by the sly old man: "Precisely because of the way Pop looked, a sensitive person might feel remorse for condemning unfairly or judging unkindly. Just because of a face? Some must have bent over backward. Then he had them" (par. 73).

It seems natural to assume that descriptions of the physical qualities or appearance of a character present the reader with a clear mental image of that character, but that's not often the case. Try to remember the appearance of even the main character in a poem, story, nonfictional prose piece, or the play in this chapter. Write it down. If you are able to draw, you might want to make a portrait of the character. Compare your description or drawing with those done by your classmates. The range of differences may astound you. You may have a very clear picture of Rhoda Schwartz's father, but someone else in your class may have quite a different image. You might want to ask what clues in the work he or she has used to make the description or drawing. Go back to the poem. You may be surprised to find that just about the only physical details are his slightness and shortness and, when young, his black curly hair.

Nor is this paucity of physical detail limited to poems. The mother is the central character in Tony Ardizzone's story, yet what do we know about her appearance? As a young girl she is skinny, as a bride slim, beautiful, and brown-haired, as an older woman brown-eyed and round like a fruit. They are the only details we are given.

Clothes or ornament often supplement or modify physical description.

In Ardizzone's story, for example, the narrator's father as a young man is muscled, tanned, with a thin waist and dark hair; when his future wife first sees him, he is wearing a sleeveless undershirt and, around his neck, "golden things glistening on a thin chain" (par. 7). Keine Lazarovitch's gold earrings make a "proud carnal assertion." The stage directions in *Family Devotions* tell us that Wilbur "is a Japanese American man, nisei, in his late thirties. His hair is permed. He wears tennis clothes"; we don't need much more.

Especially after we hear his "What's up?" and "How you doin', Mom, Auntie?" and his " *'Gao sai'* to you, too." For a character's language tells us much about him or her. Sometimes it is the lie, or the contrast between the verbal expression and what we know to be the fictional "reality," that tells us about a character. We know, for example, that Woody's father, in "A Silver Dish," is sly and devious and that he is trying to talk the charitable, religious, and naive Mrs. Skoglund into loaning him money.

> "I haven't got it [money]. If I had it, wouldn't I give it? There's bread lines and soup lines all over town. Is it just me? What I have I divvy with. I give the kids. A bad father? You think my son would bring me if I was a bad father into your house? He loves his dad, he trusts his dad, he knows his dad is a good dad. Every time I start a little business going I get wiped out. This one is a good little business, if I could hold on to that little business. Three people work for me, I meet a payroll, and three people will be on the street, too, if I close down. Missus, I can sign a note and pay you in two months. I'm a common man, but I'm a hard worker and a fellow you can trust."
>
> Woody was startled when Pop used the word "trust." It was as if from all four corners a Sousa band blew a blast to warn the entire world: "Crook! This is a crook!" (Pars. 83–84)

In characterization, action often speaks louder than words. In Rhoda Schwartz's "Old Photographs," the father's rowing across the Dnieper River in a tiny boat against all advice gives some idea of his courage, his love of life and adventure, his independence. When he comes to America he rows across the St. Lawrence in a rowboat. His habitual actions—reading hidden books in the hayloft, arguing with what he reads—also tell you something about him. The action does not have to be habitual; it can be an instance that seems signally indicative, as in Li-Young Lee's "The Gift," in which the father's soft, deep voice and tender hands as he removes a splinter from the boy's palm and presents it to him engrave themselves on the boy's memory and on his character.

Sometimes a character will act "out of character," or so it seems, only to reveal more of his or her inner self. So the father in "My Mother's Stories," who always seems to be reading the newspaper or joking, tells his son, when his wife is desperately ill, how much he loves her, what the thirty-four years of their married life have meant to him.

These are but a few of the ways and means by which an author characterizes people. He or she counts on us and on our experience to fill in some of the gaps, to bring to life in our minds a simulacrum of the image in his or hers, not the same image but one with approximately the same values and significance. To be aware of the means of characterization may make us more attentive to and appreciative of the traits, the psychological and moral suggestiveness of the people in the stories, poems, and plays we read. Such awareness may also sharpen our vision of the people we meet, even, perhaps, our understanding of ourselves.

# WRITING
# ABOUT THE READING

## PERSONAL ESSAYS AND NARRATIVES

1. What family doesn't have a thousand stories? Are you old enough to enjoy stories about yourself when you were very, very small? Like when your father and uncles used to gather in the big bathroom and smoke because your grandmother wouldn't let anyone smoke in the house, and you were two and used to knock on the door and they'd say, "Who's there?" and you'd say, "Me," and they'd say, "Who's 'me'?" and you'd say, "Me . . . me, the baby." Or stories about your mother, when she was caught coming home from violin lessons, a small girl carrying a large violin case, by the crowds demonstrating against segregation, and she was pushed and shoved here and there and almost run over by a mounted policeman. Or your uncle's stories about the Vietnam War, or your memories of a death in the family.

Write, for other family members, your favorite family stories. Or, for someone outside the family, write up the stories that best define—or explain or defend—your family.

2. Write an essay on family reunions, citing a few instances of the kinds of things that can happen based on your family's reunions over the past ten years or so. Or you could just remember one, perhaps the first one, and how excited you were and what happened. (Or you could make one up.)

3. Write a narrative depicting or honoring a parent or sibling in an incident or a series of incidents. You might want to embellish it a bit with a few made-up incidents or details or responses of your own. If you want to be true to your understanding of the character, make sure you invent episodes or details that are consistent with what you believe to be true of that person. Be aware, however, that sometimes the most revealing incidents or details are those that seem at first "out of character."

## IMITATIONS AND PARODIES

1. Using Merle Woo's "Letter to Ma" as a guide, write a letter to your own mother explaining your differences of opinion about some major issue or attitude. Use family anecdotes or stories to illustrate the differences between your attitudes and those of older generations.

2. You may want to parody Saul Bellow's—or, rather, Woody Selbst's—generosity toward Woody's father's selfish, amoral behavior by writing something like "My Rascally Father, Darth Vader."

3. Try to change the point of view in one of the poems and stories in the chapter and write a new version or a piece of a new version. How does Charlie-O's wife see him? What does she think of their marriage? What is the grown child in Naomi Madgett's "Offspring" thinking of her and of home?

4. Write the poem you imagine the mother of the SPEAKER in Jimmy Santiago Baca's "Ancestor" would write about her husband.

## ANALYTICAL PROSE

1. Choose one work, or a group of short works, from the chapter and analyze the ways in which the subjects are characterized, or compare how one story or poem characterizes—say, predominantly by actions—whereas another uses description or analysis of thoughts. It may be useful in this regard to look very closely at the selection of words and the kinds of metaphors or figures of speech that are used. Or you may be interested in analyzing all the ways in which mothers or fathers are characterized by the variety of attitudes on the part of the son or daughter.

2. Do the tributes or sketches or stories from different ethnic or cultural groups have something in common? Do they differ? If so, how?

3. Analyze the nature of family gatherings or reunions. Based on your own experience or observation, analyze the typical American (or Chinese- or Italian- or Jewish- or Afro- or Native American) family. Concern yourself with such questions as, What is the typical family size? How "close" is the family? How many aunts, uncles, cousins habitually visit? To what extent are friends and neighbors of the same background? Who "rules" the family? Are the children obedient? independent? What language is spoken in the house?

## COMPARISON-CONTRAST PAPERS

1. Compare the ways in which fathers are eulogized by these authors—the qualities their children choose to remember with love; those qualities that one would wish had been otherwise. Or compare and contrast the ways in which mothers are treated as opposed to fathers.

2. Compare the "typical" family or family dynamics of two ethnic groups that you know.

## ARGUMENTATIVE PAPER

Reread "Letter to Ma." Write a letter to one of your parents in which you try to explain, politely and lovingly, your position on some emotional issue on which you disagree. Then write a second letter in which you try to persuade the same person to change his or her position. Finally, write a third letter, on the same issue, to someone your own age, arguing the *opposite* position from the one you took in the previous letter.

## RESEARCH PAPERS

1. We hear a good deal about the breakup of the American family, the frequency of divorce, and so on. Just what are the statistics? How many "nuclear" families are there in the 1980s? Are divorce statistics skewed (some people having five or six marriages/divorces)? How do the figures break down by urban/suburban/small town/ rural setting? by ethnic group? by a combination of ethnic and urban/rural factors?

2. Interview someone of the oldest living generation in your family about the ethnic makeup of the family, in as many branches as possible.

3. Interview a classmate or friend who is from an ethnic background different from your own, and gather as much detail about the differences in your families and upbringing as possible.

# 3

# HERITAGE

Where there's a will, someone once said, there's a relative, but material possessions are not the only things we inherit. We inherit physical traits, mannerisms, attitudes, tastes, and customs. Many things we inherit from our parents, but sometimes heredity skips a generation, so that we walk more like Grandma than our mother. Once in a while we are told that we do something—smile, frown, gesture—like someone we never knew, grandmother's grandfather, perhaps. Heritage, then, goes back more than a generation or two, even beyond memory.

Some of the things that make us what we are are so pervasive in our family and our community that they cannot be attributed to some *one;* they are cultural heritages. Our "self" is something more than the space between our head and toes and the time span between our birth and death. Our identity reaches back through generations, even centuries; who we are is conditioned by our familial and cultural heritage.

Cultural heritage comes to us through the older generations of our families and our community in stories, myths, art, decoration, dress, food, all sorts of daily practices, conscious or unconscious values, traditional wisdom or "lore." Much of this we take for granted, unaware that it is an intimate part of us, part of what makes us *us.* Sometimes our culture and its lore come into conflict with that of others, with "new-fangled" ideas, and some of it, like some of our culture's language, has to be abandoned, or is rebelled against as we seek to join our peers from other cultures. We cannot comfortably cast it all aside, however; it all remains part of our being, some just below the surface of our "new" selves, much in the form of nostalgia and longing.

Heritage in the New World, the Americas, means something different from what it does in older and more stable societies. Our cultural heritage is both American and Other. Even those who are full-blooded Native Americans have a heritage that is not "American" in anything but the geographical sense: the dominant society on the American continents is not that of those who were here before 1492, whatever it may have inherited from them. Nor are those whose families came from England in the seventeenth century to settle the East Coast of what is now the United States the "real Americans," the only possessors of the "true" American heritage. Their culture, too, is a mixture of British (often Scots or Scots-Irish rather than English, by the way) and the polyglot, diverse heritage of modern America. The most recent Americans—Haitians, Vietnamese, Cubans, Mexicans, Hungarians, Iranians, and so on—are in one sense more American by their very newness: their blend of old culture and new is typical of the New World. We are a significantly mixed-up people, both as individuals and as a society. American culture is a quilt, or perhaps a tightly woven, intricate fabric.

But most of us have an affinity, if not an identity, with some Other culture, a "foreign" culture in time or space. When that heritage is fairly recent and identifiable, it sometimes has much of the same attractive power as home and family. But our American heritage, the pull toward more recent, polygenetic, American ways, is powerful, too. These contrary pulls and pushes can cause us pain or a sense of loss as well as pride and joy. We love our grandparents and often admire aspects of their old ways; yet we cannot be like them. Sometimes we feel we have gone on to better things and a better way of life, and resent their disapproval and their attempt to pull us back to a way of life they chose to abandon in coming here.

The poems, stories, and nonfiction prose pieces in this chapter focus on heritage, that which has been passed on to us from the recent and the remote past and is part of us in the present, in our identity and daily lives. Nostalgia, admiration, and pride; regret, embarrassment, and pain are all here, part of our heritage.

# Countee Cullen

A member of the Harlem Renaissance, winner of the Witter Bynner Poetry Prize and a Guggenheim Fellowship, Countee Cullen (born Countee Porter in 1903) did much to establish the canon of black literature before his untimely death in 1946.

After 300 years in this country, the speaker is still conscious of his African heritage and is torn between the two worlds.

## HERITAGE

What is Africa to me:
Copper sun or scarlet sea,
Jungle star or jungle track,
Strong bronzed men, or regal black
Women from whose loins I sprang                5
When the birds of Eden sang?
*One three centuries removed*
*From the scenes his fathers loved,*
*Spicy grove, cinnamon tree,*
*What is Africa to me?*                         10

So I lie, who all day long
Want no sound except the song
Sung by wild barbaric birds
Goading massive jungle herds,
Juggernauts of flesh that pass                 15
Trampling tall defiant grass
Where young forest lovers lie,
Plighting troth beneath the sky.
So I lie, who always hear,
Though I cram against my ear                    20
Both my thumbs, and keep them there,
Great drums throbbing through the air.
So I lie, whose fount of pride,
Dear distress, and joy allied,

In my somber flesh and skin,                                      25
With the dark blood dammed within
Like great pulsing tides of wine
That, I fear, must burst the fine
Channels of the chafing net
Where they surge and foam and fret.                               30

Africa? A book one thumbs
Listlessly, till slumber comes.
Unremembered are her bats
Circling through the night, her cats
Crouching in the river reeds,                                     35
Stalking gentle flesh that feeds
By the river brink; no more
Does the bugle-throated roar
Cry that monarch claws have leapt
From the scabbards where they slept.                              40
Silver snakes that once a year
Doff the lovely coats you wear,
Seek no covert in your fear
Lest a mortal eye should see;
What's your nakedness to me?                                      45
Here no leprous flowers rear
Fierce corollas in the air;
Here no bodies sleek and wet,
Dripping mingled rain and sweat,
Tread the savage measures of                                      50
Jungle boys and girls in love.
What is last year's snow to me,[1]
Last year's anything? The tree
Budding yearly must forget
How its past arose or set—                                        55
Bough and blossom, flower, fruit,
Even what shy bird with mute
Wonder at her travail there,
Meekly labored in its hair.
*One three centuries removed*                                     60
*From the scenes his fathers loved,*
*Spicy grove, cinnamon tree,*
*What is Africa to me?*

So I lie, who find no peace
Night or day, no slight release                                   65

---

1. An echo of the lament "Where are the snows of yesteryear?" from the fifteenth-century French poet François Villon's *Testament*.

From the unremittent beat
Made by cruel padded feet
Walking through my body's street.
Up and down they go, and back,
Treading out a jungle track.                                    70
So I lie, who never quite
Safely sleep from rain at night—
I can never rest at all
When the rain begins to fall;
Like a soul gone mad with pain                                 75
I must match its weird refrain;
Ever must I twist and squirm,
Writhing like a baited worm,
While its primal measures drip
Through my body, crying, "Strip!                                80
Doff this new exuberance.
Come and dance the Lover's Dance!"
In an old remembered way
Rain works on me night and day.

Quaint, outlandish heathen gods                                85
Black men fashion out of rods,
Clay, and brittle bits of stone,
In a likeness like their own,
My conversion came high-priced;
I belong to Jesus Christ,                                      90
Preacher of humility;
Heathen gods are naught to me.

Father, Son, and Holy Ghost,
So I make an idle boast;
Jesus of the twice-turned cheek                                95
Lamb of God, although I speak
With my mouth thus, in my heart
Do I play a double part.
Ever at Thy glowing altar
Must my heart grow sick and falter,                           100
Wishing He I served were black,
Thinking then it would not lack
Precedent of pain to guide it,
Let who would or might deride it;
Surely then this flesh would know                             105
Yours had borne a kindred woe.
Lord, I fashion dark gods, too,
Daring even to give You
Dark despairing features where,

Crowned with dark rebellious hair, 110
Patience wavers just so much as
Mortal grief compels, while touches
Quick and hot, of anger, rise
To smitten cheek and weary eyes.
Lord, forgive me if my need 115
Sometimes shapes a human creed.
*All day long and all night through,*
*One thing only must I do:*
*Quench my pride and cool my blood,*
*Lest I perish in the flood.* 120
*Lest a hidden ember set*
*Timber that I thought was wet*
*Burning like the dryest flax,*
*Melting like the merest wax,*
*Lest the grave restore its dead.* 125
*Not yet has my heart or head*
*In the least way realized*
*They and I are civilized.*

# STUDY QUESTIONS

1. The SPEAKER* says (lines 24–26) that he is both pleased and distressed by his dark skin and blood. What pleasure does he derive from his African heritage? what distress? (Note that the distress seems internal; there is very little here about the mistreatment of blacks in America.)

2. How would you describe the speaker's religious struggle (ll. 85–116)? What is his religious position?

3. The last dozen lines seem to suggest that he is struggling to repress his racial pride and anger and remain "civilized." How do you read these lines? What is their tone? This poem was written more than sixty years ago; is it "out of date" or "old-fashioned"? If so, how? How might the poem be written now?

4. How do the meter, rhythm, and language relate to what the poem says?

*Words in small capitals are defined in the glossary.

# Lorna Dee Cervantes

B orn in San Francisco in 1954, Lorna Dee Cervantes is of Mexican descent. She published her first book of poems, *Emplumada*, in 1981. She was educated at San Jose City College and San Jose State University and is the founder of Mango Publications, a small press that publishes books and a literary magazine.

The uprooted, Americanized speaker in "Heritage" searches for her roots in Mexico, but no longer fits or is accepted by the land of her ancestors, those very ancestors who "betrayed" her by moving to America.

## HERITAGE

Heritage
I look for you all day in the streets of Oaxaca.
The children run to me, laughing,
spinning me blind and silly.
They call to me in words of another language.                5
My brown body searches the streets
for the dye that will color my thoughts.

But Mexico gags
"ESPUTA"[1]
on this bland pochaseed.[2]                                 10

I didn't ask to be brought up tonta![3]
My name hangs about me like a loose tooth.
Old women know my secret,
"Es la culpa de los antepasados"[4]
Blame it on the old ones.                                   15
They give me a name
that fights me.

1. Spit; *Es puta* also means "She is a prostitute."
2. Americanized Mexican.
3. As a fool.
4. It's the fault of the ancestors.

## STUDY QUESTION

How does the language of this poem reflect the cultural situation of the SPEAKER?

# Linda Hogan

Linda Hogan, a Chickasaw, was born in Denver in 1947, grew up in Oklahoma, and earned an M.A. in English and Creative Writing from the University of Colorado. Now an associate professor of American Studies and American Indian Studies at the University of Minnesota, she has published several books of poems, including *Calling Myself Home; Daughters, I Love You; Eclipse; That House;* and *Seeing Through the Sun* (which won the 1986 American Book Award from the Before Columbus Foundation). Her first novel, *Mean Spirit*, appeared in 1989.

Hogan's heritage, physical and cultural, is American and therefore mixed, has roots in the soil and is rootless.

# HERITAGE

From my mother, the antique mirror
where I watch my face take on her lines.
She left me the smell of baking bread
to warm fine hairs in my nostrils,
she left the large white breasts that weigh down          5
my body.

From my father I take his brown eyes,
the plague of locusts that leveled our crops,
they flew in formation like buzzards.

From my uncle the whittled wood                           10
that rattles like bones
and is white
and smells like all our old houses
that are no longer there. He was the man
who sang old chants to me, the words                      15
my father was told not to remember.

From my grandfather who never spoke
I learned to fear silence.
I learned to kill a snake
when you're begging for rain.                                    20

And grandmother, blue-eyed woman
whose skin was brown,
she used snuff.
When her coffee can full of black saliva
spilled on me                                                    25
it was like the brown cloud of grasshoppers
that leveled her fields.
It was the brown stain
that covered my white shirt,
my whiteness a shame.                                            30
That sweet black liquid like the food
she chewed up and spit into my father's mouth
when he was an infant.
It was the brown earth of Oklahoma
stained with oil.                                                35
She said tobacco would purge your body of poisons.
It has more medicine than stones and knives
against your enemies.

That tobacco is the dark night that covers me.

She said it is wise to eat the flesh of deer                     40
so you will be swift and travel over many miles.
She told me how our tribe has always followed a stick
that pointed west
that pointed east.
From my family I have learned the secrets                        45
of never having a home.

# STUDY QUESTIONS

1. What are the good things the SPEAKER inherits? the undesirable things? What part of the heritage seems doubtful or ambiguous? Is the speaker proud of his or her heritage? ashamed? happy or unhappy? What, then, is the tone of the poem?

2. The grandmother uses snuff, we are told in line 23; she spits into a coffee can, and apparently there once was an accident involving the can and the speaker. How does the poem use this accident to describe how her grandmother passed on to the speaker the cultural heritage? What other brown and black things is the black saliva compared to? How do they relate to the heritage? Why is the speaker's whiteness "a shame" (l. 30)? Line 39 stands alone; what does it mean?

3. What is the nature and location of the homeland from which the speaker comes?

4. What practices or beliefs identify the culture from which the speaker comes?

# Agha Shahid Ali

Originally from Kashmir (and a graduate of the University of Kashmir), Agha moved to New Delhi and then to the United States to receive his advanced degrees (M.A., University of Delhi, 1970; M.F.A., University of Arizona, 1985; Ph.D., Penn State, 1984). He has written poetry exclusively in English since the age of ten, and he now lives in Tucson, Arizona. A scholar as well as a poet, Agha is the author of *T. S. Eliot as Editor*; his first volume of poetry, *The Half-Inch Himalayas*, was published in 1987.

This "heritage" from an unknown ancestor is not entirely desirable, but the speaker accepts it rather defiantly and almost, it seems, triumphantly.

## SNOWMEN

My ancestor, a man
of Himalayan snow,
came to Kashmir from Samarkand,
carrying a bag
of whale bones: 5
heirlooms from sea funerals.
His skeleton
carved from glaciers, his breath
arctic,
he froze women in his embrace. 10
His wife thawed into stony water,
her old age a clear
evaporation.

This heirloom,
his skeleton under my skin, passed 15
from son to grandson,
generations of snowmen on my back.
They tap every year on my window,
their voices hushed to ice.

No, they won't let me out of winter,                    20
and I've promised myself,
even if I'm the last snowman,
that I'll ride into spring
on their melting shoulders.

## STUDY QUESTION

What has the SPEAKER's ancestor bequeathed to him? What is that heirloom said to be
made out of? How does the speaker feel about his inheritance? What do you understand the speaker's promise to himself to be? What is its tone?

# Wendy Rose

Editor (*American Indian Quarterly*), anthropologist (*Aboriginal Tattooing in California*), professor (Native American studies, University of California, Berkeley),
artist, and poet (*Lost Copper*—nominated for the American Book Award in 1981—and
*Halfbreed Chronicles*), Hopi / Miwok Wendy Rose is a major force in Native American
culture.

Ancestral heritage can survive migration, new religious teachings, and new ways,
and the new generation—here a woman—is added to, or etched onto the ancestral
record.

# TO SOME FEW HOPI ANCESTORS

No longer the drifting
and falling of wind
your songs have changed;
they have become
thin willow whispers                                     5
that take us by the ankle
and tangle us up
with red mesa stone,
that keep us turned
to the round sky,                                        10

that follow us down
to Winslow, to Sherman,
to Oakland, to all the spokes
that have left earth's middle.
You have engraved yourself                                   15
with holy signs, encased yourself
in pumice, hammered on my bones
till you could no longer hear
the howl of the missions
slipping screams through                                     20
your silence, dropping dreams
from your wings.
              Is this why
              you made me
              sing and weep                       25
              for you?
Like butterflies
made to grow another way
this woman is chiseled
on the face of your world.                                   30
The badger-claw of her father
shows slightly in the stone
burrowed from her sight,
facing west from home.

## STUDY QUESTIONS

1. Who is addressed as "you"?

2. The ancestral songs, changed, grab the young "by the ankle / and tangle us up / with red mesa stone / that keep us turned / to the round sky" (lines 6–10), the poem says. What do you understand from this to be the literal influence of the old tribal songs on the young Hopi? Why is the sky described as "round"?

3. What is the "earth's middle"? What are the "spokes" (l. 13) that have left that middle?

4. The songs, the SPEAKER says, have "hammered on my bones / till you could no longer hear / the howl of the missions" (ll. 17–19); what do you understand by this to have been the literal religious influence of the old songs?

5. Trace all the IMAGES of rock and stone in the poem. Why or how is this appropriate to the SUBJECT matter and THEME?

# Cathy Song

B orn in 1955 in Hawaii, Cathy Song attended the University of Hawaii, Wellesley College (B.A., 1977), and Boston University (M.A., 1981). She is the author
of *Picture Bride* (winner of the Yale Younger Poets Award in 1982), in which the title
poem tells the story of her Korean grandmother, who was sent for as a mail-order
bride in Hawaii on the basis of her photograph. Her latest book is *Frameless Windows,
Squares of Light* (1988).

The immigrant Chinese woman finds great freedom in America, but loneliness,
too, and the need for a link to her heritage.

## LOST SISTER

*1*

In China,
even the peasants
named their first daughters
Jade—
the stone that in the far fields                                      5
could moisten the dry season,
could make men move mountains
for the healing green of the inner hills
glistening like slices of winter melon.

And the daughters were grateful:                                     10
they never left home.
To move freely was a luxury
stolen from them at birth.
Instead, they gathered patience,
learning to walk in shoes                                            15
the size of teacups,
without breaking—
the arc of their movements
as dormant as the rooted willow,
as redundant as the farmyard hens.                                   20
But they traveled far

in surviving,
learning to stretch the family rice,
to quiet the demons,
the noisy stomachs.                                          25


                              2
There is a sister
across the ocean,
who relinquished her name,
diluting jade green
with the blue of the Pacific.                                30
Rising with a tide of locusts,
she swarmed with others
to inundate another shore.
In America,
there are many roads                                         35
and women can stride along with men.

But in another wilderness,
the possibilities,
the loneliness,
can strangulate like jungle vines.                           40
The meager provisions and sentiments
of once belonging—
fermented roots, Mah-Jongg tiles and firecrackers—
set but a flimsy household
in a forest of nightless cities.                             45
A giant snake rattles above,
spewing black clouds into your kitchen.
Dough-faced landlords
slip in and out of your keyholes,
making claims you don't understand,                          50
tapping into your communication systems
of laundry lines and restaurant chains.

You find you need China:
your one fragile identification,
a jade link                                                  55
handcuffed to your wrist.
You remember your mother
who walked for centuries,
footless—
and like her,                                                60
you have left no footprints,
but only because

there is an ocean in between,
the unremitting space of your rebellion.

## STUDY QUESTIONS

1. Why do so many Chinese families name their first daughter Jade?

2. How were the girl children restricted in their movements? What did they achieve?

3. What advantages does the sister who comes to America find? What is the "giant snake" that rattles above the immigrant's household (line 46)? Why are the landlords called "dough-faced" (l. 48)?

4. Why does the "lost sister" need a "jade link" (l. 55) to China and her heritage? Why has she, like her mother, "left no footprints" (l. 61)?

# Alice Walker

Best known now for *The Color Purple* (1982), which won the Pulitzer Prize for fiction and was made into a popular movie by Steven Spielberg, Georgia-born Alice Walker (born 1944) is the author of two other novels—*The Third Life of Grange Copeland* (1970) and *Meridian* (1976)—as well as several volumes of poetry (*Revolutionary Petunias and Other Poems* [1970] and *Horses Make a Landscape Look More Beautiful* [1984]), essays (*In Search of Our Mothers' Gardens* [1983]), and short stories (*In Love and Trouble: Stories of Black Women* [1973], from which this story is taken, and *You Can't Keep a Good Woman Down* [1981]).

Here a young educated urbanized black American who feels she "has made something of herself" visits her rural Southern roots. We watch and listen from the vantage point of her mother, who is accused of not understanding her "heritage."

# EVERYDAY USE

*for your grandmama*

I will wait for her in the yard that Maggie and I made so clean and wavy yesterday afternoon. A yard like this is more comfortable than most people know. It is not just a yard. It is like an extended living room. When the hard clay is swept clean as a floor and the fine sand around the edges lined with tiny, irregular grooves, anyone can come and sit and look up into the elm tree and wait for the breezes that never come inside the house

Maggie will be nervous until after her sister goes: she will stand hope-lessly in corners, homely and ashamed of the burn scars down her arms and legs, eying her sister with a mixture of envy and awe. She thinks her sister has held life always in the palm of one hand, that "no" is a word the world never learned to say to her.

You've no doubt seen those TV shows where the child who has "made it" is confronted, as a surprise, by her own mother and father, tottering in weakly from backstage. (A pleasant surprise, of course: What would they do if parent and child came on the show only to curse out and insult each other?) On TV mother and child embrace and smile into each other's faces. Some-times the mother and father weep, the child wraps them in her arms and leans across the table to tell how she would not have made it without their help. I have seen these programs.

Sometimes I dream a dream in which Dee and I are suddenly brought together on a TV program of this sort. Out of a dark and soft-seated limou-sine I am ushered into a bright room filled with many people. There I meet a smiling, gray, sporty man like Johnny Carson who shakes my hand and tells me what a fine girl I have. Then we are on the stage and Dee is embrac-ing me with tears in her eyes. She pins on my dress a large orchid, even though she has told me once that she thinks orchids are tacky flowers.

In real life I am a large, big-boned woman with rough, man-working hands. In the winter I wear flannel nightgowns to bed and overalls during the day. I can kill and clean a hog as mercilessly as a man. My fat keeps me hot in zero weather. I can work outside all day, breaking ice to get water for washing; I can eat pork liver cooked over the open fire minutes after it comes steaming from the hog. One winter I knocked a bull calf straight in the brain between the eyes with a sledge hammer and had the meat hung up to chill before nightfall. But of course all this does not show on television. I am the way my daughter would want me to be: a hundred pounds lighter, my skin like an uncooked barley pancake. My hair glistens in the hot bright lights. Johnny Carson has much to do to keep up with my quick and witty tongue.

But that is a mistake. I know even before I wake up. Who ever knew a Johnson with a quick tongue? Who can even imagine me looking a strange white man in the eye? It seems to me I have talked to them always with one foot raised in flight, with my head turned in whichever way is farthest from them. Dee, though. She would always look anyone in the eye. Hesitation was no part of her nature.

"How do I look, Mama?" Maggie says, showing just enough of her thin body enveloped in pink skirt and red blouse for me to know she's there, almost hidden by the door.

"Come out into the yard," I say.                                                    8

Have you ever seen a lame animal, perhaps a dog run over by some    9
careless person rich enough to own a car, sidle up to someone who is ignorant
enough to be kind to him? That is the way my Maggie walks. She has been
like this, chin on chest, eyes on ground, feet in shuffle, ever since the fire
that burned the other house to the ground.

Dee is lighter than Maggie, with nicer hair and a fuller figure. She's a    10
woman now, though sometimes I forget. How long ago was it that the other
house burned? Ten, twelve years? Sometimes I can still hear the flames and
feel Maggie's arms sticking to me, her hair smoking and her dress falling off
her in little black papery flakes. Her eyes seemed stretched open, blazed open
by the flames reflected in them. And Dee. I see her standing off under the
sweet gum tree she used to dig gum out of; a look of concentration on her
face as she watched the last dingy gray board of the house fall in toward the
red-hot brick chimney. Why don't you do a dance around the ashes? I'd
wanted to ask her. She had hated the house that much.

I used to think she hated Maggie, too. But that was before we raised the    11
money, the church and me, to send her to Augusta to school. She used to
read to us without pity; forcing words, lies, other folks' habits, whole lives
upon us two, sitting trapped and ignorant underneath her voice. She washed
us in a river of make-believe, burned us with a lot of knowledge we didn't
necessarily need to know. Pressed us to her with the serious way she read,
to shove us away at just the moment, like dimwits, we seemed about to
understand.

Dee wanted nice things. A yellow organdy dress to wear to her gradu-    12
ation from high school; black pumps to match a green suit she'd made from
an old suit somebody gave me. She was determined to stare down any disaster in her efforts. Her eyelids would not flicker for minutes at a time. Often
I fought off the temptation to shake her. At sixteen she had a style of her
own: and knew what style was.

I never had an education myself. After second grade the school was    13
closed down. Don't ask me why: in 1927 colored asked fewer questions than
they do now. Sometimes Maggie reads to me. She stumbles along good-
naturedly but can't see well. She knows she is not bright. Like good looks
and money, quickness passed her by. She will marry John Thomas (who has
mossy teeth in an earnest face) and then I'll be free to sit here and I guess
just sing church songs to myself. Although I never was a good singer. Never
could carry a tune. I was always better at a man's job. I used to love to milk
till I was hooked in the side in '49. Cows are soothing and slow and don't
bother you, unless you try to milk them the wrong way.

I have deliberately turned my back on the house. It is three rooms, just    14
like the one that burned, except the roof is tin; they don't make shingle roofs
any more. There are no real windows, just some holes cut in the sides, like
the portholes in a ship, but not round and not square, with rawhide holding

the shutters up on the outside. This house is in a pasture, too, like the other one. No doubt when Dee sees it she will want to tear it down. She wrote me once that no matter where we "choose" to live, she will manage to come see us. But she will never bring her friends. Maggie and I thought about this and Maggie asked me, "Mama, when did Dee ever *have* any friends?"

She had a few. Furtive boys in pink shirts hanging about on washday after school. Nervous girls who never laughed. Impressed with her they worshiped the well-turned phrase, the cute shape, the scalding humor that erupted like bubbles in lye. She read to them.

When she was courting Jimmy T she didn't have much time to pay to us, but turned all her faultfinding power on him. He *flew* to marry a cheap city girl from a family of ignorant flashy people. She hardly had time to recompose herself.

When she comes I will meet—but there they are!

Maggie attempts to make a dash for the house, in her shuffling way, but I stay her with my hand. "Come back here," I say. And she stops and tries to dig a well in the sand with her toe.

It is hard to see them clearly through the strong sun. But even the first glimpse of leg out of the car tells me it is Dee. Her feet were always neat-looking, as if God himself had shaped them with a certain style. From the other side of the car comes a short, stocky man. Hair is all over his head a foot long and hanging from his chin like a kinky mule tail. I hear Maggie suck in her breath. "Uhnnnh," is what it sounds like. Like when you see the wriggling end of a snake just in front of your foot on the road. "Uhnnnh."

Dee next. A dress down to the ground, in this hot weather. A dress so loud it hurts my eyes. There are yellows and oranges enough to throw back the light of the sun. I feel my whole face warming from the heat waves it throws out. Earrings gold, too, and hanging down to her shoulders. Bracelets dangling and making noises when she moves her arm up to shake the folds of the dress out of her armpits. The dress is loose and flows, and as she walks closer, I like it. I hear Maggie go "Uhnnnh" again. It is her sister's hair. It stands straight up like the wool on a sheep. It is black as night and around the edges are two long pigtails that rope about like small lizards disappearing behind her ears.

"Wa-su-zo-Tean-o!" she says, coming on in that gliding way the dress makes her move. The short stocky fellow with the hair to his navel is all grinning and he follows up with "Asalamalakim, my mother and sister!" He moves to hug Maggie but she falls back, right up against the back of my chair. I feel her trembling there and when I look up I see the perspiration falling off her chin.

"Don't get up," says Dee. Since I am stout it takes something of a push. You can see me trying to move a second or two before I make it. She turns, showing white heels through her sandals, and goes back to the car. Out she peeks next with a Polaroid. She stoops down quickly and lines up picture after picture of me sitting there in front of the house with Maggie cowering behind me. She never takes a shot without making sure the house is included. When a cow comes nibbling around the edge of the yard she snaps it and me and Maggie *and* the house. Then she puts the Polaroid in the back seat of the car, and comes up and kisses me on the forehead.

Meanwhile Asalamalakim is going through motions with Maggie's hand. 23 Maggie's hand is as limp as a fish, and probably as cold, despite the sweat, and she keeps trying to pull it back. It looks like Asalamalakim wants to shake hands but wants to do it fancy. Or maybe he don't know how people shake hands. Anyhow, he soon gives up on Maggie.

"Well," I say. "Dee." 24

"No, Mama," she says. "Not 'Dee,' Wangero Leewanika Kemanjo!" 25

"What happened to 'Dee'?" I wanted to know. 26

"She's dead," Wangero said. "I couldn't bear it any longer, being named 27 after the people who oppress me."

"You know as well as me you was named after your aunt Dicie," I said. 28 Dicie is my sister. She named Dee. We called her "Big Dee" after Dee was born.

"But who was *she* named after?" asked Wangero. 29

"I guess after Grandma Dee," I said. 30

"And who was she named after?" asked Wangero. 31

"Her mother," I said, and saw Wangero was getting tired. "That's about 32 as far back as I can trace it," I said. Though, in fact, I probably could have carried it back beyond the Civil War through the branches.

"Well," said Asalamalakim, "there you are." 33

"Uhnnnh," I heard Maggie say. 34

"There I was not," I said, "before 'Dicie' cropped up in our family, so 35 why should I try to trace it that far back?"

He just stood there grinning, looking down on me like somebody 36 inspecting a Model A car. Every once in a while he and Wangero sent eye signals over my head.

"How do you pronounce this name?" I asked. 37

"You don't have to call me by it if you don't want to," said Wangero. 38

"Why shouldn't I?" I asked. "If that's what you want us to call you, 39 we'll call you."

"I know it might sound awkward at first," said Wangero. 40

"I'll get used to it," I said. "Ream it out again." 41

Well, soon we got the name out of the way. Asalamalakim had a name 42 twice as long and three times as hard. After I tripped over it two or three times he told me to just call him Hakim-a-barber. I wanted to ask him was he a barber, but I didn't really think he was, so I didn't ask.

"You must belong to those beef-cattle peoples down the road," I said. 43 They said "Asalamalakim" when they met you, too, but they didn't shake hands. Always too busy: feeding the cattle, fixing the fences, putting up salt-lick shelters, throwing down hay. When the white folks poisoned some of the herd the men stayed up all night with rifles in their hands. I walked a mile and a half just to see the sight.

Hakim-a-barber said, "I accept some of their doctrines, but farming and raising cattle is not my style." (They didn't tell me, and I didn't ask, whether Wangero [Dee] had really gone and married him.) 44

We sat down to eat and right away he said he didn't eat collards and pork was unclean. Wangero, though, went on through the chitlins and corn bread, the greens and everything else. She talked a blue streak over the sweet potatoes. Everything delighted her. Even the fact that we still used the benches her daddy made for the table when we couldn't afford to buy chairs. 45

"Oh, Mama!" she cried. Then turned to Hakim-a-barber. "I never knew how lovely these benches are. You can feel the rump prints," she said, running her hands underneath her and along the bench. Then she gave a sigh and her hand closed over Grandma Dee's butter dish. "That's it!" she said. "I knew there was something I wanted to ask you if I could have." She jumped up from the table and went over in the corner where the churn stood, the milk in it clabber by now. She looked at the churn and looked at it. 46

"The churn top is what I need," she said. "Didn't Uncle Buddy whittle it out of a tree you all used to have?" 47

"Yes," I said. 48

"Uh huh," she said happily. "And I want the dasher, too." 49

"Uncle Buddy whittle that, too?" asked the barber. 50

Dee (Wangero) looked up at me. 51

"Aunt Dee's first husband whittled the dash," said Maggie so low you almost couldn't hear her. "His name was Henry, but they called him Stash." 52

"Maggie's brain is like an elephant's," Wangero said, laughing. "I can use the churn top as a centerpiece for the alcove table," she said, sliding a plate over the churn, "and I'll think of something artistic to do with the dasher." 53

When she finished wrapping the dasher the handle stuck out. I took it for a moment in my hands. You didn't even have to look close to see where hands pushing the dasher up and down to make butter had left a kind of sink in the wood. In fact, there were a lot of small sinks; you could see where thumbs and fingers had sunk into the wood. It was a beautiful light yellow wood, from a tree that grew in the yard where Big Dee and Stash had lived. 54

After dinner Dee (Wangero) went to the trunk at the foot of my bed and started rifling through it. Maggie hung back in the kitchen over the dishpan. Out came Wangero with two quilts. They had been pieced by Grandma Dee and then Big Dee and me had hung them on the quilt frames on the front porch and quilted them. One was in the Lone Star pattern. The other was Walk Around the Mountain. In both of them were scraps of dresses Grandma Dee had worn fifty and more years ago. Bits and pieces of Grandpa Jarrell's Paisley shirts. And one teeny faded blue piece, about the size of a penny matchbox, that was from Great Grandpa Ezra's uniform that he wore in the Civil War. 55

"Mama," Wangero said sweet as a bird. "Can I have these old quilts?" 56

I heard something fall in the kitchen, and a minute later the kitchen door 57
slammed.

"Why don't you take one or two of the others?" I asked. "These old 58
things was just done by me and Big Dee from some tops your grandma
pieced before she died."

"No," said Wangero. "I don't want those. They are stitched around the 59
borders by machine."

"That'll make them last better," I said. 60

"That's not the point," said Wangero. "These are all pieces of dresses 61
Grandma used to wear. She did all this stitching by hand. Imagine!" She
held the quilts securely in her arms, stroking them.

"Some of the pieces, like those lavender ones, come from old clothes her 62
mother handed down to her," I said, moving up to touch the quilts. Dee
(Wangero) moved back just enough so that I couldn't reach the quilts. They
already belonged to her.

"Imagine!" she breathed again, clutching them closely to her bosom. 63

"The truth is," I said, "I promised to give them quilts to Maggie, for 64
when she marries John Thomas."

She gasped like a bee had stung her. 65

"Maggie can't appreciate these quilts!" she said. "She'd probably be 66
backward enough to put them to everyday use."

"I reckon she would," I said. "God knows I been saving 'em for long 67
enough with nobody using 'em. I hope she will!" I didn't want to bring up
how I had offered Dee (Wangero) a quilt when she went away to college.
Then she had told me they were old-fashioned, out of style.

"But they're *priceless!*" she was saying now, furiously; for she has a tem- 68
per. "Maggie would put them on the bed and in five years they'd be in rags.
Less than that!"

"She can always make some more," I said. "Maggie knows how to quilt." 69

Dee (Wangero) looked at me with hatred. "You just will not understand. 70
The point is these quilts, *these* quilts!"

"Well," I said, stumped. "What would *you* do with them?" 71

"Hang them," she said. As if that was the only thing you *could* do with 72
quilts.

Maggie by now was standing in the door. I could almost hear the sound 73
her feet made as they scraped over each other.

"She can have them, Mama," she said, like somebody used to never 74
winning anything, or having anything reserved for her. "I can 'member
Grandma Dee without the quilts."

I looked at her hard. She had filled her bottom lip with checkerberry 75
snuff and it gave her face a kind of dopey, hangdog look. It was Grandma
Dee and Big Dee who taught her how to quilt herself. She stood there with
her scarred hands hidden in the folds of her skirt. She looked at her sister
with something like fear but she wasn't mad at her. This was Maggie's portion. This was the way she knew God to work.

When I looked at her like that something hit me in the top of my head 76 and ran down to the soles of my feet. Just like when I'm in church and the spirit of God touches me and I get happy and shout. I did something I never had done before: hugged Maggie to me, then dragged her on into the room, snatched the quilts out of Miss Wangero's hands and dumped them into Maggie's lap. Maggie just sat there on my bed with her mouth open.

"Take one or two of the others," I said to Dee. 77

But she turned without a word and went out to Hakim-a-barber. 78

"You just don't understand," she said, as Maggie and I came out to the 79
car.

"What don't I understand?" I wanted to know. 80

"Your heritage," she said. And then she turned to Maggie, kissed her, 81
and said, "You ought to try to make something of yourself, too, Maggie. It's really a new day for us. But from the way you and Mama still live you'd never know it."

She put on some sunglasses that hid everything above the tip of her nose 82
and her chin.

Maggie smiled; maybe at the sunglasses. But a real smile, not scared. 83
After we watched the car dust settle I asked Maggie to bring me a dip of snuff. And then the two of us sat there just enjoying, until it was time to go in the house and go to bed.

## STUDY QUESTIONS

1. Why does Dee make sure she gets the house in every picture she takes (paragraph 22)?

2. "I heard something fall in the kitchen, and a minute later the kitchen door slammed" (par. 57). Who is making the noise? Why?

3. Why does Maggie let Dee have the quilts? Why does Dee want them so much?

4. What is the IRONY of Dee's accusing her mother of not understanding her heritage? What does the story imply *is* the narrator's true heritage?

5. The story clearly concerns two different black life-patterns. Which one does the story seem to prefer? How does the VOICE of the story (the first-person NARRATION) help you evaluate the different modes?

6. Why is the story called "Everyday Use"?

# Gail Y. Miyasaki

G ail Miyasaki, a third-generation Japanese-American born in Hawaii, has taught ethnic studies; she has also worked as a journalist for bilingual newspapers and as an editor for Hawaii Public Television. Her books include *Asian Women* (1971), *A Legacy of Diversity* (1975), and *Montage: An Ethnic History of Women in Hawaii* (1977).

"Obāchan" is a tender but not uncritical story of the Japanese grandmother of a Japanese-American girl, who expresses both nostalgia and disapproval of her heritage but great love for her grandmother.

## OBĀCHAN[1]

Her hands are now rough and gnarled from working in the canefields. But   1
they are still quick and lively as she sews the "futon" cover. And she would
sit like that for hours Japanese-style with legs under her, on the floor steadily
sewing.

She came to Hawaii as a "picture bride." In one of her rare self-reflecting   2
moments, she told me in her broken English-Japanese that her mother had
told her that the streets of Honolulu in Hawaii were paved with gold coins,
and so encouraged her to go to Hawaii to marry a strange man she had never
seen. Shaking her head slowly in amazement, she smiled as she recalled her
shocked reaction on seeing "Ojitchan's" (grandfather's) ill-kept room with
only lauhula mats as bedding. She grew silent after that, and her eyes had a
faraway look.

She took her place, along with the other picture brides from Japan, beside   3
her husband on the plantation's canefields along the Hamakua coast on the
island of Hawaii. The Hawaiian sun had tanned her deep brown. But the
sun had been cruel too. It helped age her. Deep wrinkles lined her face and
made her skin look tough, dry, and leathery. Her bright eyes peered out
from narrow slits, as if she were constantly squinting into the sun. Her brown
arms, though, were strong and firm, like those of a much younger woman,
and so different from the soft, white, and plump-dangling arms of so many
old teachers I had had. And those arms of hers were always moving—scrub-

1. Grandmother.

bing clothes on a wooden washboard with neat even strokes, cutting vegetables with the big knife I was never supposed to touch, or pulling the minute weeds of her garden.

I remember her best in her working days, coming home from the cane-fields at "pauhana"[2] time. She wore a pair of faded blue jeans and an equally faded navy-blue and white checked work shirt. A Japanese towel was wrapped carefully around her head, and a large straw "papale" or hat covered that. Her sickle and other tools, and her "bento-bako" or lunch-box, were carried in a khaki bag she had made on her back.

I would be sitting, waiting for her, on the back steps of her plantation-owned home, with my elbows on my knees. Upon seeing me, she would smile and say, "Tadaima" (I come home). And I would smile and say in return, "Okaeri" (Welcome home). Somehow I always felt as if she waited for that. Then I would watch her in silent fascination as she scraped the thick red dirt off her heavy black rubber boots. Once, when no one was around, I had put those boots on, and deliberately flopped around in a mud puddle, just so I could scrape off the mud on the back steps too.

Having retired from the plantation, she now wore only dresses. She called them "makule-men doresu," Hawaiian for old person's dress. They were always gray or navy-blue with buttons down the front and a belt at the waistline. Her hair, which once must have been long and black like mine, was now streaked with gray and cut short and permanent-waved.

The only time she wore a kimono was for the "Bon"[3] dance. She looked so much older in a kimono and almost foreign. It seemed as if she were going somewhere, all dressed up. I often felt very far away from her when we all walked together to the Bon dance, even if I too was wearing a kimono. She seemed almost a stranger to me, with her bent figure and her short pigeon-toed steps. She appeared so distantly Japanese. All of a sudden, I would notice her age; there seemed something so old in being Japanese.

She once surprised me by sending a beautiful "yūkata" or summer kimono for me to wear to represent the Japanese in our school's annual May Day festival. My mother had taken pictures of me that day to send to her. I have often wondered, whenever I look at that kimono, whether she had ever worn it when she was a young girl. I have wondered too what she was thinking when she looked at those pictures of me.

My mother was the oldest daughter and the second child of the six children Obāchan bore, two boys and four girls. One of her daughters, given the name of Mary by one of her school teachers, had been disowned by her for marrying a "haole" or Caucasian. Mary was different from the others, my mother once told me, much more rebellious and independent. She had refused to attend Honokaa and Hilo High Schools on the Big Island of Hawaii, but chose instead to go to Honolulu to attend McKinley High School. She

2. Drudgery, tedious work.
3. The Lantern Festival, the Buddhist's All Soul's Day.

smoked cigarettes and drove a car, shocking her sisters with such unheard of behavior. And then, after graduation, instead of returning home, Mary took a job in Honolulu. Then she met a haole sailor. Mary wrote home, telling of her love for this man. She was met with harsh admonishings from her mother.

"You go with haole, you no come home!" was her mother's ultimatum.    10

Then Mary wrote back, saying that the sailor had gone home to Amer-    11
ica, and would send her money to join him, and get married. Mary said she was going to go.

"Soon he leave you alone. He no care," she told her independent daugh-    12
ter. Her other daughters, hearing her say this, turned against her, accusing her of narrow-minded, prejudiced thinking. She could not understand the words that her children had learned in the American schools; all she knew was what she felt. She must have been so terribly alone then.

So Mary left, leaving a silent, unwavering old woman behind. Who    13
could tell if her old heart was broken? It certainly was enough of a shock that Honolulu did not have gold-paved streets. Then, as now, the emotionless face bore no sign of the grief she must have felt.

But the haole man did not leave Mary. They got married and had three    14
children. Mary often sends pictures of them to her. Watching her study the picture of Mary's daughter, her other daughters know she sees the likeness to Mary. The years and the pictures have softened the emotionless face. She was wrong about this man. She was wrong. But how can she tell herself so, when in her heart, she only feels what is right?

"I was one of the first to condemn her for her treatment of Mary," my    15
mother told me. "I was one of the first to question how she could be so prejudiced and narrow-minded." My mother looked at me sadly and turned away.

"But now, being a mother myself, and being a Japanese mother above    16
all, I *know* how she must have felt. I just don't know how to say I'm sorry for those things I said to her."

Whenever I see an old Oriental woman bent with age and walking with    17
short steps, whenever I hear a child being talked to in broken English-Japa-nese, I think of her. She is my grandmother. I call her "Obāchan."

## STUDY QUESTIONS

1. Why does the NARRATOR put on her grandmother's black rubber boots (paragraph 5)? (Make sure you take into account the last word—"too"—in the sentence describing her actions.)

2. How does the narrator's perspective of her grandmother change when "Obāchan" wears a kimono?

3. How does the reader's view of Obāchan change when we learn of her treatment of her daughter Mary? What do you understand by these two sentences: "She was

wrong. But how can she tell herself so, when in her heart, she only feels what is right?" (par. 14)?

4. Why is the narrator's mother sorry for what she said to her mother at the time of Mary's leaving home?

5. "She is my grandmother. I call her 'Obāchan' " (par. 17). Why? Why isn't the story called "Grandmother"?

# Paula Gunn Allen

Sioux-Laguna and Lebanese-Jewish, Paula Gunn Allen was born in 1939 in Cubero, New Mexico. Her family spoke five languages when she was growing up. It is to this mixture she attributes her being a poet. She believes that poetry should be useful, and that the use-full is the beauty-full. "Language, like a woman, can bring into being what was not in being; it can, like food, transform one set of materials into another set of materials." She holds a doctorate from the University of New Mexico and is chair of Native American Studies at San Francisco State University.

The speaker of this poem acknowledges the debt of life and of tradition to "grandmother" and pays the debt by following some of the old ways, remembering and preserving them. Much of its meaning is presented and held together by the image of weaving.

## GRANDMOTHER

Out of her own body she pushed
silver thread, light, air
and carried it carefully on the dark, flying
where nothing moved.

Out of her body she extruded                                   5
shining wire, life, and wove the light
on the void.

From beyond time,
beyond oak trees and bright clear water flow,
she was given the work of weaving the strands             10
of her body, her pain, her vision

into creation, and the gift of having created,
to disappear.

After her,
the women and the men weave blankets into tales of life,                15
memories of light and ladders,
infinity-eyes, and rain.
After her I sit on my laddered rain-bearing rug
and mend the tear with string.

## STUDY QUESTIONS

1. What does "Out of her own body she pushed / silver thread . . . extruded / shining wire, life, and wove the light / on the void" (lines 1–2, 5–7) mean, in your own words?

2. "After" means "patterned on the model of" as well as next in time, and this seems to be the force of the word in the final verse paragraph. But what else in the relationship of SPEAKER to grandmother is implied in the fact that the speaker is mending the rug that, apparently, the grandmother created?

# Pam Durban

*All Set About with Fever Trees* is the title story of South Carolinian Pam Durban's first volume, published in 1988. Durban won the Mary Roberts Rinehart Award in fiction in 1984. She now teaches at Georgia State University.

This rich story spans the narrator's life from childhood to motherhood; through it all threads the influence of her energetic, unorthodox grandmother, who at sixty left schoolteaching in Macon, Georgia, "to teach the children of the Presbyterian missionaries in the Belgian Congo in Africa," and who left a heritage that the narrator is passing on to her own daughter.

# ALL SET ABOUT WITH FEVER TREES

In Macon, Georgia, my grandmother, Mariah Palmer, was a famous teacher.         1
She took up this career after her husband died during the Depression, leaving her with three small children to look after. From that time on, she taught

English in the Bibb County schools and Sunday school at the First Presbyterian Church. Later, when the wine of her understanding had clarified and aged to her satisfaction, she taught the Bible at the YWCA, where all seats were filled, so I've heard, when her topic was the Book of John, that great gospel of abiding faith. Then, at sixty, she announced to us all that she'd signed on to teach the children of the Presbyterian missionaries in the Belgian Congo in Africa.

For days after she got the news, my mother went around worrying out loud to herself. Folding the laundry, she'd snap a towel and say, "Well, damn," as if she were determined to have her say, even if she'd already lost the argument. I overheard them talking once when my grandmother came to visit that summer before she left for Africa. They were sitting out on the screened porch, stringing and snapping beans for supper. My mother is a master at subtle persuasion. Not for her the direct attack. She prefers to sketch an outline of danger and to leave you to fill in the rest. Driving by a black juke joint called the Royal Peacock Club, for instance, she had recently taken to slowing down and pointing out to me the slash marks in the black vinyl door, and the men, with hats cocked low over their eyes, who were bothering women and shoving each other around outside, and though I was only eight years old I knew that this was a piece of some puzzle that I was supposed to hold onto until I was old enough to realize where it fit and what I was being warned against. 2

That particular day, Mother selected her somber colors, muddy browns and greens, and with these she painted pictures for my grandmother of the lonely life she would lead over in Africa. Then she selected the darker earth tones and with these she made her a picture of an aging, ailing body, of brittle bones, a failing mind, all set against the black background of death itself. When this was over she sighed: "I've had my say, not that it makes any difference." 3

"Good," my grandmother said. "It's always better to get these things off your chest than to keep them bottled up inside. But I will tell you, my best beloved," she said. "I have done a lot of praying in my short and happy life and I can now report to you with confidence that I have never been surer of anything. As it happens, I have heard the clear call down deep in my soul and it is summoning me to labor in the fields far from the fleshpots of civilization." 4

This was good stuff. I stood there hugging myself, feeling the goosebumps run along my arms as I imagined how her eyes must look—like Moses' eyes in her illustrated copy of the Old Testament, two points of leaden fire aimed at the idolaters as they danced around their golden calf and tended their fleshpots, where fleshy women and men with small pointed beards played tambourines and writhed around together. "Fleshpots," I said to myself, and I remembered the way the fire blazed up in the trash barrel outside the door of the Royal Peacock Club on cold winter nights, throwing shadows on the black faces, and the way the whiskey bottles flashed in that light. And I 5 wanted her to go to Africa and stay as long as she wished, as long as it took to find whatever had called her. I wanted her to go because lately I had had glimmerings in myself, intimations of some kind of destiny that was waiting for me, somewhere, with my name, Annie Vess, already written on it in big bright letters. Sometimes when I was sitting in the library at school or running in the playground or even at supper with my family, everything would get very quiet inside me and then a glowing would begin, followed by a burst of light, like a bomb going off up in the air, and I would feel that something was about to speak, to show me the way I was meant to go.

While she was gone, I kept a map of Africa thumbtacked to the wall of my room and circled her town, Lubondai, and every other place she mentioned, in red. Her letters arrived covered with stamps that featured regal black heads held high on thin necks, a white queen in her jewels, a king who looked like a walrus with his mustache and his heavy staring expression. The paper smelled sweet and dusty, the way Africa must smell, I thought, sun-warmed and lush, like hay. I imagined her writing them, alone there in the middle of the continent, in a hut late at night, with the lantern burning beside her. I saved these letters and studied them at night by flashlight under the covers before I fell asleep, speed-reading through the parts about how their houses were nice houses just like those back in the States, with plumbing and curtains and all, and about the well-mannered Christian children she was fortunate to be teaching, and hurrying on to the paragraphs that described her travels.

She wrote that she traveled by Land Rover, along roads where the vines grew so fast the driver had to get out now and then and hack the road clear. In the snapshot she sent along with one letter, the driver is naked to the waist and black as a carved onyx while she is as serene as the queen mother, her broad-brimmed straw hat lying on her lap. "On the road to Lulluraburg," the caption read, "to hear a chorus of native voices sing Bach, Handel, and Brahms." "A 50,000-acre game preserve," read another caption enclosed with a postcard that was divided into four sections and showed elephants, giraffes, lions and antelopes. "The Mountains of the Moon," she wrote, "imagine, Annie, mountains 19,000 feet high, so high that even viewed up close, they look far away." Sometimes I would dream of these places, the Mountains of the Moon and a chorus of golden lions singing as they galloped up and down the slopes.

When I showed my mother one of these letters or a postcard, she would shake her head, sigh, and say, "It certainly sounds like Mother's found what she's been looking for."

"Which is?"

She would shrug, roll her eyes. "Beats me."

I kept the faith, waiting for the day when my grandmother would come back and tell me everything she knew about clear calls and destiny. I was patient in my waiting because I believed in her. She knew things. She would not fail. She had powers that other people did not have. There is, for instance, a memory which is not a dream, which I have of her and of myself as a child in her house in Macon which will show you what I mean. In this memory, I've gone downstairs by myself at night, looking for a drink of water. The light from the streetlights comes through the tall windows and makes shapes like tall lighted doors across the floors. So I start for one and find myself standing in the corner of a room, start for another and I end up facing the wall. I've not made a sound but my grandmother comes down from upstairs, tying her bathrobe as she comes, flipping light switches until we reach the kitchen and when she flips that switch, everything is white—the enamel of the table top, the kitchen sink, the bowl of paper white narcissus just coming into bloom, her bathrobe and the ruff of white hair standing out around her head, the glass of milk she sets in front of me.

And then she lifts me and holds me so close to her face I can see the flecks of gold in her bright hazel eyes and the tiny roses etched along the gold rims of her thick glasses, and sets me down on her lap. From the shelf above the kitchen table, from beside the bowl of narcissus, she has taken down a book, the *Just So Stories* by Rudyard Kipling, and slowly, surely, as I listen to her heartbeat, and the sound of her voice humming against my back, the bewildered way I had felt as I wandered from room to room, like a small leaf floating in a cold sea of light, leaves me. And we are gone into that country on the banks of the great, gray, green, greasy Limpopo River, all set about with fever trees, where life first stirred and crawled from the mud. Where the rhino got his baggy skin, the whale his throat, the leopard his spots, where the cat walked by himself waving his wild wild tail and the humans made the first letter and then the whole alphabet. Where everything is about first causes, sources, what stirs within the seed that causes the plant to grow. "Hear and attend and listen," she reads, "for this befell and behappened and became, O My Best Beloved, when the Tame animals were wild." 12

As she reads and reads I drowse and float close to sleep, feel the house all around us, sleeping and dark, except for this room. And then I'm growing, I'm rising out through the roof and flying over the planet, searching until I find Macon, Georgia, on the banks of the Ocmulgee River, sleeping in its grove of dark pines, and in the middle of that city, I find the room where we are reading, set against the dark like the North Star. And below the windy ocean of darkness that runs around the world, that lighted room remains. 13

The summer I was twelve, my grandmother came back to the States and we went to Macon to welcome her home. I had prepared for days with a notebook full of questions to ask her. What was it in your experience which most clearly answered the call that took you there? What unusual or exciting experiences did you have that give us a clue as to the differences between people? Did anything happen to you there that has convinced you of anything or shaken any previously held beliefs? 14

Macon, Georgia, straggles along the banks of the great grave Ocmulgee River which is a broad, slow river, sluggish as its name. In the summer, the 15 sky is always white, as though a layer of smoke hangs between you and everything you want to see, and the sun burns behind this haze like a white metal disk. "The only difference between Macon, Georgia, and hell," my father said, as we drove across the bridge and into the city, "is that a river runs through Macon."

"A river runs through hell, too," I said. "If what you mean by hell is the underworld. It's called the River Styx." I knew because I had just finished reading a book called *Great Myths of the Western World* and added it to the list on my summer reading club card at the public library. 16

"Then I guess there's no difference at all," he said. 17

In the same church basement where we'd told her good-bye four years earlier, we spread the long tables with yellow tablecloths and set out platters of chicken, and potato salad, green beans, and a thickly iced cake shaped like Africa with the Belgian Congo outlined in red and centered with a small green flag in the middle of red icing that spelled out "Lubondai" to show where she'd lived. I was the one responsible for the lettering on the cake. 18

As I helped to set the tables, I kept one eye on the doorway and the excitement turned inside me like a bright whirligig going round and round. As I slid down the halls and in and out of the Sunday school rooms with my pack of cousins, I kept an ear tuned to the noise in the other room. To this day, I don't know exactly what I'd hoped to see, but when she walked through the door, something died in me with the sudden fading sound that a record makes when the plug is pulled on the machine. It was my grandmother, arms open wide to welcome everyone, and was she fat! She must have gained thirty pounds and she looked like a flour sack tied in the middle, with her black patent leather belt cinched tight around the waist of her gaudy blue-and-pink print dress. 19

I remember I tried to escape, but it was too late. She wrapped me in her flabby arms and pulled me into her bosom, where I thought I might suffocate on the smell of English Lavender cologne and Vicks Vapo-Rub. She rocked me, weeping, calling me her best beloved, the heart of her heart, the light of her life. And then I was weeping too, the whole place was weeping. She would take off her glasses, wipe her eyes, look at me, and we'd both burst into tears again. But I'll bet I wasn't weeping for the joy of seeing her again. I was weeping because I'd been betrayed. Because she'd crossed the equator and received a scroll signed by Neptune, ruler of the deep. Because she'd sailed up the Congo River as far as it might be sailed. Because she'd climbed halfway up the great Pyramid of Cheops at Giza, she'd visited the Sphinx and heard the riddle. She'd even walked the streets of Paris, France, on her way back home. Because she'd done all those things and then she'd come back fat. That was the only change, not to mention miracle, that had happened to her. 20

Now all she could do was argue and eat, eat and argue. She tore the paper table cloth with her pen, drawing maps and lines and arrows. This tribe, that tribe. What does the Mau-Mau uprising have to do with the one 21 clear call? That's what I wanted to know. Meanwhile, she ate four wedges of cornbread soaked with butter, three pieces of chicken and a biscuit. She ate fresh peach cobbler topped with two scoops of ice cream. She ate after everyone else had laid down their forks. My mother said, "My God, Mother, how could you let yourself gain all that weight?"

"Daughter mine," she said. "I did not plan it that way. I became fond of the native diet which consists mostly of starch and well, these things happen in this great world of ours."

"What do they eat?" I asked, shoving the last of my banana pudding into the potato salad.

"A root called *manioc*, my best beloved," she said, fishing for another slab of cornbread. "It's like our sweet potato. They dry this manioc root and pound it into flour and they make a bread with the flour that's called *bidia*. They dunk this bread (she dunked the cornbread into the gravy boat and held it up, dripping) in palm oil gravy, and they call it food for the hunter inside."

"That's gross," I said. She laughed and I saw all the gold fillings in her teeth. While we watched slides of Africa which consisted mostly of a dozen different views of a row of mustard-colored concrete block houses, with here and there a view of the Mountains of the Moon seen through a herd of curious giraffes, I hashed over the story about the roots. There in the land of the one clear call, in the shadow of the Mountains of the Moon, they scratched in the dirt and ate roots. From that point on, I could have cared less about anything. I imagined that I was sitting up on a high bald rock, too high even for eagles to reach, looking down on everyone as they crowded close to see the treasures she'd collected—the broad-bladed knives etched with intricate woven patterns, the hammered copper crosses, the raffia baskets and carved wooden bowls and ivory crosses, the shaman's headpiece that was covered in leopard skin and had cold eyes, a fiercely sucking mouth and perfect little ears made of clay. I watched as she lined up a troop of ivory elephants in order of descending size. The smallest was no larger than the nail of your smallest finger and each was carved in perfect detail, from the flapping ears down to the moon-shaped toes. I watched as she modeled the latest fashion from The Congo—a braided straw rope with two tassels of coarse black hair attached, to be worn around the waist like a skirt.

I watched it all from my bald rock high above the valley. But when she came to my gift I would have gladly died. I was her favorite, so they said, and when she called me to the front of the room everyone turned their tender smiling silence, their tearful happiness my way. I unwrapped the tissue paper she'd pressed into my hand, and there in my palm was a wooden pin—a brown, antelope-looking creature, carved so that the hooves, horns and nostrils, even the muscles that rippled under its coat, looked real.

"Now, my best beloved," she said, "I watched the craftsman carve it. He took great pains and I told him all about you so that he might make it especially for Annie. And that's not only beautifully carved, it's very valuable wood too," she said.

"What kind?" I felt the pin, felt along the carved muscles. My hand had warmed it and under my thumb the wood felt alive, as if the animal were about to wake up and begin breathing. 28

"That's called *stinkwood*, Annie," she said. At that, the whole adult chorus chuckled, heads bobbed, eyes were wiped, hands were patted and pressed, and my humiliation was complete. "Thank you, it's very nice," I managed to say. While they clapped and clapped, I stood staring at the broken strap of my Aunt Louise's sandal, at her toes that gripped the soles as though she were leaning into a wind that was blowing her backwards, or trying to. Restlessness, like an itch, began inside me. If my grandmother had corrected herself, said: "Oh, please excuse me, Annie, I have made a dreadful mistake, that's called *heavenwood*," I would not have been comforted. My mother pinned the thing to the front of my dress and I sat there, feeling itchy and hot inside my clothes, looking at my badge, that sleek animal all carved of stinkwood and gathered for the leap. 29

But I didn't give up. When I'd recovered a little from my embarrassment, I worked my way close to her again and asked, "How did you talk to them?" 30

"Who, my best beloved?" 31

"The people over there." I imagined sign language, shadow shows by the fire, figures scratched in the dirt with sticks, and all around, the jungle night—which was longer and scarier, somehow, than nights we knew—had gathered to listen. 32

"Some speak English," she said. 33

"Oh." 34

"And of course I learned a little of the Tschiluba language," she said. "It's a tonal language, not like ours." 35

"Say some of it." 36

She closed her eyes and began to speak, low liquid sounds, like music that asked questions, like a stream running fast over stones. On this tide, my hope returned. "Of course there were people who could talk for me too," she said. "They translated that language into English and vice versa. We had us a big talking party once, and, oh, was it grand." 37

"Do they really wear, you know, those things?" I pointed to the rope with the tassels. 38

"Why yes," she said. "Some do. I can't explain this to you, heart of my heart, but it's the most natural thing in the world to them, to go around like that. They don't give a hoot about some things we hold very dear. To them our bodies are the coverings we wear, *the beauty inside turned inside out*, they say." 39

Well, afterwards as we drove back to the motel, I turned over what she'd said like a small bead, round and polished. All that about people's bodies and 40 what she'd called the hunter and the inside. I felt that a series of small but violent explosions had dislodged certain ideas I'd held without even knowing I believed them. I was being raised Roman Catholic because this was my father's faith and Mother, a Presbyterian, had promised to turn us over to the church in return for being allowed to marry him. At least that's how she told it. So I knew all about the soul because every day in catechism class at Catholic school we pinned her wings and studied her, worried over her condition and her future. I knew that this soul was either a rippling sheet of light, cold and distantly beautiful as the *aurora borealis*, or it was spotted with decay or even entirely dark, extinguished by sin. But whatever this soul might be, its life was not with roots or stinkwood or hunters and darkness was always its death.

The summer I was sixteen, we went to a reunion of the Palmer family 41 in the mountains up near Highlands, North Carolina. The house, which belonged to my great aunt Martha, Grandmother's sister, had been added onto haphazardly and looked like a train wreck, a heap of boxcars lying every which way and covered with tar paper but no boards or shingles, and screened from the road by a line of cedar trees that ran straight along the road's edge. Behind this house, Scaley Mountain reared up out of the earth. You could actually go out and touch the place where the mountain came out of the ground and when the mountain threw its shadow over the house, it was damp and cold. Inside, the house was full of rooms where a person could go off by herself and think about things or read all afternoon without being disturbed.

In the valley between the mountain and the house, a small, cold stream 42 ran so fast it made a roaring sound, as though it were angry at being confined in such a narrow channel. Aunt Martha took her constitutional there. She'd built a small dam in the stream and every morning she descended into the stream, with her hair done in braids and wrapped over the top of her head, and for ten minutes she sat on stones below this dam and let the water pelt her shoulders. Now this water was so cold that you could not breathe when you were in it and whatever parts of your body the water touched turned red and began to ache, and then went numb as cork. Nevertheless, I had decided that Aunt Martha, who was a clairvoyant, a medium and an astrologer, famous in the family for her seances and levitations, for giving somebody the heebie-jeebies at every reunion, was more likely than my grandmother to tell me what I needed to know about clear calls, souls, destinies and all the rest. So every morning just at dawn, I put on my bathing suit and followed her into the stream and while the water poured over us like a clear cape, I gasped out my questions and she would tell me things about the psychic gifts of the Palmer side of the family, each one unique and fabulous—the gift of second sight and the ability to read destinies in the stars being first among them.

Or she would talk about what she called the spirit world and the rein- 43 carnated lives of other members of the family. My grandmother, for instance, had lived several lifetimes on the continent of Africa, which is why Martha had not been at all surprised when Grandmother had returned there since the human soul, according to Martha, gravitates toward scenes of its former unfoldings as naturally as a seed seeks the earth. I told her about the time when the idea of my search had first come to me and about those moments when I'd felt that I was bound for a destiny that no one had ever lived before. I told her about the night when my grandmother had found me and read to me and I had felt myself leave the room and fly around the planet, a disembodied spirit, searching for its home. Martha nodded as she listened. "It doesn't surprise me in the least," she said. And as I talked I imagined the clear icy water running all through me and I thought, this is how I will feel when I arrive at my destiny, this is how it will be.

Nights, the grownups gathered near the line of cedar trees beside the road to reminisce about each other. The rest of us sat around on quilts on the grass. The stories they told were about each other but it seemed to me that they all shared a common center. They were about the past but not the whole past, just special moments, those moments I was looking for, times that had been dilated somehow by a mysterious richness. Uncle Edward, they said that night, came to Macon, a scared, green boy from Statesboro, to take a job at the Bibb Mills. One day, on his lunch break, he passed the door to the weave room and looking in he saw a woman sitting with her back to him, elbows flying, working like there was no tomorrow. "Never saw her face until later," someone remembered he'd said. "Never had to." The bare light bulb suspended over her head had made the cotton dust shine in her hair, and he'd known at that very moment, as though some hindrance to sight had been struck down and he saw not just her but something essential and radiant about her, that this woman would be his wife. As it turned out, he did marry her and she died shortly after bearing him two children, but no one seemed particularly sad about that as long as they could go to the quick sweet stream of that moment when he'd first seen her and drink deeply of the life there, the life that he saw in her and cleaved to all his days, past reason, past hope. And this was the stream, I promised myself, that I would drink from too. I lay on my back and listened and watched the stars and the fireflies, which were like stars drifting down to join us, until the entire meadow and valley and sky swarmed with light. [44]

Meanwhile, Aunt Martha sat twisting the paisley scarf around her neck, rocking so hard her chair cracked each time she rocked. Finally, Uncle Edward's story was done and he was at peace, having been hauled around to funeral services in three states before coming to his final resting place among the family in the long slope of green hillside above the Ocmulgee River. Then Martha chimed in. "Now I have an interesting recollection for us about my sister, Mariah, and about her birth long ago in the south of the state of Georgia." I struggled up from the grass, pulling the damp quilt around my shoulders. My grandmother had gone to bed early. She was dizzy, she said, from [45] the blood pressure medicine she had to take six times a day. But it was better without her there; in her absence, her story expanded, took on important new dimensions.

Aunt Martha went on: "You know Mariah was born with her eyes shut tight as a kitten's and that she didn't open them for three days? I would give anything to know what wonders she witnessed during those three days." As she talked, she rocked and stared out past us all in a fixed way. Now we are getting someplace, I thought, this is more like it. And it seemed as though I'd been waiting for a long time to be there at that moment with Martha staring at the night with her enormous eyes as though she were using her second sight to carry her past the first layer of things and right on into the marrow. I turned my head slowly, the hair prickling along the tops of my arms, and looked where she was looking and saw only the fireflies and the shape of Scaley Mountain, darker than the sky. 46

"Mariah's was a special birth, attended by special signs," Martha continued. "She was born with the caul over her head." She looked at the group of us with wide, light eyes which at this moment I can still remember as the eyes of a creature staring in from somewhere outside a circle of light. "They say the caul is a sure sign that she had been granted the gift of second sight." From the line of rockers, someone protested: "Oh, Martha, go on now." 47

"You can't tell me it's not true," Aunt Martha snapped back. "I was present at her birth, and though I was only a small child, I remember it as though it were yesterday. The pity is that she's never developed this gift." 48

"But how do you know she hasn't?" I asked. Martha bent her long thin neck and smiled on me. She always encouraged us girls to use our minds and speak up when we had something to say. 49

"Hush now, Annie," someone answered. "Martha's just talking." 50

I sat up then; I sat very still. The damp quilt felt clammy against my skin so I shucked it off and stood up as if I'd remembered someplace I had to go. I ducked out through the cedars and onto the road that ran the length of the valley, pulling the cigarette I'd snitched earlier out of the waistband of my shorts. I lit up, inhaled deeply, tipped my head back and blew smoke up in a blue plume toward the stars. A gift. Martha had said there was a gift and it had to do with special powers. I held the cigarette between my teeth, put my hands on my hips and looked up at the deep blue sky. "I'm ready," I said. I thought I could hear the silence that rested there between the stars. I wondered what my gift might be. I wanted it to be clairvoyance, or something like it, because only with this gift would I be able to penetrate the layer of troubles that seemed to lie over everything like humid heat over Macon, and see into the heart of things. I wandered to the edge of the road where the rhododendron bushes grew. I stamped out my cigarette, leaned close to one of the blooms and opened my eyes very wide and stared until I started to get a headache, waiting for that flower to give up and reveal the secret of its life. I imagined that this would happen in slow motion, like time lapse photography—first the petals would unfold, then the center would break 51 open and fall away and there inside I would see it, a star-swarming stream of pure life.

I gave up on the flower and I imagined myself going back to school with these special powers, able to tell who my real friends were and my secret enemies, able to know the secrets people keep in their hearts and to help them with their darkest troubles. And I would know what it was that Mother and I fought about all the time and why Grandmother never spoke to Aunt Rachel except in a cold and formal tone of voice and why Aunt Louise, Mother's sister, only called us late at night, and why my father could sometimes be found sitting back in the kitchen at three o'clock in the morning without a single light turned on. Behind me, something scratched lightly in the gravel. I turned slowly, full of a tingling like the light shaking of a thousand small silver bells, ready for my first encounter with the spirit world, and found one of Aunt Martha's old palsied hounds that had shuffled out after me, wagging its lazy tail. From back at the house, a screen door slammed, my mother's voice called "Annie, Annie, come in now, please." The spell was broken.

Still, for most of the rest of the night, I tried not to sleep because I had discovered that sleeping on it, as you're so often advised to do, makes some of the best feelings and strongest convictions dissolve into thin air. So, up in the Hen's Nest, a narrow room under the eaves where the women and girls slept, I tried to hold onto what Aunt Martha had said about the gifts and the way I had felt out on the road waiting for mine, as though some barrier were about to crumble and I was about to see things that no human eye could see, and no tongue could tell. As it turns out, I was right about sleep. When I woke up, it seemed, I had forgotten everything. Martha had taken her constitutional without me and gone into town, so I went looking for my grandmother instead, to ask her about these gifts she was supposed to have and why she'd never developed her own as Aunt Martha had accused her of not doing.

It was then that trouble lifted its head. I wandered through the house listening for the sound of my grandmother's voice. In the living room, a picture window looked out onto Scaley Mountain. Someone had placed an ink bottle full of violets on the windowsill, right below the teardrop-shaped crystal which Martha had hung in the window. Crystals, Martha said, are excellent conductors of the life force. I tapped it and small rainbows wobbled all over the walls and ceiling.

I found them in the kitchen. My grandmother was wiping her eyes with the back of one hand and fanning a newspaper over the cakes with the other. My mother chopped cabbage on the drainboard beside the sink, her mouth as thin and set as the blade of her knife. Aunt Louise's name, like the echo of an angry outburst, hung in the air. I perched on the stool beside the table, grabbed a knife and a head of cabbage and began to chop. There were travel brochures fanned out on the table. They showed New England on a vivid autumn day, all red and orange, with a silver bus cutting cleanly down a road, beneath a sky so clear you might break chunks from it, the sun exploding off the windshield.

Grandmother was keen on taking fall foliage tours in New Hampshire  56
and Vermont. Every year she went and sent us back postcards covered with lists of the colors she'd seen which sounded to me like no colors ever seen on this earth—helianthin, saffron, beaten gold—all brought to an absolute *pinnacle* of beauty in their last days of life. If Louise could just be there and see it, surely it would do her heart good, surely she would thrive in that good clean air. Surely the trip would bring her back to herself. I tried to match this vision of Louise with the woman I knew, the one who hadn't been able to come to the reunion because she had sprained her ankle or something. The Aunt Louise who sat restlessly silent at any gathering, worrying at her hands, the woman who walked as though she were a globe turning around a bent axis. Oh, no, not that Louise. My grandmother shooed her off with the newspaper. This other Louise was revived, refreshed, she was a risen Louise who laughed like a girl, who drank all the clear sweet water she wanted to drink. "Is Aunt Louise sick?" I asked.

"Just worn down, honey," my grandmother said. "She's had such a long,  57
trying summer, you see."

"Louise has had several trying *winters* too," my mother snapped. "In  58
fact, if you ask me, her summers and winters are getting worse every single year."

"Well, it's a good thing no one's asked you," my grandmother said. She  59
flipped open a brochure and frowned at an autumn hillside. The newspaper swept back and forth across the cakes.

"Let's just look at some facts here, Mother," she said. There's no stop-  60
ping Mother when she's in full cry. As usual when Mother talked facts, I wanted to yell loud enough to drown her out. Her facts were always strong medicine, mixed in a dose equal to your high opinions of yourself and others. I cringed to see her number Louise's failures: the three lost jobs, the falls, the near accidents, the calls, the *collect* phone calls to my mother in the middle of the night. Grandmother hunched over, guarding something with her body.

"You're free to make of this what you will," she said. "Thank the Lord  61
for independent minds. But Louise is my daughter. You're not there. I am. And she needs me."

"Will somebody please tell me what's wrong with Aunt Louise?" I said.  62

My mother fixed me with her long, contemplative stare in which she  63
seems to be staring into a void full of the world's sadness. "She drinks," Mother said wearily. "She should be put in a hospital where she can get help."

"Her life is hard," my grandmother said, smacking the table hard with  64
her palm. "She has a difficult life. Her husband is dead and her children are unmanageable. And Louise will never go to a hospital as long as I'm alive."

She spoke these words so clearly it seemed she'd bitten them out of all possible words on the subject.

Backing away, my mother shrugged and bit her lower lip; then she began    65
to chop cabbage, letting the blade come too close to her hand. "Louise is a wreck," she said quietly. "It's just plain cruel not to see it."

"Louise is my daughter. It doesn't matter what she is, I'm with her."    66

I put down my knife. "Excuse me," I said and I left the kitchen, fighting    67
down the urge to run. I went and stood on the porch, blinking into the strong sunlight. Did Aunt Louise have gifts, I wondered. If so, what happened to them? What was it that wrecked inside you? Where did you go when you were lost, and where did you come back to when you were found?

That fall, as she had promised, my grandmother took Aunt Louise to    68
New England for a foliage tour. And, as my mother had predicted, the trip was a disaster. The Louise my grandmother had imagined—the revitalized, healed Louise, who would find inspiration, comfort, peace, something bright in herself to match the leaves—that Louise, when taken to the mountains, vanished from the tour. She was found two days later holed up in an expensive hotel without two dimes to rub together. "The room-service tab was all for liquor, Annie," my mother said. "Louise was dead-dog drunk." Mother's cheeks were flushed, her eyes bright. When she looks that way it's easy to imagine her on a horse, leading a crusade. The story of the crisis as it developed via the long distance telephone line was this: On the morning when they came within sight of the most spectacular gorge in the White Mountains, a deep gorge with sides so thickly wooded and blazing that the air seemed saturated with color as though the world they'd come into at last were one tall flame, Louise bolted. The last person to see her reported that she was weeping. She'd checked into the resort hotel where they found her, started drinking, and—since she couldn't pay and she couldn't leave without paying—she stayed, and kept ordering out for liquor.

The ashtray on the phone stand filled up with Mother's cigarette butts    69
as she negotiated the return of her mother and sister to Georgia. I hung around waiting for the progress reports and feeling helpless. I'd grown up believing there was always *something* you could do. She slammed down the phone: "Annie, she took Louise out and bought her a new dress and then she led her around like a little lost child, just like a little child. Can you beat that?"

I said I couldn't. It seemed some things couldn't be helped. Aunt Louise    70
was one of them. My grandmother seemed defeated by it. She telephoned us when she got home and she said: "Louise has so much to give, I wanted to remind her of that. I thought she might see it this time."

"Well, she didn't," my mother said.    71

"Why didn't it help?" I asked my grandmother. I couldn't keep the anger    72
out of my voice. After all, *she* was the one who was supposed to know about everything.

Her voice sounded tired as though she'd sunk to the bottom of a deep, 73
hollow place. "There is something in Louise that nobody can get to," she
said. "Don't ask me why."

I heard my mother take a breath. I thought I would kill her if she said 74
anything small or mean-spirited. "Well, Mother, you tried," she said finally.

"And I will continue to do so," she said. "You can count on that." 75

I didn't exactly lose touch with my grandmother after that fall, but over 76
the next six years it seemed we had to reach across a wider gap in order to
make contact. There were the letters, always, and the Christmas visits when
Louise wasn't doing too badly and my grandmother could leave Macon. But
in the November after the reunion, Martha died, the mountain house was
sold in April and after that the family split off into separate orbits, each
around a different sun.

I knew my grandmother was sick and getting sicker but it didn't seem 77
exactly real to me. I only knew that by the time I graduated from college,
my grandmother was seriously ill with angina. Her life had become a series
of risks. "Washing dishes or bathing," she wrote to me once, "are now gambles I must take. For my efforts, I'm rewarded with a freely drawn breath or
these chest pains."

Early in July, I was visiting at home when Aunt Louise was involved in 78
her second hit-and-run accident of the year and the judge gave her a choice:
she could sign herself into a hospital for alcoholics, or she could go to jail.
When my mother heard that my grandmother had consented to Louise's
hospitalization, she said: "We are going to see Mother, *today.*"

It was an edgy drive, a cord of silence tied in small knots of talk. We 79
drove down through Georgia, through Thompson and Sparta, the dusty towns
bunched around their courthouse squares, some with limp red and green
tinsel left over from Christmas, faded and unseasonable, still wrapped around
the light poles. We spoke only twice during the drive. Leaving Thompson,
she said: "You be sure to tell her you're getting married."

"Of course," I said. "Why wouldn't I?" Later, when we stopped for the 80
traffic light in Sparta, I said: "Is she very sick?" My mother gunned the
engine until the fan belt screeched.

"Yes," she said. The light changed from red to green, and she pressed 81
the accelerator firmly. I felt as though we'd spoken to each other for the first
time in years.

The apartment house where my grandmother lived hadn't changed. 82
Neither had the hill where the building stood. Only the trees lining the sidewalk had changed, their tops sawed flat to make way for the power lines. We
opened the heavy oak door that always stuck and walked inside. In the hallway, the smell of gas and bacon grease still lingered. The tea roses on the
stained wallpaper were brown.

We let ourselves into her living room. It looked like one of those rooms 83
in a museum, arranged to show the clutter and hurry of someone's everyday

life. Her books, reference books, and composition books with their black and white mottled covers, were piled beside chairs, slips of paper sprouting from between their pages. Dust lay thick on every surface and the windows were clouded, streaked with dried rain. All the walls were hung with African paintings, hammered copper crosses, the shaman's mask with its leopard-skin face motheaten and mournful as the face of a derelict.

Her nightstand was covered with pill bottles, and a chart with check marks beside the hours and the names of pills hung from a string around the bedpost. She lay dozing on the bed, one arm flung over her eyes, dressed as though she were going to a party, in a lavender print dress with purple beads and earrings to match. She'd dotted her cheeks with two bright circles of rouge and brightened her mouth with lipstick. But her feet were bare, the blue veins like a forked branch all over them, the toenails thick and stained tobacco brown. I reached for my mother's hand. And as I watched my grandmother's chest rise and fall with each breath, I realized that Mother and I were matching our breathing to hers and I thought I understood a little more about what people mean when they say, "This person is alive." They mean that the circle curves, unbroken, between what is visible and what cannot be seen and you know of its existence the same way you know currents in water by watching a boat or currents in the sky by seeing the way a hawk holds tight to the wind. I let go of Mother's hand and went to the window and yanked at the dusty blinds, forced the window open as high as it would go. The sound of a jackhammer riddled the air. Still she lay quietly, breathing from somewhere high in her chest. 84

"Mother." 85

"Grandmother." My mother and I spoke at once. For a second or two, she stared at us wildly as though we were robbers. She sat up, one cheek creased and flushed, and fumbled at the nightstand for her glasses. I helped her with her slippers and then she stood up beside the bed and reached for us. She'd lost weight and her dress hung on her in folds, like a slack flag. I was her best beloved, my mother was the light of her life. She pressed her hand to her chest and began taking small sips of air. 86

"You sit down," Mother said, her forehead tight with worry. We helped her to the armchair in the living room and she sat heavily. "I'll make us some tea," Mother said, in her voice that gets cheerful and bright whenever she's afraid. 87

"Coffee for me," I said. "Black, please." Grandmother started to protest. She leaned up in her chair, then let herself go against the cushions. And I saw that she was radically changed. It was as if I'd been looking at her from the corner of my eye and had finally gotten up the nerve to look her full in the face. And for a moment, whatever hurries us along, slipping one minute into the next to make a continuous flow of time, stopped, and I had my moment of sight, though it was no gift I would have asked for. Her face looked vivid and full of light as though her expression had become a clean window, and peace itself looked through. And then, without pause or change, 88 her face began to darken into a stillness beyond peace, beyond any power to name or know. But that light didn't just disappear—I saw it leave her. And it seemed at that moment that death was very close to us, only it wasn't silent or empty or dark. It was full of the recollection of everything I had loved about her, everything that would be lost, as though grief and love are the fruit of the same tree, the one with roots so old and tangled they can never be pulled apart.

I turned away then. I think I twisted away because she grabbed my wrist and held it. Her hand felt strong, as though she'd gathered all her strength there. "Well, sit right down," she said, "and tell me how it is." 89

"How is what?" I felt confused and let myself be pulled into the chair next to hers. 90

"Oh the wide, wide world and those who live there." 91

"It's about the same," I said. I rubbed her hand, felt the knuckles under the loose skin, moved my thumb over the joints. 92

"Now you know as well as I do that that is never so," she said. She closed her eyes, her head dropped back. I saw her face settle along the bones into that stillness. When she opened her eyes again, she looked angry and scared. "Lulluraburg," she said. She shook her head. "That name has eluded me for days." 93

"The place where they sang?" 94

She smiled. "Imagine remembering that from when you were just a little thing." 95

"I think there's lots I remember," I said. "Pieces of it come floating back to me now and then, like there's a place for them, you know what I mean?" 96

"I do indeed," she said. "I do indeed. And aren't you looking well. Your mother tells me you're just doing so well." 97

"Yes," I said, "yes I am." The sound of my voice was loud with cheerfulness, just like my mother's. "I'm getting married soon." 98

"Married?" She turned her head so quickly I thought a sound had startled her. She looked at me fiercely. "Is he a good man, and I mean day to day?" She tapped out the words on the arm of the chair with one long finger. 99

"Why, yes," I said. "Yes he is, as a matter of fact. How did you know? Now don't forget, the wedding's in August. I want to make sure you don't miss it. I'll drive down and pick you up, how would that be?" 100

"Married," she said. "Isn't that something!" She folded her arms and looked straight ahead. "The Bible says it's not good that we should be alone because if one should fall alone, who will pick him up, and if one should lie alone in the cold, who will warm him?" She picked at a loose thread on the arm of the chair. *You haven't answered my question, will you come to my wedding?* I wanted to say, but just then my mother returned with a rattle of cups and saucers, calling: "Here we are now, isn't this nice?" 101

I let go of her hand and excused myself. I went into the bathroom and stood at the window looking across what had been a trash-filled gully, now grown over in kudzu and wild Cherokee rose. The chinaberry tree was still 102 standing, hung with dull gold fruit, half choked in dead limbs. As I watched, a cardinal snagged in the upper branches and began its high sweet chirping. The Ocmulgee wound by, a thick and sluggish muddy gold, and I thought of the summers I'd spent there watching the river, following it in my mind's eye all the way down till it found the Atlantic. I used to stand there imagining myself in a small glass-covered boat drifting down the river, and when I talked to her about this trip I wanted to make, my grandmother was always ready to go. Sometimes while I helped her dry the dishes, we stocked my boat with provisions—matches in a waterproof case, canned food, a cat for good company, a map. She'd laughed. "You don't need a map."

"Well, what if the river forks?" 103

"Well, what if it does?" 104

Around five o'clock my grandmother refused for the last time to come 105 back with us to South Carolina. "This is my home," she said. "I have work to do here."

"What work?" Mother snapped. She thrust her chin out the way she 106 does and I saw how she must have looked as a child challenging someone whose protection she needed, whose power she feared.

"I have to prepare my YWCA classes for fall," my grandmother said in 107 that cold, imperious tone that allowed no words to follow.

My mother shoved a cigarette into her mouth and bustled around the 108 apartment, bullying things into place, shoving books and papers around, slapping at the dust with a rag, stirring it up so it hung in the air. When she finished and we'd collected our things, she said: "Now, Mother, for goodness' sake call us. You just worry me to death." She laughed, her mouth open, said: "Oh well, Mother, what would we do if everybody was as stubborn as you?"

"I'm glad I have a tractable nature," I said. I laughed too. 109

Grandmother hauled herself out of her chair and stood there breathing, 110 counting, as though she were poor and every breath was a dollar she was forced to spend.

"Mother, don't come out with us, we can let ourselves out," my mother 111 said. But she walked with us anyway, as far as the entrance to the building. I turned and waved as we walked down toward the car. "August," I yelled. "I'll come and pick you up. You'll like him, I promise, he's your type." She cupped her hand to her ear, nodded. At the car, I shaded my eyes and looked back, hoping to find her gone but she was still there, standing quietly and watching the clouds, the trees along the street in a shy sort of way as though she'd just noticed the size and silence of things. She stared at me as though she were looking for a bird in a tree. Then deliberately and clearly she said: "Good-bye," and she turned and walked back into the building.

It wasn't until four summers later, when Grandmother was four years 112 dead and my daughter Jesse was three, that I came to a place I recognized again as a destination on some road I had been traveling though I couldn't tell you all the twists and turns that brought me there. What happened was that Mother came down with pneumonia in the middle of August. It came on her overnight while my father was away on business in Mobile and what was so frightening was the timing of it. When she called to tell me, the sky was white, the sun glared off the sidewalks, the thermometer read 97 degrees. She couldn't say just exactly what was wrong, probably nothing, or why she hadn't called one of her friends there in town, but she was having trouble breathing and she just felt, well, weak and sort of cold, not all the time, but whenever she moved around. Why, yesterday, if I could imagine such a thing, she had gotten so dizzy that she'd just had to lie down for a minute, right there on the kitchen floor. She sounded casual about it, the way you might with a stranger in the house and you calling for help and trying not to let on that you were afraid of him.

People just don't get pneumonia in the middle of August, I said to myself as I drove to South Carolina. That's just crazy. It was close to dusk by the time I made it. When I opened the door, the heat hit me like a blast of desert air. The house must have been 80 degrees. Mother had camped out under a pile of blankets on the sofa back in the den. With the curtains drawn, the room was dark as a lair, the only light came from the television set on the table just in front of the sofa. Her eyes watched me from a shadowed place way back in her head. I put my hand on her forehead; it was so hot the heat seemed to radiate from it. "What took you so long?" she asked, her voice high and wheedling as an old woman's.

"I've been on my way ever since you called, Mother," I said. "I came as soon as I could." I yanked back the curtains, cranked open the window. As the light came into the room I saw how old she looked, how scared. I saw on her face the same dimness I had seen on my grandmother's face just before she died. It looked as though her cheekbones were throwing shadows under the skin. And I felt ashamed just then, for the trust I had put in the future, the way I always looked beyond what was right in front of me, believing that my destiny was somewhere else. For that blind burrowing trust that tunneled toward some promised land where we would all arrive someday, together and healthy and whole. For that misplaced faith in a someday when all would be well, all promises kept, all gifts given, all life lived.

"At least you're here now," she said. Her eyes closed and I pressed her hand to my cheek and held it there.

"Let's go," I said. "We're going to the emergency room right now." She was too weak to change out of her housedress but while I called her doctor to meet us at the hospital, she pulled on the fur coat my father had given her and together we went down into the August heat. There was something awful about the sheen of that healthy-looking fur wrapped around her and the way she shivered inside it as though she were shivering from a place that nothing could warm.

I called my father in Mobile. Then, for three days, while I waited for him to come home, I took prescriptions to the drug store and doled out the medicine, cleaned the house and watered the flowerbeds. For some reason I got it in my head that what she needed was fish, fresh vegetables, and clear broth with lots of ginger in it. So I went to the market and bought bunches of greens, tiny lady peas and lima beans, okra and tomatoes and corn with the milk still sweet in the kernels. Every day I bought fresh shrimp or grouper or flounder, food from the ocean, with the ocean's mineral brine in the sweet flesh. "I'm going to swim out of here by the time you get through with me," she said.

"That's the idea," I said. I watched while the shadow retreated from her face. On the third day, her fever broke, her eyes cleared. 118

The night before my father was due back from Mobile we sat up late back in the den while a summer storm moved onto us. I was paging through back issues of *Southern Living* while Mother read, an afghan across her lap to guard against the chills that still grabbed her now and then. The air thickened and grew stuffy, bringing the charge of the storm into the room to surround us. The rain blew in scattered gusts. Then, with a stumble of thunder, the tall hickory tree just outside the window bent halfway to the ground and the windows rinsed with rain as though a bucket of water had been thrown against the glass. I held the magazine up in front of my face and tried to focus my attention on the chart on the page which showed how to schedule your fall garden chores, when to take in the gladiola bulbs, how deep to plant next spring's jonquils. 119

I tried to concentrate but all I heard was the rain as it rushed around the house, around the room where we sat watching, and the wind as it bent the trees and whipped the leaves. Then a gust of wind came that was so strong it made the weatherstripping hum under the door. I dropped my magazine and looked up and that's when I saw my startled face staring back from the window. At the sight of my own scared face, something gave way inside me that had been holding firm since I'd first arrived and seen how sick my mother was. Behind me, Mother read as though she did not hear the storm, as though she would read forever. But the storm was everywhere and I thought that if I listened long enough, I might hear the sound of the rain as it came into the house and ran inside the walls like a river and the sound of the house going under that river, dissolving board by board, life by life, until all had been returned that once had been given. 120

I bowed my head again and turned through the pages, trying to find something that would hold my attention. And when I had skimmed through every page and looked up again, I saw myself again in the window glass and Mother behind me, with her book closed over one finger and her head turned toward the sound of the storm. And I saw that dullness had left her face. She was well again, and unafraid. 121

"Some storm," she said, as though she could match it, strength for strength, blow for blow. 122

"The best part of a storm is when it's over," I said. Already, the storm had wheeled away to the south. The gap lengthened between lightning and 123 its thunder. Outside, I heard the trees dripping. It was over. But when the time came, I felt no peace. I looked to my mother, trying to find comfort in her health, in the light that had returned to her face. Instead, I saw in this light everything I had ever rejoiced in, grieved over, loved. There was nothing outside it, nothing beyond. And I saw that this life I had tried to find and know and keep exists in this world in human form, and darkened by the crossing. And on the banks of that river I bowed my head, thankful for the night and the rain and the trouble, and for the darkness in which the light is kept.

Seeing Aunt Louise again is what started me thinking about all this again. I'd driven down to Macon for the day to do research in the Mercer library and she'd asked me to stop by for a visit. I hadn't seen her in years, not since Grandmother had died, so I wasn't prepared for the change in her. The Louise I remembered had been dazed and frumpy looking. But the Louise who answered the door was thin and dressed in a buff suede tunic and sweater and matching shoes. She looked thin but not starved. In fact, she looked healthy and solid, alive. I remembered what my mother had said after seeing Louise up on the dais, the guest of honor at her fourth AA birthday party. "I felt like I was celebrating right along with her," she'd said. Seeing Louise again, I felt that same kind of rejoicing, so quiet it couldn't be named, running like a stream through her life. "Louise," I said, "you're looking so well." We held each other's elbows while she considered this.

"That's because I am," she said.

Louise's place is modern and it overlooks the river. She's done it up with a lot of glass, glass shelves, glass ornaments, each set on a chosen spot and with a little pool of space around it as though everything needed room to breathe. Louise moved within a quiet space of her own. As we talked, her hands stayed calm in her lap. But it was her face that told the story. Nothing had deserted her face, not the pain and not the death. It was all there like something you could read if only you knew the language. There was the death she'd lived and the life that came after that death, all shadowed by a determination that was almost, but not quite, peace.

We sipped our coffee and traded pictures—my daughter Jesse and my husband Thomas, her grandson, William, Jr. Finally, I said: "It's getting late, Louise. Thomas and Jesse expect me for supper." But neither of us moved.

She said: "Will you look at something before you go? I found this the other day and I can't for the life of me figure it out." She hauled out her mother's African scrapbook, the one covered in woven straw and embroidered on the front with a wine-red moon, a golden sun. We flipped through the pages—past the pressed fronds and African flowers, the snapshots of the Mountains of the Moon, the scroll signed by Neptune—and stopped at a child's crayon drawing done in yellow, black, and green, of people in a jungle gathered around a snake. My grandmother was among them, the pillow-shaped person wearing black shoes and glasses. "I know that's supposed to be Mother," Louise said, "but what's that?"

"A dead snake?" 129

"I know that," she said. "I'm talking about the other thing." 130

The snake's eyes were red x's, the forked tongue lay limply on the ground. 131 Out of its middle, an animal was rising, a cross between fox and deer with wings and a fishy smile, surrounded by a globe of light. "Oh, that," I said, sorting back through the Africa stories. "Isn't that the anaconda they found that had swallowed some kind of animal?"

Louise laughed. She put her hand to her throat. "How could I forget?" 132 she said. "Of course, that's right. The animal that was alive inside the snake." She shook her head. "Now, who do you suppose made that one up? Mother was always so serious about it, too."

"Maybe she made it up." 133

"Maybe she did. She was good at that." Louise's smile tightened. "She 134 surely was."

By the time I left Macon, dusk lay thick as blue dust over the fields. It 135 was autumn then, and in the dusty green woods the sourwood leaves had already turned a lustrous red. All the way home I thought about these things, turning them over in my mind, putting one turn next to the other, watching the road they made. It seemed like one road with many turnings and the end nowhere in sight. When I got to the outskirts of Atlanta and the traffic started picking up, I turned my attention toward home and I imagined how Jesse would look, waiting for me at the front window and how she'd rush out as soon as she saw the car coming down the street and dance around me while I unloaded the car, talking a mile a minute. "What'd you bring me," I could almost hear her say. "Where'd you go, how long did it take you? What'd you bring me?"

Well, Jesse, I will say, I have those ivory elephants that march across 136 the mantel in single file, the big ones first, the little ones following. I have the wooden bowl with the people carved at the bottom, the ones who are passing the inlaid ivory bird from hand to hand. And now I have this story to tell, to keep her through the night and give her good dreams. I will say: In Africa, Jesse, your great-grandmother was walking beside the Kasai River one day and she stepped over a log lying across the path and do you know, that log was a snake? Yes it was. Well, that old snake lifted up its old scaly head and its eyes looked cold and dead, like the eyes of a very sad person. And this snake wanted to swallow her whole, it surely did. How did she know? She saw it in his eyes. When she saw the snake, why of course she yelled as loud as she could. And some men heard her and they ran out from the village and they killed the snake. Yes they did. They killed it, and they cut the snake open and do you know what they found? They found an antelope fawn that the snake had swallowed. It stood up trembling, Jesse, and do you know, that creature was alive? Yes. Down inside that dark old snake, it was alive as you or me.

# STUDY QUESTIONS

1. ". . . when the wine of her understanding had clarified and aged to her satisfaction, she taught the Bible at the YWCA . . ." (paragraph 1). Though there are no quotation marks around this in the text, it does not sound very much like the NARRATOR's language. Whose language is it, then? What other examples of such language can you find in the story?

2. Why does Annie's (the narrator's) mother slow down while driving past the Royal Peacock Club (par. 2)?

3. What is the relation between Annie's "intimations of some kind of destiny" for herself (par. 5), and her hoping Grandmother Palmer goes to Africa as planned?

4. What does Annie choose to ignore and what to concentrate on in reading her grandmother's letters from Africa?

5. Explain the title of the story.

6. What is the only change in her grandmother that Annie perceives upon her grandmother's return from Africa? Why does it make her cry?

7. Why, when everyone is watching slides of Africa, does Annie feel aloof, "looking down on everyone as they crowded close to see the treasures she'd collected" (par. 25)?

8. What present does her grandmother bring Annie, her "best beloved"? Why does her grandmother think it special? Why is Annie disappointed?

9. What does Annie hope to learn from her great-aunt Martha? Why does she think Martha may be able to teach her?

10. Describe Uncle Edward's "courtship." Why is that typical of the Palmer family stories?

11. What secrets does Annie hope to learn when she gets her "gift" (par. 52)?

12. What happens when Annie's grandmother takes Aunt Louise to New England to see the autumn foliage? This seems a defeat for her grandmother, and Annie concludes that perhaps there are some things that cannot be helped. To what extent does the story confirm, modify, or deny this conclusion?

13. Why, when Louise is hospitalized, does Annie's mother decide they must go to see Annie's grandmother in Macon that day?

14. When, on the drive to Macon, Annie asks if her grandmother is very sick, her mother says yes and guns the accelerator. "I felt as though we'd spoken to each other for the first time in years" (par. 81). Explain. Describe in a paragraph the relationship between Annie and her mother.

15. Watching her grandmother breathe, Annie understands what it means to know someone is alive. Explain.

16. What is Annie's moment of "sight" (par. 88)?

17. What does Annie mean when she says that "grief and love are the fruit of the same tree" (par. 88)?

18. Why is Annie, when she reaches her sick mother, ashamed of her trust in the future (par. 114)? What else is she ashamed of?

19. Describe Annie's feelings during the storm, and what it reveals to her about life (pars. 120–23).

20. Describe the child's crayon picture that Aunt Louise shows Annie. What story does Annie tell her daughter Jesse about that picture? What does it mean? How is it related to the story you have just read?

# Yvonne Sapia

Yvonne Sapia's family came from Puerto Rico to New York, where, in 1946, she was born. She moved to Florida in 1956 and has lived there since, attending the University of Florida and Florida State University, where she is now resident poet and editor of a humanities publication, *Woodrider*. *Valentino's Hair*, from which this poem is taken, won the Samuel French Morse Poetry Prize in 1987.

The children of immigrants never know their grandparents who have been left in the old country, the old world, the island or continent beyond the sea, and so they must learn about them from their parents.

## GRANDMOTHER, A CARIBBEAN INDIAN, DESCRIBED BY MY FATHER

Nearly a hundred when she died,
mi viejita[1]
was an open boat,
and I had no map
to show her the safe places.                               5
There was much to grieve.
Her shoulders were stooped.

---

1. My little old woman or mother. [Author's note]

Her hands were never young.
They broke jars
at the watering holes,                                                    10
like bones, like hearts.

When she was a girl,
she was given the island
but no wings.
She wanted wings,                                                         15
though she bruised
like a persimmon.
She was not ruined
before her marriage.
But after the first baby died,                                            20
she disappeared in the middle
of days to worship
her black saint,
after the second,
to sleep with a hand towel                                                25
across her eyes.

I had to take care
not to exhume
from the mound of memory
these myths, these lost ones.                                             30
Born sleek as swans
on her river, my brother,
the man you have met
who has one arm,
and I glided into the sun.                                                35
Other children poured forth,
and by the time I was sixteen
I lost my place
in her thatched house.

She let me go,                                                            40
and she did not come to the pier
the day the banana boat
pushed away from her shore
towards Nueva York
where I had heard                                                         45
there would be room for me.

## STUDY QUESTIONS

1. Who is the SPEAKER of the poem? Who is the grandchild referred to in the title in the first person ("my")? Who is addressed as "you" in line 33?

2. What does the speaker mean when he says that his mother was "an open boat" (l. 3)?

3. What were some of the things she had to grieve over? Why did she begin to sleep with "a hand towel / across her eyes" (ll. 25–26)?

4. Why was there no room at home for the speaker when he was sixteen?

# Barbara Watkins

B  arbara Watkins received an M.F.A. from the University of Massachusetts and now lives in New York City. This poem appeared in the *Pushcart Prize* series.
A photograph of Grandmother Kankovska, taken when she was fifteen, generates thoughts about her life and death.

## JOSEFA KANKOVSKA

It is a photograph of my grandmother, very young,
perhaps fifteen, standing with her family:
father, stepmother, half sisters, her brother,

standing in their country before it became
Czechoslovakia,[1] before the photographs                              5
were carried to America.
                    Their faces are stern
as if the parents knew they would take their children
to another continent and leave them, sailing the boat back
alone, as if the children knew.

---

1. Czechoslovakia became an independent country in 1918, formed from the merger of Moravia, Bohemia, and parts of Silesia and Slovakia.

                              There are other photographs:
an Atlantic City beach, 1916. Her husband                          10
lounges on the sand, her arms around his neck.
Their faces are full of sun. They are laughing.

Later came their son, and then
his father died, 1926, the day before Christmas.
Their son was only nine and could barely remember          15
how his mother tried to detach the radiator
from the wall, carry it out to the cemetery.
It was so cold.

It could have started then, the ice
that formed in her eyes, the distrust of people            20
because they disappear on ships that leave no tracks—
because they die.
                              For ten years in old age
she lived with us, carrying her closed face like a fist
but a few times in dim rooms in summer
she spoke of Europe.
                              And when in the heat of July     25
her body finally loosened, we found these photographs
carried for years like a map.

## STUDY QUESTIONS

1. How did Josefa get to America? about when?

2. Was Josefa the mother of the SPEAKER's mother or father?

3. The speaker says her grandmother distrusted people "because they disappear on
ships that leave no tracks—/ because they die" (lines 21–22). Who disappeared on
a ship? who died?

# Joseph Bruchac

Publisher of the *Greenfield Review*, poet, novelist, editor, and anthologist, Joseph
Bruchac was born in Saratoga Springs, New York, in 1942 of Slovakian and
Abnaki (Native American) heritage. He did not wander too far away to go to college,

earning a B.A. from Cornell University and an M.A. from Syracuse University. He still lives in nearby Greenfield Center, New York. Among his books are *Entering Onandaga*, *Turkey Brother*, and *There Are No Trees Inside the Prison*.

The speaker of this poem visits Ellis Island, where his paternal grandparents were admitted into the United States from central Europe, and he recalls his quite different maternal heritage.

# ELLIS ISLAND

Beyond the red brick of Ellis Island
where the two Slovak children
who became my grandparents
waited the long days of quarantine,
after leaving the sickness,                                   5
the old Empires of Europe,
a Circle Line ship slips easily
on its way to the island
of the tall woman, green
as dreams of forests and meadows                              10
waiting for those who'd worked
a thousand years
yet never owned their own.

Like millions of others,
I too come to this island,                                    15
nine decades the answerer
of dreams.

Yet only one part of my blood loves that memory.
Another voice speaks
of native lands                                               20
within this nation.
Lands invaded
when the earth became owned.
Lands of those who followed
the changing Moon,                                            25
knowledge of the seasons
in their veins.

## STUDY QUESTIONS

1. Who is the "tall woman" (line 9)?

2. Why is Ellis Island referred to in lines 16–17 as "nine decades the answerer / of dreams"?

3. What part of the SPEAKER's heritage seems the more desirable?

# R. T. Smith

R. T. Smith, Scotch-Irish and Tuscarora, was born in Washington, D.C., in 1947 and educated at the University of North Carolina at Charlotte and Appalachian State University. He is now Alumni Writer-in-Residence and director of creative writing at Auburn University. He is the author of ten books of poetry, including *Waking Under Snow* (1975), *Good Water* (1979), *Rural Route* (1981), and *Banish Misfortune* (1988), and has won many prizes for his work.

Like the speaker in Paula Gunn Allen's "Grandmother," the speaker here pays tribute to his grandmother and her old, tribal ways.

## YONOSA HOUSE

She stroked molten tones
from the heart-carved maple dulcimer.
My grandma did.
She sat like a noble sack of bones
withered within coarse skin.                                        5
rocking to snake or corn tunes,
music of passing seasons.
She sang the old songs.

Her old woman's Tuscarora uncut hair
hung like waxed flax ready to spin                                  10
till she wove it to night braids,
and two tight-knotted ropes
lay like lanyards on her shoulders.

On my young mind she wove
the myths of the race                                                    15
in fevered patterns, feathery colors:
*Sound of snow, kiss of rock,*
*the feel of bruised birch bark,*
*the call of the circling hawk.*

Her knotted hands showing slow blue rivers                               20
jerked nervously through cornbread frying,
pressed fern patterns on butter pats,
brewed sassafras tea in the hearth.
She wore her lore and old age home.

They buried Yonosa in a doeskin skirt,                                   25
beads and braids, but featherless,
like a small bird with clipped wings.
I cut hearts on her coffin lid,
wind-slain maple like the dulcimer.
The mountain was holy enough for Yonosa.                                 30
We kept our promise and raised no stone.
She sank like a root to be red Georgia clay.
No Baptist churchyard caught her bones.

I thank her hands when the maple leaves turn,
hear her chants in the thrush's song.                                    35

## STUDY QUESTIONS

1. What are the grandmother's various activities that the poem describes? Which of her activities is described first? How does that emphasis help structure the poem?

2. Why are the last four phrases of the second verse paragraph italicized?

3. What do the details of her burial suggest about her cultural attitudes and identity?

4. What clues do you have about the way the SPEAKER feels about his grandmother?

# Michael Harper

D irector of the Writing Program at Brown University and, since 1980, Kapstein
Professor there, Michael Harper (born 1938) has been active in establishing
and expanding the canon of black literature and art with such publications as *Chant
of Saints* (1973) and *The Collected Poems of Sterling Brown* (1980), in addition to volumes
of his own poetry such as *Eight Poems* (1981) and *Healing Songs for the Inner Ear* (1984).

The first verse paragraph recounts an episode in his grandfather's life, something
that resembles some of the "fences" in chapter 7, but the second paragraph is a tribute
to the memory, as the first paragraph is to the courage, of the grandfather. Here there
is not so much nostalgia for the old days or old ways as there is recognition that the
struggle for a place in American society goes on . . . and on.

## GRANDFATHER

In 1915 my grandfather's
neighbors surrounded his house
near the dayline[1] he ran
on the Hudson
in Catskill, NY                                5
and thought they'd burn
his family out
in a movie they'd just seen
and be rid of his kind:
the death of a lone black                     10
family is *the Birth*
*of a Nation*[2]
or so they thought.
His 5′4″ waiter gait
quenched the white jacket smile               15
he'd brought back from watered
polish of my father
on the turning seats,

1. Excursion-boat line.
2. Film (1915) by D. W. Griffith glorifying the Confederacy and the Ku Klux Klan.

and he asked his neighbors
up on his thatched porch                                    20
for the first blossoms of fire
that would burn him down.

They went away, his nation,
spittooning their torched necks
in the shadows of the riverboat                             25
they'd seen, posse decomposing;
and I see him on Sutter
with white bag from your
restaurant, challenged by his first
grandson to a foot-race                                     30
he will win in white clothes.
I see him as he buys galoshes
for his railed yard near Mineo's
metal shop, where roses jump
as the el circles his house                                 35
toward Brooklyn, where his rain fell;
and I see cigar smoke in his eyes,
chocolate Madison Square Garden chews
he breaks on his set teeth,
stitched up after cancer,                                   40
the great white nation immovable
as his weight wilts
and he is on a porch
that won't hold my arms,
or the legs of the race run                                 45
forwards, or the film
played backwards on his grandson's eyes.

# STUDY QUESTIONS

1. Explain how the neighbors might believe that the death of a black family would
   signify the birth of a nation. What kind of nation?
2. What is a "white jacket smile" (line 15)?
3. Where is the first scene set? Where does the grandfather live now?
4. What is the porch referred to in line 43?

# Alberto Ríos

Author of a volume of short stories (*The Iguana Killer* [1984]) and a volume of poems (*Whispering to Fool the Wind* [1981]), Alberto Ríos teaches at Arizona State University, not too far from Nogales, Arizona, where, in 1952, he was born. His father was from southern Mexico, his mother from England, and his interest in language came to him early. He has degrees in English, psychology, and creative writing and for a time attended law school.

His mixture of fantasy and reality, evident in the poem about his grandfather that follows, will remind some of Gabriel García Márquez and other modern Hispanic-American writers.

## MI ABUELO

Where my grandfather is is in the ground
where you can hear the future like an
Indian with his ear at the tracks. A
pipe leads down to him so that sometimes
he whispers what will happen to a man                                  5
in town or how he will meet the best-
dressed woman tomorrow and how the best
man at her wedding will chew the ground
next to her. Mi abuelo is the man
who talks through all the mouths in my house. An                      10
echo of me hitting the pipe sometimes
to stop him from saying "my hair is a
sieve" is the only other sound. It is a
phrase that among all others is the best,
he says, and "my hair is a sieve" is sometimes                        15
repeated for hours out of the ground
when I let him, but mostly I don't. "An
abuelo should be much more than a man
like you!" He stops then, and speaks: "I am a man
who has served ants with the attitude of a                            20
waiter, who has made each smile as only an
ant who is fat can, and they liked me best,

but there is nothing left." Yet, I know he ground
green coffee beans as a child, and sometimes
he will talk about his wife, and sometimes                    25
about when he was deaf and a man
cured him by mail and he heard ground
hogs talking, or about how he walked with a
cane he chewed on when he got hungry. At best,
mi abuelo is a liar. I see an                                 30
old picture of him at nani's with an
off-white yellow center mustache and sometimes
that's all I know for sure. He talks best
about these hills, slowest waves, and where this man
is going, and I'm convinced his hair is a                     35
sieve, that his fever is cool now in the ground.
Mi abuelo is an ordinary man.
I look down the pipe, sometimes, and see a
ripple-topped stream in its best suit, in the ground.

## STUDY QUESTIONS

1. How long does it take the reader who does not know Spanish to know what the title means?

2. Where is the SPEAKER's grandfather? What do you understand by the grandfather's speaking through a pipe in the ground? by his talking "through all the mouths in my house" (line 10)?

3. The speaker says in the middle of the poem, "An / abuelo should be much more than a man / like you" (ll. 17–19). What does that mean? How does the speaker feel at the end of the poem?

# Linda Pastan

Author of more than half a dozen volumes of poetry, including *PM/AM: New and Selected Poems*, which was nominated for the American Book Award, and *The Imperfect Paradise*, from which "Grudnow" is taken, Linda Pastan (born 1932) has received fellowships from the National Endowment for the Arts and from the Maryland Arts Council. She now lives in Potomac, Maryland.

Grudnow, in his native Poland, still lives for the grandfather and—through the grandfather—for the speaker.

# GRUDNOW

When he spoke of where he came from,
my grandfather could have been
clearing his throat
of that name, that town
sometimes Poland, sometimes Russia,                    5
the borders pencilled in
with a hand as shaky as his.
He left, I heard him say,
because there was nothing there.

I understood what he meant                             10
when I saw the photograph
of his people standing
against a landscape emptied
of crops and trees, scraped raw
by winter. Everything                                  15
was in sepia, as if the brown earth
had stained the faces,
stained even the air.

I would have died there, I think
in childhood maybe                                     20
of some fever,
my face pressed for warmth
against a cow with flanks
like those of the great aunts
in the picture. Or later                               25
I would have died of history
like the others, who dug

their stubborn heels into that earth,
heels as hard as the heels
of the bread my grandfather tore                       30
from the loaf at supper. He always
sipped his tea through a cube of sugar
clenched in his teeth, the way
he sipped his life here, noisily,
through all he remembered                              35
that might have been sweet in Grudnow.

## STUDY QUESTIONS

1. The sound of the name "Grudnow" is identified with the sound of the grandfa-ther's clearing his throat, and the frequently changing border between Russia and Poland is identified with the shaky drawing of his grandfather's hand. What other comparisons or analogies are there in this poem between the grandfather or traits or actions of the grandfather and Grudnow, Poland, the old country?

2. What does the SPEAKER say is likely to have been her fate had her grandfather not emigrated to the United States?

3. What does the last sentence suggest about how the grandfather spoke of his native land?

4. Compare the use of the photograph here with its use in Rhoda Schwartz's "Old Photographs" (chapter 2) or other poems in this collection.

# Maxine Hong Kingston

T*he Woman Warrior*, Maxine Hong Kingston's first book and the one from which "No Name Woman" is taken, won the National Book Critics Circle Award in 1976. Since then the California-born (born 1940) resident of Hawaii has published another volume, *China Men* (1980). Hers is a mixed genre or a new genre, neither fully fiction nor nonfiction, which indeterminacy pleases her, for she wants her work to be beyond or outside categories—including ethnic and feminist categories—and to be identified merely as "human."

To write about her aunt who fifty years ago committed suicide in China, the narrator has to unravel the complicated web of Chinese traditions and practices involving housing, emigration, sexual mores, marriage customs, dress, naming, storytelling, a whole way of life.

# NO NAME WOMAN

"You must not tell anyone," my mother said, "what I am about to tell you.   1
In China your father had a sister who killed herself. She jumped into the family well. We say that your father has all brothers because it is as if she had never been born.

"In 1924 just a few days after our village celebrated seventeen hurry-up weddings—to make sure that every young man who went 'out on the road' would responsibly come home—your father and his brothers and your grandfather and his brothers and your aunt's new husband sailed for America, the Gold Mountain. It was your grandfather's last trip. Those lucky enough to get contracts waved good-bye from the decks. They fed and guarded the stowaways and helped them off in Cuba, New York, Bali, Hawaii. 'We'll meet in California next year,' they said. All of them sent money home.

"I remember looking at your aunt one day when she and I were dressing; I had not noticed before that she had such a protruding melon of a stomach. But I did not think, 'She's pregnant,' until she began to look like other pregnant women, her shirt pulling and the white tops of her black pants showing. She could not have been pregnant, you see, because her husband had been gone for years. No one said anything. We did not discuss it. In early summer she was ready to have the child, long after the time when it could have been possible.

"The village had also been counting. On the night the baby was to be born the villagers raided our house. Some were crying. Like a great saw, teeth strung with lights, files of people walked zigzag across our land, tearing the rice. Their lanterns doubled in the disturbed black water, which drained away through the broken bunds. As the villagers closed in, we could see that some of them, probably men and women we knew well, wore white masks. The people with long hair hung it over their faces. Women with short hair made it stand up on end. Some had tied white bands around their foreheads, arms, and legs.

"At first they threw mud and rocks at the house. Then they threw eggs and began slaughtering our stock. We could hear the animals scream their deaths—the roosters, the pigs, a last great roar from the ox. Familiar wild heads flared in our night windows; the villagers encircled us. Some of the faces stopped to peer at us, their eyes rushing like searchlights. The hands flattened against the panes, framed heads, and left red prints.

"The villagers broke in the front and the back doors at the same time, even though we had not locked the doors against them. Their knives dripped with the blood of our animals. They smeared blood on the doors and walls. One woman swung a chicken, whose throat she had slit, splattering blood in red arcs about her. We stood together in the middle of the house, in the family hall with the pictures and tables of the ancestors around us, and looked straight ahead.

"At that time the house had only two wings. When the men came back, we would build two more to enclose our courtyard and a third one to begin a second courtyard. The villagers pushed through both wings, even your grandparents' rooms, to find your aunt's, which was also mine until the men returned. From this room a new wing for one of the younger families would grow. They ripped up her clothes and shoes and broke her combs, grinding them underfoot. They tore her work from the loom. They scattered the cooking fire and rolled the new weaving into it. We could hear them in the kitchen breaking our bowls and banging the pots. They overturned the great waist-high earthenware jugs; duck eggs, pickled fruits, vegetables burst out and mixed in acrid torrents. The old woman from the next field swept a broom through the air and loosed the spirits-of-the-broom over our heads. 'Pig.' 'Ghost.' 'Pig,' they sobbed and scolded while they ruined our house.

"When they left, they took sugar and oranges to bless themselves. They cut pieces from the dead animals. Some of them took bowls that were not broken and clothes that were not torn. Afterward we swept up the rice and sewed it back up into sacks. But the smells from the spilled preserves lasted. Your aunt gave birth in the pigsty that night. The next morning when I went for the water, I found her and the baby plugging up the family well.

"Don't let your father know that I told you. He denies her. Now that you have started to menstruate, what happened to her could happen to you. Don't humiliate us. You wouldn't like to be forgotten as if you had never been born. The villagers are watchful."

Whenever she had to warn us about life, my mother told stories that ran like this one, a story to grow up on. She tested our strength to establish realities. Those in the emigrant generations who could not reassert brute survival died young and far from home. Those of us in the first American generations have had to figure out how the invisible world the emigrants built around our childhoods fit in solid America.

The emigrants confused the gods by diverting their curses, misleading them with crooked streets and false names. They must try to confuse their offspring as well, who, I suppose, threaten them in similar ways—always trying to get things straight, always trying to name the unspeakable. The Chinese I know hide their names; sojourners take new names when their lives change and guard their real names with silence.

Chinese-Americans, when you try to understand what things in you are Chinese, how do you separate what is peculiar to childhood, to poverty, insanities, one family, your mother who marked your growing with stories, from what is Chinese? What is Chinese tradition and what is the movies?

If I want to learn what clothes my aunt wore, whether flashy or ordinary, I would have to begin, "Remember Father's drowned-in-the-well sister?" I cannot ask that. My mother has told me once and for all the useful parts. She will add nothing unless powered by Necessity, a riverbank that guides her life. She plants vegetable gardens rather than lawns; she carries the odd-shaped tomatoes home from the fields and eats food left for the gods.

Whenever we did frivolous things, we used up energy; we flew high kites. We children came up off the ground over the melting cones our parents brought home from work and the American movie on New Year's Day—*Oh, You Beautiful Doll* with Betty Grable one year, and *She Wore a Yellow Ribbon* with John Wayne another year. After the one carnival ride each, we paid in guilt; our tired father counted his change on the dark walk home.

Adultery is extravagance. Could people who hatch their own chicks and eat the embryos and the heads for delicacies and boil the feet in vinegar for party food, leaving only the gravel, eating even the gizzard lining—could such people engender a prodigal aunt? To be a woman, to have a daughter in starvation time was a waste enough. My aunt could not have been the lone romantic who gave up everything for sex. Women in the old China did not choose. Some man had commanded her to lie with him and be his secret evil. I wonder whether he masked himself when he joined the raid on the family.

Perhaps she encountered him in the fields or on the mountain where the daughters-in-law collected fuel. Or perhaps he first noticed her in the marketplace. He was not a stranger because the village housed no strangers. She had to have dealings with him other than sex. Perhaps he worked an adjoining field, or he sold her the cloth for the dress she sewed and wore. His demand must have surprised, then terrified her. She obeyed him; she always did as she was told. 16

When the family found a young man in the next village to be her husband, she stood tractably beside the best rooster, his proxy, and promised before they met that she would be his forever. She was lucky that he was her age and she would be the first wife, an advantage secure now. The night she first saw him, he had sex with her. Then he left for America. She had almost forgotten what he looked like. When she tried to envision him, she only saw the black and white face in the group photograph the men had had taken before leaving. 17

The other man was not, after all, much different from her husband. They both gave orders: she followed. "If you tell your family, I'll beat you. I'll kill you. Be here again next week." No one talked sex, ever. And she might have separated the rapes from the rest of living if only she did not have to buy her oil from him or gather wood in the same forest. I want her fear to have lasted just as long as rape lasted so that the fear could have been contained. No drawn-out fear. But women at sex hazarded birth and hence lifetimes. The fear did not stop but permeated everywhere. She told the man, "I think I'm pregnant." He organized the raid against her. 18

On nights when my mother and father talked about their life back home, sometimes they mentioned an "outcast table" whose business they still seemed to be settling, their voices tight. In a commensal tradition, where food is precious, the powerful older people made wrongdoers eat alone. Instead of letting them start separate new lives like the Japanese, who could become samurais and geishas, the Chinese family, faces averted but eyes glowering sideways, hung on to the offenders and fed them leftovers. My aunt must have lived in the same house as my parents and eaten at an outcast table. My mother spoke about the raid as if she had seen it, when she and my aunt, a daughter-in-law to a different household, should not have been living together at all. Daughters-in-law lived with their husbands' parents, not their own; a synonym for marriage in Chinese is "taking a daughter-in-law." Her husband's parents could have sold her, mortgaged her, stoned her. But they had sent her back to her own mother and father, a mysterious act hinting at 19 disgraces not told me. Perhaps they had thrown her out to deflect the avengers.

She was the only daughter; her four brothers went with her father, hus- 20
band, and uncles "out on the road" and for some years became western men.
When the goods were divided among the family, three of the brothers took
land, and the youngest, my father, chose an education. After my grandparents gave their daughter away to her husband's family, they had dispensed
all the adventure and all the property. They expected her alone to keep the
traditional ways, which her brothers, now among the barbarians, could fum-
ble without detection. The heavy, deep-rooted women were to maintain the
past against the flood, safe for returning. But the rare urge west had fixed
upon our family, and so my aunt crossed boundaries not delineated in space.

The work of preservation demands that the feelings playing about in 21
one's guts not be turned into action. Just watch their passing like cherry
blossoms. But perhaps my aunt, my forerunner, caught in a slow life, let
dreams grow and fade and after some months or years went toward what
persisted. Fear at the enormities of the forbidden kept her desires delicate,
wire and bone. She looked at a man because she liked the way the hair was
tucked behind his ears, or she liked the question-mark line of a long torso
curving at the shoulder and straight at the hip. For warm eyes or a soft voice
or a slow walk—that's all—a few hairs, a line, a brightness, a sound, a pace
she gave up family. She offered us up for a charm that vanished with tired-
ness, a pigtail that didn't toss when the wind died. Why, the wrong lighting
could erase the dearest thing about him.

It could very well have been, however, that my aunt did not take subtle 22
enjoyment of her friend, but, a wild woman, kept rollicking company. Imagining her free with sex doesn't fit, though. I don't know any woman like that,
or men either. Unless I see her life branching into mine, she gives me no
ancestral help.

To sustain her being in love, she often worked at herself in the mirror, 23
guessing at the colors and shapes that would interest him, changing them
frequently in order to hit on the right combination. She wanted him to look
back.

On a farm near the sea, a woman who tended her appearance reaped a 24
reputation for eccentricity. All the married women blunt-cut their hair in
flaps about their ears or pulled it back in tight buns. No nonsense. Neither
style blew easily into heart-catching tangles. And at their weddings they
displayed themselves in their long hair for the last time. "It brushed the backs
of my knees," my mother tells us. "It was braided, and even so, it brushed
the backs of my knees."

At the mirror my aunt combed individuality into her bob. A bun could 25
have been contrived to escape into black streamers blowing in the wind or in
quiet wisps about her face, but only the older women in our picture album
wear buns. She brushed her hair back from her forehead, tucking the flaps
behind her ears. She looped a piece of thread, knotted into a circle between
her index fingers and thumbs, and ran the double strand across her forehead.

When she closed her fingers as if she were making a pair of shadow geese bite, the string twisted together catching the little hairs. Then she pulled the thread away from her skin, ripping the hairs out neatly, her eyes watering from the needles of pain. Opening her fingers, she cleaned the thread, then rolled it along her hairline and the tops of her eyebrows. My mother did the same to me and my sisters and herself. I used to believe that the expression "caught by the short hairs" meant a captive held with a depilatory string. It especially hurt at the temples, but my mother said we were lucky we didn't have to have our feet bound when we were seven. Sisters used to sit on their beds and cry together, she said, as their mothers or their slaves removed the bandages for a few minutes each night and let the blood gush back into their veins. I hope that the man my aunt loved appreciated a smooth brow, that he wasn't just a tits-and-ass man.

Once my aunt found a freckle on her chin, at a spot that the almanac    26
said predestined her for unhappiness. She dug it out with a hot needle and washed the wound with peroxide.

More attention to her looks than these pulling of hairs and pickings at    27
spots would have caused gossip among the villagers. They owned work clothes and good clothes, and they wore good clothes for feasting the new seasons. But since a woman combing her hair hexes beginnings, my aunt rarely found an occasion to look her best. Women looked like great sea snails—the corded wood, babies, and laundry they carried were the whorls on their backs. The Chinese did not admire a bent back; goddesses and warriors stood straight. Still there must have been a marvelous freeing of beauty when a worker laid down her burden and stretched and arched.

Such commonplace loveliness, however, was not enough for my aunt.    28
She dreamed of a lover for the fifteen days of New Year's, the time for families to exchange visits, money, and food. She plied her secret comb. And sure enough she cursed the year, the family, the village, and herself.

Even as her hair lured her imminent lover, many other men looked at    29
her. Uncles, cousins, nephews, brothers would have looked, too, had they been home between journeys. Perhaps they had already been restraining their curiosity, and they left, fearful that their glances, like a field of nesting birds, might be startled and caught. Poverty hurt, and that was their first reason for leaving. But another, final reason for leaving the crowded house was the never-said.

She may have been unusually beloved, the precious only daughter, spoiled    30
and mirror gazing because of the affection the family lavished on her. When her husband left, they welcomed the chance to take her back from the in-laws; she could live like the little daughter for just a while longer. There are stories that my grandfather was different from other people, "crazy ever since the little Jap bayoneted him in the head." He used to put his naked penis on the dinner table, laughing. And one day he brought home a baby girl, wrapped up inside his brown western-style greatcoat. He had traded one of his sons, probably my father, the youngest, for her. My grandmother made him trade

back. When he finally got a daughter of his own, he doted on her. They must have all loved her, except perhaps my father, the only brother who never went back to China, having once been traded for a girl.

Brothers and sisters, newly men and women, had to efface their sexual color and present plain miens. Disturbing hair and eyes, a smile like no other threatened the ideal of five generations living under one roof. To focus blurs, people shouted face to face and yelled from room to room. The immigrants I know have loud voices, unmodulated to American tones even after years away from the village where they called their friendships out across the fields. I have not been able to stop my mother's screams in public libraries or over telephones. Walking erect (knees straight, toes pointed forward, not pigeon-toed, which is Chinese-feminine) and speaking in an inaudible voice, I have tried to turn myself American-feminine. Chinese communication was loud, public. Only sick people had to whisper. But at the dinner table, where the family members came nearest one another, no one could talk, not the outcasts nor any eaters. Every word that falls from the mouth is a coin lost. Silently they gave and accepted food with both hands. A preoccupied child who took his bowl with one hand got a sideways glare. A complete moment of total attention is due everyone alike. Children and lovers have no singularity here, but my aunt used a secret voice, a separate attentiveness.

She kept the man's name to herself throughout her labor and dying; she did not accuse him that he be punished with her. To save her inseminator's name she gave silent birth.

He may have been somebody in her own household, but intercourse with a man outside the family would have been no less abhorrent. All the village were kinsmen, and the titles shouted in loud country voices never let kinship be forgotten. Any man within visiting distance would have been neutralized as a lover—"brother," "younger brother," "older brother"—one hundred and fifteen relationship titles. Parents researched birth charts probably not so much to assure good fortune as to circumvent incest in a population that has but one hundred surnames. Everybody has eight million relatives. How useless then sexual mannerisms, how dangerous.

As it came from an atavism deeper than fear, I used to add "brother" silently to boys' names. It hexed the boys, who would or would not ask me to dance, and made them less scary and as familiar and deserving of benevolence as girls.

But, of course, I hexed myself also—no dates. I should have stood up, both arms waving, and shouted out across libraries, "Hey, you! Love me back." I had no idea, though, how to make attraction selective, how to control its direction and magnitude. If I made myself American-pretty so that the five or six Chinese boys in the class fell in love with me, everyone else—the Caucasian, Negro, and Japanese boys—would too. Sisterliness, dignified and honorable, made much more sense.

Attraction eludes control so stubbornly that whole societies designed to organize relationships among people cannot keep order, not even when they bind people to one another from childhood and raise them together. Among the very poor and the wealthy, brothers married their adopted sisters, like doves. Our family allowed some romance, paying adult brides' prices and providing dowries so that their sons and daughters could marry strangers. Marriage promises to turn strangers into friendly relatives—a nation of siblings.

In the village structure, spirits shimmered among the live creatures, bal-    37
anced and held in equilibrium by time and land. But one human being flaring up into violence could open up a black hole, a maelstrom that pulled in the sky. The frightened villagers, who depended on one another to maintain the real, went to my aunt to show her a personal, physical representation of the break she had made in the "roundness." Misallying couples snapped off the future, which was to be embodied in true offspring. The villagers punished her for acting as if she could have a private life, secret and apart from them.

If my aunt had betrayed the family at a time of large grain yields and    38
peace, when many boys were born, and wings were being built on many houses, perhaps she might have escaped such severe punishment. But the men—hungry, greedy, tired of planting in dry soil, cuckolded—had had to leave the village in order to send food-money home. There were ghost plagues, bandit plagues, wars with the Japanese, floods. My Chinese brother and sister had died of an unknown sickness. Adultery, perhaps only a mistake during good times, became a crime when the village needed food.

The round moon cakes and round doorways, the round tables of grad-    39
uated size that fit one roundness inside another, round windows and rice bowls—these talismen had lost their power to warn this family of the law: a family must be whole, faithfully keeping the descent line by having sons to feed the old and the dead, who in turn look after the family. The villagers came to show my aunt and her lover-in-hiding a broken house. The villagers were speeding up the circling of events because she was too shortsighted to see that her infidelity had already harmed the village, that waves of consequences would return unpredictably, sometimes in disguise, as now, to hurt her. This roundness had to be made coin-sized so that she would see its circumference: punish her at the birth of her baby. Awaken her to the inexorable. People who refused fatalism because they could invent small resources insisted on culpability. Deny accidents and wrest fault from the stars.

After the villagers left, their lanterns now scattering in various direc-    40
tions toward home, the family broke their silence and cursed her. "Aiaa, we're going to die. Death is coming. Death is coming. Look what you've done. You've killed us. Ghost! Dead ghost! Ghost! You've never been born." She ran out into the fields, far enough from the house so that she could no longer hear their voices, and pressed herself against the earth, her own land no more. When she felt the birth coming, she thought that she had been hurt. Her body seized together. "They've hurt me too much," she thought. "This is gall, and it will kill me." Her forehead and knees against the earth,

her body convulsed and then released her onto her back. The black well of sky and stars went out and out and out forever; her body and her complexity seemed to disappear. She was one of the stars, a bright dot in blackness, without home, without a companion, in eternal cold and silence. An agoraphobia rose in her, speeding higher and higher, bigger and bigger; she would not be able to contain it; there would be no end to fear.

Flayed, unprotected against space, she felt pain return, focusing her 41 body. This pain chilled her—a cold, steady kind of surface pain. Inside, spasmodically, the other pain, the pain of the child, heated her. For hours she lay on the ground, alternately body and space. Sometimes a vision of normal comfort obliterated reality: she saw the family in the evening gambling at the dinner table, the young people massaging their elders' backs. She saw them congratulating one another, high joy on the mornings the rice shoots came up. When these pictures burst, the stars drew yet further apart. Black space opened.

She got to her feet to fight better and remembered that old-fashioned 42 women gave birth in their pigsties to fool the jealous, pain-dealing gods, who do not snatch piglets. Before the next spasms could stop her, she ran to the pigsty, each step a rushing out into emptiness. She climbed over the fence and knelt in the dirt. It was good to have a fence enclosing her, a tribal person alone.

Laboring, this woman who had carried her child as a foreign growth 43 that sickened her every day, expelled it at last. She reached down to touch the hot, wet, moving mass, surely smaller than anything human, and could feel that it was human after all—fingers, toes, nails, nose. She pulled it up on to her belly, and it lay curled there, butt in the air, feet precisely tucked one under the other. She opened her loose shirt and buttoned the child inside. After resting, it squirmed and thrashed and she pushed it up to her breast. It turned its head this way and that until it found her nipple. There, it made little snuffling noises. She clenched her teeth at its preciousness, lovely as a young calf, a piglet, a little dog.

She may have gone to the pigsty as a last act of responsibility: she would 44 protect this child as she had protected its father. It would look after her soul, leaving supplies on her grave. But how would this tiny child without family find her grave when there would be no marker for her anywhere, neither in the earth nor the family hall? No one would give her a family hall name. She had taken the child with her into the wastes. At its birth the two of them had felt the same raw pain of separation, a wound that only the family pressing tight could close. A child with no descent line would not soften her life but only trail after her, ghostlike, begging her to give it purpose. At dawn the villagers on their way to the fields would stand around the fence and look.

Full of milk, the little ghost slept. When it awoke, she hardened her 45 breasts against the milk that crying loosens. Toward morning she picked up the baby and walked to the well.

Carrying the baby to the well shows loving. Otherwise abandon it. Turn 46 its face into the mud. Mothers who love their children take them along. It was probably a girl; there is some hope of forgiveness for boys.

"Don't tell anyone you had an aunt. Your father does not want to hear her name. She has never been born." I have believed that sex was unspeakable and words so strong and fathers so frail that "aunt" would do my father mysterious harm. I have thought that my family, having settled among immigrants who had also been their neighbors in the ancestral land, needed to clean their name, and a wrong word would incite the kinspeople even here. But there is more to this silence: they want me to participate in her punishment. And I have. 47

In the twenty years since I heard this story I have not asked for details nor said my aunt's name; I do not know it. People who can comfort the dead can also chase after them to hurt them further—a reverse ancestor worship. The real punishment was not the raid swiftly inflicted by the villagers, but the family's deliberately forgetting her. Her betrayal so maddened them, they saw to it that she would suffer forever, even after death. Always hungry, always needing, she would have to beg food from other ghosts, snatch and steal it from those whose living descendants give them gifts. She would have to fight the ghosts massed at crossroads for the buns a few thoughtful citizens leave to decoy her away from village and home so that the ancestral spirits could feast unharassed. At peace, they could act like gods, not ghosts, their descent lines providing them with paper suits and dresses, spirit money, paper houses, paper automobiles, chicken, meat, and rice into eternity—essences delivered up in smoke and flames, steam and incense rising from each rice bowl. In an attempt to make the Chinese care for people outside the family, Chairman Mao encourages us now to give our paper replicas to the spirits of outstanding soldiers and workers, no matter whose ancestors they may be. My aunt remains forever hungry. Goods are not distributed evenly among the dead. 48

My aunt haunts me—her ghost drawn to me because now, after fifty years of neglect, I alone devote pages of paper to her, though not origamied into houses and clothes. I do not think she always means me well. I am telling on her, and she was a spite suicide, drowning herself in the drinking water. The Chinese are always very frightened of the drowned one, whose weeping ghost, wet hair hanging and skin bloated, waits silently by the water to pull down a substitute. 49

# STUDY QUESTIONS

1. Paragraphs 4 through 9 describe in detail the attack on the NARRATOR's grandparents' home. What is the tone of that description? Where are your sympathies at this point?

2. What is "the invisible world the emigrants built around our childhoods" (par. 10)? How is it related to the story of the sacking of the house?

3. What is the purpose of the emigrants' using false names, living on crooked streets, trying to confuse their children (par. 11)?

4. Why does the narrator find it difficult to find out what is the Chinese tradition?

5. What does it mean that the narrator's mother is "powered by Necessity" (par. 13)? What does that have to do with the way she tells stories? with the "prodigal aunt"? with the way her Chinese people eat chicken?

6. How were young women married in China? What was the "outcast table" (par. 19)? How did the moral standards for young men and women differ?

7. How did Chinese women get a smooth brow? What did the narrator's aunt do when she found a freckle on her chin? What does the narrator imagine her aunt's position in the family might have been before her "fall"?

8. How did the narrator's grandfather get the little girl baby he brought back inside his raincoat one day (par. 30)? How did he feel about his daughter (the narrator's aunt) when she was a little girl and while she was growing up?

9. What effect did the housing arrangement—"five generations living under one roof" (par. 31)—have on the way young people dressed, fixed their hair, looked at each other, spoke? What is the effect on mores of everybody having "eight million relatives" (par. 33)?

10. How did the Chinese villages attempt to control sexual relationships? What were the economic and social conditions among the Chinese at the time the aunt "fell"? How did the living arrangements, the sexual taboos, and the contemporary conditions contribute to the fierceness of the attack on the narrator's aunt? How did the family treat her after the raid?

11. Why did the aunt go to the pigsty to give birth?

12. Why does the narrator feel that she has participated in her aunt's punishment? What was the aunt's "real punishment"?

13. What paper offerings are given to the dead? What paper offering does the narrator give her dead aunt?

# Peter Blue Cloud

Peter Blue Cloud/Aroniawenrate, born in 1927 on Caughnawaga Reservation, Quebec, is a Mohawk, a member of the Turtle clan, and an ironworker turned poet and editor. He has published several volumes of poetry, including *Coyote and*

*Friends* (1976), *Turtle, Bear & Wolf* (1976), *Back Then Tomorrow* (1978), *White Corn Sister* (1979), and *Elderberry Flute Song* (1982).

Planting time brings back memories of the departed, the speaker's old herb-doctor aunt, who could make medicine and foresee when she herself would die, and who was a good companion for the speaker when he was a little boy.

# TO-TA TI-OM
# (FOR AN AUNT)

my aunt was an herb doctor, one-eyed with crooked yellow teeth
    the Christians called her pagan witch
    and their children taunted her
    or ran in fear of their bible lives
      at her approach,        5
her house of barn lumber leaned into the wind as if toppling
    in winter it grew squat with snow
    and bright sparks from the wood stove
    hissed the snowflakes into steam
      icing the roof,        10
"when my body dies it will be in winter just in time to see the spring"
    she told this while rolling leaves
    to powder between her boney hands
    for her duty as a medicine person
      was to cure,        15
in early summer grandfather and i would begin planting
    the corn and beans and squash
    just behind my aunt's house
    and she'd hobble over to help
      plant the tobacco,        20
as the first green shoots emerged into sunlight
    she would sit on the steps
    grating dried roots into a bowl
    stopping every so often to gaze
      at the garden,        25
when the time of tobacco curing came she'd be there
    feeling and smelling and tasting
    and every season she would approve
    then later sit by the woodstove
      smoking her pipe,        30
"Come," she would say to me, "the time for onanoron is here,"
    and she would walk to the pond

```
        and she would point out strong plants
        for me to wade to and slowly pull
            those medicine roots,                               35
we strung the roots of twisted brown above the woodstove
        to preserve their sacred power
        to be released as needed
        by those who had need
            of such strength,                                   40
tiny bundles were made of the roots with bits of string
        then she named the persons
        i was to take onanoron to
        and tied all in a blue bandana
            and said, "go,"                                     45
this is for Kaienwaktatse and this for Kaerine
        Lives Close to Town
        and She Bends the Boughs
        a penny or two and bread and jam
            I shyly ate,                                        50
the pennies slowly filled the glass jar on the table
        until my aunt went to the store
        a block of salt pork one finger square
        a nutmeg, salt and four candies
            just for me,                                        55
sitting there by the woodstove I would steal a glance
        at her tired wrinkled face
        and I'd want to shout loud
        feeling a tightening in my throat
            and maybe cry,                                      60
"she was sitting at her table with a bowl in her lap
        and it was just turning Spring,"
        my grandfather wrote this to me
        and i went somewhere to be alone
            and just sat,                                       65
it's planting time again and all done except tobacco
        grandfather's leaning on the hoe
        and looking at my aunt's house
        then he smiles and I smile back
            lonely, like crying.                                70
```

# STUDY QUESTIONS

1. How does the SPEAKER's aunt make her living?

2. When is it that he particularly misses her? Why?

# Michael Ondaatje

B orn in Sri Lanka (then called Ceylon) in 1943 to a family of mixed Dutch, Sin-
halese, and Tamil ancestry, Michael Ondaatje left at the age of eleven, settling
in Canada in 1962. He now teaches at Glendon College of York University in Toronto.
He is the author of several books, including *The Collected Works of Billy the Kid* (1970),
*Coming Through Slaughter* (1976), and the autobiographical *Running in the Family* (1982).
His books have twice won the Governor General's Award. *There's a Trick with a Knife
I'm Learning to Do: Poems 1963–78*, from which "Light" is taken, was published in
1979.

Old photographs trigger memories of this most crazy, exotic family.

## LIGHT

*for Doris Gratiaen*

Midnight storm. Trees walking off across the fields in fury
naked in the spark of lightning.
I sit on the white porch on the brown hanging cane chair
coffee in my hand midnight storm midsummer night.
The past, friends and family, drift into the rain shower.      5
Those relatives in my favourite slides
re-shot from old minute photographs so they now stand
complex ambiguous grainy on my wall.

This is my Uncle who turned up to his marriage
on an elephant. He was a chaplain.      10
This shy looking man in the light jacket and tie was infamous,
when he went drinking he took the long blonde beautiful hair
of his wife and put one end in the cupboard and locked it
leaving her tethered in an armchair.
He was terrified of her possible adultery      15
and this way died peaceful happy to the end.
My Grandmother, who went to a dance in a muslin dress
with fireflies captured and embedded in the cloth, shining

and witty. This calm beautiful face
organised wild acts in the tropics.                                    20
She hid the mailman in her house
after he had committed murder and at the trial
was thrown out of the court for making jokes at the judge.
Her son became a Q.C.[1]
This is my brother at 6. With his cousin and his sister               25
and Pam de Voss who fell on a pen-knife and lost her eye.
My Aunt Christie. She knew Harold MacMillan[2] was a spy
communicating with her through pictures in the newspapers.
Every picture she believed asked her to forgive him,
his hound eyes pleading.                                              30
Her husband Uncle Fitzroy a doctor in Ceylon had a memory
sharp as scalpels into his 80's
though I never bothered to ask him about anything
—interested then more in the latest recordings of Bobby Darin.

And this is my Mother with her brother Noel in fancy dress.           35
They are 7 and 8 years old, a hand-coloured photograph,
it is the earliest picture I have. The one I love most.
A picture of my kids at Halloween
has the same contact and laughter.
My Uncle dying at 68, and my Mother a year later dying at 68.         40
She told me about his death and the day he died
his eyes clearing out of illness as if seeing
right through the room the hospital and she said
he saw something so clear and good his whole body
for a moment became youthful and she remembered               45
when she sewed badges on his trackshirts.
Her voice joyous in telling me this, her face light and clear.
(My firefly Grandmother also dying at 68.)

These are the fragments I have of them, tonight
in this storm, the dogs restless on the porch.                       50
They were all laughing, crazy, and vivid in their prime.
At a party my drunk Father
tried to explain a complex operation on chickens
and managed to kill them all in the process, the guests
having dinner an hour later while my Father slept                    55
and the kids watched the servants clean up the litter
of beaks and feathers on the lawn.

1. Queen's Counsel; a lawyer selected to serve the British crown.
2. British prime minister 1957–1963.

These are their fragments, all I remember,
wanting more knowledge of them. In the mirror and in my kids
I see them in my flesh. Wherever we are                                          60
they parade in my brain and the expanding stories
connect to the grey grainy pictures on the wall,
as they hold their drinks or 20 years later
hold grandchildren, pose with favourite dogs,
coming through the light, the electricity, which the storm              65
destroyed an hour ago, a tree going down by the highway
so that now inside the kids play dominoes by candlelight
and out here the thick rain static the spark of my match
                                                  to a cigarette
and the trees across the fields leaving me, distinct                          70
lonely in their own knife scars and cow-chewed bark
frozen in the jagged light as if snapped in their run
the branch arms waving to what was a second ago the dark sky
when in truth like me they haven't moved.
Haven't moved an inch from me.                                                       75

# STUDY QUESTIONS

1. How does the SETTING contribute to the poem? What has the SPEAKER done to preserve and improve his old photographs? What does that suggest about his attitude toward and feelings about his family, the subjects of the photographs? Why are they "complex ambiguous grainy on my wall" (line 8)?

2. What is the relationship between outward appearance and behavior in Uncle and Grandmother (ll. 9–24)?

3. What relationship is there between moral conventions and actions, actions and happiness, contentment and acceptability? What seems to be the attitude of the speaker toward his relations? What is the TONE of the poem?

4. What picture does the speaker like best? Why? What does the picture of the speaker's children suggest about their heritage?

5. How does his father fit into this weird family?

# William Saroyan

Author of stories—his first collection, *The Daring Young Man on the Flying Trapeze*, was published in 1934; plays—*The Time of Your Life* won the Pulitzer Prize in 1939, though he refused the award on principle (he did not believe in literary "prizes"); and novels—the best known of which is *The Human Comedy* (1943); William Saroyan (1908–81) was born in Fresno, California. His belief in the basic goodness of man, his positive pictures of the innocence of the poor, popular in the socially conscious 1930s and early 1940s, seemed untenable in the darker days of World War II and the Cold War that followed, but there are recent signs of a revival of interest in Saroyan's works.

Whether you will learn how to live with a snake may be open to question, but if you read closely and with interest, as you surely will, you will learn how to tell a story, and perhaps a little bit about stories and heritage.

## NAJARI LEVON'S OLD COUNTRY ADVICE TO THE YOUNG AMERICANS ON HOW TO LIVE WITH A SNAKE

Najari Levon went to Aram's house on Van Ness Avenue for some legal advice about a private matter, but Aram hadn't come home yet, so the old man with the gargoyle face was asked to make himself at home somewhere. 1

He saw Aram's two small sons and two small daughters on the linoleum floor of a glassed-in porch, playing a board game and keeping score on a small pad with a small pencil, and so he went there and sat down to watch. 2

A metal arrow at the center of the large board was spun, and if it stopped in the space where there was a picture of a bright star, for instance, the player was given ten points, but just beside the picture of the star, there was a space in which there was a picture of a small green snake, and if the needle stopped there, ten points were taken away from the player's score. 3

The scorekeeper was Aram's firstborn, a boy of ten or eleven. 4

"Star," Aram's secondborn, a daughter, said, but the scorekeeper told his sister the needle was on the *line*, and *nearer* to the snake than to the star. 5

"Snake," he said, picking up the small pencil to put the score on the 6

pad. His sister knocked the pad and pencil out of his hand, saying, "Star."
And they began to fight.

Najari Levon said in Armenian, "In our house in Bitlis lived a very large 7
black snake, which was our family snake."

The fighters stopped to listen, and he said. "No proper family was with- 8
out its proper snake. A house was not complete without a snake, because the
long snake crawling back of the walls held the house together."

The fighters relaxed, and he said, "Our snake had great wisdom. It was 9
the oldest house snake in Bitlis."

The scorekeeper sprawled belly down on the floor, not far from the 10
corner of the room where the small pencil had fallen during the fight.

"Did you *see* the snake?" he said. 11

The storyteller glanced at the small green pencil and then at the boy, 12
and he said, "Yes, I saw the snake. His door into the house was at the top of
the stone wall in the room where I slept, a door just big enough for the snake
to pass through, about the size of a saucer. In the evening as soon as I got
into my bed, I looked up at the snake's door, and there I would see him
looking down at me."

"*How much* of him would you see?" 13

"Only the head, because it was nighttime now, and he would soon go 14
to sleep, too."

"Did you ever see *all* of him?" 15

"Oh, yes." 16

"How big was he?" 17

"As big around as a saucer, with a very sensitive face, very large eyes— 18
not the little eyes of English people, but the large eyes of Armenian people.
And Kurdish people. And a very thoughtful mouth, like the mouth of John
D. Rockefeller, but of course with a different kind of tongue, although I can't
be sure of this, because I have seen in a newspaper only a picture of John D.
Rockefeller, but not a picture of his tongue."

"Did you see the snake's tongue?" 19

"Many times, in and out, like words, but of course in his own language, 20
not ours."

"How long was he?" 21

"Ten times the length of a walking stick. He was not small." 22

"What would he do back there?" 23

"He lived there. His house was on that side of the stone wall, our house 24
was on our side. But of course there was no such thing as his and ours. The
whole house was ours and the whole house was his, but he *lived* back of the
wall. In the wintertime I would not see him, and I would almost forget he
was there. And then one evening in the springtime I would look up at his
door, and there he would be again. He would speak, but I would say, 'Not
now, because it's night and time to sleep, but in the morning come down and
I will bring you something to eat.' So in the morning . . ."

"What did he eat?"                                                                                       25

"Milk. In the morning I filled a bowl with milk—not one of those little   26
bowls soup is served in for a small man, but one of those large bowls for a
large man. My mother asked where I was taking the bowl of milk, and I said,
'Mama, I am taking the bowl of milk to the snake.' Everybody in our family,
every man, every woman, and every child comes to my room to see the
snake, because to have a snake in a house is baracat.[1] Everybody stands in
the room and waits to see the snake. Thirty-three men, women, and children, instead of thirty-four, because during the winter my grandfather Setrak
died."

"Did the snake come out?" the boy sprawled on the floor said.              27

"I took the bowl of milk, and put it in the corner straight across from    28
the snake's door so that all of the snake would be able to come out of the
door, down the wall, and across the floor. And then the thirty-three of us
would be able to see *all* of the snake, from the head with the mouth like John
D. Rockefeller's mouth, and with the eyes that are not the little eyes of English
people, but the large eyes of Armenian people, and Kurdish people. I put
the bowl down and look up at the snake's door, but the snake is not there, so
I speak to the snake, I say to him, 'Sevavor, I have put the bowl of milk on
the floor in the corner of the room, so come out of your door and down the
wall and across the floor and have something to eat; it is no longer wintertime, it is springtime.' "

"Did he come down?"                                                         29

"The snake came to the door to see who it was who was speaking to          30
him, he came to see, he came to see who it was, was it me or was it somebody
else, so when he came to see, I said, 'Don't worry, Sevavor, it is me, Levon,
your friend. I am the one who is speaking, Najari Levon.' The snake looked
at me, and then he looked at each of the others in the room, but he did not
come down, the snake did not come down because we had been thirty-four
and now were thirty-three, so the snake did not come down. I said, 'Sevavor,
in the wintertime my grandfather Setrak died—that is why we are no longer
thirty-four, we are now only thirty-three, but two of the wives are pregnant
and in August we will be more than thirty-four, we will be thirty-five, and
if one of the wives has twins, we will be thirty-six, and if both of the wives
have twins, we will be thirty-seven, the Najari people will be thirty-seven,
Sevavor, so come out of the door, and down the wall, and across the floor to
the bowl of milk in the corner.' "

"Did he?"                                                                   31

"Very slowly, like this, like my arm, the snake came out of the door,      32
slowly, down the wall, like this, one walking-stick length of the black body
like this, slowly, down the wall, two walking-stick lengths, very hungry,
very old, very wise, three walking-stick lengths, very black, four lengths,

---

1. "Baracat" is "good fortune" in Arabic. [Author's note]

five lengths, six lengths, and now the snake's head is on the floor like this, but his tail is still behind the wall, and all of the Najari people are watching and waiting, and slowly the snake pushes himself forward on the floor a little nearer to the bowl of milk in the corner, seven lengths out of the door, seven lengths down the wall, eight lengths, nine lengths, and now all thirty-three of the Najari people are almost not breathing, to see better the Najari snake, the snake of the Najari people, from the head to the tail, and now there is only one more length. As soon as the snake moves one more length toward the bowl of milk in the corner, every man, woman, and child in the room will see *all* of the snake of our house, of our family, of the Najari people. But the snake stops. With only one more length to go the black snake moving to the white bowl of milk in the corner stops.

"Why?" the boy said, and the storyteller said, "An old snake who does [33] not see an old man in the springtime because the old man is dead, an old snake who does not see an old man he saw in the summertime, because in the wintertime the old man died, an old snake stops to think about a thing like that. I said, 'Sevavor, do not be unhappy about my grandfather Setrak who died in the cold of wintertime; it is good for an old man to go to sleep in the snow, it is good for him to go home; if nobody went to sleep, if nobody went home, the house would soon be crowded and there would not be food enough for everybody. Do not be sorry for the old man, he is asleep, he has gone home, go and have the milk I have put in the bowl for you.' "

"Did he go?" [34]

"The snake did not move, the black snake with his head and two walk- [35] ing-stick lengths on the floor, and seven lengths up the wall, and one length behind the wall, did not move, because when my grandfather Setrak was born the snake saw him, and every year of Setrak's life the snake saw him, but now the old man was dead, and the snake was on his way to the bowl of milk in the corner, but the snake did not want to move any more and all of the Najari people did not want to breathe. I said, 'Sevavor, do not worry about the old man, he is home, he is asleep, he is a small boy again running in the meadows, go and have your milk.' And then the snake, slowly, like a big black snake with eyes not like the little eyes of English people . . .'"

"Yes, Yes," the boy said. "Don't stop." [36]

The old storyteller glanced at the small stub of green pencil on the floor, [37] and then back at the boy, directly this time, scaring him a little, and then in English he said, "Dat your pancil?"

At that moment Aram came in and said, "What is it, Levon?" [38]

The old man got up and chuckled deeply in the manner for which he [39] was famous all over Fresno, and he said, "Aram Sevavor, I came for advice about a private matter. I came all the way from my house on L Street to your house on Van Ness Avenue, past the place where they have those red fire engines, all the way up Eye Street, where the police have their building, all the way up Forthcamp Avenue, I came, Aram Sevavor, one foot after the other, from my house to your house, I came, and now I go, I go all the way back, Aram Sevavor, because I can't remember the question I came to ask."

He went out the back, and down the alley, and the boy with the green 40
pencil stood in the alley and watched him go, taking with him forever the
end of the story about the snake.

# STUDY QUESTIONS

1. "Snake" is mentioned in the title. Where does the first reference to a snake appear in the story? How does it lead (or mislead) your expectations of how a snake will figure in the story?

2. Why does Levon tell the story of the snake? What is its immediate effect upon the children? What sort of questions does the boy "scorekeeper" ask? Do these questions imply a certain amount of skepticism about the story? What skeptical or challenging questions does the boy *not* ask?

3. Why, according to Levon, does the snake, at one point, not come down to get his milk? How does Levon convince him to come down? Why, according to Levon, does the snake stop with only one length of a walking stick yet to go?

4. Describe the actions that Levon is demonstrating when he says "like this . . . like this" (paragraph 32).

5. What is the effect of the repetitions in the story? In paragraph 35, Levon begins to repeat again, "with eyes not like the little eyes of English people . . . ," but he is interrupted by the boy. What seems to have been the effect of the repetition on the boy? Why does he not want to hear it now?

6. In paragraph 37, Levon says, *in English*, "Dat your pancil?" This suggests, of course, that until now he has been speaking in Armenian. Compare the language of the story with the language in paragraph 39, when he tells Aram Sevavor that he forgot what he came for, a passage that also must have been spoken in Armenian. Compare the broken English to the language of the story. Can you see "foreign" elements in it—rhythms, for example? What does the contrast in language suggest about language and heritage?

   Look back at the title. Notice "Advice to the Young *Americans*." What is Levon's "advice"? How should one live with a snake? What does it seem to suggest about old country and American ways? In what sense is Levon passing on a "heritage"?

# TONE

"In Macon, Georgia, my grandmother, Mariah Palmer, was a famous teacher. She took up this career after her husband died during the Depression, leaving her with three small children to look after." So Pam Durban begins her story "All Set About with Fever Trees." We could call such a TONE "flat," or "matter-of-fact," or some such term.

Passages in which the meaning is almost inseparable from the feeling or tone are not all the same. Even those that seem "straightforward" are not always also "flat." The following straightforward passage in the mouth of the NARRATOR of Alice Walker's "Everyday Use," for example, seems stronger than flat, something like "forthright" or "forceful," "neutral" or "objective":

> In the winter I wear flannel nightgowns to bed and overalls during the day. I can kill and clean a hog as mercilessly as a man. My fat keeps me hot in zero weather. I can work outside all day, breaking ice to get water for washing; I can eat pork liver cooked over the open fire minutes after it comes steaming from the hog. One winter I knocked a bull calf straight in the brain between the eyes with a sledge hammer and had the meat hung up to chill before nightfall. (Paragraph 5)

Some might hear pride in this rather than straightforward forcefulness, others bragging, still others exaggeration (though I wouldn't want to be the one who tells this narrator she's lying).

Tone is almost inseparable from the literal MEANING in most cases, but tone can modify meaning—in this case by questioning whether these forcefully direct statements may not be exaggerations. Tone is to some extent a matter of interpretation. Different readers may interpret the same line, passage, or work differently, just as different actors may interpret the same part differently. We have some latitude in exploring or defining the tone of a passage, but we cannot make things mean just any old thing we choose for them to mean. There are guidelines and limits set by the definitions of words, the grammar and syntax of the English language, and the social and historical CONTEXT. These controls rule out of order the more fanciful or eccentric readings.

Words, then, do not always "speak" for themselves. We must be aware in reading that there may be overtones or undertones that could modulate the literal statement of the words we are reading. If we want to read the words of a text aloud (or speak them silently in the theater of our minds as we read silently), we are often faced with choices. In the first and last sentences of the opening stanza of Countee Cullen's poem "Heritage," the SPEAKER asks "What is Africa to me?" How do you read that? As a straightforward question whose answer may be discovered in the course of the poem? As if the answer were "not much"? Or as if the answer were "everything"? The speaker himself seems pulled in opposite directions, toward Africa and toward America, Western culture, Christianity. You will be able to identify the tone when you decide on the meaning, and you will be able to pin down its meaning when you can identify its tone.

It is not only questions whose meanings or implications depend on whether you let the literal statements stand or see them modified by tone. How literally, for example, do you read the last lines of this same poem:

> One thing only must I do:
> Quench my pride and cool my blood,
> Lest I perish in the flood.
> . . . . . . . . . . . .
> Not yet has my heart or head
> In the least way realized
> They and I are civilized.

Is "civilized" said with contempt? Is it IRONIC—is there a discrepancy between the intended meaning and the dictionary definition of the word? Or does he really mean that he is struggling to overcome his African heritage, which he thinks of as "savage," and become more Westernized, American, Christian, "civilized"?

The same kind of ambivalence in situation and detail challenges the reader to "listen" carefully for the appropriate tone in the last lines of Linda Hogan's "Heritage": "From my family I have learned the secrets / of never having a home." Is that a proud statement or a bitter one?

Tone is not always difficult to determine. Sometimes the language of a work will suddenly change. It is as if you are listening to one voice when suddenly another, distinctly different voice takes its place, almost as if a passage should be in quotation marks, though there is no punctuation to guide us. In the very first paragraph of the Pam Durban story, for example, after we are told in two somewhat flat-toned sentences that the narrator's grandmother was a famous teacher in her community and how it was that she came to teach school, we get further details of her career: "From that time on, she taught English in the Bibb County schools and Sunday school at the First Presbyterian Church. Later, when the wine of her understanding had clarified and aged to her satisfaction, she taught the Bible at the YWCA." The beginning of the second sentence here seems to be in a different register from both what has gone before and what comes right after. When, three paragraphs later, we hear the grandmother say, " 'As it happens, I have heard the clear call down deep in my soul and it is summoning me to labor in the fields far from the fleshpots of civilization,' " we know whose voice it was we heard. The function of tone in that second sentence, then, is not to modulate its meaning or even to reinforce its meaning so much as it is to deny those words the narrator's authority. Without shifting FOCUS or "officially" shifting VOICE through quotation marks or similar devices, we can hear the tone of the narrative voice change.

Tone is a transaction between the author and reader through the language of the text. Though we cannot always be sure that the author intended the particular tone and thus the modulation of literal statement that we hear, this does not mean that we must take everything at face value, literally, and ignore the possible qualifications created by tone. Nor does it mean that we can unilaterally determine the tone. The tone, like the meanings of words, is largely determined by common sense and context, both the context within the work and the context of history, tradition, and the larger world reflected or suggested in the text.

The exaggeration that we thought we saw in "Everyday Use" is unquestionably there in Agha Shahid Ali's "Snowmen." His ancestor's skeleton, the speaker tells us, "carved from glaciers, his breath / arctic, / he froze women in his embrace" (lines 8–10). The purpose of the *overstatement* or HYPERBOLE, the words saying more than they could literally mean, is here not intended to mock the speaker or the ancestor but to magnify him. When hyperbole is used to mock a subject or a work by treating common or "low" things in high-flown, lofty language, it is called PARODY. UNDERSTATEMENT, as its name implies, says less than is meant, portrays something as lesser than it is or seems to be, as when Alberto Ríos says, "Mi abuelo is an ordinary man" (l. 37), though we have heard enough about him earlier in the poem "Mi Abuelo" to know that this is an underevaluation. Under- and overstatement are actually variants of the most familiar of the devices whereby the literal statement of a word, phrase, passage, or work is modified by tone: IRONY, which is usually thought of as a tone that suggests that the word or phrase or passage "really" means the opposite of what it seems to say. Irony's modulation need not be to suggest the exact opposite; it can be oblique, deviating from the sense indirectly rather than directly. When it is simple, snide, and polarly opposed to the literal, it becomes SARCASM: in "Everyday Use," when Dee stood watching her house burn down and her mother carrying her badly burned sister, the speaker says she wanted to ask her, "Why don't you do a dance around the ashes?" (par. 10).

Tone, then, is a part of the meaningful structure of a work, which— through sounds, syntax, context—reinforces, modifies, or even, at times, reverses what seems to be the literal meaning of any verbal passage, from a word to a work. It is thus part of the total meaning of a work, but, equally important, it is part of the emotional effect and effectiveness of literature.

# WRITING
# ABOUT THE READING

## PERSONAL ESSAYS AND NARRATIVES

1. Construct a family tree. Go as far as you can yourself, and then consult the oldest living relative on either side of your family. Ask about the characters of your forebears, strange or interesting incidents in their lives, ethnic or national backgrounds. Any surprises? interesting new information?

   With this as a base, write a tribute to one or more of your forebears. Note that in several of the pieces the subject is not perfect—Miyasaki's obāchan, for example, seems a little narrow, old-fashioned, rigid; "mi abuelo" is "at best" an ordinary man—yet the portraits of them are touching, even loving.

   Your essay may be a general character sketch, like "Obāchan," or stress a single revealing incident or series of incidents, like "All Set About with Fever Trees."

2. If you chose to honor or depict a forebear in one or a series of incidents, you could write a narrative. You might even want to embellish it a bit with a few made-up incidents or responses of your own. If you want to be true to your understanding of the CHARACTER, make sure you invent episodes or details that are consistent with what you believe to be true of the person.

3. Look through a family album for the oldest family photographs you can find, preferably those of grandparents, great-grandparents, or other forebears who lived in a different country, region, or environment from yours. Try to reconstruct something of their lives and what it meant for them and you to have moved from their / your "roots" to where you live now.

## IMITATIONS AND PARODIES

1. Change the point of view in one of the poems or stories and write a new version. How would Annie's mother view the people depicted in "All Set About with Fever Trees"? How might Yvonne Sapia's Caribbean Indian grandmother describe her son? How about telling the story of "Everyday Use" from the point of view of Dee / Wangero or Hakim-a-barber?

2. Write a conversation with a grandparent in the grave, in PARODY of Ríos's poem. Or imitate Agha's poem; you may inherit some attribute from ancestors other than snow and ice—from "Flabmen," for example.

3. Finish Najari Levon's story of the snake in the style of the existing narrative. In a separate paragraph, or in two, discuss the difference in MEANING between the unfinished tale and your completed one.

## ANALYTICAL PROSE

1. What do you think of as your own "heritage"? Do you identify with one particular branch of your family tree? Do you think of yourself as "American" through and through—without any sense of roots or even tentacles entangled with another culture? Or are you so "hybrid" that you feel you almost define what it is to be American by the diversity of your heritage?

2. Write a descriptive or analytical essay about your family tree, or an essay called "Heritage," or an analysis of your own character as you understand it in terms of heredity, deducing the heredity factors from what you know of your forebears.

## ARGUMENTATIVE PAPERS

1. Young people should cherish the values and traditions of their cultural traditions.

2. Young people should be free to ignore old values and old traditions in building a new society.

## RESEARCH PAPER

What *is* the ethnic mix of America? How many first-generation immigrants are there in the United States? Canada? Of those who have been in America since World War I or earlier, what percentage have "pure" ethnic family lines?

What studies have been made of cultural heritage? What characteristics, other than physical, seem to be heredity? What studies have there been on cultural or vocational choices by adopted children whose parentage is known?

# 4

# TRIBE

Beyond home, family, and ancestry, loyalties of a somewhat larger kind affect our daily lives and habits almost as strongly. These loyalties have to do with groups we belong to by birth and tradition though not necessarily by direct blood lines—ethnic groups, nationalities, groups bonded by common languages and customs—and they may be powerful, involving strong emotional ties to customs and traditions treasured by large communities of people and passed down from generation to generation. Such loyalties to "tribe"—to a group with whom we share traditions and values and with whom we are likely to share a strong sense of the past—have different names among different peoples, but for most of us our personal relationship to "our own people" is likely to have shaped firmly our individual sense of self.

Some of us like to think of ourselves as tradition-free, unaffected by the place of our "tribe's" origins and the customs that over the years have provided our people a sense of definition, identity, and stability. We may cast our lot with the future and try to free ourselves from the powers of the past, rebelling against—or just ignoring—the insistences of tribe. Others of us are intensely loyal to our tribe and make every conscious effort to carry on habits, customs, rituals, beliefs, and myths because we like continuity and believe in the past and its power to shape the present and future. We may feel our character to have been molded, perhaps irrevocably, by our tribal (as well as our parental and ancestral) origins. If we take pride in the places of our origin and the characteristic habits of the people who reared and nurtured us, there is something quite wonderful in the power of the past and the distinctiveness of tribal identity.

Perhaps most of us are caught in between, respectful of values of the past associated with our national and ethnic heritage but anxious as well to establish individual identities that break with old habits and customs and look toward new models in the future. Most Americans, whether newly arrived from another culture or the product of several generations on this soil, have mixed loyalties galore, sometimes because we have moved from one kind of place to another, sometimes because our families have set up in a neighborhood with traditions foreign to us, sometimes because home and work provide totally different environments and expectations, sometimes because even within our families there are two or more different national or ethnic traditions. All cultures, of course, experience conflict based on different expectations; but, because the Americas have become so much a melting pot, the excitement and stress of change, conflict, and divided loyalties have been an especially important fact for Americans of all kinds and backgrounds in the twentieth century. Writers, especially the ones included in this chapter, seem particularly drawn to situations and events in which people find their loyalties divided and their feelings uncertain.

In the selections that follow, you will find stories about people searching for their roots in homelands abroad, poems about the power of a tradition to determine future generations, a play about what happens when the habits, customs, and values of one group come into conflict with those of another. Here are opportunities to see ourselves and to know others who, while different from us, participate as well in some larger drama of humanity and human history.

# Jamaica Kincaid

B orn in St. John's, Antigua (an island in the West Indies north of Guadeloupe), Jamaica Kincaid now lives in New York, where she is a staff writer for *The New Yorker*. She is the author of a novel, *Annie John* (1985), and a volume of short stories, *At the Bottom of the River* (1984), from which the following selection is taken.

In "Girl," which is a kind of MONOLOGUE* about the process of growing up, a young girl hears the voice of a long tradition of information and advice from older generations.

## GIRL

Wash the white clothes on Monday and put them on the stone heap; wash the color clothes on Tuesday and put them on the clothesline to dry; don't walk barehead in the hot sun; cook pumpkin fritters in very hot sweet oil; soak your little cloths right after you take them off; when buying cotton to make yourself a nice blouse, be sure that it doesn't have gum on it, because that way it won't hold up well after a wash; soak salt fish overnight before you cook it; is it true that you sing benna¹ in Sunday school?; always eat your food in such a way that it won't turn someone else's stomach; on Sundays try to walk like a lady and not like the slut you are so bent on becoming; don't sing benna in Sunday school; you mustn't speak to wharf-rat boys, not even to give directions; don't eat fruits on the street—flies will follow you; *but I don't sing benna on Sundays at all and never in Sunday school*; this is how to sew on a button; this is how to make a buttonhole for the button you have just sewed on; this is how to hem a dress when you see the hem coming down and so to prevent yourself from looking like the slut I know you are so bent on becoming; this is how you iron your father's khaki shirt so that it doesn't have a crease; this is how you iron your father's khaki pants so that they don't have a crease; this is how you grow okra—far from the house, because okra tree harbors red ants; when you are growing dasheen, make sure it gets plenty of water or else it makes your throat itch when you are eating it; this is how you sweep a corner; this is how you sweep a whole

*Words in small capitals are defined in the glossary.
1. Sing popular music, calypso.

house; this is how you sweep a yard; this is how you smile to someone you don't like too much; this is how you smile to someone you don't like at all; this is how you smile to someone you like completely; this is how you set a table for tea; this is how you set a table for dinner; this is how you set a table for dinner with an important guest; this is how you set a table for lunch; this is how you set a table for breakfast; this is how to behave in the presence of men who don't know you very well, and this way they won't recognize immediately the slut I have warned you against becoming; be sure to wash every day, even if it is with your own spit; don't squat down to play marbles—you are not a boy, you know; don't pick people's flowers—you might catch something; don't throw stones at blackbirds, because it might not be a blackbird at all; this is how to make a bread pudding; this is how to make doukona;[2] this is how to make pepper pot; this is how to make a good medicine for a cold; this is how to make a good medicine to throw away a child before it even becomes a child; this is how to catch a fish; this is how to throw back a fish you don't like, and that way something bad won't fall on you; this is how to bully a man; this is how a man bullies you; this is how to love a man, and if this doesn't work there are other ways, and if they don't work don't feel too bad about giving up; this is how to spit up in the air if you feel like it, and this is how to move quick so that it doesn't fall on you; this is how to make ends meet; always squeeze bread to make sure it's fresh; *but what if the baker won't let me feel the bread?*; you mean to say that after all you are really going to be the kind of woman who the baker won't let near the bread?

## STUDY QUESTIONS

1. Who is the main CHARACTER in this story? What kind of voice does the girl continually hear? What clues are there about the person whose voice it is?

2. What THEMES and ideas are repeated in the MONOLOGUE? What phrases? What effect does this repetition produce? What do you make of the tendency of the voice to put the girl down and suggest that her future is somewhat clouded?

3. What indications are there that the advice comes from more than one generation? How much of the information and advice seems to have been passed down from generation to generation? Does the phrasing suggest that information has traditionally been passed along orally or in writing? What evidence can you cite for your answer?

4. What suggestions are there in the story that customs and beliefs were developed as a part of the definition of family? of the culture more generally?

2. A spicy pudding, often made from plantain and wrapped in a plantain or banana leaf.

5. What customs seem basic to the culture behind the voice in the story? What values does the culture support? Characterize the "tribe" implied in the story.

6. In what sense does "Girl" tell a story? Do you think it is proper to call it a short story? With whose view of things do you identify? Why?

# Muriel Rukeyser

B orn in New York City in 1913, Muriel Rukeyser was an aviator and journalist as well as a poet. She was in Spain to report on the Spanish Civil War, and she was one of the reporters arrested at the famous Scottsboro Trial (1931), a crucial moment in the history of American race relations. Rukeyser's poems often reflect both her Jewish heritage and her powerful concerns for human rights. She died in 1980.

"To Be a Jew" was written during World War II; it has been included in *The Service of the Heart* (London), the new Reform Jewish prayer book. In this poem, Rukeyser equates the "full life" of twentieth-century Jews with "full agony."

# TO BE A JEW IN THE TWENTIETH CENTURY

To be a Jew in the twentieth century
Is to be offered a gift.   If you refuse,
Wishing to be invisible, you choose
Death of the spirit, the stone insanity.
Accepting, take full life, full agonies:                    5
Your evening deep in labyrinthine blood
Of those who resist, fail and resist; and God
Reduced to a hostage among hostages.
The gift is torment.   Not alone the still
Torture, isolation; or torture of the flesh.              10
That may come also.   But the accepting wish,
The whole and fertile spirit as guarantee
For every human freedom, suffering to be free,
Daring to live for the impossible.

## STUDY QUESTIONS

1. What, according to the poem, distinguishes being a Jew in the twentieth century from previous centuries? Why does the poem refuse to be specific about agonies, blood, and torture? What kinds of sufferings are suggested by these terms? What events does the poem seem to have in mind? What kinds of information are readers assumed already to have before reading the poem?

2. What does it mean to "refuse" the gift to be "invisible" (lines 2–3)? Why is the blood described as "labyrinthine" (l. 6)? What does it mean for God to be "reduced to a hostage" (l. 8)? What ideals does the poem express most forcibly?

3. Why does the poem become more direct and explicit beginning with line 9? How do the final six lines relate to the first eight? What words are repeated in the poem? Explain the effect of every instance of a repeated word.

4. What pattern of rhymes does the poem have? Where are the major structural breaks in the poem's organization? How are the breaks in thought signaled?

# John Fante

Born in Colorado in 1909, John Fante was the author of a number of screenplays and books, including *Dago Red* (1940), a collection of short stories; the novel *Brotherhood of the Grape* (1977); and a tetralogy of novels published over more than forty years, the general title of which is *The Saga of Arturo Bandini*.

"The Odyssey of a Wop" explores the feelings of an Italian-American boy toward his nationality, tracing his attitudes toward his Italian family from early confusion to embarrassment and deep resentment and finally to pride in what he comes to understand is a significant part of his personal identity.

# THE ODYSSEY OF A WOP

I pick up little bits of information about my grandfather. My grandmother tells me of him. She tells me that when he lived he was a good fellow whose goodness evoked not admiration but pity. He was known as a good little Wop. Of an evening he liked to sit at a table in a saloon sipping a tumbler of anisette, all by himself. He sat there like a little girl nipping an ice-cream cone. The old boy loved that green stuff, that anisette. It was his passion, and when folks saw him sitting alone it tickled them, for he was a good little Wop.

One night, my grandmother tells me, my grandfather was sitting in the saloon, he and his anisette. A drunken teamster stumbled through the swinging doors, braced himself at the bar, and bellowed: 2

"All right, everybody! Come an' get 'em! They're on me!" 3

And there sat my grandfather, not moving, his old tongue coquetting with the anisette. Everyone but he stood at the bar and drank the teamster's liquor. The teamster swung round. He saw my grandfather. He was insulted. 4

"You too, Wop!" said he. "Come up and drink!" 5

Silence. My grandfather arose. He staggered across the floor, passed the teamster, and then what did he do but go through the swinging doors and down the snowy street! He heard laughter coming after him from the saloon and his chest burned. He went home to my father. 6

"*Mamma mia!*" he blubbered. "Tummy Murray, he calla me Wopa." 7

"*Sangue della Madonna!*"[1] 8

Bareheaded, my father rushed down the street to the saloon. Tommy Murray was not there. He was in another saloon half a block away, and there my father found him. He drew the teamster aside and spoke under his breath. A fight! Immediately blood and hair began to fly. Chairs were drawn back. The customers applauded. The two men fought for an hour. They rolled over the floor, kicking, cursing, biting. They were in a knot in the middle of the floor, their bodies wrapped around each other. My father's head, chest, and arms buried the teamster's face. The teamster screamed. My father growled. His neck was rigid and trembling. The teamster screamed again, and lay still. My father got to his feet and wiped blood from his open mouth with the back of his hand. On the floor the teamster lay with a loose ear hanging from his head. . . . This is the story my grandmother tells me. 9

I think about the two men, my father and the teamster, and I picture them struggling on the floor. Boy! *Can* my father fight! 10

I get an idea. My two brothers are playing in another room. I leave my grandmother and go to them. They are sprawled on the rug, bent over crayons and drawing-paper. They look up and see my face flaming with my idea. 11

"What's wrong?" one asks. 12

"I dare you to do something!" 13

"Do what?" 14

"I dare you to call me a Wop!" 15

My youngest brother, barely six, jumps to his feet, and dancing up and down, screams: "Wop! Wop! Wop! Wop!" 16

I look at him. Pooh! He's too small. It's that other brother, that bigger brother, I want. He's got ears too, he has. 17

"I bet *you're* afraid to call me Wop." 18

1. Blood of the Madonna!

But he senses the devil in the woodpile.                                    19

"Nah," says he. "I don't wanna."                                            20

"Wop! Wop! Wop! Wop!" screams the little brother.                           21

"Shut your mouth, you!"                                                     22

"I won't, neither. You're a Wop! Wop. Woppedy Wop!"                         23

My older brother's box of crayons lies on the floor in front of his nose.   24
I put my heel upon the box and grind it into the carpet. He yells, seizing my
leg. I back away, and he begins to cry.

"Aw, that was sure dirty," he says.                                         25

"I dare you to call me a Wop!"                                              26

"Wop!"                                                                      27

I charge, seeking his ear. But my grandmother comes into the room            28
flourishing a razor strop.

## II

From the beginning, I hear my mother use the words Wop and Dago              29
with such vigor as to denote violent distaste. She spits them out. They leap
from her lips. To her, they contain the essence of poverty, squalor, filth. If
I don't wash my teeth, or hang up my cap, my mother says: "Don't be like
that. Don't be a Wop." Thus, as I begin to acquire her values, Wop and
Dago to me become synonymous with things evil. But she's consistent.

My father isn't. He's loose with his tongue. His moods create his judg-      30
ments. I at once notice that to him Wop and Dago are without any distinct
meaning, though if one not an Italian slaps them onto him, he's instantly
insulted. Christopher Columbus was the greatest Wop who ever lived, says
my father. So is Caruso. So is this fellow and that. But his very good friend
Peter Ladonna is not only a drunken pig, but a Wop on top of it; and of
course all his brothers-in-law are good-for-nothing Wops.

He pretends to hate the Irish. He really doesn't, but he likes to think      31
so, and he warns us children against them. Our grocer's name is O'Neil.
Frequently and inadvertently he makes errors when my mother is at his store.
She tells my father about short weights in meats, and now and then of a stale
egg.

Straightway my father grows tense, his lower lip curling. "This is the       32
last time that Irish bum robs me!" And he goes out, goes to the grocery-
store, his heels booming.

Soon he returns. He's smiling. His fists bulge with cigars. "From now        33
on," says he, "everything's gonna be all right."

I don't like the grocer. My mother sends me to his store every day, and      34
instantly he chokes up my breathing with the greeting: "Hello, you little
Dago! What'll you have?" So I detest him, and never enter his store if other
customers are to be seen, for to be called a Dago before others is a ghastly,
almost a physical, humiliation. My stomach expands and contracts, and I
feel naked.

I steal recklessly when the grocer's back is turned. I enjoy stealing from   35 him—candy bars, cookies, fruit. When he goes into his refrigerator I lean on his meat scales, hoping to snap a spring; I press my toe into egg baskets. Sometimes I pilfer too much. Then, what a pleasure it is to stand on the curb, my appetite gorged, and heave *his* candy bars, *his* cookies, *his* apples into the high yellow weeds across the street! . . . "Damn you, O'Neil, you can't call me a Dago and get away with it!"

His daughter is of my age. She's cross-eyed. Twice a week she passes    36
our house on her way to her music lesson. Above the street, and high in the branches of an elm tree, I watch her coming down the sidewalk, swinging her violin case. When she is under me, I jeer in sing-song:

> *Martha's crooooooss-eyed!*
> *Martha's crooooooss-eyed!*
> *Martha's crooooooss-eyed!*

### III

As I grow older, I find out that Italians use Wop and Dago much more    37
than Americans. My grandmother, whose vocabulary of English is confined to the commonest of nouns, always employs them in discussing contemporary Italians. The words never come forth quietly, unobtrusively. No; they bolt forth. There is a blatant intonation, and then the sense of someone being scathed, stunned.

I enter the parochial school with an awful fear that I will be called Wop.    38
As soon as I find out why people have such things as surnames, I match my own against such typically Italian cognomens as Bianchi, Borello, Pacelli— the names of other students. I am pleasantly relieved by the comparison. After all, I think, people will say I am French. Doesn't my name sound French? Sure! So thereafter, when people ask me my nationality, I tell them I am French. A few boys begin calling me Frenchy. I like that. It feels fine.

Thus I begin to loathe my heritage. I avoid Italian boys and girls who    39
try to be friendly. I thank God for my light skin and hair, and I choose my companions by the Anglo-Saxon ring of their names. If a boy's name is Whitney, Brown, or Smythe, then he's my pal; but I'm always a little breathless when I am with him; he may find me out. At the lunch hour I huddle over my lunch pail, for my mother doesn't wrap my sandwiches in wax paper, and she makes them too large, and the lettuce leaves protrude. Worse, the bread is homemade; not bakery bread, not "American" bread. I make a great fuss because I can't have mayonnaise and other "American" things.

The parish priest is a good friend of my father's. He comes strolling    40
through the school grounds, watching the children at play. He calls to me and asks about my father, and then he tells me I should be proud to be studying about my great countrymen, Columbus, Vespucci, John Cabot. He speaks in a loud, humorous voice. Students gather around us, listening, and I bite my lips and wish to Jesus he'd shut up and move on.

Occasionally now I hear about a fellow named Dante. But when I find    41 out that he was an Italian I hate him as if he were alive and walking through the classrooms, pointing a finger at me. One day I find his picture in a dictionary. I look at it and tell myself that never have I seen an uglier bastard.

We students are at the blackboard one day, and a soft-eyed Italian girl whom I hate but who insists that I am her beau stands beside me. She twitches and shuffles about uneasily, half on tiptoe, smiling queerly at me. I sneer and turn my back, moving as far away from her as I can. The nun sees the wide space separating us and tells me to move nearer the girl. I do so, and the girl draws away, nearer the student on her other side. 42

Then I look down at my feet, and there I stand in a wet, spreading spot. I look quickly at the girl, and she hangs her head and looks at me in a way that begs me to take the blame for her. We attract the attention of others, and the classroom becomes alive with titters. Here comes the nun. I think I am in for it again, but she embraces me and murmurs that I should have raised two fingers and of course I would have been allowed to leave the room. But, says she, there's no need for that now; the thing for me to do is go out and get the mop. I do so, and amid the hysteria I nurse my conviction that only a Wop girl, right out of a Wop home, would ever do such a thing as this. 43

Oh, you Wop! Oh, you Dago! You bother me even when I sleep. I dream of defending myself against tormentors. One day I learn from my mother that my father went to the Argentine in his youth, and lived in Buenos Aires for two years. My mother tells me of his experiences there, and all day I think about them, even to the time I go to sleep. That night I come awake with a jerk. In the darkness I grope my way to my mother's room. My father sleeps at her side, and I awaken her gently, so that he won't be aroused. 44

I whisper: "Are you sure Papa wasn't *born* in Argentina?" 45
"No. Your father was born in Italy." 46
I go back to bed, disconsolate and disgusted. 47

### IV

During a ball game on the school grounds, a boy who plays on the opposing team begins to ridicule my playing. It is the ninth inning, and I ignore his taunts. We are losing the game, but if I can knock out a hit our chances of winning are pretty strong. I am determined to come through, and I face the pitcher confidently. The tormentor sees me at the plate. 48

"Ho! Ho!" he shouts. "Look who's up! The Wop's up. Let's get rid of the Wop!" 49

This is the first time anyone at school has ever flung the word at me, and I am so angry that I strike out foolishly. We fight after the game, this boy and I, and I make him take it back. 50

Now school days become fighting days. Nearly every afternoon at 3:15 a crowd gathers to watch me make some guy take it back. This is fun; I am getting somewhere now, so come on, you guys, I dare you to call me a Wop! 51

When at length there are no more boys who challenge me, insults come to me by hearsay, and I seek out the culprits. I strut down the corridors. The smaller boys admire me. "Here he comes!" they say, and they gaze and gaze. My two younger brothers attend the same school, and the smallest, a little squirt seven years old, brings his friends to me and asks me to roll up my sleeve and show them my muscles. Here you are, boys. Look me over.

My brother brings home furious accounts of my battles. My father listens avidly, and I stand by, to clear up any doubtful details. Sadly happy days! My father gives me pointers: how to hold my fist, how to guard my head. My mother, too shocked to hear more, presses her temples and squeezes her eyes and leaves the room. <sub>52</sub>

I am nervous when I bring friends to my house; the place looks so Italian. Here hangs a picture of Victor Emmanuel, and over there is one of the cathedral of Milan, and next to it one of St. Peter's, and on the buffet stands a wine pitcher of medieval design; it's forever brimming, forever red and brilliant with wine. These things are heirlooms belonging to my father, and no matter who may come to our house, he likes to stand under them and brag. <sub>53</sub>

So I begin to shout to him. I tell him to cut out being a Wop and be an American once in a while. Immediately he gets his razor strop and whales hell out of me, clouting me from room to room and finally out the back door. I go into the woodshed and pull down my pants and stretch my neck to examine the blue slices across my rump. A Wop, that's what my father is! Nowhere is there an American father who beats his son this way. Well, he's not going to get away with it; some day I'll get even with him. <sub>54</sub>

I begin to think that my grandmother is hopelessly a Wop. She's a small, stocky peasant who walks with her wrists crisscrossed over her belly, a simple old lady fond of boys. She comes into the room and tries to talk to my friends. She speaks English with a bad accent, her vowels rolling out like hoops. When, in her simple way, she confronts a friend of mine and says, her old eyes smiling: "You lika go the Seester scola?" my heart roars. *Mannaggia!*[2] I'm disgraced; now they all know that I'm an Italian. <sub>55</sub>

My grandmother has taught me to speak her native tongue. By seven, I know it pretty well, and I always address her in it. But when friends are with me, when I am twelve and thirteen, I pretend ignorance of what she says, and smirk stiffly; my friends daren't know that I can speak any language but English. Sometimes this infuriates her. She bristles, the loose skin at her throat knits hard, and she blasphemes with a mighty blasphemy. <sub>56</sub>

## V

When I finish in the parochial school my people decide to send me to a Jesuit academy in another city. My father comes with me on the first day. Chiseled into the stone coping that skirts the roof of the main building of the <sub>57</sub>

2. Damn!

academy is the Latin inscription: *Religioni et Bonis Artibus.*[3] My father and I stand at a distance, and he reads it aloud and tells me what it means.

I look up at him in amazement. Is this man my father? Why, look at him! Listen to him! He reads with an Italian inflection! He's wearing an Italian mustache. I have never realized it until this moment, but he looks exactly like a Wop. His suit hangs carelessly in wrinkles upon him. Why the deuce doesn't he buy a new one? And look at his tie! It's crooked. And his shoes: they need a shine. And, for the Lord's sake, will you look at his pants! They're not even buttoned in front. And oh, damn, damn, damn, you can see those dirty old suspenders that he won't throw away. Say, Mister, are you really my father? You there, why, you're such a little guy, such a runt, such an old-looking fellow! You look exactly like one of those immigrants carrying a blanket. You can't be *my* father! Why, I thought . . . I've always thought . . . 58

I'm crying now, the first time I've ever cried for any reason excepting a licking, and I'm glad he's not crying too. I'm glad he's as tough as he is, and we say good-by quickly, and I go down the path quickly, and I do not turn to look back, for I know he's standing there and looking at me. 59

I enter the administration building and stand in line with strange boys who also wait to register for the autumn term. Some Italian boys stand among them. I am away from home, and I sense the Italians. We look at one another and our eyes meet in an irresistible amalgamation, a suffusive consanguinity; I look away. 60

A burly Jesuit rises from his chair behind the desk and introduces himself to me. Such a voice for a man! There are a dozen thunderstorms in his chest. He asks my name, and writes it down on a little card. 61

"Nationality?" he roars. 62

"American." 63

"Your father's name?" 64

I whisper it: "Guido." 65

"How's that? Spell it out. Talk louder." 66

I cough. I touch my lips with the back of my hand and spell out the name. 67

"Ha!" shouts the registrar. "And still they come! Another Wop! Well, young man, you'll be at home here! Yes, sir! Lots of Wops here! We've even got Kikes! And, you know, this place reeks with shanty Irish!!" 68

*Dio!*[4] How I hate that priest! 69

He continues: "Where was your father born?" 70

"Buenos Aires, Argentina." 71

"Your mother?" 72

At last I can shout with the gusto of truth. 73

"Denver!" Aye, just like a conductor. 74

3. (Devoted to) Religion and the Good Arts.
4. God!

Casually, by way of conversation, he asks: "You speak Italian?"  75
"Nah! Not a word."  76
"Too bad," he says.  77
"You're nuts," I think.  78

### VI

That semester I wait on table to defray my tuition fee. Trouble ahead;  79
the chef and his assistants in the kitchen are all Italians. They know at once
that I am of the breed. I ignore the chef's friendly overtures, loathing him
from the first. He understands why, and we become enemies. Every word
he uses has a knife in it. His remarks cut me to pieces. After two months I
can stand it no longer in the kitchen, and so I write a long letter to my
mother; I am losing weight, I write; if you don't let me quit this job, I'll get
sick and flunk my tests. She telegraphs me some money and tells me to quit
at once; oh, I feel so sorry for you, my boy; I didn't dream it would be so
hard on you.

I decide to work just one more evening, to wait on table for just one  80
more meal. That evening, after the meal, when the kitchen is deserted save
for the cook and his assistants, I remove my apron and take my stand across
the kitchen from him, staring at him. This is my moment. Two months I
have waited for this moment. There is a knife stuck into the chopping block.
I pick it up, still staring. I want to hurt the cook, square things up.

He sees me, and he says: "Get out of here, Wop!"  81
An assistant shouts: "Look out, he's got a knife!"  82
"You won't throw it, Wop," the cook says. I am not thinking of throw-  83
ing it, but since he says I won't, I do. It goes over his head and strikes the
wall and drops with a clatter to the floor. He picks it up and chases me out
of the kitchen. I run, thanking God I didn't hit him.

That year the football team is made up of Irish and Italian boys. The  84
linemen are Irish, and we in the backfield are four Italians. We have a good
team and win a lot of games, and my team-mates are excellent players who
are unselfish and work together as one man. But I hate my three fellow-
players in the backfield; because of our nationality we seem ridiculous. The
team makes a captain of me, and I call signals and see to it my fellow-Italians
in the backfield do as little scoring as possible. I hog the play.

The school journal and the town's sports pages begin to refer to us as  85
the Wop Wonders. I think it an insult. Late one afternoon, at the close of an
important game, a number of students leave the main grandstand and group
themselves at one end of the field, to improvise some yells. They give three
big ones for the Wop Wonders. It sickens me. I can feel my stomach move;
and after that game I turn in my suit and quit the team.

I am a bad Latinist. Disliking the language, I do not study, and therefore  86
I flunk my examinations regularly. Now a student comes to me and tells me
that it is possible to drop Latin from my curriculum if I follow his suggestion,

which is that I fail deliberately in the next few examinations, fail hopelessly. If I do this, the student says, the Jesuits will bow to my stupidity and allow me to abandon the language.

This is an agreeable suggestion. I follow it out. But it backtracks, for the Jesuits are wise fellows. They see what I'm doing, and they laugh and tell me that I am not clever enough to fool them, and that I must keep on studying Latin, even if it takes me twenty years to pass. Worse, they double my assignments and I spend my recreation time with Latin syntax. Before examinations in my junior year the Jesuit who instructs me calls me to his room and says:

"It is a mystery to me that a thoroughbred Italian like yourself should have any trouble with Latin. The language is in your blood and, believe me, you're a darned poor Wop."

*Abbastanza!*[5] I go upstairs and lock my door and sit down with my book in front of me, my Latin book, and I study like a wild man, tearing crazily into the stuff until, lo, what is this? What am I studying here? Sure enough, it's a lot like the Italian my grandmother taught me so long ago—this Latin, it isn't so hard, after all. I pass the examination. I pass it with such an incredibly fine grade that my instructor thinks there is knavery somewhere.

Two weeks before graduation I get sick and go to the infirmary and am quarantined there. I lie in bed and feed my grudges. I bite my thumbs and ponder old grievances. I am running a high fever, and I can't sleep. I think about the principal. He was my close friend during my first two years at the school, but in my third year, last year, he was transferred to another school. I lie in bed thinking of the day we met again in this, the last year. We met again on his return that September, in the principal's room. He said hello to the boys, this fellow and that, and then he turned to me, and said:

"And you, the Wop! So you're still with us."

Coming from the mouth of the priest, the word had a lumpish sound that shook me all over. I felt the eyes of everyone, and I heard a giggle. So that's how it is! I lie in bed thinking of the priest and now of the fellow who giggled.

All of a sudden I jump out of bed, tear the fly-leaf from a book, find a pencil, and write a note to the priest. I write: "Dear Father: I haven't forgotten your insult. You called me a Wop last September. If you don't apologize right away there's going to be trouble." I call the brother in charge of the infirmary and tell him to deliver the note to the priest.

After a while I hear the priest's footsteps rising on the stairs. He comes to the door of my room, opens it, looks at me for a long time, not speaking, but only looking querulously. I wait for him to come in and apologize, for this is a grand moment for me. But he closes the door quietly and walks away. I am astonished. A double insult!

I am well again on the night of graduation. On the platform the principal

5. Enough!

makes a speech and then begins to distribute the diplomas. We're supposed to say: "Thank you," when he gives them to us. So thank you, and thank you, and thank you, everyone says in his turn. But when he gives me mine, I look squarely at him, just stand there and look, and I don't say anything, and from that day we never speak to each other again.

The following September I enroll at the university. 96

"Where was your father born?" asks the registrar. 97

"Buenos Aires, Argentina." 98

Sure, that's it. The same theme, with variations. 99

## VII

Time passes, and so do school days. I am sitting on a wall along the 100 plaza in Los Angeles, watching a Mexican *fiesta* across the street. A man comes along and lifts himself to the wall beside me, and asks if I have a cigarette. I have, and, lighting the cigarette, he makes conversation with me, and we talk of casual things until the *fiesta* is over. Then we get down from the wall and, still talking, go walking through the Los Angeles Tenderloin. This man needs a shave and his clothes do not fit him; it's plain that he's a bum. He tells one lie upon another, and not one is well told. But I am lonesome in this town, and a willing listener.

We step into a restaurant for coffee. Now he becomes intimate. He has 101 bummed his way from Chicago to Los Angeles, and has come in search of his sister; he has her address, but she is not at it, and for two weeks he has been looking for her in vain. He talks on and on about this sister, seeming to gyrate like a buzzard over her, hinting to me that I should ask some questions about her. He wants me to touch off the fuse that will release his feelings.

So I ask: "Is she married?" 102

And then he rips into her, hammer and tongs. Even if he does find her, 103 he will not live with her. What kind of a sister is she to let him walk these streets without a dime in his pocket, and she married to a man who has plenty of money and can give him a job? He thinks she has deliberately given him a false address so that he will not find her, and when he gets his hands on her he's going to wring her neck. In the end, after he has completely demolished her, he does exactly what I think he is going to do.

He asks: "Have *you* got a sister?" 104

I tell him yes, and he waits for my opinion of her; but he doesn't get it. 105

We meet again a week later. 106

He has found his sister. Now he begins to praise her. She has induced 107 her husband to give him a job, and tomorrow he goes to work as a waiter in his brother-in-law's restaurant. He tells me the address, but I do not think more of it beyond the fact that it must be somewhere in the Italian quarter.

And so it is, and by a strange coincidence I know his brother-in-law, 108 Rocco Saccone, an old friend of my people and a *paesano*[6] of my father's. I

6. Countryman; someone from the same region or village.

am in Rocco's place one night a fortnight later. Rocco and I are speaking in Italian when the man I have met on the plaza steps out of the kitchen, an apron over his legs. Rocco calls him and he comes over, and Rocco introduces him as his brother-in-law from Chicago. We shake hands.

"We've met before," I say, but the plaza man doesn't seem to want this 109 known, for he let's go my hand quickly and goes behind the counter, pretending to be busy with something back there. Oh, he's bluffing; you can see that.

In a loud voice, Rocco says to me: "That man is a skunk. He's ashamed 110 of his own flesh and blood." He turns to the plaza man. "Ain't you?"

"Oh, yeah?" the plaza man sneers. 111

"How do you mean—he's ashamed? How do you mean?" 112

"Ashamed of being an Italian," Rocco says. 113

"Oh, yeah?" from the plaza man. 114

"That's all he knows," Rocco says. "Oh, yeah? That's all he knows. Oh, 115 yeah? Oh, yeah? Oh, yeah? That's all he knows."

"Oh, yeah?" the plaza man says again. 116

"Yah," Rocco says, his face blue. *"Animale codardo!"*[7] 117

The plaza man looks at me with peaked eyebrows, and he doesn't know 118 it, he standing there with his black, liquid eyes, he doesn't know that he's as good as a god in his waiter's apron; for he is indeed a god, a miracle worker; no, he doesn't know; no one knows; just the same, he is that—he, of all people. Standing there and looking at him, I feel like my grandfather and my father and the Jesuit cook and Rocco; I seem to have come home, and I am surprised that this return, which I have somehow always expected, should come so quietly, without trumpets and thunder.

"If I were you, I'd get rid of him," I say to Rocco. 119

"Oh, yeah?" the plaza man says again. 120

I'd like to paste him. But that won't do any good. There's no sense in 121 hammering your own corpse.

## STUDY QUESTIONS

1. How old is the NARRATOR of the story at the beginning? How can you tell? What evidence is there that the anecdote about the grandfather is invented? Why is it important to the narrator, at his young age, to believe the anecdote?

2. How does the boy's image of his father change over the years? Trace the different steps in his feelings. At which stages is he reverent? respectful? dismissive? embarrassed?

3. What does the narrator learn when he is very young about the uses of terms like "wop" and "dago"? How can he tell when the terms are honorific? In what ways

7. Cowardly animal!

does the use of such terms inside the family help to solidify the sense of tribe and the pride in Italianness?

4. How do the encounters with the Irish dramatize the sense of separate identity felt by the Italians? by the narrator specifically? What STEREOTYPES do the encounters between the Italians and the Irish depend on? What stereotype is the narrator's attempt to pass himself off as French based on?

5. What different episodes demonstrate the determination of his elders to demonstrate the dignity of his heritage to the narrator? How is the parish priest characterized? What attitudes does the narrator express toward the church more generally?

6. Trace the narrator's developing relationships with his brothers. How important to the story is the sense of brotherhood? In what ways is the THEME of brotherhood related to the story's preoccupation with family rituals?

7. Physical fights dominate much of the story's action. How important are they to the narrator's sense of himself? Why? In what different ways does the narrator's physical strength save his self-conception when it is under threat? In what sense is his quitting the football team a turning point in his dependence on physical skills?

8. Explain how the final scene works. Why is it important that Rocco is someone the narrator knows through his family?

9. Why does the story begin with an anecdote about older generations? How important is it to the story's effects that three generations are encompassed in the story? that its action takes place over a number of years? How many years, approximately, are covered in the story?

10. What does the last sentence of the story mean?

# Ana Castillo

Born in Chicago of Aztec heritage, Ana Castillo is the author of a novel, *The Mixquiahala Letters* (1986), and several collections of poetry, including *Women Are Not Roses* (1984).

The following poem looks back into the past to remember the days of Amerindian peoples before the coming of Europeans, and it chronicles the changes in customs and values once the invasion has taken place.

# OUR TONGUE WAS NAHUATL

You.
We have never met
yet
we know each other
well.                                                    5
I recognized
your high
              set
                    cheekbones,
slightly rounded                                         10
                    nose,
the deep brownness
of your hardened face—
soft full lips.

Your near-slanted eyes                                  15
follow me—
sending flashback memories
to your so-called
primitive mind.
And I know                                              20
you remember . . .

It was a time
of turquoise blue-greenness,
sky-topped mountains,
god-suns /                                              25
wind-swept rains;
oceanic deities
naked children running
in the humid air.

I ground corn                                           30
upon a slab of stone,
while you bargained
at the market
dried skins
and other things                                        35
that were our own.

I would watch
our small sons
chase behind your bare legs
when you came home those days.                    40
We would sit—
                eat;
Give thanks to our
                rich golden
                        Earth.                    45
Our tongue was Nahuatl.

We were content—
With the generosity
of our gods
            and our kins;                         50
knowing nothing
            of a world
across the bitter waters—
Until they came . . .

White foreign strangers                            55
riding high
            on four-legged
                creatures;
that made us bow to them.
In our ignorance to the                            60
                    unknown
they made us bow.

They made us bow—
until our skin became
the color of caramel                               65
and nothing anymore
was our own.

Raped of ourselves—
Our civilization—
Even our gods turned away                           70
from us in shame . . .

Yet we bowed,
                as we do now—
On buses
            going to factories                      75
where "No-Help Wanted" signs

laugh at our faces,
stare at our hungry eyes.

Yet we bow . . .
>WE BOW!                                   80

But I remember you
                        still—
It was a time
much different
                        than now . . .           85

## STUDY QUESTIONS

1. Who is the "You" of line 1? In the course of the poem, how much do we learn about this "You"? In what time and place does the "You" exist? How can it be that the SPEAKER has "never met" the "You," and yet both the speaker and the "You" remember each other (ll. 21 and 81)?

2. What parts of her people's history concern the speaker most? In what ways did the coming of "white foreign strangers" (l. 55) change the speaker's people? What were the people like before the "strangers" came? What values did they have that now seem to have been lost?

3. Why does the speaker make so much of the act of bowing? What, exactly, does bowing come to mean in the poem? What does bowing seem to symbolize to the speaker?

4. What is Nahuatl? What is the meaning of "our" in the title?

# Virginia Cerenio

A second-generation Filipino-American, Virginia Cerenio grew up in San Francisco and received her B.A. from San Francisco State University. She is a member of the Kearny Street Workshop and has published both poems and fiction. She defines art as "a fusion of art and politics."

The following poem describes a powerful sense of continuity between generations of women.

# [WE WHO CARRY
# THE ENDLESS SEASONS]

we who carry the endless seasons
    of tropical rain in our blood
still weep our mother's tears
feel the pain of their birth
        their growing                               5
        as women in america

we wear guilt for their minor sins
            singing lullabies
            in foreign tongue
                ". . . o ilaw sa gabing madilim    10
                wangis mo'y bituin sa langit . . ."[1]
     their desires
            wanting us
            their daughters
            to marry only                    15
                ". . . a boy from the islands . . .
                ang guapo lalake[2] . . . and
                from a good family too. . . ."

   like shadows
   attached to our feet                          20
   we cannot walk away

though we are oceans and dreams apart
waves carry the constant clicking of their rosary beads
                        like heartbeats
                        in our every breathing    25

## STUDY QUESTIONS

1. Why are different generations said to be "oceans" apart (line 22)? "dreams" apart? Why can't the present generation walk away from the past? Explain how the shadow IMAGE (ll. 19–21) works.

1. Light in the middle of the night / your face like stars in the sky.

2. A handsome man.

2. What different connections between generations does the poem articulate? Explain why the Filipino phrases are inserted in a poem that is primarily in English.

3. Describe the fundamental attitude the poem takes to the past. What is the poem's basic TONE?

# Marcela Christine Lucero-Trujillo

B orn in Westminster, Colorado, Marcela Christine Lucero-Trujillo (1931–1984) received her Ph.D. in 1981 from the University of Minnesota with a thesis called *Colorado Chicanos: Their History, Their Literature*. Her poetry has appeared in a variety of publications (such as *La Luz*) and has been included in such anthologies as *The Third Woman*.

The poem that follows looks back nostalgically to a time when musicians composed and sang songs about the heritage of the people of Capulín.

## THE MUSICOS FROM CAPULÍN

MANY SUMMER MOUNTAIN NIGHTS AGO.
   LOS VIEJITOS[1] WITH SQUEAKY VIOLINS,
CAME TO THE VALLEY FOR WEDDING DANCES,
   THOSE WERE THE MUSICOS[2] FROM CAPULÍN.
THEY PLAYED AND COMPOSED ORIGINAL VERSES     5
   TO ALL LA RAZA[3] PRESENT.
THEY TRACED THE LINEAGE OF FAMILY TREES
   AND TIED OUR BLOOD TO GREAT DESCENDANTS.
THE RAZA TAPPED THEIR FEET
     TO THE REPETITIOUS BEAT     10
AND THE GENERATIONS PRESENT,
     GRATEFULLY THREW MONEY AT THEIR FEET.
THEIR "VERSOS"[4] WERE CUSTOMS OF ANOTHER AGE,
LEARNED BY ORAL TRADITION, OR SO THEY SAY.

---

1. The little old men.
2. Musicians.
3. People of the same heritage.
4. Verses.

A MOUNTAIN SOUL IN VIOLIN STRINGS,                        15
SYNCHRONIZED TO A MOUNTAIN SPRING.

THEY'RE GONE NOW, THESE OLD MEN,
AND YOU CAN'T FIND OTHERS LIKE THEM IN CAPULÍN,
OR MONTE VISTA OR EVEN SAN LUIS,
  IT PASSED INTO OBLIVION,                                20
  THIS CULTURAL RITE
  OF ANOTHER AGE
  MANY MOUNTAIN NIGHTS.

## STUDY QUESTIONS

1. Why were "wedding dances" the setting for the kinds of songs the "musicos" sang? What, exactly, were the songs about? To whom were the songs addressed? What kind of "cultural rite" (line 21) do the songs represent?

2. Why has the music disappeared? What other changes seem to have occurred in the community of Capulín?

3. How far from Capulín is Monte Vista? San Luis? How large is each place? What is the history of the area? What is implied by the mention of the three places?

4. Why are Spanish terms used at key points in the poem? Examine carefully each of these terms, and explain the particular effect produced by each. How would the effect be different if an English word had been used in each case? How do you account for the fact that the entire poem is written in capital letters?

5. How much do we know about the SPEAKER of the poem? What attitudes does the speaker express toward the past? toward the present?

# Richard Olivas

The following poem uses a homey, personal experience to raise questions about the relevance, to "new" Americans, of the old American myths.

# [I'M SITTING IN MY HISTORY CLASS]

I'm sitting in my history class,
The instructor commences rapping,
I'm in my U.S. History class,
And I'm on the verge of napping.

The Mayflower landed on Plymouth Rock.          5
Tell me more! Tell me more!
Thirteen colonies were settled.
I've heard it all before.

What did he say?
Dare I ask him to reiterate?          10
Oh why bother
It sounded like he said,
George Washington's my father.

I'm reluctant to believe it,
I suddenly raise my mano.[1]          15
If George Washington's my father,
Why wasn't he Chicano?

## STUDY QUESTIONS

1. What special effects are created by the mixture of formal and colloquial language in the poem? Explain the IRONIES in using the term "rapping" to describe the instructor's talk.

2. Why does the poem repeat the simplest "facts" from class, then jump to the level of METAPHOR and MYTH in its reference to George Washington? What does the poem imply about the process of classroom education?

3. How much do we know about the NARRATOR of the poem? Describe the poem's TONE.

1. Hand.

# Toni Morrison

Born in 1931, Toni Morrison grew up in Lorrain, Ohio, and was educated at Howard and Cornell universities. For many years, she was an editor at Random House; she taught at Howard and Texas Southern universities, held the prestigious Albert Schweitzer Chair at the State University of New York, Albany, and now teaches at Princeton. Her most recent novel, *Beloved*, won the Pulitzer Prize in 1988; her earlier novels include *The Bluest Eye* (1969), *Sula* (1973, from which the following selection is taken), *Song of Solomon* (1977), and *Tar Baby* (1981).

"1920" tells the story of Nel Wright's growing up and of her relationship to her family and its past.

## 1920

It had to be as far away from the Sundown House as possible. And her grandmother's middle-aged nephew who lived in a Northern town called Medallion was the one chance she had to make sure it would be. The red shutters had haunted both Helene Sabat and her grandmother for sixteen years. Helene was born behind those shutters, daughter of a Creole whore who worked there. The grandmother took Helene away from the soft lights and flowered carpets of the Sundown House and raised her under the dolesome eyes of a multicolored Virgin Mary, counseling her to be constantly on guard for any sign of her mother's wild blood.

So when Wiley Wright came to visit his Great Aunt Cecile in New Orleans, his enchantment with the pretty Helene became a marriage proposal—under the pressure of both women. He was a seaman (or rather a lakeman, for he was a ship's cook on one of the Great Lakes lines), in port only three days out of every sixteen.

He took his bride to his home in Medallion and put her in a lovely house with a brick porch and real lace curtains at the window. His long absences were quite bearable for Helene Wright, especially when, after some nine years of marriage, her daughter was born.

Her daughter was more comfort and purpose than she had ever hoped to find in this life. She rose grandly to the occasion of motherhood—grateful, deep down in her heart, that the child had not inherited the great beauty that was hers: that her skin had dusk in it, that her lashes were substantial but not undignified in their length, that she had taken the broad flat nose of Wiley (although Helene expected to improve it somewhat) and his generous lips.

Under Helene's hand the girl became obedient and polite. Any enthusiasms that little Nel showed were calmed by the mother until she drove her daughter's imagination underground.

Helene Wright was an impressive woman, at least in Medallion she was. Heavy hair in a bun, dark eyes arched in a perpetual query about other people's manners. A woman who won all social battles with presence and a conviction of the legitimacy of her authority. Since there was no Catholic church in Medallion then, she joined the most conservative black church. And held sway. It was Helene who never turned her head in church when latecomers arrived; Helene who established the practice of seasonal altar flowers; Helene who introduced the giving of banquets of welcome to returning Negro veterans. She lost only one battle—the pronunciation of her name. The people in the Bottom refused to say Helene. They called her Helen Wright and left it at that.

All in all her life was a satisfactory one. She loved her house and enjoyed manipulating her daughter and her husband. She would sigh sometimes just before falling asleep, thinking that she had indeed come far enough away from the Sundown House.

So it was with extremely mixed emotions that she read a letter from Mr. Henri Martin describing the illness of her grandmother, and suggesting she come down right away. She didn't want to go, but could not bring herself to ignore the silent plea of the woman who had rescued her.

It was November. November, 1920.[1] Even in Medallion there was a victorious swagger in the legs of white men and a dull-eyed excitement in the eyes of colored veterans.

Helene thought about the trip South with heavy misgiving but decided that she had the best protection: her manner and her bearing, to which she would add a beautiful dress. She bought some deep-brown wool and three-fourths of a yard of matching velvet. Out of this she made herself a heavy but elegant dress with velvet collar and pockets.

Nel watched her mother cutting the pattern from newspapers and moving her eyes rapidly from a magazine model to her own hands. She watched her turn up the kerosene lamp at sunset to sew far into the night.

The day they were ready, Helene cooked a smoked ham, left a note for her lake-bound husband, in case he docked early, and walked head high and arms stiff with luggage ahead of her daughter to the train depot.

It was a longer walk than she remembered, and they saw the train steaming up just as they turned the corner. They ran along the track looking for the coach pointed out to them by the colored porter. Even at that they made a mistake. Helene and her daughter entered a coach peopled by some twenty

---

1. Second anniversary of the armistice ending World War I.

white men and women. Rather than go back and down the three wooden steps again, Helene decided to spare herself some embarrassment and walk on through to the colored car. She carried two pieces of luggage and a string purse; her daughter carried a covered basket of food.

As they opened the door marked COLORED ONLY, they saw a white con- 14 ductor coming toward them. It was a chilly day but a light skim of sweat glistened on the woman's face as she and the little girl struggled to hold the door open, hang on to their luggage and enter all at once. The conductor let his eyes travel over the pale yellow woman and then stuck his little finger into his ear, jiggling it free of wax. "What you think you doin', gal?"

Helene looked up at him. 15

So soon. So soon. She hadn't even begun the trip back. Back to her 16 grandmother's house in the city where the red shutters glowed, and already she had been called "gal." All the old vulnerabilities, all the old fears of being somehow flawed gathered in her stomach and made her hands tremble. She had heard only that one word; it dangled above her wide-brimmed hat, which had slipped, in her exertion, from its carefully leveled placement and was now tilted in a bit of a jaunt over his eye.

Thinking he wanted her tickets, she quickly dropped both the cowhide 17 suitcase and the straw one in order to search for them in her purse. An eagerness to please and an apology for living met in her voice. "I have them. Right here somewhere, sir . . ."

The conductor looked at the bit of wax his fingernail had retrieved. 18 "What was you doin' back in there? What was you doin' in that coach yonder?"

Helene licked her lips. "Oh . . . I . . ." Her glance moved beyond the 19 white man's face to the passengers seated behind him. Four or five black faces were watching, two belonging to soldiers still in their shit-colored uniforms and peaked caps. She saw their closed faces, their locked eyes, and turned for compassion to the gray eyes of the conductor.

"We made a mistake, sir. You see, there wasn't no sign. We just got in 20 the wrong car, that's all. Sir."

"We don't 'low no mistakes on this train. Now git your butt on in there." 21

He stood there staring at her until she realized that he wanted her to 22 move aside. Pulling Nel by the arm, she pressed herself and her daughter into the foot space in front of a wooden seat. Then, for no earthly reason, at least no reason that anybody could understand, certainly no reason that Nel understood then or later, she smiled. Like a street pup that wags its tail at the very doorjamb of the butcher shop he has been kicked away from only moments before, Helene smiled. Smiled dazzlingly and coquettishly at the salmon-colored face of the conductor.

Nel looked away from the flash of pretty teeth to the other passengers. 23 The two black soldiers, who had been watching the scene with what appeared to be indifference, now looked stricken. Behind Nel was the bright and blazing light of her mother's smile; before her the midnight eyes of the soldiers.

She saw the muscles of their faces tighten, a movement under the skin from blood to marble. No change in the expression of the eyes, but a hard wetness that veiled them as they looked at the stretch of her mother's foolish smile.

As the door slammed on the conductor's exit, Helene walked down the aisle to a seat. She looked about for a second to see whether any of the men would help her put the suitcases in the overhead rack. Not a man moved. Helene sat down, fussily, her back toward the men. Nel sat opposite, facing both her mother and the soldiers, neither of whom she could look at. She felt both pleased and ashamed to sense that these men, unlike her father, who worshiped his graceful, beautiful wife, were bubbling with a hatred for her mother that had not been there in the beginning but had been born with the dazzling smile. In the silence that preceded the train's heave, she looked deeply at the folds of her mother's dress. There in the fall of the heavy brown wool she held her eyes. She could not risk letting them travel upward for fear of seeing that the hooks and eyes in the placket of the dress had come undone and exposed the custard-colored skin underneath. She stared at the hem, wanting to believe in its weight but knowing that custard was all that it hid. If this tall, proud woman, this woman who was very particular about her friends, who slipped into church with unequaled elegance, who could quell a roustabout with a look, if *she* were really custard, then there was a chance that Nel was too.

It was on that train, shuffling toward Cincinnati, that she resolved to be on guard—always. She wanted to make certain that no man ever looked at her that way. That no midnight eyes or marbled flesh would ever accost her and turn her into jelly.

For two days they rode; two days of watching sleet turn to rain, turn to purple sunsets, and one night knotted on the wooden seats (their heads on folded coats), trying not to hear the snoring soldiers. When they changed trains in Birmingham for the last leg of the trip, they discovered what luxury they had been in through Kentucky and Tennessee, where the rest stops had all had colored toilets. After Birmingham there were none. Helene's face was drawn with the need to relieve herself, and so intense was her distress she finally brought herself to speak about her problem to a black woman with four children who had got on in Tuscaloosa.

"Is there somewhere we can go to use the restroom?"

The woman looked up at her and seemed not to understand. "Ma'am?" Her eyes fastened on the thick velvet collar, the fair skin, the high-tone voice.

"The restroom," Helene repeated. Then, in a whisper, "The toilet."

The woman pointed out the window and said, "Yes, ma'am. Yonder."

Helene looked out of the window halfway expecting to see a comfort station in the distance; instead she saw gray-green trees leaning over tangled grass. "Where?"

"Yonder," the woman said. "Meridian. We be pullin' in direc'lin." Then she smiled sympathetically and asked, "Kin you make it?"

Helene nodded and went back to her seat trying to think of other things—

for the surest way to have an accident would be to remember her full bladder.

At Meridian the women got out with their children. While Helene looked about the tiny stationhouse for a door that said COLORED WOMEN, the other woman stalked off to a field of high grass on the far side of the track. Some white men were leaning on the railing in front of the stationhouse. It was not only their tongues curling around toothpicks that kept Helene from asking information of them. She looked around for the other woman and, seeing just the top of her head rag in the grass, slowly realized where "yonder" was. All of them, the fat woman and her four children, three boys and a girl, Helene and her daughter, squatted there in the four o'clock Meridian sun. They did it again in Ellisville, again in Hattiesburg, and by the time they reached Slidell, not too far from Lake Pontchartrain, Helene could not only fold leaves as well as the fat woman, she never felt a stir as she passed the muddy eyes of the men who stood like wrecked Dorics[2] under the station roofs of those towns.

The lift in spirit that such an accomplishment produced in her quickly disappeared when the train finally pulled into New Orleans.

Cecile Sabat's house leaned between two others just like it on Elysian Fields. A Frenchified shotgun house,[3] it sported a magnificent garden in the back and a tiny wrought-iron fence in the front. On the door hung a black crepe wreath with purple ribbon. They were too late. Helene reached up to touch the ribbon, hesitated, and knocked. A man in a collarless shirt opened the door. Helene identified herself and he said he was Henri Martin and that he was there for the settin'-up.[4] They stepped into the house. The Virgin Mary clasped her hands in front of her neck three times in the front room and once in the bedroom where Cecile's body lay. The old woman had died without seeing or blessing her granddaughter.

No one other than Mr. Martin seemed to be in the house, but a sweet odor as of gardenias told them that someone else had been. Blotting her lashes with a white handkerchief, Helene walked through the kitchen to the back bedroom where she had slept for sixteen years. Nel trotted along behind, enchanted with the smell, the candles and the strangeness. When Helene bent to loosen the ribbons of Nel's hat, a woman in a yellow dress came out of the garden and onto the back porch that opened into the bedroom. The two women looked at each other. There was no recognition in the eyes of either. Then Helene said, "This is your . . . grandmother, Nel." Nel looked at her mother and then quickly back at the door they had just come out of.

"No. That was your great-grandmother. This is your grandmother. My mother . . ."

---

2. Heavy Greek columns.

3. House in which all the rooms are in line front to back. Elysian Fields is a major street running through the poor section of New Orleans.

4. Wake; a watch held over the body prior to the funeral.

Before the child could think, her words were hanging in the gardenia air. "But she looks so young." [39]

The woman in the canary-yellow dress laughed and said she was forty-eight, "an old forty-eight." [40]

Then it was she who carried the gardenia smell. This tiny woman with the softness and glare of a canary. In that somber house that held four Virgin Marys, where death sighed in every corner and candles sputtered, the gardenia small and canary-yellow dress emphasized the funeral atmosphere surrounding them. [41]

The woman smiled, glanced in the mirror and said, throwing her voice toward Helene, "That your only one?" [42]

"Yes," said Helene. [43]

"Pretty. A lot like you." [44]

"Yes. Well. She's ten now." [45]

"Ten? Vrai?[5] Small for her age, no?" [46]

Helene shrugged and looked at her daughter's questioning eyes. The woman in the yellow dress leaned forward. "Come. Come, chère." [47]

Helene interrupted. "We have to get cleaned up. We been three days on the train with no chance to wash or . . ." [48]

"Comment t'appelle?" [49]

"She doesn't talk Creole." [50]

"Then you ask her." [51]

"She wants to know your name, honey." [52]

With her head pressed into her mother's heavy brown dress, Nel told her and then asked, "What's yours?" [53]

"Mine's Rochelle. Well. I must be going on." She moved closer to the mirror and stood there sweeping hair up from her neck back into its halo-like roll, and wetting with spit the ringlets that fell over her ears. "I been here, you know, most of the day. She pass on yesterday. The funeral tomorrow. Henri takin' care." She struck a match, blew it out and darkened her eyebrows with the burnt head. All the while Helene and Nel watched her. The one in a rage at the folded leaves she had endured, the wooden benches she had slept on, all to miss seeing her grandmother and seeing instead that painted canary who never said a word of greeting or affection or . . . [54]

Rochelle continued, "I don't know what happen to de house. Long time paid for. You be thinkin' on it? Oui?"[6] Her newly darkened eyebrows queried Helene. [55]

"Oui." Helene's voice was chilly. "I be thinkin' on it." [56]

"Oh, well. Not for me to say . . ." [57]

Suddenly she swept around and hugged Nel—a quick embrace tighter and harder than one would have imagined her thin soft arms capable of. [58]

" 'Voir! 'Voir!" and she was gone. [59]

5. Is that the truth? Below: chère—dear; Comment t'appelle—What's your name?
6. Will you? (literally, Yes?) Below: 'Voir (and "vwah"), short for Au revoir—see you again.

In the kitchen, being soaped head to toe by her mother, Nel ventured 60
an observation. "She smelled so nice. And her skin was so soft."

Helene rinsed the cloth. "Much handled things are always soft." 61

"What does 'vwah' mean?" 62

"I don't know," her mother said. "I don't talk Creole." She gazed at her 63
daughter's wet buttocks. "And neither do you."

When they got back to Medallion and into the quiet house they saw the 64
note exactly where they had left it and the ham dried out in the icebox.

"Lord, I've never been so glad to see this place. But look at the dust. 65
Get the rags, Nel. Oh, never mind. Let's breathe awhile first. Lord, I never
thought I'd get back here safe and sound. Whoo. Well it's over. Good and
over. Praise His name. Look at that. I told that old fool not to deliver any
milk and there's the can curdled to beat all. What gets into people? I told him
not to. Well, I got other things to worry 'bout. Got to get a fire started. I left
it ready so I wouldn't have to do nothin' but light it. Lord, it's cold. Don't
just sit there, honey. You could be pulling your nose . . ."

Nel sat on the red-velvet sofa listening to her mother but remembering 66
the smell and the tight, tight hug of the woman in yellow who rubbed burned
matches over her eyes.

Late that night after the fire was made, the cold supper eaten, the sur- 67
face dust removed, Nel lay in bed thinking of her trip. She remembered
clearly the urine running down and into her stockings until she learned how
to squat properly; the disgust on the face of the dead woman and the sound
of the funeral drums. It had been an exhilarating trip but a fearful one. She
had been frightened of the soldiers' eyes on the train, the black wreath on
the door, the custard pudding she believed lurked under her mother's heavy
dress, the feel of unknown streets and unknown people. But she had gone on
a real trip, and now she was different. She got out of bed and lit the lamp to
look in the mirror. There was her face, plain brown eyes, three braids and
the nose her mother hated. She looked for a long time and suddenly a shiver
ran through her.

"I'm me," she whispered. "Me." 68

Nel didn't know quite what she meant, but on the other hand she knew 69
exactly what she meant.

"I'm me. I'm not their daughter. I'm not Nel. I'm me. Me." 70

Each time she said the word me there was a gathering in her like power, 71
like joy, like fear. Back in bed with her discovery, she stared out the window
at the dark leaves of the horse chestnut.

"Me," she murmured. And then, sinking deeper into the quilts, "I want 72
. . . I want to be . . . wonderful. Oh, Jesus, make me wonderful."

The many experiences of her trip crowded in on her. She slept. It was 73
the last as well as the first time she was ever to leave Medallion.

For days afterward she imagined other trips she would take, alone though, 74
to faraway places. Contemplating them was delicious. Leaving Medallion

would be her goal. But that was before she met Sula, the girl she had seen for five years at Garfield Primary but never played with, never knew, because her mother said Sula's mother was sooty. The trip, perhaps, or her new found me-ness, gave her the strength to cultivate a friend in spite of her mother.

When Sula first visited the Wright house, Helene's curdled scorn turned to butter. Her daughter's friend seemed to have none of the mother's slackness. Nel, who regarded the oppressive neatness of her home with dread, felt comfortable in it with Sula, who loved it and would sit on the red-velvet sofa for ten to twenty minutes at a time—still as dawn. As for Nel, she preferred Sula's woolly house, where a pot of something was always cooking on the stove; where the mother, Hannah, never scolded or gave directions; where all sorts of people dropped in; where newspapers were stacked in the hallway, and dirty dishes left for hours at a time in the sink, and where a one-legged grandmother named Eva handed you goobers from deep inside her pockets or read you a dream.

75

# STUDY QUESTIONS

1. Why does the story begin with so much detail about different generations of Nel Wright's background? What importance does that background come to have in Nel's self-discovery?

2. When Nel begins to assert her own sense of self ("I'm me. . . . Me" [paragraph 68]), what is she differentiating herself from? How important is it to her sense of self that she is aware of different personalities in her family? different characters? different geographical backgrounds? different traditions of language and culture? different moral codes?

3. How is each of the strands of tradition introduced to Nel? Why does the story center at first on Helene's relationship with her own grandmother and mother?

4. Trace the different times when a new generation shows itself to be ashamed of an older generation. What instances are there of pride in the past?

5. How much of the family's history has been kept from Nel early in her life? How can you tell?

6. How important to the story is geographical location? What are the cultural differences between Ohio and Louisiana, as presented in the story? How important to the family's identity is religion?

7. Describe Nel's feelings toward her mother. What does she fear most about her mother? What does she least understand? In what ways do her feelings change in the course of the story?

8. In what ways does the use of Creole language come to stand for differences between the traditions Nel is trying to understand? In what ways do the religious objects

confronted in Louisiana stand for the "foreignness" of parts of the family tradition to Nel?

9. What is the central conflict in the story? How do the other conflicts in the story relate to the central one? In what ways is the date of the story, as revealed in the title, important?

# Ray A. Young Bear

Born in Tama, Iowa, in 1950, Ray A. Young Bear is from the Sauk and Fox tribe of Iowa, better known as the Mesquakies, and has been writing poetry since the age of sixteen. He is the author of two collections of poems, *Winter of the Salamander* (1980) and *The Bumblebee Is the Bear King* (1985).

In the following poem, recurring memories of childhood experiences help the speaker to clarify his feelings about his grandfather and ultimately help him to define his larger relationship to the tribe.

# IN THE FIRST PLACE OF MY LIFE

in the first place of my life
something which comes before all others
there is the sacred and holylike
recurring memory of an old teethless
bushy white-haired man                                   5
gesturing with his wrinkled hands
and squinty eyes for me to walk to him
sitting on the edge of his wooden
summer bed

being supported and guided along               10
like a newborn spotted fawn
who rises to the cool and minty wind
i kept looking at his yellow
and cracked fingernails
they moved back and forth against the stove    15

and they shined against the kerosene
                              darkened
kitchen and bedroom walls

i floated over the floor towards him
and he smiled as he lifted me up to the                    20
                              cardboard
ceiling and on there were symbols i later read
as that of emily
her scratched-in name alongside the face
of a lonely softball player                                25

remembrance two: it was shortly after he
                              held me
or else it was a day
or a couple of months

or a couple of years later when i saw him next            30
the bodies of three young men leaned against him
as he staggered out towards the night

i never knew what closed him
why i never saw him again
he was on the floor with a blanket                        35
over his still and quiet body
above me there was a mouth moving
it was the face of a woman who had opened
the door for the three young men
she pointed to his body                                   40
this is your grandfather

and then i remember the daylight
with the bald-headed man in overalls
he too mentioned the absence
of my grandfather                                        45
i understood them both
i picture the appletree and its shade
as he was talking to me i saw a group
of people on the green grass
on the ground were table and linen cloths               50
with bowls and dishes of fruits and meats

the bald-headed man in overalls stood
in the brilliance of the summer daylight

his eyebrows made his face look concerned
or worried                                                                          55

later he stood on the same grass
he had been chosen to fill my grandfather's
empty place

the new colored blankets around his waist
and chest glistened with the fresh                                          60
fibrous wool
the beads reflected the good weather
the earth and its people stood and danced
with the beautifully clothed man
who was my grandfather                                                      65
standing in between time
watching the daylight pass through
his eyes

from then on i only saw him occasionally
he would stand on his tractor                                               70
waving to each passing car on the road
as he drove home from
the soybean fields
or else he would converse with my two uncles
that the blood which ran through their                                   75
                                      father's veins
and theirs was unlike the rest of the tribe
in that it came from the beginnings
unlike ours

# STUDY QUESTIONS

1. What does "the first place of my life" seem to represent? Is it a literal place? a state of mind? a relationship to others? How far, would you estimate, is the SPEAKER removed from the central events in the poem? Why do the memories have such a power for the speaker?

2. What accounts for the dreamlike quality of the poem? Notice how many vivid details the poem presents. How do the various details relate to one another?

3. List all of the things we know about the grandfather. What do we know about the bald-headed man in overalls? the three young men? the woman whose hand opened the door? Emily? the speaker? When in the poem do we first become aware that the "teethless / bushy white-haired man" (lines 4–5) is kin to the speaker?

4. Describe the organization of the poem. How does the poem make the move from two quite specific memories in time to a more general consideration of tribal relationships?

# Paula Gunn Allen

Sioux-Laguna and Lebanese-Jewish, Paula Gunn Allen was born in 1939 in Cubero, New Mexico. Her family spoke five languages when she was growing up. It is to this mixture she attributes her being a poet. She believes that poetry should be useful, and that the use-full is the beauty-full. "Language, like a woman, can bring into being what was not in being; it can, like food, transform one set of materials into another set of materials." She holds a doctorate from the University of New Mexico and is chair of Native American studies at San Francisco State University.

The following poem describes an encounter between mother and daughter at a powwow in a gymnasium.

## POWWOW 79, DURANGO

haven't been to one in almost three years
there's six drums and 200 dancers a few
booths piled with jewelry and powwow stuff
some pottery and oven bread
everyone gathers                                        5
stands for the grand entry
two flag songs
and the opening prayer by some guy
works for the BIA[1]
who asks our father                                    10
to bless our cars
to heal our hearts
to let the music here tonight
make us better, cool
hurts and unease                                       15
in his son's name, amen.
my daughter arrives, stoned,

---

1. Bureau of Indian Affairs.

brown face ashy from the weed,
there's no toilet paper
in the ladies room she accuses me                         20
there's never any toilet paper
in the *ladies* room at a powwow she glares
changes
calms
it's like being home after a long time                   25
are you gonna dance I ask
here's my shawl
not dressed right she says
the new beaded ties I bought her swing
from her long dark braids                                 30
why not you have dark blue on I say
look.
we step inside the gym
eyes sweep the rubber floor
jackets, jeans, down-filled vests,                        35
sweatshirts all dark blue.
have to look close to pick out
occasional brown or red on older folks
the dark brown faces rising on the bleachers
the dark hair on almost every head                        40
ever see so many Indians
you're dressed right
we look at the bleachers
quiet like shadows
the people sit watching the floor below                   45
where dancers circle the beating drums
exploding color in the light.

# STUDY QUESTIONS

1. How much does the poem tell us about the SPEAKER? List all of the facts we are given. What else can we infer from the way she talks about the powwow and about the daughter?

2. How much do we know about the daughter? How does she relate to the event? How do you interpret her remarks about the lack of toilet paper? about the shawl? Where is the blame being cast by the daughter? What differences are there in the mother's and daughter's feelings about tradition? How can you tell? What is the speaker's attitude toward the opening prayer?

3. Why do "older" folks have on brown or red clothes in the sea of dark blue ones? What other differences between generations does the poem articulate?

# Leslie Marmon Silko

Born in 1948 in Albuquerque, New Mexico, Leslie Marmon Silko grew up on the Laguna Pueblo reservation. Her heritage is mixed—part Laguna, part Mexican, part white—and she refuses to apologize for it, believing that her storytelling ability "rise[s] out of this source." She is a graduate of the University of New Mexico and now teaches at the University of Arizona. Her best-known work, *Storyteller* (1981), is a collection of many of her best poems and stories. Her writing, in both prose and poetry, is highly regarded, and she is the recipient of a prestigious MacArthur Fellowship.

Silko often draws, as in the selection that follows, on her wide knowledge of languages and traditions. Here, a family feud over the borders between yards leads to a range of individual vignettes that add up to a revealing community portrait.

## PRIVATE PROPERTY

All Pueblo Tribes have stories about such a person—a young child, an orphan. Someone has taken the child and has given it a place by the fire to sleep. The child's clothes are whatever the people no longer want. The child empties the ashes and gathers wood. The child is always quiet, sitting in its place tending the fire. They pay little attention to the child as they complain and tell stories about one another. The child listens although it has nothing to gain or lose in anything they say. The child simply listens. Some years go by and great danger stalks the village—in some versions of the story it is a drought and great famine, other times it is a monster in the form of a giant bear. And when all the others have failed and even the priests doubt the prayers, this child, still wearing old clothes, goes out. The child confronts the danger and the village is saved. Among the Pueblo people the child's reliability as a narrator is believed to be perfect.

Etta works with the wind at her back. Sand and dust roll down the road. She feels scattered drops of rain and sometimes flakes of snow. What they have been saying about her all these years is untrue. They are angry because she left. Old leaves and weed stalks lie in gray drifts at the corners of the old fence. Part of an old newspaper is caught in the tumbleweeds; the wind presses it into brittle yellow flakes. She rakes the debris as high as her belly.

They continue with stories about her. Going away has changed her. Living with white people has changed her. Fragments of glass blink like animal eyes. The wind pushes the flames deep into the bones and old manure heaped under the pile of dry weeds. The rake drags out a shriveled work shoe and then the sleeve torn from a child's dress. They burn as dark and thick as hair. The wind pushes her off balance. Flames pour around her and catch the salt bushes. The yard burns bare. The sky is the color of stray smoke. The next morning the wind is gone. The ground is crusted with frost and still the blackened bones smolder.

The horses trot past the house before dawn. The sky and earth are the same color then—dense gray of the night burned down. At the approach of the sun, the east horizon bleeds dark blue. Reyna sits up in her bed suddenly and looks out the window at the horses. She has been dreaming she was stolen by Navajos and was taken away in their wagon. The sound of the horses' hooves outside the window had been the wagon horses of her dreams. The white one trots in the lead, followed by the gray. The little sorrel mare is always last. The gray sneezes at their dust. They are headed for the river. Reyna wants to remember this, and gets up. The sky is milky. Village dogs are barking in the distance. She dresses and finds her black wool cardigan. The dawn air smells like rain but it has been weeks since the last storm. The crickets don't feel the light. The mockingbird is in the pear tree. The bare adobe yard is swept clean. A distance north of the pear tree there is an old wire fence caught on gray cedar posts that lean in different directions. Etta has come back after many years to live in the little stone house.

    The sound of the hammer had been Reyna's first warning. She blames herself for leaving the old fence posts and wire. The fence should have been torn down years ago. The old wire had lain half-buried in the sand that had drifted around the posts. Etta was wearing men's gloves that were too large for her. She pulled the strands of wire up and hammered fence staples to hold the wire to the posts. Etta has made the fence the boundary line. She has planted morning glories and hollyhocks all along it. She waters them every morning before it gets hot. Reyna watches her. The morning glories and hollyhocks are all that hold up the fence posts anymore.

Etta is watching Reyna from the kitchen window of the little stone house. She fills the coffee pot without looking at the level of water. Reyna is walking the fence between their yards. She paces the length of the fence as if she can pull the fence down with her walking. They had been married to brothers, but the men died long ago. They don't call each other "sister-in-law" anymore. The fire in the cookstove is cracking like rifle shots. She bought a pick-up load of pinon wood from a Navajo. The little house has one room, but the walls are rock and adobe mortar two feet thick. The one who got the big house got the smaller yard. That is how Etta remembers it. Their mother-in-law had been a kind woman. She wanted her sons and daughters-in-law to live happily with each other. She followed the old ways. She believed houses and fields must always be held by the women. There had been no nieces or daughters. The old woman stood by the pear tree with the daughters-in-law and gave them each a house, and the yard to divide. She pointed at the little stone house. She said the one who got the little house got the bigger share of the yard. Etta remembers that.

Cheromiah drives up in his white Ford pick-up. He walks to the gate smiling. He wears his big belly over his Levi's like an apron. Reyna is gathering kindling at the woodpile. The juniper chips are hard and smooth as flint. She rubs her hands together although there is no dust. "They came through this morning before it was even daylight." She points in the direction of the river. "They were going down that way." He frowns, then he smiles. "I've been looking for them all week," he says. The old woman shakes her head. "Well, if you hurry, they might still be there." They are his horses. His father-in-law gave him the white one when it was a colt. Its feet are as big around as pie pans. The gray is the sorrel mare's colt. The horses belong to Cheromiah, but the horses don't know that. "Nobody told them," that's what people say and then they laugh. The white horse leans against corral planks until they give way. It steps over low spots in old stone fences. The gray and little sorrel follow.

"The old lady said to share and love one another. She said we only make use of these things as long as we are here. We don't own them. Nobody owns anything." Juanita nods. She listens to both of her aunts. The two old women are quarreling over a narrow strip of ground between the two houses. The earth is hard-packed. Nothing grows there. Juanita listens to her Aunt Reyna and agrees that her Aunt Etta is wrong. Too many years living in Winslow. Aunt Etta returns and she wants to make the yard "private property" like white people do in Winslow. Juanita visits both of her aunts every day. She visits her Aunt Etta in the afternoon while her Aunt Reyna is resting. Etta and Reyna know their grandniece must visit both her aunts. Juanita has no husband or family to look after. She is the one who looks after the old folks. She is not like her brothers or sister who have wives or a husband. She doesn't forget. She looked after Uncle Joe for ten years until he finally died. He always told her she would have the house because women should have the houses. He didn't have much. Just his wagon horses, the house and a pig. He was the oldest and believed in the old ways. Aunt Reyna was right. If her brother Joe were alive he would talk to Etta. He would remind her that this is the village, not Winslow, Arizona. He would remind Etta how they all must share. Aunt Reyna would have more space for her woodpile then.

Most people die once, but "old man Joe he died twice," that's what people said, and then they laughed. Juanita knew they joked about it, but still she held her head high. She was the only one who even tried to look after the old folks. That November, Uncle Joe had been sick with pneumonia. His house smelled of Vicks and Ben-Gay. She checked on him every morning. He was always up before dawn the way all the old folks were. They greeted the sun and prayed for everybody. He was always up and had a fire in his little pot belly stove to make coffee. But that morning she knocked and there was no answer. Her heart was beating fast because she knew what she would find. The stove was cold. She stood by his bed and watched. He did not move. She touched the hand on top of the blanket and the fingers were as cold as the room. Juanita ran all the way to Aunt Reyna's house with the news. They sent word. The nephews and the clansmen came with picks and shovels. Before they went to dress him for burial, they cooked the big meal always prepared for the gravediggers. Aunt Reyna rolled out the tortillas and cried. Joe had always been so good to her. Joe had always loved her best after their parents died.

Cheromiah came walking by that morning while Juanita was getting 9 more firewood. He was dragging a long rope and leather halter. He asked if she had seen any sign of his horses. She shook her head and then she told him Uncle Joe had passed away that morning. Tears came to her eyes. Cheromiah stood quietly for a moment. "I will miss the old man. He taught me everything I know about horses." Juanita nodded. Her arms were full of juniper wood. She looked away toward the southeast. "I saw your gray horse up in the sandhills the other day." Cheromiah smiled and thanked her. Cheromiah's truck didn't start in cold weather. He didn't feel like walking all the way up to the sand hills that morning. He took the road around the far side of the village to get home. It took him past Uncle Joe's place. The pig was butting its head against the planks of the pen making loud smacking sounds. The wagon horses were eating corn stalks the old man had bundled up after harvest for winter feed. Cheromiah wondered which of the old man's relatives was already looking after the livestock. He heard someone chopping wood on the other side of the house. The old man saw him and waved in the direction of the river. "They were down there last evening grazing in the willows." Cheromiah dropped the halter and rope and gestured with both hands. "Uncle Joe! They told me you died! Everyone thinks you are dead! They already cooked the gravediggers lunch!"

From that time on Uncle Joe didn't get up before dawn like he once did. 10 But he wouldn't let them tease Juanita about her mistake. Behind her back, Juanita's cousins and in-laws were saying that she was in such a hurry to collect her inheritance. They didn't think she should get everything. They thought all of it should be shared equally. The following spring, Uncle Joe's wagon horses went down Paguate Hill too fast and the wagon wheel hit a big rock. He was thrown from the wagon and a sheepherder found him. Uncle Joe was unconscious for two days and then he died. 'This time he really *is* dead, poor thing," people would say and then they'd smile.

The trouble over the pig started on the day of the funeral. Juanita caught 11 her brother's wife at the pig pen. The wife held a large pail in both hands. The pail was full of a yellowish liquid. There were bones swimming in it.

Corn tassels floated like hair. She looked Juanita in the eye as she dumped the lard pail into the trough. The pig switched its tail and made one push through the liquid with its snout. It looked up at both of them. The snout kept moving. The pig would not eat. Juanita had already fed the pigs scraps from the gravediggers' plates. She didn't want her brothers' wives feeding the pig. They would claim, they had fed the pig more than she had. They would say that whoever fed the pig the most should get the biggest share of meat. At butchering time they would show up to collect half. "It won't eat slop," Juanita said, "don't be feeding it slop."

The stories they told about Etta always came back to the same thing.               12

While the other girls learn cooking and sewing at the Indian School, Etta   13
works in the greenhouse. In the evenings the teacher sits with her on the sofa. They repeat the names of the flowers. She teaches Etta the parts of the flower. On Saturdays while the dormitory matrons take the others to town, Etta stays with the teacher. Etta kneels beside her in the garden. They press brown dirt over the gladiola bulbs. The teacher runs a hot bath for her. The teacher will not let her return to the dormitory until she has cleaned Etta's fingernails. The other girls tell stories about Etta.

The white gauze curtains are breathing in and out. The hollyhocks bend   14
around the fence posts and lean over the wire. The buds are tight and press between the green lips of the sheath. The seed had been saved in a mason jar. Etta found it in the pantry behind a veil of cobwebs. She planted it the length of the fence to mark the boundary. She had only been a child the first time, but she can still remember the colors—reds and yellows swaying above her head, tiny black ants in the white eyes of pollen. Others were purple and dark red, almost black as dried blood. She planted the seeds the teacher had given her. She saved the seeds from the only year the hollyhocks grew. Etta doesn't eat pork. She is thinking about the row of tamarisk trees she will plant along the fence so people cannot see her yard or house. She does not want to spend her retirement with everyone in the village minding her business the way they always have. Somebody is always fighting over something. The years away taught her differently. She knows better now. The yard is hers. They can't take it just because she had lived away from the village all those years. A person could go away and come back again. The village people don't understand fences. At Indian School she learned fences tell you where you stand. In Winslow, white people built fences around their houses, otherwise something might be lost or stolen. There were rumors about her the whole time she lived in Winslow. The gossip was not true. The teacher had written to her all the years Etta was married. It was a job to go to after her husband died. The teacher was sick and old. Etta went because she loved caring for the flowers. It was only a job, but people like to talk. The teacher was sick for a long time before she died.

"What do you want with those things," the clanswoman scolded, "wast-  15
ing water on something we can't eat." The old woman mumbled to herself
all the way across the garden. Etta started crying. She sat on the ground by
the hollyhocks she had planted, and held her face. She pressed her fingers
into her eyes. The old woman had taken her in. It was the duty of the clan
to accept orphans.

Etta tells her she is not coming back from Indian School in the summer. She  16
has a job at school caring for the flowers. She and the clanswoman are cleaning a sheep stomach, rinsing it under the mulberry tree. The intestines are
coiled in a white enamel pan. They are bluish gray, the color of the sky
before snow. Strands of tallow branch across them like clouds. "You are not
much good to me anyway. I took you because no one else wanted to. I have
tried to teach you, but the white people at that school have ruined you. You
waste good water growing things we cannot eat."

The first time Etta returned from Winslow for a visit, Reyna confided  17
there was gossip going on in the village. Etta could tell by the details that her
sister-in-law was embroidering stories about her too. They did not speak to
each other after that. People were jealous of her because she had left. They
were certain she preferred white people. But Etta spoke only to the teacher.
White people did not see her when she walked on the street.

The heat holds the afternoon motionless. The sun does not move. It has  18
parched all color from the sky and left only the fine ash. The street below is
empty. Down the long dim hall there are voices in English and, more distantly, the ticking of a clock. The room is white and narrow. The shade is
pulled. It pulses heat the texture of pearls. The water in the basin is the color
of garnets. Etta waits in a chair beside the bed. The sheets are soaked with
her fever. She murmurs the parts of the flowers—she whispers that the bud
is swelling open, but that afternoon was long ago.

Ruthie's husband is seeing that other woman in the cornfield. The cornfield  19
belongs to her and to her sister, Juanita. Their mother left it to both of them.
In the morning her husband walks to the fields with the hoe on his shoulder.
Not long after, the woman appears with a coal bucket filled with stove ashes.
The woman follows the path toward the trash pile, but when she gets to the
far corner of the cornfield she stops. When she thinks no one is watching she
sets the bucket down. She gathers up the skirt of her dress and steps over the
fence where the wire sags.

Ruthie would not have suspected anything if she had not noticed the  20
rocks. He was always hauling rocks to build a new shed or corral. But this
time there was something about the colors of the sandstone. The reddish
pink and orange yellow looked as if they had been taken from the center of
the sky as the sun went down. She had never seen such intense color in
sandstone. She had always remembered it being shades of pale yellow or

peppered white-colors for walls and fences. But these rocks looked as if rain had just fallen on them. She watched her husband. He was unloading the rocks from the old wagon and stacking them carefully next to the woodpile. When he had finished it was dark and she could not see the colors of the sandstone any longer. She thought about how good-looking he was, the kind of man all the other women chase.

Reyna goes with them. She takes her cane but carries it ready in her     21
hand like a rabbit club. Her grandnieces have asked her to go with them. Ruthie's husband is carrying on with another woman. The same one as before. They are going after them together—the two sisters and the old aunt. Ruthie told Juanita about it first. It was their mother's field and now it is theirs. If Juanita had a husband he would work there too. "The worst thing is them doing it in the cornfield. It makes the corn sickly, it makes the beans stop growing. If they want to do it they can go down to the trash and lie in the tin cans and broken glass with the flies," that's what Reyna says.

They surprise them lying together on the sandy ground in the shade of     22
the tall corn plants. Last time they caught them together they reported them to the woman's grandmother, but the old woman didn't seem to care. They told that woman's husband too. But he has a job in Albuquerque, and men don't bother to look after things. It is up to women to take care of everything. He is supposed to be hoeing weeds in their field, but instead he is rolling around on the ground with that woman, killing off all their melons and beans.

Her breasts are long and brown. They bounce against her like potatoes.     23
She runs with her blue dress in her hand. She leaves her shoes. They are next to his hoe. Ruthie stands between Juanita and Aunt Reyna. They gesture with their arms and yell. They are not scolding him. They don't even look at him. They are scolding the rest of the village over husband-stealing and corn that is sickly. Reyna raps on the fence post with her cane. Juanita calls him a pig. Ruthie cries because the beans won't grow. He kneels to lace his work shoes. He kneels for a long time. His fingers move slowly. They are not talking to him. They are talking about the other woman. The red chili stew she makes is runny and pale. They pay no attention to him. He goes back to hoeing weeds. Their voices sift away in the wind. Occasionally he stops to wipe his forehead on his sleeve. He looks up at the sky or over the sand hills. Off in the distance there is a man on foot. He is crossing the big sand dune above the river. He is dragging a rope. The horses are grazing on yellow rice grass at the foot of the dune. They are down wind from him. He inches along, straining to crouch over his own stomach. The big white horse whirls suddenly, holding its tail high. The gray half-circles and joins it, blowing loudly through its nostrils. The little sorrel mare bolts to the top of the next dune before she turns.

Etta awakens and the yard is full of horses. The gray chews a hollyhock. Red petals stream from its mouth. The sorrel mare watches her come out the door. The white horse charges away, rolling his eyes at her nightgown. Etta throws a piece of juniper from the woodpile. The gray horse presses hard against the white one. They tremble in the corner of the fence, strings of blue morning glories trampled under their hooves. Etta yells and the sorrel mare startles, crowding against the gray. They heave forward against the fence, and the posts make slow cracking sounds. The wire whines and squeaks. It gives way suddenly and the white horse stumbles ahead tangled in wire. The sorrel and the gray bolt past, and for an instant the white horse hesitates, shivering at the wire caught around its forelegs and neck. Then the white horse leaps forward, rusty wire and fence posts trailing behind like a broken necklace.

## STUDY QUESTIONS

1. Twice in the story, people are said to follow the "old ways." What are the "old ways"? What values do they represent? Which characters in the story embody the "old ways" most fully?

2. In what different ways do Etta's habits and values differ from those of others in the story? What in her life history accounts for those differences? Do you think that the village people are right to assume that her "foreign" experience has corrupted her? Which characteristics of hers are least attractive? Which are most attractive? How does the narrator of the story seem to feel about Etta? How can you tell?

3. What strategies does the author use to characterize each of the people in the story?

4. Who is responsible for the fences? What do the fences mean to the different characters in the story? How effective are the fences in dealing with people's feelings of ownership and sharing? How effective are they in containing the animals?

5. Why does the NARRATOR tell us directly that the rumors about Etta at school were untrue?

6. What does the episode about the catching of Ruthie's husband with another woman in the cornfield have to do with the central THEME of the story? Why do the people who have caught the husband in the act ignore him once their mission is completed? What kinds of roles do men play in the story?

7. What does the first paragraph of the story have to do with the rest of it?

# Arthur Laurents

Born in Brooklyn in 1918, Arthur Laurents began writing plays for radio in 1939 and later turned primarily to stage and screen writing. *West Side Story* (with a score by Leonard Bernstein and lyrics by Stephen Sondheim) is his best-known play, but he has written many other successful plays, including *The Turn of the Cuckoo* (1952), *Gypsy* (1959), and *Hallelujah Baby!* (1967). He also wrote for several radio series, including "Dr. Christian," "The Thin Man," and "This Is Your FBI."

*West Side Story*, adapted into a film that won ten Academy Awards, depicts gang wars in New York City in the 1950s, and (using motifs from *Romeo and Juliet*) sets a cross-cultural love story against bitter feuding between the groups to which the lovers belong.

# WEST SIDE STORY

The action takes place on the West Side of New York City during the last days of summer.

## ACT I

### Scene 1

*5:00 P.M. The street.*
*A suggestion of city streets and alleyways; a brick wall.*

*The opening is musical: half-danced, half-mimed, with occasional phrases of dialogue. It is primarily a condensation of the growing rivalry between two teen-age gangs, the Jets and the Sharks, each of which has its own prideful uniform. The boys—sideburned, long-haired—are vital, restless, sardonic; the Sharks are Puerto Ricans, the Jets an anthology of what is called American.*

*The action begins with the Jets in possession of the area: owning, enjoying, loving their "home." Their leader is* RIFF: *glowing, driving, intelligent, slightly whacky. His lieutenant is* DIESEL: *big, slow, steady, nice. The youngest member of the gang is* BABY JOHN: *awed at everything, including that he is a Jet, trying to act the big man. His buddy is* A-RAB: *an explosive little ferret who enjoys everything and understands the seriousness of nothing. The most aggressive is* ACTION: *a catlike ball of fury. We will get to know these boys better later, as well as* SNOWBOY: *a bespectacled self-styled expert.*

*The first interruption of the Jets' sunny mood is the sharply punctuated entrance of the leader of the Sharks,* BERNARDO: *handsome, proud, fluid, a chip on his sardonic shoulder. The Jets, by far in the majority, flick him off. He returns with other Sharks: they, too, are flicked off. But the numerical supremacy, the strength of the Jets, is gradually being threatened. The beginnings of warfare are mild at first: a boy being tripped up, or being sandbagged with a flour sack or even being spit on—all with overly elaborate apologies.*

*Finally,* A-RAB *comes across the suddenly deserted area, pretending to be an airplane. There is no sound as he zooms along in fancied flight. Then over the wall drops* BERNARDO. *Another Shark, another and another appear, blocking* A-RAB'S *panicky efforts at escape. They close in, grab him, pummel him, as a Shark on top of the wall is stationed as lookout. Finally,* BERNARDO *bends over* A-RAB *and makes a gesture (piercing his ear); the lookout whistles; Jets tear on, Sharks tear on, and a free-for-all breaks out.* RIFF *goes at once to* A-RAB, *like a protective father. The fight is stopped by a police whistle, louder and louder, and the arrival of a big goonlike cop,* KRUPKE, *and a plain-clothes man,* SCHRANK. SCHRANK *is strong, always in command; he has a charming, pleasant manner, which he often employs to cover his venom and his fear.*

KRUPKE: Knock it off! Settle down.

SCHRANK: All right: *kill each other!* . . . But not on my beat.

RIFF: [*Such innocence*] Why if it isn't Lieutenant Schrank!

SEVERAL JETS: [*Dancing-class manners*] Top of the day, Lieutenant Schrank.

BERNARDO: [*One with Riff*] And Officer Krupke!

SEVERAL SHARKS: Top of the day, Officer Krupke.

SCHRANK: Boy, what you Puerto Ricans have done to this neighborhood. Which one of 'em clobbered ya, A-rab?

[A-RAB *looks to* RIFF, *who takes over with great helpful seriousness.*]

RIFF: As a matter of factuality, sir, we suspicion the job was done by a cop.

SNOWBOY: Two cops.

A-RAB: Oh, at least!

KRUPKE: Impossible!

SCHRANK: Didn't nobody tell ya there's a difference between bein' a stool pigeon and co-operatin' with the law?

RIFF: You told us the difference, sir. And we all chipped in for a prize for the first guy who can figure it out.

ACTION: [*Indicating* SCHRANK] Maybe buddy boy should get the prize.

SCHRANK: Don't buddy boy me, Action! I got a hot surprise for you: you hoodlums don't own the streets. There's been too much raiding between you and the PRs. All right, Bernardo, get your trash outa here. (*Mock charm*) Please.

BERNARDO: Let's go, Sharks.

[*They exit.*]

SCHRANK: [*To the* JETS] If I don't put down the roughhouse, I get put down—on a traffic corner. Your friend don't like traffic corners. So you buddy boys are gonna play ball with me. I gotta put up with them and so do you. *You're gonna make nice with them PRs from now on.* Because otherwise I'm gonna beat the crap outa every one of ya and *then* run ya in. Say good-bye to the nice boys, Krupke.

KRUPKE: Good-bye, boys. [*He follows* SCHRANK *out.*]

SNOWBOY: [*Imitating* KRUPKE] Good-bye, boys.

A-RAB: They make a very nice couple.

ACTION: [*Bitterly*] "You hoodlums don't own the streets."

SNOWBOY: Go play in the park!

ACTION: Keep off the grass!

BABY JOHN: Get outa the house!

ACTION: Keep off the block!

A-RAB: Get outa *here!*

ACTION: Keep off the world! A gang that don't own a street is nuthin'!

RIFF: WE DO OWN IT! Jets—square off! Acemen: [DIESEL, ACTION *and* SNOWBOY *line up at attention*] Rocketmen: [*Three others line up*] Rank-and-file: [*Sheepishly,* A-RAB *trudges into position,* BABY JOHN *behind him.*]

BABY JOHN: [*Shocked, to* A-RAB] Gee, your ear's got blood on it!

A-RAB: [*Proudly*] I'm a casual, Baby John.

BABY JOHN: [*Examining the ear*] Them PRs! They branded you!

SNOWBOY: That makes you a Puerto Rican tomato. Cha-cha-cha señorita?

RIFF: Cut the frabbajabba. Which one of the Sharks did it?

A-RAB: Bernardo. 'Cause I heard him say: "Thees ees for stink bombin' my old man's store." [*He makes the same gesture* BERNARDO *made when he pierced his ear.*]

BABY JOHN: Ouch!

ACTION: You shoulda done worse. Them PRs're the reason my old man's gone bust.

RIFF: Who says?

ACTION: My old man says.

BABY JOHN: [*To* A-RAB] My old man says his old man woulda gone bust anyway.

ACTION: Your old man says what?

BABY JOHN: My old man says them Puerto Ricans is ruinin' free ennaprise.

ACTION: And what're we doin' about it?

[*Pushing through the gang comes a scrawny teen-age girl, dressed in an outfit that is a pathetic attempt to imitate that of the Jets. Perhaps we have glimpsed her in the fracas before the police came in. Her name is* ANYBODYS.]

ANYBODYS: Gassin', crabbin'—

ACTION: You still around?

ANYBODYS: Listen, I was a smash in that fight. Oh, Riff, Riff, I was murder!

RIFF: Come on, Anybodys—

ANYBODYS: Riff, how about me gettin' in the gang now?

A-RAB: How about the gang gettin' in—ahhh, who'd wanta!

ANYBODYS: You cheap beast! [*She lunges for* A-RAB, *but* RIFF *pulls her off and pushes her out.*]

RIFF: The road, little lady, the road. [*In a moment of bravado, just before she goes,* ANYBODYS *spits—but cautiously*] Round out! [*This is* RIFF's *summoning of the gang, and they surround him*] We fought hard for this territory and it's ours. But with those cops servin' as cover, the PRs can move in right under our noses and take it away. *Unless* we speed fast and clean 'em up in one all-out fight!

ACTION: [*Eagerly*] A rumble! [*A jabbing gesture*] Chung! Chung!

RIFF: Cool, Action boy. The Sharks want a place, too, and *they are tough.* They might ask for bottles or knives or zip guns.

BABY JOHN: Zip guns . . . Gee!

RIFF: I'm not finalizin' and sayin' they will: I'm only sayin' they might and we gotta be prepared. Now, what's your mood?

ACTION: I say go, go!!

SNOWBOY: But if they say knives or guns—

BABY JOHN: I say let's forget the whole thing.

DIESEL: What do you say, Riff?

RIFF: I say this turf is small, *but it's all we got.* I wanna hold it like we always held it: with skin! But if they say switchblades, I'll get a switchblade. I say I want the Jets to be Number One, to sail, to hold the sky!

DIESEL: Then rev us off. [*A punching gesture*] Voom-va voom!

ACTION: Chung chung!

A-RAB: Cracko, jacko!

SNOWBOY: Riga diga dum!

BABY JOHN: Pam pam!!

RIFF: O.K., buddy boys, we rumble! (*General glee*) Now protocality calls for a war council to decide on weapons. I'll make the challenge to Bernardo.

SNOWBOY: You gotta take a lieutenant.

ACTION: That's me!

RIFF: That's Tony.

ACTION: Who needs Tony?

[*Music starts.*]

RIFF: Against the Sharks we need every man we got.

ACTION: Tony don't belong any more.

RIFF: Cut it, Action boy. I and Tony started the Jets.

ACTION: Well, he acts like he don't wanna belong.

BABY JOHN: Who wouldn't wanna belong to the Jets!

ACTION: Tony ain't been with us for over a month.

SNOWBOY: What about the day we clobbered the Emeralds?

A-RAB: Which we couldn't have done without Tony.

BABY JOHN: He saved my ever lovin' neck.

RIFF: Right. He's always come through for us and he will now.

> [*He sings*]
> When you're a Jet,
> You're a Jet all the way
> From your first cigarette
> To your last dyin' day.
> When you're a Jet,
> If the spit hits the fan,
> You got brothers around,
> You're a family man!
> You're never alone,
> You're never disconnected!
> You're home with your own—
> When company's expected,
> You're well protected!
> Then you are set
> With a capital J,
> Which you'll never forget
> Till they cart you away.
> When you're a Jet,
> You stay
> A jet!

[*He speaks*] I know Tony like I know me. I guarantee you can count him in.

ACTION: In, out, let's get crackin'.

A-RAB: Where you gonna find Bernardo?

RIFF: At the dance tonight at the gym.

BIG DEAL: But the gym's neutral territory.

RIFF: [*Sweet innocence*] I'm gonna make nice there! I'm only gonna challenge him.

A-RAB: Great, Daddy-O!

RIFF: So everybody dress up sweet and sharp. Meet Tony and me at ten. And walk tall! [*He runs off.*]

A-RAB: We always walk tall!

BABY JOHN: We're Jets!

ACTION: The greatest!

> [*He sings with* BABY JOHN]
> When you're a Jet,
> You're the top cat in town,

You're the gold-medal kid
With the heavyweight crown!

[A-RAB, ACTION, BIG DEAL *sing*]
When you're a Jet,
You're the swingin'est thing.
Little boy, you're a man;
Little man, you're a king!

[ALL]
The Jets are in gear,
Our cylinders are clickin'!
The Sharks'll steer clear
'Cause every Puerto Rican
'S a lousy chicken!

Here come the Jets
Like a bat out of hell—
Someone gets in our way,
Someone don't feel so well!
Here come the Jets:
Little world, step aside!
Better go underground,
Better run, better hide!
We're drawin' the line,
So keep your noses hidden!
We're hangin' a sign
Says "Visitors forbidden"—
And we ain't kiddin'!
Here come the Jets,
Yeah! And we're gonna beat
Every last buggin' gang
On the whole buggin' street!

[DIESEL *and* ACTION]
On the whole!

[ALL]
Ever—!
Mother—!
Lovin'—!
Street!

*The lights black out.*

SCENE 2

5:30 P.M. *A back yard.*

*On a small ladder, a good-looking sandy-haired boy is painting a vertical sign that will say: Doc's. Below,* RIFF *is haranguing.*

RIFF: Riga tiga tum tum. Why not? . . . You can't say ya won't, Tony boy, without sayin' why not?

TONY: [*Grins*] Why not?

RIFF: Because it's me askin': Riff. Womb to tomb!

TONY: Sperm to worm! [*Surveying the sign*] You sure this looks like skywritin'?

RIFF: It's brilliant.

TONY: Twenty-seven years the boss has had that drugstore. I wanna surprise him with a new sign.

RIFF: [*Shaking the ladder*] Tony, this is important!

TONY: Very important: Acemen, Rocketmen.

RIFF: What's with you? Four and one-half years I live with a buddy and his family. Four and one-half years I think I know a man's character. Buddy boy, I am a victim of disappointment in you.

TONY: End your sufferin', little man. Why don't you pack up your gear and clear out?

RIFF: 'Cause your ma's hot for me. [TONY *grabs his arm and twists it*] No! 'Cause I hate livin' with my buggin' uncle uncle UNCLE!

[TONY *releases him and climbs back up the ladder.*]

TONY: Now go play nice with the Jets.

RIFF: The Jets are the greatest!

TONY: Were.

RIFF: Are. You found somethin' better?

TONY: No. But—

RIFF: But what?

TONY: You won't dig it.

RIFF: Try me.

TONY: O.K. . . . Every single damn night for the last month, I wake up— and I'm reachin' out.

RIFF: For what?

TONY: I don't know. It's right outside the door, around the corner. But it's comin'!

RIFF: *What* is? Tell me!

TONY: I don't know! It's—like the kick I used to get from bein' a Jet.

RIFF: [*Quietly*] . . . Or from bein' buddies.

TONY: We're still buddies.

RIFF: The kick comes from people, buddy boy.

TONY: Yeah, but not from being a Jet.

RIFF: No? Without a gang you're an orphan. With a gang you walk in two's, three's, four's. And when your gang is the best, when you're a Jet, buddy boy, you're out in the sun and home free home!

TONY: Riff, I've had it. [*Pause.*]

RIFF: Tony, the trouble is large: the Sharks bite hard! We got to stop them now, and we need *you!* [*Pause. Quietly*] I never asked the time of day from a clock, but I'm askin' you: Come to the dance tonight . . . [TONY *turns away*] . . . I already told the gang you'd be there.

TONY: [*After a moment, turns to him with a grin*] What time?

RIFF: Ten?

TONY: Ten it is.

RIFF: Womb to tomb!

TONY: Sperm to worm! And I'll live to regret this.

RIFF: Who knows? Maybe what you're waitin' for'll be twitchin' at the dance! [*He runs off.*]

TONY: Who knows?

> [*Music starts and he sings*]
> Could be! . . .
> Who knows? . . .
> There's something due any day;
> I will know right away
> Soon as it shows.
> It may come cannonballin' down through the sky,
> Gleam in its eye,
> Bright as a rose!
> Who knows? . . .
> It's only just out of reach,
> Down the block, on a beach,
> Under a tree.
> I got a feeling there's a miracle due,
> Gonna come true,
> Coming to me!
>
> Could it be? Yes, it could.
> Something's coming, something good,
> If I can wait!
> Something's coming, I don't know what it is
> But it is
> Gonna be great!
>
> With a click, with a shock,
> Phone'll jingle, door'll knock,
> Open the latch!

Something's coming, don't know when, but it's soon—
Catch the moon,
One-handed catch!

Around the corner,
Or whistling down the river,
Come on—deliver
To me!

Will it be? Yes, it will.
Maybe just by holding still
It'll be there!
Come on, something, come on in, don't be shy,
Meet a guy,
Pull up a chair!

The air is humming,
And something great is coming!
Who knows?
It's only just out of reach,
Down the block, on a beach . . .
Maybe tonight . . .

*The lights dim.*

SCENE 3

*6:00 P.M. A bridal shop.*
*A small section, enough to include a table with sewing machine, a chair or two.*
ANITA, *a Puerto Rican girl with loose hair and slightly flashy clothes, is finishing remaking what was a white communion dress into a party dress for an extremely lovely, extremely young girl:* MARIA. ANITA *is knowing, sexual, sharp.* MARIA *is an excited, enthusiastic, obedient child, with the temper, stubborn strength and awareness of a woman.*

MARIA: [*Holding out scissors*] *Por favor*,[1] Anita. Make the neck lower!
ANITA: Stop it, Maria.
MARIA: One inch. How much can one little inch do?
ANITA: Too much.
MARIA: [*Exasperated*] Anita, it is now to be a dress for dancing, no longer for kneeling in front of an altar.
ANITA: With those boys you can start in dancing and end up kneeling.
MARIA: *Querida*, one little inch; *una poca poca*—[2]

1. Please.
2. Dear . . . one little little.

ANITA: Bernardo made me promise—

MARIA: *Ai!* Bernardo! One month have I been in this country—do I ever even touch excitement? I sew all day, I sit all night. For what did my fine brother bring me here?

ANITA: To marry Chino.

MARIA: When I look at Chino, nothing happens.

ANITA: What do you expect to happen?

MARIA: I don't know: something. What happens when you look at Bernardo?

ANITA: It's when I don't look that it happens.

MARIA: I think I will tell Mama and Papa about you and 'Nardo in the balcony of the movies.

ANITA: I'll rip this to shreds!

MARIA: No. But if you perhaps could manage to lower the neck—

ANITA: Next year.

MARIA: Next year I will be married and no one will care if it is down to here!

ANITA: Down to where?

MARIA: Down to here [*Indicates her waist*] I hate this dress!

ANITA: Then don't wear it and don't come with us to the dance.

MARIA: Don't come! [*Grabs the dress*] Could we not dye it red, at least?

ANITA: No, we could not. [*She starts to help* MARIA *into the dress.*]

MARIA: White is for babies. I will be the only one there in a white—

ANITA: Well???

MARIA: Ahhhh—*sí!* It is a beautiful dress: I love you!

[*As she hugs* ANITA, BERNARDO *enters, followed by a shy, gentle, sweet-faced boy:* CHINO.]

BERNARDO: Are you ready?

MARIA: Come in, 'Nardo. [*Whirls in the dress*] Is it not beautiful?

BERNARDO: [*Looking only at* MARIA's *face*] Yes. [*Kisses her*] Very.

ANITA: I didn't quite hear . . .

BERNARDO: [*Kissing* ANITA *quite differently*] Very beautiful.

MARIA: [*Watches them a second, then turns to* CHINO] Come in, Chino. Do not be afraid.

CHINO: But this is a shop for ladies.

BERNARDO: Our ladies!

MARIA: 'Nardo, it is most important that I have a wonderful time at the dancing tonight.

BERNARDO: [*As* ANITA *hooks up* MARIA] Why?

MARIA: Because tonight is the real beginning of my life as a young lady of America!

[*She begins to whirl in the dress as the shop slides off and a flood of gaily colored streamers pours down. As* MARIA *begins to turn and turn, going offstage, Shark girls, dressed for the dance, whirl on, followed by Jet girls, by boys from both gangs. The streamers fly up again for the next scene.*]

## SCENE 4

10:00 P.M. *The gym.*

*Actually, a converted gymnasium of a settlement house, at the moment being used as a dancehall, disguised for the occasion with streamers and bunting.*

*Both gangs are jitterbugging wildly with their bodies, but their faces, although they are enjoying themselves, remain cool, almost detached. The line between the two gangs is sharply defined by the colors they wear: the Jets, girls as well as boys, reflecting the colors of the Jet jackets; the same is true of the Sharks. The dancing is a physical and emotional release for these kids.*

MARIA *enters with* CHINO, BERNARDO *and* ANITA. *As she looks around, delighted, thrilled by this, her first dance, the Jets catch sight of* BERNARDO, *who is being greeted by* PEPE, *his lieutenant, and other Sharks. As the music peters away, the Jets withdraw to one side of the hall, around* RIFF. *The Sharks, seeing this, draw to their side, around* BERNARDO. *A brief consultation, and* RIFF *starts across—with lieutenants—to make his challenge to* BERNARDO, *who starts—with his lieutenants—to meet him. The moment is brief but it would be disastrous if a smiling, overly cheerful young man of about thirty did not hurry forward. He is called* GLAD HAND, *and he is a "square."*

GLAD HAND: [*Beaming*] All right, boys and girls! Attention, please! [*Hum of talk*] Attention! [KRUPKE *appears behind* GLAD HAND: *the talk stops*] Thank you. It sure is a fine turnout tonight. [*Ad libs from the kids*] We want you to make friends here, so we're going to have a few get-together dances. [*Ad libs; "Oh, ginger peachy," etc.*] You form two circles: boys on the outside, girls on the inside.

SNOWBOY: Where are you?

GLAD HAND: [*Tries to laugh at this*] All right. Now when the music stops, each boy dances with whichever girl is opposite. O.K.? O.K. Two circles, kids. [*The* KIDS *clap their hands back at him and ad lib: "Two circles, kids," etc., but do not move*] Well, it won't hurt you to try.

SNOWBOY: [*Limping forward*] Oh, it hurts; it hurts; it—

[KRUPKE *steps forward.* SNOWBOY *straightens up and meekly returns to his place.* RIFF *steps forward and beckons to his girl,* VELMA. *She is terribly young, sexy, lost in a world of jive. She slithers forward to take her place with* RIFF. *The challenge is met by* BERNARDO, *who steps forward, leading* ANITA *as though he were presenting the most magnificent lady in all the world. The other kids follow, forming the two circles* GLAD HAND *requested.*]

GLAD HAND: That's it, kids. Keep the ball rolling. Round she goes and where she stops, nobody knows. All right: here we go!

[*Promenade music starts and the circles start revolving.* GLAD HAND, *whistle to his mouth, is in the center with* KRUPKE. *He blows the whistle and the music stops, leaving Jet boys opposite Shark girls, and vice versa. There is a moment of tenseness, then* BERNARDO *reaches across the Jet girl opposite for* ANITA'S *hand,*

*and she comes to him.* RIFF *reaches for* VELMA; *and the kids of both gangs follow suit. The "get-together" has failed, and each gang is on its own side of the hall as a mambo starts. This turns into a challenge dance between* BERNARDO *and* ANITA—*cheered on by the Sharks—and* RIFF *and* VELMA—*cheered on by the Jets. During it,* TONY *enters and is momentarily embraced by* RIFF, *who is delighted that his best friend did turn up. The dance builds wilder and wilder, until, at the peak, everybody is dancing and shouting, "Go, Mambo!" It is at this moment that* TONY *and* MARIA—*at opposite sides of the hall—see each other. They have been cheering on their respective friends, clapping in rhythm. Now, as they see each other, their voices die, their smiles fade, their hands slowly go to their sides. The lights fade on the others, who disappear into the haze of the background as a delicate cha-cha begins and* TONY *and* MARIA *slowly walk forward to meet each other. Slowly, as though in a dream, they drift into the steps of the dance, always looking at each other, completely lost in each other; unaware of anyone, any place, any time, anything but one another.*)

TONY: You're not thinking I'm someone else?

MARIA: I know you are not.

TONY: Or that we have met before?

MARIA: I know we have not.

TONY: I felt, I *knew* something-never-before was going to happen, had to happen. But this is—

MARIA: [*Interrupting*] My hands are cold. [*He takes them in his*] Yours, too. [*He moves her hands to his face*] So warm. [*She moves his hands to her face.*]

TONY: Yours, too.

MARIA: But of course. They are the same.

TONY: It's so much to believe—you're not joking me?

MARIA: I have not yet learned how to joke that way. I think now I never will.

[*Impulsively, he stops to kiss her hands; then tenderly, innocently, her lips. The music bursts out, the lights flare up, and* BERNARDO *is upon them in an icy rage.*]

BERNARDO: Go home, "American."

TONY: Slow down, Bernardo.

BERNARDO: Stay away from my sister!

TONY: . . . Sister?

[RIFF *steps up.*]

BERNARDO: [*To* MARIA] Couldn't you see he's one of them?

MARIA: No; I saw only him.

BERNARDO: [*As* CHINO *comes up*] I told you: there's only one thing they want from a Puerto Rican girl!

TONY: That's a lie!

RIFF: Cool, boy.

CHINO: [*To* TONY] Get away.

TONY: You keep out, Chino. [*To* MARIA] Don't listen to them!

BERNARDO: She will listen to her brother before—

RIFF: [*Overlapping*] If you characters want to settle—

GLAD HAND: Please! Everything was going so well! Do you fellows get pleasure out of making trouble? Now come on—it won't hurt you to have a good time.

[*Music starts again.* BERNARDO *is on one side with* MARIA *and* CHINO; ANITA *joins them.* TONY *is on the other with* RIFF *and* DIESEL. *Light emphasizes the first group.*]

BERNARDO: I warned you—

CHINO: Do not yell at her, 'Nardo.

BERNARDO: You yell at babies.

ANITA: And put ideas in the baby's head.

BERNARDO: Take her home, Chino.

MARIA: 'Nardo, it is my first dance.

BERNARDO: Please. We are family, Maria. Go.

[MARIA *hesitates, then starts out with* CHINO *as the light follows her to the other group, which she passes.*]

RIFF: [*To* DIESEL, *indicating* TONY *happily*] I guess the kid's with us for sure now.

[TONY *doesn't even hear; he is staring at* MARIA, *who stops for a moment.*]

CHINO: Come, Maria.

[*They continue out.*]

TONY: Maria . . . [*He is unaware that* BERNARDO *is crossing toward him, but* RIFF *intercepts.*]

BERNARDO: I don't want you.

RIFF: I want you, though. For a war council—Jets and Sharks.

BERNARDO: The pleasure is mine.

RIFF: Let's go outside.

BERNARDO: I would not leave the ladies here alone. We will meet you in half an hour.

RIFF: Doc's drugstore? [BERNARDO *nods*] And no jazz before then.

BERNARDO: I understand the rules—Native Boy.

[*The light is fading on them, on everyone but* TONY.]

RIFF: Spread the word, Diesel.

DIESEL: Right, Daddy-o.

RIFF: Let's get the chicks and kick it. Tony?

TONY: Maria . . .

[*Music starts.*]

RIFF: [*In darkness*] Tony!

DIESEL: [*In darkness*] Ah, we'll see him at Doc's.

TONY: [*Speaking dreamily over the music—he is now standing alone in the light*]
Maria . . .

> [*Singing softly*]
> The most beautiful sound I ever heard.

> [VOICES *off stage*]
> Maria, Maria, Maria, Maria . . .

> [TONY]
> All the beautiful sounds of the world in a single word:

> [VOICES *off stage*]
> Maria, Maria, Maria, Maria . . .
> [*Swelling in intensity*]
> Maria, Maria . . .

> [TONY]
> Maria!
> I've just met a girl named Maria,
> And suddenly that name
> Will never be the same
> To me.
>
> Maria!
> I've just kissed a girl named Maria,
> And suddenly I've found
> How wonderful a sound
> Can be!
>
> Maria!
> Say it loud and there's music playing—
> Say it soft and it's almost like praying—
> Maria . . .
> I'll never stop saying
> Maria!

> [CHORUS, *offstage, against* TONY's *obbligato*]
> I've just met a girl named Maria,
> And suddenly that name
> Will never be the same
> To me.

MARIA: [*Touching his face*] I see you.

TONY: See only me.

Maria—
I've just kissed a girl named Maria,
And suddenly I've found
How wonderful a sound
Can be!

[TONY]

Maria—
Say it loud and there's music playing—
Say it soft and it's almost like praying—
Maria—
I'll never stop saying Maria!
The most beautiful sound I ever heard—
Maria.

[*During the song, the stage behind* TONY *has gone dark; by the time he has finished, it is set for the next scene.*]

Scene 5

*11:00* P.M. *A back alley.*
*A suggestion of buildings; a fire escape climbing to the rear window of an unseen flat.*
*As* TONY *sings, he looks for where* MARIA *lives, wishing for her. And she does appear, at the window above him, which opens onto the fire escape. Music stays beneath most of the scene.*

[TONY *sings*]
Maria, Maria . . .

MARIA: Ssh!
TONY: Maria!!
MARIA: Quiet!
TONY: Come down.
MARIA: No.
TONY: Maria . . .
MARIA: Please. If Bernardo—
TONY: He's at the dance. Come down.
MARIA: He will soon bring Anita home.
TONY: Just for a minute.
MARIA: [*Smiles*] A minute is not enough.
TONY: [*Smiles*] For an hour, then.
MARIA: I cannot.
TONY: Forever!

MARIA: Ssh!

TONY: Then I'm coming up.

WOMAN'S VOICE: [*From the offstage apartment*] Maria!

MARIA: *Momentito,*[3] Mama . . .

TONY: [*Climbing up*] Maria, Maria—

MARIA: *Cállate!* [*Reaching her hand out to stop him*] Ssh!

TONY: [*Grabbing her hand*] Ssh!

MARIA: It is dangerous.

TONY: I'm *not* "one of them."

MARIA: You are; but to me, you are not. Just as I am one of them— [*She gestures toward the apartment.*]

TONY: To me, you are all the—

[*She covers his mouth with her hand.*]

MAN'S VOICE: [*From the unseen apartment*] Maruca!

MARIA: *Si, ya vengo,*[4] Papa.

TONY: Maruca?

MARIA: His pet name for me.

TONY: I like him. He will like me.

MARIA: No. He is like Bernardo: afraid. [*Suddenly laughing*] Imagine being afraid of you!

TONY: You see?

MARIA: [*Touching his face*] I see you.

TONY: See only me.

[MARIA *sings*]
Only you, you're the only thing I'll see forever.
In my eyes, in my words and in everything I do,
Nothing else but you
Ever!

[TONY]
And there's nothing for me but Maria,
Every sight that I see is Maria.

[MARIA]
Tony, Tony . . .

[TONY]
Always you, every thought I'll ever know,
Everywhere I go, you'll be.

3. A brief moment. *Cállate:* Hush!

4. Yes, I'm coming.

[MARIA]

All the world is only you and me!
[*And now the buildings, the world fade away,
leaving them suspended in space*]
Tonight, tonight,
It all began tonight,
I saw you and the world went away.
Tonight, tonight,
There's only you tonight,
What you are, what you do, what you say.

[TONY]

Today, all day I had the feeling
A miracle would happen—
I know now I was right.
For here you are
And what was just a world is a star
Tonight!

[BOTH]

Tonight, tonight,
The world is full of light,
With suns and moons all over the place.
Tonight, tonight,
The world is wild and bright,
Going mad, shooting sparks into space.
Today the world was just an address,
A place for me to live in,
No better than all right,
But here you are
And what was just a world is a star
Tonight!

MAN'S VOICE: [*Offstage*] Maruca!
MARIA: Wait for me! [*She goes inside as the buildings begin to come back into place.*]

[TONY *sings*]

Tonight, tonight,
It all began tonight,
I saw you and the world went away.

MARIA: [*Returning*] I cannot stay. Go quickly!
TONY: I'm not afraid.
MARIA: They are strict with me. Please.
TONY: [*Kissing her*] Good night.

MARIA: *Buenas noches.*[5]

TONY: I love you.

MARIA: Yes, yes. Hurry. [*He climbs down*] Wait! When will I see you? [*He starts back up*] No!

TONY: Tomorrow.

MARIA: I work at the bridal shop. Come there.

TONY: At sundown.

MARIA: Yes. Good night.

TONY: Good night. [*He starts off.*]

MARIA: Tony!

TONY: Ssh!

MARIA: Come to the back door.

TONY: *Sí.* [*Again, he starts out.*]

MARIA: Tony! [*He stops. A pause*] What does Tony stand for?

TONY: Anton.

MARIA: *Te adoro,*[6] Anton.

TONY: *Te adoro,* Maria.

> [*Both sing as music starts again*]
> Good night, good night,
> Sleep well and when you dream,
> Dream of me
> Tonight.

[*She goes inside; he ducks out into the shadows just as* BERNARDO *and* ANITA *enter, followed by* INDIO *and* PEPE *and their girls. One is a bleached-blond, bangled beauty:* CONSUELO. *The other, more quietly dressed, is* ROSALIA. *She is not too bright.*]

BERNARDO: [*Looking up to the window*] Maria?

ANITA: She *has* a mother. Also a father.

BERNARDO: They do not know this country any better than she does.

ANITA: You do not know it at all! Girls here are free to have fun. She-is-in-America-now.

BERNARDO: [*Exaggerated*] But Puerto-Rico-is-in-America-now!

ANITA: [*In disgust*] Ai!

BERNARDO: [*Cooing*] Anita Josefina Teresita—

ANITA: It's plain Anita now—

BERNARDO: [*Continuing through*] —Beatriz del Carmen Margarita, etcetera, etcetera—

ANITA: Immigrant!

BERNARDO: [*Pulling her to him*] Thank God, you can't change your hair!

PEPE: [*Fondling* CONSUELO's *bleached mop*] Is that possible?

---

5. Good night.
6. I adore you.

CONSUELO: In the U.S.A., everything is real.

BERNARDO: [*To* CHINO, *who enters*] Chino, how was she when you took her home?

CHINO: All right. 'Nardo, she was only dancing.

BERNARDO: With an "*American.*" Who is really a Polack.

ANITA: Says the Spic.

BERNARDO: You are not so cute.

ANITA: That Tony is.

ROSALIA: And he works.

CHINO: A delivery boy.

ANITA: And what are you?

CHINO: An assistant.

BERNARDO: *Sí!* And Chino makes half what the Polack makes—the Polack is American!

ANITA: Ai! Here comes the whole commercial! [*A burlesque oration in mock Puerto Rican accent.* BERNARDO *starts the first line with her*] The mother of Tony was born in Poland; the father still goes to night school. Tony was born in America, so that makes him an American. But us? Foreigners!

PEPE *and* CONSUELO: Lice!

PEPE, CONSUELO, ANITA: Cockroaches!

BERNARDO: Well, it is true! You remember how we were when we first came! Did we even think of going back?

BERNARDO *and* ANITA: No! We came ready, eager—

ANITA: [*Mocking*] With our hearts open—

CONSUELO: Our arms open—

PEPE: You came with your pants open.

CONSUELO: *You* did, pig! [*Slaps him*] You'll go back with handcuffs!

BERNARDO: I am going back with a Cadillac!

CHINO: Air-conditioned!

BERNARDO: Built-in bar!

CHINO: Telephone!

BERNARDO: Television!

CHINO: Compatible color!

BERNARDO: And a king-sized bed. [*Grabs* ANITA] Come on.

ANITA: [*Mimicking*] Come on.

BERNARDO: Well, are you or aren't you?

ANITA: Well, are you or aren't you?

BERNARDO: Well, are you?

ANITA: You have your big, important war council. The council or me?

BERNARDO: First one, then the other.

ANITA: [*Breaking away from him*] I am an American girl now. I don't wait.

BERNARDO: [*To* CHINO] Back home, women know their place.

ANITA: Back home, little boys don't have war councils.

BERNARDO: You want me to be an American. [*To the boys*] *Vámonos, chicos, es tarde.*[7] [*A mock bow*] *Buenos noches,* Anita Josefina del Carmen, etcetera, etcetera, etcetera. [*He exits with the boys.*]

ROSALIA: That's a very pretty name: Etcetera.

ANITA: Ai!

CONSUELO: She means well.

ROSALIA: We have many pretty names at home.

ANITA: [*Mimicking*] At home, at home. If it's so nice "at home," why don't you go back there?

ROSALIA: I would like to—[*A look from* ANITA]—just for a successful visit.

[*She sings nostalgically*]
Puerto Rico . . .
You lovely island . . .
Island of tropical breezes.
      Always the pineapples growing.
      Always the coffee blossoms blowing . . .

[ANITA *sings sarcastically*]
Puerto Rico . . .
You ugly island . . .
Island of tropic diseases.
      Always the hurricanes blowing,
      Always the population growing . . .
      And the money owing,
      And the babies crying,
      And the bullets flying.
I like the island Manhattan—
Smoke on your pipe and put that in!

[ALL, *except* ROSALIA]
I like to be in America!
O.K. by me in America!
Everything free in America
For a small fee in America!

[ROSALIA]
I like the city of San Juan—

[ANITA]
I know a boat you can get on.

[ROSALIA]
Hundreds of flowers in full bloom—

7. Let's go, guys, it's late.

[ANITA]
Hundreds of people in each room!

[ALL, *except* ROSALIA]
Automobile in America,
Chromium steel in America,
Wire-spoke wheel in America—
Very big deal in America!

[ROSALIA]
I'll drive a Buick through San Juan—

[ANITA]
If there's a road you can drive on.

[ROSALIA]
I'll give my cousins a free ride—

[ANITA]
How you get all of them inside?

[ALL, *except* ROSALIA]
Immigrant goes to America,
Many hellos in America;
Nobody knows in America
Puerto Rico's in America.
[*The girls whistle and dance.*]

[ROSALIA]
When I will go back to San Juan—

[ANITA]
When you will shut up and get gone!

[ROSALIA]
I'll give them new washing machine—

[ANITA]
What have they got there to keep clean?

[ALL *except* ROSALIA]
I like the shores of America!
Comfort is yours in America!
Knobs on the doors in America,
Wall-to-wall floors in America!
[*They whistle and dance.*]

[ROSALIA]
I'll bring a TV to San Juan—

[ANITA]
If there's a current to turn on.

[ROSALIA]
Everyone there will give big cheer!

[ANITA]
Everyone there will have moved here!
[*The song ends in a joyous dance.*]

*The lights black out.*

Scene 6

*Midnight. The drugstore.*
*A suggestion of a run-down, musty general store which, in cities, is called a drugstore. A door leading to the street outside; another leading to the cellar below.*
BABY JOHN *is reading a comic book;* A-RAB *is playing solitaire;* ANYBODYS *is huddled by the juke box;* ACTION *is watching the street door. The atmosphere is tense, jumpy.* ACTION *slams the door and strides to the dart board.*

ACTION: Where the devil are they? Are we havin' a war council tonight or ain't we? [*He throws a dart savagely.*]
BABY JOHN: He don't use knives. He don't even use an atomic ray gun.
A-RAB: Who don't?
BABY JOHN: Superman. Gee, I love him.
SNOWBOY: So marry him.
ANYBODYS: I ain't never gonna get married: too noisy.
A-RAB: You ain't never gonna get married: too ugly.
ANYBODYS: [*"Shooting" him*] Pow pow!
A-RAB: Cracko, jacko! [*Clutching his belly, he spins to the floor*] Down goes a teen-age hoodlum.
BABY JOHN: Could a zip gun make you do like that?

[*A second of silence. Then* SNOWBOY *slams into the room and they all jump.*]

ACTION: What the hell's a matter with you?
SNOWBOY: I got caught sneakin' outa the movies.
A-RAB: Sneakin' *out?* Wadd'ya do that for?
SNOWBOY: I sneaked in.
ACTION: A war council comin' up and he goes to the movies.
ANYBODYS: And you let him be a Jet!
BABY JOHN: Ah, go walk the streets like ya sister.

ANYBODYS: [*Jumping him*] Lissen, jail bait, I licked you twice and I can do it again.

[*From the doorway behind the counter a little middle-aged man enters:* DOC.]

DOC: Curfew, gentlemen. And lady. Baby John, you should be home in bed.
BABY JOHN: We're gonna have a war council here, Doc.
DOC: A who?
A-RAB: To decide on weapons for a big-time rumble!
SNOWBOY: We're gonna mix with the PRs.
DOC: Weapons. You couldn't play basketball?
ANYBODYS: Get with it, buddy boy.
DOC: War councils—
ACTION: Don't start, Doc.
DOC: Rumbles . . .
ACTION: Doc—
DOC: Why, when I was your age—
ACTION: When you was my age; when my old man was my age; when my brother was my age! *You was never my age, none a you!* The sooner you creeps get hip to that, the sooner you'll dig us.
DOC: I'll dig your early graves, that's what I'll dig.
A-RAB: Dig, dig, dig—
DOC: What're you gonna be when you grow up?
ANYBODYS: [*Wistfully*] A telephone call girl!

[*The store doorbell tinkles as* RIFF *enters with* VELMA.]

SNOWBOY: Riff, hey!
ACTION: Are they comin'?
RIFF: Unwind, Action. Hey, Doc, Tony here?
DOC: No, Riff, it's closing time.
ACTION: [*To* RIFF] What d'ya think they're gonna ask for?
A-RAB: Just rubber hoses, maybe, huh?
RIFF: Cool, little men. Easy, freezy cool.
VELMA: Oo, oo, ooblee—oo.

[DIESEL *enters with a would-be grand number:* GRAZIELLA.]

DIESEL: They're comin' any minute now!
ACTION: Chung chung!
A-RAB: Cracko, jacko!
VELMA: Ooblee-oo.
RIFF: [*Sharply*] Cool!
ANYBODYS: Riff—in a tight spot you need every man you can—
RIFF: No.
GRAZIELLA: [*Indicating* ANYBODYS *to* VELMA] An American tragedy.
ANYBODYS: ["*Shooting*" her] Pow.
GRAZIELLA: Poo.
VELMA: Ooblee-pooh.

[*They giggle.*]

RIFF: Now when the victims come in, you chicks cut out.

GRAZIELLA: We might, and then again we might not.

DIESEL: This ain't kid stuff, Graziella.

GRAZIELLA: I and Velma ain't kid stuff, neither. Are we, Vel?

VELMA: No thank you-oo, ooblee-oo.

GRAZIELLA: And you can punctuate it?

VELMA: Ooo!

[*They giggle again.*]

ACTION: [*to* RIFF] What're we poopin' around with dumb broads?

GRAZIELLA: [*Enraged*] I and Velma ain't dumb!

ACTION: We got important business comin'.

DOC: Makin' trouble for the Puerto Ricans?

SNOWBOY: They make trouble for us.

DOC: Look! He almost laughs when he says it. For you, trouble is a relief.

RIFF: We've got to stand up to the PRs, Doc. It's important.

DOC: Fighting over a little piece of the street is so important?

ACTION: To us, it is.

DOC: To hoodlums, it is. [*He goes out through the cellar doorway as* ACTION *lunges for him.*]

ACTION: Don't you call me hoodlum!

RIFF: [*Holding him*] Easy, Action! Save your steam for the rumble.

A-RAB: He don't want what we want, so we're hoodlums!

BABY JOHN: I wear a jacket like my buddies, so my teacher calls me hoodlum!

ACTION: I swear the next creep who calls me hoodlum—

RIFF: *You'll laugh!* Yeah. Now you all better dig this and dig it the most. No matter who or what is eatin' at you, you show it, buddy boys, and *you are dead.* You are cuttin' a hole in yourselves for them to stick in a red hot umbrella and open it. Wide. You wanna live? You play it cool.

[*Music starts.*]

ACTION: I wanna get even!

RIFF: Get cool.

A-RAB: I wanna bust!

RIFF: Bust cool.

BABY JOHN: I wanna go!

RIFF: *Go cool!*

[*He sings*]
Boy, boy, crazy boy—
Get cool, boy!
Got a rocket in your pocket—
Keep coolly cool, boy!
Don't get hot,

'Cause, man, you got
Some high times ahead.
Take it slow and, Daddy-o,
You can live it up and die in bed!
Boy, boy, crazy boy—
Stay loose, boy!
Breeze it, buzz it, easy does it—
Turn off the juice, boy!
Go man, go,
But not like a yo-
Yo school boy—
Just play it cool, boy,
Real cool!

Easy, Action.
Easy.

[*This leads into a frenetic dance in which the boys and girls release their emotions and get "cool." It finishes, starts again when a Jet bounces in with the gang whistle. Everyone but* RIFF *and* VELMA *stops dancing. A moment, then* BERNARDO, CHINO, PEPE *and* INDIO *enter. The tinkle of the doorbell brings a worried* DOC *back in. Tension—but* RIFF *dances a moment longer. Then he pats* VELMA *on her behind. Followed by* GRAZIELLA, *she runs out, slithering past the Sharks.* ANYBODYS *is back, huddled by the juke box, but* RIFF *spots her. She gives him a pleading let-me-stay look, but he gestures for her to go. Unlike the other girls, as she exits,* ANYBODYS *shoves the Sharks like a big tough man.*]

RIFF: Set 'em up, Doc. Cokes all around.
BERNARDO: Let's get down to business.
RIFF: Bernardo hasn't learned the procedures of gracious livin'.
BERNARDO: I don't like you, either. So cut it.
RIFF: Kick it, Doc.
DOC: Boys, couldn't you maybe all talk it—
RIFF: Kick it!

[DOC *goes out. The two gangs take places behind their leaders.*]

RIFF: We challenge you to a rumble. All out, once and for all. Accept?
BERNARDO: On what terms?
RIFF: Whatever terms you're callin', buddy boy. You crossed the line once too often.
BERNARDO: You started it.
RIFF: Who jumped A-rab this afternoon?
BERNARDO: Who jumped me the first day I moved here?
ACTION: Who asked you to move here?
PEPE: Who asked you?
SNOWBOY: Move where you're wanted!

A-RAB: Back where ya came from!

ACTION: Spics!

PEPE: Micks!

INDIO: Wop!

BERNARDO: *We accept!*

RIFF: Time:

BERNARDO: Tomorrow?

RIFF: After dark. [*They shake*] Place:

BERNARDO: The park.

RIFF: The river.

BERNARDO: Under the highway.

[*They shake.*]

RIFF: Weapons:

[*The doorbell tinkles as* TONY *bursts in, yelling.*]

TONY: Hey, Doc! [*He stops as he sees them. Silence. Then he comes forward.*]

RIFF: Weapons!

[DOC *enters.*]

BERNARDO: Weapons . . .

RIFF: You call.

BERNARDO: Your challenge.

RIFF: Afraid to call?

BERNARDO: . . . . Sticks.

RIFF: . . . . Rocks.

BERNARDO: . . . Poles.

RIFF: . . . Cans.

BERNARDO: . . . Bricks.

RIFF: . . Bats.

BERNARDO: . Clubs.

RIFF: Chains.

TONY: Bottles, knives, guns! [*They stare*] What a coop full of chickens!

ACTION: Who you callin' chicken?

BERNARDO: Every dog knows his own.

TONY: I'm callin' all of you chicken. The big tough buddy boys have to throw bricks! Afraid to get close in? Afraid to slug it out? Afraid to use plain skin?

BABY JOHN: Not even garbage?

ACTION: That ain't a rumble.

RIFF: Who says?

BERNARDO: You said call weapons.

TONY: A rumble can be clinched by a fair fight. If you have the guts to risk that. Best man from each gang to slug it out.

BERNARDO: [*Looking at* TONY] I'd enjoy to risk that. O.K.! Fair fight!

PEPE: What?

ACTION: [*Simultaneously*] No!

RIFF: The commanders say yes or no. [*To* BERNARDO] Fair fight.

[*They shake.*]

BERNARDO: [*To* TONY] In two minutes you will be like a fish after skinnin'.

RIFF: Your best man fights our best man—and we pick him. [*Claps* DIESEL *on the shoulder.*]

BERNARDO: But I thought I would be—

RIFF: We shook on it, Bernardo.

BERNARDO: Yes. I shook on it.

ACTION: [*Quickly*] Look, Bernardo, if you wanna change your mind, maybe we could all—

[*One of the Jets near the door suddenly whistles. Instantly, they shift positions so they are mixed up: no segregation. Silence; then in comes* SCHRANK. *During the following, the gangs are absolutely silent and motionless, unless otherwise indicated.*]

DOC: [*Unhappily*] Good evening, Lieutenant Schrank. I and Tony was just closing up.

SCHRANK: [*Lifting a pack of cigarettes*] Mind?

DOC: I have no mind. I am the village idiot.

SCHRANK: [*Lighting a cigarette*] I always make it a rule to smoke in the can. And what else is a room with half-breeds in it, eh, Riff? [BERNARDO'S *move is checked by* RIFF. SCHRANK *speaks again, pleasantly*] Clear out, Spics. Sure; it's a free country and I ain't got the right. But it's a country with laws: and I can find the right. I got the badge, you got the skin. It's tough all over. Beat it!

[*A second. Then* RIFF *nods once to* BERNARDO, *who nods to his gang. Slowly, they file out.* BERNARDO *starts to whistle "My Country 'Tis of Thee" as he exits proudly. His gang joins in, finishing a sardonic jazz lick offstage.*]

SCHRANK: [*Still pleasant*] From their angle, sure. Say, where's the rumble gonna be? Ah, look: I know regular Americans don't rub with the gold-teeth otherwise. The river? The park? [*Silence*] I'm for *you*. I want this beat cleaned up and you can do it for me. I'll even lend a hand if it gets rough. Where ya gonna rumble? The playground? Sweeney's lot? [*Angered by the silence*] Ya think I'm a lousy stool pigeon? I wanna help ya get rid of them! Come on! Where's it gonna be? . . . Get smart, you stupid hoodlums! I oughta fine ya for litterin' the streets. You oughta be taken down the station house and have your skulls mashed to a pulp! You and the tin-horn immigrant scum you come from! How's your old man's d.t.'s, A-rab? How's the action on your mother's mattress, Action? [ACTION *lunges for him but is tripped up by* RIFF. SCHRANK *crouches low, ready for him. Quiet now*] Let him go, buddy boy, just let him go. [ACTION *starts to his feet but* DIESEL *holds him*] One of these days there won't be nobody to hold you. [RIFF *deliberately starts for the door, followed by the others, except* TONY] I'll find out where ya gonna rumble. But be sure to finish each other off. Because if you don't, I will! [RIFF *has stayed at the door until the others have passed through. Now he just looks at* SCHRANK *and cockily saunters out. Silence.* SCHRANK *looks at* DOC] Well, you try keepin' hoodlums in line and see what it does to you. [*He exits.*]

DOC: [*Indicating* SCHRANK] It wouldn't give me a mouth like his.

TONY: Forget him. From here on in, everything goes my way. [*He starts to clean up, to turn out the lights.*]

DOC: You think it'll really be a fair fight.

TONY: Yeah.

DOC: What have you been takin' tonight?

TONY: A trip to the moon. And I'll tell you a secret. It isn't a man that's up there, Doc. It's a girl, a lady. [*Opens the door*] Buenas noches, señor.

DOC: *Buenas noches?!* So that's why you made it a fair fight. [TONY *smiles*] . . . Tony . . . things aren't tough enough?

TONY: Tough? Doc, I'm in love.

DOC: How do you know?

TONY: Because . . . there isn't any other way I could feel.

DOC: And you're not frightened?

TONY: Should I be? [*He opens door, exits.*]

DOC: Why? I'm frightened enough for both of you. [*He turns out the last light.*]

*The stage is dark.*

## Scene 7

*5:30 P.M. The next day. The bridal shop.*

*Hot late-afternoon sun coloring the workroom. One or two sewing machines. Several dressmaker dummies, male and female, in bridal-party garb.*

MARIA, *in a smock, is hand-sewing a wedding veil as* ANITA *whirls in whipping off her smock.*

ANITA: She's gone! That old bag of a *bruja*[8] has gone!

MARIA: *Bravo!*

ANITA: The day is over, the jail is open, home we go!

MARIA: You go, *querida.* I will lock up.

ANITA: Finish tomorrow. Come!

MARIA: But I am in no hurry.

ANITA: I am. I'm going to take a bubble bath all during supper: Black Orchid.

MARIA: You will not eat?

ANITA: After the rumble—with 'Nardo.

MARIA: [*Sewing, angrily*] That rumble, why do they have it?

_____
8. Witch.

ANITA: You saw how they dance: like they have to get rid of something, quick. That's how they fight.

MARIA: To get rid of what?

ANITA: Too much feeling. And they get rid of it: after a fight, that brother of yours is so healthy! Definitely: Black Orchid.

[*There is a knock at rear door, and* TONY *enters.*]

TONY: *Buenas noches!*

ANITA: [*Sarcastically, to* MARIA] "You go, *querida.* I will lock up." [*To* TONY] It's too early for *noches. Buenas tardes.*⁹

TONY: [*Bows*] *Gracias. Buenas tardes.*

MARIA: He just came to deliver aspirin.

ANITA: You'll need it.

TONY: No, we're out of the world.

ANITA: You're out of your heads.

TONY: We're twelve feet in the air.

MARIA: [*Gently taking his hand*] Anita can see all that. [*To* ANITA] You will not tell?

ANITA: Tell what? How can I hear what goes on twelve feet over my head? [*Opens door. To* MARIA] You better be home in fifteen minutes. [*She goes out.*]

TONY: Don't worry. She likes us!

MARIA: But she is worried.

TONY: She's foolish. We're untouchable; we *are* in the air; we have magic!

MARIA: Magic is also evil and black. Are you going to that rumble?

TONY: No.

MARIA: Yes.

TONY: Why??

MARIA: You must go and stop it.

TONY: I have stopped it! It's only a fist fight. 'Nardo won't get—

MARIA: *Any* fight is not good for us.

TONY: Everything is good for us and we are good for everything.

MARIA: Listen and *hear* me. You must go and stop it.

TONY: Then I will.

MARIA: [*Surprised*] Can you?

TONY: You don't want even a fist fight? There won't be any fight.

MARIA: I believe you! You *do* have magic.

TONY: Of course, I have you. You go home and dress up. Then tonight, I will come by for you.

MARIA: You cannot come by. My mama . . .

TONY: [*After a pause*] Then I will take you to my house—

MARIA: [*Shaking her head*] *Your* mama . . .

---

9. Good afternoon or evening.

[*Another awkward pause. Then he sees a female dummy and pushes it forward.*]

TONY: She will come running from the kitchen to welcome you. She lives in the kitchen.

MARIA: Dressed so elegant?

TONY: I told her you were coming. She will look at your face and try not to smile. And she will say: Skinny—but pretty.

MARIA: She is plump, no doubt.

TONY: [*Holding out the waist of dummy's dress*] Fat!

MARIA: [*Indicating another female dummy*] I take after my mama; delicate-boned. [*He kisses her*] Not in front of Mama! [*He turns the dummy around as she goes to a male dummy*] Oh, I would like to see Papa in this! Mama will make him ask about your prospects, if you go to church. But Papa—Papa *might* like you.

TONY: [*Kneeling to the "father" dummy*] May I have your daughter's hand?

MARIA: He says yes.

TONY: *Gracias!*

MARIA: And your mama?

TONY: I'm afraid to ask her.

MARIA: Tell her she's not getting a daughter; she's getting rid of a son!

TONY: She says yes.

MARIA: She has good taste.

[*She grabs up the wedding veil and puts it on as* TONY *arranges the dummies.*]

TONY: Maid of honor!

MARIA: That color is bad for Anita.

TONY: Best man!

MARIA: That is my papa!

TONY: Sorry, Papa. Here we go, Riff: womb to tomb! [*He takes hat off dummy.*]

MARIA: Now you see, Anita, I told you there was nothing to worry about.

[*Music starts as she leaves the dummy and walks up to* TONY. *They look at each other—and the play acting vanishes. Slowly, seriously, they turn front, and together kneel as before an altar.*]

TONY: I, Anton, take thee, Maria . . .

MARIA: I, Maria, take thee, Anton . . .

TONY: For richer, for poorer . . .

MARIA: In sickness and in health . . .

TONY: To love and to honor . . .

MARIA: To hold and to keep . . .

TONY: From each sun to each moon . . .

MARIA: From tomorrow to tomorrow . . .

TONY: From now to forever . . .

MARIA: Till death do us part.

TONY: With this ring, I thee wed.
MARIA: With this ring, I thee wed.

[TONY *sings*]
Make of our hands one hand,
Make of our hearts one heart,
Make of our vows one last vow:
Only death will part us now.

[MARIA]
Make of our lives one life,
Day after day, one life.

[BOTH]
Now it begins, now we start
One hand, one heart—
Even death won't part us now.

[*They look at each other, then at the reality of their "game." They smile tenderly, ruefully, and slowly put the dummies back into position. Though brought back to earth, they continue to sing.*]

Make of our lives one life,
Day after day, one life.
Now it begins, now we start
One hand, one heart—
Even death won't part us now.

[*Very gently, he kisses her hand.*]

*The lights fade out.*


Scene 8

*6:00 to 9:00* P.M. *The neighborhood.*
*Spotlights pick out* RIFF *and the Jets,* BERNARDO *and the Sharks,* ANITA, MARIA *and* TONY *against small sets representing different places in the neighborhood. All are waiting expectantly for the coming of night, but for very different reasons.*

[JETS *sing*]
The Jets are gonna have their day
Tonight.

[SHARKS]
The Sharks are gonna have their way
Tonight.

[JETS]
The Puerto Ricans grumble,
"Fair fight,"
But if they start a rumble,
We'll rumble 'em right.

[SHARKS]
We're gonna hand 'em a surprise
Tonight.

[JETS]
We're gonna cut 'em down to size
Tonight.

[SHARKS]
We said, "O.K., no rumpus,
No tricks"—
But just in case they jump us,
We're ready to mix
Tonight!

[BOTH GANGS]
We're gonna rock it tonight,
We're gonna jazz it up and have us a ball.
They're gonna get it tonight;
The more they turn it on, the harder they'll fall!

[JETS]
Well, they began it—

[SHARKS]
Well, they began it—

[BOTH GANGS]
And we're the ones to stop 'em once and for all,
Tonight!

[ANITA]
Anita's gonna get her kicks
Tonight.
We'll have our private little mix
Tonight.
He'll walk in hot and tired,
So what?
Don't matter if he's tired,

As long as he's hot
Tonight!

[TONY]

Tonight, tonight
Won't be just any night,
Tonight there will be no morning star.

Tonight, tonight,
I'll see my love tonight.
And for us, stars will stop where they are.

Today
The minutes seem like hours,
The hours go so slowly,
And still the sky is light . . .

Oh moon, grow bright,
And make this endless day endless night!

[RIFF, *to* TONY]

I'm counting on you to be there
Tonight.
When Diesel wins it fair and square
Tonight.

That Puerto Rican punk'll
Go down.
And when he's hollered Uncle
We'll tear up the town
Tonight!

[MARIA]

Tonight, tonight
Won't be just any night . . .

[*She reprises the same chorus* TONY *has just sung.*]

[RIFF]

So I can count on you, boy?

[TONY]

All right.

[RIFF]

We're gonna have us a ball.

[TONY]

All right . . .
   [*Regretting his impatience*]
Womb to tomb!

[RIFF]

Sperm to worm!
I'll see you there about eight . . .

[TONY]

Tonight . . .

[BERNARDO *and* SHARKS]
We're gonna rock it tonight!!!

[ANITA]

Tonight . . .

[*All have been singing at once, reprising the choruses they sang before.*]

[BERNARDO *and* SHARKS]
We're gonna jazz it tonight
They're gonna get it tonight—tonight.
They began it—they began it
And we're the ones
To stop 'em once and for all!
The Sharks are gonna have their way,
The Sharks are gonna have their day,
We're gonna rock it tonight—
Tonight!

[ANITA]

Tonight,
Late tonight,
We're gonna mix it tonight.
Anita's gonna have her day,
Anita's gonna have her day
Bernardo's gonna have his way
Tonight—tonight.
Tonight—this very night,
We're gonna rock it tonight,
Tonight!

[RIFF *and* JETS]
They began it.
They began it.

We'll stop 'em once and for all
The Jets are gonna have their day,
The Jets are gonna have their way,
We're gonna rock it tonight.
Tonight!

[MARIA]
Tonight there will be no morning star.
Tonight, tonight, I'll see my love tonight.
When we kiss, stars will stop where they are.

[TONY *and* MARIA]
Today the minutes seem like hours.
The hours go so slowly,
And still the sky is light.
Oh moon, grow bright,
And make this endless day endless night,
Tonight!

[*The lights build with the music to the climax, and then blackout at the final exultant note.*]


Scene 9

9:00 P.M. *Under the highway.*
*A dead end: rotting plaster-and-brick walls and mesh wire fences. A street lamp.*
*It is nightfall. The almost-silhouetted gangs come in from separate sides: climbing over the fences or crawling through holes in the walls. There is silence as they fan out on opposite sides of the cleared space. Then* BERNARDO *and* DIESEL *remove their jackets, handing them to their seconds:* CHINO *and* RIFF.

BERNARDO: Ready.
CHINO: Ready!
DIESEL: Ready.
RIFF: Ready! Come center and shake hands.
BERNARDO: For what?
RIFF: That's how it's done, buddy boy.
BERNARDO: More gracious living? Look: I don't go for that pretend crap you all go for in this country. Every one of you hates every one of us, and we hate you right back. I don't drink with nobody I hate, I don't shake hands with nobody I hate. Let's get at it.
RIFF: O.K.
BERNARDO: [*Moving toward center*] Here we go.

[DIESEL *begins to move toward him. There are encouragements called from each side. The "fair fight" is just beginning when there is an interruption.*]

TONY: Hold it! [*He leaps over a fence and starts toward* BERNARDO.]

RIFF: Get with the gang.

TONY: No.

RIFF: What're you doin'?

BERNARDO: Maybe he has found the guts to fight his own battles.

TONY: [*Smiling*] It doesn't take guts if you *have* a battle. But we haven't got one, 'Nardo. [*He extends his hand for* BERNARDO *to shake it.* BERNARDO *knocks the hand away and gives* TONY *a shove that sends him sprawling.*]

BERNARDO: *Ber*nardo.

RIFF: [*Quiet, strong*] The deal is a fair fight between you and Diesel. [*To* TONY, *who has gotten up*] Get with the gang.

[*During the following,* BERNARDO *flicks* TONY'S *shirt, pushes his shoulder, pinches his cheek.*]

BERNARDO: [*To* TONY] I'll give you a battle, Kiddando.

DIESEL: You've got one.

BERNARDO: I'll take pretty boy on as a warm-up. Afraid, pretty boy? Afraid, chicken? Afraid, gutless?

RIFF: Cut that—

TONY: I don't want to, Bernardo . . .

BERNARDO: I'm sure.

TONY: Bernardo, you've got it wrong.

BERNARDO: Are you chicken?

TONY: You *won't* understand!

BERNARDO: What d'ya say, chicken?

ACTION: Get him, Tony!

BERNARDO: He *is* chicken.

DIESEL: Tony—

A-RAB: Get him!

TONY: Bernardo, *don't.*

BERNARDO: Don't what, pretty little chicken?

RIFF: Tony, don't just stand—

BERNARDO: Yellow-bellied chicken—

RIFF: TONY!

ACTION: Murder him!

SNOWBOY: Kill him!

TONY: DON'T PUSH ME!

BERNARDO: Come on, you yellow-bellied Polack bas—

[*He never finishes, for* RIFF *hauls off and hits him. Immediately, the two gangs alert, and the following action takes on the form of a dance. As* BERNARDO *reels back to his feet, he reaches for his back pocket.* RIFF *reaches for his back pocket, and at the same instant each brings forth a gleaming knife. They jockey for position, feinting, dueling; the two gangs shift position, now and again temporarily obscuring the fighters.* TONY *tries to get between them.*]

RIFF: Hold him!

[DIESEL *and* ACTION *grab* TONY *and hold him back. The fight continues.* RIFF *loses his knife, is passed another by a Jet. At last, he has* BERNARDO *in a position where it seems that he will be able to run him through.* TONY *breaks from* DIESEL *and, crying out, moves to stop* RIFF.]

TONY: Riff, don't! [RIFF *hesitates a moment; the moment is enough for* BERNARDO— *whose hand goes forward with a driving motion, running his knife into* RIFF. TONY *leaps forward to catch* RIFF. *He breaks his fall, then takes the knife from his hand. A free-for-all has broken out as* TONY, RIFF'S *knife in hand, leaps at the triumphant* BERNARDO. *All this happens terribly fast; and* TONY *rams his knife into* BERNARDO. *The free-for-all continues a moment longer. Then there is a sharp police whistle. Everything comes to a dead stop—dead silence. Then a distant police siren: the kids waver, run one way, another, in panic, confusion. As the stage is cleared,* TONY *stands, horrified, over the still bodies of* RIFF *and* BERNARDO. *He bends over* RIFF'S *body; then he rolls* BERNARDO'S *body over— and stares. Then* TONY *raises his voice in an anguished cry*] MARIA!

[*Another police whistle, closer now, but he doesn't move. From the shadows,* ANYBODYS *appears. She scurries to* TONY *and tugs at his arm. A siren, another whistle, then a searchlight cuts across the playground.* ANYBODYS' *insistent tugging brings* TONY *to the realization of the danger. He crouches, starts to run with her to one escapeway. She reaches it first, goes out—but the searchlight hits it just as he would go through. He stops, runs the other way. He darts here, there, and finally gets away as a distant clock begins to boom.*]

*The curtain falls.*

# ACT II

## Scene 1

9:15 P.M. *A bedroom.*
*Part of a parlor is also visible. The bedroom has a window opening onto the fire escape, a bed on a wall, a small shrine to the Virgin, and a curtained doorway, rear. There is a door between bedroom and the parlor.*
*Gay music for* CONSUELO, *who is examining herself in the mirror, and for* ROS-ALIA, *who is on the bed, finishing her nails.*

CONSUELO: This is my last night as a blonde.
ROSALIA: No loss.
CONSUELO: A gain! The fortune teller told Pepe a dark lady was coming into his life.
ROSALIA: So that's why he's not taking you out after the rumble!

[*The music becomes festively, humorously Spanish as* MARIA *enters through the curtained doorway. She is finishing getting very dressed up.*]

MARIA: There is not going to be a rumble.

ROSALIA: Another fortune teller.

CONSUELO: Where is Chino escorting you after the rumble-that-is-not-going-to-be-a-rumble?

MARIA: Chino is escorting me no place.

ROSALIA: She is just dolling up for us. *Gracias, querida.*

MARIA: No, not for you. Can you keep a secret?

CONSUELO: I'm hot for secrets!

MARIA: Tonight is my wedding night!

CONSUELO: The poor thing is out of her mind.

MARIA: I am: crazy!

ROSALIA: She might be at that. She looks somehow different.

MARIA: I do?

ROSALIA: And I think she is up to something tonight.

MARIA: I am?

CONSUELO: "I do?" "I am?" What is going on with you?

[MARIA *sings*]

I feel pretty,
Oh, so pretty,
I feel pretty, and witty and bright,
And I pity
Any girl who isn't me tonight.

I feel charming,
Oh, so charming—
It's alarming how charming I feel,
And so pretty
That I hardly can believe I'm real.

See the pretty girl in that mirror there:
Who can that attractive girl be?
Such a pretty face,
Such a pretty dress,
Such a pretty smile,
Such a pretty me!

I feel stunning
And entrancing—
Feel like running and dancing for joy,
For I'm loved
By a pretty wonderful boy!

[ROSALIA *and* CONSUELO]
Have you met my good friend Maria,
The craziest girl on the block?
You'll know her the minute you see her—
She's the one who is in an advanced state of shock.

She thinks she's in love.
She thinks she's in Spain.
She isn't in love,
She's merely insane.

It must be the heat
Or some rare disease
Or too much to eat,
Or maybe it's fleas.

Keep away from her—
Send for Chino!
This is not the Mar-
Ia we know!

Modest and pure
Polite and refined,
Well-bred and mature
And out of her mind!

[MARIA]
I feel pretty,
Oh, so pretty,
That the city should give me its key.
A committee
Should be organized to honor me.

I feel dizzy,
I feel sunny,
I feel fizzy and funny and fine,
And so pretty,
Miss America can just resign!

See the pretty girl in that mirror there:

[ROSALIA *and* CONSUELO]
What mirror where?

[MARIA]
Who can that attractive girl be?

[ROSALIA *and* CONSUELO]
Which? What? Where? Whom?

[MARIA]
Such a pretty face,
Such a pretty dress,
Such a pretty smile,
Such a pretty me!

[ALL]
I feel stunning
And entrancing—
Feel like running and dancing for joy,
For I'm loved
By a pretty wonderful boy!

CHINO: [*Offstage*] Maria!
CONSUELO: It's Chino.
ROSALIA: The happy bridegroom.
CHINO: [*Closer*] Maria!
MARIA: Please—
CONSUELO: Yes, little bride, we're going. [*She exits.*]
ROSALIA: They have a quaint old-fashioned custom in this country, Maria: they get married here *before* the wedding night.

[*She follows* CONSUELO *out as* CHINO *enters from offstage. His clothes are dirty and torn from the fight; his face is smeared. They shake their heads at him and flounce out. He closes the outer door.*]

CHINO: Maria? . . .
MARIA: I'm in here. I was just getting ready to—

[*She is hurriedly trying to put a bathrobe over her dress.* CHINO *comes in before she can finish, so that she leaves it over her shoulders, holding it closed with her hand.*]

CHINO: Where are your parents?
MARIA: At the store. If I had known you were—You have been fighting, Chino.
CHINO: Yes. I am sorry.
MARIA: That is not like you.
CHINO: No.
MARIA: Why, Chino?
CHINO: I don't know why. It happened so fast.
MARIA: You must wash up.
CHINO: Maria—
MARIA: You can go in there.
CHINO: In a minute. Maria . . . at the rumble—

MARIA: There was no rumble.

CHINO: There was.

MARIA: You are wrong.

CHINO: No; there was. Nobody meant for it to happen . . .

MARIA: . . . Tell me.

CHINO: It's bad.

MARIA: Very bad?

CHINO: [Nods] You see . . . [He moves closer to her, helplessly.]

MARIA: It will be easier if you say it very fast.

CHINO: [Nods] There was a fight—[She nods] And 'Nardo—[She nods] And somehow a knife—and 'Nardo and someone— [He takes her hand.]

MARIA: Tony. What happened to Tony? [The name stops CHINO. He drops her hand: the robe opens] Tell me! [Crudely, CHINO yanks off the robe, revealing that she is dressed to go out] Chino, is Tony all right?!

CHINO: He killed your brother.

[He walks into the parlor, slamming the door behind him. A pause.]

MARIA: You are lying. [CHINO has started to leave the parlor, but turns back now. Swiftly searching behind furniture, he comes up with an object wrapped in material the same color as Bernardo's shirt. From the bedroom, MARIA's voice calls out, louder] You are lying, Chino! [Coldly, CHINO unwraps a gun which he puts in his pocket. There is the sound of a police siren at a distance. He goes out. During this, MARIA has knelt before the shrine on the wall. She rocks back and forth in prayer, some of it in Spanish, some of it in English] Make it not be true . . . please make it not be true. . . . I will do anything: make me die. . . . Only, please—make it not be true. [As she prays, TONY appears at the fire-escape window and quietly climbs in. His shirt is ripped, half-torn off. He stands still, limp, watching her. Aware that someone is in the room, she stops her prayers. Slowly, her head turns; she looks at him for a long moment. Then, almost in one spring, she is on him, her fists beating his chest] Killer killer killer killer killer—

[But her voice breaks with tears, her arms go about him, and she buries her face in his chest, kissing him. She begins to slide down his body. He supports her as, together, they go to the floor, he cradling her body in his arms. He pushes her hair back from her face; kisses her hair, her face, between the words that tumble out.]

TONY: I tried to stop it; I did try. I don't know how it went wrong. . . . I didn't mean to hurt him; I didn't want to; I didn't know I had. But Riff . . . Riff was like my brother. So when Bernardo killed him—[She lifts her head] 'Nardo didn't mean it, either. Oh, I know he didn't! Oh, no. I didn't come to tell you. Just for you to forgive me so I could go to the police—

MARIA: No!

TONY: It's easy now—

MARIA: No . . .

TONY: Whatever you want, I'll do—
MARIA: Stay. Stay with me.
TONY: I love you so much.
MARIA: Tighter.

[*Music starts.*]

TONY: We'll be all right. I know it. We're really together now.
MARIA: But it's not us! It's everything around us!
TONY: Then we'll find some place where nothing can get to us; not one of them, not anything. And—

> [*He sings*]
> I'll take you away, take you far far away out of here,
> Far far away till the walls and the streets disappear,
> Somewhere there must be a place we can feel we're free,
> Somewhere there's got to be some place for you and for me.

[*As he sings, the walls of the apartment begin to move off, and the city walls surrounding them begin to close in on them. Then the apartment itself goes, and the two lovers begin to run, battering against the walls of the city, beginning to break through as chaotic figures of the gangs, of violence, flail around them. But they do break through, and suddenly—they are in a world of space and air and sun. They stop, looking at it, pleased, startled, as boys and girls from both sides come on. And they, too, stop and stare, happy, pleased. Their clothes are soft pastel versions of what they have worn before. They begin to dance, to play: no sides, no hostility now; just joy and pleasure and warmth. More and more join, making a world that* TONY *and* MARIA *want to be in, belong to, share their love with. As they go into the steps of a gentle love dance, a voice is heard singing.*]

> [OFFSTAGE VOICE *sings*]
> There's a place for us,
> Somewhere a place for us.
> Peace and quiet and room and air
> Wait for us
> Somewhere.
>
> There's a time for us,
> Someday a time for us,
> Time together with time to spare,
> Time to learn, time to care
> Someday!
>
> Somewhere
> We'll find a new way of living,
> We'll find a way of forgiving

Somewhere,
Somewhere . . .

There's a place for us,
A time and place for us.
Hold my hand and we're halfway there.
Hold my hand and I'll take you there
Someday,
Somehow,
Somewhere!

[*The lovers hold out their hands to each other; the others follow suit: Jets to Sharks; Sharks to Jets. And they form what is almost a procession winding its triumphant way through this would-be world, as they sing the words of the song with wonderment. Then, suddenly, there is a dead stop. The harsh shadows, the fire escapes of the real, tenement world cloud the sky, and the figures of* RIFF *and* BERNARDO *slowly walk on. The dream becomes a nightmare: as the city returns, there are brief re-enactments of the knife fight, of the deaths.* MARIA *and* TONY *are once again separated from each other by the violent warring of the two sides.* MARIA *tries to reach* BERNARDO, TONY *tries to stop* RIFF; *the lovers try to reach each other, but they cannot. Chaotic confusion and blackness, after which they find themselves back in the bedroom, clinging to each other desperately. With a blind refusal to face what they know must be, they reassure each other desperately as they sing.*]

[TONY *and* MARIA]
Hold my hand and we're halfway there.
Hold my hand and I'll take you there
Someday,
Somehow,
Somewhere!

[*As the lights fade, together they sink back on the bed.*]

### Scene 2

10:00 P.M. *Another alley.*
*A fence with loose boards; angles between buildings.*
*Softly, from behind the fence, the Jet gang whistle. A pause, then the answering whistle, softly, from offstage or around a corner. Now a loose board flips up and* BABY JOHN *wriggles through the fence. He whistles again, timidly, and* A-RAB *comes on.*

A-RAB: They get you yet?
BABY JOHN: No. You?
A-RAB: Hell, no.

BABY JOHN: You seen Tony?

A-RAB: Nobody has.

BABY JOHN: Geez . . .

A-RAB: You been home yet?

BABY JOHN: Uh uh.

A-RAB: Me, either.

BABY JOHN: Just hidin' around?

A-RAB: Uh huh.

BABY JOHN: A-rab . . . did you get a look at 'em?

A-RAB: Look at who?

BABY JOHN: Ya know. At the rumble. Riff and Bernardo.

[*Pause.*]

A-RAB: I wish it was yesterday.

BABY JOHN: Wadaya say we run away?

A-RAB: What's a matter? You scared?

BABY JOHN: . . . Yeah.

A-RAB: You cut it out, ya hear? You're only makin' me scared and that scares me! [*Police whistle. He grabs* BABY JOHN] Last thing ever is to let a cop know you're scared or anythin'.

KRUPKE: [*Offstage*] Hey, you two!

A-RAB: Play it big with the baby blues.

BABY JOHN: [*Scared*] O.K.

A-RAB: [*Gripping him*] Big, not scared, big!

[*Again a whistle. Elaborately casual, they start sauntering off as* KRUPKE *appears.*]

KRUPKE: Yeah, you.

[*They stop, so surprised.*]

A-RAB: Why it *is* Officer Krupke, Baby John.

BABY JOHN: [*Quaking*] Top of the evening, Officer Krupke.

KRUPKE: I'll crack the top of your skulls if you punks don't stop when I whistle.

A-RAB: But we stopped the very moment we heard.

BABY JOHN: We got twenty-twenty hearing.

KRUPKE: You wanna get hauled down to the station house?

BABY JOHN: Indeed not, sir.

KRUPKE: I'll make a little deal. I know you was rumblin' under the highway—

BABY JOHN: We was at the playground, sir.

A-RAB: We like the playground. It keeps us deprived kids off the foul streets.

BABY JOHN: It gives us comradeship—

A-RAB: A place for pleasant pastimes—And for us, born like we was on the hot pavements—

KRUPKE: O.K., wise apples, down to the station house.

BABY JOHN: Which way?

A-RAB: This way! [*He gets down on all fours,* BABY JOHN *pushes* KRUPKE, *so that he tumbles over* A-RAB. BABY JOHN *starts off one way,* A-RAB *the other.* KRUPKE *hesitates, then runs after one of them, blowing his whistle like mad. The moment he is off,* A-RAB *and* BABY JOHN *appear through the fence, followed by the other Jets.*] Look at the brass-ass run!

BABY JOHN: I hope he breaks it!

ACTION: Get the lead out, fat boy!

DIESEL: Easy. He'll come back and drag us down the station house.

ACTION: I already been.

SNOWBOY: We both already been.

A-RAB: What happened?

SNOWBOY: A big fat nuthin'!

A-RAB: How come?

SNOWBOY: Cops believe everythin' they read in the papers.

ACTION: To them we ain't human. We're cruddy juvenile delinquents. So that's what we give 'em.

SNOWBOY: [*Imitating* KRUPKE] Hey, you!

ACTION: Me, Officer Krupke?

SNOWBOY: Yeah, you! Gimme one good reason for not draggin' ya down the station house, ya punk.

[ACTION *sings*]
Dear kindly Sergeant Krupke,
You gotta understand—
It's just our bringin' upke
That gets us out of hand.
Our mothers all are junkies,
Our fathers all are drunks.

[ALL]
Golly Moses—natcherly we're punks!

Gee, Officer Krupke, we're very upset;
We never had the love that every child oughta get.
We ain't no delinquents,
We're misunderstood.
Deep down inside us there is good!

[ACTION]
There is good!

[ALL]
There is good, there is good,
There is untapped good.
Like inside, the worst of us is good.

[SNOWBOY, *imitating* KRUPKE]
That's a touchin' good story.

[ACTION]
Lemme tell it to the world!

[SNOWBOY *imitating* KRUPKE]
Just tell it to the judge.

[ACTION, *to* DIESEL]
Dear kindly Judge, your Honor,
My parents treat me rough.
With all their marijuana,
They won't give me a puff.
They didn't wanna have me,
But somehow I was had.
Leapin' lizards—that's why I'm so bad!

[DIESEL, *imitating a judge*]
Right!
Officer Krupke, you're really a square;
This boy don't need a judge, he needs a analyst's care!
It's just his neurosis that oughta be curbed—
He's psychologically disturbed!

[ACTION]
I'm disturbed!

[ALL]
We're disturbed, we're disturbed,
We're the most disturbed.
Like we're psychologically disturbed.

DIESEL: [*Speaks, still acting part of the judge*] Hear ye, Hear ye! In the opinion of this court, this child is depraved on account he ain't had a normal home.
ACTION: Hey, I'm depraved on account I'm deprived!
DIESEL: [*As judge*] So take him to a headshrinker.

[ACTION, *to* A-RAB]
My father is a bastard,
My ma's an S.O.B.
My grandpa's always plastered,
My grandma pushes tea.
My sister wears a mustache,

My brother wears a dress.
Goodness gracious, that's why I'm a mess!

[A-RAB, *as psychiatrist*]

Yes!
Officer Krupke, you're really a slob.
This boy don't need a doctor, just a good honest job.
Society's played him a terrible trick,
And sociologically he's sick!

[ACTION]

I am sick!

[ALL]

We are sick, we are sick,
We are sick sick sick,
Like we're sociologically sick!

A-RAB: [*Speaks as psychiatrist*] In my opinion, this child don't need to have his head shrunk at all. Juvenile delinquency is purely a social disease.
ACTION: Hey, I got a social disease!
A-RAB: [*As psychiatrist*] So take him to a social worker!

[ACTION, *to* BABY JOHN]

Dear kindly social worker,
They say go earn a buck,
Like be a soda jerker,
Which means like be a schmuck.
It's not I'm antisocial,
I'm only antiwork.
Glory Osky, that's why I'm a jerk!

[BABY JOHN, *as female social worker*]

Eek!
Officer Krupke, you've done it again.
This boy don't need a job, he needs a year in the pen.
It ain't just a question of misunderstood;
Deep down inside him, he's no good!

[ACTION]

I'm no good!

[ALL]

We're no good, we're no good,
We're no earthly good,
Like the best of us is no damn good!

[DIESEL, *as judge*]
The trouble is he's crazy,

[A-RAB, *as psychiatrist*]
The trouble is he drinks.

[BABY JOHN, *as social worker*]
The trouble is he's lazy.

[DIESEL, *as judge*]
The trouble is he stinks.

[A-RAB, *as psychiatrist*]
The trouble is he's growing.

[BABY JOHN, *as social worker*]
The trouble is he's grown!
[ALL]
Krupke, we got troubles of our own!

Gee, Officer Krupke,
We're down on our knees,
'Cause no one wants a fella with a social disease.
Gee, Officer Krupke,
What are we to do?
Gee, Officer Krupke—
Krup you!

[*At the end of the song,* ANYBODYS *appears over the fence.*]

ANYBODYS: Buddy boys!
ACTION: Ah! Go wear a skirt.
ANYBODYS: I got scabby knees. Listen—
ACTION: [*To the gang*] Come on, we gotta make sure those PRs know we're on
    top.
DIESEL: Geez, Action, ain't we had enough?
ANYBODYS: [*Going after them*] Wotta buncha Old Man Rivers: they don't know
    nuthin' and they don't say nuthin'.
ACTION: Diesel, the question ain't whether we had enough—
ANYBODYS: The question is: Where's Tony and what party is lookin' for him.
ACTION: What do you know?
ANYBODYS: I know I gotta get a skirt. [*She starts off, but* DIESEL *stops her.*]
DIESEL: Come on, Anybodys, tell me.
SNOWBOY: Ah, what's that freak know?
ANYBODYS: Plenty. I figgered somebody oughta infiltrate PR territory and
    spy around. I'm very big with shadows, ya know. I can slip in and out
    of 'em like wind through a fence.

SNOWBOY: Boy, is she ever makin' the most of it!

ANYBODYS: You bet your fat A, I am!

ACTION: Go on. Wadd'ya hear?

ANYBODYS: I heard Chino tellin' the Sharks somethin' about Tony and Bernardo's sister. And then Chino said, "If it's the last thing I do, I'm going to get Tony."

ACTION: What'd I tell ya? Them PRs won't stop!

SNOWBOY: Easy, Action!

DIESEL: It's bad enough now—

BABY JOHN: Yeah!

ACTION: You forgettin'? Tony came through for us Jets. We gotta find him and protect him from Chino.

A-RAB: Right!

ACTION: O.K. then! Snowboy—cover the river! [SNOWBOY *runs off*] A-rab—get over to Doc's.

BABY JOHN: I'll take the back alleys.

ACTION: Diesel?

DIESEL: I'll cover the park.

ACTION: Good boy! [*He begins to run off.*]

ANYBODY'S: What about me?

ACTION: You? You get a hold of the girls and send 'em out as liaison runners so we'll know who's found Tony where.

ANYBODYS: Right! [*She starts to run off.*]

ACTION: Hey! [*She stops*] You done good, buddy boy.

ANYBODYS: [*She has fallen in love.*] Thanks, Daddy-o.

[*They both run off.*]

*The lights black out.*

## Scene 3

*11:30 P.M. The bedroom.*

*The light is, at first, a vague glow on the lovers, who are asleep on the bed. From offstage, faint at first, there is the sound of knocking. It gets louder; TONY stirs. At a distance a police siren sounds, and the knocking is now very loud. TONY bolts upright. ANITA comes in from outside and goes to the bedroom door—which is locked—tries the knob.*

ANITA: [*Holding back tears*] Maria? . . . Maria? [TONY *is reaching for his shirt when* MARIA *sits up. Quickly, he puts his hand, then his lips, on her lips*] Maria, it's Anita. Why are you locked in?

MARIA: I didn't know it was locked.

ANITA: Open the door. I need you.

[MARIA *reaches for the knob,* TONY *stops her.*]

MARIA: [*A whisper*] Now you are afraid, too.

ANITA: What?

MARIA: [*Loud*] One moment.

TONY: [*Whispering*] Doc'll help. I'll get money from him. You meet me at his drugstore.

[*In the other room,* ANITA *is aware of voices but unsure of what they are saying.*]

MARIA: At Doc's, yes. [*Aloud*] Coming, Anita!

TONY: [*Kisses her*] Hurry!

[*He scrambles out the window as* MARIA *hastily puts a bathrobe on over her slip. In the other room* ANITA *has stiffened and moved away from the door. She stands staring at it coldly as* MARIA *prattles to her through the door.*]

MARIA: Did you see Chino? He was here before, but he left so angry I think maybe he . . . [*She opens the door and sees* ANITA'S *look. A moment, then* ANITA *pushes her aside: looks at the bed, at the window, then turns accusingly to* MARIA] All right: now you know.

ANITA: [*Savagely*] And you still don't know: *Tony is one of them!*

> [*She sings bitterly*]
> A boy like that who'd kill your brother,
> Forget that boy and find another!
> One of your own kind—
> Stick to your own kind!
>
> A boy like that will give you sorrow—
> You'll meet another boy tomorrow!
> One of your own kind,
> Stick to your own kind!
>
> A boy who kills cannot love,
> A boy who kills has no heart.
> And he's the boy who gets your love
> And gets your heart—
> Very smart, Maria, very smart!
>
> A boy like that wants one thing only,
> And when he's done he'll leave you lonely.
> He'll murder your love; he murdered mine.
> Just wait and see—
> Just wait, Maria,
> Just wait and see!
>
> [MARIA *sings*]
> Oh no, Anita, no—
> Anita, no!
> It isn't true, not for me,

It's true for you, not for me,
I hear your words—
And in my head
I know they're smart,
But my heart, Anita,
But my heart
Knows they're wrong

[ANITA *reprises the chorus she has just sung, as* MARIA *continues her song*]

And my heart
Is too strong,
For I belong
To him alone, to him alone,
One thing I know:
I am his,
I don't care what he is.
I don't know why it's so,
I don't want to know.
Oh no, Anita, no—you should know better!
You were in love—or so you said.
You should know better . . .

I have a love, and it's all that I have.
Right or wrong, what else can I do?
I love him; I'm his,
And everything he is
I am, too.
I have a love and it's all that I need,
Right or wrong, and he needs me too.
I love him, we're one;
There's nothing to be done,
Not a thing I can do
But hold him, hold him forever,
Be with him now, tomorrow
And all of my life!

[BOTH]
When love comes so strong,
There is no right or wrong,
Your love is your life!

ANITA: [*Quietly*] Chino has a gun . . . He is sending the boys out to hunt for
   Tony—
MARIA: [*Tears off her bathrobe*] If he hurts Tony—If he touches him—I swear
to you, I'll—

ANITA: [*Sharply*] You'll do what Tony did to Bernardo?
MARIA: I love Tony.
ANITA: I know. I loved Bernardo.

[SCHRANK *comes into the outer room.*]

SCHRANK: Anybody home? [*Goes to bedroom door. Pleasantly*] Sorry to disturb you. Guess you're disturbed enough.
MARIA: [*Gathering her robe*] Yes. You will excuse me, please. I must go to my brother.
SCHRANK: There are just a coupla questions—
MARIA: Afterwards, please. Later.
SCHRANK: It'll only take a minute.
ANITA: Couldn't you wait until—
SCHRANK: [*Sharply*] No! [*A smile to* MARIA] You were at the dance at the gym last night.
MARIA: Yes.
SCHRANK: Your brother got in a heavy argument because you danced with the wrong boy.
MARIA: Oh?
SCHRANK: Who was the boy?
MARIA: Excuse me. Anita, my head is worse. Will you go to the drugstore and tell them what I need?
SCHRANK: Don't you keep aspirin around?
MARIA: This is something special. Will you go for me, Anita?
ANITA: [*Hesitates, looks at* MARIA, *then nods*] Shall I tell him to hold it for you till you come?
MARIA: [*To* SCHRANK] Will I be long?
SCHRANK: As long as it takes.
MARIA: [*To* ANITA] Yes. Tell him I will pick it up myself. [ANITA *goes out*] I'm sorry. Now you asked?
SCHRANK: [*As the lights dim*] I didn't ask, I told you. There was an argument over a boy. Who was that boy?
MARIA: Another from my country.
SCHRANK: And his name?
MARIA: José.

*The lights are out.*


SCENE 4

*11:40 P.M. The drugstore.*
A-RAB *and some of the Jets are there as* ANYBODYS *and other Jets run in.*

ACTION: Where's Tony?
A-RAB: Down in the cellar with Doc.

DIESEL: Ya warn him about Chino?

A-RAB: Doc said he'd tell him.

BABY JOHN: What's he hidin' in the cellar from?

SNOWBOY: Maybe he can't run as fast as you.

ACTION: Cut the frabbajabba.

ANYBODYS: Yeah! The cops'll get hip, if Chino and the PRs don't.

ACTION: Grab some readin' matter; play the juke. Some of ya get outside and if ya see Chino or any PR—

[*The shop doorbell tinkles as* ANITA *enters. Cold silence, then slowly she comes down to the counter. They all stare at her. A long moment. Someone turns on the juke box; a mambo comes on softly.*]

ANITA: I'd like to see Doc.

ACTION: He ain't here.

ANITA: Where is he?

A-RAB: He's gone to the bank. There was an error in his favor.

ANITA: The banks are closed at night. Where is he?

A-RAB: You know how skinny Doc is. He slipped in through the night-deposit slot.

ANYBODYS: And got stuck halfway in.

ACTION: Which indicates there's no tellin' when he'll be back. *Buenas noches, señorita.*

[ANITA *starts to go toward the cellar door.*]

DIESEL: Where you goin'?

ANITA: Downstairs—to see Doc.

ACTION: Didn't I tell ya he ain't here?

ANITA: I'd like to see for myself.

ACTION: [*Nastily*] Please.

ANITA: [*Controlling herself*] . . . Please.

ACTION: *Por favor.*

ANITA: Will you let me pass?

SNOWBOY: She's too dark to pass.

ANITA: [*Low*] Don't.

ACTION: *Please* don't.

SNOWBOY: *Por favor.*

DIESEL: *Non comprende.*

A-RAB: *Gracias.*

BABY JOHN: *Di nada.*

ANYBODYS: Ai! Mambo! Ai!

ANITA: Listen, you— [*She controls herself.*]

ACTION: We're listenin'.

ANITA: I've got to give a friend of yours a message. I've got to tell Tony—

DIESEL: He ain't here.

ANITA: I know he is.

ACTION: Who says he is?

A-RAB: Who's the message from?

ANITA: Never mind.

ACTION: Couldn't be from Chino, could it?

ANITA: I want to stop Chino! I want to help!

ANYBODYS: Bernardo's girl wants ta help?

ACTION: Even a greaseball's got feelings.

ANYBODYS: But she wants to help get Tony!

ANITA: No!

ACTION: Not much—Bernardo's tramp!

SNOWBOY: Bernardo's pig!

ACTION: Ya lyin' Spic—!

ANITA: Don't do that!

BABY JOHN: Gold tooth!

DIESEL: Pierced ear!

A-RAB: Garlic mouth!

ACTION: Spic! Lyin' Spic!

[*The taunting breaks out into a wild, savage dance, with epithets hurled at* ANITA, *who is encircled and driven by the whole pack. At the peak, she is shoved so that she falls in a corner.* BABY JOHN *is lifted up high and dropped on her as* DOC *enters from the cellar door and yells.*]

DOC: *Stop it!* . . . What've you been doing now?

[*Dead silence.* ANITA *gets up and looks at them.*]

ANITA: [*Trying not to cry*] Bernardo was right . . . If one of you was bleeding in the street, I'd walk by and spit on you. [*She flicks herself off and makes her way toward the door.*]

ACTION: Don't let her go!

DIESEL: She'll tell Chino that Tony—

[SNOWBOY *grabs her; she shakes loose.*]

ANITA: Let go! [*Facing them*] I'll give you a message for your American buddy! Tell the murderer Maria's *never* going to meet him! Tell him Chino found out and—and shot her! [*She slams out. There is a stunned silence.*]

DOC: What does it take to get through to you? When do you stop? *You make this world lousy!*

ACTION: That's the way we found it, Doc.

DOC: Get out of here!

[*Slowly, they start to file out.*]

*The lights fade.*

## SCENE 5

*11:50 P.M. The cellar.*

*Cramped: a box or crate; stairs leading to the drugstore above; a door to the outside.*

*TONY is sitting on a crate, whistling "Maria" as DOC comes down the stairs, some bills in his hand.*

TONY: Make a big sale?

DOC: No.

TONY: [*Taking the money that* DOC *is holding*] Thanks. I'll pay you back as soon as I can.

DOC: Forget that.

TONY: I won't; I couldn't. Doc, you know what we're going to do in the country, Maria and me? We're going to have kids and we'll name them all after you, even the girls. Then when you come to visit—

DOC: [*Slapping him*] *Wake up!* [*Raging*] Is that the only way to get through to you? Do just what you all do? Bust like a hot-water pipe?

TONY: Doc, what's gotten—

DOC: [*Overriding angrily*] Why do you live like there's a war on? [*Low*] Why do you kill?

TONY: I told you how it happened, Doc. Maria understands. Why can't you?

DOC: I never had a Maria.

TONY: [*Gently*] I have, and I'll tell you one thing, Doc. Even if it only lasts from one night to the next, it's worth the world.

DOC: That's all it did last.

TONY: What?

DOC: That was no customer upstairs, just now. That was Anita. [*Pause*] Maria is dead. Chino found out about you and her—and shot her.

[*A brief moment.* TONY *looks at* DOC, *stunned, numb. He shakes his head, as though he cannot believe this.* DOC *holds out his hands to him, but* TONY *backs away, then suddenly turns and runs out the door. As he does, the set flies away and the stage goes dark. In the darkness, we hear* TONY'S *voice.*]

TONY: Chino? *Chino?* Come and get me, too, Chino.

## SCENE 6

*Midnight. The street.*

*The lights come up to reveal the same set we saw at the beginning of Act I—but it is now jagged with shadows.* TONY *stands in the emptiness, calling, whirling around as a figure darts out of the shadows and then runs off again.*

TONY: Chino? . . . COME ON: GET ME, TOO!

ANYBODYS: [*A whisper from the dark*] Tony . . .

TONY: [*Swings around*] Who's that?

ANYBODYS: [*Darting on*] Me: Anybodys.

TONY: Get outa here. HEY, CHINO! COME GET ME, DAMN YOU!

ANYBODYS: What're you doin', Tony?

TONY: I said get outa here! CHINO!

ANYBODYS: Look, maybe if you and me just—

TONY: [*Savagely*] It's not playing any more! Can't any of you get that?

ANYBODYS: But the gang—

TONY: You're a girl: *be a girl!* Beat it. [*She retreats*] CHINO, I'M CALLING FOR YOU, CHINO! HURRY! IT'S CLEAR NOW. THERE'S NOBODY BUT ME. COME ON! Will you, please. I'm waiting for you. I want you to— [*Suddenly, all the way across the stage from him, a figure steps out of the dark. He stops and peers as light starts to glow on it. He utters an unbelieving whisper*] Maria . . . Maria?

MARIA: Tony . . .

[*As she holds out her arms toward him, another figure appears:* CHINO.]

TONY: MARIA! [*As they run to each other, there is a gun shot.* TONY *stumbles, as though he has tripped.* MARIA *catches him and cradles him in her arms as he falters to the ground. During this* BABY JOHN *and* A-RAB *run on; then* PEPE *and* INDIO *and other Sharks.* CHINO *stands very still, bewildered by the gun dangling from his hand. More Jets and Sharks, some girls run on, and* DOC *comes out to stare with them*] I didn't believe hard enough.

MARIA: Loving is enough.

TONY: Not here. They won't let us be.

MARIA: Then we'll get away.

TONY: Yes, we can. We *will*.

[*He shivers, as though a pain went through him. She holds him closer and begins to sing—without orchestra.*]

[MARIA]
Hold my hand and we're halfway there.
Hold my hand and I'll take you there,
Someday,
Somehow . . .

[*He has started to join in on the second line. She sings harder, as though to urge him back to life, but his voice falters and he barely finishes the line. She sings on, a phrase or two more, then stops, his body quiet in her arms. A moment, and then, as she gently rests* TONY *on the floor, the orchestra finishes the last bars of the song. Lightly, she brushes* TONY's *lips with her fingers. Behind her,* ACTION, *in front of a group of Jets, moves to lead them toward* CHINO. MARIA *speaks, her voice cold, sharp*]

MARIA: Stay back. [*The shawl she has had around her shoulders slips to the ground as she gets up, walks to* CHINO *and holds out her hand. He hands her the gun. She speaks again, in a flat, hard voice*] How do you fire this gun, Chino? Just by pulling this little trigger? [*She points it at him suddenly; he draws back. She has all of them in front of her now, as she holds the gun out and her voice gets stronger with anger and savage rage*] How many bullets are left, Chino? Enough for you? [*Pointing at another*] And you? [*At* ACTION] All of you? WE ALL KILLED HIM; and my brother and Riff. I, too. I CAN KILL NOW BECAUSE *I* HATE NOW. [*She has been pointing the gun wildly, and they have all been drawing back. Now, again, she holds it straight out at* ACTION] How many can I kill, Chino? How many—and still have one bullet left for me? [*Both hands on the gun, she pushes it forward at* ACTION. *But she cannot fire, and she breaks into tears, hurls the gun away and sinks to the ground.* SCHRANK *walks on, looks around and starts toward* TONY'S *body. Like a madwoman,* MARIA *races to the body and puts her arms around it, all-embracing, protecting, as she cries out*] DON'T YOU TOUCH HIM! [SCHRANK *steps back.* KRUPKE *and* GLAD HAND *have appeared in the shadows behind him.* MARIA *now turns and looks at* CHINO, *holds her hand out to him. Slowly he comes and stands by the body. Now she looks at* ACTION, *holds out her hand to him. He, too, comes forward, with* DIESEL, *to stand by the body.* PEPE *joins* CHINO. *Then* MARIA *leans low over* TONY'S *face. Softly, privately*] Te adoro, Anton.

[*She kisses him gently. Music starts as the two Jets and two Sharks lift up* TONY'S *body and start to carry him out. The others, boys and girls, fall in behind to make a procession, the same procession they made in the dream ballet, as* BABY JOHN *comes forward to pick up* MARIA'S *shawl and put it over her head. She sits quietly, like a woman in mourning, as the music builds, the lights start to come up and the procession makes its way across the stage. At last, she gets up and, despite the tears on her face, lifts her head proudly, and triumphantly turns to follow the others. The adults—*DOC, SCHRANK, KRUPKE, GLAD HAND—*are left bowed, alone, useless.*]

*The curtain falls.*

# STUDY QUESTIONS

1. How quickly are individuals characterized? What strategies are used to make CHARACTERS distinct individuals? How important are their names? How does the fact that most of the characters are members of gangs complicate the process of distinguishing them as individuals? How are members of the same gang distinguished from one another? What role do habits of speech play in characterization here? Why is Tony characterized, from the beginning, as different from the others?

2. In what specific ways are the two policemen important to the PLOT? How do the two differ from each other? What attitudes do they hold in common? In what ways do they represent the attitudes of the community? How do you feel about the policemen? Why?

3. What aspects of the stage SETTING seem to you most important to the play's effects? What kinds of lighting would you use if you were directing the play? What kinds of body movements and hand gestures would you have the actors use in common?

4. In what ways do the gangs represent attitudes of the larger community? Which attitudes of gang members are explicitly said to be derived from their parents? Which speeches made by gang members sound like clichés that might be uttered by "ordinary" members of the community? What ethnic and nationalistic prejudices are directly expressed here?

5. Why do the Jets believe they "own" the street? How, exactly, do they regard the Sharks in relation to their own ownership? What traits do they attribute to Puerto Ricans? What ethnic slurs do the Sharks hurl at the Jets?

6. How much of the language of the play seems "topical" to the times? Which expressions used by gang members do you not understand? How much is the play "dated" by its use of popular slang? Is the play a realistic portrayal of gangs as they are today? as they were when the play was written?

7. Which of the song lyrics read best as "poems"? Listen to a tape of the music from the movie sound track: which of the songs is most impressive as a song? How do you account for the differences in effect? In what specific ways does the music affect the TONE of the play?

8. What does Maria mean (end of Act I, scene 3) when she describes tonight as "the real beginning of my life as a young lady of America"? What other signs of aspiration to be "American" do you find among the Puerto Rican characters? How frequent are such references among the Jets and their girls? How do you account for the differences?

9. Why does Bernardo call Riff "Native Boy" (I, 4)? What other nicknames or derogatory terms express feelings of frustration or envy?

10. Why is the language of the first love scene between Tony and Maria so otherworldly (I, 5)? How consistently is such language maintained later in the play when the two are together? What explicit reminders of *Romeo and Juliet* do you see in the play? How does the language of love relate to the violence that dominates the play near the end? Describe as precisely as you can the way the contrast between language and action works.

11. What is implied by Anita's comment (I, 5) that Maria is now free to have fun? What role has Bernardo been playing for her? How does the plot of the play comment on that role? What is the tone of the nostalgia for Puerto Rico in the song at the end of the scene?

12. Why does Action claim that his father, his brother, and Doc were "never" the age he is now? How much generational tension is portrayed in the play?

13. Describe the tone achieved when Bernardo whistles "My Country 'Tis of Thee" (I, 6). How much of the effect of Bernardo's whistling is produced by your memory of the words of the song?

14. Explain the scene (I, 7) in which Tony and Maria use dummies to act out their own feelings and situation. Why do the stage directions refer self-consciously to what they do as "play acting"? Exactly what is accomplished in this scene?

15. How do the stage directions for changing the scenery to reflect earlier moments in the play affect the tone of the play? the meaning?

16. Describe the central CONFLICTS in the play. How does each develop onstage? Chart the RISING ACTION of the play. Where do the conflicts between gangs and between love and loyalty to ethnic backgrounds come most dramatically into focus?

17. Whose story is this? Who are the leading characters? What is the central conflict? How do the various settings reflect the central themes of the play?

# Francine du Plessix Gray

Born in France in 1930, Francine du Plessix Gray moved to the United States with her parents (her father was a diplomat) in 1941. Among her novels are *Lovers and Tyrants* (1976), in which this story appeared, and *World Without End* (1981).

"Tribe" describes the "return" to Europe of someone who has lived in America for more than a quarter of a century without going back to the ancestral home.

## TRIBE

"What about Suez?" Aunt Charlotte asked. "What about Algeria? What about Vietnam? Twenty years! We have a lot of catching up to do. How curious of you not to have returned sooner!"

A very heavy woman, her flesh accreted like uncontrolled lava, was welcoming me back to Saint-Seran. I had finally gathered the courage to visit my father's family again. Aunt Charlotte's silvery hair tumbled over an exorbitantly pink face, she held on her lap a piece of tapestry work and a large album of collected stamps. Inured by age and willful isolation, her mind swung giddily among historical cataclysms and recitations of family chronicles. All of my father's brothers, including her husband, Uncle Jean, were now dead.

"Are there roads in America?" she continued. "Do you eat bread in America? What kind of bread? What is the speed limit on your roads? Did you do your studies in English or in American? Do you remember how you used to skim the foam off the raspberry jam in our kitchen before the war? Do you think you could send me some African stamps from the United States? Possibly you could find me some from Zaïre. . . . Listen, dear child, we have all the room in the world for you."

And she pointed to the proliferation of bedding scattered about her living room and the entire house. It was the most startling feature of this dwelling I had not entered since the age of fifteen; it made my long absence seem all the odder. There were army cots stood up helter-skelter against the eighteenth-century *boiseries*[1] of the old library, folding beds crammed in the hallways, sleeping bags strewn about the little dining room to which Aunt Charlotte hobbled to take her meals, more beds stacked against the delicate Louis XIII staircase that wound upstairs from the front entrance hall. This proliferation of sleeping arrangements contrasted bizarrely with the bleak gray walls hung with portraits of ancestors, the forbidding crucifixes dominating a wall of every room, the austerity of gray stone floors left uncarpeted since the German occupation. It gave Saint-Seran a warm and profligate bohemianism, testifying to the enormous number of grandchildren, great-grandchildren, nephews, nieces who flocked back here every summer with an eagerness which I found mysterious, seeing how terrified I had been of my own return. When my father was shot down over Gibraltar from the Spanish coast, presumably by German gunfire, he had been buried in the British cemetery. Nine years later his body had been brought back to France and reburied in the family vault near Saint-Seran. I had never dared to visit his grave. I had spent a good part of my life denying the reality of his death. And now as I sat finally facing Aunt Charlotte I was crippled by another fear that had haunted me for decades: that my family would bear me too much rancor after my long absence for any return to be bearable, that I could never return. 4

Rancor? Quite the contrary! My aunt's gentle, inquisitive eyes seemed filled with gratitude at my visit. She lived all year long in this ancient house where I had spent some of my happiest childhood holidays. Seventy-six years old, rooted to the first floor of the dwelling by her great weight, she was as frenetically curious about contemporary events as she was reluctant to witness them at first hand. And she treated my arrival as if it were the most precious of gifts—a marvelously riskless exposure to the modern world. 5

"Don't you dare think I'm out of touch," she announced emphatically, pointing to her large RCA television set, "even though I've not once been to Paris since World War Two. It's only a three hours' train ride from Nantes nowadays, but there is something about the capital which most of our family has always disliked and feared—the many new ideas perhaps . . . the modernism . . . the size . . . the craze for novelty . . . the foreign visitors . . ." 6

Her fingers fidgeting with a corner of her stamp album, her cane tapping agitatedly on the floor, she stared at her foreign visitor with the furtive, taunting excitement with which we sometimes stare at a tiger safely caged in a zoo. 7

"You're not going to tell *me*, in *this* house," she challenged me within ten minutes of our first embrace, "that Algerian independence was not a monstrosity. Just think of your great-great-granduncle, General de Lamoricière, who dedicated his life to conquering Algeria for France, and your father's 8

1. Woodwork.

brother, Uncle André, whom independence left totally destitute at the age of sixty-seven. And now it's the Algerians who are bankrupt; we gave them freedom much too early for their own good, not even to speak of ours. What's all this idea of liberty for children who don't even know how to read, who barely know how to make a little camel drawing instead of their signature, how can they vote? That's one point on which I broke totally with our great de Gaulle, but God bless his soul, he may have been forced into it, he's beyond reproach on all else. Tell me, aren't you afraid of an invasion of Chinese into the United States?"

No, I said, there were many things to fear, but that was not one of them.     9

"Well, I'd watch out if I were you, I think you're overly optimistic.    10
They just might turn out to be like the Africans in England or the Arabs here, drive you out of job and home. And what about Vietnam, what could you think of that atrocity? How did you manage not to learn a lesson from our history and immediately get out? What a frightful decade you must be living through!"

Yes, I said, I had been arrested once for taking part in a demonstration     11
against the war in Vietnam.

She clapped her plump little hands, and appeared to feel increasingly    12
safe in my company. "Bravo, bravo! You're one of us down to the last straw, that's just what many of us would have done. Risk! Acting out one's conscience always entails some risk. I must tell you that several of your second cousins who were in the underground have never really recovered from their experience in concentration camps even twenty years later. Foreigners tend to forget how scarred we still are by the war, how many generations it takes for these wounds to heal. By the way, I suppose you're going to visit your father's grave tomorrow or the day after?"

Yes, I said, it had been very much on my mind to do that.    13

"Well, Stéphanie, there is something you do not know about him that is    14
very important for you to know. You see, after we saw you here last we heard from the chaplain in Gibraltar that all the men on your father's plane were still conscious when they crashed upon the beach, that they were all able to receive Extreme Unction."

She watched my face closely, waiting to be rewarded with an expression    15
of gratitude, which did not come. For the first time, she seemed irritated with me.

"But you live in a world of delusions, my dear! You don't seem to realize    16
what joy it gave us to know that he had received the last sacrament! Just think how ghastly it would have been if the plane he was on had fallen into the sea like the others, if we hadn't been able to eventually bring his body here. You see, God always gives us something to be grateful for, if you look at life in the right way." And she crossed herself with great cheerfulness.

I stared at the crucifix hanging above the television set alongside a pic-    17
ture of de Gaulle, and the family's hallowed dead, thinking yes, this was the kind of grim detail I must be prepared to face here, that I had felt incapable

of facing up to now. At such times my mind took refuge from her chatter in safely historical, encyclopedic meditations on the verdant countryside about me: "Vendée, a maritime department of western France adjoining the southeast boundary of Brittany, one of France's most conservative districts, was the region which most fiercely resisted the Revolution in 1793. The Chouans, peasant bands well documented in the Balzac novel named after them, instigated a series of Royalist insurrections which lasted well into the nineteenth century. . . ." The landscape out of Aunt Charlotte's window was as flat as any in my memory, there was not a hillock, not a rock, to disturb the monotonous platitude of its horizon. A serene, dead-straight alley of luxuriant chestnut trees stretched from the little castle to the country road. To the left stood some dilapidated buildings that had once served as stables and servants' quarters. The old greenhouse to the right of the entrance had also been abandoned since the war, when the family fortune declined sharply. In the flower beds circling about the castle's entrance only the simplest and most tenacious of flowers—hydrangeas, geraniums—fought their way nobly through tall clumps of weeds.

"Now for the family albums," Aunt Charlotte was saying. "Let's start with 1936, we'll do 'thirty-seven in the afternoon, and perhaps 'thirty-eight after tea if we're not too tired. Well, here you are, aged five, with your cousin Daniel, who's coming from Nantes to lunch with you. There you are with Louise, your oldest cousin, who is coming from Paris tomorrow to see you. And look at that sweet picture of you with Catherine, who is coming to meet you here this afternoon. Ah, here's one of you with your father and all five of your Saint-Seran cousins, mercy how they adored him, he was their hero. . . ." She lingered with particular affection upon a photo of my father surrounded by a pack of children—we were swarming and climbing up his limbs as if he were a huge oak tree, gamboling on the stoop of the ancestral door which I had avoided for so long. Cousins, cousins, I never knew anyone could possess as many as I did. Throughout the day they tumbled out of Aunt Charlotte's albums as prolifically as the camp beds set out to accommodate them, testifying to the redoubtable fact that in other parts of France my father's other three brothers had each borne a minimum of five children, most of whom had also had five or six of their own, and that all thirty or forty of them came back here every summer. It was awesome, this proliferation of shared protoplasm, to someone who had been brought up kinless in the New World. Every few hours some new batch of my tribesmen would arrive, each greeting me with different tones of curiosity, irony, emotion.

"It's very nice of you to come back after all these years," my cousin 19 Daniel hollered at me from the front door, by way of greeting, "awfully good of you to finally come back!"

I stared back at him with particular curiosity, for he was depicted in one 20 of the few childhood photographs that had followed me to America. It showed us together at the age of eight or nine, both sucking on lollipops and dressed in white for someone's First Communion. My arm was linked through his, and he looked miserable under my possessive embrace—I had been madly in love with him at that age. He was now a tall, angular businessman in his thirties with great fangs of tobacco-stained teeth.

"You could have given us some sign of life earlier, you know," he continued to roar. "Awfully strange behavior. Strange notion of family you have in the United States. We've always heard you had no great sense of family or of the past. Well, my dear, you're a living proof. So you've finally decided to come back. We were never about to spank you or anything for staying away. Your father was one of my best friends when I was a child. A hero to us all, God knows. Every few years our magazines still ask for a picture of him to illustrate another story on the early days of the Resistance. I'd have recognized you in a crowd a hundred yards away! Ah, well, give us a kiss, it's good to have you back!"

And he embraced me powerfully, exhaling pungent odors of Gitanes.[2] It was almost time for lunch. On this August holiday—the Feast of the Assumption of Mary—young cousins from Nantes, from Rennes, from Brest, kept flocking unannounced to the family house, arriving on motorcycles and in *quatre chevaux*[3] with the suddenness with which a lover surprises his mistress on an idle afternoon.

"Yes, here they are," Daniel said pointedly, "*they*'ve got a sense of family. Properly brought up people. You can't keep them away."

The helter-skelter village girl in charge of Aunt Charlotte's housekeeping scurried about, peeling more potatoes, picking more tomatoes.

"It's always like this in the summers," Aunt Charlotte grumbled good-naturedly as she hobbled about, masterminding the frantic resetting of the table, "sometimes we're three, sometimes eighteen. I wish they'd let me know with a little phone call, I who try to build my life around accurate and precise reception of world news, lunch at twelve sharp so I can get the one o'clock *informations*,[4] dinner punctually at seven so I can see the best of the evening reports. . . ."

With an entrancing blend of formality and confusion, a long series of courses—melon, fish, chicken, a vegetable, salad, cheese, fruit—were served separately, on seven changes of slightly chipped two-hundred-year-old family china.

"We hear you're a writer. So what do you write about in America?" Daniel shouted over the table. "Oh, my God, current events? I don't know how you can keep up with them, where you live."

"Where's Dayton, Ohio?" asked a young cousin who had arrived from Nantes on his motorcycle. "In the center of your country or on the coast?"

"You have only two children? Why such a small family?"

2. French cigarettes.
3. Small Renaults; literally, "four horses."
4. News.

"Do your sons play soccer, rugby, or football?"                                     30

"Hasn't Dr. Spock had a terribly pernicious influence on your young     31
people?"

"What are the speed limits on your roads?"                                          32

"Absolutely monstrous of you to pressure your President Johnson with     33
those filthy antiwar demonstrations," Daniel broadcast over the fish course.
"You elect him with the greatest plurality in history, and then you make life
hell for him. What's all this hysteria? I repeat, you have no sense of history.
You should have avoided the whole mess by profiting by our example, but
once you're in, full steam ahead. All your puritanical nonsense about corrup-
tion in South Vietnam, it's so naïve. What do you think politics are all about?
Did anyone raise an eyebrow when Napoleon pillaged Italy?" He washed
down his fish with a large mouthful of Montrachet.[5] "Did anyone protest
when Louis XIII had his opponents jailed? How else can you run a country?
In messing up your Johnson you're thinking of yourselves, not of world order,
it's very selfish, it's not very elegant."

It was the hottest day of the summer. Some twelve of us were crowded     34
into the tiny dining room furnished with frayed, weathered Louis XV chairs
and piles of sleeping bags. All the windows were tightly shut. The crucifix
hanging over the door to the kitchen was ornamented with dried palm and
bay and surmounted a receptacle for holy water. Everyone except me had
gone to Mass that morning. The three nieces I had acquired at lunch that
day were large and pretty, with that high-toned, Irishlike complexion typical
of the Vendée and Brittany. The prettiest—one of Daniel's daughters—wore
a thin-strapped mini-skirted gingham dress that looked like an elongated bathing
suit.

"You should have put something on top of that décolleté today," her     35
father grumbled. "Monsieur le curé[6] almost had a stroke when he gave you
Communion this morning."

"Don't worry, Papa," she minced saucily, putting her arms over her     36
large and beautiful breasts, "I crossed my hands over them so that the Host
wouldn't fall in between."

Her father guffawed. What an unpredictable lot, I thought, I rather like     37
them. I fancied their blend of conservatism and earthiness, their extraordinary fear of fresh air. Halfway through coffee, almost fainting from the heat,
I pleaded the beauty of the midday light on the castle's façade and went out
to take a photograph and breathe. The pretty niece followed me.

"Stop, stop, don't take it yet!" she cried as I focused the camera. "There's     38
a window open on the second floor, it looks so awful!"

She ran up to close it and quickly ran back. "*Now* take it," she ordered,     39
staring beatifically at the pale symmetrical structure surmounted by silvery
slopes of gray mansarded roofs.

5. A fine white wine.
6. The parish priest.

I obeyed. *Click:* my ancestors' home. With all its windows shut, the little 40 castle, glimpsed through its alley of chestnut trees, looked as impervious to the flow of history as to currents of air, like a structure out of a Perrault fairy tale, like a picture in a coloring book which each of us could fill in with our particular obsessions. Papa had spent his childhood here, had helped to nurse his mother through a dreadfully lingering cancer. I had learned that detail only today. The Benjamin of the lot, he had been nine when she died, the same age I was at his death, and had remained alone with his older sister Colette while his father and brothers were away at the First World War. Had those years of sorrow and of solitude helped to shape his need for heroism, for early death? Here we had slept in the same bed, during some weeks of each summer, in that second-floor room which I refused to visit. And two years ago the last of my surviving uncles had died here, quietly sitting in his armchair; a wave of sorrow suddenly filled me for not having seen him one last time, there was no one left now of my father's generation except Aunt Colette, whom I was to visit tomorrow. Too late; always too late; perhaps not always totally too late. . . .

The pretty cousin hollered to a bevy of her contemporaries, and we all 41 took a walk in the park. It struck me that there was literally nothing to do at Saint-Seran but wallow in family history and walk through forests. There was not a pond or a river to bathe in or a movie to go to, no horses, no tennis, no town to shop in within a half hour's driving distance, nothing, nothing, nothing. Nothing but *la promenade dans le beau parc.*[7] And here were these hordes of young persons in their late teens and early twenties who had the means to go to the mountains or to the Côte d'Azur, but who preferred to lounge about this sweet dormant structure; with nothing else to do but study Aunt Charlotte's family albums, glue into them the weddings and baptisms of the year, or walk through alleys of trees, commenting on the beauty of sunlight as it hit the oaks, a stand of elms, a cluster of chestnuts, a grove of pines or poplars. Occasionally, when filled with a sense of adventure, they employed themselves by cutting down some brush to enlarge the park's old alleys, or began the grave task of tracing the beginnings of a new one.

"So you come here every summer for your vacation?" I asked the pretty 42 cousin.

"Of course," she exclaimed, as if I were mad to ask such a question. She 43 worked as a bank clerk in Brest, and had five brothers.

"You like it better than the sea, or the mountains?" 44

"We come here to recapture our childhoods," she said as if announcing 45 something totally uncontestable. "Don't you like to recall your childhood? What is there more beautiful than bathing in the past?" she added dreamily, hitching up a strap of her bathing suit–church dress. "Oh, I can't tell you how attached we all are to this place, every single one of us. Look, it is so pretty from here, why don't you take a photo now?" She squinted her eyes

7. A stroll in the beautiful park.

to admire the silvery structure, whose gray slate roofs sloped gently down to its long, narrow closed windows.

History, loyalty, continuity. It would take me some time to realize that my cousins' attachment to Saint-Seran was dictated by a quest for roots that was also a reassurance of immortality, that they achieved some peace by bathing in the aura of the ancestral dead. And if there were an occasional glance of defiance, of irritation, admixed with the burning curiosity my cousins bestowed upon me, it was because I was the only descendant who had refused to continue this linkage, who had once attempted to scrub myself clean of family memories, who had tried to forge a false innocence by shutting myself off from the griefs of the past. Destroy, New World immigrant, destroy, destroy, destroy. Destroy the forests, destroy the past, be free again from the pain of history.

There is a recurring nightmare that has haunted me in various forms, over the years, since my father died. I dream that he is still alive somewhere, and hiding; that he is avoiding me, that he has just reasserted his refusal ever to communicate with me again. The dream recurs one night that very summer in Nantes, where I have taken a hotel room, twenty minutes from Saint-Seran. I dream that my Aunt Colette and I are on a plane that has made a crash landing. We are not hurt but seem to be the only survivors, and massive debris is scattered all about us. We receive a message that my father is alive and well in some distant country, that he is crippled and confined to a wheelchair but still strong and magnificent, that he is happily married to a much younger woman and refuses more adamantly than ever to communicate with us. "Traitor!" Colette and I scream together upon receiving the news. "Traitor, traitor!"

On the morning after this dream—the day I was to see Aunt Colette again for the first time in twelve years—I took a long walk on the banks of the Loire to shake off the obsessions of the night. And I tried to remember that time twenty years ago, after the war's end, when I had returned to Saint-Seran and found my father's absence there so insupportable, and had fled after twenty-four hours. During the war years in the United States I had romanticized the family house—the way my cousins did now—as that place where reality was unsurpassed in its perfection. And I had rushed there alone as soon as traveling became possible. I was fifteen, childishly unaware of my relatives' suffering or of the toll of the war. The pain of the visit was bound to be augmented by the fact that my mother's anxiety about the past had kept her from ever mentioning my father to me, and that I doggedly continued to believe he was still hiding in the Resistance underground long after I had learned he was dead. And pain still reduces my memory of the visit to images of catatonic brevity: Saint-Seran is a crumbling structure set in a stretch of stagnant fields. My Uncle Jean is thin. My Aunt Charlotte is fat. One of my cousins is in the colonies. Another one is trying to leave for the colonies. The oldest cousin, the wan pious Cécile whom I used to visit in her tower room, had died a few days before she was scheduled to enter a convent. Nantes is one of the three French towns most brutally destroyed in World War II. Aunt Colette lives in one pathetic room overlooking the rubble of the bombed-out port. We sit down to a prisonlike supper of watery soup in which float stony hunks of dry bread. The next morning I am taken to visit the place where my father will be buried when his body is brought home from Gibraltar. The cemetery is overgrown with brush, and the dank family chapel is filled with the tombs of ancestors whose history is meaningless to me. I remember little but the high grass, the dampness of the chapel's stone walls, my dumb pain and anger. With anger I stared at what would be his final resting place, raging at him: Why, why did you abandon me? I think I needed to break down right there and accept the reality of his death, I needed to lie on his tomb and flail my limbs about in some grim but necessary exorcism of emotion, demanding to pierce into the earth, to be reunited with his bones. But they were not even there. The absence of his body was like a double treason, further augmenting the treason that was his death. I had insisted on taking the next train back to Paris and had wept for days, refusing to eat, unable to stop crying, not knowing precisely why I was crying—a minor breakdown, perhaps.

When I had come to live in Paris eight years later, at twenty-three, I 49 had steeped myself in my mother's world and elaborately steered clear of any contact with my father's immediate family, as my mother always had. Eventually I ran into Aunt Colette, the adored older sister who had taken care of him when their parents died and who had been one of the idols of my own childhood. I met her by accident at the home of distant cousins. Since it was her only trip to Paris since 1947, when she had come to receive a Legion of Honor for her work in the Resistance, I suppose she had come in great part to try to see me. She was very poor. The trip was difficult for her. Her eyes had devoured me across the room. I did not have the honesty or kindness to return her gaze. I was terrified of this proud, gentle woman who had worn mourning since my father's death, who was my last link to my total childhood. "It would be so nice to see you, even here," she had said, intimating that she would prolong her stay in Paris if I could grant her a few hours. But I had lied and said that I was going away that same evening to Italy. Those were the years when I could not bear to hear the mention of my father's name. And I had rejected her as crassly as I had avoided the rest of his family—more crassly, since she was so totally alone in the world, since along with me she had mourned him more deeply than anyone else.

Walking through Nantes today toward Aunt Colette's apartment on a 50 summer day in the nineteen-sixties. Past the great castle of Anne of Brittany, where white swans glide tranquilly in deep lily-filled moats. Past the monument to Jules Verne, born in this city, past the factory which manufactures the nice biscuits Petit Beurre Lu, Lu Lustucru. The city is bathed in that silvery light of the upper Atlantic coast, we are in Gaelic, Celtic country here, the light is like the gleam on a pear, all seems spun in webs of fragile silver. Past the docks famous for the drownings of the Revolution, when some two thousand Royalists, their hands bound to their sides, were marched into boats that were sunk in the River Loire. Past the house where Aunt Colette and my father were born. My grandmother was a great beauty and painted with talent; during World War I, my grandfather died of typhoid; I am thirty-five and have learned that only yesterday. I suddenly need to see and own a picture of them, very well, all's easy now, I'll ask Aunt Colette. A student in theatrical peasant costume hands me a pamphlet on the Breton liberation movement. Another Breton liberationist, incongruous in blue jeans and formal white lace headdress, hands me an antiabortion pamphlet in Gaelic. Three hippies with angelically long blond hair sit on the sidewalk in the morning sunshine, washing their feet in the gutter as they would on a summer day in any town in Europe. World War II had ended, Dien Bien Phu, Suez, Algeria, have come and gone, and the dead are coming home from Vietnam, and I am walking down a street called Cours John Kennedy. Some new courage buttresses me this morning, making all kinds of new emotions and meetings possible, as if this visit has finally thrust me out of childhood. I come to the address Aunt Colette has given me, to the door of a ground-floor apartment in a pale seventeenth-century building a block from the cathedral.

An extraordinary face stares at me through the window. A delicate face $51$ as fragile and carefully painted as a moth's, ruled by enormous and melancholy eyes. All over the moth's face large furry tufts of silvery hair grow in mad, erratic spurts, as they might on some wood sprite, on a creature half human, half tree. Aunt Colette so clearly has my father's and my eyes—ironic, sad, gay eyes with deeply chiseled lids—that this is the way one of my cousins had found me at the airport: she had simply walked up to me, extended her hand, and said, "You have Aunt Colette's gaze." The moth's face leaves the window, and a few seconds later a person weighing some seventy pounds, with the frail, erect, boyish body of an aging ballerina, opens the door. She is eighty years old. She has still a different way of greeting me. She falls into my arms, her body shaking, her face shaking, yet some stoicism keeps her eyes quite dry. "Well, here you are at last," she says during our long embrace.

I am shaking, too. "Forgive me," I want to cry, "forgive me for my lies $52$ and my evasions." But I know that I can never use such terms with her, that this frail, subtle, solid woman prefers not to resort to words, that everything between us will be accomplished as in a choreography of insects.

Very soon thereafter we sit down to lunch. One must always eat. Among $53$ the decorous, the diffident, the French, much pain and joy is punctuated by appropriate mundanities over the solemnity of a five-course meal.

"Did you do your studies in British or in American?" she asks, her eyes $54$ devouring me, our gaze meeting straightforwardly across the table laden with fragile Saint-Seran china. "Do you eat much bread in America? What color is the bread? Do you have Trotskyists in America? How many of them do you have? They are responsible for many of our troubles here, aren't they responsible for your black uprisings? What do you think of the Pope? I hear from Aunt Charlotte that you receive dissident priests for tea, it has become much the fashion here too, deplorably. Have you reread Sainte-Beuve lately? Don't you agree with him that the progress of civilization is accompanied by a terrible degeneration of morals in mankind? Is your stepfather Catholic? Oh, he is Jewish. Ah, well, the Pope has forgiven them. . . ."

In this willfully remote province, reality seems to filter through prisms that block out many aspects of modern civilization yet enlarge others into obsessive proportions—Trotskyists, speed limits, the color of bread. Aunt Colette's voice is as light and striking as her person, thin but powerful, with a silvery tint to it recalling the light that bathes her city, frequently punctuated with pealing, boyish laughs, She retired fifteen years ago from her work as a librarian, and lives in a modest but dainty three-room flat filled with remnants of Saint-Seran as frail as her body: odd teacups, residues of Sèvres porcelain, miniatures of ancestors on fragile Louis XVI tables, spindly chairs covered in worn petit-point rose patterns that seem as if they could support no more than her weight. Even the crucifix hanging on the wall by the inevitable photograph of de Gaulle is spindly and ethereal. She shares her flat with a childhood friend, also a spinster, and by pooling their resources they have somehow reconstituted comfort out of their postwar poverty. And I rejoice in Colette's ease and her lack of solitude, as if these amenities—those of her own resourcefulness—could reduce my guilt. 55

Perhaps desiring to emphasize our birthright to decorousness, she feasts me, as Aunt Charlotte has done, with a procession of courses served on five different sets of china. I protest, in midmeal, that one could eat the vegetables *with* the meat instead of separately, wouldn't it make her dishwashing easier? "Oh, no," she rebuts, her voice crackling with indignation, "eat like the Germans, who heap meat and potatoes and vegetables on the same plate? The most disgusting custom I know. Why, even when we go on picnics in the forest we bring at least four changes of china." 56

I am regaled by tales of her frequent trips to the country, of her vociferous reading, of her prodigious passion for bridge. She plays bridge at least four afternoons a week, being, like most members of our family, "of a nature driven to excess." She frequently entertains groups of ten friends in her flat for two-table bridge parties; since they are all quite old, she explains, there are always two players dropping out and napping in the other room, resting up for their turn to play. She goes every August to vacation on the island of Oléron with a few friends her age. Over the years they have chosen a particular hotel for its proximity to beautiful trees and also to a church where they can go to Mass every morning. "I adore forests," she says, "the joy of my life is to walk in lovely parks like that of Saint-Seran or Oléron, and observe the play of sunlight on different kinds of trees. In Oléron we always carry a folding card table into the forest and spend the afternoon playing our bridge 57 match there, enjoying the effect of afternoon sunlight on the leaves. . . . Tell me, do you have insomnia?"

Yes, deplorably so, ever since a certain period of the war.                                58

"Bravo, then you're really one of us!" she exclaims, acknowledging the      59
reference to my father's death with a wise, sad look but preferring not to
dwell upon it. (For she, who knows more about him than anyone else, never
offers any detail more telling than "He hated his braces as a child," or "He
passed his exams marvelously.") "You might even have had insomnia *without*
the war," she continues. "That's a trait from the Lamoricière side which
plagues most of us. For instance, your grandfather, a colonel in the professional Army, read and reread Taine through the night, whether he was stationed in Annecy or in Algeria. Your Uncle Jean used to read Michelet from
two to six A.M., he slept three or four hours a night and hunted five hours
each day; he lunched at ten and dined at four . . . as for my white nights, I
reread de Gaulle's memoirs."

"Why this anxiety?" I ask. "Are we romantics?"                                        60

She nods her head emphatically with an ironic smile. "Oh, yes, indeed,      61
we've always been romantics."

"In what sense?"                                                                          62

"We're concerned with heroism," she ventures slowly, "and the future      63
of our actions, and how they relate to the past. Oh, by the way, have you
been there yet? No? You are going tomorrow, with your cousin Catherine?
Very well. Do you like de Gaulle?" she asks hurriedly, as if to get ourselves
back on safer ground.

"A great man," I answered carefully, "perhaps a little astigmatic, more      64
skilled at seeing long-range consequences than immediate ones."

"But you *do* think he is great?"                                                      65

"Oh yes."                                                                                66

"Thank God," she simply says. "All these modern trends, I just don't      67
know about them . . . these Cabinet ministers whose wives allow themselves
to be photographed in bathing suits . . . these birth-control pills handed out
by the state to anyone . . . those hooligans who salute you with clenched
fists. . . ."

She noticed, before lunch, that I looked longingly at a photograph of      68
my father on her bedside table. And after taking a brief nap to rest for the
afternoon excursion we have planned, she comes out of her bedroom, swiftly
handing me an envelope. She gives it to me between one room and another,
with an air of contraband and one of those infinitely sad, wise looks of hers.
Our sorrows flutter, hover about each other like languorous moths. We look
at each other with that melancholy, ironic gaze that belongs to her, to him,
to me. We link arms and start on our walk. We stroll in the Botanical Gardens, and admire the play of sunlight on its elms and oaks. She wears a gown
of watered silk, a sweater reaching halfway to her knees, long pearls, her legs
are like matchsticks, her nails are painted the color of fading tea roses. She
helps me to feed the swans in the moated castle of Anne of Brittany, as she

did when I was a child. I take her photograph on the cathedral steps as she clutches her extraordinarily flowered hat in a gust of wind, saying, proudly, "We have the highest nave of any church after Beauvais."

At day's end we drive to visit distant maiden aunts of mine whom even 69 Colette refers to as "the guardians of the past." They have lived totally alone since the end of World War I—when both their parents died—in a magnificent Louis XIII castle they have dedicated their lives to preserving. Smell of damp wood, splendor of moldings not painted since the war of 1870, resplendent alleys in a park designed by LeNôtre.[8] One aunt is seventy, the other is eighty. Bent and elflike and totally eccentric, too poor to employ a servant, they live and cook, each one for herself, in different floors of the great house, keeping vastly different hours and savoring totally different styles of life. One cultivates the flower garden and sweeps the castle's thirty-six uninhabited rooms, the other spends her day doing the heavy outdoor work, maintaining LeNôtre's alleys with a John Deere garden tractor. They have not been to Nantes in three, four years. It is a twenty-minute ride away. Before an array of harps and harpsichords, the peeling dank walls of the grand salon—which they open only every few years for special guests—are hung with pictures of great dead Frenchmen. We are briefly left to ourselves while our cousins make tea.

"Ah, look, there's de Gaulle," Aunt Colette jubilates as she advances 70 slowly into the salon, unfolding her lorgnette.

"No, Aunt Colette, it's Pétain,"[9] I correct her. 71

"*Merde alors,*" she exclaims, "I must admit that I haven't been in this 72 room for years and that I've never mentioned de Gaulle's name to them, they might think I'm a Communist."

After tea we stroll out into the park and walk in the alleys designed by 73 LeNôtre. "Look, what an exquisite oak, of the species *Quercus virginiana,*" Aunt Colette murmurs, "and what a noble elm, of the *Ulmus procera* species." Our seventy-year-old relative rides past us on her electric carriage, dressed in boots and ancient riding jodhpurs, a khaki army hat sat cockily on her head. "What dedication, what sacrifice," Aunt Colette says. "This house is their child, their martyrdom, their immortality. You see, perhaps that's why we're such insomniacs in the family. We're romantic enough to dedicate our *lives* to any cause we believe in, however small or great."

"Do you believe in grace?" my cousin Catherine asked me as we drove 74 through the flat, flat countryside outside Nantes in the direction of the family chapel where my father was buried. It was her way of being mundane, I suppose, of diverting me from the trouble that might lie ahead. She was a

8. (1613–1700), a famous designer of gardens and parks.

9. (1856–1951), World War I hero who was leader of the French puppet government during the Nazi occupation of World War II; at war's end he was condemned to death for treason, but his sentence was commuted by de Gaulle to life imprisonment. De Gaulle (1890–1970) led the French Resistance against the Nazis and was president of France at the time of the story. *Merde alors:* Well, shit!

singular woman, this husky, serious cousin who had undertaken to accompany me on my first visit to my father's grave: the only spinster of her generation in the family, tall, powerful, with short gray hair brushed back in mannish fashion and steel-rimmed glasses framing the family's melancholy, straightforward eyes. She was the cousin who had met me at the airport, and I had immediately sensed that as the spinster of the family she assigned herself the more disagreeable and awesome family tasks: helping to cook and keep house for her aging mother, my Aunt Charlotte, meeting strangers at airports, accompanying them on delicate missions such as this one. As if it were her way of punishing herself, within this family hell-bent on procreation, for failing to reproduce God's image. She was a government social worker, with a fairly high-placed job in the federal system which entailed attending a monthly meeting in Paris. And she was utterly consumed by her duty toward others. She lived in a phoneless two-room flat in Nantes. Anyone attempting to find her there in the evening would learn that instead of going home to put her feet up and do her laundry, as she constantly announced she was about to do, she had gone to check on some particularly bereaved family in the suburbs, or rushed to Saint-Seran to make sure that her mother's dinner was properly taken care of. Her manner had that balance that characterizes the finest members of her profession—those equipped with enough diplomacy and toughness to deal adequately with drunks, drug addicts, the orphaned, the handicapped. And she had asked me, in that diverting tone appropriate for the day's excursion, whether I believed in grace.

"I'm not sure that we would see eye to eye on that." I was trying to avoid the severe cultural shock that some of my answers evoked among my relatives. "I mean I've quite lost my faith in Christ as the exclusive vehicle of salvation. I think grace can be attained through the visions of many other great religions, and also outside of them." How flat the countryside was on the way to the chapel.

My answer seemed startling and novel to her, but not totally shocking. "Ah, how interesting, Stéphanie," she exclaimed. "You do *not* believe in Christ as the hinge, the joint that relates God to man—you think one can reach grace through Buddha, or the Hindu deities, or some curious Moslem sect?"

"And why not *without* them, since they all stress that He is in us already? I think there are many persons untaught in any religion who have grace because they are able to live totally for the other."

"Total sacrifice for the other, certainly, as you find in all our saints," she agreed. "But how would you recognize a state of grace among the unbaptized?"

"Well, their sainthood might remain quite obscure, totally unrecognized. I can't think of any surer sign than their willingness to risk going into death for others. And I'm not sure that such grace can be reached without the most scrupulous self-knowledge, and it is this knowledge, this total givingness, that is of the essence, not the contact with any religious system."

She was frowning. 80

"Look at all the lies we invent to protect our self-esteem and self-respect," 81
I continued. "I talk about this a lot with a great Jesuit friend of mine. He's
always stressing our unwillingness to face the reality of death, our arrogance
in thinking that we are Godlike and immortal."

"What do you mean, *thinking* that we are immortal? We *are* all immortal! 82
I am immortal! You are immortal! That is precisely how we differ from
animals! What does our catechism say? 'Because I have an immortal soul'!"
("Really," her eyes were saying to me, "you Americans go too far, even your
priests!")

"Well, perhaps our beliefs are more similar than you think, and we just 83
phrase them differently. I'd say that we differ from animals by our awareness
of death, and that this awareness of death might be the sign of our potential
for some form of immortality, a manifestation of some kind of immortal world
soul."

Stopping at a red light, still frowning, she offered me a package of lico- 84
rice and mint candy drops which she kept in a pouch in her car—along with
comic books and a manual for self-defense—for the adolescents she had to
transport back and forth to the rehabilitation home.

"To get back to grace," I continued, trying to soothe her back into the 85
conversation, "I am trying to document a story about a humble nineteenth-
century servant girl who rescued a child and then died herself as a result.
She was so devoid of illusions, so completely willing to cross into death for
the sake of another human being, that she was a perfect example of a state of
true grace. Do you get to see any Ingmar Bergman films in Nantes?"

"Oh, we get very few foreign films," she said. "As a matter of fact we 86
get very few ideas of any kind from the outside. While you in America, on
the contrary, must be veritably swamped, inundated, by fresh and novel
ideas. How curious that must feel!" She ran her large hand through the stubby
hair with a gesture that communicated impatience, some envy. "Doesn't this
profusion of new ideas, this perennial invasion, sometimes make you feel . . .
out of balance? To be perpetually bombarded by such a stream of novelty?"

"Yes. It's a country where it's sometimes hard to keep track of reality. 87
Everything flows by us so very swiftly—fads, allegiances. Your brother Daniel loves to attack me for our lack of any sense of history."

"Do you know, Stéphanie, that in the ten years I have had to make 88
monthly trips to Paris I have spent the night there only once?" She said this
with a certain pride. "Even though it's only three hours by train, I did it only
once, when my sister Louise offered me a ticket for a performance of the
*Saint Matthew Passion* in Notre-Dame. But I felt so guilty for having offered
myself this luxury that I took the six A.M train back to Nantes, and then I
worked for twenty-four hours around the clock to get rid of my unease."

I stared at her with the same intense curiosity with which my French 89
cousins often stared at me. "You see, darling," Aunt Colette had said, "we
are all so nutty, so excessive. . . ."

"Go on, talk some more," Catherine said, "you're such a breath of fresh 90
air. Tell me how you really feel about this place, why you finally came back
when you did."

We would be arriving at the chapel soon. The ancient fear gripped me. 91
I sensed that I could talk freely to her.

"Well, I'll tell you, I've been terrified of this visit to Papa's grave. It's as 92
if . . . well, as if he could drag me down with him, as if he had the power to
force me to join him in death. And so I was too much of a coward and a
louse, too small and ungenerous to honor his memory. It's as if—to get back
to what we were saying a minute ago—as if I dared to think I could never be
touched by death, and refused to acknowledge any aspect of it. If it weren't
for the advice of my Jesuit friend, Father Gregory, I'd never have dared come
back. I was equally fearful of some ill will on the part of the family here,
fearful that they might bear me a grudge for never coming back. And every
year it grew worse, every year I feared it more. That part of it was silly,
you've been so marvelous to me."

She gave me a proud, forthright grin. "Well, perhaps we're more under- 93
standing than you thought we'd be. Not necessarily about Buddhism or foreign films, but about things like pain and death and a child's emotions toward
them. Do you know, I understand your fears totally. Someone once wrote—
who could it have been, Mauriac perhaps?—that upon the death of a parent,
a child is like a reed bent by a heavy storm. He may straighten up in time,
or he may not. He may have to live perpetually in a stooped position, in a
condition of enfeeblement. Also, what happened in your particular instance
is quite clear—a child who is not properly acquainted with the facts of a
parent's death may suffer from powerful delusions, complex feelings of guilt.
One, you feel guilty that you did not join him in death. Two, you feel guilty
that in some vague sense you are responsible for his death. Three, because
you were not given the chance of going through the proper rituals of mourning—these things exist for the sanity of the survivor, you know—in some
sense you may still refuse to believe that he is dead."

Her conciseness stunned me. Cartesian clarity, one, two, three, like a 94
prize-winning French high-school essay. And so much briefer, clearer, cheaper
than the shrink. I could not speak.

"What about life after death?" she asked in the same conversational 95
mundane tone with which she had ventured into grace. "Or the resurrection
of the body, things like that? In a system of thought as progressive as yours,
what would you have to say?"

"Oh, I don't have any great problems with it. It's the *transfigured* body, 96
after all. I've always been absolutely obsessed with that concept. Remember
how in catechism we used to ask, 'What is the transfigured body?' and they'd
answer, 'Ah, my child, that is a mystery.' I don't admire the notion because
the Church teaches it but because it's such a brilliant historical solution; after
all those centuries of pre-Christian quibbling about body versus soul, they
had the genius to come along and say, 'You can take your body too.' Any-

way, there might well be a residuum of self that is not reducible to material quantities, the nature of which science may never be able to decipher. And if so, why not a continuity, or even a resurrection, of this selfhood?"

"Well, speaking of *that*, here we are," she said, putting on her wide, comforting social worker's smile. "Here's the town where they're all buried." 97

It had come earlier than I had thought, a bare half hour from Nantes and Saint-Seran. I felt a kind of numbness. That blunt wisdom of Catherine's had made everything much easier than I had expected. 98

"Look," I said, "I might break down, okay? I just don't know yet. I hope you'll understand." 99

She made a casual gesture of dismissal, as if to say, "If you only knew the real breakdowns I see everyday." 100

My great-great-granduncle General Louis-Christophe-Léon Juchault de Lamoricière,[1] who helped complete France's conquest of Algeria and briefly served as its governor, is so revered in his native Vendée that no one is quite sure which part of him is buried where. His heart—that much is certain—is preserved within a gigantic black marble cenotaph in the north nave of the Nantes cathedral. It is said that at the insistence of the very first colonialists another parcel of his mortal body was buried in Algeria. One of my aunts suggests that still another slice of the General reposes in a Paris church. But whatever remains of him after these cannibalistic acts of veneration is buried in his native village of Saint-Philbert-de-Grand-Lieu, in a family chapel built by the General's sisters. It was here that my father came to rest some seventeen years ago. 101

As one drives into Saint-Philbert, the General's connection with that town is announced by a twelve-foot-high bronze statue that shows him striding into battle, his bearded intense face—not unlike Lenin's—surmounted by a towering kepi, his long sword held high to the sky as if giving the signal of attack. Below him a Zouave soldier in native robes bows in deference and blows his war trumpet. At the General's feet sits Marianne, symbol of French glory and justice, naked to the waist, her large and perfect breasts surmounting the noble flow of classical draperies below. And to the left of Marianne an Arab woman kneels in tribute, offering her a large basket of native fruit and flowers—the fruits of the Algerian colonies for France. The family's burial chapel stands two blocks from this martial statue, in a village cemetery dotted with marble or stone crosses of varying degrees of grandeur, and with the purple and crimson ceramic flowers that adorn many French tombs. It was this site, this building, which I had been trying to avoid for over twenty years. 102

What a goddam bitch reality is, I thought as I walked in, will she always remain as elusive and stingy with her symbols? Entering the chapel that day with Catherine, I experienced the same anger that had swept over me two decades ago, when I had come here before my father's body had been brought 103

1. (1806–1865), a historical figure.

back. For I was looking forward to a physical sign of his death, I wanted a tomb, an indenture in the earth, a sarcophagus, a glimpse of his coffin even, something real, something tangible, something that would knock me over the head with the reality of his death. The chapel offered none of that. It was simply a sea of names engraved from top to bottom of each wall, gold letters on black marble slabs, and the dead were buried below or around it. I did not know which at first. The only change from my last visit was that my father's name had been added to the left wall, near the entrance, underneath the names of his parents. First came his father's name: *"Mort pour la France,[2] 1918."* And then my father's: *"Mort pour la France, 1940."*

"So here we are," Catherine said cheerfully. "Would you like to be alone?" 104

"No, no, no, no." And I wandered about the chapel with the casual air 105 of a museum visitor, whispering the musical names of ancestors commemorated on its walls: "Marie-Laure de Hauterive . . . Clotilde du Maistre . . . ah, yes, Anne-Marie de La Laurencie . . ." Would there never be an end to my cycle of anger, delusion, anger? He might not be here. He simply might not be anywhere to be found. He might have abandoned me even more totally than I had thought. What a cheat life is, always to be deceiving me that way. I would go, I must go to whatever place his body really lies in, to make absolutely sure, to see the coffin bearing his name. I wanted to break down in the presence of his corpse, to affirm the reality of my grief, to confirm my sorrow to him and to myself, and here there was nothing but names, a sea of names, there was no one to cry to, no one to talk to, and inside me there was an anger that verged on boredom, on void.

"So," I asked Catherine, "where are they?" 106

"Below, naturally. Actually, if I remember accurately, your father is 107 almost underneath and to the right of the sealing stone, just a few coffins away from the General. As for Papa—his oldest brother—he is to the left, and their mother is directly above them. Over toward the apse you have the Montmorencys," she continued, as if seating a dinner party, "the du Maistres, the Saint-Marceaus, the branches of the family that have become a little more distant. You're sure you don't want to be alone?"

"No, please stay. What does it look like downstairs? How are they bur- 108 ied?"

"It's not unlike the . . . you know, the cubicles in which you check your 109 bags at the railroad station," she said, pushing her spectacles onto her nose. "A long deep recess in the wall into which the coffin is placed lengthwise, with a plaque outside."

"How does one get down there?" 110

"Right through here." She gave a familiar pat to a large stone in the 111 floor, just to the right of the entrance. It had a large, rusting metal handle.

"Can't we go downstairs?" My voice sounded faint and piping, like that 112 of a child fighting back its tears.

"Certainly not, my poor girl, that's a very complex proposition," she 113

2. Died for France.

exclaimed, lifting an arm up toward the sky to indicate a very annoying chapter of family history. "We are never supposed to go down there except in the company of a witness—a judge, a clerk of the court, an official of that order. It's a very difficult business, breaking all that cement around the stone, unsealing it, then lifting it. I know all about it, I'm the only old maid in the family, and I get all the wretched jobs. Ten years ago the vault became totally filled and we realized that to be practical we'd have to do some clearing out, some pruning and weeding if you will. And wouldn't you know it, I was the one who had to get the stone unsealed and go down into the burial vault with a witness." She gave a little shudder.

"*Merde alors, tu sais, c'était très impressionant.*[3] It was dark in there, very dark, and . . . Listen, are you sure you don't want to be alone for a moment? All right. It was dark, it was not a pleasant task. We had held a family council the night before and decided exactly whom to get rid of. We decided not to stick to chronology, that would have been a bit didactic. We simply got rid of those strains of the family we like the least—the Cassons, the Du Bourgs, all distant cousins, and there were a few bad marriages in those branches of the family anyhow. We did some selecting, in other words, and put them into the common grave still farther underneath. What else can you do, when you get so crowded? The whole planet is getting to be that way. Can you imagine what it will be like at resurrection time?" she added gaily. "Not an inch of elbow room! What a mess!"

She was twisting and turning her car keys now, eager to go, as if she really had seen quite enough of the place. "I think we're all right down there for another twenty years or so. But you just wait and see," she added, throwing the car keys defiantly into the air. "If ever it gets filled up again, I'm the one who'll end up having to go down there again!"

And with that we drove back to Saint-Seran for tea. On the drive back my husky Charon had the brisk and tender manner of those nurses assigned the midnight shift to deal with the more complex textures of loneliness and pain. "You're quite all right, aren't you?" she would say, giving a reassuring, sideways look. "Would you like a licorice, a comic book? Ah, I forget, you're too old for that, in my mind you're always my little cousin. An aspirin? I always keep them for the drunks I have to transport to the tribunal. I haven't told you, have I, that Nantes has the highest percentage of alcoholics in any city in Europe. Worse than Dublin, can you imagine? Actually we're so alike, we and the Irish, all wild Celts. So. Tell me more about America. Did you do your studies in English or in American? What do you do for your insomnia? I find Teilhard good at those moments. I hear you do not eat lunch in America. How is that possible? What do you do all that time, from twelve to two? Perhaps it's why you get so much accomplished over there, you're less sleepy in the afternoon. Does France seem like a very small country in comparison?"

114

115

116

---

3. Shit, you know, it was very impressive.

And she said that her oldest sister, Louise, who was waiting for me at 117
Saint-Seran, swore she remembered and loved me like a sister, and had driven
from Paris a day ahead of schedule to catch me before I flew back to New
York.

Alone, alone, I thought, as Catherine's chatter lulled me like a midnight 118
hypodermic. I must go back there tomorrow alone.

Louise was waiting for me at the front door, an enormous woman with 119
the body of the *Venus of Lespugue*.[4] Having rushed toward me as I got out of
her sister's car, she cupped my face in her hands and stared at me intently,
exhaling strong odors of garlic sausage.

"After twenty years I would have recognized you from a hundred yards 120
away," she cried, "from two hundred yards away, do you hear, if I had so
much as passed you on a street in Paris!"

And she leaned back to study me more attentively, smiling beatifically 121
at her little cousin. She had a round and shiny face, abundant brown hair
pulled back in a messy bun, yellowed teeth that went at crazy angles to each
other, an expression of great kindness. Her enormous breasts were barely
covered by a flimsy printed challis dress. "Well what's taken you so long?
What's the idea? Oh, if you knew what a shining memory we all have of your
father! He was our hero, you know that. What an extraordinary man! What
brilliance! What charm! The best-looking man of his generation, on top of
everything else! What an impression he made on us! How he stamped our
memory! How indelibly, in-del-ib-ly he marked us all! How he adored you!
And how you adored him! Do you remember him well?"

"Very," I said faintly. 122

"And, of course, you're one of us down to the tip of your little fingers! 123
Well, welcome, welcome!" And she hugged me to her large chest, rocking
me back and forth like a small baby. Behind her stood a bevy of her children,
a new batch of nephews and nieces for me to meet—five sons and daughters
between the ages of nineteen and twenty-four who had come to spend the
week at Saint-Seran.

"Yes, how he adored you, how you adored him," she repeated. "What 124
a pretty couple you made, always hugging and kissing, never separated, he
couldn't stand to have you out of his sight for five minutes, and you couldn't
stand to ever let go of his hand. No one else really mattered for you when
you were little, isn't that right? No, I know, no one, no one! How you must
miss him!"

She squeezed me again to her bountiful chest and began to whimper, 125
quite genuinely. The sweet bitch, I thought, when will she stop? "Poor little
Stéphanie," she moaned, "left alone at such an early age, and by such an
extraordinary man, by such an extraordinary parent. How different, how

---

4. Paleolithic statuette (about 20000–18000 B.C.) of a female figure with exaggerated breasts, buttocks, and
thighs.

different things would have been if he had not died—what a different destiny you would have had! Even our own destinies might have been changed, too. Do you remember when he took us all to Nantes to see *Three Little Pigs?*"

"No, I don't, quite." 126

"You don't remember *Three Little Pigs?*" she wailed. "But how could you forget? I was fifteen, Catherine was twelve, you and Daniel were eight. Then do you remember that time he took us all to the circus in Nantes?" 127

"No, not quite." 128

"But how can you not remember? There was this lovely clown you enjoyed so, but when he came toward us and your father said, 'Don't you want to shake hands with the clown?' you burst into tears and said, 'No, I can't, we haven't been introduced.'" 129

She laughed uproariously, shaking my body back and forth. 130

"You were always such a formal child, always so strictly brought up by that governess. Almost too strictly, I'd say. A very complex child, that's for sure, very precise, very sensitive. I remember you used to brush your hair one hundred times in the morning and one hundred times at night even when you were eight years old. You were always our little princess, even though you didn't come back all this time, you've remained our little princess in America. Oh, my God I haven't even shown you the photographs of my daughters' weddings! Such marvelous weddings! How could you have stayed away!" 131

An album was already set upon the table next to us, carefully prepared for my perusal. 132

"Ah, here's the wedding of my oldest daughter, Poupette. Yes, how could you have stayed away from such a fine event? We sent you all our wedding announcements, we all did, for years, and you never responded to them. She married a very good name. Not that much money, but a very old name, that's still what counts, after all. And an excellent piece of land in Picardy. The wedding at a private chapel of the bridegroom's parents' castle. Not many of us have that anymore, a private chapel! Four priests officiating. Dominicans. Can you imagine! *Four* Dominicans! Then an orchestra from Amiens played Strauss waltzes. Six attendants in Alençon lace, carrying bouquets of roses and stephanotis. How could you not have come back to such a splendid wedding?" 133

"Oh, my little treasure. Hello, my sweetie, sweetie, sweetheart." Louise's daughter is already wheeling a baby carriage at the end of a stroll in the park. Aunt Charlotte, my cousin Daniel, Aunt Colette very slowly walk alongside her, making pretty noises at the baby. More celebration of the propagation of protoplasm. Another offspring to revere Saint-Seran, to come back each summer to admire its shuttered windows, its mysterious and sleeping air. 134

"Oh the beautiful little doll, the beautiful little soldier," Aunt Colette is cooing into the carriage. "Don't you love babies when they're tiny tiny, when they can almost fit into the palm of your hand? Look at those teeny teeny 135 hands, those teeny teeny feet. Can you imagine, even de Gaulle once had feet as teeny as those."

The family gathers about the beautiful chipped porcelain. Tea is brought out. Debate rages about the chocolate cake. The recipe has not left the family for two hundred years.    136

"You do *not* add the egg yolks to it, you only put in the whites," storms Aunt Charlotte. "I know that our cousins on the Lamoricière side add the yolks, but that's a deformation of principle. Yolks make it too heavy, I assure you."    137

"Maman, I agree about the yolks," Louise rebuts, "but I don't agree about the flour. Some of our cousins put in five tablespoons of flour and you don't put any in, but I compromise and put in three tablespoons for measure. It needs the binder."    138

"My sweet sweet dolly," Aunt Colette continues to purr at the baby, as she may have purred at me in my carriage, "my rabbit, my little treasure . . ."    139

One last family picture, outside the pale dwelling bathed in the shimmering Vendée light. *Click:* here they are, poised for my own slim slice of eternity.    140

Aunt Colette in her watery silks, her tufted face pointed in the direction of the forest, says in her twinkling voice, "We had a glorious stroll this afternoon, the afternoon sunlight is so beautiful today on the stands of elms at the northwest corner of the park."    141

"Mozambique," Aunt Charlotte says, pouring tea out of the gilt and crested Empire tea pot, her album of stamps on her lap. "Listen, dear child, you're going back to America tomorrow, surely you can find me one from Mozambique. And listen, next time you return, there's more than one bed for you, we expect you back next summer."    142

"So you're going to go back and give more hell to your President on some other silly puritanical principle," Daniel roars across the tea table. "Did anyone raise an eyebrow when Napoleon pillaged Egypt? A little more high-handed authority, that's what the modern world needs."    143

Catherine is looking anxiously at her watch, straightening her spectacles, saying, "I really must get back to Nantes by five, there's a very disturbed child in an alcoholic family. . . ."    144

I almost do not get there—back to the chapel alone. I feel an ambivalence of desire and terror toward that last visit which is more confusing than any emotion I have ever known. Yet I manage to go. I am booked on a one-o'clock plane from Nantes to Paris which connects with a three-o'clock flight back to New York. I hire a car for the morning and set off very early, my bags in the trunk, for Saint-Philbert. I am possessed by one principal fear: that I shall again feel emptiness, the absence of him, the absence of pain, the same numb hollowness I felt before, the void and boredom that so artfully mask rage. I find my way without difficulty. Turn right at the post office,    145 turn left at the bakery, turn right again at the General two blocks away from the Saint-Philbert cemetery. On the side wall of the bakery is an enormous sign: *"Gordon's Gin."* The General looks fiercer than ever in this morning's sunny light, his sword rising threateningly above the bands of petunias, for-get-me-nots, geraniums, that grow in impeccable circles about his feet.

One more block and I am at the graveyard. I park the car, walk out and take a picture of the cemetery. The ceramic flowers blaze crimson and purple about the gray monument. An albinic light envelops it all. Once inside the chapel I walk up the tiny nave, reach into my pocket for a notebook, and feel driven to take notes on my ancestors' names. So and so and so and so and so and so, Amélie de Pommery, Isabelle de La Varende, such pretty names, names of champagne and musketeers. The notebook is a hedge, a chastity belt, a haven of safety. Stephanie's the reporter, she always takes notes on whatever comes within her range of sight, she's seldom moved by the subject matter at hand. Still, they all had insomnia, that's very touching. Grand-father reading his Taine, Uncle Jean his Michelet, Colette her de Gaulle, my father spending seven years of his white nights authoring a tract on the rad-ical reform of the European economy. He lost the only copy in the back of someone's car. Whence this anxiety, dear history nuts, whence this agita-tion? Here you sleep at last, new friends, sweet insomniacs, here you sleep at last after centuries of turning in your beds. . . .

A woman in dun-colored dress walks into the chapel, quietly comes up the nave, crosses herself and starts to trim the gladioli and dahlias at the altar with slow deliberate strokes of her pruning shears. She bows again, returns to a back pew and sits down. I am scribbling, scribbling. The gold letters announce that one of our great-granduncles died in 1838 while directing the French Navy's assault on Vera Cruz, Mexico; that the General, after leaving his post in Algeria, was exiled from France for opposing Napoleon III's Ital-ian campaign, and chose to serve on the other side—as head of the Papal troops. Militarists, imperialists, colonialists, just the men I would take part in protest marches against, and yet I am beginning to understand them, to be proud of them. What a good tribe I was born into, defiant, eccentric, pigheaded. Created for violence and romance, for heroism and early death. Nantes—the highest percentage of royalists of any city in France, the highest percentage of alcoholics of any city in Europe, perhaps the highest percent-age of insomniacs. The Brittany liberation movement is trying to make it the capital of a new independent state. . . . I sense by the silence behind me that the woman with the pruning shears is praying, that she must be a nun. I hear her footsteps retreating, I sense by some slight rustling of her clothes that she is making the sign of the cross as she leaves the chapel.

I put my notebook back into my pocket. I don't quite know what to do next. Now that I am alone again I turn around and walk down the nave toward the back pew. The nuns must come to tend the flowers every day, there is a heavy but clean scent of roses on the air. Outside the chapel the light is fresh, inviting, bland. Shall I leave now, exit into the sunlight before it happens? But through some instinct made possible by the rituals of child-hood, I kneel down on the sealing stone which stands between me and the dead, the stone I had so desired to break open the day before, the stone that separates his body from mine. I kneel on the stone, scratching shyly at the cement that seals me off from below. It resembles all the other bands of cement that intersect the gray flagstones of the chapel floor, but it is slightly darker, different in texture. There is some difference, some difference that makes me keep on scratching, scratching, to make sure that it is indeed as immutable as Catherine said, to make sure that I cannot break through it. And then suddenly my liberation comes. I am free now, kneeling on the stone, suddenly free and shaking, my head resting against the rusty metal handle that could be lifted for our reunion. I weep, I shake, I pound at the floor with my head, I kick it, I beat it with my hands. I feel no unease or shame at my behavior, I know that society is sick for forbidding us such liberations any more, for obstructing the channels of our grief, for not letting us properly mourn the dead. I know that I am inconquerably sane and that society is mad. I lie prone on the floor for a half hour, crying abundantly, my hands bruised by my knocking, my head aching from hitting it against the stone, my jeans drenched as if I had sailed a boat into a storm. Yet I do not feel any more rage. Nor do I feel void, or fear. I am ready to die, but not now, not in a violent or untimely way, I simply have no more fear of dying, I want to die the way I want to live, I have conquered some fear of both. I am crying my heart out, free at last. He is there, he is there, he is there. I finally know that he is there, down below. But that is not the point. He is both there and not there. Above all else he is now allowed to live in my memory, totally restored and whole now, as if resurrected, the reality of his death accepted, faced. After some time I begin to raise myself up to my knees. I have no more need to hammer at the floor, I know he is there, may he sleep at last. May he rest in peace. May he sleep at last.

As I start to get up I see that a plaque above my head, a few feet away, **149** commemorates one Julie de Lamoricière, wife of that martial conqueror whose remains were so voraciously preserved by his admirers. It says:

> Julie-Amélie d'Abeslard de Lamoricière
> Died in Paris the 26th of April 1885
> Her body reposes here
> Next to that of her husband and her children
> Awaiting the resurrection.

Think of that.　　**152**

# STUDY QUESTIONS

1. Describe Aunt Charlotte. How much do we know about the way she looks? To what extent is she characterized by her attitudes? by the questions she asks? by the opinions she has about family? by her appearance? To what extent does her knowledge of America condition our response to her? How important to the story is she as a CHARACTER? What function does she perform for the narrator? for the story? How does the NARRATOR feel about her? How can you tell?

2. Describe the range of attitudes represented in the story about Johnson and the antiwar demonstrations. To what extent are the different people characterized by how they respond to that situation? What do their opinions on that subject reveal about their politics? their ideas about law? their ideas about tradition? their sense of the past? their cultural values?

3. How is the narrator characterized? How important to the story is the place where the narrator is from? Are there any points where you doubt the narrator's veracity? Do you assume right away that the narrator is a female because the author is female? The story first appeared in *The New Yorker*, where authorship is revealed at the end of the story, often buried in labyrinthine pages of advertisements and continued text; if you had read it there (without authorship specified at the beginning), do you think you would have begun by assuming the narrator to be male? Why or why not? What "facts" in the story bear on the issue of the narrator's gender? How early in the story can you actually be sure of the narrator's gender?

4. Describe the castle of Saint-Seran. How important is the castle to the family? How important is the SETTING to the THEME of the story? In what way is the weather important?

5. Material things play an important role at a number of points in the story. Which objects are especially important for characterization? for establishing the character of the family more generally?

6. What does the narrator miss most in Saint-Seran? What factors seem most important to the narrator's sense of home?

7. The narrator early on speaks of all the family relatives as "tribesmen." Why is that term significant? How extensive are the implications of the idea of the "tribe" articulated here? How many different "tribes" are represented in the story?

8. Often a particular word seems very carefully chosen for its specific impact. Daniel, for example, responding to a witty remark by his daughter, is said to have "guffawed" (paragraph 37). Explain the meaning of the term. Explain the connotations. To what extent is Daniel characterized by that one word?

9. In paragraph 40, a child is described as "the Benjamin of the lot." What does the ALLUSION mean? What does it contribute to the characterization? to the sense of "tribe" in the theme of the story? (You can look up Benjamin in a dictionary of the Bible or a concordance.) What does the reference, in the same paragraph, to a Perrault fairy tale contribute to the richness of the story? Why do you think the

story contains so many references to other well-known pieces of writing from previous centuries? What do such references have to do with the character of the family? with the themes of the story? What other words or phrases seem to you especially carefully chosen?

10. At several points in the story, the immediate moment is recorded by a photograph. What functions does the photograph-taking perform for the family? for the narrator? for the sense of pastness in the story? for the story's theme?

11. How much of the difference between parts of the family is attributed, in the story, to "old" world/"new" world differences? What distinctions are made between different countries in the old world?

12. How do you interpret the dream in paragraph 47? What does it have to do with the themes of the story?

13. How important to the story are the conversations about religious belief? How do they relate to the character of Aunt Charlotte? to our understanding of the narrator? to the question of tradition and family history? to the themes of the story?

14. Much of the story is about searches for knowledge—on the part of various characters and on the part of the narrator. What kind of knowledge does the narrator seek? In what sense does the narrator's search become identical to the reader's search for interpretation and certainty? How much of the search for knowledge involves the past? Compare the desire to know the past here with the same desire in Agha's poem "Postcard from Kashmir" (chapter 1).

# POINT OF VIEW

No two people see things exactly alike, and in a piece of writing everything depends on whose point of view we are given. Ordinarily, a story is not just a story; it is *someone's* story. That is, it is told by someone in particular so that rather than a story that is "objective," it is some particular person's *version* of a story. Someone else might see events differently, someone else might emphasize different things, someone else might even draw different conclusions, making the same events add up to a wholly different story. Essays, too, are usually someone's in particular; often an author feels free to be quite visible and personal in an essay in a way that he or she would not be when the distancing of fiction is used. Even in poems, which sometimes do not tell a story or seem to involve the interaction of different people, there is usually a distinctive voice or point of view that we as readers need to identify. Words never exist in a pure vacuum, without a context. They always belong to some VOICE that speaks them to us as readers. The kind of voice portrayed therefore influences what the words seem to say, how we interpret them, from what angle of vision their "facts" or feelings come. And the better we become at identifying that voice and its characteristic features, the better we become at interpretation.

In plays, the action takes place before our eyes, and we "know" what "really" happens: we see for ourselves. But even in a play, different perspectives on the action quickly become important. Some action takes place offstage, and we are told about it by a CHARACTER whose reliability we have to evaluate. The words we hear are the words of the author, but they are spoken by actors who have chosen to interpret (perhaps with the aid of a director) the words, their roles, the whole play. And even the action we actually see involves our INTERPRETATION, built on the interpretations of director and actors as well as the playwright, of the words and gestures of the characters. By the *way* characters (or actors) express themselves, they influence what we see and what conclusions we draw about actions and events.

As soon as characters begin to speak, interpretations of actions, attitudes, and feelings assert themselves. The attributes of characters affect how we respond to them. The acting is important. So are the voice, the gestures, the words spoken, the lighting, the set. All these things help determine how we interpret and what we conclude about what is going on and why. As observers ourselves, we are influenced not just by what we see for ourselves and what we hear from others, but how we see and how we "read" what we are told. Do we believe Oka's account of his relationship with his wife in *And the Soul Shall Dance?* Often, as here, what we come to know about the marriage and the specifics of the marriage involve putting together what we see with what characters say or report. Do we accept the social and cultural opinions of Officer Schrank in *West Side Story?* Almost never, even in a play or a film, are we allowed to "see" purely. Words, gestures, people intervene to color what we see, to give us a fuller, more resonant, and sometimes contradictory account to put against the testimony of our own eyes and ears. We have to interpret, we have to sort.

Stories, though, are much more specifically dependent on who tells us what, for we have no eyes of our own. There, words are the only means we have of visualizing, and what we visualize depends completely on what someone tells us to see. The reliability of the NARRATOR, therefore, is all-important, and so is the angle he or she has on the central action. Often, in stories, a character tells a story about himself or herself. We are probably least reliable when we speak of ourselves, for there is where our greatest biases exist. We are far less likely to tell something damaging about ourselves than we are to divulge negative information about someone else. People who talk about themselves, in stories as in life, are thus always somewhat suspect. It may turn out, of course, that they are telling the truth—even the basest of people may be capable of being truthful—but we have to be on our guard. We cannot, at first, be sure whether they speak the truth or judge matters properly. In Jamaica Kincaid's "Girl," for example, we hear a mother's voice, not necessarily as it was but just as an adolescent girl would hear it, and we have to judge not only the truth of what the voice itself expresses but what the girl hearing the voice is like. How accurate a description of her does it provide? She has to judge, and so do we.

Guardedness is, in fact, a good rule of thumb for accepting the validity of anything we are told in a piece of writing. It may, of course, turn out to be absolutely true (sometimes everything we are told in a story has finally to be taken exactly at face value), but it is usually a good idea to start out with doubt, to ask basic questions about the grounds for believing. The reliability, then, of the person speaking can be a major issue for interpretation in a story, in the dialogue of a play, in an essay, or even in a poem. For poems are not always "spoken" directly by the poet; often a kind of "character" is created in a poem to speak the words; that is, the voice in the poem is sometimes that of a fictional person the poet creates, not necessarily the voice of the poet.

Often, of course, the voice in the poem is not very distinct from the voice of the poet her- or himself, and often the SPEAKER of the poem (that is, the person who speaks the poem's words) cannot be distinguished, except technically, from the voice of the poet. In Paula Gunn Allen's "Powwow 79, Durango," for example, or Ray A. Young Bear's "in the first place of my life," there is little reason to think that the speaker is not someone very like the poet, for the events described there might well have happened exactly that way to Allen and Young Bear. But it is still a good idea to get in the habit of thinking of the words in a poem as being spoken by a "speaker" rather than by the "poet," for often there is a distinction. Besides, even a very personal poem such as Ana Castillo's "Our Tongue Was Nahuatl" sometimes becomes something larger than the representation of a single personal voice. "Our Tongue Was Nahuatl" is not only the personal statement of a poet but a kind of litany that represents the voice of a whole people, and the speaker may just as easily be said to be the voice of a people as that of Ana Castillo.

Sometimes, especially in stories, writers adopt an independent or "objective" stance so that the authority of the facts will not be questioned. In such cases, they may "follow" a particular character very closely, in effect virtually seeing things through the eyes of that character, but avoiding the issue of "reliability" and "subjective judgment" by not telling the story in that character's voice. Thus, in Norma Rosen's "A Thousand Tears" (chapter 9), the "facts" of the story are never in doubt; we do not have to decide whether Sandra Loeb is telling the truth because she is not telling the story. In Francine du Plessix Gray's "Tribe," however, the narrator has to be judged continually; it is "her" story—both about her and hers to tell—and a key part of our response to the story involves our sorting out of the facts and opinions the narrator offers us. There are, of course, advantages in either approach; sometimes it is part of an author's strategy to have readers raise questions about reliability; sometimes it is not. It depends on the aims of the story. When a story is told directly by a character, it is said to be a *first-person* story. When a distant or "objective" view is used but the action of the story follows a single character throughout, the story is said to be *focused* on that character, or that character is said to be the FOCUS of the story. *Focus* is the viewing aspect of the story; *voice* is the verbal aspect.

Knowing who it is who speaks to us in a work of literature—recognizing the voice for what it is or what it presents itself to be—is important to understanding and interpretation. Asking basic questions about the voice we hear, who the person seems to be, what we know about him or her, the accents and nuances of the voice speaking to us, is a valuable skill to learn. Often it helps us in reading, as such a skill does also in life, to sort and decide—to know how to "read" books as well as people.

# WRITING
# ABOUT THE READING

## PERSONAL ESSAYS AND NARRATIVES

1. What characteristic habit or feature of your own personality seems to you to have come most directly from your ethnic or national origins? Write a brief description of yourself as a member of a specific ethnic or national group. Try to account for the ways you differ from others in the group, and indicate the most powerful sources of influence from the group. Did particular members of the group who were not members of your family provide models for your behavior and values? Did the largest influence of the group on you come through your family upbringing? through religion? through language? through stories that were told in the group? through games and rituals?

2. Write a short essay of no more than 500 words describing the person you most admire who comes from your own ethnic or national background. Be sure to indicate what characteristics of that person you admire most. Give examples of things he or she has accomplished that lead to your high evaluation. What values does the person embody? In what ways are those values related to the "tribe" he or she comes from?

3. Describe the moment in your life when you first remember meeting someone whose background was very different from yours. What differences did you notice most vividly at the time? How were you made aware of the differences between the two of you? Write a brief paragraph describing, as precisely as you can remember them, your responses at the time. Did you experience the meeting as conflict? Did it seem threatening to your sense of identity? How does the episode now seem different to you than it did at the time? How much of the difference derives from difference in age and knowledge? How much just because time has gone by and you have had a chance to reflect on the experience and put your emotions into perspective? Write another paragraph in which you describe your present reflections on the episode.

4. Write a *story* about the episode you have described in #3 above.

5. Reread John Fante's "Odyssey of a Wop." What words heard in your early childhood had special meanings within your family or "tribe"? Recreate a scene from your early life in which friends or members of your family used words or described events that you did not understand. Present as much of the scene as you can in DIALOGUE.

# IMITATION AND PARODY

Using Jamaica Kincaid's "Girl" as a guide, write a monologue of advice as if spoken by your mother or father.

# ARGUMENTATIVE PAPER

With *West Side Story* in mind, write two arguments of equal length and conviction: only love can bring people of different ethnic backgrounds together; people of different backgrounds can never really be brought together.

# RESEARCH PAPERS

1. In the reference section of the library, look up (in a dictionary of slang or unconventional English) some derogatory word you have heard used about a national, ethnic, or religious group. Compare your own sense of the word, from your experience in hearing it, with the dictionary "definitions." Have you ever heard the word used affectionately or as a term of admiration by someone within that group? In what kind of situation? How could you tell the difference between the intentions?

2. With the help of a reference librarian, find three or four reliable books that provide basic factual information about the coming to America of your own national, or ethnic, or tribal group. Write a paper tracing the history of your "tribe" in America.

3. Interview someone from an older generation, preferably your great-grandmother or great-grandfather or someone you know from their generation. Ask them questions about things they remember from their childhood and early life, especially events that helped shape their personal identity or that involve their moving from one place to another. Take notes on the interview. Choose what you think is the most interesting story the person tells you, and write it in narrative form. Then rate yourself as an interviewer: How good were you at getting the person to tell stories? How did you do it? What would you do differently on another similar occasion? Write a brief "how to" guide for interviewing people about their life experiences, complete with a list of good questions to ask and ones to avoid.

# 5

# DANGER:
# FOREIGN TONGUE

Human misunderstandings take many forms, but they often arise from people not speaking the same language. Even with the best intentions, people who do not understand one another cannot communicate adequately. There are in the world enough difficulties and potential conflicts about real differences in needs and values without the added hazards of broken communication. Even when human beings understand one another perfectly, different attitudes, different needs and wants, and different interests provide grounds for plenty of disagreement and conflict. And when basic inability to communicate underlies a human situation, conflict is almost inevitable. Much of the distrust that exists between different cultures derives from a fundamental unease about different ways of considering things, different terminology about values, or languages that are totally incompatible.

Limitations of language lie at the heart of difficulties between nations, regions, families, or even individuals. Some words do not readily translate from one language to another, and expressions translated literally often mean something quite different from the intention in their original language. But most difficulties of language go beyond technical problems. Expertise is usually available to take care of difficulties that are genuinely built into different languages if there is the will to find and use it. But good will is not always available when people need to communicate across language lines, sometimes because there are misapprehensions or misperceptions to begin with, sometimes because the different languages represent cultural or political barriers that are even more difficult to get over.

Language difference often represents cultural difference, and suspicion, uncertainty, or even prejudice runs high when there are unknown ("foreign," "alien," or even just "different") ways to deal with. Sometimes people do not want to understand someone who speaks, or thinks, or acts differently from what they are used to, and the "foreign tongue" that person speaks comes to stand for a whole range of unacceptable values. Thus, a Spanish-speaking family may be reluctant to accept the friends of a son or daughter who speak English or Chinese, and parents from New York City may be resistant to a potential son- or daughter-in-law from a part of the country where a different dialect is spoken or where voices have a different accent: Southerners or Midwesterners or Californians or even New Englanders or upstate New Yorkers may seem "foreign" in their ways—just because they use different terms for familiar things, or express their feelings in a different way, or have different ways of pronouncing *r*'s or of giving rhythm to their sentences. People can be very difficult with one another when their expectations are upset or their familiar routines are interrupted. And when language difficulty combines with other ready areas of misunderstanding—between generations, between people of different religions, between people with different habits or customs—major conflicts often develop and major intolerances become evident.

The selections that follow illustrate a variety of problems—some minor, some humorous, some serious—that occur when language barriers intrude into human situations. In the "one world" of America, with its mix of cultures, customs, habits, and backgrounds, the mix of languages sometimes seems like the Tower of Babel realized in modern dress, but the challenges of linguistic difference sometimes bring out the best and most tolerant in human beings, too, as anyone who has been treated compassionately in a "foreign" nation can testify. Unfortunately, not all collisions of language result in compassionate encounters, but they do often illustrate poignantly the differences between cultural values that lie beneath language differences. Writers often find it a challenge to use language to make sense of conflicts that derive from language itself.

# Mark Singer

B orn in Tulsa, Oklahoma, Mark Singer is a graduate of Yale. He now lives in
New York City, where, since 1974, he has been a staff writer for *The New Yorker*.

The following selection, part of a 1987 "Talk of the Town" column in *The New Yorker*, describes an unusual combination of families, their languages, and their tastes.

## TYPICAL

At the Peking Duck House, on Mott Street, one recent Saturday evening, the Schwartzman family (Papa Fred, Mama Kyoko, sons Harry and Daniel) got together with the Xu family (Papa Jian-Guo, Mama Jun Cai, daughter Ran) for dinner (prawns in garlic sauce, spicy bean curd, Peking duck, mu-shu pork, sea bass, double-fried pork cutlets, pickled cabbage, and beef with snow peas and bamboo shoots) and conversation (Japanese, Chinese, English, and Yiddish). They shared a big round corner table on the second floor of the restaurant.

The Schwartzmans are one of those typical Manhattan families in which the father, a native of the city who is an entertainment lawyer, has since the birth of his sons (Harry is ten, Daniel is eight) spoken to them only in Yiddish and the mother, a native of Tokyo, has spoken to them only in Japanese. (When Harry grows up, he wants to be "a producer, director, and movie scriptwriter, and also a lawyer, so I won't have to pay a lot of legal fees." Harry gets a kick out of saying this in the presence of his father's clients. Daniel wants to be "a football player, an inventor, or an Air Force pilot." Harry and Daniel learned their English in school.)

The Xus are one of those typical Woodside, Queens, families in which the father is an abstract painter and former set designer for the Shanghai Opera who, in September, 1984, emigrated from the People's Republic of China with forty dollars in his pocket, was bitten by a dog his first night in America, worked as a delivery boy, eventually got discovered by the Carolyn Hill Gallery, in SoHo, and, in time, managed to sell enough of his paintings to send for his wife and daughter. Four months ago, Mrs. Xu, who is a ballerina, and Ran arrived in America. Ran, eight years old and in the second grade at P.S. 11 in Queens, is the only student in her class whose native tongue is Mandarin. When Ran was four years old, she briefly attended an English-language school in Shanghai. Absorbing the intricacies of English has therefore been less of a challenge for her than it has for her mother. When a Cantonese-speaking waiter materialized, Mr. Xu conferred with his wife in Mandarin, and then, addressing the waiter in English ordered dinner for everyone.

Waiting for the meal to arrive, the Schwartzmans had one of their typical three-way dinner-table conversations. In Japanese, Mrs. Schwartzman asked Harry whether he thought he would like prawns in garlic sauce. In Yiddish, Mr. Schwartzman informed Harry and Daniel that, because dinner with the Xus was a special occasion, it was all right for them to order Coca-Colas. (This was a compromise; Daniel had said he would prefer a beer.) When Daniel slouched in his chair, his father said, *"Daniel, kenst zitzen vi a mensch?"* ("Daniel, can you sit like a human being?"), and Daniel sat upright. When the pancakes for the Peking duck were brought to the table, Harry said that they reminded him of matzos. He also said that his favorite sandwich was one that his mother invented—cream cheese with Japanese codfish roe, on rye or a bagel. (His second-favorite sandwich filling is *natto*, fermented soybean paste, mixed with mustard and soy sauce or with dried seaweed and scallions.)  4

The Schwartzmans became friendly with Mr. Xu two years ago, after meeting him during a reception at Urasenke, a school that teaches the Japanese tea ceremony, on Sixty-ninth Street between Lexington and Third. "When Mr. Xu's wife and daughter arrived in New York, last January, we invited them over for dinner," Fred Schwartzman said. "It was their first meal in an American household—if ours is an American household." Inviting the Schwartzmans to dinner at the Peking Duck House was Mr. Xu's way of reciprocating.  5

During a break between the mu-shu pork and the beef with snow peas and bamboo shoots, Mr. Schwartzman mentioned that Mr. Xu had donated a painting titled "Meditation on the Homeless" to the National Mental Health Association to be auctioned at its big fund-raising gala in Washington in early June, and that Mr. Xu would be a guest of honor. Modestly, Mr. Xu acknowledged that this was true. In a burst of paternal pride, Mr. Schwartzman also mentioned the brilliant term paper Harry had recently written for his fifth-grade class at P.S. 6—ten pages on the types of weaponry used during the Mexican Revolution of 1810.  6

There was a digression into horror movies; Harry and Daniel are tireless Stephen King loyalists.  7

Daniel asked, *"Tate, kennen mir zehen 'Creepshow 2'?"* ("Dad, can we see " 'Creepshow 2'?")  8

*"Vos is 'Creepshow 2'?"*  9

Daniel said that it was a movie that he thought had something to do with black mummies.  10

"Do you appreciate grossness?" Harry asked us. "You should. It's a ₁₁ major part of life." Then he began to read to Ran his favorite passages from the 1987 edition of the "Guinness Book of World Records": coffin dimensions for the burial of the fattest person in the world; longest fingernails; smallest waist; most miserly miser; worst possible writing ("The lovely woman-child Kaa was mercilessly chained to the cruel post of the warrior chief Beast with his barbarian tribe now stacking wood at her nubile feet").

Because the restaurant was crowded, it was hard to sustain conversation ₁₂ above the din. At one point, Mr. Xu asked Mr. Schwartzman to repeat something. "Excuse me," Mr. Schwartzman said. "My English is not so good."

When Mr. Schwartzman offered a platter of food to Daniel, they had ₁₃ another exchange in Yiddish.

"What did you just say to each other?" we asked Daniel. ₁₄

"He asked me if I wanted a pork chop," Daniel said. "And I said, 'No ₁₅ way, José.' "

## STUDY QUESTIONS

1. What does the title of the essay imply? Of what, exactly, is the dinner in China-town "typical"? In what sense, as described in paragraphs 2 and 3, is each family "typical"?

2. How do the habits of each family reflect their eclectic national and ethnic back-grounds? Explain the appropriateness of Coca-Cola being allowed on this special occasion. How does the mention of Coca-Cola function in the essay? How do the subjects of conversation at dinner reflect the mix of human backgrounds?

3. Why is Daniel's response at the end particularly amusing in the context of this essay? What other idioms or trendy expressions can you think of that depend on "ethnic" names?

4. Imagine a "typical" scene in a restaurant in your community. What kinds of people would be there? What kind of conversation would there be? What foods would be most popular? What different "languages," dialects, and local habits of speech would be heard? Try to characterize the "languages" of different neighborhoods, social groups, genders, occupations, and age groups. What difficulties of "translation" or of understanding one another would be evident?

# Leo C. Rosten

Born in Poland in 1908, Leo Rosten was educated at the University of Chicago and the London School of Economics. He has written about a wide variety of subjects—films, politics, art, and religion among them—but he is most famous for his fictional explorations of how people use language.

The following lighthearted account of linguistic misunderstandings among tourists plays with the similarities between very different words and expressions in a variety of languages—and notes with wry humor the way people tend to go out of their way to seem both "natural" and "sophisticated" in order to impress strangers.

## DANGER: FOREIGN TONGUE!

The guidebooks urge any American venturing abroad to learn the basic phrases of a foreign language. Tourist tip-sheets assure you that natives just adore hearing a visitor roll his tongue around theirs. Well, I hate to say this, but the advice is cockeyed, and if you fall for it, you'll end up to your armpits in the treacherous quicksands of phonetics.

Suppose you're in Uzbek (that's just an example) and, spying an itinerant Uzbekian, utter a debonair "Hello, Charley!" in Kurdish. That will certainly flatter the most Kurdish of Kurds, but it makes him think you understand his ghoulish lingo; so his eyes light up and he answers you—in a burst of colloquial gibberish. This not only dumbfounds an American; it fills him with dismay and shame anent his linguistic inferiority.

No, brave voyager, take my advice: *Never try to speak a foreign language.* Speak English. The natives, spotting you for the illiterate you are, will knock themselves out to help you; and their joyous cries and gestures and pigeon-prattle will be oodles easier for you to comprehend than the flapdoodle which would follow your breezy *"Où est le john, frère Jacques?"* or *"Haben Sie ein Autojack?"*

The terrible truth is that the slightest slip in pronouncing one little vowel, in any language, can throw you straight into bedlam. Take English. Our *mama-loshn*[1] is sheer torture for a foreigner to pronounce. The difference between "Call me" and "Kill me," for instance, is only $\frac{1}{64}$ of an inch of air

---

1. Yiddish for "mother-tongue."

space, so a greenhorn in a hurry can wind up being throttled by an American eager to oblige a customer from abroad.

I was once accosted in Washington by a gent in a dashiki who, with a courtly bow and the sweetest of smiles, exclaimed: "Hollow Sarah!" Only quick thinking kept me from defending both my solidity and my manhood: the poor wretch *thought* he was producing the proper noises for "Hello, sir."

Or take a simple, straightforward sentence such as: "I want my meat well-done." Naively uttered by, say, a Papuan, that sentence comes out, "I want my mate walled in." Very few restaurants will brick up your wife on such short notice.

The same booby traps await the Americano who is fool enough to plunge into the jungle of an alien argot. One morning in Paris (pronounced "Paree"), my wife drove the hotel's *concierge* into a squirrel cage when she complained about the feeble amount of heat (the Gauls call it *chauffage*) coming out of our radiator. What Madame Rosten actually *said*, in her revised, unstandard version of French, was: "Attention! Chauffeurs are missing from my radiant editor!"

The *concierge* replied that Madame's radiant editor (me) had ordered a car and chauffeur for 11, and it was now only 7:40.

My wife wailed that she had been shivering with cold since 6:20 and wanted the chauffeur turned up *immédiatement.*

The *concierge* exclaimed that he would telephone the garage at once.

My wife cried: "Stop trying to cut expenses by borrowing a heater from a garage! Just rouse your lazy janitor, who is probably napping, or your greedy superintendent, who goofs off, and turn up the heat—or I shall report you *to the police!*"

The *concierge* promptly phoned a superintendent of the police and demanded he broadcast a search for a chauffeur who had been kidnapped by a lazy janitor.

Semantic snafus like that can just about unhinge you. In Tokyo, I carefully read aloud (from a phrase-book called *You, Too, Can Speak Japanese*) the phonetic syllables for "I—would—like—a—massage." To this the Oriental attendant replied, with ceremonial hisses of joy and abnegation: "I would be honored to carry you there on my back, exalted thimble, but the cat is already late for the wedding."

I think I had misled him. Either that, or he was relying on his vest-pocket copy of *You, Too, Can Spoke Engrish.*

Occidental places can be just as disorienting. I once entered a splashy men's store in Madrid and, in buoyant high-school Spanish, informed the clerk that I wanted to purchase a pair of gloves and an umbrella. The oaf turned white, whinnied, and dashed off, bleating for his superior.

To this person in a morning-coat and striped trousers, I calmly repeated: "I want—a—pair—of—men's—gloves—and an umbrella."

The superior Iberian flinched. "But, *señor*," he quavered, "why do you wish to wallop yon horse with a parachute?" Oh, it was jolly.

What happened, as I reconstruct the linguistic mish-mosh, was this: the  18
Spanish for umbrella is *paraguas*, which I mangled into *paracas*, which they
took to mean *paracaídas*, which means parachute. Gentleman is *caballero*, which
I blithely rendered as *caballo*, which means horse. It was a cinch to nose-dive
from *guante* (glove) to *guantada* (wallop), even though I have never laid a glove
on a horse, much less walloped one with a parachute. I have never even
chastised a Chihuahua. Not with so much as a feather, which is *pluma*, much
less a *plancha*, which is flatiron.

So, I don't care *how* easy the guidebooks tell you it is to toss off a few  19
fruity phrases in Flemish or Khasi or Plattdeutsch. The depressing truth is
that any language simply bulges with laryngeal pitfalls and idiomatic ambushes.

The first time I went to Paris, I was 19—an age in which omniscience  20
and obnoxiousness are mixed in equal portions. I spurned the provincialism
of the typical tourist (the very word triggered sneers). I knew the deeper
rewards that await a cultivated American who uses the patois of the natives.
So I strode into a modest neighborhood bistro and hailed the *propriétaire* with
a grand "Ah, M'sieur, but I am very hungry tonight!"

That, at least, is what I thought I was saying. What I actually uttered  21
was, "Ah, but I shall have many a female tonight."

You can hardly blame the astounded *patron* for hustling me to a far and  22
shadowy corner where my rampaging lust would cause no trouble. On the
other hand, you can hardly blame me for having fallen victim to the treacherous nasalities of French, where the ever-so-slight difference in sound between
*faim* and *femme* had converted a hungry adolescent into a sex maniac.

My greater downfall as a *manqué* Frenchman came about when I went  23
to a railway station to inquire about trains to Nice. I came armed with a
charming "Guide to Conversational French" I had picked up at a bargain (it
was published in 1880) in a picturesque bookstall on the romantic Left Bank.

The charade between men and the cretin behind the bars took this form—  24
to which I reserve all rights:

I (smiling): Bonjour, M'sieur! Is not this day reliable?
TICKET AGENT: You speak *French!* (he salutes): What joys! *Vive* the States
    United! May I wax your elbow?
I (modestly): *Voilà!* To affairs?
TICKET AGENT (beaming): Advance.
I (chuckling): I demand you: When, dear Amy (*cher ami*), do gentleman trains
    go toward Lady Nice?
TICKETEER (enthusiastic): They are *very* nice chemises of iron, wet knight.
I (clearing throat): I fear I have been soft. What I intended to choke you is:
    "Pray recount such trains' *schedule!*"
TICKETEER (crying): Who can blame you? Do you ponder *I* perceive those
    swearing schedules? They are a sponge on French honor! They rife!
    They glut! They snore—
I: Please! What—*time*—does—the—train—

TICKETEER (slapping forehead): The *time?!* Smite my neck for buttering your confusion. It takes twelve hours from Paris.

I: No, no! I do not want the interval between farewelling Paris and helloing Nice. What I chattered was: "When—*when*—"

TICKETEER (excited): *Always* it occupies twelve hours! Saturdays, Sundays, apricots—bread pains—

I (moaning): Please, dear backache, speak *slower*.

TICKETEER: Slower, marches our *local* chemises! Naturally, the wagons are of diminished luxury—

I (shouting): Who denies: Merely recite! When shrink the trains from Paris to the south—*la Sud*—

TICKETEER (flinging hands heavenward): Ahh, a thousand apologies for my porcupine! Let us banish error once and for alright. Tray of beans: to reach the Sudan, you approximate Marseilles—

I: The *south*—

TICKETEER (puzzled): But the Sudan *is* south of dirty Marseilles!

I: —of *France!*

TICKETEER: It is south of France also! From Marseilles, you eat the bark off a boat—

I (hollering): Arrest! I do not gnaw vessels! I thirst but one dainty piece of entirely different *in-for-ma-tion!*

Fourteen hours later, I was in Innsbruck. Hold on: "Innsbruck" does begin with "in" and *is* a small piece of an entirely different nation.   25

*Alors*, then, my innocents, profit from my porcupine. Shun the natives' own locutions. Dodge the sly cedilla, the *accent grave*, the umbrageous umlaut. If you want to buy a drink in Budapest, just say: "Booze—on the rocks." To see a movie in Russia, hail a *muzhik*: "Sasha, which way to the RKO Lenin?" If you're lost in Mozambique, stop any yokel with a bright "Blessings from your patron saint, and how do I get to the flea market?" Five will get you twenty if the peon doesn't take you by the hand and lead you there himself.   26

In the name of American mercy, why drive the locals *loco* by asking them to wallop yon horse with a parachute?   27

## STUDY QUESTIONS

1. Rosten's essay begins by pretending to be very chauvinistic about the English language. How quickly do you become aware that the stance is only a pretense? What clues does the essay offer?

2. How "serious" do you think Rosten is about the dangers of miscommunication when people attempt to speak a language they do not know? Analyze one of his examples of a misunderstood phrase. How likely is such a chain of mispronunciations and mishearings to occur? Why does he exaggerate? What is the effect of his exaggeration? Would the difficulty be erased if everyone spoke English?

3. Describe the TONE* of Rosten's essay. Describe the author's attitude to his audience. What sort of audience does the author seem to have in mind for his essay?
How can you tell?

4. Describe the kind of person whose voice you hear in the essay. What kind of
"voice" does the author assume here? What kind of PERSONA or CHARACTER does
the author create for himself (that is, what kind of person is the narrator made to
seem to be)? What are the advantages of portraying "himself" in such a way?

5. What views of the translatability of language underlie Rosten's essay? Is there
evidence that the *author* understands the complexities of language and linguistic
theory more fully than the NARRATOR pretends to?

# Noel Perrin

B orn in 1927, Noel Perrin has taught for many years at Dartmouth College. He
is the author of several books, including three collections of "essays of a sometime farmer." It was in the first of these, *First Person Rural* (1978), that the following
selection appeared.

This amusing account of how people describe animal sounds illustrates the way
different languages choose to transliterate sounds that, presumably, we all hear more
or less in the same way.

## OLD MACBERLITZ HAD A FARM

As a former student of nightingales' cries, I have long known that men hear    1
things differently. Set a few poets to transcribing nightingale notes, and one
man's *jug-jug* is another man's *tereu* and a third's *whit-whit-whit*. Yes, and a
fourth careful listener's *zucküt, zicküt, zidiwick, zifizigo*. If you grant even a
moderate consistency to what nightingales actually sing, you are forced to
conclude that the human ear operates on remarkably low fidelity.

Just how low-fi it can get, though, I didn't realize myself until I hap-    2
pened to stop off between planes in Singapore a couple of years ago. Most of
my two days there I spent visiting a friend from college, a young Chinese
scholar who lives over toward the campus of the University of Malaya. This
man owns a good-sized white bulldog, and we were out walking it. It was
making a spectacle of itself.

*Words in small capitals are defined in the glossary.

"Listen to him," Henry said proudly. "He'll go *wang-wang* at anything on four legs." 3

"He'll bark at anything, you mean?" 4

"Sure. Bark. *Wang-wang-wang*. Look at that Pekinese run." 5

I did look, but my mind had leaped to matters of fidelity. "Henry," I said, "I want to ask you something. Have you ever heard a cow m—I mean, call to another cow?" 6

"Sure. Why?" 7

"What did it sound like?" 8

"Cows go *hou*," said Henry. "The outcry is especially noticeable when there's an active bulldog about. Why?" 9

"What about sheep?" 10

"Sheep go *mieh*. Why do you ask? Are you writing a book for children?" 11

"Just curious. Goats?" 12

"Goats go *mieh*, too. And, for your information, cats say *miao*, and ducks *kua-kua*. Furthermore, there's a mosquito about to light on your neck and *he's* going *hêng-hêng*. Slap him and tell me about this book." 13

I'm not writing any children's book, and I have no plans to, but it's true I've been reading a good many since I got home. I've also been sending letters to foreign farmers and consulting endless bilingual dictionaries. I am now ready to report my findings. They are going to come as a nasty shock to those raised on the belief that dogs the world over really do go "bow-wow," or that mosquitoes go "zzz," or that all cows "moo," or even that a stone drops into water with a sound resembling "plop." Such innocents are going to feel as lost and miserable as the Chinese nightingale in a poem Henry quoted me: "While *ying* is its cry, seeking with its voice its companion." 14

Dogs are the place to start. Dogs have no consistency at all. As far as I can tell, even Henry's bulldog hardly sounds alike to any two people in Singapore. "That damned *gong-gong* night and day is driving me crazy," one of Henry's Indonesian colleagues told me, and he was not speaking of temple bells. There is a Dutch businessman in Henry's circle, and he confessed that to his Netherlandish ear bulldogs appear to say *waf-waf*. Before I left, Henry himself got interested in the vocal proficiency of his dog, and he dug up an old Spaniard who informed us that a mind shaped in Barcelona would invariably hear a bulldog bark as *guau!* Frenchmen you find everywhere, and the one I questioned in Singapore said with a patronizing smile that any literate man should know the verb "to bark" is *faire ouâ-ouâ*. 15

Little more pattern emerged when I got home and began to consult the children's books and farmers and dictionaries. It's true that the Polish *hau-hau* does not differ much from the Latvian *vau! vau!* And I grant that all dogs in Scandinavia, irrespective of nationality, raise their muzzles on moonlit nights and let out a noise something like *vov-vov*. On the other hand, you have only to follow the path of King Ivar the Boneless from southern Norway over to Ireland to discover that the inhabitants of the former Free State have wolfhounds and terriers and even white bulldogs which bark in Irish, 16 *amh-amh.* Swing down to Turkey, and while some Turkish dogs will set up a sedate chorus of *hav-hav,* others apparently come up yelping *kuçu-kuçu.* Read a dictionary of the sacred Pali language of Ceylon, and you find that those old Vedic Aryans called their dogs *bho-bhu-kaas,* which translates *bhu-bhu*-maker. My one real disappointment is the dogs of Japan. A bamboo importer in New York told me they bark *ming-ming.* My research shows it's not true. A Japanese dog actually barks *wan-wan,* which is much duller, and would not even faintly surprise anyone who had been to Singapore. I am only consoled by thinking of the word *pyee* in the Shangana-Tsonga language of the Bantu group; it means "the cry a dog makes after being kicked."

Cows are a good deal more stable than dogs. Cows have a reassuring sameness. Right there among the Shangana-Tsonga, to whose ears the sound of a gun doing off—our plain English "bang"—is best represented by the word *gibii,* even to the Shangana-Tsonga the voice of a cow seems to be saying *mhoo.* (The reply of her calf is a high-pitched *dwee,* but that's another matter.) German cows softly go *muh.* French cows elegantly if nasally bawl *meu.* Spanish cows make a noise that Spaniards spell *mu.* Russian cows say simply *moo,* and in Poland (where the winters are probably worse), it's *mooo.* Practically the only deviants I know are the versatile Hungarian cows, who call *mu-bu;* the Norse cows, who say *bø* and the fat cows of Ireland, who, when in Gaelic mood, are able to produce a sound that their masters put into the Roman alphabet as *geim.*

Pigs are like dogs, only more so. Pigs vary. A man could travel the world over, nearly, and hear nothing even close to a friendly *oink.* Certainly not in Portugal, for example. Portuguese swine are much given to lolling in the mud, letting out little cries of *cué, cué.* In Poland, on the other hand, from identical positions in similar mud, the pigs—the younger ones, at least—call out *kwick-kwick.* Across the border in Russia, they roll their eyes and go *khru.* Not one of these words would kindle any recognition in the mind of a Hungarian swineherd, who knows very well that pigs go *röff-röff.* (Except, of course, in Japan where they go *buu-buu;* in Finland, where the cry is *snöf-snöf;* and in Italy, where the sound you hear down by the sty at swill-time is a frantic *fron-fron-fron.*)

As for sheep, the problem is to separate them from the goats. It is not easy. In China, where *mieh* is the solitary bleat uttered by either, people obviously don't even try. Nor do they in Spain, where both sheep and goats cry *bee.* And in Onitsha Province of Nigeria, it must take a keen ear to tell the *nmáa* of a sheep from the *nmée* of a goat. Things are clearer in France. There the sheep cry *bê!* and the goats *mê!* When one turns to Russia and finds that the sheep are calling *beh* and the goats *meh,* hope soars. One begins immediately to work out a theory of *b*'s to tell sheep and *m*'s to tell goats. One soon abandons it. Turkish sheep, calling out *mee-mee,* don't fit the b-for-sheep theory. Turkish goats, with their steady *bö-bö,* don't fit the m-for-goats theory. German goats, bleating *meck-meck,* fit in, but German sheep, whimpering *mäh-mäh,* ruin everything. Perhaps one had better say the hell with

17

18

19

sheep and goats and go join the Norwegian cavalry, so as to hear the horses calling *knegg-knegg*, each to each.

    I could keep on with this roster more or less forever. I want to. I want to tell how even the familiar "cock-a-doodle-doo" of a crowing rooster is not the reliable thing one supposes. (Dutch roosters, for example, stand on their dunghills shouting *kuke-leku*, which Dutch dictionaries explain as their *victoriege-kraai*, while across the border, in Germany, the roosters pronounce it *kikeriki*. I would like to report the music-hall phrase *coin-coin*, believed by Frenchmen to be the cry uttered by ducks. And the sound one hears from turkey gobblers in Poland, which is *gool-gool-gool*. It pains me that as for mosquitoes I can only mention that from pole to pole, wherever Japanese is spoken, these sober insects advance on picnics humming *bun-bun*. I had even hoped to stage a quick Iberian invasion of Norway, so as to startle those shaggy northern horses with a Portuguese cavalry squadron, every steed in it going *ri-lin-chin-chin*.

    But the loud *bimbam!* and *klingklang!* of the German bells in the Lutheran church tell me that my time is growing short, an impression confirmed by the musical *cing-e-bing* coming from the little Albanian Orthodox chapel around the corner. I shall hardly have time to imagine a few coins dropping *zblunk*, *zblunk* into a Czechoslovakian fountain and to meditate that in Turkey those same coins would strike with a heavy sound of *cumberlop, cumberlop*. In less time than it would take a Swedish farm cart to rumble *mullra, bullra* past my window, I must be off. I'm going to Africa, on sub-safari. I want to visit the Shangana-Tsonga. If *pyhakavaka* really and truly represents the noise made in that part of Africa when a naked person falls seated into the mud, I may settle down in that onomatopoeic paradise. If it isn't I'm coming home by way of Japan. I've always wanted to hear a nightingale that could sing *hoo-hokekyo*.

## STUDY QUESTIONS

1. Why does the difference among individual ears finally fail to account for the different ways that animal sounds are transcribed? What patterns do you see in this account of how animal sounds are recorded in different languages? What does the fact that different languages use totally different sound patterns to record the "same" sounds "prove" about linguistic differences?

2. Describe the NARRATOR's attitude toward different nationalities; toward linguistic difference; toward his audience; toward himself. What is the TONE of the essay? How serious does the author seem to be about his SUBJECT? What kinds of research lie behind the essay? What kinds of views of language underlie the essay?

# Gloria Naylor

Gloria Naylor is the author of three highly acclaimed novels—*The Women of Brewster Place* (1982, for which she won the American Book Award for first fiction), *Linden Hills* (1985), and *Mama Day* (1988)—and she has been awarded a Guggenheim Fellowship for 1988–89. She is a native of New York City, where she still lives, and was educated at Brooklyn College and Yale. She has taught at George Washington University, New York University, and Boston University. Her novels have dealt with black people and black traditions in a variety of settings—urban, suburban, and, in her most recent novel, on an island off the coast of Georgia and South Carolina.

The essay that follows uses a poignant childhood moment to explore how language is given specific meaning by the way a community of speakers and hearers *agree* on specific values, seizing a word for their own uses.

## "MOMMY, WHAT DOES 'NIGGER' MEAN?"

Language is the subject. It is the written form with which I've managed to keep the wolf away from the door and, in diaries, to keep my sanity. In spite of this, I consider the written word inferior to the spoken, and much of the frustration experienced by novelists is the awareness that whatever we manage to capture in even the most transcendent passages falls far short of the richness of life. Dialogue achieves its power in the dynamics of a fleeting moment of sight, sound, smell and touch.

I'm not going to enter the debate here about whether it is language that shapes reality or vice versa. That battle is doomed to be waged whenever we seek intermittent reprieve from the chicken and egg dispute. I will simply take the position that the spoken word, like the written word, amounts to a nonsensical arrangement of sounds or letters without a censensus that assigns "meaning." And building from the meanings of what we hear, we order reality. Words themselves are innocuous; it is the consensus that gives them true power.

I remember the first time I heard the word "nigger." In my third-grade class, our math tests were being passed down the rows, and as I handed the papers to a little boy in back of me, I remarked that once again he had received a much lower mark than I did. He snatched his test from me and spit out that word. Had he called me a nymphomaniac or a necrophiliac, I couldn't have been more puzzled. I didn't know what a nigger was, but I knew that whatever it meant, it was something he shouldn't have called me. This was verified when I raised my hand, and in a loud voice repeated what he had said and watched the teacher scold him for using a "bad" word. I was later to go home and ask the inevitable question that every black parent must face—"Mommy, what does 'nigger' mean?"

And what exactly did it mean? Thinking back, I realize that this could        4
not have been the first time the word was used in my presence. I was part of a large extended family that had migrated from the rural South after World War II and formed a close-knit network that gravitated around my maternal grandparents. Their ground-floor apartment in one of the buildings they owned in Harlem was a weekend mecca for my immediate family, along with count-less aunts, uncles and cousins who brought along assorted friends. It was a bustling and open house with assorted neighbors and tenants popping in and out to exchange bits of gossip, pick up an old quarrel or referee the ongoing checkers game in which my grandmother cheated shamelessly. They were all there to let down their hair and put up their feet after a week of labor in the factories, laundries and shipyards of New York.

Amid the clamor, which could reach deafening proportions—two or three       5
conversations going on simultaneously, punctuated by the sound of a baby's crying somewhere in the back rooms or out on the street—there was still a rigid set of rules about what was said and how. Older children were sent out of the living room when it was time to get into the juicy details about "you-know-who" up on the third floor who had gone and gotten herself "p-r-e-g-n-a-n-t!" But my parents, knowing that I could spell well beyond my years, always demanded that I follow the others out to play. Beyond sexual miscon-duct and death, everything else was considered harmless for our young ears. And so among the anecdotes of the triumphs and disappointments in the various workings of their lives, the word "nigger" was used in my presence, but it was set within contexts and inflections that caused it to register in my mind as something else.

In the singular, the word was always applied to a man who had distin-      6
guished himself in some situation that brought their approval for his strength, intelligence or drive:

"Did Johnny really do that?"       7

"I'm telling you, that nigger pulled in $6,000 of overtime last year. Said        8
he got enough for a down payment on a house."

When used with a possessive adjective by a woman—"my nigger"—it        9
became a term of endearment for husband or boyfriend. But it could be more than just a term applied to a man. In their mouths it became the pure essence of manhood—a disembodied force that channeled their past history of strug-gle and present survival against the odds into a victorious statement of being: "Yeah, that old foreman found out quick enough—you don't mess with a nigger."

In the plural, it became a description of some group within the com-      10 munity that had overstepped the bounds of decency as my family defined it: Parents who neglected their children, a drunken couple who fought in public, people who simply refused to look for work, those with excessively dirty mouths or unkempt households were all "trifling niggers." This particular circle could forgive hard times, unemployment, the occasional bout of depression—they had gone through all of that themselves—but the unforgivable sin was lack of self-respect.

A woman could never be a "nigger" in the singular, with its connotation of confirming worth. The noun "girl" was its closest equivalent in that sense, but only when used in direct address and regardless of the gender doing the addressing. "Girl" was a token of respect for a woman. The one-syllable word was drawn out to sound like three in recognition of the extra ounce of wit, nerve or daring that the woman had shown in the situation under discussion. 11

"G-i-r-l, stop. You mean you said that to his face?" 12

But if the word was used in a third-person reference or shortened so that it almost snapped out of the mouth, it always involved some element of communal disapproval. And age became an important factor in these exchanges. It was only between individuals of the same generation, or from an older person to a younger (but never the other way around), that "girl" would be considered a compliment. 13

I don't agree with the argument that use of the word nigger at this social stratum of the black community was an internalization of racism. The dynamics were the exact opposite: the people in my grandmother's living room took a word that whites used to signify worthlessness or degradation and rendered it impotent. Gathering there together, they transformed "nigger" to signify the varied and complex human beings they knew themselves to be. If the word was to disappear totally from the mouths of even the most liberal of white society, no one in that room was naïve enough to believe it would disappear from white minds. Meeting the word head-on, they proved it had absolutely nothing to do with the way they were determined to live their lives. 14

So there must have been dozens of times that the word "nigger" was spoken in front of me before I reached the third grade. But I didn't "hear" it until it was said by a small pair of lips that had already learned it could be a way to humiliate me. That was the word I went home and asked my mother about. And since she knew that I had to grow up in America, she took me in her lap and explained. 15

## STUDY QUESTIONS

1. Why does the author, as a third grader, at first misunderstand a word she has heard so many times before? What is there about the word, as she hears it at school, that is different? According to Naylor, what controls the meaning of a particular word?

2. How does Naylor explain what happens when a community decides to take over a word and renegotiate its meaning?

3. What devices does Naylor use to suggest, in writing, the *oral* nuances of a word? How does her attempt to duplicate oral speech relate to the themes of her essay? Why, according to Naylor, is oral speech superior to writing?

4. Describe the organization of the essay. What function does the childhood anecdote perform? Why does the essay move from large generalization to specific anecdote to an again more general account of communal usage? How does the form of Naylor's essay reflect her view of how language works?

# Mary TallMountain

A native of Alaska although she now lives in San Francisco, Mary TallMountain is part Russian and Scots-Irish as well as Athabaskan. She is the author of *Nine Poems* (1979) and *There Is No Word for Goodbye* (1981), of which the following is the title poem.

This poem suggests subtleties of language that express subtleties of behavior and feeling.

# THERE IS NO WORD FOR GOODBYE

Sokoya,[1] I said, looking through
    the net of wrinkles into
    wise black pools
    of her eyes.

What do you say in Athabaskan          5
    when you leave each other?
    What is the word
    for goodbye?

A shade of feeling rippled
    the wind-tanned skin.          10
    Ah, nothing, she said,
    watching the river flash.

---

1. Maternal aunt.

She looked at me close.
    We just say, Tlaa. That means,
    See you.               15
    We never leave each other.
    When does your mouth
    say goodbye to your heart?

She touched me light
    as a bluebell.           20
    You forget when you leave us,
    You're so small then.
    We don't use that word.

We always think you're coming back,
    but if you don't,        25
    we'll see you some place else.
    You understand.
          There is no word for goodbye.

## STUDY QUESTIONS

1. Who is Sokoya? What details do we know about Sokoya?

2. What do lines 17–18 mean? What does the "small[ness]" of line 22 suggest? What does the promise to "see you some place else" (l. 26) imply?

3. What, according to the poem, do the words available imply about a language's culture? What values of the culture described here are emphasized most strongly?

# Sherley Williams

Born in Bakersfield, California, in 1944, Sherley Williams was educated at California State University at Fresno, Howard University, and Brown University. She has taught at Federal City College, California State University at Fresno, and the University of California, San Diego, where she is now professor of literature and chair of the department. A highly regarded poet, she is author of *Give Birth to Brightness* (1972), *The Peacock Poems* (1975), and the novel *Dessa Rose* (1986).

In the following poem, the speaker describes a recurrent song that is cyclical but ultimately unexpected, predictable but unpleasant.

# THE COLLATERAL ADJECTIVE

I sing my song in
a cycle a round
spiral up spiral
down the adjective
has little to do                              5
with the noun

            The round
is showy and loud
proud like the noun it
designates person                             10
place thing. To find *place*
call name (and thing is
a greased pole). So much
to gain and nothing
to lose: the noun has                         15
all the lines and the
lines, they cover all
the pain.

            Spiral up
spiral down. Cycle                            20
the round circle the
song. Without a drum
that sings soprano
the tongue's only a
wagging member in                             25
the void of the mouth
speechless in the face
of what it has said.
I never never
thought to sing this song.                    30
The adjective the
noun—This is not my
idea of a game.

## STUDY QUESTIONS

1. How many different forms of repetition does the poem contain? How does the repetitiveness relate to the THEMES of the poem?

2. How much do we know about the SPEAKER of the poem? What attitudes expressed in the poem might lead us to make inferences about the qualities of her life? about the kinds of experiences she has had? about her maturity?

3. How does the grammar described in the poem relate to the grammar the poem itself uses? What do you make of the paradoxes in the final stanza—the concept of "a drum / that sings soprano" (lines 22–23), for example? What does the final statement mean? What do lines 4–6 mean? How do lines 31–32 relate to lines 4–6?

# Lorna Dee Cervantes

Born in San Francisco in 1954, Lorna Dee Cervantes is of Mexican descent. She published her first book of poems, *Emplumada*, in 1981. She was educated at San Jose City College and San Jose State University and is the founder of Mango Publications, a small press that publishes books and a literary magazine.

"Refugee Ship" describes an experience of alienation based on language deprivation.

## REFUGEE SHIP

like wet cornstarch
I slide past *mi abuelita's*[1] eyes
bible placed by her side
she removes her glasses
the pudding thickens                                      5

*mamá* raised me with no language
I am an orphan to my spanish name
the words are foreign, stumbling on my tongue

1. My grandmother's.

I stare at my reflection in the mirror
brown skin, black hair                                                    10

I feel I am a captive
aboard the refugee ship
a ship that will never dock
a ship that will never dock

## STUDY QUESTIONS

1. What does it mean to be "an orphan to my spanish name" (line 7)? to be "a captive /
   aboard the refugee ship" (ll. 11–12)?

2. Explain the "cornstarch" image in line 1. What does the fifth line mean?

3. What is the source of the SPEAKER's alienation? Why will the ship "never dock" (ll.
   13–14)?

4. What does the reflection in the mirror (ll. 9–10) mean? Explain the meaning of the
   objects in lines 3 and 4.

# Richard Rodriguez

B orn in San Francisco in 1944 of Mexican heritage, Richard Rodriguez received a
   B.A. from Stanford and an M.A. from Columbia. He is the author of *Hunger
of Memory: The Education of Richard Rodriguez* (1982), in which a different version of the
following essay appeared.

In this "memoir" of his childhood, Rodriguez remembers his first days at school,
where, after an intimate family life in which only Spanish was spoken, he encountered an impersonal world where only English was spoken.

# ARIA: A MEMOIR OF A BILINGUAL
# CHILDHOOD

I remember, to start with, that day in Sacramento, in a California now nearly        1
thirty years past, when I first entered a classroom—able to understand about
fifty stray English words. The third of four children, I had been preceded

by my older brother and sister to a neighborhood Roman Catholic school. But neither of them had revealed very much about their classroom experiences. They left each morning and returned each afternoon, always together, speaking Spanish as they climbed the five steps to the porch. And their mysterious books, wrapped in brown shopping-bag paper, remained on the table next to the door, closed firmly behind them.

An accident of geography sent me to a school where all my classmates were white and many were the children of doctors and lawyers and business executives. On that first day of school, my classmates must certainly have been uneasy to find themselves apart from their families, in the first institution of their lives. But I was astonished. I was fated to be the "problem student" in class.

The nun said, in a friendly but oddly impersonal voice: "Boys and girls, this is Richard Rodriguez." (I heard her sound it out: *Rich-heard Road-ree-guess*.) It was the first time I had heard anyone say my name in English. "Richard," the nun repeated more slowly, writing my name down in her book. Quickly I turned to see my mother's face dissolve in a watery blur behind the pebbled-glass door.

Now, many years later, I hear of something called "bilingual education"—a scheme proposed in the late 1960s by Hispanic-American social activists, later endorsed by a congressional vote. It is a program that seeks to permit non-English-speaking children (many from lower-class homes) to use their "family language" as the language of school. Such, at least, is the aim its supporters announce. I hear them, and am forced to say no: It is not possible for a child, any child, ever to use his family's language in school. Not to understand this is to misunderstand the public uses of schooling and to trivialize the nature of intimate life.

Memory teaches me what I know of these matters. The boy reminds the adult. I was a bilingual child, but of a certain kind: "socially disadvantaged," the son of working-class parents, both Mexican immigrants.

In the early years of my boyhood, my parents coped very well in America. My father had steady work. My mother managed at home. They were nobody's victims. When we moved to a house many blocks from the Mexican-American section of town, they were not intimidated by those two or three neighbors who initially tried to make us unwelcome. ("Keep your brats away from my sidewalk!") But despite all they achieved, or perhaps because they had so much to achieve, they lacked any deep feeling of ease, of belonging in public. They regarded the people at work or in crowds as being very distant from us. Those were the others, *los gringos*. That term was interchangeable in their speech with another, even more telling: *los americanos*.

I grew up in a house where the only regular guests were my relations. On a certain day, enormous families of relatives would visit us, and there would be so many people that the noise and the bodies would spill out to the backyard and onto the front porch. Then for weeks no one would come. (If the doorbell rang, it was usually a salesman.) Our house stood apart—gaudy yellow in a row of white bungalows. We were the people with the noisy dog, the people who raised chickens. We were the foreigners on the block. A few neighbors would smile and wave at us. We waved back. But until I was seven years old, I did not know the name of the old couple living next door or the names of the kids living across the street.

In public, my father and mother spoke a hesitant, accented, and not 8 always grammatical English. And then they would have to strain, their bodies tense, to catch the sense of what was rapidly said by *los gringos*. At home, they returned to Spanish. The language of their Mexican past sounded in counterpoint to the English spoken in public. The words would come quickly, with ease. Conveyed through those sounds was the pleasing, soothing, consoling reminder that one was at home.

During those years when I was first learning to speak, my mother and 9 father addressed me only in Spanish; in Spanish I learned to reply. By contrast, English *(inglés)* was the language I came to associate with gringos, rarely heard in the house. I learned my first words of English overhearing my parents speaking to strangers. At six years of age, I knew just enough words for my mother to trust me on errands to stores one block away—but no more.

I was then a listening child, careful to hear the very different sounds of 10 Spanish and English. Wide-eyed with hearing, I'd listen to sounds more than to words. First, there were English (gringo) sounds. So many words still were unknown to me that when the butcher or the lady at the drugstore said something, exotic polysyllabic sounds would bloom in the midst of their sentences. Often the speech of people in public seemed to me very loud, booming with confidence. The man behind the counter would literally ask, "What can I do for you?" But by being so firm and clear, the sound of his voice said that he was a gringo; he belonged in public society. There were also the high, nasal notes of middle-class American speech—which I rarely am conscious of hearing today because I hear them so often, but could not stop hearing when I was a boy. Crowds at Safeway or at bus stops were noisy with the birdlike sounds of *los gringos*. I'd move away from them all— all the chirping chatter above me.

My own sounds I was unable to hear, but I knew that I spoke English 11 poorly. My words could not extend to form complete thoughts. And the words I did speak I didn't know well enough to make distinct sounds. (Listeners would usually lower their heads to hear better what I was trying to say.) But it was one thing for *me* to speak English with difficulty; it was more troubling to hear my parents speaking in public: their high-whining vowels and guttural consonants; their sentences that got stuck with "eh" and "ah" sounds; the confused syntax; the hesitant rhythm of sounds so different from the way gringos spoke. I'd notice, moreover, that my parents' voices were softer than those of gringos we would meet.

I am tempted to say now that none of this mattered. (In adulthood I am 12 embarrassed by childhood fears.) And, in a way, it didn't matter very much that my parents could not speak English with ease. Their linguistic difficulties had no serious consequences. My mother and father made themselves understood at the county hospital clinic and at government offices. And yet, in another way, it mattered very much. It was unsettling to hear my parents struggle with English. Hearing them, I'd grow nervous, and my clutching trust in their protection and power would be weakened.

There were many times like the night at a brightly lit gasoline station (a blaring white memory) when I stood uneasily hearing my father talk to a teenage attendant. I do not recall what they were saying, but I cannot forget the sounds my father made as he spoke. At one point his words slid together to form one long word—sounds as confused as the threads of blue and green oil in the puddle next to my shoes. His voice rushed through what he had left to say. Toward the end, he reached falsetto notes, appealing to his listener's understanding. I looked away at the lights of passing automobiles. I tried not to hear any more. But I heard only too well the attendant's reply, his calm, easy tones. Shortly afterward, headed for home, I shivered when my father put his hand on my shoulder. The very first chance that I got, I evaded his grasp and ran on ahead into the dark, skipping with feigned boyish exuberance.

But then there was Spanish: *español*, the language rarely heard away from the house; *español*, the language which seemed to me therefore a private language, my family's language. To hear its sounds was to feel myself specially recognized as one of the family, apart from *los otros*.[1] A simple remark, an inconsequential comment could convey that assurance. My parents would say something to me and I would feel embraced by the sounds of their words. Those sounds said: *I am speaking with ease in Spanish. I am addressing you in words I never use with* los gringos. *I recognize you as someone special, close, like no one outside. You belong with us. In the family. Ricardo.*

At the age of six, well past the time when most middle-class children no longer notice the difference between sounds uttered at home and words spoken in public, I had a different experience. I lived in a world compounded of sounds. I was a child longer than most. I lived in a magical world, surrounded by sounds both pleasing and fearful. I shared with my family a language enchantingly private—different from that used in the city around us.

Just opening or closing the screen door behind me was an important experience. I'd rarely leave home all alone or without feeling reluctance. Walking down the sidewalk, under the canopy of tall trees, I'd warily notice the (suddenly) silent neighborhood kids who stood warily watching me. Nervously, I'd arrive at the grocery store to hear there the sounds of the gringo, reminding me that in this so-big world I was a foreigner. But if leaving home was never routine, neither was coming back. Walking toward our house, climbing the steps from the sidewalk, in summer when the front door was

1. The others.

open, I'd hear voices beyond the screen door talking in Spanish. For a second or two I'd stay, linger there listening. Smiling, I'd hear my mother call out, saying in Spanish, "Is that you, Richard?" Those were her words, but all the while her sounds would assure me: *You are home now. Come closer inside. With us.* "*Sí*," I'd reply.

Once more inside the house, I would resume my place in the family. 17 The sounds would grow harder to hear. Once more at home, I would grow less conscious of them. It required, however, no more than the blurt of the doorbell to alert me all over again to listen to sounds. The house would turn instantly quiet while my mother went to the door. I'd hear her hard English sounds. I'd wait to hear her voice turn to soft-sounding Spanish, which assured me, as surely as did the clicking tongue of the lock on the door, that the stranger was gone.

Plainly it is not healthy to hear such sounds so often. It is not healthy 18 to distinguish public from private sounds so easily. I remained cloistered by sounds, timid and shy in public, too dependent on the voices at home. And yet I was a very happy child when I was at home. I remember many nights when my father would come back from work, and I'd hear him call out to my mother in Spanish, sounding relieved. In Spanish, his voice would sound the light and free notes that he never could manage in English. Some nights I'd jump up just hearing his voice. My brother and I would come running into the room where he was with our mother. Our laughing (so deep was the pleasure!) became screaming. Like others who feel the pain of public alien- ation, we transformed the knowledge of our public separateness into a con- soling reminder of our intimacy. Excited, our voices joined in a celebration of sounds. *We are speaking now the way we never speak out in public— we are together*, the sounds told me. Some nights no one seemed willing to loosen the hold that sounds had on us. At dinner we invented new words that sounded Spanish, but made sense only to us. We pieced together new words by tak- ing, say, an English verb and giving it Spanish endings. My mother's instruc- tions at bedtime would be lacquered with mock-urgent tones. Or a word like *sí*, sounded in several notes, would convey added measures of feeling. Tongues lingered around the edges of words, especially fat vowels. And we happily sounded that military drum roll, the twirling roar of the Spanish *r*. Family language, my family's sounds: the voices of my parents and sisters and brother. Their voices insisting: *You belong here. We are family members. Related. Special to one another. Listen!* Voices singing and sighing, rising and straining, then surging, teeming with pleasure which burst syllables into fragments of laugh- ter. At times it seemed there was steady quiet only when, from another room, the rustling whispers of my parents faded and I edged closer to sleep.

Supporters of bilingual education imply today that students like me miss 19 a great deal by not being taught in their family's language. What they seem not to recognize is that, as a socially disadvantaged child, I regarded Spanish as a private language. It was a ghetto language that deepened and strengthened my feeling of public separateness. What I needed to learn in school was that I had the right, and the obligation, to speak the public language. The odd truth is that my first-grade classmates could have become bilingual, in the conventional sense of the word, more easily than I. Had they been taught early (as upper middle-class children often are taught) a "second language" like Spanish or French, they could have regarded it simply as another public language. In my case, such bilingualism could not have been so quickly achieved. What I did not believe was that I could speak a single public language.

Without question, it would have pleased me to have heard my teachers address me in Spanish when I entered the classroom. I would have felt much less afraid. I would have imagined that my instructors were somehow "related" to me; I would indeed have heard their Spanish as my family's language. I would have trusted them and responded with ease. But I would have delayed—postponed for how long?—having to learn the language of public society. I would have evaded—and for how long?—learning the great lesson of school: that I had a public identity.     20

Fortunately, my teachers were unsentimental about their responsibility. What they understood was that I needed to speak public English. So their voices would search me out, asking me questions. Each time I heard them I'd look up in surprise to see a nun's face frowning at me. I'd mumble, not really meaning to answer. The nun would persist. "Richard, stand up. Don't look at the floor. Speak up. Speak to the entire class, not just to me!" But I couldn't believe English could be my language to use. (In part, I did not want to believe it.) I continued to mumble. I resisted the teacher's demands. (Did I somehow suspect that once I learned this public language my family life would be changed?) Silent, waiting for the bell to sound, I remained dazed, diffident, afraid.     21

Because I wrongly imagined that English was intrinsically a public language and Spanish was intrinsically private, I easily noted the difference between classroom language and the language of home. At school, words were directed to a general audience of listeners. ("Boys and girls . . .") Words were meaningfully ordered. And the point was not self-expression alone, but to make oneself understood by many others. The teacher quizzed: "Boys and girls, why do we use that word in this sentence? Could we think of a better word to use there? Would the sentence change its meaning if the words were differently arranged? Isn't there a better way of saying much the same thing?" (I couldn't say. I wouldn't try to say.)     22

Three months passed. Five. A half year. Unsmiling, ever watchful, my teachers noted my silence. They began to connect my behavior with the slow progress my brother and sisters were making. Until, one Saturday morning, three nuns arrived at the house to talk to our parents. Stiffly they sat on the blue living-room sofa. From the doorway of another room, spying on the visitors, I noted the incongruity, the clash of two worlds, the faces and voices of school intruding upon the familiar setting of home. I overheard one voice     23 gently wondering, "Do your children speak only Spanish at home, Mrs. Rodriguez?" While another voice added, "That Richard especially seems so timid and shy."

*That Rich-heard!*  24

With great tact, the visitors continued, "Is it possible for you and your  25
husband to encourage your children to practice their English when they are home?" Of course my parents complied. What would they not do for their children's well-being? And how could they question the Church's authority which those women represented? In an instant they agreed to give up the language (the sounds) which had revealed and accentuated our family's close-ness. The moment after the visitors left, the change was observed. *"Ahora, speak to us only en inglés,"*[2] my father and mother told us.

At first, it seemed a kind of game. After dinner each night, the family  26
gathered together to practice "our" English. It was still then *inglés*, a language foreign to us, so we felt drawn to it as strangers. Laughing, we would try to define words we could not pronounce. We played with strange English sounds, often over-anglicizing our pronunciations. And we filled the smiling gaps of our sentences with familiar Spanish sounds. But that was cheating, some-body shouted, and everyone laughed.

In school, meanwhile, like my brother and sisters, I was required to  27
attend a daily tutoring session. I needed a full year of this special work. I also needed my teachers to keep my attention from straying in class by calling out, *"Rich-heard!"*—their English voices slowly loosening the ties to my other name, with its three notes, *Ri-car-do*. Most of all, I needed to hear my mother and father speak to me in a moment of seriousness in "broken"—suddenly heartbreaking—English. This scene was inevitable. One Saturday morning I entered the kitchen where my parents were talking, but I did not realize that they were talking in Spanish until, the moment they saw me, their voices changed and they began speaking English. The gringo sounds they uttered startled me. Pushed me away. In that moment of trivial misunderstanding and profound insight, I felt my throat twisted by unsounded grief. I simply turned and left the room. But I had no place to escape to where I could grieve in Spanish. My brother and sisters were speaking English in another part of the house.

Again and again in the days following, as I grew increasingly angry, I  28
was obliged to hear my mother and father encouraging me: "Speak to us *en inglés*." Only then did I determine to learn classroom English. Thus, some-time afterward it happened: one day in school, I raised my hand to volunteer an answer to a question. I spoke out in a loud voice and I did not think it remarkable when the entire class understood. That day I moved very far from being the disadvantaged child I had been only days earlier. Taken hold at last was the belief, the calming assurance, that I *belonged* in public.

Shortly after, I stopped hearing the high, troubling sounds of *los gringos*.  29

2. Now . . . in English.

A more and more confident speaker of English, I didn't listen to how strangers sounded when they talked to me. With so many English-speaking people around me, I no longer heard American accents. Conversations quickened. Listening to persons whose voices sounded eccentrically pitched, I might note their sounds for a few seconds, but then I'd concentrate on what they were saying. Now when I heard someone's tone of voice—angry or questioning or sarcastic or happy or sad—I didn't distinguish it from the words it expressed. Sound and word were thus tightly wedded. At the end of each day I was often bemused, and always relieved, to realize how "soundless," though crowded with words, my day in public had been. An eight-year-old boy, I finally came to accept what had been technically true since my birth: I was an American citizen.

But diminished by then was the special feeling of closeness at home. 30 Gone was the desperate, urgent, intense feeling of being at home among those with whom I felt intimate. Our family remained a loving family, but one greatly changed. We were no longer so close, no longer bound tightly together by the knowledge of our separateness from *los gringos*. Neither my older brother nor my sisters rushed home after school any more. Nor did I. When I arrived home, often there would be neighborhood kids in the house. Or the house would be empty of sounds.

Following the dramatic Americanization of their children, even my par- 31 ents grew more publicly confident—especially my mother. First she learned the names of all the people on the block. Then she decided we needed to have a telephone in our house. My father, for his part, continued to use the word gringo, but it was no longer charged with bitterness or distrust. Stripped of any emotional content, the word simply became a name for those Americans not of Hispanic descent. Hearing him, sometimes, I wasn't sure if he was pronouncing the Spanish word *gringo*, or saying gringo in English.

There was a new silence at home. As we children learned more and 32 more English, we shared fewer and fewer words with our parents. Sentences needed to be spoken slowly when one of us addressed our mother or father. Often the parent wouldn't understand. The child would need to repeat himself. Still the parent misunderstood. The young voice, frustrated, would end up saying, "Never mind"—the subject was closed. Dinners would be noisy with the clinking of knives and forks against dishes. My mother would smile softly between her remarks; my father, at the other end of the table, would chew and chew his food while he stared over the heads of his children.

My mother! My father! After English became my primary language, I 33 no longer knew what words to use in addressing my parents. The old Spanish words (those tender accents of sound) I had earlier used—*mamá* and *papá*—I couldn't use any more. They would have been all-too-painful reminders of how much had changed in my life. On the other hand, the words I heard neighborhood kids call their parents seemed equally unsatisfactory. "Mother" and "father," "ma," "papa," "pa," "dad," "pop" (how I hated the all-American sound of that last word)—all these I felt were unsuitable terms of address for *my* parents. As a result, I never used them at home. Whenever I'd speak to my parents, I would try to get their attention by looking at them. In public conversations, I'd refer to them as my "parents" or my "mother" and "father."

My mother and father, for their part, responded differently, as their [34] children spoke to them less. My mother grew restless, seemed troubled and anxious at the scarceness of words exchanged in the house. She would question me about my day when I came home from school. She smiled at my small talk. She pried at the edges of my sentences to get me to say something more. ("What . . .?") She'd join conversations she overheard, but her intrusions often stopped her children's talking. By contrast, my father seemed to grow reconciled to the new quiet. Though his English somewhat improved, he tended more and more to retire into silence. At dinner he spoke very little. One night his children and even his wife helplessly giggled at his garbled English pronunciation of the Catholic "Grace Before Meals." Thereafter he made his wife recite the prayer at the start of each meal, even on formal occasions when there were guests in the house.

Hers became the public voice of the family. On official business it was [35] she, not my father, who would usually talk to strangers on the phone or in stores. We children grew so accustomed to his silence that years later we would routinely refer to his "shyness." (My mother often tried to explain: both of his parents died when he was eight. He was raised by an uncle who treated him as little more than a menial servant. He was never encouraged to speak. He grew up alone—a man of few words.) But I realized my father was not shy whenever I'd watch him speaking Spanish with relatives. Using Spanish, he was quickly effusive. Especially when talking with other men, his voice would spark, flicker, flare alive with varied sounds. In Spanish he expressed ideas and feelings he rarely revealed when speaking English. With firm Spanish sounds he conveyed a confidence and authority that English would never allow him.

The silence at home, however, was not simply the result of fewer words [36] passing between parents and children. More profound for me was the silence created by my inattention to sounds. At about the time I no longer bothered to listen with care to the sounds of English in public, I grew careless about listening to the sounds made by the family when they spoke. Most of the time I would hear someone speaking at home and didn't distinguish his sounds from the words people uttered in public. I didn't even pay much attention to my parents' accented and ungrammatical speech—at least not at home. Only when I was with them in public would I become alert to their accents. But even then their sounds caused me less and less concern. For I was growing increasingly confident of my own public identity.

I would have been happier about my public success had I not recalled, [37] sometimes, what it had been like earlier, when my family conveyed its intimacy through a set of conveniently private sounds. Sometimes in public, hearing a stranger, I'd hark back to my lost past. A Mexican farm worker approached me one day downtown. He wanted directions to some place. "*Hijito*, . . ."[3] he said. And his voice stirred old longings. Another time I was standing beside my mother in the visiting room of a Carmelite convent, before the dense screen which rendered the nuns shadowy figures. I heard several of them speaking Spanish in their busy, singsong, overlapping voices, assuring my mother that, yes, yes, we were remembered, all our family was remembered, in their prayers. Those voices echoed faraway family sounds. Another day a dark-faced old woman touched my shoulder lightly to steady herself as she boarded a bus. She murmured something to me I couldn't quite comprehend. Her Spanish voice came near, like the face of a never-before-seen relative in the instant before I was kissed. That voice, like so many of the Spanish voices I'd hear in public, recalled the golden age of my childhood.

Bilingual educators say today that children lose a degree of "individuality" by becoming assimilated into public society. (Bilingual schooling is a program popularized in the seventies, that decade when middle-class "ethnics" began to resist the process of assimilation—the "American melting pot.") But the bilingualists oversimplify when they scorn the value and necessity of assimilation. They do not seem to realize that a person is individualized in two ways. So they do not realize that, while one suffers a diminished sense of *private* individuality by being assimilated into public society, such assimilation makes possible the achievement of *public* individuality.    38

Simplistically again, the bilingualists insist that a student should be reminded of his difference from others in mass society, of his "heritage." But they equate mere separateness with individuality. The fact is that only in private—with intimates—is separateness from the crowd a prerequisite for individuality; an intimate "tells" me that I am unique, unlike all others, apart from the crowd. In public, by contrast, full individuality is achieved, paradoxically, by those who are able to consider themselves members of the crowd. Thus it happened for me. Only when I was able to think of myself as an American, no longer an alien in gringo society, could I seek the rights and opportunities necessary for full public individuality. The social and political advantages I enjoy as a man began on the day I came to believe that my name is indeed *Rich-heard Road-ree-guess*. It is true that my public society today is often impersonal; in fact, my public society is usually mass society. But despite the anonymity of the crowd, and despite the fact that the individuality I achieve in public is often tenuous—because it depends on my being one in a crowd—I celebrate the day I acquired my new name. Those middle-class ethnics who scorn assimilation seem to me filled with decadent self-pity, obsessed by the burden of public life. Dangerously, they romanticize public separateness and trivialize the dilemma of those who are truly socially disadvantaged.    39

3. Little boy, little son.

If I rehearse here the changes in my private life after my Americaniza-   40
tion, it is finally to emphasize a public gain. The loss implies the gain. The
house I returned to each afternoon was quiet. Intimate sounds no longer
greeted me at the door. Inside there were other noises. The telephone rang.
Neighborhood kids ran past the door of the bedroom where I was reading
my schoolbooks—covered with brown shopping-bag paper. Once I learned
the public language, it would never again be easy for me to hear intimate
family voices. More and more of my day was spent hearing words, not sounds.
But that may only be a way of saying that on the day I raised my hand in
class and spoke loudly to an entire roomful of faces, my childhood started to
end.

I grew up the victim of a disconcerting confusion. As I became fluent in   41
English, I could no longer speak Spanish with confidence. I continued to
understand spoken Spanish, and in high school I learned how to read and
write Spanish. But for many years I could not pronounce it. A powerful
guilt blocked my spoken words; an essential glue was missing whenever I
would try to connect words to form sentences. I would be unable to break a
barrier of sound, to speak freely. I would speak, or try to speak, Spanish,
and I would manage to utter halting, hiccuping sounds which betrayed my
unease. (Even today I speak Spanish very slowly, at best.)

When relatives and Spanish-speaking friends of my parents came to the   42
house, my brother and sisters would usually manage to say a few words
before being excused. I never managed so gracefully. Each time I'd hear
myself addressed in Spanish, I couldn't respond with any success. I'd know
the words I wanted to say, but I couldn't say them. I would try to speak,
but everything I said seemed to me horribly anglicized. My mouth wouldn't
form the sounds right. My jaw would tremble. After a phrase or two, I'd
stutter, cough up a warm, silvery sound, and stop.

My listeners were surprised to hear me. They'd lower their heads to   43
grasp better what I was trying to say. They would repeat their questions in
gentle, affectionate voices. But then I would answer in English. No, no, they
would say, we want you to speak to us in Spanish *("en español")*. But I couldn't
do it. Then they would call me *pocho*. Sometimes playfully, teasing, using
the tender diminutive—*mi pochito*. Sometimes not so playfully but mockingly, *pocho*. (A Spanish dictionary defines that word as an adjective meaning
"colorless" or "bland." But I heard it as a noun, naming the Mexican-American who, in becoming an American, forgets his native society.) *"¡Pocho!"*
my mother's best friend muttered, shaking her head. And my mother laughed,
somewhere behind me. She said that her children didn't want to practice
"our Spanish" after they started going to school. My mother's smiling voice
made me suspect that the lady who faced me was not really angry at me. But
searching her face, I couldn't find the hint of a smile.

Embarrassed, my parents would often need to explain their children's   44
inability to speak fluent Spanish during those years. My mother encountered

the wrath of her brother, her only brother, when he came up from Mexico one summer with his family and saw his nieces and nephews for the very first time. After listening to me, he looked away and said what a disgrace it was that my siblings and I couldn't speak Spanish, "*su propria idioma*."[4] He made that remark to my mother, but I noticed that he stared at my father.

One other visitor from those years I clearly remember: a long-time friend of my father from San Francisco who came to stay with us for several days in late August. He took great interest in me after he realized that I couldn't answer his questions in Spanish. He would grab me, as I started to leave the kitchen. He would ask me something. Usually he wouldn't bother to wait for my mumbled response. Knowingly, he'd murmur, "*¿Ay pocho, pocho, dónde vas?*"[5] And he would press his thumbs into the upper part of my arms, making me squirm with pain. Dumbly I'd stand there, waiting for his wife to notice us and call him off with a benign smile. I'd giggle, hoping to deflate the tension between us, pretending that I hadn't seen the glittering scorn in his glance.

I recount such incidents only because they suggest the fierce power that Spanish had over many people I met at home, how strongly Spanish was associated with closeness. Most of those people who called me a *pocho* could have spoken English to me, but many wouldn't. They seemed to think that Spanish was the only language we could use among ourselves, that Spanish alone permitted our association. (Such persons are always vulnerable to the ghetto merchant and the politician who have learned the value of speaking their clients' "family language" so as to gain immediate trust.) For my part, I felt that by learning English I had somehow committed a sin of betrayal. But betrayal against whom? Not exactly against the visitors to the house. Rather, I felt I had betrayed my immediate family. I knew that my parents had encouraged me to learn English. I knew that I had turned to English with angry reluctance. But once I spoke English with ease, I came to feel guilty. I sensed that I had broken the spell of intimacy which had once held the family so close together. It was this original sin against my family that I recalled whenever anyone addressed me in Spanish and I responded, confounded.

Yet even during those years of guilt, I was coming to grasp certain consoling truths about language and intimacy—truths that I learned gradually. Once, I remember playing with a friend in the backyard when my grandmother appeared at the window. Her face was stern with suspicion when she saw the boy (the *gringo* boy) I was with. She called out to me in Spanish, sounding the whistle of her ancient breath. My companion looked up and watched her intently as she lowered the window and moved (still visible) behind the light curtain, watching us both. He wanted to know what she had said. I started to tell him, to translate her Spanish words into English.

4. Their own language.
5. *Pocho*, where are you?

The problem was, however, that though I knew how to translate exactly what she had told me, I realized that any translation would distort the deepest meaning of her message; it had been directed only to me. This message of intimacy could never be translated because it did not lie in the actual words she had used but passed through them. So any translation would have seemed wrong; the words would have been stripped of an essential meaning. Finally I decided not to tell my friend anything—just that I didn't hear all she had said.

This insight was unfolded in time. As I made more and more friends  48
outside my house, I began to recognize intimate messages spoken in English in a close friend's confidential tone or secretive whisper. Even more remarkable were those instances when, apparently for no special reason, I'd become conscious of the fact that my companion was speaking *only to me*. I'd marvel then, just hearing his voice. It was a stunning event to be able to break through the barrier of public silence, to be able to hear the voice of the other, to realize that it was directed just to me. After such moments of intimacy outside the house, I began to trust what I heard intimately conveyed through my family's English. Voices at home at last punctured sad confusion. I'd hear myself addressed as an intimate—in English. Such moments were never as raucous with sound as in past times, when we had used our "private" Spanish. (Our English-sounding house was never to be as noisy as our Spanish-sounding house had been.) Intimate moments were usually moments of soft sound. My mother would be ironing in the dining room while I did my homework nearby. She would look over at me, smile, and her voice sounded to tell me that I was her son. *Richard.*

Intimacy thus continued at home; intimacy was not stilled by English.  49
Though there were fewer occasions for it—a change in my life that I would never forget—there were also times when I sensed the deep truth about language and intimacy: *Intimacy is not created by a particular language; it is created by intimates.* Thus the great change in my life was not linguistic but social. If, after becoming a successful student, I no longer heard intimate voices as often as I had earlier, it was not because I spoke English instead of Spanish. It was because I spoke public language for most of my day. I moved easily at last, a citizen in a crowded city of words.

As a man I spend most of my day in public, in a world largely devoid  50
of speech sounds. So I am quickly attracted by the glamorous quality of certain alien voices. I still am gripped with excitement when someone passes me on the street, speaking in Spanish. I have not moved beyond the range of the nostalgic pull of those sounds. And there is something very compelling about the sounds of lower-class blacks. Of all the accented versions of English that I hear in public, I hear theirs most intently. The Japanese tourist stops me downtown to ask me a question and I inch my way past his accent to concentrate on what he is saying. The eastern European immigrant in the neighborhood delicatessen speaks to me and, again, I do not pay much atten-

tion to his sounds, nor to the Texas accent of one of my neighbors or the Chicago accent of the woman who lives in the apartment below me. But when the ghetto black teenagers get on the city bus, I hear them. Their sounds in my society are the sounds of the outsider. Their voices annoy me for being so loud—so self-sufficient and unconcerned by my presence, but for the same reason they are glamorous: a romantic gesture against public acceptance. And as I listen to their shouted laughter, I realize my own quietness. I feel envious of them—envious of their brazen intimacy.

I warn myself away from such envy, however. Overhearing those teenagers, I think of the black political activists who lately have argued in favor of using black English in public schools—an argument that varies only slightly from that of foreign-language bilingualists. I have heard "radical" linguists make the point that black English is a complex and intricate version of English. And I do not doubt it. But neither do I think that black English should be a language of public instruction. What makes it inappropriate in classrooms is not something in the language itself but, rather, what lower-class speakers make of it. Just as Spanish would have been a dangerous language for me to have used at the start of my education, so black English would be a dangerous language to use in the schooling of teenagers for whom it reinforces feelings of public separateness.

This seems to me an obvious point to make, and yet it must be said. In recent years there have been many attempts to make the language of the alien a public language. "Bilingual education, two ways to understand . . ." television and radio commercials glibly announce. Proponents of bilingual education are careful to say that above all they want every student to acquire a good education. Their argument goes something like this: Children permitted to use their family language will not be so alienated and will be better able to match the progress of English-speaking students in the crucial first months of schooling. Increasingly confident of their ability, such children will be more inclined to apply themselves to their studies in the future. But then the bilingualists also claim another very different goal. They say that children who use their family language in school will retain a sense of their ethnic heritage and their family ties. Thus the supporters of bilingual education want it both ways. They propose bilingual schooling as a way of helping students acquire the classroom skills crucial for public success. But they likewise insist that bilingual instruction will give students a sense of their identity apart from the English-speaking public.

Behind this scheme gleams a bright promise for the alien child: one can become a public person while still remaining a private person. Who would not want to believe such an appealing idea? Who can be surprised that the scheme has the support of so many middle-class ethnic Americans? If the barrio or ghetto child can retain his separateness even while being publicly educated, then it is almost possible to believe that no private cost need be paid for public success. This is the consolation offered by any of the number of current bilingual programs. Consider, for example, the bilingual voter's ballot. In some American cities one can cast a ballot printed in several languages. Such a document implies that it is possible for one to exercise that most public of rights—the right to vote—while still keeping oneself apart, unassimilated in public life.

It is not enough to say that such schemes are foolish and certainly doomed. 54 Middle-class supporters of public bilingualism toy with the confusion of those Americans who cannot speak standard English as well as they do. Moreover, bilingual enthusiasts sin against intimacy. A Hispanic-American tells me, "I will never give up my family language," and he clutches a group of words as though they were the source of his family ties. He credits to language what he should credit to family members. This is a convenient mistake, for as long as he holds on to certain familiar words, he can ignore how much else has actually changed in his life.

It has happened before. In earlier decades, persons ambitious for social 55 mobility, and newly successful, similarly seized upon certain "family words." Workingmen attempting to gain political power, for example, took to calling one another "brother." The word as they used it, however, could never resemble the word (the sound) "brother" exchanged by two people in intimate greeting. The context of its public delivery made it at best a metaphor; with repetition it was only a vague echo of the intimate sound. Context forced the change. Context could not be overruled. Context will always protect the realm of the intimate from public misuse. Today middle-class white Americans continue to prove the importance of context as they try to ignore it. They seize upon idioms of the black ghetto, but their attempt to appropriate such expressions invariably changes the meaning. As it becomes a public expression, the ghetto idiom loses its sound, its message of public separateness and strident intimacy. With public repetition it becomes a series of words, increasingly lifeless.

The mystery of intimate utterance remains. The communication of inti- 56 macy passes through the word and enlivens its sound, but it cannot be held by the word. It cannot be retained or ever quoted because it is too fluid. It depends not on words but on persons.

My grandmother! She stood among my other relations mocking me when 57 I no longer spoke Spanish. *Pocho*, she said. But then it made no difference. She'd laugh, and our relationship continued because language was never its source. She was a woman in her eighties during the first decade of my life— a mysterious woman to me, my only living grandparent, a woman of Mexico in a long black dress that reached down to her shoes. She was the one relative of mine who spoke no word of English. She had no interest in gringo society and remained completely aloof from the public. She was protected by her daughters, protected even by me when we went to Safeway together and I needed to act as her translator. An eccentric woman. Hard. Soft.

When my family visited my aunt's house in San Francisco, my grand- 58 mother would search for me among my many cousins. When she found me, she'd chase them away. Pinching her granddaughters, she would warn them away from me. Then she'd take me to her room, where she had prepared for my coming. There would be a chair next to the bed, a dusty jellied candy nearby, and a copy of *Life en Español* for me to examine. "There," she'd say. And I'd sit content, a boy of eight. *Pocho*, her favorite. I'd sift through the pictures of earthquake-destroyed Latin-American cities and blonde-wigged Mexican movie stars. And all the while I'd listen to the sound of my grandmother's voice. She'd pace around the room, telling me stories of her life. Her past. They were stories so familiar that I couldn't remember when I'd heard them for the first time. I'd look up sometimes to listen. Other times she'd look over at me, but she never expected a response. Sometimes I'd smile or nod. (I understood exactly what she was saying.) But it never seemed to matter to her one way or the other. It was enough that I was there. The words she spoke were almost irrelevant to that fact. We were content. And the great mystery remained: intimate utterance.

I learn nothing about language and intimacy listening to those social activists who propose using one's family language in public life. I learn much more simply by listening to songs on a radio, or hearing a great voice at the opera, or overhearing the woman downstairs at an open window singing to herself. Singers celebrate the human voice. Their lyrics are words, but, animated by voice, those words are subsumed into sounds. (This suggests a central truth about language: all words are capable of becoming sounds as we fill them with the "music" of our life.) With excitement I hear the words yielding their enormous power to sound, even though their meaning is never totally obliterated. In most songs, the drama or tension results from the way that the singer moves between words (sense) and notes (song). At one moment the song simply "says" something; at another moment the voice stretches out the words and moves to the realm of pure sound. Most songs are about love: lost love, celebrations of loving, pleas. By simply being occasions when sounds soar through words, however, songs put me in mind of the most intimate moments of life. 59

Finally, among all types of music, I find songs created by lyric poets most compelling. On no other public occasion is sound so important for me. Written poems on a page seem at first glance a mere collection of words. And yet, without musical accompaniment, the poet leads me to hear the sounds of the words that I read. As song, a poem moves between the levels of sound and sense, never limited to one realm or the other. As a public artifact, the poem can never offer truly intimate sound, but it helps me to recall the intimate times of my life. As I read in my room, I grow deeply conscious of being alone, sounding my voice in search of another. The poem serves, then, as a memory device; it forces remembrance. And it refreshes; it reminds me of the possibility of escaping public words, the possibility that awaits me in intimate meetings. 60

The child reminds the adult: to seek intimate sounds is to seek the company of intimates. I do not expect to hear those sounds in public. I would 61 dishonor those I have loved, and those I love now, to claim anything else. I would dishonor our intimacy by holding on to a particular language and calling it my family language. Intimacy cannot be trapped within words; it passes through words. It passes. Intimates leave the room. Doors close. Faces move away from the window. Time passes, and voices recede into the dark. Death finally quiets the voice. There is no way to deny it, no way to stand in the crowd claiming to utter one's family language.

The last time I saw my grandmother I was nine years old. I can tell you 62 some of the things she said to me as I stood by her bed, but I cannot quote the message of intimacy she conveyed with her voice. She laughed, holding my hand. Her voice illumined disjointed memories as it passed them again. She remembered her husband—his green eyes, his magic name of Narcissio, his early death. She remembered the farm in Mexico, the eucalyptus trees nearby (their scent, she remembered, like incense). She remembered the family cow, the bell around its neck heard miles away. A dog. She remembered working as a seamstress, how she'd leave her daughters and son for long hours to go into Guadalajara to work. And how my mother would come running toward her in the sun—in her bright yellow dress—on her return. "MMMMAAAAMMMMMÁÁÁÁÁ," the old lady mimicked her daughter (my mother) to her daughter's son. She laughed. There was the snap of a cough. An aunt came into the room and told me it was time I should leave. "You can see her tomorrow," she promised. So I kissed my grandmother's cracked face. And the last thing I saw was her thin, oddly youthful thigh, as my aunt rearranged the sheet on the bed.

At the funeral parlor a few days after, I remember kneeling with my 63 relatives during the rosary. Among their voices I traced, then lost, the sounds of individual aunts in the surge of the common prayer. And I heard at that moment what since I have heard very often—the sound the women in my family make when they are praying in sadness. When I went up to look at my grandmother, I saw her through the haze of a veil draped over the open lid of the casket. Her face looked calm—but distant and unyielding to love. It was not the face I remembered seeing most often. It was the face she made in public when the clerk at Safeway asked her some question and I would need to respond. It was her public face that the mortician had designed with his dubious art.

## STUDY QUESTIONS

1. To what extent was Rodriguez's early life defined by the intimacy of the family? How was "family" defined? What role did language play in the family's self-definition? To what extent was his identity defined by the hostility of "los gringos"? In what ways was his family different from others in the neighborhood? Why is "los Americanos" a more "telling" term than "los gringos" (paragraph 6)?

2. In what ways does the language used, by Rodriguez and others, in the early paragraphs of this memoir help to define the problems of living in self-contained worlds? How does Rodriguez describe the sounds of the language used in his house? How does he connect sound to the sense of security he felt in his family? Explain what he means later in the memoir, about the sounds of the outsider (par. 50). How do you reconcile these two observations?

3. How did the young Rodriguez react to his parents' efforts to speak English? Explain why he comes to think of Spanish as a "private" language. How accurate does the distinction turn out to be for him in later life? How does his opinion of "bilingual education" relate to his initial experiences at school? to his view of the difference between public and private language?

4. What does the difference between the way people call his name—"Rich-heard" or "Ri-car-do"—come to mean to Rodriguez as a boy? How does his acceptance of himself as "Rich-heard" later help him to define stages in his life?

5. Why does Rodriguez, as a boy, think that English is "intrinsically" a public language? How does his view change as he grows older? Why does it change?

6. Why does the family become more silent as the children learn more and more English? What seems to happen psychologically to the mother and father?

7. How does Rodriguez define the "necessity" (par. 38) of assimilation? List all of the arguments and examples he uses to support his position. What counterarguments can you think of?

8. What effect does the gradual loss of Spanish have on Rodriguez? Why does he call the speaking of English the "original sin against my family" (par. 46)?

9. Explain fully what Rodriguez means when he describes the "deep truth" (par. 49) about language and intimacy.

10. Explain the statement "Context will always protect the realm of the intimate from public misuse" (par 55).

11. Why is the "sound of my grandmother's voice" (par. 58) so important to Rodriguez, even many years later when he remembers his childhood experiences from such a distance? Why does the sound blur or drown out other perceptions? How do you explain the preoccupation with sound and aural IMAGES throughout the memoir? Do you agree with Rodriguez that "a poem moves between the levels of sound and sense, never limited to one realm or the other"? On what principles does he base his argument?

12. Beyond his sensitivity to sound, Rodriguez is also a keen visual observer. Explain how he gives meaning to the visual image (par. 63) of his grandmother's face in the casket. Explain the meaning of the image (par. 3) of his mother's face dissolving behind the door. What other visual images in the memoir seem to you especially effective? How does each one work?

13. In what different ways are people's names important in this selection?

# Rita Dove

**B**orn in 1952 in Akron, Ohio, Rita Dove is from a family that replicated the
mythic migration of Southern blacks to the North. She is a *summa cum laude*
graduate of Miami University (Ohio), holds an M.F.A. from the Writers' Workshop
at the University of Iowa, and was a Fulbright Fellow at the University of Tübingen,
Germany. She has been both a Guggenheim Fellow and a Fellow of the National
Endowment for the Arts, and she now teaches at Arizona State University. Her
books include *The Yellow House on the Corner* (1980), *Museum* (1983), and *Thomas and
Beulah* (1986), for which she won the Pulitzer Prize.

The following poem describes the persecution of people who, because of their
ethnic background and linguistic habits, are unable to pronounce a particular sound.

## PARSLEY[1]

### *1. The Cane Fields*

There is a parrot imitating spring
in the palace, its feathers parsley green.
Out of the swamp the cane appears

to haunt us, and we cut it down. El General
searches for a word; he is all the world                5
there is. Like a parrot imitating spring,

we lie down screaming as rain punches through
and we come up green. We cannot speak an R—
out of the swamp, the cane appears

and then the mountain we call in whispers *Katalina.*[2]   10
The children gnaw their teeth to arrowheads.
There is a parrot imitating spring.

---

1. On October 2, 1957, Rafael Trujillo (1891–1961), dictator of the Dominican Republic, ordered 20,000
blacks killed because they could not pronounce the letter "r" in *perejil*, the Spanish word for parsley.
[Author's note]
2. I.e., "Katarina."

El General has found his word: *perejil.*
Who says it, lives. He laughs, teeth shining
out of the swamp. The cane appears                    15

in our dreams, lashed by wind and streaming.
And we lie down. For every drop of blood
there is a parrot imitating spring.
Out of the swamp the cane appears.

### 2. The Palace

The word the general's chosen is parsley.             20
It is fall, when thoughts turn
to love and death; the general thinks
of his mother, how she died in the fall
and he planted her walking cane at the grave
and it flowered, each spring stolidly forming         25
four-star blossoms. The general

pulls on his boots, he stomps to
her room in the palace, the one without
curtains, the one with a parrot
in a brass ring. As he paces he wonders               30
Who can I kill today. And for a moment
the little knot of screams
is still. The parrot, who has traveled

all the way from Australia in an ivory
cage, is, coy as a widow, practising                  35
spring. Ever since the morning
his mother collapsed in the kitchen
while baking skull-shaped candies
for the Day of the Dead,[3] the general
has hated sweets. He orders pastries                  40
brought up for the bird; they arrive

dusted with sugar on a bed of lace.
The knot in his throat starts to twitch;
he sees his boots the first day in battle
splashed with mud and urine                           45
as a soldier falls at his feet amazed—
how stupid he looked!—at the sound
of artillery. *I never thought it would sing*

3. All Souls' Day, November 1.

the soldier said, and died. Now
the general sees the fields of sugar                                50
cane, lashed by rain and streaming.
He sees his mother's smile, the teeth
gnawed to arrowheads. He hears
the Haitians sing without R's
as they swing the great machetes:                                  55
*Katalina*, they sing, *Katalina*,


*mi madle, mi amol en muelte.*[4] God knows
his mother was no stupid woman; she
could roll an R like a queen. Even
a parrot can roll an R! In the bare room                           60
the bright feathers arch in a parody
of greenery, as the last pale crumbs
disappear under the blackened tongue. Someone


calls out his name in a voice
so like his mother's, a startled tear                              65
splashes the tip of his right boot.
*My mother, my love in death.*
The general remembers the tiny green sprigs
men of his village wore in their capes
to honor the birth of a son. He will                              70
order many, this time, to be killed


for a single, beautiful word.

# STUDY QUESTIONS

1. Why is "El General" said to be "all the world / there is" (lines 5–6)? Why does he keep a parrot in the palace? Why does the parrot imitate spring?

2. What does the general's hatred of sweets (l. 40) have to do with "The Cane Fields" section? How much do we know about the general? What details are especially important in characterizing him?

3. How important to the poem's TONE are the greenness and lush tropical setting? Beyond the contrast between the fields and the palace, what other sharp contrasts does the poem contain? Why are the parrot's feathers said to be "a parody / of greenery" (ll. 61–62)?

4. What effects are produced by the repeated contrasts between beauty and ugliness?

---

4. See line 67 for a translation.

5. Why are the "we," juxtaposed with "he" in the first section of the poem, not mentioned explicitly in the second section? Why are the repeated, ritualistic phrases used in the first section? How is the second section of the poem structured?

6. Beyond the inability of the blacks to pronounce *r*'s, in what other ways is language important to the poem?

# Louise Erdrich

Although primarily known as a novelist and writer of prose sketches, Louise Erdrich is also a poet of distinction. She is of Chippewa and German-American descent; she grew up in North Dakota and now lives in New Hampshire with her husband and five children. Her best-known novel, *Love Medicine* (1984), won the National Book Critics Circle Award and was a national best-seller. It was followed by *The Beet Queen* (1986) and *Tracks* (1988). Philip Roth called her "the most interesting new American novelist to have appeared in years."

The following poem describes a special moment of illumination when a couple is discovered in the woods.

## JACKLIGHT

> The same Chippewa word is used both for flirting and hunting game, while another Chippewa word connotes both using force in intercourse and also killing a bear with one's bare hands.
>
> —Dunning 1959

We have come to the edge of the woods,
out of brown grass where we slept, unseen,
out of knotted twigs, out of leaves creaked shut,
out of hiding.

At first the light wavered, glancing over us.          5
Then it clenched to a fist of light that pointed,
searched out, divided us.
Each took the beams like direct blows the heart answers.
Each of us moved forward alone.

We have come to the edge of the woods,                    .          10
drawn out of ourselves by this night sun,
this battery of polarized acids,
that outshines the moon.

We smell them behind it
but they are faceless, invisible.                                      15
We smell the raw steel of their gun barrels,
mink oil on leather, their tongues of sour barley.
We smell their mother buried chin-deep in wet dirt.

We smell their fathers with scoured knuckles,
teeth cracked from hot marrow.                                        20
We smell their sisters of crushed dogwood, bruised apples,
of fractured cups and concussions of burnt hooks.

We smell their breath steaming lightly behind the jacklight.
We smell the itch underneath the caked guts on their clothes.
We smell their minds like silver hammers                              25
cocked back, held in readiness
for the first of us to step into the open.

We have come to the edge of the woods,
out of brown grass where we slept, unseen,
out of leaves creaked shut, out of our hiding.                        30
We have come here too long.

It is their turn now,
their turn to follow us. Listen,
they put down their equipment.
It is useless in the tall brush.                                      35
And now they take the first steps, not knowing
how deep the woods are and lightless.
How deep the woods are.

## STUDY QUESTIONS

1. What is "jacklight"? Who are "we"? Who are "they"? How does the poem make
   the differences between the two groups clear?

2. What do the woods represent to the SPEAKER and companion? What are the others
   afraid of? What sort of threat do the others represent? How is the threat represented in the poem's images?

3. What does the EPIGRAPH of the poem mean? How does it relate to the body of the
   poem?

# Salli Benedict

S alli Benedict (Kawennotakie) is director of the Akwesasne Museum on the reserve of the Mohawk Nation in upstate New York.

The following selection not only is about highly self-conscious and odd language, but it also *uses* language in a peculiar way itself.

## TAHOTAHONTANEKENT-SERATKERONTAKWENHAKIE

Deep in the woods, there lived a man and his wife, and their newborn baby boy. The baby was so young that his parents had not yet given him a name. Hunting was very bad that winter and they had very little to eat. They were very poor.  1

One day around suppertime, a little old man came to their door. He was selling rabbits.  2

"Do you wish to buy a rabbit for your supper?" he asked.  3

The woman who met him at the door replied that they were very poor and had no money to buy anything.  4

It was growing dark and the man looked very tired. The woman knew that he had travelled very far just to see if they would buy a rabbit from him. She invited him to stay for supper and share what little they had to eat.  5

"What is your name?" the husband asked as he got up to meet the old man.  6

"I have no name," the little man replied. "My parents were lost before they could name me. People just call me Tahotahontanekentseratkeron-takwenhakie which means, 'He came and sold rabbits.' "  7

The husband laughed. "My son has not been named yet either. We just call him The Baby."  8

The old man said, "You should name him so that he will know who he is. There is great importance in a name." The old man continued, "I will give you this last rabbit of mine for a good supper, so that we may feast in honor of the birth of your new son."  9

In the morning, the old man left. The parents of the baby still pondered over a name for the baby.  10

"We shall name the baby after the generous old man who gave him a     11
feast in honor of his birth. But he has no name," the mother said.

"Still, we must honor his gift to our son," the husband replied. "We will     12
name our son after what people call the old man, Tahotahontanekentseratkerontakwenhakie which means, 'He came and sold rabbits.' "

"What a long name that is," the mother said. "Still, we must honor the     13
old man's wish for a name for our son and his feast for our son."

So the baby's name became Tahotahontanekentseratkerontakwenhakie     14
which means, "He came and sold rabbits," in honor of the old man.

The baby boy grew older and became very smart. He had to be, to be     15
able to remember his own name. Like all other children he was always trying
to avoid work. He discovered that by the time his mother had finished calling
his name for chores, he could be far, far away.

Sometimes his mother would begin telling him something to do, "Ta-     16
hotahontanekentseratkerontakwenhakie . . . hmmmm . . ." She would forget what she wanted to have him do, so she would smile and tell him to go
and play.

Having such a long important name had its disadvantages too. When his     17
family travelled to other settlements to visit friends and other children, the
other children would leave him out of games. They would not call him to
play or catch ball. They said that it took more energy to say his name than
it did to play the games.

News of this long, strange name travelled to the ears of the old man,     18
Tahotahontanekentseratkerontakwenhakie. "What a burden this name must
be for a child," the old man thought. "This name came in gratitude for my
feast for the birth of the boy. I must return to visit them."

The old man travelled far to the family of his namesake, Tahotahonta-     19
nekentseratkerontakwenhakie. The parents met the old man at the door and
invited him in. He brought with him food for another fine meal.

"You are very gracious to honor me with this namesake," he said. "But     20
we should not have two people wandering this world, at the same time, with
the same name. People will get us confused, and it may spoil my business.
Let us call your son Oiasosonaion which means, 'He has another name.' If
people wish to know his other name, then he can tell them."

Oiasosonaion smiled and said, "I will now have to call you Tahotahon-     21
tanekentseratkerontakwenhakie tanon Oiasahosonnon which means, 'He came
and sold rabbits and gave the boy another name.' "

Everyone laughed.     22

## STUDY QUESTIONS

1. What do you think the point of the story is? Is the story an ALLEGORY? a FABLE? a
   PARABLE? a fairy tale? Can you think of a more appropriate label to describe the
   story's mode?

2. What does the story imply about the importance of names? What is the significance of the lack of names for the little man and the baby at the story's beginning? In what ways are the names invented here like "real" names in English or in another language you know? What traditions of naming are suggested by the process of naming depicted here?

3. Describe the TONE of the story. In what places is the story funny? Against whom is the laughter at the end directed? Are the poor people without names ever made fun of?

# Linda Hogan

Linda Hogan, a Chickasaw, was born in Denver in 1947, grew up in Oklahoma, and earned an M.A. in English and creative writing from the University of Colorado. Now an associate professor of American studies and American Indian studies at the University of Minnesota, she has published several books of poems, including *Calling Myself Home; Daughters, I Love You; Eclipse; That House;* and *Seeing Through the Sun* (which won the 1986 American Book Award from the Before Columbus Foundation). Her first novel, *Mean Spirit*, appeared in 1989.

The following poem celebrates both a name and the act of naming.

## SONG FOR MY NAME

Before sunrise
think of brushing out an old woman's
dark braids.
Think of your hands,
fingertips on the soft hair.                                    5

If you have this name,
your grandfather's dark hands
lead horses toward the wagon
and a cloud of dust follows,
ghost of silence.                                              10

That name is full of women
with black hair

and men with eyes like night.
It means no money
tomorrow.                                                     15

Such a name my mother loves
while she works gently
in the small house.
She is a white dove
and in her own land                                           20
the mornings are pale,
birds sing into the white curtains
and show off their soft breasts.

If you have a name like this,
there's never enough water.                                   25
There is too much heat.
When lightning strikes, rain
refuses to follow.
It's my name,
that of a woman living                                        30
between the white moon
and the red sun, waiting to leave.
It's the name that goes with me
back to earth
no one else can touch.                                        35

## STUDY QUESTIONS

1. List all of the things the SPEAKER's name means. What emotions does it provoke in those who have it? What sensuous experiences does it suggest? What history does it seem to have?

2. How much do we know about the poem's speaker? Why do you think the speaker does not give more direct information about herself? How do you know that the speaker in the poem is a woman?

3. What aspects of heritage seem attached to the name? What does the name mean to the speaker? Why does the speaker refuse to say what the name is?

# Nora Dauenhauer

A native Alaskan, Nora Dauenhauer comes from a family of noted carvers and beadwork artists. She is a linguist and author of instructional materials in her own native language, Tlingit. A collection of her poems, *The Drowning Shaman*, has recently been published.

The poem that follows is a CONCRETE POEM shaping Tlingit words on the page to portray an object.

## TLINGIT CONCRETE POEM

```
                                    t ' a   n
                                  a                i
                              a      k
              x'aax'x'aax'x 'aax'x ' aax'x'aax
            aax'x'aax'x'aax'x 'aax'x ' aax'x'aax'x
          'x'aax'x'aax'x'aax'x 'aax'x ' aax'x'aax'x'a
        x'x'aax'x'aax'x'aax'x 'aax'x ' aax'x'aax'x'aax
      aax'x'aax'x'aax'x'aax'x 'aax'x ' aax'x'aax'x'aax'
      'aax'x'aax'x'aax'x'aax'x 'aax'x ' aax'x'aax'x'aax'x
    x'aax'x'aax'x'aax'x'aax'x 'aax'x ' aax'x'aax'x'aax'x'
    'x'aax'x'aax'x'aax'x'aax'x 'aax'x ' aax'x'aax'x'aax'x'
    'x'aax'x'aax'x'aax'x'aax'x 'aax'x ' aax'x'aax'x'aax'x'a
    'x'aax'x'aax'x'aax'x'aax'x 'aax'x ' aax'x'aax'x'aax'x'a
  x'x'aax'x'aax'x'aax'x'aax'x 'aax'x ' aax'x'aax'x'aax'x'a
  x'x'aax'x'aax'x'aax'x'aax'x 'aax'x ' aax'x'aax'x'aax'x'a
  x'x'aax'x'aax'x'aax'x'aax'x 'aax'x ' aax'x'aax'x'aax'x'a
  x'x'aax'x'aax'x'aax'x'aax'x 'aax'x ' aax'x'aax'x'aax'x'a
  'x'aax'x'aax'x'aax'x'aax'x 'aax'x ' aax'x'aax'x'aax'x'a
  'x'aax'x'aax'x'aax'x'aax'x 'aax'x ' aax'x'aax'x'aax'x'
  'x'aax'x'aax'x'aax'x'aax'x 'aax'x ' aax'x'aax'x'aax'x'
  x'aax'x'aax'x'aax'x'aax'x 'aax'x ' aax'x'aax'x'aax'x'
    'aax'x'aax'x'aax'x'aax'x 'aax'x ' aax'x'aax'x'aax'x
    'aax'x'aax'x'aax'x'aax'x 'aax'x ' aax'x'aax'x'aax'
    aax'x'aax'x'aax'x'aax'x 'aax'tl'uk w x'aax'x'aax'
      ax'x'aax'x'aax'x'aax'x 'aax'x ' aax'x'aax'x'aax
      x'x'aax x'aax'x'aax'x'aax'x ' aax'x'aax'x'aa
        'x'aax'x'aax'x'aax'x'aax'x ' aax'x'aax'x'a
        'aax'x'aax'x'aax'x'aax'x ' aax'x'aax'x
          ax'x'aax'x'aax'x'aax'x ' aax'x'aax
          'x'aax'x'aax'x'aax'x ' aax'x'a
            'aax'x'aax'x'aax'x ' aax'x'
              'x'aax'x'aax'x ' aa
                'x'aa
```

Akat'ani = stem
x'aax' = apple
tl'ukwx = worm

## STUDY QUESTIONS

1. How long did it take you to spot the worm? Do you need to know anything about the Tlingit language to "understand" this poem? What do you think it "means"?

2. Would the poem have a different effect if it were composed in a different language? What traditional meanings of apples seem to be alluded to in the poem? What traditions do they come from?

3. Describe the emotional effect the poem has on you. Does its effect have anything to do with its linguistic tradition? its visual appearance? religious beliefs? MYTH?

# Li-Young Lee

Li-Young Lee was born in 1957 in Jakarta, Indonesia, to Chinese parents "who were classically educated and in the habit of reciting literally hundreds of ancient Chinese poems." His father was jailed by then-dictator Sukarno for nineteen months, seventeen of them in a leper colony. After his escape, the family fled from country to country, and then settled in western Pennsylvania, where his father became a Presbyterian minister. Lee has published a volume of poems called *Rose* (1986). "I . . . believe the King James Bible to contain some of the greatest poetry in the world," he says, "and I hope to own some of its simplicity, glory, and mystery in my own writing one day."

In the following poem, a childhood incident becomes the basis for an investigation of different languages and what they stand for in the human observation of objects, events, and values.

# PERSIMMONS

In sixth grade Mrs. Walker
slapped the back of my head
and made me stand in the corner
for not knowing the difference
between *persimmon* and *precision*.          5
How to choose

persimmons. This is precision.
Ripe ones are soft and brown-spotted.
Sniff the bottoms. The sweet one

will be fragrant. How to eat:                                                    10
put the knife away, lay down newspaper.
Peel the skin tenderly, not to tear the meat.
Chew the skin, suck it,
and swallow. Now, eat
the meat of the fruit,                                                           15
so sweet,
all of it, to the heart.

Donna undresses, her stomach is white.
In the yard, dewy and shivering
with crickets, we lie naked,                                                     20
face-up, face-down.
I teach her Chinese.
Crickets:   *chiu chiu*. Dew:   I've forgotten.
Naked:   I've forgotten.
*Ni, wo:*   you and me.                                                          25
I part her legs,
remember to tell her
she is beautiful as the moon.

Other words
that got me into trouble were                                                    30
*fight* and *fright, wren* and *yarn.*
Fight was what I did when I was frightened,
fright was what I felt when I was fighting.
Wrens are small, plain birds,
yarn is what one knits with.                                                     35
Wrens are soft as yarn.
My mother made birds out of yarn.
I loved to watch her tie the stuff;
a bird, a rabbit, a wee man.

Mrs. Walker brought a persimmon to class                                         40
and cut it up
so everyone could taste
a *Chinese apple.* Knowing
it wasn't ripe or sweet, I didn't eat
but watched the other faces.                                                     45

My mother said every persimmon has a sun
inside, something golden, glowing,
warm as my face.

Once, in the cellar, I found two wrapped in newspaper,
forgotten and not yet ripe.                                                      50

I took them and set both on my bedroom windowsill,
where each morning a cardinal
sang, *The sun, the sun.*

Finally understanding
he was going blind,                                                      55
my father sat up all one night
waiting for a song, a ghost.
I gave him the persimmons,
swelled, heavy as sadness,
and sweet as love.                                                      60

This year, in the muddy lighting
of my parents' cellar, I rummage, looking
for something I lost.
My father sits on the tired, wooden stairs,
black cane between his knees,                                            65
hand over hand, gripping the handle.

He's so happy that I've come home.
I ask how his eyes are, a stupid question.
*All gone,* he answers.

Under some blankets, I find a box.                                       70
Inside the box I find three scrolls.
I sit beside him and untie
three paintings by my father:
Hibiscus leaf and a white flower.
Two cats preening.                                                       75
Two persimmons, so full they want to drop from the cloth.

He raises both hands to touch the cloth,
asks, *Which is this?*

*This is persimmons, Father.*

*Oh, the feel of the wolftail on the silk,*                              80
*the strength, the tense*
*precision in the wrist.*
*I painted them hundreds of times*
*eyes closed. These I painted blind.*
*Some things never leave a person:*                                     85
*scent of the hair of one you love,*
*the texture of persimmons,*
*in your palm, the ripe weight.*

## STUDY QUESTIONS

1. What different things do persimmons represent to the SPEAKER? What different characteristics of persimmons does the poem mention? What is the significance of each to the effect of the poem?

2. How much do we know about Mrs. Walker? What is ironic about her punishment of the speaker? What does she not know about persimmons? Why does the speaker watch the other faces when the persimmon is cut up? What other instances are there in the poem of watching reactions? Why is the THEME of being a spectator appropriate to the total poem?

3. What different voices are heard in the poem? What different languages does the poem record? In what different ways are the responses of one person communicated to another? How does the cardinal's song relate to the issue of communication? How is the sight of the cardinal related to other central objects in the poem?

4. How are the various CHARACTERS in the poem—Mrs. Walker, Donna, the father, and the speaker—related to the central themes of the poem?

# Pat Mora

Born in El Paso, Pat Mora writes poems in which her Chicana heritage and Southwestern background are central. Her first book, *Chants* (which won the Southwest Book Award), is largely composed of what she calls "desert incantations." Her second, *Borders* (from which the following poem is taken), describes the two cultures that create her own "border" life.

The poem explores the different languages spoken by women and men.

# BORDERS

*My research suggests that men and women may speak different languages that they assume are the same.*

Carol Gilligan

If we're so bright,
why didn't we notice?

*I*

The side-by-side translations
were the easy ones.
Our tongues tasted *luna*                                    5
chanting, chanting to the words
it touched; our lips circled
*moon* sighing its longing.
We knew: similar but different.

*II*

And we knew of grown-up talk,                               10
how even in our own home
like became unlike,
how the child's singsong

                  I want, I want

burned our mouth                                            15
when we whispered in the dark.

*III*

But us? You and I
who've talked for years
tossing words back and forth

                *success, happiness*     20

back and forth
over coffee, over wine
at parties, in bed
and I was sure you heard,
    u n d e r s t o o d ,                25
though now I think of it
I can remember screaming
to be sure.

So who can hear
the words we speak                                          30
you and I, like but unlike,
and translate us to us
side by side?

# STUDY QUESTIONS

1. To whom is the poem addressed? Who are the "we" in line 2? the "us" in line 17?

2. Who is Carol Gilligan? Why is an EPIGRAPH from her study especially significant to this poem?

3. What are "side-by-side translations" (l. 3)? Why are they "easy" compared with difficulties of translation when both people use the same word differently, as in section III?

4. According to the poem, what differences are there between the talk of children and that of adults? What, exactly, are the differences between women's language and men's, according to the poem? What illustrations does the poem offer?

5. In what specific ways do the examples of speech illustrated by "luna" and "moon" contribute to the sense of intimacy and companionship in the poem? How do they contribute to the atmosphere of the poem? Contrast the TONES of sections II and III. What accounts for the differences? What is the mythological connection between women and the moon? Does the poem challenge traditional mythological associations in any way?

6. How does the sense of audience projected by the poem relate to the central problem the poem poses? In what sense does a conception of audience provide a solution?

# Maya Angelou

Maya Angelou's ongoing autobiography has now reached five volumes, and she is still a relatively young woman. But no wonder. Besides writing the autobiography, three volumes of poetry, and a ten-part television series (which she also produced), Angelou has toured Europe and Africa as an actress (in *Porgy and Bess*), studied and taught dance, served as the Northern coordinator for the Southern Christian Leadership Conference, and served on the Commission of International Women's Year and on the Board of Trustees of the American Film Institute. She was understandably named "Woman of the Year" by the *Ladies Home Journal* in 1975.

"The Languages of Home" (editors' title), from *Gather Together in My Name*, describes two trips Angelou made to Stamps, Arkansas: one when she was four years old, to be reared by her grandmother ("Momma"), and a second when, after a number of years in California, she was in a position to notice the customs, rituals, and languages of the culture.

## THE LANGUAGES OF HOME

There is a much-loved region in the American fantasy where pale white women     1
float eternally under black magnolia trees, and white men with soft hands
brush wisps of wisteria from the creamy shoulders of their lady loves. Har-

monious black music drifts like perfume through this precious air, and nothing of a threatening nature intrudes.

The South I returned to, however, was flesh-real and swollen-belly poor. 2 Stamps, Arkansas, a small hamlet, had subsisted for hundreds of years on the returns from cotton plantations, and until World War I, a creaking lumbermill. The town was halved by railroad tracks, the swift Red River and racial prejudice. Whites lived on the town's small rise (it couldn't be called a hill), while blacks lived in what had been known since slavery as "the Quarters."

After our parents' divorce in California, our father took us from Mother, 3 put identification and destination tags on our wrists, and sent us alone, by train, to his mother in the South. I was three and my brother four when we first arrived in Stamps. Grandmother Henderson accepted us, asked God for help, then set about raising us in His way. She had established a country store around the turn of the century, and we spent the Depression years minding the store, learning Bible verses and church songs, and receiving her undemonstrative love.

We lived a good life. We had some food, some laughter and Momma's 4 quiet strength to lean against. During World War II the armed services drew the town's youth, black and white, and Northern war plants lured the remaining hale and hearty. Few, if any, blacks or poor whites returned to claim their heritage of terror and poverty. Old men and women and young children stayed behind to tend the gardens, the one paved block of stores and the long-accepted way of life.

In my memory, Stamps is a place of light, shadow, sounds and entranc- 5 ing odors. The earth smell was pungent, spiced with the odor of cattle manure, the yellowish acid of the ponds and rivers, the deep pots of greens and beans cooking for hours with smoked or cured pork. Flowers added their heavy aroma. And above all, the atmosphere was pressed down with the smell of old fears, and hates, and guilt.

On this hot and moist landscape, passions clanged with the ferocity of 6 armored knights colliding. Until I moved to California at thirteen I had known the town, and there had been no need to examine it. I took its being for granted and now, five years later, I was returning, expecting to find the shield of anonymity I had known as a child.

Along with other black children in small Southern villages, I had accepted 7 the total polarization of the races as a psychological comfort. Whites existed, as no one denied, but they were not present in my everyday life. In fact, months often passed in my childhood when I only caught sight of the thin hungry po' white trash (sharecroppers), who lived sadder and meaner lives than the blacks I knew. I had no idea that I had outgrown childhood's protection until I arrived back in Stamps.

Momma took my son in one arm and folded the other around me. She 8 held us for one sweet crushing moment. "Praise God Almighty you're home safe."

She was already moving away to keep her crying private. 9

"Turned into a little lady. Sure did." My Uncle Willie examined me 10 with his quiet eyes and reached for the baby. "Let's see what you've got there."

He had been crippled in early childhood, and his affliction was never 11 mentioned. The right side of his body had undergone severe paralysis, but his left arm and hand were huge and powerful. I laid the baby in the bend of his good arm.

"Hello, baby. Hello. Ain't he sweet?" The words slurred over his tongue 12 and out of the numb lips. "Here, take him." His healthy muscles were too strong for a year-old wriggler.

Momma called from the kitchen, "Sister, I made you a little something 13 to eat."

We were in the Store; I had grown up in its stronghold. Just seeing the 14 shelves loaded with weenie sausages and Brown Plug chewing tobacco, salmon and mackerel and sardines all in their old places softened my heart and tears stood at the ready just behind my lids. But the kitchen, where Momma with her great height bent to pull cakes from the wood-burning stove and arrange the familiar food on well-known plates, erased my control and the tears slipped out and down my face to plop onto the baby's blanket.

The hills of San Francisco, the palm trees of San Diego, prostitution 15 and lesbians and the throat hurting of Curly's departure disappeared into a never-could-have-happened land. I was home.

"Now what you crying for?" Momma wouldn't look at me for fear my 16 tears might occasion her own. "Give the baby to me, and you go wash your hands. I'm going to make him a sugar tit. You can set the table. Reckon you remember where everything is."

The baby went to her without a struggle and she talked to him without 17 the cooing most people use with small children. "Man. Just a little man, ain't you? I'm going to call you Man and that's that."

Momma and Uncle Willie hadn't changed. She still spoke softly and her 18 voice had a little song in it.

"Bless my soul, Sister, you come stepping up here looking like your 19 daddy for the world."

Christ and Church were still the pillars of her life. 20

"The Lord my God is a rock in a weary land. He is a great God. Brought 21 you home, all in one piece. Praise His name."

She was, as ever, the matriarch. "I never did want you children to go to 22 California. Too fast that life up yonder. But then, you all's their children, and I didn't want nothing to happen to you, while you're in my care. Jew was getting a little too big for his britches."

Five years before, my brother had seen the body of a black man pulled 23 from the river. The cause of death had not been broadcast, but Bailey (Jew was short for Junior) had seen that the man's genitals had been cut away. The shock caused him to ask questions that were dangerous for a black boy in 1940 Arkansas. Momma decided we'd both be better off in California where lynchings were unheard of and a bright young Negro boy could go places. And even his sister might find a niche for herself.

Despite the sarcastic remarks of Northerners, who don't know the region (read Easterners, Westerners, North Easterners, North Westerners, Midwesterners), the South of the United States can be so impellingly beautiful that sophisticated creature comforts diminish in importance. 24

For four days I waited on the curious in the Store, and let them look me over. I was that rarity, a Stamps girl who had gone to the fabled California and returned. I could be forgiven a few siditty[1] airs. In fact, a pretension to worldliness was expected of me, and I was too happy to disappoint. 25

When Momma wasn't around, I stood with one hand on my hip and my head cocked to one side and spoke of the wonders of the West and the joy of being free. Any listener could have asked me: if things were so grand in San Francisco, what had brought me back to a dusty mote of Arkansas? No one asked, because they all needed to believe that a land existed somewhere, even beyond the Northern Star, where Negroes were treated as people and whites were not the all-powerful ogres of their experience. 26

For the first time the farmers acknowledged my maturity. They didn't order me back and forth along the shelves but found subtler ways to make their wants known. 27

"You all have any long-grain rice, Sister?" 28

The hundred-pound sack of rice sat squidged down in full view. 29

"Yes, ma'am, I believe we do." 30

"Well then, I'll thank you for two pounds." 31

"Two pounds? Yes, ma'am." 32

I had seen the formality of black adult equals all my youth but had never considered that a time would come when I, too, could participate. The customs are as formalized as an eighteenth-century minuet, and a child at the race's knee learns the moves and twirls by osmosis and observation. 33

Values among Southern rural blacks are not quite the same as those existing elsewhere. Age has more worth than wealth, and religious piety more value than beauty. 34

There were no sly looks over my fatherless child. No cutting insinuations kept me shut away from the community. Knowing how closely my grandmother's friends hewed to the Bible, I was surprised not to be asked to confess my evil ways and repent. Instead, I was seen in the sad light which had been shared and was to be shared by black girls in every state in the country. I was young, yes, unmarried, yes—but I was a mother, and that placed me nearer to the people. 35

I was flattered to receive such acceptance from my betters (seniors) and strove mightily to show myself worthy. 36

Momma and Uncle Willie noted my inclusion into the adult stratum, 37

1. Or "sidy": conceited.

and on my fourth day they put up no resistance when I said I was going for a night on the town. Since they knew Stamps, they knew that any carousing I chose to do would be severely limited. There was only one "joint" and the owner was a friend of theirs.

Age and travel had certainly broadened me and obviously made me more attractive. A few girls and boys with whom I'd had only generalities in common, all my life, asked me along for an evening at Willie Williams' café. The girls were going off soon to Arkansas Mechanical and Technical College to study Home Economics and the boys would be leaving for Tuskegee Institute in Alabama to learn how to farm. Although I had no education, my California past and having a baby made me equal to an evening with them. 38

When my escorts walked into the darkened Store, Momma came from the kitchen, still wearing her apron, and joined Uncle Willie behind the counter. 39

"Evening, Mrs. Henderson. Evening, Mr. Willie." 40

"Good evening, children." Momma gathered herself into immobility. 41

Uncle Willie leaned against the wall. "Evening, Philomena, and Harriet and Johnny Boy and Louis. How you all this evening?" 42

Just by placing their big still bodies in the Store at that precise time, my grandmother and uncle were saying, "Be good. Be very very good. Somebody is watching you." 43

We squirmed and grinned and understood. 44

The music reached out for us when we approached the halfway point. A dark throbbing bass line whonked on the air lanes, and our bodies moved to tempo. The steel guitar urged the singer to complain 45

> "Well, I ain't got no
> special reason here.
> No, I ain't got no
> special reason here.
> I'm going leave
> 'cause I don't feel welcome here . . ."

The Dew Drop In café was a dark square outline, and on its wooden exterior, tin posters of grinning white women divinely suggested Coca-Cola, R.C. Cola and Dr. Pepper for complete happiness. Inside the one-room building, blue bulbs hung down precariously close to dancing couples, and the air moved heavily like stagnant water. 46

Our entrance was noted but no one came rushing over to welcome me or ask questions. That would come, I knew, but certain formalities had first to be observed. We all ordered Coca-Cola, and a pint bottle of sloe gin appeared by magic. The music entered my body and raced along my veins with the third syrupy drink. Hurry, I was having a good time. I had never had the chance to learn the delicate art of flirtation, so now I mimicked the other girls at the table. Fluttering one hand over my mouth, while laughing as hard as 47

I could. The other hand waved somewhere up and to my left as if I and it had nothing to do with each other.

"Marguerite?" 48

I looked around the table and was surprised that everyone was gone. I 49 had no idea how long I had sat there laughing and smirking behind my hand. I decided they had joined the dancing throng and looked up to search for my, by now, close but missing friends.

"Marguerite." L. C. Smith's face hung above me like the head of a body- 50 less brown ghost.

"L. C., how are you?" I hadn't seen him since my return, and as I 51 waited for his answer a wave of memory crashed in my brain. He was the boy who had lived on the hill behind the school who rode his own horse and at fifteen picked as much cotton as the grown men. Despite his good looks he was never popular. He didn't talk unless forced. His mother had died when he was a baby, and his father drank moonshine, even during the week. The girls said he was womanish, and the boys that he was funny that way.

I commenced to giggle and flutter and he took my hand. 52

"Come on. Let's dance." 53

I agreed and caught the edge of the table to stand. Half erect, I noticed 54 that the building moved. It rippled and buckled as if a nest of snakes were mating beneath the floors. I was concerned, but the sloe gin had numbed my brain and I couldn't panic. I held on to the table and L. C.'s hand, and tried to straighten myself up.

"Sit down. I'll be right back." He took his hand away and I plopped 55 back into the chair. Sometime later he was back with a glass of water.

"Come on. Get up." His voice was raspy like old corn shucks. I set my 56 intention on getting up and pressed against the iron which had settled in my thighs.

"We're going to dance?" My words were thick and cumbersome and 57 didn't want to leave my mouth.

"Come on." He gave me his hand and I stumbled up and against him 58 and he guided me to the door.

Outside, the air was only a little darker and a little cooler, but it cleared 59 one corner of my brain. We were walking in the moist dirt along the pond, and the café was again a distant outline. With soberness came a concern for my virtue. Maybe he wasn't what they said.

"What are you going to do?" I stopped and faced him, readying myself 60 for his appeal.

"It's not me. It's you. You're going to throw up." He spoke slowly. 61 "You're going to put your finger down your throat and tickle, then you can puke."

With his intentions clear, I regained my pose. 62

"But I don't want to throw up. I'm not in the least—" 63

He closed a hand on my shoulder and shook me a little. "I say, put your 64 finger in your throat and get that mess out of your stomach."

I became indignant. How could he, a peasant, a nobody, presume to lecture me? I snatched my shoulder away. 65

"Really, I'm fine. I think I'll join my friends," I said and turned toward the café. 66

"Marguerite." It was no louder than his earlier tone but had more force than his hand. 67

"Yes?" I had been stopped. 68

"They're not your friends. They're laughing at you." He had mis-judged. They couldn't be laughing at me. Not with my sophistication and city ways. 69

"Are you crazy?" I sounded like a San Francisco-born debutante. 70

"No. You're funny to them. You got away. And then you came back. What for? And with what to show for your travels?" His tone was as soft as the Southern night and the pond lapping. "You come back swaggering and bragging that you've just been to paradise and you're wearing the very clothes everybody here wants to get rid of." 71

I hadn't stopped to think that while loud-flowered skirts and embroi-dered white blouses caused a few eyebrows to be raised in San Diego, in Stamps they formed the bulk of most girls' wardrobes. 72

L. C. went on, "They're saying you must be crazy. Even people in Texarkana dress better than you do. And you've been all the way to Califor-nia. They want to see you show your butt outright. So they gave you extra drinks of sloe gin." 73

He stopped for a second, then asked, "You don't drink, do you?" 74

"No." He had sobered me. 75

"Go on, throw up. I brought some water so you can rinse your mouth after." 76

He stepped away as I began to gag. The bitter strong strong fluid gur-gled out of my throat, burning my tongue. And the thought of nausea brought on new and stronger contractions. 77

After the cool water we walked back past the joint, and the music, still heavy, throbbed like gongs in my head. He left the glass by the porch and steered me in the direction of the Store. 78

His analysis had confused me and I couldn't understand why I should be the scapegoat. 79

He said, "They want to be free, free from this town, and crackers, and farming, and yes-sirring and no-sirring. You never were very friendly, so if you hadn't gone anywhere, they wouldn't have liked you any more. I was born here, and will die here, and they've never liked me." He was resigned and without obvious sorrow. 80

"But, L. C., why don't you get away?" 81

"And what would my poppa do? I'm all he's got." He stopped me before I could answer, and went on, "Sometimes I bring home my salary and he drinks it up before I can buy food for the week. Your grandmother knows. She lets me have credit all the time." 82

We were nearing the Store and he kept talking as if I weren't there. I  83
knew for sure that he was going to continue talking to himself after I was
safely in my bed.

"I've thought about going to New Orleans or Dallas, but all I know is  84
how to chop cotton, pick cotton and hoe potatoes. Even if I could save the
money to take Poppa with me, where would I get work in the city? That's
what happened to him, you know? After my mother died he wanted to leave
the house, but where could he go? Sometimes when he's drunk two bottles
of White Lightning, he talks to her. 'Reenie, I can see you standing there.
How come you didn't take me with you, Reenie? I ain't got no place to go,
Reenie. I want to be with you, Reenie.' And I act like I don't even hear him."

We had reached the back door of the Store. He held out his hand.  85

"Here, chew these Sen-sen. Sister Henderson ought not know you've  86
been drinking. Good night, Marguerite. Take it easy."

And he melted into the darker darkness. The following year I heard that  87
he had blown his brains out with a shotgun on the day of his father's funeral.

## STUDY QUESTIONS

1. What different contrasts are involved between the "American fantasy" described
   in paragraph 1 and the realities the NARRATOR finds in the South she returns to?
   How much of the difference involves black life under segregation? What kind of
   language is used to describe the fantasy in paragraph 1? What STEREOTYPES are
   involved? What RITUALS?

2. Why is memory described primarily in terms of sense impressions? Which sense
   memories seem especially vivid? How do sense impressions become associated with
   feelings, ideas, and principles?

3. Describe the language used to greet the new baby when the narrator returns to
   Arkansas as an adult with a newborn child in her arms. Out of what customs does
   the language derive? out of what values? What contrasts between life in Arkansas
   and California is the narrator immediately aware of? What differences does she
   come to understand later? What, precisely, brings about her later recognitions?

4. How dependent is the language of the narrator's family on their religious habits
   and beliefs? What Store customs demonstrate a dependence on ritual and on a
   careful sorting out of behavioral conventions? On what distinctions is such behavior based? How does the language used in the Store depend on established rituals?
   How is the body language related to the words spoken?

5. How do the verbal exchanges between the older people and young people before
   the evening on the town demonstrate contrasts between generational values? How
   do the events in the Dew Drop In Café relate to those contrasts? To what kinds of
   language do the narrator's values belong?

6. How many different "languages" can you define in this brief account? What are
   the distinct characteristics of each? Which are associated with region? with com-

munity? with race? with age? On what specific kinds of values does each language depend?

# Toshio Mori

Born in California of Japanese ancestry in 1910, Toshio Mori is the author of the novel *Woman from Hiroshima* (1979). He is, however, best known for his short stories, which have been collected in the volumes *Yokohama, California* (1949) and *The Chauvinist and Other Stories* (1979).

The following story describes a young (but gradually growing older) man whose only ambition is to become a Shakespearean actor.

## JAPANESE HAMLET

He used to come to the house and ask me to hear him recite. Each time he handed me a volume of *The Complete Works of William Shakespeare*. He never forgot to do that. He wanted me to sit in front of him, open the book, and follow him as he recited his lines. I did willingly. There was little for me to do in the evenings so when Tom Fukunaga came over I was ready to help out almost any time. And as his love for Shakespeare's plays grew with the years he did not want anything else in the world but to be a Shakespearean actor.

Tom Fukunaga was a schoolboy in a Piedmont home. He had been one since his freshman days in high school. When he was thirty-one he was still a schoolboy. Nobody knew his age but he and the relatives. Every time his relatives came to the city they put up a roar and said he was a good-for-nothing loafer and ought to be ashamed of himself for being a schoolboy at this age.

"I am not loafing," he told his relatives. "I am studying very hard."

One of his uncles came often to the city to see him. He tried a number of times to persuade Tom to quit stage hopes and schoolboy attitude. "Your parents have already disowned you. Come to your senses," he said. "You should go out and earn a man's salary. You are alone now. Pretty soon even your relatives will drop you."

"That's all right," Tom Fukunaga said. He kept shaking his head until his uncle went away.

When Tom Fukunaga came over to the house he used to tell me about     6
his parents and relatives in the country. He told me in particular about the
uncle who kept coming back to warn and persuade him. Tom said he really
was sorry for Uncle Bill to take the trouble to see him.

"Why don't you work for someone in the daytime and study at night?"     7
I said to Tom.

"I cannot be bothered with such a change at this time," he said. "Besides,     8
I get five dollars a week plus room and board. That is enough for me. If I
should go out and work for someone I would have to pay for room and board
besides carfare so I would not be richer. And even if I should save a little
more it would not help me become a better Shakespearean actor."

When we came down to the business of recitation there was no recess.     9
Tom Fukunaga wanted none of it. He would place a cup of water before him
and never touch it. "Tonight we'll begin with Hamlet," he said many times
during the years. Hamlet was his favorite play. When he talked about Shakespeare to anyone he began by mentioning Hamlet. He played parts in other
plays but always he came back to Hamlet. This was his special role, the role
which would establish him in Shakespearean history.

There were moments when I was afraid that Tom's energy and time     10
were wasted and I helped along to waste it. We were miles away from the
stage world. Tom Fukunaga had not seen a backstage. He was just as far
from the stagedoor in his thirties as he was in his high school days. Sometimes as I sat holding Shakespeare's book and listening to Tom I must have
looked worried and discouraged.

"Come on, come on!" he said. "Have you got the blues?"     11

One day I told him the truth: I was afraid we were not getting any-     12
where, that perhaps we were attempting the impossible. "If you could contact the stage people it might help," I said. "Otherwise we are wasting our
lives."

"I don't think so," Tom said. "I am improving every day. That is what     13
counts. Our time will come later."

That night we took up Macbeth. He went through his parts smoothly.     14
This made him feel good. "Some day I'll be the ranking Shakespearean actor,"
he said.

Sometimes I told him I liked best to hear him recite the sonnets. I thought     15
he was better with the sonnets than in the parts of Macbeth or Hamlet.

"I'd much rather hear you recite his sonnets, Tom." I said.     16

"Perhaps you like his sonnets best of all," he said. "Hamlet is my forte.     17
I know I am at my best playing Hamlet."

For a year Tom Fukunaga did not miss a week coming to the house.     18
Each time he brought a copy of Shakespeare's complete works and asked me
to hear him say the lines. For better or worse he was not a bit downhearted.
He still had no contact with the stage people. He did not talk about his uncle
who kept coming back urging him to quit. I found out later that his uncle
did not come to see him any more.

In the meantime Tom stayed at the Piedmont home as a schoolboy. He 19 accepted his five dollars a week just as he had done years ago when he was a freshman at Piedmont High. This fact did not bother Tom at all when I mentioned it to him. "What are you worrying for?" he said. "I know I am taking chances. I went into this with my eyes open so don't worry."

But I could not get over worrying about Tom Fukunaga's chances. Every 20 time he came over I felt bad for he was wasting his life and for the fact that I was mixed in it. Several times I told him to go somewhere and find a job. He laughed. He kept coming to the house and asked me to sit and hear him recite Hamlet.

The longer I came to know Tom the more I wished to see him well off 21 in business or with a job. I got so I could not stand his coming to the house and asking me to sit while he recited. I began to dread his presence in the house as if his figure reminded me of my part in the mock play that his life was, and the prominence that my house and attention played.

One night I became desperate. "That book is destroying you, Tom. 22 Why don't you give this up for awhile?"

He looked at me curiously without a word. He recited several pages and 23 left early that evening.

Tom did not come to the house again. I guess it got so that Tom could 24 not stand me any more than his uncle and parents. When he quit coming I felt bad. I knew he would never abandon his ambition. I was equally sure that Tom would never rank with the great Shakespearean actors, but I could not forget his simple persistence.

One day, years later, I saw him on the Piedmont car at Fourteenth and 25 Broadway. He was sitting with his head buried in a book and I was sure it was a copy of Shakespeare's. For a moment he looked up and stared at me as if I were a stranger. Then his face broke into a smile and he raised his hand. I waved back eagerly.

"How are you, Tom?" I shouted. 26

He waved his hand politely again but did not get off, and the car started 27 up Broadway.

## STUDY QUESTIONS

1. How much do we know about Tom Fukunaga? about the NARRATOR? about their relationship beyond the reading of Shakespeare? How much do we know about Tom's family? about other aspects of his life?

2. This story was first published in 1939. What facts in the story are explained by the temporal SETTING? Piedmont is a town between Oakland and Berkeley that could, in the 1930s, be reached by streetcar from San Francisco. What does the setting in San Francisco have to do with the story's situation? Why is the place where the narrator sees Tom at the end significant?

3. What function does Tom's uncle perform in the story? How powerful a force does Tom's family represent? Why does the uncle's prediction (paragraph 4) that "pretty soon even your relatives will drop you" come true?

4. How significant is Tom's age? his allowance as a schoolboy?

5. Why doesn't the narrator say more about Tom's ability as an actor? What role does language play in the story? in Tom's dreams? in the family's attitudes? in the narrator's feelings?

6. Why does Tom refuse to become acquainted with the realities of stage production? Why might he be especially attracted to *Hamlet?* How important is Tom to the narrator? the narrator to Tom?


# James Alan McPherson


James Alan McPherson was born in Savannah, Georgia, in 1943 and educated at Harvard Law School. His stories have been collected in *Hue and Cry* (1969) and *Elbow Room* (1977), the latter of which won a Pulitzer Prize.

In the following story, a black American couple become aware of suspicious behavior in a small London hotel and discover that the room next to theirs, occupied by two Japanese students, has been burglarized. The story records a welter of cross-cultural misunderstandings and suspicions, and much of its effect is produced by an insistence on stereotyping that interferes repeatedly with even the best-intentioned attempts to communicate.


## I AM AN AMERICAN


It was not the kind of service one would expect, considering the quality of the hotel. At eight o'clock both Eunice and I were awakened by a heavy pounding on the door of our room that sounded once, loud and authoritatively, then decreased into what seemed a series of pulsing echoes. I staggered across the dirty rug, feeling loose grit underfoot, and opened the door. Halfway down the hall a rotund little man, seeming no more than a blur of blue suit and red tie, was pounding steadily on another door and shouting, "American girlies, wake up! Breakfast!"

"Telephone?" I called to him.

"Breakfast!" he shouted cheerily, turning his face only slightly in my direction. I could not see the details of his face, although it seemed to me his nose was large and red, and his hair was close-cropped and iron gray. For some reason, perhaps because of the way his suit was cut, I nursed the intuition that he was a Bulgarian, although there are many other eastern Europeans who wear the same loose style of suit. Just then the door before him opened. "Breakfast, American girlies!" he called into the room. From where I stood in my own doorway, stalled by sleepiness as much as by lingering curiosity, I glimpsed a mass of disarranged blond hair leaning out the door toward the man. "We'll be right down," a tired voice said. But the man was already moving down the hall toward the next door.

"Who was it?" Eunice asked from the bed.                                              4

"Time for breakfast," I said, and slammed the door. I had been expect-    5
ing something more than a call for breakfast. We had come over from Paris to London in hopes of making a connection. All during the hot train ride the previous afternoon, from Gare du Nord to Calais, from Dover to Paddington Station, we had built up in our imaginations X, our only local connection, into a personage of major importance and influence in matters of London tourism. But so far he had not called.

While Eunice unpacked fresh clothes, I sat on the bed smoking a ciga-    6
rette and assessed our situation. We could wander about the city on our own, call X again, or wait politely for him to call on us. But the thought of waiting in the room through the morning was distasteful. Looking around, I saw again what I had been too reluctant to perceive when we checked in the evening before. The room was drab. Its high ceiling, watermarked and cracked in places, seemed a mocking reminder of the elegance that might have once characterized the entire building. The rug was dusty and footworn from tramping tourists and the sheer weight of time. The thin mattress, during the night, had pressed into my back the history of many bodies it had borne. This was not Dick Whittington's magic London.

"Hurry up!" Eunice ordered. "They stop serving breakfast at nine o'clock."    7
She opened the door, pulling her robe close about her neck. "I'll use that john down the hall, and then you get out until after I wash up in the face bowl." As she went out, I glanced over at the yellowing face bowl. The sight of it provided another reason for giving up the room. After digging out my toothbrush from my suitcase, I stood over the bowl brushing my teeth and trying to remember just why we had come to London.

One reason might have been our having grown tired of being mere tour-    8
ists. In the Louvre two mornings before, among a crowd of American tourists standing transfixed before the Old Masters of Renaissance painting, I had suddenly found myself pointing a finger and exclaiming to Eunice, "Hey, didn't they name a cheese after that guy?"

"Leroy, they did no such a-thing!" Eunice had hissed.                              9

The other tourists had laughed nerviously.                                        10

Eunice had pulled me out of the Louvre, though not by the ear.                    11

That same morning I had decided to wire one of a list of London people    12
suggested to us by friends back home in Atlanta. Their advice had been the

usual in such matters: "Be sure to look up X. We're good friends. He showed us a good time when we were in London, and we showed him a good time when he came to Atlanta. Be sure to tell him all the news about us." My wire to X had been humble: "We are Leroy and Eunice Foster from Atlanta, friends of Y and Z. Will be in London on weekend. Would like to see you." X's reply, which arrived the next morning, was efficient: "Call at home on arrival. X." And so we had raced from Paris to London. Upon arrival, as I instructed, I called up X.

"Y and Z who?" he asked, after I introduced myself.                13

I gave their full names. "They send warm regards from Atlanta," I added   14
smoothly.

"Yes," X said. "They're fine people. I always regretted I never got to   15
know them well."

"They're fine people," I said.                                           16

"Yes," X allowed. "I've got a bit of a flu right now, you know."         17

So we were in London. We located a room a few blocks from the train      18
station and were content to let be. The room was in a neat, white Georgian house that, at some point during that time when American tourists first began arriving en masse, had been converted into a hotel. Such places abound in London; many of them are quite pleasant. But the interior of this one was bleak, as was the room we secured on the fourth floor. To compound our displeasure, the landlady had insisted that we declare exactly how long we planned to stay, and then pay for that period in advance. This was one of those periodic lapses of faith in the American dollar. American tourists suffered with it. But watchful landlords from Lyons to Wales refused to show the slightest mercy. "These are class rooms, love," the landlady had declared, inspecting our faces over the tops of her glasses. She was a plump woman who fidgeted impatiently inside a loose gray smock. "There's lots of people callin' for rooms," she reminded us. "All the time," she added.

We had been in no position to haggle. Having entered London on the       19
eve of a bank holiday weekend, we had no choice but to cash more traveler's checks and pay rent through the following Monday morning. Only then did the landlady issue us a single set of keys: one for the street door, which was always locked, and one for our room. To further frustrate us, I found that the lobby pay telephone did not work. This required me to walk back to the station to ring up X and supply him with our address. He did not seem enthusiastic about getting it, but said he might call on us the next day, if his flu showed signs of abating. Discovering, finally, that the toilet on our floor barely flushed, and that the bathtub was unhealthily dirty, we went to bed with curses rumbling in us and the dust of the road still clinging to our skins.

Considering the many little frustrations that marred our arrival in Lon-  20
don, we were very pleased to have been awakened for breakfast by the house porter. After Eunice returned to the room, I went out into the hall and waited in line for my turn in the john. I was not even perturbed that the two Orientals, occupying the room next to ours, took long chances at the toilet.

While one occupied the stall, the other stood outside the door as if on guard. Standing behind him, I noted that he was tall and slim and conservatively dressed in a white shirt and black trousers. He seemed aloof, even reserved, though not inscrutable. This I could tell from the way his brows lifted and his ears perked, like mine, each time his companion made a vain attempt to flush the slowly gurgling toilet. Indeed, the two of us outside the door tried with the companion: we strained to apply our own pressures to the loose handle, to join in his anticipation of a solid and satisfying flush. But, unlike me, the Oriental did not shift from foot to foot each time his companion's failure was announced by strained gurgles and hisses from behind the closed door. Standing straight as a Samurai, he seemed more intent on studying my movements, without seeming to, than on commandeering the john. I wanted to communicate with him, but did not want to presume that he spoke English. To further compound the problem, I could not tell if he was Japanese or Chinese. In Paris I had seen Chinese tourists, but they had been uniformed in the colors of Chairman Mao. This fellow wore western clothes. The problem became academic, however, when I recalled that the only Oriental phrases I knew were derived from a few sessions in a class in Mandarin I had once attended. I could never hope to master the very intricate and delicate degrees of inflection required, but I had managed to bring away from the class a few phrases lodged in memory, one of which was a greeting and the other introducing me as an American.

"Ni hau ma?" I inquired with a broad smile.                                              21

At first the Oriental stared at me in silence. Then he pointed a finger at       22
his chest. "I next," he said. Then he pointed a finger at my chest. "You next."

He was right. I shifted from one foot to the other until finally there           23
came the welcome sound of his companion's mastery of English hydraulics. As the companion stepped out of the stall and my acquaintance went in, I wanted to caution him that he need not be as concerned with a matter as ephemeral as decorum. But the desire died aborning. I did not have the language, and could only continue to shift from foot to foot. And sadly, very shortly afterward, while the second Oriental waited by the stairs, there came the same dry, strained sound of the very same difficulty. The situation was hopeless. I brushed past the companion and raced down the stairs to the third floor. But that stall too was in use. The one on the second floor offered even less hope: an elderly couple and a young man stood shifting in front of it.

On the ground floor, off the lobby, I ran into the same little man, still        24
seeming to me like nothing if not a Bulgarian, still knocking on doors and shouting, "Americans! Americans! Get up for breakfast!" When he saw me he turned, again ever so slightly, and said, "That way," pointing toward the door to the street. "Hurry! Hurry! Only served from eight to nine." I nodded my thanks and, seeing no stall on that floor, raced back up the stairs. Just below the third floor the two Orientals passed me on their way down. "Ni hau ma?" I called to them. They stopped and looked at each other, then

at me. The taller man spoke in a high, hurried tone to the other. Then his companion nodded enthusiastically and said, "Oh!" He looked at me, pointed a finger up the stairs and said, "Open now."

He was right.                                                                                                      25

Going down for breakfast, finally, Eunice and I passed the little blue-   26
suited man in the lobby. He seemed about to go out the door, but as we approached he stepped aside and held the portal open for us. "Breakfast that way," he said, smiling. "In the basement." We thanked him and walked out the door, along a few feet of pavement, and down into the basement of the adjoining house. The little room was dank and smelled of rancid bacon. About a score of people, mostly Americans, were seated at the cloth-covered tables. We could tell they were Americans by the way they avoided eye contact. One girl was speaking halting French with a West Texas accent to two male companions who only listened. Over against the wall a middle-aged couple was poring over a *Herald-Tribune* stretched out beside their plates of bacon and eggs. "You just wait till we get back," the man was saying in a loud voice. "I'll *get* the sonofbitches for doin' this to me!" His wife kept looking up from her reading and saying, "Now Bob . . . now Bob . . ." Eunice and I went to a table at the far side of the room. At the table next to ours a rather attractive girl was eating rapidly and saying to the young man with her, "Cadiz was an utter bore. Madrid was an utter bore. . . . There's too many kids in Copenhagen. . . . Italian men are the *nastiest* men on earth! . . . "

"Aw, shut up and eat," her friend said.                                                                            27

Across the room, seemingly at a distance, the two Orientals ate their   28
meal in silence, looking only at each other.

The landlady's assistant brought our plates out from the kitchen. She   29
was pale and dumpy, with dull auburn hair done up in a ragged bun. She seemed immune to all of us in the room. She slid two plates onto our table, plunked down a dish of jam, and sashayed back into the kitchen.

"You know," Eunice said, inspecting the food, "it's kind of funny."      30
"What?" I asked.                                                                                                   31
"That a place as sloppy as this can afford to have somebody wake you   32
up for breakfast. This kind of place, the more people miss breakfast, the more food they save."

"You know," I said, after reflecting a moment, "it *is* kind of funny that   33
that little Bulgarian was heading *out* the door when we came down, but stepped back *inside* the second we went out."

Eunice laid down her fork. "It's more than funny," she said. "It's pure-   34
dee suspicious."

"It's more than suspicious," I added. "It could be downright slick."       35
Both of us looked around the room. Everyone was eating.                    36
"I been telling you, Leroy," Eunice said. "It's good sense to riff in a   37
place where you don't know the score." She fished the keys from her purse. "Which one of us go'n go up?"

But I had already eased out of my seat and was on my way. In a few   38 seconds I had unlocked the front door and stepped quickly into the hall. Although I ran up the three flights of stairs on tiptoe, the aged boards betrayed my presence. And just as I reached the fourth floor landing, I saw the little blue-suited man backing quickly out the door of the room next to ours. I paused. He turned and smiled at me, shutting the door and giving a theatrical turn to the doorknob. Then he walked calmly over to the linen closet, opened it, and peered inside. At first he frowned in exasperation, then he patted a stack of folded sheets and smiled reassuringly at me. Turning, he waltzed slowly to the stairs and went down. By this time I had opened my own door. Nothing in the room seemed to have been disturbed. I checked our suitcases. Eunice's camera was still there, as were the gifts she had purchased in Paris. But my suspicions were not eased. After locking the door, I rushed down to the breakfast room and directly to the table where the two Orientals were eating their meals. "Ni hau mau?" I said hurriedly. Again they stared at each other, then at me. "Not open?" the one who had the better command of English, the shorter of the two, said to me. He was dressed like his companion, except that his short-sleeved shirt was light green. And he carried a row of pens on a plastic clip in the breast pocket of his shirt.

"I think you had better check your room," I said as slowly as my excitement would allow. "I-think-you-had-better-check-your-room," I repeated even more slowly. "I-just-saw-a-man-com-ing-out-of-it." 39

He screwed up his face. "English is not good to us," he said. "Please to speak more slow." 40

I pointed to my keys and then raised a finger in the direction of the other building. "I-think-your-room-may-have-been-*robbed!*" I said. 41

"*Rob?*" he said. 42

"I saw a man come out of there." 43

"Rob," he repeated slowly to his companion. 44

To avoid seeming to caricature a fine and extremely proud people, I will not attempt to relate the development of their conversation after that point. They consulted extensively across the table in their own language. From their gestures and eye movements I could tell that the discussion included references to me, Eunice, the landlady, the quality of the meal, and the lazy toilet way up on the fourth floor. Then one word of their own language, sounding like "New Sunday," seemed to come suddenly into focus. It bounded back and forth between them across the table. The word excited them, made them anxious, perhaps even angry. The spokesman repeated "New Sunday" to me with sufficient force to make me know that my suspicion had been absorbed, and then run through their own language until it settled around a corresponding thought. "New Sunday—*robbed*," I said in answer, nodding my head. 45

Both of them leaped up from the table and rushed toward the door. Most people in the room turned to look after them. Only after the two had vanished did the tourists turn their eyes on me. I slipped back to where Eunice waited at our table. By this time my eggs had hardened into a thin 46 layer of yellow mush encrusted in bacon fat. I sipped the cup of cold tea and waited.

"Leroy, maybe it was a false alarm," Eunice said. 47

"Those Chinese don't think so," I told her. 48

Eunice frowned. "Those aren't Chinese." 49

"Well, they ain't Koreans," I observed. 50

"They're Japanese," Eunice said. "How could you be so dumb?" 51

"How can *you* be so sure?" 52

"All you have to do is *look* at them," Eunice told me. "Japanese are like 53 upper-class people down home. They don't look around much because they *know* who *they* are in relation to everybody else."

"Bullshit," I said. "They're Chinese. Whoever saw Japanese without 54 cameras?"

"Leroy, you're a black bigot," Eunice told me. "And a *dumb* one at that," 55 she added.

"But not in *public!*" I whispered through my teeth. Over at the next 56 table the young man was watching us intently. But soon he turned back to his companion and her complaints—this time against Etruscan art.

We waited. 57

In a few minutes the two Orientals came rushing back into the room. 58 The taller one pointed at me and spoke hurriedly to his companion. Then the two of them came over to our table. "Please to say Japanese students are . . . rob in hotel."

"New Sundayed?" I asked. 59

The young man nodded. 60

I said I was sorry to hear it. 61

"You see doorrobber?" He breathed excitedly. 62

I admitted that both of us had seen the man, although I was careful not 63 to say that to me he seemed to be a Bulgarian.

The taller student spoke to his companion. 64

"He complains for police," the spokesman translated. 65

I agreed that should be done. Leaving Eunice at the table gloating pride- 66 fully over the sharpness of her insight, I led the two students back into the kitchen. The landlady was scraping bacon fat off the top of her black range. She glanced up at the three of us over her glasses and said, "What you want, love?"

The man in the green shirt, the shorter of the two, attempted to explain; 67 but he seemed unable to muster sufficient English, or sufficient interest on the landlady's part, to make her appreciate how seriously he viewed the sit- uation. While he was speaking, the service lady came in from the breakfast room with a stack of plates. She squeezed past the three of us, further upset- ting the student in his recital. "Pity what these blokes does to the language," she muttered.

At this point I interrupted the student with a bow intended to be polite. 68 I explained to the landlady the ploy used in the robbery and a description of the man whom I suspected of the deed. But I did not volunteer my suspicion that he looked to me to be a Bulgarian.

"What was took off you?" the landlady asked the two, and I thought I detected suspicion in her voice. They did not understand, so I translated as best I could, using sign language and the smallest part of pig Latin. Between the three of us it was finally determined that the thief had taken two Eurail passes, two Japanese passports, and about one hundred dollars in traveler's checks drawn on the bank of Tokyo. 69

"Shssss!" whispered the landlady. "Don't talk so *loud*, love! You want the other guests to hear?" Then she turned to the service lady, who leaned against a cupboard with her thick arms folded, and said, "Think they'd know enough to lock up their valuables." Then she faced the three of us again and said. "We can't be *responsible* for all that, duckies. There's signs on all the doors tellin' you to keep valuables under padlock. Regulations, you know." 70

Even without understanding fully what had been said, both students seemed to sense they could make more progress into the theft on their own. "Go search doorrobber," the short man said. 71

The electricity of their excitement sparked into me. As they left the basement I stepped quickly behind them, recalling all the scenes dealing with personal honor I had viewed in Japanese movies. I had the feeling of being part of a posse. As one of the students was unlocking the door, his companion suddenly gave out a shrill cry and jumped several feet in the air. He kept repeating, "*Aa! Aa! Aa!*" and pointed down the street with a quick movement of his arm. I looked immediately where he pointed, but did not see the man whom I suspected of being the thief. But the other student looked in the same direction, and what he saw made him shout back to his comrade. Looking again, I saw the cause of their excitement: a rather chubby Oriental man was walking up the street toward us. The two students rushed toward the man. After greeting him, and after a few gestures, the three of them, shouting something that sounded like "Waa Waa! Waa!" swept past me and into the building. The spokesman paused beside me long enough to say, "Please to watch door." 72

Waiting excitedly on the bottom step, I imagined them searching the building from attic to basement, peering into keyholes, dark stairwells, the johns on each floor, trying doors, linen closets, open windows. I pictured the little Bulgarian cornered in the hall, trying to understand what they could possibly mean when they said in cultured Japanese, "You have dishonored the hospitality of this house. You will please commit hara-kiri." And the little fellow, sneak thief that he was, would echo the countercode: "*Why?* I want to *live!*" I expected to see at any moment the little blue-suited fellow come pumping out the door, his red tie trailing in the wind he made, with the three Japanese in hot pursuit. When Eunice came up from the basement, I urged her to take a long walk around the block. I advised that I anticipated 73 horrors from which her modesty should be protected. But Eunice refused to budge from where she stood on the sidewalk.

"Leroy, you're overreacting," she said. 74

Eunice was right as usual. 75

Instead of three samurai bearing the head of the thief, only the two 76 Japanese students and their newfound tourist ally emerged from the building. They sighed and looked up and down the street, perhaps looking for additional samurai, perhaps looking for bobbies. I sighed, and looked with them. But there was nothing else on the street we could add to our resources. The three conversed among themselves in Japanese, and then the stranger turned to me. "This Japanese salaryman from Osaka," the English-speaking student announced.

"Ni hau ma?" I said, offering my hand as the man bowed smartly. 77

"You are African?" the man asked, smiling pleasantly as we shook. 78 "Nigerian, yes?"

"Woo sh Meei-gworen," I said. 79

He looked perplexed. "I do not know this tribe," he confessed finally. 80 "But now I must go. They should get the officials to help them," he told me. He turned and made a short statement to the students in Japanese. Then he shook my hand again, bowed smartly to the students, and went on his way up the block.

"What was that foolishness you were talking?" Eunice asked. 81

The English-speaking student strolled closer to me. He looked deep into 82 my face and said, "All *open* upstair."

"You ought to be horsewhipped for carryin' on such foolishness at a 83 serious time like this," Eunice said.

Of course Eunice was right. 84

For the second time we crowded into the kitchen to register our com- 85 plaint with the landlady. "Pipe *down*, love!" she muttered. "We don't want the others to hear, now do we?"

"Why not?" I asked. 86

She stood with her back against the black gas range. "What can *I* do?" 87

"Call up the bobbies." 88

She mumbled some more to herself, gave us a cold stare, then fished 89 around in the pocket of her gray smock and produced a shilling and a few pence for the telephone. As we passed again through the breakfast room, the other tourists stared at us as though we were entertainers employed by the landlady to make the breakfast hour less monotonous. I wondered how many of them had been robbed while they sat leisurely over their bacon and eggs. And I wondered whether the little Bulgarian had anticipated they would have this blind spot.

I glanced at the table Eunice and I had occupied. It had been cleared 90 and another couple, who looked German, now occupied it. They ate in silence and looked only at each other. But at the next table the little brunette was still preaching over cold tea to her companion: "Spain was *so* depressing. The French ignore you in August. Zurich looks like a big computer. Greek men . . ."

We were inside the lobby before I remembered the telephone did not work.                                                                                      91

After getting directions from a passerby and advising Eunice to wait outside, lest the Bulgarian should be lurking in our room, the two Japanese and I walked toward a bobby station, said to be about a mile from the hotel. During the walk they managed to communicate to me their names and the outline of their dilemma. The spokesman's name was Toyohiko Kageyama. His tall companion, who apparently knew little English, was Yoshitsune Hashima. I told them to call me Lee. Toyohiko explained that without the traveler's checks, passports and rail passes they could not get to Amsterdam, where their flight back to Japan would depart in a few days. And with the bank holiday in effect, they would not be able to obtain more traveler's checks until Monday, when the banks reopened. Unfortunately, Monday was also the day their flight was to leave Amsterdam.                                                92

They talked between themselves in Japanese, working through the problem. They decided that with help from the Japanese embassy they might be able to obtain money for a flight to Amsterdam. But there was still the matter of the missing passports. I did not learn this by listening to their conversation, but through the pains taken by Toyohiko Kageyama to explain the problem to me in English. So far as I could tell, neither of them made any unkind remarks about the thief. Instead, they seemed to have accepted the loss and were working toward solution of the problem it caused. As we talked, Yoshitsune Hashima looked at the two of us, nodding occasional, though hesitant, agreement with whatever Kageyama said to me. But neither one of them smiled.                                                                          93

When we arrived at the bobby station, a bleak little building containing almost no activity, I excused myself and sat in the waiting room while the two Japanese stood at the reception desk and reported the robbery to the desk officer. He was a pale, elderly man with a gray-speckled pencil-line mustache. He listened carefully, occasionally drumming his pen on a report form, while suggesting words to Toyohiko Kageyama. The student had difficulty making the bobby recognize the name of the hotel and the street on which it was located, as well as the items that had been stolen. After many trials and errors by the bobby, Kageyama came over to me. "Please tell," he said.                                                                                       94

I went to the desk and reported to the bobby as much as I knew about the robbery. I gave him a description of the man whom I suspected of being the thief, but I did not volunteer my suspicion that to me he seemed to be a Bulgarian. The bobby wrote it all down on a report form, then questioned us again for corroboration. Afterward, he wrote something of his own at the                  95 bottom of the form, perhaps a private comment, perhaps his own name. Then the students and I sat in the waiting room, while a pair of bobbies was summoned to accompany us back to the hotel. These were somewhat younger men, although one of them sported the same kind of thin mustache as the bobby at the desk. The other was plump, with tufts of bright red hair showing beneath his tall hat. He had a cold manner that became evident when he motioned us out of the building and into the back seat of their patrol car. The gesture was one of professional annoyance.

During the drive back to the hotel, the students and I were silent, but the two bobbies in the front seat discussed a recent rally of homosexuals in Trafalgar Square.   96

"What a hellish sight that one was," the redhead observed.   97

"No doubt," the other said. "No doubt."   98

"At least five hundred of them parading round like the Queens of Elfin."   99

"No doubt," said the other. "Any trouble?"   100

The redhead laughed. "No," he said grimly.   101

The two Japanese students sat next to each other, their eyes looking past the bobbies and through the windshield of the car. Only I concentrated on the conversation. And after a while, I found myself wondering about how I had come to be driving through the streets of London in the back seat of a bobby car listening to commentary on a rally of homosexuals, when my major purpose in coming over from Paris had been to contact X, that elusive knower of London nightlife, and give him the warm regards of Y and Z, friends of his who lived in Atlanta.   102

The two bobbies searched the hotel from top to bottom, but they did not find the man. No one else had reported anything missing. The landlady flitted around with a great show of sympathy, explaining to the bobbies that this sort of thing had not happened in her place since the boom in American tourists back in '65. Both bobbies were cool and efficient, asking questions in a manner that suggested their suspicion of everyone and of no one in particular. But the redhead, it seemed to me, was more than probing in his questions concerning the part Eunice and I had played in the drama. He said finally, "There's little else we can do now except get a notice out. You'll have to go over to the station for the Paddington district and make a report there. This isn't our district, you know; so they'll need a bit of a report over there."   103

"People should be careful of these things," the landlady said, wiping her hands on her apron.   104

"It's ten-thirty," Eunice said. "We want to go sightseeing."   105

The redhead smiled cryptically. "He'll have to go along to make a proper description," he advised Eunice. "It would be quite helpful to these two chaps here."   106

"I'm sick and tired of all the running around," Eunice said.   107

The bobby smiled.   108

The two Orientals stood watching all of us.   109

The drive to the other district station was short. The bobbies did not   110
talk more about the rally of homosexuals. They let us out in front of the
station and wished us luck. I wished them a happy bank holiday. Inside the
station the routine was the same as before: while the students explained their
predicament as best they could, I stayed in the waiting room until I was
needed. Waiting, I amused myself by studying the wanted posters on the
bulletin board hanging between the windows. Walking close to the board for
a closer inspection, I saw that four of the seven wanted men were black.
Moreover, one of them, a hardcase named Wimberly Lane, priced at fifty
pounds and wanted for extortion, looked somewhat familiar. I studied his
face. Lane had high cheekbones, prominent eyes, and a dissolute look about
him. I looked closer and saw that he resembled, especially in profile, my
cousin Freddy Tifton back home in Atlanta. But Lane was a desperado,
probably hiding out in the London underworld, and my cousin was a world
away in Atlanta, probably at the moment eating fried chicken on Hunter
Street.

"Please tell about . . . doorrobber," someone said. Toyohiko Kageyama   111
was standing behind me.

I turned and followed him back to the desk. This bobby's pale blue eyes   112
flickered over my face. He and another man, a clerk who had obviously been
helping him piece together the story told by the students, glanced quickly at
each other and then back at me. "You saw the alleged robber?" the bobby
asked.

"I did."   113

"Can you describe him?"   114

I gave what I thought was an accurate description. But this time I was   115
sure not to venture my suspicion that he seemed to me to be a Bulgarian.
The bobby wrote with his left hand. He wrote beautiful script with his pen
turned inward toward his wrist. I watched his hands.

The two students stood behind me, one on each side.   116

"Just what is your relation to the complainants?" the bobby asked.   117

"I am an American," I said. "My room is next to theirs."   118

The bobby stopped writing and frowned. "You are the only person who   119
actually *saw* this man, you know?" His eyes narrowed.

"What about it?" I said.   120

"A friend indeed, what?" the clerk said. He looked at the bobby and   121
winked.

The two students stood behind me, conversing between themselves.   122

"Not let's go through this *once* more," the bobby said.   123

Suddenly Yoshitsune Hashima stepped from behind me and up to the   124
desk. "Lee . . . good . . . de*tail*," he said, pointing firmly at me. "Japanese
students . . . take *Lee* detail . . . *doorrobber*."

The bobby stopped smiling and began writing again. He wrote a beau-   125
tiful script.

Yoshitsune Hashima did not speak again.   126

The bobby advised them to go quickly to the Japanese embassy.    127
I wanted to go quickly and see the rest of London.    128

We saw the two students again in the late afternoon at Madame Tus-    129
saud's. Eunice and I had wandered down into one of the lower chambers
with exhibits commemorating the French Revolution. When I saw them I
was standing beside a rusty guillotine that had been used to behead Marie
Antoinette. The Japanese were standing together, peering into a lighted
showcase containing wax replicas of famous murderers who had once plagued
London. I motioned to Eunice, then walked over and touched Kageyama on
the shoulder. He started, as if intruded upon too much by the mood of the
place. But when they saw who we were, both of them smiled nervously and
bowed. Toyohiko Kageyama reported that the Japanese embassy had secured
temporary passports for them, had ordered the checks cancelled, and had
lent them enough money for living expenses and a flight to Amsterdam. Now
that business had been taken care of, they were seeing the sights of London.
Both of them thanked us for our help. Kageyama in English and Hashima in
Japanese. Both of them bowed politely. Then Yoshitsune Hashima pulled a
notebook from the pocket of his trousers, leafed through it to a certain page,
and read in a slow voice, "Please-to-give-Japanese-students-name-and-house-
number."

I wrote them for him.    130

Yoshitsune Hashima accepted back the notebook, leafed through several    131
more pages, and read in an uncertain voice: "I thank you kindness at New
Sunday to help Japanese students. . . . I hope Lee visit Nihon one day. . . .
Please visit home of Yoshitsune Hashima in suburb of Tokyo."

Then he handed me a packet of Japanese stamps.    132

The two of them bowed again.    133

"You see?" Eunice said, as we walked away. "The Japanese ain't nothing    134
but part-time Southerners."

I had to concede that once again Eunice was right.    135

But it was too dark inside the wax museum. The colored lights shining    136
on the exhibits did not improve the mood of the place. "Let's get out," I said
to Eunice.

Toward dusk we stood in a crowd of tourists on a green outside the
Tower of London. We had spent about ten minutes inside the tower. Before
us on the green was an old man, encased in a white sack crisscrossed with
chains and padlocks. He wriggled and moaned inside the sack while the crowd
laughed. Standing beside him was a muscular, bald-headed man who beat
himself on the naked chest with a sledge-hammer. In certain respects this
man resembled the thief, but he not at all resembled a Bulgarian. From time
to time this strong man marched with a tin cup around the inside of the
circle, holding it out to onlookers. He collected pence and shillings from
some of those standing closest to the recreation. He said things like, "Me old
daddy left near a thousand pound when he died; but I ain't yet found out

where he left it." When the crowd laughed, he laughed with them. But he cursed those who put slugs and very small change in his cup. He seemed to be a foreigner, but he spoke with the accents of the British lower class. "A man 'as got to live!" he shouted at us while rattling the cup. "The old man there can't get out the sack till you pay up."

"Leroy," Eunice said beside me. "I don't think X will ever call. Now that we've seen London, let's please go home." 138

As usual, Eunice was right. 139

# STUDY QUESTIONS

1. If you only knew Americans from those in the breakfast room, what would your impressions of Americans be? What do Leroy and Eunice become suspicious of at breakfast? Why? What does Eunice mean when she says that it is "good sense to riff in a place where you don't know the score" (paragraph 37)?

2. What is the first indication you have of the ethnic identity of Leroy and Eunice? Does that make you reevaluate in any way what has gone before in the story? Does it change your anticipation of what is to come?

3. Explain the title of the story. Why does the NARRATOR, long after he recognizes that the two students are not Chinese, continue to use the only Mandarin phrases he knows?

4. Why does the narrator insist, repeatedly, that Eunice is right? About what in particular is Eunice always right? Why does the narrator keep repressing his conclusion that the burglar is Bulgarian? On what different STEREOTYPES of behavior does the plot depend?

5. Why does the story put so much emphasis on people watching other people? How self-conscious is the narrator about his observations of others? How conscious is he that he moves toward national stereotypes based on his observations? Explain the force of the policemen's suspicion about him.

6. How fully does the narrator ultimately communicate with the Japanese students? When words fail, what other kinds of language do the three men use? What eye, face, and body gestures reinforce the meanings of the words they speak?

7. In how many different situations does the narrator have difficulty communicating with other people who speak English? What are the sources of difficulty? What conventions of language are illuminated by the miscommunications with X? Is the narrator more comfortable speaking to the Japanese students than to other native speakers of English? If so, why?

8. Explain the IRONY of the service lady's observation "Pity what these blokes does to the language" (par. 67).

9. Explain the irony that the plot turns on unexpected behavior, given the fact that stereotypical behavior is under examination throughout the story.

# Israel Horovitz

B orn in Wakefield, Massachusetts, in 1939, Israel Horovitz was educated at the Royal Academy of Dramatic Art in London, the New School for Social Research, and the City University of New York. He has been playwright-in-residence with the Royal Shakespeare Company and has written television plays and screenplays in addition to plays for the stage.

*The Indian Wants the Bronx* was first produced off Broadway in 1968, ran for 177 performances, and won three Obie Awards. The play dramatizes a "game" that two insecure but boisterous youths play with an East Indian who is waiting for a bus in Manhattan. The Indian understands no English and the New Yorkers, who understand no Hindi, refuse to try to understand even the most elementary body language when the Indian asks for help. This language "barrier" comes to stand here not just for the inability of people from different worlds to understand one another but also for willful misunderstanding and a cruel refusal to satisfy basic human needs for relationship and security.

# THE INDIAN WANTS THE BRONX

### CHARACTERS

GUPTA, *an East Indian*
MURPH
JOEY

*Place: A bus stop on upper Fifth Avenue in New York City.*
*Time: A chilly September's night.*

*As the curtains open the lights fade up, revealing* GUPTA, *an East Indian. He is standing alone, right of center stage, near a bus stop sign. An outdoor telephone booth is to his left; several city-owned litter baskets are to his right.*

GUPTA *is in his early fifties. Although he is swarthy in complexion, he is anything but sinister. He is, in fact, meek and visibly frightened by the city.*

*He is dressed in traditional East Indian garb, appropriately for mid-September.*

*As* GUPTA *strains to look for a bus on the horizon, the voices of two boys can be heard in the distance, singing. They sing a rock-'n'-roll song, flatly, trying to harmonize.*

[FIRST BOY]
I walk the lonely streets at night,
A-lookin' for your door,
I look and look and look and look,
But, baby, you don't care.
Baby, you don't care.
Baby, no one cares.

SECOND BOY: [*Interrupting*] Wait a minute, Joey. I'll take the harmony. Listen.

[*Singing*]
But, baby, you don't care.
Baby, you don't care.
Baby, no one cares.

[*Confident that he has fully captured the correct harmony, boasting*] See? I've got a knack for harmony. You take the low part.

[BOYS *sing together*]
I walk . . . the lonely, lonely street . . .
A-listenin' for your heartbeat,
Listening for your love.
But, baby, you don't care.
Baby, you don't care.
Baby, no one cares.

[*They appear on stage.* FIRST BOY *is* JOEY. SECOND BOY *is* MURPH. JOEY *is slight, baby-faced, in his early twenties.* MURPH *is stronger, long-haired, the same age*]
[MURPH *singing*]
The lonely, lonely, streets, called out for lovin',
But there was no one to love . . .
'Cause, baby, you don't care . . .

[JOEY *joins in the singing*]
Baby, you don't care . . .

[JOEY AND MURPH *singing together*]
Baby, you don't care.
Baby, you don't care.
Baby, no one cares.
Baby, no one cares.

MURPH: [*Calls out into the audience, to the back row: across to the row of apartment houses opposite the park*] Hey, Pussyface! Can you hear your babies singing? Pussyface. We're calling you.

JOEY: [*Joins in*] Pussyface. Your babies are serenading your loveliness.

[*They laugh*]

MURPH: Baby, no one cares.

> [MURPH AND JOEY *singing together*]
> Baby, no one cares.
> Baby, no one cares.

MURPH: [*Screams*] Pussyface, you don't care, you Goddamned idiot! [*Notices the* INDIAN] Hey. Look at the Turk.

[JOEY *stares at the* INDIAN *for a moment, then replies*]

JOEY: Just another pretty face. Besides. That's no Turk. It's an Indian.

> [MURPH *continues to sing*]
> Baby, no one cares.

[*Dances to his song, strutting in the* INDIAN's *direction. He then turns back to* JOEY *during the completion of his stanza and feigns a boxing match*]

> I walk the lonely, lonely streets.
> A-callin' out for loving,
> But, baby, you don't give a Christ for
> Nothin' . . . not for nothin'.

[*Pretends to swing a punch at* JOEY, *who backs off laughing*] You're nuts. It's a Turk!

JOEY: Bet you a ten spot. It's an Indian.
MURPH: It's a Turk, schmuck. Look at his fancy hat. Indians don't wear fancy hats. [*Calls across the street, again*] Hey, Pussyface. Joey thinks we got an Indian. [*Back to* JOEY] Give me a cigarette.
JOEY: You owe me a pack already, Murphy.
MURPH: So I owe you a pack. Give me a cigarette.
JOEY: Say "please," maybe?
MURPH: Say "I'll bust your squash if you don't give me a cigarette!"
JOEY: One butt, one noogie.
MURPH: First the butt.
JOEY: You're a Jap, Murphy.

[*As* JOEY *extends the pack,* MURPH *grabs it*]

MURPH: You lost your chance, baby. [*To the apartment block*] Pussyface! Joey lost his chance!
JOEY: We made a deal. A deal's a deal. You're a Jap, Murphy. A rotten Jap. [*To the apartment*] Pussyface, listen to me! Murphy's a rotten Jap and just

Japed my whole pack. That's unethical, Pussyface. He owes me noo-gies, too!

MURPH: Now I'll give you twenty noogies, so we'll be even.

[*He raps* JOEY *on the arm. The* INDIAN *looks up as* JOEY *squeals*]

JOEY: Hey. The Indian's watching.

MURPH: [*Raps* JOEY *sharply again on the arm*] Indian's a Turkie.

JOEY: [*Grabs* MURPH'*s arm and twists it behind his back*] Gimme my pack and it's an Indian, right?

MURPH: I'll give you your head in a minute, jerkoff.

JOEY: Indian? Indian? Say, Indian!

MURPH: Turkie? Turkie?

JOEY: Turkie. Okay. Let go. [MURPH *lets him up and laughs.* JOEY *jumps up and screams*] Indian! [*Runs a few steps*] Indian!

MURPH: [*Laughing*] If your old lady would have you on Thanksgiving you'd know what a turkey was, ya' jerk. [*Hits him on the arm again*] Here's another noogie, Turkie-head!

[*The* INDIAN *coughs*]

JOEY: Hey, look. He likes us. Shall I wink?

MURPH: You sexy beast, you'd wink at anything in pants.

JOEY: Come on. Do I look like a Murphy?

MURPH: [*Grabs* JOEY *and twists both of his arms*] Take that back.

JOEY: Aw! ya' bastard. I take it back.

MURPH: You're a Turkie-lover, right?

JOEY: Right.

MURPH: Say it.

JOEY: I'm a Turkie-lover.

MURPH: You're a Turkie-humper, right?

JOEY: *You're* a Turkie-humper.

MURPH:Say, *I'm* a Turkie-humper.

JOEY: That's what I said. You're a Turkie-humper. [MURPH *twists his arms a bit further*] Oww, ya' dirty bastard! All right, I'm a Turkie-humper! Now, leggo! [JOEY *pretends to laugh*]

MURPH: You gonna hug him and kiss him and love him up like a mother?

JOEY: Whose mother?

MURPH: Your mother. She humps Turkies, right?

JOEY: Owww! All right, Yeah. She humps Turkies. Now leggo!

MURPH: [*Lets go*] You're free.

JOEY: [*Breaks. Changes the game*] Where's the bus?

MURPH: Up your mother.

JOEY: My old lady's gonna' kill me. It must be late as hell.

MURPH: So why don't you move out?

JOEY: Where to?

MURPH: Maybe we'll get our own place. Yeah. How about that, Joey?

JOEY: Yeah, sure. I move out on her and she starves. You know that.

MURPH: Let her starve, the Turkie-humper.

JOEY: [*Hits* MURPH *on the arm and laughs*] That's my mother you're desecrating, you nasty bastard.

MURPH: How do you desecrate a whore? Call her a lady?

JOEY: Why don't you ask *your* mother?

MURPH: [*Hits* JOEY *on the arm*] Big mouth, huh?

JOEY: Hey! Why don't you pick on som'body your own size, like Turkie, there.

MURPH: Leave Turkie out of this. He's got six elephants in his pocket, probably.

JOEY: [*Laughs at the possibility*] Hey, Turkie, you got six elephants in your pocket?

MURPH: Hey, shut up, Joey. [*Glances in the* INDIAN'*s direction and the* INDIAN *glances back*] Shut up.

JOEY: Ask him for a match.

MURPH: You ask him.

JOEY: You got the butts.

MURPH: Naw.

JOEY: Chicken. Want some seeds to chew on?

MURPH: I'll give you somethin' to chew on.

JOEY: Go on, ask him. I ain't never heard an Indian talk Turkie-talk.

MURPH: He's a Turkie, I told ya'. Any jerk can see that he's a definite Turk!

JOEY: You're a definite jerk, then. 'Cause I see a definite Indian!

MURPH: I'll show you.

[*Walks toward the* INDIAN *slowly, taking a full minute to cross the stage. He slithers from side to side and goes through pantomime of looking for matches*]

JOEY: Hey, Murph. You comin' for dinner? We're havin' turkey tonight! Hey! Tell your Turkie to bring his elephants.

MURPH: Schmuck! How's he going to fit six elephants in a rickshaw?

JOEY: [*Flatly*] Four in front. Three in back.

[*He reaches the* INDIAN]

MURPH: Excuse me. May I borrow a match?

INDIAN: [*Speaking in Hindi*] Mai toom-haree bo-lee nrh-hee bol sak-tah. Mai tum-hah-ree bah-sha nah-hee sah-maj-tah. [*I cannot speak your language. I don't understand.*]

MURPH: [*To* JOEY, *does a terrific "take," then speaks, incredulous*] He's got to be kidding.

[ JOEY *and* MURPH *laugh*]

INDIAN: Moo-jhay mahaf kar-nah mai toom-hah-ree bah-art nah-hee sah-maj sak-tah. [*I'm sorry. I don't understand you.*]

MURPH: No speak English, huh? [*The* INDIAN *looks at him blankly. Louder*] You can't speak English, huh?

[*The* INDIAN *stares at him, confused by the increase in volume*]

JOEY: [*Flatly*] Son of a bitch. Hey, Murph. Guess what? Your Turkie only speaks Indian.

MURPH: [*Moves in closer, examining the* INDIAN] Say something in Indian, big mouth.

JOEY: [*Holds up his hand*] How's your teepee? [*The* INDIAN *stares at him. He laughs*] See.

[*The* INDIAN *welcomes* JOEY's *laugh and smiles. He takes their hands and "shakes" them*]

MURPH: [*Catches on as to why the* INDIAN *has joined the smile and feigns a stronger smile until they all laugh aloud.* MURPH *cuts off the laughter as he shakes the* INDIAN's *hand and says*] You're a fairy, right?

INDIAN: [*Smiles harder than before*] Mai toom-haree bah-at nah-hee sah-maj-tah. Mai ap-nay lah-kay kah gha-r dhoo-nd rah-haw hooh. Oos-nay moo-jhay mil-nah tar pahr nah-jah-nay woh cah-hah hai. Mai oos-kah mah-kan dhoo-nd rah-hah hoon. Oos-kah pah-tah yeh rah-hah k-yah. [*I don't understand you. I'm looking for my son's home. We were supposed to meet, but I could not find him. I'm looking for his home. This is his address. Am I headed in the correct direction?*]

[*The* INDIAN *produces a slip of paper with an address typed on it. And a photograph*]

MURPH: Gupta. In the Bronx. Big deal. [*To the* INDIAN] Indian, right? You an Indian, Indian? [*Shakes his head up and down, smiling. The* INDIAN *smiles, confused*] He don't know. [*Pauses, studies the picture, smiles*] This picture must be his kid. Looks like you, Joe.

JOEY: [*Looks at the picture*] Looks Irish to me. [*He hands the picture to* MURPH]

BOTH: Ohhh.

MURPH: Yeah. Why'd you rape all those innocent children? [*Pause*] I think he's the wrong kind of Indian. [*To the* INDIAN] You work in a restaurant? [*Pauses. Speaks with a homosexual's sibilant "s"*] It's such a shame to kill these Indians. They do such superb beaded work.

[MURPH *shakes his head up and down again, smiling*]

INDIAN: [*Follows* MURPH's *cue*] Mai—ay ap-nay lar-kay koh su-bah say nah-hee day-kha. Toom-hara shah-har bah-hoot bee barah hai. [*I haven't seen my son all day. Your city is so big and so busy.*]

JOEY: Ask him to show you his elephants.

MURPH: You ask. You're the one who speaks Turkie-Indian.

JOEY: White man fork with tongue. Right? [*The* INDIAN *stares at him blankly*] Naw, he don't understand me. You ask. You got the right kind of accent.

All you foreigners understand each other good.

MURPH: You want another noogie?

JOEY: Maybe Turkie wants a noogie or six?

MURPH: [*Shaking his head*] You want a noogie, friend?

INDIAN: [*Agrees*] Moo-jhay mahaf kar-nah. Moo-jay. Yah-han aye zyah-da sah-may na-hee hoo-ah. [*I'm sorry. I haven't been here long.*]

MURPH: Give him his noogie.

JOEY: Naw. He's your friend. You give it to him. That's what friends are for.

MURPH: [*Looks at the paper and photograph, gives them back*] Jesus, look at that for a face.

JOEY: Don't make it.

MURPH: Don't make it. Prem Gupta. In the Bronx. Jesus, this is terrific. The Indian wants the Bronx.

JOEY: [*Sits on a trash can*] He ain't gonna find no Bronx on this bus.

MURPH: Old Indian, pal. You ain't going to find the Bronx on this bus, unless they changed commissioners again. Now I've got a terrific idea for fun and profit. [*Pauses*]

INDIAN: K-yah kah-ha toom-nay. [*Excuse me?*]

MURPH: Right. Now why don't you come home and meet my mother? Or maybe you'd like to meet Pussyface, huh? [*To* JOEY] Should we bring him over to Pussyface?

JOEY: He don't even know who Pussyface is. You can't just go getting Indians blind dates without giving him a breakdown.

MURPH: Okay, Chief. Here's the breakdown on Pussyface. She's a pig. She lives right over there. See that pretty building? [*Points over the audience to the back row of seats*] That one. The fancy one. That's Pussyface's hideaway. She's our social worker.

JOEY: That's right.

MURPH: Pussyface got assigned to us when we were tykers, right, Joe?

JOEY: Just little fellers.

MURPH: Pussyface was sent to us by the city. To watch over us. And care for us. And love us like a mother. Not because she wanted to. Because we were bad boys. We stole a car.

JOEY: We stole two cars.

MURPH: We stole two cars. And we knifed a kid.

JOEY: You knifed a kid.

MURPH: [*To* JOEY] Tell it to the judge, Fella! [*He takes a pocketknife from his pocket and shows it to the* INDIAN, *who pulls back in fear*]

JOEY: The Chief thinks you're going to cut him up into a totem pole.

MURPH: Easy, Chief. I've never cut up an Indian in my life.

JOEY: You've never *seen* an Indian in your life.

MURPH: Anyway, you got a choice. My mother—who happens to have a terrific personality. Or Pussyface, our beloved social lady.

JOEY: Where's the bus?

MURPH: It's coming.

JOEY: So's Christmas.

MURPH: Hey. Show Turkie my Christmas card for Pussyface. [*To the* INDIAN] Pussyface gives us fun projects. I had to make Christmas cards last year. [*Back to* JOEY] Go on. Show the Chief the card.

[JOEY *fishes through his wallet, finds a dog-eared photostat, hands it to the* INDIAN, who accepts it curiously]

INDIAN: Yeh k-yah hai. [*What is this?*]

MURPH: I made that with my own two cheeks. Tell him, Joe.

JOEY: Stupid, he don't speak English.

MURPH: It don't matter. He's interested, ain't he?

JOEY: You're a fink-jerk.

MURPH: Oooo. I'll give you noogies up the kazzooo. [*Takes the card away from the* INDIAN *and explains*] This is a Christmas card. I made it! I made it! Get me? Pussyface got us Christmas jobs last year. She got me one with the city. With the war on poverty. I ran the Xerox machines.

JOEY: Jesus. You really are stupid. He don't understand one word you're saying.

MURPH: [*Mimes the entire scene, slowly*] He's interested, ain't he? That's more than I can say for most of them. [*To the* INDIAN] Want to know how you can make your own Christmas cards with your simple Xerox 2400? It's easy. Watch. [*He mimes*] First you lock the door to the stat room, so no one can bust in. Then you turn the machine on. Then you set the dial at the number of people you want to send cards to. Thirty, forty.

JOEY: Three or four

MURPH: Right, fella. Then you take off your pants. And your underpants that's underneath. You sit on the glass. You push the little button. The lights flash. When the picture's developed, you write "Noel" across it! [*Pauses*] That's how you make Christmas cards. [*Waits for a reaction from the* INDIAN, *then turns back to* JOEY, *dismayed*] He's waiting for the bus.

JOEY: Me too. Jesus. Am I ever late!

MURPH: Tell her to stuff it. You're a big boy now.

JOEY: She gets frightened, that's all. She really don't care how late I come in, as long as I tell her when I'm coming. If I tell her one, and I don't get in until one-thirty, she's purple when I finally get in. [*Pauses*] She's all right. Where's the Goddamned bus, huh? [*Calls across the park*] Pussyface, did you steal the bus, you dirty old whore? Pussyface, I'm calling you! [*Pauses*] She's all right, Murph. Christ, she's my mother. I didn't ask for her. She's all right.

MURPH: Who's all right? That Turkie-humper? [*To the* INDIAN] His old lady humps Turkies, you know that? [*Smiles, but the* INDIAN *doesn't respond*] Hey, Turkie's blowin' his cool a little. Least you got somebody waitin'. My old lady wouldn't know if I was gone a year.

JOEY: What? That Turkie-humper?

MURPH: [*To the* INDIAN] Hey! [*The* INDIAN *jumps, startled.* MURPH *laughs*] You got any little Indians runnin' around your teepee? No? Yeah? No? Aw, ya' stupid Indian. Where is the Goddamn bus?

JOEY: Let's walk it.

MURPH: Screw that. A hundred blocks? Besides, we gotta keep this old Turkie company, right? We couldn't let him stand all alone in this big ole city. Some nasty boys might come along and chew him up, right?

JOEY: We can walk it. Let the Indian starve.

MURPH: So walk it, jerk. I'm waiting with the Chief. [MURPH *stands next to the* INDIAN]

JOEY: Come on, we'll grab the subway.

MURPH: Joe, the trains are running crazy now. Anyway, I'm waitin' with my friend the Chief, here. You wanna go, go. [*Murmurs*] Where is it, Chief? Is that it? Here it comes, huh?

JOEY: [*Consider it*] Yeah, we gotta watch out for Turkie.

[JOEY *stands on the other side of the* INDIAN, *who finally walks slowly back to the bus stop area*]

MURPH: See that, Turkie, little Joe's gonna keep us company. That's nice, huh? [*The* INDIAN *looks for the bus*] You know, Joey, this Turk's a pain in my ass. He don't look at me when I talk to him.

JOEY: He oughta look at you when you talk. He oughta be polite.

[*They pass the card in a game. The* INDIAN *smiles*]

MURPH: I don't think he learned many smarts in Indiana. Any slob knows enough to look when they're being talked to. Huh?

JOEY: This ain't just any slob. This is a definite Turkie-Indian slob.

[*They pass the card behind their backs*]

MURPH: He's one of them commie slobs, probably. Warmongering bastard. [*Flatly*] Pinko here rapes all the little kids.

JOEY: Terrible thing. Too bad we can't give him some smarts. Maybe he could use a couple.

[*The game ends.* JOEY *has the card as in a magic act*]

MURPH: We'll give him plenty of smarts. [*Calling him upstage*] Want some smarts? Chief?

INDIAN: Bna-ee mai toom-maree bah-at nah-Hee sah-maj-sak-tah. Bus yah-han kis sa-may a-tee haj. K-yah mai sa-hee BUS STOP par shoon! [*I can't understand you. Please? When is the bus due here? Am I at the right station?*]

JOEY: Hey, look. He's talking out of the side of his mouth. Sure, that's right . . . Hey, Murph. Ain't Indian broads s'posed to have sideways breezers? Sure.

MURPH: [*Grins*] You mean chinks, Joey.

JOEY: Naw. Indian broads too. All them foreign broads. Their breezers are sideways. That's why them foreign cars have the back seat facing the side, right?

MURPH: Is that right, Turkie? Your broads have horizontal snatches?

INDIAN: [*Stares at him nervously*] Mai toom-haree bah-at nah-hee sah-maj sak-tah. [*I can't understand you.*]

MURPH: [*Repeating him in the same language*] Toom-haree bah-at nah-hee sah-maj sak-tah.

INDIAN: [*Recognizing the language finally. He speaks with incredible speed*] Toom-haree bah-sha nah-hee sah-maj-tah. Moo-jhay mah-Af kar-nah par ah-bhee moo-jhay tomm-ha-ray desh aye kuh-Chah hee din toh Hu-yay hain. Moo-jhay toom-ha-ree bah-sha see-kh-nay kah ah-bhee sah-mai hee nah-hee milah. Mai ahp-nay lar-kay say bih-chur gah-ya hoon. Oos-say toh toom-ha-ray desh may rah-tay chai sah-al hoh Gah-ye hain. Jah-b doh mah-hee-nay pah-lay oos-kee mah kah inth-kahl moo-ah toh oos-nay moo-jhay ya-han booh-lah bheh-jha or mai ah gah-hay. Woh bah-ra hon-har lar-ka hai. Moo-jhay mah-af kar-nah kee majh-nay ah-bhee toom-ha-ree bah-sha na-hee see-kiee par mai see-kh loon-gha. [*Yes, that's correct. I can't understand your language. I'm sorry, but I've only been in your country for a few days. I haven't had time to understand your language. Please forgive me. I'm separated from my son. He's been living in your country for six years. When his mother died two months ago, he sent for me. I came immediately. He's a good son to his father. I'm sorry I haven't learned your language yet, but I shall learn.*]

MURPH: [*Does a take. Flatly*] This Turkie's a real pain in the ass.

JOEY: Naw. I think he's pretty interesting. I never saw an Indian before.

MURPH: Oh. It's fascinating. It's marvelous. This city's a regular melting pot. Turkies. Kikes like you. [*Pause*] I even had me a real French lady once. [*Looks at the ground. Pauses*] I thought I saw a dime here. [*Ponders*] I knew it. [*He picks up a dime and pockets it proudly*]

JOEY: A French lady, huh?

MURPH: Yep. A real French broad.

JOEY: [*Holds a beat*] You been at your mother again?

MURPH: [*Hits him on the arm*] Wise-ass. Just what nobody likes. A wise-ass.

JOEY: Where'd you have this French lady, huh?

MURPH: I found her in the park over there. [*Points*] Just sitting on a bench. She was great. [*Boasts*] A real *talent*.

JOEY: Yeah, sure thing. [*Calls into the park*] Hello, talent. Hello, talent! [*Pauses*] I had a French girl, too. [*Turns to avoid* MURPH's *eyes, caught in a lie*] Where the hell's that bus?

MURPH: [*Simply*] Sure you did. Like the time you had a mermaid?

JOEY: You better believe I did. She wasn't really French. She just lived there a long time. I went to first grade with her. Geraldine. She was my first girl friend. [*Talks very quickly*] Her old man was in the Army or something, 'cause they moved to France. She came back when we were in high school.

MURPH: Then what happened?

JOEY: Nothin'. She just came back, that's all.

MURPH: I thought you said you *had* her . . .

JOEY: No, she was just my girl friend.

MURPH: In high school?

JOEY: No, ya stoop. In the first grade. I just told you.

MURPH: You had her in the first grade?

JOEY: Jesus, you're stupid. She was my girl friend. That's all.

MURPH: [*Feigns excitement*] Hey . . . that's a *sweet little story.* [*Flatly*] What the hell's wrong with you?

JOEY: What do ya' mean?

MURPH: First you say you had a French girl, then you say you had a girl friend in first grade, who went to France. What the hell kind of story's that?

JOEY: It's a true one, that's all. Yours is full of crap.

MURPH: What's full of crap?

JOEY: About the French lady in the park. You never had any French lady, unless you been at your own old lady again. Or maybe you've been at Pussyface?

MURPH: Jesus, you're lookin' for it, aren't you?

[*They pretend to fistfight*]

JOEY: I mean, if you gotta tell lies to your best buddy, you're in bad shape, that's all.

MURPH: [*Gives* JOEY *a "high-sign"*] Best buddy? You?

[*The sign to the* INDIAN. *He returns the obscene gesture, thinking it a berserk American sign of welcome*]

JOEY: Is that how it is in Ceylon, sir?

MURPH: Say-lon? What the hell is say-long?

JOEY: See, ya jerk, Ceylon's part of India. That's where they grow tea.

MURPH: No kiddin'? Boy it's terrific what you can learn just standin' here with a schmuck like you. Tea, huh? [*To the* INDIAN *he screams*] Hey! [*The* INDIAN *turns around, startled*] How's your teabags? [*No response*] No? [*To* JOEY] Guess you're wrong again. He don't know teabags.

JOEY: Look at the bags under his eyes. That ain't chopped liver.

[*This is the transition scene:* MURPH *screams "Hey!"—the* INDIAN *smiles. They dance a war dance around him, beating a rhythm on the trashcans, hissing and cat-calling for a full minute.* MURPH *ends the dance with a final "Hey!" The* INDIAN *jumps in fear. Now that they sense his fear, the comedy has ended*]

MURPH: Turkie looks like he's getting bored.

JOEY: Poor old Indian. Maybe he wants to play a game.

MURPH: You know any poor old Indian games?

JOEY: We could burn him at the stake. [*He laughs*] That ain't such a terrible idea, you know. Maybe make an Indian stew.

MURPH: Naw, we couldn't burn a nice fellow like Turkie. That's nasty.

JOEY: We got to play a game. Pussyface always tells us to play games. [*To the apartment, the back of the audience*] Ain't that right, Pussyface? You always want us to play games.

MURPH: I know a game . . .

JOEY: Yeah?

MURPH: Yeah. [*Screams at the* INDIAN] "Indian, Indian, Where's the Indian?"

JOEY: That's a sweet game. I haven't played that for years.

MURPH: Wise-ass. You want to play a game, don't you?

JOEY: Indian-Indian. Where's the Indian?

MURPH: Sure. It's just like ring-a-leave-eo. Only with a spin.

JOEY: That sounds terrific.

MURPH: Look. I spin the hell out of you until you're dizzy. Then you run across the street and get Pussyface. I'll grab the Indian and hide him. Then Pussyface and you come over here and try to find us.

JOEY: We're going to spin, huh?

MURPH: Sure.

JOEY: Who's going to clean up after you? Remember the Ferris wheel, big shot? All those happy faces staring up at you?

MURPH: I ain't the spinner. You're the spinner. I'll hide the Chief. Go on. Spin.

JOEY: How about if we set the rules as we go along? [*To the* INDIAN] How does that grab you, Chief?

INDIAN: Moo-jhay mah-af kar-nah. Mai toom-nakee bah-sha na-hee sah-maj sak-ta. [*I'm sorry, but I can't understand your language.*]

MURPH: He's talking Indian again. He don't understand. Go on. Spin. I'll grab the Chief while you're spinning . . . count to ten . . . hide the Chief, while you're after Pussyface. Go on. Spin.

JOEY: I ain't going to spin. I get sick.

MURPH: Ain't you going to play?

JOEY: I'll play. But I can't spin any better than you can. I get sick. You know that. How about if you spin and I hide the Chief? You can get Pussyface. She likes you better than me, anyhow.

MURPH: Pussyface ain't home. You know that. She's in New Jersey.

JOEY: Then what the hell's the point of this game, anyway?

MURPH: It's just a game. We can pretend.

JOEY: You can play marbles for all I care. I just ain't going to spin, that's all. And neither are you. So let's forget the whole game.

MURPH: [*Fiercely*] Spin! Spin!

JOEY: You spin.

MURPH: Hey. I told you to spin.

[MURPH *squares off against* JOEY *and slaps him menacingly.* JOEY *looks* MURPH *straight in the eye for a moment*]

JOEY: Okay. Big deal. So I'll spin. Then I get Pussyface, right? You ready to get the Chief?

MURPH: Will you stop talking and start spinning?

JOEY: All right. All right. Here I go. [JOEY *spins himself meekly, as* MURPH *goes toward the* INDIAN *and the trash can.* JOEY *giggles as he spins ever so slowly.* MURPH *glances at* JOEY *as* JOEY *pretends.* MURPH *is confused*] There. I spun. Is that okay?

MURPH: That's a spin?

JOEY: Well, it wasn't a fox trot.

MURPH: I told you to spin! Any slob knows that ain't no spin? Now spin. God damn it! Spin!

JOEY: This is stupid. You want to play games. You want a decent spin. You spin.

[*He walks straight to* MURPH—*a challenge.* JOEY *slaps* MURPH. *He winces*]

MURPH: [*Squares off viciously. Raises his arms. Looks at* JOEY *cruelly. Orders*] Spin me.

[JOEY *brings* MURPH's *arms behind* MURPH's *back and holds* MURPH's *wrists firmly so that he is helpless.* JOEY *spins him. Slowly at first. Then faster. Faster.* JOEY's *hostility is released; he laughs*]

JOEY: You wanted to spin. Spin. Spin.

[JOEY *spins* MURPH *frantically. The* INDIAN *watches in total horror, not knowing what to do; he cuddles next to the bus stop sign, his island of safety*]

MURPH: [*Screaming*] Enough, you little bastard.

JOEY: [*Continues to spin him*] Now *you* get Pussyface. Go on. [*Spins* MURPH *all the faster as in a grotesque dance gone berserk*] I'll hide the Chief. This is your game! This is your game. *You* get Pussyface. I'll hide the Chief. Go on, Murphy. You want some more spin? [JOEY *has stopped the spinning now, as* MURPH *is obviously ill*] You want to spin some more?

MURPH: Stop it, Joey. I'm sick.

JOEY: [*Spins* MURPH *once more around*] You want to spin some more, or are you going to get Pussyface and come find the Chief and me?

MURPH: You little bastard.

JOEY: [*Spins* MURPH *once again, still holding* MURPH *helpless with his arms behind his back*] I'll hide the Chief. *You* get Pussyface and find us. Okay? Okay? Okay?

MURPH: Okay . . . you bastard . . . okay.

JOEY: Here's one more for good luck.

[JOEY *spins* MURPH *three more times, fiercely, then shoves him offstage.* MURPH *can be heard retching, about to vomit, during the final spins.* JOEY *then grabs the* INDIAN, *who pulls back in terror*]

INDIAN: Na-hee bha-yee toom ah-b k-yah kah-rogay? [*No, please, what are you going to do?*]

JOEY: Easy, Chief. It's just a game. Murph spun out on us. It's just a game. I've got to hide you now.

[MURPH's *final puking sounds can be heard well in the distance*]

INDIAN: Na-hee na-hee bha-yee. Mai mah-afee mah-ng-ta. Hoon. [*No. No. Please. I beg you.*]

JOEY: Easy, Chief. Look. I promise you, this ain't for real. This is only a game. A game. Get it? It's all a game! Now I got to count to ten. [*Grabs the INDIAN and forces him down behind a city litter basket. He covers the INDIAN's scream with his hand, as he slaps the INDIAN—a horrifying sound*] One. Two. Three. Murphy? [*He laughs*] Four. Five. Murph? Come get us. Six. Seven. Pussyface is waiting. Eight. Nine. [*Pauses*] Murphy? Murph? Hey, buddy. [*Stands up. Speaks*] Ten. [*Lights are narrowing on JOEY and the INDIAN. The INDIAN tries to escape. JOEY subdues him easily. JOEY turns slowly back to the INDIAN, who responds with open fear*] Get up. Up. [*No response*] Get up, Turkie. [*Moves to the INDIAN, who recoils sharply. JOEY persists and pulls the INDIAN to his feet. The INDIAN shudders, stands and faces his captor. The INDIAN shakes from fear and from a chill. There is a moment's silence as JOEY watches. He removes his own sweater and offers it to the INDIAN*] Here. Here. Put it on. It's okay. [*The INDIAN is bewildered, but JOEY forces the sweater into his hands*] Put it on. [*The INDIAN stares at the sweater. JOEY takes it from his hands and begins to cover the INDIAN, who is amazed*] I hope I didn't hurt you too much. You okay? [*No response*] You ain't sick too bad, huh? [*Pause*] Huh? [*Checks the INDIAN for cuts*] You look okay. You're okay, huh? [*No response*] I didn't mean to rough you up like that, but . . . you know. Huh? [*The INDIAN raises his eyes to meet JOEY's. JOEY looks down to avoid the stare*] I hope you ain't mad at me or nothin'. [*Pause*] Boy it's gettin' chilly. I mean, it's cold, right? Sure is quiet all of a sudden. Kind of spooky, huh? [*Calls*] Hey, Murphy! [*Laughs aloud*] Murph ain't a bad guy. He's my best buddy, see? I mean, he gets kinda crazy sometimes, but that's all. Everybody gets kind of crazy sometime, right? [*No response*] Jesus, you're a stupid Indian. Can't you speak any English? No? Why the hell did you come here, anyway? Especially if you can't talk any English. You ought to say something. Can't you even say "Thank you"?

[*The INDIAN recognizes those words, finally, and mimics them slowly and painfully*]

INDIAN: [*In English, very British and clipped*] Thank you.

JOEY: I'll be Goddamned! You're welcome. [*Slowly, indicating for the INDIAN to follow*] You're welcome.

[*He waits*]

INDIAN: [*In English*] You are welcome.

JOEY: That's terrific. You are welcome. [*Smiles, as though all is forgiven. In relief*] How are you?

INDIAN: You are welcome.

JOEY: No. How are ya? [JOEY *is excited. The* INDIAN *might be a second friend*]

INDIAN: [*In English—very "Joey"*] How are ya?

JOEY: [*Joyously*] Jesus. You'll be talking like us in no time! You're okay, huh? You ain't bleeding or anything. I didn't wanna hurt you none. But Murph gets all worked up. You know what I mean. He gets all excited. This ain't the first time, you know. No, sir!

INDIAN: [*In English*] No, sir.

JOEY: That's right. He's especially crazy around broads.

INDIAN: [*In English*] Broads.

JOEY: [*Forgetting that the* INDIAN *is only mimicking*] That's right. Broads. [*Pauses and remembers, deeply*] What am I yakking for? Tell me about India, huh? I'd like to go to India sometime. Maybe I will. You think I'd like India? India? [*No response. The* INDIAN *recognizes the word, but doesn't understand the question*] That's where you're from, ain't it? Jesus, what a stupid Indian. India! [*Spells the word*] I-N-D-I-A. Nothin'. Schmuck. *India!*

INDIAN: [*A stab in the dark*] Hindi?

JOEY: Yeah! Tell me about India! [*Long pause as they stand staring at each other*] No? You're not talking, huh? Well, what do you want to do? Murph oughta be back soon. [*Discovers a coin in his pocket*] You wanna flip for quarters? Flip? No? Look, a Kennedy half! [*Goes through three magic tricks with the coin:* (1) *He palms the coin, offers the obvious choice of hand, then uncovers the coin in his other hand. The Indian raises his hand to his turban in astonishment*] Like that, huh? [(2) *Coin is slapped on his breast*] This hand right? Is it this hand, this hand? No, it's *this* hand! Back to your dumb act? Here. Here's the one you liked! [*Does* (1). *This time the* INDIAN *points to the correct hand instantly*] You're probably some kind of hustler. Okay. Double or nothing. [*Flips*] Heads, you live. Tails, you die. Okay? [*Uncovers the coin*] I'll be a son of a bitch. You got Indian luck. Here. [*He hands the coin to the* INDIAN]

INDIAN: [*Stares in question*] Na-hff? [*No?*]

JOEY: [*Considers cheating*] Take it. You won. No, go ahead. Keep it. I ain't no Indian giver. [*Pause. He laughs at his own joke. No response*] You ain't got no sense of humor, that's what. [*Stares upstage*] Murph's my best buddy, you know? Me and him were buddies when we were kids. Me and Murph, all the time. And Maggie. His kid sister. [*Pause*] I had Maggie once. Sort of. Well, kind of. Yeah, I had her. That's right. Murph don't know. Makes no difference now. She's dead, Maggie. [*Sings*] "The worms crawl in, the worms crawl out." [*Speaks*] What the hell difference does it make? *Right?*

INDIAN: [*In English*] No, sir.

JOEY: [*Without noticing*] That's why Murph is crazy. That's why he gets crazy, I mean. She died seventeen, that's all. Seventeen. Just like *that*. Appendix. No one around. There was no one around. His old lady? Forget it! The old man took off years ago. All there was really was just Murph and Maggie. That's why he could take it. At home. You think my old lady's bad? She's nothing. His old lady's a pro. You know? She don't even make a living at it, either. That's the bitch of it. Not even a living. She's a dog. I mean, *I* wouldn't even pay her a nickel. Not a nickel. Not that I'd screw around with Murphy's old lady. Oh! Not that she doesn't try. She tries. Plenty. [*His fantasy begins*] That's why I don't come around to his house much. She tries it all the time. She wouldn't charge me anything, probably. But it ain't right screwing your best buddy's old lady, right? I'd feel terrible if I did. She ain't that bad, but it just ain't right. I'd bet she'd even take Murph on. She probably tries it with him, too. That's the bitch of it. She can't even make a living. His own God-damned mother. The other one—Pussyface. You think Pussyface is a help? That's the biggest joke yet. [*The* INDIAN *is by now thoroughly confused on all counts. He recognizes the name "Pussyface," and reacts slightly. Seeing* JOEY's *anxiety, he cuddles him. For a brief moment they embrace—an insane father-and-son tableau. Note: Be careful here*] Pussyface. There's a brain. You see what she gave us for Christmas? [*Fishes his knife out of his pocket*] Knives. Brilliant, huh? Murph's up on a rap for slicing a kid, and she gives us knives for Christmas. To whittle with. She's crazier than Murphy. Hah. [*Flashes his open knife at the* INDIAN, *who misinterprets the move as spelling disaster. The* INDIAN *waits, carefully scrutinizing* JOEY, *until* JOEY *begins to look away.* JOEY *now wanders to the spot where he pushed* MURPH *offstage*] Hey, Murph! [*The* INDIAN *moves slowly to the other side of the stage.* JOEY *sees his move at once and races after him, thinking the* INDIAN *was running away*] Hey. Where are you going? [*The* INDIAN *knows he'll be hit. He tries to explain with mute gestures and attitude. It's futile. He knows at once and hits* JOEY *as best he can and races across the stage.* JOEY *recovers from the blow and starts after him, as the* INDIAN *murmurs one continuous frightening scream.* JOEY *dives after the* INDIAN *and tackles him on the other side of the stage. The* INDIAN *fights more strongly than ever, but* JOEY's *trance carries him ferociously into this fight. He batters the* INDIAN *with punches to the body. The* INDIAN *squeals as* JOEY *sobs*] You were gonna run off. Right? Son of a bitch. You were gonna tell Murphy.

[*The* INDIAN *makes one last effort to escape and runs the length of the stage, screaming a bloodcurdling, anguished scream.* MURPH *enters, stops, stares incredulously as the* INDIAN *runs into his open arms.* JOEY *races to the* INDIAN *and strikes a karate chop to the back of his neck.* JOEY *is audibly sobbing. The* INDIAN *drops to the stage as a bull in the ring, feeling the final thrust of the sword . . .* JOEY *stands frozen above him.* MURPH *stares, first at* JOEY *and then at the* INDIAN]

MURPH: Pussyface isn't home yet. She's still in New Jersey. Ring-a-leave-eo.
JOEY: [*Sobbing, senses his error*] Indians are dumb.
MURPH: [*Stares again at* JOEY. *Then to the* INDIAN. *Spots* JOEY's *sweater on the* INDIAN. *Fondles it, then stares at* JOEY *viciously*] Pussyface isn't home. I rang

her bell. She don't answer. I guess she's still on vacation. She ruined our game.

JOEY: [*Sobbing*] Oh, jumping Jesus Christ. Jesus, Jesus. Jesus. Indians are dumb.

MURPH: Pussyface ruins everything. She don't really care about our games. She ruins our games. Just like Indians. They don't know how to play our games either.

JOEY: Indians are dumb. Dumb.

[*He sobs.* MURPH *slaps* JOEY *across the face. He straightens up and comes back to reality*]

MURPH: What the hell's going on?

JOEY: He tried to run. I hit him.

MURPH: Yeah. I saw that. You hit him, all right. [*Stares at the* INDIAN] Is he alive?

[*The* INDIAN *groans, pulls himself to his knees*]

JOEY: He was fighting. I hit him.

MURPH: Okay, you hit him.

[*The* INDIAN *groans again. Then he speaks in a plea*]

INDIAN: [*Praying*] Moo-jhay or nah sah-tao. Maih-nay toom-hara k-yah bigarah hai. Moo-jhay or nah sah-tao. Moo-jhay in-seh. [*Please. Don't hurt me anymore. What have I done? Please don't hurt me. Don't let them hurt me*]

MURPH: He's begging for something. Maybe he's begging for his life. Maybe he is. Sure, maybe he is.

JOEY: [*Embarrassed, starts to help the* INDIAN *to his feet*] C'mon there, Chief. Get up and face the world. C'mon, Chief. Everything's going to be all right.

MURPH: What's got into you, anyway?

JOEY: C'mon, Chief. Up at the world. Everything's okay.

[*The* INDIAN *ad libs words of pleading and pain*]

MURPH: Leave him be. [*But* JOEY *continues to help the* INDIAN] Leave him be. What's with you? Hey, Joey! I said leave him be!

[MURPH *pushes* JOEY *and the* INDIAN *pulls back with fear*]

JOEY: Okay, Murph. Enough's enough.

MURPH: Just tell me what the hell's wrong with you?

JOEY: He tried to run away, that's all. Change the subject. Change the subject. It ain't important. I hit him, that's all.

MURPH: Okay, so you hit him.

JOEY: Okay! Where were you? Sick. Were you a little bit sick? I mean, you couldn't have been visiting, 'cause there ain't no one to visit, right?

MURPH: What *do* you mean?

JOEY: Where the hell were you? [*Looks at* MURPH *and giggles*] You're a little green there, Irish.

MURPH: You're pretty funny. What the hell's so funny?

JOEY: Nothing's funny. The Chief and I were just having a little pow-wow, and we got to wondering where you ran off to. Just natural for us to wonder, ain't it? [*To the* INDIAN] Right, Chief.

MURPH: Hey, look at that. Turkie's got a woolly sweater just like yours. Ain't that a terrific coincidence. You two been playing strip poker?

JOEY: Oh, sure. Strip poker. The Chief won my sweater and I won three of his feathers and a broken arrow. [*To the* INDIAN, *he feigns a deep authoritative voice*] You wonder who I am, don't you? Perhaps this silver bullet will help to identify me? [*Extends his hand. The* INDIAN *peers into* JOEY's *empty palm quizzically. As he does,* MURPH *quickly taps the underside of* JOEY's *hand, forcing the hand to rise and slap the* INDIAN's *chin sharply. The* INDIAN *pulls back at the slap.* JOEY *turns on* MURPH, *quickly*] What the hell did you do that for, ya' jerk. The Chief didn't do nothing.

MURPH: Jesus, you and your Chief are pretty buddy-buddy, ain't you? [*Mimics* JOEY] "The Chief didn't do nothing." Jesus. You give him your sweater. Maybe you'd like to have him up for a beer . . .

JOEY: Drop it, Murph. You're giving me a pain in the ass.

MURPH: [*Retorts fiercely*] You little pisser. Who the hell do you think you're talking to?

[*The telephone rings in the booth. They are all startled, especially the* INDIAN, *who senses hope*]

JOEY: [*After a long wait, speaking the obvious flatly*] It's the phone.

MURPH: [*To the* INDIAN] The kid's a whiz. He guessed that right away.

[*The phone rings a second time*]

JOEY: Should we answer it?

MURPH: What for? Who'd be calling here? It's a wrong number.

[*The phone rings menacingly a third time. Suddenly the* INDIAN *darts into the phone booth and grabs the receiver.* JOEY *and* MURPH *are too startled to stop him until he has blurted out his hopeless plea, in his own language*]

INDIAN: Prem k-yah woh may-rah ar-kah hai. Prem (Pray-em) bay-tah moo-jhay bachah-low. Mai fah ns ga-yah boon yeh doh goon-day moo-jhay mar ra-hay hain. Mai ba-hoot ghah-bara gaya hoon. Pray-em. [*Prem? Is this my son? Prem? Please help me. I'm frightened. Please help me. Two boys are hurting me . . . I'm frightened. Please. Prem?*]

[*The* INDIAN *stops talking sharply and listens. He crumbles as the voice drones the wrong reply. He drops the receiver and stares with horror at the boys.* MURPH *realizes the* INDIAN's *horror and begins to laugh hysterically.* JOEY *stares silently. The* INDIAN *begins to mumble and weep. He walks from the phone booth. The voice is heard as a drone from the receiver. The action freezes*]

MURPH: [*Laughing*] What's the matter, Turkie? Don't you have a dime? Give Turkie a dime, Joe. Give him a dime.

JOEY: Jesus Christ. I'd hate to be an Indian.

MURPH: Hey, the paper! C'mon, Joey, get the paper from him. We'll call the Bronx.

JOEY: Cut it out, Murph. Enough's enough.

MURPH: Get the frigging piece of paper. What's the matter with you, anyway?

JOEY: I just don't think it's such a terrific idea, that's all.

MURPH: You're chicken. That's what you are.

JOEY: Suppose his son has called the police. What do you think? You think he hasn't called the police? He knows the old man don't speak any English. He called the police. Right? And they'll trace our call.

MURPH: You're nuts. They can't trace any phone calls. Anyway, we'll be gone from here. You're nuts.

JOEY: I don't want to do it.

MURPH: For Christ's sake. They can't trace nothing to nobody. Who's going to trace. Get the paper.

JOEY: Get it yourself. Go on. Get it yourself. I ain't going to get it.

MURPH: C'mon, Joey. It's not real. This is just a game. It ain't going to hurt anybody. You know that. It's just a game.

JOEY: Why don't we call somebody else? We'll call somebody else and have the Indian talk. That makes sense. Imagine if an Indian called you up and talked to you in Indian. I bet the Chief would go for that all right. Jesus, Murphy.

MURPH: Get the paper and picture.

INDIAN: Ah-b toom k-yah kah-rogay. Moo-jhay mah-af kar-doh bha-yee maih-nay soh-cha tah key woh may-rah bay-tah pray-em hai. Moo-jhay tele-phone kar raha. Mai-nay soh-chah thah sha-yahd woh. Pray-em hoh. [*What are you going to do now? I'm sorry. I thought that was my son, Prem. I thought that it might be Prem calling me on the telephone. Prem. That's who I thought it was. Prem.*]

MURPH: Prem. That's the name. [*Plays the rhyme*]

INDIAN: Pray-aim. [*Prem?*]

MURPH: Yes, Prem. I want to call Prem. Give me the paper with his name.

INDIAN: Toom pray-aim kay ba-ray may k-yah hah ra-hay. Ho toom-nay pray-aim koh kyah key-yah. Toom oos-kay bah-ray may k-yah jan-tay ho k-yah toom jan-tay ho woh kah-han hai. [*What are you saying about Prem? Prem is my son. What have you done to Prem? What do you know about him? Do you know where he is?*]

MURPH: Shut up already and give me the paper.

JOEY: Jesus, Murph.

MURPH: [*Turning the INDIAN around so that they face each other*] This is ridiculous. [*Searches the INDIAN, who resists a bit at first, and then not at all. Finally, MURPHY finds the slip of paper*] I got it. I got it. Terrific. "Prem Gupta." In the Bronx. In the frigging Bronx. This is terrific. [*Pushes the* INDIAN *to* JOEY] Here. Hold him.

INDIAN: Toom k-yah kar ra-hay ho k-yah toom pray-aim k-oh boo-lah ra-hay ho. [*What are you doing? Are you going to call my son?*]

MURPH: Shut him up. [*Fishes for a dime*] Give me a dime, God damn it. This is terrific.

JOEY: [*Finds the coins in his pocket*] Here's two nickels. [*Hands them over*] I think this is a rotten idea, that's what I think. [*Pauses*] And don't forget to pay me back those two nickels either.

MURPH: Just shut up. [*Dials the information operator*] Hello. Yeah, I want some information . . . I want a number up in the Bronx . . . Gupta . . . G-U-P-T-A . . . an Indian kid . . . His first name's Prem . . . P-R-E-M . . . No . . . I can't read the street right . . . Wait a minute. [*Reads the paper to himself*] For Christ's sake. How many Indians are up in the Bronx? There must be only one Indian named Gupta.

JOEY: What's she saying?

MURPH: There are two Indians named Gupta. [*To the operator*] Is the two of them named Prem? [*Pauses*] Well, that's what I told you . . . Jesus . . . wait a minute . . . okay . . . Okay. Say that again . . . Okay . . . Okay . . . Right. Okay . . . thanks. [*Hurries quickly to return the coins to the slot.* GUPTA *mumbles. To* JOEY] Don't talk to me. [*Dials*] Six . . . seven-four. Oh. One. Seven, seven. [*Pauses*] It's ringing. It's ringing. [*Pauses*] Hello. [*Covers the phone with his hand*] I got him! Hello! Is this Prem Gupta? Oh swell. How are you? [*To* JOEY] I got the kid!

[*The* INDIAN *breaks from* JOEY's *arms and runs to the telephone . . .* MURPH *sticks out his leg and holds the* INDIAN *off. The* INDIAN *fights, but seems weaker than ever*]

INDIAN: [*Screams*] Cree-payah moo-jhay ad-nay lar-kay say bah-at kar-nay doh. [*Please let me talk to my son.*]

[MURPH *slams the* INDIAN *aside violently.* JOEY *stands frozen, watching. The* INDIAN *wails and finally talks calmly, as in a trance*]

INDIAN: Cree-payah moo-jhay ahd-nay lar-kay say bah-at kar-nay doh. Mai toom-haray hah-th jor-tah hoom mai toom-hay joh mango-gay doon-gar bus moo-jhay oos-say bah-at kar-nay doh. [*Please let me talk to my son. Oh, Prem. Please, I beg of you. Please. I'll give you anything at all. Just tell me what you want of me. Just let me talk with my son. Won't you, please?*]

[MURPH *glares at the* INDIAN, *who no longer tries to interfere, as it becomes obvious that he must listen to even the language he cannot understand*]

MURPH: Just listen to me, will you, Gupta? I don't know where the hell your old man is, that's why I'm calling. We found an old elephant down here in Miami and we thought it must be yours. You can't tell for sure whose elephant is whose. You know what I mean? [MURPH *is laughing now*] What was that? Say that again. I can't hear you too well. All the distance between us, you know what I mean? It's a long way down here, you follow me? No. I ain't got no Indian. I just got an elephant. And he's eating all my peanuts. Gupta, you're talking too fast. Slow down.

INDIAN: Pray-aim bhai-yah moo-jhay ah-kay lay ja-oh moo-jhay ap-nay lar-kay say bah-at kar-nay doh moo-jhay oos-say bah-at k-yohn nah-hee kar-nay day-tay. [*Prem! Prem! Please come and get me. Please let me talk to my son, mister. Why don't you let me talk to my son?*]

[JOEY *leaps on the* INDIAN; *tackles him, lies on top of him in front of the telephone booth*]

MURPH: That was the waiter. I'm in an Indian restaurant. [*Pauses*] Whoa. Slow down, man. That was nobody. That was just a myth. Your imagination. [*Pauses. Screams into the receiver*] Shut up, damn you! And listen. Okay? Okay. Are you listening? [MURPH *tastes the moment. He silently clicks the receiver back to the hook. To* JOEY] He was very upset. [*To the* INDIAN] He was very upset. [*Pauses*] Well, what the hell's the matter with you? I only told him we found an elephant, that's all. I thought maybe he lost his elephant.

[*The* INDIAN *whimpers*]

INDIAN: Toom-nay ai-saw k-yohn ki-yah toom-nay may-ray lar-kay koh k-yah ka-hah hai. [*Why have you done this? What have you said to my son?*]

MURPH: You don't have to thank me, Turkie. I only told him your elephant was okay. He was probably worried sick about your elephant. [MURPH *laughs*] This is terrific, Joey. Terrific. You should have heard the guy jabber. He was so excited he started talking in Indian just like the Chief. He said that Turkie here and him got separated today. Turkie's only been in the city one day. You're pretty stupid, Turkie. One day in the city . . . and look at the mess you've made. You're pretty stupid. He's stupid, right?

JOEY: Yeah. He's stupid.

MURPH: Hold him. We'll try again. Sure.

[*The* INDIAN *jumps on* MURPH. *He tries to strangle* MURPH]

MURPH: [*Screaming*] Get him off of me! [JOEY *pulls the* INDIAN *down to the ground as* MURPH *pounds the booth four times, screaming hideous sounds of aggression. With this tension released he begins to call, fierce but controlled, too controlled.* MURPH *takes the dime from his pocket, shows it to* JOEY, *and recalls the number. Talking into receiver. He dials number again and waits for reply*] Hello? Is this Gupta again? Oh, hello there . . . I'm calling back to complain about your elephant . . . hey, slow down, will you? Let me do the talking. Okay? Your elephant is a terrific pain in the balls to me, get it? Huh? Do you follow me so far? [*Pauses*] I don't know what you're saying, man . . . how about if I do the talking, all right? . . . Your elephant scares hell out of me and my pal here. We don't like to see elephants on the street. Spiders and snakes are okay, but elephants scare us. Elephants . . . yea, that's right. Don't you get it, pal? . . . Look, we always see spiders and snakes. But we never expect to see an elephant . . . What do you mean "I'm crazy"? I don't know nothing about your old man . . . I'm talking about your elephant. Your elephant offends the hell out of me. So why don't you be a nice Indian kid and come pick him up . . . that's right . . . wait a minute . . . I'll have to check the street sign. [*Covers the receiver*] This is terrific. [*Talks again into the telephone*] Jesus, I'm sorry about that. There don't seem to be no street sign . . . that's a bitch. I guess you lose your elephant . . . well, what do you expect me to do, bring your elephant all the way up to the Bronx? Come off it, pal. You wouldn't ever bring my elephant home. I ain't no kid, you know! I've lost a couple of elephants in my day. [*Listens*] Jesus, you're boring me now . . . I don't know what the hell you're talking about. Maybe you want to talk to your elephant . . . huh? [*Turns to the* INDIAN] Here, come talk to your "papoose."

[*He offers the telephone. The* INDIAN *stares in disbelief, then grabs the telephone from* MURPH'S *hands and begins to chatter wildly*]

INDIAN: Pray-aim, bhai-yah Pray-aim moo-jhay ah-kay lay jah-oh k-Yah? moo-jhay nah-hee pa-tah mai kah-han hoo-n moo-jhay ah-hp-nay gha-ar lay chah-low ya-hahn do-ah bad-mash lar-Kay. Jo bah-hoot kha-tar-nahk hai-don-say mai nah-hee bah-cha sak-tah ah-pa-nay koh toom aik-dam moo-jhay ah-kay. [*Prem? Oh, Prem. Please come and take me away . . . what? I don't know where I am . . . Please come and take me to your house . . . please? There are two bad people. Two young men. They are dangerous. I cannot protect myself from them. Please . . . You must come and get me.*]

[MURPH *takes his knife from his pocket, cuts the line. The* INDIAN *almost falls flat on his face as the line from the receiver to the phone box is cut, since he has been leaning away from* MURPH *and* JOEY *during his plea*]

MURPH: You've had enough, Chief. [MURPH *laughs aloud*]

INDIAN: [*Not at once realizing the line must be connected, continues to talk into the telephone in Hindi*] Pray-aim, Pray-aim, ya-hahn aa-oh sah-rak kah nah-am hai—yeh toom-nay k-yah key-yah. [*Prem. Prem. Please come here. The street sign reads . . .*]

[*He now realizes he has been cut off and stares dumbly at the severed cord as* MURPH *waves the severed cord in his face*]

INDIAN: Toom-nay yeh k-yoh key-yah? [*What have you done?*]

MURPH: There it is, Turkie. Who you talkin' to?

INDIAN: [*To* JOEY, *screaming a father's fury and disgust*] Toom-nay yeh k-yohn key-yah cri-payah may-ree mah-dah-d kah-roho. [*Why have you done this? Please. Please help me.*]

[JOEY *has been standing throughout the entire scene, frozen in terror and disgust. He walks slowly toward* MURPH, *who kicks the* INDIAN. JOEY *bolts from the stage, muttering one continuous droning sob*]

MURPH: [*Screaming*] Go ahead, Joey. Love him. Love him like a mother. Hey? Joey? What the hell's the matter? C'mon, buddy? [*Turns to the* INDIAN, *takes his knife and cuts the* INDIAN'*s hand, so blood is on the knife*] Sorry, Chief. This is for my buddy, Joey. And for Pussyface. [*Calls offstage*] Joey! Buddy! What the hell's the matter? [*Races from the stage after* JOEY] Joey! Wait up. Joey! I killed the Indian!

[*He exits. The* INDIAN *stares dumbly at his hand, dripping blood. He then looks to the receiver and talks into it*]

INDIAN: Pray-aim, Pray-aim, mai ah-pa-nay lar-kay key ah-wah-az k-yon nah-hee soon sak-tah Pray-aim! Toom-nay may-ray sah-ahth aih-saw k-yohn key-yaw bay-tah Pray-aim, k-yah toom ho? [*Prem. Prem.*] [*He walks center stage, well way from the telephone booth*] [*Why can I not hear my son, Prem? Why have you done this to me?*] [*Suddenly the telephone rings again. Once. Twice. The* INDIAN *is startled. He talks into the receiver, while he holds the dead line in his bleeding hand*] [*Prem? Is that you? Prem?*] [*The telephone rings a third time*] Pray-aim, Pray-aim, bay-tah k-yah toom ho—[*Prem. Prem? Is that you?*] [*A fourth ring. The* INDIAN *knows the telephone is dead*] Pray-aim Pray-aim—moo-jhay bah-chald Pray-aim. [*Prem. Prem. Help me. Prem.*]

[*As the telephone rings a fifth time, in the silence of the night, the sounds of two boys' singing is heard*]

[FIRST BOY:]
I walk the lonely streets at night,
A-lookin' for your door . . .
[SECOND BOY:]
I look and look and look and look . . .
[FIRST BOY *and* SECOND BOY:]
But, baby, you don't care.
But, baby, no one cares.
But, baby, no one cares.

[*Their song continues to build as they repeat the lyrics, so the effect is one of many, many voices. The telephone continues its unanswered ring. The* INDIAN *screams a final anguished scream of fury to the boys offstage. The telephone rings a final ring as the* INDIAN *screams*]

INDIAN: [*Desperately, holding the telephone to the audience as an offer. He speaks in English into the telephone. The only words he remembers are those from his lesson*] How are you? You're welcome. You're welcome. Thank you. [*To the front*] Thank you!

*Blackout.*

# STUDY QUESTIONS

1. How much do we know about the background of Joey and Murph? What personal traits do the two share? How do they differ from each other? How important are their different ethnic backgrounds? Why is it important to the play's effect that they act so much alike?

2. What does the horseplay between the two suggest about their friendship? about their feelings? about their sense of identity and security? What does the opening song suggest about their relationship?

3. How much accurate information do we have about Murph's mother? about Pussyface? How can you tell what is fact and what is fiction about the two women? Why do the boys keep calling to them or addressing them as if they were just offstage? What conclusions do you draw about Murph and Joey themselves from the way they talk about the two women?

4. Besides their abuse of Gupta, how many different other ethnic or racial slurs do Murph and Joey utter? Why do they argue about whether Gupta is an Indian or a Turk? What is the point of their mixing up Gupta's heritage with other heritages, especially that of American Indians? What indications are there that they know better? What is implied by the blurring of distinctions? What does the generalized lumping together of ethnic slurs imply about the two boys? What does the undifferentiated language of abuse imply about the CONFLICTS in the play? How does the blurring of terms used to describe or address "foreigners" relate to the identity of the two boys? to their CHARACTER? to the THEMES of the play?

5. If you were staging the play, how would you indicate to the audience what Gupta is saying (note that the English translation of the Hindi included in parentheses in the printed text would not be available to an audience)? How "serious" would you make the fight scene? How would you distinguish between the tone of the violence between the boys and that between Joey and Gupta? How would you stage the spinning scene? What feelings toward the boys would you try to arouse in that scene?

6. How does the cutting of Gupta's hand affect your feelings toward the boys? How do you respond to their teasing of each other? to their verbal abuse of Gupta early in the play? How fully do you identity with Gupta's feelings? Why? At what point do you feel the most empathy with him? Do you ever identify with the feelings, attitudes, or values of Murph and Joey? If so, when? Why?

7. What is the central conflict in the play? How much of the conflict in the play occurs within the characters? How are the internal conflicts externalized? In what ways does the language of each character reflect his internal conflict? In what ways does the language reflect the larger conflicts in the play?

8. Describe the language spoken by Murph and Joey. In what ways is it distinctive? What indications are there that the two have developed a special language that has "private" meanings only for the two of them? How do the physical horseplay

and the fighting relate to the language they share? Does the fact that Gupta speaks virtually no English put more emphasis or less on the language the boys use? How does Gupta's lack of knowledge of English affect his body language and gestures?

9. How does the cutting of the telephone line relate to the major THEMES of the play? Describe the effect on Gupta of his inability to respond to words that urgently demand his response. Describe the effect on the audience.

10. How many different kinds of broken communication are represented in the play? How do the difficulties in communication relate to the frustrations about relationships felt by each of the characters? Compare ways the different characters respond to their frustrations.

11. What effect does the fact that Gupta is a stranger in the city have on his ability to understand what is happening to him? What other factors, besides his lack of understanding of English, affect his sense of disorientation?

12. Besides Hindi and English, what other human "languages" are used in the play—that is, by what other means do people try to communicate? How important is body language? gesture? facial expression? physical intimidation? physical touching? other physical rituals? communication through eye contact? verbal sparring? the verbal blurring of distinctions between people? the refusal to call people by their correct names? the staking out of physical territory?

# LANGUAGE

Words perhaps never mean quite the same thing to someone who hears them as they do to the person speaking them. They disappear into thin air, and we may misremember, or we may have misheard in the first place. Or the speaker may have misspoken or not gotten the emphasis just right. And even words firmly printed on a page do not always have definitive, discoverable, unimpeachable meaning. Nuances in the ways words are spoken change things; hearers filter words through their own consciousness, sometimes hearing only what they want to hear and sometimes mistaking intentions.

Writers work hard to make their meanings clear and solid, but often the words do not exactly express what writers wanted to say or thought they wanted to say. Words are, by definition, ambiguous. Every individual word, in any language, means more than one simple, specifiable thing, and when we string words together in phrases, sentences, and paragraphs, their possible meanings multiply and ramify. The process sounds hopeless when we think about all the things that can go wrong. And those things *do* often go wrong—in conversation, in writing, or in reading what someone else has written. Interpretations become ambiguous; confusions occur; misunderstandings result. The world of words, in life or in art, is often a frustrating and uncertain place.

But it is also exciting. The excitement results in part from uncertainties and ambiguities, in part from the creative challenge. Communication does sometimes, miraculously, take place; speakers and writers, formally or in a conversation or a letter, find ways to get to us, to touch us. Words are power; they are explosive, sometimes dangerous. Conversations often give joy, sometimes great joy, as minds meet or something new is discovered because someone else has pushed us or led us in a new direction. And reading provides pleasures that can be very satisfying indeed—in spite of uncertainties and ambiguities, sometimes in fact because of them. Good writing puts readers to work, not only reading but hearing, sorting, interpreting.

The challenge in reading or writing is to find the common denominator, what it is that a writer and reader—or speaker and audience—share. Language is based on the fundamental idea of communality, a conviction that people with interests and values in common need to—and can—share thoughts and feelings. Language at its base is thus an intimate thing, something shared between people who already have something in common. At its best, language is almost private, for it only "works" between people who share something important—feelings, values, traditions, conventions, a history, a culture. Sharing is crucial. Language is a way out of the prison of the self, yet by definition it has a limited audience; it is only available to those already within the circle. Thus, it limits the sharing, protects the self from invasion by an utterly hostile other. Language—any single language— is open only to a finite number of receivers. That is, in one sense, its power and glory, but in another sense, it is also the source of its failures and the human frustrations that result.

To speak of language in the abstract, though that may be necessary in order to suggest its power and ubiquity, is to be somewhat misleading, for although language is universal in human cultures, no single language is universal or even close to it. Over the centuries, there have been a series of well-meaning attempts to create a universal language. Such visionary projects are foolish because they fundamentally misunderstand the nature of language as a system for drawing upon shared experience. Many things— things that need to be articulated and communicated—are not universally shared, though they are shared within a particular group that can develop a language to express them. Outsiders may not be able to break the code and thus may find the group impossible to understand.

Trying to read words on a page in a language one doesn't understand is not only frustrating but absurd. We can't translate if we haven't a clue about what the words mean or about the nature of the language. It is equally frustrating to recognize the words but to have no idea what ideas or events they represent because there is a cultural or social barrier between us and the words on the page or on someone's lips. If we do not share at least a basic understanding of values and referents, we cannot begin to read because we do not know the "language." The value of having many different languages lies in what they can do for the commonality of those who are in a particular system.

When we talk about the language someone speaks, we usually literally mean Spanish, or French, or Russian, or Japanese, or English. But those who know well any one of these major languages know that within each are dozens, perhaps hundreds, of distinct variations. "American" is different from the "English" of England, and both are different from "Canadian" or "Caribbean." But there are other refinements as well. People from Boston speak one way, people from San Antonio another. People from Toronto one way, from Vancouver another. Jamaica one way, Barbados another. Some of the difference involves urban versus rural distinctions, some involves regionalism. And there are differences, in speech and in written language, of race, class, occupation, neighborhood, income group.

There is a language of farmers and one of truckers; computer technicians use a very different language, not just because they need special terms for things other people may not talk about at all, but because they think differently and share a particular system of expression that depends on shared values. There is a language of Valley girls, of mobsters, rock musicians, disc jockeys, fraternity men, black preachers, car salesmen, beach bums; there is street language, rap, the language of family, of church, of "the club" (whatever club it may be), of the classroom, the museum, the ballpark, the playground, the factory, the dance class, the game show, the kindergarten, the singles bar. All of us speak several of these languages, in addition to the English or Spanish or Arabic that we regard as our native language. We speak one way when we speak to people we know to be from a particular group—school friends, concertgoers, cousins, or lovers—and another way when we speak to others, not because we are phony with some people and not with others, but because it takes different words, different syntax, different uses of the voice to communicate with some people from those it takes with others. People come from different places, literally and emotionally, and to communicate with anyone we have to find a language in common.

But words can be treacherous as well as friendly. In some cultures, particular words—or even the processes of naming and articulating in themselves—carry a mystical or supernatural power: as curse, creative force, spell, or hex. But even without assuming that their force involves a special kind of energy, we can readily see that they have powerful effects on hearers. Politicians use them to persuade people about a particular notion—or to mislead people into mistaking one set of interests for another. Teachers use words to clarify matters in the common fund of knowledge, to stimulate new thinking, or to proselytize students to a particular way of looking at things. Preachers use them to try to change people's minds or lives—or to raise money for their projects. Businessmen use them to make deals, lawyers to argue and persuade, physicians to explain a process or clarify a diagnosis, scientists to discover new facts or develop new theories. Men use them to seduce women, and women to seduce men; parents to instruct or discipline children, children to coax favors or justify themselves to adults. Without language we are lost as human beings, and yet with it we are often confused and perplexed, feeling just a bit as if we are doing something dishonest or misleading in using words at all.

The process of reading is a process of becoming self-conscious about words, of learning their limits, their hazards, the ways they can be misused as well as the ways they can help us to be more human and lead richer and more connected emotional and intellectual lives. Some of the misunderstandings words cause in life are from carelessness, the using of words without adequate consideration or control. In the selections in this chapter and throughout the book, the writers have ordinarily thought through very carefully exactly what they want to say and what they want to do. This does not mean that what they have written is perfect in every detail, but it does mean that the words have been carefully chosen and their effects upon us as readers have been planned, one might even say calculated.

The formal study of how language works is called RHETORIC. One can speak of the rhetoric of a given story—what effects it is calculated to produce—or more generally of the rhetoric of an author (what particular strategies of persuasion he or she uses) or the rhetoric of fiction or poetry (the way a particular literary mode uses language to accomplish its particular ends). Within rhetoric, certain standard features develop over a period of time, and when such features become commonly accepted and frequently imitated, they are called CONVENTIONS. There is, for example, a convention of giving descriptive or suggestive or symbolic names to CHARACTERS (Lily Goode, Dr. Stern) in order to give readers some idea of what they may be like. In life, nicknames often actually work the same way, but in literature, writers sometimes take a certain *license* with names, inventing names that help to characterize a person. Too egregious a use of descriptive or symbolic names would, of course, seem overdone, artificial, or just plain silly, and writers tend to husband such tricks carefully, if they are wise, so that readers will still find their work believable and enjoyable.

Writers, even the best professional writers, do sometimes make mistakes—either calculating their effects too precisely and becoming overingenious, or planning them insufficiently and becoming careless. But it is a good rule of thumb to assume that a good writer always has a reason for doing a particular thing—that every word is carefully chosen, and that the word used is exactly the one needed to make a particular point rather than some other almost equivalent word. Paying close attention to the language of a story, play, essay, or poem is usually quite rewarding, and one of the best habits a reader can develop is to ask, repeatedly, the questions: Why this word? Why in this place? What would the difference be if another word were used instead?

Words are the building blocks of writers, and writers with pride in their craft use what they have in the best possible way. The selections here have been chosen with an eye to finding examples of writing that show how language can be used effectively, how it can be used to make particular points, and, more important, how it can make us as readers feel, as well as think, in a particular way.

# WRITING
# ABOUT THE READING

## PERSONAL NARRATIVE

What forbidden words were considered most shocking in your home? in your community? in your school? among your friends? What kinds of people were willing to violate the taboo? What were their motivations? What price did they pay for the violation? What kinds of violations were most severely punished? Under what conditions, if any, were people allowed to use these forbidden words?

Choose one incident from your childhood or teenage years in which community standards of language were violated. Describe the episode in detail, making clear just what kinds of standards—religious, moral, ethnic, or standards of "good" taste—were at issue in the incident.

## IMITATION AND PARODY

Using Gloria Naylor's essay as a model, discuss STEREOTYPICAL words or phrases that your own national, ethnic, or community group finds the most offensive when used by someone *outside* the group.

## ARGUMENTATIVE PAPER

On the basis of your own experiences or those of your friends, write an essay attacking Richard Rodriguez's position on the use of English in American schools. Be sure you read the Rodriguez piece carefully and understand exactly what his position is before you begin. Make clear what kinds of human values are at stake in the controversy.

Alternative essay: Write an essay based on your own experiences in which you support Rodriguez.

## ANALYTICAL ESSAY

Using *The Indian Wants the Bronx*, "The Language of Home," and "Borders" as examples, analyze the relationship between the uses of language and the everyday behavior that goes with the language use. In an essay of no more than 1,000 words, show how behavior and words are linked in the portrayal of CHARACTERS in these selections, and suggest what psychological insights are explored in the way these characters are presented.

## RESEARCH PAPER

List ten "forbidden" words from your childhood—words that family, friends, church groups, or school officials considered offensive. Using dictionaries of slang and other materials that reference librarians can help you find, look up the words' etymologies. Attempt to discover which words, if any, have always been considered objectionable and which, if any, have changed in their acceptability.

# 6

# THE MAN FROM MARS

Not all of the people we meet are part of our tribe; not all share our heritage, or speak our language. Some, in fact, are so very different that it sometimes seems they might as well be men or women from Mars.

Such encounters are common in the American experience. Think of what the Native Americans must have thought when they first saw Columbus and his men or Cortés or de Soto. Think of what some New Yorkers of a hundred years ago must have thought as they saw the stream of Eastern and central Europeans pour onto the streets of the city from Ellis Island, or what Californians a little earlier must have been thinking when Chinese were brought in to build the railroads.

But even today, someone with dreadlocks or earlocks or someone wearing a turban, a sari, or a dashiki can turn heads in many towns and on many campuses. Though television and movies have made us more or less familiar with everyone from Watusi to Laplanders, and many of them with us, there is often something unsettling when someone from a dramatically different culture walks into our everyday lives. These dramatic differences in language, dress, and customs may create all kinds of misunderstanding or problems. The Japanese, for example, make the kind of slurping noises when they eat that many American mothers send children away from the table for making, though in Japan such behavior is perfectly acceptable. On the other hand, the Japanese (and Chinese as well) cannot stand the smell or taste of butter or cheese and wonder how we can manage to eat such loath-some stuff. To them, many Americans—big, blond, hairy, and boister-ous—must seem a bit like creatures from outer space.

"Aliens"—what we call such space creatures—is also what we call for-eigners among us; but in the United States, Canada, and elsewhere in the hemisphere, aliens may be "naturalized" and become Americans. Indeed, all but a few of us are from families that came to this continent as "aliens," no matter whether that was last year, or fifty, a hundred, or four hundred years ago or whether our people came as explorers, settlers, missionaries, refugees, draft evaders, or slaves. Meeting "aliens" is part of our everyday American experience; America has been a favorite landing place for Mar-tians.

But the "aliens" we meet may not be aliens in fact. They may be as American as we are but from a different background and heritage, living a life so remote from ours it seems as if they inhabited another planet, but living still what is an American life. Have you ever walked into a strange neighborhood in a city, perhaps your own city, and suddenly noticed that all the older women were wearing black? Or, in another neighborhood, that all the men had beards and hair curled around their ears and were wearing round black hats and all black clothes? Or, when you visited another neigh-borhood, city, or region, that everyone seemed to be yelling at the tops of their voices, or in another that no one said "Hi" or smiled?

When you first meet someone from another culture, these differences may be exotic, exciting, and attractive, but they are just as likely to be puz-zling, frightening, or offensive. These strange encounters interrupt our rou-tines, our ordinary ways of speaking and behaving. Putting into question things we have taken for granted, they can be occasions for growth and expansion of our horizons. But sometimes they seem threatening, and we back off or reject the invader. Or, instead of responding to the new experi-ence—positively or negatively, but as a new experience—we may fall back on what we have read or been told. We may have a ready-made attitude generated by a STEREOTYPE* that does not open us up to the new but closes us off from the other. For, more often than not, these stereotypes are not very flattering or reassuring, unless it is to flatter ourselves and reassure ourselves of our inherent superiority.

The poems, stories, and nonfiction prose pieces here offer a range of encounters: Americans abroad who learn wonderful or troubling things

---

*Words in small capitals are defined in the glossary.

about another "planet"; Americans who go abroad to find their roots only to discover that they are considered by their relatives not as siblings but as Americans, creatures from another planet; foreigners who come here as conquerors or as refugees and meet various receptions; Americans of various ethnic groups who confront other Americans from other groups with anxiety, insensitivity, or perplexity.

American society is so complex and so fluid we are all Martians to some other Americans, and we encounter Martians every day.

# Diane Burns

A painter and illustrator, Diane Burns was educated at the Institute of American Indian Art in Santa Fe, New Mexico, and at Barnard College. Her first volume of poetry, *Riding the One-Eyed Ford* (1981), was nominated for the William Carlos Williams Award. She belongs to the Third World Writers Association and the Feminist Writers Guild.

The answer to the personal question is Anishinabe (Ojibwa) and Cheemehuevi Indian, but if you ask the question, you'd better duck.

## SURE YOU CAN ASK ME A PERSONAL QUESTION

How do you do?
    No, I am not Chinese.
No, not Spanish.
    No, I am American Indi-uh, Native American.
No, not from India.                        5
    No, not Apache.
No, not Navajo.
    No, not Sioux.
No, we are not extinct.
    Yes, Indin.                        10
Oh?
    So that's where you got those high cheekbones.
Your great grandmother, huh?
    An Indian Princess, huh?
Hair down to there?                      15
    Let me guess. Cherokee?
Oh, so you've had an Indian friend?
    That close?
Oh, so you've had an Indian lover?
    That tight?                        20
Oh, so you've had an Indian servant?
    That much?

Yeah, it was awful what you guys did to us.
    It's real decent of you to apologize.
No, I don't know where you can get peyote. 25
    No, I don't know where you can get Navajo rugs real cheap.
No, I didn't make this. I bought it at Bloomingdale's.
    Thank you. I like your hair too.
I don't know if anyone knows whether or not Cher is really Indian.
    No, I didn't make it rain tonight. 30
Yeah. Uh-huh. Spirituality.
    Uh-huh. Yeah. Spirituality. Uh-huh. Mother
Earth. Yeah. Uh'huh. Uh'huh. Spirituality.
    No, I didn't major in archery.
Yeah, a lot of us drink too much. 35
    Some of us can't drink enough.
This ain't no stoic look.
    This is my face.

## STUDY QUESTIONS

1. Identify which lines are spoken by the "I" and which by someone else.

2. What are some of the STEREOTYPES indicated by the implied questions?

# Mitsuye Yamada

Born in Japan, raised in Seattle, interned with her family in a concentration camp in Idaho during World War II, Mitsuye Yamada teaches at Cypress College in California. She and the Chinese-American poet Nellie Wong were the subjects of a National Public Broadcasting Service documentary on Asian-American women.

"Looking Out," from *Camp Notes and Other Poems* (1976), is typical of Yamada's understated dry wit and bite. Cover up all but the first three lines. What do you think the speaker's response will be to what "he was saying?"

# LOOKING OUT

It must be odd
to be a minority
he was saying.
I looked around
and didn't see any.                                        5
So I said
Yeah
it must be.

## STUDY QUESTIONS

1. Why doesn't the SPEAKER see any minority?

2. What does the title mean?

# Tess Slesinger

Author of two books—the novel *The Unpossessed* (1934) and the short story collection from which "White on Black" is taken, *On Being Told That Her Second Husband Has Taken His First Lover and Other Stories* (1935)—Tess Slesinger (1905–45) wrote screenplays and fiction during the last ten years of her life. In the small number of works she has produced, she displays a distinct voice, keen perception, and sharp wit.

This story—although it was written in 1931 and its action is set twenty years before that, and despite its use of words, such as "Negro," that are no longer current—might easily be set in the 1980s.

# WHITE ON BLACK

One of the private schools attended by the "nice" children of the West Side     1
some twenty years ago followed not only the liberal practice of mixing rich
and poor, Gentile and Jew, but made a point also of including Negroes. Not
many, of course—just enough so that when the eye of a visiting parent roved
down the rows of pink and white faces collected for the Harvest Festival or
the Easter Play, it stumbled complacently here and there—perhaps three or
four times in all the auditorium—on an equally scrubbed black one sticking
out like a solitary violet in a bed of primroses. For, except in the case of two
sisters, or of a brother and sister, these black children never made friends
among themselves, seldom even to the extent of choosing seats side by side
in assemblies.

I suppose that the effect upon the rest of us was, as it was intended to     2
be, on the whole good. It must have taught us well-bred little boys and girls
at the least the untruth of the common slander that Negroes have an unpleasant odor; for certainly none of the Wilsons and Whites and Washingtons in
our school ever smelt of anything but soap. And we were brought up, through
weekly ethics lessons and the influence of the inevitable elderly lady teacher
who had never got Harriet Beecher Stowe out of her mind, to the axiom that
all men were created equal.

The few scattered colored children in clean clothes, then, contributed     3
practically to our liberal education. But what effect we, in our more than
clean, our often luxurious clothes and with our pink and white faces, had in
turn upon them, it is impossible for one of us to judge. Although I can tell
you today what has happened since to a number of my old schoolmates, even
to those in whom I have long ceased to be interested, and although I run
every year across gossip concerning still others, none of us has any idea what
happened to our colored classmates. Some of them left school before the
high-school years were over; some of them were graduated and stood at our
elbows with their rolled-up diplomas; but all of them have equally dropped
out of our common knowledge since. Where are they now? Did they drift
back to Harlem, those Wilsons and Washingtons and Whites? How do they
look back upon their ten years' interlude with white children? I cannot imagine. But I remember vividly the school careers of the two who were in my
class.

The Wilsons, brother and sister, joined us in the sixth grade. Paul was     4
exquisitely made, his face chiselled and without fault; a pair of delicately
dilated nostrils at the end of a short fine nose, and an aureole of dim black
curls. Elizabeth was bigger, coarser, more negroid; darker, her lips were

thick, her nose less perfect; but still she was a beautiful child, luxuriously made, and promising to develop into a type of the voluptuous Negro woman at her best. Elizabeth was older than Paul; but her brain, like her nose, was less sharp, and both were put into the same class.

For the first week or two our kind teachers paid them the surplus attention which was always extended to Negro, or crippled, or poverty-stricken children. They suggested that Paul be chosen when the boys were choosing up sides; they asked the girls to take Elizabeth as partner. The children stood off from them no more than they stood off from any newcomers. We were not adultly snobbish; we merely glared at all newcomers in our world until they should prove themselves worthy. But by the end of the month, there was no longer any question of choosing Paul: Paul himself was the chooser and the permanently chosen; likewise Elizabeth was besieged with requests for the seats on either side of her in assembly, and it became an honor to have a seat in the same row; and the teachers turned round, and were given rather to suppressing the colored Wilsons than to bringing them out.

For after a certain natural humility had worn off, Paul and Elizabeth were not merely taken into the group; they took over the group. Including the faculty. They were a smashing success. For one thing, they feared nothing; furthermore, they proved marvelous athletes; and they were born leaders. Electing Paul to the captaincy of the basketball team was a mere formality; even if he hadn't richly deserved it, he would have permitted no one else to hold it. Elizabeth was as strong as a horse, less skilful, less graceful than he, but easily outshining, by her animal strength and fearlessness, all the white girls in the class. Beside their athletic prowess, which alone would have won them popularity in a class of eleven-year-olds, both of them were gifted with an over-powering jubilancy and a triumphant bullying wit, which inevitably made them czars.

They ruled the class with a rod of iron, chose their intimates, played with them, dropped them, and patronized the teachers. Their power spread to politics; by the end of the first year Paul was president of the class, and Elizabeth, who could not spell, secretary. Their class-meetings were masterpieces of irreverent wit and bedlam, subtly dominated by the tacitly authoritative Paul. The teachers turned over to them the difficult business of controlling the class after recess, and Paul, in his double capacity of legal president and illegal czar, easily succeeded where they had long failed. Even his sister, who was no small power among the girls, feared and adored him. If her authority was for one moment questioned, she had only to say, "I'll call Paul. . . ."

I remember myself—and probably not a few others of the dazzled little white girls did the same in secret—going home to dream about marrying Paul and taking Elizabeth to live with us. I remember a moment of certainly unprecedented and of almost unsurpassed voluptuous pleasure on an occasion when Paul, twisting his wiry body into one of those marvelous knots from which he unrolled himself to shoot a basket, stretched so far that his shirt left his trousers and revealed a few inches of coffee-colored skin glistening with sweat, which caused me to gasp with delight. We girls chose to play against the boys of the class rather than among ourselves, and I was surely not the only girl who had voted favorably for the pure delight of being tossed on the ground and swung round the hips by the jubilant Paul, who had, beside his lovely body and fierce little nostrils, not the slightest inhibition.

For two years the noisy Wilsons demoralized the entire class into a raucous group that was never tired of wrestling, playing basketball, shouting jokes, and merrily defying the teachers. Not even the famous Seventh Grade Trouble, which involved the Wilsons as central figures, subdued them. Not even the visit, upon that terrifying occasion, of their mother. All of us made a point of walking past the principal's office to view Mrs Wilson, who sat there, dressed in black and with her face held low and ashamed as though she were the culprit herself. We whispered afterward, among ourselves, of what a lady Mrs Wilson was; we had never before seen a colored lady. 9

The high-school years loomed ahead. We were to be joined by another section of the same grade, and we were determined to maintain our solidarity with Paul at our head. Our reputation as a champion class had preceded us; but with it, we soon noticed, a reputation for rowdiness. Paul was instantly elected captain of the basketball team. But he was just nosed out of the presidency by a white boy belonging to the other section, who must have gained some treacherous votes from among our own. Although the other boy occupied the chair, Paul managed, for half a year, to bully even the new section into slowly waning submission to the last echoes of his power. 10

Elizabeth's popularity remained limited to the girls in our own old section. The others adopted her at first as a novelty, but they had not been trained to her loud hearty jokes and her powerful wrestling, and soon tired of her and left her to her old companions. These dwindled slowly, as we girls gained consciousness of our status as girls and wished to dissociate ourselves from anything rowdy. Of course it was our fault—we could have pushed Elizabeth forward and remained loyal to her—but we had so many things to think of in those days. And I think something of the sort was bound to happen to Elizabeth anyway; she did not have the native personality to warrant and sustain the unlimited popularity which had fallen on her partly because of her strength and partly because she was her brother's sister. There was a quiet girl in our class, less mature than the rest of us—who were, in that first year of high-school, more fiercely mature than some of us are today, which is ten years later. This girl, Diana, fastened upon Elizabeth as a chum, and from now on the curious pair were inseparable. 11

I remember the early days when it became the thing for the boys to take the girls to the corner soda-store after basketball games, and for each boy to treat one girl to a fudge sundae. We couldn't help noticing that the boys, so eager to rough-house with Elizabeth in the classroom, hesitated among themselves as to which should treat her, and that the same one never treated her twice. We noticed too, that the soda-clerk stared at the dark blemish in our 12 small white group. Elizabeth never seemed to notice anything; she developed a habit of kidding the soda-clerk in a loud professional voice, and soon our indignation was shifted to her, and we told her to lower her voice and not fool around with soda-clerks. Toward the end of the year Diana and Elizabeth dissociated themselves from our group, and began to occupy a little table by themselves in a corner. Here they would sit and pretend to be alone, and we could hear them giggling and whispering happily. Paul, of course, was still too young and too "manly" ever to join these parties.

In the course of that first year in high-school many things beside the soda-parties happened to us. Wrestling between boys and girls was outlawed, the girls began to loop their hair in buns over the ears, and the boys began to appear in navy-blue long trousers. 13

I remember Paul in his first longies. Instead of navy-blue, he appeared in a sleek suit of light Broadway tan, nicely nipped in at the waist, which harmonized with his clear mocha skin and showed off his dapper little figure to perfection. But it didn't quite fit in our school. I noticed that day, standing in line behind him to buy lunch tickets, that he wore brand new shoes: they were long and very pointed, and polished a brilliant ochre; they were button shoes, with cloth tops; they squeaked like nothing else in the world. I remember staring at them, and wondering where I had seen shoes like those before: was it in the elevator at home? 14

We were so grown-up that year that instead of shooting baskets in the twenty-minute recess that followed lunch, we got one girl to play the piano and the rest of us danced. Only about half of the boys were bold enough to dance; Paul still belonged to the group which stood in a corner and laughed and imitated their bolder friends, waiting for younger girls to be imported into the high-school department next year. With one boy to every pair of girls, it was not surprising that Elizabeth danced more than half of her dances with her friend Diana. The rest of us paired off with our girl-friends equally often. 15

But for no reason that anyone could see, Elizabeth's friends still diminished week by week. She had occasional spurts of her old popularity, but these were chiefly occasioned by reaction against some more stable idol, who would soon be restored to her post. Elizabeth's one permanent friend was Diana, the quiet little blonde girl who had no other friends. As far as I know, Diana was the only girl who ever invited Elizabeth to her house, and it was rumored that Diana was the only one who had seen the inside of the Wilson house, but Diana could be made neither to say whether it was true, nor what it was like if she had seen it. As for the rest of us, we were a little uncomfortable about omitting Elizabeth at afternoon parties at our homes; but somebody's mother settled it for us by saying that she thought it would be an unkindness to the little colored girl to invite her to a home where there would be none of her own people. This conflicted, of course, with the lesson 16 of our ethics classes, but we were thirteen-going-on-fourteen, and we had too much to think about, so we let it go at that.

Meanwhile Paul, who had remained captain all the first year, failed to be elected for the second. Some of his classmates started propaganda to the effect that, while still their best player, he was no good as a captain, and they self-righteously elected the second-best player in his stead. Paul took out his anger in refusing to coöperate with the team, and developed into a poor sport, that worst of anathemas in school, successfully hogging the ball so that no one else had a chance. The epithet poor sport began to be whispered about the classroom, and when class elections for the second year were held, Paul was not even nominated for an office. Our section had sworn to stand by him when we had suffered defeat at the beginning of the year, but when the time came we simply sat and held our tongues, and elected another boy from the hostile section.

When the Wilsons returned for the second year after vacation, they looked a little different to us. Paul had turned into something resembling an uptown beau, and Elizabeth's face had grown coarser. Elizabeth joined her friend Diana at once, and their companionship remained unbroken. Paul, however, held in considerably less esteem, remained aloof, making no effort to regain his lost popularity, and pursued his way sullenly and almost defiantly among us. He met our reproaches with indifference.

That year evening dances broke out among us. For the sake of girls who might never be asked, there was a rule that everyone must come unescorted and unescorting. It was easy enough, of course, to break the rule. Most of the girls came regularly attended by boys from the upper classes. Elizabeth came the first few times with her brother, which was as good as coming unattended. Paul stood in a corner with the stags; Elizabeth sat with the other girls who had come unattended or attended by brothers, looking very dark and strange in her short-sleeved light dresses, and accepted gratefully her few opportunities to dance.

There began to be whispers among us of what we would do if Paul asked one of us to come to a dance with him, or offered a treat to a soda. We admitted to feeling uncomfortable at the thought of being seen on the street with him. At the same time we realized that what we were contemplating was horribly unfair. But Evelyn—Evelyn, who led our class in social matters because at fourteen she wore rouge and baby French heels—said, "School is school; it's not the World; it's not our Real Lives," and we let it go at that. As we had tacitly adopted policies toward Elizabeth, we now officially adopted one toward Paul; we were to be extra nice to him, but not in the way that one treats a boy; and we were to dance with him when he asked us, but very kindly refuse his invitations to escort us anywhere outside the school walls. Fortunately for our peace of mind, ethics lessons were that year changed to weekly lessons in elocution for the girls, and public speaking for the boys.

But none of us was given the chance to refuse him. So far as I know, he never asked a girl to go anywhere with him, never left the stag-line at our Friday night dances, and after the first half-dozen, he never even came with Elizabeth. He scrupulously avoided even the careless physical contacts in the elevator, of which the other boys took modest advantage. Also, when we followed our policy of being nice to him in school, we found ourselves politely ignored. Paul grew increasingly sullen, even occasionally rude, and one girl reported that he had passed her on the street and pretended not to see her, neglecting to lift his elegant tan felt hat.

In the middle of that year Elizabeth's friend Diana was withdrawn from the school by her parents and sent to a boarding-school in the South, rumor said to get her away from the black girl and teach her a proper sense of color. 22

With her friend gone, Elizabeth picked up smaller fry and dazzled them, because, unlike Paul, she seemed to want never to be alone. But even with these she learned to disappear at the school door, or at most to walk no further with a white classmate than the end of the school block. There, making some excuse about having to hurry, or going in another direction, she would dash away with a good-humored smile. I remember watching her running away from us once and wondering to what strange world she disappeared every day after school. 23

Of course, not one of the nice girls in our school would have dreamed of hurting Elizabeth's feelings by suggesting that she leave us on the street, but there must have been some hesitating on the corner before Elizabeth so effectively learned that her position with her white schoolmates ended with the school door. Or could it have been that dark lady, who had sat in the principal's office with her head lowered as though she were the culprit, that time of the Seventh Grade Trouble? But no matter, we were in our third year of high-school now, and had forgotten the seventh grade as we had forgotten the famous trouble, and were used now to seeing our dark classmate hurry off after school and run down the long block, leaving us standing on the corner, discussing our this and that, which was so awfully important to us. . . . 24

In the third year of high-school, Paul simply did not appear. We were, I suppose, faintly relieved, in so far as we thought about him at all. He removed, after all, such uncomfortable questions as playing other schools with a Negro on our first team. And our own old section, our merry, rowdy section, of which Paul had once been undisputed king, had imperceptibly melted away, the boundary line was wavery, our old loyalty vague, a thing of the past; Paul, so far as he was anything in our minds, was a memory belonging to our lost section. When we asked Elizabeth what had happened to him, she told us he was going to another school because he didn't like girls and considered our private school sissy. She carried it off rather well, I think. One or two of us suggested that he might have been fired, because we all knew that his work had gone off badly in that last year. 25

Elizabeth herself, in those last two years, toned down considerably. Her 26 prowess in studies had never been great, and she seemed now to be devoting more time to them. Her athletic ability had not lived up to its promise, because she had been after all primarily interested in rough-neck play, and seemed unable or unwilling to tame her strength and spirits into rules and skill. She abandoned the bright colors she had worn as a child, and came to school in neat and modest dresses. She dropped without reluctance into the common order of students, learned to toady as she had once been toadied to, and managed to keep up a decent sober reputation which ensured her a mild amount of companionship, restricted, of course, to within the school walls. On committees Elizabeth volunteered for unpleasant jobs and carried them out cheerfully and efficiently. She grew generous and sweet-tempered, and a little like a servant; and like a servant, she was thanked for her services and forgotten.

Paul had dropped out of our existence.  27

The last time I saw either of them was at our graduation dance. Eliza-  28
beth had long ago given up coming alone to our dances, but she came, of course, to this one, looking rather too burly and black in the prescribed white dress, with bare arms which hung like bones from her ungainly shoulders. She was the whole of the committee on refreshments, and all during the first part of the evening she stood behind a table with her diploma tucked on a rack over her head—nobody from her family had come to see her be gradu-ated—and cheerfully dispensed sandwiches and ice-cream.

Everybody was mingling proudly in the big assembly room, waiting for  29
the chairs to be removed for dancing; everybody was very nice to Elizabeth and even took down her address as a matter of form, but in the rush of taking addresses that really meant something and comparing notes about future col-leges, she was forgotten, and if it hadn't been for a teacher who came to her rescue, she might have been completely alone. When the dancing began, the teacher led her away from the buffet table with her arm around her, to bring her to the row of chairs where girls sat waiting for partners.

Some of us must have had compunctions—I know I did—floating by  30
her in our partners' arms, for on that night the least popular girl had achieved a faithful escort, if only by importing boys from classes below who felt it an honor to be there at all. But none of us felt badly enough to urge our partners to leave us and dance with Elizabeth. Later one or two boys danced a waltz with her, because a waltz was the least difficult thing to sacrifice. She sat all evening and talked cheerfully to the teacher. She looked uncomplaining, as though she had quietly learned her place. She even seemed to enjoy watching the rest of us dance.

The evening broke up on a high-note of "See you again," "Don't forget,"  31
and "Oh, the most marvelous time!" and I remember emerging from the dance-room in a fever of happiness, walking on winged feet. I pushed my way through the gay crowd outside the door. Somebody tapped me on the

arm: "Miss!" I turned and saw, for the first time in three years, Paul Wilson, the king of our old section! I smiled eagerly, delighted to see him again. "Why Paul!" I exclaimed, holding out my hand.

He was as beautiful as he had been three years before, but his face was different, hardened perhaps, so that the dapper tan clothes he wore made him cheap and flashy. He still wore pointed button shoes with cloth tops. He was standing by the wall with his hat pulled down over his eyes. "Why, Paul!" I said.

32

He looked up, caught my eye, and shifted his away as though he had failed to recognize me. He looked down at the floor and spoke in a low voice. "Miss, would you mind finding my sister Elizabeth Wilson inside and say her brother is waiting for her?" He stuck his hands suddenly into his pockets with something of his old sullen gesture.

33

I remember turning from him with an overpowering sense of guilt to spare him embarrassment, and going back with tears burning my eyes to find Elizabeth. I left him standing there against the wall, with his hat over his eyes, snubbing his former classmates, while they passed their former god and leader, some of them too happy to distinguish his features under that hat, others no doubt turning from him to prevent his embarrassment, and even, on that happy night, to spare themselves. . . . This should have been his graduation.

34

## STUDY QUESTIONS

1. Why do the parents look "complacently" on the few black faces at the school functions (paragraph 1)?

2. By the end of the first nine paragraphs, the two Wilsons, especially Paul, are triumphant athletically, politically, and socially in the school. At that point, as they are about to enter high school, what do you expect to happen? Why?

3. Why does Elizabeth's popularity begin to slip once the students merge classes and enter high school?

4. What are some of the changes in behavior among all the students when they enter high school? How do you expect those changes to alter the status of Paul and Elizabeth?

5. How does Paul dress in high school? Why does he not seem to "fit"? What does the NARRATOR mean by the last sentence in paragraph 14: "I remember staring at them, and wondering where I had seen shoes like those before: was it in the elevator at home?"

6. How do the liberal mothers justify not inviting Elizabeth Wilson to their homes?

7. How does Paul react to his not being elected captain of the basketball team in his second year? How does this affect his school political career? How does he react to his loss of popularity in the second year? How do the girls resolve to treat Paul? What does he do before the third year begins?

8. How does Elizabeth fare during her third year? How do you account for the fact that she succeeds, in her fashion, at the school, whereas Paul, the handsomer and brighter, drops out? What does she do at the graduation dance? What commentary does that seem to make on how blacks could manage to succeed in the racist society? How does it affect Paul?

# Marcela Christine Lucero-Trujillo

B orn in Colorado, Marcela Christine Lucero-Trujillo (1931–84) taught Chicano studies at the University of Minnesota. Her poetry has appeared in a variety of publications (such as *La Luz*) and has been included in such anthologies as *The Third Woman*.

These strangers eat beans every day, their wondering neighbors believe.

## ROSEVILLE, MINN., U.S.A.

In Roseville, one notices
    a speck on a white wall
    a moustache on a brown face
and listens to right wing dilemmas
    of another race.          5
Turn that corrido[1] record down,
    walk softly in ponchos,
Speak Spanish in whispers
    or they'll approach you to say,
    "I've been to Spain too, ¡Ole!"     10
    (even if you never have),
In Roseville, U.S.A.

Start the stove fan,
    close the windows on a summer day,
    'cause the neighbors might say,     15
    "Do they eat beans every day, even on Sundays?"
In Roseville, U.S.A.

1. Border folksong.

At the sign of the first snowflake
    Inquiring eyes will pursue you,
    asking why you haven't returned with the migrant stream    20
    that went back in June, or even in September,
In Roseville, U.S.A.

My abuela[2] would turn in her grave
    to think that the culmination
    of her cultural perpetuation    25
    is Marcela at Target's food section
    searching desperately for flour tortillas,
No way—I live in ROSEVILLE, U.S.A.
My modus vivendi
of New Mexico piñon and green chili    30
and my Colorado Southwest mentality
are another reality
in ROSEVILLE, U.S.A.

## STUDY QUESTIONS

1. What facets of "racial perpetuation" are endangered in Roseville?
2. How does Marcela respond?

# Jack G. Shaheen

Born in 1935 in Pittsburgh, Jack G. Shaheen teaches mass communications at Southern Illinois University, Edwardsville. The recipient of two Fulbright-Hays Lectureship grants, he is the author of *The TV Arab* and *Nuclear War Films 1978*.

The Arab is the new whipping boy of the media, stereotyped as a terrorist, and the caricatures hurt Arab-Americans, who have to explain to their children that ethnic stereotypes of any kind are false and harmful.

2. Grandmother.

# THE MEDIA'S IMAGE OF ARABS

America's bogyman is the Arab. Until the nightly news brought us TV pictures of Palestinian boys being punched and beaten, almost all portraits of Arabs seen in America were dangerously threatening. Arabs were either billionaires or bombers—rarely victims. They were hardly ever seen as ordinary people practicing law, driving taxis, singing lullabies or healing the sick. Though TV news may portray them more sympathetically now, the absence of positive media images nurtures suspicion and stereotype. As an Arab-American, I have found that ugly caricatures have had an enduring impact on my family.

I was sheltered from prejudicial portraits at first. My parents came from Lebanon in the 1920s; they met and married in America. Our home in the steel city of Clairton, Pa., was a center for ethnic sharing—black, white, Jew and gentile. There was only one major source of media images then, at the State movie theater where I was lucky enough to get a part-time job as an usher. But in the late 1940s, Westerns and war movies were popular, not Middle Eastern dramas. Memories of World War II were fresh, and the screen heavies were the Japanese and the Germans. True to the cliché of the times, the only good Indian was a dead Indian. But when I mimicked or mocked the bad guys, my mother cautioned me. She explained that stereotypes blur our vision and corrupt the imagination. "Have compassion for all people, Jackie," she said. "This way, you'll learn to experience the joy of accepting people as they are, and not as they appear in films. Stereotypes hurt."

Mother was right. I can remember the Saturday afternoon when my son, Michael, who was seven, and my daughter, Michele, six, suddenly called out: "Daddy, Daddy, they've got some bad Arabs on TV." They were watching that great American morality play, TV wrestling. Akbar the Great, who liked to hear the cracking of bones, and Abdullah the Butcher, a dirty fighter who liked to inflict pain, were pinning their foes with "camel locks." From that day on, I knew I had to try to neutralize the media caricatures.

It hasn't been easy. With my children, I have watched animated heroes Heckle and Jeckle pull the rug from under "Ali Boo-Boo, the Desert Rat," and Laverne and Shirley stop "Sheik Ha-Mean-Ie" from conquering "the U.S. and the world." I have read comic books like the "Fantastic Four" and "G.I. Combat" whose characters have sketched Arabs as "lowlifes" and "human hyenas." Negative stereotypes were everywhere. A dictionary informed my youngsters that an Arab is a "vagabond, drifter, hobo and vagrant." Whatever happened, my wife wondered, to Aladdin's good genie?

To a child, the world is simple: good versus evil. But my children and others with Arab roots grew up without ever having seen a humane Arab on the silver screen, someone to pattern their lives after. Is it easier for a camel to go through the eye of a needle than for a screen Arab to appear as a genuine human being?

Hollywood producers must have an instant Ali Baba kit that contains    6
scimitars, veils, sunglasses and such Arab clothing as *chadors* and *kufiyahs*. In the mythical "Ay-rabland," oil wells, tents, mosques, goats and shepherds prevail. Between the sand dunes, the camera focuses on a mock-up of a palace from "Arabian Nights"—or a military air base. Recent movies suggest that Americans are at war with Arabs, forgetting the fact that out of 21 Arab nations, America is friendly with 19 of them. And in "Wanted Dead or Alive," a movie that starred Gene Simmons, the leader of the rock group Kiss, the war comes home when an Arab terrorist comes to the United States dressed as a rabbi and, among other things, conspires with Arab-Americans to poison the people of Los Angeles. The movie was released last year.

The Arab remains American culture's favorite whipping boy. In his    7
memoirs, Terrel Bell, Ronald Reagan's first secretary of education, writes about an "apparent bias among mid-level, right-wing staffers at the White House" who dismissed Arabs as "sand niggers." Sadly, the racial slurs continue. At a recent teacher's conference, I met a woman from Sioux Falls, S.D., who told me about the persistence of discrimination. She was in the process of adopting a baby when an agency staffer warned her that the infant had a problem. When she asked whether the child was mentally ill, or physically handicapped, there was silence. Finally, the worker said: "The baby is Jordanian."

To me, the Arab demon of today is much like the Jewish demon of    8
yesterday. We deplore the false portrait of Jews as a swarthy menace. Yet a similar portrait has been accepted and transferred to another group of Semites—the Arabs. Print and broadcast journalists have started to challenge this stereotype. They are now revealing more humane images of Palestinian Arabs, a people who traditionally suffered from the myth that Palestinian equals terrorist. Others could follow that lead and retire the stereotypical Arab to a media Valhalla.

It would be a step in the right direction if movie and TV producers    9
developed characters modeled after real-life Arab-Americans. We could then see a White House correspondent like Helen Thomas, whose father came from Lebanon, in "The Golden Girls," a heart surgeon patterned after Dr. Michael DeBakey on "St. Elsewhere," or a Syrian-American playing tournament chess like Yasser Seirawan, the Seattle grandmaster.

Politicians, too, should speak out against the cardboard caricatures. They    10
should refer to Arabs as friends, not just as moderates. And religious leaders could state that Islam like Christianity and Judaism maintains that all mankind is one family in the care of God. When all imagemakers rightfully begin to treat Arabs and all other minorities with respect and dignity, we may begin to unlearn our prejudices.

## STUDY QUESTIONS

1. Can you remember IMAGES of Arabs in recent movies that fit Shaheen's accusations? Can you remember any who were portrayed sympathetically? Watch television news for the next two or three evenings; what Arabs are shown there? How are they shown?

2. What Arab-Americans do you know or know of? What have they achieved? What mistreatment or misunderstanding have they suffered?

3. What STEREOTYPES other than those Arab ones Shaheen describes have you seen recently in films? on television?

# James Fallows

James Fallows is Washington editor for *The Atlantic* but is currently based in Kuala Lumpur, Malaysia, where he has been writing a series of articles on Asia for the magazine.

The Japanese economic "miracle" has engendered lots of discussion about the organization of the Japanese economy and the larger society. This look at the culture behind the miracle may not please the more fervid nationalists in either country.

# THE JAPANESE ARE DIFFERENT FROM YOU AND ME

Japan is turning me into Mrs. Trollope. She was the huffy Englishwoman who viewed the woolly American society of the 1820s and found it insufficiently refined. ("The total and universal want of good, or even pleasing, manners, both in males and females, is so remarkable, that I was constantly endeavoring to account for it," and so forth.) Her mistake, as seems obvious in retrospect, was her failure to distinguish between things about America that were merely different from the ways of her beloved England and things that were truly wrong. The vulgar American diction that so offended her belongs in the first category, slavery in the second.

I will confess that this distinction—between different and wrong— 2
sometimes eludes me in Japan. Much of the time I do keep it in mind. I
observe aspects of Japanese life, note their difference from standard practice
in the West, and serenely say to myself, who cares? Orthodontia has never
caught on in Japan, despite seemingly enormous potential demand, because
by the local canon of beauty overlapping and angled-out teeth look fetching,
especially in young girls. It was barely a century ago that Japanese women
deliberately blackened their teeth in the name of beauty. The delicate odor
of decaying teeth was in those days a standard and alluring reference in
romantic poetry. This is not how it's done in Scarsdale, but so what? For
their part, the Japanese can hardly conceal their distaste for the "butter smell"
that they say wafts out of Westerners or for our brutish practice of wearing
the same shoes in the dining room and the toilet.

Similarly, child psychologists and family therapists have told me that 3
the Japanese parent's way of persuading his children to stop doing something
is not to say "It's wrong" or "It's unfair" but rather to tell the child, "People
will laugh at you." This is not my idea of a wholesome child-rearing philosophy, but I'm not preparing my children for membership in a society that
places such stress on harmonious social relations. Several American psychologists have recently claimed that the Japanese approach may in fact equip
children for more happiness in life than American practices do. Americans
are taught to try to control their destiny; when they can't, they feel they've
failed. Japanese children, so these psychologists contend, are taught to adjust
themselves to an externally imposed social order, which gives them "secondary control"—that is, a happy resignation to fate.

Now that Japan has become so notoriously successful, American visitors 4
often cannot help feeling, This is different—and better. Practically anything
that has to do with manufacturing and economic organization falls into this
category. Recently I toured a Nissan factory an hour outside Tokyo, escorted
by a manager who seemed almost embarrassed by the comparisons I asked
him to make between his company's standards and GM's or Ford's. Yes,
Nissan did insist on a higher grade of steel for its cars. No, the foreign companies had not matched its level of automation. Yes, the gap between managers' earnings and those of assembly workers was tiny compared with that
in Detroit. No, the company did not expect trouble surmounting the challenge of the higher yen.

From what I have seen, a tight-knit, almost tribal society like Japan is 5
better set up for straightforward productive competition than is the West. It
places less emphasis on profit than on ensuring that every company and every
worker will retain a place in the economic order. (Apart from raw materials
and American movies, most Japanese would be content, I think, if the country imported nothing at all. Who cares about high prices, as long as everyone
is at work?) Its politics is ridden with factions—because of certain peculiari-
ties of the electoral system, politicians can win seats in the Diet with only 10
or 12 percent of their district's vote. (Each district elects several representa-

tives to the Diet, but each voter has only one vote. In a four-member district, for example, the leading candidate might get 35 percent of the total vote, and the next three might get 15, 12, and 8 percent. All four of them would be winners.) But there are few seriously divisive political issues, and the country has a shared sense of national purpose, as the United States last did between 1941 and 1945.

Even beyond the measurable signs of its productive success, Japan seems  6
different and better in those details of daily life that reflect consideration and duty. During my first week here another American journalist told me that only when I had left would I realize how thoroughly Japan had had me. At the time, I was still reeling from exchange-rate shock and thought she was crazy. But I am beginning to understand what she meant. A thousand times a day in modern society your life is made easier or harder, depending on the care with which someone else has done his job. Are the newspapers delivered on time? Are vending machines fixed when they break? Are the technocrats competent? Do the captains of industry really care about their companies, not just about feathering their own nests? In general, can you count on others to do their best? In Japan you can. Mussolini gave trains that ran on time a bad name. After seeing Japan, I think that on this one point Mussolini had the right idea.

From bureaucrats at the Ministry of Foreign Affairs (who, I am told,  7
average six hours of overtime a *day*) to department-store package-wrappers, the Japanese seem immune against the idea that discharging their duty to others might be considered "just a job." Tipping is virtually unknown in Japan; from the Japanese perspective it seems vulgar, because it implies that the recipient will not do his best unless he is bribed. The no-tipping custom is something you get used to very quickly, because it seems so much more dignified and honorable, not—at least in Japan—because it's a way of gypping the working class. Japan is famous for the flatness of its income distribution. Year in and year out more than 90 percent of the Japanese tell pollsters that they think of themselves as "middle class"—and here the perception seems accurate, not a delusion as it might be in the United States. Indeed, from the Japanese perspective America seems fantastically wrapped up in and bound by class. American commercials are basically targeted along class lines: one kind of person drinks Miller beer, another buys Steuben glass. Japanese commercials are not—or so I am told by people who produce them. They may aim at different age groups—new mothers, teenage boys, and so forth—but otherwise they address the Japanese as one.

I can't say exactly, but I would bet that 100,000 people live within half  8
a mile of the apartment where I live with my family. Yet in the evening, when I walk home through the alleyways from the public baths, the neighborhoods are dead quiet—unless my own children are kicking a can along the pavement or noisily playing tag. The containedness and reserve of Japanese life can seem suffocating if you're used to something different, but they are also admirable, and necessary, if so many people are to coexist so har-

moniously in such close quarters. Because the Japanese have agreed not to get on one another's nerves (and because so much of Tokyo is built only two or three stories high), the city, though intensely crowded, produces nothing like the chronic high-anxiety level of New York. The very low crime rate obviously has something to do with this too. "Is this not, truly, Japan's golden age?" one American businessman exclaimed, spreading his arms in non-Japanese expansiveness and nearly knocking over the passersby, as we walked near the Imperial Place on a brilliant sunny day recently. Everyone was working, Japan was taking a proud place in the world, there were no serious domestic divisions, and the drugs, dissoluteness, and similar disorders that blight the rest of the world barely existed here. Wasn't it obvious that Japan had figured out what still puzzled everybody else?

On the whole, I had to agree. What most Americans fear about Japan is precisely that it works so well. Foreigners who have lived for years in Japan tell me that the legendary Japanese hospitality toward visitors suddenly disappears when you stop being an "honored guest" and slide into the "resident alien" category. In effect, the country is like an expensive, very well run hotel, making the guest comfortable without ever tempting him to think he's found a home. But while it lasts, the hospitality is a delight. Those I interview at least feign more attention and courtesy than their counterparts in the United States have done. A few people have moved beyond the tit-for-tat ritualistic exchange of favors to displays of real generosity. Still, after making all appropriate allowances for the debts I owe them, and all disclaimers about the perils of generalizing after a few months on the scene, I find that two aspects of Japanese life bring out the Mrs. Trollope in me. 9

One is the prominence of pornography in daily life. I realize that no one from the land that created *Hustler* and *Deep Throat* can sound pious about obscene material. The difference is the degree of choice. In the United States pornography did not enter my life unless I invited it in, and I had no trouble keeping it from my grade-school children. Here it enters unbidden all the time. 10

Like most other residents of Tokyo, I spend a lot of time on the trains— about three hours a day. There I am surrounded not just by people but also by printed matter—advertising placards all over the trains, and books, magazines, and newspapers in everyone's hands. The dedicated literacy of Japan is yet another cause for admiration, but the content of the reading matter— especially on the trains, where no one knows his neighbor and in principle everyone is unobserved—is not. Some of the men are reading books, but more are reading either "sports papers" or thick volumes of comics, the size of telephone books, known as *manga*. What these two media have in common is the porno theme. Sports papers carry detailed coverage of baseball games or sumo tournaments on the outside pages and a few spreads of nearly nude women inside. (The only apparent restriction is that the papers must not display pubic hair.) The comic books, printed on multicolored paper and 11 popular with every segment of the population, are issued weekly and sell in the millions. They run from innocent kids' fare to hard-core pornography.

To some degree the sports papers and the more prurient *manga* exist to display female bodies, no more and no less, and they differ from their counterparts in other cultures only in the carefree spirit with which men read them in public. I don't know whether Japanese men consume any more pornography than American ones, but in the United States men look guilty as they slink out of dirty movies, and they rarely read skin magazines in front of women. Japanese men are far less inhibited—perhaps because of the anonymity of the crowded train car, or perhaps because their society is, as often claimed, more matter-of-fact about sex. In any case, the trains and subways are awash in pornography, as are television shows starting as early as 8 P.M. My sons, ages nine and six, very quickly figured out this new aspect of Japanese culture. On train rides they stare goggle-eyed at the lurid fare now available to them.

In addition to its pervasiveness, Japanese subway pornography differs from the *Playboys* and *Penthouses* of the West in the graphic nastiness of its themes. Voyeurism plays a big part in the *manga*, and in a lot of advertisements too. One new publication recently launched a huge advertising campaign billing itself as "the magazine for watchers." Its posters showed people peeping out from under manhole covers or through venetian blinds. In the comics women—more often, teenage girls—are typically peeped up at, from ground level. A major weekly magazine recently published two pages of telephoto-lens shots of couples in advanced stages of love-making in a public park. Most of the teenage girls in Japan spend their days in severe, dark, sailor-style school uniforms, with long skirts. As in Victorian-era fantasies, in the comics the skirts are sure to go. But before the garments are ripped off, the girls are typically spied upon by ecstatic men.

The comics are also quite violent. Women are being accosted, surprised, tied up, beaten, knifed, tortured, and in general given a hard time. Many who are so treated are meant to be very young—the overall impression is as if the Brooke Shields of five years ago had been America's exclusive female sexual icon, with no interference from Bo Derek or other full-grown specimens. One advertising man, who has been here for ten years and makes his living by understanding the Japanese psyche, says that everything suddenly fell into place for him when he thought of a half-conscious, low-grade pedophilia as the underlying social motif. It affects business, he said, where each year's crop of fresh young things, straight out of high school, are assigned seats where the senior managers can look at them—until the next year, when a newer and younger crop are brought in. It affects TV shows and commercials, which feature girls with a teenage look. The most sought-after description in Japan is *kawaii*, or "cute" (as opposed to "beautiful" or "sexy"), often pronounced in a way equivalent to "Cuu-uuuute!" The *kawaii* look is dominant on television and in advertising, giving the impression that Japanese masculinity consists primarily of yearning for a cute little thing about fifteen years old. "A director can shoot an act of sodomy or rape for a TV drama programmed for the dinner hour with impunity so long as he allows no pubic hair to be shown," a recent article by Saran Brickman in the *Far Eastern Economic Review* said. "He is, of course, particularly assured of immunity from legal repercussions if the female star of the scene is prepubescent."

A few years ago Ian Buruma, a Dutch writer who had lived here for    15
years and has a Japanese wife, published *Behind the Mask*, a wonderful book that closely analyzed the *manga*, soap operas, low-brow movies, and other aspects of Japanese popular culture. He richly illustrated how the Japanese, in many ways so buttoned up and contained, sought outlandish fantasy releases. Buruma attempted to trace the oddities of *manga*-style fantasy to the deep bond between Japanese boys and their mothers, who typically raise their children with little help from the father. I don't know enough to judge Buruma's theory, or otherwise to make sense of Japan's standards of pornographic display. My point is that they rest on theories and values at odds with the West's. According to the *Far Eastern Review* article, the director-general of Japan's Agency for Cultural Affairs once endorsed physical exercise this way: "When asked my reasons for jogging, I used to answer 'although it is shameful for a gentleman to rape a woman, it is also shameful for a man not to have the physical strength necessary to rape a woman!' "

In the United States more and more people are claiming that pornogra-    16
phy contributes to sex crimes. If you look at Japan—with its high level of violent stimulation but reportedly low incidence of rape and assault—you have your doubts. But even if it leads to few indictable offenses, and even if Japanese women themselves do not complain, the abundance of violent pornography creates an atmosphere that gives most Westerners the creeps.

The other off-putting aspect of Japan is the ethnic—well, racial—exclu-    17
sion on which the society is built. I hesitated to say "racial" or "racist," because the terms are so loaded and so irritating to the Japanese. I can understand why they are annoyed. In their dealings with the West the Japanese have traditionally seen themselves as the objects of racial discrimination—the little yellow men looked down on by the great white fathers. A new book by the historian John W. Dower, called *War Without Mercy*, provides hair-raising illustrations of the racism with which both Japanese and Japanese-Americans were viewed during the war. For instance, Ernie Pyle explained to the readers of his famous battlefront column that the difference between the Germans and the Japanese was that the Germans "were still people."

Rather than talking about race—as white Americans did when enslaving    18
blacks and excluding "inferior" immigrants—the Japanese talk about "purity." Their society is different from others in being purer; it consists of practically none but Japanese. What makes the subject so complicated is the overlap between two different kinds of purity, that of culture and that of blood.

That the Japanese have a distinct culture seems to me an open-and-shut    19 case. Some economists here have given me little speeches about the primacy of economic forces in determining people's behavior. Do the Japanese save more, stick with their companies longer, and pay more attention to quality? The explanations are all to be found in tax incentives, the "lifetime-employment" policy at big firms, and other identifiable economic causes. I'm sure there is something to this outlook, but I am also impressed by what it leaves out. We do not find it remarkable that the past 250 years of American history, which include revolution, settling the frontier, subjugating Indians, creating and then abolishing slavery, and absorbing immigrant groups, have given the United States a distinctive set of values. Is it so implausible that 2,500 years of isolation on a few small islands might have given the Japanese some singular traits?

Japan is different from certain "old" Western cultures because it has      20
been left to itself so much. In the same 2,500 years the British Isles were invaded by Romans, Angles, Saxons, and Normans—and after that the British themselves went invading and exploring. Blood was mixed, and culture was opened up. During all that time the Japanese sat at home, uninvaded and disinclined to sail off to see what the rest of the world might hold. The effect of this long isolation was a distinctive culture *and* the isolation of a "pure" racial group, which tempted people to think that race and culture were the same.

I'm sure that someone could prove that the Japanese are not really mono-      21
racial, or not clearly separate from the Koreans or the Chinese. The significant point is that as far as the Japanese are concerned, they *are* inherently different from other people, and are all bound together by birth and blood. The standard Japanese explanation for their horror of litigation and their esteem for consensus is that they are a homogenous people, who understand one another's needs. When I've asked police officials and sociologists why there is so little crime, their explanations have all begun, "We are a homogenous race . . ." Most people I have interviewed have used the phrase "We Japanese . . ." I have rarely heard an American say "We Americans . . ."

The Japanese sense of separateness rises to the level of race because the      22
Japanese system is closed. The United States is built on the principle of voluntary association; in theory anyone can become an American. A place in Japanese society is open only to those who are born Japanese.

When I say "born," I mean with the right racial background, not merely      23
on rocky Japanese soil. One of Japan's touchiest problems is the second- or even third-generation Koreans, descended from people who were brought to Japan for forced labor in the fascist days. They are still known as Koreans even though they were born here, speak the language like natives, and in many cases are physically indistinguishable from everyone else. They have long-term "alien residence" permits but are not citizens—and in principle they and their descendants never will be. (Obtaining naturalized Japanese citizenship is not impossible but close to it.) They must register as aliens and

be fingerprinted by the police. The same prospect awaits the handful of Vietnamese refugees whom the Japanese, under intense pressure from the United States, have now agreed to accept for resettlement.

The Japanese public has a voracious appetite for *Nihonjinron*—the study    24
of traits that distinguish them from everyone else. Hundreds of works of self-examination are published each year. This discipline involves perfectly reasonable questions about what makes Japan unique as a social system, but it easily slips into inquiries about what makes the Japanese people special as a race. Perhaps the most lunatic work in this field is *The Japanese Brain*, by a Dr. Tadanobu Tsunoda, which was published to wide acclaim and vast sales in the late 1970s. The book contends that the Japanese have brains that are organized differently from those of the rest of humanity, their internal wiring optimized for the requirements of the Japanese language. (Tsunoda claims that all non-Japanese—including "Chinese, Koreans, and almost all Southeast Asian peoples"—hear vowels in the right hemispheres of their brains, while the Japanese hear them in the left. Since the Japanese also handle consonants in the left hemisphere, they are able to attain a higher unity and coherence than other races.)

I haven't heard anyone restate the theory in precisely this form. And in    25
fairness, during the war British scientists advanced a parallel unique-Japanese-brain theory (as John Dower points out), asserting that Japanese thought was permanently impaired by the torture of memorizing Chinese characters at an early age. But British scientists don't say this any longer, while Tsunoda is still a prominent, non-ridiculed figure in Japan. Whatever the Japanese may think of his unique-brain theory, large numbers of them seem comfortable with the belief that not just their language but also their thoughts and emotions are different from those of anyone else in the world.

The Japanese language is the main evidence for this claim. It is said to    26
foster the understatement for which the Japanese are so famous, and to make them more carefully attuned to nuance, nature, unexpressed thoughts, and so forth, than other people could possibly be. Most of all, it is a convenient instrument of exclusion. Mastering it requires considerable memory work. Japanese businessmen posted to New York or London often fret about taking their children with them, for fear that three or four years out of the Japanese school system will leave their children hopelessly behind. It's not that the overall intellectual standards are so different but that in Japan children spend much of their time memorizing the Chinese characters, *kanji*, necessary for full literacy—and for success on the all-important university-entrance tests.

Until a few years ago only a handful of foreigners had bothered to become    27
fully fluent in Japanese, and they could be written off as exceptions proving the general rule: that Japanese was too complicated and subtle for non-Japanese to learn. Now the situation is changing—many of the Americans I meet here are well into their Japanese-language training—but the idea of uniqueness remains. Four years ago an American linguist named Roy Andrew Miller published a splenetic book titled *Japan's Modern Myth*, designed to explode

the idea that Japanese was unique, any more than Urdu or German or other languages are. Edward Seidensticker, a renowned translator of Japanese literature, makes the point concisely: " 'But how do you manage the nuances of Japanese?' the Japanese are fond of asking, as if other languages did not have nuances, and as if there were no significance in the fact that the word 'nuance' had to be borrowed from French."

As Roy Miller pointed out, the concept of an unlearnable language offers a polite outlet for a more deeply held but somewhat embarrassing belief in racial uniqueness. In a passage that illustrated this book's exasperated tone but also his instinct for the home truth, Miller wrote:    28

> Japanese race consists in using the Japanese language. But how does one become a member of the Japanese race? By being born into it, of course, just as one becomes a member of any other race. . . . But what if someone not a Japanese by right of race . . . does manage to acquire some proficiency in the Japanese language? Well, in that case, the system literally makes no intellectual provision at all for his or her very existence. Such a person is a nonperson within the terms and definitions of Japanese social order. . . . The society's assumption [is] that the Japanese-speaking foreigner is for some unknown reason involved in working out serious logical contradictions in his or her life. . . . He or she had better be watched pretty carefully; obviously something is seriously amiss somewhere, otherwise why would this foreigner be speaking Japanese?

As applied to most other races of the world—especially other Asians, with whom the Japanese have been in most frequent contact—the Japanese racial attitude is unambiguous: Southeast Asians and Koreans are inferior to Japanese. Koreans are more closely related to the Japanese than are any other Asians, but they are held in deep racial contempt by the Japanese. (A hilarious, long-running controversy surrounds excavations in central Honshu that seemed to indicate that the Imperial Family was originally . . . Korean! The digs were soon closed up, for reasons that are continually debated in the English-language but not, I am told, the Japanese-language press.) Recent opinion polls show that the nation the Japanese most fear is not the United States, on which they depend for their export market, nor the Soviet Union, which still occupies four of their northern islands, but Korea—which threatens to beat them at their own hard-work game and which fully reciprocates Japan's ill will. China—the source of Japan's written language and the model for much of its traditional culture—presents a more difficult case. The Australian journalist Murray Sayle offers the model of China as the "wastrel older brother," who forfeited his natural right of prominence through his dissolute behavior, placing the family burden on the steadfast younger brother, Japan. This is one reason why stories of Chinese opium dens were so important in pre-war Japan: the older brother had gone to hell and needed the discipline of Japanese control.    29

For Westerners the racial question is more confusing than even for the    30

Chinese. For a few weeks after arrival I seized on the idea that being in Japan might, for a white American, faintly resemble the experience of being black in America. That is, my racial identity was the most important thing about me, and it did not seem to be a plus.

I am just beginning to understand how complicated the racial attitude toward Westerners really is. Whereas Southeast Asians in Japan are objects of unrelieved disdain, Westerners are seen as both better and worse than the Japanese. One timeless argument in Japan is whether the Japanese feel inferior to Westerners, or superior to them, or some combination of the two. Feeling equal to them—different in culture, but equal as human beings—somehow does not emerge as a possibility, at least in the talks I have had so far.

There is evidence for both propositions—that the Japanese feel superior to Westerners, and that they feel inferior to them. On the one hand, Japanese culture is simply awash in Western—mainly American—artifacts. The movies and music are imported straight from America; the fashion and commercial models are disproportionately Caucasian; the culture seems to await its next signal from the other side of the Pacific. A hundred years ago, Japan began its Meiji-era drive to catch up with the West's industrial achievements. Prominent figures urged Japanese to interbreed with Westerners, so as to improve the racial stock, and to dump the character-based Japanese language in favor of English, which was the mark of a more advanced race. To judge by the styles they affect and the movies and music they favor, today's young Japanese seem to take Europe as the standard of refinement and America as the source of pop-cultural energy. Even when nothing earthshaking is happening in America, the TV news has extensive what's-new-in-New-York segments.

Herbert Passin, a professor of sociology at Columbia University, who came to Japan during the Occupation and has been here off and on ever since, contends that the sense of inferiority is so deep-seated that a few years of economic victories cannot really have dislodged it. The longer I have been here, and the better I've gotten to know a few Japanese, the more frequently I've seen flashes of the old, nagging fear of inferiority. Americans often talk, with good reason, about the defects of their "system." Many Japanese take pride in their economic and social system but still act as if something is wrong with them as a race. I talked with a group of teenage entrepreneurs, who had set up a mildly rebellious magazine. We talked about Japan's economic success, and then one of them burst out: "We're just like a bunch of ants. We all teem around a biscuit and carry it off. That's the only way we succeed." A famous scientist who has directed successful research projects for the Ministry of International Trade and Industry—precisely the kind of man American industrialists most fear—described Japan's impressive scientific work-in-progress. Then he sighed and said, "Still, my real feeling is, Everything new comes from the States. We can refine it and improve it, but the firsts always come from outside."

On the other hand, many Japanese can barely conceal their disdain for the West's general loss of economic vigor. Many people I have interviewed have talked about the United States the way many Americans talk about England: it had its day, but now that's done. One influential businessman in his early forties told me that members of his generation were not even daunted by the wartime defeat. Our fathers were beaten, he told me with a fierce look—not us. This is shaping up as the year of "economic-adjustment" plans: every week a new ministry comes out with a scheme for reducing Japan's trade surplus. I have yet to see the word *fairness* in the English versions of these documents. Instead they are all designed to promote "harmony." The stated premise is that Japan has to give foreigners a break, so that it doesn't make needless enemies overseas. The unstated but obvious corollary is that Japan could crush every indolent Western competitor if it tried. Even the things some Japanese still claim to admire about America suggest racial condescension. Among the American virtues that Japanese have mentioned to me are a big army, a sense of style and rhythm, artistic talent and energy, and raw animal (and supposedly sexual) strength. In their eyes we are big, potent, and hairy. 34

The Japanese have obviously profited, in purely practical terms, from their racial purity. Many of the things that are most admirable about the society—its shared moral values, its consideration for all its members' interests, the attention people pay to the collective well-being as well as to their own—are easier to create when everyone is ethnically the same. Three years ago, at a commemoration for those killed by the atomic bomb at Hiroshima, Prime Minister Nakasone made this point as crudely as possible. He said, "The Japanese have been doing well for as long as 2,000 years because there are no foreign races." 35

I have always thought that, simply in practical terms, the United States had a big edge because it tried so hard, albeit inconsistently and with limited success, to digest people from different backgrounds and parts of the world. Didn't the resulting cultural collisions give us extra creativity and resilience? Didn't the ethnic mixture help us at least slightly in our dealings with other countries? The Japanese in contrast, have suffered grievously from their lack of any built-in understanding of foreign cultures. Sitting off on their own, it is easy for them to view the rest of the world as merely a market—an attitude harder to hold if your population contains a lot of refugees and immigrants. This perspective has as much to do with "trade frictions" as does their admirable management style. I am exaggerating for effect here—the most cosmopolitan Japanese I have met have a broader view than most people I know in America—but in general a homogeneous population with no emotional ties to the rest of the world acts even more narcissistically than do others. When the United States threatened to drown the world in its trade surpluses, it 36 started the Marshall Plan. The Japanese, to put it mildly, have been less eager to share their wealth.

Practicalities aside, the United States, like the rest of Western society, 37 has increasingly in the twentieth century considered it morally "right" to rise above differences of race, inconvenient and uncomfortable as that may sometimes be. Few Western societies, and few people, may succeed in so rising—but they feel guilty when they fail. The Japanese do not.

The integrationist dream has few supporters in this half of the globe. 38 The Japanese are unusual in having so large a population with so little racial diversity, but their underlying belief that politics and culture should run on racial lines is held in many other parts of Asia. Directly or indirectly, the politics of most Asian countries revolve around racial or tribal divisions, especially those between the numerous Chinese expatriates and the Malays, Vietnamese, Indonesians, and others among whom the Chinese live. It's hard to think of a really stable or happy multi-racial Asian state. Asians look at the Hindu-Moslem partition of India and see acquiescence to fate. Japanese look at America and see a mongrel race.

Edward Seidensticker, now a professor at Columbia, lived here for many 39 years after the war—and then, in 1962, announced his intention to depart. "The Japanese are just like other people," he wrote in a *sayonara* newspaper column. "But no. They are not like other people. They are infinitely more clannish, insular, parochial, and one owes it to one's self-respect to preserve a feeling of outrage at the insularity. To have the sense of outrage go dull is to lose the will to communicate; and that, I think, is death. So I am going home."

I've just gotten here, but I think I understand what Seidensticker was 40 talking about. And it is connected with my only real reservation about the Japanese economic miracle. Even as Japan steadily rises in influence, the idea that it should be the new world model is hard for me to swallow. I know it is not logical to draw moral lessons from economics. But everyone does it—why else did Richard Nixon brag to Nikita Khrushchev about our big refrigerators—and the Japanese are naturally now drawing lessons of their own. Their forty-year recovery represents the triumph of a system and a people, but I think many Japanese see it as the victory of a *pure* people, which by definition no inferior or mixed-blood race can match. The Japanese have their history and we have ours, so it would not be fair to argue that they "should" be a multi-racial, immigrant land. Most of the world, with greater or lesser frankness, subscribes to the Japanese view that people must be ethnically similar to get along. But to me, its ethic of exclusion is the least lovable thing about this society. And I hope, as the Japanese reflect upon their victories, that they congratulate themselves for diligence, sacrifice, and teamwork, not for remaining "pure."

## STUDY QUESTIONS

1. What things did Mrs. Trollope fail to distinguish in her criticism of America in the 1820s?

2. How do Japanese and American attitudes toward teeth and toward butter differ?

3. Why do Japanese parents tell their children, "People will laugh at you" rather than "It's unfair" or "It's wrong"?

4. What are some of the differences between Japanese and American automobile production according to the Nissan factory manager?

5. What are some of the ways in which details of daily life seem better in Japan than in America? What are the two aspects of Japanese life about which Fallows is most critical?

6. What do the sports pages and the thick comic books (*manga*) have in common? What is the *kawaii* look, and what is it symptomatic of in Japanese popular culture? To what in the Japanese culture does the Dutch writer Ian Buruma attribute the *manga*-style fantasies?

7. What do the Japanese mean when they speak of national "purity"? How is that accounted for historically? What is *Nihonjinron?* What effect does Dr. Tadanobu Tsunoda say the Japanese language has had on the Japanese brain? What happens to Japanese theories of the uniqueness and impossible difficulty of their language, according to Roy Miller, when a foreigner manages to learn Japanese well?

8. What is the Japanese attitude toward Korea and Koreans? What is the Japanese attitude toward the West, especially America? What is the Japanese STEREOTYPE of an American?

9. Is the Japanese assumption that politics and culture should be run on racial lines unique in Asia?

10. What is the basic CONFLICT between the American and Japanese ways of life?


# Mark Salzman


Interested in Chinese martial arts, calligraphy, and ink paintings from the age of thirteen, Mark Salzman graduated with highest honors from Yale in 1982 with a degree in Chinese language. His senior essay, a translation of Chinese poems, won a prize for the best paper on an East Asian subject. He taught English at Hunan Medical College in Changsha from 1982 to 1984 and at that time studied with various martial arts masters, returning to China in 1985 by invitation to participate with honor in the National Martial Arts Competition and Conference.

This piece, taken from his book *Iron and Silk* (1986), epitomizes his persistence, dedication, and triumph over cultural barriers in pursuing his love of excellence in the martial arts.

# TEACHER WEI

I did not like riding the buses in Changsha; they were always terribly crowded,    1
sometimes with passengers squeezed partway out of the doors and windows. I once rode a bus which stopped at a particularly crowded streetcorner. Women were holding their children above their heads so they would not be crushed in the shoving, and I saw a man desperately grab onto something inside the bus while most of his body was not yet on board. The bus attendant screamed at him to let go, but he would not, so she pressed the button operating the doors and they crashed shut on him, fixing him exactly half inside and half out. The bus proceeded to its destination, whereupon the doors opened and the man stepped down, cheerfully paid the attendant half the usual fare, and went on his way.

To avoid having to ride the buses, I decided to follow the example of    2
the three senior Yale-China teachers in Changsha, Bill, Bob and Marcy, and buy a bicycle. Because I was a foreigner, I was allowed to choose the model I wanted, pay for it on the spot with foreign currency certificates and take it home right away. I walked it out of the store with most of the store following me, got on, and rode away feeling acutely self-conscious, as if I had walked into a car dealer, paid for a Porsche in cash, and driven it out of the show-room right through the floor-to-ceiling windows.

When I got back to the house I felt grimy from all the dust on the roads,    3
so I went upstairs to take a bath. Foreigners were not supposed to take show-ers in the public bathhouse, so our building was equipped with its own bath-tub on the second floor, with an electric water heater attached to the wall above it. The hot water passed from the tank, which was at head level, through an iron pipe into the tub. The first time I used the tub, not realizing that the iron pipe conducted the heat of the heating element, I leaned my backside against it while drying off. As soon as the pain struck I reached out and grabbed the only object within reach—the wire supplying electricity to the heater, which stretched across the room over the tub. As soon as I had pulled myself free, I remembered my parents' command never to touch wires or electrical devices when standing in a bathtub. I let go in a panic, lost my balance and fell back onto the pipe. After that I got in the habit of drying off in my room.

This time, as I ran downstairs with a towel around my waist, I was met in my room by Teacher Wu and a silver-haired lady who looked about the same age as Teacher Wu, but was very thin and had fiercely bright eyes. Teacher Wu, who seemed not to notice that I was half-naked and dripping wet, introduced us. 4

"Mark, this is Teacher Wei, my colleague. The college has assigned her to be your teacher, in case you would like to continue your study of Chinese. Since you have a background in classical Chinese, she offered to teach you; she taught classical Chinese in our middle school here for many years. She is a very good teacher." Teacher Wei shook her head and said, "No, no. I'm a bad teacher," but she grinned. Teacher Wu wanted to arrange a schedule then and there, but Teacher Wei pulled her out of the room saying, "He's wet now. I will come again some other time." She looked at me. "I will come tomorrow and bring the books you will need." 5

After they left I remembered that I had met Teacher Wei before, at a welcoming party thrown the day after I arrived. One of the Middle-Aged English Teachers had taken me aside and said, "Teacher Wei is a widow and has the reputation of being the strictest teacher in our college. It is said that she never smiles and has never laughed out loud!" 6

I did not have much time to worry about how I would get along with mirthless Teacher Wei, however—that night I was scheduled to give a lecture for which I had yet to prepare. My predecessors at the college had begun a Wednesday night "Western Culture Lecture Series" held in the largest hall in the college and open to anyone interested in learning English. Virtually everyone in our college was interested in learning English, so we usually drew a crowd of three to five hundred. Past topics had ranged from "Medical Schools in America" to "The American Legal System," and each lecture, an hour and a half in length, was given twice—once to the doctors and teachers and once to the students. I was to give my first lecture that night to the doctors and teachers; my topic was "E.T." 7

For starters, I wrote out the events of the movie as I remembered them. Then I figured out what vocabulary I would have to introduce—like "spaceship," "alien," "ouch," and "phone home." I adopted a distinct facial expression, walk, or tone of voice for each character, to make it easier for the audience to know right away who was who, and decided to alternate between narrating and acting out the scenes. I worried that the audience might not appreciate this sort of storytelling and think it childish or uninteresting, but I did not have to worry long. When I introduced E.T. by jumping on the lab table and hopping the length of it with my knees under my chin and my hands dragging on the table, the audience rose to its feet and cheered. 8

The next day Teacher Wei arrived after xiuxi[1] with a cloth bag and her glasses case. She walked into my room, sat down and accepted a cup of tea, put on her glasses, and took a book from her bag. 9

---

1. The Chinese version of siesta. [Author's note]

"We'll begin with this collection of classical essays prepared for Chinese 10
high school students." She handed it to me and took out another copy for
herself. I noticed that her copy was filled with pencil notes, smudged from
her habit of following the text with her fingertip as she read.

"We'll begin with an essay by Tao Qian. You are familiar with him, 11
aren't you? Then of course you know that he was a hermit and a famous
drinker, almost fifteen hundred years ago. Most of the great Chinese authors
were drinkers and dreamers."

She stopped, took off her glasses, and looked closely at me. 12

"I saw your lecture last night, the one called 'E.T.' You are a very naughty 13
boy!" She took from her bag a small medicine jar and handed it to me. I
opened it and found that it contained a shot of *baijiu*—Chinese rice liquor.

"Since we will be reading the works of drinkers and dreamers, and since 14
you are clearly an eccentric yourself, I think it only fitting that you appreciate their essays like this. From now on I will bring a small bottle of baijiu
when I come. You will finish it, then we will have our lesson."

I thought she was kidding, so I laughed, but she really meant for me to 15
drink it. She reached into her bag and pulled out a container of fried peanuts,
still warm from the wok.

"You must have something to eat with it, of course. I brought some 16
peanuts for you. If you don't finish the wine, no lesson for you."

I finished the baijiu and peanuts, to her great satisfaction. Then she put 17
on her glasses and began the lesson.

Not long after our first lesson Teacher Wei happened to walk by our 18
house while I was practicing *wushu* out front. *Wushu* is the Chinese word for
martial arts, and refers to any of hundreds of schools of armed and unarmed
combat practiced in China for more than two thousand years. These schools
range from the slow, graceful Taijiquan, or T'ai Chi Ch'uan, to the explosive
Northern and Southern schools of Shaolin boxing. In the West, Chinese
martial arts are called "kung fu" or "gong fu," but the word *gong fu* actually
means skill that transcends mere surface beauty. A martial artist whose technique is decorative but without power "has no gong fu," whereas, say, a
calligrapher whose work is not pretty to look at but reflects a strong, austere
taste certainly "has gong fu."

Teacher Wei walked over and asked what I was doing. When I told her 19
that wushu had been an interest of mine for many years, she nodded with
approval.

"In classical Chinese we have a saying that to be a true gentleman it is 20
important to be 'well-versed in the literary and the martial.' Wushu is an
excellent sport. Have you found a teacher here yet?"

At this I became very excited. I told her that I would love to find a 21
teacher but had no idea where to look for one, and that even if I found one,
I wouldn't know how to approach him. I also expressed my doubts that a
wushu teacher would accept a foreign student, as I had heard that they were

usually secretive and old-fashioned in their thinking. She shook her head vigorously.

"That may be true of the mediocre fighters, but you will find that the best fighters in China are not superstitious or close-minded. If you want to learn wushu, you will have a teacher—I can guarantee it, because you are a friendly boy. That is most important. Besides,"—she allowed herself a giggle—"you are exotic. Your big nose alone will open doors! You have blond hair, blue eyes, and you are very strong—you're a 'model foreigner!' Teachers will find you." I asked her if she knew anyone who might be able to help me, but she just smiled and said to be patient, then continued on her way.

As I walked back into the house to take a bath and have breakfast, I noticed a man with close-cropped white hair squatting on the steps of our building. I said good morning to him and he answered politely, complimenting my Chinese. I asked him if he had come to see one of the American teachers, and he said no, then explained that he was staying in the one empty room in our building, which the college offered to guests when the regular guest house was full. He was a doctor of rehabilitative therapy and traditional Chinese medicine at a hospital on the outskirts of the city, and had come to represent his specialty at a conference our college was sponsoring. His name was Dr. Li. When he stood up to introduce himself, I noticed that he was taller than I, had broad shoulders, and held back his head slightly, which gave him an extraordinarily distinguished appearance.

"I saw you exercising," he said, "and overheard your conversation with the lady. There are several good teachers in Hunan."

"Do you know any of them?"

"Yes, I know one or two."

"Do you think any of them would be willing to teach me?"

"Hard to say," he said, then wished me good morning and left for breakfast.

Dr. Li stayed for one week. Every morning he squatted in front of the house, watched me exercise, talked for a little while, then left to get breakfast. The afternoon before he left he happened to return to the house while I was sitting out front working on a charcoal and ink sketch. He sat next to me until I finished, then took it in his hands to have a better look. He seemed to like it, so I asked him please to keep it.

"Thank you very much—it is a beautiful drawing," he said, then got up to leave. "Will you be exercising tomorrow morning?" he asked casually.

"Probably."

"I'll tell you something. The reason you haven't seen anyone practicing wushu is that you get up too late. You are out here at 6:30 every morning. The wushu people have already finished practicing by then! Get up a little earlier tomorrow; you might see something then." He thanked me again for the drawing and went into the house.

At five o'clock the next morning my alarm went off. I scrambled outside and sat down on the steps. It was still dark out, and I didn't see anyone else up yet, much less practicing wushu. Then it occurred to me how unlikely it would be for a wushu expert to choose to practice in the north campus of Hunan Medical College, and I cursed myself for not asking Dr. Li where I should go. I stood up to go back to bed when I noticed an unfamiliar shape next to a bamboo tree planted against the south end of the house. I walked over and saw that it was Dr. Li, balanced on one leg in an impossible posture, his body so still I could not even see him breathe.

After an interminable length of time he suddenly straightened up, nodding to acknowledge my presence. He then practiced a Taijiquan form that lasted some twenty minutes. He moved so slowly I felt hypnotized watching him. When he finished, he gestured for me to stand next to him.  34

"Of the wushu I practice," he said, "my favorite is called the Xuan Men Sword. *Xuan* means dark, or mysterious; *men* means gate." He had me stay put while he quickly found two sticks of equal length, perhaps two and a half feet long, then gave one to me.  35

"Do what I do," he said, and began teaching me the form.  36

After half an hour or so, he said it was time for breakfast and told me that this was the last day he would be living in our house, so unfortunately he could not teach me every morning.  37

"But I will come here every three days or so until you learn the form. Wait for me here, in front of your house, early in the morning."  38

He kept his promise and I was able to learn all the movements of the form in a month, but he insisted that something was still missing. Although I performed the techniques well, he could see I was not concentrating in a manner appropriate for the form: "You look good, but you have no gong fu." At last he invited me to his home for dinner, saying that he could teach me better there. When I followed the directions he gave me to his house, I realized that he had been riding forty-five mintues each way to teach me for the past month. He lived well outside the center of the city on a small hill surrounded by lush, irrigated fields. As soon as I arrived his wife offered me a hot towel to wipe the dust off my hands and face. The three of us sat down to a simple but delicious meal of pork strips over noodles in broth, steamed fish, and plenty of rice.  39

When we had finished, Dr. Li's wife took what was left over and carried it into the adjacent bedroom where, I discovered, his son and two daughters, all in their teens or twenties, were sitting. When I asked why they hadn't eaten with us, Dr. Li seemed puzzled. "That would be rude, wouldn't it? You are our guest, after all."  40

He apparently sensed my discomfort, because he invited them to join us for dessert—a few oranges and apples, and more tea. Dr. Li's children were far too shy to carry on a conversation with me, but one of them did manage to ask me if American food was the same as Chinese food. I tried to describe a typical American meal for them, but it proved difficult: how do  41 you explain pizza to someone who has never seen cheese, tomato sauce, or a pie crust?

After dessert Dr. Li took two swords from another room, tied them together with some string, and asked me to follow him. We got on our bicycles and rode to nearby Mawangdui, the site of the hole that had contained the two-thousand-year-old corpse.[2] We walked past that hole to a second mound, which Dr. Li told me was supposed to contain the tomb of either the marquise's husband or her son. The top of the mound was nearly flat and had patches of grass growing here and there on its packed dirt surface. As Dr. Li unfastened the two swords and handed me one, I realized that the flat part of the mound was just the right size for the form he had taught me. 42

The sun had not yet gone down, and it cast a glittering reflection over the Xiang River a few miles away. The vegetable plots in all directions around us caught the light as well and glowed brightly, in sharp contrast to the deep red earth of the paths between the fields. 43

"Just think," he said, "under your feet is so much history! There are all sorts of treasures in this mound—probably even swords like these, only real ones that were used in ancient wars. With all this history under you, don't you feel moved? Now, practice the form, and this time don't fuss over the technique. Just enjoy it, as if this mound gave you power. That is the kind of feeling that makes wushu beautiful—it is tradition passing through you. Isn't that a kind of power?" 44

After the lesson at Mawangdui Dr. Li said there was no need for him to come in the mornings to teach me anymore, but that if I wanted any further information I could visit him anytime. Since very few people in China have telephones, about the only way to arrange to visit someone is to walk to his house and knock on the door. If it's a friend, you can often dispense with the knocking and just walk in. My students told me again and again that if I ever wanted to see them I could walk into their homes any time of day or night. 45

"But what if you are busy?" 46

"It doesn't matter! If you come, I won't be busy anymore!" 47

"But what if you are asleep?" 48

"Then wake me up!" 49

No matter how often I was given these instructions, though, I could not bring myself to follow them. Whenever someone banged on my door unexpectedly, or simply appeared in my room, I always felt slightly nervous, and I only visited my friends when I felt I had a good reason. 50

So I did not call upon Dr. Li for more lessons, but contented myself with practicing the Xuan Men Sword and trying to recreate the feeling invoked by dancing with the sword on the Han dynasty tomb. 51

By that time Teacher Wei was helping me through a classical novel, *The* 52

---

2. The body of a Changsha noblewoman who died about 2100 years ago. Sealed in a series of six airtight coffins, it was so well preserved that scientists were able to perform an autopsy, which was filmed and shown throughout China in 1973.

*Water Margin*, the story of a hundred and eight renegade heroes, all martial arts experts, who band together and perform deeds similar to those of Robin Hood and the men of Sherwood Forest. Teacher Wei and I agreed that our favorite character was Lu Zhishen, known as the Phony Monk, a man with a righteous soul but a powerful temper, who was on the run from the law after killing an evil merchant to redress an injustice. To escape execution he became a Buddhist monk, but was unsuited to the monk's abstemious way of life. He would sneak out of the monastery at night to drink superhuman amounts of baijiu and eat roast dogs, bones and all, then return to the monastery where the other monks would scold him for drinking and eating meat. In a drunken rage, he would beat them all up, reduce a few buildings to rubble, then throw up in the meditation hall. Of course, the next day he would feel very bad and fix everything he had broken.

My lessons with Teacher Wei had come to involve more than reading 53 and writing assignments. She was a teacher in the Chinese tradition, taking responsibility not only for my academic progress but for my development as a person. She had advice for me concerning my family and friends, my diet, my clothing, my study and exercise habits, and my attitude toward life. At times I got impatient with her and explained that in America, children become adults around the time they leave for college and like to make decisions for themselves after that. She was appalled. "Don't your parents and teachers care about you?"

"Of course they do, but—" 54

"Then how can they leave you stranded when you are only a child?" 55

"Well, we—" 56

"And how can you possibly think you understand everything? You are 57 only twenty-two years old! You are so far away from home, and I am your teacher; if I don't care about you, won't you be lonely?"

She pointed out that the close relationship between teacher and student 58 has existed in China since before the time of Confucius and should not be underestimated—besides, she was older than me and knew better. I couldn't help respecting her conviction, and she seemed to get such pleasure out of trying to figure and then to straighten me out that I stopped resisting and let her educate me.

I learned how to dress to stay comfortable throughout the year (a useful 59 skill in a place without air conditioning or heat in most buildings), how to prevent and treat common illness, how to behave toward teachers, students, strangers and bureaucrats, how to save books from mildew and worms, and never to do anything to excess.

"Mark, you laugh a great deal during your lectures. Why?" 60

"Because, Teacher Wei, I am having fun." 61

"I see. Laugh less. It seems odd that a man laughs so hard at his own 62 jokes. People think you are a bit crazy, or perhaps choking."

"Teacher Wei, do you think it is bad to laugh?" 63

"No, not at all. In fact, it is healthy to laugh. In Chinese we have a 64 saying that if you laugh you will live long. But you shouldn't laugh too much, or you will have digestive problems."

Teacher Wei also encouraged me to travel. She knew I was homesick; 65
she said that travel gives experience, helps cope with sadness, and in any case is fun. I disagreed with her. My last trip, from Hong Kong to Changsha, had given me unwelcome experience and was no fun at all. She let the issue drop until I told her one day that Bob, Marcy and Bill were planning a trip to Wuhan to spend a holiday weekend with the Yale-China teachers living there. Actually, I had already decided to join them, but I did not want to rob Teacher Wei of the opportunity to talk me into it. After I promised her that I would go to Wuhan if she really thought I should, she wanted to know who was going to arrange our travel.

"Teacher Wei, it is only a six-hour train ride." 66
"Yes, but who will buy the tickets for you? Who will see you to the 67
train station? Who will see to it that you get seats?"
"Teacher Wei, we will just take the bus to the station, get in line, buy 68
the tickets, and find seats ourselves."
She could not understand why I would not allow her to get all of her 69
relatives in Changsha and Wuhan to arrange our passage.
"It is my duty to help you!" 70
"We will be all right, Teacher Wei. It is only for a weekend." 71
"Well, when will you be back?" 72
"Monday night." 73
"Which train will you take?" 74
"Probably this one—the one that arrives at dinner time." 75
"I see." 76
The weekend in Wuhan turned out to be fun, although I did not enjoy 77
the train ride either way. Going up we sat on pieces of newspaper on the floor between two cars, knee to knee with three exhausted men traveling from South to North China. On the way down it was so crowded there was not even room on the floor between cars, so we stood, packed like cattle, with our faces pressed against a mountain of cabbages stacked up to the ceiling of the train. Bob had the clever idea of anchoring his arms in the pile of cabbages and leaning against it so he could sleep, so I followed his example and managed to doze for a few hours. When we got back to Changsha we stopped at a shop for some noodles in broth as the sun went down, before going home.

By the time we reached the gate of our college it was nearly dark. As I 78
passed through it I heard someone calling my name and turned to see Teacher Wei waving at me from under a tree. I walked over and asked if she was on her way somewhere.

"No—I am waiting for you." 79
"Why are you waiting for me?" 80

"This was your first trip in China. How shameful it would be if no one    81
greeted you when you came home."

# STUDY QUESTIONS

1. What do you conclude about Chinese life and attitudes from the opening episode about the crowded buses in Changsha? (Be sure you take into account the words "cheerfully" and "half" in the final sentence of the first paragraph.) What do you expect the attitude of the writer to be toward things Chinese after reading this first paragraph?

2. What is Salzman's topic for his lecture on Western culture? How does it compare with the topics of previous lectures that he mentions? What does it reveal about his CHARACTER? What did you expect the response to be? What is it? What does that suggest about the Chinese doctors and teachers who make up the audience? What does Teacher Wei think of it? of him? Is her opinion of him justified? How does she begin the lesson? What is your impression of her at this point (pars. 9–17)?

3. What does *gong fu* ("kung fu") mean literally in Chinese? How is the term used? What, according to Teacher Wei, is the attitude of the best fighters in China toward foreigners who want to learn the sport? Compare this attitude with the Japanese attitude toward foreigners learning their language and toward foreigners in general as James Fallows describes those attitudes in "The Japanese Are Different from You and Me."

4. What is there about Salzman that Teacher Wei finds "exotic"?

5. When Salzman asks Teacher Wei if she knows anyone who might teach him the martial arts, she just smiles and asks him to be patient; when he asks Dr. Li, the doctor responds, "Hard to say" (par. 28). What did you think of their friendliness at that point? What did you expect to happen? What does happen? Who teaches him? What does he discover his teacher must do to come to teach him? What do you make of the reticence and the silent, almost secret effort to be helpful? What qualities in the Chinese character or culture does that suggest?

6. Why do Li's son and daughters not eat with their parents and Salzman when he is a guest? What is the Chinese practice when coming to someone's door to visit (pars. 45–50)? What do you feel about these practices? Do they surprise you? Do you admire them? dislike them? Do they make you uncomfortable? Is there an implied conflict between their practices and manners and the Western reader's? Does it make you think about our customs?

7. When Dr. Li and Salzman go to practice on the mound at Mawangdui, what does Li advise him to do? What does he claim makes the martial arts (wushu) beautiful?

8. What is the Phony Monk in the classical Chinese novel *The Water Margin* like (par. 52)? Why do you think he is the favorite character of Salzman and Teacher Wei (remember what Teacher Wei said about Salzman after hearing his lecture)? What impression of their characters does their choice of favorite give you?

9. What are Chinese parents' and teachers' attitude and behavior toward grown-up children, people in their twenties, for example?

10. What does Salzman learn about laughter?

11. What is your final impression about Chinese attitudes and manners? How would you compare them with our own?

# Countee Cullen

A member of the Harlem Renaissance, winner of the Witter Bynner Poetry Prize and a Guggenheim Fellowship, Countee Cullen (born Countee Porter in 1903) did much to establish the canon of black literature before his untimely death in 1946.

A border city, Baltimore was the North to many blacks from the Deep South, and the South to many white residents who knew they lived below the Mason-Dixon Line.

## INCIDENT

Once riding in old Baltimore,
    Heart-filled, head-filled with glee,
I saw a Baltimorean
    Keep looking straight at me.

Now I was eight and very small,                 5
    And he was no whit bigger,
And so I smiled, but he poked out
    His tongue and called me, "Nigger."

I saw the whole of Baltimore
    From May until December:              10
Of all the things that happened there
    That's all that I remember.

## STUDY QUESTION

This ugly little incident is reported in ballad form (abcb rhymes and alternating four-beat and three-beat lines). Does the somewhat jaunty verse form trivialize the incident? make it seem funny? emphasize the childishness of the incident? lend it the air of folk music?

# Sharon Olds

Born in San Francisco in 1942 and educated at Stanford and Columbia universities, Sharon Olds has published three volumes of poetry, *Satan Says* (1980), *The Dead and the Living* (1983), and *The Gold Cell* (1987). She has won many awards, including the National Book Critics Circle Award, a National Endowment for the Arts Grant, and a Guggenheim Foundation Fellowship.

"On the Subway," from her most recent volume, recounts, in her direct, aware, concerned way, ordinary fears and extraordinary sympathies during a rather common encounter. Stop reading after the first nine lines; what do you expect to happen? Stop again after twenty-one lines; have your expectations intensified? changed?

## ON THE SUBWAY

The boy and I face each other.
His feet are huge, in black sneakers
laced with white in a complex pattern like a
set of intentional scars. We are stuck on
opposite sides of the car, a couple of                                    5
molecules stuck in a rod of light
rapidly moving through darkness. He has the
casual cold look of a mugger,
alert under hooded lids. He is wearing
red, like the inside of the body                                          10
exposed. I am wearing dark fur, the
whole skin of an animal taken and
used. I look at his raw face,

he looks at my fur coat, and I don't
know if I am in his power—                                    15
he could take my coat so easily, my
briefcase, my life—
or if he is in my power, the way I am
living off his life, eating the steak
he does not eat, as if I am taking                            20
the food from his mouth. And he is black
and I am white, and without meaning or
trying to I must profit from his darkness,
the way he absorbs the murderous beams of the
nation's heart, as black cotton                               25
absorbs the heat of the sun and holds it. There is
no way to know how easy this
white skin makes my life, this
life he could take so easily and
break across his knee like a stick the way his               30
own back is being broken, the
rod of his soul that at birth was dark and
fluid and rich as the heart of a seedling
ready to thrust up into any available light.

## STUDY QUESTIONS

1. Why does the SPEAKER call the boy's face "raw" (line 13)?

2. The boy is obviously bigger and stronger than the speaker, and so she is "in his power" (l. 15); in what sense, however, is he in her power? What does she mean by "without meaning or / trying to I must profit from his darkness" (ll. 22–23)? What did you anticipate would happen?

3. Is the CONFLICT in the poem between the boy and the speaker? within the speaker herself? neither? both? Define that conflict. How did you expect it to come out?

4. List the IMAGES and figures of speech from "like a / set of intentional scars" in lines 3–4 to "the heart of a seedling" in the next-to-last line. What categories do they fall into? What one or two categories predominate? How do these images contribute to the TONE and effect of the poem?

# Leslie Marmon Silko

Born in 1948 in Albuquerque, New Mexico, Leslie Marmon Silko grew up on the Laguna Pueblo reservation. Her heritage is mixed—part Laguna, part Mexican, part white—and she refuses to apologize for it, believing that her storytelling ability "rise[s] out of this source." She is a graduate of the University of New Mexico and now teaches at the University of Arizona. Her best-known work, *Storyteller* (1981), is a collection of many of her best poems and stories. Her writing, in both prose and poetry, is highly regarded, and she is the recipient of a prestigious MacArthur Fellowship.

The comic-strip character Pogo used to say, "We have met the enemy, and they is us"; white readers may feel that way reading this poem.

## [LONG TIME AGO]

Long time ago
in the beginning
there were no white people in this world
there was nothing European.
And this world might have gone on like that          5
except for one thing:
witchery.
This world was already complete
even without white people.
There was everything          10
including witchery.

Then it happened.
These witch people got together.
Some came from far far away
across oceans          15
across mountains.
Some had slanty eyes
others had black skin.
They all got together for a contest
the way people have baseball tournaments nowadays          20
except this was a contest
in dark things.

So anyway
they all got together
witch people from all directions                    25
witches from all the Pueblos
and all the tribes.
They had Navajo witches there,
some from Hopi, and a few from Zuni.
They were having a witches' conference,              30
that's what it was
Way up in the lava rock hills
north of Cañoncito
they got together
to fool around in caves                              35
with their animal skins.
Fox, badger, bobcat, and wolf
they circled the fire
and on the fourth time
they jumped into that animal's skin.                 40


But this time it wasn't enough
and one of them
maybe a Sioux or some Eskimos
started showing off.
"That wasn't anything,                               45
watch this."


The contest started like that.
Then some of them lifted the lids
on their big cooking pots,
calling the rest of them over                        50
to take a look:
dead babies simmering in blood
circles of skull cut away
all the brains sucked out.
Witch medicine                                       55
to dry and grind into powder
for new victims.


Others untied skin bundles of disgusting objects:
dark flints, cinders from burned hogans where the
                    dead lay                          60
Whorls of skin
cut from fingertips
sliced from the penis end and clitoris tip.

Finally there was only one
who hadn't shown off charms or powers.                                    65
The witch stood in the shadows beyond the fire
and no one ever knew where this witch came from
which tribe
or if it was a woman or a man.
But the important thing was                                               70
this witch didn't show off any dark thunder charcoals
or red ant-hill beads.
This one just told them to listen:
"What I have is a story."

At first they all laughed                                                 75
but this witch said
*Okay*
*go ahead*
*laugh if you want to*
*but as I tell the story*                                                 80
*it will begin to happen.*

*Set in motion now*
*set in motion by our witchery*
*to work for us.*

*Caves across the ocean*                                                  85
*in caves of dark hills*
*white skin people*
*like the belly of a fish*
*covered with hair.*

*Then they grow away from the earth*                                      90
*then they grow away from the sun*
*then they grow away from the plants and animals.*
*They see no life*
*When they look*
*they see only objects.*                                                  95
*The world is a dead thing for them*
*the trees and rivers are not alive*
*the mountains and stones are not alive.*
*The deer and bear are objects*
*They see no life.*                                                       100

*They fear*
*They fear the world.*
*They destroy what they fear.*
*They fear themselves.*

The wind will blow them across the ocean                    105
   thousands of them in giant boats
     swarming like larva
   out of a crushed ant hill.

     They will carry objects
     which can shoot death                    110
   faster than the eye can see.

They will kill the things they fear
     all the animals
   the people will starve.

     They will poison the water                    115
   they will spin the water away
   and there will be drought
   the people will starve.

   They will fear what they find
     They will fear the people                    120
   They kill what they fear.

Entire villages will be wiped out
They will slaughter whole tribes.
     Corpses for us
      Blood for us                    125
Killing killing killing killing.

   And those they do not kill
     will die anyway
   at the destruction they see
      at the loss                    130
   at the loss of the children
   the loss will destroy the rest.

   Stolen rivers and mountains
   the stolen land will eat their hearts
and jerk their mouths from the Mother.                    135
     The people will starve.

   They will bring terrible diseases
   the people have never known.
    Entire tribes will die out
    covered with festered sores                    140
     shitting blood

*vomiting blood.*
*Corpses for our work*

*Set in motion now*
*set in motion by our witchery*                                    145
*set in motion*
*to work for us.*

*They will take this world from ocean to ocean*
*they will turn on each other*
*they will destroy each other*                                     150
*Up here*
*in these hills*
*they will find the rocks,*
*rocks with veins of green and yellow and black.*
*They will lay the final pattern with these rocks*                 155
*they will lay it across the world*
*and explode everything.*

*Set in motion now*
*set in motion*
*To destroy*                                                       160
*To kill*
*Objects to work for us*
*objects to act for us*
*Performing the witchery*
*for suffering*                                                    165
*for torment*
*for the stillborn*
*the deformed*
*the sterile*
*the dead.*                                                        170

*Whirling*
*Whirling*
*Whirling*
*Whirling*
*set into motion now*                                              175
*set into motion.*

So the other witches said
"Okay you win; you take the prize,
but what you said just now—
it isn't so funny                                                  180
It doesn't sound so good.

We are doing okay without it
we can get along without that kind of thing.
Take it back.
Call that story back." 185

But the witch just shook its head
at the others in their stinking animal skins, fur
and feathers.
*It's already turned loose.*
*It's already coming.* 190
*It can't be called back.*

## STUDY QUESTIONS

1. There are some very "flat," "unpoetic" lines in this poem, like "So anyway" (line 23). Find others. What seems to be their function?

2. How is the location of the "witches' conference" in southern Colorado made use of—and how does it become ominous—later in the poem?

3. If the "white skin people" are to be the scourge, the destroyers, why are the practices of the dark-skinned people, or their witches, shown in such horrific detail (ll. 52–63, for example)?

4. What are the effect and implication of the fact that the identity of the witch who tells the prize-winning story is unknown? that the prize-winning witchcraft is a story?

5. What are the "rocks with veins of green and yellow and black" (l. 154)? What is the effect of the fact that some of the "prophecy" in the story—such as the coming of the white men, guns, diseases, etc.—is already history, but that the terrible ending is not . . . yet?

6. Can you make anything out of the strange shape of this poem?

# Maxine Hong Kingston

*The Woman Warrior*, Maxine Hong Kingston's first book, won the National Book Critics Circle Award in 1976. Since then, the California-born (born 1940) resident of Hawaii has published another volume, *China Men* (1980), from which "The Wild Man of the Green Swamp" is taken. Hers is a mixed genre or a new genre, neither fully fiction nor nonfiction, which indeterminacy pleases her, for she wants

her work to be beyond or outside categories—including ethnic and feminist categories—and to be identified merely as "human."

Try stopping after you read the title and first paragraph and write down what
you think will happen next.

# THE WILD MAN OF THE GREEN SWAMP

For eight months in 1975, residents on the edge of Green Swamp, Florida,     1
had been reporting to the police that they had seen a Wild Man. When they
stepped toward him, he made strange noises as in a foreign language and ran
back into the saw grass. At first, authorities said the Wild Man was a mass
hallucination. Man-eating animals lived in the swamp, and a human being
could hardly find a place to rest without sinking. Perhaps it was some kind
of a bear the children had seen.

In October, a game officer saw a man crouched over a small fire, but as     2
he approached, the figure ran away. It couldn't have been a bear because the
Wild Man dragged a burlap bag after him. Also, the fire was obviously man-
made.

The fish-and-game wardens and the sheriff's deputies entered the swamp     3
with dogs but did not search for long; no one could live in the swamp. The
mosquitoes alone would drive him out.

The Wild Man made forays out of the swamp. Farmers encountered     4
him taking fruit and corn from the turkeys. He broke into a house trailer,
but the occupant came back, and the Wild Man escaped out a window. The
occupant said that a bad smell came off the Wild Man. Usually, the only
evidence of him were his abandoned campsites. At one he left the remains of
a four-foot-long alligator, of which he had eaten the feet and tail.

In May a posse made an air and land search; the plane signaled down to     5
the hunters on the ground, who circled the Wild Man. A fish-and-game war-
den "brought him down with a tackle," according to the news. The Wild
Man fought, but they took him to jail. He looked Chinese, so they found a
Chinese in town to come translate.

The Wild Man talked a lot to the translator. He told him his name. He     6
said he was thirty-nine years old, the father of seven children, who were in
Taiwan. To support them, he had shipped out on a Liberian freighter. He
had gotten very homesick and asked everyone if he could leave the ship and
go home. But the officers would not let him off. They sent messages to China
to find out about him. When the ship landed, they took him to the airport
and tried to put him on an airplane to some foreign place. Then, he said, the
white demons took him to Tampa Hospital, which is for insane people, but
he escaped, just walked out and went into the swamp.

The interpreter asked how he lived in the swamp. He said he ate snakes,    7
turtles, armadillos, and alligators. The captors could tell how he lived when
they opened up his bag, which was not burlap but a pair of pants with the
legs knotted. Inside, he had carried a pot, a piece of sharpened tin, and a
small club, which he had made by sticking a railroad spike into a section of
aluminum tubing.

The sheriff found the Liberian freighter that the Wild Man had been    8
on. The ship's officers said that they had not tried to stop him from going
home. His shipmates had decided that there was something wrong with his
mind. They had bought him a plane ticket and arranged his passport to send
him back to China. They had driven him to the airport, but there he began
screaming and weeping and would not get on the plane. So they had found
him a doctor, who sent him to Tampa Hospital.

Now the doctors at the jail gave him medicine for the mosquito bites,    9
which covered his entire body, and medicine for his stomachache. He was
getting better, but after he'd been in jail for three days, the U.S. Border
Patrol told him they were sending him back. He became hysterical. That
night, he fastened his belt to the bars, wrapped it around his neck, and hung
himself.

In the newspaper picture he did not look very wild, being led by the    10
posse out of the swamp. He did not look dirty, either. He wore a checkered
shirt unbuttoned at the neck, where his white undershirt showed; his shirt
was tucked into his pants; his hair was short. He was surrounded by men in
cowboy hats. His fingers stretching open, his wrists pulling apart to the extent
of the handcuffs, he lifted his head, his eyes screwed shut, and cried out.

There was a Wild Man in our slough too, only he was a black man. He    11
wore a shirt and no pants, and some mornings when we walked to school,
we saw him asleep under the bridge. The police came and took him away.
The newspaper said he was crazy; it said the police had been on the lookout
for him for a long time, but we had seen him every day.

## STUDY QUESTIONS

1. In the first three paragraphs, there is a conflict of probabilities: a man has been
   seen in the swamp; no one can live in the swamp. What expectations does that
   conflict trigger?

2. How do you feel about the wild man? Is there something wrong with his mind, as
   his shipmates believe (par. 8)?

3. What is the effect of the matter-of-fact tone with which the man's history and death
   are described? How do the details of the newspaper picture modify your feelings
   toward and judgment of the "Wild Man"?

4. What does the final paragraph add to the story? Compare the two "Wild Men."
   What relevance is there, if any, to the fact that both belong to ethnic minorities?

# Katherine Anne Porter

K atherine Anne Porter's life (1890–1980) was long, but her career as a writer of short stories and short novels was brief. Her first volume, *Flowering Judas*, made up of stories that had appeared in magazines in the previous decade, was published in 1930; her last, *The Leaning Tower*, in 1944. (Her *Collected Stories*, which appeared in 1966, added only works from this early period.) Yet almost entirely on the basis of these works, she assured herself of a high and permanent place among the writers of her generation (a generation that included Faulkner, Fitzgerald, and Hemingway). Among her many awards were the Gold Medal of the National Institute of Arts and Letters and the Pulitzer Prize.

The first-person narrator of "Holiday" (Porter often warns us not to insist on identifying her narrators with herself) finds in the deep blackland Texas farm country near the Louisiana border an isolated and alien family, and within the family an individual even more alien and isolated.

# HOLIDAY

At that time I was too young for some of the troubles I was having, and I had not yet learned what to do with them. It no longer can matter what kind of troubles they were, or what finally became of them. It seemed to me then there was nothing to do but run away from them, though all my tradition, background, and training had taught me unanswerably that no one except a coward ever runs away from anything. What nonsense! They should have taught me the difference between courage and foolhardiness, instead of leaving me to find it out for myself. I learned finally that if I still had the sense I was born with, I would take off like a deer at the first warning of certain dangers. But this story I am about to tell you happened before this great truth impressed itself upon me—that we do not run from the troubles and dangers that are truly ours, and it is better to learn what they are earlier than later, and if we don't run from the others, we are fools.

I confided to my friend Louise, a former schoolmate about my own age, not my troubles but my little problem: I wanted to go somewhere for a spring holiday, by myself, to the country, and it should be very simple and nice and, of course, not expensive, and she was not to tell anyone where I had gone; but if she liked, I would send her word now and then, if anything interesting was happening. She said she loved getting letters but hated answering them; and she knew the very place for me, and she would not tell anybody anything. Louise had then—she has it still—something near to genius for making improbable persons, places, and situations sound attractive. She told amusing stories that did not turn grim on you until a little while later, when by chance you saw and heard for yourself. So with this story. Everything was just as Louise had said, if you like, and everything was, at the same time, quite different.

"I know the very place," said Louise, "a family of real old-fashioned German peasants, in the deep blackland Texas farm country, a household in real patriarchal style—the kind of thing you'd hate to live with but is very nice to visit. Old father, God Almighty himself, with whiskers and all; Old mother, matriarch in men's shoes; endless daughters and sons and sons-in-law and fat babies falling about the place; and fat puppies—my favourite was a darling little black thing named Kuno—cows, calves, and sheep and lambs and goats and turkeys and guineas roaming up and down the shallow green hills, ducks and geese on the ponds. I was there in the summer when the peaches and watermelons were in—" 3

"This is the end of March," I said, doubtfully. 4

"Spring comes early there," said Louise. "I'll write to the Müllers about you, you just get ready to go." 5

"Just where is this paradise?" 6

"Not far from the Louisiana line," said Louise. "I'll ask them to give you my attic—oh, that was a sweet place! It's a big room, with the roof sloping to the floor on each side, and the roof leaks a little when it rains, so the shingles are all stained in beautiful streaks, all black and grey and mossy green, and in one corner there used to be a stack of dime novels, *The Duchess*, Ouida, Mrs. E.D.E.N. Southworth, Ella Wheeler Wilcox's poems—one summer they had a lady boarder who was a great reader, and she went off and left her library. I loved it! And everybody was so healthy and good-hearted, and the weather was perfect. . . . How long do you want to stay?" 7

I hadn't thought of this, so I said at random, "About a month." 8

A few days later I found myself tossed off like an express package from a dirty little crawling train onto the sodden platform of a country station, where the stationmaster emerged and locked up the waiting room before the train had got round the bend. As he clumped by me he shifted his wad of tobacco to his cheek and asked, "Where you goin'?" 9

"To the Müller farm," I said, standing beside my small trunk and suit-case with the bitter wind cutting through my thin coat. 10

"Anybody meet you?" he asked, not pausing. 11

"They *said* so." 12

"All right," he said, and got into his little ragged buckboard with a sway-backed horse and drove away. 13

I turned my trunk on its side and sat on it facing the wind and the desolate mud-colored shapeless scene and began making up my first letter to 14

Louise. First I was going to tell her that unless she was to be a novelist, there was no excuse for her having so much imagination. In daily life, I was going to tell her, there are also such useful things as the plain facts that should be stuck to, through thick and thin. Anything else led to confusion like this. I was beginning to enjoy my letter to Louise when a sturdy boy about twelve years old crossed the platform. As he neared me, he took off his rough cap and bunched it in his thick hand, dirt-stained at the knuckles. His round cheeks, his round nose, his round chin were a cool, healthy red. In the globe of his face, as neatly circular as if drawn in bright crayon, his narrow, long, tip-tilted eyes, clear as pale-blue water, seemed out of place, as if two incompatible strains had collided in making him. They were beautiful eyes, and the rest of the face was not to be taken seriously. A blue woollen blouse buttoned up to his chin ended abruptly at his waist as if he would outgrow it in another half hour, and his blue drill breeches flapped about his ankles. His old clodhopper shoes were several sizes too big for him. Altogether, it was plain he was not the first one to wear his clothes. He was a cheerful, detached, self-possessed apparition against the tumbled brown earth and ragged dark sky, and I smiled at him as well as I could with a face that felt like wet clay.

He smiled back slightly without meeting my eye, motioning for me to take up my suitcase. He swung my trunk to his head and tottered across the uneven platform, down the steps slippery with mud where I expected to see him crushed beneath his burden like an ant under a stone. He heaved the trunk into the back of his wagon with a fine smash, took my suitcase and tossed it after, then climbed up over one front wheel while I scrambled my way up over the other.

The pony, shaggy as a wintering bear, eased himself into a grudging trot, while the boy, bowed over with his cap pulled down over his ears and eyebrows, held the reins slack and fell into a brown study. I studied the harness, a real mystery. It met and clung in all sorts of unexpected places; it parted company in what appeared to be strategic seats of jointure. It was mended sketchily in risky places with bits of hairy rope. Other seemingly unimportant parts were bound together irrevocably with wire. The bridle was too long for the pony's stocky head, so he had shaken the bit out of his mouth at the start, apparently, and went his own way at his own pace.

Our vehicle was an exhausted specimen of something called a spring wagon, who knows why? There were no springs, and the shallow enclosed platform at the back, suitable for carrying various plunder, was worn away until it barely reached midway of the back wheels, one side of it steadily scraping the iron tire. The wheels themselves spun not dully around and around in the way of common wheels, but elliptically, being loosened at the hubs, so that we proceeded with a drunken, hilarious swagger, like the rolling motion of a small boat on a choppy sea.

The soaked brown fields fell away on either side of the lane, all rough with winter-worn stubble ready to sink and become earth again. The scanty leafless woods ran along an edge of the field nearby. There was nothing beautiful in those woods now except the promise of spring, for I detested bleakness, but it gave me pleasure to think that beyond this there might be something else beautiful in its own being, a river shaped and contained by its banks, or a field stripped down to its true meaning, ploughed and ready for the seed. The road turned abruptly and was almost hidden for a moment, and we were going through the woods. Closer sight of the crooked branches assured me that spring was beginning, if sparely, reluctantly: the leaves were budding in tiny cones of watery green besprinkling all the new shoots; a thin sedate rain began again to fall, not so opaque as a fog, but a mist that merely deepened overhead, and lowered, until the clouds became rain in one swathing, delicate grey.

As we emerged from the woods, the boy roused himself and pointed 19 forward, in silence. We were approaching the farm along the skirts of a fine peach orchard, now faintly colored with young bud, but there was nothing to disguise the gaunt and aching ugliness of the farmhouse itself. In this Texas valley, so gently modulated with small crests and shallows, "rolling country" as the farmers say, the house was set on the peak of the barest rise of ground, as if the most infertile spot had been thriftily chosen for building a shelter. It stood there staring and naked, an intruding stranger, strange even beside the barns ranged generously along the back, low-eaved and weathered to the color of stone.

The narrow windows and the steeply sloping roof oppressed me; I wished 20 to turn away and go back. I had come a long way to be so disappointed, I thought, and yet I must go on, for there could be nothing here for me more painful than what I had left. But as we drew near the house, now hardly visible except for the yellow lamplight in the back, perhaps in the kitchen, my feelings changed again toward warmth and tenderness, or perhaps just an apprehension that I could feel so, maybe, again.

The wagon drew up before the porch, and I started climbing down. No 21 sooner had my foot touched ground than an enormous black dog of the detestable German shepherd breed leaped silently at me, and as silently I covered my face with my arms and leaped back. "Kuno, down!" shouted the boy, lunging at him. The front door flew open and a young girl with yellow hair ran down the steps and seized the ugly beast by the scruff. "He does not mean anything," she said seriously in English. "He is only a dog."

Just Louise's darling little puppy Kuno, I thought, a year or so older. 22 Kuno whined, apologized by bowing and scraping one front paw on the ground, and the girl holding his scruff said, shyly and proudly, "I teach him that. He has always such bad manners, but I teach him!"

I had arrived, it seemed, at the moment when the evening chores were 23 about to begin. The entire Müller household streamed out of the door, each man and woman going about the affairs of the moment. The young girl walked with me up the porch and said, "This is my brother Hans," and a young man paused to shake hands and passed by. "This is my brother Fritz," she said, and Fritz took my hand and dropped it as he went. "My sister Annetje," said the young girl, and a quiet young woman with a baby draped loosely like a scarf over her shoulder smiled and held out her hand. Hand after hand went by, their palms variously younger or older, broad or small, male or female, but all thick hard decent peasant hands, warm and strong. And in every face I saw again the pale, tilted eyes, on every head that taffy-colored hair, as though they might all be brothers and sisters, though Annetje's husband and still another daughter's husband had gone by after greeting me. In the wide hall with a door at front and back, full of cloudy light and the smell of soap, the old mother, also on her way out, stopped to offer her hand. She was a tall strong-looking woman wearing a three-cornered black wool shawl on her head, her skirts looped up over a brown flannel petticoat. Not from her did the young ones get those water-clear eyes. Hers were black and shrewd and searching, a band of hair showed black streaked with grey, her seamed dry face was brown as seasoned bark, and she walked in her rubber boots with the stride of a man. She shook my hand briefly and said in German English that I was welcome, smiling and showing her blackened teeth.

"This is my girl Hatsy," she told me, "and she will show you to your room." Hatsy took my hand as if I were a child needing a guide. I followed her up a flight of steps steep as a ladder, and there we were, in Louise's attic room, with the sloping roof. Yes, the shingles were stained all the colors she had said. There were the dime novels heaped in the corner. For once, Louise had got it straight, and it was homely and familiar, as if I had seen it before. "My mother says we could give you a better place on the downstairs," said Hatsy, in her soft blurred English, "but *she* said in her letter you would like it so." I told her indeed I did like it so. She went down the steep stairs then, and her brother came up as if he were climbing a tree, with the trunk on his head and the suitcase in his right hand, and I could not see what kept the trunk from crashing back to the bottom, as he used the left hand to climb with. I wished to offer help but feared to insult him, having noted well the tremendous ease and style with which he had hurled the luggage around before, a strong man doing his turn before a weakling audience. He put his burden down and straightened up, wriggling his shoulders and panting only a little. I thanked him and he pushed his cap back and pulled it forward again, which I took for some sort of polite response, and clattered out hugely. Looking out of my window a few minutes later, I saw him setting off across the fields carrying a lighted lantern and a large steel trap.

I began changing my first letter to Louise. "I'm going to like it here. I don't quite know why, but it's going to be all right. Maybe I can tell you later—"

The sound of the German speech in the household below was part of the pleasantness, for they were not talking to me and did not expect me to answer. All the German I understood then was contained in five small deadly sentimental songs of Heine's, learned by heart; and this was a very different tongue, Low German corrupted by three generations in a foreign country.

A dozen miles away, where Texas and Louisiana melted together in a rotting swamp whose sluggish under-tow of decay nourished the roots of pine and cedar, a colony of French emigrants had lived out two hundred years of exile, not wholly incorruptible, but mystically faithful to the marrow of their bones, obstinately speaking their old French by then as strange to the French as it was to the English. I had known many of these families during a certain long summer happily remembered, and here again, listening to another language nobody could understand except those of this small farming community, I knew that I was again in a house of perpetual exile. These were solid, practical, hard-bitten, land-holding German peasants, who struck their mattocks into the earth deep and held fast wherever they were, because to them life and the land were one indivisible thing; but never in any wise did they confuse nationality with habitation.

I liked the thick warm voices, and it was good not to have to understand    27
what they were saying. I loved that silence which means freedom from the constant pressure of other minds and other opinions and other feelings, that freedom to fold up in quiet and go back to my own center, to find out again, for it is always a rediscovery, what kind of creature it is that rules me finally, makes all the decisions no matter who thinks they make them, even I; who little by little takes everything away except the one thing I cannot live without, and who will one day say, "Now I am all you have left—take me." I paused there a good while listening to this muted unknown language which was silence with music in it; I could be moved and touched but not troubled by it, as by the crying of frogs or the wind in the trees.

The catalpa tree at my window would, I noticed, when it came into    28
leaf, shut off my view of the barns and the fields beyond. When in bloom the branches would almost reach through the window. But now they were a thin screen through which the calves, splotchy red and white, moved prettily against the weathered darkness of the sheds. The brown fields would soon be green again; the sheep washed by the rains and become clean grey. All the beauty of the landscape now was in the harmony of the valley rolling fluently away to the wood's edge. It was an inland country, with the forlorn look of all unloved things; winter in this part of the south is a moribund coma, not the northern death sleep with the sure promise of resurrection. But in my south, my loved and never-forgotten country, after her long sickness, with only a slight stirring, an opening of the eyes between one breath and the next, between night and day, the earth revives and bursts into the plenty of spring with fruit and flowers together, spring and summer at once under the hot shimmering blue sky.

The freshening wind promised another light sedate rain to come at eve-    29
ning. The voices below stairs dispersed, rose again, separately calling from the yards and barns. The old woman strode down the path toward the cow sheds, Hatsy running behind her. The woman wore her wooden yoke, with the milking pails covered and closed with iron hasps, slung easily across her shoulders, but her daughter carried two tin milking pails on her arm. When

they pushed back the bars of cedar which opened onto the fields, the cows came through lowing and crowding, and the calves scampered each to his own dam with reaching, opened mouths. Then there was the battle of separating the hungry children from their mothers when they had taken their scanty share. The old woman slapped their little haunches with her open palm, Hatsy dragged at their halters, her feet slipping wide in the mud, the cows bellowed and brandished their horns, the calves bawled like rebellious babies. Hatsy's long yellow braids whisked around her shoulders, her laughter was a shrill streak of gaiety above the angry cow voices and the raucous shouting of the old woman.

From the kitchen porch below came the sound of splashing water, the creaking of the pump handle, and the stamping boots of men. I sat in the window watching the darkness come on slowly, while all the lamps were being lighted. My own small lamp had a handle on the oil bowl, like a cup's. There was also a lantern with a frosted chimney hanging by a nail on the wall. A voice called to me from the foot of my stairs and I looked down into the face of a dark-skinned, flaxen-haired young woman, far advanced in pregnancy, and carrying a prosperous year-old boy on her hip, one arm clutching him to her, the other raised above her head so that her lantern shone upon their heads. "The supper is now ready," she said, and waited for me to come down before turning away.

In the large square room the whole family was gathering at a long table covered with a red checkered cotton cloth, with heaped-up platters of steaming food at either end. A crippled and badly deformed servant girl was setting down pitchers of milk. Her face was so bowed over it was almost hidden, and her whole body was maimed in some painful, mysterious way, probably congenital, I supposed, though she seemed wiry and tough. Her knotted hands shook continually, her wagging head kept pace with her restless elbows. She ran unsteadily around the table scattering plates, dodging whoever stood in her way; no one moved aside for her, or spoke to her, or even glanced after her when she vanished into the kitchen.

The men then moved forward to their chairs. Father Müller took his patriarch's place at the head of the table, Mother Müller looming behind him like a dark boulder. The younger men ranged themselves about on one side, the married ones with their wives standing back of their chairs to serve them, for three generations in this country had not made them self-conscious or disturbed their ancient customs. The two sons-in-law and three sons rolled down their shirt sleeves before beginning to eat. Their faces were polished with recent scrubbing and their open collars were damp.

Mother Müller pointed to me, then waved her hand at her household, telling off their names rapidly. I was a stranger and a guest, so was seated on the men's side of the table, and Hatsy, whose real name turned out to be Huldah, the maiden of the family, was seated on the children's side of the board, attending to them and keeping them in order. These infants ranged from two years to ten, five in number—not counting the one still straddling his mother's hip behind his father's chair—divided between the two married daughters. The children ravened and gorged and reached their hands into the sugar bowl to sprinkle sugar on everything they ate, solemnly elated over their food and paying no attention to Hatsy, who struggled with them only a little less energetically than she did with the calves, and ate almost nothing. She was about seventeen years old, pale-lipped and too thin, and her sleek fine butter-yellow hair, streaked light and dark, real German peasant hair, gave her an air of fragility. But she shared the big-boned structure and the enormous energy and animal force that was like a bodily presence itself in the room; and seeing Father Müller's pale-grey deep-set choleric eyes and high cheekbones, it was easy to trace the family resemblance around the table: it was plain that poor Mother Müller had never had a child of her own—black-eyed, black-haired South Germany people. True, she had borne them, but that was all; they belonged to their father. Even the tawny Gretchen, expecting another baby, obviously the pet of the family, with the sly smiling manner of a spoiled child, who wore the contented air of a lazy, healthy young animal, seeming always about to yawn, had hair like pulled taffy and those slanted clear eyes. She stood now easing the weight of her little boy on her husband's chair back, reaching with her left arm over his shoulder to refill his plate from time to time.

Annetje, the eldest daughter, carried her newly born baby over her shoulder, where he drooled comfortably down her back, while she spooned things from platters and bowls for her husband. Whenever their eyes met, they smiled with a gentle, reserved warmth in their eyes, the smile of long and sure friendship. 34

Father Müller did not in the least believe in his children's marrying and leaving home. Marry, yes, of course; but must that take a son or daughter from him? He always could provide work and a place in the household for his daughters' husbands, and in time he would do the same for his sons' wives. A new room had lately been built on, to the northeast, Annetje explained to me, leaning above her husband's head and talking across the table, for Hatsy to live in when she should be married. Hatsy turned very beautifully pink and ducked her head almost into her plate, then looked up boldly and said, "Jah, jah, I am marrit now soon!" Everybody laughed except Mother Müller, who said in German that girls at home never knew when they were well off—no, they must go bringing in husbands. This remark did not seem to hurt anybody's feelings, and Gretchen said it was nice that I was going to be here for the wedding. This reminded Annetje of something, and she spoke in English to the table at large, saying that the Lutheran pastor had advised her to attend church oftener and put her young ones in Sunday school, so that God would give her a blessing with her fifth child. I counted around again, and sure enough, with Gretchen's unborn, there were eight children at that table under the age of ten; somebody was going to need a blessing in all that crowd, no doubt. Father Müller delivered a short speech to his daughter in German, then turned to me and said, "What I say iss, it iss all craziness 35 to go to church and pay a preacher goot money to talk his nonsense. Say rather that he pay me to come and lissen, then I vill go!" His eyes glared with sudden fierceness above his square speckled grey and yellow beard that sprouted directly out from the high cheekbones. "He thinks, so, that my time maybe costs nothing? That iss goot! Let him pay me!"

Mother Müller snorted and shuffled her feet. "Ach, you talk, you talk. Now you vill make the pastor goot and mad if he hears. Vot ve do, if he vill not chrissen the babies?" [36]

"You give him goot money, he vill chrissen," shouted Father Müller. "You vait und see!" [37]

"Ah sure, dot iss so," agreed Mother Müller. "Only do not let him hear!" [38]

There was a gust of excited talk in German, with much rapping of knife handles on the table. I gave up trying to understand, but watched their faces. It sounded like a pitched battle, but they were agreeing about something. They were united in their tribal scepticisms, as in everything else. I got a powerful impression that they were all, even the sons-in-law, one human being divided into several separate appearances. The crippled servant girl brought in more food and gathered up plates and went away in her limping run, and she seemed to me the only individual in the house. Even I felt divided into many fragments, having left or lost a part of myself in every place I had travelled, in every life mine had touched, above all, in every death of someone near to me that had carried into the grave some part of my living cells. But the servant, she was whole, and belonged nowhere. [39]

I settled easily enough into the marginal life of the household ways and habits. Day began early at the Müllers', and we ate breakfast by yellow lamplight, with the grey damp winds blowing with spring softness through the open windows. The men swallowed their last cups of steaming coffee standing, with their hats on, and went out to harness the horses to the ploughs at sunrise. Annetje, with her fat baby slung over her shoulder, could sweep a room or make a bed with one hand, all finished before the day was well begun; and she spent the rest of the day outdoors, caring for the chickens and the pigs. Now and then she came in with a shallow boxful of newly hatched chickens, abject dabs of wet fluff, and put them on a table in her bedroom where she might tend them carefully on their first day. Mother Müller strode about hugely, giving orders right and left, while Father Müller, smoothing his whiskers and lighting his pipe, drove away to town with Mother Müller calling out after him final directions and instructions about household needs. He never spoke a word to her and appeared not to be listening, but he always returned in a few hours with every commission and errand performed exactly. After I had made my own bed and set my attic in order, there was nothing at all for me to do, and I walked out of this enthusiastic bustle into the lane, feeling extremely useless. But the repose, the almost mystical inertia of their minds in the midst of this muscular life, communicated itself to me little by little, and I absorbed it gratefully in silence and [40] felt all the hidden knotted painful places in my own mind beginning to loosen. It was easier to breathe, and I might even weep, if I pleased. In a very few days I no longer felt like weeping.

One morning I saw Hatsy spading up the kitchen garden plot, and my offer to help, to spread the seeds and cover them, was accepted. We worked at this for several hours each morning, until the warmth of the sun and the stooping posture induced in me a comfortable vertigo. I forgot to count the days, they were one like the other except as the colors of the air changed, deepening and warming to keep step with the advancing season, and the earth grew firmer underfoot with the swelling tangle of crowding roots.

The children, so hungry and noisy at the table, were peaceable little folk who played silent engrossed games in the front yard. They were always kneading mud into loaves and pies and carrying their battered dolls and cotton rag animals through the operations of domestic life. They fed them, put them to bed; they got them up and fed them again, set them to their chores making more mud loaves; or they would harness themselves to their carts and gallop away to a great shady chestnut tree on the opposite side of the house. Here the tree became the *Turnverein*, and they themselves were again human beings, solemnly ambling about in a dance and going through the motions of drinking beer. Miraculously changed once more into horses, they harnessed themselves and galloped home. They came at call to be fed and put to sleep with the docility of their own toys or animal playmates. Their mothers handled them with instinctive, constant gentleness; they never seemed to be troubled by them. They were as devoted and caretaking as a cat with her kittens.

Sometimes I took Annetje's next to youngest child, a baby of two years, in her little wagon, and we would go down through the orchard, where the branches were beginning to sprout in cones of watery green, and into the lane for a short distance. I would turn again into a smaller lane, smoother because less travelled, and we would go slowly between the aisle of mulberry trees where the fruit was beginning to hang and curl like green furry worms. The baby would sit in a compact mound of flannel and calico, her pale-blue eyes tilted and shining under her cap, her two lower teeth showing in a rapt smile. Sometimes several of the other children would follow along quietly. When I turned, they all turned without question, and we would proceed back to the house as sedately as we had set out.

The narrow lane, I discovered, led to the river, and it became my favorite walk. Almost every day I went along the edge of the naked wood, passionately occupied with looking for signs of spring. The changes there were so subtle and gradual I found one day that branches of willows and sprays of blackberry vine alike were covered with fine points of green; the color had changed overnight, or so it seemed, and I knew that tomorrow the whole valley and wood and edge of the river would be quick and feathery with golden green blowing in the winds.

And it was so. On that day I did not leave the river until after dark and came home through the marsh with the owls and nightjars crying over my head, calling in a strange and broken chorus in the woods until the farthest answering cry was a ghostly echo. When I went through the orchard the trees were all abloom with fireflies. I stopped and looked at it for a long time, then walked slowly, amazed, for I had never seen anything that was more beautiful to me. The trees were freshly budded out with pale bloom, the branches were immobile in the thin darkness, but the flower clusters shivered in a soundless dance of delicately woven light, whirling as airily as leaves in a breeze, as rhythmically as water in a fountain. Every tree was budded out with this living, pulsing fire as fragile and cool as bubbles. When I opened the gate their light shone on my hands like fox fire. When I looked back, the shimmer of golden light was there, it was no dream.

Hatsy was on her knees in the dining room, washing the floor with heavy dark rags. She always did this work at night, so the men with their heavy boots would not be tracking it up again and it would be immaculate in the morning. She turned her young face to me in a stupor of fatigue. "Ottilie! Ottilie!" she called, loudly, and before I could speak, she said, "Ottilie will give you supper. It is waiting, all ready." I tried to tell her that I was not hungry, but she wished to reassure me. "Look, we all must eat. Now or then, it's no trouble." She sat back on her heels, and raising her head, looked over the window sill at the orchard. She smiled and paused for a moment and said happily, "Now it is come spring. Every spring we have that." She bent again over the great pail of water with her mops.                   46

The crippled servant came in, stumbling perilously on the slippery floor,      47
and set a dish before me, lentils with sausage and red chopped cabbage. It was hot and savory and I was truly grateful, for I found I was hungry, after all. I looked at her—so her name was Ottilie?—and said, "Thank you." "She can't talk," said Hatsy, simply stating a fact that need not be emphasized. The blurred, dark face was neither young nor old, but crumpled into criss cross wrinkles, irrelevant either to age or suffering; simply wrinkles, pattern-less blackened seams as if the perishable flesh had been wrung in a hard cruel fist. Yet in that mutilated face I saw high cheekbones, slanted water-blue eyes, the pupils very large and strained with the anxiety of one peering into a darkness full of danger. She jarred heavily against the table as she turned, her bowed back trembling with the perpetual working of her withered arms, and ran away in aimless, driven haste.

Hatsy sat on her heels again for a moment, tossed her braids back over      48
her shoulder and said, "That is Ottilie. She is not sick now. She is only like that since she was sick when she was a baby. But she can work so well as I can. She cooks. But she cannot talk so you can understand." She went up on her knees, bowed over, and began to scrub again, with new energy. She was really a network of thin taut ligaments and long muscles elastic as woven steel. She would always work too hard, and be tired all her life, and never know that this was anything but perfectly natural; everybody worked all the time, because there was always more work waiting when they had finished

what they were doing then. I ate my supper and took my plate to the kitchen and set it on the table. Ottilie was sitting in a kitchen chair with her feet in the open oven, her arms folded and her head waggling a little. She did not see or hear me.

At home, Hatsy wore an old brown corduroy dress and galoshes with-   49
out stockings. Her skirts were short enough to show her thin legs, slightly crooked below the knees, as if she had walked too early. "Hatsy, she's a good, quick girl," said Mother Müller, to whom praising anybody or anything did not come easily. On Saturdays, Hatsy took a voluminous bath in a big tub in the closet back of the kitchen, where also were stored the extra chamber pots, slop jars, and water jugs. She then unplaited her yellow hair and bound up the crinkled floss with a wreath of pink cotton rosebuds, put on her pale-blue China silk dress, and went to the *Turnverein* to dance and drink a seidel of dark-brown beer with her suitor, who resembled her brothers enough to be her brother, though I think nobody ever noticed this except myself, and I said nothing because it would have been the remark of a stranger and hopeless outsider. On Sundays, the entire family went to the *Turnverein* after copious washings, getting into starched dresses and shirts, and getting the baskets of food stored in the wagons. The servant, Ottilie, would rush out to see them off, standing with both shaking arms folded over her forehead, shading her troubled eyes to watch them to the turn of the lane. Her muteness seemed nearly absolute; she had no coherent language of signs. Yet three times a day she spread that enormous table with solid food, freshly baked bread, huge platters of vegetables, immoderate roasts of meat, extravagant tarts, strudels, pies—enough for twenty people. If neighbors came in for an afternoon on some holiday, Ottilie would stumble into the big north room, the parlor, with its golden oak melodeon, a harsh-green Brussels carpet, Nottingham lace curtains, crocheted lace antimacassars on the chair backs, to serve them coffee with cream and sugar and thick slices of yellow cake.

Mother Müller sat but seldom in her parlor, and always with an air of   50
formal unease, her knotted big fingers cramped in a cluster. But Father Müller often sat there in the evenings, where no one ventured to follow him unless commanded; he sometimes played chess with his elder son-in-law, who had learned a good while ago that Father Müller was a good player who abhorred an easy victory, and he dared not do less than put up the best fight he was able, but even so, if Father Müller felt himself winning too often, he would roar, "No, you are not trying! You are not doing your best. Now we stop this nonsense!" and son-in-law would find himself dismissed in temporary disgrace.

Most evenings, however, Father Müller sat by himself and read *Das*   51
*Kapital*.[1] He would settle deeply into the red plush base rocker and spread the volume upon a low table before him. It was an early edition in blotty

1. Critique of capitalism by Karl Marx (1818–83).

black German type, stained and ragged in its leather cover, the pages falling apart, a very bible. He knew whole chapters almost by heart, and added nothing to, took nothing from, the canonical, once-delivered text. I cannot say at that time of my life I had never heard of *Das Kapital*, but I had certainly never known anyone who had read it, though if anyone mentioned it, it was always with profound disapproval. It was not a book one had to read in order to reject it. And here was this respectable old farmer who accepted its dogma as a religion—that is to say, its legendary inapplicable precepts were just, right, proper, one must believe in them, of course, but life, everyday living, was another and unrelated thing. Father Müller was the richest man in his community; almost every neighboring farmer rented land from him, and some of them worked it on the share system. He explained this to me one evening after he had given up trying to teach me chess. He was not surprised that I could not learn, at least not in one lesson, and he was not surprised either that I knew nothing about *Das Kapital*. He explained his own arrangements to me thus: "These men, they cannot buy their land. The land must be bought, for Kapital owns it, and Kapital will not give back to the worker the land that is his. Well, somehow, I can always buy land. Why? I do not know. I only know that with my first land here I made good crops to buy more land, and so I rent it cheap, more than anybody else I rent it cheap, I lend money so my neighbors do not fall into the hands of the bank, and so I am not Kapital. Someday these workers, they can buy land from me, for less than they can get it anywhere else. Well, that is what I can do, that is all." He turned over a page, and his angry grey eyes looked out at me under his shaggy brows. "I buy my land with my hard work, all my life, and I rent it cheap to my neighbors, and then they say they will not elect my son-in-law, my Annetje's husband, to be sheriff because I am atheist. So then I say, all right, but next year you pay more for your land or more shares of your crops. If I am atheist I will act like one. So, my Annetje's husband is sheriff, that is all."

He had put a stubby forefinger on a line to mark his place, and now he sank himself into his book, and I left quietly without saying good night. 52

The *Turnverein* was an octagonal pavilion set in a cleared space in a patch of woods belonging to Father Müller. The German colony came here to sit about in the cool shade, while a small brass band played cloppity country dances. The girls danced with energy and direction, their starched petticoats rustling like dry leaves. The boys were more awkward, but willing; they clutched their partners' waists and left crumpled sweaty spots where they clutched. Here Mother Müller took her ease after a hard week. Her gaunt limbs would relax, her knees spread squarely apart, and she would gossip over her beer with the women of her own generation. They would cast an occasional caretaking glance at the children playing nearby, allowing the younger mothers freedom to dance or sit in peace with their own friends. 53

On the other side of the pavilion, Father Müller would sit with the sober 54 grandfathers, their long curved pipes wagging on their chests as they discussed local politics with profound gravity, their hard peasant fatalism tempered only a little by a shrewd worldly distrust of all officeholders not personally known to them, all political plans except their own immediate ones. When Father Müller talked, they listened respectfully, with faith in him as a strong man, head of his own house and his community. They nodded slowly whenever he took his pipe from his mouth and gestured, holding it by the bowl as if it were a stone he was getting ready to throw. On our way back from the *Turnverein* one evening, Mother Müller said to me, "Well, now, by the grace of Gott it is all settled between Hatsy and her man. It is next Sunday by this time they will be marrit."

All the folk who usually went to the *Turnverein* on Sundays came instead  55
to the Müller house for the wedding. They brought useful presents, mostly bed linen, pillow covers, a white counterpane, with a few ornaments for the bridal chamber—a home-braided round rug in many colors, a brass-bottomed lamp with a round pink chimney decorated with red roses, a stone china wash-bowl and pitcher also covered with red roses; and the bridegroom's gift to the bride was a necklace, a double string of red coral twigs. Just before the short ceremony began, he slipped the necklace over her head with trembling hands. She smiled up at him shakily and helped him disentangle her short veil from the coral, then they joined hands and turned their faces to the pastor, not letting go until time for the exchange of rings—the widest, thickest, reddest gold bands to be found, no doubt—and at that moment they both stopped smiling and turned a little pale. The groom recovered first, and bent over—he was considerably taller than she—and kissed her on the forehead. His eyes were a deep blue, and his hair not really Müller taffy color, but a light chestnut; a good-looking, gentle-tempered boy, I decided, and he looked at Hatsy as if he liked what he saw. They knelt and clasped hands again for the final prayer, then stood together and exchanged the bridal kiss, a very chaste reserved one, still not on the lips. Then everybody came to shake hands and the men all kissed the bride and the women all kissed the groom. Some of the women whispered in Hatsy's ear, and all burst out laughing except Hatsy, who turned red from her forehead to her throat. She whispered in turn to her husband, who nodded in agreement. She then tried to slip away quietly, but the watchful young girls were after her, and shortly we saw her running through the blossoming orchard, holding up her white ruffled skirts, with all the girls in pursuit, shrieking and calling like excited hunters, for the first to overtake and touch her would be the next bride. They returned, breathless, dragging the lucky one with them, and held her against her ecstatic resistance, while all the young boys kissed her.

The guests stayed on for a huge supper, and Ottilie came in, wearing a  56
fresh blue apron, sweat beaded in the wrinkles of her forehead and around her formless mouth, and passed the food around the table. The men ate first and then Hatsy came in with the women for the first time, still wearing her square little veil of white cotton net bound on her hair with peach blossoms

shattered in the bride's race. After supper, one of the girls played waltzes and polkas on the melodeon, and everyone danced. The bridegroom drew gallons of beer from a keg set up in the hall, and at midnight everybody went away, warmly emotional and happy. I went down to the kitchen for a pitcher of hot water. The servant was still setting things to rights, hobbling between table and cupboard. Her face was a brown smudge of anxiety, her eyes were wide and dazed. Her uncertain hands rattled among the pans, but nothing could make her seem real, or in any way connected with the life around her. Yet when I set my pitcher on the stove, she lifted the heavy kettle and poured the scalding water into it without spilling a drop.

The clear honey green of the early morning sky was a mirror of the bright earth. At the edge of the woods there had sprung a reticent blooming of small white and pale-colored flowers. The peach trees were now each a separate nosegay of shell rose and white. I left the house, meaning to take the short path across to the lane of mulberries. The women were deep in the house, the men were away to the fields, the animals were turned into the pastures, and only Ottilie was visible, sitting on the steps of the back porch peeling potatoes. She gazed in my direction with eyes that fell short of me, and seemed to focus on a point midway between us, and gave no sign. Then she dropped her knife and rose, her mouth opened and closed several times, she strained toward me, motioning with her right hand. I went to her, her hands came out and clutched my sleeve, and for a moment I feared to hear her voice. There was no sound from her, but she drew me along after her, full of some mysterious purpose of her own. She opened the door of a dingy bitter-smelling room, windowless, which opened off the kitchen, beside the closet where Hatsy took her baths. A lumpy narrow cot and chest of drawers supporting a blistered looking-glass almost filled the space. Ottilie's lips moved, struggling for speech, as she pulled and tumbled over a heap of rubbish in the top drawer. She took out a photograph and put it in my hands. It was in the old style, faded to a dirty yellow, mounted on cardboard elaborately clipped and gilded at the edges.

I saw a girl child about five years old, a pretty smiling German baby, looking curiously like a slightly elder sister of Annetje's two-year-old, wearing a frilled frock and a prodigious curl of blonde hair, called a roach, on the crown of her head. The strong legs, round as sausages, were encased in long white ribbed stockings, and the square firm feet were laced into old-fashioned soft-soled black boots. Ottilie peered over the picture, twisted her neck, and looked up into my face. I saw the slanted water-blue eyes and the high cheekbones of the Müllers again, mutilated, almost destroyed, but unmistakable. This child was what she had been, and she was without doubt the elder sister of Annetje and Gretchen and Hatsy; in urgent pantomime she insisted that this was so—she patted the picture and her own face, and strove terribly to speak. She pointed to the name written carefully on the back, Ottilie, and touched her mouth with her bent knuckles. Her head wagged in her perpet-

57

58

ual nod; her shaking hand seemed to flap the photograph at me in a roguish humor. The bit of cardboard connected her at once somehow to the world of human beings I knew; for an instant some filament lighter than cobweb spun itself out between that living center in her and in me, a filament from some center that held us all bound to our unescapable common source, so that her life and mine were kin, even a part of each other, and the painfulness and strangeness of her vanished. She knew well that she had been Ottilie, with those steady legs and watching eyes, and she was Ottilie still within herself. For a moment, being alive, she knew she suffered, for she stood and shook with silent crying, smearing away her tears with the open palm of her hand. Even while her cheeks were wet, her face changed. Her eyes cleared and fixed themselves upon that point in space which seemed for her to contain her unaccountable and terrible troubles. She turned her head as if she had heard a voice and disappeared in her staggering run into the kitchen, leaving the drawer open and the photograph face downward on the chest.

At midday meal she came hurrying and splashing coffee on the white floor, restored to her own secret existence of perpetual amazement, and again I had been a stranger to her like all the rest but she was no stranger to me, and could not be again. 59

The youngest brother came in, holding up an opossum he had caught in his trap. He swung the furry body from side to side, his eyes fairly narrowed with pride as he showed us the mangled creature. "No, it is cruel, even for the wild animals," said gentle Annetje to me, "but boys love to kill, they love to hurt things. I am always afraid he will trap poor Kuno." I thought privately that Kuno, a wolfish, ungracious beast, might well prove a match for any trap. Annetje was full of silent, tender solicitudes. The kittens, the puppies, the chicks, the lambs and calves were her special care. She was the only one of the women who caressed the weanling calves when she set the pans of milk before them. Her child seemed as much a part of her as if it were not yet born. Still, she seemed to have forgotten that Ottilie was her sister. So had all the others. I remembered how Hatsy had spoken her name but had not said she was her sister. Their silence about her was, I realized, exactly that—simple forgetfulness. She moved among them as invisible to their imaginations as a ghost. Ottilie their sister was something painful that had happened long ago and now was past and done for; they could not live with that memory or its visible reminder—they forgot her in pure self-defense. But I could not forget her. She drifted into my mind like a bit of weed carried in a current and caught there, floating but fixed, refusing to be carried away. I reasoned it out. The Müllers, what else could they have done with Ottilie? By a physical accident in her childhood she had been stripped of everything but her mere existence. It was not a society or a class that pampered its invalids and the unfit. So long as one lived, one did one's share. This was her place, in this family she had been born and must die; did she suffer? No one asked, no one looked to see. Suffering went with life, suffering and labor. While one lived one worked, that was all, and without complaints, for no 60 one had time to listen, and everybody had his own troubles. So, what else could they have done with Ottilie? As for me, I could do nothing but promise myself that I would forget her, too; and to remember her for the rest of my life.

Sitting at the long table, I would watch Ottilie clattering about in her tormented haste, bringing in that endless food that represented all her life's labors. My mind would follow her into the kitchen where I could see her peering into the great simmering kettles, the crowded oven, her whole body a mere machine of torture. Straight up to the surface of my mind the thought would come urgently, clearly, as if driving time toward the desired event: Let it be now, let it be *now*. Not even tomorrow, no, today. Let her sit down quietly in her rickety chair by the stove and fold those arms, and let us find her there like that, with her head fallen forward on her knees. She will rest then. I would wait, hoping she might not come again, ever again, through that door I gazed at with wincing eyes, as if I might see something unendurable enter through it. Then she would come, and it was only Ottilie, after all, in the bosom of her family, and one of its most useful and competent members; and they with a deep right instinct had learned to live with her disaster on its own terms, and hers; they had accepted and then made use of what was for them only one more painful event in a world full of troubles, many of them much worse than this. So, a step at a time, I followed the Müllers as nearly as I could in their acceptance of Ottilie, and the use they made of her life, for in some way that I could not quite explain to myself, I found great virtue and courage in their steadiness and refusal to feel sorry for anybody, least of all for themselves.

Gretchen bore her child, a son, conveniently between the hours of supper and bedtime, one evening of friendly and domestic-sounding rain. The next day brought neighboring women from miles around, and the child was bandied about among them as if he were a new kind of medicine ball. Sedate and shy at dances, emotional at weddings, they were ribald and jocose at births. Over coffee and beer the talk grew broad, the hearty gutturals were swallowed in the belly of laughter; those honest hard-working wives and mothers saw life for a few hours as a hearty low joke, and it did them good. The baby bawled and suckled like a young calf, and the men of the family came in for a look and added their joyful improprieties.

Cloudy weather drove them home earlier than they had meant to go. The whole sky was lined with smoky black and grey vapor hanging in ragged wisps like soot in a chimney. The edges of the woods turned dull purple as the horizon reddened slowly, then faded, and all across the sky ran a deep shuddering mumble of thunder. All the Müllers hurried about getting into rubber boots and oilcloth overalls, shouting to each other, making their plan of action. The youngest boy came over the ridge of the hill with Kuno helping him to drive the sheep down into the fold. Kuno was barking, the sheep were baaing and bleating, the horses freed from the ploughs were excited;

they whinnied and trotted at the lengths of their halters, their ears laid back. The cows were bawling in distress and the calves cried back to them. All the men went out among the animals to round them up and quiet them and get them enclosed safely. Even as Mother Müller, her half-dozen petticoats looped about her thighs and tucked into her hip boots, was striding to join them in the barns, the cloud rack was split end to end by a shattering blow of lightning, and the cloudburst struck the house with the impact of a wave against a ship. The wind broke the windowpanes and the floods poured through. The roof beams strained and the walls bent inward, but the house stood to its foundations. The children were huddled into the inner bedroom with Gretchen. "Come and sit on the bed with me now," she told them calmly, "and be still." She sat up with a shawl around her, suckling the baby. Annetje came then and left her baby with Gretchen, too; and standing at the doorsteps with one arm caught over the porch rail, reached down into the furious waters which were rising to the very threshold and dragged in a half-drowned lamb. I followed her. We could not make ourselves heard above the cannonade of thunder, but together we carried the creature into the hall under the stairs, where we rubbed the drowned fleece with rags and pressed his stomach to free him from the water and finally got him sitting up with his feet tucked under him. Annetje was merry with triumph and kept saying in delight, "Alive, alive! look!"

We left him there when we heard the men shouting and beating at the kitchen door and ran to open it for them. They came in, Mother Müller among them, wearing her yoke and milk pails. She stood there with the water pouring from her skirts, the three-cornered piece of black oilcloth on her head dripping, her rubber boots wrinkled down with the weight of her petticoats stuffed into them. She and Father Müller stood near each other, looking like two gnarled lightning-struck old trees, his beard and oilcloth garments streaming, both their faces suddenly dark and old and tired, tired once for all; they would never be rested again in their lives. Father Müller suddenly roared at her, "Go get yourself dry clothes. Do you want to make yourself sick?"

"Ho," she said, taking off her milk yoke and setting the pails on the floor. "Go change yourself. I bring you dry socks." One of the boys told me she had carried a day-old calf on her back up a ladder against the inside wall of the barn and had put it safely in the hayloft behind a barricade of bales. Then she had lined up the cows in the stable, and, sitting on her milking stool in the rising water, she had milked them all. She seemed to think nothing of it.

"Hatsy!" she called, "come help with this milk!" Little pale Hatsy came flying barefoot because she had been called in the midst of taking off her wet shoes, her thick yellow and silver braids thumping on her shoulders as she ran. Her new husband followed her, rather shy of his mother-in-law.

"Let me," he said, wishing to spare his dear bride such heavy work, and started to lift the great pails. "No!" shouted Mother Müller, so the poor young man nearly jumped out of his shirt, "not you. The milk is not business for a man." He fell back and stood there with dark rivulets of mud seeping from his boots, watching Hatsy pour the milk into pans. Mother Müller started to follow her husband to attend him, but said at the door, turning back, "Where is Ottilie?" and no one knew, no one had seen her. "Find her," said Mother Müller, going. "Tell her we want supper now."

Hatsy motioned to her husband, and together they tiptoed to the door  68
of Ottilie's room and opened it silently. The light from the kitchen showed them Ottilie, sitting by herself, folded up on the edge of the bed. Hatsy threw the door wide open for more light and called in a high penetrating voice as if to a deaf person or one at a great distance, "Ottilie! Suppertime. We are hungry!" and the young pair left the kitchen to look under the stairway to see how Annetje's lamb was getting on. Then Annetje, Hatsy, and I got brooms and began sweeping the dirty water and broken glass from the floors of the hall and dining room.

The storm lightened gradually, but the flooding rain continued. At sup-  69
per there was talk about the loss of animals and their replacement. All the crops must be replanted, the season's labor was for nothing. They were all tired and wet, but they ate heartily and calmly, to strengthen themselves against all the labor of repairing and restoring which must begin early tomorrow morning.

By morning the drumming on the roof had almost ceased; from my  70
window I looked upon a sepia-colored plain of water moving slowly to the valley. The roofs of the barns sagged like the ridge poles of a tent, and a number of drowned animals floated or were caught against the fences. At breakfast Mother Müller sat groaning over her coffee cup. "Ach," she said, "what it is to have such a pain in the head. Here too," she thumped her chest. "All over. Ach, Gott, I'm sick." She got up sighing hoarsely, her cheeks flushed, calling Hatsy and Annetje to help her in the barn.

They all came back very soon, their skirts draggled to the knees, and  71
the two sisters were supporting their mother, who was speechless and could hardly stand. They put her to bed, where she lay without moving, her face scarlet. Everybody was confused, no one knew what to do. They tucked the quilts about her, and she threw them off. They offered her coffee, cold water, beer, but she turned her head away. The sons came in and stood beside her, and joined the cry: "*Mutterchen, Mutti, Mutti*, what can we do? Tell us, what do you need?" But she could not tell them. It was impossible to ride the twelve miles to town for a doctor; fences and bridges were down, the roads were washed out. The family crowded into the room, unnerved in panic, lost unless the sick woman should come to herself and tell them what to do for her. Father Müller came in and, kneeling beside her, he took hold of her hands and spoke to her most lovingly, and when she did not answer him he broke out crying openly in a loud voice, the great tears rolling, "Ach, Gott, Gott. A hundert tousand tollars in the bank"—he glared around at his family and spoke broken English to them, as if he were a stranger to himself and

had forgotten his own language—"and tell me, tell, what goot does it do?"

This frightened them, and all at once, together, they screamed and called    72
and implored her in a tumult utterly beyond control. The noise of their grief
and terror filled the place. In the midst of this, Mother Müller died.

In the midafternoon the rain passed, and the sun was a disc of brass in    73
a cruelly bright sky. The waters flowed thickly down to the river, leaving
the hill bald and brown, with the fences lying in a flattened tangle, the young
peach trees stripped of bloom and sagging at the roots. In the woods had
occurred a violent eruption of ripe foliage of a jungle thickness, glossy and
burning, a massing of hot peacock green with cobalt shadows.

The household was in such silence, I had to listen carefully to know that    74
anyone lived there. Everyone, even the younger children, moved on tiptoe
and spoke in whispers. All afternoon the thud of hammers and the whine of
a saw went on monotonously in the barn loft. At dark, the men brought in a
shiny coffin of new yellow pine with rope handles and set it in the hall. It
lay there on the floor for an hour or so, where anyone passing had to step
over it. Then Annetje and Hatsy, who had been washing and dressing the
body, appeared in the doorway and motioned: "You may bring it in now."

Mother Müller lay in state in the parlor throughout the night, in her    75
black silk dress with a scrap of white lace at the collar and a small lace cap
on her hair. Her husband sat in the plush chair near her, looking at her face,
which was very contemplative, gentle, and remote. He wept at intervals,
silently, wiping his face and head with a big handkerchief. His daughters
brought him coffee from time to time. He fell asleep there toward morning.

The light burned in the kitchen nearly all night, too, and the sound of    76
Ottilie's heavy boots thumping about unsteadily was accompanied by the
locust whirring of the coffee mill and the smell of baking bread. Hatsy came
to my room. "There's coffee and cake," she said, "you'd better have some,"
and turned away crying, crumbling her slice in her hand. We stood about
and ate in silence. Ottilie brought in a fresh pot of coffee, her eyes bleared
and fixed, her gait as aimless-looking and hurried as ever, and when she
spilled some on her own hand, she did not seem to feel it.

For a day longer they waited; then the youngest boy went to fetch the    77
Lutheran pastor, and a few neighbors came back with them. By noon many
more had arrived, spattered with mud, the horses heaving and sweating. At
every greeting the family gave way and wept afresh, as naturally and openly
as children. Their faces were drenched and soft with their tears; there was a
comfortable relaxed look in the muscles of their faces. It was good to let go,
to have something to weep for that nobody need excuse or explain. Their
tears were at once a luxury and a cure of souls. They wept away the hard
core of secret trouble that is in the heart of each separate man, secure in a
communal grief; in sharing it, they consoled each other. For a while they
would visit the grave and remember, and then life would arrange itself again
in another order, yet it would be the same. Already the thoughts of the living

were turning to tomorrow, when they would be at the work of rebuilding and replanting and repairing—even now, today, they would hurry back from the burial to milk the cows and feed the chickens, and they might weep again and again for several days, until their tears could heal them at last.

On that day I realized, for the first time, not death, but the terror of dying. When they took the coffin out to the little country hearse and I saw that the procession was about to form, I went to my room and lay down. Staring at the ceiling, I heard and felt the ominous order and purpose in the movements and sounds below—the creaking harness and hoofbeats and grating wheels, the muted grave voices—and it was as if my blood fainted and receded with fright, while my mind stayed wide awake to receive the awful impress. Yet when I knew they were leaving the yard, the terror began to leave me. As the sounds receded, I lay there not thinking, not feeling, in a mere drowse of relief and weariness. 78

Through my half-sleep I heard the howling of a dog. It seemed to be a dream, and I was troubled to awaken. I dreamed that Kuno was caught in the trap; then I thought he was really caught, it was no dream and I must wake, because there was no one but me to let him out. I came broad awake, the cry rushed upon me like a wind, and it was not the howl of a dog. I ran downstairs and looked into Gretchen's room. She was curled up around her baby, and they were both asleep. I ran to the kitchen. 79

Ottilie was sitting in her broken chair with her feet on the edge of the open oven, where the heat had died away. Her hands hung at her sides, the fingers crooked into the palm; her head lay back on her shoulders, and she howled with a great wrench of her body, an upward reach of the neck, without tears. At sight of me she got up and came over to me and laid her head on my breast, and her hands dangled forward a moment. Shuddering, she babbled and howled and waved her arms in a frenzy through the open window over the stripped branches of the orchard toward the lane where the procession had straightened out into formal order. I took hold of her arms where the unnaturally corded muscles clenched and strained under her coarse sleeves; I led her out to the steps and left her sitting there, her head wagging. 80

In the barnyard there remained only the broken-down spring wagon and the shaggy pony that had brought me to the farm on the first day. The harness was still a mystery, but somehow I managed to join pony, harness, and wagon not too insecurely, or so I could only hope; and I pushed and hauled and tugged at Ottilie and lifted her until she was in the seat and I had the reins in hand. We careened down the road at a grudging trot, the pony jolting like a churn, the wheels spinning elliptically in a truly broad comedy swagger. I watched the jovial antics of those wheels with attention, hoping for the best. We slithered into round pits of green mud, and jogged perilously into culverts where small bridges had been. Once, in what was left of the main road, I stood up to see if I might overtake the funeral train; yes, there it was, going inch-meal up the road over the little hill, a bumbling train of black beetles crawling helter-skelter over clods. 81

Ottilie, now silent, was doubled upon herself, slipping loosely on the 82 edge of the seat. I caught hold of her stout belt with my free hand, and my fingers slipped between her clothes and bare flesh, ribbed and gaunt and dry against my knuckles. My sense of her realness, her humanity, this shattered being that was a woman, was so shocking to me that a howl as doglike and despairing as her own rose in me unuttered and died again, to be a perpetual ghost. Ottilie slanted her eyes and peered at me, and I gazed back. The knotted wrinkles of her face were grotesquely changed, she gave a choked little whimper, and suddenly she laughed out, a kind of yelp but unmistakably laughter, and clapped her hands for joy, the grinning mouth and suffering eyes turned to the sky. Her head nodded and wagged with the clownish humor of our trundling lurching progress. The feel of the hot sun on her back, the bright air, the jolly senseless staggering of the wheels, the peacock green of the heavens: something of these had reached her. She was happy and gay, and she gurgled and rocked in her seat, leaning upon me and waving loosely around her as if to show me what wonders she saw.

Drawing the pony to a standstill, I studied her face for a while and 83 pondered my ironical mistake. There was nothing I could do for Ottilie, selfishly as I wished to ease my heart of her; she was beyond my reach as well as any other human reach, and yet, had I not come nearer to her than I had to anyone else in my attempt to deny and bridge the distance between us, or rather, her distance from me? Well, we were both equally the fools of life, equally fellow fugitives from death. We had escaped for one day more at least. We would celebrate our good luck, we would have a little stolen holiday, a breath of spring air and freedom on this lovely, festive afternoon.

Ottilie fidgeted, uneasy at our stopping. I flapped the reins, the pony 84 moved on, we turned across the shallow ditch where the small road divided from the main travelled one. I measured the sun westering gently; there would be time enough to drive to the river down the lane of mulberries and to get back to the house before the mourners returned. There would be plenty of time for Ottilie to have a fine supper ready for them. They need not even know she had been gone.

## STUDY QUESTIONS

1. What EXPECTATIONS are created by the opening paragraph? by the second paragraph? In what ways does the opening paragraph instruct you in how to read the story? What do you learn or infer about the NARRATOR from the opening paragraph? What does the rest of the story confirm or modify in these opening remarks?

2. How does Louise's description of the "holiday" place in paragraphs 3 and 7 fit the narrator's description of Louise and her stories in paragraph 2?

3. In paragraphs 16 and 17, there are rather lengthy descriptions of what seem to be trivial matters—the harness and the spring wagon. What do these contribute to your expectations? to your understanding of the Müllers?

4. In paragraphs 14 through 17, there are a number of SIMILES, figures of speech involving comparisons of essentially unlike things—"a face that felt like wet clay"; "crushed . . . like an ant under a stone"; "shaggy as a wintering bear." What do clay, ant, and bear have in common? What other similes can you find in the story? What do they contribute to your image of the narrator and her life? to the SET-TING? to the effect of the story?

5. Paragraphs 1 and 20 hint darkly at something painful in the narrator's recent past; what other hints do you find? What "possible trouble" do you imagine? Which of these do you reject as you read along? Why? Which do you find more and more confirmed as you read along? What do the troubles have to do with the main episode of the story of the "holiday"?

6. What does it mean that the Müllers' is "a house of perpetual exile" and that they do not "confuse nationality with habitation" (par. 26)? What are mealtime habits that the Müllers brought from Germany generations ago? Why are so many of the Müllers living in the same house? How do the household activity and family attitudes affect the narrator (par. 40)? Hatsy's suitor looks very much like her brother, but only the narrator seems to notice (par. 49); why? Which members of the family look somewhat different from the others?

7. What does the narrator think of as her "center" (par. 27)? Do you think of your "center" in the same way?

8. "But the servant, she was whole, and belonged nowhere" (par. 39). Explain. Trace the gradual emergence of information about and interest in Ottilie. How does the narrator discover who Ottilie is? The narrator says she realizes that Ottilie's life "and mine were kin" and she would never forget her; explain. Why have Ottilie's brothers and sisters "forgotten" she was kin? What "use" do the Müllers make of Ottilie's life?

9. What do the chess games (par. 50) tell you about Father Müller? How much is positive (good) and how much is negative (bad)? How did Annetje's husband become sheriff?

10. What does Mother Müller do during the storm? What happens to her afterward?

11. "They wept away the hard core of secret trouble that is in the heart of each separate man, secure in a communal grief" (par. 77); explain. What is the relevance of this to the narrator? to the story as a whole? How does Father Müller take his wife's death? What is "the howling of a dog" the narrator hears (par. 79)? Why does the narrator almost howl herself (par. 82)? Why does Ottilie laugh?

12. The narrator says she "selfishly" wants to help Ottilie but cannot (par. 83). Why is her desire to help "selfish"? "We were both equally the fools of life" (par. 83). Explain.

13. Explain the title and its significance as fully as possible.

14. Who is (are) the "Martian(s)" in this story?

# Carter Revard

Born into an Osage and white family in Oklahoma in 1931, Carter Revard—whose Indian name, Nompewathe, means "fear-inspiring"—won a Rhodes Scholarship to Oxford and earned a doctorate at Yale. He now teaches at Washington University in St. Louis. His poetry is widely published in a variety of magazines and anthologies. His volume *Ponca War Dances* was published in 1980.

The strangers in the poem below are almost literally men from Mars, but despite their green skins, scarlet eyes, and antennae, they are revealed to be uncomfortably like certain humans. What do you expect to be the outcome of this poem?

## DISCOVERY OF THE NEW WORLD

The creatures that we met this morning
        marveled at our green skins
            and scarlet eyes.
    They lack antennae
        and can't be made to grasp                               5
            your proclamation that they are
    our lawful food and prey and slaves,
            nor can they seem to learn
        their body-space is needed to materialize
            our oxygen absorbers—                                10
    which they conceive are breathing
        and thinking creatures whom they implore
at first as angels or (later) as devils
        when they are being snuffed out
            by an absorber swelling                              15
                into their space.
    Their history bled from one this morning
        while we were tasting his brain
            in holographic rainbows
        which we assembled into quite an interesting            20
                set of legends—
            that's all it came to, though
    the colors were quite lovely before we

poured them into our time;
the blue shift bleached away                                                    25
meaningless circumstance and they would not fit
any of our truth-matrices—
there was, however,
a curious visual echo in their history
of our own coming to their earth;                                              30
a certain General Sherman
had said concerning a group of them
exactly what we were saying to you
about these creatures:
it is our destiny to asterize this planet,                                      35
and they will not be asterized,
so they must be wiped out.
We need their space and oxygen
which they do not know how to use,
yet they will not give up their gas unforced,                                   40
and we feel sure,
whatever our "agreements" made this morning,
we'll have to kill them all:
the more we cook this orbit,
the fewer next time around.                                                     45
We've finished burning all their crops
and killed their cattle.
They'll have to come into our pens
and then we'll get to study
the way our heart attacks and cancers spread among them,                        50
since they seem not immune to these.
If we didn't have this mission it might be sad
to see such helpless creatures die,
but never fear,
the riches of this place are ours                                               55
and worth whatever pain others may have to feel.
We'll soon have it cleared
as in fact it is already, at the poles.
Then we will be safe, and rich, and happy here forever.

# STUDY QUESTIONS

1. What do you understand by "their body-space is needed to materialize / our oxygen absorbers" (lines 9–10)? What do the creatures these green-skinned beings have
met think the oxygen absorbers are? What do you expect to happen in this encounter?

2. What appeared in "holographic rainbows" (ll. 17–21)?

3. What do these lines mean: "the blue shift bleached away / meaningless circumstance and they would not fit / any of our truth-matrices" (ll. 25–27)?

4. Does the invaders' talk about not keeping "agreements" (l. 42) remind you of the actions of any other discoveries of new worlds?

5. In what way is the final line of the poem IRONIC?

6. What is the literal CONFLICT in the poem? What past conflict is implied? What side are you on in each? If your heritage is European, how do you feel about the conflict? If your heritage is other than European, how do *you* feel about the conflict? about the Europeans?

# Margaret Atwood

Born in Ottawa in 1939, Margaret Atwood was educated at Victoria College of the University of Toronto and at Harvard University. Best known for her six novels, including the widely admired *Surfacing* (1972) and the best-selling *The Handmaid's Tale* (1985), she has published more than a dozen other books: poetry, nonfiction, short stories, and books for children. Her collection of poetry *The Circle Game* (1966) received the Governor-General's Award.

"The Man from Mars" is an eerie story, increasingly disturbing to the very end.

# THE MAN FROM MARS

A long time ago Christine was walking through the park. She was still wearing her tennis dress; she hadn't had time to shower and change, and her hair was held back with an elastic band. Her chunky reddish face, exposed with no softening fringe, looked like a Russian peasant's, but without the elastic band the hair got in her eyes. The afternoon was too hot for April; the indoor courts had been steaming, her skin felt poached.

The sun had brought the old men out from wherever they spent the winter: she had read a story recently about one who lived for three years in a manhole. They sat weedishly on the benches or lay on the grass with their heads on squares of used newspaper. As she passed, their wrinkled toadstool faces drifted towards her, drawn by the movement of her body, then floated away again, uninterested.

The squirrels were out too, foraging; two or three of them moved towards her in darts and pauses, eyes fixed on her expectantly, mouths with the rat-like receding chins open to show the yellowed front teeth. Christine walked faster, she had nothing to give them. People shouldn't feed them, she thought, it makes them anxious and they get mangy.

Halfway across the park she stopped to take off her cardigan. As she bent over to pick up her tennis racquet again someone touched her on her freshly-bared arm. Christine seldom screamed; she straightened up suddenly, gripping the handle of her racquet. It was not one of the old men, however: it was a dark-haired boy of twelve or so.

"Excuse me," he said, "I search for Economics Building. It is there?" He motioned towards the west.

Christine looked at him more closely. She had been mistaken: he was not young, just short. He came a little above her shoulder, but then, she was above the average height; "statuesque," her mother called it when she was straining. He was also what was referred to in their family as "a person from another culture": oriental without a doubt, though perhaps not Chinese. Christine judged he must be a foreign student and gave him her official welcoming smile. In high school she had been President of the United Nations Club; that year her school had been picked to represent the Egyptian delegation at the Mock Assembly. It had been an unpopular assignment—nobody wanted to be the Arabs—but she had seen it through. She had made rather a good speech about the Palestinian refugees.

"Yes," she said, "that's it over there. The one with the flat roof. See it?"

The man had been smiling nervously at her the whole time. He was wearing glasses with transparent plastic rims, through which his eyes bulged up at her as though through a goldfish bowl. He had not followed where she was pointing. Instead he thrust towards her a small pad of green paper and a ballpoint pen.

"You make map," he said.

Christine set down her tennis racquet and drew a careful map. "We are here," she said, pronouncing distinctly. "You go this way. The building is here." She indicated the route with a dotted line and an X. The man leaned close to her, watching the progress of the map attentively; he smelled of cooked cauliflower and an unfamiliar brand of hair grease. When she had finished Christine handed the paper and pen back to him with a terminal smile.

"Wait," the man said. He tore the piece of paper with the map off the pad, folded it carefully and put it in his jacket pocket; the jacket sleeves came down over his wrists and had threads at the edges. He began to write something; she noticed with a slight feeling of revulsion that his nails and the ends of his fingertips were so badly bitten they seemed almost deformed. Several of his fingers were blue from the leaky ballpoint.

"Here is my name," he said, holding the pad out to her.

Christine read an odd assemblage of G's, Y's and N's, neatly printed in   13
block letters. "Thank you," she said.

"You now write *your* name," he said, extending the pen.   14

Christine hesitated. If this had been a person from her own culture she   15
would have thought he was trying to pick her up. But then, people from her
own culture never tried to pick her up: she was too big. The only one who
had made the attempt was the Moroccan waiter at the beer parlour where
they sometimes went after meetings, and he had been direct. He had just
intercepted her on the way to the Ladies' Room and asked and she said no;
that had been that. This man was not a waiter though but a student; she
didn't want to offend him. In his culture, whatever it was, this exchange of
names on pieces of paper was probably a formal politeness, like saying Thank
You. She took the pen from him.

"That is a very pleasant name," he said. He folded the paper and placed   16
it in his jacket pocket with the map.

Christine felt she had done her duty. "Well, goodbye," she said, "it was   17
nice to have met you." She bent for her tennis racquet but he had already
stooped and retrieved it and was holding it with both hands in front of him,
like a captured banner.

"I carry this for you."   18

"Oh no, please. Don't bother, I am in a hurry," she said, articulating   19
clearly. Deprived of her tennis racquet she felt weaponless. He started to
saunter along the path; he was not nervous at all now, he seemed completely
at ease.

"Vous parlez français?"[1] he asked conversationally.   20

"Oui, un petit peu," she said. "Not very well." How am I going to get   21
my racquet away from him without being rude, she was wondering.

"Mais vous avez un bel accent." His eyes goggled at her through the   22
glasses: was he being flirtatious? She was well aware that her accent was
wretched.

"Look," she said, for the first time letting her impatience show, "I really   23
have to go. Give me my racquet please."

He quickened his pace but gave no sign of returning the racquet. "Where   24
are you going?"

"Home," she said. "My house."   25

"I go with you now," he said hopefully.   26

"*No,*" she said: she would have to be firm with him. She made a lunge   27
and got a grip on her racquet; after a brief tug of war it came free.

"Goodbye," she said, turning away from his puzzled face and setting off   28
at what she hoped was a discouraging jog-trot. It was like walking away from
a growling dog, you shouldn't let on you were frightened. Why should she
be frightened anyway? He was only half her size and she had the tennis
racquet, there was nothing he could do to her.

---

1. Do you speak French? . . . Yes, a little bit. . . . But you have a good accent.

Although she did not look back she could tell he was still following. Let   29
there be a streetcar, she thought, and there was one, but it was far down the
line, stuck behind a red light. He appeared at her side, breathing audibly, a
moment after she reached the stop. She gazed ahead, rigid.

"You are my friend," he said tentatively.   30

Christine relented: he hadn't been trying to pick her up after all, he was   31
a stranger, he just wanted to meet some of the local people; in his place she
would have wanted the same thing.

"Yes," she said, doling him out a smile.   32

"That is good," he said, "My country is very far."   33

Christine couldn't think of an apt reply. "That's interesting," she said.   34
"Très intéressant."[2] The streetcar was coming at last; she opened her purse
and got out a ticket.

"I go with you now," he said. His hand clamped on her arm above the   35
elbow.

"You . . . stay . . . *here*," Christine said, resisting the impulse to shout   36
but pausing between each word as though for a deaf person. She detached
his hand—his hold was quite feeble and could not compete with her tennis
biceps—and leapt off the curb and up the streetcar steps, hearing with relief
the doors grind shut behind her. Inside the car and a block away she permitted herself a glance out a side window. He was standing where she had left
him; he seemed to be writing something on his little pad of paper.

When she reached home she had only time for a snack, and even then   37
she was almost late for the Debating Society. The topic was, "Resolved:
That War Is Obsolete." Her team took the affirmative, and won.

Christine came out of her last examination feeling depressed. It was not   38
the exam that depressed her but the fact that it was the last one: it meant the
end of the school year. She dropped into the coffee shop as usual, then went
home early because there didn't seem to be anything else to do.

"Is that you, dear?" her mother called from the livingroom. She must   39
have heard the front door close. Christine went in and flopped on the sofa,
disturbing the neat pattern of the cushions.

"How was your exam, dear?" her mother asked.   40

"Fine," said Christine flatly. It had been fine, she had passed. She was   41
not a brilliant student, she knew that, but she was conscientious. Her pro-
fessors always wrote things like "A serious attempt" and "Well thought out
but perhaps lacking in *élan*" on her term papers; they gave her B's, the occasional B$^+$. She was taking Political Science and Economics, and hoped for a
job with the Government after she graduated; with her father's connections
she had a good chance.

"That's nice."   42

Christine felt, resentfully, that her mother had only a hazy idea of what   43

2. Very interesting.

an exam was. She was arranging gladioli in a vase; she had rubber gloves on to protect her hands as she always did when engaged in what she called "housework." As far as Christine could tell her housework consisted of arranging flowers in vases: daffodils and tulips and hyacinths through gladioli, iris and roses, all the way to asters and mums. Sometimes she cooked, elegantly and with chafing-dishes, but she thought of it as a hobby. The girl did everything else. Christine thought it faintly sinful to have a girl. The only ones available now were either foreign or pregnant; their expressions usually suggested they were being taken advantage of somehow. But her mother asked what they would do otherwise, they'd either have to go into a Home or stay in their own countries, and Christine had to agree this was probably true. It was hard anyway to argue with her mother, she was so delicate, so preserved-looking, a harsh breath would scratch the finish.

"An interesting young man phoned today," her mother said. She had finished the gladioli and was taking off her rubber gloves. "He asked to speak with you and when I said you weren't in we had quite a little chat. You didn't tell me about him, dear." She put on the glasses which she wore on a decorative chain around her neck, a signal that she was in her modern, intelligent mood rather than her old-fashioned whimsical one.  44

"Did he leave his name?" Christine asked. She knew a lot of young men but they didn't often call her, they conducted their business with her in the coffee shop or after meetings.  45

"He's a person from another culture. He said he would call back later."  46

Christine had to think a moment. She was vaguely acquainted with several people from other cultures, Britain mostly; they belonged to the Debating Society.  47

"He's studying Philosophy in Montreal," her mother prompted. "He sounded French."  48

Christine began to remember the man in the park. "I don't think he's French, exactly," she said.  49

Her mother had taken off her glasses again and was poking absentmindedly at a bent gladiolus. "Well, he sounded French." She meditated, flowery sceptre in hand. "I think it would be nice if you had him to tea."  50

Christine's mother did her best. She had two other daughters, both of whom took after her. They were beautiful, one was well married already and the other would clearly have no trouble. Her friends consoled her about Christine by saying, "She's not fat, she's just big-boned, it's the father's side," and "Christine is so healthy." Her other daughters had never gotten involved in activities when they were at school, but since Christine could not possibly ever be beautiful even if she took off weight, it was just as well she was so athletic and political, it was a good thing she had interests. Christine's mother tried to encourage her interests whenever possible. Christine could tell when she was making an extra effort, there was a reproachful edge to her voice.  51

She knew her mother expected enthusiasm but she could not supply it. "I don't know, I'll have to see," she said dubiously.  52

"You look tired, darling," said her mother. "Perhaps you'd like a glass   53
of milk."

Christine was in the bathtub when the phone rang. She was not prone   54
to fantasy but when she was in the bathtub she often pretended she was a
dolphin, a game left over from one of the girls who used to bathe her when
she was small. Her mother was being bell-voiced and gracious in the hall;
then there was a tap at the door.

"It's that nice young French student, Christine," her mother said.   55

"Tell him I'm in the bathtub," Christine said, louder than necessary.   56
"He isn't French."

She could hear her mother frowning. "That wouldn't be very polite,   57
Christine. I don't think he'd understand."

"Oh all right," Christine said. She heaved herself out the bathtub, swathed   58
her pink bulk in a towel and splattered to the phone.

"Hello," she said gruffly. At a distance he was not pathetic, he was a   59
nuisance. She could not imagine how he had tracked her down: most likely
he went through the phone book, calling all the numbers with her last name
until he hit on the right one.

"It is your friend."   60

"I know," she said, "How are you?"   61

"I am very fine." There was a long pause, during which Christine had a   62
vicious urge to say, "Well, goodbye then," and hang up; but she was aware
of her mother poised figurine-like in her bedroom doorway. Then he said, "I
hope you also are very fine."

"Yes," said Christine. She wasn't going to participate.   63

"I come to tea," he said.   64

This took Christine by surprise. "You do?"   65

"Your pleasant mother ask me. I come Thursday, four o'clock."   66

"Oh," Christine said, ungraciously.   67

"See you then," he said, with conscious pride of one who has mastered   68
a difficult idiom.

Christine set down the phone and went along the hall. Her mother was   69
in her study, sitting innocently at her writing desk.

"Did you ask him to tea on Thursday?"   70

"Not exactly, dear," her mother said. "I did mention he might come   71
round to tea *some*time, though."

"Well, he's coming Thursday. Four o'clock."   72

"What's wrong with that?" her mother said serenely. "I think it's a very   73
nice gesture for us to make. I do think you might try to be a little more co-
operative." She was pleased with herself.

"Since you invited him," said Christine, "you can bloody well stick around   74
and help me entertain him. I don't want to be left making nice gestures all
by myself."

"Christine *dear*," her mother said, above being shocked. "You ought to   75
put on your dressing gown, you'll catch a chill."

After sulking for an hour Christine tried to think of the tea as a cross     76
between an examination and an executive meeting: not enjoyable, certainly,
but to be got through as tactfully as possible. And it *was* a nice gesture. When
the cakes her mother had ordered arrived from *The Patisserie* on Thursday
morning she began to feel slightly festive; she even resolved to put on a dress,
a good one, instead of a skirt and blouse. After all, she had nothing against
him, except the memory of the way he had grabbed her tennis racquet and
then her arm. She suppressed a quick impossible vision of herself pursued
around the livingroom, fending him off with thrown sofa cushions and vases
of gladioli; nevertheless she told the girl they would have tea in the garden.
It would be a treat for him, and there was more space outdoors.

She had suspected her mother would dodge the tea, would contrive to     77
be going out just as he was arriving: that way she could size him up and then
leave them alone together. She had done things like that to Christine before;
her mother carefully mislaid her gloves and located them with a faked murmur of joy when the doorbell rang. Christine relished for weeks afterwards
the image of her mother's dropped jaw and flawless recovery when he was
introduced: he wasn't quite the foreign potentate her optimistic, veil-fragile
mind had concocted.

He was prepared for celebration. He had slicked on so much hair cream     78
that his head seemed to be covered with a tight black patent-leather cap, and
he had cut the threads off his jacket sleeves. His orange tie was overpower-
ingly splendid. Christine noticed however as he shook her mother's sud-
denly-braced white glove that the ballpoint ink on his fingers was indelible.
His face had broken out, possibly in anticipation of the delights in store for
him; he had a tiny camera slung over his shoulder and was smoking an exotic-
smelling cigarette.

Christine led him through the cool flowery softly-padded livingroom     79
and out by the French doors into the garden. "You sit here," she said. "I will
have the girl bring tea."

This girl was from the West Indies: Christine's parents had been enrap-     80
tured with her when they were down at Christmas and had brought her back
with them. Since that time she had become pregnant, but Christine's mother
had not dismissed her. She said she was slightly disappointed but what could
you expect, and she didn't see any real difference between a girl who was
pregnant before you hired her and one who got that way afterward. She
prided herself on her tolerance; also there was a scarcity of girls. Strangely
enough, the girl became progressively less easy to get along with. Either she
did not share Christine's mother's view of her own generosity, or she felt she
had gotten away with something and was therefore free to indulge in contempt. At first Christine had tried to treat her as an equal. "Don't call me
'Miss Christine,' " she had said with an imitation of light, comradely laughter. "What you want me to call you then?" the girl had said, scowling. They
had begun to have brief, surly arguments in the kitchen, which Christine
decided were like the arguments between one servant and another: her moth-

er's attitude towards each of them was similar, they were not altogether satisfactory but they would have to do.

The cakes, glossy with icing, were set out on a plate and the teapot was    81
standing ready; on the counter the electric kettle boiled. Christine headed for it, but the girl, till then sitting with her elbows on the kitchen table and watching her expressionlessly, made a dash and intercepted her. Christine waited until she had poured the water into the pot. Then, "I'll carry it out, Elvira," she said. She had just decided she didn't want the girl to see her visitor's orange tie; already, she knew, her position in the girl's eyes had suffered because no-one had yet attempted to get *her* pregnant.

"What you think they pay me for, Miss Christine?" the girl said inso-    82
lently. She swung toward the garden with the tray; Christine trailed her, feeling lumpish and awkward. The girl was at least as big as she was but she was big in a different way.

"Thank you, Elvira," Christine said when the tray was in place. The    83
girl departed without a word, casting a disdainful backward glance at the frayed jacket sleeves, the stained fingers. Christine was now determined to be especially kind to him.

"You are very rich," he said.    84

"No," Christine protested, shaking her head; "we're not." She had never    85
thought of her family as rich, it was one of her father's sayings that nobody made any money with the Government.

"Yes," he repeated, "You are very rich." He sat back in his lawn chair,    86
gazing about him as though dazed.

Christine set his cup of tea in front of him. She wasn't in the habit of    87
paying much attention to the house or the garden; they were nothing special, far from being the largest on the street; other people took care of them. But now she looked where he was looking, seeing it all as though from a different height: the long expanses, the border flowers blazing in the early-summer sunlight, the flagged patio and walks, the high walls and the silence.

He came back to her face, sighing a little. "My English is not good," he    88
said, "but I improve."

"You do," Christine said, nodding encouragement.    89

He took sips of his tea, quickly and tenderly as though afraid of injuring    90
the cup. "I like to stay here."

Christine passed him the cakes. He took only one, making a slight face    91
as he ate it; but he had several more cups of tea while she finished the cakes. She managed to find out from him that he had come over on a Church fellowship—she could not decode the denomination—and was studying Philosophy or Theology, or possibly both. She was feeling well-disposed towards him: he had behaved himself, he had caused her no inconvenience.

The teapot was at last empty. He sat up straight in his chair, as though    92
alerted by a soundless gong. "You look this way, please," he said. Christine saw that he had placed his miniature camera on the stone sundial her mother had shipped back from England two years before: he wanted to take her picture. She was flattered, and settled herself to pose, smiling evenly.

He took off his glasses and laid them beside his plate. For a moment she 93
saw his myopic, unprotected eyes turned towards her, with something tremulous and confiding in them she wanted to close herself off from knowing
about. Then he went over and did something to the camera, his back to her.
The next instant he was crouched beside her, his arm around her waist as far
as it could reach, his other hand covering her own hands which she had
folded in her lap, his cheek jammed up against hers. She was too startled to
move. The camera clicked.

He stood up at once and replaced his glasses, which glittered now with 94
a sad triumph. "Thank you, Miss," he said to her. "I go now." He slung the
camera back over his shoulder, keeping his hand on it as though to hold the
lid on and prevent escape. "I send to my family; they will like."

He was out the gate and gone before Christine had recovered; then she 95
laughed. She had been afraid he would attack her, she could admit it now,
and he had; but not in the usual way. He had raped, *rapeo, rapere, rapui, to
seize and carry off*, not herself but her celluloid image, and incidentally that of
the silver tea service, which glinted mockingly at her as the girl bore it away,
carrying it regally, the insignia, the official jewels.

Christine spent the summer as she had for the past three years: she was 96
the sailing instructress at an expensive all-girls camp near Algonquin Park.
She had been a camper there, everything was familiar to her; she sailed almost
better than she played tennis.

The second week she got a letter from him, postmarked Montreal and 97
forwarded from her home address. It was printed in block letters on a piece
of the green paper, two or three sentences. It began, "I hope you are well,"
then described the weather in monosyllables and ended, "I am fine." It was
signed "Your friend." Each week she got another of these letters, more or
less identical. In one of them a colour print was enclosed: himself, slightly
crosseyed and grinning hilariously, even more spindly than she remembered
him against her billowing draperies, flowers exploding around them like firecrackers, one of his hands an equivocal blur in her lap, the other out of sight;
on her own face, astonishment and outrage, as though he was sticking her in
the behind with his hidden thumb.

She answered the first letter, but after that the seniors were in training 98
for the races. At the end of the summer, packing to go home, she threw all
the letters away.

When she had been back for several weeks she received another of the 99
green letters. This time there was a return address printed at the top which
Christine noted with foreboding was in her own city. Every day she waited
for the phone to ring; she was so certain his first attempt at contact would be
a disembodied voice that when he came upon her abruptly in mid-campus
she was unprepared.

"How are you?" 100

His smile was the same, but everything else about him had deteriorated. 101
He was, if possible, thinner; his jacket sleeves had sprouted a lush new crop

of threads, as though to conceal hands now so badly bitten they appeared to have been gnawed by rodents. His hair fell over his eyes, uncut, ungreased; his eyes in the hollowed face, a delicate triangle of skin stretched on bone, jumped behind his glasses like hooked fish. He had the end of a cigarette in the corner of his mouth and as they walked he lit a new one from it.

"I'm fine," Christine said. She was thinking, I'm not going to get involved again, enough is enough, I've done my bit for internationalism. "How are you?"

"I live here now," he said. "Maybe I study Economics."

"That's nice." He didn't sound as though he was enrolled anywhere.

"I come to see you."

Christine didn't know whether he meant he had left Montreal in order to be near her or just wanted to visit her at her house as he had done in the spring; either way she refused to be implicated. They were outside the Political Science building. "I have a class here," she said. "Goodbye." She was being callous, she realized that, but a quick chop was more merciful in the long run, that was what her beautiful sisters used to say.

Afterwards she decided it had been stupid of her to let him find out where her class was. Though a timetable was posted in each of the colleges: all he had to do was look her up and record her every probable movement in block letters on his green notepad. After that day he never left her alone.

Initially he waited outside the lecture rooms for her to come out. She said Hello to him curtly at first and kept on going, but this didn't work; he followed her at a distance, smiling his changeless smile. Then she stopped speaking altogether and pretended to ignore him, but it made no difference, he followed her anyway. The fact that she was in some way afraid of him— or was it just embarrassment?—seemed only to encourage him. Her friends started to notice, asking her who he was and why he was tagging along behind her; she could hardly answer because she hardly knew.

As the weekdays passed and he showed no signs of letting up, she began to jog-trot between classes, finally to run. He was tireless, and had an amazing wind for one who smoked so heavily: he would speed along behind her, keeping the distance between them the same, as though he was a pull-toy attached to her by a string. She was aware of the ridiculous spectacle they must make, galloping across campus, something out of a cartoon short, a lumbering elephant stampeded by a smiling, emaciated mouse, both of them locked in the classic pattern of comic pursuit and flight; but she found that to race made her less nervous than to walk sedately, the skin on the back of her neck crawling with the feel of his eyes on it. At least she could use her muscles. She worked out routines, escapes: she would dash in the front door of the Ladies' Room in the coffee shop and out the back door, and he would lose the trail, until he discovered the other entrance. She would try to shake him by detours through baffling archways and corridors, but he seemed as familiar with the architectural mazes as she was herself. As a last refuge she could head for the women's dormitory and watch from safety as he was skid-

ded to a halt by the receptionist's austere voice: men were not allowed past
the entrance.

Lunch became difficult. She would be sitting, usually with other mem-  110
bers of the Debating Society, just digging nicely into a sandwich, when he
would appear suddenly as though he'd come up through an unseen manhole.
She then had the choice of barging out through the crowded cafeteria, sandwich half-eaten, or finishing her lunch with him standing behind her chair,
everyone at the table acutely aware of him, the conversation stilting and
dwindling. Her friends learned to spot him from a distance; they posted
lookouts. "Here he comes," they would whisper, helping her collect her
belongings for the sprint they knew would follow.

Several times she got tired of running and turned to confront him. "What  111
do you want?" she would ask, glowering belligerently down at him, almost
clenching her fists; she felt like shaking him, hitting him.

"I wish to talk with you."  112

"Well, here I am," she would say. "What do you want to talk about?"  113

But he would say nothing; he would stand in front of her, shifting his  114
feet, smiling perhaps apologetically (though she could never pinpoint the
exact tone of that smile, chewed lips stretched apart over the nicotine-yel-
lowed teeth, rising at the corners, flesh held stiffly in place for an invisible
photographer), his eyes jerking from one part of her face to another as though
he saw her in fragments.

Annoying and tedious though it was, his pursuit of her had an odd  115
result: mysterious in itself, it rendered her equally mysterious. No-one had
ever found Christine mysterious before. To her parents she was a beefy
heavyweight, a plodder, lacking in flair, ordinary as bread. To her sisters she
was the plain one, treated with an indulgence they did not give to each other:
they did not fear her as a rival. To her male friends she was the one who
could be relied on. She was helpful and a hard worker, always good for a
game of tennis with the athletes among them. They invited her along to drink
beer with them so they could get into the cleaner, more desirable Ladies and
Escorts side of the beer parlour, taking it for granted she would buy her share
of the rounds. In moments of stress they confided to her their problems with
women. There was nothing devious about her and nothing interesting.

Christine had always agreed with these estimates of herself. In child-  116
hood she had identified with the False Bride or the ugly sister; whenever a
story had begun, "Once there was a maiden as beautiful as she was good,"
she had known it wasn't her. That was just how it was, but it wasn't so bad.
Her parents never expected her to be a brilliant social success and weren't
overly disappointed when she wasn't. She was spared the manoeuvering and
anxiety she witnessed among others her age, and she even had a kind of
special position among men: she was an exception, she fitted none of the
categories they commonly used when talking about girls, she wasn't a cock-
teaser, a cold fish, an easy lay or a snarky bitch; she was an honorary person.
She had grown to share their contempt for most women.

Now however there was something about her that could not be explained. 117
A man was chasing her, a peculiar sort of man, granted, but still a man, and
he was without doubt attracted to her, he couldn't leave her alone. Other
men examined her more closely than they ever had, appraising her, trying to
find out what it was those twitching bespectacled eyes saw in her. They
started to ask her out, though they returned from these excursions with their
curiosity unsatisfied, the secret of her charm still intact. Her opaque dump-
ling face, her solid bear-shaped body became for them parts of a riddle no-
one could solve. Christine knew this and began to use it. In the bathtub she
no longer imagined she was a dolphin; instead she imagined she was an elusive water-nixie, or sometimes, in moments of audacity, Marilyn Monroe.
The daily chase was becoming a habit; she even looked forward to it. In
addition to its other benefits she was losing weight.

All those weeks he had never phoned her or turned up at the house. He 118
must have decided however that his tactics were not having the desired result,
or perhaps he sensed she was becoming bored. The phone began to ring in
the early morning or late at night when he could be sure she would be there.
Sometimes he would simply breathe (she could recognize, or thought she
could, the quality of his breathing), in which case she would hang up. Occasionally he would say again that he wanted to talk to her, but even when she
gave him lots of time nothing else would follow. Then he extended his range:
she would see him on her streetcar, smiling at her silently from a seat never
closer than three away; she could feel him tracking her down her own street,
though when she would break her resolve to pay no attention and would
glance back he would be invisible or in the act of hiding behind a tree or
hedge.

Among crowds of people and in daylight she had not really been afraid 119
of him; she was stronger than he was and he had made no recent attempt to
touch her. But the days were growing shorter and colder, it was almost
November, often she was arriving home in twilight or a darkness broken only
by the feeble orange streetlamps. She brooded over the possibility of razors,
knives, guns; by acquiring a weapon he could quickly turn the odds against
her. She avoided wearing scarves, remembering the newspaper stories about
girls who had been strangled by them. Putting on her nylons in the morning
gave her a funny feeling. Her body seemed to have diminished, to have become
smaller than his.

Was he deranged, was he a sex maniac? He seemed so harmless, yet it 120
was that kind who often went berserk in the end. She pictured those ragged
fingers at her throat, tearing at her clothes, though she could not think of
herself as screaming. Parked cars, the shrubberies near her house, the drive-
ways on either side of it, changed as she passed them from unnoticed background to sinisterly-shadowed foreground, every detail distinct and harsh:
they were places a man might crouch, leap out from. Yet every time she saw
him in the clear light of morning or afternoon (for he still continued his old
methods of pursuit), his aging jacket and jittery eyes convinced her that it

was she herself who was the tormentor, the persecuter. She was in some sense responsible; from the folds and crevices of the body she had treated for so long as a reliable machine was emanating, against her will, some potent invisible odour, like a dog's in heat or a female moth's, that made him unable to stop following her.

Her mother, who had been too preoccupied with the unavoidable fall entertaining to pay much attention to the number of phone calls Christine was getting or to the hired girl's complaints of a man who hung up without speaking, announced that she was flying down to New York for the weekend; her father decided to go too. Christine panicked: she saw herself in the bathtub with her throat slit, the blood drooling out of her neck and running in a little spiral down the drain (for by this time she believed he could walk through walls, could be everywhere at once). The girl would do nothing to help; she might even stand in the bathroom door with her arms folded, watching. Christine arranged to spend the weekend at her married sister's.

When she arrived back Sunday evening she found the girl close to hysterics. She said that on Saturday she had gone to pull the curtains across the French doors at dusk and had found a strangely contorted face, a man's face, pressed against the glass, staring in at her from the garden. She claimed she had fainted and had almost had her baby a month too early right there on the livingroom carpet. Then she had called the police. He was gone by the time they got there but she had recognized him from the afternoon of the tea; she had informed them he was a friend of Christine's.

They called Monday evening to investigate, two of them; they were very polite, they knew who Christine's father was. Her father greeted them heartily; her mother hovered in the background, fidgeting with her porcelain hands, letting them see how frail and worried she was. She didn't like having them in the livingroom but they were necessary.

Christine had to admit he'd been following her around. She was relieved he'd been discovered, relieved also that she hadn't been the one to tell, though if he'd been a citizen of the country she would have called the police a long time ago. She insisted he was not dangerous, he had never hurt her.

"That kind don't hurt you," one of the policemen said. "They just kill you. You're lucky you aren't dead."

"Nut cases," the other one said.

Her mother volunteered that the thing about people from another culture was that you could never tell whether they were insane or not because their ways were so different. The policeman agreed with her, deferential but also condescending, as though she was a royal halfwit who had to be humoured.

"You know where he lives?" the first policeman asked. Christine had long ago torn up the letter with his address on it; she shook her head.

"We'll have to pick him up tomorrow then," he said. "Think you can keep him talking outside your class if he's waiting for you?"

After questioning her they held a murmured conversation with her father in the front hall. The girl, clearing away the coffee cups, said if they didn't lock him up she was leaving, she wasn't going to be scared half out of her skin like that again.

Next day when Christine came out of her Modern History lecture he was there, right on schedule. He seemed puzzled when she did not begin to run. She approached him, her heart thumping with treachery and the prospect of freedom. Her body was back to its usual size; she felt herself a giantess, self-controlled, invulnerable. 131

"How are you?" she asked, smiling brightly. 132

He looked at her with distrust. 133

"How have you been?" she ventured again. His own perennial smile faded; he took a step back from her. 134

"This the one?" said the policeman, popping out from behind a notice board like a Keystone Cop and laying a competent hand on the worn jacket shoulder. The other policeman lounged in the background; force would not be required. 135

"Don't *do* anything to him," she pleaded as they took him away. They nodded and grinned, respectful, scornful. He seemed to know perfectly well who they were and what they wanted. 136

The first policeman phoned that evening to make his report. Her father talked with him, jovial and managing. She herself was now out of the picture; she had been protected, her function was over. 137

"What did they *do* to him?" she asked anxiously as he came back into the livingroom. She was not sure what went on in police stations. 138

"They didn't do anything to him," he said, amused by her concern. "They could have booked him for Watching and Besetting, they wanted to know if I'd like to proffer charges. But it's not worth a court case: he's got a visa that says he's only allowed in the country as long as he studies in Montreal, so I told them to just ship him up there. If he turns up here again they'll deport him. They went around to his rooming house, his rent's two weeks overdue; the landlady said she was on the point of kicking him out. He seems happy enough to be getting his back rent paid and a free train ticket to Montreal." He paused. "They couldn't get anything out of him though." 139

"*Out* of him?" Christine asked. 140

"They tried to find out why he was doing it; following you, I mean." Her father's eyes swept her as though it was a riddle to him also. "They said when they asked him about that he just clammed up. Pretended he didn't understand English. He understood well enough, but he wasn't answering." 141

Christine thought this was the end, but somehow between his arrest and the departure of the train he managed to elude his escort long enough for one more phone call. 142

"I see you again," he said. He didn't wait for her to hang up. 143

Now that he was no longer an embarrassing present reality he could be talked about, he could become an amusing story. In fact he was the only 144 amusing story Christine had to tell, and telling it preserved both for herself and for others the aura of her strange allure. Her friends and the men who continued to ask her out speculated about his motives. One suggested he had wanted to marry her so he could remain in the country; another said that oriental men were fond of well-built women: "It's your Rubens quality."

Christine thought about him a lot. She had not been attracted to him, 145 rather the reverse, but as an idea only he was a romantic figure, the one man who had found her irresistible; though she often wondered, inspecting her unchanged pink face and hefty body in her full-length mirror, just what it was about her that had done it. She avoided whenever it was proposed the theory of his insanity: it was only that there was more than one way of being sane.

But a new acquaintance, hearing the story for the first time, had a dif- 146 ferent explanation. "So he got you too," he said, laughing. "That has to be the same guy who was hanging around our day camp a year ago this summer. He followed all the girls like that. A short guy, Japanese or something, glasses, smiling all the time."

"Maybe it was another one," Christine said. 147

"There couldn't be two of them, everything fits. This was a pretty 148 weird guy."

"What . . . *kind* of girls did he follow?" Christine asked. 149

"Oh, just anyone who happened to be around. But if they paid any 150 attention to him at first, if they were nice to him or anything, he was unshakeable. He was a bit of a pest, but harmless."

Christine ceased to tell her amusing story. She had been one among 151 many, then. She went back to playing tennis, she had been neglecting her game.

A few months later the policeman who had been in charge of the case 152 telephoned her again.

"Like you to know, Miss, that fellow you were having the trouble with 153 was sent back to his own country. Deported."

"What for?" Christine asked. "Did he try to come back here?" Maybe 154 she had been special after all, maybe he had dared everything for her.

"Nothing like it," the policeman said. "He was up to the same tricks in 155 Montreal but he really picked the wrong woman this time—a Mother Superior of a convent. They don't stand for things like that in Quebec—had him out of here before he knew what happened. I guess he'll be better off in his own place."

"How old was she?" Christine asked, after a silence. 156

"Oh, around sixty, I guess." 157

"Thank you very much for letting me know," Christine said in her best 158 official manner. "It's such a relief." She wondered if the policeman had called to make fun of her.

She was almost crying when she put down the phone. What *had* he 159 wanted from her then? A Mother Superior. Did she really look sixty, did she look like a mother? What did convents mean? Comfort, charity? Refuge?

Was it that something had happened to him, some intolerable strain just from being in this country; her tennis dress and exposed legs too much for him, flesh and money seemingly available everywhere but withheld from him wherever he turned, the nun the symbol of some final distortion, the robe and the veil reminiscent to his nearsighted eyes of the women of his home-land, the ones he was able to understand? But he was back in his own coun-try, remote from her as another planet; she would never know.

He hadn't forgotten her though. In the spring she got a postcard with a foreign stamp and the familiar block-letter writing. On the front was a pic-ture of a temple. He was fine, he hoped she was fine also, he was her friend. A month later another print of the picture he had taken in the garden arrived, in a sealed manila envelope otherwise empty.

Christine's aura of mystery soon faded; anyway, she herself no longer believed in it. Life became again what she had always expected. She gradu-ated with mediocre grades and went into the Department of Health and Wel-fare; she did a good job, and was seldom discriminated against for being a woman because nobody thought of her as one. She could afford a pleasant-sized apartment, though she did not put much energy into decorating it. She played less and less tennis; what had been muscle with a light coating of fat turned gradually to fat with a thin substratum of muscle. She began to get headaches.

As the years were used up and the war began to fill the newspapers and magazines, she realized which eastern country he had actually been from. She had known the name but it hadn't registered at the time, it was such a minor place; she could never keep them separate in her mind.

But though she tried, she couldn't remember the name of the city, and the postcard was long gone—had he been from the North or the South, was he near the battle zone or safely far from it? Obsessively she bought the magazines and poured over the available photographs, dead villagers, soldiers on the march, colour blowups of frightened or angry faces, spies being exe-cuted; she studied maps, she watched the late-night newscasts, the distant country and terrain becoming almost more familiar to her than her own. Once or twice she thought she could recognize him but it was no use, they all looked like him.

Finally she had to stop looking at the pictures. It bothered her too much, it was bad for her; she was beginning to have nightmares in which he was coming through the French doors of her mother's house in his shabby jacket, carrying a packsack and a rifle and a huge bouquet of richly-coloured flowers. He was smiling in the same way but with blood streaked over his face, partly blotting out the features. She gave her television set away and took to reading nineteenth century novels instead; Trollope and Galsworthy were her favourites. When, despite herself, she would think about him, she would tell herself that he had been crafty and agile-minded enough to survive, more or less, in her country, so surely he would be able to do it in his own, where he knew the language. She could not see him in the army, on either side; he wasn't the type, and to her knowledge he had not believed in any particular ideology. He would be something nondescript, something in the background, like herself; perhaps he had become an interpreter.

# STUDY QUESTIONS

1. When you finish the story, go back and look at the first four words; why does the story begin that way?

2. Christine's face is described in the first paragraph—it "looked like a Russian peasant's." She is there being seen from the outside; both FOCUS and VOICE are someone else's, that is, a NARRATOR's. In the second paragraph, we learn that she had read a story about an old man who had lived in a manhole, so we are inside her mind. When the old men look at her as she's passing, their faces float "away again, uninterested." Is this an authoritative statement by the narrator, or is it Christine's opinion? If it is Christine's, what does it tell you about her? Look in the story for other places where the focus and voice seem to move from narrator to character or to be partly the narrator's, partly Christine's.

3. Christine remembers that her mother calls her "statuesque" "when she was straining" (par. 6). Straining for what? How would Christine describe herself?

4. Why does Christine give the stranger her name?

5. Why is Christine frightened (par. 28)?

6. That first day, Christine's team wins a debate in which they argue that war is obsolete (par. 37). Having read the story to the end, you may want to think about why that detail is included.

7. What does the description of Christine's mother's "housework" and how the house is run contribute to the story? How is it related to the central incident, the advent of "the man from Mars"?

8. Why does Christine's mother invite the stranger to tea?

9. What is Christine's mother's reaction when the stranger comes to the door? Why?

10. What is the relationship between the maid Elvira and Christine?

11. When "the man from Mars" takes off his glasses, Christine sees "his myopic, unprotected eyes turned towards her, with something tremulous and confiding in them she wanted to close herself off from knowing about" (par. 93). What do you think that "something" is? Why does Christine want not to know about it?

12. When the stranger returns to Christine's city, he follows her around; when her friends ask her why, "she could hardly answer because she hardly knew" (par. 108). Does the reader know? Or are we so confined to Christine's focus that we are as puzzled as she? What are the possible reasons? Which seem more likely?

13. Christine begins running between classes, taking evasive shortcuts, does everything to avoid him, with no results; she confronts him but can get him neither to

stop nor explain. At that point, paragraphs 115–17, there is a surprising twist. What happens to Christine's image in the eyes of the other students, especially male students, and of her friends?

14. Trace the stages both of the stranger's pursuit of Christine and of her feelings and yours about his actions.

15. When Elvira calls in the police, Christine is relieved, glad she did not have to do so herself, but admits to herself that "if he'd been a citizen of the country she would have called the police a long time ago" (par. 124). Why? What does this suggest about Christine's feelings about "Martians," those "from another culture"?

16. In what sense is the stranger "a romantic figure" (par. 145)?

17. Why is he deported? When Christine is told the reason he is deported, what is the effect on her?

18. The story does not end with "the man from Mars" being deported. Why? What would be the difference in the meaning and effect of the story had it ended there?

19. What country is the man from? How do you know? Why is it not mentioned earlier in the story? Why is it not specifically identified even at the end? Which part of that country do you think he comes from? What difference would that make? How does the final section of the story, in which the man does not himself appear at all, nevertheless change Christine's attitude toward him? your own?

20. The last clause in the story is "perhaps he had become an interpreter." Is there a sense in which that is true?

AFTERWORD

# EXPECTATION

Reading is a *re-creational activity*. A text should stir your mind into activity from the time you read the title, even if you are just reading the title of a chapter in a textbook: "The Man from Mars."

What do you do when your interest is aroused, your curiosity piqued? You read on, of course, but, whether you are aware of it or not, your mind probably scans the possible meanings of that which has aroused it. You mentally flip through other reading experiences that might have to do with Mars or Martians, and you remember what has gone before in the text. The preceding chapters, you recall, have concerned such things as home, heritage, foreign languages. What sort of pattern does that suggest? The most obvious pattern seems to consist in a movement away both in space and time: farther and farther from home toward the remote, the foreign. If the pattern holds, the chapter called "The Man from Mars" will no doubt leave the earth and the present for space and the future; there will probably be lots of science fiction.

All of this speculation happens, if it does happen—and not everyone's mind works exactly the same way—in a matter of seconds, and, unless you're watching yourself actively read, it happens without your being aware of it. You will be aware, however, of what it is you anticipate.

Meanwhile, or in a few heartbeats, you are reading on. When you read the headnote, you might not be too sure about the science fiction: there are other kinds of "aliens," the headnote reminds you—foreign, but earthmen and -women. If you then read through the works in the order in which they appear, by the time you get to the last couple of selections you have probably long abandoned the notion that the chapter will be about Martians; the strangers or "aliens" have so far been human: a black on a subway, Chicanos in Minnesota, a Chinese hiding out in a swamp—all seen by white Americans—Japanese, Arabs, and so on. When you read the title of the next work, Carter Revard's poem "Discovery of the New World," you are probably ready for some sort of account about the Europeans' first encounter with Native Americans centuries ago.

Surprise! This time there are Martians, or at least aliens in the space-fiction sense. You glance at the title of the next and last selection, "The Man from Mars." It may be time to adjust your projected pattern: thinking back quickly and perhaps unconsciously, you may detect what appears to be a new pattern: the selections seem to have moved more or less consistently from the strange to the foreign to the space alien.

Surprise again!

Reading a literary work is a much richer experience than reading the table of contents of a chapter in an anthology of literary works, but the activity of reading is in outline much the same. There is anticipation or EXPECTATION generated by the words you are reading (even when they are just titles), recollection of what you read before, and the tentative formation of a pattern out of the past and present so that you can project it forward to anticipate what will be coming next. Reading *is* an activity; and it does *re-create*.

The activity of reading a tightly woven literary text is more complex than a simple recording, recalling, anticipating. Because of the complexity of the work and of the process, reading beyond the title is a much more global and mentally muscular activity. And there is even more to the process of reading and anticipating along with the text than just absorbing, recalling, and projecting on the basis of the words and determining signals in the text. Each of us understands the words in a slightly different way; each of us recalls selectively, and projects differently. We have had different reading and different life experiences, and it is these as well as the words of the text that trigger expectations and condition our interpretations of the text. This does not mean that we cannot learn from a text, that we can only extract from it what we already know or feel. Nor does this mean that we can make the text say anything we want. There are grossly distortive, "wrong" readings; there just is not one right and only reading.

No single account of a reading, therefore, will be applicable to everyone, but, in order to bring our unconscious act of reading to consciousness, let us look very briefly and selectively at how one reader might engage a piece of one work.

Look at the beginning of "The Man from Mars." The first words of the story are "A long time ago." How long ago? At first we may still be beguiled by the title; the present of the story may be far in the future, and the story may be being told by a Martian years and years from now. But Christine's coming away from playing tennis, wearing a tennis dress, her hair held back by an elastic band, makes it seem not so long ago—our present or recent past, perhaps (the story was published in 1977).

We probably dismiss those first four words after a while; they seem totally irrelevant. But they are stored somewhere at the back of our mind. We have been prepared, whether we know it or not, to recognize what nation it is that is "Mars," though the name of that nation is never given in the story.

The function of holding the revelation—not, notice, just an event or action or matter of plot—to near the end is not only to intensify the surprise for its own sake but to intensify its power to engage our deepest feelings. Some of us will have felt repulsed by "the man from Mars"; his annoying relentlessness and his increasingly threatening presence will have engendered something close to disgust, perhaps mixed with a little fear and something approaching hate. But in the end, after he has been shipped back to his own country, we can imagine what he is facing or going through. The hatred is replaced by pity, the disgust with understanding. And, note, the story makes it clear that it is not going to specify whether he is our ally, from the South, or our designated enemy, from the North—for the man's plight and behavior and our responses are not to be partisan, are to be political only in the sense of deploring the inhumanity of war. Sympathy transcends argument, human feeling transcends even patriotism.

Expectation, recall, patterning, surprise or modification of expectations, new expectations and new patterning—this dynamics of reading does not only operate on details that embrace the whole work or its central themes or emotional impact. It operates locally, on smaller issues and effects, and on other tangential though important contributing concerns. In the second paragraph of Atwood's story, for example, Christine passes the old men sunning themselves: "their wrinkled toadstool faces drifted towards her, drawn by the movement of her body, then floated away again, uninterested." Almost casually we are led to expect there may be a sexual encounter of some sort; at the same time, we are made aware of Christine's lack of sexual attractiveness, which later we will recall. It will make the pursuit by "the man from Mars" more incomprehensible, even mysterious, and will arouse our curiosity. Because she is not used to sexual attention, she may be more vulnerable when "the man from Mars" pursues her, and the reader wishing her well will be more apprehensive about what might happen to her.

The third paragraph describes the squirrels foraging in the park: "two or three of them moved towards her in darts and pauses, eyes fixed on her expectantly, mouths with the ratlike receding chins open to show the yellowed front teeth. Christine walked faster, she had nothing to give them. People shouldn't feed them, she thought, it makes them anxious and they get mangy." Some will want to say that the squirrels "symbolize" "the man from Mars," but it seems more useful to see them as preparing the reader for expectations of the ominous and the threatening, and to reveal Christine's skittishness. The squirrels do not reappear in the story; they have served their purpose. They are immediately replaced by "the man from Mars," the stranger who touches her on the arm, a man she and her mother do feed.

It is necessary to concentrate on one piece and a small section of that piece—in this case, the first three paragraphs of a story—in order to show the scope, nature, interaction, and complexity of expectations in a literary work. To pull out for examination only one thread, no matter how central or important, is to misrepresent the reading experience. For we respond moment by moment to detail after detail, sometimes word after word, taking words and details in, threading them together with what has gone before and projecting the pattern forward. But there is not just one pattern we project; and some projections are more conscious and enduring than others. Here we "store" or keep in the background "A long time ago," while we keep close to the forefront of our minds the sexual attention—or inattention—of the old men, and transfer immediately our, and Christine's, response to the squirrels from them to the touch on her arm and the man who touches her. We weave and unweave the story through the expectations aroused, much as Penelope unweaves at night what she weaves during the day until Ulysses comes home and the story is over.

In the rather superficial example of trying to guess what kind of story, essay, poem, or play is coming next in the chapter, you probably noticed that the "education" of your expectations did not always do you much good—that is, it did not help you guess correctly what was going to come next. And the title of Atwood's story is in many ways as misleading in indicating what that story is to be about as the title of the chapter is in preparing you for what the chapter is going to be about. But guessing wrong often yields the greater rewards in the reading experience.

The effect of a wrong guess is surprise, but surprise not just in the sense of an unexpected turn of events—though we enjoy being outwitted by a clever plot—but also in the sense of a revelation or shock of recognition, an intensification of our attention to details, a new way of looking at things. Thus Revard's poem gets you to expect something about the discovery of America, gets you to put aside that expectation when the poem opens with space creatures, and then gets you to return to the initial expectation that you pushed into the background but were not entirely able to dismiss from your mind—the poem has something to do with the discovery of America. Surprise, then, at the beginning and at the end makes you see the discovery and settling of America in a new light—new to those who are not Native Americans, that is—and to *feel* the inhumanity of the settling of the Americas in a way no argument and probably no documentary history could achieve. Similarly, "A long time ago," pushed into the background by the events of the Atwood story, may resurface when you recognize that the man is not literally from Mars, that the unnamed country he comes from was the setting for a war that changed our world. The time before that war now seems another epoch, a long time ago, and that unnamed country another world, another planet.

# WRITING
# ABOUT THE READING

## PERSONAL ESSAYS AND NARRATIVES

1. Recount your experiences with strangers whose national, ethnic, or cultural origins you could not at first determine. Include encounters in which you never determined the cultural identity of your man or woman from Mars. Be honest about your responses, from puzzlement to impatience, repulsion, sentimental patronizing, etc. What did you expect to happen or think or fear or hope might happen? How did it turn out?

2. Describe in detail your thoughts and feelings in an encounter—whether casual, social, or other—with a stranger from a different cultural, national, or ethnic background (not necessarily a strange or rare one), using, if you wish, Sharon Olds's poem "On the Subway" as a model, and concentrating on your expectations.

3. Recount or invent an experience in which you met someone whose national, ethnic, or cultural background puzzled you, and tell how the relationship developed. (You can be either "the man from Mars" or the one "visited" by him or her.)

## IMITATIONS AND PARODIES

1. In a short short story, rewrite Atwood's "The Man from Mars" as if you were the man. You need not conclude the story with the episode in Montreal or even with the war but, if you wish, with details, episodes, and explanations of your own invention. Try to keep your reader guessing.

2. Imagine (if necessary) yourself a member of a rare minority in an ethnically homogeneous town like "Roseville, Minn., U.S.A." (you need not imagine the same ethnic majority). Write a brief poem, essay, or story about your life there.

## ANALYTICAL ESSAYS

1. "The _____ Are Different." Using James Fallows's article as a possible model, write an essay on a national, cultural, or ethnic group.

2. Basing your understanding of Chinese culture on the Salzman selection, compare Chinese customs to those of the Japanese as described by Fallows, to those of Americans, or to those of any culture with which you are familiar.

## ARGUMENTATIVE ESSAY

Defend the position that in "Holiday" the narrator is the Martian. Or that Ottilie is the alien. Or that all the Müllers are the aliens.

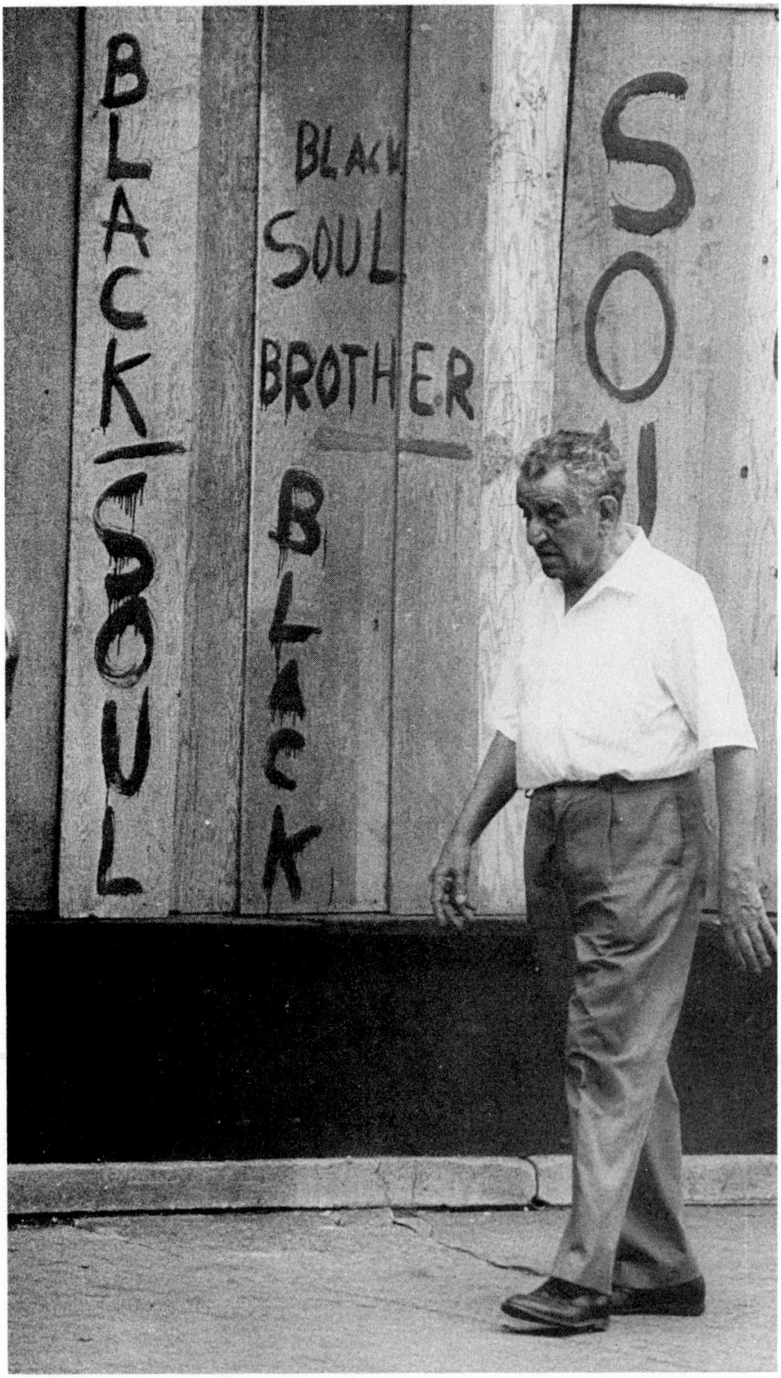
BLACK
SOUL
BLACK
SOUL
BROTHER
BLACK

# 7

# FENCES

"Good fences make good neighbors," a crusty old New England character says in one of Robert Frost's poems, reflecting a common sense of keeping things straight and insisting on distances between people so that they don't become confused about boundaries. Fences mark things—private yards from public sidewalks, pastures from fields, my property from yours—and the marking may feel good or ill depending on how satisfied we are with our own property and place or how desirous of exploring or conquering other worlds. But once fences are constructed, it is hard to pull them down, for even if they are only symbolic objects, they create difference as well as mark it.

The "fences" we construct to separate our own kind from others, even though mainly intended to keep out strangers or someone different from ourselves, also hold us in. Feelings of being confined, cut off, fenced in, are often felt especially strongly by those of us who want adventure, novelty, new experience. Families, ethnic groups, nationality groups, tribes, social and religious groups, gangs, fraternities and sororities, neighborhood groups, political parties, our "circles" of friends—all build fences around themselves both to keep others out and to keep "members" in. Often these fences are constructed for laudable motives of identity or loyalty, but sometimes they end up seeming, even to the people they are meant to benefit with security and identity, horribly confining and limiting.

Fences—literal fences—do not actually prevent the crossing of borders.

Hunters can climb over fences, and predatory beasts get over, under, or through. And cattle find holes or sometimes knock down the fence. Fences intimidate more than they actually repel or contain. The function of a fence is to underline the border and discourage crossing it. It is a sign to outsiders not to enter, an impediment to invaders, a restraint upon insiders, a reminder to anyone who tends to ignore borders or resist control. It is not a wall, a bar, an absolute barrier. A fence *articulates* difference, insists on the recognition between us and them, mine and yours, what is "in" and what is "out": it draws a line.

The risk in crossing a fence is always substantial, perhaps the more so when fences are social and metaphoric rather than physical and actual. The outsider who dares to marry into a family or ethnic group that has fenced out outsiders takes a very large risk. So does an insider who dares to leave the farm or village to try life in a big city or a foreign country. But history is full of individuals who have dared to challenge barriers and cross lines, sometimes because they were courageous and heroic, sometimes because they were just headstrong and foolish. The selections in chapter 8 will explore what happens when people cross fences.

The poems, stories, essays, and play in this chapter sometimes celebrate barriers as providing protection and definition; sometimes they denounce them as authoritarian and constricting. Mainly, though, they explore the reasons that we construct barriers, whether to keep our "own kind" in or the "other kind" out. The human conflicts described here are considerable, and the difficulties run deep. Every human step out of an ordinary path challenges, in one way or another, the limits of all established paths and patterns, and if such challenges represent necessary human growth, they also represent the crucial battlegrounds of human history.

# Ralph Ellison

B orn in Oklahoma City in 1914, Ralph Ellison was educated at Tuskegee Institute and began to publish short stories in 1939. His famous novel *Invisible Man* was published in 1953 and garnered a series of awards including the National Book Award and the American Academy of Rome Prize. Ellison has taught at Bard College, the University of Chicago, Rutgers, the University of California at Los Angeles, Yale, and New York University.

The following story, which ultimately became the first chapter of *Invisible Man*, was first published in *Horizon* in 1947. The narrator here describes the complex feelings associated with a humiliating early experience during which his grandfather's dying advice suddenly becomes meaningful.

## BATTLE ROYAL

It goes a long way back, some twenty years. All my life I had been looking for something, and everywhere I turned someone tried to tell me what it was. I accepted their answers too, though they were often in contradiction and even self-contradictory. I was naïve. I was looking for myself and asking everyone except myself questions which I, and only I, could answer. It took me a long time and much painful boomeranging of my expectations to achieve a realization everyone else appears to have been born with: That I am nobody but myself. But first I had to discover that I am an invisible man!

And yet I am no freak of nature, nor of history. I was in the cards, other things having been equal (or unequal) eight-five years ago. I am not ashamed of my grandparents for having been slaves. I am only ashamed of myself for having at one time been ashamed. About eighty-five years ago they were told that they were free, united with others of our country in everything pertaining to the common good, and, in everything social, separate like the fingers of the hand. And they believed it. They exulted in it. They stayed in their place, worked hard, and brought up my father to do the same. But my grandfather is the one. He was an odd old guy, my grandfather, and I am told I take after him. It was he who caused the trouble. On his deathbed he called my father to him and said, "Son, after I'm gone I want you to keep up the good fight. I never told you, but our life is a war and I have been a traitor all my born days, a spy in the enemy's country ever since I give up my gun back in the Reconstruction. Live with your head in the lion's mouth. I want you to overcome 'em with yeses, undermine 'em with grins, agree 'em to death and destruction, let 'em swoller you till they vomit or bust wide open." They thought the old man had gone out of his mind. He had been the meekest of men. The younger children were rushed from the room, the shades drawn and the flame of the lamp turned so low that it sputtered on the wick like the old man's breathing. "Learn it to the younguns," he whispered fiercely; then he died.

But my folks were more alarmed over his last words than over his dying. It was as though he had not died at all, his words caused so much anxiety. I was warned emphatically to forget what he had said and, indeed, this is the first time it has been mentioned outside the family circle. It had a tremendous effect upon me, however. I could never be sure of what he meant. Grandfather had been a quiet old man who never made any trouble, yet on his deathbed he had called himself a traitor and a spy, and he had spoken of his meekness as a dangerous activity. It became a constant puzzle which lay unanswered in the back of my mind. And whenever things went well for me I remembered my grandfather and felt guilty and uncomfortable. It was as though I was carrying out his advice in spite of myself. And to make it worse, everyone loved me for it. I was praised by the most lily-white men of the town. I was considered an example of desirable conduct—just as my grandfather had been. And what puzzled me was that the old man had defined it as *treachery*. When I was praised for my conduct I felt a guilt that in some way I was doing something that was really against the wishes of the white folks, that if they had understood they would have desired me to act just the opposite, that I should have been sulky and mean, and that that really would have been what they wanted, even though they were fooled and thought they wanted me to act as I did. It made me afraid that some day they would look upon me as a traitor and I would be lost. Still I was more afraid to act any other way because they didn't like that at all. The old man's words were like a curse. On my graduation day I delivered an oration in which I showed that humility was the secret, indeed, the very essence of progress. (Not that I believed this—how could I, remembering my grandfather?—I only believed that it worked.) It was a great success. Everyone praised me and I was invited to give the speech at a gathering of the town's leading white citizens. It was a triumph for our whole community.

It was in the main ballroom of the leading hotel. When I got there I discovered that it was on the occasion of a smoker, and I was told that since I was to be there anyway I might as well take part in the battle royal to be fought by some of my schoolmates as part of the entertainment. The battle royal came first.

All of the town's big shots were there in their tuxedoes, wolfing down the buffet foods, drinking beer and whiskey and smoking black cigars. It was a large room with a high ceiling. Chairs were arranged in neat rows around three sides of a portable boxing ring. The fourth side was clear, revealing a gleaming space of polished floor. I had some misgivings over the battle royal, by the way. Not from a distaste for fighting, but because I didn't care too much for the other fellows who were to take part. They were tough guys who seemed to have no grandfather's curse worrying their minds. No one could mistake their toughness. And besides, I suspected that fighting a battle royal might detract from the dignity of my speech. In those pre-invisible days I visualized myself as a potential Booker T. Washington. But the other fellows didn't care too much for me either, and there were nine of them. I felt superior to them in my way, and I didn't like the manner in which we were all crowded together into the servants' elevator. Nor did they like my being there. In fact, as the warmly lighted floors flashed past the elevator we had words over the fact that I, by taking part in the fight, had knocked one of their friends out of a night's work.

We were led out of the elevator through a rococo hall into an anteroom and told to get into our fighting togs. Each of us was issued a pair of boxing gloves and ushered out into the big mirrored hall, which we entered looking cautiously about us and whispering, lest we might accidentally be heard above the noise of the room. It was foggy with cigar smoke. And already the whiskey was taking effect. I was shocked to see some of the most important men of the town quite tipsy. They were all there—bankers, lawyers, judges, doctors, fire chiefs, teachers, merchants. Even one of the more fashionable pastors. Something we could not see was going on up front. A clarinet was vibrating sensuously and the men were standing up and moving eagerly forward. We were a small tight group, clustered together, our bare upper bodies touching and shining with anticipatory sweat; while up front the big shots were becoming increasingly excited over something we still could not see. Suddenly I heard the school superintendent, who had told me to come, yell, "Bring up the shines, gentlemen! Bring up the little shines!"

We were rushed up to the front of the ballroom, where it smelled even more strongly of tobacco and whiskey. Then we were pushed into place. I almost wet my pants. A sea of faces, some hostile, some amused, ringed around us, and in the center, facing us, stood a magnificent blonde—stark naked. There was dead silence. I felt a blast of cold air chill me. I tried to back away, but they were behind me and around me. Some of the boys stood with lowered heads, trembling. I felt a wave of irrational guilt and fear. My teeth chattered, my skin turned to goose flesh, my knees knocked. Yet I was strongly attracted and looked in spite of myself. Had the price of looking been blindness, I would have looked. The hair was yellow like that of a circus kewpie doll, the face heavily powdered and rouged, as though to form an abstract mask, the eyes hollow and smeared a cool blue, the color of a baboon's butt. I felt a desire to spit upon her as my eyes brushed slowly over her body. Her breasts were firm and round as the domes of East Indian temples, and I stood so close as to see the fine skin texture and beads of pearly perspiration glistening like dew around the pink and erected buds of her nipples. I wanted at one and the same time to run from the room, to sink through the floor, or go to her and cover her from my eyes and the eyes of the others with my body; to feel the soft thighs, to caress her and destroy her, to love her and murder her, to hide from her, and yet to stroke where below the small American flag tattooed upon her belly her thighs formed a capital V. I had a notion that of all in the room she saw only me with her impersonal eyes.

And then she began to dance, a slow sensuous movement; the smoke of a hundred cigars clinging to her like the thinnest of veils. She seemed like a fair bird-girl girdled in veils calling to me from the angry surface of some gray and threatening sea. I was transported. Then I became aware of the clarinet playing and the big shots yelling at us. Some threatened us if we looked and others if we did not. On my right I saw one boy faint. And now a man grabbed a silver pitcher from a table and stepped close as he dashed ice water upon him and stood him up and forced two of us to support him as his head hung and moans issued from his thick bluish lips. Another boy began to plead to go home. He was the largest of the group, wearing dark red fighting trunks much too small to conceal the erection which projected from him as though in answer to the insinuating low-registered moaning of the clarinet. He tried to hide himself with his boxing gloves.

And all the while the blonde continued dancing, smiling faintly at the big shots who watched her with fascination, and faintly smiling at our fear. I noticed a certain merchant who followed her hungrily, his lips loose and drooling. He was a large man who wore diamond studs in a shirtfront which swelled with the ample paunch underneath, and each time the blonde swayed her undulating hips he ran his hand through the thin hair of his bald head and, with his arms upheld, his posture clumsy like that of an intoxicated panda, wound his belly in a slow and obscene grind. This creature was completely hypnotized. The music had quickened. As the dancer flung herself about with a detached expression on her face, the men began reaching out to touch her. I could see their beefy fingers sink into the soft flesh. Some of the others tried to stop them and she began to move around the floor in graceful circles, as they gave chase, slipping and sliding over the polished floor. It was mad. Chairs went crashing, drinks were spilt, as they ran laughing and howling after her. They caught her just as she reached a door, raised her from the floor, and tossed her as college boys are tossed at a hazing, and above her red, fixed-smiling lips I saw the terror and disgust in her eyes, almost like my own terror and that which I saw in some of the other boys. As I watched, they tossed her twice and her soft breasts seemed to flatten against the air and her legs flung wildly as she spun. Some of the more sober ones helped her to escape. And I started off the floor, heading for the anteroom with the rest of the boys.

Some were still crying and in hysteria. But as we tried to leave we were stopped and ordered to get into the ring. There was nothing to do but what we were told. All ten of us climbed under the ropes and allowed ourselves to be blindfolded with broad bands of white cloth. One of the men seemed to feel a bit sympathetic and tried to cheer us up as we stood with our backs against the ropes. Some of us tried to grin. "See that boy over there?" one of the men said. "I want you to run across at the bell and give it to him right in the belly. If you don't get him, I'm going to get you. I don't like his looks." Each of us was told the same. The blindfolds were put on. Yet even then I had been going over my speech. In my mind each word was as bright as flame. I felt the cloth pressed into place, and frowned so that it would be loosened when I relaxed.

But now I felt a sudden fit of blind terror. I was unused to darkness. It was as though I had suddenly found myself in a dark room filled with poisonous cottonmouths. I could hear the bleary voices yelling insistently for the battle royal to begin.

"Get going in there!"

"Let me at that big nigger!"

I strained to pick up the school superintendent's voice, as though to squeeze some security out of that slightly more familiar sound.

"Let me at those black sonsabitches!" someone yelled.

"No, Jackson, no!" another voice yelled. "Here, somebody, help me hold Jack."

"I want to get at that ginger-colored nigger. Tear him limb from limb," the first voice yelled.

I stood against the ropes trembling. For in those days I was what they called ginger-colored, and he sounded as though he might crunch me between his teeth like a crisp ginger cookie.

Quite a struggle was going on. Chairs were being kicked about and I could hear voices grunting as with a terrific effort. I wanted to see, to see more desperately than ever before. But the blindfold was tight as a thick skin-puckering scab and when I raised my gloved hands to push the layers of white aside a voice yelled, "Oh, no you don't, black bastard! Leave that alone!"

"Ring the bell before Jackson kills him a coon!" someone boomed in the sudden silence. And I heard the bell clang and the sound of the feet scuffling forward.

A glove smacked against my head. I pivoted, striking out stiffly as someone went past, and felt the jar ripple along the length of my arm to my shoulder. Then it seemed as though all nine of the boys had turned upon me at once. Blows pounded me from all sides while I struck out as best I could. So many blows landed upon me that I wondered if I were not the only blindfolded fighter in the ring, or if the man called Jackson hadn't succeeded in getting me after all.

Blindfolded, I could no longer control my motions. I had no dignity. I stumbled about like a baby or a drunken man. The smoke had become thicker and with each new blow it seemed to sear and further restrict my lungs. My saliva became like hot bitter glue. A glove connected with my head, filling my mouth with warm blood. It was everywhere. I could not tell if the moisture I felt upon my body was sweat or blood. A blow landed hard against the nape of my neck. I felt myself going over, my head hitting the floor. Streaks of blue light filled the black world behind the blindfold. I lay prone, pretending that I was knocked out, but felt myself seized by hands and yanked to my feet. "Get going, black boy! Mix it up!" My arms were like lead, my head smarting from blows. I managed to feel my way to the ropes and held on, trying to catch my breath. A glove landed in my mid-section and I went over again, feeling as though the smoke had become a knife jabbed into my guts. Pushed this way and that by the legs milling around me, I finally pulled erect and discovered that I could see the black, sweat-washed forms weaving in the smoky-blue atmosphere like drunken dancers weaving to the rapid drum-like thuds of blows.

Everyone fought hysterically. It was complete anarchy. Everybody fought everybody else. No group fought together for long. Two, three, four, fought one, then turned to fight each other, were themselves attacked. Blows landed below the belt and in the kidney, with the gloves open as well as closed, and with my eye partly opened now there was not so much terror. I moved carefully, avoiding blows, although not too many to attract attention, fighting from group to group. The boys groped about like blind, cautious crabs crouching to protect their mid-sections, their heads pulled in short against their shoulders, their arms stretched nervously before them, with their fists testing the smoke-filled air like the knobbed feelers of hypersensitive snails. In one corner I glimpsed a boy violently punching the air and heard him scream in pain as he smashed his hand against a ring post. For a second I saw him bent over holding his hand, then going down as a blow caught his unprotected head. I played one group against the other, slipping in and throwing a punch then stepping out of range while pushing the others into the melee to take the blows blindly aimed at me. The smoke was agonizing and there were no rounds, no bells at three minute intervals to relieve our exhaustion. The room spun round me, a swirl of lights, smoke, sweating bodies surrounded by tense white faces. I bled from both nose and mouth, the blood spattering upon my chest. [23]

The men kept yelling, "Slug him, black boy! Knock his guts out!" [24]

"Uppercut him! Kill him! Kill that big boy!" [25]

Taking a fake fall, I saw a boy going down heavily beside me as though we were felled by a single blow, saw a sneaker-clad foot shoot into his groin as the two who had knocked him down stumbled upon him. I rolled out of range, feeling a twinge of nausea. [26]

The harder we fought the more threatening the men became. And yet, I had begun to worry about my speech again. How would it go? Would they recognize my ability? What would they give me? [27]

I was fighting automatically when suddenly I noticed that one after another of the boys was leaving the ring. I was surprised, filled with panic, as though I had been left alone with an unknown danger. Then I understood. The boys had arranged it among themselves. It was the custom for the two men left in the ring to slug it out for the winner's prize. I discovered this too late. When [28] the bell sounded two men in tuxedoes leaped into the ring and removed the blindfold. I found myself facing Tatlock, the biggest of the gang. I felt sick at my stomach. Hardly had the bell stopped ringing in my ears than it clanged again and I saw him moving swiftly toward me. Thinking of nothing else to do I hit him smash on the nose. He kept coming, bringing the rank sharp violence of stale sweat. His face was a black blank of a face, only his eyes alive—with hate of me and aglow with a feverish terror from what had happened to us all. I became anxious. I wanted to deliver my speech and he came at me as though he meant to beat it out of me. I smashed him again and again, taking his blows as they came. Then on a sudden impulse I struck him lightly and as we clinched, I whispered, "Fake like I knocked you out, you can have the prize."

"I'll break your behind," he whispered hoarsely. 29

"For *them?*" 30

"For *me*, sonofabitch!" 31

They were yelling for us to break it up and Tatlock spun me half around 32 with a blow, and as a joggled camera sweeps in a reeling scene, I saw the howling red faces crouching tense beneath the cloud of blue-gray smoke. For a moment the world wavered, unraveled, flowed, then my head cleared and Tatlock bounced before me. That fluttering shadow before my eyes was his jabbing left hand. Then falling forward, my head against his damp shoulder, I whispered,

"I'll make it five dollars more." 33

"Go to hell!" 34

But his muscles relaxed a trifle beneath my pressure and I breathed, 35 "Seven?"

"Give it to your ma," he said, ripping me beneath the heart. 36

And while I still held him I butted him and moved away. I felt myself 37 bombarded with punches. I fought back with hopeless desperation. I wanted to deliver my speech more than anything else in the world, because I felt that only these men could judge truly my ability, and now this stupid clown was ruining my chances. I began fighting carefully now, moving in to punch him and out again with my greater speed. A lucky blow to his chin and I had him going too—until I heard a loud voice yell, "I got my money on the big boy."

Hearing this, I almost dropped my guard. I was confused: Should I try 38 to win against the voice out there? Would not this go against my speech, and was not this a moment for humility, for nonresistance? A blow to my head as I danced about sent my right eye popping like a jack-in-the-box and settled my dilemma. The room went red as I fell. It was a dream fall, my body languid and fastidious as to where to land, until the floor became impatient and smashed up to meet me. A moment later I came to. An hypnotic voice said FIVE emphatically. And I lay there, hazily watching a dark red spot of my own blood shaping itself into a butterfly, glistening and soaking into the soiled gray world of the canvas.

When the voice drawled TEN I was lifted up and dragged to a chair. I     39
sat dazed. My eye pained and swelled with each throb of my pounding heart
and I wondered if now I would be allowed to speak. I was wringing wet, my
mouth still bleeding. We were grouped along the wall now. The other boys
ignored me as they congratulated Tatlock and speculated as to how much
they would be paid. One boy whimpered over his smashed hand. Looking
up front, I saw attendants in white jackets rolling the portable ring away and
placing a small square rug in the vacant space surrounded by chairs. Perhaps,
I thought, I will stand on the rug to deliver my speech.

Then the M.C. called to us, "Come on up here boys and get your money."     40

We ran forward to where the men laughed and talked in their chairs,     41
waiting. Everyone seemed friendly now.

"There it is on the rug," the man said. I saw the rug covered with coins     42
of all dimensions and a few crumpled bills. But what excited me, scattered
here and there, were the gold pieces.

"Boys, it's all yours," the man said. "You get all you grab."     43

"That's right, Sambo," a blond man said, winking at me confidentially.     44

I trembled with excitement, forgetting my pain. I would get the gold     45
and the bills, I thought. I would use both hands. I would throw my body
against the boys nearest me to block them from the gold.

"Get down around the rug now," the man commanded, "and don't any-     46
one touch it until I give the signal."

"This ought to be good," I heard.     47

As told, we got around the square rug on our knees. Slowly the man     48
raised his freckled hand as we followed it upward with our eyes.

I heard, "These niggers look like they're about to pray!"     49

Then, "Ready," the man said. "Go!"     50

I lunged for a yellow coin lying on the blue design of the carpet, touch-     51
ing it and sending a surprised shriek to join those rising around me. I tried
frantically to remove my hand but could not let go. A hot, violent force tore
through my body, shaking me like a wet rat. The rug was electrified. The
hair bristled up on my head as I shook myself free. My muscles jumped, my
nerves jangled, writhed. But I saw that this was not stopping the other boys.
Laughing in fear and embarrassment, some were holding back and scooping
up the coins knocked off by the painful contortions of the others. The men
roared above us as we struggled.

"Pick it up, goddamnit, pick it up!" someone called like a bass-voiced     52
parrot. "Go on, get it!"

I crawled rapidly around the floor, picking up the coins, trying to avoid     53
the coppers and to get greenbacks and the gold. Ignoring the shock by laughing, as I brushed the coins off quickly, I discovered that I could contain the
electricity—a contradiction, but it works. Then the men began to push us
onto the rug. Laughing embarrassedly, we struggled out of their hands and
kept after the coins. We were all wet and slippery and hard to hold. Suddenly I saw a boy lifted into the air, glistening with sweat like a circus seal,

and dropped, his wet back landing flush upon the charged rug, heard him yell and saw him literally dance upon his back, his elbows beating a frenzied tattoo upon the floor, his muscles twitching like the flesh of a horse stung by many flies. When he finally rolled off, his face was gray and no one stopped him when he ran from the floor amid booming laughter.

"Get the money," the M.C. called. "That's good hard American cash!"    54

And we snatched and grabbed, snatched and grabbed. I was careful not    55
to come too close to the rug now, and when I felt the hot whiskey breath descend upon me like a cloud of foul air I reached out and grabbed the leg of a chair. It was occupied and I held on desperately.

"Leggo, nigger! Leggo!"    56

The huge face wavered down to mine as he tried to push me free. But    57
my body was slippery and he was too drunk. It was Mr. Colcord, who owned a chain of movie houses and "entertainment palaces." Each time he grabbed me I slipped out of his hands. It became a real struggle. I feared the rug more than I did the drunk, so I held on, surprising myself for a moment by trying to topple *him* upon the rug. It was such an enormous idea that I found myself actually carrying it out. I tried not to be obvious, yet when I grabbed his leg, trying to tumble him out of the chair, he raised up roaring with laughter, and, looking at me with soberness dead in the eye, kicked me viciously in the chest. The chair leg flew out of my hand and I felt myself going and rolled. It was as though I had rolled through a bed of hot coals. It seemed a whole century would pass before I would roll free, a century in which I was seared through the deepest levels of my body to the fearful breath within me and the breath seared and heated to the point of explosion. It'll all be over in a flash, I thought as I rolled clear. It'll all be over in a flash.

But not yet, the men on the other side were waiting, red faces swollen    58
as though from apoplexy as they bent forward in their chairs. Seeing their fingers coming toward me I rolled away as a fumbled football rolls off the receiver's fingertips, back into the coals. That time I luckily sent the rug sliding out of place and heard the coins ringing against the floor and the boys scuffling to pick them up and the M.C. calling, "All right, boys, that's all. Go get dressed and get your money."

I was limp as a dish rag. My back felt as though it had been beaten with    59
wires.

When we had dressed the M.C. came in and gave us each five dollars,    60
except Tatlock, who got ten for being last in the ring. Then he told us to leave. I was not to get a chance to deliver my speech, I thought. I was going out into the dim alley in despair when I was stopped and told to go back. I returned to the ballroom, where the men were pushing back their chairs and gathering in groups to talk.

The M.C. knocked on a table for quiet. "Gentlemen," he said, "we almost    61
forgot an important part of the program. A most serious part, gentlemen. This boy was brought here to deliver a speech which he made at his graduation yesterday . . ."

"Bravo!"                                                                                    62

"I'm told that he is the smartest boy we've got out there in Greenwood.     63
I'm told that he knows more big words than a pocket-sized dictionary."

Much applause and laughter.                                                         64

"So now, gentlemen, I want you to give him your attention."              65

There was still laughter as I faced them, my mouth dry, my eye throb-    66
bing. I began slowly, but evidently my throat was tense, because they began
shouting, "Louder! Louder!"

"We of the younger generation extol the wisdom of that great leader and     67
educator," I shouted, "who first spoke these flaming words of wisdom: 'A
ship lost at sea for many days suddenly sighted a friendly vessel. From the
mast of the unfortunate vessel was seen a signal: "Water, water; we die of
thirst!" The answer from the friendly vessel came back: "Cast down your
bucket where you are." The captain of the distressed vessel, at last heeding
the injunction, cast down his bucket, and it came up full of fresh sparkling
water from the mouth of the Amazon River.' And like him I say, and in his
words, 'To those of my race who depend upon bettering their condition in a
foreign land, or who underestimate the importance of cultivating friendly
relations with the Southern white man, who is his next-door neighbor, I
would say: "Cast down your bucket where you are"—cast it down in making
friends in every manly way of the people of all races by whom we are surrounded . . .' "

I spoke automatically and with such fervor that I did not realize that the     68
men were still talking and laughing until my dry mouth, filling up with blood
from the cut, almost strangled me. I coughed, wanting to stop and go to one
of the tall brass, sand-filled spittoons to relieve myself, but a few of the men,
especially the superintendent, were listening and I was afraid. So I gulped it
down, blood, saliva and all, and continued. (What powers of endurance I
had during those days! What enthusiasm! What a belief in the rightness of
things!) I spoke even louder in spite of the pain. But still they talked and still
they laughed, as though deaf with cotton in dirty ears. So I spoke with greater
emotional emphasis. I closed my ears and swallowed blood until I was nau-
seated. The speech seemed a hundred times as long as before, but I could
not leave out a single word. All had to be said, each memorized nuance
considered, rendered. Nor was that all. Whenever I uttered a word of three
or more syllables a group of voices would yell for me to repeat it. I used the
phrase "social responsibility" and they yelled:

"What's that word you say, boy?"                                                69

"Social responsibility," I said.                                                70

"What?"                                                                              71

"Social . . ."                                                                        72

"Louder."                                                                            73

". . . responsibility."                                                              74

"More!"                                                                              75

"Respon—"                                                                          76

"Repeat!"

"—sibility."

The room filled with the uproar of laughter until, no doubt, distracted by having to gulp down my blood, I made a mistake and yelled a phrase I had often seen denounced in newspaper editorials, heard debated in private.

"Social . . ."

"What?" they yelled.

". . . equality—"

The laughter hung smokelike in the sudden stillness. I opened my eyes, puzzled. Sounds of displeasure filled the room. The M.C. rushed forward. They shouted hostile phrases at me. But I did not understand.

A small dry mustached man in the front row blared out. "Say that slowly, son!"

"What, sir?"

"What you just said!"

"Social responsibility, sir," I said.

"You weren't being smart, were you, boy?" he said, not unkindly.

"No, sir!"

"You sure that about 'equality' was a mistake?"

"Oh, yes, sir," I said. "I was swallowing blood."

"Well, you had better speak more slowly so we can understand. We mean to do right by you, but you've got to know your place at all times. All right, now, go on with your speech."

I was afraid. I wanted to leave but I wanted also to speak and I was afraid they'd snatch me down.

"Thank you, sir," I said, beginning where I had left off, and having them ignore me as before.

Yet when I finished there was a thunderous applause. I was surprised to see the superintendent come forth with a package wrapped in white tissue paper, and, gesturing for quiet, address the men.

"Gentlemen, you see that I did not overpraise this boy. He makes a good speech and some day he'll lead his people in the proper paths. And I don't have to tell you that that is important in these days and times. This is a good, smart boy, and so to encourage him in the right direction, in the name of the Board of Education I wish to present him a prize in the form of this . . ."

He paused, removing the tissue paper and revealing a gleaming calfskin brief case.

". . . in the form of this first-class article from Shad Whitmore's shop."

"Boy," he said, addressing me, "take this prize and keep it well. Consider it a badge of office. Prize it. Keep developing as you are and some day it will be filled with important papers that will help shape the destiny of your people."

I was so moved that I could hardly express my thanks. A rope of bloody saliva forming a shape like an undiscovered continent drooled upon the leather and I wiped it quickly away. I felt an importance that I had never dreamed.

"Open it and see what's inside," I was told.                     101

My fingers a-tremble, I complied, smelling the fresh leather and finding    102
an official-looking document inside. It was a scholarship to the state college
for Negroes. My eyes filled with tears and I ran awkwardly off the floor.

I was overjoyed; I did not even mind when I discovered that the gold    103
pieces I had scrambled for were brass pocket tokens advertising a certain
make of automobile.

When I reached home everyone was excited. Next day the neighbors    104
came to congratulate me. I even felt safe from grandfather, whose deathbed
curse usually spoiled my triumphs. I stood beneath his photograph with my
brief case in hand and smiled triumphantly into his solid black peasant's face.
It was a face that fascinated me. The eyes seemed to follow everywhere I
went.

That night I dreamed I was at a circus with him and that he refused to    105
laugh at the clowns no matter what they did. Then later he told me to open
my brief case and read what was inside and I did, finding an official envelope
stamped with the state seal; and inside the envelope I found another and
another, endlessly, and I thought I would fall of weariness. "Them's years,"
he said. "Now open that one." And I did and in it I found an engraved
document containing a short message in letters of gold. "Read it," my grandfather said. "Out loud!"

"To Whom It May Concern," I intoned. "Keep This Nigger-Boy Run-    106
ning."

I awoke with the old man's laughter ringing in my ears.    107

(It was a dream I was to remember and dream again for many years    108
after. But at that time I had no insight into its meaning. First I had to attend
college.)

## STUDY QUESTIONS

1. How much are we told about the NARRATOR's* present situation? From what perspective does he seem to be looking back? What attitudes does his family hold?
   How does the position of his grandfather change in the family tradition after his
   "embarrassing" deathbed remarks?

2. What is the effect of the narrator's admission, before the delivery of his speech to
   the "smoker," that he does not believe in his speech on humility? What effect does
   the behavior of the town dignitaries, before the speech, have on your attitudes
   toward the narrator? What actions of the white audience do you find most disgusting? Why? What language seems to you the most reprehensible?

3. What justification is given for asking the narrator to participate in the battle royal?
   What are the real motives? What actions preceding the battle make those motives
   clear?

*Words in small capitals are defined in the glossary.

4. How do you respond to the narrator's effort to bribe his opponent? Why? How does the story establish its moral principles?

5. How do you interpret the dream at the end of the story? In what way does the story set up how we, as readers, interpret the dream?

# Leo Romero

Born in Chacon, New Mexico, in 1950, Leo Romero graduated from the University of New Mexico with a degree in English. His poetry has been widely anthologized.

The following poem describes the power of rumor and of envy, telling a story of the community response to a beautiful young girl whose leg had to be amputated.

## WHAT THE GOSSIPS SAW

Everyone pitied Escolastica, her leg
had swollen like a watermelon in the summer
It had practically happened over night
She was seventeen, beautiful and soon
to be married to Guillermo who was working                5
in the mines at Terreros, eighty miles away
far up in the mountains, in the wilderness
Poor Escolastica, the old women would say
on seeing her hobble to the well with a bucket
carrying her leg as if it were the weight              10
of the devil, surely it was a curse from heaven
for some misdeed, the young women who were
jealous would murmur, yet they were grieved too
having heard that the doctor might cut
her leg, one of a pair of the most perfect legs          15
in the valley, and it was a topic of great
interest and conjecture among the villagers
whether Guillermo would still marry her
if she were crippled, a one-legged woman—
as if life weren't hard enough for a woman               20
with two legs—how could she manage

Guillermo returned and married Escolastica
even though she had but one leg, the sound
of her wooden leg pounding down the wooden aisle
stayed in everyone's memory for as long                     25
as they lived, women cried at the sight
of her beauty, black hair so dark
that the night could get lost in it, a face
more alluring than a full moon

Escolastica went to the dances with her husband            30
and watched and laughed but never danced
though once she had been the best dancer
and could wear holes in a pair of shoes
in a matter of a night, and her waist had been
as light to the touch as a hummingbird's flight            35
And Escolastica bore five children, only half
what most women bore, yet they were healthy
In Escolastica's presence, no one would mention
the absence of her leg, though she walked heavily          40
And it was not long before the gossips
spread their poison, that she must be in cohorts
with the devil, had given him her leg
for the power to bewitch Guillermo's heart
and cloud his eyes so that he could not see
what was so clear to them all                              45

# STUDY QUESTIONS

1. Explain the importance of the word "saw" in the title. How important are appearances in the world of the poem? Why is it appropriate, given the community's values, that the gossips accuse Escolastica of the power to cloud Guillermo's eyes?

2. Why do you think the poet refuses to account medically for the cause of Escolastica's affliction? Why is the idea of a "curse" (line 11) introduced into the poem? How important is Escolastica's beauty to the community's responses to her?

3. Why do we learn so little about Guillermo and his feelings? What is the significance of the details about Escolastica's energy?

4. What ATTITUDE does the poem develop toward communal opinions? Why are the members of the community, except for Escolastica and Guillermo, not differentiated in the poem?

5. Why does the poem refuse to use conventional punctuation? How does the rejection of CONVENTIONS in language reflect THEMES in the poem itself?

# R. T. Smith

R. T. Smith, Scotch-Irish and Tuscarora, was born in Washington, D.C., in 1947 and educated at the University of North Carolina at Charlotte and Appalachian State University. He is now Alumni Writer-in-Residence and director of creative writing at Auburn University. He is the author of ten books of poetry, including *Waking Under Snow* (1975), *Good Water* (1979), *Rural Route* (1981), and *Banish Misfortune* (1988), and has won many prizes for his work.

The following poem captures the anger of being trapped in the squalor, frustration, and hopelessness of life on reservations.

## RED ANGER

The reservation school is brown and bleak
with bugs' guts mashed against walls
and rodent pellets reeking in corners.
Years of lies fade into the black chalk board.
A thin American flag with 48 stars                           5
hangs lank over broken desks.
The stink of stale piss haunts the halls.

Tuscarora.

My reservation home is dusty.
My mother grows puffy with disease,                          10
her left eye infected open forever.
Outside the bedroom window
my dirty, snotty brother Roy
claws the ground,
scratching like the goat who gnaws the garden.              15

Choctaw.

My father drinks
pale moonshine whiskey
and gambles recklessly at the garage,
kicks dust between weeds in the evening                      20

and dances a fake-feathered rain dance
for tourists and a little cash.
Even the snakes have left.
Even the sun cannot stand to watch.

Cherokee.                                                                25

Our limping dog sniffs a coil of hot shit
near the outhouse where
my sister shot herself with a .22.
So each day I march
two miles by meagre fields                                               30
to work in a tourist lunch stand
in their greasy aprons.
I nurse my anger like a seed,
and the whites would wonder why
I spit in their hamburgers.                                              35

Tuscarora, Choctaw, Cherokee . . .
the trail of tears never ends.

## STUDY QUESTIONS

1. Why does the American flag have only forty-eight stars? What other outdated and leftover objects are mentioned in the first STANZA? What does the presence of such objects imply about government attitudes toward Native Americans?

2. What kinds of IMAGES characterize lines 9–15? How do they differ from those in the first stanza? What patterns and images unify the different activities described in lines 17–24? in lines 26–35?

3. Which lines suggest the most powerful emotions of the SPEAKER? What kinds of incidents or situations seem to generate the strongest feelings? Explain the image of "nurs[ing] anger like a seed" (l. 33).

# Donna Kate Rushin

Donna Kate Rushin lives in Boston, Massachusetts, and teaches theater and creative writing at South Boston High School. "The Bridge Poem" appeared in *This Bridge Called My Back: Writings by Radical Women of Color*, edited by Cherríe Moraga and Gloria Anzaldúa (second edition, 1983).

The poem expresses the frustrations of someone who repeatedly finds herself a token, the only "bridge" between different kinds of people, attitudes, and values.

# THE BRIDGE POEM

I've had enough
I'm sick of seeing and touching
Both sides of things
Sick of being the damn bridge for everybody

Nobody                                                 5
can talk to anybody
Without me
Right?

I explain my mother to my father my father to my little sister
My little sister to my brother my brother to the white feminists     10
The white feminists to the Black church folks the Black church folks
To the ex-hippies the ex-hippies to the Black separatists the
Black separatists to the artists the artists to my friends' parents . . .

Then
I've got to explain myself                                         15
To everybody

I do more translating
Than the Gawdamn U.N.

Forget it
I'm sick of it                                            20

I'm sick of filling in your gaps

Sick of being your insurance against
The isolation of your self-imposed limitations
Sick of being the crazy at your holiday dinners
Sick of being the odd one at your Sunday Brunches             25
Sick of being the sole Black friend to 34 individual white people

Find another connection to the rest of the world
Find something else to make you legitimate
Find some other way to be political and hip

I will not be the bridge to your womanhood                    30
Your manhood
Your human-ness

I'm sick of reminding you not to
Close off too tight for too long

I'm sick of mediating with your worst self               35
On behalf of your better selves

I am sick
of having to remind you
To breathe
Before you suffocate                                          40
Your own fool self

Forget it
Stretch or drown
Evolve or die

The bridge I must be                                          45
Is the bridge to my own power
I must translate
My own fears
Mediate
My own weaknesses                                             50

I must be the bridge to nowhere
But my true self
And then
I will be useful

# STUDY QUESTIONS

1. List all the frustrations the SPEAKER mentions about her status as a "bridge." How does the TONE of the poem change? Which experiences seem to frustrate the speaker most? How does the poem communicate the intensifying feelings of frustration? What role does the repetition of words play in the poem?

2. Characterize the speaker as fully as you can. To whom is the poem addressed?

3. What positive kind of "bridging" does the speaker desire?

# Pat Mora

B orn in El Paso, Pat Mora writes poems in which her Chicana heritage and South-western background are central. Her first book, *Chants* (which won the Southwest Book Award), is largely composed of what she calls "desert incantations." Her second, *Borders* (from which the following poem is taken), describes the two cultures that create her own "border" life.

"Sonrisas" dramatizes, through the description of two groups of women, basic differences in cultural and human values between the heritage of Anglo-Americans and that of Mexican-Americans.

## SONRISAS

I live in a doorway
between two rooms, I hear
quiet clicks, cups of black
coffee, *click, click* like facts
    budgets, tenure, curriculum,      5
from careful women in crisp beige
suits, quick beige smiles
that seldom sneak into their eyes.

I peek
in the other room señoras      10
in faded dresses stir sweet
milk coffee, laughter whirls
with steam from fresh *tamales*
    *sh, sh, mucho ruido,*[1]
they scold one another,      15
press their lips, trap smiles
in their dark, Mexican eyes.

---

1. A lot of noise.

## STUDY QUESTIONS

1. What is the SPEAKER's relationship to the two worlds described in the poem? How much are we told about the speaker specifically? Why do we not need to know more? What does it mean that the speaker "lives[s] in a doorway" (line 1)?

2. How precise are the contrasts between activities in the two STANZAS? Compare the differences in word choice between the two stanzas. Why are the Anglo women said to have "beige" (l. 7) smiles? Why, in stanza one, do smiles "sneak," whereas the women "trap" smiles into their eyes in stanza two? Why are the eyes in stanza two "dark," while the eyes in stanza one have no color? Compare the syntax in the two stanzas: Why do the women in stanza one perform no specific actions? What differences are suggested in the way the two groups take their coffee?

3. Which world seems to the poet to have superior human values? How can you tell? What specific values are ascribed to each world?

# Edward Corsi

Edward Corsi was born in Italy and came to the United States at the age of ten early in the twentieth century. From 1931 to 1934, he was commissioner of immigration at the Port of New York and was stationed at Ellis Island.

The following selection includes chapters 1 and 6 of his autobiographical account *In the Shadow of Liberty* (1935).

## I BEHOLD AMERICA

The swelling caravan of immigration reached its record volume in 1907 when the incoming tide brought to America 1,285,349 aliens. I was one of them, a ten year old boy.

My first impressions of the new world will always remain etched in my memory, particularly that hazy October morning when I first saw Ellis Island. The steamer *Florida*, fourteen days out of Naples, filled to capacity with sixteen hundred natives of Italy, had weathered one of the worst storms in our captain's memory; and glad we were, both children and grown-ups, to leave the open sea and come at last through the Narrows into the Bay.

My mother, my stepfather, my brother Giuseppe, and my two sisters, Liberta and Helvetia, all of us together, happy that we had come through the storm safely, clustered on the foredeck for fear of separation and looked with wonder on this miraculous land of our dreams. 3

Giuseppe and I held tightly to stepfather's hands, while Liberta and Helvetia clung to mother. Passengers all about us were crowding against the rail. Jabbered conversation, sharp cries, laughs and cheers—a steadily rising din filled the air. Mothers and fathers lifted up the babies so that they too could see, off to the left, the Statue of Liberty. 4

I looked at that statue with a sense of bewilderment, half doubting its reality. Looming shadowy through the mist, it brought silence to the decks of the *Florida*. This symbol of America—this enormous expression of what we had all been taught was the inner meaning of this new country we were coming to—inspired awe in the hopeful immigrants. Many older persons among us, burdened with a thousand memories of what they were leaving behind, had been openly weeping ever since we entered the narrower waters on our final approach toward the unknown. Now somehow steadied, I suppose, by the concreteness of the symbol of America's freedom, they dried their tears. 5

Directly in front of the *Florida*, half visible in the faintly-colored haze, rose a second and even greater challenge to the imagination. 6

"Mountains!" I cried to Giuseppe. "Look at them!" 7

"They're strange," he said, "why don't they have snow on them?" He was craning his neck and standing on tiptoe to stare at the New York skyline. 8

Stepfather looked toward the skyscrapers, and, smiling, assured us that they were not mountains but buildings—"the highest buildings in the world." 9

On every side the harbor offered its marvels: tugs, barges, sloops, lighters, sluggish freighters and giant ocean liners—all moving in different directions, managing, by what seemed to us a miracle, to dart in and out and up and down without colliding with one another. They spoke to us through the varied sounds of their whistles, and the *Florida* replied with a deep echoing voice. Bells clanged through our ship, precipitating a new flurry among our fellow-passengers. Many of these people had come from provinces far distant from ours, and were shouting to one another in dialects strange to me. Everything combined to increase our excitement, and we rushed from deck to deck, fearful lest we miss the smallest detail of the spectacle. 10

Finally the *Florida* veered to the left, turning northward into the Hudson River, and now the incredible buildings of lower Manhattan came very close to us. 11

The officers of the ship, mighty and unapproachable beings they seemed to me, went striding up and down the decks shouting orders and directions and driving the immigrants before them. Scowling and gesturing, they pushed and pulled the passengers, herding us into separate groups as though we were animals. A few moments later we came to our dock, and the long journey was over. 12

A small boat, the *General Putnam* of the Immigration Service, carried us   13
from the pier to Ellis Island. Luckily for us, we were among the first to be
transferred to the tiny vessel, and so were spared the long ordeal of waiting
that occasionally stretched, for some immigrants, into several days and nights.

During this ride across the bay, as I watched the faces of the people   14
milling about me, I realized that Ellis Island could inspire both hope and
fear. Some of the passengers were afraid and obviously dreading the events
of the next few hours; others were impatient, anxious to get through the
inspection and be off to their destinations. I have never forgotten the scene.
Impelled they may all have been, my parents and all the others alike, by a
single desire—to make a fresh start in a free country; nevertheless they were
a strange and motley company. Crowded together upon the little deck of the
*General Putnam*, each family huddled over its trunks and boxes, suitcases or
bundles wrapped in bedding. Some were guarding grimy piles of worn bedding wound about with string or rope or wire. Among the horde of bewildered peasants were some with their pitiful, paltry personal belongings, all
they had in the world, tied up in old blue or red bandannas, which they
clutched anxiously as they peered over the rail toward the tiny island where
their fate would be decided.

So they had shuffled aboard at the Italian port, forsaking the arduous   15
security of their villages among the vineyards, leaving behind the friends of
their youth, of their maturity, or their old age. The young accepted the
challenge with the daring of youth; the old pressed forward without a hope
of return. But both saw in the future, through their shadowy dreams, what
they believed was an earthly paradise. They did not weigh the price of their
coming against the benefits of the New World. They were convinced, long
before they left Italy, that America had enough and more for all who wished
to come. It was only a question of being desired by the strong and wealthy
country, of being worthy to be admitted.

I was not thinking of all this then, as the boat bore down toward Ellis   16
Island. I was watching our fellow-passengers, some of whom were weeping,
some still shouting, others whispering to each other their hopes and fears. I
began to pity with something like the confidence of a superior those whose
faces showed alarm. Then I heard stepfather tell mother anxiously that we
might not be permitted to enter the country—that we might be sent back to
Italy.

"What!" I cried angrily. "After we came all the way across the ocean?"   17

I suddenly remembered that I had heard stepfather say to mother, early   18
in the voyage, that he had spent almost all our money on the second day out
of Naples so that mother's passage might be exchanged from steerage to a
cabin. I wondered if this was the reason for his sudden doubt.

He confirmed my fears by replying that one could not enter America   19
without some money, and perhaps we would not have enough. Ahead of us
loomed Ellis Island, and its buildings of red brick and gray stone seemed to
grow more grim every instant.

"Why wouldn't they let us in?" Liberta asked passionately. "Aren't we like everyone else, even without money?"                                                              20

Mother patted my little sister's curly head. For the first time during the voyage I saw tears in mother's eyes. What sort of world was this, where people were judged by the amount of money they had?                                          21

I felt resentment toward this Ellis Island ahead of us, where we could already see many people crowded into a small enclosure. It could not be a good place. It would have been better if we had stayed in our comfortable home in the Abruzzi, back in Italy. To come here made mother cry. I looked around the deck and saw that many women were crying.                                22

Our little vessel coasted into the slip at Ellis Island. The passengers began to move. We moved with them and as we stepped from the gangplank to the land, all silent and subdued, I knew that my parents were thinking as I was, "What is next?"                                                                   23

\*   \*   \*

Ellis Island in 1907 represented a cross section of all the races in the world. Five thousand persons disembarked on that October day when my mother, my stepfather, and we four children landed there from the *General Putnam*.                                                                                24

We took our places in the long line and went submissively through the routine of answering interpreters' questions and receiving medical examinations. We were in line early and were told that our case would be considered in a few hours, so we avoided the necessity of staying overnight, an ordeal which my mother had long been dreading. Soon we were permitted to pass through America's Gateway.                                                         25

My stepfather's brother was waiting for us. It was from him that the alluring accounts of opportunities in the United States had come to our family in Italy, and we looked to him for guidance.                                       26

Crossing the harbor on the ferry, I was first struck by the fact that American men did not wear beards. In contrast with my own fellow-countrymen I thought they looked almost like women. I felt that we were superior to them. Also on this boat I saw my first negro. But these wonders melted into insignificance when we arrived at the Battery[1] and our first elevated trains appeared on the scene. There could be nothing in America superior to these!                                                                              27

Carrying our baggage, we walked across lower Manhattan and then climbed the steps leading to one of these marvellous trains. We were going, my uncle said, to the upper East Side, where he had rented an apartment in a tenement for us.                                                                   28

On this train I saw a Chinaman, queue and all! It had been a day of breath-taking surprises from the time of our entry into New York harbor, and by the time we started on our journey to Harlem I decided that anything could happen—anything might be true in this strange country.                      29

1. Park at the southern tip of Manhattan named for the Dutch and English fortifications there.

I liked the din and bustle, the hurrying crowds on every hand, but I could see that my mother was bewildered. They were in startling contrast to the peaceful routine of life back in the Abruzzi. It had never occurred to me that any language except Italian was spoken anywhere, because it was the only one I had ever heard even in Switzerland. Here there were strange tongues on every side. I began to feel dazed and lost, but it gave me a new grip on myself to arrive in Harlem's little Italy and see and hear all about me people of my own nationality.

Our new home was a sad disappointment. We were not strangers to hardship, and our cottage in Lugano had been a contrast to the beautiful home where I was born; but here we found ourselves paying what seemed an enormous price for four sordid tenement rooms. There was, I remember, but one outside window, and this looked down on a dingy street. My mother was discouraged by the sight of the apartment the moment she stepped into it, and she never overcame the repulsion.

Back in Italy, I had seen her sit and gaze for long hours at the quiet beauty of Sulmona's countryside and the towering grandeur of Monte Majella. She loved quiet, and hated noise and confusion. Here she never left the house unless she had to. She spent her days, and the waking hours of the nights, sitting at that one outside window staring up at the little patch of sky above the tenements. She was never happy here and, though she tried, could not adjust herself to the poverty and despair in which we had to live.

My stepfather had no special training except his military service, and had to take employment at manual labor in a piano factory. He earned eleven dollars a week which was barely enough to keep our bodies and souls together. He was brave and did all he could for us, but at the end of three years my mother, who had become ill, went back to Italy. When she could no longer write us, others wrote for her, and she constantly begged me not to forget the ideals of my father. She lived only one year after returning to Sulmona.

I am sure our life on the East Side was typical of the lives of thousands upon thousands of immigrant families. It was a continuous struggle. There were many times when we had nothing to eat in the house. There was one period when my stepfather was out of work for eighteen months.

Those who lived in our tenement had to furnish their own heat, and during the times when there was no money for food or fuel, Giuseppe and I went out into the New York Central freight yards and gathered lumps of coal that had fallen from the cars. On one cold winter day we went there as usual, and crawled under a standing train of cars which had not moved for many weeks. I finished sooner than Giuseppe, and was waiting for him on the other side when suddenly the cars were set in motion. I heard him cry out sharply once, and then there was no sound. The cars moved on, and I saw him lying on the ground, one of his arms torn and mangled and hanging half-severed just above the elbow. Frightened and sick, I somehow got him back to our flat. A doctor came and amputated the arm, and my stepfather had to go out on a borrowing expedition to pay the doctor. Friends induced him to bring legal action against the railroad company, but the lawyer who handled the case managed, in some mysterious way, to settle it for two hundred dollars.

## STUDY QUESTIONS

1. How do the author's memories of Italy change once he has settled into his new home? Compare his first impressions of America with his observations of his new neighborhood.

2. What disappointments in America are the most powerful? How do family relationships change? What evidence does the author present to suggest that environment alters behavior?

3. What kinds of barriers—economic, social, political, personal—does the author discover in the new world? What barriers seem the most difficult?

4. Describe the TONE of Corsi's account of his new life. How does his sense of "home" change? In what ways are his expectations of America altered?

# James Seilsopour

James Seilsopour was born in California in 1962, the son of an Iranian father. He spent most of his early life in Iran but returned to the United States with his family in 1979 at the time when the Ayatollah Khomeini came to power.

Seilsopour was in high school in California during the "hostage crisis" that began in 1979 when Iranians took control of the American embassy in Teheran. The following autobiographical essay describes his experiences as a high school student during the crisis.

# I FORGOT THE WORDS TO THE NATIONAL ANTHEM

The bumper sticker read, "Piss on Iran."                                              1

To me, a fourteen-year-old living in Teheran, the Iranian revolution          2
was nothing more than an inconvenience. Although the riots were just around

the corner, although the tanks lined the streets, although a stray bullet went through my sister's bedroom window, I was upset because I could not ride at the Royal Stable as often as I used to. In the summer of 1979 my family— father, mother, brothers, sister, aunt, and two cousins—were forced into exile. We came to Norco, California.

In Iran, I was an American citizen and considered myself an American, even though my father was Iranian. I loved baseball and apple pie and knew the words to the "Star-Spangled Banner." That summer before high school, I was like any other kid my age; I listened to rock'n'roll, liked fast cars, and thought Farrah Fawcett was a fox. Excited about going to high school, I was looking forward to football games and school dances. But I learned that it was not meant to be. I was not like other kids, and it was a long, painful road I traveled as I found this out.

The American embassy in Iran was seized the fall I started high school. I did not realize my life would be affected until I read that bumper sticker in the high school parking lot which read, "Piss on Iran." At that moment I knew there would be no football games or school dances. For me, Norco High consisted of the goat ropers, the dopers, the jocks, the brains, and one quiet Iranian.

I was sitting in my photography class after the hostages were taken. The photography teacher was fond of showing travel films. On this particular day, he decided to show a film about Iran, knowing full well that my father was Iranian and that I grew up in Iran. During the movie, this teacher encouraged the students to make comments. Around the room, I could hear "Drop the bomb" and "Deport the mothers." Those words hurt. I felt dirty, guilty. However, I managed to laugh and assure the students I realized they were just joking. I went home that afternoon and cried. I have long since forgiven those students, but I have not and can never forgive that teacher. Paranoia set in. From then on, every whisper was about me: "You see that lousy son of a bitch? He's Iranian." When I was not looking, I could feel their pointing fingers in my back like arrows. Because I was absent one day, the next day I brought a note to the attendance office. The secretary read the note, then looked at me. "So you're Jim Seilsopour?" I couldn't answer. As I walked away, I thought I heard her whisper to her co-worker, "You see that lousy son of a bitch? He's Iranian." I missed thirty-five days of school that year.

My problems were small compared to those of my parents. In Teheran, my mother had been a lady of society. We had a palatial house and a maid. Belonging to the women's club, she collected clothes for the poor and arranged Christmas parties for the young American kids. She and my father dined with high government officials. But back in the States, when my father could not find a job, she had to work at a fast-food restaurant. She was the proverbial pillar of strength. My mother worked seventy hours a week for two years. I never heard her complain. I could see the toll the entire situation was taking on her. One day my mother and I went grocery shopping at

Stater Brothers Market. After an hour of carefully picking our food, we proceeded to the cashier. The cashier was friendly and began a conversation with my mother. They spoke briefly of the weather as my mother wrote the check. The cashier looked at the check and casually asked, "What kind of name is that?" My mother said, "Italian." We exchanged glances for just a second. I could see the pain in her eyes. She offered no excuses; I asked for none.

Because of my father's birthplace, he was unable to obtain a job. A 7 naturalized American citizen with a master's degree in aircraft maintenance engineering from the Northrop Institute of Technology, he had never been out of work in his life. My father had worked for Bell Helicopter International, Flying Tigers, and McDonnell Douglas. Suddenly, a man who literally was at the top of his field was unemployable. There is one incident that haunts me even today. My mother had gone to work, and all the kids had gone to school except me. I was in the bathroom washing my face. The door was open, and I could see my father's reflection in the mirror. For no particular reason I watched him. He was glancing at a newspaper. He carefully folded the paper and set it aside. For several long moments he stared blankly into space. With a resigned sigh, he got up, went into the kitchen, and began doing the dishes. On that day, I know I watched a part of my father die.

My father did get a job. However, he was forced to leave the country. 8 He is a quality control inspector for Saudi Arabian Airlines in Jeddah, Saudi Arabia. My mother works only forty hours a week now. My family has survived, financially and emotionally. I am not bitter, but the memories are. I have not recovered totally; I can never do that.

And no, I have never been to a high school football game or dance. The 9 strike really turned me off to baseball. I have been on a diet for the last year, so I don't eat apple pie much anymore. And I have forgotten the words to the national anthem.

# STUDY QUESTIONS

1. Describe the authors' social and political background. Do his habits and affluent life-style make his adjustment to American life more or less difficult? In what ways does he feel that he fits in? In what ways is he "different"?

2. Who seems to be responsible for the barriers raised against Seilsopour in high school? Who is responsible for the bumper sticker and the comments following the taking of hostages at the American embassy?

3. Why does Seilsopour feel "dirty, guilty" (paragraph 5)? Describe his attitude toward his Iranian heritage.

4. How do you account for the calm TONE of his description of a bullet passing through his sister's room? Which events are the most upsetting to him? Why?

5. What does learning "The Star-Spangled Banner" mean to Seilsopour? What does his "forgetting" the words mean to him? In what other ways has he changed by the end of the essay?

# Michelle Cliff

Born in Kingston, Jamaica, Michelle Cliff was educated at Wagner College and the Warburg Institute (London). A novelist, poet, and essayist, she has been a MacDowell Fellow, an Eli Kantor Fellow at Yaddo, and a Fellow of the National Endowment for the Arts. She has also worked as a reporter, researcher, and editor, and has taught at the New School for Social Research, Hampshire College, the University of Massachusetts at Amherst, and Vista College. She now lives in Santa Cruz, California.

In the following autobiographical essay, Cliff describes aspects of her life in Jamaica, London, and the United States and shows us the complex emotions and loyalties she feels in encountering a number of different "fences."

## IF I COULD WRITE THIS IN FIRE I WOULD WRITE THIS IN FIRE[1]

*I*

We were standing under the waterfall at the top of Orange River. Our chests were just beginning to mound—slight hills on either side. In the center of each were our nipples, which were losing their sideways look and rounding into perceptible buttons of dark flesh. Too fast it seemed. We touched each other, then, quickly and almost simultaneously, raised our arms to examine the hairs growing underneath. Another sign. Mine was wispy and light-brown. My friend Zoe had dark hair curled up tight. In each little patch the river-water caught the sun so we glistened.

The waterfall had come about when my uncles dammed up the river to bring power to the sugar mill. Usually, when I say "sugar mill" to anyone not familiar with the Jamaican countryside or for that matter my family, I can tell their minds cast an image of tall smokestacks, enormous copper cauldrons, a man in a broad-brimmed hat with a whip, and several dozens of

---

1. For this piece I owe a debt to Ama Ata Aidoo and her brilliant book *Our Sister Killjoy or Reflections from a Black-Eyed Squint* (Lagos and New York: Nok Publishers, 1979). [Author's note]

slaves—that is, if they have any idea of how large sugar mills once operated. It's a grandiose expression—like plantation, verandah, outbuilding. (Try substituting farm, porch, outside toilet.) To some people it even sounds romantic.

Our sugar mill was little more than a round-roofed shed, which contained a wheel and woodfire. We paid an old man to run it, tend the fire, and then either bartered or gave the sugar away, after my grandmother had taken what she needed. Our canefield was about two acres of flat land next to the river. My grandmother had six acres in all, one donkey, a mule, two cows, some chickens, a few pigs, and stray dogs and cats who had taken up residence in the yard.

Her house had four rooms, no electricity, no running water. The kitchen was a shed in the back with a small pot-bellied stove. Across from the stove was a mahogany counter, which had a white enamel basin set into it. The only light source was a window, a small space covered partly by a wooden shutter. We washed our faces and hands in enamel bowls with cold water carried in kerosene tins from the river and poured from enamel pitchers. Our chamber pots were enamel also, and in the morning we carefully placed them on the steps at the side of the house where my grandmother collected them and disposed of their contents. The outhouse was about thirty yards from the back door—a "closet" as we called it—infested with lizards capable of changing color. When the door was shut it was totally dark, and the lizards made their presence known by the noise of their scurrying through the torn newspaper, or the soft shudder when they dropped from the walls. I remember most clearly the stench of the toilet, which seemed to hang in the air in that climate.

But because every little piece of reality exists in relation to another little piece, our situation was not that simple. It was to our yard that people came with news first. It was in my grandmother's parlor that the Disciples of Christ held their meetings.

Zoe lived with her mother and sister on borrowed ground in a place called Breezy Hill. She and I saw each other almost every day on our school vacations over a period of three years. Each morning early—as I sat on the cement porch with my coffee cut with condensed milk—she appeared: in her straw hat, school tunic faded from blue to gray, white blouse, sneakers hanging around her neck. We had coffee together, and a piece of hard-dough bread with butter and cheese, waited a bit and headed for the river. At first we were shy with each other. We did not start from the same place.

There was land. My grandparents' farm. And there was color. (My family was called "red." A term which signified a degree of whiteness. "We's just a

flock of red people," a cousin of mine said once.) In the hierarchy of shades
I was considered among the lightest. The countrywomen who visited my
grandmother commented on my "tall" hair—meaning long. Wavy, not curly.
I had spent the years from three to ten in New York and spoke—at first—     8
like an American. I wore American clothes: shorts, slacks, bathing suit. Because
of my American past I was looked upon as the creator of games. Cowboys
and Indians. Cops and Robbers. Peter Pan.

(While the primary colonial identification for Jamaicans was English, Amer-     9
ican colonialism was a strong force in my childhood—and of course continues
today. We were sent American movies and American music. American aluminum companies had already discovered bauxite on the island and were
shipping the ore to their mainland. United Fruit bought our bananas. White
Americans came to Montego Bay, Ocho Rios, and Kingston for their vacations and their cruise ships docked in Port Antonio and other places. In some
ways America was seen as a better place than England by many Jamaicans.
The farm laborers sent to work in American agribusiness came home with
dollars and gifts and new clothes; there were few who mentioned American
racism. Many of the middle class who emigrated to Brooklyn or Staten Island
or Manhattan were able to pass into the white American world—saving their
blackness for other Jamaicans or for trips home; in some cases, forgetting it
altogether. Those middle-class Jamaicans who could not pass for white managed differently—not unlike the Bajans in Paule Marshall's *Brown Girl,
Brownstones*—saving, working, investing, buying property. Completely separate in most cases from Black Americans.)

I was someone who had experience with the place that sent us triple features     10
of B-grade westerns and gangster movies. And I had tall hair and light skin.
And I was the granddaughter of my grandmother. So I had power. I was the
cowboy, Zoe was my sidekick, the boys we knew were Indians. I was the
detective, Zoe was my "girl," the boys were the robbers. I was Peter Pan,
Zoe was Wendy Darling, the boys were the lost boys. And the terrain around
the river—jungled and dark green—was Tombstone, or Chicago, or Never-
Never Land.

This place and my friendship with Zoe never touched my life in Kingston.     11
We did not correspond with each other when I left my grandmother's home.

I never visited Zoe's home the entire time I knew her. It was a given: never     12
suggested, never raised.

———

Zoe went to a state school held in a country church in Red Hills. It had been     13
my mother's school. I went to a private all-girls school where I was taught
by white Englishwomen and pale Jamaicans. In her school the students were
caned as punishment. In mine the harshest punishment I remember was being

sent to sit under the *lignum vitae* to "commune with nature." Some of the girls were out-and-out white (English and American), the rest of us were colored—only a few were dark. Our uniforms were blood-red gabardine, heavy and hot. Classes were held in buildings meant to recreate England: damp with stone floors, facing onto a cloister, or quad as they called it. We began each day with the headmistress leading us in English hymns. The entire school stood for an hour in the zinc-roofed gymnasium.

Occasionally a girl fainted, or threw up. Once, a girl had a grand mal seizure. 14 To any such disturbance the response was always "keep singing." While she flailed on the stone floor, I wondered what the mistresses would do. We sang "Faith of Our Fathers," and watched our classmate as her eyes rolled back in her head. I thought of people swallowing their tongues. This student was dark—here on a scholarship—and the only woman who came forward to help her was the gamesmistress, the only dark teacher. She kneeled beside the girl and slid the white web belt from her tennis shorts, clamping it between the girl's teeth. When the seizure was over, she carried the girl to a tumbling mat in a corner of the gym and covered her so she wouldn't get chilled.

Were the other women unable to touch this girl because of her darkness? I 15 think that now. Her darkness and her scholarship. She lived on Windward Road with her grandmother; her mother was a maid. But darkness is usually enough for women like those to hold back. Then, we usually excused that kind of behavior by saying they were "ladies." (We were constantly being told we should be ladies also. One teacher went so far as to tell us many people thought Jamaicans lived in trees and we had to show these people they were mistaken.) In short, we felt insufficient to judge the behavior of these women. The English ones (who had the corner on power in the school) had come all this way to teach us. Shouldn't we treat them as the missionaries they were certain they were? The creole Jamaicans had a different role: they were passing on to those of us who were light-skinned the creole heritage of collaboration, assimilation, loyalty to our betters. We were expected to be willing subjects in this outpost of civilization.

The girl left school that day and never returned. 16

After prayers we filed into our classrooms. After classes we had games: ten- 17 nis, field hockey, rounders (what the English call baseball), netball (what the English call basketball). For games we were divided into "houses"—groups named for Joan of Arc, Edith Cavell, Florence Nightingale, Jane Austen. Four white heroines. Two martyrs. One saint. Two nurses. (None of us knew then that there were black women with Nightingale at Scutari.) One novelist. Three involved in white men's wars. Two dead in white men's wars. *Pride and Prejudice.*

Those of us in Cavell wore red badges and recited her last words before a    18
firing squad in W.W. I: "Patriotism is not enough. I must have no hatred or
bitterness toward anyone."

*Sorry to say I grew up to have exactly that.*    19

———

*Looking back:* To try and see when the background changed places with the    20
foreground. To try and locate the vanishing point: where the lines of perspective converge and disappear. Lines of color and class. Lines of history
and social context. Lines of denial and rejection. When did *we* (the light-
skinned middle-class Jamaicans) take over for *them* as oppressors? I need to
see when and how this happened. When what should have been reality was
overtaken by what was surely unreality. When the house nigger became master.

"What's the matter with you? You think you're white or something?"    21
"Child, what you want to know 'bout Garvey for? The man was nothing but
a damn fool."
"They not our kind of people."

Why did we wear wide-brimmed hats and try to get into Oxford? Why did    22
we not return?

*Great Expectations:* a novel about origins and denial. about the futility and    23
tragedy of that denial. about attempting assimilation. We learned this novel
from a light-skinned Jamaican woman—she concentrated on what she called
the "love affair" between Pip and Estella.

*Looking back:* Through the last page of *Sula.* "And the loss pressed down on    24
her chest and came up into her throat. "We was girls together,' she said as
though explaining something." It was Zoe, and Zoe alone, I thought of. She
snapped into my mind and I remembered no one else. Through the greens
and blues of the riverbank. The flame of red hibiscus in front of my grandmother's house. The cracked grave of a former landowner. The fruit of the
ackee which poisons those who don't know how to prepare it.

*"What is to become of us?"*    25
We borrowed a baby from a woman and used her as our dolly. Dressed and
undressed her. Dipped her in the riverwater. Fed her with the milk her mother
had left with us: and giggled because we knew where the milk had come
from.

———

*A letter:* "I am desperate. I need to get away. I beg you one fifty-dollar."    26

I send the money because this is what she asks for. I visit her on a trip back home. Her front teeth are gone. Her husband beats her and she suffers blackouts. I sit on her chair. She is given birth-control pills which aggravate her "condition." We boil up sorrel and ginger. She is being taught by Peace Corps volunteers to embroider linen mats with little lambs on them and gives me one as a keepsake. We cool off the sorrel with a block of ice brought from the shop nearby. The shopkeeper immediately recognizes me as my grandmother's granddaughter and refuses to sell me cigarettes. (I am twenty-seven.) We sit in the doorway of her house, pushing back the colored plastic strands which form a curtain, and talk about Babylon and Dred. About Manley and what he's doing for Jamaica. About how hard it is. We walk along the railway tracks—no longer used—to Crooked River and the post office. Her little daughter walks beside us and we recite a poem for her: "Mornin' buddy/Me no buddy fe wunna/Who den', den' I saw?" and on and on. 27

I can come and go. And I leave. To complete my education in London. 28

## II

Their goddam kings and their goddam queens. Grandmotherly Victoria spreading herself thin across the globe. Elizabeth II on our t.v. screens. We stop what we are doing. We quiet down. We pay our respects. 29

1981: In Massachusetts I get up at 5 a.m. to watch the royal wedding. I tell myself maybe the IRA will intervene. It's got to be better than starving themselves to death. Better to be a kamikaze in St. Paul's Cathedral than a hostage in Ulster. And last week Black and white people smashed storefronts all over the United Kingdom. But I really don't believe we'll see royal blood on t.v. I watch because they once ruled us. In the back of the cathedral a Maori woman sings an aria from Handel and I notice that she is surrounded by the colored subjects. 30

To those of us in the commonwealth the royal family was the perfect symbol of hegemony. To those of us who were dark in the dark nations the prime minister, the parliament barely existed. We believed in royalty—we were convinced in this belief. Maybe it played on some ancestral memories of West Africa—where other kings and queens had been. Altars and castles and magic. 31

The faces of our new rulers were everywhere in my childhood. Calendars, newsreels, magazines. Their presences were often among us. Attending test matches between the West Indians and South Africans. They were our landlords. Not always absentee. And no matter what Black leader we might elect—were we to choose independence—we would be losing something almost holy in our impudence. 32

WE ARE HERE BECAUSE YOU WERE THERE          33
BLACK PEOPLE AGAINST STATE BRUTALITY
BLACK WOMEN WILL NOT BE INTIMIDATED
WELCOME TO BRITAIN ... WELCOME TO SECOND-CLASS
CITIZENSHIP
(slogans of the Black movement in Britain)

Indian women cleaning the toilets in Heathrow airport. This is the first thing   34
I notice. Dark women in saris trudging buckets back and forth as other dark
women in saris—some covered by loosefitting winter coats—form a line to
have their passports stamped.

The triangle trade: molasses/rum/slaves. Robinson Crusoe was on a slave-   35
trading journey. Robert Browning was a mulatto. Holding pens. Jamaica
was a seasoning station. Split tongues. Sliced ears. Whipped bodies. The
constant pretense of civility against rape. Still. Iron collars. Tinplate masks.
The latter a precaution: to stop the slaves from eating the sugar cane.

A pregnant woman is to be whipped—they dig a hole to accommodate her   36
belly and place her face down on the ground. Many of us became light-
skinned very fast. Traced ourselves through bastard lines to reach the duke
of Devonshire. The earl of Cornwall. The lord of this and the lord of that.
Our mothers' rapes were the thing unspoken.

You say: But Britain freed her slaves in 1834. Yes.   37

Tea plantations in India and Ceylon. Mines in Africa. The Cape-to-Cairo   38
Railroad. Rhodes scholars. Suez Crisis. The white man's bloody burden.
Boer War. Bantustans. Sitting in a theatre in London in the seventies. A play
called *West of Suez*. A lousy play about British colonials. The finale comes
when several well-known white actors are machine-gunned by several lesser-
known Black actors. (As Nina Simone says: "This is a show tune but the
show hasn't been written for it yet.")

The red empire of geography classes. "The sun never sets on the British   39
empire and you can't trust it in the dark." Or with the dark peoples. "Because
of the Industrial Revolution European countries went in search of markets
and raw materials." Another geography (or was it a history) lesson.

Their bloody kings and their bloody queens. Their bloody peers. Their bloody   40
generals. admirals. explorers. Livingstone. Hillary. Kitchener. All the bwanas.
And all their beaters, porters, sherpas. Who found the source of the Nile.
Victoria Falls. The tops of mountains. Their so-called discoveries reek of
untruth. How many dark people died so they could misname the physical
features in their blasted gazetteer. A statistic we shall never know. Dr. Livingstone, I presume you are here to rape our land and enslave our people.

There are statues of these dead white men all over London.                                          41

An interesting fact: The swearword "bloody" is a contraction of "by my          42
lady"—a reference to the Virgin Mary. They do tend to use their ladies.
Name ages for them. Places for them. Use them as screens, inspirations,
symbols. And many of the ladies comply. While the national martyr Edith
Cavell was being executed by the Germans in Belgium in 1915 (Belgium was
called "poor little Belgium" by the allies in the war), the Belgians were engaged
in the exploitation of the land and peoples of the Congo.

And will we ever know how many dark peoples were "imported" to fight in        43
white men's wars. Probably not. Just as we will never know how many hearts
were cut from African people so that the Christian doctor might be a success—i.e., extend a white man's life. Our Sister Killjoy observes this from
her black-eyed squint.

Dr. Schweitzer—humanitarian, authority on Bach, winner of the Nobel Peace     44
Prize—on the people of Africa: "The Negro is a child, and with children
nothing can be done without the use of authority. We must, therefore, so
arrange the circumstances of our daily life that my authority can find expression. With regard to Negroes, then, I have coined the formula: 'I am your
brother, it is true, but your elder brother.' " (On the Edge of the Primeval Forest,
1961)

They like to pretend we didn't fight back. We did: with obeah, poison, rev-    45
olution. It simply was not enough.

"Colonies . . . these places where 'niggers' are cheap and the earth is rich."—    46
W. E. B. DuBois, "The Souls of White Folk"

A cousin is visiting me from M.I.T. where he is getting a degree in engi-      47
neering. I am learning about the Italian Renaissance. My cousin is recognizably Black and speaks with an accent. I am not and I do not—unless I am
back home, where the "twang" comes upon me. We sit for some time in a
bar in his hotel and are not served. A light-skinned Jamaican comes over to
our table. He is an older man—a professor at the University of London.
"Don't bother with it, you hear. They don't serve us in this bar." A run-of-
the-mill incident for all recognizably Black people in this city. But for me it
is not.

Henry's eyes fill up, but he refuses to believe our informant. "No, man, the   48
girl is just busy." (The girl is a fifty-year-old white woman, who may just be
following orders. But I do not mention this. I have chosen sides.) All I can
manage to say is, "Jesus Christ, I hate the fucking English." Henry looks at
me. (In the family I am known as the "lady cousin." It has to do with how I
look. And the fact that I am twenty-seven and unmarried—and for all they

know, unattached. They do not know that I am really the lesbian cousin.) Our informant says—gently, but with a distinct tone of disappointment— "My dear, is that what you're studying at the university?"

You see—the whole business is very complicated.                    49

Henry and I leave without drinks and go to meet some of his white colleagues    50
at a restaurant I know near Covent Garden Opera House. The restaurant caters to theatre types and so I hope there won't be a repeat of the bar scene— at least they know how to pretend. Besides, I tell myself, the owners are Italian *and* gay; they *must* be halfway decent. Henry and his colleagues work for an American company which is paying their way through M.I.T. They mine bauxite from the hills in the middle of the island and send it to the United States. A turnaround occurs at dinner: Henry joins the white men in a sustained mockery of the waiters: their accents and the way they walk. He whispers to me: "Why you want to bring us to a battyman's den, lady?" (*Battyman = faggot* in Jamaican.) I keep quiet.

We put the white men in a taxi and Henry walks me to the underground    51
station. He asks me to sleep with him. (It wouldn't be incest. His mother was a maid in the house of an uncle and Henry has not seen her since his birth. He was taken into the family. She was let go.) I say that I can't. I plead exams. I can't say that I don't want to. Because I remember what happened in the bar. But I can't say that I'm a lesbian either—even though I want to believe his alliance with the white men at dinner was forced: not really him. He doesn't buy my excuse. "Come on, lady, let's do it. What's the matter, you 'fraid?" I pretend I am back home and start patois to show him somehow I am not afraid, not English, not white. I tell him he's a mar-ried man and he tells me he's a ram goat. I take the train to where I am staying and try to forget the whole thing. But I don't. I remember our dif-ferent skins and our different experiences within them. And I have a hard time realizing that I am angry with Henry. That to him—no use in pretend-ing—a queer is a queer.

———

1981: I hear on the radio that Bob Marley is dead and I drive over the Mohawk    52
Trail listening to a program of his music and I cry and cry and cry. Someone says: "It wasn't the ganja that killed him, it was poverty and working in a steel foundry when he was young."

I flashback to my childhood and a young man who worked for an aunt I lived    53
with once. He taught me to smoke ganja behind the house. And to peel an orange with the tip of a machete without cutting through the skin—"Love" it was called: a necklace of orange rind the result. I think about him because I heard he had become a Rastaman. And then I think about Rastas.

We are sitting on the porch of an uncle's house in Kingston—the family and 54
I—and a Rastaman comes to the gate. We have guns but they are locked
behind a false closet. We have dogs but they are tied up. We are Jamaicans
and know that Rastas mean no harm. We let him in and he sits on the side
of the porch and shows us his brooms and brushes. We buy some to take
back to New York. "Peace, missis."

There were many Rastas in my childhood. Walking the roadside with their 55
goods. Sitting outside their shacks in the mountains. The outsides painted
bright—sometimes with words. Gathering at Palisadoes Airport to greet the
Conquering Lion of Judah. They were considered figures of fun by most
middle-class Jamaicans. Harmless: like Marcus Garvey.

Later: white American hippies trying to create the effect of dred in their 56
straight white hair. The ganja joint held between their straight white teeth.
"Man, the grass is good." Hanging out by the Sheraton pool. Light-skinned
Jamaicans also dredlocked, also assuming the ganja. Both groups moving to
the music but not the words. Harmless. "Peace, brother."

### III

My grandmother: "Let us thank God for a fruitful place." My grandfather: 57
"Let us rescue the perishing world."

This evening on the road in western Massachusetts there are pockets of fog. 58
Then clear spaces. Across from a pond a dog staggers in front of my headlights. I look closer and see that his mouth is foaming. He stumbles to the
side of the road—I go to call the police.

I drive back to the house, radio playing "difficult" piano pieces. And I think 59
about how I need to say all this. This is who I am. I am not what you allow
me to be. Whatever you decide me to be. In a bookstore in London I show
the woman at the counter my book and she stares at me for a minute, then
says: "You're a Jamaican." "Yes." "You're not at all like our Jamaicans."

Encountering the void is nothing more nor less than understanding invisibil- 60
ity. Of being fogbound.

It is up to me to sort out these connections—to employ anger and take the 61
consequences. To choose not to be harmless. To make it impossible for them
to think me harmless.

*Then:*  It was never a question of passing. It was a question of hiding. Behind 62
Black and white perceptions of who we were—who they thought we
were. Tropics. Plantations. Calypso. Cricket. We were the people with
the musical voices and the coronation mugs on our parlor tables. I

would be whatever figure these foreign imaginations cared for me to be. It would be so simple to let others fill in for me. So easy to startle them with a flash of anger when their visions got out of hand—but never to sustain the anger for myself.

It could become a life lived within myself. A life cut off. I know who I am but you will never know who I am. I may in fact lose touch with who I am.

I hid from my real sources. But my real sources were hidden from me.   63

*Now:*  It is not a question of relinquishing privilege. It is a question of grasp-   64
ing more of myself. I have found that in the real sources are concealed my survival. My speech. My voice. To be colonized is to be rendered insensitive. To have those parts necessary to sustain life numbed. And this is in some cases—in my case—perceived as privilege. The test of a colonized person is to walk through a shantytown in Kingston and not bat an eye. This I cannot do. Because part of me lives there—and as I grasp more of this part I realize what needs to be done with the rest of my life.

———

Sometimes I used to think we were like the Marranos—the Sephardic Jews   65
forced to pretend they were Christians. The name was given to them by the Christians, and meant "pigs." But once out of Spain and Portugal, they became Jews openly again. Some settled in Jamaica. They knew who the enemy was and acted for their own survival. But they remained Jews always.

We also knew who the enemy was—I remember jokes about the English.   66
Saying they stank. saying they were stingy. that they drank too much and couldn't hold their liquor. that they had bad teeth. were dirty and dishonest. were limey bastards. and horse-faced bitches. We said the men only wanted to sleep with Jamaican women. And that the women made pigs of themselves with Jamaican men.

But of course this was seen by us—the light-skinned middle class—with a   67
double vision. We learned to cherish that part of us that was them—and to deny the part that was not. Believing in some cases that the latter part had ceased to exist.

None of this is as simple as it may sound. We were colorists and we aspired   68
to oppressor status. (Of course, almost any aspiration instilled by western civilization is to oppressor status: success, for example.) Color was the sym-bol of our potential: color taking in hair "quality," skin tone, freckles, nose-width, eyes. We did not see that color symbolism was a method of keeping us apart: in the society, in the family, between friends. Those of us who were light-skinned, straight-haired, etc., were given to believe that we could

actually attain whiteness—or at least those qualities of the colonizer which made him superior. We were convinced of white supremacy. If we failed we were not really responsible for our failures: we had all the advantages—but it was that one persistent drop of blood, that single rogue gene that made us unable to conceptualize abstract ideas, made us love darkness rather than despise it, which was to be blamed for our failure. Our dark part had taken over: an inherited imbalance in which the doom of the creole was sealed.

I am trying to write this as clearly as possible, but as I write I realize that what I say may sound fabulous, or even mythic. It is. It is insane. 69

Under this system of colorism—the system which prevailed in my childhood in Jamaica, and which has carried over to the present—rarely will dark and light people co-mingle. Rarely will they achieve between themselves an intimacy informed with identity. (I should say here that I am using the categories light and dark both literally and symbolically. There are dark Jamaicans who have achieved lightness and the "advantages" which go with it by their successful pursuit of oppressor status.) 70

Under this system light and dark people will meet in those ways in which the light-skinned person imitates the oppressor. But imitation goes only so far: the light-skinned person becomes an oppressor in fact. He / she will have a dark chauffeur, a dark nanny, a dark maid, and a dark gardener. These employees will be paid badly. Because of the slave past, because of their dark skin, the servants of the middle class have been used according to the traditions of the slavocracy. They are not seen as workers for their own sake, but for the sake of the family who has employed them. It was not until Michael Manley became prime minister that a minimum wage for houseworkers was enacted—and the indignation of the middle class was profound. 71

During Manley's leadership the middle class began to abandon the island in droves. Toronto. Miami. New York. Leaving their houses and businesses behind and sewing cash into the tops of suitcases. Today—with a new regime— they are returning: "Come back to the way things used to be" the tourist advertisement on American t.v. says. "Make it Jamaica again." "Make it your own." 72

But let me return to the situation of houseservants as I remember it: They will be paid badly, but they will be "given" room and board. However, the key to the larder will be kept by the mistress in her dresser drawer. They will spend Christmas with the family of their employers and be given a length of English wool for trousers or a few yards of cotton for dresses. They will see their children on their days off: their extended family will care for the children the rest of the time. When the employers visit their relations in the country, the servants may be asked along—oftentimes the servants of the 73 middle class come from the same part of the countryside their employers have come from. But they will be expected to work while they are there. Back in town, there are parts of the house they are allowed to move freely around; other parts they are not allowed to enter. When the family watches the t.v. the servant is allowed to watch also, but only while standing in a doorway. The servant may have a radio in his / her room, also a dresser and a cot. Perhaps a mirror. There will usually be one ceiling light. And one small square louvered window.

*A true story:* One middle-class Jamaican woman ordered a Persian rug from Harrod's in London. The day it arrived so did her new maid. She was going downtown to have her hair touched up, and told the maid to vacuum the rug. She told the maid she would find the vacuum cleaner in the same shed as the power mower. And when she returned she found that the fine nap of her new rug had been removed. 74

The reaction of the mistress was to tell her friends that the "girl" was backward. She did not fire her until she found that the maid had scrubbed the teflon from her new set of pots, saying she thought they were coated with "nastiness." 75

———

The houseworker / mistress relationship in which one Black woman is the oppressor of another Black woman is a cornerstone of the experience of many Jamaican women. 76

I remember another true story: In a middle-class family's home one Christmas, a relation was visiting from New York. This woman had brought gifts for everybody, including the housemaid. The maid had been released from a mental institution recently, where they had "treated" her for depression. This visiting light-skinned woman had brought the dark woman a bright red rayon blouse, and presented it to her in the garden one afternoon, while the family was having tea. The maid thanked her softly, and the other woman moved toward her as if to embrace her. Then she stopped, her face suddenly covered with tears, and ran into the house, saying, "My God, I can't, I can't." 77

———

We are women who come from a place almost incredible in its beauty. It is a beauty which can mask a great deal, and which has been used in that way. But that the beauty is there is a fact. I remember what I thought the freedom of my childhood, in which the fruitful place was something I took for granted. Just as I took for granted Zoe's appearance every morning on my school vacations—in the sense that I knew she would be there. That she would always be the one to visit me. The perishing world of my grandfather's graces at the table, if I ever seriously thought about it, was somewhere else. 78

Our souls were affected by the beauty of Jamaica, as much as they were affected by our fears of darkness. 79

There is no ending to this piece of writing. There is no way to end it. As I    80
read back over it, I see that we / they / I may become confused in the mind
of the reader: but these pronouns have always co-existed in my mind. The
Rastas talk of the "I and I"—a pronoun in which they combine themselves
with Jah. Jah is a contraction of Jahweh and Jehova, but to me always sounds
like the beginning of Jamaica. I and Jamaica is who I am. No matter how far
I travel—how deep the ambivalence I feel about ever returning. And Jamaica
is a place in which we/they/I connect and disconnect—change place.

## STUDY QUESTIONS

1. In what ways, according to the author, did her family and its traditions influence
   her later life and attitudes? How important was the influence of childhood friends?
   childhood experiences? social standing? the physical beauty of Jamaica? the traditions of social hierarchy?

2. What experiences in London and the United States seem, in retrospect, the most
   memorable? Describe the author's attitude toward England; toward the United
   States; toward Jamaica.

3. What specific effects are accomplished by the following writing strategies?
   —the use of many anecdotes, told succinctly and quickly
   —the rapid pace of the essay, with its refusal to dwell long on individual experi-
     ences
   —the extraordinary willingness to talk about strong feelings of distrust and dislike
   —the extensive allusions to historical events and political figures
   —the extensive allusions to books
   —the frequent use of quotations

4. Which anecdote seems to you most powerful in its effects? Analyze carefully how
   the story is told. What devices account for the power of the anecdote?

5. What "fences" encountered by the author seem to have produced the most bitter
   memories? the most powerful results?

# nila northSun

B orn in Schurz, Nevada, in 1951 of Shoshoni-Chippewa heritage, nila northSun
is coauthor of *After the Drying Up of the Water* and *Diet Pepsi and Nacho Cheese.*
  The following poem describes some of the ironies of success beyond the reservation.

# up & out

we total it up for
income tax
hoping to get a little
something back
but it seems we've moved ourselves          5
out of the poverty level
we made more money than
we've ever made before
but felt poorer
we made better money cause we               10
moved to the city
left the reservation where
there were no jobs
the city had jobs but
it also had high rent                       15
high food high medical
high entertainment
we made better money but
it got sucked up by
the city by cable tv                        20
by sparklettes water by
lunches in cute places
by drinking in quaint bars
instead of home like we did
on the reservation                          25
there we lived in gramma's old house
no rent
the wood stove saved electricity &
heating bills
we only got one tv channel but             30
we visited with relatives more
there was no place to eat on the res
'cept a pool hall with chips & coke
there was only one movie house in town
& nothing good ever showed                 35
we got government commodities that
tasted like dog food but
it was free

we got government doctors at i.h.s.[1]
that graduated last in their class                    40
but they were free
if a car broke down there was the
old pick-up truck or a cousin with
a little mechanical know-how
god how i hated living on the reservation            45
but now
it doesn't look so bad.

## STUDY QUESTIONS

1. What positive values does life on the reservation have, according to the poem? what frustrations? What indications are there that the speaker's attitudes are colored by nostalgia?

2. What does the image of getting sucked up by modern civilization (line 19) suggest about alien values? In what specific ways are the customs and values of the city contrasted with those of the reservation?

3. About what specific matters does the speaker feel most strongly?

# Dwight Okita

Dwight Okita was born in Chicago in 1958 and educated at the University of Illinois at Chicago. Active in that city's performance/poetry community, he has written music and written for the theatre.

During World War II, both his parents were sent to relocation camps for Japanese-Americans. His father gained his release by agreeing to fight in Europe with other Japanese-Americans in the famous 442nd Battalion. His mother stayed in the camp; the following poem is written in her voice.

1. Indian Health Services.

# IN RESPONSE TO EXECUTIVE ORDER 9066: ALL AMERICANS OF JAPANESE DESCENT MUST REPORT TO RELOCATION CENTERS

Dear Sirs:
Of course I'll come. I've packed my galoshes
and three packets of tomato seeds. Janet calls them
"love apples." My father says where we're going
they won't grow.                                                        5

I am a fourteen-year-old girl with bad spelling
and a messy room. If it helps any, I will tell you
I have always felt funny using chopsticks
and my favorite food is hot dogs.
My best friend is a white girl named Denise—          10
we look at boys together. She sat in front of me
all through grade school because of our names:
O'Connor, Ozawa. I know the back of Denise's head very well.
I tell her she's going bald. She tells me I copy on tests.
We're best friends.                                                   15

I saw Denise today in Geography class.
She was sitting on the other side of the room.
"You're trying to start a war," she said, "giving secrets away
to the Enemy, Why can't you keep your big mouth shut?"
I didn't know what to say.                                          20
I gave her a packet of tomato seeds
and asked her to plant them for me, told her
when the first tomato ripens
to miss me.

## STUDY QUESTIONS

1. What details do we know about the SPEAKER of the poem? Which of them emphasize her Japanese heritage? Which emphasize her likeness to "typical" American
   teenagers?

2. Describe the speaker's relationship to Denise. What details in the poem provide evidence that the speaker and Denise are "best friends"? What seems to be responsible for Denise's accusation in line 18?

3. What possessions are most important to the speaker? Why are the tomato seeds significant for her? Explain the appropriateness of her final gift to Denise.

# August Wilson

Born in 1945, August Wilson grew up in a poor family in Pittsburgh and dropped out of school at the age of sixteen. While working at menial jobs, he began to write poetry. In 1968, he founded the Black Horizons Theatre Company in St. Paul, Minnesota, but he continued to think of himself primarily as a poet until he started writing for the theater in the 1980s. In 1982, his first short play, *Jitney*, was produced in Pittsburgh, and two years later *Ma Rainey's Black Bottom* opened on Broadway after a trial run at the Yale Repertory Theatre. *Fences* was produced at Yale in 1985 and then opened on Broadway in 1987, winning several awards, including the Tony Award for best play and the Pulitzer Prize for drama. A new play, *Joe Turner's Come and Gone*, opened on Broadway in 1988.

Wilson has often been quoted as saying that his parents, representatives of earlier generations of deprived blacks, had life much harder than they ever let on to their six children, and Wilson's plays are sensitive to the different problems of different generations. In *Fences*, the tension between generations is only one among several conflicts based on circumstances and individual human needs. Here, the fence that is planned but remains unbuilt through most of the play represents both fears and desires, and for different characters it means different things.

# FENCES

## CHARACTERS

TROY MAXON
JIM BONO, Troy's friend
ROSE, Troy's wife
LYONS, Troy's oldest son by previous marriage
GABRIEL, Troy's brother
CORY, Troy and Rose's son
RAYNELL, Troy's daughter

## SETTING

The setting is the yard that fronts the only entrance to the MAXON household, an ancient two-story brick house set back off a small alley in a big-city neighborhood. The entrance to the house is gained by two or three steps leading to a wooden porch badly in need of paint.

A relatively recent addition to the house and running its full width, the porch lacks congruence. It is a sturdy porch with a flat roof. One or two chairs of dubious value sit at one end where the kitchen window opens onto the porch. An old-fashioned icebox stands silent guard at the opposite end.

The yard is a small dirt yard, partially fenced, except for the last scene, with a wooden sawhorse, a pile of lumber, and other fence-building equipment set off to the side. Opposite is a tree from which hangs a ball made of rags. A baseball bat leans against the tree. Two oil drums serve as garbage receptacles and sit near the house at right.

## THE PLAY

Near the turn of the century, the destitute of Europe sprang on the city with tenacious claws and an honest and solid dream. The city devoured them. They swelled its belly until it burst into a thousand furnaces and sewing machines, a thousand butcher shops and bakers' ovens, a thousand churches and banks and hospitals and funeral parlors. The city grew. It nourished itself and offered each man a partnership limited only by his talent, his guile, and his willingness and capacity for hard work. For the immigrants of Europe, a dream dared and won true.

The descendants of African slaves were offered no such welcome or participation. They came from places called the Carolinas and the Virginias, Georgia, Alabama, Mississippi, and Tennessee. They came strong, eager, searching. The city rejected them and they fled and settled along the riverbanks and under bridges in shallow, ramshackle houses made of sticks and tar paper. They collected rags and wood. They sold the use of their muscles and their bodies. They cleaned houses and washed clothes, they shined shoes, and in quiet desperation and vengeful pride, they stole, and lived in pursuit of their own dream: that they could breathe free, finally, and stand to meet life with the force of dignity and whatever eloquence the heart could call upon.

By 1957, the hard-won victories of the European immigrants had solidified the industrial might of America. War had been confronted and won with new energies that used loyalty and patriotism as its fuel. Life was rich, full, and flourishing. The Milwaukee Braves won the World Series, and the hot winds of change that would make the sixties a turbulent, racing, dangerous, and provocative decade had not yet begun to blow full.

# ACT I

## Scene 1

*It is 1957.* TROY *and* BONO *enter the yard engaged in conversation.* TROY *is fifty-three years old, a large man with thick heavy hands; it is this largeness that he strives to fill out and make an accommodation with. Together with his blackness, his largeness informs his sensibilities and the choices he has made in his life. Of the two men,* BONO *is obviously the follower. His commitment to their friendship of thirty-odd years is rooted in his admiration of* TROY'S *honesty, capacity for hard work, and his strength, which* BONO *seeks to emulate.*

*It is Friday night, payday, and the one night of the week the two men engage in a ritual of talk and drink.* TROY *is usually the most talkative and at times he can be crude and almost vulgar, though he is capable of rising to profound heights of expression. The men carry lunch buckets and wear or carry burlap aprons and are dressed in clothes suitable to their jobs as garbage collectors.*

BONO: Troy, you ought to stop that lying!

TROY: I ain't lying! The nigger had a watermelon this big. [TROY *indicates with his hands.*] Talking about . . . "What watermelon, Mr. Rand?" I liked to fell out! "What watermelon, Mr. Rand?" . . . And it sitting there big as life.

BONO: What did Mr. Rand say?

TROY: Ain't said nothing. Figure if the nigger too dumb to know he carrying a watermelon, he wasn't gonna get much sense out of him. Trying to hide that great big old watermelon under his coat. Afraid to let the white man see him carry it home.

BONO: I'm like you . . . I ain't got no time for them kind of people.

TROY: Now what he look like getting mad 'cause he see the man from the union talking to Mr. Rand?

BONO: Well, as long as you got your complaint filed, they can't fire you. That's what one of them white fellows tell me.

TROY: I ain't worried about them firing me. They gonna fire me 'cause I asked a question? That's all I did. I went to Mr. Rand and asked him why. "Why you got the white mens driving and the colored lifting?" Told him, "What's the matter, don't I count? You think only white fellows got sense enough to drive a truck. That ain't no paper job! Hell, anybody can drive a truck. How come you got all whites driving and the colored lifting?" He told me take it to the union. Well, hell, that's what I done! Now they wanna come up with this pack of lies.

BONO: I told Brownie if the man come and ask him any questions . . . just tell the truth! It ain't nothing but something they done trumped up on you 'cause you filed a complaint on them.

TROY: Brownie don't understand nothing. All I want them to do is change the job description. Give everybody a chance to drive the truck. Brownie can't see that. He ain't got that much sense.

BONO: How you figure he making out with that gal be up at Taylor's all the time . . . that Alberta gal?

TROY: Same as you and me. Getting just as much as we is. Which is to say nothing.

BONO: It is, huh? I figure you doing a little better than me . . . and I ain't saying what I'm doing.

TROY: Aw, nigger, look here . . . I know you. If you had got anywhere near that gal, twenty minutes later you gonna be looking to tell somebody. And the first one you gonna tell . . . that you gonna want to brag to . . . is gonna be me.

BONO: I ain't saying that. I see where you be eyeing her.

TROY: I eye all the women. I don't miss nothing. Don't never let nobody tell you Troy Maxson don't eye the women.

BONO: You been doing more than eyeing her. You done bought her a drink or two.

TROY: Hell yeah, I bought her a drink! What that mean? I bought you one, too. What that mean 'cause I buy her a drink? I'm just being polite.

BONO: It's all right to buy her one drink. That's what you call being polite. But when you wanna be buying two or three . . . that's what you call eyeing her.

TROY: Look here, as long as you known me . . . you ever known me to chase after women?

BONO: Hell yeah! Long as I done known you. You forgetting I knew you when.

TROY: Naw, I'm talking about since I been married to Rose?

BONO: Not since you been married to Rose. That's the truth. I can say that.

TROY: All right then! Case closed.

BONO: I see you be walking up around Alberta's house.

TROY: What you watching where I'm walking for? I ain't watching after you.

BONO: I seen you walking around there more than once.

TROY: Hell, you liable to see me walking anywhere! That don't mean nothing 'cause you see me walking around there.

BONO: Where she come from anyway? She just kinda showed up one day.

TROY: Tallahassee. You can look at her and tell she one of them Florida gals. They got some big healthy women down there. Grow them right up out the ground. Got a little bit of Indian in her. Most of them niggers down in Florida got some Indian in them.

BONO: I don't know about that Indian part. But she damn sure big and healthy. Woman wear some big stockings. Got them great big old legs and hips as wide as the Mississippi River.

TROY: Legs don't mean nothing. You don't do nothing but push them out of the way. But them hips cushion the ride.

BONO: Troy, you ain't got no sense.

TROY: It's the truth! Like you riding on Goodyears!

[ROSE *enters from the house. She is ten years younger than* TROY, *and her devotion to him stems from her recognition of the possibilities of her life without him: a succession of abusive men and their babies, a life of partying and running the streets, the church, or aloneness with its attendant pain and frustration. She recognizes* TROY'*s spirit as a fine and illuminating one and she either ignores or forgives his faults, only some of which she recognizes. Though she doesn't drink, her presence is an integral part of the Friday-night rituals. She alternates between the porch and the kitchen, where supper preparations are under way.*]

ROSE: What you all out here getting into?

TROY: What you worried about what we getting into for? This is men talk, woman.

ROSE: What I care what you are talking about? Bono, you gonna stay for supper?

BONO: I thank you, Rose. But Lucille say she cooking up a pot of pig feet.

TROY: Pig feet! Hell, I'm going home with you! Might even stay the night if you got some pig feet. You got something in there to top them pig feet, Rose?

ROSE: I'm cooking up some chicken. I got some chicken and collard greens.

TROY: Well, go on back in the house and let me and Bono finish what we was talking about. This is men talk. I got some talk for you later. You know what kind of talk I mean. You go on and powder it up.

ROSE: Troy Maxson, don't you start that now!

TROY: [*Puts his arm around* ROSE.] Aw, woman . . . come here. Look here, Bono . . . when I met this woman . . . I got out that place, say, "Hitch up my pony, saddle up my mare . . . there's a woman out there for me somewhere." I looked here. Looked there. Saw Rose and latched on to her. I latched on to her and told her—I'm gonna tell you the truth—I told her, "Baby, I don't wanna marry, I just wanna be your man." Rose told me . . . Tell him what you told me, Rose.

ROSE: I told him if he wasn't the marrying kind, then move out the way so the marrying kind could find me.

TROY: That's what she told me. "Nigger, you in my way. You blocking the view! Move out the way so I can find me a husband." I thought it over two or three days. Come back—

ROSE: [*Interrupting.*] Ain't no two or three days nothing. You was back the same night.

TROY: Come back, told her, "Okay, baby . . . but I'm gonna buy me a banty rooster and put him out there in the backyard, and when he see a stranger come, he'll flap his wings and crow . . ." Look here, Bono, I could watch the front door by myself; it was that backdoor I was worried about.

ROSE: Troy, you ought not talk like that. Troy ain't doing nothing but telling a lie.

TROY: Only thing is, when we first got married—forget the rooster—we ain't had no yard!

BONO: I hear you tell it. Me and Lucille was staying down there on Logan Street. Had two rooms with the outhouse in the back. I ain't mind the outhouse none. But when that goddamn wind blow through there in the winter, that's what I'm talking about! To this day I wonder why in the hell I ever stayed down there for six long years. But see, I didn't know I could do better. I thought only white folks had inside toilets and things.

ROSE: There's a lot of people don't know they can do better than they doing now. That's just something you got to learn. A lot of folks still shop at Bella's.

TROY: Ain't nothing wrong with shopping at Bella's. She got fresh food.

ROSE: I ain't said nothing about if she got fresh food. I'm talking about what she charge. She charge ten cents more than the A&P.

TROY: The A&P ain't never done nothing for me. I spends my money where I'm treated right. I go down to Bella, say, "I need a loaf of bread, I'll pay you on Friday," she give it to me. What sense that make when I got money to go and spend it somewhere else and ignore the person who done right by me? That ain't in the Bible.

ROSE: We ain't talking about what's in the Bible. What sense it make to shop there when she overcharge?

TROY: You shop where you want to. I'll do my shopping where the people been good to me.

ROSE: Well, I don't think it's right for her to overcharge. That's all I was saying.

BONO: Look here . . . I got to get on. Lucille going be raising all kind of hell.

TROY: Where you going, nigger? We ain't finished this pint. Come on, finish this pint.

BONO: Well, hell, I am . . . if you ever turn the bottle loose.

TROY: [Hands him the bottle.] The only thing I say about the A&P is I'm glad Cory got that job down there. Help him take care of his school clothes and things. Gabe done moved out and things getting tight around here. He got that job. He can start to look out for himself.

ROSE: Cory done went and got recruited by a college football team.

TROY: I told that boy about that football stuff. The white man ain't gonna let him get nowhere with that football. I told him when he first come to me with it. Now you come telling me he done went and got more tied up in it. He need to go and get recruited in how to fix cars or something where he can make a living.

ROSE: He ain't talking about making no living playing football. It's just something the boys in school do. They gonna send a recruiter by to talk to you. He'll tell you he ain't talking about making no living playing football. It's a honor to be recruited.

TROY: It ain't gonna get him nowhere. Bono'll tell you that.

BONO: If he be like you in the sports, he's gonna be all right. Ain't but two men ever played baseball as good as you. That's Babe Ruth and Josh Gibson. Thems the only two men hit a baseball farther than you.

TROY: What it ever get me? Ain't got a pot to piss in or a window to throw it out of.

ROSE: Times have changed since you was playing baseball, Troy. That was before the war. Times have changed a lot since then.

TROY: It's the same now as it was then. The white man ain't gonna let him get nowhere with that football.

ROSE: They got lots of colored boys playing ball now. Baseball and football.

BONO: You right about that, Rose. Times have changed. Troy just come along too early.

TROY: There ought not never have been no time called too early! Now you take that fellow . . . What's that fellow they had playing left field for the Yankees back then? You know who I'm talking about, Bono. Used to play left field for the Yankees?

ROSE: Selkirk?

TROY: Selkirk! That's it! Man batting .269, understand? .269. What kind of sense that make? I was hitting .432 with thirty-seven home runs! Man batting .269 and playing left field for the Yankees! I saw Josh Gibson's daughter yesterday. She walking around with raggedy shoes on her feet. Now I bet you Selkirk's daughter ain't walking around with raggedy shoes. I bet you that!

ROSE: They got a lot of colored baseball players now. Jackie Robinson was the first. Folks had to wait for Jackie Robinson.

TROY: I done seen a hundred niggers play baseball better than Jackie Robinson. Hell, I know some teams Jackie Robinson couldn't even make! What you talking about Jackie Robinson. Jackie Robinson wasn't nobody. I'm talking about if you could play ball, then they ought to have let you play. Don't care what color you were. Come telling me I come along too early. If you could play, then they ought to have let you play. [TROY *takes a long drink from the bottle.*]

ROSE: You gonna drink yourself to death. You don't need to be drinking like that.

TROY: Death ain't nothing. I done seen him, done wrestled with him. You can't tell me nothing about death. Death ain't nothing but a fastball on the outside corner. And you know what I'll do to that! Look here, Bono . . . am I lying? You get one of them fastballs about waist high over the outside corner of the plate where you can get the meat of the bat on it . . . and good God! You can kiss it good-bye. Now, am I lying?

BONO: Naw, you telling the truth there. I seen you do it.

TROY: If I'm lying, that's 450 feet worth of lying! [*Pause.*] That's all death is to me. A fastball on the outside corner.

ROSE: I don't know why you want to get on talking about Death.

TROY: Ain't nothing wrong with talking about Death. That's part of life. Everybody gonna die. You gonna die, I'm gonna die, Bono's gonna die. Hell, we all gonna die.

ROSE: But you ain't got to talk about it. I don't like to talk about it.

TROY: You the one brought it up. Me and Bono was talking about baseball . . . you tell me I'm gonna drink myself to Death. Ain't that right, Bono? You know I don't drink this but one night out of the week. That's Friday night. I'm gonna drink just enough to where I can handle it. Then I cuts it loose. I leave it alone. So don't you worry about me drinking myself to death. 'Cause I ain't worried about Death. I done seen him. I done wrestled with him. Look here, Bono . . . I looked up one day and Death was marching straight at me. Like Soldiers on Parade! The Army of Death marching straight at me. The middle of July, 1941. It got real cold just like to be winter. It seem like Death himself reached out and touched me on the shoulder. He touch me just like I touch you. I got cold as ice and Death standing there grinning at me.

ROSE: Troy, why don't you hush that talk.

TROY: I say, "What you want, Mr. Death? You be wanting me? You done brought your army to be getting me?" I looked him dead in the eye. I wasn't fearing nothing. I was ready to tangle. Just like I'm ready to tangle now. The Bible say be ever vigilant. That's why I don't get but so drunk. I got to keep watch.

ROSE: Troy was right down there in Mercy Hospital. You remember he had pneumonia? Laying there with a fever talking plumb out of his head.

TROY: Death, he ain't said nothing. He just stared at me. He had a thousand men to do his bidding and he wasn't going to get a thousand and one. Not then! Hell, I wasn't but thirty-seven years old. [*Pause.*] Death standing there staring at me . . . carrying that sickle in his hand. Finally he say, "You want bound over for another year?" See, just like that . . . "You want bound over for another year?" I told him, "Bound over hell! Let's settle this now!" It seem like he kinda fell back when I said that, and all the cold went out of me. I reached out and grabbed that sickle and threw it just as far as I could throw it . . . and me and him commenced to wrestling. We wrestled for three days and three nights. I can't say where I found the strength from. Every time it seemed like he was gonna get the best of me, I'd reach way down deep inside myself and find the strength to do him one better.

ROSE: Every time Troy tell that story he find different ways to tell it. Different things to make up about it.

TROY: I ain't making up nothing. I'm telling you the facts of what happened. I wrestled with Death for three days and three nights and I'm standing here to tell you about it. [*Pause.*] All right. At the end of the third night we done weakened each other to where both of us could hardly move. Death stood up, throwed on his robe . . . had him a white robe with a hood on it. He throwed on that robe and went off to look for his sickle.

Say, "I'll be back." Just like that, "I'll be back." I told him, say, "You gonna have to find me!" I wasn't no fool. I wasn't going looking for him. Death ain't nothing to play with. And I know he's gonna get me. I know I got to join his army. . . . his camp followers. But as long as I keep my strength and see him coming, as long as I keep up my vigilance, he's gonna have to fight to get me. I ain't going easy.

BONO: Well, look here, since you got to keep up your vigilance . . . let me have the bottle.

TROY: Aw hell, I shouldn't have told you that part. I should have left out that part. That vigilance part.

ROSE: Troy be talking that stuff and half the time don't even know what he be talking about.

TROY: Bono know me better than that. He know I don't talk nothing lessen I got a good handle on it as the truth. Ain't that right, Bono?

BONO: That's right. I know you. I know you got some Uncle Remus in your blood. You got more stories than the devil got sinners.

TROY: Aw hell, I done seen him too! Done talked with the devil.

ROSE: Troy, don't nobody wanna be hearing all that stuff.

[LYONS *enters the yard from the street. Thirty-four years old,* TROY's *son by a previous marriage, he sports a neatly trimmed goatee, sport coat, white shirt, tieless and buttoned at the collar. Though he fancies himself a musician, he is more caught up in the rituals and "idea" of being a musician than in the actual practice of the music. The music offers him a "life-style and stance from which he can ignore the sociological context of his existence and celebrate the music's ability to provide a maintenance of equilibrium despite the precarious circumstances of day-to-day living." He has come to borrow money from* TROY, *and while he knows he will be successful, he is uncertain as to what extent his life-style will be held up to scrutiny and ridicule.*]

LYONS: Hey, Pop.

TROY: What you come Hey, Popping me for?

LYONS: How you doing, Rose? [*He kisses her.*] Mr. Bono, how you doing?

BONO: Hey, Lyons, how you been?

TROY: He must have been doing all right. I ain't seen him around here last week.

ROSE: Troy, leave the boy alone. He come by to see you and you wanna start all that nonsense.

TROY: I ain't bothering Lyons. [*Offers him the bottle.*] Here . . . get you a drink. We got an understanding. I know why he come by to see me and he know I know.

LYONS: Come on, Pop . . . I just stopped by to say hi, see how you was doing.

TROY: You ain't stopped by yesterday.

ROSE: You gonna stay for supper, Lyons? I got some chicken cooking in the oven.

LYONS: No, Rose . . . thanks. I was just in the neighborhood and thought I'd stop by for a minute.

TROY: You was in the neighborhood all right, nigger. You telling the truth there. You was in the neighborhood 'cause it's my payday.

LYONS: Well, hell, since you mentioned it, let me have ten dollars.

TROY: I'll be damned! I'll die and go to hell and play blackjack with the devil before I give you ten dollars.

BONO: That's what I wanna know about . . . this devil you done seen.

LYONS: What? Pop done seen the devil? You too much, Pops.

TROY: Yeah, I done seen him. Talked to him too!

ROSE: You ain't seen no devil. I done told you that man ain't had nothing to do with the devil. Anything you can't understand, you want to call it the devil.

TROY: Look here, Bono . . . I went down to see Hertzberger about some furniture. Got three rooms for two-ninety-eight. That what it say on the radio. Three rooms . . . two-ninety-eight. Even made up a little song about it. Go down there . . . man tell me I can't get no credit. I'm working every day and can't get no credit. What to do? I got an empty house with some raggedy furniture in it. Cory ain't got no bed. He's sleeping on a pile of rags on the floor. Working every day and can't get no credit. Come back home—Rose'll tell you—madder than hell. Sit down, try to figure what I'm gonna do. Come a knock on the door. Ain't been living here but three days. Who know I'm here? Open the door . . . devil standing there bigger than life. White fellow . . . got on good clothes and everything. Standing there with a clipboard in his hand. I ain't had to say nothing. First words come out of his mouth was "I understand you need some furniture and can't get no credit." I liked to fell over. He say I'll give you all the credit you want, but you got to pay the interest on it. I told him give me three rooms worth and charge whatever you want. Next day a truck pulled up here and two men unloaded them three rooms. Man what drove the truck give me a book. Say send ten dollars a month to the address in the book and everything will be all right. Say if I miss a payment the devil was coming back and it'll be hell to pay. That was fifteen years ago. To this day, the first of the month I send my ten dollars, Rose'll tell you.

ROSE: Troy lying.

TROY: I ain't never seen that man since. Now, you tell me who else that could have been but the devil? I ain't sold my soul or nothing, you understand. I wouldn't have truck with the devil about nothing like that. He ain't mentioned nothing like that. I just got my furniture and pays my ten dollars the first of the month just like clockwork.

BONO: How long you say you been paying this ten dollars a month?

TROY: Fifteen years!

BONO: Hell, ain't you finished paying for it yet? How much the man done charged you.

TROY: Aw hell, I done paid for it. I done paid for it ten times over! The fact is I'm scared to stop paying it.

ROSE: Troy lying. We got that furniture from Mr. Glickman. He ain't paying no ten dollars a month to nobody.

TROY: Aw hell, woman. Bono know I ain't that big a fool.

LYONS: I was just getting ready to say . . . I know where there's a bridge for sale.

TROY: Look here, I'll tell you this . . . it don't matter to me if he was the devil. It don't matter if the devil give credit. Somebody has got to give it.

ROSE: It ought to matter. You going around talking about having truck with the devil . . . God's the one you gonna have to answer to. He's the one gonna be at the judgment.

LYONS: Yeah, well, look here, Pop . . . let me have that ten dollars. I'll give it back to you. Bonnie got a job working at the hospital.

TROY: What I tell you, Bono? The only time I see this nigger is when he wants something. That's the only time I see him.

LYONS: Come on, Pop, Mr. Bono don't want to hear all that. Let me have the ten dollars. I told you Bonnie working.

TROY: What that mean to me? "Bonnie working." I don't care if she working. Go ask her for the ten dollars if she working. Talking about Bonnie working . . . why ain't you working?

LYONS: Aw, Pop, you know I can't find no decent job. Where am I gonna get a job at? You know I can't get no job.

TROY: I told you I know some people down there. I can get you on the rubbish if you want to work. I told you that the last time you came by here asking me for something.

LYONS: Naw, Pop . . . thanks. That ain't for me. I don't wanna be carrying nobody's rubbish. I don't wanna be punching nobody's time clock.

TROY: What's the matter? You too good to carry rubbish? Where you think that ten dollars you talking about come from? I'm just supposed to haul people's rubbish and give my money to you 'cause you too lazy to work. You too lazy to work and wanna know why you ain't got what I got.

ROSE: What hospital Bonnie working at? Mercy?

LYONS: She's down at Passavant working in the laundry.

TROY: Ain't got nothing as it is. I give you that ten dollars and I got to eat beans the rest of the week. Naw, you ain't getting no ten dollars here.

LYONS: You ain't got to be eating no beans. I don't know why you wanna say that.

TROY: I ain't got no extra money. Gabe done moved over to Miss Pearl's paying her the rent and things done got tight around here. I can't afford to be giving you every payday.

LYONS: I ain't asked you to give me nothing. I asked you to loan me ten dollars. I know you got ten dollars.

TROY: Yeah, I got it. Why you think I got it? 'Cause I don't throw my money away out there in the streets. You living the fast life, wanna be a musician, running around in them clubs and things . . . then you learn to take care of yourself. You ain't gonna find me going and asking nobody for nothing. I done spent too many years without.

LYONS: You and me is two different people, Pop.

TROY: I done learned my mistake and learned to do what's right by it. You still trying to get something for nothing. Life don't owe you nothing. You owe it to yourself. Ask Bono. He'll tell you I'm right.

LYONS: You got your way of dealing with the world . . . I got mine. The only thing that matters to me is the music.

TROY: Hell, I can see that! It don't matter how you gonna eat, where your next dollar is coming from. You telling the truth there.

LYONS: I know I got to eat. But I got to live too. I need something that gonna help me to get out of the bed in the morning. Make me feel like I belong in the world. I don't bother nobody. I just stay with my music 'cause that's the only way I can find to live in the world. Otherwise there ain't no telling what I might do. Now I don't come by here criticizing you and the way you live. I just come by to ask you for ten dollars. I don't wanna hear all that about how I live.

TROY: Boy, your mama did a hell of a job raising you.

LYONS: You can't change me, Pop. I'm thirty-four years old.

ROSE: Let the boy have ten dollars, Troy.

TROY: [*To* LYONS.] What the hell you looking at me for? I ain't got no ten dollars. You know what I do with my money. [*To* ROSE.] Give him ten dollars if you want him to have it.

ROSE: I will. Just as soon as you turn it loose.

TROY: [*Handing* ROSE *the money.*] There it is. Seventy-six dollars and forty-two cents. You see this, Bono? Now, I ain't gonna get but six of that back.

ROSE: You ought to stop telling that lie. Here, Lyons. [*She hands him the money.*]

LYONS: Thanks, Rose. Look . . . I got to run. I'll see you later.

TROY: Wait a minute. You gonna say, "Thanks, Rose," and ain't gonna look to see where she got that ten dollars from?

LYONS: I know she got it from you, Pop. Thanks. I'll give it back to you.

TROY: There he go telling another lie. Time I see that ten dollars he'll be owed me thirty more.

LYONS: See you, Mr. Bono. Thanks, Pop. I'll see you again. [LYONS *exits the yard.*]

TROY: I don't know why he don't go and get him a decent job and take care of that woman he got.

BONO: He'll be all right, Troy. The boy's still young.

TROY: The boy is thirty-four years old.

ROSE: Let's not get off into all that.

BONO: Look here . . I got to be going. I got to be getting on. Lucille gonna be waiting.

TROY: [*Puts his arm around* ROSE.] See this woman, Bono? I love this woman.

I love this woman so much it hurts. I love her so much . . . I done run out of ways to love her. So I got to go back to basics. Don't you come by my house Monday morning talking about time to go to work . . . 'cause I'm still gonna be stroking!

ROSE: Troy! Stop it now!

BONO: I ain't paying him no mind, Rose. That ain't nothing but gin-talk. Go on, Troy. I'll see you Monday.

TROY: Don't you come by my house, nigger! I done told you what I'm gonna be doing.

[*The lights go down to black.*]

## Scene 2

*The lights come up on* ROSE *hanging up clothes. She hums and sings softly to herself.* TROY *enters from the house. It is the following morning.*

ROSE: 'Morning. You ready for breakfast? I can fix it soon as I finish hanging up these clothes?

TROY: I got the coffee on. That'll be all right. I'll just drink some of that this morning.

ROSE: That 642 hit yesterday. That's the second time this month. Miss Pearl hit for a dollar . . . seem like those that need the least always get lucky. Poor folks can't get nothing.

TROY: Them numbers don't know nobody. I don't know why you fool with them. You and Lyons both.

ROSE: It's something to do.

TROY: You ain't doing nothing but throwing your money away.

ROSE: Troy, you know I don't play foolishly. I just play a nickel here and a nickel there.

TROY: That's two nickels you done thrown away.

ROSE: Now I hit sometimes . . . that makes up for it. It always comes in handy when I do hit. I don't hear you complaining then.

TROY: I ain't complaining. I just say it's foolish. Trying to guess out of six hundred ways which way the number gonna come. If I had all the money niggers throw away on numbers for one week—just one week—I'd be a rich man.

ROSE: Well, you wishing and calling it foolish ain't gonna stop folks from playing numbers. That's one thing for sure. Besides, some good things come from playing numbers. Look where Pope done bought him that restaurant off of numbers.

TROY: I can't stand niggers like that. Man ain't had two dimes to rub together. He walking around with his shoes all run over bumming money for cigarettes. All right. Got lucky there and hit the numbers—

ROSE: Troy, I know all about it.

TROY: Had good sense, I'll say that for him. He ain't throwed his money away. I seen niggers hit the numbers and go through two thousand dollars in four days. Man bought him that restaurant down there, fixed it up real nice, and then didn't want nobody to come in it! A Negro go in there and can't get no kind of service. I seen a white fellow come in there and order a bowl of stew. Pope picked all the meat out the pot for him. Man ain't had nothing but a bowl of meat! Negro come behind him and ain't got nothing but the potatoes and carrots. Talking about what numbers do for people you picked a wrong example. Ain't done nothing but make him a worse fool than he was before. [*Pause.*] Where's Cory? Cory in the house? [*Calls.*] Cory?

ROSE: He gone out.

TROY: Out, huh? He gone out 'cause he know I want him to help me with this fence. I know how he is. That boy afraid of work. He ain't done a lick of work in his life.

ROSE: He had to go to football practice. Coach wanted them to get in a little extra practice before the season start.

TROY: I got his practice . . . running out of here before he get his chores done.

ROSE: Troy, what is wrong with you this morning? Don't nothing set right with you. Go on back in there and go to bed . . . get up on the other side.

TROY: Why something got to be wrong with me? I ain't said nothing wrong with me.

ROSE: You got something to say about everything. First it's the numbers, then it's the way the man runs his restaurant, then you done got on Cory. What's it gonna be next? Take a look up there and see if the weather suits you . . . or is it gonna be how you gonna put up the fence with the clothes hanging in the yard.

TROY: You hit the nail on the head there! Damn if that wasn't what I was thinking.

ROSE: I know you like I know the back of my hand. Go on in there and get you some coffee . . . see if that straighten you up. 'Cause you ain't right this morning.

[GABRIEL *is heard singing off stage.* TROY's *brother, he is seven years younger than* TROY. *Injured in World War II, he has a metal plate in his head. He carries an old trumpet tied around his waist and believes with every fiber of his being that he is the Archangel Gabriel. He carries a chip basket with an assortment of discarded fruits and vegetables he has picked up in the strip district and which he attempts to sell.*]

[GABRIEL *singing.*]
Yes mam I got plums
You ask me how I sell them.

TROY: [*Hearing* GABRIEL.] Just what I need this morning.

[GABRIEL *singing.*]
Oh ten cents apiece
Three for a quarter
Come and buy now
'Cause I'm here today
And tomorrow I'll be gone

[GABRIEL *enters.*]

GABRIEL: Hey, Rose!

ROSE: How you doing, Gabe?

GABRIEL: There's Troy. Hey, Troy!

TROY: Hey, Gabe.

ROSE: [*To* GABRIEL.] What you got there?

GABRIEL: You know what I got, Rose. I got fruits and vegetables.

ROSE: [*Looking in basket.*] Where's all these plums you talking about?

GABRIEL: I ain't got no plums today, Rose. I was just singing that. Have some
    tomorrow. Put me in a big order for plums. Have enough plums tomor-
    row for St. Peter and everybody. [*To* ROSE.] Troy's mad at me.

TROY: I ain't mad at you. What I got to be mad at you about? You ain't done
    nothing to me.

GABRIEL: I just moved over to Miss Pearl's to keep out from in your way. I
    ain't mean no harm by it.

TROY: Who said anything about that? I ain't said nothing about that.

GABRIEL: You ain't mad at me, is you?

TROY: Naw, I ain't mad at you Gabe. If I was mad at you I'd tell you about
    it.

GABRIEL: Got me two rooms. In the basement. Got my own door too. Wanna
    see my key? [*He holds up a key.*] That's my own key! Ain't nobody else
    got a key like that. That's my key! My two rooms!

TROY: Well, that's good, Gabe. You got your own key . . . that's good.

ROSE: You hungry, Gabe? I was just fixing to cook Troy his breakfast.

GABRIEL: You got some biscuits? I'll take some biscuits. Did you know when
    I was in heaven, every morning me and St. Peter would sit down by the
    gate and eat some big fat biscuits? Oh, yeah! We had us a good time.
    We'd eat us them biscuits and then St. Peter would go off to sleep and
    tell me to wake him up when it's time to open the gates for the judg-
    ment.

ROSE: Well, come on . . . I'll make up a batch of biscuits. [ROSE *exits into the
    house.*]

GABRIEL: Troy, St. Peter got your name in the book. I seen it. It say, "Troy
    Maxson." I say, "I know him! He got the same name like what I got.
    That's my brother!"

TROY: How many times you gonna tell me that, Gabe? He got your name in there too?

GABRIEL: Ain't got my name in the book. Don't have to have my name. I done died and went to heaven. He got your name, though. One morning St. Peter was looking at his book, marking it up for the judgment, and he let me see your name. Got it in there under M. Got Rose's name too. I ain't seen it like I seen yours, but I know it's in there. Great big book. Got everybody's name what was ever been born. That's what he told me. But I seen your name. Seen it with my own eyes.

TROY: Go on in the house there. Rose going to fix you something to eat.

GABRIEL: Oh, I ain't hungry. I done had breakfast with Aunt Jemima. She come by and cooked me up a whole mess of flapjacks. Remember how we used to eat them flapjacks?

TROY: Yeah, I remember. Go on in the house and get you something to eat now.

GABRIEL: I got to go sell my plums. I done sold some tomatoes. Got me two quarters. Wanna see? [*He shows* TROY *his quarters.*] I'm gonna save them and buy me a new horn so St. Peter can hear me when it's time to open the gates. [GABRIEL *stops suddenly. Listens.*] Hear that? That's the hell-hounds. I got to chase them out of here. Go on get out of here! Get out!

[GABRIEL *exits singing.*]
Better get ready for the judgment
Better get ready for the judgment
My lord is coming down
Better get ready for the judgment
Better get ready for the judgment morning
Better get ready for the judgment
My god is coming down

[ROSE *enters from the house.*]

TROY: He gone off somewhere.

ROSE: He ain't eating right. Miss Pearl say she can't get him to eat nothing.

TROY: What you want me to do about it, Rose? I done did everything I can for the man. I can't make him get well. Man got half his head blown away . . . what you expect?

ROSE: Seem like something ought to be done to help him.

TROY: Man don't bother nobody. He just mixed up from that metal plate he got in his head. Ain't no sense for him to go back into the hospital.

ROSE: Least he be eating right. They can help him take care of himself.

TROY: Don't nobody wanna be locked up, Rose. What you wanna lock him up for? Man go over there and fight the war, get half his head blown off, and they give him a lousy three thousand dollars. And I had to swoop down on that.

ROSE: Is you fixing to go into that again?

TROY: That's the only way I got a roof over my head . . . 'cause of that metal plate.

ROSE: Ain't no sense you blaming yourself for nothing. You done what was right by him. Can't nobody say you ain't done what was right by him. Look how long you took care of him . . . till he wanted to have his own place and moved over there with Miss Pearl.

TROY: That ain't what I'm saying, woman! I'm just stating the facts. If my brother didn't have that metal plate in his head, I wouldn't have a pot to piss in or a window to throw it out of. And I'm fifty-three years old. Now you try and understand that! [TROY *gets up from the porch and starts to exit the yard.*]

ROSE: Where you going off to? You been running out of here every Saturday for weeks. I thought you was gonna work on this fence?

TROY: I'm gonna walk down to Taylor's. Listen to the ballgame. I'll be back in a bit. I'll work on it when I get back.

[TROY *exits the yard. The lights go to black.*]

### Scene 3

*The lights come up on the yard. It is four hours later.* ROSE *is taking down the clothes from the line.* CORY *enters carrying his football equipment.*

ROSE: Your daddy liked to had a fit with you running out of here this morning without doing your chores.

CORY: I told you I had to go to practice.

ROSE: He say you were supposed to help him with this fence.

CORY: He always say that every Saturday and then he don't never do nothing. Did you tell him about the recruiter?

ROSE: Yeah, I told him.

CORY: What he say?

ROSE: He ain't said nothing too much. You go in there and get started on your chores before he gets back. Go on and scrub down them steps before he gets back here hollering and carrying on.

CORY: I'm hungry. What you got to eat, Mama?

ROSE: Go on and get started on your chores. I got some meat loaf in there. Go on and make you a sandwich . . . and don't leave no mess in there.

[CORY *exits into the house.* ROSE *continues to take down the clothes.* TROY *enters the yard and sneaks up and grabs her from behind.*]

Troy! Go on, now. You liked to scared me to death. What was the score of the game? Lucille had me on the phone and I couldn't keep up with it.

TROY: What I care about the game? Come here, woman. [*He tries to kiss her.*]

ROSE: I thought you went down Taylor's to listen to the game. Go on, Troy! You supposed to be putting up this fence.

TROY: [*Attempting to kiss her again.*] I'll put it up when I finish with what is at hand.

ROSE: Go on, Troy. I ain't studying you.

TROY: [*Chasing after her.*] I'm studying you . . . fixing to do my homework!

ROSE: Troy, you better leave me alone.

TROY: Where's Cory? That boy brought his butt home yet?

ROSE: He's in the house doing his chores.

TROY: [*Calling.*] Cory! Get your butt out here, boy!

[ROSE *exits into the house with the laundry.* TROY *goes over to the pile of wood, picks up a board, and starts sawing.* CORY *enters from the house.*]

TROY: You just now coming in here from leaving this morning?

CORY: Yeah, I had to go to football practice.

TROY: Yeah, what? What kind of talk is that?

CORY: Yessir.

TROY: I ain't but two seconds off you noway. The garbage sitting in there overflowing . . . you ain't done none of your chores . . . and you come in here talking about, "Yeah."

CORY: I was just getting ready to do my chores now.

TROY: Your first chore is to help me with this fence on Saturday. Everything else come after that. Now get that saw and cut them boards.

[CORY *takes the saw and begins cutting the boards.* TROY *continues working. There is a long pause.*]

CORY: The Pirates done won five in a row.

TROY: I ain't thinking about the Pirates. Got an all-white team. Got that boy . . . that Puerto Rican boy . . . Clemente. Don't even half-play him. That boy could be something if they give him a chance. Play him one day and sit him on the bench the next.

CORY: He gets a lot of chances to play.

TROY: I'm talking about playing regular. Playing every day so you can get your timing. That's what I'm talking about.

CORY: They got some white guys on the team that don't play every day. You can't play everybody at the same time.

TROY: If they got a white fellow sitting on the bench, you can bet your last dollar he can't play! The colored guy got to be twice as good before he get on the team. That's why I don't want you to get all tied up in them sports. Man on the team and what it get him? They got colored on the team and don't play them. Same as not having them. All them teams the same.

CORY: The Braves got Hank Aaron and Wes Covington. Hank Aaron hit two home runs today. That makes forty-three.

TROY: Hank Aaron ain't nobody. That's the way you supposed to do. That's how you supposed to play the game. Ain't nothing to it. It's just a matter of timing . . . getting the right follow-through. Hell, I can hit forty-three home runs right now!

CORY: Not off no major-league pitching you couldn't.

TROY: We had better pitching in the Negro League. I hit seven home runs off of Satchel Paige. You can't get no better than that!

CORY: Sandy Koufax. He's leading the league in strikeouts.

TROY: I ain't thinking of no Sandy Koufax nothing.

CORY: You got Warren Spahn and Lew Burdette. I bet you couldn't hit no home runs off of Warren Spahn.

TROY: I'm through with it now. You go on and get them boards cut. [*Pause.*] Your mama tells me you got recruited by a college football team? Is that right?

CORY: Yeah. Coach Zellman say the recruiter gonna be coming by to talk to you. Get you to sign the permission papers.

TROY: I thought you supposed to be working down there at the A&P. Ain't you supposed to be working down there after school?

CORY: Mr. Stawicki say he gonna hold my job for me until after the football season. Say starting next week I can work weekends.

TROY: I thought we had an understanding about this football stuff? You suppose to keep up with your chores and hold that job down at the A&P. Ain't been around here all day on a Saturday. Ain't none of your chores done . . . and now you telling me you done quit your job.

CORY: I'm gonna be working weekends.

TROY: You damn right you are! And ain't no need for nobody coming around here to talk to me about signing nothing.

CORY: Hey, Pop, you can't do that. He's coming all the way from North Carolina.

TROY: I don't care where he coming from. The white man ain't gonna let you get nowhere with that football no way. You go and get your book-learning where you can learn to do something besides carrying people's garbage.

CORY: I get good grades, Pop. That's why the recruiter wants to talk with you. You got to keep up your grades to get recruited. This way I'll be going to college. I'll get a chance—

TROY: You gonna get your butt down there to the A&P and get your job back.

CORY: Mr. Stawicki done already hired somebody else 'cause I told him I was playing football.

TROY: You a bigger fool than I thought . . . to let somebody take away your job so you can play some football. That's downright foolishness. Where you gonna get your money to take out your girlfriend and whatnot? What kind of foolishness is that to let somebody take away your job?

CORY: I'm still gonna be working weekends.

TROY: Naw . . . naw. You getting your butt out of here and finding you another job.

CORY: Come on, Pop! I got to practice. I can't work after school and play football too. Coach Zellman say the team needs me—say—

TROY: I don't care what nobody else say. I'm the boss . . . you understand? I'm the boss around here. I do the only saying what counts.

CORY: Come on, Pop!

TROY: I asked you. Did you understand?

CORY: Yeah . . . Yessir.

TROY: You go down there to that A&P and see if you can get your job back. If you can't do both, then you quit the football team. You've got to take the crooked with the straights.

CORY: Yessir. [*Pause.*] Can I ask you a question?

TROY: What the hell you wanna ask me? Mr. Stawicki the one you got the questions for.

CORY: How come you ain't never liked me?

TROY: Liked you? Who the hell say I got to like you? What law is there say I got to like you? Wanna stand up in my face and ask a damn fool-ass question like that. Talking about liking somebody. Come here, boy, when I talk to you.

[CORY *comes over to where* TROY *is working. He stands slouched over and* TROY *shoves him on his shoulder.*] Straighten up, goddammit! I asked you a question. What law is there say I got to like you?

CORY: None.

TROY: Well, all right then! Don't you eat every day? [*Pause.*] Answer me when I talk to you! Don't you eat every day?

CORY: Yeah.

TROY: Nigger, as long as you in my house you put that sir on the end of it when you talk to me!

CORY: Yes . . . sir.

TROY: You eat every day. Got a roof over your head. Got clothes on your back.

CORY: Yessir.

TROY: Why you think that is?

CORY: 'Cause of you.

TROY: Aw, hell I know it's 'cause of me . . . but why do you think that is?

CORY: [*Hesitant.*] 'Cause you like me.

TROY: Like you? I go out of here every morning, bust my butt, putting up with them crackers every day . . . 'cause I like you? You about the biggest fool I ever saw. [*Pause.*] It's my job. It's my responsibility! You understand that? A man got to take care of his family. You live in my house, sleep you behind on my bedclothes, fill you belly up with my food . . . 'cause you my son. You my flesh and blood. Not 'cause I like you! 'Cause I owe a responsibility to you! 'Cause it's my duty to take care of you. Let's get this straight right here—before it go along any further—I ain't got to like you. Mr. Rand don't give me my money come payday 'cause he likes me. He gives me 'cause he owe me. I done give you everything I had to give you. I gave you your life! Me and your mama worked that out between us. And liking your black ass wasn't part of the bargain. Don't you try and go through life worrying about if somebody like you or not. You best be making sure they doing right by you. You understand what I'm saying, boy?

CORY: Yessir.

TROY: Then get the hell out of my face, and get on down to that A&P.

[ROSE *has been standing behind the screen door for much of the scene. She enters as* CORY *exits.*]

ROSE: Why don't you let the boy go ahead and play football, Troy? Ain't no harm in that. He's just trying to be like you with the sports.

TROY: I don't want him to be like me! I want him to move as far away from my life as he can get. You the only decent thing that ever happened to me. I wish him that. But I don't wish him a thing else from my life. I decided seventeen years ago that boy wasn't getting involved in no sports. Not after what they did to me in the sports.

ROSE: Troy, why don't you admit you was too old to play in the major leagues? For once . . . why don't you admit that?

TROY: What do you mean too old? Don't come telling me I was too old. I just wasn't the right color. Hell, I'm fifty-three years old and I can do better than Selkirk's .269 right now!

ROSE: How was you gonna play ball when you was over forty? Sometimes I can't get no sense out of you.

TROY: I got good sense, woman. I got sense enough not to let my boy get hurt over playing no sports. You been mothering that boy too much. Worried about if people like him.

ROSE: Everything that boy do he do for you. He wants you to say "Good job, son." That's all.

TROY: Rose, I ain't got time for that. He's alive. He's healthy. He's got to make his own way. I made mine. Ain't nobody gonna hold his hand when he get out there in that world.

ROSE: Times have changed from when you was young, Troy. People change. The world's changing around you and you can't even see it.

TROY: [*Slow, methodical.*] Woman . . . I do the best I can do. I come in here every Friday. I carry a sack of potatoes and a bucket of lard. You all line up at the door with your hands out. I give you the lint from my pockets. I give you my sweat and my blood. I ain't got no tears. I done spent them. We go upstairs in that room at night and I fall down on you and try to blast a hole into forever. I get up Monday morning . . . find my lunch on the table. I go out. Make my way. Find my strength to carry me through to the next Friday. [*Pause.*] That's all I got, Rose. That's all I got to give. I can't give nothing else.

[TROY *exits into the house. The lights go down to black.*]

## Scene 4

*It is Friday, two weeks later.* CORY *enters from the house carrying his football equipment. The phone rings.*

CORY: [*Calling.*] I got it! [*He answers the phone and stands in the screendoor talking.*] Hello? Hey, Jesse. Naw . . . I was just leaving now.

ROSE: [*Calling from inside the house.*] Cory!

CORY: I told you man, them spikes is all tore up. You can use them if you want but they ain't no good. Earl got some spikes.

ROSE: [*Calling.*] Cory!

CORY: Size nine, I think. [*Calling to* ROSE] Mam? I'm talking to Jesse. [*Into phone.*] When she say that? Aw, you lying, man. I'm gonna tell her you said that.

ROSE: [*Calling.*] Cory, don't you go nowhere!

CORY: I got to go to the game, Ma! [*Into the phone.*] Yeah, hey look, I'll talk to you later. Yeah, I'll meet you over Earl's house. [*He hangs up the phone and calls to* ROSE] Bye, Ma!

[ROSE *enters from the house.*]

ROSE: Cory, where you going off to? You got all that stuff pulled out and thrown all over your room.

CORY: I was looking for my spikes. Jesse wanted to borrow my spikes.

ROSE: Get up there and get that cleaned up before your daddy gets back in here.

CORY: I got to go. I'll clean it up when I get back. [CORY *exits.*]

ROSE: That's all he need to do is see that room all messed up.

[ROSE *exits into the house as* TROY *and* BONO *enter the yard.* TROY *is dressed in clothes other than his work clothes.*]

BONO: He told him the same thing he told you. Take it to the union.

TROY: Brownie ain't got that much sense. Man wasn't thinking about nothing. He wait until I confront them on it, then he wanna come crying seniority. [*Calls.*] Hey, Rose!

BONO: I wish I could have seen Mr. Rand's face when he told you.

TROY: He couldn't get it out of his mouth! Liked to bit his tongue! When they called me down there to the commissioner's office, he thought they was gonna fire me . . . like everybody else.

BONO: I didn't think they was gonna fire you . . . I thought they was gonna put you on the warning paper.

TROY: Hey, Rose! [*To* BONO.] Yeah . . .Mr. Rand like to bit his tongue. [TROY *breaks the seal on the bottle, takes a drink, and hands it to* BONO.] Hey, Rose!

ROSE: [*Entering from the house.*] Hush all that hollering man! I know you out here. What they say down there at the commissioner's office?

TROY: You supposed to come when I call you, woman. Bono'll tell you that. [*To* BONO.] Don't Lucille come when you call her?

ROSE: Man, hush your mouth. I ain't no dog . . . talk about come when you call me.

TROY: [*Puts his arm around* ROSE.] You hear this, Bono? I had me an old dog used to get uppity like that. You say, comere, Blue . . . and he just lay there and look at you. End up getting a stick and chasing him away trying to make him come.

ROSE: I ain't studying you and your dog. I remember you used to sing that old song.

[TROY *sings.*]
I had a dog his name was Blue
You know Blue was mighty true
You know Blue was a good old dog
Blue treed a possum in a hollow log.

ROSE: Don't nobody wanna hear you sing that old song. Used to have Cory running around here singing that song.

BONO: Hell, I remember that myself.

TROY: That was my daddy's song. My daddy made up that song.

ROSE: I don't care who made it up. Don't nobody wanna hear you sing it.

TROY: [*Makes a song like calling a dog.*] Come here, woman.

ROSE: You come in here carrying on, I reckon they ain't fired you. What they say down there at the commissioner's office?

TROY: Look here, Rose . . . Mr. Rand called me into his office today when I got back from talking to them people down there. It come from up top . . . he called me in and told me they was making me a driver.

ROSE: Troy, you kidding!

TROY: No I ain't. Ask Bono.

ROSE: Well, that's great, Troy. Now you don't have to hassle them people no more.

TROY: Brownie got mad when he heard about . . . run to Mr. Rand talking about he got seniority. Tell her what Mr. Rand told him, Bono.

BONO: Told him take it to the union . . . same as he told Troy.

[LYONS *enters from the street.*]

TROY: Aw hell, I wasn't looking to see you today. I thought you was in jail. Got it all over the front page of the *Courier* about them raiding Sefus' place . . . where you be hanging out with all them thugs.

LYONS: Hey, Pop . . . that ain't got nothing to do with me. I don't go down there gambling. I go down there to sit in with the band. I ain't got nothing to do with the gambling part. They got some good music down there.

TROY: They got some rogues . . . is what they got.

LYONS: How you been, Mr. Bono? Hi, Rose.

BONO: I see where you playing down at the Crawford Grill tonight.

ROSE: How come you ain't brought Bonnie like I told you. You should have brought Bonnie with you, she ain't been over in a month of Sundays.

LYONS: I was just in the neighborhood . . . thought I'd stop by.

TROY: Here he come with that I-was-in-the-neighborhood stuff.

BONO: Your daddy got a promotion on the rubbish. He's gonna be the first colored driver. Ain't got to do nothing but sit up there and read the paper like them white fellows.

LYONS: Hey, Pop . . . if you knew how to read you'd be all right.

TROY: What you care if I can read or not? I read about all them thugs you be hanging out with. I read about them going to jail. I read that.

BONO: Naw . . . naw . . . you mean if the nigger knew how to *drive* he'd be all right. Been fighting with them people about driving and ain't even got a license. Mr. Rand know you ain't got no driver's license?

TROY: Driving ain't nothing. All you do is point the truck where you want it to go and keep from hitting the rest of them cars and things out there. Driving ain't nothing.

BONO: Do Mr. Rand know you ain't got no driver's license? That's what I'm talking about. I ain't asked if driving was easy. I asked if Mr. Rand know you ain't got no driver's license.

TROY: He ain't got to know. The man ain't got to know my business.

LYONS: [*Going into his pocket.*] Say, look here, Pop . . .

TROY: I knew it was coming. Didn't I tell you, Bono? I know what kind of "Look here, Pop" that was. The nigger fixing to ask me for some money. It's Friday night. It's my payday. All them rogues down there on the avenue—the ones that ain't in jail—and Lyons is hopping in his shoes to get down there with them.

LYONS: See, Pop . . . if you give somebody else a chance to talk sometime, you'd see that I was fixing to pay you back your ten dollars like I told you. Here . . . told you I'd pay you when Bonnie got paid.

TROY: Naw . . . you go ahead and keep that ten dollars. Put it in the bank. The next time you feel like you wanna come by here and ask me for something, you go on down there and get that.

LYONS: Here's your ten dollars, Pop. I told you I don't want you to give me nothing. I just wanted to borrow ten dollars.

TROY: Naw . . . you go on and keep that for the next time you want to ask me.

LYONS: Come on, Pop . . . here go your ten dollars.

ROSE: Why don't you go on and let the boy pay you back, Troy?

LYONS: Here you go, Rose. If you don't take it I'm gonna have to hear about it for the next six months. [*He hands her the money.*]

ROSE: You can hand yours over here too, Troy.

TROY: You see this, Bono. You see how they do me.

BONO: Yeah, Lucille do me the same way.

[GABRIEL *is heard singing off stage. He enters.*]

GABRIEL: Hey! Hey! There's Troy's boy!

LYONS: How you doing, Uncle Gabe?

GABRIEL: Lyons . . . the King of the Jungle! Rose . . . hey, Rose. Got a flower for you. [*He takes a rose from his pocket.*] Picked it myself. That's the same rose like what you is!

ROSE: That's right nice of you, Gabe.

LYONS: What you been doing, Uncle Gabe?

GABRIEL: Oh, I been chasing hellhounds and waiting on the time to tell St. Peter to open the gates.

LYONS: You been chasing hellhounds, huh? Well, you doing the right thing, Uncle Gabe. Somebody got to chase them.

GABRIEL: Oh, yeah . . . I know it. The devil's strong. The devil ain't no pushover. Hellhounds snipping at everybody's heels. But I got my trumpet waiting on the judgment time.

LYONS: Waiting on the battle of Armageddon, huh?

GABRIEL: Ain't gonna be too much of a battle when God get to waving that judgment sword. But the peoples gonna have a hell of a time trying to get into heaven if them gates ain't open.

LYONS: [*Putting his arm around* GABRIEL.] You hear this, Pop. Uncle Gabe, you all right!

GABRIEL: [*Laughing with* LYONS.] Lyons! King of the Jungle.

ROSE: You gonna stay for supper, Gabe. Want me to fix you a plate?

GABRIEL: I'll take a sandwich, Rose. Don't want no plate. Just wanna eat with my hands. I'll take a sandwich.

ROSE: How about you, Lyons? You staying? Got some short ribs cooking.

LYONS: Naw, I won't eat nothing till after we finished playing. [*Pause.*] You ought to come down and listen to me play, Pop.

TROY: I don't like that Chinese music. All that noise.

ROSE: Go on in the house and wash up, Gabe . . . I'll fix you a sandwich.

GABRIEL: [*To* LYONS *as he exits.*] Troy's mad at me.

LYONS: What you mad at Uncle Gabe for, Pop.

ROSE: He thinks Troy's mad at him 'cause he moved over to Miss Pearl's.

TROY: I ain't mad at the man. He can live where he want to live at.

LYONS: What he move over there for? Miss Pearl don't like nobody.

ROSE: She don't mind him none. She treats him real nice. She just don't allow all that singing.

TROY: She don't mind that rent he be paying . . . that's what she don't mind.

ROSE: Troy, I ain't going through that with you no more. He's over there 'cause he want to have his own place. He can come and go as he please.

TROY: Hell, he could come and go as he please here. I wasn't stopping him. I ain't put no rules on him.

ROSE: It ain't the same thing, Troy. And you know it. [GABRIEL *comes to the door.*] Now, that's the last I wanna hear about that. I don't wanna hear nothing else about Gabe and Miss Pearl. And next week . . .

GABRIEL: I'm ready for my sandwich, Rose.

ROSE: . . . when that recruiter come from that school, I want you to sign that paper and go on and let Cory play football. Then that'll be the last I have to hear about that.

TROY: [*To* ROSE *as she exits into the house.*] I ain't thinking about Cory nothing.

LYONS: What? Cory got recruited? What school he going to?

TROY: That boy walking around here smelling his piss, thinking he's grown. Thinking he's gonna do what he want irrespective of what I say. Look here, Bono . . . I left the commissioner's office and went down to the A&P—that boy ain't working down there. He lying to me all the time. Telling me he got his job back, telling me he working weekends, telling me he working after school. Mr. Stawicki tell me he ain't working down there at all!

LYONS: Cory just growing up. He's just busting at the seams trying to fill out your shoes.

TROY: I don't care what he's doing. When he get to the point where he wanna disobey me . . . then it's time for him to move on. Bono'll tell you that. I bet he ain't never disobeyed his daddy without paying the consequences.

BONO: I ain't never had a chance. My daddy came on through, but I ain't never knew him to see him . . . or what he had on his mind or where he went. Just moving on through. Searching for the New Land. That's what the old folks used to call it. See a fellow moving around from place to place, woman to woman, called it searching for the New Land. I can't say if he ever found it. I come along, didn't want no kids. Didn't know if I was gonna be in one place long enough to fix on them right as their daddy. I figured I was going searching too. As it turned out, I been hooked up with Lucille near about as long as your daddy been with Rose. Going on sixteen years.

TROY: Sometimes I wish I hadn't known my daddy. My daddy ain't cared nothing about no kids. A kid to him wasn't nothing. All he wanted was for you to learn how to walk so he could start you to working. When it come time for eating, he ate first. If there was anything left over, that's what you got. Man would sit down and eat two chickens and give you the wing.

LYONS: You ought to stop that, Pop. Everybody feed their kids. No matter how hard times is, everybody care about their kids. Make sure they have something to eat.

TROY: The only thing my daddy cared about was getting them bales of cotton in to Mr. Lubin. That's the only thing that mattered to him. Sometimes

I used to wonder why he was living. Wonder why the devil hadn't come and got him. Get them bales in to Mr. Lubin and find out he owe him money . . . and don't do nothing but walk around cussing for the next two months. That was the worse time to cross his path. Seem like he was mad at the world and would strike out at anything underfoot.

LYONS: He should have just went on and left when he saw he couldn't get nowhere. That's what I would have done.

TROY: How he gonna leave with eleven kids? And where he gonna go? He ain't knew how to do nothing but farm. No, he was trapped, and I think he knew it. But I'll say this for him: he felt a responsibility toward us. Maybe he ain't treated us the way I felt he should have, but without that responsibility he could have walked off and left us, made his own way.

BONO: A lot of them did. Back in those days what you talking about, niggers used to travel all over. They get up one day and see where the day ain't sitting right with them and they walk out their front door and just take on down one road or another and keep on walking.

LYONS: There you go! That's what I'm talking about.

BONO: Ain't owned nothing but what was on their back, so you didn't have to worry about leaving nothing behind or carrying nothing with you for that matter. Just walk on till you come to something else. Ain't you never heard of nobody having the walking blues? Well, that's what you call it when you just take off like that.

TROY: My daddy ain't had them walking blues what you talking about. He stayed right there with his family. But he was just as evil as he could be. My mama couldn't stand him . . . couldn't stand that evilness. She run off when I was about eight. She sneaked off one night after he had gone to sleep. Told me she was coming back for me. I ain't never seen her no more. All his women run off and left him. He wasn't good for nobody. When my turn come to head out, I was fourteen and got to sniffing around Joe Canewell's daughter. Had us an old mule we called Greyboy. My daddy sent me out to do some plowing and I tied up Greyboy and went to fooling around with Joe Canewell's daughter. We done found us a nice little spot, got real cozy with each other. She about thirteen and we done figured we was grown anyway, so we down there enjoying ourselves . . . ain't thinking about nothing. We didn't know Greyboy had got loose and wandered back to the house and my daddy was looking for me. We down there by the creek enjoying ourselves when my daddy come up on us, surprised us. He had them leather straps off the mule and commenced to whupping me like there was no tomorrow. I jumped up, mad and embarrassed. I was scared of my daddy. When he commenced to whupping on me, quite naturally I run to get out of the way. [Pause.] Now I thought he was mad 'cause I ain't done my work. But I see where he was chasing me off so he could have the gal for himself. When I see what the matter of it was, I lost all fear of my daddy. Right there is where I become a man . . . at fourteen years of age. [*Pause.*] Now it was my turn to run him off. I picked up the same reins that he had used on me. I picked up them reins and commenced to whupping on him. The gal jumped up and run off, and when my daddy turned to face me, I could see why the devil had never come to get him: 'cause he was the devil himself. I don't know what happened. When I woke up I was laying right there by the creek and Blue—this old dog we had—was licking my face. I thought I was blind. I couldn't see nothing. Both my eyes were swollen shut. I layed there and cried. I didn't know what I was gonna do. The only thing I knew was the time had come for me to leave my daddy's house. And right there the world suddenly got big. And it was a long time before I could cut it down to where I could handle it. Part of that cutting down was when I got to the place where I could feel him kicking in my blood and knew that the only thing that separated us was the matter of a few years.

[GABRIEL *enters from the house with a sandwich.*]

LYONS: What you got there, Uncle Gabe?

GABRIEL: Got me a ham sandwich. Rose gave me a ham sandwich.

TROY: I don't know what happened to him. I done lost touch with everybody except Gabriel. But I hope he's dead. I hope he found some peace.

LYONS: That's a heavy story, Pop. I didn't know you left home when you was fourteen?

[*The telephone rings.*]

TROY: And didn't know nothing. The only part of the world I knew was the forty-two acres of Mr. Lubin's land. That's all I knew about life.

LYONS: Fourteen's kinda young to be out on your own. I don't even think I was ready to be out on my own at fourteen. I don't know what I would have done.

TROY: I got up from the creek and walked on down to Mobile. I was through with farming. Figured I could do better in the city. So I walked the two hundred miles to Mobile.

LYONS: Wait a minute . . . you ain't walked no two hundred miles, Pop. Ain't nobody gonna walk no two hundred miles. You talking about some walking there.

BONO: That's the only way you got anywhere back in them days.

LYONS: Shhh. Damn if I wouldn't have hitched a ride with somebody.

TROY: Who you gonna hitch it with? They ain't had no cars and things like they got now. We talking about 1918.

ROSE: [*Entering.*] What you all out here getting into?

TROY: [*To* ROSE.] I'm telling Lyons how good he got it. He don't know nothing about this I'm talking.

ROSE: Lyons, that was Bonnie on the phone. She say you supposed to pick her up.

LYONS: Yeah, okay, Rose.

TROY: I walked on down to Mobile and hitched up with some of them fellows that was heading this way. Got up here and found out not only couldn't you get a job, you couldn't find no place to live. I thought I was in freedom. Shhh. Colored folks living down there on the riverbanks in whatever kind of shelter they could make for themselves. Right down there under the Brady Street Bridge. Living in shacks made of sticks an' tar paper. Messed around there and went from bad to worse. Started stealing. First it was food. Then I figured, hell, if I steal money I can buy me some food. Buy me some shoes, too. One thing led to another. Met your mama—I was young and anxious to be a man—met your mama and had you. What I do that for? Now I got to worry about feeding you and her. Got to steal three times as much. Went out one day looking for somebody to rob . . . That's what I was, a robber. I'll tell you the truth. I'm ashamed of it today. But it's the truth. Went to rob this fellow— pulled out my knife, and he pulled out a gun. Shot me in the chest. It felt just like somebody had taken a hot branding iron and laid it on me. When he shot me, I jumped at him with my knife. They tell me I killed him. They put me in the penitentiary and locked me up for fifteen years. That's where I met Bono. That's where I learned how to play baseball. Got out that place and your mama had taken you and went on to make life without me. Fifteen years was a long time for her to wait. But that fifteen years cured me of that robbing stuff. Rose'll tell you. She asked me when I met her if I had gotten all that foolishness out of my system. And I told her, "Baby, it's you and baseball all what count with me." You hear me, Bono? I meant it too. She say, "Which one comes first?" I told her, "Baby, there ain't no doubt it's baseball, but you stick and get old with me and we'll both outlive this baseball." Am I right, Rose? And it's true.

ROSE: Man, hush your mouth. You ain't said no such thing. Talking about, "Baby, you know you'll always be number one with me." That's what you was talking.

TROY: You hear that, Bono? That's why I love her.

BONO: Rose'll keep you straight. You get off the track, she'll straighten you up.

ROSE: Lyons, you better get on home and get Bonnie. She waiting on you.

LYONS: [*Getting up to go.*] Hey, Pop, why don't you come down to the Grill and hear me play?

TROY: I ain't' going down there. I got to get up in the morning. I'm too old to be sitting around in them clubs.

LYONS: You ain't got to stay long.

TROY: Naw, I'm gonna get my supper and go on to bed.

LYONS: Well, I got to go. I'll see you again.

TROY: Don't you come around here on my payday!

ROSE: Pick up the phone and let somebody know you coming. And bring

Bonnie with you. You know I'm always glad to see her.

LYONS: Yeah, I'll do that, Rose. You take care now. See you, Pop. See you, Mr. Bono. See you, Uncle Gabe.

GABRIEL: Lyons! King of the Jungle!

[LYONS *exits*.]

TROY: Is supper ready, woman? Me and you got some business to take care of. I'm gonna tear it up too!

ROSE: Troy, I done told you now!

TROY: [*Puts his arm around* BONO.] Aw hell, woman . . . this is Bono. Bono like family. I done known this nigger since . . . How long I done know you?

BONO: It's been a long time.

TROY: I done known this nigger since Skippy was a pup. Me and him done been through some times.

BONO: You sure right about that.

TROY: Hell, I done know him longer than I known you. And we still standing shoulder to shoulder. Hey, look here, Bono . . . a man can't ask for no more than that. [*Drinks to him.*] I love you, nigger.

BONO: Hell, I love you too, but I got to get home to see my woman. You got yours. I got to go get mine.

[BONO *starts to exit as* CORY *enters the yard dressed in his football uniform. He gives* TROY *a hard, uncompromising look.*]

CORY: What you do that for, Pop? [*He throws his helmet down in the direction of* TROY.]

ROSE: What's the matter? Cory, what's the matter?

CORY: Papa done went up to the school and told Coach Zellman I can't play football no more. Wouldn't even let me play the game. Told him to tell the recruiter not to come.

ROSE: Troy—

TROY: What you Troying me for. Yeah, I did it. And the boy know why I did it.

CORY: Why you wanna do that to me? This the one chance I had.

ROSE: Ain't nothing wrong with Cory playing football, Troy.

TROY: The boy lied to me, Rose. I told the nigger if he wanna play football to keep up his chores and hold down that job at the A&P. That was the conditions. Stopped down there to see Mr. Stawicki—

CORY: I can't work after school during football season, Pop! I tried to tell you that Mr. Stawicki's holding my job for me. You don't ever want to listen to nobody. And then you wanna go and do this to me!

TROY: I ain't done nothing to you. You done it to yourself.

CORY: Just 'cause you didn't have a chance! You just scared I'm gonna be better than you, that's all.

TROY: Come here.

ROSE: Troy—

[CORY *reluctantly crosses over to* TROY.]

TROY: All right! See. You done made a mistake.

CORY: I didn't even do nothing!

TROY: I'm gonna tell you what your mistake was. See . . . you swung at the
ball and didn't hit it. That's strike one. See, you in the batter's box now.
You swung and you missed. That's strike one. Don't you strike out!

[*Lights fade to black.*]

# ACT II

## Scene 1

*The following morning.* CORY *is at the tree hitting the ball with the bat. He tries to
mimic* TROY, *but his swing is awkward, less sure.* ROSE *enters from the house.*

ROSE: Cory, I want you to help me with this cupboard.

CORY: I ain't quitting the team. I don't care what Poppa say.

ROSE: I'll talk to him when he gets back. He had to go see about your Uncle
Gabe. The police done arrested him. Say he was disturbing the peace.
He'll be back directly. Come on in here and help me clean out the top
of this cupboard.

[CORY *exits into the house.* ROSE *sees* TROY *and* BONO *coming down the alley.*]

Troy, what they say down there?

TROY: Ain't said nothing. I give them fifty dollars and they let him go. I'll
talk to you about it. Where's Cory?

ROSE: He's in there helping me clean out these cupboards.

TROY: Tell him to get his butt out here.

[ROSE *exits into the house.* TROY *and* BONO *go over to the pile of wood.* BONO
*picks up the saw and begins sawing.*]

TROY: All they want is the money. That makes six or seven times I done went
down there and got him out. See me coming they stick out their hands.

BONO: Yeah, I know what you mean. That's all they care about is that money.
They don't care about what's right. [*Pause.*] Nigger, why you got to go
and get some hard wood? You ain't doing nothing but building a little
old fence. Get you some soft pine wood. That's all you need.

TROY: I know what I'm doing. This is outside wood. You put pine wood
inside the house. Pine wood is inside wood. This here is outside wood.
Now you tell me where the fence is gonna be?

BONO: You don't need this wood. You can put it up with pine wood and it'll stand as long as you gonna be here looking at it.

TROY: How you know how long I'm gonna be here, nigger? Hell, I might just live forever. Live longer than old man Horsely.

BONO: That's what Magee used to say.

TROY: Magee was a damn fool. Now you tell me who you ever heard of gonna pull their own teeth with a pair of rusty pliers?

BONO: The old folks . . . my granddaddy used to pull his teeth with pliers. They ain't had no dentists for the colored folks back then.

TROY: Get clean pliers! You understand? Clean pliers! Sterilize them! Besides we ain't living back then. All Magee had to do was walk over to Doc Goldblums.

BONO: I see you and that Tallahassee gal—that Alberta—I see you all done got tight.

TROY: What you mean "got tight"?

BONO: I see where you be laughing and joking with her all the time.

TROY: I laughs and jokes with all of them, Bono. You know me.

BONO: That ain't the kind of laughing and joking I'm talking about.

[CORY *enters from the house.*]

CORY: How you doing, Mr. Bono?

BONO: How you doing, Cory?

TROY: Get that saw from Bono and cut some wood. He talking about the wood's too hard to cut. Stand back there, Jim, and let that young boy show you how it's done.

BONO: He's sure welcome to it.

[CORY *takes the saw and begins to cut the wood.*]

Look at that. Big old strong boy. Look like Joe Louis. Hell, I must be getting old the way I'm watching that boy whip through that wood.

CORY: I don't see why Mama want a fence around the yard noways.

TROY: Damn if I know either. What the hell she keeping out with it? She ain't got nothing nobody want.

BONO: Some people build fences to keep people out . . . and some people build fences to keep people in. Rose wants to hold on to you all. She loves you.

TROY: Hell, nigger, I don't need nobody to tell me my wife loves me. Cory, go on in the house and see if you can find that other saw.

CORY: Where's it at?

TROY: I said find it! Look for it till you find it.

[CORY *exits into the house.*]

What's that supposed to mean? Wanna keep us in?

BONO: Troy, I done known you seem like damn near all my life. You and

Rose both. I done known both of you all for a long time. I remember when you met Rose. When you was hitting them baseballs out the park. A lot of them old gals was after you then, You had the pick of the litter. When you picked Rose, I was happy for you. That was the first time I knew you had any sense. I said, "My man Troy knows what he's doing; I'm gonna follow this nigger, he might take me somewhere." I been following you too. I done learned a whole heap of things about life watching you. I done learned how to tell where the shit lies, how to tell it from the alfalfa. You done learned me a lot of things. You showed me how to not make the same mistakes, to take life as it comes along and keep putting one foot in front of the other. [*Pause.*] Rose a good woman, Troy.

TROY: Hell, nigger, I know she a good woman. I been married to her for eighteen years. What you got on your mind, Bono?

BONO: I just say she a good woman. Just like I say anything. I ain't got to have nothing on my mind.

TROY: You just gonna say she a good woman and leave it hanging out there like that? Why, you telling me she a good woman?

BONO: She loves you, Troy. Rose loves you.

TROY: You saying I don't measure up. That's what you trying to say. I don't measure up 'cause I'm seeing this other gal. I know what you trying to say.

BONO: I know what Rose means to you, Troy. I'm just trying to say I don't want to see you mess up.

TROY: Yeah, I appreciate that, Bono. If you was messing around on Lucille, I'd be telling you the same thing.

BONO: Well, that's all I got to say. I just say that because I love you both.

TROY: Hell, you know me . . . I wasn't out there looking for nothing. You can't find a better woman than Rose. I know that. But seems like this woman just stuck on to me where I can't shake her loose. I done wrestled with it, tried to throw her off me, but she just stuck tighter. Now she's stuck on for good.

BONO: You's in control . . . that's what you tell me all the time. You responsible for what you do.

TROY: I ain't ducking the responsibility of it. As long as it sets right in my heart, then I'm okay. 'Cause that's all I listen to. It'll tell me right from wrong every time. And I ain't talking about doing Rose no bad turn. I love Rose. She done carried me a long ways and I love and respect her for that.

BONO: I know you do. That's why I don't want to see you hurt her. But what you gonna do when she find out? What you got then? If you try and juggle both of them, sooner or later you gonna drop one of them. That's common sense.

TROY: Yeah, I hear what you saying, Bono. I been trying to figure a way to work it out.

BONO: Work it out right, Troy. I don't want to be getting all up between you and Rose's business, but work it so it come out right.

TROY: Aw hell, I get all up between you and Lucille's business. When you gonna get that woman that refrigerator she been wanting? Don't tell me you ain't got no money now. I know who your banker is. Mellon don't need that money bad as Lucille want that refrigerator. I'll tell you that.

BONO: Tell you what I'll do. When you finish building this fence for Rose, I'll buy Lucille that refrigerator.

TROY: You done stuck your foot in your mouth now!

[TROY *grabs up a board and begins to saw.* BONO *starts to walk out the yard.*]

Hey, nigger . . . where you going?

BONO: I'm going home. I know you don't expect me to help you now. I'm protecting my money. I wanna see you put that fence up by yourself. That's what I want to see. You'll be here another six months without me.

TROY: Nigger, you ain't right.

BONO: When it comes to my money, I'm right as fireworks on the Fourth of July.

TROY: All right, we gonna see now. You better get out your bank book.

[BONO *exits, and* TROY *continues to work.* ROSE *enters from the house.*]

ROSE: What they say down there? What's happening with Gabe?

TROY: I went down there and got him out. Cost me fifty dollars. Say he was disturbing the peace. Judge set up a hearing for him in three weeks. Say to show cause why he shouldn't be recommitted.

ROSE: What was he doing that cause them to arrest him?

TROY: Some kids was teasing him and he run them off home. Say he was howling and carrying on. Some folks seen him and called the police. That's all it was.

ROSE: Well, what'd you say? What'd you tell the judge?

TROY: Told him I'd look after him. It didn't make no sense to recommit the man. He stuck out his big greasy palm and told me to give him fifty dollars and take him on home.

ROSE: Where's he at now? Where'd he go off to?

TROY: I ain't the man's keeper. He's gone on about his business. He don't need nobody to hold his hand.

ROSE: Well, I don't know. Seem like that would be the best place for him if they did put him into the hospital. I know what you're gonna say. But that's what I think would be best.

TROY: I'm gonna go down there and show cause all right. The man done had his life ruined fighting for what? And they wanna take and lock him up. Let him be free. He don't bother nobody.

ROSE: Well, everybody got their own way of looking at it, I guess. Come on and get your lunch. I got a bowl of lima beans and some cornbread in the oven. Come on get something to eat. Ain't no sense you fretting over Gabe. [ROSE *turns to go into the house.*]

TROY: Rose, I got something to tell you.

ROSE: Well, come on, wait till I get this food on the table.

TROY: Rose!

[*She stops and turns around.*]

I don't know how to say this. [*Pause.*] I can't explain it none. It just sort of grows on you till it gets out of hand. It starts out like a little bush . . . and the next thing you know it's a whole forest.

ROSE: Troy . . . what are you talking about?

TROY: I'm talking, woman, let me talk. I'm trying to find a way to tell you . . . I'm gonna be a daddy. I'm gonna be somebody's daddy.

ROSE: Troy . . you're not telling me this? You're gonna be . . . what?

TROY: Rose . . . now . . . see . . .

ROSE: You telling me you gonna be somebody's daddy? You telling your *wife* this?

[GABRIEL *enters from the street. He carries a rose in his hand.*]

GABRIEL: Hey, Troy! Hey, Rose!

ROSE: I have to wait eighteen years to hear something like this.

GABRIEL: Hey, Rose . . . got a flower for you. [*He hands it to her.*] That's a rose. Same rose like what you is.

ROSE: Thanks, Gabe.

GABRIEL: Troy, you ain't mad at me, is you? Them bad mens come and put me away. You ain't mad at me, is you?

TROY: Naw, Gabe, I ain't mad at you.

ROSE: Eighteen years and you wanna come with this.

GABRIEL: [*Takes a quarter out of his pocket.*] See what I got? Got a brand-new quarter.

TROY: Rose, it's just—

ROSE: Ain't nothing you can say, Troy. Ain't no way of explaining that.

GABRIEL: Fellow that give me this quarter had a whole mess of them. I'm gonna keep this quarter till it stops shining.

ROSE: Gabe, go on in the house there. I got some watermelon in the frigidaire. Go on and get you a piece.

GABRIEL: Say, Rose . . . you know I was chasing hellhounds and them bad mens come and get me and take me away. Troy helped me. He come down there and told them they better let me go before he beat them up. Yeah, he did!

ROSE: You go on and get you a piece of watermelon, Gabe. Them bad mens is gone now.

GABRIEL: Okay, Rose . . . gonna get me some watermelon. The kind with the stripes on it. [GABRIEL *exits into the house.*]

ROSE: Why, Troy? Why? After all these years to come dragging this in to me now. It don't make no sense at your age. I could have expected this ten or fifteen years ago, but not now.

TROY: Age ain't got nothing to do with it, Rose.

ROSE: I done tried to be everything a wife should be. Everything a wife could be. Been married eighteen years and I got to live to see the day you tell me you been seeing another woman and done fathered a child by her. And you know I ain't never wanted no half-nothing in my family. My whole family is half. Everybody got different fathers and mothers . . . my two sisters and my brother. Can't hardly tell who's who. Can't never sit down and talk about Papa and Mama. It's your papa and your mama and my papa and my mama—

TROY: Rose, stop it now.

ROSE: I ain't never wanted that for none of my children. And now you wanna drag your behind in here and tell me something like this.

TROY: You ought to know. It's time for you to know.

ROSE: Well, I don't want to know, goddamn it!

TROY: I can't just make it go away. It's done now. I can't wish the circumstances of the thing away.

ROSE: And you don't want to either. Maybe you want to wish me and my boy away. Maybe that's what you want? Well, you can't wish us away. I've got eighteen years of my life invested in you. You ought to have stayed upstairs in my bed, where you belong.

TROY: Rose, now listen to me, we can get a handle on this thing. We can talk this out, come to an understanding.

ROSE: All of a sudden it's "we." Where was "we" at when you was down there rolling around with some Godforsaken woman? "We" should have come to an understanding before you started making a damn fool of yourself. You're a day late and a dollar short when it comes to an understanding with me.

TROY: It's just . . . She gives me a different idea, a different understanding about myself. I can step out of this house and get away from the pressures and problems . . . be a different man. I ain't got to wonder how I'm gonna pay the bills or get the roof fixed. I can just be a part of myself that I ain't never been.

ROSE: What I want to know is, do you plan to continue seeing her? That's all you can say to me.

TROY: I can sit up in her house and laugh. Do you understand what I'm saying. I can laugh out loud . . . and it feels good. It reaches all the way down to the bottom of my shoes. [*Pause.*] Rose, I can't give that up.

ROSE: Maybe you ought to go on and stay down there with her . . . if she a better woman than me.

TROY: It ain't about nobody being a better woman or nothing. You ain't the blame, Rose. A man couldn't ask for no woman to be a better wife than you've been. I'm responsible for it. I done locked myself into a pattern trying to take care of you all that I forgot about myself.

ROSE: What the hell was I there for? That was my job, not somebody else's.

TROY: Rose, I done tried all my life to live decent . . . to live a clean, hard, useful life. I tried to be a good husband to you. In every way I knew. Maybe I come into the world backwards, I don't know. But you born with two strikes on you before you come to the plate. You got to guard it closely . . . looking for the curveball on the inside corner. You can't afford to let none get past you. You can't afford a call strike. If you going down, you going down swinging. Everything lined up against you. What you gonna do? I fooled them, Rose. I bunted. When I found you and Cory and a halfway decent job, I was safe. Couldn't nothing touch me. I wasn't gonna strike out no more. I wasn't going back to the penitentiary. I wasn't gonna lay in the streets with a bottle of wine. I was safe. I had me a family. A job. I wasn't gonna get that last strike. I was on first looking for one of them boys to knock me in. To get me home.

ROSE: You should have stayed in my bed, Troy.

TROY: Then, when I saw that gal, she firmed up my backbone. And I got to thinking that if I tried, I just might be able to steal second. Do you understand . . . after eighteen years I wanted to steal second.

ROSE: You should have held me tight. You should have grabbed me and held on.

TROY: I stood on first base for eighteen years and I thought . . . Well, goddamn it, go on for it!

ROSE: We're not talking about baseball! We're talking about you going off to lay in bed with another woman . . . and then bring it home to me. That's what we're talking about. We ain't talking about baseball.

TROY: Rose, you're not listening to me. I'm trying the best I can to explain it to you. It's not easy for me to admit that I been standing in the same place for eighteen years.

ROSE: I been standing with you! I been right here with you, Troy. I got a life too. I gave eighteen years of my life to stand in the same spot with you. Don't you think I ever wanted other things? Don't you think I had dreams and hopes? What about my life? What about me? Don't you think it ever crossed my mind to want to know other men? That I wanted to lay up somewhere and forget about my responsibilities? That I wanted someone to make me laugh so I could feel good? You not the only one who's got wants and needs. But I held on to you, Troy. I took all my feelings, my wants and needs, my dreams, and I buried them inside you. I planted a seed and watched and prayed over it. I planted myself inside you and waited to bloom. And it didn't take me no eighteen years to find out the soil was hard and rocky and it wasn't never gonna bloom. But I held on to you, Troy. I held you tighter. You was my husband. I owed you everything I had. Every part of me I could find to give you. And upstairs in that room, with the darkness falling in on me, I gave everything I had to try and erase the doubt that you wasn't the finest man in the world. And wherever you was going I wanted to be there with you. 'Cause you was my husband, 'cause that's the only way I was gonna survive as your wife. You always talking about what you give and what you don't have to give. But you take too. You take and don't even know nobody's giving!

[ROSE *turns to exit into the house;* TROY *grabs her arm.*]

TROY: You're gonna listen to me. It ain't like what you saying!
ROSE: Troy, let go of my arm. You're hurting me.
TROY: You say I take and don't give.
ROSE: Troy, you're hurting my arm. Let go.
TROY: I done give you everything I got. Don't you tell me about not taking and giving. Don't you tell that lie on me.
ROSE: Troy!
TROY: Don't you tell that lie on me!

[CORY *enters from the house.*]

CORY: Mama!
ROSE: Troy, you're hurting me.
TROY: Don't you tell me about no taking and giving.

[CORY *comes up behind* TROY *and grabs him.* TROY, *surprised, is thrown off balance just as* CORY *throws a glancing blow that catches him on the chest and knocks him down.* TROY *is stunned, as is* CORY.]

ROSE: Troy. Troy. NO!

[TROY *gets to his feet and starts at* CORY.]

Troy . . . no. Please! Troy!

[ROSE *pulls on* TROY *to hold him back.* TROY *stops himself.*]

TROY: [*To* CORY.] All right. That's strike two. You stay away from around me, boy. Don't you strike out. You living with a full count. Don't you strike out.

[TROY *exits out the yard as the lights go down.*]

Scene 2

*It is six months later, early afternoon.* TROY *enters from the house and starts to exit the yard.* ROSE *enters from the house.*

ROSE: Troy, I want to talk to you.
TROY: All of a sudden, after all this time, you want to talk to me, huh? You ain't wanted to talk to me for months. You ain't wanted to talk to me

last night. You ain't wanted no part of me then. What you wanna talk to me about now?

ROSE: Tomorrow's Friday.

TROY: I know what day tomorrow is. You think I don't know tomorrow's Friday? My whole life I ain't done nothing but look to see Friday coming, and you got to tell me it's Friday.

ROSE: I want to know if you're coming home.

TROY: I always come home, Rose. You know that. There ain't never been a night I ain't come home.

ROSE: That ain't what I mean, Troy, and you know it. I want to know if you're coming straight home after work.

TROY: I figure I'd cash my check, hang out at Taylor's with the fellows . . . maybe play a game of checkers.

ROSE: Troy, I can't live like this. I won't live like this. It's been going on six months now you ain't been coming home.

TROY: I be here every night. Every night of the year. That's 365 days.

ROSE: I want you to come home tomorrow after work.

TROY: Rose, I don't mess up my pay. You know that now. I take my pay and I give it to you. I don't have no money but what you give me back. I just want to have a little time to myself . . . a little time to enjoy life.

ROSE: What about me? When's my time to enjoy life?

TROY: I don't know what to tell you, Rose. I'm doing the best I can do.

ROSE: You ain't been home from work but time enough to change your clothes and run out . . . and you wanna call that the best you can do?

TROY: I'm going over to the hospital to see Alberta. She went into the hospital this afternoon. Look like she might have the baby early. I won't be gone long.

ROSE: Well, you ought to know. . . . They went over to Miss Pearl's and got Gabe today. She said you told them to go ahead and lock him up.

TROY: I ain't said no such thing. Whoever told you that is a liar. Miss Pearl ain't doing nothing but telling a big fat lie.

ROSE: She ain't had to tell me. I read it on the papers.

TROY: I ain't told them nothing of the kind.

ROSE: I saw it right there on the papers.

TROY: What it say, huh? What it say?

ROSE: It said you told them to take him.

TROY: They got that all screwed up. The way they screw up everything. I ain't worried about what they got on the paper.

ROSE: Say the government send part of his check to the hospital and the other part to you.

TROY: I ain't got nothing to do with that if that's the way it works. I ain't made up the rules about how it work.

ROSE: You did Gabe just like you did Cory. You wouldn't sign the paper for Cory, but you signed for Gabe. You signed that paper.

[*The telephone is heard ringing inside the house.*]

TROY: I told you I ain't signed nothing, woman. The only thing I signed was the release form. I ain't signed nothing about sending Gabe away.

ROSE: I said send him to the hospital—you said let him be free—now you done went down there and signed him to the hospital for half his money. You went back on yourself, Troy. You gonna have to answer for that. [ROSE *exits into the house to answer the phone.*]

TROY: [*Calling after her.*] See now . . . you been over there talking to Miss Pearl. She done got mad 'cause she ain't getting Gabe's rent money. That's all it is. She's liable to say anything.

ROSE: [*From inside the house.*] Troy, I seen where you signed the paper.

TROY: What she doing got papers on my brother anyway? Miss Pearl telling a big fat lie. And I'm gonna tell her about it too!

[TROY *paces about the yard. Presently* ROSE *enters.*]

You ain't seen nothing I signed.

ROSE: Troy, that was the hospital. Alberta had the baby.

TROY: What she have? What is it?

ROSE: It's a girl.

TROY: I better get on down to the hospital to see her.

ROSE: Troy . . .

TROY: Rose, I got to go see her now. That's only right. What's the matter? The baby's all right, ain't it?

ROSE: Alberta died having the baby.

TROY: Died? You say she's dead? Alberta's dead?

ROSE: They said they done all they could. They couldn't do nothing for her.

TROY: The baby? How's the baby?

ROSE: They say it's healthy.

TROY: [*More to himself than* ROSE.] I had that sickle in my hand. I just didn't throw it far enough.

ROSE: I wonder who's gonna bury her?

TROY: She had family, Rose. She wasn't living in the world by herself.

ROSE: I know she wasn't living in the world by herself.

TROY: Next thing you gonna want to know if she had any insurance.

ROSE: Troy, you ain't got to talk like that.

TROY: That's the first thing that jumped out your mouth. "Who's gonna bury her?" Like I'm fixing to take on that task for myself.

ROSE: I am your wife. Don't push me away.

TROY: I ain't pushing nobody away. Just give me some space. That's all. Just give me some room to breathe.

[ROSE *exits into the house.* TROY *walks about the yard.*]

TROY: [*With a quiet rage that threatens to consume him.*] All right, Mr. Death. See now . . . I'm gonna tell you what I'm gonna do. I'm gonna take and build me a fence around this yard. See? I'm gonna build me a fence around what belongs to me. And then I want you to stay on the other side. See? You stay over there until you're ready for me. Then you come on. Bring your army. Bring your sickle. Bring your wrestling clothes. I ain't gonna fall down on my vigilance this time. You ain't gonna sneak up on me no more. When you ready for me, when the top of your list say Troy Maxson, that's when you come around here. You come up and knock on the front door and ask for me. Then we gonna find out what manner of man you are. Ain't nobody else got nothing to do with this. This is between you and me. Man to man. You stay on the other side of that fence until you ready for me. Then you come up and knock on the front door. Anytime you want. I'll be ready for you.

[*The lights go down to black.*]


Scene 3

*The lights come up on the porch. It is late evening three days later.* ROSE *sits listening to the ball game waiting for* TROY. *The final out of the game is made and* ROSE *switches off the radio and enters the house. Presently* TROY: *enters the yard carrying an infant wrapped in blankets. He stands back from the house and calls.*

TROY: Rose . . . Rose!

[ROSE *enters and stands on the porch. There is a long, awkward silence, the weight of which grows heavier with each passing second.*]

Rose . . . I'm standing here with my daughter in my arms. She ain't but a wee bitty little old thing. She don't know nothing about grown-ups' business. She innocent . . . and she ain't got no mamma.
ROSE: What you telling me for, Troy? [*She turns and exits into the house.*]
TROY: Well . . . I guess we'll just sit out here on the porch. [*He sits down on the porch. There is an awkward indelicateness about the way he handles the baby. His largeness engulfs and seems to swallow it. He speaks loud enough for* ROSE *to hear.*] A man's got to do what's right for him. I ain't sorry for nothing I done. It felt right in my heart, and if it set right there, a man can't be blamed. [*To the baby.*] Ain't that right? What you smiling at? You smiling 'cause your daddy's telling the truth? Your daddy's a big man. Got these great big old hands. But sometimes he's scared. And right now your daddy's scared 'cause we sitting out here and ain't got no home. Oh, I been homeless before. I ain't had no little baby with me. But I been homeless. You just be out on the road by your lonesome and you see one of them trains coming and you just kinda go like this.

[*He sings as a lullaby.*]
Please, Mr. Engineer, let a man ride the line

Please, Mr. Engineer, let a man ride the line
I ain't got no ticket, please let me ride the blinds

[ROSE *enters from the house.* TROY, *hearing her steps behind him, stands and faces her.*]

She's my daughter, Rose. My own flesh and blood. I can't deny her no more than I can deny them boys. We's the same. They my children. [*Pause.*] You and them boys is my family. You and them and this child is all I got in the world. World get so big sometimes a man can't hardly wrestle with it none. He need some help. This here little bitty thing is my daughter. I don't know too much about babies. So I guess what I'm saying is, I'd appreciate it if you'd help me take care of her.

ROSE: Okay, Troy. You're right. I'll take care of your baby for you 'cause, like you say, she's innocent and you can't visit the sins of the father upon the child. A motherless child has got a hard time. [*She takes the baby from him.*] From right now . . . this child got a mother. But you a womanless man.

[ROSE *turns and exits into the house with the baby. Lights go down to black.*]

## Scene 4

*It is two months later.* LYONS *enters from the street. He knocks on the door and calls.*

LYONS: Hey, Rose! [*Pause.*] Rose!
ROSE: [*From inside the house.*] Stop all that hollering. You gonna wake up Raynell. I just got her to sleep.
LYONS: I just stopped by to pay Papa this twenty dollars I owe him. Where's everybody at?
ROSE: He should be here in a minute. I'm getting ready to go down to the church. Sit down and wait on him.
LYONS: I got to go pick up Bonnie over her mother's house.
ROSE: Well, sit it down there on the table. He'll get it.
LYONS: [*Enters the house and sets the money on the table.*] Tell Papa I said thanks. I'll see you again.
ROSE: All right, Lyons. We'll see you.

[LYONS *starts to exit as* CORY *enters.*]

CORY: Hey, Lyons.
LYONS: What's happening, Cory. Say man, I'm sorry I missed your graduation. You know I had a gig and couldn't get away. Otherwise you know I would have been there. So what you doing?
CORY: I'm trying to find a job.
LYONS: I know how that go. It's rough out here. Jobs are scarce.
CORY: Yeah, I know. I been looking all over.

LYONS: Look here, I got to run. Talk to Papa . . . he know some people. He'll be able to help get you a job. Talk to him . . . see what he say.

CORY: Yeah, okay, Lyons.

LYONS: You take care. I'll talk to you soon. We'll find some time to talk.

[LYONS *exits the yard.* CORY *wanders over to the tree, picks up the bat and assumes a batting stance. He studies an imaginary pitcher and swings. Dissatisfied with the result, he tries again.* TROY *enters. They eye each other for a beat.* CORY *puts the bat down and exits the yard.* TROY *starts into the house as* ROSE *exits with* RAYNELL. *She is carrying a cake.*]

TROY: I'm coming in and everybody's going out.

ROSE: I'm taking this cake down to the church for the bake sale. Lyons was by to see you. He stopped by to pay you your twenty dollars. It's laying in there on the table.

TROY: [*Going into his pocket.*] Well, here go this money.

ROSE: Put it there on the table, Troy. I'll get it.

TROY: What time you coming back?

ROSE: Ain't no use in you studying me. It don't matter what time I come back.

TROY: I just asked you a question, woman. What's the matter . . . can't I ask you a question?

ROSE: Troy, I don't want to go into it. Your dinner's in there on the stove. All you got to do is heat it up. And don't you be eating the rest of them cakes in there. I'm coming back for them. We having a bake sale at the church tomorrow.

[ROSE *exits the yard.* TROY *sits down on the steps, takes a pint bottle from his pocket, opens it, and drinks. He begins to sing.*]

[TROY]
Had an old dog his name was Blue
You know Blue was a good old dog
Blue treed a possum in a hollow log
You know from that he was a good old dog.

[BONO *enters the yard.*]

BONO: Hey, Troy.

TROY: Hey, what's happening, Bono?

BONO: I just thought I'd stop by to see you.

TROY: What you stop by and see me for? You ain't stopped by in a month of Sundays. Hell, I must owe you money or something.

BONO: Since you got your promotion I can't keep up with you. Used to see you every day. Now I don't even know what route you working.

TROY: They keep switching me around. Got me out in Greentree now . . . hauling white folks' garbage.

BONO: Greentree, huh? Well, at least you ain't got to be lifting them barrels. Damn if they ain't getting heavier. I'm gonna put in my two years and call it quits.

TROY: I'm thinking about retiring myself. How's Lucille?

BONO: She all right. Her arthritis get to acting up on her sometime. Saw Rose on my way in. She going down to the church, huh?

TROY: Yeah, she took up going down there. All them preachers looking for somebody to fatten their pockets. [*Pause.*] Got some gin here.

BONO: Naw, thanks. I just stopped by to say hello.

TROY: Hell, nigger, you can take a drink. I ain't never known you to say no to a drink. You ain't got to work tomorrow.

BONO: I just stopped by. I'm fixing to go over to Skinner's. We got us a domino game going over his house every Friday.

TROY: Nigger, you can't play no dominoes. I used to whup you four games out of five.

BONO: Well, that learned me. I'm getting better.

TROY: Yeah? Well, that's all right. You sure had a good teacher.

BONO: Look here . . . I got to be getting on. Stop by sometime, huh?

TROY: Yeah, I'll do that, Bono. Lucille told Rose you bought her a new refrigerator.

BONO: Yeah, I finally broke down on that score.

TROY: I knew you would. I knew she'd get you.

BONO: Yeah . . . okay. I'll be talking to you.

TROY: Yeah, take care, Bono. Good to see you. I'm gonna stop over.

BONO: Yeah, okay, Troy. [BONO *exits.*]

> [TROY *drinks from the bottle and sings.*]
> Old Blue's feets was big and round
> Never 'llowed a possum to touch the ground
> Old Blue died and I dig his grave
> Let him down with a golden chain
> Every night when I hear old Blue bark
> I know Blue treed a possum in Noah's Ark.

[CORY *enters the yard. They eye each other for a beat.* TROY *is sitting in the middle of the steps.* CORY *walks over.*]

CORY: I got to get by.

TROY: Say what? What's you say?

CORY: You in my way. I got to get by.

TROY: You got to get by where? This is my house. Bought and paid for. In full. Took me fifteen years. And if you wanna go in my house and I'm sitting on the steps you say excuse me. Like your mama taught you.

CORY: Come on, Pop . . . I got to get by.

[CORY *starts to maneuver his way past* TROY. TROY *grabs his leg and shoves him back.*]

TROY: You just gonna walk over top of me?

CORY: I live here too!

TROY: [*Advancing toward him.*] You just gonna walk over top of me in my own house?

CORY: I ain't scared of you.

TROY: I ain't asked if you was scared of me. I asked you if you was fixing to walk over top of me in my own house? That's the question. You ain't gonna say excuse me? You just gonna walk over top of me?

CORY: If you wanna put it like that.

TROY: How else am I gonna put it?

CORY: I was walking by you to go into the house 'cause you sitting on the steps drunk, singing to yourself. You can put it like that.

TROY: Without saying excuse me?

[CORY *doesn't respond.*]

I asked you a question. Without saying excuse me?

CORY: I ain't got to say excuse me to you. You don't count around here no more.

TROY: Oh, I see . . . I don't count around here no more. You ain't got to say excuse me to your daddy. All of a sudden you done got so grown that your daddy don't count around here no more. Around here in his own house and yard that he done paid for with the sweat of his brow. You done got so grown to where you gonna take over. You gonna take over my house. Is that right? You gonna wear my pants. You gonna go in there and stretch out on my bed. You ain't got to say excuse me 'cause I don't count around here no more. Is that right?

CORY: That's right. You always talking this dumb stuff. Now, why don't you just get out my way.

TROY: I guess you got someplace to sleep and something to put in your belly. You got that, huh? You got that? That's what you need. You got that, huh?

CORY: You don't know what I got. You ain't got to worry about what I got.

TROY: You right! You one hundred percent right! I done spent the last seventeen years worrying about what you got. Now it's your turn, see? I'll tell you what you do. You grown . . . we done established that. You a man. Now, let's see you act like one. Turn your behind around and walk out this yard. And when you get out there in the alley, you can forget about this house. See? 'Cause this is my house. You go on and be a man and get your own house. You can forget about this. 'Cause this is mine. You go on and get yours 'cause I'm through with doing for you.

CORY: You talking about what you did for me . . . What'd you ever give me?

TROY: Them feet and bones! That pumping heart! I give you more than anybody else is ever gonna give you.

CORY: You ain't never gave me nothing. You ain't never done nothing but hold me back. Afraid I was gonna be better than you. All you ever did was try and make me scared of you. I used to tremble every time you called my name. Every time I heard your footsteps in the house. Wondering all the time, What's Papa gonna say if I do this? What's he gonna say if I do that? What's Papa gonna say if I turn on the radio? And Mama, too—she tries, but she's scared of you.

TROY: You leave your mama out of this. She ain't got nothing to do with this.

CORY: I don't know how she stands you . . . after what you did to her.

TROY: I told you to leave your mama out of this! [*He advances toward* CORY.]

CORY: What you gonna do . . . give me a whupping? You can't whup me no more. You're too old. You just an old man.

TROY: [*Shoves him on his shoulder.*] Nigger! That's what you are. You just another nigger on the street to me!

CORY: You crazy! You know that?

TROY: Go on now! You got the devil in you. Get on away from me!

CORY: You just a crazy old man . . . talking about I got the devil in me.

TROY: Yeah, I'm crazy! If you don't get on the other side of that yard, I'm gonna show you how crazy I am! Go on . . . get out my yard.

CORY: It ain't your yard. You took Uncle Gabe's money he got from the army to buy the house . . . and then you put him out.

TROY: [*Advances to him.*] You get your black ass out my yard!

[TROY's *advance backs* CORY *up against the tree.* CORY *grabs up the bat.*]

CORY: I ain't going nowhere! Come on . . . put me out! I ain't scared of you.

TROY: That's my bat! Put my bat down!

CORY: Come on! Put me out.

[TROY *stops his advance.*]

CORY: What's the matter? You so bad . . . put me out!

TROY: That's strike three. You done struck out now. All right! Let's see what you gonna do now!

CORY: [*Backing up.*] Come on! Come on!

TROY: You gonna have to use it. You want to draw back that bat on me . . . you gonna have to use it.

[CORY *has retreated to the alley as* ROSE *enters carrying the baby.*]

ROSE: Cory! What you doing with that bat?

TROY: [*To* CORY.] Go on . . . don't you come around here no more.

ROSE: Troy, what's going on?

TROY: Rose, this boy don't live here no more. If he want to come back in here, he's gonna have to use that bat. [*To* CORY.] Go on! Get on away from around my house.

CORY: [*Throws the bat down in* TROY's *direction.*] I'll be back for my things, Mama.

TROY: They better be out there on the other side of that yard.

[CORY *exits down the alley.* TROY *watches after him.*]

ROSE: Cory! Troy, you just can't put the boy out like that.

TROY: I don't want to hear it, Rose, I promised myself when the day come that boy want to get up in my face and challenge me, he going on away from here. So I don't want to hear nothing you got to say.

[ROSE *turns and exits into the house.*]

'Cause it don't matter no more. I can't taste nothing. Hallelujah! I can't taste nothing no more!

[*The lights fade to black.*]

## Scene 5

*The time is 1965. An unpainted, weather-beaten fence surrounds the house.* RAYNELL, *a rather tall, gangly girl of seven, barefoot and wearing a flannel nightgown, enters the yard and crosses over to a small plot of ground off to the side. The screen door bangs shut.* ROSE *calls from the house.*

ROSE: Raynell!

RAYNELL: Mam?

ROSE: What you doing out there?

RAYNELL: Nothing.

ROSE: [*Coming to the door.*] Girl, get in here and get your shoes on. What you doing?

RAYNELL: Seeing if my garden growed.

ROSE: I told you it ain't gonna grow overnight. You got to wait.

RAYNELL: It don't look like it never gonna grow, dag!

ROSE: I told you a watched pot never boils. Get in here and get your shoes on.

RAYNELL: This ain't even no pot, Mama!

ROSE: You got to give it a chance. It'll grow. Now you come on and do what I told you. We got to be getting ready. This ain't no morning to be playing around. Hear me?

RAYNELL: Yes, mam.

[ROSE *turns and goes into the house.* RAYNELL *pokes at her garden with a stick.* CORY *enters. He is dressed in a Marine sergeant's uniform and carries a duffel bag. His posture is that of a military man and his speech has a clipped sternness.*]

CORY: Hi. [*Pause.*] I bet your name is Raynell.

RAYNELL: Uh huh.

CORY: Is your mama home?

[RAYNELL *runs up on the porch to the screen door.*]

RAYNELL: Mama . . . there's some man out here. Mama?

[ROSE *comes to the door.*]

ROSE: Cory? Lord have mercy! [ROSE *and* CORY *embrace in a tearful reunion.*] Look at you. My goodness . . . just look at you.

CORY: How have you been, Mama? It's good to see you.

ROSE: If you ain't a sight for sore eyes! Done got all grown up.

CORY: Don't cry, Mama. What you crying about?

ROSE: I'm just so glad to see you. I didn't know if you was gonna make it or not. What took you so long?

CORY: You know how the Marines are, Mama. They have to have all their paperwork straight before they let you do anything.

ROSE: You seen Raynell? Isn't she grown? Raynell?

RAYNELL: Mam?

ROSE: Come here and say hello to your brother. Come on . . . this is your brother, Cory. You remember Cory?

RAYNELL: No, mam.

CORY: She don't remember me, Mama.

ROSE: Well, we talk about you. She heard us talk about you. [*To* RAYNELL.] This is your brother, Cory. Come on and say hello.

RAYNELL: Hi.

CORY: Hi. So you're Raynell. Mama told me a lot about you.

ROSE: Now, you go on in there and put your shoes on and lay out that dress like I told you.

RAYNELL: Mama, it's too big. Can't I wear the other one with the bow?

ROSE: Don't you give me no sass now. You go on and do what I told you.

RAYNELL: [*As she exits.*] Yes, mam.

ROSE: She's a good girl. She give me a little back talk every now and then. But she's a good child. [*Pause.*] I was hoping you'd bring your girlfriend so I could get a chance to meet her.

CORY: She had to work. She told me to tell you hello and she'd meet you some other time.

ROSE: Well, I'm sure glad you made it. I done called up there about Lyons. They say they gonna let him come. Gabriel's still in the hospital. I don't know if they gonna let him come or not. If it wasn't for Jim Bono and Miss Pearl I don't know how I would have made it these past few days. Ain't had nobody but me. And Raynell . . . she too young to understand. I try to get down to see Lyons every chance I get. But with working and taking care of Raynell and going to church and whatnot . . . there just ain't that many hours in the day.

CORY: I didn't know you was working, Mama.

ROSE: Ain't been but about a year or so. Your daddy retired and I got tired of sitting in the house doing nothing. The ward chairman got me on down there cleaning up at the courthouse. I could have got Miss Pearl to write and tell you, but her arthritis got so bad I hate to ask her anymore.

CORY: I see you got your fence built.

ROSE: Oh, that's been up there ever since Raynell wasn't but a wee little bitty old thing. Your daddy finally got around to putting that up to keep her in the yard. The thing's near about fallen down now. Ain't too much else changed. He still got that old piece of rag tied to that tree. He was out here swinging that bat. I was just ready to go back in the house. He swung that bat and then he just fell over. Seem like he swung it and stood there with this grin on his face . . . and then he just fell over. They carried him on down to the hospital, but I knew there wasn't no need.

CORY: Mama . . . I don't know how to tell you this, but I've got to tell you. I'm not going to Papa's funeral.

ROSE: Boy, hush your mouth. That's your daddy you're talking about. I don't wanna hear that kind of talk this morning. I done raised you to come to this? You standing there all healthy and grown talking about you ain't going to your daddy's funeral?

CORY: Mama, listen . . .

ROSE: I don't want to hear it, Cory. You just get that thought out your head.

CORY: I can't drag Papa with me everywhere I go. I've got to say no to him. One time in my life I've got to say no.

ROSE: Don't nobody have to listen to nothing like that. I know you and your daddy ain't seen eye to eye, but I ain't got to listen to that kind of talk this morning. Whatever was between you and your daddy . . . the time has come to put it aside. Just take it and set it over there on the shelf and forget about it. Disrespecting your daddy ain't gonna make you a man, Cory. You got to find a way to come to that on your own. Not going to your daddy's funeral ain't gonna make you a man.

CORY: The whole time I was growing up, living in his house, Papa was like a shadow that followed you everywhere. It weighed on you and sunk in your flesh. It would wrap around you and lay there until you couldn't tell which one was you anymore. That shadow digging in your flesh. Trying to crawl in. Trying to live through you. Everywhere I looked Troy Maxson was staring back at me: hiding under the bed, in the closet. I'm just saying I've got to find a way to get rid of that shadow, Mama.

ROSE: You just like him. You got him in you good.

CORY: Don't tell me that, Mama.

TROY: You Troy Maxson all over again.

CORY: I don't want to be Troy Maxson. I want to be me.

ROSE: You can't be nobody but who you are, Cory. That shadow wasn't nothing but you growing into yourself. You either got to grow into it or cut it down to fit you. But that's all you got to make life with. That's all you got to measure yourself against that world out there. Your daddy wanted you to be everything he wasn't . . . and at the same time he tried to make you into everything he was. I don't know if he was right or wrong, but I know he meant to do more good than he meant to do harm. He wasn't always right. Sometimes when he touched, he bruised. And sometimes when he took me in his arms, he cut. When I first met your daddy I thought, Here is a man I can lay down with and make a baby. That's the first thing I thought when I seen him. I was thirty years old and had done seen my share of men. But when he walked up to me and said, "I can dance a waltz that'll make you dizzy," I thought, Rose Lee, here is a man that you can open yourself up to and be filled to bursting. Here is a man that can fill all them empty spaces you been tipping around the edges of. One of them empty spaces was being some-body's mother. I married your daddy and settled down to cooking his supper and keeping clean sheets on the bed. When your daddy walked through the house, he was so big he filled it up. That was my first mistake. Not to make him leave some room for me, for my part in the matter. But at that time I wanted that. I wanted a house that I could sing in. And that's what your daddy gave me. I didn't know to keep up his strength I had to give up little pieces of mine. I did that. I took on his life as mine and mixed up the pieces so that you couldn't hardly tell which was which anymore. It was my choice. It was my life and I didn't have to live it like that. But that's what life offered me in the way of being a woman, and I took it. I grabbed hold of it with both hands. After a while he didn't seem so big no more. Sometimes I'd catch him just sitting and staring at his hands, just sitting there staring like he was watching the silence eat away at them. By the time Raynell came into the house, me and your daddy had done lost touch with each other. I didn't want to make my blessing off of nobody's misfortune, but I took on to Raynell like she was all them babies I had wanted and never had. Like I'd been blessed to relive a part of my life. And if the Lord see fit to keep up my strength, I'm gonna do her just like your daddy did you . . . I'm gonna give her the best of what's in me.

[RAYNELL *enters from the house.*]

RAYNELL: Mama, can I wear my white shoes? This here hurt my feet.

ROSE: Well, they just gonna have to hurt your feet for a while. You ain't said they hurt your feet when you went down there to the store and got them.

RAYNELL: They ain't hurt then. My feet done got bigger.

ROSE: You leave them shoes on your feet and go back in there and get that black belt like I told you.

RAYNELL: I can't find it. These here look all right to me.

ROSE: Girl, go on back in that house and get that belt like I told you!

RAYNELL: [*As she exits.*] Dag! I told you I don't know where to find it.

ROSE: Don't you give me no back talk. You look around and find that belt. Look in that drawer upstairs.

[LYONS *enters from the street.*]

LYONS: Hey . . . hey, look here . . . is that Cory?

CORY: Hey, Lyons.

ROSE: [*Embracing* LYONS.] Lord have mercy.

LYONS: It'll be all right, Rose. Everything's gonna be all right. Looking at Cory standing there. He done come home. Standing there all big and grown. It's gonna be all right now. [LYONS *and* CORY *embrace awkwardly.*] Look at you, man. Look at you. A sergeant in the United States Marines! How you been, man?

CORY: I been all right.

LYONS: You look good. Don't he look good, Rose.

ROSE: Yeah . . . He come in a little while ago. A sight for sore eyes.

LYONS: Where's Uncle Gabe? He in the house?

ROSE: They don't know if they gonna let him come or not. I just talked to them a little while ago.

LYONS: Where's Raynell? Cory, you seen Raynell?

CORY: Yeah, she was in the yard when I came in.

LYONS: Ain't she precious? She gonna break a whole lot of hearts.

ROSE: You all come on in the house and let me fix you some breakfast . . . keep your strength up.

CORY: I ain't hungry, Mama.

LYONS: You can fix me something, Rose. I'll be in there in a minute. I'm gonna stay out here and talk to Cory a minute.

ROSE: Cory, you sure you don't want nothing? I know they ain't feeding you right.

CORY: No, Mama . . . thanks. I don't feel like eating. I'll get something later.

[ROSE *exits into the house.*]

LYONS: So how you been?

CORY: I been doing okay.

LYONS: Yeah. So when you get in?

CORY: A little while ago. This morning.

LYONS: Look at you . . . Got them sergeant stripes! [*Pause.*] I heard you thinking about getting married?

CORY: Yeah, I am. I figure it's about time.

LYONS: Me and Bonnie been split up about four years now. I guess she just got tired of all the changes I was putting her through. [*Pause.*] The Marines, huh? Sergeant. I knew you was gonna make something of yourself. Your head always was in the right direction. You gonna stay in. You gonna make it a career? Put in your twenty years?

CORY: I don't know. I got six in already. I think that's enough.

LYONS: Stick with Uncle Sam and retire early. There ain't nothing out here. I guess Rose told you what happened to me. They got me down the workhouse.

CORY: Yeah, she told me.

LYONS: You got to take the crooked with the straight. That's what Papa used to say. I thought I was being slick cashing other people's checks.

CORY: How much time you doing?

LYONS: They gave me three years. I got that beat now. I ain't got but nine months. It ain't so bad. You just learn to deal with it like anything else.

CORY: You still playing?

LYONS: Hey, you know I'm gonna do that. There's some fellows down there . . . we got us a band. We gonna stay together when we get out and see if we can make something out of it. But, yeah, I'm still playing. It still help me to get out of the bed in the morning. As long as it do that, I'm gonna be right there playing to make some sense out of it.

ROSE: [*At the screen door.*] Lyons, I got these eggs in the pan.

LYONS: Let me go get these eggs, man. Go eat and get ready to bury Papa. [LYONS *starts toward the house. He stops at the door and salutes.*] Sergeant! [*To* RAYNELL.] Hey, precious!

[LYONS *exits into the house.* CORY *walks about the yard. He goes over to the tree and picks up* TROY's *bat.* RAYNELL *enters from the house.*]

RAYNELL: You in the Army or the Marines?

CORY: The Marines.

RAYNELL: Papa said it was the Army. [*Pause.*] Did you know Blue?

CORY: Blue? Who's Blue?

RAYNELL: Papa's dog what he sing about all the time.

[*After a long pause,* CORY *begins singing.*]

[CORY]
I had a dog his name was Blue
You know how Blue was mighty true
You know Blue was a good old dog
Blue treed a possum in a hollow log
You know from that he was a good old dog.

[RAYNELL *joining the singing.*]

[CORY *and* RAYNELL]
Blue treed a possum out on a limb
Blue looked at me and I looked at him
Grabbed that possum and put him in a sack
Blue stayed there till I came back
Old Blue's feets was big and round
Never allowed a possum to touch the ground.

Old Blue died and I dug his grave
I dug his grave with a silver spade
Let him down with a golden chain
And every night I call his name
Go on, Blue, you good dog, you!
Go on, Blue, you good dog, you!

Old Blue laid down and died like a man
Now he's treeing possums in the Promised Land.
I'm gonna tell you this to let you know:
Blue's gone where the good dogs go.
When I hear old Blue bark
When I hear old Blue bark

Blue treed a possum in Noah's Ark
Blue treed a possum in Noah's Ark.

ROSE: [*Comes to the door and calls.*] Raynell. Get in here and get them other shoes like I told you.
RAYNELL: I'll be back.

[RAYNELL *exits into the house.* ROSE *comes out into the yard.*]

ROSE: Cory, we gonna be ready to go in a few minutes.

[GABRIEL *enters waving his trumpet. He is dressed in a crumpled suit, shirt and tie, and a battered hat.*]

GABRIEL: Hey, Rose! I'm here, Rose. Hey, Rose. I'm here!
ROSE: Gabe? Lord . . . look here Lyons!

[LYONS *enters from the house, followed by* RAYNELL.]

GABRIEL: Hey, Rose. It's time. It's time to tell St. Peter to open the gates. Troy, you ready? You ready, Troy? I'm gonna tell St. Peter to open the gates. You get ready now.

[*With great fanfare, he braces himself to blow. The trumpet is without a mouth-piece. He puts the end of it into his mouth and blows with great force, like a man who has been waiting some twenty-odd years for this single moment. No sound comes out of the trumpet. He braces himself and blows again with the same result. A third time he blows. There is a weight of impossible description that falls away and leaves him bare and exposed to a frightful realization. It is a trauma that a sane and normal mind would be unable to withstand. He begins to dance. A slow, strange dance, eerie and life-giving. A dance of atavistic signature and ritual. He begins to howl in what is an attempt at song, or perhaps a song turning back into itself in an attempt at speech. He finishes his dance and the gates of heaven stand open as wide as God's closet.*]

That's the way that go!

# STUDY QUESTIONS

1. How does the SETTING relate to the play's title? If you were staging the play, how prominent would you make the fence-building materials? How would you indicate, visually, their temporariness and potential to add another dimension to the scene? What other visual aspects of the setting help to set up the THEMES of the play? Why do you think the author takes the trouble to describe the setting in so much detail? What does each of the items mentioned in the description of setting suggest about the CHARACTERS in the play?

2. Why is each of the characters described, in the list of characters, strictly in his or her relationship to Troy? What other indications are there, early on, that Troy is to be considered the center of the play? How much of the ACTION do we experience from Troy's POINT OF VIEW? What early indications are there of Troy's weakness? of flaws in his perceptions of reality?

3. What events from the past seem to have been most important in shaping Troy's character? What indications are there in the text that Troy's treatment of Cory replicates patterns of previous generations? Describe fully Troy's character; what aspects of his character and personality are explicable in terms of his past experiences? How important is family history in explaining his behavior? How important are economic and social conditions?

4. In what ways does the language of the play reflect Troy's past life? How thoroughly does the past infiltrate conceptions of the present in the play's language? What indications are there that behavior is passed down from generation to generation?

5. What characteristics of Troy are held in common by all of his children? What position does the play seem to take on the question of inherited characteristics? What gender roles seem to be important to the play's sorting out of issues? In what ways is history important to the behavior of the various characters?

6. In what ways are the characters' ages important to events in the play? How fully do different characters seem to reflect roles "characteristic" of their age groups? How are age behaviors distinguished from actions dependent on individual character?

7. What STEREOTYPES of white behavior are referred to in the play? How are these stereotypes represented? Which of the stereotypes seem to be upheld by the play's action? Which are undercut or corrected? What kind of attitude does the play take toward stereotypes based on race? on social position? on age? on economic conditions?

8. What different CONFLICTS does the play represent? Which ones seem most important to the play's dramatic focus? How do the conflicts reflect one another? What seems to you to be the central conflict of the play? Who is the central character? How can you tell?

9. What function does the idea of the fence perform for the central characters? How do their notions of the significance of the fence differ from one another? How

does the function of the fence change as the play goes on? By the end, what significance does the fence take on? Whose ideas of "fencing" does the play ultimately seem to support?

10. What value does Troy's life seem to have had by the play's end? What characters seem most closely to embody the play's human values? What attitude does the play ultimately establish toward Lyons? toward Gabriel? toward Bono? toward men? toward women?

11. On what principles are Troy's values based? What attitude does the total play take toward those values? How important is the past to the behavior of the various characters? According to the play, how does one free oneself from the influence of the past? In what ways are the themes treated here like those in Arthur Miller's *Death of a Salesman?*

12. Which characters in the play are the most attractive? What characteristics make them attractive? What kinds of behavior are we, as audience, led to disapprove of most fully? How are we made to disapprove? What values does the play ultimately seem to support most fully? What values does it disapprove of? How can you tell?

13. In what ways are the values of the white world brought to bear on the lives of the people in the play? What attitudes does the play support toward these values? How responsible do the characters in the play seem for their own destiny? What results seem to have been determined by larger social forces?

14. Toward what characters do you feel most sympathetic by the end of the play? Toward which do you feel the least sympathetic? What accounts for your feelings?

15. Describe the TONE of the ending of the play. What does the repetition of the song suggest about attitudes toward Troy? What issues are resolved satisfactorily by the death of Troy? What issues are left unresolved?

# CONFLICT AND STRUCTURE

C onflict, however unpleasant, seems a constant in human history, perhaps a part of human nature. Most people try hard to avoid conflict, preferring that their lives be serene and their relationships with other people smooth and without complication. No one, however, escapes conflict for long. Even without wars or large-scale disagreements among nations or religions or ethnic groups or political parties or gangs, human beings seldom are successful in avoiding conflict in their daily lives. In school, the desire to learn or excel quickly becomes competition among people; in the marketplace, people compete for jobs or profits or success. Men find themselves in conflict with the interests of women, blacks in conflict with the interests of whites, Native Americans with Hispanics, Chinese-Americans with Vietnamese-Americans, poor with rich, people from one part of town with people from another, Cub fans with White Sox fans, pedestrians with drivers, teachers with students, children with parents, friends with friends. Even those who avoid conflict with others at all cost—those who are solitary or who stay passive in the face of any difficulty or opposition—find conflict, if not between themselves and another, then within themselves. Many psychologists think that conflict is necessary, if not to life itself, at least to growth, change, and emotional development. Necessary or not, it is a part of the human condition as we know it.

And literature thrives on it. Conflict is at the base of almost all literature—at least narrative and dramatic literature. Plots are structured on the
basis of conflict, and emotional identifications with characters in literature
almost always depend on the reader's choosing someone's side in a disagreement. In plays, one can usually chart, quite regularly and predictably,
where the conflict will occur. The introduction of conflict (and other elements of an unfolding plot) is so predictable in a play that it has become
conventional to speak of plays as having five regular units or steps:

1. Exposition, in which the situation at the beginning of the play is explained,
   characters are introduced and their interrelationships explained, the setting is presented, and the plot begins to be introduced.
2. Rising Action, in which a series of events occur to complicate the original
   situation and create conflict among the characters.
3. Climax (sometimes called Turning Point). During the rising action, the
   flow or movement of the play is in one direction; the climax introduces
   some crucial moment that changes the direction of the action.
4. Falling Action, in which the complications begin to unwind.
5. Conclusion (also sometimes called Catastrophe or Denouement), in which
   a stable situation is reestablished so that the drama may end.

Ordinarily, in a five-act play, the acts correspond (at least roughly) to
these five units. When a play is divided into two or three acts, as most modern plays are, the five stages are included but divided up differently. Some
plays use multiple scenes rather than "acts" as such, but almost always one
can trace a progressive movement rather like that described in the five units
above.

In the conventional organization of plays, the centrality of conflict is
readily apparent. Nothing much gets started until conflict develops; conflict
is at the heart of the action, and in fact no action of any meaningful sort
takes place until some conflict is introduced. Conflict is just as crucial to
short stories and to other kinds of narrative, such as autobiography. Poems,
too, are often (though not always) characterized by conflict; conflict there,
however, may just as easily involve a conflict within a person's mind as conflict that manifests itself in physical confrontation or overt action.

Other, more formal features may also help to STRUCTURE a piece of
writing. Just as the act and scene divisions in a play or the dialogue between
characters provides visual divisions on a page (divisions that have a visual
and aural counterpart onstage when the play is produced), so stories,

essays, and poems have visible divisions into paragraphs and sections, lines and stanzas.

Paragraph division, like the sentence division from which it follows as a logical extension, helps to mark the stages of transition in an argument or discourse and in a story provides breaks (rather like scene divisions in a play) in the narrative that may mark changes in time, place, mood, or perspective. In poems, lines are often "broken" at what seem to be illogical places (if one regards "logic" as strictly a function of meaning), recording instead sounds and rhythms, the cadences of a human voice. Poetry is closely related to music and often is structured by sound in addition to content. Poems, in fact, often play off against one another their crucial elements of sound and sense, creating their effects through a tension between meaning and musical vehicle. Line breaks and the way words are arranged on the page provide a guide to reading. To an experienced reader, they are like a musical score that signals the reader where to pause, how fast to proceed, and what tone to strike, offering a visual equivalent of the rhythms of the human voice.

Writers, in fact, use all kinds of devices to organize their materials in ways that will produce in their audience a certain effect, for they are concerned not only to "make sense" but to produce feelings in readers, to drive them to conclusions, to persuade them to hold new attitudes, sometimes even to take some kind of action. The strategies of persuasion that literature uses are collectively called RHETORICAL DEVICES, and the rhetoric of a poem, story, essay, or play crucially involves the work's structure—the sum of all the devices of organization and shape. Some of those devices are logical (involving meaning), some are formal (involving shape, visual or otherwise). All are important in determining the way a work affects us as we read it from beginning to end.

# WRITING
# ABOUT THE READING

## PERSONAL ESSAYS AND NARRATIVES

1. What "fences" have you encountered in your school, community, church, clubs, or social groups? Have you ever felt excluded from some group you wished to be in because of race, nationality, or gender? because of personal characteristics that were considered odd or undesirable? because of your economic status, political beliefs, or social class? because of language or your lack of knowledge of "the code"? How did you sort out the reasons for your exclusion? How could you tell what the "real" reasons were? Did you try to change yourself or hide facts about yourself to make you more suitable to the group you wished to join? How did you feel about the incident? In what ways would you handle it differently if a similar thing were to happen again?

   To get some perspective on the effects—emotional, personal, psychological, and social—of the episode, create a CHARACTER who is in some crucial way different from yourself, and write a short story about an episode similar to the one in your own life. Tell the story from the POINT OF VIEW of the character who is excluded, and try to make clear the complexities of the sorting-out process as the character assesses the reasoning of the in-group and the feelings he or she experiences as a result of the exclusion.

2. What experiences have you had as the excluder? Consider episodes in which, for one reason or another, you have kept someone out of a social organization, and choose one such episode to concentrate on. What was the person you excluded like? What were your reasons for excluding him or her? Did you have second thoughts about the exclusion? Did you ever distrust your reasons? suspect yourself of some categorical kind of prejudice? regret your decision?

   Write a straightforward autobiographical NARRATIVE of the episode in which you try to explain yourself and indicate what kind of long-range effects the episode had on your self-analysis and on your behavior.

## IMITATIONS AND PARODIES

1. Using R. T. Smith's "Red Anger" as your model, write a short poem in which you explore some powerful emotion you have experienced as a member of a particular national, ethnic, religious, or other group.

2. Using Ralph Ellison's "Battle Royal" as a model, write a story in which a well-meaning and idealistic character is humiliated by being made to participate in a

degrading activity—in a fraternity, club, gang, social group, church group, or job experience.

# ARGUMENTATIVE PAPER

Construct both sides of a debate on the following topic: Resolved, that a church or political group organized primarily for religious or political purposes has no right to exclude people who do not agree with its goals and should be legally prosecuted for such exclusions.

# RESEARCH PAPERS

1. How were Iranians treated in North America during and after the hostage crisis of 1979–81? Using newspaper and magazine articles in your library (a reference librarian can show you how to use the appropriate indexes), find out as much as you can about the public and private treatment of people of Iranian descent. How much anger did Americans express about Iran's actions? In what ways did the anger manifest itself toward individuals who seemed to be of Iranian descent? How did Iranians in America respond?

2. Using the guidelines in #1, do the same kind of research on:

    a) the treatment of people of Japanese or Italian descent in the United States or Canada during World War II.

    b) the treatment of people of German descent in the United States or Canada during World War I.

    c) the treatment of people of Russian descent in the late 1950s in the United States or Canada.

# 8

# CROSSING

Whether a group is as small as a family or a fraternity or as large and diverse as a nation or ethnic community, the sense of togetherness, familiarity, and belonging is comforting. Within the group we feel secure, for we know its customs, rules, and rituals, its language and its limits. Within the group we know our place; we know who we are. Other members are like us, "our kind of people." Our very sense of who we are is bound up with our place in the group.

An outsider is an unknown quantity, *not* like us, *not* one of "our people," a threat not only to the group but to our sense of ourselves. For our safety and sanity and sense of self, then, as well as for the protection of the homogeneity of the group, it sometimes seems necessary to repel the outsider who tries to cross over the boundary line and into our group, even if we have to use force. At its worst, this fear of the Other becomes prejudice against all outsiders, or even xenophobia—fear or hatred of anything or anyone "foreign." It is the dangerous other side of feelings of familiarity and security within the group.

In growing up, however, it is often necessary to rebel against the familiar and secure, to assert our own sense of individuality, freedom, difference, by separating ourselves from our parents, and to define ourselves by our differences from them. The more adventurous—or rebellious—of us, or those with the greater opportunity, often step across the boundaries of the larger group: the neighborhood, the ethnic or cultural community. If we attempt to cross the fences, however, we must be prepared not only to be criticized, restrained, perhaps even cast out by our own, but to be rebuffed and ridiculed, even attacked, by the group toward which we are reaching out. In leaving the "narrow" and "provincial" tribe, we may think of ourselves as seeking growth, breadth of experience, and knowledge. We may see ourselves as generously "tolerating" the differences of the Other, and therefore entitled to admiration by our own who stay at home and the Other whom we flatter with our acceptance and attention. That may be what we think, but it may not be what others think of our venturing abroad; indeed, we risk rootlessness and rejection.

Not all rebellion arises from curiosity, adventurousness, or generous motives. Rejection of those nearest to us—parents, friends, compatriots— may at times be the result of callow notions of greener grass on the other side, or of conceited notions of our own importance and potential being restricted by the ignorance of those around us. If we were only free, we think, of the foolish restraints of "home," we would at last be treated in the manner we know we deserve.

But "crossing" is not only the action of the strong, adventurous individual defying the repressive power of the group. For there are societies, from families to tribes, that may need to be strengthened by bringing in new ideas and blood. The young in such a society must sometimes be kicked out of the nest; they may be permitted to marry, for example, only outside the tribe or group.

Courtship and marriage are, of course, the ultimate and thus most controversial of crossing experiences. Most of the pieces in this chapter, therefore, have to do with sexual relationships. When the most intimate and emotional of private feelings clash with the most primordial sense of the group, the conflict may threaten the security and identity of both the individual and the group. Both sides will fight with passionate intensity.

# O. Henry

O. Henry was born William Sydney Porter in North Carolina in 1862. He left school at fifteen and worked in a drugstore, on a ranch in Texas, and in a bank. He began to write short stories, some of which appeared in newspapers. Arrested for stealing funds from the bank, he served three years in prison, during which time he wrote and published several short stories. When he was released, he went to New York to work on a newspaper and to write short stories. By the time he died—in 1910—he had written fourteen volumes of stories; the best known of his stories is "The Gift of the Magi." O. Henry is noted for surprise endings and for otherwise creating expectations that often will need to be revised.

You may want to pay particular attention in this story to what you are expecting to happen next and how that expectation is fulfilled or revised or completely overturned. In paragraphs 6–8, Maggie announces she has a date but refuses to say what he is like, making her friend Anna and the reader wait to find out. You might stop there and think of the possibilities. And once you meet him, you may want to stop periodically to ask yourself what you are curious about and what you think will happen next.

## THE COMING-OUT OF MAGGIE

Every Saturday night the Clover Leaf Social Club gave a hop in the hall of the Give and Take Athletic Association on the East Side. In order to attend one of these dances you must be a member of the Give and Take—or, if you belong to the division that starts off with the right foot in waltzing, you must work in Rhinegold's paper-box factory. Still, any Clover Leaf was privileged to escort or be escorted by an outsider to a single dance. But mostly each Give and Take brought the paper-box girl that he affected; and few strangers could boast of having shaken a foot at the regular hops.

Maggie Toole, on account of her dull eyes, broad mouth, and left-handed style of footwork in the two-step, went to the dances with Anna McCarty and her "fellow." Anna and Maggie worked side by side in the factory, and were the greatest chums ever. So Anna always made Jimmy Burns take her by Maggie's house every Saturday night so that her friend could go to the dance with them.

The Give and Take Athletic Association lived up to its name. The hall    3
of the Association in Orchard Street was fitted out with muscle-making
inventions. With the fibres thus builded up the members were wont to engage
the police and rival social and athletic organizations in joyous combat. Between
these more serious occupations the Saturday night hops with the paper-box
factory girls came as a refining influence and as an efficient screen. For sometimes the tip went 'round, and if you were among the elect that tiptoed up
the dark back stairway you might see as neat and satisfying a little welter-
weight affair to a finish as ever happened inside the ropes.

On Saturdays Rhinegold's paper-box factory closed at 3 P.M. On one    4
such afternoon Anna and Maggie walked homeward together. At Maggie's
door Anna said, as usual: "Be ready at seven, sharp, Mag; and Jimmy and
me'll come by for you."

But what was this? Instead of the customary humble and grateful thanks    5
from the non-escorted one there was to be perceived a high-poised head, a
prideful dimpling at the corners of a broad mouth, and almost a sparkle in a
dull brown eye.

"Thanks, Anna," said Maggie; "but you and Jimmy needn't bother    6
tonight. I've a gentleman friend that's coming 'round to escort me to the
hop."

The comely Anna pounced upon her friend, shook her, chided and    7
beseeched her. Maggie Toole catch a fellow! Plain, dear, loyal, unattractive
Maggie, so sweet as a chum, so unsought for a two-step or a moonlit bench
in the little park. How was it? When did it happen? Who was it?

"You'll see to-night," said Maggie, flushed with the wine of the first    8
grapes she had gathered in Cupid's vineyard. "He's swell all right. He's two
inches taller than Jimmy, and an up-to-date dresser. I'll introduce him, Anna,
just as soon as we get to the hall."

Anna and Jimmy were among the first Clover Leafs to arrive that eve-    9
ning, Anna's eyes were brightly fixed upon the door of the hall to catch the
first glimpse of her friend's "catch."

At 8:30 Miss Toole swept into the hall with her escort. Quickly her    10
triumphant eye discovered her chum under the wing of her faithful Jimmy.

"Oh, gee!" cried Anna, "Mag ain't made a hit—oh, no! Swell fellow?    11
well, I guess! Style? Look at 'um."

"Go as far as you like," said Jimmy, with sandpaper in his voice. "Cop    12
him out if you want him. These new guys always win out with the push.
Don't mind me. He don't squeeze all the limes, I guess. Huh!"

"Shut up, Jimmy. You know what I mean. I'm glad for Mag. First fel-    13
low she ever had. Oh, here they come."

Across the floor Maggie sailed like a coquettish yacht convoyed by a    14
stately cruiser. And truly, her companion justified the encomiums of the
faithful chum. He stood two inches taller than the average Give and Take
athlete; his dark hair curled; his eyes and his teeth flashed whenever he

bestowed his frequent smiles. The young men of the Clover Leaf Club pinned not their faith to the graces of person as much as they did to its prowess, its achievements in hand-to-hand conflicts, and its preservation from the legal duress that constantly menaced it. The member of the association who would bind a paper-box maiden to his conquering chariot scorned to employ Beau Brummel airs. They were not considered honourable methods of warfare. The swelling biceps, the coat straining at its buttons over the chest, the air of conscious conviction of the supereminence of the male in the cosmogony of creation, even a calm display of bow legs as subduing and enchanting agents in the gentle tourneys of Cupid—these were the approved arms and ammunition of the Clover Leaf gallants. They viewed, then, the genuflexions and alluring poses of this visitor with their chins at a new angle.

"A friend of mine, Mr. Terry O'Sullivan," was Maggie's formula of introduction. She led him around the room, presenting him to each new-arriving Clover Leaf. Almost was she pretty now, with the unique luminosity in her eyes that comes to a girl with her first suitor and a kitten with its first mouse.   15

"Maggie Toole's got a fellow at last," was the word that went round among the paper-box girls. "Pipe Mag's floor-walker"—thus the Give and Take expressed their indifferent contempt.   16

Usually at the weekly hops Maggie kept a spot on the wall warm with her back. She felt and showed so much gratitude whenever a self-sacrificing partner invited her to dance that his pleasure was cheapened and diminished. She had even grown used to noticing Anna joggle the reluctant Jimmy with her elbow as a signal for him to invite her chum to walk over his feet through a two-step.   17

But to-night the pumpkin had turned to a coach and six. Terry O'Sullivan was a victorious Prince Charming, and Maggie Toole winged her first butterfly flight. And though our tropes of fairyland be mixed with those of entomology they shall not spill one drop of ambrosia from the rose-crowned melody of Maggie's one perfect night.   18

The girls besieged her for introductions to her "fellow." The Clover Leaf young men, after two years of blindness, suddenly perceived charms in Miss Toole. They flexed their compelling muscles before her and bespoke her for the dance.   19

Thus she scored; but to Terry O'Sullivan the honours of the evening fell thick and fast. He shook his curls; he smiled and went easily through the seven motions for acquiring grace in your own room before an open window ten minutes each day. He danced like a faun; he introduced manner and style and atmosphere; his words came trippingly upon his tongue, and—he waltzed twice in succession with the paper-box girl that Dempsey Donovan brought.   20

Dempsey was the leader of the association. He wore a dress suit, and could chin the bar twice with one hand. He was one of "Big Mike" O'Sullivan's lieutenants, and was never troubled by trouble. No cop dared to arrest   21 him. Whenever he broke a pushcart man's head or shot a member of the Heinrick B. Sweeney Outing and Literary Association in the kneecap, an officer would drop around and say:

"The Cap'n 'd like to see ye a few minutes round to the office whin ye have time, Dempsey, me boy." 22

But there would be sundry gentlemen there with large gold fob chains and black cigars; and somebody would tell a funny story, and then Dempsey would go back and work half an hour with the six-pound dumbbells. So, doing a tightrope act on a wire stretched across Niagara was a safe terpsichorean performance compared with waltzing twice with Dempsey Donovan's paper-box girl. At 10 o'clock the jolly round face of "Big Mike" O'Sullivan shone at the door for five minutes upon the scene. He always looked in for five minutes, smiled at the girls, and handed out real perfectos to the delighted boys. 23

Dempsey Donovan was at his elbow instantly, talking rapidly. "Big Mike" looked carefully at the dancers, smiled, shook his head and departed. 24

The music stopped. The dancers scattered to the chairs along the walls. Terry O'Sullivan, with his entrancing bow, relinquished a pretty girl in blue to her partner, and started back to find Maggie. Dempsey intercepted him in the middle of the floor. 25

Some fine instinct that Rome must have bequeathed to us caused nearly every one to turn and look at them—there was a subtle feeling that two gladiators had met in the arena. Two or three Give and Takes with tight coat sleeves drew nearer. 26

"One moment, Mr. O'Sullivan," said Dempsey. "I hope you're enjoying yourself. Where did you say you lived?" 27

The two gladiators were well matched. Dempsey had, perhaps, ten pounds of weight to give away. The O'Sullivan had breadth with quickness. Dempsey had a glacial eye, a dominating slit of a mouth, an indestructible jaw, a complexion like a belle's, and the coolness of a champion. The visitor showed more fire in his contempt and less control over his conspicuous sneer. They were enemies by the law written when the rocks were molten. They were each too splendid, too mighty, too incomparable to divide preëminence. One only must survive. 28

"I live on Grand," said O'Sullivan, insolently; "and no trouble to find me at home. Where do you live?" 29

Dempsey ignored the question. 30

"You say your name's O'Sullivan," he went on. "Well, 'Big Mike' says he never saw you before." 31

"Lots of things he never saw," said the favourite of the hop. 32

"As a rule," went on Dempsey, huskily sweet, "O'Sullivans in this district know one another. You escorted one of our lady members here, and we want a chance to make good. If you've got a family tree let's see a few historical O'Sullivan buds come out on it. Or do you want us to dig it out of you by the roots?" 33

"Suppose you mind your own business," suggested O'Sullivan blandly. 34

Dempsey's eye brightened. He held up an inspired forefinger as though 35 a brilliant idea had struck him.

"I've got it now," he said cordially. "It was just a little mistake. You 36 ain't no O'Sullivan. You are a ring-tailed monkey. Excuse us for not recognizing you at first."

O'Sullivan's eye flashed. He made a quick movement, but Andy Geo- 37 phan was ready and caught his arm.

Dempsey nodded at Andy and William McMahan, the secretary of the 38 club, and walked rapidly toward a door at the rear of the hall. Two other members of the Give and Take Association swiftly joined the little group. Terry O'Sullivan was now in the hands of the Board of Rules and Social Referees. They spoke to him briefly and softly, and conducted him out through the same door at the rear.

This movement on the part of the Clover Leaf members requires a word 39 of elucidation. Back of the association hall was a smaller room rented by the club. In this room personal difficulties that arose on the ballroom floor were settled, man to man, with the weapons of nature, under the supervision of the board. No lady could say that she had witnessed a fight at a Clover Leaf hop in several years. Its gentlemen members guaranteed that.

So easily and smoothly had Dempsey and the board done their prelim- 40 inary work that many in the hall had not noticed the checking of the fascinating O'Sullivan's social triumph. Among these was Maggie. She looked about for her escort.

"Smoke up!" said Rose Cassidy. "Wasn't you on? Demps Donovan picked 41 a scrap with your Lizzie-boy, and they've waltzed out to the slaughter room with him. How's my hair look done up this way, Mag?"

Maggie laid a hand on the bosom of her cheesecloth waist. 42

"Gone to fight with Dempsey!" she said, breathlessly. "They've got to 43 be stopped. Dempsey Donovan can't fight him. Why, he'll—he'll kill him!"

"Ah, what do you care?" said Rose. "Don't some of 'em fight every 44 hop?"

But Maggie was off, darting her zig-zag way through the maze of dancers. 45 She burst through the rear door into the dark hall and then threw her solid shoulder against the door of the room of single combat. It gave way, and in the instant that she entered her eye caught the scene—the board standing about with open watches; Dempsey Donovan in his shirt sleeves dancing, light-footed, with the wary grace of the modern pugilist, within easy reach of his adversary; Terry O'Sullivan standing with arms folded and a murderous look in his dark eyes. And without slacking the speed of her entrance she leaped forward with a scream—leaped in time to catch and hang upon the arm of O'Sullivan that was suddenly uplifted, and to whisk from it the long, bright stiletto that he had drawn from his bosom.

The knife fell and rang upon the floor. Cold steel drawn in the rooms of 46 the Give and Take Association! Such a thing had never happened before.

Every one stood motionless for a minute. Andy Geoghan kicked the stiletto with the toe of his shoe curiously, like an antiquarian who has come upon some ancient weapon unknown to his learning.

And then O'Sullivan hissed something unintelligible between his teeth. 47 Dempsey and the board exchanged looks. And then Dempsey looked at O'Sullivan without anger, as one looks at a stray dog, and nodded his head in the direction of the door.

"The back stairs, Giuseppi," he said, briefly. "Somebody'll pitch your 48 hat down after you."

Maggie walked up to Dempsey Donovan. There was a brilliant spot of 49 red in her cheeks, down which slow tears were running. But she looked him bravely in the eye.

"I knew it, Dempsey," she said, as her eyes grew dull even in their tears. 50 "I knew he was a Guinea. His name's Tony Spinelli. I hurried in when they told me you and him was scrappin'. Them Guineas always carries knives. But you don't understand, Dempsey. I never had a fellow in my life. I got tired of comin' with Anna and Jimmy every night, so I fixed it with him to call himself O'Sullivan, and brought him along. I knew there'd be nothin' doin' for him if he came as a Dago. I guess I'll resign from the club now."

Dempsey turned to Andy Geoghan. 51

"Chuck that cheese slicer out of the window," he said, "and tell 'em 52 inside that Mr. O'Sullivan has had a telephone message to go down to Tammany Hall."

And then he turned back to Maggie. 53

"Say, Mag," he said, "I'll see you home. And how about next Saturday 54 night? Will you come to the hop with me if I call around for you?"

It was remarkable how quickly Maggie's eyes could change from dull to 55 a shining brown.

"With you, Dempsey?" she stammered. "Say—will a duck swim?" 56

# STUDY QUESTIONS

1. In paragraph 1, what is meant by "if you belong to the division that starts off with the right foot in waltzing"? If you did not understand the clause immediately, is there anything later in the paragraph that helps explain it? Toward the end of the paragraph is a somewhat similar clause, though one more easily understood on first reading—"few strangers could boast of having shaken a foot at the regular hops." Find a half dozen or so similar expressions in the story. What seems to be the purpose or effect of such indirect or roundabout phrases or sentences? Does the author seem to be imitating the language of the characters in the story, or is he speaking to the reader "over the heads" of the characters, or some combination of the two? Use some of the examples you found as evidence to support your conclu-

sion. How do such expressions set the TONE* of the story? the ATTITUDE of the narrator? How do these expressions condition the response of the reader?

2. In paragraph 14, the narrator refers to "the swelling biceps, the coat straining at its buttons over the chest, the air of conscious conviction of the supereminence of the male in the cosmogony of creation," and in the next paragraph to "the unique luminosity in [Maggie's] eyes that comes to a girl with her first suitor and a kitten with its first mouse." What seems to be the attitude of the narrator in this 1906 story to gender roles? Can you distinguish between the characters' attitudes and those of the narrator?

3. When are you first aware of the ethnic makeup of the Give and Take Association? Trace the emergence of the ethnic theme through the story.

4. Why does Maggie interrupt the fight? What does she expect might happen? Why? Where are her primary loyalties, to Terry or the club? Why?

5. How are Terry's actions during the fight "typical" of the Give and Take Association's STEREOTYPE of his ethnic group? Does the story, then, affirm the prejudices of the club? How else can you explain or justify Terry's actions? Might he not act as the story suggests? Discuss the truth, falsity, usefulness, and dangers of ethnic stereotypes.

# Gabrielle Roy

Winner of three Governor-General's Awards, for novels and short stories written in French, Gabrielle Roy was born in Manitoba in 1909, and, after two years in London and Paris and five years in Montreal, settled in 1947 in Quebec City.

Wilhelm is from Holland, the first sentence tells us, and we soon learn that the O'Neills are from County Cork, Ireland; it takes a while to learn the narrator's ethnic identity, unless the author's name is a tip-off. And it takes even longer to learn how these ethnic distinctions are important in the story.

## WILHELM

My first suitor came from Holland. He was called Wilhelm and his teeth were too regular; he was much older than I; he had a long, sad face . . . at least thus it was that others made me see him when they had taught me to

*Words in small capitals are defined in the glossary.

consider his defects. As for me, at first I found his face thoughtful rather than long and peaked. I did not yet know that his teeth—so straight and even—were false. I thought I loved Wilhelm. Here was the first man who, through me, could be made happy or unhappy; here was a very serious matter.

I had met him at our friends' the O'Neills', who still lived not far from us in their large gabled house on Rue Desmeurons. Wilhelm was their boarder; for life is full of strange things: thus this big, sad man was a chemist in the employ of a small paint factory then operating in our city, and—as I have said—lodged with equally uprooted people, the O'Neills, formerly of County Cork in Ireland. A far journey to have come merely to behave, in the end, like everyone else—earn your living, try to make friends, learn our language, and then, in Wilhelm's case, love someone who was not for him. Do adventures often turn out so tritely? Obviously enough, though, in those days I did not think so.

Evenings at the O'Neills' were musical. Kathleen played "Mother Machree," while her mother, seated on a sofa, wiped her eyes, trying the while to avert our attention, to direct it away from herself, for she did not like people to believe her so deeply stirred by Irish songs. Despite the music, Elizabeth kept right on digging away at her arithmetic; she still was utterly indifferent to men. But Kathleen and I cared a great deal. We feared dreadfully to be left on the shelf; we feared we should fail to be loved and to love with a great and absolutely unique passion.

When Mrs. O'Neill requested it of me—"to relieve the atmosphere," as she put it—I played Paderewski's "Minuet"; then Wilhelm would have us listen to Massenet on a violin of choice quality. Afterward he would show me in an album scenes of his country, as well as his father's house and the home of his uncle, his father's partner. I think he was anxious to convey to me that his family was better off than you might think if you judged by him—I mean by his having had to quit his native land and come live in our small city. Yet he need have had no fear that I should form an opinion on the basis of silly social appearances; I wanted to judge people in strict accordance with their noble personal qualities. Wilhelm would explain to me how Ruisdael had really most faithfully rendered the full, sad sky of the Low Countries; and he asked me whether I thought I should like Holland enough one day to visit it. Yes, I replied; I should much like to see the canals and the tulip fields.

Then he had had sent to me from Holland a box of chocolates, each one of which was a small vial containing a liqueur.

But one evening he had the ill-starred notion of accompanying me back home, as far as our front door, though it was only two steps away and darkness had not wholly fallen. He was chivalrous: he insisted that a man should not let a woman go home all alone, even if that woman only yesterday had still been playing with hoops or walking on stilts.

Alas! The moment his back was turned, Maman asked me about my 7
young man. "Who is that great beanstalk?"

I told her it was Wilhelm of Holland, and all the rest of it: the box of 8
chocolates, the tulip fields, the stirring sky of Wilhelm's country, the wind-
mills. . . . Now all that was fine and honorable! But why, despite what I
thought of appearances, did I believe myself obliged also to speak of the uncle
and the father, partners in a small business which . . . which . . . made a lot
of money?

My mother at once forbade me to return to the O'Neills, so long, said 9
she, as I had not got over the idea of Wilhelm.

But Wilhelm was clever. One or two days each week he finished work 10
early; on those days he waited for me at the convent door. He took over my
great bundle of books—Lord, what homework the Sisters piled on us in those
days!—my music sheets, my metronome, and he carried all these burdens to
the corner of our street. There he would lower upon me his large and sad
blue eyes and say to me, "When you are bigger, I'll take you to the opera, to
the theater. . . ."

I still had two years of the convent ahead of me; the opera, the theater 11
seemed desperately far away. Wilhelm would tell me that he longed to see
me in an evening gown; that then he would at last remove from its moth-
proof bag his dress clothes and that we should go in style to hear symphonic
music.

My mother ultimately learned that Wilhelm had the effrontery to carry 12
my books, and it annoyed her very much. She forbade me to see him.

"Still," said I to Maman, "I can hardly prevent his walking next to me 13
along the pavement."

My mother cut through that problem. "If he takes the same sidewalk as 14
you, mind you, cross right over to the other."

Now, she must have sent a message of rebuke to Wilhelm and told him, 15
as she had me, precisely which sidewalk he should take, for I began seeing
him only on the opposite side of the street, where he would stolidly await
my passage. All the while I was going by, he held his hat in his hand. The
other young girls must have been horribly envious of me; they laughed at
Wilhelm's baring his head while I was passing. Yet I felt death in my soul at
seeing Wilhelm so alone and exposed to ridicule. He was an immigrant, and
Papa had told me a hundred times that you could not have too much sympathy, too much consideration for the uprooted, who have surely suffered
enough from their expatriation without our adding to it through scorn or
disdain. Why then had Papa so completely changed his views, and why was
he more set even than Maman against Wilhelm of Holland? True enough, no
one at home, since Georgianna's marriage, looked favorably upon love. Perhaps because as a whole we had already had too much to suffer from it. But
I—presumably—I had not yet suffered enough at its hands. . . .

And then, as I have said, Wilhelm was clever. Maman had forbidden 16 him to speak to me on the street, but she had forgotten letters. Wilhelm had made great progress in English. He sent me very beautiful epistles which began with: "My own beloved child . . ." or else "Sweet little maid. . . ." Not to be outdone, I replied: "My own dearest heart. . . ." One day my mother found in my room a scrawl on which I had been practicing my handwriting and in which I expressed to Wilhelm a passion that neither time nor cruel obstacles could bend. . . . Had my mother glanced into the volume of Tennyson lying open upon my table, she would have recognized the whole passage in question, but she was far too angry to listen to reason. I was enjoined from writing to Wilhelm, from reading his letters, if, by a miracle, one of them succeeded in penetrating the defenses thrown up by Maman; I was even enjoined from thinking of him. I was allowed only to pray for him, if I insisted upon it.

Until then I had thought that love should be open and clear, cherished by all and making peace between beings. Yet what was happening? Maman was turned into something like a spy, busy with poking about in my wastebasket; and I then thought that she was certainly the last person in the world to understand me! So that was what love accomplished! And where was that fine frankness between Maman and me! Does there always arise a bad period between a mother and her daughter? Is it love that brings it on? . . . And what, what is love? One's neighbor? Or some person rich, beguiling? 17

During this interval Wilhelm, unable to do anything else for me, sent me many gifts; and at the time I knew nothing of them, for the moment they arrived, Maman would return them to him: music scores, tulip bulbs from Amsterdam, a small collar of Bruges lace, more liqueur-filled chocolates. 18

The only means left to us by which to communicate was the telephone. Maman had not thought of that. Obviously she could not think of everything; love is so crafty! Then, too, during her loving days the telephone did not exist, and this, I imagine, was why Maman forgot to ban it for me. Wilhelm often called our number. If it was not I who answered, he hung up gently. And many a time did Maman then protest, "What's going on? . . . I shall write the company a letter; I'm constantly being bothered for nothing. At the other end I can barely hear a sort of sighing sound." Naturally she could not foresee how far the tenacity of a Wilhelm would extend. 19

But when it was I who answered, Wilhelm was scarcely better off. There could be between us no real conversation without its exposing us to the discovery of our secret and consequent prohibition of the telephone. Moreover, we neither of us had any taste for ruses; Gervais employed them when he had on the wire the darling of his heart, to whom he spoke as though she were another schoolboy. But Wilhelm and I—without blaming Gervais, for love is love, and when it encounters obstacles, is even more worthy!—we strove to be noble in all things. Thus Wilhelm merely murmured to me, from afar, "Dear heart . . ." after which he remained silent. And I listened to his silence for a minute or two, blushing to the roots of my hair. 20

One day, though, he discovered an admirable way to make me under- 21 stand his heart. As I was saying "Allo!" his voice begged me to hold the wire; then I made out something like the sound of a violin being tuned, then the opening bars of "Thaïs."[1] Wilhelm played me the whole composition over the phone. Kathleen must have been accompanying him. I heard piano chords somewhere in the distance, and—I know not why—this put me out a trifle, perhaps at thinking that Kathleen was in on so lovely a secret. It was the first time, however, that Wilhelm put me out at all.

Our phone was attached to the wall at the end of a dark little hallway. At first no one was surprised at seeing me spend hours there, motionless and in the most complete silence. Only little by little did the people at home begin to notice that at the telephone I uttered no word. And from then on, when I went to listen to "Thaïs" the hall door would open slightly; someone hid there to spy on me, motioning the others to advance one by one and watch me. Gervais was the worst, and it was very mean on his part, for I had respected his secret. He manufactured reasons for making use of the hall; as he went by he tried to hear what I could be listening to. At first, however, I held the receiver firmly glued to my ear. Then I must already have begun to find "Thaïs" very long to hear through. One evening I allowed Gervais to listen for a moment to Wilhelm's music; perhaps I hoped that he would have enough enthusiasm to make me myself admire the composition. But Gervais choked with mirth; later on I saw him playing the fool in front of the others, at the far end of the living room, bowing an imaginary violin. Even Maman laughed a little, although she tried to remain angry. With a long, sad countenance which—I knew not how—he superimposed upon his own features, Gervais was giving a fairly good imitation of Wilhelm in caricature. I was a little tempted to laugh. For it is a fact that there is something quite comic in seeing a sad person play the violin. 22

When you consider it, it is astonishing that all of them together should not have thought much sooner of parting me from Wilhelm by the means they so successfully employed from that night forward. 23

All day long, when I went by, someone was whistling the melody of "Thaïs." 24

My brother grossly exaggerated the Dutchman's slightly solemn gait, his habit of keeping his eyes lifted aloft. They discovered in him the mien of a Protestant minister, dry—said they—and in the process of preparing a sermon. Maman added that the "Netherlander" had a face as thin as a knife blade. This was the way they now referred to him: the "Netherlander" or the "Hollander." My sister Odette—I should say Sister Edouard—who had been informed and was taking a hand in the matter, even though she had renounced the world, my pious Odette herself told me to forget the "foreigner" . . . that a foreigner is a foreigner. . . . 25

One evening as I listened to "Thaïs," I thought I must look silly, stand- 26

---

1. Opera (1894) by the French composer Jules Massenet (1842–1912).

ing thus stock still, the receiver in my hand. I hung up before the end of the performance.

Thereafter, Wilhelm scarcely crossed my path again. 27

A year later, perhaps, we learned that he was returning to Holland. 28

My mother once more became the just and charitable pre-Wilhelm per- 29 son I had loved so dearly. My father no longer harbored anything against Holland. Maman admitted that Mrs. O'Neill had told her concerning Wilhelm that he was the best man in the world, reliable, a worker, very gentle. . . . And Maman hoped that Wilhelm, in his own country, among his own people, would be loved . . . as, she said, he deserved to be.

## STUDY QUESTIONS

1. The NARRATOR's name is not mentioned; is it Gabrielle? The narrative mode of the story is that of a reminiscence—is it real or fictional reminiscence? Does it matter? Do you read nonfictional narrative with different expectations, different demands from those with which you read fiction?

2. The story begins, "My first suitor came from Holland," but the "defects" in Wilhelm that "others" point out to the narrator (paragraph 1) are not specifically related to his nationality, nor is that brought up directly in her mother's disapproval (pars. 7–9). What other causes for disapproval seem to be implied in the story? When do nationality and religion, ethnic and cultural differences rise to the surface as the major cause of parental disapproval?

3. Opening and closing sentences in a story bear special weight of emphasis; how do you interpret the full force of the final sentence here? What does the mother mean? What is the implied ATTITUDE of the narrator toward the mother's meaning?

# Jeffery Paul Chan

As teacher, writer, editorial consultant, and educational activist, Jeffery Paul Chan (born in California in 1942) has long championed the inclusion of Asian-American literature in the American literature canon.

There are clear ethnic labels in his story reprinted here, but you may have to look hard to find stereotypes, or even many discriminating cultural or traditional characteristics, values, or other identifying traces.

# THE CHINESE IN HAIFA

Bill dreamed he heard the cry of starving children in Asia bundled together    1
in a strangely familiar school yard. They pressed up tightly against a Cyclone
fence and they were dressed in quilted black uniforms that reached down to
the ground with wide sleeves they used for handkerchiefs dabbling at their
flat brown noses, a mosaic of fingers and faces reaching toward him through
the squares of wire. Their gaping figures settled into the grain of the vestibule door of his grandfather's house. It was solid oak with cleverly fashioned
brass mullions molded to the likeness of Taoist household deities, blending
wheat chaff and shoots of new rice into the bodies of farm animals, with the
toothless smile of Hotai[1] and a border of tiny lion dogs snatching at tails and
paws or locked jaw to jaw in a faceless struggle. The frieze was grimy with
age and a narrow green cuticle outlined the hole where the brass met the
wood and where the clear lacquer had begun to flake and crack. The door
swung back and instead of his children he saw what might have been the
fleeting figure of his wife driving a line of coolies down a dark hallway. Take
everything, take everything, she screamed. Then his father appeared, oversized on a stretch of bright green fairway. He was wearing his powder blue
slacks and his favorite alpaca sweater, white with dark blue piping up the
sleeves. Bill caught sight of a golf ball nestled in a clump of dandelions. His
father was intent on the ball, lining up a second shot to the green. Bill felt
apprehension tighten his throat. His hands trembled as his father suddenly
relaxed his pose. He looked over his shoulder, straight into Bill's eyes. He
winked and casually pushed the ball clear of the weeds. The ball exposed
was incandescent, each dimple seemed to catch fire until it shone brilliant
white and the glare made Bill turn away but he could not escape it because
he was not there.

The movers finally managed to wedge their van under the carport roof.    2
At first Bill Wong kept to his study. He heard his wife out on the driveway
and avoided her, avoided the squabble she'd promised when she phoned the
night before from "The Chickencoop," his name for his sister-in-law's duplex
in Chinatown. Last night on the phone he heard the television hissing the
news and there was the brittle sizzling of a wok in the kitchen. His wife was
calling from the living room. He suspected the conversation was being overheard. He pictured his sister-in-law, her husband, the oldest daughter with
her hand over her mouth, all perched around the extension, three monkeys
listening intently. He politely inquired about the children who now lived in

1. The god of the kitchen; the image is part of a mosaic of popular, Taoist household duties.

Hong Kong with their grandmother. They were happy. "Of course they're happy," she snapped. "They like their grandma." Her sister was happy to get the furniture, the linen, the dishes. Bill resisted the urge to ask where in the hell she would put it. But she read his mind. "You got the house. I get everything else tomorrow, Bill, everything." The emphasis was like everything else in their marriage, awkward, unnecessary. Would the kids drop him a postcard? There was a pause, then his sister-in-law answered from the kitchen.

"Bill? This is Mamie," she said abruptly. Now Bill was sure her husband was listening, too. His wife fumbled with the receiver in the living room, then hung up.    3

"Goddamn it, put Alice back on the phone." He tried to sound testy, but it came out like a whine. All of Alice's family could read his mind.    4

"I'm still here," Mamie said.    5

"That's swell."    6

"Now, Bill. Alice and us think it's better if the kids don't think about you for a while," she began.    7

"Mamie, this is none of your goddamned . . . oh, shit . . ." How in the hell would they accomplish that? Horrible Chinese tortures? A water cure? Prefrontal lobotomy?    8

"You know they're learning to write Chinese? By Christmas, they can write to you in Chinese."    9

Her twisted optimism and the smell of bait rising from her unctuous tones made him sick. "Gee, that's terrific, Mamie. How am I supposed to read it?"    10

"Now don't you be selfish, Bill. You let your own ignorance rob your kids of their heritage. That's your way."    11

"Terrific, Mamie," he said, letting his voice drop to a whisper.    12

"What did you say? What, Bill?" he heard as he slammed the receiver against the wall. It had bounced on the linoleum twice, then swung by the cord, emitting shrill angry squeals.    13

There was nothing left to hear. The following day he sat in the shade by the side of the house sipping from the hose and smelling bay leaves. He watched his wife with the toaster under her arm struggle down the steep driveway to her car. She had come in the company of the moving men. Mamie had her kids to look after.    14

Her atrocious green knit dress was tight around the sleeves and her arms looked creased and damp with sweat. She'd gained some weight in the few months since the divorce. She looked vulnerable. She avoided seeing him, and she left before the van finally rolled down the hill at dusk, followed by a pack of neighborhood dogs that barked and snapped. The engine exploded as the muffler tore against the pavement. He watched the truck make its way down the narrow road. Then there was nothing left to see.    15

The lights of his neighbor's garage beamed through the tangle of ivy that had begun to climb the window of his study. He smiled at his reflection.    16

"Let's get stoned," he invited himself. He yanked his desk drawer open, found the dope, and rolled a joint. Without thinking, he looked over his shoulder, then examined his reflection again. Paranoia, he thought. No one here to tell him not to smoke, no children around to be corrupted. He studied himself, one eyebrow raised, peering out from a frame of ivy. He swept the stray crumbs of pot from his desk blotter into a plastic bag, then tucked the cigarette papers and bag into a manila envelope marked "interdepartmental mail," snapped a rubber band around it, and set the package into his filing cabinet under "D" for dope. He ignored the papers he was supposed to correct, neatly stacked on his desk. The top page was stained red where he had spilled wine the night before.

Alice had thrown everything that was his into the long narrow corridor behind the laundry room. She'd stuck it all into paper cartons, filled boxes with his books and clothes and jumbled them on top of one another, a precarious pile threatened with momentary collapse. But there was nothing unusual about the room's disorder. The cold and damp creeping through the unheated walls had already warped the unpainted pine bookshelf he had built after the collapse of his marrige. Overdue notices from the school library were sandwiched between pictures drawn by his daughter that curled out from his bulletin board with her name and date of execution. They were nearly a year old.

He clenched the joint tightly between his teeth, touched a match to the end without inhaling the flame, then filled his lungs with smoke. He felt petulant and self-indulgent. It was all clear. His wife was a vampire, and now she watched him from every dark window in the empty house. Soy sauce dribbled down her jaws. Now that he was starting to relax, settled down with his smoke, she wanted to make love. Afraid? There was nothing to be afraid of.

In the kitchen someone had taken a chicken pie out of the refrigerator and left it to thaw on the counter top. He pulled a chair from the study and sat at the backdoor, listening to the chicken pie drip into the sink and the sounds of the neighborhood settling into evening. He could still hear birds slapping against the curtain of eucalyptus trees in the grove at the bottom of the driveway. The night had turned cold and a thick cloud cover erased the last lights in the sky. He finished his smoke, pinched the last ember between his fingers, then swallowed the roach. Supper. The taste of ash and paper, the alfalfa smell of it all, shut his lips against a mouthful of saliva he could feel welling up from his throat. But there was no place to spit. He stripped his shirt off and washed and drank from the garden hose. "God in heaven, I'm free," he said. His voice was tentative and hoarse. He went back in the house and fell asleep on the carpet in the empty living room.

The morning sun had just broken over the ridge of hills, burning away the fog trapped in the crown of redwood trees behind the house. Bill finished his shower, then dripped water down the hall to the linen closet where he discovered she had taken every towel from the shelves. He remembered her words, "Everything. Everything." He rubbed himself dry with an old sweat-shirt he found in a bag of garbage in the kitchen that smelled of rotting chicken pie. Peering out the window at the trees, he wondered what time it was. She had taken the clock radio that always rested on the kitchen table. The table was gone, for that matter. He walked into the living room and kicked the front door open. The warm, steamy air began to condense on the windows near the floor, and he drew a stick figure with his big toe on a frosted pane of glass. He heard someone crunching up the path. The hair on his legs rose in the chill and he remembered he was naked. He wrapped the still damp sweatshirt around his waist.

Herb Greenberg carried a thermos bottle in his hand and the morning paper tucked under his arm. The sleeves of his old work shirt were wet from the heavy dew on the shrubs and his hands and fingers were white with cold. He had a transistor radio stuck in his shirt pocket with the earphone plugged into his ear so that he looked like he was wearing a hearing aid. He clumped heavily up the stairs, slapped the paper and thermos down on the porch rail, and pulled two coffee mugs from his back pockets. They looked at one another for a moment before Herb broke into an embarrassed grin, his wide walrus mustache twitching with what looked like dried toothpaste at the ends. 21

"Listen," he said. "My mother started at five-thirty this morning making blintzes 'cause she's flying to Haifa today, the Japs just bombed an Israeli airliner in Rome, and I just left the kids at the Hauptmanns. Let's get the hell out of here and go fishing." He walked past Bill to eye the empty living room. "Oh, man," he shouted. "Alice took everything, huh?" 22

"Morning, Herb." Bill opened the thermos and filled both cups. "Hey, the coffee smells fine. Thanks." 23

"That, my friend, is genuine Kenya Blue. Real coffee! None of this MJB[2] crap. Ethel was in the city yesterday picking up my mom at the air-port." Herb stepped out on the porch and took his mug in both hands, blow-ing a cloud of steam. "She saw Alice and the moving van yesterday afternoon and she guessed you didn't have a coffeepot anymore." 24

"Listen, I had to towel off with a roll of toilet paper!" Bill laughed and ran his hand through his hair, rubbing his damp scalp. "What time is it anyway? It must be early because I'm still out of my mind. Kenya Blue sounds like something I smoked last night." 25

Herb held his hands up, signaling Bill to be quiet. "Goddamn Japs," he whispered. "Good God in heaven, did you hear that?" 26

Bill put one finger in his ear. "No." 27

"I been following it on the news," he said. "Three Japanese terrorists opened up on passengers getting on an Israeli jetliner in Rome. Machine guns and hand grenades. Can you imagine that! And here my mother's going to Israel today. Christ on his everlovin' crutch! What in the hell do the Japs have against us?" 28

2. M. J. Brandenstein, a good San Francisco coffee. *Kenya Blue:* a gourmet coffee.

Bill was confused. "Japanese disguised as Arab guerrillas?" He tried not to smile. "To do in your mother?"                                                            29

"No, no. They were Japs, dressed like Japs," Herb said bitterly.          30

Bill wanted nothing to do with the conversation they were having. If     31
Herb wanted to rage about Japs, that was his business. "Listen, thank Ethel
for me. The coffee and all, that's very thoughtful."

Herb removed the plug from his ear and coiled the wire into his pocket.   32
"Thank her yourself. I think she's all hot to find you a nice Jewish girl."

"What, are you inviting me home to meet your sister?"                     33

Herb waggled a finger in his face. "My *mother*," he said. Bill sat back on  34
an aluminum garden chair and stuck his feet out over the railing. The coffee
cut through the hangover and he squinted in the sunlight, looking over the
wet trees and the ribbon of road that led out of the canyon to the town that
sat by the freeway that went to the city where his wife, his children, and the
Chinese were forever distant strangers. His feet were cold, his toes were
numb. He pushed the chair back, tipping. Herb grabbed his naked shoulder
from behind and Bill nearly fell over backward.

"Yeah, Wong, I'm inviting you to lunch if you can catch it. There's a     35
low tide at nine we can make." He caught the chair and held it, threatening
Bill.

"How can I refuse?"                                                       36

Herb set him upright. "All right. You see? I saved your life again. I     37
should adopt you since you obviously don't know how to take care of yourself." He laughed, pointing into the empty house. "Today's agenda calls for
rock fishing till noon."

"You sure you want me in the house with your mother around? I don't      38
want her to get the idea that I might be a terrorist in disguise." The sweat-
shirt had slipped off, and he hoped Ethel wasn't looking out from the garage.

"Nahh. You're no Jap." Herb grinned. "You're a Chinaman. I explained     39
that all to you already. Go on now and get your pants."

Bill dressed quickly, and together they walked across the hill to Herb's  40
house. He saw Ethel peering from the kitchen window and he waved. Herb
continued to rave about the Japs as they tied his long bamboo fishing poles
to the side of the car. Ethel appeared, wiping her hands on her apron.

"Good morning, Bill."                                                     41

"Morning, Ethel."                                                         42

"Herb," she said.                                                         43

Herb answered, "Good morning, Ethel."                                     44

"Please take out the garbage before you leave."                          45

"Where's Mama?" he said, turning toward the kitchen.                      46

"She went back to bed. Don't make so much noise." She turned to look      47
at Bill as he wrapped twine around the aerial to hold the fishing poles. "Did
you hear what time we had to get up this morning?"

"Yes, I heard." Bill looked at her face. She wasn't wearing any make-     48
up. She had that clean, well-scrubbed, early in the morning look she wore

after the kids had gone to school when the three of them would have coffee in their kitchen before he drove Herb to the bus stop on his way to class. "I am a Japanese terrorist this morning. I fell asleep on the rug last night and my back hurts. It's awful. I want to shoot up an airport and scream at people in Japanese."

"Well, you do look a little awful," she offered, teasing. 49

"Just put your finger there." He indicated a knot he wanted held down. 50

"Catch something we can eat for lunch and we'll cook it Chinese style." 51

She stood next to him, her finger on the twine. With her other hand she massaged his back. "Sure. Ahhh. Sure." Bill tensed and glanced back at her. She smiled coyly. 52

"Does the little terrorist want me to walk on his back?" 53

A short blast from the horn startled him, and he saw Herb behind the wheel. He leaned over and remonstrated, "She's too small, Wong. Throw her back and we'll catch a bigger one." 54

"Yes, boss," he said. 55

Bill stood up on the gray knuckle of rock. His tennis shoes were friction-less along the face of the tide pool. He stepped where the water was shallow-est and barely touched the green slime of algae surrounding every foothold. Tiny crabs skipped and fell before him off the rocks and skittered like gravel into the water before his feet slipped past them. Every rock seemed to be covered with crabs. The sound of the breakers steadied in his ears like his own breathing, like meditation. He lit a cigarette while his hands were still dry enough to strike a match. The imperceptible movement of the tide washed over the rock he stood on and he could feel water seep into his shoes. His feet felt warm and scummy. He slipped along a carpet of purple seaweed knee deep into the water and made his way along a submerged granite shelf, groping with the tip of his pole behind a ribbon of kelp into a long, deep fissure. He pulled back a fraction to let the hook dangle without getting tan-gled around the pole. Something nibbled at his bait, a slight bump and a nudge. It reminded him of his wife making love. "Come out, Alice," he crooned. 56

And whether it was the excitement of the catch or the weary energy he drew from the roach digesting in his stomach from the night before, he knew for certain it was his wife tucked warily in the dark crack, guarding his chil-dren from him, her arms and legs wedged against the tight walls of her watery cave. Come out, Alice, he sang, come on out of there. He eased the tip of his pole in another inch. 57

Why do you waste your time fishing for that stuff, she used to say. I can buy it for you cheap. For a dollar in Chinatown, she used to say. 58

He shortened his grip and with both hands set the hook with a quick jerk, and he had her, he had this fish passing for his wife. He felt a violent current of energy running the length of the fishing pole. Whatever it was, it 59 was big. He looked behind him, judging the distance to the beach. The water was too deep to wade straight across, so he edged around the pool to the last visible foothold and stood out of the water. He jammed both feet tight against a clump of mussel shell, trying to steady himself. His pants pockets poured sea water down his legs. He braced himself, then pulled hard, wrenching the fish from its hiding place. She pushed off from the shallow bottom, nearly jerking the pole out of his hand. The weight of her snapped at the short line, snapped the tip of his pole back and forth, and he felt his shoes scrape against the sharp edges of the shells, then pull away. He landed on both feet in water up to his waist. Now the violence was real for him. Too real. The fish pushed off from the shallow bottom and jumped clear of the water. The pole slipped from his hands and hit him. He stepped backward, green water and kelp and foam splashing in his face, his feet slipping on the rocky bottom. His feet came out from under him and he landed hard on the dry gravel. The pole lay between his legs. The fish on the end of it panted in the brackish puddle.

To hell with her, he didn't want her any more. The hook must have passed through the roof of her mouth. Blood flooded the white of one bulging eyeball. He stood up and kicked the pole into the water. "Hey, that's my pole!" Herb shouted from behind him. "And that's our lunch!" His soaking pants had nearly fallen off, and sea water stung the cuts on his hands and arms. He sat on a piece of driftwood and watched the fish twist over slowly, propped up by a hard ridge of bone on the top of its head, and he could see the flesh on its belly was a bright blue. Die, Alice, he thought to himself. The tail swept back and forth in a mimickry of agony, its gill plates snapped open and shut forcing air through its lungs and strangling it. Red fiddler crabs scurried around the fish, plucking delicately at the fins. Again it rolled over, its face impaled on the hook, the barb gleaming out of its one bloodshot eye. There was an impish expression on its face. A smile suggested by its thick purple lips, the fishing line pulling up against the mouth, became a sneer that belonged to his wife, his ex-wife. She seemed pleased. Why not? She'd just eaten. 60

Herb appeared on the bluff directly behind him and he laughed with excitement. "That damn thing must weigh ten pounds! Man, it sure is ugly, Wong!" Bill looked up at him and waved. He remembered now that the fish was for Ethel. They would cook it, Chinese style. He laughed to himself. 61

"That's my wife you're talking about." 62

Herb came leaping down from the rocks. "What did you say?" 63

"That's a capizone. Not known for their beauty." Bill took the end of the pole and heaved it out of the water, letting the fish roll in the dirt. 64

Herb was out on the patio picking coriander for the fish and Bill and Ethel were cooking in the kitchen. Bill watched him wander past the straw flowers Ethel had gathered on the windowsill just over the sink, pinpoints of startling amethyst and ruby in smoke glass bottles. Tiny ceramic miniatures 65 of farm animals Ethel bought in Chinatown pastured around a can of cleanser. Ethel padded barefoot across the kitchen floor and dipped hot oil over the fish laid on a bed of bean cake. "I hope I'm doing this right," she said.

"What we need is a piece of window screen stretched across some sort of frame. That way you wouldn't waste so much oil." He took the spoon from her hand.

"Did you cook for Alice?"

"Sure. I cooked. I even made a screen for frying the fish."

"But she took it." Ethel cocked her head, catching his words as they fell. "Everything," they said simultaneously. "Alice took everything!" They laughed.

The kitchen was redolent of garlic and ginger. The fish sent up clouds of thick steam as the oil crisped its flesh, drawing blisters of juice where the body had split apart.

"Careful!" Bill caught her by the shoulder as the oil exploded, sending a hot shower down around her legs. She danced back a pace from the stove.

"Ooh, I think I got the oil too hot."

"That's all right, but you better stand out of the way." Her eyes are positively green, he thought, they seem to change color in the sunlight coming through the open door.

"I saw the moving people yesterday. Was that the refrigerator going down the driveway?" She balanced her head against her hand, a finger stuck in her mouth, gnawing on her wedding ring.

"I went into the kitchen after everybody was gone," Bill said, "and found my frozen dinner in the sink. It was so sad, my dinner, all thawed out and starting to smell."

"Poor baby. You can put all the frozen dinners you want in our freezer, and we'll even give you a key for your very own." She heaped green onions and tomatoes on a chopping board. As she brushed past him he caught the aroma of lilac and garlic and something else like home permanent solution in her hair, her tight blonde curls turning limp and feathery in the humid kitchen. She wore one of Herb's old shirts with the tails wrapped around her waist. When she held herself to attention slicing tomatoes at the counter, he marveled at her legs, tanned to the ankles. Her faded denims were cut off and rolled up to where the pockets stuck out around her thighs like the uncreased tabs on a paper doll. Her toenails were brushed with blue polish.

Herb appeared at the kitchen door just as a covey of jets from the Naval Air Station laid a vapor trail across the sky. A clap of thunder rattled the dishes and silverware on the table. He stood there clutching the coriander wetly in one hand and watched the planes disappear.

"Leave the door open, Herbie. I don't want the smoke to settle into the walls." She smiled warmly at Bill, a guileless and direct smile that made him conscious of his eyes lowering to her knees, to her bare brown feet. "You must be starving to death," still a lax affectionate smile, a lopsided complexity as she rubbed the corners of her eyes tearing in the clouds of oily smoke.

He looked at Herb. "I think it's done."  79

Herb settled into his chair. "Where's Mama? Still asleep?" He put a  80
stalk of green onion in his mouth and clipped the stems from the coriander
with a pair of scissors. Bill swung the plate to the table with a flourish of
Ethel's pot holder. Herb deliberately sprinkled the leaves of coriander over
the steaming fish, and they all sat back in their chairs. It was a moment of
respect reserved for some unspoken grace. Ethel whispered, "I think she's
still asleep."

"Let her sleep then. Look," he said with mock awe. "Look at it." All  81
three groaned loudly, Herb beating on the table with his fork. "Let's eat it!"

Ethel started spooning fish onto Bill's plate. "Herbie, are you sure you  82
want to drive her to the airport? You know you're going to hit all that weekend traffic."

"Sure, sure. It's me or you, and I'd rather it be me. You're the mommy.  83
You can have the kids when they get home. That's why we have a successful
marriage, Bill. Sharing and caring."

Bill waited until Ethel was settled into her chair. Then he said, "You  84
can't sit down yet. Give me a fish eye."

Herb looked around the table, then went to the refrigerator for horse-  85
radish. Ethel leaned back and maneuvered a gallon of wine over her head
from the counter to the table and filled their glasses, spilling as much as she
poured. "No, no," she said. "The eyes are for Mama Greenberg."

Their knees touched under the table. Bill was sure it was an accident,  86
as sure as he knew there were bony ridges just beneath her kneecaps. He
could almost feel them. He finished his wine. "More, please," he said, holding out his glass.

"I think all this hijacking nonsense is ridiculous. You know your sister  87
had her handbag searched in Los Angeles when she took Mama to the airport." She bit into a tomato wedge and the juice ran down her chin.

Herb spooned horseradish over his fish. "It wasn't a hijacking. They  88
didn't even ask for anything, no demands, nothing, just opened up with their
Soviet," stressing the word *Soviet*, "machine guns, and blasted away. One's
still alive. I hope they castrate the bastard so he doesn't breed any more like
him. Fire with fire."

Ethel brought her eyebrows together and took a sip of wine. "That would  89
be a bucket of cold water."

Bill stood up as Herb's mother suddenly appeared in the kitchen. She  90
was tall like her son, the same dark brown hair and dark eyes, slightly puffed
with sleep, glazed, framed with waxy mascara. "So. When do we leave?" she
said excitedly.

"Mama, you should have slept longer," Herb said as he leaned across  91
the table to kiss her cheek.

"I can sleep on the plane." She turned her head to accept the kiss, reach-  92
ing at the same time to take Bill's hand. "You must be Bill. My son and
daughter say nice things about you."

"How do you do," Bill began, but her smile suddenly vanished. She 93 stood awkwardly over the table, Bill's hand in her own, and sniffed at what she saw in front of her. She completed the smile, let go of his hand, and picked at the fish with a teaspoon. "Very tasty, dear, but you know it's not nice to look at the whole thing. It looks right up at you."

They all stared down at it. The eyes were a solid milky white. A clove 94 of garlic protruded from its mouth and Ethel pushed it back, giggling.

"Is it fresh?" she demanded. 95

"Bill caught it this morning, Mama," Herb told her. 96

"Where?" she inquired suspiciously. 97

"In the ocean, Mama, in the ocean. We went fishing this morning, after 98 you went back to sleep."

She prowled around the kitchen replacing dishes. She snatched a dish- 99 towel from the back of Herb's chair and put it through the handle of the dishwasher, then took a sponge and wiped up spilled oil from the counter top. "Where are the children now, Ethel?"

"Mrs. Hauptmann's got them, Mama. She gives them their lunch today." 100 Ethel delicately removed a bone from between her lips. "They don't like fish either."

"So who can blame them?" She began laughing at herself, caught Bill's 101 eye and stopped. "All right, food is food. Is this the way the Chinese cook fish, Bill?" He nodded. She heaved a sigh. "Bill, you just have to put up with me. I have to know everything, don't I, Herbie?"

"Herb said you made blintzes this morning, Mrs. Greenberg." 102

"You like blintzes? Ethel, you give Bill some blintzes from out of the 103 freezer."

"I love blintzes," Bill said. 104

She sat down between Herb and Ethel and motioned to Bill. "Eat." She 105 was too excited to eat. "You have that house with the steep driveway right next door? You must get a lot of sun up there. You have a garden?"

Bill nodded through an exchange of questions and a barrage of small 106 talk. Now and again he caught Ethel smiling. She began to imitate his every nod. When he folded his arms, she folded hers. Mrs. Greenberg explained that she would fly to Tell Aviv, then to Haifa. Her niece had married an Israeli engineer. Bill poured wine for her, and she allowed for a second glass, then a third. She described an enormous family as she talked, and she reached out with her hands to touch her son. She held his hand to her cheek, and rapped the knuckles of her other hand on the table for luck. "We have big families," she said with a great deal of satisfaction. She reached for Ethel and patted her on the arm. "You must know about big families, Bill. The Chinese always have big families, like Jews. Herbie and Ethel are waiting for what I don't know. Two beautiful children, but just two. Did you come from a big family, Bill?"

"No," Bill said. "I was an only child." 107

"You know, I can tell. You don't know how to talk through an old lady. 108

You're too quiet. That's a good thing sometimes, but sometimes a good thing is too much."

"My mother had a large family." 109

"Yes?" she said. "How many?" 110

"Nine." 111

"Nine? Nine is a good size. We had eleven, but one died." 112

"Who, Mama?" Herb carried his plate to the sink. 113

"I had a sister and she died of pneumonia when she was four. She was Miriam. I was only five, but I remember her." 114

"My mother had a sister who died when she was young," Bill confided. 115

"Yes?" She beamed across the remains of the fish. "There, you see?" 116

Bill thought it was a strange issue to make an alliance from. But he was drawn to her, hostile, then open, testy like a peacock and at once glorious. "But I never heard them speak of her," he offered. "I saw her picture once in a photo album my uncle kept." 117

"But that's the way. They had nine to take care of, your grandparents." 118

"Yes," he said. 119

"That's what families are for," she said. 120

"What are they for?" 121

"So when you lose one, you have more." 122

"Wouldn't it be the same if you never had one, never started?" 123

"Started what? Everybody's got a family. What do you mean? You come from one family, you make another." 124

Bill didn't know whether to laugh or not. He was confused. Maybe she was drunk. 125

"Now you, Bill, you're not young but you're not old, either. When you're as old as me, maybe you want to sit in one place. Stand still, maybe. Maybe. Me, I don't want to wait around to die." 126

Ethel was at the sink listening to them talk. "Mama's got one foot in the grave." 127

"No! That's a bad joke! I'm not dying, not yet! I'm only being practical. Who wants me to die on them? Who wants to walk into my room and find me home, but not home. It would kill my friends, I mean, they're not chickens. So I keep moving. Maybe I'll go in the airplane or someplace maybe where they can send a body home, but they pack me up. It's easier. I fall down and maybe I won't scare somebody to death. I don't know. Maybe you're right. If you never start—how can that be? Everybody has family." She stopped abruptly. Finishing the rest of her wine, she started to laugh. "You made me talk and I don't even know what I'm talking about, Bill." 128

Herb roused himself from the half-sleep he had fallen into while his mother was talking, and got up from the table. "It's about time. Let's get your luggage, Mama." 129

Bill rose, smiling. He steadied himself on the table. He began, "I'm glad we got drunk together." 130

But she put her hands to his lips. She leaned across the table and whis- 131 pered in his ear. "Who would have me," she hissed, "who wants an old lady around the house after a few days?"

"Come live with me, Mama," Bill said softly.                                        132

She stood back and smiled at him. "You should have children, Bill."                 133

And before he could reply, Herb lied. "Bill's a confirmed bachelor,                 134
Mama."

"Well, not confirmed," Bill said.                                                    135

She nodded as if she understood. She straightened herself up and began              136
to talk energetically. "I stick my nose into everybody's business. But I'm a
great-grandmother once over so it's forgivable. You'll pardon me, but I'm
sure your mama would say the same thing. You should marry, have children." She indicated Herb and Ethel with a wave of her hand. "Have a big
family. My speech is over." She laughed, and Bill heard a faint edge of contempt in her laughter.

Ethel winked at Bill from over her shoulder. "Maybe you can find Bill               137
a nice Jewish girl, Mama, in Haifa."

"Are there Chinese in Haifa?" Herb asked.                                          138

"The Jews and the Chinese," she said, standing in the middle of the                139
room and weaving her eyes back and forth from her son to his wife, "they're
the same." She walked to the door and Herb followed. "You know there are
Jews in China, there must be Chinese in Haifa. It's all the same, even in Los
Angeles." She went out the door.

They stood in the garage together while Herb put her suitcases in the              140
trunk and started the car. Mrs. Greenberg gave Ethel a long hug, then walked
up to Bill. "You have a safe journey Mrs. Greenberg. I'm glad to have met
you."

"So polite you are." She shook his hand. "I was glad to meet you, too.             141
You're too quiet, though." Then, loudly, over the noise of the car, she said,
"Ethel, you get him married. You get married before I come back."

He nodded.                                                                         142

"Drive carefully, Herbie," Ethel shouted as the car backed slowly out             143
of the garage. She waved as the station wagon turned the corner and disappeared.

Ethel breathed a sigh of relief. They stood together in the driveway. A           144
riot of fuchsias hung from the redwood baskets suspended over their heads.
The sound of bees flew around their ears. "Thank you, Ethel. Lunch was
fine."

"Oh, Bill." She stretched her arms and yawned deliberately in his face.           145
"Mama's right, you're so polite." She crossed over the driveway, tracing little
dance steps on the concrete. Then, setting her foot on a tricycle, she pushed
off up the path littered with empty paint cans and discarded lumber that
connected their houses, coasting to a stop against some loose cinder blocks
scattered in the weeds. She looked over her shoulder at him. "Bet you can't
catch me," she shouted.

Bill felt such irony in the confession he made to himself as he slowly            146 followed her through the trees. He probably couldn't catch her. His feet struck the hard pan and he nearly stumbled over the exposed roots of creosote bushes that held the hill together during the long wet winters he would spend in his empty house, alone with his neighbor's wife. He found his footing in the eroded path the rain cut in the earth. He gathered his energies together and took the hill at a jog. He could see Ethel's head, just visible beyond his driveway. He followed her path, marked by a cloud of fine yellow dust that hung in his face and caught in his nose and throat.

She was standing on the porch pouring herself a cup of coffee from the thermos he'd forgotten to return. He stood for a moment at the bottom of the stairs, catching his breath. She saw him, smiled, then wandered uncertainly through the open doorway. He found her in the living room, her back to him, staring at the blank walls. She refused to turn around even as he wrapped his arms around her from behind.

"Got ya!" he said, his tone a shade too jovial. Herb's shirt was already unbuttoned. He untied the shirt tails and gently kissed the nape of her neck.

"You didn't chase me," she complained in a whisper as his hands covered both of her breasts.

Bill spent the rest of the evening in his study. He had thrown the window open to let the stale air escape, and he heard the Greenberg children's noisy return just before nightfall. He watched the lights of Herb's station wagon as it pulled up the road a few minutes later, saw the momentary red afterglow of the brake lights, heard the engine sputter to a stop and the garage door slide shut. His hands went searching through his desk drawer and found a nail clipper. He pared methodically at his fingernails, scraping bits of dry fish scale from under the cuticles. He licked his thumb and tasted the salty wrinkles that lined the back of his hands. Tiny cracks appeared where he'd cut himself on the rocks, and they stung as he scratched away the dried skin.

It was cold now, and he closed the window. A few shreds of ivy caught in it and hung inside the frame. He could see fog gathering along the lowest ridges of the hillside, caught in the brittle blue glare of a street lamp. He pulled the filing cabinet open, shook out some dope and rolled a joint, carefully brushing the stems and seeds into an ashtray. He snapped his desk light on and lit the joint, the smoke easing down his throat and filling his lungs. He held his breath for a moment, then blew a white cloud billowing around the lamp. There was an initial disappointment, a change that he could taste as chemistry blunting his mind, the acrid combustion of cigarette paper and spit. But suddenly the taste was gone. His mouth was dry. A premonition that Ethel was looking over his shoulder made him glance into the darkened window to catch her reflection behind him. But he was alone. His hand held the burning joint in front of his mouth, the smoke curling undisturbed across his face. A vague collection of swarthy Japanese in mufti crowding around Herb's station wagon at the airport grew in his mind's eye.

# STUDY QUESTIONS

1. Ethel does wok cooking; Bill likes blintzes; since there are Jews in China, there must be Chinese in Haifa. Is this the realization of the American dream of the melting pot? Where has Bill's ex-wife gone? Where does her sister live? Is there any implied relationship between integration or assimilation and positive values? Can we assume the story or author agrees with Bill and the Greenbergs? (Note that the only stereotypical elements seem to be the family names—"typical" Chinese, "Wong"; typical Jewish, "Greenberg.")

2. The author and the main CHARACTER, through whose eyes and mind we see and understand the story, are both youngish Chinese-American men and college teachers living in California. Can we assume the two are the same? or that Bill Wong speaks for and has the full sympathy of the author? Do you like Bill Wong? approve of his actions and values? have hostile or mixed feelings about him?

3. What does the opening dream sequence have to do with the story? Do all elements of the dream figure in the ACTION or meaning of the story? The final sentence is also in Bill's mind or "mind's eye": how do its details reflect what has gone before in the story? What does the imagined scene suggest about Bill's desires?

4. Were you prepared for the chase scene and what follows it in the story? What hints were there earlier of what was to come?

# Paula Gunn Allen

Sioux-Laguna and Lebanese-Jewish, Paula Gunn Allen was born in 1939 in Cubero, New Mexico. Her family spoke five languages when she was growing up. It is to this mixture she attributes her being a poet. She believes that poetry should be useful, and that the use-full is the beauty-full. "Language, like a woman, can bring into being what was not in being; it can, like food, transform one set of materials into another set of materials." She holds a doctorate from the University of New Mexico and is chair of Native American studies at San Francisco State University.

We traditionally think of Pocahontas, the Indian maid who saved both Captain John Smith and John Rolfe, whom she married, as a noble savage, good but rather simple, and the men she saved and served as "civilized," and therefore wiser and more sophisticated. This poem puts a rather different slant on things.

# POCAHONTAS TO HER ENGLISH HUSBAND, JOHN ROLFE

Had I not cradled you in my arms,
oh beloved    perfidious one,
you would have died.
And how many times did I pluck you
from certain death in the wilderness—                                      5
my world through which you stumbled
as though blind?
Had I not set you tasks
your masters far across the sea
would have abandoned you—                                                 10
did abandon you, as many times they
left you to reap the harvest of their lies;
still you survived    oh my fair husband
and brought them gold
wrung from a harvest I taught you                                          15
to plant: Tobacco.    It
is not without irony that by this crop
your descendants die, for other powers
than those you know take part in this.
And indeed I did rescue you                                               20
not once but a thousand thousand times
and in my arms you slept, a foolish child,
and beside me you played,
chattering nonsense about a God
you had not wit to name;                                                  25
and wondered you at my silence—
simple foolish wanton maid you saw,
dusky daughter of heathen sires
who knew not the ways of grace—
no doubt, no doubt.                                                       30
I spoke little, you said.
And you listened less.
But played with your gaudy dreams
and sent ponderous missives to the throne
striving thereby to curry favor                                           35
with your king.    I saw you well.    I
understood the ploy and still protected you,

going so far as to die in your keeping—
a wasting, putrifying death, and you,
deceiver, my husband, father of my son,                    40
survived, your spirit bearing crop
slowly from my teaching, taking
certain life from the wasting of my bones.


## STUDY QUESTIONS

1. When is Pocahontas speaking this poem?

2. What did Pocahontas die of?

3. How would you describe the TONE of this speech to her husband? (You may want
   to try reading it aloud, as if you were acting the part.)


# Wendy Rose


Editor *(American Indian Quarterly)*, anthropologist *(Aboriginal Tattooing in Califor-nia)*, professor (Native American studies, University of California, Berkeley), artist, and poet *(Lost Copper*—nominated for the American Book Award in 1981—and *Halfbreed Chronicles*, from which "Julia" is taken), Hopi/Miwok Wendy Rose is a major force in Native American culture.

This dramatic monologue created out of a horrible and pathetic reality challenges our sympathetic imagination.


# JULIA

Julia Pastrana, 1832–60, was a singer and dancer billed in the circus as "The Ugliest Woman in the World" or "Lion Lady." She was a Mexican Indian, born with a deformed bone structure of the face and hair growing from her entire body. Her manager, in an attempt to maintain control over her professional life, married her. She believed in him and was heard to say on the morning of her wedding, "I know he loves me for my own sake." When she gave birth to her son, she saw that he had inherited her own deformities plus some lethal gene that killed him at the age of six hours. In less than a week, Julia also died. Her husband, unwilling to abandon his

financial investment, had Julia and her infant son stuffed and mounted in a
wood and glass case. As recently as 1975 they were exhibited at locations in
the United States and Europe.

Tell me it was just a dream,
my husband, a clever trick
made by some tin-faced village god
or ghost-coyote pretending
to frighten me with his claim    5
that our marriage is made
of malice and money. Oh tell me again
how you admire my hands, how
my jasmine tea is rich and strong,
my singing sweet, my eyes so dark    10
you would lose yourself swimming,
man into flesh, as you mapped the pond
you would own. That was not all.
The room grew cold
as if to joke with these    15
warm days; the curtains blew out
and fell back against
the moon-painted sill.
I rose from my bed like a spirit
and, not a spirit at all, floated    20
slowly to my great glass oval
to see myself reflected
as the burnished bronze woman,
skin smooth and tender,
I know myself to be in the dark    25
above the confusion
of French perfumes and
I was there in the mirror
and I was not.
I had become hard    30
as the temple stones of Otomi,
hair grown over my ancient face
like black moss, gray
as jungle fog soaking green
the tallest tree tops.    35
I was frail as
the breaking dry branches
of my winter wand canyons
standing so still as if

to stand forever. Oh                                          40
such a small room—
no bigger than my elbows outstretched
and just as tall as my head.
A small room from which
to sing open the doors                                        45
with my cold graceful mouth,
my rigid lips, silences
dead as yesterday, cruel as what
the children say, cold
as the coins that glitter                                     50
in your pink fist.
And another terrifying magic
in the cold of that tall box: in my arms
or standing next to me
on a tall table by my right shoulder                          55
a tiny doll that
looked like me . . . oh my husband
tell me again
this is only a dream
I wake from warm                                              60
and today is still today,
summer sun and quick rain;
tell me, husband, how you love me
for my self one more time.
It scares me so                                               65
to be with child
lioness
with cub.


# STUDY QUESTIONS

1. To what does "it" in the first line refer?

2. How does Julia in the dark imagine herself to be?

3. Explain lines 28–29—"I was there in the mirror / and I was not."

4. In lines 53–57, Julia says there's a doll that looks like her standing near her; who or what is that "doll"? In the last four lines of the poem, Julia says she is with child. Is that true? When is the poem being spoken by Julia? Where is she?

# Gary Soto

C alifornian Gary Soto (born 1952), who writes fiction, nonfiction, and poetry, has won many awards, including a Guggenheim Fellowship, the Academy of American Poets Award, Discovery—The Nation Prize, *Poetry*'s Bess Hoskins Prize, and, in 1985, the American Book Award for his volume of recollections, *Living Up the Street*. That was the same year *Small Faces*, from which this selection is taken, was published. Soto teaches Chicano studies and English at the University of California, Berkeley.

Soto goes to meet his Japanese girlfriend's family and is relieved to find that they are like Mexicans—only different.

## LIKE MEXICANS

My grandmother gave me bad advice and good advice when I was in my early teens. For the bad advice, she said that I should become a barber because they made good money and listened to the radio all day. "Honey, they don't work como burros," she would say every time I visited her. She made the sound of donkeys braying. "Like that, honey!" For the good advice, she said that I should marry a Mexican girl. "No Okies, hijo"—she would say—"Look, my son. He marry one and they fight every day about I don't know what and I don't know what." For her, everyone who wasn't Mexican, black, or Asian were Okies. The French were Okies, the Italians in suits were Okies. When I asked about Jews, whom I had read about, she asked for a picture. I rode home on my bicycle and returned with a calendar depicting the important races of the world. "Pues si, son Okies tambien!"[1] she said, nodding her head. She waved the calendar away and we went to the living room where she lectured me on the virtues of the Mexican girl: first, she could cook and, second, she acted like a woman, not a man, in her husband's home. She said she would tell me about a third when I got a little older.

I asked my mother about it—becoming a barber and marrying Mexican. She was in the kitchen. Steam curled from a pot of boiling beans, the radio was on, looking as squat as a loaf of bread. "Well, if you want to be a barber—they say they make good money." She slapped a round steak with a

1. Well yes, they're Okies too.

knife, her glasses slipping down with each strike. She stopped and looked up. "If you find a good Mexican girl, marry her of course." She returned to slapping the meat and I went to the backyard where my brother and David King were sitting on the lawn feeling the inside of their cheeks.

"This is what girls feel like," my brother said, rubbing the inside of his cheek. David put three fingers inside his mouth and scratched. I ignored them and climbed the back fence to see my best friend, Scott, a second-generation Okie. I called him and his mother pointed to the side of the house where his bedroom was a small aluminum trailer, the kind you gawk at when they're flipped over on the freeway, wheels spinning in the air. I went around to find Scott pitching horseshoes.

I picked up a set of rusty ones and joined him. While we played, we talked about school and friends and record albums. The horseshoes scuffed up dirt, sometimes ringing the iron that threw out a meager shadow like a sundial. After three argued-over games, we pulled two oranges apiece from his tree and started down the alley still talking school and friends and record albums. We pulled more oranges from the alley and talked about who we would marry. "No offense, Scott," I said with an orange slice in my mouth, "but I would never marry an Okie." We walked in step, almost touching, with a sled of shadows dragging behind us. "No offense, Gary," Scott said, "but I would *never* marry a Mexican." I looked at him: a fang of orange slice showed from his munching mouth. I didn't think anything of it. He had his girl and I had mine. But our seventh-grade vision was the same: to marry, get jobs, buy cars and maybe a house if we had money left over.

We talked about our future lives until, to our surprise, we were on the downtown mall, two miles from home. We bought a bag of popcorn at Penneys and sat on a bench near the fountain watching Mexican and Okie girls pass. "That one's mine," I pointed with my chin when a girl with eyebrows arched into black rainbows ambled by. "She's cute," Scott said about a girl with yellow hair and a mouthful of gum. We dreamed aloud, our chins busy pointing out girls. We agreed that we couldn't wait to become men and lift them onto our laps.

But the woman I married was not Mexican but Japanese. It was a surprise to me. For years, I went about wide-eyed in my search for the brown girl in a white dress at a dance. I searched the playground at the baseball diamond. When the girls raced for grounders, their hair bounced like something that couldn't be caught. When they sat together in the lunchroom, heads pressed together, I knew they were talking about us Mexican guys. I saw them and dreamed them. I threw my face into my pillow, making up sentences that were good as in the movies.

But when I was twenty, I fell in love with this other girl who worried my mother, who had my grandmother asking once again to see the calendar of the Important Races of the World. I told her I had thrown it away years before. I took a much-glanced-at snapshot from my wallet. We looked at it together, in silence. Then grandma reclined in her chair, lit a cigarette, and said, "Es pretty." She blew and asked with all her worry pushed up to her forehead: "Chinese?"

I was in love and there was no looking back. She was the one. I told my mother who was slapping hamburger into patties. "Well, sure if you want to marry her," she said. But the more I talked, the more concerned she became. Later I began to worry. Was it all a mistake? "Marry a Mexican girl," I heard my mother say in my mind. I heard it at breakfast. I heard it over math problems, between Western Civilization and cultural geography. But then one afternoon while I was hitchhiking home from school, it struck me like a baseball in the back: my mother wanted me to marry someone of my own social class—a poor girl. I considered my fiancee, Carolyn, and she didn't look poor, though I knew she came from a family of farm workers and pull-yourself-up-by-your-bootstraps ranchers. I asked my brother, who was marrying Mexican poor that fall, if I should marry a poor girl. He screamed "Yeah" above his terrible guitar playing in his bedroom. I considered my sister who had married Mexican. Cousins were dating Mexican. Uncles were remarrying poor women. I asked Scott, who was still my best friend, and he said, "She's too good for you, so you better not." 8

I worried about it until Carolyn took me home to meet her parents. We drove in her Plymouth until the houses gave way to farms and ranches and finally her house fifty feet from the highway. When we pulled into the drive, I panicked and begged Carolyn to make a U-turn and go back so we could talk about it over a soda. She pinched my cheek, calling me a "silly boy." I felt better, though, when I got out of the car and saw the house: the chipped paint, a cracked window, boards for a walk to the back door. There were rusting cars near the barn. A tractor with a net of spiderwebs under a mulberry. A field. A bale of barbed wire like children's scribbling leaning against an empty chicken coop. Carolyn took my hand and pulled me to my future mother-in-law who was coming out to greet us. 9

We had lunch: sandwiches, potato chips, and iced tea. Carolyn and her mother talked mostly about neighbors and the congregation at the Japanese Methodist Church in West Fresno. Her father, who was in khaki work clothes, excused himself with a wave that was almost a salute and went outside. I heard a truck start, a dog bark, and then the truck rattle away. 10

Carolyn's mother offered another sandwich, but I declined with a shake of my head and a smile. I looked around when I could, when I was not saying over and over that I was a college student, hinting that I could take care of her daughter. I shifted my chair. I saw newspapers piled in corners, dusty cereal boxes and vinegar bottles in corners. The wallpaper was bubbled from rain that had come in from a bad roof. Dust. Dust lay on lamp shades and window sills. These people are just like Mexicans, I thought. Poor people. 11

Carolyn's mother asked me through Carolyn if I would like a *sushi*. A plate of black and white things were held in front of me. I took one, wide-eyed, and turned it over like a foreign coin. I was biting into one when I saw a kitten crawl up the window screen over the sink. I chewed and the kitten 12 opened its mouth of terror as she crawled higher, wanting in to paw the leftovers from our plates. I looked at Carolyn who said that the cat was just showing off. I looked up in time to see it fall. It crawled up, then fell again.

We talked for an hour and had apple pie and coffee, slowly. Finally, we 13 got up with Carolyn taking my hand. Slightly embarrassed, I tried to pull away but her grip held me. I let her have her way as she led me down the hallway with her mother right behind me. When I opened the door, I was startled by a kitten clinging to the screen door, its mouth screaming "cat food, dog biscuits, *sushi*. . . ." I opened the door and the kitten, still holding on, whined in the language of hungry animals. When I got into Carolyn's car, I looked back: the cat was still clinging. I asked Carolyn if it were possibly hungry, but she said the cat was being silly. She started the car, waved to her mother, and bounced us over the rain-poked drive, patting my thigh for being her lover baby. Carolyn waved again. I looked back, waving, then gawking at a window screen where there were now three kittens clawing and screaming to get in. Like Mexicans, I thought. I remembered the Molinas and how the cats clung to their screens—cats they shot down with squirt guns. On the highway, I felt happy, pleased by it all. I patted Carolyn's thigh. Her people were like Mexicans, only different.

# STUDY QUESTIONS

1. Why does the NARRATOR's grandmother want him to become a barber? Who, according to her, are Okies? Why does Soto say, in the first paragraph, that his grandmother's advice to marry a Mexican girl was good advice? What is his mother's advice? Why does she seem so uninterested?

2. What is Soto's mother's advice when he says he wants to marry a Japanese girl? How does that advice seem to conflict with what he hears her voice saying inside him? How does he reconcile the conflicting advice?

3. Why is he worried about visiting his girlfriend's parents? Why does he feel "better" when he sees the chipped paint, cracked windows, and boards used as a walkway to the back door?

4. How are Carolyn's people "like Mexicans"? How are they different?

# Alice Childress

H er 1955 play *Trouble in Mind* won an Obie Award and her novel *A Hero Ain't Nothing but a Sandwich* was nominated for both the Newbery Medal and the National Book Award, yet Alice Childress (born in Charleston, South Carolina, in 1920) still seems relatively neglected.

*Wedding Band* is set in 1918, during World War I, when, after decades of Jim Crow racist laws, blacks expected that their service in the war would earn them greater rights at war's end. The play was first performed (at the University of Michigan) in 1966, in the middle of the Vietnam War and just after the passage of the Civil Rights Act of 1965, which raised similar hopes for the future of racial harmony and justice in America. It was performed in New York, directed by the author and Joseph Papp, in 1972 and the following year was on national television (ABC).

Childress's earlier plays were scathing indictments of white "liberal" racism and class prejudice within the black community. She seemed to see in ordinary people more wisdom and humanity than she found in those who were more comfortably off and more removed from the reality of the life of the majority. The power and wisdom of the ordinary is evident here, too, in a play that is hopeful but tough, where virtue and vice are not parceled out neatly, one to each race. The separate but equal power of the monologues Herman and Julia speak more or less to themselves and to each other in the final scene is an emblem, perhaps, of the hope and the difficulties, the possibilities of love and of hate, in human relationships.

# WEDDING BAND

## A LOVE/HATE STORY IN BLACK AND WHITE

### CHARACTERS
### *(In Order of Appearance)*

| | |
|---|---|
| JULIA AUGUSTINE | THE BELL MAN |
| TEETA | PRINCESS |
| MATTIE | HERMAN |
| LULA GREEN | ANNABELLE |
| FANNY JOHNSON | HERMAN'S MOTHER |
| NELSON GREEN | |

# ACT I

## Scene 1

TIME: *Summer 1918 . . . Saturday morning. A city by the sea . . . South Carolina, U.S.A.*

SCENE: *Three houses in a backyard. The center house is newly painted and cheery looking in contrast to the other two which are weather-beaten and shabby. Center house is gingerbready . . . odds and ends of "picked up" shutters, picket railing, wrought iron railing, newel posts, a Grecian pillar, odd window boxes of flowers . . . every-thing clashes with a beautiful, subdued splendor; the old and new mingle in defiance of style and period. The playing areas of the houses are raised platforms furnished accord-ing to the taste of each tenant. Only one room of each house is visible.* JULIA AUGUS-TINE *(tenant of the center house) has recently moved in and there is still unpacking to be done. Paths are worn from the houses to the front yard entry. The landlady's house and an outhouse are offstage. An outdoor hydrant supplies water.*

JULIA *is sleeping on the bed in the center house.* TEETA, *a girl about eight years old, enters the yard from the Stage Right house. She tries to control her weeping as she examines a clump of grass. The muffled weeping disturbs* JULIA's *sleep. She starts up, half rises from her pillow, then falls back into a troubled sleep.* MATTIE, TEETA's *mother, enters carrying a switch and fastening her clothing. She joins the little girl in the search for a lost quarter. The search is subdued, intense.*

MATTIE: You better get out there and get it! Did you find it? Gawd, what've I done to be treated this way! You gon' get a whippin' too.

FANNY: [*Enters from the front entry. She is landlady and the self-appointed, fifty-year-old representative of her race.*] Listen, Mattie . . . I want some quiet out here this mornin'.

MATTIE: Dammit, this gal done lost the only quarter I got to my name.

[LULA *enters from the direction of the outhouse carrying a covered slop jar. She is forty-five and motherly.*]

"Teeta," I say, "Go to the store, buy three cent grits, five cent salt pork, ten cent sugar; and keep your hand closed 'roun' my money." How I'm gonna sell any candy if I got no sugar to make it? You little heifer! [*Goes after* TEETA *who hides behind* LULA.]

LULA: Gawd, help us to find it.

MATTIE: Your daddy is off sailin' the ocean and you got nothin' to do but lose money! *I'm gon' put you out in the damn street, that's what!*

[TEETA *cries out.* JULIA *sits up in the bed and cries out.*]

JULIA: No . . . no . . .

FANNY: You disturbin' the only tenant who's paid in advance.

LULA: Teeta, retrace your steps. Show Lula what you did.

TEETA: I hop-hop-hop . . . [*Hops near a post-railing of* JULIA's *porch.*]

MATTIE: What the hell you do that for?

LULA: There 'tis! That's a quarter . . . down in the hole . . . Can't reach it . . .

[JULIA *is now fully awake. Putting on her house-dress over her camisole and petticoat.* MATTIE *takes an axe from the side of the house to knock the post out of the way.*]

MATTIE: Aw, *move*, move! That's all the money I got. I'll tear this damn house down and you with it!

FANNY: And I'll blow this police whistle.

[JULIA *steps out on the porch. She is an attractive brown woman about thirty-five years old.*]

MATTIE: Blow it . . . blow it . . . blow it . . . hot damn—[*Near tears. She decides to tell* JULIA *off also.*] I'll tear it down—that's right. If you don't like it—come on down here and whip me.

JULIA: [*Nervous but determined to present a firm stand.*] Oh, my . . . Good mornin' ladies. My name is Julia Augustine. I'm not gonna move.

LULA: My name is Lula. Why you think we wantcha to move?

FANNY: Miss Julia, I'm sorry your first day starts like this. Some people are ice cream and others just cow-dung. I try to be ice cream.

MATTIE: Dammit, I'm ice cream, too. Strawberry. [*Breaks down and cries.*]

FANNY: That's Mattie. She lost her last quarter, gon' break down my house to get it.

JULIA: [*Gets a quarter from her dresser.*] Oh my, dear heart, don't cry. Take this twenty-five cents, Miss Mattie.

MATTIE: No thank you, ma'm.

JULIA: And I have yours under my house for good luck.

FANNY: Show your manners.

TEETA: Thank you. You the kin'est person in the worl'.

[LULA *enters her house.* TEETA *starts for home, then turns to see if her mother is coming.*]

MATTIE: [*To* JULIA.] I didn't mean no harm. But my husband October's in the Merchant Marine and I needs my little money. Well, thank you. [*To* TEETA.] Come on, honey bunch.

[*She enters her house Stage Right.* TEETA *proudly follows.* LULA *is putting* NELSON's *breakfast on the table at Stage Left.*]

FANNY: [*Testing strength of post.*] My poor father's turnin' in his grave. He built these rent houses just 'fore he died . . . And he wasn't a carpenter. Shows what the race can do when we wanta. [*Feels the porch railing and tests its strength.*] That loud-mouth Mattie used to work in a white cat-house.

JULIA: A what?

FANNY: Sportin' house, house of . . . A whore house. Know what she used to do?

JULIA: [*Embarrassed.*] Not but so many things *to* do, I guess.

[FANNY *wants to follow her in the house but* JULIA *fends her off.*]

FANNY: Used to wash their joy-towels. Washin' joy-towels for one cent apiece. I wouldn't work in that kinda place—would you?

JULIA: Indeed not.

FANNY: Vulgarity.

JULIA: [*Trying to get away.*] I have my sewing to do now, Miss Fanny.

FANNY: I got a lovely piece-a blue serge. Six yards. [*She attempts to get into the house but* JULIA *deftly blocks the door.*]

JULIA: I don't sew for people. [FANNY *wonders why not.*] I do homework for a store . . . hand-finishin' on ladies' shirt-waists.

FANNY: You 'bout my age . . . I'm thirty-five.

JULIA: [*After a pause.*] I thought you were younger.

FANNY: [*Genuinely moved by the compliment.*] Thank you. But I'm not married 'cause nobody's come up to my high standard. Where you get them expensive-lookin', high-class shoes?

JULIA: In a store. I'm busy now, Miss Fanny.

FANNY: Doin' what?

JULIA: First one thing then another. Good-day.

[*Thinks she has dismissed her. Goes in the house.* FANNY *quickly follows into the room . . . picks up a teacup from the table.*]

FANNY: There's a devil in your teacup . . . also prosperity. Tell me 'bout yourself, don't be so distant.

JULIA: It's all there in the tea-leaves.

FANNY: Oh, go on! I'll tell you somethin' . . . that sweet-face Lula killed her only child.

JULIA: No, she didn't.

FANNY: In a way-a speakin'. And then Gawd snatched up her triflin' husband. One nothin' piece-a man. Biggest thing he ever done for her was to lay down and die. Poor woman. Yes indeed, then she went and adopted this fella from the colored orphan home. Boy grew too big for a lone woman to keep in the house. He's a big, strappin', over-grown man now. I wouldn't feel safe livin' with a man that's not blood kin, 'doption or no 'doption. It's 'gainst nature. Oughta see the muscles on him.

JULIA: [*Wearily.*] Oh, my . . . I think I hear somebody callin' you.

FANNY: Yesterday the white-folks threw a pail-a dirty water on him. A black man on leave got no right to wear his uniform in public. The crackers don't like it. That's flauntin' yourself.

JULIA: Miss Fanny, I don't talk about people.

FANNY: Me neither. [*Giving her serious advice.*] We high-class, quality people oughta stick together.

JULIA: I really do stay busy.

FANNY: Doin' what? Seein' your beau? You have a beau haven't-cha?

JULIA: [*Realizing she must tell her something in order to get rid of her.*] Miss Johnson . . .

FANNY: Fanny.

JULIA: [*Managing to block her toward the door.*] My mother and father have long gone on to Glory.

FANNY: Gawd rest the dead and bless the orphan.

JULIA: Yes, I do have a beau . . . But I'm not much of a mixer. [*She now has* FANNY *out on the porch.*]

FANNY: Get time, come up front and see my parlor. I got a horsehair settee and a four piece, silver-plated tea service.

JULIA: Think of that.

FANNY: The first and only one to be owned by a colored woman in the United States of America. Salesman told me.

JULIA: Oh, just imagine.

[MATTIE *enters wearing a blue calico dress and striped apron.*]

FANNY: My mother was a genuine, full-blooded, qualified, Seminole Indian.

TEETA: [*Calls to her mother from the doorway.*] Please . . . Mama . . . Mama . . . Buy me a hair ribbon.

MATTIE: All right! I'm gon' buy my daughter a hair ribbon.

FANNY: Her hair is so short you'll have to nail it on. [FANNY *exits to her house.*]

MATTIE: That's all right about that, Fanny. Your father worked in a stinkin' phosphate mill . . . yeah, and didn't have a tooth in his head. Then he went and married some half Portuguese woman. I don't call that bein' in no damn society. I works for my livin'. I makes candy and I takes care of a little white girl. Hold this nickel 'til I get back. Case of emergency I don't like Teeta to be broke.

JULIA: I'll be busy today, lady.

MATTIE: [*As she exits carrying a tray of candy.*] Thank you, darlin'.

TEETA: Hey lady, my daddy helps cook food on a big war boat. He peels potatoes. You got any children?

JULIA: No . . . Grace-a Gawd. [*Starts to go in house.*]

TEETA: Hey, lady! Didja ever hear of Philadelphia? After the war that's where we're goin' to live. Philadelphia!

JULIA: Sounds like heaven.

TEETA: Jesus is the President of Philadelphia.

[TEETA *sweeps in front of* JULIA'S *house. Lights come up in* LULA'S *house.* NELSON *is eating breakfast. He is a rather rough-looking muscly fellow with a soft voice and a bittersweet sense of humor. He is dressed in civilian finery and his striped silk shirt seems out of place in the drab little room.* LULA *makes paper flowers, and the colorful bits of paper are seen everywhere as finished and partially finished flowers and stems, also a finished funeral piece. A picture of Abraham Lincoln hangs on the upstage wall.* LULA *is brushing* NELSON's *uniform jacket.*]

LULA: Last week the Bell Man came to collect the credit payment he says . . . "Auntie, whatcha doin' with Abraham Lincoln's pitcher on the wall? He was such a poor president."

NELSON: Tell the cracker to mind his damn business.

LULA: It don't pay to get mad. Remember yesterday.

NELSON: [*Studying her face for answers.*] Mama, you supposed to get mad when somebody throw a pail-a water on you.

LULA: It's their country and their uniform, so just stay out the way.

NELSON: Right. I'm not goin' back to work in that coal-yard when I get out the army.

LULA: They want you back. A bird in the hand, y'know.

NELSON: A bird in the hand ain't always worth two in the bush.

LULA: This is Saturday, tomorrow Sunday . . . thank Gawd for Monday; back to the army. That's one thing . . . Army keeps you off the street.

[*The sound of the* SHRIMP MAN *passing in the street.*]

SHRIMP MAN: [*Offstage.*] Shrimp-dee-raw . . . I got raw shrimp.

[NELSON *leaves the house just as* JULIA *steps out on her porch to hang a rug over the rail.* TEETA *enters* GREEN *house.*]

NELSON: Er . . . howdy-do, er . . . beg pardon. My name is Nelson. Lula Green's son, if you don't mind. Miss . . . er . . . Mrs.?

JULIA: [*After a brief hesitation.*] Miss . . . Julia Augustine.

NELSON: Miss Julia, you the best-lookin' woman I ever seen in my life. I declare you look jus' like a violin sounds. And I'm not talkin' 'bout pretty. You look like you got all the right feelin's, you know?

JULIA: Well, thank you, Mr. Nelson.

NELSON: See, you got me talkin' all outta my head.

[LULA *enters,* TEETA *follows eating a biscuit and carrying a milk pail . . . she exits toward street.*]

Let's got for a walk this evenin', get us a lemon phosphate.

JULIA: Oh, I don't care for any, Mr. Nelson.

LULA: That's right. She say stay home.

JULIA: [*To* NELSON.] I'm sorry.

NELSON: Don't send me back to the army feelin' bad 'cause you turn me down. Orange-ade tonight on your porch. I'll buy the oranges, you be the sugar.

JULIA: No, thank you.

NELSON: Let's make it—say—six o'clock.

JULIA: No, I said no!

LULA: Nelson, go see your friends. [*He waves goodbye to* JULIA *and exits through the back entry.*] He's got a lady friend, her name is Merrilee Jones. And he was just tryin' to be neighborly. That's how me and Nelson do. But you go on and stay to yourself. [*Starts toward her house.*]

JULIA: Miss Lula! I'm sorry I hurt your feelin's. Miss Lula! I have a gentleman friend, that's why I said no.

LULA: I didn't think-a that. When yall plan to cut the cake?

JULIA: Not right now. You see . . . when you offend Gawd you hate for it to be known. Gawd might forgive but people never will. I mean . . . when a man and a woman are not truly married . . .

LULA: Oh, I see.

JULIA: I live by myself . . . but he visits . . . I declare I don't know how to say . . .

LULA: Everybody's got some sin, but if it troubles your heart you're a gentle sinner, just a good soul gone wrong.

JULIA: That's a kind thought.

LULA: My husband, Gawd rest the dead, used to run 'round with other women; it made me kind-a careless with my life. One day, many long years ago, I was sittin' in a neighbor's house tellin' my troubles; my only child, my little boy, wandered out on the railroad track and got killed.

JULIA: That must-a left a fifty pound weight on your soul.

LULA: It did. But if we grow stronger . . . and rise higher than what's pullin' us down . . .

JULIA: Just like Climbin' Jacob's Ladder . . . [*Sings.*] Every round goes higher and higher . . .

LULA: Yes, rise higher than the dirt . . . that fifty pound weight will lift and you'll be free, free without anybody's by-your-leave. Do something to wash out the sin. That's why I got Nelson from the orphanage.

JULIA: And now you feel free?

LULA: No, no yet. But I believe Gawd wants me to start a new faith; one that'll make our days clear and easy to live. That's what I'm workin' on now. Oh, Miss Julia, I'm glad you my neighbor.

JULIA: Oh, thank you, Miss Lula! Sinners or saints, didn't Gawd give us a beautiful day this mornin'!

[*The sound of cow-bells clanking and the thin piping of a tin and paper flute.* TEETA *backs into the yard carefully carrying the can of milk.* THE BELL MAN *follows humming "Over There" on the flute. He is a poor white about thirty years old but time has dealt him some hard blows. He carries a large suitcase; the American flag painted on both sides, cowbells are attached.* THE BELL MAN *rests his case on the ground. Fans with a very tired-looking handkerchief. He cuts the fool by dancing and singing a bit of a popular song as he turns corners around the yard.*]

THE BELL MAN: [*As* LULA *starts to go in the house.*] Stay where you at, Aunty! You used to live on Thompson Street. How's old Thompson Street?

JULIA: [*A slightly painful memory.*] I moved 'bout a year ago, moved to Queen Street.

THE BELL MAN: Move a lot, don'tcha? [*Opens suitcase.*] All right, everybody stay where you at! [*Goes into a fast sales spiel.*] Lace-trim ladies' drawers! Stockin's, ladies stockin's . . . gottem for the knock-knees and the bow-legs too . . . white, black and navy blue! All right, no fools no fun! The joke's on me! Here we go! [*As he places some merchandise in front of the* WOMEN, *does a regular minstrel walk-around.*] Anything in the world . . . fifty cent a week and one long, sweet year to pay . . . Come on, little sister!

[TEETA *doing the walk-around with* THE BELL MAN.]

> And a-ring-ting-tang
> And-a shimmy-she-bang
> While the sun am a-shinin' and the sky am blue . . .
> And a-ring-ting-tang
> And-a shimmy-she-bang
> While the sun am a-shinin' and the sky am blue . . .

LULA: [*Annoyed with* TEETA'*s dancing with* THE BELL MAN.] Stop all that shimmy she-bang and get in the house! [*Swats at* TEETA *as she passes.*]

THE BELL MAN: [*Coldly.*] Whatcha owe me, Aunty?

LULA: Three dollars and ten cent. I don't have any money today.

THE BELL MAN: When you gon' pay?

LULA: Monday, or better say Wednesday.

JULIA: [*To divert his attention from* LULA.] How much for sheets?

THE BELL MAN: For you they on'y a dollar.

[JULIA *goes to her house to get the money.* THE BELL MAN *moves toward her house as he talks to* LULA.]

Goin' to the Service Men's parade Monday?

LULA: Yes sir. My boy's marchin'. [*She exits.*]

THE BELL MAN: Uh-huh, I'll getcha later. Lord, Lord, Lord, how'dja like to trot 'round in the sun beggin' the poorest people in the world to buy somethin' from you. This is nice. Real nice. [*To* JULIA.] A good friend-a mine was a nigra boy. Me 'n' him was jus' like that. Fine fella, he couldn't read and he couldn't write.

JULIA: [*More to herself than to him.*] When he learns you're gon' lose a friend.

THE BELL MAN: But talkin' serious, what is race and color? Put a paper bag over your head and who'd know the difference. Tryin' to remember me ain'tcha. I seen you one time coming out that bakery shop on Thompson Street, didn' see me.

JULIA: Is that so?

THE BELL MAN: [*Sits on the bed and bounces up and down.*] Awwww, Great Gawd-a-mighty! I haven't been on a high-built bed since I left the back woods.

JULIA: Please don't sit on my bed!

THE BELL MAN: Old country boy, that's me! Strong and healthy country boy . . . [*Not noticing any rejection.*] Sister, Um in need for it like I never been before. Will you 'commodate me? Straighten me, fix me up, will you? Wouldn't take but five minutes. Um quick like a jack rabbit. Wouldn't nobody know but you and me.

[*She backs away from him as he pants and wheezes out his admiration.*]

Um clean, too. Clean as the . . . Board-a Health. Don't believe in dippin' inta everything. I got no money now, but Ladies always need stockin's.

JULIA: [*Trying to keep her voice down, throws money at his feet.*] Get out of my house! Beneath contempt, that's what you are.

THE BELL MAN: Don't be lookin' down your nose at me . . . actin' like you Mrs. Martha Washington . . . Throwin' one chicken-shit dollar at me and goin' on . . .

JULIA: [*Picking up wooden clothes hanger.*] Get out! Out, before I take a stick to you.

THE BELL MAN: [*Bewildered, gathering his things to leave.*] Hell, what I care who you sleep with! It's your nooky. Give it 'way how you want to. I don't own no run-down bakery shop but I'm good as those who do. A baker ain' nobody . . .

JULIA: I wish you was dead, you just oughta be dead, stepped on and dead.

THE BELL MAN: Bet that's what my mama said first time she saw me. I was a fourteenth child. Damn women! . . . that's all right . . . Gawd bless you, Gawd be with you and let his light shine on you. I give you good for evil . . . God bless you! [*As he walks down the porch steps.*] She must be goin' crazy. Unfriendly, sick-minded bitch!

[TEETA *enters from* LULA's *house.* THE BELL MAN *takes a strainer from his pocket and gives it to* TEETA *with a great show of generosity.*]

Here, little honey. You take this sample. You got nice manners.

TEETA: Thank you, you the kin'est person in the world.

[THE BELL MAN *exits to the tune of clanking bells, and* LULA *enters.*]

JULIA: I hate those kind-a people.

LULA: You mustn't hate white folks. Don'tcha believe in Jesus? He's white.

JULIA: I wonder if he believes in me.

LULA: Gawd says we must love everybody.

JULIA: Just lovin' and lovin', no matter what? There are days when I love, days when I hate.

FANNY: Mattie, Mattie, mail!

JULIA: Your love is worthless if nobody wants it.

[FANNY *enters carrying a letter. She rushes over to Mattie's house.*]

FANNY: I had to pay the postman two cent. No stamp.

TEETA: [*Calls to* JULIA.] Letter from Papa! Gimmie my mama's five cents!

FANNY: [*To* TEETA.] You gon' end your days in the Colored Women's Jail-house.

[PRINCESS, *a little girl, enters skipping and jumping. She hops, runs and leaps across the yard.* PRINCESS *is six years old.* TEETA *takes money from* JULIA's *outstretched hand and gives it to* FANNY.]

MATTIE: [*To* MATTIE.] Letter from Papa! Gotta pay two cent!

FANNY: Now I owe you three cent . . . or do you want me to read the letter?

[PRINCESS *gets wilder and wilder, makes Indian war whoops.* TEETA *joins the noise-making. They climb porches and play follow-the-leader.* PRINCESS *finally lands on* JULIA's *porch after peeping and prying into everything along the way.*]

PRINCESS: [*Laughing merrily.*] Hello . . . hello . . . hello.

JULIA: [*Overwhelmed by the confusion.*] Well—hello.

FANNY: Get away from my new tenant's porch!

PRINCESS: [*Is delighted with* FANNY's *scolding and decides to mock her.*] My new tennis porch!

[MATTIE *opens the letter and removes a ten-dollar bill. Lost in thought she clutches the letter to her bosom.*]

FANNY: [*To* MATTIE.] Ought-a mind w-h-i-t-e children on w-h-i-t-e property!

PRINCESS: [*Now swinging on* JULIA's *gate.*] . . . my new tennis porch!

FANNY: [*Chases* PRINCESS *around the yard.*] You Princess! Stop that!

[JULIA *laughs but she is very near tears.*]

MATTIE: A letter from October.

FANNY: Who's gon' read it for you?

MATTIE: Lula!

PRINCESS: My new tennis porch!

FANNY: Princess! Mattie!

MATTIE: Teeta! In the house with that drat noise!

FANNY: It'll take Lula half-a day. [*Snatches letter.*] I won't charge but ten cent. [*Reads.*] "Dear, Sweet Molasses, My Darlin' Wife . . ."

MATTIE: No, I don't like how you make words sound. You read too rough.

[*Sudden offstage yells and screams from* TEETA *and* PRINCESS *as they struggle for possession of some toy.*]

PRINCESS: [*Offstage.*] Give it to me!

TEETA: No! It's mine!

MATTIE: [*Screams.*] Teeta! [*The* CHILDREN *are quiet.*]

FANNY: Dear, Sweet Molasses—how 'bout that?

JULIA: [*To* FANNY.] Stop that! Don't read her mail.

FANNY: She can't read it.

JULIA: She doesn't want to. She's gonna go on holdin' it in her hand and never know what's in it . . just 'cause it's hers!

FANNY: Forgive 'em Father, they know not.

JULIA: Another thing, you told me it's quiet here! You call this quiet? I can't stand it!

FANNY: When you need me come and humbly knock on my *back* door. [*She exits.*]

MATTIE: [*Shouts to* FANNY.] I ain't gonna knock on no damn back door! Miss Julia, can you read? [*Offers the letter to* JULIA.] I'll give you some candy when I make it.

JULIA: [*Takes the letter.*] All right.

[LULA *takes a seat to enjoy a rare social event. She winds stems for the paper flowers as* JULIA *reads.*]

Dear, sweet molasses, my darlin' wife.

MATTIE: Yes, honey. [*To* JULIA.] Thank you.

JULIA: [*Reads.*] Somewhere, at sometime, on the high sea, I take my pen in hand . . . well, anyway, this undelible pencil.

LULA: Hope he didn't put it in his mouth.

JULIA: [*Reads.*] I be missin' you all the time.

MATTIE: And we miss you.

JULIA: [*Reads.*] Sorry we did not have our picture taken.

MATTIE: Didn't have the money.

JULIA: [*Reads.*] Would like to show one to the men and say this is my wife and child . . . They always be showin' pictures.

MATTIE: [*Waves the ten-dollar bill.*] I'm gon' send you one, darlin'.

JULIA: [*Reads.*] I recall how we used to take a long walk on Sunday afternoon . . . [*Thinks about this for a moment.*] . . . then come home and be lovin' each other.

MATTIE: I recall.

JULIA: [*Reads.*] The Government people held up your allotment.

MATTIE: Oh, do Jesus.

JULIA: [*Reads.*] They have many papers to be sign, pink, blue and white also green. Money can't be had 'til all papers match. Mine don't match.

LULA: Takes a-while.

JULIA: [*Reads.*] Here is ten cash dollars I hope will not be stole.

MATTIE: [*Holds up the money.*] I got it.

JULIA: [*Reads.*] Go to Merchant Marine office and push things from your end.

MATTIE: Monday. Lula, le's go Monday.

LULA: I gotta see Nelson march in the parade.

JULIA: [*Reads.*] They say people now droppin' in the street, dying' from this war-time influenza. Don't get sick—buy tonic if you do. I love you.

MATTIE: Gotta buy a bottle-a tonic.

JULIA: [*Reads.*] Sometimes people say hurtful things 'bout what I am, like color and race . . .

MATTIE: Tell 'em you my brown-skin Carolina daddy, that's who the hell you are. Wish I was there.

JULIA: [*Reads.*] I try not to hear 'cause I do want to get back to your side. Two things a man can give the woman he loves . . . his name and his protection . . . The first you have, the last is yet to someday come. The war is here, the road is rocky. I am *ever* your lovin' husband, October.

MATTIE: So-long, darlin'. I wish I had your education.

JULIA: I only went through eighth grade. Name and protection. I know you love him.

MATTIE: Yes'm I do. If I was to see October in bed with another woman, I'd never doubt him 'cause I trust him more than I do my own eyesight. Bet yall don't believe me.

JULIE: I know how much a woman can love. [*Glances at the letter again.*] Two things a man can give . . .

MATTIE: Name and protection. That's right, too. I wouldn't live with no man. Man got to marry me. Man that won't marry you thinks nothin' of you. Just usin' you.

JULIA: I've never allowed anybody to *use* me!

LULA: [*Trying to move her away Stage Right.*] Mattie, look like rain.

MATTIE: A man can't use a woman less she let him.

LULA: [*To* MATTIE.] You never know when to stop.

JULIA: Well, I read your letter. Good day.

MATTIE: Did I hurtcha feelin's? Tell me, what'd I say.

JULIA: I—I've been keepin' company with someone for a long time and . . . we're not married.

MATTIE: For how long?

LULA: [*Half-heartedly tries to hush* MATTIE *but she would also like to know.*] Ohhh, Mattie.

JULIA: [*Without shame*]. Ten years today, ten full, faithful years.

MATTIE: He got a wife?

JULIA: [*Very tense and uncomfortable.*] No.

MATTIE: Oh, a man don't wanta get married, work on him. Cut off piece-a his shirt-tail and sew it to your petticoat. It works. Get Fanny to read the tea leaves and tell you how to move. She's a old bitch but what she sees in a teacup is true.

JULIA: Thank you, Mattie.

LULA: Let's pray on it, Miss Julia. Gawd bring them together, in holy matrimony.

JULIA: Miss Lula, please don't . . . You know it's against the law for black and white to get married, so Gawd nor the tea leaves can help us. My friend is white and that's why I try to stay to myself.

[*After a few seconds of silence.*]

LULA: Guess we shouldn't-a disturbed you.

JULIA: But I'm so glad you did. Oh, the things I can tell you 'bout bein' lonesome and shut-out. Always movin', one place to another, lookin' for some peace of mind. I moved out in the country . . . Pretty but quiet as the graveyard; so lonesome. One year I was in such a *lovely* colored neighborhood but they couldn't be bothered with me, you know? I've lived near sportin' people . . . they were very kindly but I'm not a sporty type person. Then I found this place hid way in the backyard so quiet, didn't see another soul . . . And that's why I thought yall wanted to tear my house down this mornin' . . . 'cause you might-a heard 'bout me and Herman . . . and some people are . . . well, they judge, they can't help judgin' you.

MATTIE: [*Eager to absolve her of wrong doing.*] Oh, darlin', we all do things we don't want sometimes. You grit your teeth and take all he's got; if you don't somebody else will.

LULA: No, no, you got no use for 'em so don't take nothin' from 'em.

MATTIE: He's takin' somethin' from her.

LULA: Have faith, you won't starve.

MATTIE: Rob him blind. Take it all. Let him froth at the mouth. Let him die in the poorhouse—bitter, bitter to the gone!

LULA: A white man is somethin' else. Everybody knows how that low-down slave master sent for a different black woman every night . . . for his pleasure. That's why none of us is the same color.

MATTIE: And right now today they're mean, honey. They can't help it; their nose is pinched together so close they can't get enough air. It makes 'em mean. And their mouth is set back in their face so hard and flat . . . no roundness, no sweetness, they can't even carry a tune.

LULA: I couldn't stand one of 'em to touch me intimate no matter what he'd give me.

JULIA: Miss Lula, you don't understand. Mattie, the way you and your husband feel that's the way it is with me 'n' Herman. He loves me . . . We love each other, that's all, we just love each other. [*After a split second of silence.*] And someday, as soon as we're able, we have to leave here and go where it's right . . . Where it's legal for everybody to marry. That's what we both want . . . to be man and wife—like you and October.

LULA: Well I have to cut out six dozen paper roses today. [*Starts for her house.*]

MATTIE: And I gotta make a batch-a candy and look after Princess so I can feed me and Teeta 'til October comes back. Thanks for readin' the letter. [*She enters her house.*]

JULIA: But Mattie, Lula—I wanted to tell you why it's been ten years—and why we haven't—

LULA: Good day, Miss Julia. [*Enters her house.*]

JULIA: Well, that's always the way. What am I doing standin' in a backyard explainin' my life? Stay to yourself, Julia Augustine. Stay to yourself. [*Sweeps her front porch.*]

I got to climb my way to glory
Got to climb it by myself
Ain't nobody here can climb it for me
I got to climb it for myself.

*Curtain.*

## Scene 2

TIME: *That evening. Cover closed Scene 1 curtain with song and laughter from* MAT-
TIE, LULA *and* KIDS.

*As curtain opens,* JULIA *has almost finished the unpacking. The room now looks
quite cozy. Once in a while she watches the clock and looks out of the window.* TEETA
*follows* PRINCESS *out of* MATTIE's *house and ties her sash.* PRINCESS *is holding a jump-
rope.*

[MATTIE *offstage. Sings.*]

My best man left me, it sure do grieve my mind
When I'm laughin', I'm laughin' to keep from cryin' . . .

PRINCESS: [*Twirling the rope to one side.*] Ching, ching, China-man eat dead
rat . . .
TEETA: [*As* PRINCESS *jumps rope.*] Knock him in the head with a baseball bat . . .
PRINCESS: You wanta jump?
TEETA: Yes.
PRINCESS: Say "Yes, M'am."
TEETA: No.
PRINCESS: Why?
TEETA: You too little.
PRINCESS: [*Takes bean bag from her pocket.*] You can't play with my bean bag.
TEETA: I 'on care, play it by yourself.
PRINCESS: [*Drops rope, tosses the bag to* TEETA.] Catch.

[TEETA *throws it back.* HERMAN *appears at the back-entry. He is a strong, forty-
year-old working man. His light brown hair is sprinkled with gray. At the
present moment he is tired.* PRINCESS *notices him because she is facing the back
fence. He looks for a gate or opening but can find none.*]

Hello.
TEETA: Mama! Mama!
HERMAN: Hello, children. Where's the gate?

[HERMAN *passes several packages through a hole in the fence; he thinks of climbing
the fence but it is very rickety. He disappears from view.* MATTIE *dashes out of
her house, notices the packages, runs into* LULA's *house, then back into the yard.*
LULA *enters in a flurry of excitement; gathers a couple of pieces from the clothesline.* MATTIE *goes to inspect the packages.*]

LULA: Don't touch 'em, Mattie. Might be dynamite.

MATTIE: Well, I'm gon' get my head blowed off, 'cause I wanta see.

[NELSON *steps out wearing his best civilian clothes; neat fitting suit, striped silk shirt and bulldog shoes in ox-blood leather. He claps his hands to frighten* MATTIE.]

MATTIE: Oh, look at him. Where's the party?

NELSON: Everywhere! The ladies have heard Nelson's home. They waitin' for me!

LULA: Don't get in trouble. Don't answer anybody that bothers you.

NELSON: How come it is that when I carry a sack-a coal on my back you don't worry, but when I'm goin' out to enjoy myself you almost go crazy.

LULA: Go on! Deliver the piece to the funeral.

[*Hands him a funeral piece.* MATTIE *proceeds to examine the contents of a paper bag.*]

NELSON: Fact is, I was gon' stay home and have me some orange drink, but Massa beat me to it. None-a my business no-how, dammit.

[MATTIE *opens another bag.* HERMAN *enters through the front entry.* FANNY *follows at a respectable distance.*]

MATTIE: Look, rolls and biscuits!

LULA: Why'd he leave the food in the yard?

HERMAN: Because I couldn't find the gate. Good evening. Pleasant weather. Howdy do. Cool this evenin'. [*Silence.*] Err—I see where the Allies suffered another set-back yesterday. Well, that's the war, as they say.

[*The* WOMEN *answer with nods and vague throat clearings.* JULIA *opens her door, he enters.*]

MATTIE: That's the lady's husband. He's a light colored man.

PRINCESS: What is a light colored man?

[CHILDREN *exit with* MATTIE *and* NELSON. FANNY *exits by front entry,* LULA *to her house.*]

JULIA: Why'd you pick a conversation? I tell you 'bout that.

HERMAN: Man gotta say somethin' stumblin' round in a strange back yard.

JULIA: Why didn't you wear your good suit? You know how people like to look you over and sum you up.

HERMAN: Mama and Annabelle made me so damn mad tonight. When I got home Annabelle had this in the window. [*Removes a cardboard sign from the bag . . . printed with red, white and blue crayon . . .* WE ARE AMERICAN CITIZENS . . .]

JULIA: We are American Citizens. Why'd she put it in the window?

HERMAN: Somebody wrote cross the side of our house in purple paint . . . "Krauts . . . Germans live here"! I'd-a broke his arm if I caught him.

JULIA: It's the war. Makes people mean. But didn't she print it pretty.

HERMAN: Comes from Mama boastin' 'bout her German grandfather, now it's no longer fashionable. I snatched that coward sign outta the window . . . Goddamit, I says . . . Annabelle cryin', Mama hollerin' at her. Gawd save us from the ignorance, I say . . . Why should I see a sign in the window when I get home? That Annabelle got flags flyin' in the front yard, the backyard . . . and red, white and blue flowers in the grass . . . confound nonsense . . . Mama is an ignorant woman . . .

JULIA: Don't say that . . .

HERMAN: A poor ignorant woman who is mad because she was born a sharecropper . . . outta her mind 'cause she ain't high class society. We're red-neck crackers, I told her, that's what.

JULIA: Oh, Herman . . . no you didn't . . .

HERMAN: I did.

JULIA: [Standing.] But she raised you . . . loaned you all-a-her three thousand dollars to pour into that bakery shop. You know you care about her.

HERMAN: Of course I do. But sometimes she makes me so mad . . . Close the door, lock out the world . . . all of 'em that ain't crazy are coward. [Looks at sign.] Poor Annabelle—Miss War-time Volunteer . . .

JULIA: She's what you'd call a very Patriotic Person, wouldn't you say?

HERMAN: Well, guess it is hard for her to have a brother who only makes pies in time of war.

JULIA: A brother who makes pies and loves a nigger!

HERMAN: Sweet Kerist, there it is again!

JULIA: Your mama's own words . . . according to you—I'll never forget them as long as I live. Annabelle, you've got a brother who makes pies and loves a nigger.

HERMAN: How can you remember seven or eight years ago, for Gawd's sake? Sorry I told it.

JULIA: I'm not angry, honeybunch, dear heart. I just remember.

HERMAN: When you say honeybunch, you're angry. Where do you want your Aunt Cora?

JULIA: On my dresser!

HERMAN: An awful mean woman.

JULIA: Don't get me started on your mama and Annabelle. [Pause.]

HERMAN: Julia, why did you move into a backyard?

JULIA: [Goes to him.] Another move, another mess. Sometimes I feel like fightin' . . . and there's nobody to fight but you . . .

HERMAN: Open the box. Go on. Open it.

JULIA: [Opens the box and reveals a small but ornate wedding cake with a bride and groom on top and ten pink candles.] Ohhh, it's the best one ever. Tassels, bells, roses . . .

HERMAN: . . . Daffodils and silver sprinkles . . .

JULIA: You're the best baker in the world.

HERMAN: [As she lights the candles.] Because you put up with me . . .

JULIA: Gawd knows that.

HERMAN: . . . because the palms of your hands and the soles of your feet are pink and brown . . .

JULIA: Jus' listen to him. Well, go on.

HERMAN: Because you're a good woman, a kind, good woman.

JULIA: Thank you very much, Herman.

HERMAN: Because you care about me.

JULIA: Well, I do.

HERMAN: Happy ten years . . . Happy tenth year.

JULIA: And the same to you.

> [HERMAN *tries a bit of soft barbershop harmony.*]
>
> I love you as I never loved before [JULIA *joins him.*]
> When first I met you on the village green
> Come to me ere my dream of love is o'er
> I love you as I loved you
> When you were sweet—Take the end up higher—
> When you were su-weet six-ateen.
> Now blow!

*[They blow out the candles and kiss through a cloud of smoke.]*

JULIA: [*Almost forgetting something.*] Got something for you. Because you were my only friend when Aunt Cora sent me on a sleep-in job in the white-folks kitchen. And wasn't that Miss Bessie one mean white woman? [*Gives present to* HERMAN.]

HERMAN: Oh, Julia, just say she was mean.

JULIA: Well yes, but she was white too.

HERMAN: A new peel, thank you. A new pastry bag. Thank you.

JULIA: [*She gives him a sweater.*] I did everything right but one arm came out shorter.

HERMAN: That's how I feel. Since three o'clock this morning, I turned out twenty ginger breads, thirty sponge cakes, lady fingers, Charlotte Russe . . . loaf bread, round bread, twist bread and water rolls . . . and—

JULIA: Tell me about pies. Do pies!

HERMAN: Fifty pies. Open apple, closed apple, apple-crumb, sweet potato and pecan. And I got a order for a large wedding cake. They want it in the shape of a battleship. [HERMAN *gives* JULIA *ring box.* JULIA *takes out a wide, gold wedding band—it is strung on a chain.*] It's a wedding band . . . on a chain . . . To have until such time as . . . It's what you wanted, Julia. A damn fool present.

JULIA: Sorry I lost your graduation ring. If you'd-a gone to college what do you think you'd-a been?

HERMAN: A baker with a degree.

JULIA: [*Reads.*] Herman and Julia 1908 . . . and now it's . . . 1918. Time runs away. A wedding band . . . on a chain. [*She fastens the chain around her neck.*]

HERMAN: A damn fool present. [JULIA *drops the ring inside of her dress.*]

JULIA: It comforts me. It's your promise. You hungry?

HERMAN: No.

JULIA: After the war, the people across the way are goin' to Philadelphia.

HERMAN: I hear it's cold up there. People freeze to death waitin' for a trolley car.

JULIA: [*Leans back beside him, rubs his head.*] In the middle of the night a big bird flew cryin' over this house—then he was gone, the way time goes flyin' . . .

HERMAN: Julia, why did you move in a back yard? Out in the country the air was so sweet and clean. Makes me feel shame . . .

JULIA: [*Rubbing his back.*] Crickets singin' that lonesome evenin' song. Any kind-a people better than none a-tall.

HERMAN: Mama's beggin' me to hire Greenlee again, to help in the shop, "Herman, sit back like a half-way gentleman and just take in money."

JULIA: Greenlee! When white-folks decide . . .

HERMAN: People, Julia, people.

JULIA: When people decide to give other people a job, they come up with the biggest Uncle Tom they can find. The *people* I know call him a "white-folks-nigger." It's a terrible expression so don't you ever use it.

HERMAN: He seems dignified, Julia.

JULIA: Jus' 'cause you're clean and stand straight, that's not dignity. Even speakin' nice might not be dignity.

HERMAN: What's dignity? Tell me. Do it.

JULIA: Well, it . . . it . . . It's a feeling—It's a spirit that rises higher than the dirt around it, without any by-your-leave. It's not proud and it's not 'shamed . . . Dignity "Is" . . . and it's never Greenlee . . . I don't know if it's us either, honey.

HERMAN: [*Standing.*] It still bothers my mother that I'm a baker. "When you gonna rise in the world!" A baker who rises . . . [*Laughs and coughs a little.*] Now she's worried 'bout Annabelle marryin' a sailor. After all, Annabelle is a concert pianist. She's had only one concert . . . in a church . . . and not many people there.

JULIA: A sailor might just persevere and become an admiral. Yes, an admiral and a concert pianist.

HERMAN: Ten years. If I'd-a known what I know now, I wouldn't-a let Mama borrow on the house or give me the bakery.

JULIA: Give what? Three broken stoves and all-a your papa's unpaid bills.

HERMAN: I *got* to pay her back. And I can't go to Philadelphia or wherever the hell you're saying to go. I can hear you thinkin', Philadelphia, Philadelphia, Phil . . .

JULIA: [*Jumping up. Pours wine.*] Oh damnation! The hell with that!

HERMAN: All right, not so much hell and damn. When we first met you were so shy.

JULIA: Sure was, wouldn't say "dog" 'cause it had a tail. In the beginnin' nothin' but lovin' and kissin' . . . and thinkin' 'bout you. Now I worry 'bout gettin' old. I do. Maybe you'll meet somebody younger. People do get old, y'know. [*Sits on bed.*]

HERMAN: There's an old couple 'cross from the bakery . . . "Mabel," he yells, "where's my keys!" . . . Mabel has a big behind on her. She wears his carpet slippers. "All right, Robbie, m'boy," she says . . . Robbie walks kinda one-sided. But they're havin' a pretty good time. We'll grow old together both of us havin' the same name. [*Takes her in his arms.*] Julia, I love you . . . you know it . . . I love you . . . [*After a pause.*] Did you have my watch fixed?

JULIA: [*Sleepily.*] Uh-huh, it's in my purse. [*Getting up.*] Last night when the bird flew over the house—I dreamed 'bout the devil's face in the fire . . . He said "I'm comin' to drag you to hell."

HERMAN: [*Sitting up.*] There's no other hell, honey. Celestine was sayin' the other day—

JULIA: How do you know what Celestine says?

HERMAN: Annabelle invited her to dinner.

JULIA: They still trying to throw that white widow-woman at you? Oh, Herman, I'm gettin' mean . . . jumpin' at noises . . . and bad dreams.

HERMAN: [*Brandishing bottle.*] Dammit, this is the big bird that flew over the house!

JULIA: I don't go anywhere, I don't know anybody, I gotta do somethin'. Sometimes I need to have company—to say . . . "Howdy-do, pleasant evenin', do drop in." Sometimes I need other people. How you ever gonna pay back three thousand dollars? Your side hurt?

HERMAN: Schumann came in to see me this mornin'. Says he'll buy me out, ten cents on the dollar, and give me a job bakin' for him . . . it's an offer—can get seventeen hundred cash.

JULIA: Don't do it. Herman. That sure wouldn't be dignity.

HERMAN: He makes an American flag outta gingerbread. But they sell. Bad taste sells. Julia, where do you want to go? New York, Philadelphia, where? Let's try their dignity. Say where you want to go.

JULIA: Well, darlin', if folks are freezin' in Philadelphia, we'll go to New York.

HERMAN: Right! You go and size up the place. Meanwhile I'll stay here and do like everybody else, make war money . . . battleship cakes, cannonball cookies . . . chocolate bullets . . . they'll sell. Pay my debts. Less than a year, I'll be up there with money in my pockets.

JULIA: Northerners talk funny—"We're from New Yorrrk."

HERMAN: I'll getcha train ticket next week.

JULIA: No train. I wanta stand on the deck of a Clyde Line boat, wavin' to the people on the shore. The whistle blowin', flags flyin' . . . wavin' my handkerchief . . . So long, so long, look here—South Carolina . . . so long, hometown . . . goin' away by myself—[*Tearfully blows her nose.*]

HERMAN: You gonna like it. Stay with your cousin and don't talk to strangers.
[JULIA *gets dress from her hope chest.*]

JULIA: Then, when we do get married we can have a quiet reception. My cut glass punch bowl . . . little sandwiches, a few friends . . . Herman? Hope my weddin' dress isn't too small. It's been waitin' a good while. [*Holds dress in front of her.*] I'll use all of my hope chest things. Quilts, Irish linens, the silver cups . . . Oh, Honey, how are you gonna manage with me gone?

HERMAN: Buy warm underwear and a woolen coat with a fur collar . . . to turn against the northern wind. What size socks do I wear?

JULIA: Eleven, eleven and a half if they run small.

HERMAN: . . . what's the store? Write it down.

JULIA: Coleridge. And go to King Street for your shirts.

HERMAN: Coleridge. Write it down.

JULIA: Keep payin' Ruckheiser, the tailor, so he can start your new suit.

HERMAN: Ruckheiser. Write it down.

JULIA: Now that I know I'm goin' we can take our time.

HERMAN: No, rush, hurry, make haste, do it. Look at you . . . like your old self.

JULIA: No, no, not yet—I'll go soon as we get around to it. [*Kisses him.*]

HERMAN: That's right. Take your time . . .

JULIA: Oh, Herman.

[MATTIE *enters through the back gate with* TEETA. *She pats and arranges* TEE-TA's *hair.* FANNY *enters from the front entry and goes to* JULIA's *window.*]

MATTIE: You goin' to Lula's service?

FANNY: A new faith. Rather be a Catholic than somethin' you gotta make up. Girl, my new tenant and her—

MATTIE: [*Giving* FANNY *the high-sign to watch what she says in front of* TEETA.] . . . and her husband.

FANNY: I gotcha. She and her husband was in there havin' a orgy. Singin', laughin', screamin', crying' . . . I'd like to be a fly on that wall.

[LULA *enters the yard wearing a shawl over her head and a red band on her arm. She carries two chairs and places them beside two kegs.*]

LULA: Service time!

[MATTIE, TEETA *and* FANNY *enter the yard and sit down.* LULA *places a small table and a cross.*]

FANNY: [*Goes to* JULIA's *door and knocks.*] Let's spread the word to those who need it. [*Shouts.*] Miss Julia, don't stop if you in the middle-a somethin'. We who love Gawd are gatherin' for prayer. Got any time for Jesus?

ALL: [*Sing.*] When the roll is called up yonder.

JULIA: Thank you, Miss Fanny.

[FANNY *flounces back to her seat in triumph.* JULIA *sits on the bed near* HERMAN.]

HERMAN: Dammit, she's makin' fun of you.

JULIA: [*Smooths her dress and hair.*] Nobody's invited me anywhere in a long time . . . so I'm goin'.

HERMAN: [*Standing.*] I'm gonna buy you a Clyde Line ticket for New York City on Monday . . . this Monday.

JULIA: Monday?

HERMAN: As Gawd is my judge. That's dignity. Monday.

JULIA: [*Joyfully kissing him.*] Yes, Herman! [*She enters yard.*]

LULA: My form-a service opens with praise. Let us speak to Gawd.

MATTIE: Well, I thang Gawd that—that I'm livin' and I pray my husband comes home safe.

TEETA: I love Jesus and Jesus loves me.

ALL: Amen.

FANNY: I thang Gawd that I'm able to rise spite-a-those who try to hold me down, spite-a those who are two-faceted, spite-a those in my own race who jealous 'cause I'm doin' so much better than the rest of 'em. He preparest a table for me in the presence of my enemies. Double-deal Fanny Johnson all you want but me 'n' Gawd's gonna come out on top.

[ALL *look to* JULIA.]

JULIA: I'm sorry for past sin—but from Monday on through eternity—I'm gonna live in dignity accordin' to the laws of God and man. Oh, Glory!

LULA: Glory Halleluhjah!

[NELSON *enters a bit unsteadily . . . struts and preens while singing.*]

NELSON: Come here black woman . . . whoooo . . . eee . . . on daddy's knee . . . etc.

LULLA: [*Trying to interrupt him.*] We're testifyin' . . .

NELSON: [*Throwing hat on porch.*] Right! Testify! Tonight I asked the prettiest girl in Carolina to be my wife; and Merrilee Jones told me . . . I'm sorry but you got nothin' to offer. She's right! I got nothin' to offer but a hard way to go. Merrilee Jones . . . workin' for the rich white folks and better off washin' their dirty drawers than marryin' me.

LULA: Respect the church! [*Slaps him.*]

NELSON: [*Sings.*] Come here, black woman (*etc.*) . . .

JULIA: Oh, Nelson, respect your mother!

NELSON: Respect your damn self, Julia Augustine! [*Continues singing.*]

LULA: How we gonna find a new faith?

NELSON: [*Softly.*] By tellin' the truth, Mama. Merrilee ain't no liar. I got nothin' to offer, just like October.

MATTIE: You keep my husband's name outta your mouth.

NELSON: [*Sings.*] Come here, black woman . . .

FANNY AND CONGREGATION: [*Sing.*]

> Ain't gon let nobody turn me round, turn me round,
>     turn me round
> Ain't gon let nobody turn me round . . .

HERMAN: [*Staggers out to porch.*] Julia, I'm going now, I'm sorry . . . I don't feel well . . . I don't know . . . [*Slides forward and falls.*]
JULIA: Mr. Nelson . . . won'tcha please help me . . .
FANNY: Get him out of my yard.

[NELSON AND JULIA *help* HERMAN *in to bed. Others freeze in yard.*]

# ACT II

## Scene 1

TIME: *Sunday morning.*
SCENE: *The same as Act One except the yard and houses are neater. The clothes line is down. Off in the distance someone is humming a snatch of a hymn. Church bells are ringing.* HERMAN *is in a heavy, restless sleep. The bed covers indicate he has spent a troubled night. On the table Downstage Right are medicine bottles, cups and spoons.* JULIA *is standing beside the bed, swinging a steam kettle; she stops and puts it on a trivet on top of her hope chest.*

FANNY: [*Seeing her.*] Keep usin' the steam-kettle.

[HERMAN *groans lightly.*]

MATTIE: [*Picks up scissors.*] Put the scissors under the bed, open, It'll cut the pain.
FANNY: [*Takes scissors from* MATTIE.] That's for childbirth.
JULIA: He's had too much paregoric. Sleepin' his life away. I want a doctor.
FANNY: Over my dead body. It's against the damn law for him to be layin' up in a black woman's bed.
MATTIE: A doctor will call the police.
FANNY: They'll say I run a bad house.
JULIA: I'll tell 'em the truth.
MATTIE: We don't tell things to police.
FANNY: When Lula gets back with his sister, his damn sister will take charge.
MATTIE: That's his family.
FANNY: Family is family.
JULIA: I'll hire a hack and take him to a doctor.
FANNY: He might die on you. That's police. That's the work-house.
JULIA: I'll say I found him on the street!
FANNY: Walk into the jaws of the law—they'll chew you up.

JULIA: Suppose his sister won't come?

FANNY: She'll be here. [FANNY *picks up a teacup and turns it upside down on the saucer and twirls it.*] I see a ship, a ship sailin' on the water.

MATTIE: Water clear or muddy?

FANNY: Crystal clear.

MATTIE: [*Realizing she's late.*] Oh, I gotta get Princess so her folks can open their ice cream parlor. Take care-a Teeta.

FANNY: I see you on your way to Miami, Florida, goin' on a trip.

JULIA: [*Sitting on window seat.*] I know you want me to move. I will, Fanny.

FANNY: Julia, it's hard to live under these mean white-folks . . . but I've done it. I'm the first and only colored they let buy land' round here.

JULIA: They all like you, Fanny. Only one of 'em cares for me . . . just one.

FANNY: Yes, I'm thought highly of. When I pass by they can say . . . "There she go, Fanny Johnson, representin' her race in-a approved manner" . . . 'cause they don't have to worry 'bout my next move. I can't afford to mess that up on account-a you or any-a the rest-a these hard-luck, better-off-dead, triflin' niggers.

JULIA: [*Crossing up Right.*] I'll move. But I'm gonna call a doctor.

FANNY: Do it, we'll have a yellow quarantine sign on the front door . . . "INFLUENZA." Doctor'll fill out papers for the law . . . address . . . race . . .

JULIA: I . . . I guess I'll wait until his sister gets here.

FANNY: No, you call a doctor, Nelson won't march in the parade tomorrow or go back to the army, Mattie'll be outta work, Lula can't deliver flowers . . .

JULIA: I'm sorry, so very sorry. I'm the one breakin' laws, doin' wrong.

FANNY: I'm not judgin' you. High or low, nobody's against this if it's kept quiet. But when you pickin' white . . . pick a wealthy white. It makes things easier.

JULIA: No, Herman's not rich and I've never tried to beat him out of anything.

FANNY: [*Crossing to JULIA.*] Well, he just ought-a be and you just should-a. A colored woman needs money more than anybody else in this world.

JULIA: You sell yours.

FANNY: All I don't sell I'm going to keep.

HERMAN: Julia?

FANNY: [*Very genial.*] Well, well, sir, how you feelin', Mr. Herman? This is Aunt Fanny . . . Miss Julia's landlady. You lookin' better, Mr. Herman. We've been praying for you. [FANNY *exits to* TEETA's *house.*]

JULIA: Miss Lula—went to get your sister.

HERMAN: Why?

JULIA: Fanny made me. We couldn't wake you up.

[*He tries to sit up in bed to prepare for leaving. She tries to help him. He falls back on the pillow.*]

HERMAN: Get my wallet . . . see how much money is there. What's that smell?

[*She takes the wallet from his coat pocket. She completes counting the money.*]

JULIA: Eucalyptus oil, to help you breathe; I smell it, you smell it and Anna-belle will have to smell it too! Seventeen dollars.

HERMAN: A boat ticket to New York is fourteen dollars—Ohhh, Kerist! Pain . . . pain . . . Count to ten . . . one, two . . . [JULIA *gives paregoric water to him. He drinks. She puts down glass and picks up damp cloth from bowl on tray and wipes his brow.*] My mother is made out of too many . . . little things . . . the price of carrots, how much fat is on the meat . . . little things make people small. Make ignorance—y'know?

JULIA: Don't fret about your people, I promise I won't be surprised at any-thing and I won't have unpleasant words no matter what.

HERMAN: [*The pain eases. He is exhausted.*] Ahhh, there . . . All men are born which is—utterly untrue.

[NELSON *steps out of the house. He is brushing his army jacket.* HERMAN *moans slightly.* JULIA *gets her dress-making scissors and opens them, places the scissors under the bed.*]

FANNY: [*To* NELSON *as she nods towards* JULIA'*s house.*] I like men of African descent, myself.

NELSON: Pitiful people. They pitiful.

FANNY: They common. Only reason I'm sleepin' in a double bed by myself is 'cause I got to bear the standard for the race. I oughta run her outta here for the sake-a the race too.

NELSON: It's your property. Run us all off it, Fanny.

FANNY: Plenty-a these hungry, jobless, bad-luck colored men, just-a itchin' to move in on my gravy-train. I don't want 'em.

NELSON: [*With good nature.*] Right, Fanny! We empty-handed, got nothin' to offer.

FANNY: But I'm damn tired-a ramblin' round in five rooms by myself. House full-a new furniture, the icebox forever full-a goodies. I'm a fine cook and I know how to pleasure a man . . . he wouldn't have to step outside for a thing . . . food, fun and finance . . . all under one roof. Nelson, how'd you like to be my business advisor? Fix you up a little office in my front parlor. You wouldn't have to work for white folks . . . and Lula wouldn't have to pay rent. The war won't last forever . . . then what you gonna do? They got nothin' for you but haulin' wood and cleanin' toilets. Let's you and me pitch in together.

NELSON: I know you just teasin', but I wouldn't do a-tall. Somebody like me ain't good enough for you no-way, but you a fine-lookin' woman, though. After the war I might hit out for Chicago or Detroit . . . a rollin' stone gathers no moss.

FANNY: Roll on. Just tryin' to help the race.

[LULA *enters by front entry, followed by* ANNABELLE, *a woman in her thirties. She assumes a slightly mincing air of fashionable delicacy. She might be graceful if she were not ashamed of her size. She is nervous and fearful in this strange atmosphere. The others fall silent as they see her,* ANNABELLE *wonders if* PRINCESS *is her brother's child. Or could it be* TEETA, *or both?*]

ANNABELLE: Hello there . . . er . . . children.

PRINCESS: [*Can't resist mocking her.*] Hello there, er . . . children. [*Giggles.*]

ANNABELLE: [*To* TEETA.] Is she your sister? [ANNABELLE *looks at* NELSON *and draws her shawl a little closer.*]

TEETA: You have to ask my mama.

NELSON: [*Annoyed with* ANNABELLE'*s discomfort.*] Mom, where's the flat-iron? [*Turns and enters his house.* LULA *follows.* MATTIE *and* CHILDREN *exit.*]

FANNY: I'm the landlady. Mr. Herman had every care and kindness 'cept a doctor. Miss Juliaaaa! That's the family's concern. [FANNY *opens door, then exits.*]

ANNABELLE: Sister's here. It's Annabelle.

JULIA: [*Shows her to a chair.*] One minute he's with you, the next he's gone. Paregoric makes you sleep.

ANNABELLE: [*Dabs at her eyes with a handkerchief.*] Cryin' doesn't make sense a-tall. I'm a volunteer worker at the Naval hospital . . . I've nursed my mother . . . [*Chokes with tears.*]

JULIA: [*Pours a glass of water for her.*] Well, this is more than sickness. It's not knowin' 'bout other things.

ANNABELLE: We've known for years. He is away all the time and when old Uncle Greenlee . . . He's a colored gentleman who works in our neighborhood . . . and he said . . . he told . . . er, well, people do talk. [ANNABELLE *spills water,* JULIA *attempts to wipe the water from her dress.*] Don't do that . . . It's all right.

HERMAN: Julia?

ANNABELLE: Sister's here. Mama and Uncle Greenlee have a hack down the street. Gets a little darker we'll take you home, call a physician . . .

JULIA: Can't you do it right away?

ANNABELLE: 'Course you could put him out. Please let us wait 'til dark.

JULIA: Get a doctor.

ANNABELLE: Our plans are made, thank you.

HERMAN: Annabelle, this is Julia.

ANNABELLE: Hush.

HERMAN: This is my sister.

ANNABELLE: Now be still.

JULIA: I'll call Greenlee to help him dress.

ANNABELLE: No. Dress first. The colored folk in *our* neighborhood have great respect for us.

HERMAN: Because I give away cinnamon buns, for Kerist sake.

ANNABELLE: [*To* JULIA.] I promised my mother I'd try and talk to you. Now—
you look like one-a the nice coloreds . . .

HERMAN: Remember you are a concert pianist, that is a very dignified calling.

ANNABELLE: Put these on. We'll turn our backs.

JULIA: He can't.

ANNABELLE: [*Holds the covers in a way to keep his midsection under wraps.*] Hold
up. [*They manage to get the trousers up as high as his waist but they are twisted
and crooked.*] Up we go! There . . . [*They are breathless from the effort of
lifting him.*] Now fasten your clothing.

[JULIA *fastens his clothes.*]

I declare, even a dead man oughta have enough pride to fasten himself.

JULIA: You're a volunteer at the Naval hospital?

HERMAN: [*As another pain hits him.*] Julia, my little brown girl . . . Keep singing . . .

[JULIA.]
We are climbin' Jacob's ladder, We are climbin' Jacob's ladder,
We are climbin' Jacob's ladder, Soldiers of the Cross . . .

HERMAN: The palms of your hands . . .

[JULIA *singing*]

Every round goes higher and higher . . .

HERMAN: . . . the soles of your feet are pink and brown.

ANNABELLE: Dammit, hush. Hush this noise. Sick or not sick, hush! It's ugliness. [*To* JULIA.] Let me take care of him, please, leave us alone.

JULIA: I'll get Greenlee.

ANNABELLE: No! You hear me? No.

JULIA: I'll be outside.

ANNABELLE: [*Sitting on bed.*] If she hadn't-a gone I'd-a screamed. [JULIA *stands
on the porch.* ANNABELLE *cries.*] I thought so highly of you . . . and here
you are in somethin' that's been festerin' for years. [*In disbelief.*] One of
the finest women in the world is pinin' her heart out for you, a woman
who's pure gold. Everything Celestine does for Mama she's really doin'
for you . . . to get next to you . . . But even a Saint wants some reward.

HERMAN: I don't want Saint Celestine.

ANNABELLE: [*Standing.*] Get up! [*Tries to move* HERMAN.] At the Naval hospital
I've seen influenza cases tied down to keep 'em from walkin'. What're
we doin' here? How do you meet a black woman?

HERMAN: She came in the bakery on a rainy Saturday evening.

ANNABELLE: [*Giving in to curiosity.*] Yes?

MATTIE: [*Offstage. Scolding* TEETA *and* PRINCESS.] Sit down and drink that lem-
onade. Don't bother me!

HERMAN: "I smell rye bread baking." Those were the first words . . . Every day . . . Each time the bell sounds over the shop door I'm hopin' it's the brown girl . . . pretty shirt-waist and navy blue skirt. One day I took her hand . . . "Little lady, don't be afraid of me" . . . She wasn't. . . . I've never been lonesome since.

ANNABELLE: [*Holding out his shirt.*] Here, your arm goes in the sleeve. [*They're managing to get the shirt on.*]

HERMAN: [*Beginning to ramble.*] Julia? Your body is velvet . . . the sweet blackberry kisses . . . you are the night-time, the warm, Carolina night-time in my arms . . .

ANNABELLE: [*Bitterly.*] Most excitement I've ever had was takin' piano lessons.

JULIA: [*Calls from porch.*] Ready?

ANNABELLE: No. Rushin' us out. A little longer, please. [*Takes a comb from her purse and nervously combs his hair.*] You nor Mama put yourselves out to understand my Walter when I had him home to dinner. Yes, he's a common sailor . . . I wish he was an officer. I never liked a sailor's uniform, tight pants and middy blouses . . . but they are in the service of their country . . . He's taller than I am. You didn't even stay home that one Sunday like you promised. Must-a been chasin' after some-a them blackberry kisses you love so well. Mama made a jackass outta Walter. You know how she can do. He left lookin' liked a whipped dog. Small wonder he won't live down here. I'm crazy-wild 'bout Walter even if he is a sailor. Marry Celestine. She'll take care-a Mama and I can go right on up to the Brooklyn Navy Yard. I been prayin' so hard . . . You marry Celestine and set me free. And Gawd knows I don't want another concert.

HERMAN: [*Sighs.*] Pain, keep singing.

ANNABELLE: Dum-dum-blue Danube.

[*He falls back on the pillow. She bathes his head with a damp cloth.*]

JULIA: [*As NELSON enters the yard.*] Tell your mother I'm grateful for her kindness. I appreciate . . .

NELSON: Don't have so much to say to me. [*Quietly, in a straightforward manner.*] They set us on fire 'bout their women. String us up, pour on kerosene and light a match. Wouldn't I make a bright flame in my new uniform?

JULIA: Don't be thinkin' that way.

NELSON: I'm thinkin' 'bout black boys hangin' from trees in Little Mountain, Elloree, Winnsboro.

JULIA: Herman never killed anybody. I couldn't care 'bout that kind-a man.

NELSON: [*Stepping, turning to her.*] How can you account for carin' 'bout him a-tall?

JULIA: In that place where I worked, he was the only one who cared . . . who really cared. So gentle, such a gentle man . . . "Yes, Ma'am," . . . "No, Ma'am," "Thank you, Ma'am . . ." In the best years of my youth, my Aunt Cora sent me out to work on a sleep-in job. His shop was near that place where I worked. . . . Most folks don't have to *account* for why they love.

NELSON: You ain't most folks. You're down on the bottom with us, under his foot. A black man got nothin' to offer you . . .

JULIA: I wasn't lookin' for anybody to do for me.

NELSON: . . . and *he's* got nothin' to offer. The one layin' on your mattress, not even if he's kind as you say. He got nothin' for you . . . but some meat and gravy or a new petticoat . . . or maybe he can give you mer-iny-lookin' little bastard chirrun for us to take in and raise up. We're the ones who feed and raise 'em when it's like this . . . They don't want 'em. They only too glad to let us have their kin-folk. As it is, we sup-portin' half-a the slave-master's offspring right now.

JULIA: Go fight those who fight you. He never threw a pail-a water on you. Why didn't you fight them that did? Takin' it out on me 'n' Herman 'cause you scared of 'em . . .

NELSON: Scared? What scared! If I gotta die I'm carryin' one 'long with me.

JULIA: No you not. You gon' keep on fightin' me.

NELSON: . . . Scared-a what? I look down on 'em, I spit on 'em.

JULIA: No, you don't. They throw dirty water on your uniform . . . and you spit on me!

NELSON: Scared, what scared!

JULIA: You fightin' me, me, me, not them . . . never them.

NELSON: Yeah, I was scared and I'm tougher, stronger, a better man than any of 'em . . . but they won't letcha fight one or four or ten. I was scared to fight a hundred or a thousand. A losin' fight.

JULIA: I'd-a been afraid too.

NELSON: And you scared right now, you let the woman run you out your house.

JULIA: I didn't want to make trouble.

NELSON: But that's what a fight is . . . trouble.

LULA: [*In her doorway.*] Your mouth will kill you. [*To* JULIA.] Don't tell Mr. Herman anything he said . . . or I'll hurt you.

JULIA: Oh, Miss Lula.

LULA: Anyway, he didn't say nothin'.

[HERMAN'S MOTHER *enters the yard. She is a "poor white" about fifty-seven years old. She has risen above her poor farm background and tries to assume the airs of "quality." Her clothes are well-kept-shabby. She wears white shoes, a shirt-waist and skirt, drop earrings, a cameo brooch, a faded blue straw hat with a limp bit of veiling. She carries a heavy-black, oil-cloth bag. All in the yard give a step backward as she enters. She assumes an air of calm well-being. Almost as though visiting friends, but anxiety shows around the edges and underneath.* JULIA *approaches and* HERMAN'S MOTHER *abruptly turns to* MATTIE.]

HERMAN'S MOTHER: How do.

[MATTIE, TEETA *and* PRINCESS *look at* HERMAN'S MOTHER. HERMAN'S MOTHER *is also curious about them.*]

MATTIE: [*In answer to a penetrating stare from the old woman.*] She's mine. I take care-a her. [ *Speaking her defiance by ordering the children.*] Stay inside 'fore y'all catch the flu!

HERMAN'S MOTHER: [*To* LULA.] You were very kind to bring word . . . er . . .

LULA: Lula, Ma'am.

HERMAN'S MOTHER: The woman who nursed my second cousin's children . . . she had a name like that . . . Lul*u* we called her.

LULA: My son, Nelson.

HERMAN'S MOTHER: Can see that.

[MATTIE *and the children exit.* FANNY *hurries in from the front entry. Is most eager to establish herself on the good side of* HERMAN'S MOTHER. *With a slight bow. She is carrying the silver tea service.*]

FANNY: Beg pardon, if I may be so bold, I'm Fanny, the owner of all this property.

HERMAN'S MOTHER: [*Definitely approving of* FANNY.] I'm . . . er . . . Miss Anna-belle's mother.

FANNY: My humble pleasure . . . er . . . Miss er . . .

HERMAN'S MOTHER: [*After a brief, thoughtful pause.*] Miss Thelma.

[*They move aside but* FANNY *makes sure others hear.*]

FANNY: Miss Thelma, this is not Squeeze-gut Alley. We're just poor, hum-ble, colored people . . . and everybody knows how to keep their mouth shut.

HERMAN'S MOTHER: I thank you.

FANNY: She wanted to get a doctor. I put my foot down.

HERMAN'S MOTHER: You did right. [*Shaking her head, confiding her troubles.*] Ohhhh, you don't know.

FANNY: [*With deep understanding.*] Ohhhh, yes, I do. She moved in on me yesterday.

HERMAN'S MOTHER: Friend Fanny, help me to get through this.

FANNY: I will. Now this is Julia, she's the one . . .

[HERMAN'S MOTHER *starts toward the house without looking at* JULIA. FANNY *decides to let the matter drop.*]

HERMAN'S MOTHER: [*To* LULA.] Tell Uncle Greenlee not to worry. He's holdin' the horse and buggy.

NELSON: [*Bars* LULA's *way.*] Mama. I'll do it.

[LULA *exits into her house.* FANNY *leads her to the chair near* HERMAN's *bed.*]

ANNABELLE: Mama, if we don't call a doctor Herman's gonna die.

HERMAN'S MOTHER: Everybody's gon' die. Just a matter of when, where and how. A pretty silver service.

FANNY: English china. Belgian linen. Have a cup-a tea?

HERMAN'S MOTHER: [*As a studied pronouncement.*] My son comes to deliver baked goods and the influenza strikes him down. Sickness, it's the war.

FANNY: [*Admiring her cleverness.*] Yes, Ma'am, I'm a witness. I saw him with the packages.

JULIA: Now please call the doctor.

ANNABELLE: Yes, please, Mama. No way for him to move 'less we pick him up bodily.

HERMAN'S MOTHER: Then we'll pick him up.

HERMAN: About Walter . . . your Walter . . . I'm sorry . . .

[JULIA *tries to give* HERMAN *some water.*]

HERMAN'S MOTHER: Annabelle, help your brother. [ANNABELLE *gingerly takes glass from* JULIA.] Get that boy to help us. I'll give him a dollar. Now gather his things.

ANNABELLE: What things?

HERMAN'S MOTHER: His possessions, anything he owns, whatever is his. What you been doin' in here all this time?

[FANNY *notices* JULIA *is about to speak, so she hurries her through the motions of going through dresser drawers and throwing articles into a pillow case.*]

FANNY: Come on, sugar, make haste.

JULIA: Don't go through my belongings.

[*Tears through the drawers, flinging things around as she tries to find his articles.* FANNY *neatly piles them together.*]

FANNY: [*Taking inventory.*] Three shirts . . . one is kinda soiled.

HERMAN'S MOTHER: That's all right, I'll burn 'em.

FANNY: Some new undershirts.

HERMAN'S MOTHER: I'll burn them too.

JULIA: [*To* FANNY.] Put 'em down. I bought 'em and they're not for burnin'.

HERMAN'S MOTHER: [*Struggling to hold her anger in check.*] Fanny, go get that boy. I'll give him fifty cents.

FANNY: You said a dollar.

HERMAN'S MOTHER: All right, dollar it is. [FANNY *exits toward the front entry. In tense, hushed, excited tones, they argue back and forth.*] Now where's the bill-fold . . . there's papers . . . identity . . . [*Looks in* HERMAN's *coat pockets.*]

ANNABELLE: Don't make such-a to-do.

HERMAN'S MOTHER: You got any money of your own? Yes, I wanta know where's his money.

JULIA: I'm gettin' it.

HERMAN'S MOTHER: In her pocketbook. This is why the bakery can't make it.

HERMAN: I gave her the Gawd-damned money!

JULIA: And I know what Herman wants me to do . . .

HERMAN'S MOTHER: [*With a wry smile.*] I'm sure you know what he wants.

JULIA: I'm not gonna match words with you. Furthermore, I'm too much of a lady.

HERMAN'S MOTHER: A lady oughta learn how to keep her dress down.

ANNABELLE: Mama, you makin' a spectacle outta yourself.

HERMAN'S MOTHER: You a big simpleton. Men have nasty natures, they can't help it. A man would go with a snake if he only knew how. They cleaned out your wallet.

HERMAN: [*Shivering with a chill.*] I gave her the damn money.

[JULIA *takes it from her purse.*]

HERMAN'S MOTHER: Where's your pocket-watch or did you give that too? Annabelle, get another lock put on that bakery door.

HERMAN: I gave her the money to go—to go to New York.

[JULIA *drops the money in* HERMAN'S MOTHER'S *lap. She is silent for a moment.*]

HERMAN'S MOTHER: All right. Take it and go. It's never too late to undo a mistake. I'll add more to it. [*She puts the money on the dresser.*]

JULIA: I'm not goin' anywhere.

HERMAN'S MOTHER: Look here, girl, you leave him 'lone.

ANNABELLE: Oh, Mama, all he has to do is stay away.

HERMAN'S MOTHER: But he can't do it. Been years and he can't do it.

JULIA: I got him hoo-dooed, I sprinkle red pepper on his shirt-tail.

HERMAN'S MOTHER: I believe you.

HERMAN: I have a black woman . . . and I'm gon' marry her. I'm gon' marry her . . . got that? Pride needs a paper, for . . . for the sake of herself . . . that's dignity—tell me, what is dignity—Higher than the dirt it is . . . dignity is . . .

ANNABELLE: Let's take him to the doctor, Mama.

HERMAN'S MOTHER: When it's dark.

JULIA: Please!

HERMAN'S MOTHER: Nightfall. [JULIA *steps out on the porch but hears every word said in the room.*]

I had such high hopes for him. [*As if* HERMAN *is dead.*] All my high hopes. When he wasn't but five years old I had to whip him so he'd study his John C. Calhoun speech. Oh, Calhoun knew 'bout niggers. He said, "*MEN* are not born . . . equal, or any other kinda way . . . MEN are *made*" . . . Yes, indeed, for recitin' that John C. Calhoun speech . . . Herman won first mention and a twenty dollar gold piece . . . at the Knights of The Gold Carnation picnic.

ANNABELLE: Papa changed his mind about the Klan. I'm glad.

HERMAN'S MOTHER: Yes, he was always changin' his mind about somethin'. But I was proud-a my men-folk that day. He spoke that speech . . . The officers shook my hand. They honored me . . . "That boy a-yours gonna be somebody." A poor baker-son layin' up with a nigger woman, a overgrown daughter in heat over a common sailor. I must be payin' for somethin' I did. Yesiree, do a wrong, God'll ship you.

ANNABELLE: I wish it was dark.

HERMAN'S MOTHER: I put up with a man breathin' stale whiskey in my face every night . . . pullin' and pawin' at me . . . always tired, inside and out . . . [*Deepest confidence she has ever shared.*] Gave birth to seven . . . five-a them babies couldn't draw breath.

ANNABELLE: [*Suddenly wanting to know more about her.*] Did you love Papa, Mama? Did you ever love him? . . .

HERMAN'S MOTHER: Don't ask me 'bout love . . . I don't know nothin' about it. Never mind love. This is my harvest . . .

HERMAN: Go home. I'm better.

[HERMAN'S MOTHER's *strategy is to enlighten* HERMAN *and also wear him down. Out on the porch,* JULIA *can hear what is being said in the house.*]

HERMAN'S MOTHER: There's something wrong 'bout mismatched things, be they shoes, socks, or people.

HERMAN: Go away, don't look at us.

HERMAN'S MOTHER: People don't like it. They're not gonna letcha do it in peace.

HERMAN: We'll go North.

HERMAN'S MOTHER: Not a thing will change except her last name.

HERMAN: She's not like others . . . she's not like that . . .

HERMAN'S MOTHER: All right, sell out to Schumann. I want my cash-money . . . You got no feelin' for me, I got none for you . . .

HERMAN: I feel . . . I feel what I feel . . . I don't know what I feel . . .

HERMAN'S MOTHER: Don't need to feel. Live by the law. Follow the law— law, law of the land. Obey the law!

ANNABELLE: We're not obeyin' the law. He should be quarantined right here. The city's tryin' to stop an epidemic.

HERMAN'S MOTHER: Let the city drop dead and you 'long with it. *Rather* be dead than disgraced. Your papa gimme the house and little money . . . I want my money back. [*She tries to drag* HERMAN *up in the bed.*] I ain't payin' for this. [*Shoves* ANNABELLE *aside.*] Let Schumann take over. A man who knows what he's doin'. Go with her . . . Take the last step against your own! Kill us all. Jesus, Gawd, save us or take us—

HERMAN: [*Screams.*] No! No! No! No!

HERMAN'S MOTHER: Thank Gawd, the truth is the light. Oh, Blessed Savior . . . [HERMAN *screams out, starting low and ever going higher. She tries to cover his mouth.* ANNABELLE *pulls her hand away.*] Thank you, Gawd, let the fire go out . . . this awful fire.

[LULA *and* NELSON *enter the yard.*]

ANNABELLE: You chokin' him. Mama . . .

JULIA: [*From the porch.*] It's dark! It's dark. Now it's very dark.

HERMAN: One ticket on the Clyde Line . . . Julia . . . where are you? Keep singing . . . count . . . one, two . . . three. Over there, over there . . . send the word, send the word . . .

HERMAN'S MOTHER: Soon be home, son.

[HERMAN *breaks away from the men, staggers to* MATTIE'*s porch and holds on.* MATTIE *smothers a scream and gets the children out of the way.* FANNY *enters.*]

HERMAN: Shut the door . . . don't go out . . . the enemy . . . the enemy . . . [*Recites the Calhoun speech.*] Men are not born, infants are born! They grow to all the freedom of which the condition in which they were born permits. It is a great and dangerous error to suppose that all people are equally entitled to liberty.

JULIA: Go home— Please be still.

HERMAN: It is a reward to be earned, a reward reserved for the intelligent, the patriotic, the virtuous and deserving; and not a boon to be bestowed on a people too ignorant, degraded and vicious . . .

JULIA: You be still now, shut up.

HERMAN: . . . to be capable either of appreciating or of enjoying it.

JULIA: [*Covers her ears.*] Take him . . .

HERMAN: A black woman . . . not like the others . . .

JULIA: . . . outta my sight . . .

HERMAN: Julia, the ship is sinking . . .

[HERMAN'S MOTHER *and* NELSON *help* HERMAN *up and out.*]

ANNABELLE: [*To* JULIA *on the porch.*] I'm sorry . . . so sorry it had to be this way. I can't leave with you thinkin' I uphold Herman, and blame you.

HERMAN'S MOTHER: [*Returning.*] You the biggest fool.

ANNABELLE: I say a man is responsible for his own behavior.

HERMAN'S MOTHER: And you, you oughta be locked up . . . workhouse . . . jail! Who you think you are!?

JULIA: I'm your damn daughter-in-law, you old bitch! The Battleship Bitch! The bitch who destroys with her filthy mouth. They could win the war with your killin' mouth. The son-killer, man-killer bitch . . . She's killin' him 'cause he loved me more than anybody in the world.

[FANNY *returns.*]

HERMAN'S MOTHER: Better off . . . He's better off dead in his coffin than live with the likes-a you . . . black thing! [*She is almost backing into* JULIA'*s house.*]

JULIA: The black thing who bought a hot water bottle to put on your sick, white self when rheumatism threw you flat on your back . . . who bought flannel gowns to warm your pale, mean body. He never ran up and down King Street shoppin' for you . . . I bought what he took home to you . . .

HERMAN'S MOTHER: Lies . . . tear outcha lyin' tongue.

JULIA: . . . the lace curtains in your parlor . . . the shirt-waist you wearin'—I made them.

FANNY: Go *on* . . . I got her. [*Holds* JULIA.]

HERMAN'S MOTHER: Leave 'er go! The undertaker will have-ta unlock my hands off her black throat!

FANNY: Go on, Miss Thelma.

JULIA: Miss Thelma my ass! Her first name is Frieda. The Germans are here . . . in purple paint!

HERMAN'S MOTHER: Black, sassy nigger!

JULIA: Kraut, knuckle-eater, red-neck . . .

HERMAN'S MOTHER: Nigger whore . . . he used you for a garbage pail . . .

JULIA: White trash! Sharecropper! Let him die . . . let 'em all die . . . Kill him with your murderin' mouth—sharecropper bitch!

HERMAN'S MOTHER: Dirty black nigger . . .

JULIA: . . . If I wasn't black with all-a Carolina 'gainst me I'd be mistress of your house! [*To* ANNABELLE.] Annabelle, you'd be married livin' in Brooklyn, New York . . . [*To* HERMAN'S MOTHER.] . . . and I'd be waitin' on Frieda . . . cookin' your meals . . . waterin' that damn red white and blue garden!

HERMAN'S MOTHER: Dirty black bitch.

JULIA: Daughter of a bitch!

ANNABELLE: Leave my mother alone! She's old . . . and sick.

JULIA: But never sick enough to die . . . dirty ever-lasting woman.

HERMAN'S MOTHER: [*Clinging to* ANNABELLE, *she moves toward the front entry.*] I'm as high over you as Mount Everest over the sea. White reigns supreme . . . I'm white, you can't change that.

[*They exit.* FANNY *goes with them.*]

JULIA: Out! Out! Out! And take the last ten years-a my life with you and . . . when he gets better . . . keep him home. Killers, murderers . . . Kinsmen! Klansmen! Keep him home. [*To* MATTIE.] Name and protection . . . he can't gimme either one. [*To* LULA.] I'm gon' get down on my knees and scrub where they walked . . . what they touched . . . [*To* MATTIE.] . . . with brown soap . . . hot lye-water . . . scaldin' hot . . . [*She dashes into the house and collects an armful of bedding . . .*] Clean! . . . Clean the whiteness outta my house . . . clean everything . . . even the memory . . . no more love . . . Free . . . free to hate-cha for the rest-a my life. [*Back to the porch with her arms full.*] When I die I'm gonna keep on hatin' . . . I don't want any whiteness in my house. Stay out . . . out . . . [*Dumps the things in the yard.*] . . . out . . . out . . . out . . . and leave me to my black self!

*Blackout.*

## Scene 2

TIME: *Early afternoon the following day.*
PLACE: *The same.*

*In* JULIA's *room, some of the hope chest things are spilled out on the floor, bed-
spread, linens, silver cups. The half-emptied wine decanter is in a prominent spot. A
table is set up in the yard. We hear the distant sound of a marching band. The excitement of a special day is in the air.* NELSON's *army jacket hangs on his porch.* LULA
*brings a pitcher of punch to table.* MATTIE *enters with* TEETA *and* PRINCESS; *she is
annoyed and upset in contrast to* LULA's *singing and gala mood. She scolds the children,
smacks* TEETA's *behind.*

MATTIE: They was teasin' the Chinaman down the street 'cause his hair is
    braided. [*To* CHILDREN.] If he ketches you, he'll cook you with onions
    and gravy.
LULA: [*Inspecting* NELSON's *jacket.*] Sure will.
TEETA: Can we go play?
MATTIE: A mad dog might bite-cha.
PRINCESS: Can we go play?
MATTIE: No, you might step on a nail and get lockjaw.
TEETA: Can we go play?
MATTIE: Oh, go on and play! I wish a gypsy would steal both of 'em!

[JULIA *enters her room.*]

LULA: What's the matter, Mattie?
MATTIE: Them damn fool people at the Merchant Marine don't wanta give
    me my 'lotment money.
JULIA: [*Steps out on her porch with deliberate, defiant energy. She is wearing her
    wedding dress . . . carrying a wine glass. She is over-demonstrating a show of
    carefree abandon and joy.*] I'm so happy! I never been this happy in all my
    life! I'm happy to be alive, alive and livin' for my people.
LULA: You better stop drinkin' so much wine. [LULA *enters her house.*]
JULIA: But if you got no feelin's they can't be hurt!
MATTIE: Hey, Julia, the people at the Merchant Marine say I'm not married
    to October.
JULIA: Getcha license, honey, show your papers. Some of us, thang Gawd,
    got papers!
MATTIE: I don't have none.
JULIA: Why? Was October married before?
MATTIE: No, but I was. A good for nothin' named Delroy . . . I hate to call
    his name. Was years 'fore I met October. Delroy used to beat the hell
    outta me . . . tried to stomp me, grind me into the ground . . . callin'

me such dirty names . . . Got so 'til I was shame to look at myself in a mirror. I was glad when he run off.

JULIA: Where'd he go?

MATTIE: I don't know. Man at the office kept sayin' . . . "You're not married to October" . . . and wavin' me 'way like that.

JULIA: Mattie, this state won't allow divorce.

MATTIE: Well, I never got one.

JULIA: You shoulda so you could marry October. You have to be married to get his benefits.

MATTIE: We was married. On Edisto Island. I had a white dress and flowers . . . everything but papers. We couldn't get papers. Elder Burns knew we was doin' best we could.

JULIA: You can't marry without papers.

MATTIE: What if your husband run off? And you got no money? Readin' from the Bible makes people married, not no piece-a paper. We're together eleven years, that oughta-a be legal.

JULIA: [Puts down glass.] No, it doesn't go that way.

MATTIE: October's out on the icy water, in the war-time, worryin' 'bout me 'n Teeta. I say he's my husband. Gotta pay Fanny, buy food. Julia, what must I do?

JULIA: I don't know.

MATTIE: What's the use-a so much-a education if you don't know what to do?

JULIA: You may's well just lived with October. Your marriage meant nothin'.

MATTIE: [Standing angry.] It meant somethin' to me if not to anybody else. It means I'm ice cream, too, strawberry. [MATTIE heads for her house.]

JULIA: Get mad with me if it'll make you feel better.

MATTIE: Julia, could you lend me two dollars?

JULIA: Yes, that's somethin' I can do besides drink this wine.

[JULIA goes into her room, to get the two dollars. Enter FANNY, TEETA and PRINCESS.]

FANNY: Colored men don't know how to do nothin' right. I paid that big black boy cross the street . . . thirty cents to paint my sign . . . [Sign reads . . . GOODBYE COLORED BOYS . . . on one side; the other reads . . . FOR GOD AND CONTRY.] But he can't spell. I'm gon' call him a dumb darky and get my money back. Come on, children! [CHILDREN follow laughing.]

LULA: Why call him names!?

FANNY: 'Cause it makes him mad, that's why.

[FANNY exits with TEETA and PRINCESS. JULIA goes into her room. THE BELL MAN enters carrying a display board filled with badges and flags . . . buttons, red and blue ribbons attached to the buttons . . . slogans . . . THE WAR TO END ALL WARS. He also carries a string of overseas caps (paper) and wears one. Blows a war tune on his tin flute. LULA exits.]

BELL MAN: "War to end all wars . . ." Flags and badges! Getcha emblems! Hup-two-three . . . Flags and badges . . . hup-two-three! Hey, Aunty! Come back here! Where you at?

[*Starts to follow* LULA *into her house.* NELSON *steps out on the porch and blocks his way.*]

NELSON: My mother is in her house. You ain't to come walkin' in. You knock.

BELL MAN: Don't letcha uniform go to your head, Boy, or you'll end your days swingin' from a tree.

LULA: [*Squeezing past* NELSON *dressed in skirt and open shirt-waist.*] Please, Mister, he ain't got good sense.

MATTIE: He crazy, Mister.

NELSON: Fact is, you stay out of here. Don't ever come back here no more.

BELL MAN: [*Backing up in surprise.*] He got no respect. One them crazies. I ain't never harmed a bareassed soul but, hot damn, I can get madder and badder than you. Let your uniform go to your head.

LULA: Yessir, he goin' back in the army today.

BELL MAN: Might not get there way he's actin'.

MATTIE: [*As* LULA *takes two one dollar bills from her bosom.*] He sorry right now, Mister, his head ain' right.

BELL MAN: [*Speaks to* LULA *but keeps an eye on* NELSON.] Why me? I try to give you a laugh but they say, "Play with a puppy and he'll lick your mouth." Familiarity makes for contempt.

LULA: [*Taking flags and badges.*] Yessir. Here's somethin' on my account . . . and I'm buyin' flags and badges for the children. Everybody know you a good man and do right.

BELL MAN: [*To* LULA.] You pay up by Monday. [*To* NELSON.] Boy, you done cut off your Mama's credit.

LULA: I don't blame you, Mister. [BELL MAN *exits.*]

NELSON: Mama, your new faith don't seem to do much for you.

LULA: [*Turning to him.*] Nelson, go on off to the war 'fore somebody kills you. I ain't goin' to let nobody spoil my day.

[LULA *puts flags and badges on punchbowl table.* JULIA *comes out of her room, with the two dollars for* MATTIE—*hands it to her. Sound of Jenkins Colored Orphan Band is heard (Record: "Ramblin" by Bunk Johnson).*]

JULIA: Listen, Lula . . . Listen, Mattie . . . it's Jenkin's Colored Orphan Band . . . Play! Play, you Orphan boys! Rise up higher than the dirt around you! Play! That's struttin' music, Lula!

LULA: It sure is!

[LULA *struts, arms akimbo, head held high.* JULIA *joins her; they haughtily strut toward each other, then retreat with mock arrogance . . . exchange cold, hostile looks . . . A Carolina folk dance passed on from some dimly remembered African beginning. Dance ends strutting.*]

JULIA: [*Concedes defeat in the dance.*] All right, Lula, strut me down! Strut me right on down! [*They end dance with breathless laughter and cross to* LULA's *porch.*]

LULA: Julia! Fasten me! Pin my hair.

JULIA: I'm not goin' to that silly parade, with the colored soldiers marchin' at the end of it.

[LULA *sits on the stool.* JULIA *combs and arranges her hair.*]

LULA: Come on, we'll march behind the white folks whether they want us or not. Mister Herman's people got a nice house . . . lemon trees in the yard, lace curtains at the window.

JULIA: And red, white and blue flowers all around.

LULA: That Uncle Greenlee seems to be well-fixed.

JULIA: He works for the livery stable . . . cleans up behind horses . . . in a uniform.

LULA: That's nice.

JULIA: Weeds their gardens . . . clips white people's pet dogs . . .

LULA: Ain't that lovely? I wish Nelson was safe and nicely settled.

JULIA: Uncle Greenlee is a well-fed, tale-carryin' son-of-a-bitch . . . and that's the only kind-a love they want from us.

LULA: It's wrong to hate.

JULIA: They say it's wrong to love too.

LULA: We got to show 'em we're good, got to be three times as good, just to make it.

JULIA: Why? When they mistreat us who cares? We mistreat each other, who cares? Why we gotta be so good jus' for them?

LULA: Dern you, Julia Augustine, you hard-headed thing, 'cause they'll kill us if we not.

JULIA: They doin' it anyway. Last night I dreamed of the dead slaves—all the murdered black and bloody men silently gathered at the foot-a my bed. Oh, that awful silence. I wish the dead could scream and fight back. What they do to us . . . and all they want is to be loved in return. Nelson's not Greenlee. Nelson is a fighter.

LULA: [*Standing.*] I know. But I'm tryin' to keep him from findin' it out.

[NELSON, *unseen by* LULA, *listens.*]

JULIA: Your hair looks pretty.

LULA: Thank you. A few years back I got down on my knees in the court-house to keep him off-a the chain gang. I crawled and cried, "Please white folks, yall's everything. I'se nothin, yall's everything." The court laughed—I meant for 'em to laugh . . . then they let Nelson go.

JULIA: [*Pitying her.*] Oh, Miss Lula, a lady's not supposed to crawl and cry.

LULA: I was savin' his life. Is my skirt fastened? Today might be the last time I ever see Nelson. [NELSON *goes back in house.*] Tell him how life's gon' be better when he gets back. Make up what *should* be true. A man can't fight a war on nothin' . . . would you send a man off—to die on nothin'?

JULIA: That's sin, Miss Lula, leavin' on a lie.

LULA: That's all right—some truth has no nourishment in it. Let him feel good.

JULIA: I'll do my best.

[MATTIE *enters carrying a colorful, expensive parasol. It is far beyond the price range of her outfit.*]

MATTIE: October bought it for my birthday 'cause he know I always wanted a fine-quality parasol.

[FANNY *enters through the back entry,* CHILDREN *with her. The mistake on the sign has been corrected by pasting* OU *over the error.*]

FANNY: [*Admiring* MATTIE's *appearance.*] Just shows how the race can look when we wanta. I called Rusty Bennet a dumb darky and he wouldn't even get mad. Wouldn't gimme my money back either. A black Jew.

[NELSON *enters wearing his private's uniform with quartermaster insignia. He salutes them.*]

NELSON: Ladies. Was nice seein' you these few days. If I couldn't help, 'least I didn't do you no harm, so nothin' from nothin' leaves nothin'.

FANNY: [*Holds up her punch cup;* LULA *gives* JULIA *high sign.*] Get one-a them Germans for me.

JULIA: [*Stands on her porch.*] Soon, Nelson, in a little while . . . we'll have whatsoever our hearts desire. You're comin' back in glory . . . with honors and shining medals . . . And those medals and that uniform is gonna open doors for you . . . and for October . . . for all, all of the servicemen. Nelson, on account-a you we're gonna be able to go in the park. They're gonna take down the no-colored signs . . . and Rusty Bennet's gonna print new ones . . . Everybody welcome . . . Everybody welcome . . .

MATTIE: [*To* TEETA.] Hear that? We gon' go in the park.

FANNY: Some of us ain't ready for that.

PRINCESS: Me too?

MATTIE: You can go now . . . and me too if I got you by the hand.

PRINCESS: [*Feeling left out.*] Ohhhhh.

JULIA: We'll go to the band concerts, the museums . . . we'll go in the library and draw out books.

MATTIE: And we'll draw books.

FANNY: Who'll read 'em to you?

MATTIE: My Teeta!

JULIA: Your life'll be safe, you and October'll be heroes.

FANNY: [*Very moved.*] Colored heroes.

JULIA: And at last we'll come into our own.

[ALL *cheer and applaud.* JULIA *steps down from porch.*]

NELSON: Julia, can you look me dead in the eye and say you believe all-a that?

JULIA: If you just gotta believe somethin', it may's well be that.

[*Applause.*]

NELSON: [*Steps up on* JULIA's *porch to make his speech.*] Friends, relatives and all other well-wishers. All-a my fine ladies and little ladies—all you good-lookin', tantalizin', pretty-eyed ladies—yeah, with your *kind* ways and your *mean* ways. I find myself a thorn among six lovely roses. Sweet little Teeta . . . the merry little Princess. Mattie, she so pretty 'til October better hurry up and come on back here. Fanny—uh—tryin' to help the race . . . a race woman. And Julia—my good friend. Mama—the only mama I got, I wanta thank you for savin' my life from time to time. What's hard ain't the goin', it's the comin' back. From the bottom-a my heart, I'd truly like to see y'all, each and every one-a you . . . able to go in the park and all that. I really would. So, with a full heart and a loaded mind, I bid you, as the French say, Adieu.

LULA: [*Bowing graciously, she takes* NELSON's *arm and they exit.*] Our humble thanks . . . my humble pleasure . . . gratitude . . . thank you . . .

[CHILDREN *wave their flags.*]

FANNY: [*To the* CHILDREN.] Let's mind our manners in front-a the downtown white people. Remember we're bein' judged.

PRINCESS: Me too?

MATTIE: [*Opening umbrella.*] Yes, you too.

FANNY: [*Leads the way and counts time.*] Step, step, one, two, step, step.

[MATTIE, FANNY *and the* CHILDREN *exit.* HERMAN *enters yard by far gate, takes two long steamer tickets from his pocket.* JULIA *senses him, turns. He is carelessly dressed and sweating.*]

HERMAN: I bought our tickets. Boat tickets to New York.

JULIA: [*Looks at tickets.*] Colored tickets. You can't use yours. [*She lets tickets flutter to the ground.*]

HERMAN: They'll change and give one white ticket. You'll ride one deck, I'll ride the other . . .

JULIA: John C. Calhoun really said a mouthful—men are not born—men are made. Ten years ago—that's when you should-a bought tickets. You chained me to your mother for ten years.

HERMAN: [*Kneeling, picking up tickets.*] Could I walk out on 'em? . . . Ker-ist sake. I'm that kinda man like my father was . . . a debt-payer, a plain, workin' man—

JULIA: He was a member in good standin' of The Gold Carnation. What kinda robes and hoods did those plain men wear? For downin' me and mine. You won twenty dollars in gold.

HERMAN: I love you . . . I love work, to come home in the evenin' . . . to enjoy the breeze for Gawd's sake . . . But no, I never wanted to go to New York. The hell with Goddamn bread factories . . . I'm a stony-broke, half-dead, half-way gentleman . . . But I'm what I wanta be. A baker.

JULIA: You waited 'til you was half-dead to buy those tickets. I don't want to go either . . . Get off the boat, the same faces'll be there at the dock. It's that shop. It's that shop!

HERMAN: It's mine. I did want to keep it.

JULIA: Right . . . people pick what they want most.

HERMAN: [Indicating the tickets.] I did . . . you threw it in my face.

JULIA: Get out. Get your things and get out of my life. [The remarks become counterpoint. Each rides through the other's speech. HERMAN goes in house.] Must be fine to own somethin'—even if it's four walls and a sack-a flour.

HERMAN: [JULIA has followed him into the house.] My father labored in the street . . . liftin' and layin' down cobblestone . . . liftin' and layin' down stone 'til there was enough money to open a shop . . .

JULIA: My people . . . relatives, friends and strangers . . . they worked and slaved free for nothin' for some-a the biggest name families down here . . . Elliots, Lawrences, Ravenals . . .

[HERMAN is wearily gathering his belongings.]

HERMAN: Great honor, working for the biggest name families. That's who you slaved for. Not me. The big names.

JULIA: . . . the rich and the poor . . . we know you . . . all of you . . . Who you are . . . where you came from . . . where you goin' . . .

HERMAN: What's my privilege . . . Good mornin', good afternoon . . . pies are ten cents today . . . and you can get 'em from Schumann for eight . . .

JULIA: "She's different" . . . I'm no different . . .

HERMAN: I'm white . . . did it give me favors and friends?

JULIA: . . . "Not like the others" . . . We raised up all-a these Carolina children . . . white and the black . . . I'm just like all the rest of the colored women . . . like Lula, Mattie . . . Yes, like Fanny!

HERMAN: Go here, go there . . . Philadelphia . . . New York . . . Schumann wants me to go North too . . .

JULIA: We nursed you, fed you, buried your dead . . . grinned in your face—cried 'bout your troubles—and laughed 'bout ours.

HERMAN: Schumann . . . Alien robber . . . waitin' to buy me out . . . My father . . .

JULIA: Pickin' up cobblestones . . . left him plenty-a time to wear bed-sheets in that Gold Carnation Society . . .

HERMAN: He never hurt anybody.

JULIA: He hurts me. There's no room for you to love him and me too . . . [Sits.] it can't be done—

HERMAN: The ignorance . . . he didn't know . . . the ignorance . . . mama . . . they don't know.

JULIA: But *you* know. My father was somebody. He helped put up Roper Hospital and Webster Rice Mills after the earthquake wiped the face-a this Gawd-forsaken city clean . . . a fine brick-mason he was . . . paid him one-third-a what they paid the white ones . . .

HERMAN: We were poor . . . No big name, no quality.

JULIA: Poor! My Gramma was a slave wash-woman bustin' suds for free! Can't get poorer than that.

HERMAN: [*Trying to shut out the sound of her voice.*] Not for me, she didn't!

JULIA: We the ones built the pretty white mansions . . . for free . . . the fishin' boats . . . for free . . . made your clothes, raised your food . . . for free . . . and I loved you—for free.

HERMAN: A Gawd-damn lie . . . nobody did for me . . . you know it . . . you know how hard I worked—

JULIA: If it's anybody's home down here it's mine . . . everything in the city is mine—why should I go anywhere . . . ground I'm standin' on—it's mine.

HERMAN: [*Sitting on foot of the bed.*] It's the ignorance . . . Lemme be, lemme rest . . . Ker-ist sake . . . It's the ignorance . . .

JULIA: After ten years you still won't look. All-a my people that's been killed . . . It's your people that killed 'em . . . all that's been in bondage— your people put 'em there—all that didn't go to school—your people kept 'em out.

HERMAN: But I didn't do it. Did I do it?

JULIA: They killed 'em . . . all the dead slaves . . . buried under a blanket-a this Carolina earth, even the cotton crop is nourished with hearts' blood . . . roots-a that cotton tangled and wrapped 'round my bones.

HERMAN: And you blamin' me for it . . .

JULIA: Yes! . . . For the one thing we never talk about . . . white folks killin' me and mine. You wouldn't let me speak.

HERMAN: I never stopped you . . .

JULIA: Every time I open my mouth 'bout what they do . . . you say . . . "Ker-ist, there it is again . . ." Whenever somebody was lynched . . . you 'n'me would eat a very silent supper. It hurt me not to talk . . . what you don't say you swallow down . . . [*Pours wine.*]

HERMAN: I was just glad to close the door 'gainst what's out there. You did all the givin' . . . I failed you in every way.

JULIA: You nursed me when I was sick . . . paid my debts . . .

HERMAN: I didn't give my name.

JULIA: You couldn't . . . was the law . . .

HERMAN: I shoulda walked 'til we came to where it'd be all right.

JULIA: You never put any other woman before me.

HERMAN: Only Mama, Annabelle, the customers, the law . . . the ignorance . . . I honored them while you waited and waited—

JULIA: You clothed me . . . you fed me . . . you were kind, loving . . .

HERMAN: I never did a damn thing for you. After ten years look at it—I never did a damn thing for you.

JULIA: Don't low-rate yourself . . . leave me something.

HERMAN: When my mother and sister came . . . I was ashamed. What am I doin' bein' ashamed of us?

JULIA: When you first came in this yard I almost died-a shame . . . so many times you was nothin' to me but white . . . times we were angry . . . damn white man . . . times I was tired . . . damn white man . . . but most times you were my husband, my friend, my lover . . .

HERMAN: Whatever is wrong, Julia . . . not the law . . . *me*; what I didn't do, with all-a my faults, spite-a all that . . . You gotta believe I love you . . . 'cause I do . . . That's the one thing I know . . . I love you . . . I love you.

JULIA: Ain't too many people in this world that get to be loved . . . really loved.

HERMAN: We gon' take that boat trip . . . You'll see, you'll never be sorry.

JULIA: To hell with sorry. Let's be glad!

HERMAN: Sweetheart, leave the ignorance outside . . . [*Stretches out across the bed.*] Don't let that doctor in here . . . to stand over me shakin' his head.

JULIA: [*Pours water in a silver cup.*] Bet you never drank from a silver cup. Carolina water is sweet water . . . Wherever you go you gotta come back for a drink-a this water. Sweet water, like the breeze that blows 'cross the battery.

HERMAN: [*Happily weary.*] I'm gettin' old, that ain' no joke.

JULIA: No, you're not. Herman, my real weddin' cake . . . I wanta big one . . .

HERMAN: Gonna bake it in a wash-tub . . .

JULIA: We'll put pieces of it in little boxes for folks to take home and dream on.

HERMAN: . . . But let's don't give none to your landlady . . . Gon' get old and funny-lookin' like Robbie m'boy and . . . and . . .

JULIA: And Mable . . .

HERMAN: [*Breathing heavier.*] Robbie says "Mable, where's my keys" . . . Mable—Robbie—Mable—

[*Lights change, shadows grow longer.* MATTIE *enters the yard.*]

MATTIE: Hey, Julia! [*Sound of carriage wheels in front of the main house.* MATTIE *enters* JULIA's *house. As she sees* HERMAN.] They 'round there, they come to get him, Julia.

[JULIA *takes the wedding band and chain from around her neck, gives it to* MATTIE *with tickets.*]

JULIA: Surprise. Present.

MATTIE: For me?

JULIA: Northern tickets . . . and a wedding band.

MATTIE: I can't take that for nothing.

JULIA: You and Teeta are my people.

MATTIE: Yes.

JULIA: You and Teeta are my family. Be my family.

MATTIE: We your people whether we blood kin or not. [MATTIE *exits to her own porch.*]

FANNY: [*Offstage.*] No . . . No, Ma'am. [*Enters with* LULA. LULA *is carrying the wilted bouquet.*] Julia! They think Mr. Herman's come back.

[HERMAN'S MOTHER *enters with* ANNABELLE. *The old lady is weary and subdued.* ANNABELLE *is almost without feeling.* JULIA *is on her porch waiting.*]

JULIA: Yes, Fanny, he's here. [LULA *retires to her doorway.* JULIA *silently stares at them, studying each* WOMAN, *seeing them with new eyes. She is going through that rising process wherein she must reject them as the molders and dictators of her life.*] Nobody comes in my house.

FANNY: What kind-a way is that?

JULIA: Nobody comes in my house.

ANNABELLE: We'll quietly take him home.

JULIA: You can't come in.

HERMAN'S MOTHER: [*Low-keyed, polite and humble simplicity.*] You see my condition. Gawd's punishin' me . . . Whippin' me for somethin' I did or didn't do. I can't understand this . . . I prayed, but ain't no understandin' Herman's dyin'. He's almost gone. It's right and proper that he should die at home in his own bed. I'm askin' humbly . . . or else I'm forced to get help from the police.

ANNABELLE: Give her a chance . . . She'll do right . . . won'tcha?

[HERMAN *stirs. His breathing becomes harsh and deepens into the sound known as the "death rattle."* MATTIE *leads the* CHILDREN *away.*]

JULIA: [*Not unkindly.*] Do whatever you have to do. Win the war. Represent the race. Call the police. [*She enters her house, closes the door and bolts it.* HERMAN'S MOTHER *leaves through the front entry.* FANNY *slowly follows her.*] I'm here, do you hear me? [*He tries to answer but can't.*] We're standin' on the deck-a that Clyde Line Boat . . . wavin' to the people on the shore . . . Your mama, Annabelle, my Aunt Cora . . . all of our friends . . . the children . . . all wavin' . . . "Don't stay 'way too long . . . Be sure and come back . . . We gon' miss you . . . Come back, we need you" . . . But we're goin' . . . The whistle's blowin', flags wavin' . . . We're takin' off, ridin' the waves so smooth and easy . . . There now . . . [ANNABELLE *moves closer to the house as she listens to* JULIA.] . . . the bakery's fine . . . all the orders are ready . . . out to sea . . . on our way . . . [*The weight has lifted, she is radiantly happy. She helps him gasp out each remaining breath. With each gasp he seems to draw a step nearer to a wonderful goal.*] Yes . . . Yes . . . Yes . . . Yes . . . Yes . . . Yes . . .

*Curtain.*

# STUDY QUESTIONS

1. Early in the first scene, Mattie picks up an axe to knock the post out of the way so she can get to the quarter that she had given Teeta to get some things at the store but that Teeta had dropped. When Julia, not knowing what is going on, steps out on the porch, Mattie thinks she is trying to stop her and says, "If you don't like it—come down here and whip me." Julia "(*Nervous but determined to present a firm stand.*)" says, "Oh, my . . . Good mornin' ladies. My name is Julia Augustine. I'm not gonna move." Why does she say that?

2. What image of Julia and her CHARACTER do you get from her giving Mattie the quarter and saying that she has Mattie's quarter under the house for good luck, and from Julia's conversation with Fanny that follows?

3. What elements of humor do you find in the first scene?

4. When Nelson meets Julia, he tells her she's "the best-lookin' woman I ever seen in my life." What EXPECTATIONS do you have about their relationship? How do your expectations change or shift or grow as the play progresses? How late in the play do you think they may still get together?

5. What issues and expectations does the scene with the Bell Man introduce? How does the appearance of Princess reinforce some of these?

6. Now that you've read the whole play, what is there in October's letter that ominously foreshadows what is to happen later? Do you remember whether you particularly noticed the detail that will be important when you first read the passage? Do you think this detail, dropped in so inconspicuously, helped prepare the way for your acceptance of the later event, even if you didn't notice it? As you read the scene a second time, what is the difference in effect between your two readings? What significance does this sentence from the letter have later: "Two things a man can give the woman he loves . . . his name and his protection"?

7. The first scene ends with the situation clear—Julia is in love with a white man; they have been lovers for ten years but cannot marry because of laws against miscegenation in South Carolina at the time. Yet the fact of the relationship is not dropped dramatically—at the curtain—but almost a page earlier. Is this a weakness or a strength in the play? What is the effect of the relatively undramatic (or untheatrical) timing of the curtain?

8. Early in Act I, scene 2, Lula tells Nelson to "Go on!" He says, "Fact is, I was gon' stay home and have me some orange drink, but Massa beat me to it. None-a my business no-how, dammit." What does he mean by all that?

9. What image of Herman's mother do you get from his first conversation with Julia? What aspects of social class are touched upon in the play, and how do these interact with the racial issues?

10. What elements in the first lengthy conversation between Herman and Julia (through the celebration of their tenth "anniversary") help define their relationship for you? Can you describe that relationship in your own words, in a paragraph, perhaps?

11. In what sense does "a wedding band . . . on a chain" encapsulate their situation?

12. Which of the two seems the more "racist"? Is this confirmed or qualified later in the play?

13. Julia defines dignity as "a spirit that rises higher than the dirt around it, without any by-your-leave. It's not proud and it's not 'shamed"; why is she uncertain whether she and Herman have dignity?

14. The first act ends more dramatically than the first scene did, with Herman collapsing, but the last line, Fanny's "Get him out of my yard," splashes the cold water of reality on its theatricality. What did you think was wrong with Herman? What did you think was going to happen in Act II?

15. Why doesn't Fanny want a doctor called in?

16. Why, after Herman wakes, takes more medicine, and groans, does Julia put her open dressmaking scissors under his bed?

17. In the first act, we learn that "the people across the way" are going to Philadelphia after the war, and early in Act II, Nelson thinks he "might hit out for Chicago or Detroit" after the war. How does this reflect on the conditions of blacks in the South? on their vision of conditions in the North? on their expectations of how things will change after the end of World War I? In Act II, scene 2, what does Lula ask Julia to tell Nelson as he heads back to active duty? What do you infer that she believes will happen after the war? What does Julia say about what Lula wants her to tell Nelson? What does she actually tell him? Can you relate the situation in 1918 to that in 1966 when the play was first performed?

18. Julia asks Annabelle to get Herman to a doctor right away; Annabelle insists on waiting until dark. What is each woman's motivation? Who is right?

19. Why does Annabelle want Herman to marry Celestine?

20. What is the relationship between Fanny and Herman's mother? Why?

21. How does Herman's mother plan to explain why Herman is where he is?

22. What is Herman's mother's attitude toward men? Why?

23. What was the gift of Herman's speech on John C. Calhoun at the Gold Carnation picnic? How old was he? What is Julia's reaction when he begins reciting it in his delirium? How much of her further actions and words are the result of his recitation?

24. What does Julia reveal to Herman's mother about what she, Julia, has done for her in the past? How does Herman's mother respond?

25. How does Act II, scene 1, end?

26. What do Herman and Julia reveal about their childhood and families and their place and experience in society in the scene in which they speak in "counterpoint" (Act II, scene 2)?

27. The "counterpoint" scene begins in hostility and with accusations and grievances. When and how does it turn around to a love scene? Is the turn effective?

28. How is the end of the play an affirmation? What is it an affirmation of? How would you project Julia's future for the next few days? years? the rest of her life?

# nila northSun

Born in Schurz, Nevada, in 1951 of Shoshoni-Chippewa heritage, nila northSun is coauthor of *After the Drying Up of the Water* and *Diet Pepsi and Nacho Cheese*.

In this poem, there is not only a speaker—gramma—but also someone "behind" the speaker who can call her gramma. A member of one generation quotes a member of an older one who recalls a still older one.

## what gramma said about her grandpa

he was white grandpa
his name jim butler
he's good irish man
he was nice talk our
language                                                5
big man with moustache
boss of town
tonopah
he found silver mine
we still on reservation they                           10
come tell us "your grandpa
found mine" so
we move to tonopah
he say "buy anything you want
don't buy just little things                           15
don't buy just candy
buy something big"
that's what he used to say
4th of july he make
a great long table                                     20
put sheet over it
then put all kinds of food on it
he say "get your plate &

help yourselves"
he fed all the indians                                     25
he was good man
but then
he marry white woman
& we go back to reservation

## STUDY QUESTIONS

1. Other than quotation marks, there is no punctuation in this poem. Occasionally a sentence will end in the middle of a line but without a period, apparently to capture the rhythm of the grandmother's speech. This may cause some difficulty unless you read attentively. Find several instances of such lines.

2. Gramma says Jim Butler, her grandpa, was a nice man, a good man. Was he?

3. If you were reading this poem aloud, acting the part of gramma, what tone of voice would you use? If you were telling the story of gramma's grandpa in your own words and voice, how would you read it (or "play" it)?

# Gogisgi

Born in Oklahoma City in 1927, Carroll Arnett (who often writes under his Cherokee name, "Gogisgi") was educated at Beloit College, the University of Oklahoma, and the University of Texas. He has taught at Knox College, Stephens College, Wittenberg University, and Nasson College; he is now professor of English at Central Michigan University. He is the author of ten volumes of poetry and has been awarded a National Endowment for the Arts Fellowship.

The following short poem wittily describes the difficulties of feeling caught between worlds.

## SONG OF THE BREED

Don't offend
the fullbloods,
don't offend

the whites,
stand there in                                        5
the middle
of the god-
damned road
and get hit.


## STUDY QUESTIONS

1. To whom is the poem addressed? What do the "fullbloods" (line 2) and the "whites" (l. 4) have in common, as far as the narrator is concerned?

2. Describe the frustrations the NARRATOR feels. Does the fact that we have no particulars about his circumstances diminish the poem's potential effect? How much can we justifiably infer about the narrator's circumstances? What indications are there of his strength of feeling?


# Cyn. Zarco

C yn. Zarco was born in Manila, Philippines, in 1950 but now lives in California. She won the Before Columbus Foundation's American Book Award in 1986 for her book *Cir'cum-nav'i-ga'tion.*

The real-surreal imagery and the satiric, flip, somewhat threatening tone of "Flipochinos" are common to the writers loosely affiliated with Ishmael Reed, so watch your step.


# FLIPOCHINOS

when a brown person
gets together
with a yellow person
it is something like
the mating of a chico[1] and a banana            5

---

1. Greasewood; a thorny plant with fleshy leaves and dry papery fruit found in the deserts of the American West.

the brown meat of the chico
plus the yellow skin of the banana
take the seed of the chico for eyes
peel the banana for sex appeal
lick the juice from your fingers                                    10
and watch your step

## STUDY QUESTIONS

1. Like the nila northSun poem in this chapter, "Flipochinos" is not punctuated; unlike that poem, however, here the line endings do serve as punctuation in some cases. Where would you end the sentences in this poem? If you look closely, you will notice that many of the lines are parallel—lines 1 and 3, for example: "w——a brown person," "w—— a yellow person." What other parallel structures can you find? How do these structures reflect the subject matter of the poem?

2. Who is the "you" in the poem ("your," in final line)?

# Barbara Thompson

B orn in Los Angeles not long before World War II, Barbara Thompson grew up there and in Wisconsin. After graduating from Wellesley College, she worked for the *Washington Post*, married a Pakistani government official and went to live in Pakistan, did some book reviewing in newspapers and on radio, and tinkered with handicrafts; but she did not write about Pakistan until she left there (in 1976). She has published a number of stories in recent years, several of them, including "Crossing," winning awards or being anthologized. She writes a number of drafts of each story, gradually "coming to know who these people [are]. . . . The early drafts are exploratory, finding out what I know. Then it's a matter of telling someone else the way it was."

Two marriages across cultural borders have different results, but the children of those marriages may have other borders to cross in this quiet but exciting, compassionate but probing, story.

# CROSSING

"Memsahib?" The tap at her door is light, tentative, like the scratch of a bird   1
on a windowpane. Only bird cries and an occasional bicycle bell have interrupted the afternoon silence since an hour ago when the call to prayer rasped
out from the loudspeaker at the neighboring mosque. It is an April Friday in
the early Seventies in the old British part of Lahore. The willows that brush
against the roshandon windows[1] of Anne's dressing room were planted at the
behest of some colonial official forty years ago. And the old habits too persist:
in westernized households like this, only the menservants are at prayer in the
mosque; the sahibs sleep in their beds after a heavy lunch.

Not Anne. She is American and even after twelve years she can rarely   2
sleep in the daytime. For some minutes now she has been standing absently
over an open suitcase, rummaging through a pile of woolens. Above her head
the ceiling fan orbits slowly, making a sound like a drowsy insect.

"Memsahib?" Noiselessly the little maidservant pushes the door inward   3
with the edge of a brass tray on which the telephone rests, its receiver beside
it. "Trunk call from Karachi," she says softly. "From Libby Memsahib."

Anne takes the phone out into the passageway, away from the room in   4
which her husband, Iqbal, is sleeping. Behind her the servant secures the
connecting doors. She is young, hardly more than a child, but Anne is conscious how swift and purposeful she is, her bare feet gliding like silk over the
parquet floor, the brass latches closing with one muted click. Anne feels
again the hint of unacknowledged conspiracy between them, mistress and
maidservant, against the hegemony of men. She has tacitly endorsed the
girl's presumption by waiting these long moments before picking up the
receiver.

"Libby?" Anne braces herself. Libby has a way of careening through   5
other people's lives like a charge of static electricity, rendering everything
momentarily more vivid but trailing a wake of confusion.

"There's been a balls up, Anne. Our Afghan visas aren't ready."   6

"But we're supposed to leave tomorrow morning!"   7

"That's all right, you have yours, and I've worked it so—"   8

"But there's no point in our going without Masood!"   9

"You *won't* go without Masood! Stop interrupting, Anne, I've fixed   10
everything. I'll put Masood on the plane to Peshawar on Sunday morning
just as we planned, only I won't be with him. You pick him up and drive to
Kabul as scheduled and I'll collect both passports Monday morning and fly

---

1. Small ventilating windows just under the eaves. [The editors wish to thank Barbara Thompson for her help
with these footnotes.]

there straight. No one can stop *me*. It'll be fine. I made a hell of a row at the Afghan Consulate and they swore they'd give them Monday whether or not the authorization came from Kabul. OK?" Libby's voice is louder than necessary, higher pitched, and she is talking very fast. Anne is conscious she is meant to be overwhelmed.

"How can Masood cross the border without his passport?" she asks wearily.    11

"He'll have to use Sheriyar's. No one ever looks at kids."    12

"I'm *taking* Sheriyar, Libby. You know I'm taking both boys, that was    13
the whole excuse for the trip. No one even knows about you and Masood."

"Stop fussing, Anne. Make something up. Tell Sher you'll bring him    14
something wonderful from Kabul, a tribesman's banduq[2] with an inlaid barrel, for Christ's sake. You'll think of something."

"I can't," she says sullenly.    15

"Anne, are you there? Damn it, this bloody telephone must be bugged.    16
I can't hear a word you're saying."

"Then how do you know I'm saying anything?" Anne says. "Where are    17
you, Libby? At your office?"

"I'm at a friend's flat. Listen, let's get this all straight before the line    18
really dies. You collect Masood Sunday morning at the Peshawar airport and I'll catch up with you at the Kabul Hotel as soon as I can manage it, OK? Don't get fussed, Annie. Just make something up." There is a long pause in which Anne says nothing, and then Libby, her voice gentler, supplicating, adds, "you know how much it matters, Annie." And the phone goes dead. But not before Anne thinks she has heard another voice in the background, a man's deep laughter.

She goes back to her dressing room and takes up the packing, all her old    19
hesitancies revived by Libby's call. It was a harebrained scheme from the beginning, based on lies and precisely synchronized movements, but Anne had been persuaded weeks ago that only with her help, and by these baroque means, could Libby get her twelve-year-old son away from his father. Koranic law gives Anwer custody and he is not one to negotiate against his own advantage.

There was too much risk in a direct escape by plane from the Karachi    20
airport: the international departure lounge is full of people you meet at dinner, who know your private business and are given to meddling. If someone notified Anwer and he intercepted them, Libby would never have a second chance. And so they agreed that Libby would use the long Sunday she is permitted with Masood to fly with him to Peshawar where Anne would collect them for the drive across the border to Afghanistan—two ordinary American women on fourteen day tourist visas taking their children on a spring holiday.

2. Gun.

But now Anne is supposed to do it alone, and she wants to balk. Libby 21
is not that particular a friend. They have little in common beyond the bare
fact that in the late Fifties each had married the Pakistani student she met at
college and come here to raise children whose blood is mixed. The substance
of their lives is very different, Anne's as tranquil and domestic as her mother's back in Indiana where Anne grew up. She does not think Pakistan has
changed her very much except in superficial ways, matters of form—the routine of her day, the language she speaks to servants and shopkeepers, the
clothes she wears. Even these changes came gradually. She gave up western
dress only after her second son, Timmy, was born. It had become a bother,
having her mother send things like shoes and pantyhose; and in the summer
heat she felt buttoned up and clunky among the Pakistani women in their
flowing silks and cottons.

Libby had come to Pakistan two years before her, embracing from the 22
start every possible transformation of herself. She had met Anwer getting a
graduate degree at Columbia in anthropology and she likes to say she is the
only foreign wife she ever met who came here with both eyes open. She
landed in Karachi knowing Urdu and a smattering of Gujerati and how to
make a passable curry grinding her own spices. She wore local dress from
the beginning, never bothering with the safety pin at the waist of her sari, as
Anne still does. And when she left Anwer she had her right nostril pierced:
a symbolically neutral way of wearing her engagement diamond, she said.

When Anne met her, Libby had just given birth to Masood, born as his 23
father had been on a rope cot set in the middle of the women's courtyard to
catch the sea breeze. A year later Anne went home in the early months of
her own first confinement to be delivered of Sheriyar by the old doctor who
had attended her own birth. Iqbal had understood without being told that at
such a time she would want her own mother.

She had been surprised in those early years how well Iqbal understood 24
her needs without any explanation. At first she tested him: does he mind her
wearing sleeveless blouses in spite of the Koran? should she give in to his
mother's insistence that she have a wet-nurse for the baby? does it embarrass
him when she takes his hand, touches him, in the presence of others? But
she soon saw that the questions made him uneasy, even when he answered,
as he almost always did, the way she wanted him to. She was emphasizing
differences between them that he did not wish to acknowledge. He often
says that the lives of women are only superficially affected by culture—and
then only to their detriment. A virtuous wife and mother is the same everywhere and forever.

How Anne wishes she could call Libby back. Why hadn't she insisted 25
they postpone the trip to the following weekend? But how could she explain
that to Iqbal, now that all the arrangements had been made, dinner parties
declined on her behalf, Sher and Timmy given makeup assignments for this
particular week of school. Anyhow there is no hope of reaching Libby today
at any telephone number she knows.

Besides, through all her anxiety, Libby's last words throb like a pulse:   26
Anne *does* know how much it matters that Masood should not be left where
he is, at the mercy of his negligent father and the father's new young wife,
running barefoot, eating with his hands, speaking pidgin English like a servant . . . And she goes on, mindlessly filling her case with a jumble of woolens and a few summer shifts leftover from visits to America. Libby has
persuaded her they will be less conspicuous in their own old clothes than in
the saris or shelwar kameezes[3] that single them out as the wives or chattal of
Pakistanis. She shakes out a yellow dress. Like everything else it smells of
camphor and salty dust from years in tin trunks. She holds it up against
herself and switches on the light over the long mirror.

She sees a tall thinnish woman, someone who would be called rangy if   27
her movements were less instinctively cautious. The lemony yellow is too
strong now for her pale skin and gray-smudged chestnut hair. It gives her
the look of being unwell. In her youth she was on the verge of real beauty,
and it is likely that in age she will regain it, with her fine bones and classical
symmetries, but just now in her mid-thirties she has the diminished pretti-
ness of a cut flower left too long in the sun.

Anne has never been particularly vigorous or energetic. She knows it is   28
a wonder to Iqbal how capably she manages her household, controlling the
often devious and contentious servants better than he dreamed a foreign woman
could, better than his own mother does, though he would not admit it. And
unlike his mother she never raises her voice.

Only once in their marriage has Anne come near setting herself against   29
him, and that was—quite unexpectedly—in the matter of their children's
religious upbringing. They had begun in full accord, Anne and Iqbal, the
educated secularized offspring of devout parents. They chose to be married
in the German Lutheran Church where Anne had been baptized and confirmed, because she had always imagined herself in the slipper-satin dress
with the long train and her sorority sisters in attendance, but also because it
reassured her parents, who were troubled that however decent and devoted
he seemed, Iqbal came from a religion that allowed him four wives.

He was glad to pledge monogamy before their altar, in their words. And   30
Anne, in the same concessionary spirit and with as little reflection, agreed
that it would be best for their children to grow up like everybody else in
Pakistan, which meant as Muslims. It would be sufficiently complicating to
have a foreign mother.

But by the time her second son, Timur, was born, Anne had become   31
uncomfortable with the laxness of Iqbal's observance. He is the Islamic
equivalent of the Easter communicant, his sacramental impulses fully satisfied by abstention from pork and the formal prayers at the two major Eid[4]
celebrations. She saw Sher and Timmy growing up without any ordering

3. Trouser and tunic.
4. Celebration that ends the month of fasting.

beliefs, and with a decisiveness that surprised her she released herself from her promise. Every Sunday now she takes them to the watered-down Wesleyan service at the missionary college.

She steeled herself for a struggle, but Iqbal has never mentioned it or tried to deflect her. Perhaps he thinks she is acting out of devotional urgencies that she could not have anticipated, that it is something that happens to women when they have children. Perhaps he regrets not having followed his mother's admonition and insisted on her conversion. But it would have been out of character for him. He prized her foreignness.

Very little in their lives now proclaims her foreignness—certainly not the house in which they live. A single-story white bungalow from the heyday of the Raj, it was the choice Iqbal made when he returned to Lahore the month after their marriage, leaving Anne behind to spare her the first summer's heat. It is a house made for summer, a warren of high-ceilinged interconnecting rooms set along a stemlike corridor, each room with its cooling veranda. He furnished it with things from his mother's go-downs—carved walnut pieces which he had upholstered in rich dark colors, floorlamps that rise like giant silkcapped mushrooms fringed with iridescent beads. When Anne arrived in October she found the house gloomy and talked of lightening it with cane and wicker, fresher colors. But she had more pressing concerns—the language, Iqbal's mother, politics among the servants, her first pregnancy—and when she finally got around to it, the impulse had almost passed. She hung a few landscapes instead of the glum family portraits, taught the mali[5] not to crush the flowers together in tight nosegays, and gave in to the dense Edwardian comfort.

There are guests tonight and Anne must consult with the cook. He has been in the family longer than she has and although he can concoct a baked Alaska that looks like a marble war memorial with meringue doves, she suspects that when she is not around he reverts to his old method of suspending the meat between his toes to pare away the fat and gristle. She makes a mild clatter as she goes down the corridor and when she pushes open the kitchen door, the old man is waiting for her in a clean apron, his hookah tucked away behind the charcoal brazier.

Mangoes are beginning to come into the bazaar, and Anne dictates a recipe for Mango Fool, translating it from an old issue of *Queen*. He takes it down laboriously in a mysterious shorthand. Watching his cramped fingers form the curly symbols that must mean "castor sugar," she feels suddenly dizzy, dislocated. It is more than the script, the Babel of Tongues. There are things she is trying not to think of now.

She wanders back through the hall into the drawing room, cool and dusky, its light an eerie blue from the navy linings of the bamboo shades that cover the tall windows. In the far corner a carved walnut game-table is set out with a half-finished jigsaw puzzle, Monet's water garden at Giverny. She

5. Gardener.

lets herself down into the dimness, the intricate modulations of blue and green. Under her feet the Persian carpet is navy and dun, like an abstraction of mountain streams flowing past granite.

The afternoon falls away as other afternoons have since she discovered this way of summoning up and holding that inner stillness that other westerners have sought here in yoga and drugs. At the game-table, over a jigsaw puzzle or one of her intricate varieties of solitaire, she can withdraw into a velvet darkness beyond thought. She is not aware that the grayish arch among the greens is a bridge, she is conscious only of matching shape and color. When Iqbal comes into the room an hour later she does not look up until his hands are on her shoulders. She sees from his slight smile that he finds her absorption charming: he has said with that same smile that if the house were burning Anne would finish her game of Patience. 37

She rings for tea and they sit together on the plum settee, talking of this and that—dinner parties, a holiday in August—the domestic conversation of the peacefully married who no longer need talk of intimate things, who have the perfect courtesy of strangers. But when the tea is poured she broaches the matter of Sheriyar's remaining behind. At first Iqbal hardly listens. He likes to say that the children are her department, though Anne wonders what that means when they both know that if he determines a vital interest is at stake he will prevail. 38

"I wonder if it isn't too close to his examination, Iqi," she says, tentatively. "I know this year isn't the decisive one, but—" 39

"What are you saying, Anne?" He is suddenly in full focus. 40

"Well, next year he'll be getting ready for Chief's College, and I thought . . ." Her voice trails off. 41

"I thought you cleared everything with the school," he says sharply. 42

"I did. I'm just having second thoughts." 43

"I wish you had come to me earlier," he says. "I would not have thought you would jeopardize his acceptance for a holiday." 44

"He's only eleven," she says. 45

"Exactly. He's almost a man." 46

They are interrupted by the tap of a walking stick against the door, Iqbal's old uncle—his father's only brother—who turns up periodically for a cup of tea to see how the foreign woman is rearing his nephew's sons. In spite of three marriages, he is childless; Sher and Timmy are all his family's future. Anne finds herself pulling the loose edge of her sari over her hair as she settles him into an armchair and rings for more tea. She knows he is embarrassed on Iqbal's behalf that she does not keep purdah like the women of his household. Once fresh tea and samosas[6] are provided, she can leave the men to their own talk and find the ayah to tell her that only Timmy's things are to be packed for the next day's journey. Tonight when she tucks 47

6. Fried turnovers filled with meat or vegetable mixtures.

Sheriyar into bed she will find some way of explaining to him why he cannot go.

The moment comes: Anne is sitting on the edge of his bed on a scarlet silk quilt that Iqbal's mother had made for her when she came as a bride. The lights are out in the room and a single beam from the hallway throws her narrowed silhouette, twice longer than life, on the wall over Sheriyar's head. He himself is only a smudgy shadow with an aureole of unruly black hair against the white pillow.

She begins confidently—he has his examinations next month, someone should stay behind with Daddy. But when Sheriyar never questions, never dissents, she falters, spills out a rush of promises: gifts, a journey with her to Delhi or the Vale of Kashmir, the two of them alone. Her palms are damp, the shadow on the wall twists.

"Is there any other reason I can't go, Mummy?" he asks quietly, his voice so old in its tact and gentleness that for a minute she wonders if he knows something. But of course there is no way he could; and so she reassures him and kisses him, glad that in the darkness their eyes need not meet with anything like understanding.

The journey begins the next morning without any of the domestic ceremony that customarily attends a major departure. Even though it is Saturday, Iqbal has gone to his office and Sher is out on the polo grounds exercising his pony. Nor have the servants lined up for salaams as they do when she travels with Iqbal: is it their way of expressing disapproval that she is traveling unescorted? Only Fazal Dad, the driver, is here, sulkily polishing the already immaculate yellow Triumph, obviously hoping that at the last minute she will decide to take him along, at least as far as Peshawar, where his family is.

She honks the horn several times before Timmy scuffles out, the ayah trailing him with a wicker hamper of lunch, muttering ineffectually in Punjabi that his shirt tail is hanging out. He gets into the car without looking at Anne, but manages the obligatory "Good morning, Mummy" in a cross voice that she decides not to notice.

The sun is brilliant this morning, the first forewarning of the heat to come. Here on the plains spring is no more than ten April days, a temperate mirage of yellowy green and fragrant blossom before the blazing summer. Last night they had a wood fire in the grate, and now as Anne drives between the iron gateposts she sees in the rear-view mirror the servants assembling ladders to take the air conditioners down from their niches for spring cleaning.

Timmy hangs out of the car window, angling for a last look back.

"Well, we're off," she says with a heartiness that sounds false even to her.

"I don't see why Sher couldn't come."

"Daddy didn't want want him to miss school, Timmy." 57

"How come you just decided yesterday?" he says half under his breath, 58
glaring out of the window as though he doesn't really expect an answer.

There is only one road up-country, one way to cross the Ravi River, 59
and that is the Grand Trunk Road which the British built a century ago to
connect the Bay of Bengal with the frontier of Afghanistan. As it cuts through
Lahore it takes on many guises, mirroring the peculiarly disconnected districts of the city. Here where Anne joins it, it is the old Imperial Mall, lined
by the walls and gardens of Government House, the colonial clubs and the
botanical garden. The streets are clean and placid, empty except for a few
cars and the odd cyclist in a crisp white servant's uniform. Here and there
through ornate gates one catches sight of a mali brushing fallen leaves from
a well-tended lawn with his broom of twigs.

But at the chawk,[7] where a wedding-cake gazebo once housed a marble 60
statue of Victoria, everything changes: the road becomes a trading street, the
prosperous bazaar of the rich. Here pharmacies are air conditioned and the
restaurants have deep awnings. Over the moon-door of the Cantonese restaurant a gilded dragon breathes scarlet flame. Beggars whine among the flower
sellers and importune passers-by, but they do not follow or jostle them. Each
seems to have his own agreed-upon station beside a doorway or parking place,
and each his own unique affliction—the thin girl suckling the infant, the boy
on the oversized skateboard whose legs stump at the knees, the humpback
with the twisted face. . . .

In a few blocks the dragons and air conditioners are gone, the structures 61
more tentative, exposed to the street, their paint peeling. Beggars wander
randomly among the fruit and vegetable stalls, pushing spatulate fingers at
the black-shrouded purdah women. The women shuffle along in pairs like
nuns or are guided by a servant boy. Anne is alert to their movements; blink-
ered as they are, they sometimes panic and rush the traffic.

Nearer the University some younger women walk unveiled, with only 62
muslin dopattas[8] covering their head and breasts. Even they move as though
conscious of peril, and none sit among the cigarette-smoking boys who lounge
in the open-air tea stalls. One of these is built against the broken tomb of the
little courtesan Anarkali whose Moghul lover had her immured alive for smiling at his eldest son.

The traffic is chaotic now, a flood of ill-assorted vehicles with no com- 63
mon rhythm. Anne's knuckles are white on the wheel. Suddenly, in front of
the High Court, a wizened old man in a dhoti, crazed maybe, hurls himself
in front of them—their fender strikes some part of his body with the dead
sound of a palm on a metal drum—but he never slows down, only continues
his frenzied weaving among the moving obstacles.

7. Traffic intersection.
8. Scarves.

Anne brakes reflexively and kills the motor. The cars behind her set up    64
a din of horns and curses, and at her left a villager perched atop a load of logs
contemplates her with detached contempt. Timmy is ramrod stiff; she knows
he is wishing he were somewhere else.

She manages to start the car without flooding it, and the shouts and    65
hooting stop. They have come to the city wall now, its ancient mud-bricks
festooned with bright silk beddings put out to air. The wall is breached in
many places but it still defines the original city which has hardly changed in
five centuries, still a maze of lanes that meander and cross and come to abrupt
conclusions at open drains or the entrance to a courtyard of blue tile. Anne
has never come there alone.

She rarely goes anywhere alone here. That is partly a matter of custom    66
but also of populous households and elastic time: anyone who mentions a
destination is likely to gain a companion. Anne prefers company. A foreign
woman alone is always conspicious, however modest her demeanor, especially if she is still half-young. Timmy is a comfort to her, even his tentative
masculinity is a shield, but when she planned this journey it was on Sheriyar's quiet strength that she had implicitly depended. He is the true native
of this place, more Punjabi than his father, even—Iqbal willed some of that
self away during his years abroad. Sher bears no sign at all of the foreign
admixture, and Anne knows that she has come to invest him with a special
authority, almost magical, that this society confers only upon its men. Timmy
is frailer, still only a child, and he looks like her.

From these jumbled reflections a question arises: why was Iqbal so com-    67
placent about her setting out on this long journey with only the children? He
would think it highly eccentric, unseemly even, for his sister to do such a
thing. What does he think about Anne that makes it acceptable? Is it only
her foreignness?

"Why do you think Daddy—" She stops. "That's Datta-Sahib's shrine    68
over there," she says. "Daddy went there after your birth to offer prayers.
There's a neem tree somewhere in the courtyard with a little packet of your
baby hair." She thinks she is telling the truth. She remembers distinctly that
Iqbal gave alms and made an offering of the shaved birth hair for Sheriyar,
the firstborn.

Finally, beside the blood-colored minarets of Aurangzeb's great mosque,    69
Anne catches sight of the bridge. They are underway. On the other side she
will tell Timmy the first part, that tomorrow morning they will collect Masood
Amin at the airport and take him with them to Kabul.

He studies her as she says it. "When did you decide that?"    70
"A while ago," she says.    71
"Yesterday?"    72
"No, weeks ago when Libby and Masood were in Lahore."    73
"Is his sister coming too?"    74
Anne has been trying not to think about Yasmin, the little daughter    75
Libby is leaving behind. "Not now," she says. "It would be too hard." The

logistics, she means; Libby said there was no way she could take them both at one time without arousing suspicion. Besides, she can come back for Yasmin, she said. The Koran gives mothers the custody of female children until they are twelve. Even if they are foreigners, infidels, kidnappers?

"What about his mother?"                                                      76

"She'll meet us in Kabul Monday or Tuesday," Anne says. She doesn't        77
want to go through the rigamarole about the visas.

"Why didn't you tell us before?"                                              78

He is still thinking of Sher. "I don't know," she says lamely. "Would it     79
have mattered?"

She had told no one at all. This trip was presented as a fancy of hers, a    80
celebration of spring, a tracing of history. The almond trees would be in
bloom, pink against the immaculate snow of the Pamirs. She would show
Sher and Timmy a different world—empty, with immeasurable sky. The
harsh landscape tinted only in muted tones of dun and silver; infinite distance
from the rich clutter of Lahore, where the hand of man is on everything.

Somewhere along the way they will cross the path of the Powindahs          81
returning from winter on the plains of India. They have made this trek for a
thousand years at least, cutting through passes of their own choosing, indifferent to roads and national boundaries. Their women are unveiled and powerful as men, striding along beside their camels burdened with grain, their
flocks kept close by dogs as large and fierce as wolves. . . . She would show
them the high plateaus from which the Moghuls swept down upon the Indian
subcontinent and changed its face. Iqbal's family has an Afghan thread, a
grandmother on his father's side with slate-blue eyes, the story goes. Timmy's eyes, maybe. But she knew Iqbal would never dream of coming with
them. He prefers his holidays in the West or its counterfeit in Beirut. He has
no hankering for his ancestral past, heroic and dismal.

They are in open country now, except for the small factories and one-       82
room shops that line the road. There is little traffic, lorries mainly, but there
are wandering goats to watch out for, and chickens, and an occasional darting
child. In the empty spaces between settlements unglazed red pottery dries in
the sun. Timmy has fallen asleep, his head taps loosely against the windowpane at each rut in the road.

She wonders why he is so cranky. He loves to be alone with her; she        83
has always thought it is the second child's deepest hunger to be singled out,
to have his mother to himself. Of course there is Masood, but he didn't know
that until an hour ago.

It has grown colder and Anne rolls up her window. But after a time she      84
realizes that there is no single weather along this stretch of open road. It is
as variable as her own spirits, changing as the angle of the road changes.
From the Salt Range to the southwest comes a mild, spicy wind, bringing
with it the first gritty heat from the wakening desert. And from the north
and east the winds bring a dustless chill drawn from the melting snows of

the Karakorams. Anne makes a game of it, opening and closing windows and sunroof, covering and uncovering Timmy with their cardigans. His nose is runny, he seems to have caught a cold. He snuffles in his sleep, and he sleeps or at least keeps his eyes closed until long after they have passed his favorite part of the journey, the gently rocking boat-bridge over the River Jhelum.

They are leaving the village behind now, and the lonely spires of Angli-  85
can churches in the old cantonment towns. The road climbs through undu-lating fields, between softly rounded hills, as though this landscape was formed long ago by cyclonic winds or lashing waters. It is greener here, and in the distance Anne sees a grove of jacaranda trees in bloom, fountains of tumbling mauve. They are her favorite of all Indian trees, and they have the briefest flowering, as brief as spring itself. She half-consciously pushes away the sud-den memory the jacarandas call up of the same mauve-colored wisteria vine that clings to the porch of the white wooden house where she grew up.

When Timmy wakes they stop for their picnic. He is better-tempered  86
now, half-drugged from sleep in the enclosed car with the sun beating in. They speculate amiably about the pocked and gullied terrain. It looks like the ruin of a mud city, the rectilinear excavations of Harappa or Mohenja-daro. She is grateful to be back in her usual maternal role, teaching him about the things of the world. All morning in some indefinable way she has felt him to be the one in control.

At nightfall they check into Dean's Hotel in Peshawar. The old clerk  87
remembers her from other visits and pretends to remember Timmy whom he has never seen. Timmy starts to correct him, but Anne cuts him off, and after a minute he understands that she is asking him not to embarrass the old man in his harmless flattery. Then, united by their consciousness of behav-ing decently, they go off to eat a good dinner of Peshawari rice and mutton, and sleep the heavy sleep of the reconciled in their white beds in the tall white hotel room.

When in the morning Anne comes out of the bathroom dressed in an  88
eight-year-old summer shift, Timmy makes a face like a disapproving old Punjabi matriarch. "You're awfully white," he says, looking at her legs.

He means naked. "So are you," she snaps, sounding, she knows, like a  89
taunted child. But he *is* very light-skinned. It has always been an ambiguous blessing here where fairness is the most prized attribute of a newborn baby or a potential spouse, but where too light a skin can alienate, raise questions about your belonging. Timmy still looks more like an American than like his brother's brother, even now that his hair has lost its first gold and turned a burnished brown. And he has those slate-colored eyes. Anne has come to feel their common fairness a form of vulnerability.

At the airport he won't get out of the car, though in Lahore he and Sher  90
often straggle in hours late from school, having cozened Fazal Dad into driv-ing home by way of the airfield so they can watch the planes take off and

land. He loves especially the small ones, the Dakotas and Fokkers that PIA[9] uses on these up-country runs. "I'd rather stay here," he says.

"Look, he's a nice boy, Tim. You'll like having him along." She can hear the plane circling overhead for a landing. "Remember? He has one blue eye and one brown one." She doesn't know why she said that, and she doesn't want to hear what Timmy will retort if he does, so she slams her door and hurries out to the landing strip. Whatever she meant to say, those mismatched eyes are Masood's most haunting feature—one a cold cyanic blue, the other the lambent brown of Moghul miniatures. At close range you can hardly look at anything else.

But now, watching him pick his way down the rickety metal steps, Anne thinks how beautiful he is, and at the same time how overburdened his thin twelve-year-old body seems by the large head of golden-brown curls. He reminds her of a statue of David she and Iqbal saw somewhere in Italy, spare and solemn, somehow androgynous. The boy's leanness is emphasized by the voluminous clothing he wears, a long tunic over baggy trousers; tissue-thin from washing on stones, and starched to the consistency of paper, they stand away from his body like a carapace. He wears dirty tennis shoes and no socks and he is empty-handed. Except for his coloring he could be the child of any one of Anne's servants, leaving for Urdu school with a dusty slate under his arm. This is what he has come to since Libby left his father's house.

"Here I am, Masood." Anne reaches out to touch his sleeve.

"Ussalam uleikum, Auntie." He bobs his head in an abbreviation of the formal greeting.

"Salaam uleikum, Masood," she says, hearing in her mind Sheriyar's patient voice correcting her: "No, Mummy, you must say, 'valeikum ussalam' when it's a reply."

"Where is Sheriyar?"

"He couldn't come. You have to use his passport. Didn't your mother tell you?"

"No, Auntie, she didn't tell me anything. When she came to get me this morning she told Abu—she told my father—she would be taking me out to the beach hut at Hawk's Bay and would keep me very late. And then when we got into the taxi she told the driver to go to the airport, that I was going to my grandmother in America."

"It's all very complicated, Masood. I'm going to drive you as far as Kabul. Your mother was afraid—" Something in her resists saying Libby is afraid of anything. "She thought if she tried to take you straight from Karachi someone at the airport might see you and your father might stop her. So I said I'd drive you across to Kabul because no one bothers about people just going over for a holiday, especially women and children—"

"Is Ammi really coming, Auntie?"

9. Pakistan International Airlines.

"Of course she is. Your visas weren't ready, and she had to wait to pick them up tomorrow. She'll meet us in Kabul. But we had to travel on Sunday when you could be away the whole day. We have to be out of Pakistan before the border closes at sundown." 101

"What will Abu do?" 102

"He'll be furious, I guess. But I don't think there's anything he can do once you're out of the country. Are you sorry, Masood? I thought you wanted to go." 103

"Oh sure," he says, and for the first time his voice is like her own children's voices: under the singsong Anglo-Indian rhythm, a strong American beat. "I hate it back there." 104

They are walking toward the old hangar that has been converted to a baggage shed. The early morning mist has burned off but the wind is still sharp. The feel of it against her arms and legs reminds her how bare she must seem to the people around her. Because this is Peshawar, not Lahore, the men do not smile hungrily as they stare at her; their eyes are as solemnly judgmental as the eyes of their womenfolk peering through the embroidered lattice-work of their white burqas. There are no other foreigners. Anne pulls the cardigan over her upper arms as the Koran demands. 105

"Do you remember America at all, Masood?" 106

"I remember the room I slept in had dark blue walls with white rabbits on them with very big teeth. I was afraid of them. But everything else was soft—my bed was soft and the seats in the drawing room. My grandmother's bathroom had mirrors all around and bottles that were cut like diamonds, and you could have anything you wanted to eat." He speaks as if by rote, as though he has repeated this litany to himself over and over again. 107

The coolies are dragging the baggage carts in now, a jumble of metal and cardboard suitcases, rolled-up beddings, and rush baskets of citrus fruit and early mangoes from outside Karachi. Anne looks to Masood to identify his things. 108

"I don't have any samaan, Auntie." He uses the Urdu word for luggage. 109

"But you have to have clothes to cross the border. Your mother said she'd have a bag packed for you. It's going to be freezing tomorrow in the Gorge and colder in Kabul—" And dressed this way he's conspicuous. For God's sake, Libby could at least have done that. 110

In the car Timmy is pretending to be asleep. Anne leans over to kiss him and his eyelids flutter. "Hi, darling," she says, "Masood's here." 111

He rouses himself with elaborate yawns. "Hi, Masood," he says coolly. 112

"Ussalam uleikum, Timur." 113

"Where's your mother?" 114

"In Karachi." 115

"When's she coming?" 116

"I don't know." 117

Because it is Sunday the shops are closed in the cantonment, but in the 118 street of the cloth-sellers off the Qissakhani Anne finds a tailor who has some readymade clothes; she buys Masood a pair of khakis and a white shirt unsuitably appliqued with a blue duck but the only one that fits him, and a heavy olive-drab cardigan that looks to have been stolen from an army go-down. And, in case of trouble on the road, a red plaid blanket.

Before they leave the old city she buys apples and dried fruit and monkey nuts for the journey. At breakfast she had filled their thermos flasks with boiled water and milky tea. "We'll get kebabs and nan[1] at the border, but we have to get across as quickly as we can. I want to be in Jallalabad before dark." 119

They fill the gas tank and start out confidently on the last stretch of the Grand Trunk Road. But here, at the extent of the empire, the road suddenly branches out like fingers of a hand. Choosing the logic of the central member leads Anne twice into the barren countryside—once to the new sugar mills, once to a Canadian dam project—before she gives up. With the sun making a longer shadow of the car she hurries back to the airport road to ask directions; even Timmy, whose Urdu and Punjabi are second-nature, can follow only the drift of the Pashtu: right, left, the number of miles, the names of the villages and check-points. 120

When they find it, the road to the Khyber Pass is unmarked, as though anyone who has any business there already knows where it is. Anne herself has been here before, but Fazal Dad was driving and Iqbal was in charge. Another time she came with a woman friend to Landhikotal, the smuggler's bazaar halfway along the road that the Government more or less officially tolerates as an informal subsidy to the Tribal Area. The Westinghouse refrigerator she bought that day turned up a month later in the middle of the night after a journey by camel and bullock cart and lorry. These passes have been the site of illegal and violent transit for a thousand years. 121

The Khyber Road does not cut through the actual Khyber Pass at all. The British, assessing its historical indefensibility, built their own border-crossing at another cut slightly to the east. For good measure they set out all along the subsidiary passes and dry gullies emplacements of dragon's teeth to hinder attempted invasion—from this high road they look like rows of lump sugar. 122

There is little traffic in either direction this Sunday. Once a brilliantly painted truck with Mianwalli license plates passes her on a downhill grade with a heavy load of pale pink rock salt. She catches up to it again when the grade reverses. The paint is fresh, its circus-poster images precise: the gold-maned Lion of Kashmir, scimitar in paw, lounges before the lotus-studded Dal Lake; hawks soar among cotton-candy clouds; and an old fashioned bridge arches over a river in which giant fishes leap. These are the icons of people who live in the plains: images of coolness, freedom and power. 123

The children are so quiet that she wonders if they are sick from the 124

---

1. A kind of bread.

winding road, a pattern of hairpin turns. But as she is about to ask them if they need to stop, she sees around a broad curve the green-and-white flag of the border post, and then, clustered against the steep hillside, three or four freshly-whitewashed offices and sheds, their paths lined with blossoming spring bulbs. Its an Englishman's idea of a hostile border, she thinks. Not a soldier in sight except the one posted ceremonially at the flag. But behind them, all along the twisting road, she had been aware of stone lookouts, of deceptively empty-looking fortresses and parade grounds.

She parks at the side of the road and climbs the neat stone path to the bungalow marked Customs. She has never done this before: Iqbal has always been in charge of such things. She takes Timmy with her for moral support. 125

"Three passports here. Third passenger?" The official is polite but indifferent. American passports do not excite attention; Americans are tourists, not smugglers or fugitives. 126

"That's my other son. He's not feeling well, he's in the car." 127

"I will have to see the car." He is studying Anne's passport photograph. It is three years old and was flattering even then. "Chai pienge?" He motions to a coolie lounging by the door. "You will take a cup of tea?" 128

"No, thank you. We're rather in a hurry. I want to be in Jallalabad by dark." 129

He looks at her again. "You have a Muslim name, Memsahib." 130

"Yes, my husband is Pakistani." 131

"How does he permit you to travel unattended? Quite unsafe for ladies to travel unattended in the Tribal Area." He is annoyed. "You should have a servant." 132

"Oh, we'll be met at the border," she lies. "There was a . . . There was a death in the family." 133

His hauteur disappears. Death explains anything. "Your mummy or daddy?" he asks kindly, murmuring the prescribed blessing on the soul of the dead. 134

She is lost for a moment. "No, my husband's mummy," she says. Timmy's eyes are on her, watching the ease with which she lies. 135

"*He* is not coming?" The customs official is offended to the heart. 136

"Oh, he went ahead by plane." Yes, that is what he would do. 137

The customs man walks with her down the path to compare the description and identification numbers with those on the carnet.[2] Following behind Timmy, he riffles the boy's light hair. "He is very fair. He looks like you, yes?" 138

Anne wonders how well he has taken in the image of Sheriyar on the third passport. Snapped on his tenth birthday, it shows him round-cheeked, laughing, his dark skin glowing—one of those plump, rosy children of Punjabi motion pictures, where the chief aesthetic is abundance and the sleek, round bodies that personify it. She has told Masood to keep his eyes closed 139

2. Documents of automobile ownership and registration necessary when crossing a border.

and to stay under the blanket in the back seat, but the Triumph is too narrow for his long body and he is jackknifed like a grasshopper, his bright curls pressed against the sunny window.

"Sheriyar?" The customs man speaks gently, reaching through the front window to touch the boy's shoulder. "Sheriyar?" He makes music of the long vowels, pronouncing the name as Anne has never been able.                                    140

"Ji?" the boy responds, opening his wonderful eyes.                                    141

"Teek-tock?" asks the man. "Are you all right, baccha?"[3]                                    142

"Teek-tock, officer-sahib," the boy affirms, and closes his eyes again.                                    143

"Thank you very much, Mukhtar-sahib," Anne says, remembering the name plate on his table. If he would only move away from the door so she could get in.                                    144

Mukhtar-sahib returns her documents. "You don't worry about him," he says, indicating with a motion of his head the boy in the back seat. "He'll be first-class when he sees his father." As she starts the motor he adds, "Very tall boy for ten years old, Ma'sh'Allah."                                    145

"My husband is very tall," Anne says, waving to him as she drives out of the manicured oasis into the barbed-wired-and rock-lined corridor of no-man's-land and the Kingdom of Afghanistan.                                    146

Here everything is different. She follows the sign marked Customs into a dingy shed full of people—mostly hippies of various nationalities—who are apparently being detained and have been allowed this place as a caravanserai or flophouse. Some few have chairs or benches, but the majority have made themselves as comfortable as they can on the cement floor, their goods about them. The air is heavy with tobacco, hashish, and cooking charcoal. Near the door a young blonde girl in a dirty sari is preparing a makeshift meal for herself and the dreamy-looking boy beside her. The room is peculiarly silent. Anne can't bring herself to ask for directions, but stumbles on to the next building, where a few dishevelled men in gray uniforms sit under bare light bulbs at tables strewn with teacups and official forms. Someone takes her passports and stamps them without even looking at her. It is clear that no one has the least interest in the identity of three American tourists who carry no threat of becoming a public charge.                                    147

The automobile is another matter. Anne waits for more than an hour while various officials debate among themselves the means of preventing her from taking the little yellow car into Kabul and selling it for an exorbitant sum to a tribal malik[4] without the government's receiving its proper tax. She cannot understand a word, but she knows that is what they are saying because every now and then one of them will snatch up the carnet and storm out to study the car again, as if its smooth yellow body contains the answer to their dilemma. She does not try to interfere, partly because she cannot imagine                                    148

---

3. Boy. *Teek-tock:* okay.

4. Head man of a tribe or village.

any way of being effective. So she sits quietly, grateful she has a chair when others, waiting as long, are still standing. The room smells of sour milk and dust. At length they give her several forms to sign—there is no English translation, she could be pledging anything—stamp her papers, and indicate that she is free to go, required to return within fourteen days to this same border crossing.

"Did they make trouble about me?" Masood asks when they are on their way again. 149

"Only about the car," she says. "It wouldn't matter except I didn't want to be on this road after dark." 150

"Why did we have to come?" Timmy's voice is so low she can't tell whether he is being sullen or is about to cry. 151

"Because Masood's mother wants him to go to America, where he can have a better life, and his father won't let him go." Neither of them says anything. "We're only driving him across the border, Timmy. His mother will get to Kabul tomorrow and you and I will have fun and see everything and buy presents for Daddy and Sher. Maybe we'll buy Sher a rifle. Would you like that?" 152

"Does Daddy know what we're doing?" 153

"Not yet. I didn't want him to have to lie or be embarrassed if Masood's father should get in touch with him or anything. But we'll tell him everything when we get home. He knows how unhappy Masood has been, Timmy." She is almost pleading. 154

Masood *has* been unhappy since the divorce. Or—Anne corrects herself—since Libby left her husband's house; it is not clear even now if Anwer ever divorced her. Though certainly he has taken a second wife, a girl of eighteen with a reputation as a folk singer, who came from a tribe of gypsies. He did so, Libby told Anne at the time, because the girl's father planned to marry her off to a rich old landowner who would lock her up and never let her sing again. 155

Libby said it as though she believed Anwer was just doing the girl a favor at the expense of no one. Libby, after all, would be the senior wife, dominant in her household: the mother of Anwer's son. Why should she mind fixing up a small room at the back of the house for another needy woman? Iqbal's comment was that Libby couldn't get malaria without claiming she'd done it on purpose for the sake of the hallucinations. He doesn't care for Libby: he says she is a stereotypical willful American woman who reflects badly on others, like Anne, who are so different. 156

Anne's feelings have always been mixed: she admires Libby's courage and zest, deplores her taste for dubious adventures, and sometimes, sheepishly and in private, pities her. Libby would not stand for pity, but it is pity nonetheless that brings Anne today to this desolate road: she cannot imagine a worse privation than the loss of a child. 157

Once Libby finally left Anwer she had no way of caring for a child. Apparently she never thought of going home then because the first year alone 158 she went through half a dozen jobs ranging from handling up-country tours for a travel agency to acting as liaison for an Italian motion picture company. She left each of them in a mysterious flurry. Iqbal maintained it was always trouble with men, but Anne saw only how brave and uncomplaining she was, that when she could, she would swoop in on Sunday and carry Masood off to the beach, or to picnic where Metrovista was filming out near the blue ruins of Thatta.

How different this journey would be if Libby were here now. She would 159 already have picked out a local guide from among the tribesmen they'd passed walking along the road, and by the time they reached Jallalabad tonight, they would have known all the lore of these barren passes through which Anne and the children are blindly driving—these undifferentiated peaks and strange wildflowers and seasonal rivers they will never have names for. The Afghan might have taken them to his village for a meal; he might have fallen in love with her—all the things Anne would never risk, she whose most passionate desire this deepening twilight is to reach Jallalabad in safety.

"Can you change a tire, Masood?" 160

"I don't know, Auntie. Abu doesn't keep a car." 161

"I know how," Timmy snaps. "I've helped Fazal Dad a million times." 162

"Don't be cross, Timmy. We won't get a flat. The road's fine. This is 163 the one the Americans built. It goes all the way to Kabul. The Russians are building another one, from Kabul to the Russian border."

"Why would they want to?" Timmy says, peering out at the bleak dun- 164 and-gray moonscape, the sheer black rocks.

"Is Ammi—is my mother—really coming for me?" Masood asks. 165

"Of course she is. Look at all the trouble she's gone to, just to get you 166 here." All the trouble I've gone to, Anne thinks.

"What will happen to Yasmin?" 167

Yasmin. It is unfair that Anne should have to explain to him about Yas- 168 min. There is something altogether wrong with Yasmin's being left behind, in spite of any explanation. "Your mother thought it would be impossible to take you both at one time, that your father would be suspicious if she tried."

Masood is silent. 169

"She can come back for Yasmin. She has the right to Yasmin until she's 170 twelve, you know."

"Ji, Auntie," he says politely. 171

"Yasmin's so little, Masood. Your mother says Yasmin hardly even 172 remembers her, that she's very fond of Bano and Bano is very kind to her. Isn't that so?" She stumbles over some of the words.

"Ji, Auntie," Masood says slowly. "Yasmin's very clever. When Bano 173 comes in from the bazaar or the recording studio, Yasmin will be waiting for her, to press her feet. She knows Bano likes that."

Timmy sniffs loudly like an outraged old woman. 174

"Yasmin is very strong-headed for a little girl," he goes on. "After Ammi 175 went away I would cry sometimes in the night, but Yasmin never cried even though she was only three. She would come to my room and press me until I fell asleep. I would pretend Ammi had come back, that the glass bangles were hers, not Yasmin's."

"Someday she'll come to America too," Anne says.                                          176

"No, she won't, Auntie. Ammi doesn't like her."                                          177

"I'm sure you're wrong. Masood. Mothers always love their children."                     178

"She doesn't like Yasmin because she's dark. She says Yasmin can be                       179
Bano's child."

Anne has no answer to such enormity. She wonders if what he says is                       180
true. Perhaps Libby blames the child for Anwer's disaffection—she was carrying Yasmin when Anwer met Bano. Or has it to do with the Cleveland
grandmother? Anne knows she deplored Anwer as much for his color as for
his presumed calculations about Libby's eventual inheritance. After the marriage she had nothing to do with her daughter until Libby sent a photograph
of Masood as a blonde curly-haired infant; her mother responded with tickets
for a summer visit home. And after that there were regular gifts, carefully
chosen not to constitute support or be convertible to cash. The Christmas
Libby finally left Anwer, her mother had sent Masood—air mail from F.A.O.
Schwarz—a full-sized bubble gum machine that would dispense its gumballs
only after insertion of a U.S. penny. The customs duty equalled a week of
Anwer's pay. There was no gift for Yasmin.

"Yasmin can't go because she's black," Masood says, his voice almost a                    181
whisper.

"So are you!" Timmy says.                                                                 182

"I am not!"                                                                               183

"Inside you are. Your father is!"                                                         184

"So is yours!"                                                                            185

"I never said he wasn't!" Timmy is heaving, sobbing with rage.                            186

"Stop it, both of you. I can't drive if you go on this way. Please, let's                 187
just get to Jallalabad, we'll have tikka kebabs⁵ and nice hot baths and everything will be all right. *Please.*"

They subside into angry silence, each withdrawing into a shadowed                         188
corner. And huddled apart that way they drive one last dark hour before
Anne sees in the distance the smoky yellow light of Jallalabad.

"Now we could walk," she whispers to herself—hollow relief, for she                       189
has no idea how to find the hotel beyond its name and a vague location at the
western edge of the city. But after the bleak and menacing passes even this
strange city seems hospitable.

Her comfort is brief. Somewhere she has taken a false turn and the hard-                  190
surfaced road dwindles into a rutted city street with little shops pressing in
at either side. Some are shuttered and dark, some lighted by a single dangling
bulb or a sputtering acetylene lantern that throws grotesque dancing shadows over the car. There are no women anywhere.

---

5. Small pieces of grilled meat.

Finally, they reach the intersection of a broad well-surfaced street. At 191 one corner, like a warrant of welcome, is a large plateglass window crowded with giant scarlet geraniums, their heavy foliage pressed against the sweating glass like something tropical. It must be a restaurant, with great brass hamams[6] of tea and boiling water. She yearns for the warmth and light.

The boys are awake now, silent and alert, searching with her for the 192 column of street lights that will indicate a main thoroughfare. But when they find it, all the traffic is coming towards them. They can read nothing now, and there are no international symbols to reassure her that the road is two-way until, finally, far ahead, Timmy sees two donkey carts jogging along as they are, toward the north and west.

But it reminds her that all the great movements were in the opposite 193 direction, since Babur made his first encampment here. Jallalabad has always been a staging platform, where tribes and armies paused to collect themselves for the assault on the subcontinent. Like tonight's traffic, they came from the north and west. Anne and the children are following the path of the defeated, of broken units withdrawing through the passes to their powdery steppes to renew themselves; north to the thinner air and sparse food, water so cold it hurts your teeth.

She feels soft and unequal to anything, even, now that they have finally 194 found it, to going into this sprawling hotel to ask for rooms. In spite of a few scattered lights visible through the windows, it has the look of having been abandoned long ago. Since she came to Pakistan, Anne has never until last night gone into a hotel alone. She feels vulnerable, obliquely ashamed, as though she is doing something immoral.

The desk-clerk is slack and vague, with a stubble of beard and only 195 rudimentary English, and the neon-lit lobby is dim with settled dust, but they have plenty of vacant rooms. She takes two, intending to put the boys together and have a room to herself for once. But Timmy, who is carrying her overnight case as well as his own green PIA flight bag, goes straight to the double room and defiantly drops them both on the huge hard bed. After a minute she hands Masood the two paper bags with the clothes he arrived in and the toilet articles she bought him in Peshawar, and lets him go to the small room across the hall. She doesn't feel up to a quarrel and she doesn't really want to be alone.

The water in the tap is tepid and brown and they dry their hands and 196 faces on the edge of the bedsheet because there are no towels, but they are grateful to be here. It is with a certain weary peace that they go down to the dining room off the lobby.

They are alone in the domed cavernous room though there is evidence— 197 a greasy teacup, a still-shiny turmeric stain on the cloth of the adjacent table— that someone was here earlier. Only a few tables are set up for dining, the rest are pushed against the walls with their chairs upended on them so that

6. Vessels in which liquids are boiled or heated.

in the stark central light they cast shadows like giant spiders. Anne wonders what the season is in Jallalabad. It is hard to imagine that the bitter, dry winter would be pleasanter than this dusty spring, but she has the vague recollection that in some earlier time this was the winter capital of the Afghan royal house.

She orders the simplest of local food. The old waiter brings them grilled chunks of stringy mutton and flat rounds of bread. They split the bread and fill it with meat and onion and minted yogurt, and eat with their hands. The boys drink warm Coke and Anne tiny pots of pink Kashmiri tea from a mended porcelain cup. She tries to make conversation but her voice echoes mockingly in the domed room and the boys answer her in polite monosyllables. [198]

Afterwards they are all too restless to go up to bed, so they retrieve their heavy sweaters and the plaid blanket from the car and set out to walk the cramps from their bodies in the garden they had seen through the dining room windows. [199]

They reach it at the end of a winding cinder path, a stark geometrical park of dusty grass surrounded by brambly rose-trees just beginning to leaf out; in the darkness they look like the barbed-wire netting of no-man's-land. Beyond is a denser thicket of gray twisting branches that will in summer be a grape arbor. Timmy has seen something white in the distance—perhaps the reflection of the moon in an ornamental pool—and sets off with Masood in search of it. Their high-pitched voices are muffled and distorted in the vast emptiness. They seem to have patched up their quarrel in the subterranean way of children, without speaking of it again. [200]

Anne doubles up the blanket and makes herself a seat at the center of the lawn, thinking this is where the sun-dial would be if the British had come this far. But of course they did, two or three times. She remembers an old etching of a lone man—Dr. Brydon it was—coming into Jallalabad slung over the back of his pony, the only survivor of his garrison. He had been ambushed again and again in the narrow passes, the river gorge between here and Kabul. [201]

After a while she unfolds the blanket and lies back, gazing up at the immense indigo bowl of sky; the stars seem farther away than ever, though their pattern has never been so clear. The lemon-colored gibbous moon is halfway to the horizon, pierced by the bare branches of a cottonwood tree. The children's voices drift back intermittently like waves of ground fog. Anne occupies herself with the physical world as though it were a mantra; the black dome of sky, the circle of thorns around her resting place, the crisp, bittersweet odor of a nearby citrus grove in early blossom. But dark thoughts crowd back on her like bats that have lost their bearings and press in, brushing with agitated wings the very thing that is driving them away. [202]

Far to the south Sheriyar is going to sleep. He has finished his schoolwork, and visited the stables to see his gray pony before going to bed. His golden labrador sleeps next to him on the scarlet silk quilt, having outlasted [203] the objections of the old ayah that the touch of dog is dirty and un-Islamic. The room is clear in every detail, down to the glass of water on the bedside table with its crocheted dust-cover weighted down by blue beads. But she cannot see Sher's face, only a dark shadow against the pillow, as it was the night she left him. She feels a terrible thrill of love for him, but it imposes itself like a portent, the love you feel for something you are losing.

"But I've lost nothing," her rational mind says. Anne says it aloud, for reassurance. Iqbal will be angry, she can admit that now. Not because he thinks Masood should have been left where he was, or that Libby could ever have obtained his custody by reason or recourse to law, but because it was Anne who lied and plotted, who exposed her husband as someone who is not in control of his wife. She has shown him that she is more than the mild, agreeable woman he trusts as simply as if she were a native woman. That she is capable of acting by stealth, reckoning for herself the hazards. It will be a long time before Iqbal sees her in the old way again. 204

But perhaps there will be no reckoning, no public acknowledgement of Anne's part in this. Libby is sure Anwer will do nothing, once the boy is irretrievably beyond his reach; anything else would be a public display of impotence. "Like announcing you've been cuckolded," Libby said. Anne will be able to explain everything to Iqbal first. It will be weeks before the whole story is known, if it ever is. Masood traveled from Karachi on a variant of his name, itself as common as sand; he never technically crossed the border at all—the passport Libby brings tomorrow will register neither exit or entry. And that kind border official, if he ever comes to recognize his error, will lie to save himself. 205

But it will not come to that. In this place events do not flow to such clearly defined conclusions. The habit of mind is not toward sharp discriminations or clear assessments of gain or loss, except where honor is at stake. There is only the drift of things, a narrowing or broadening of possibility. As the country roads are at one place smooth and substantial, laid over a deep bed of crushed stone, but further on may dwindle to the width of a single vehicle or disappear altogether at the foothills or the edge of the desert, only to emerge a hundred miles beyond as mysteriously as a river gone underground. This is a country of few crossroads; nothing here happens once and for all time. 206

But as these thoughts pass through her mind, the threading of a maze to some eventual conclusion, the deeper part of Anne's consciousness holds a single, still image: the grave face of her elder son, his full lips and heavy-lidded eyes framed by the tall cerise-and-gold turban he wore at the great dinner to celebrate his circumcision. The image is like a miniature in an oval frame, confined and complete, never to be altered. Anne shivers, not entirely from the cold, and calls the children in to bed. 207

They are subdued when they return, and for the first time since Peshawar seem kindly disposed toward one another. At Masood's room she unlocks 208 the door and goes in to check the blankets and the light by his bed. As she turns to go, she thinks how confused he must be as he goes to sleep tonight, and impulsively kisses him in promise of something she has not defined. Then Timmy, with a little low howl, hurls himself at Masood in a clumsy embrace, and bolts to the hall. Masood turns his back. Anne knows he is crying but she has no words to help him.

She makes Timmy brush his teeth and tucks him in pajamas and clean socks into his side of the broad bed. Then she takes the flask of Murree gin from her overnight bag and makes herself a weak gin-and-water. She switches out the light and puts on her flannel nightgown, drawing the plaid blanket around her like a cloak as she stands at the window with her drink, looking out at the pale lawn, and the black sky with its bleak field of stars.

The wind is coming up. It tears at the shutters, shifting the loose panels. The dry wood rubbing together makes a sound like crying.

"She tried to get Sheriyar to do this," Timmy says. Anne looks back and sees that his eyes are wide open, he is staring up at the ceiling. She puts her drink on the sill and goes over to sit next to him. He doesn't make room for her.

"What do you mean, Timmy?"

"When they were in Lahore at Easter she tried to get Sheriyar to take Masood across the desert to India. She said Fazal Dad would do it if Sher gave the order. She said she'd give Sher her watch, the one with all the dials the pilot gave her."

"Why didn't you tell me?"

"We didn't think you'd be so dumb." He is crying now.

They didn't think she'd be so dumb. . . . So they had discussed it, Sher and Timmy, had speculated about this journey to Afghanistan, but had decided she couldn't be so dumb as not to know what sort of woman Libby is. That she can't be trusted, that she is capable of sending two little boys and a half-baked driver out into a desert full of border patrols, two irritable armies facing each other in terrain with no clear line of demarcation.

Even if they made it past the pickets, what reception would they have found in India? Libby might have arranged for Masood, but what about Sher and Fazal Dad, who would still have had the journey back? Every month there are reports of villagers who stray too near the border and are shot; the military says they are smuggling gold or grain.

"They could have been shot," she says.

"Yeah."

She tries to put her arms around him, but he has rolled himself into a ball, rigid and sealed against her. Now she understands what his tight little body has been showing her for two days, that he no longer trusts the perfect wisdom and benevolence of mothers.

Sher could be dead. Anne sees in her mind's eye the jeep bounding breakneck over the dunes. Fazal Dad keening tribal songs at the top of his lungs. She knows he takes bhang. He would have done whatever Sher asked. Twice last winter he took Sher deep into the Thar[7] in search of antelope. He would make no distinctions. At least once, he had let Sher urge him within sight of Bikaner State. . . . Iqbal had threatened to sack him.

"But it didn't happen," she says, as much to herself as Timmy. "And tomorrow everything will be over. Libby will meet us in Kabul, and—" [222]

"She won't come. Masood says she won't. She's got some man. She won't come, and we'll never be able to go back." He is sobbing hard, silently except for an occasional hiccough. "It's your fault, you took him. You took him instead of Sheriyar." [223]

She lies on the bed holding the rigid little form, as though there were a windstorm or some other violence of nature against which she can shield him only with her body. She will not think of what he is saying now. Masood has to be wrong. Libby is wayward but she is not evil: she will turn up tomorrow, or the day after or the day after that, getting off the plane in her proprietary way with the pilot carrying her bag. The bag will be filled with clean, warm clothes for Masood and clever gifts for her family in America. . . . [224]

But for Anne there is still the journey. Timmy is asleep now, and she disengages herself from him and goes back to her place at the window. The wind tonight is full of rain. The road through the Gorge tomorrow will be narrow and slippery, the sky only a thin, gray ribbon a thousand stony feet above them. She feels it now, the damp shale walls of the chasm pressing in on the small yellow car, the two sun-haired children, herself in her inappropriate summer dress. [225]

She will go through the Gorge tomorrow because . . . because she gave her word, because they have come so far already and there is no easy way to turn back. Because in her heart she believes, she thinks she believes, that Libby will come. [226]

Anne pours herself another gin and climbs into bed, under the thin coarse blanket that smells of dust and hashish. If Libby doesn't come, what will she do here in this alien place with someone else's child, with false papers, a handful of traveler's checks and one suitcase and no one to turn to? [227]

With an angry husband too far away for explanations, a man whose pride has been humbled. What would Iqbal do if Anwer went to him, made it a point of honor between men? He has Sher, the eldest son, the one who looks like the portrait of his grandfather. Is he capable of abandoning her to the limbo she has made for herself, of leaving her to drift here until she finds her way back to her own people, the alien woman with her light-eyed son. Is that what Timmy thinks? [228]

She lies in the dark listening to his deep breathing, interrupted now and then in sleep by a small reflexive sob. There is no hope or purpose in these [229]

---

7. The great desert bordering Pakistan and India. *Bikaner State* (below): a small Indian administrative unit previously under the control of a maharajah.

speculations and she puts them away from her, and makes a conscious effort to empty her mind, to concentrate on natural things, the steady beat of her heart, the susurration of their two breaths.

After a time she is aware that her breathing has regulated itself to match his. She listens to the soft animal noises with which he lets himself drift into a deeper slumber where there are no sobs. She too is calmer but no nearer sleep. The deepest part of her is straining for an impossible certainty: that she will hear again those basal rhythms of the soft dark child she left behind.

230

# STUDY QUESTIONS

1. In what way is the opening telephone conversation the true beginning of the story? Are there any other points at which the story might have begun? What differences in the meaning and effect of the story would these alternative beginnings have made? What suspense or expectations are set up by the opening conversation? How much of the situation can you infer from the first section of the story? What is the effect of this first section closing with "Anne thinks she has heard another voice in the background, a man's deep laughter"? How does the dramatic presentation—we mostly hear the conversation without narrative explanation—engage us in the story? What CONFLICT is involved in this opening section?

2. "Anne's [life is] as tranquil and domestic as her mother's back in Indiana" (paragraph 21); "Libby had come to Pakistan two years before her, embracing from the start every possible transformation of herself" (par. 22). Libby's son was born "as his father had been on a rope cot in the women's courtyard"; "Anne went home [to Indiana] in the early months of her own first confinement to be delivered of Sheriyar [her son] by the old doctor who had attended her own birth" (par. 23). What is the irony, then, in their present situations?

3. What is the lone conflict between Anne and her husband Iqbal? What clues do you have to the CHARACTER of Iqbal?

4. It is some time before the story reverts to the conflict between Anne and Libby; what occupies our attention during that time? What is the effect of the "digression" on your suspense about the conflict? Are there any ways in which the details about Iqbal, Anne's marriage, the dinner party planned for that evening, and so on can be obliquely related to the conflict? Do they help define the terms of the conflict? or help you take sides?

5. Interpret this sentence from paragraph 35: "There are things she is trying not to think of now."

6. Anne has found a way of achieving serenity or "stillness" that other Westerners look for in yoga and drugs (par. 37). What is it?

7. In paragraph 4, Anne seems to "conspire" with her servant girl "against the hegemony of men." In paragraph 66, Anne seems to have given her son Sheriyar "a special authority, almost magical, that this society confers only upon its men."

Can your reconcile these attitudes of Anne's? If so, how? Is there any relation between her attitude(s) and the nature of her husband and her marriage?

8. The conflict between Anne and Libby has its counterpart in Anne's own life and mind and is related to the whole issue of "crossing" as it is used in this chapter— that is, relationships, especially love and marriage, across ethnic, cultural, and racial lines. How is this internal conflict embodied in the story? What incidents are closely related to Anne's conflict within herself?

9. How do you account for the British expressions—such as "balls up," "lorries," "go-down"—in this story, which focuses on an American woman?

10. Anne, in paragraph 85, "pushes away the sudden memory . . . of the . . . house where she grew up." Why does she push the memory away? What does that tell you about her feelings of "crossing" to Pakistan?

11. What is the conflict between Anne and Timmy? What do you expect to develop or happen in the story out of that conflict?

12. Why does Anne, in remembering Sheriyar back home, have a sense of loss (pars. 202–3)?

13. Timmy says Libby will not show up in Kabul. She has not packed clothes for Masood (par. 110). Does that make you fear that Timmy is right? Might neglecting to do so merely be part of Libby's character or behavior? Substantiate your answers with other passages from the text of the story. (See also pars. 223–24, 226.)

14. What is Iqbal's perception of Libby? What evidence do we have to substantiate or contradict his vision of Libby's "willfulness"? What is Anne's attitude toward what Iqbal sees as willfulness? *Is* Libby, as Iqbal assumes, a stereotypical American woman?

15. "This is a country of few crossroads; nothing here happens once and for all time" (par. 206). How does this view of the geography, topography, and history of Afghanistan (and Pakistan) relate to the plot to get Masood away from his Pakistani father and to the whole concept of "crossing" in this story? Does it suggest anything about what will happen to Anne if Libby does not show up?

16. What has Anne's image of Sher (par. 207) to do with her thoughts of smuggling Masood into Afghanistan and its consequences? Why is Masood crying (par. 208)?

17. Why doesn't Anne want her son Timmy to be very light-skinned (par. 89)? What other indications are there in the story of "placing" people by skin color? What does the social value of skin color have to do with the major conflicts in the story? Timmy, Masood, and Anne are "sun-haired" (par. 225); they have crossed into Afghanistan. Sheriyar is a "soft dark child" (par. 230); he, his dark father, and Masood's father are left in Pakistan. How do these spatial locations at the end of the story relate to the theme of "crossing"?

# THEME

Literary works are, of course, about *something*. A work is always "about" something concrete: Barbara Thompson's story "Crossing" is about smuggling the son of a Pakistani father out of the country on behalf of his American mother. That is its SUBJECT. But literature is also about things other than *specific* events and details. "Crossing" is about cross-cultural marriages and the special problems raised by children in such marriages. This, too, is the *subject*, but stated more generally. It is therefore important to be clear when you are talking about the *specific subject* and when about the *general subject*.

You will have noticed that once we get beyond the particulars and into generalization, readers begin to have a larger and larger role in formulating just what the general subject is. For every generalization leaves out some details and consequently emphasizes others. Some will insist that any statement of the general subject of "Crossing" will have to mention the problems of cultural "adaptation"—the stance toward the differences in food, clothing, gender roles, and so on.

At some point we begin to talk less about the concrete things in the "real" world that the work points to than we do about its "ideas." As we move from the things the work points toward to the stance or position it takes about those things, we move from subject to THEME. "Crossing" may be said to have as its theme the necessity of loving accommodation in marriage (the cultural subject then is merely an intensification of marriage in general: cultural differences put a strain on marriage that requires unusual or special mutual toleration and accommodation). When we get to the realm of ideas and theme, the reader plays an even greater part in selecting and defining; for theme, or the articulation of theme, is virtually an INTERPRETATION of the work.

That does not mean, of course, that readers "own" the work and can extract or impose any theme they choose, though there may be—indeed, probably will be—different wordings or versions of the theme of a work. Another "version" of the theme of Barbara Thompson's story, for example, may go something like this: "Crossing" is about the difficulty of crossing borders in marriage. Formulating a fuller statement of the theme by bringing these two versions together means not just spinning out of our own head and experience what *we* mean by love, marriage, accommodation, and tolerance, but going back to the story itself. In doing so, with a tentative model of the theme in mind, we may discover the relevance of many details that we may have overlooked earlier, from the title of the story to Masood's having one blue and one brown eye. We will also have to adjust our earlier brief statements. For example, Libby "accommodated" to marrying a Pakistani more quickly than did Anne: she wore a sari from the beginning, spoke Urdu and a smattering of Gujerati from the time she arrived in Karachi, made her own curry, and gave birth to Masood on a rope cot in the women's courtyard as was traditional. Anne wore Western clothes for years and went home to Indiana to have her baby. Yet Libby is leaving her husband and taking her son with her, and Anne is happily married still. Perhaps total cultural accommodation is not necessary. As Anne's husband says, "The lives of women are only superficially affected by culture—and then only to their detriment. A virtuous wife and mother is the same everywhere and forever" (paragraph 24).

Has Iqbal articulated the theme of the story? It certainly is *a* theme, and it embraces many aspects of the story: Libby's unreliable character and flightiness versus Anne's devoted integrity. But this is slightly to the side of the chief subject of the story, the smuggling of Masood out of Pakistan, and the uncertainty of the ending: has Anne—by helping Libby, violating Koranic law, and putting her husband in an extremely difficult position—abandoned "the soft dark child she left behind" (par. 230)?

It is worth struggling on for the best possible statement of the theme, testing it as it evolves against the particulars of the story, for you will learn more and more about more and more details and implications of the story.

But you will never be able to frame a theme that will be a substitute for the richness of the story. That is a major reason why the term "theme" seems better than *moral* or *message*, terms that inevitably lead to oversimplification and give the illusion that a work of literature exists for its statement, that it is something like a Chinese fortune cookie that tempts you with sweetness of story, drama, or verse to get to the real "meaning" inside.

Another important reason for avoiding the term "moral" and "message" is the model of literary communication they imply: the author encodes a message that you "receive," open the envelope, and read; or the author sees a great truth, which he teaches you by example. There are, in fact, such things as FABLES and PARABLES, which are short, usually familiar stories that do have as their major aim to teach a moral or religious message. There are ALLEGORIES, narratives in which every detail has reference to another structure of events or ideas. Even so subtle a writer and critic as Henry James spoke of "the figure in the carpet," that is, a structural or thematic pattern, a pattern that controls every particular, every comma, of a work, which may seem to convey something like "hidden meaning" or a formal equivalent of "message." All of these literary examples assume the same model: (encoding) Sender-(encoded) Message-(decoding) Receiver.

There is a certain attraction, a certain clarity and common sense, even a certain amount of truth in this model. But besides having to carry such baggage as "moral," "message," "encoded message," and such embarrassingly presumptuous assertions as "what Shakespeare is trying to say," the model inevitably suggests that there is only *one* "meaning," *one* "interpretation" of a work, and it is the function of criticism and literary study to find that "true meaning."

Some nonfiction works do have something like a message. Personal essays or narratives, such as Gary Soto's "Like Mexicans," often make points that approach mere message—likeness of economic class is more important than ethnic identity in marriage—but they more nearly resemble fictional narrative in the importance of theme rather than message. The essays by Elena Padilla (chapter 1) and James Fallows (chapter 6) do aim to inform and convince in a more direct way than most stories, poems, or plays.

Perhaps another way of looking at the difference between theme and message is that while message seeks to inform or convince, theme seeks to have you comprehend and empathize, so that the information or the ideas are less directly articulated, or more broadly accessible. It is difficult to read

Wendy Rose's "Julia," for example, without feeling, and the feeling is not empty of significance; it feels as if it means. What, precisely, does it mean? That ugly-grotesque-horrific people are nonetheless human, capable of strong human emotions and therefore also worthy of our attempting to understand them and sympathize with those strong emotions? Yes, but is that a message? Are there not other ways of coming at this poem, through the monstrous greed and inhumanity of Julia's husband, for example, another instance of the bestiality humans are capable of? Or, combining both: there are monsters with human feelings and humans with monstrous appetites. There are clearly meaning and emotions here, but not necessarily a message.

Most poets, playwrights, fiction writers—and even many essayists—do not think in terms of their messages, some easy "conclusion" that can be simply stated or summarized. Their "meaning" is their vision. They embody that vision in a language that does not belong to the author but to the community and in a literary form that, whatever the work may do that is innovative and original, is part of a literary tradition. The embodied vision or perception, once put before the public, is then the property of its readers. Of course the readers, too, are constrained by the "rules" of the language, the definitions of words, the cultural assumptions of what "makes sense," and what constitutes or has constituted literature. So the readers even now do not "own" the work to make of it whatever they might fancy. But every reader, in translating the communal language back to his or her individual understanding and experience, will inevitably and legitimately have a somewhat different "reading."

Try to think of a literary work not as a telegram, but as a musical score. For a work cannot mean until it is read, any more than a musical score can be music until it is played. And all readings and all performances are unique. No two performances of Beethoven's Fifth Symphony will be identical (even when performed by the same orchestra led by the same conductor on consecutive nights). But it will not sound like "You Ain't Nothin' but a Hound Dog," no matter who plays it. Wildly eccentric readings are constrained by the language, history, and communally agreed upon standards of reasonableness. Before you can perform a work, you have to know the score.

If one reason to concern yourself with seeking out the theme of a work and articulating it as best you can is to reimmerse yourself in the details of the work and alert yourself to relationships and implications, another is to apprehend its concerns in such a way that you can relate it to your own experience. If you find the theme of "Wilhelm" to be something like "If you befriend an outsider, you may be surprised at the prejudice it brings out in people you thought reasonable and liberal," that story may strike home to you even though your experience has not been exactly like that of the girl in the story. That is not the "message" of the story, necessarily; it certainly is not an adequate substitute for the richness of the story. (The story also raises interesting questions about the narrator's involvement with Wilhelm, for example: she did not like him all that much and certainly did not love him or think of marrying him.) But the theme does help you relate to the story and to relate the story to you. It also may help you both to connect and to differentiate the handling and implications of the theme here and in works with similar themes, such as "The Coming-Out of Maggie," or variants on the theme, such as *Wedding Band*, where prejudice, even of Herman's mother and sister, gives way slightly in the face of the committed love of Herman and Julie.

Though a work and its details—like Masood's blue eye and dark eye—do not exist solely to embody a theme (Masood's eyes function in the plot, generating suspense: if the border guard notices them, the attempt to smuggle Masood across the border on Sher's passport will fail), theme is a useful instrument for digging into a story, poem, play, or essay. Habitual attention to theme will reveal similarities among works that you may not have noticed otherwise, and comparing how works handle similar themes will differentiate them, perhaps even help you evaluate them.

You must remember to put Humpty-Dumpty together again, however. A work of literature is not an embellished theme; a thematic statement is not a work of literature. Of all the elements of literature, however, theme is the most inclusive, and you will probably get closer to the performed score of the work in trying to frame its theme as precisely and fully as possible than you will by exploring any other single element.

# WRITING
# ABOUT THE READING

## PERSONAL ESSAYS AND NARRATIVES

1. Write a short paper—1,000–1,500 words—on an experience in which you were either the outsider intentionally or unintentionally invading another's turf, or a group member whose turf was being invaded by an outsider.

2. Describe a situation you have witnessed in which someone else was attempting to "cross." You may have belonged to one of the groups or you may have been a disinterested observer. Try to relate the feelings of both sides with equal sympathy.

## IMITATIONS AND PARODIES

1. Write a story or poem based on "The Coming-Out of Maggie," taking either the perspective of the "invader" or that of a "loyal" member of the group.

2. Imitate "what gramma said about her grandpa" to produce a poem or sketch about an ancestor of yours.

## ANALYTICAL AND ARGUMENTATIVE PAPER

Analyze the issues of community solidarity versus cosmopolitan openness. For example, should there be Irish-American clubs, or White Only (or Blacks Only) or Men Only private social organizations or schools? Is there a difference between a Whites Only club and a Blacks or Asians or Hispanics Only one?

## RESEARCH PAPERS

1. Find figures and dates for Irish and Italian immigration, either for the United States as a whole or New York City or another city where the numbers are significant (Boston or Chicago, for example). Find documentation of the kinds of relationships and hostility involving the two groups in the 1920s or thereabouts. (You might want to glance back at the Fante piece in chapter 4.) Use what you have learned to supply a context for "The Coming-Out of Maggie."

Or search out other works of fiction in the period between World Wars I and II involving Irish and/or Italian immigrants.

2. How many blacks served in the armed forces during World War I? What efforts, if any, were made by blacks to avoid serving on political grounds? What promises or expectations were there about how race relations would change after World War I? What can you find in newspapers or magazines of the late 1960s about the Vietnam War, black servicemen and -women, and what they might expect after the war was over?

3. What are the legends and the historical facts surrounding Pocahontas and her relations with whites?

4. Trace the history of miscegenation laws since 1900. What races or ethnic groups were not allowed to marry in the South, the Far West, the Northeast, in 1900, 1914, 1920, 1929, 1941, 1950, and 1964?

Or trace the history and nature of such laws in your region.

Or trace the history of the debate over miscegenation in a relevant decade or period, detailing the arguments on both sides.

# 9

# IN THE AMERICAN
# SOCIETY

Whoever we are and whatever we bring with us, the journey to a
new place or the entry into a new culture is full of surprises. No
other way of life is exactly like ours; no two cultures have exactly the same
customs, habits, rituals, and expectations. Making the adjustment can be
painful or exciting—or both. Learning the new rules is one thing; discovering what the way of life is really like, with all its built-in values and
assumptions, is something else again. No one brings along to a life in a new
place exactly what is needed and expected there, and old ways and new
expectations—like exotic new possessions and treasured old ones—remain
continually in contrast, often in deep conflict. The "I" that a person discovers in a new world is often a revelation—a new identity only partly
descended from the old.

There is, of course, no single "American" society—no single set of cultural assumptions that covers the geography from Alaska to Puerto Rico or
the ethnography from Native American to Hispanic to Jew to Moslem to
Afro-American to Cambodian. Every location is different, every town,
every neighborhood, every block, every group of families. And every story
of American life is essentially an individual story, modified by the heritages
and desires of an individual who lives out his or her own narrative in some

particular location. We all invent our own stories as we go, but what we have the power to invent is conditioned by our individual identities and what we bring with us from our separate pasts, as well as by what happens to us in new situations. America—the United States, Canada, the Caribbean—is a melting pot not because the character that people bring to it becomes mixed and hopelessly confused, but because it provides a common meeting place for great varieties of people who can come together in a more or less neutral setting so that their various values can compete legitimately.

"Neutral" the setting never truly is, of course, in an absolute way. Somebody gets there first, somebody sets the rules; the talents, language skills, and material possessions give some competitors advantages and others liabilities. And people or backgrounds never do "melt"; individuals, as well as peoples, carry their baggage with them, for better or worse. The "American Society" is a series of different societies made up of different kinds of Americans of different origins, traditions, and histories, somehow intermingled. Here is where "home" comes to be after long struggle. Here is where we confront the "fences" and negotiate the "crossings"; here is where self meets other, where the old forces of family, ancestry, and language are confronted with new situations, where challenge is lived out in everyday life and work.

The writings in this chapter suggest some of the many varieties of American experience that result from the steady confrontations of culture and of self that *are* America at its most basic. Sometimes that America is an admirable place, approaching that ideal culture that its Idea—its Dream—represents at its best. Sometimes it falls far short of its ideals. The stories that result from the lives lived within it are of varied kinds and moods—there are tragedies, farces, success stories, narratives of heartbreak and disappointment, poems of aspiration and despair. All such tones and all such literary "kinds" reflect actuality as well as the desires and fears of those writing them. The history of America is a collection of the stories of individual drives and conflicts, confrontations between individual and family or heritage, customs coming up against other customs, anxieties of belonging up against stubborn retentions of selves defined as old habits and rules. Most stories approach America in a spirit of hopefulness and idealism at the beginning; how that hope fares is the focus of most stories about American life.

# Gish Jen

The child of Chinese immigrants, Gish Jen grew up in New York and was educated at Harvard University and the Iowa Writers' Workshop. Her stories have appeared in numerous quarterlies and have been anthologized in *The New Generation* and *Best American Short Stories*. She is at work on a novel.

The following story describes the persistent "old country" views of a Chinese father who tries to adapt so that his family can fully be a part of "the American Society" but who finds himself stubbornly returning to familiar behavior.

# IN THE AMERICAN SOCIETY

## *I. His Own Society*

When my father took over the pancake house, it was to send my little sister Mona and me to college. We were only in junior high at the time, but my father believed in getting a jump on things. "Those Americans always saying it," he told us. "Smart guys thinking in advance." My mother elaborated, explaining that businesses took bringing up, like children. They could take years to get going, she said, years.

In this case, though, we got rich right away. At two months we were breaking even, and at four, those same hotcakes that could barely withstand the weight of butter and syrup were supporting our family with ease. My mother bought a station wagon with air conditioning, my father an oversized, red vinyl recliner for the back room; and as time went on and the business continued to thrive, my father started to talk about his grandfather and the village he had reigned over in China—things my father had never talked about when he worked for other people. He told us about the bags of rice his family would give out to the poor at New Year's, and about the people who came to beg, on their hands and knees, for his grandfather to intercede for the more wayward of their relatives. "Like that Godfather in the movie," he would tell us as, his feet up, he distributed paychecks. Sometimes an employee would get two green envelopes instead of one, which meant that Jimmy needed a tooth pulled, say, or that Tiffany's husband was in the clinker again.

"It's nothing, nothing," he would insist, sinking back into his chair. "Who else is going to take care of you people?"

My mother would mostly just sigh about it. "Your father thinks this is   4
China," she would say, and then she would go back to her mending. Once
in a while, though, when my father had given away a particularly large sum,
she would exclaim, outraged, "But this here is the U—S—of—A!"—this
apparently having been what she used to tell immigrant stock boys when
they came in late.

She didn't work at the supermarket anymore; but she had made it to the   5
rank of manager before she left, and this had given her not only new words
and phrases, but new ideas about herself, and about America, and about
what was what in general. She had opinions, now, on how downtown should
be zoned; she could pump her own gas and check her own oil; and for all she
used to chide Mona and me for being "copycats," she herself was now interested in espadrilles, and wallpaper, and most recently, the town country
club.

"So join already," said Mona, flicking a fly off her knee.   6

My mother enumerated the problems as she sliced up a quarter round   7
of watermelon: There was the cost. There was the waiting list. There was
the fact that no one in our family played either tennis or golf.

"So what?" said Mona.   8

"It would be waste," said my mother.   9

"Me and Callie can swim in the pool."   10

"Plus you need that recommendation letter from a member."   11

"Come *on*," said Mona. "Annie's mom'd write you a letter in a *sec*."   12

My mother's knife glinted in the early summer sun. I spread some more   13
newspaper on the picnic table.

"*Plus* you have to eat there twice a month. You know what that means."   14
My mother cut another, enormous slice of fruit.

"No, I *don't* know what that means," said Mona.   15

"It means Dad would have to wear a jacket, dummy," I said.   16

"Oh! Oh! Oh!" said Mona, clasping her hand to her breast. "Oh! Oh!   17
Oh! Oh! Oh!"

We all laughed: my father had no use for nice clothes, and would wear   18
only ten-year-old shirts, with grease-spotted pants, to show how little he
cared what anyone thought.

"Your father doesn't believe in joining the American society," said my   19
mother. "He wants to have his own society."

"So go to dinner without him." Mona shot her seeds out in long arcs   20
over the lawn. "Who cares what he thinks?"

But of course we all did care, and knew my mother could not simply up   21
and do as she pleased. For in my father's mind, a family owed its head a
degree of loyalty that left no room for dissent. To embrace what he embraced
was to love; and to embrace something else was to betray him.

He demanded a similar sort of loyalty of his workers, whom he treated   22
more like servants than employees. Not in the beginning, of course. In the

beginning all he wanted was for them to keep on doing what they used to do, and to that end he concentrated mostly on leaving them alone. As the months passed, though, he expected more and more of them, with the result that for all his largesse, he began to have trouble keeping help. The cooks and busboys complained that he asked them to fix radiators and trim hedges, not only at the restaurant, but at our house; the waitresses that he sent them on errands and made them chauffeur him around. Our head waitress, Gertrude, claimed that he once even asked her to scratch his back.

"It's not just the blacks don't believe in slavery," she said when she quit.     23

My father never quite registered her complaint, though, nor those of the     24 others who left. Even after Eleanor quit, then Tiffany, then Gerald, and Jimmy, and even his best cook, Eureka Andy, for whom he had bought new glasses, he remained mostly convinced that the fault lay with them.

"All they understand is that assembly line," he lamented. "Robots, they     25 are. They want to be robots."

There *were* occasions when the clear running truth seemed to eddy, when     26 he would pinch the vinyl of his chair up into little peaks and wonder if he was doing things right. But with time he would always smooth the peaks back down; and when business started to slide in the spring, he kept on like a horse in his ways.

By the summer our dishboy was overwhelmed with scraping. It was no     27 longer just the hashbrowns that people were leaving for trash, and the service was as bad as the food. The waitresses served up French pancakes instead of German, apple juice instead of orange, spilt things on laps, on coats. On the Fourth of July some greenhorn sent an entire side of fries slaloming down a lady's *massif centrale*. Meanwhile in the back room, my father labored through articles on the economy.

"What is housing starts?" he puzzled. "What is GNP?"     28

Mona and I did what we could, filling in as busgirls and bookkeepers     29 and, one afternoon, stuffing the comments box that hung by the cashier's desk. That was Mona's idea. We rustled up a variety of pens and pencils, checked boxes for an hour, smeared the cards up with coffee and grease, and waited. It took a few days for my father to notice that the box was full, and he didn't say anything about it for a few days more. Finally, though, he started to complain of fatigue; and then he began to complain that the staff was not what it could be. We encouraged him in this—pointing out, for instance, how many dishes got chipped—but in the end all that happened was that, for the first time since we took over the restaurant, my father got it into his head to fire someone. Skip, a skinny busboy who was saving up for a sportscar, said nothing as my father mumbled on about the price of dishes. My father's hands shook as he wrote out the severance check; and he spent the rest of the day napping in his chair once it was over.

As it was going on midsummer, Skip wasn't easy to replace. We hung a     30 sign in the window and advertised in the paper, but no one called the first week, and the person who called the second didn't show up for his interview. The third week, my father phoned Skip to see if he would come back, but a friend of his had already sold him a Corvette for cheap.

Finally a Chinese guy named Booker turned up. He couldn't have been 31 more than thirty, and was wearing a lighthearted seersucker suit, but he looked as though life had him pinned: his eyes were bloodshot and his chest sunken, and the muscles of his neck seemed to strain with the effort of holding his head up. In a single dry breath he told us that he had never bussed tables but was willing to learn, and that he was on the lam from the deportation authorities.

"I do not want lie to you," he kept saying. He had come to the United 32 States on a student visa, had run out of money, and was now in a bind. He was loath to go back to Taiwan, as it happened—he looked up at this point, to be sure my father wasn't pro-KMT[1]—but all he had was a phony social security card and a willingness to absorb all blame, should anything untoward come to pass.

"I do not think, anyway, that it is against law to hire me, only to be 33 me," he said, smiling faintly.

Anyone else would have examined him on this, but my father conceived 34 of laws as speed bumps rather than curbs. He wiped the counter with his sleeve, and told Booker to report the next morning.

"I will be good worker," said Booker. 35

"Good," said my father. 36

"Anything you want me to do, I will do." 37

My father nodded. 38

Booker seemed to sink into himself for a moment. "Thank you," he said 39 finally. "I am appreciate your help. I am very, very appreciate for everything." He reached out to shake my father's hand.

My father looked at him. "Did you eat today?" he asked in Mandarin. 40

Booker pulled at the hem of his jacket. 41

"Sit down," said my father. "Please, have a seat." 42

My father didn't tell my mother about Booker, and my mother didn't 43 tell my father about the country club. She would never have applied, except that Mona, while over at Annie's, had let it drop that our mother wanted to join. Mrs. Lardner came by the very next day.

"Why, I'd be honored and delighted to write you people a letter," she 44 said. Her skirt billowed around her.

"Thank you so much," said my mother. "But it's too much trouble for 45 you, and also my husband is . . ."

"Oh, it's no trouble at all, no trouble at all. I tell you." She leaned 46 forward so that her chest freckles showed. "I know just how it is. It's a secret

1. Kuomintang ("National People's party"); forced from mainland China by the Communists, it has ruled Taiwan since 1949.

of course, but you know, my natural father was Jewish. Can you see it? Just look at my skin."

"My husband," said my mother.                                                   47

"I'd be honored and delighted," said Mrs. Lardner with a little wave of        48
her hands. "Just honored and delighted."

Mona was triumphant. "See, Mom," she said, waltzing around the kitchen          49
when Mrs. Lardner left. "What did I tell you? 'I'm just honored and delighted,
just honored and delighted.' " She waved her hands in the air.

"You know, the Chinese have a saying," said my mother. "To do noth-            50
ing is better than to overdo. You mean well, but you tell me now what will
happen."

"I'll talk Dad into it," said Mona, still waltzing. "Or I bet Callie can.       51
He'll do anything Callie says."

"I can try, anyway," I said.                                                    52

"Did you hear what I said?" said my mother. Mona bumped into the               53
broom closet door. "You're not going to talk anything; you've already made
enough trouble." She started on the dishes with a clatter.

Mona poked diffidently at a mop.                                                54

I sponged off the counter. "Anyway," I ventured, "I bet our name'll            55
never even come up."

"That's if we're lucky," said my mother.                                        56

"There's all these people waiting," I said.                                     57

"Good," she said. She started on a pot.                                         58

I looked over at Mona, who was still cowering in the broom closet. "In         59
fact, there's some black family's been waiting so long, they're going to sue,"
I said.

My mother turned off the water. "Where'd you hear that?"                        60

"Patty told me."                                                                61

She turned the water back on, starting to wash a dish, then put it back        62
down and shut the faucet.

"I'm sorry," said Mona.                                                         63

"Forget it," said my mother. "Just forget it."                                  64

Booker turned out to be a model worker, whose boundless gratitude              65
translated into a willingness to do anything. As he also learned quickly, he
soon knew not only how to bus, but how to cook, and how to wait table, and
how to keep the books. He fixed the walk-in door so that it stayed shut,
reupholstered the torn seats in the dining room, and devised a system for
tracking inventory. The only stone in the rice was that he tended to be sickly;
but, reliable even in illness, he would always send a friend to take his place.
In this way we got to know Ronald, Lynn, Dirk, and Cedric, all of whom,
like Booker, had problems with their legal status and were anxious to please.
They weren't all as capable as Booker, though, with the exception of Cedric,
whom my father often hired even when Booker was well. A round wag of a
man who called Mona and me *shou hou*—skinny monkeys—he was a pro-

fessed nonsmoker who was nevertheless always begging drags off of other people's cigarettes. This last habit drove our head cook, Fernando, crazy, especially since, when refused a hit, Cedric would occasionally snitch one. Winking impishly at Mona and me, he would steal up to an ashtray, take a quick puff, and then break out laughing so that the smoke came rolling out of his mouth in a great incriminatory cloud. Fernando accused him of stealing fresh cigarettes too, even whole packs.

"Why else do you think he's weaseling around in the back of the store all the time," he said. His face was blotchy with anger. "The man is a frigging thief." 66

Other members of the staff supported him in this contention and joined in on an "Operation Identification," which involved numbering and initialing their cigarettes—even though what they seemed to fear for wasn't so much their cigarettes as their jobs. Then one of the cooks quit; and rather than promote someone, my father hired Cedric for the position. Rumors flew that he was taking only half the normal salary, that Alex had been pressured to resign, and that my father was looking for a position with which to placate Booker, who had been bypassed because of his health. 67

The result was that Fernando categorically refused to work with Cedric. 68

"The only way I'll cook with that piece of slime," he said, shaking his huge tattooed fist, "is if it's his ass frying on the grill." 69

My father cajoled and cajoled, to no avail, and in the end was simply forced to put them on different schedules. 70

The next week Fernando got caught stealing a carton of minute steaks. My father would not tell even Mona and me how he knew to be standing by the back door when Fernando was on his way out, but everyone suspected Booker. Everyone but Fernando, that is, who was sure Cedric had been the tip-off. My father held a staff meeting in which he tried to reassure everyone that Alex had left on his own, and that he had no intention of firing anyone. But though he was careful not to mention Fernando, everyone was so amazed that he was being allowed to stay that Fernando was incensed nonetheless. 71

"Don't you all be putting your bug eyes on me," he said. "*He's* the frigging crook." He grabbed Cedric by the collar. 72

Cedric raised an eyebrow. "Cook, you mean," he said. 73

At this Fernando punched Cedric in the mouth; and the words he had just uttered notwithstanding, my father fired him on the spot. 74

With everything that was happening, Mona and I were ready to be getting out of the restaurant. It was almost time: the days were still stuffy with summer, but our window shade had started flapping in the evening as if gearing up to go out. That year the breezes were full of salt, as they sometimes were when they came in from the East, and they blew anchors and docks through my mind like so many tumbleweeds, filling my dreams with wherries and lobsters and grainy-faced men who squinted, day in and day out, at the sky. 75

It was time for a change, you could feel it; and yet the pancake house was the same as ever. The day before school started my father came home with bad news.

"Fernando called police," he said, wiping his hand on his pant leg.                77

My mother naturally wanted to know what police; and so with much        78
coughing and hawing, the long story began, the latest installment of which had the police calling immigration, and immigration sending an investigator. My mother sat stiff as whalebone as my father described how the man summarily refused lunch on the house and how my father had admitted, under pressure, that he knew there were "things" about his workers.

"So now what happens?"                79

My father didn't know. "Booker and Cedric went with him to the jail,"        80
he said. "But me, here I am." He laughed uncomfortably.

The next day my father posted bail for "his boys" and waited apprehen-        81
sively for something to happen. The day after that he waited again, and the day after that he called our neighbor's law student son, who suggested my father call the immigration department under an alias. My father took his advice; and it was thus that he discovered that Booker was right: it was illegal for aliens to work, but it wasn't to hire them.

In the happy interval that ensued, my father apologized to my mother,        82
who in turn confessed about the country club, for which my father had no choice but to forgive her. Then he turned his attention back to "his boys."

My mother didn't see that there was anything to do.                83

"I like to talking to the judge," said my father.                84

"This is not China," said my mother.                85

"I'm only talking to him. I'm not give him money unless he wants it."        86

"You're going to land up in jail."                87

"So what else I should do?" My father threw up his hands. "Those are        88
my boys."

"Your boys!" exploded my mother. "What about your family? What        89
about your wife?"

My father took a long sip of tea. "You know," he said finally, "in the        90
war my father sent our cook to the soldiers to use. He always said it—the province comes before the town, the town comes before the family."

"A restaurant is not a town," said my mother.                91

My father sipped at his tea again. "You know, when I first come to the        92
United States, I also had to hide-and-seek with those deportation guys. If people did not helping me, I'm not here today."

My mother scrutinized her hem.                93

After a minute I volunteered that before seeing a judge, he might try a        94
lawyer.

He turned. "Since when did you become so afraid like your mother?"        95

I started to say that it wasn't a matter of fear, but he cut me off.        96

"What I need today," he said, "is a son."                97

My father and I spent the better part of the next day standing in lines at        98 the immigration office. He did not get to speak to a judge, but with much persistence he managed to speak to a judge's clerk, who tried to persuade him that it was not her place to extend him advice. My father, though, shamelessly plied her with compliments and offers of free pancakes until she finally conceded that she personally doubted anything would happen to either Cedric or Booker.

"Especially if they're 'needed workers,'" she said, rubbing at the red marks her glasses left on her nose. She yawned. "Have you thought about sponsoring them to become permanent residents?"  99

Could he do that? My father was overjoyed. And what if he saw to it right away? Would she perhaps put in a good word with the judge?  100

She yawned again, her nostrils flaring. "Don't worry," she said. "They'll get a fair hearing."  101

My father returned jubilant. Booker and Cedric hailed him as their savior, their Buddha incarnate. He was like a father to them, they said; and laughing and clapping, they made him tell the story over and over, sorting over the details like jewels. And how old was the assistant judge? And what did she say?  102

That evening my father tipped the paperboy a dollar and bought a pot of mums for my mother, who suffered them to be placed on the dining room table. The next night he took us all out to dinner. Then on Saturday, Mona found a letter on my father's chair at the restaurant.  103

> Dear Mr. Chang,
> You are the grat boss. But, we do not like to trial, so will runing away now. Plese to excus us. People saying the law in America is fears like dragon. Here is only $140. We hope some day we can pay back the rest bale. You will getting intrest, as you diserving, so grat a boss you are. Thank you for every thing. In next life you will be burn in rich family, with no more pancaks.
>
> Yours truley,
> Booker + Cedric

In the weeks that followed my father went to the pancake house for crises, but otherwise hung around our house, fiddling idly with the sump pump and boiler in an effort, he said, to get ready for winter. It was as though he had gone into retirement, except that instead of moving South, he had moved to the basement. He even took to showering my mother with little attentions, and to calling her "old girl," and when we finally heard that the club had entertained all the applications it could for the year, he was so sympathetic that he seemed more disappointed than my mother.  104

### II. In the American Society

Mrs. Lardner tempered the bad news with an invitation to a bon voyage bash she was throwing for a friend of hers who was going to Greece for six months.  105

"Do come," she urged. "You'll meet everyone, and then, you know, if things open up in the spring . . ." She waved her hands.

My mother wondered if it would be appropriate to show up at a party for someone they didn't know, but "the honest truth" was that this was an annual affair. "If it's not Greece, it's Antibes," sighed Mrs. Lardner. "We really just do it because his wife left him and his daughter doesn't speak to him, and poor Jeremy just feels so *unloved.*"

She also invited Mona and me to the goings on, as *"demi-*guests" to keep Annie out of the champagne. I wasn't too keen on the idea, but before I could say anything, she had already thanked us for so generously agreeing to honor her with our presence.

"A pair of little princesses, you are!" she told us. "A pair of princesses!"

The party was that Sunday. On Saturday, my mother took my father out shopping for a suit. As it was the end of September, she insisted that he buy a worsted rather than a seersucker, even though it was only ten, rather than fifty percent off. My father protested that it was as hot out as ever, which was true—a thick Indian summer had cozied murderously up to us— but to no avail. Summer clothes, said my mother, were not properly worn after Labor Day.

The suit was unfortunately as extravagant in length as it was in price, which posed an additional quandary, since the tailor wouldn't be in until Monday. The salesgirl, though, found a way of tacking it up temporarily.

"Maybe this suit not fit me," fretted my father.

"Just don't take your jacket off," said the salesgirl.

He gave her a tip before they left, but when he got home refused to remove the price tag.

"I like to asking the tailor about the size," he insisted.

"You mean you're going to *wear* it and then return it?" Mona rolled her eyes.

"I didn't say I'm return it," said my father stiffly. "I like to asking the tailor, that's all."

The party started off swimmingly, except that most people were wearing bermudas or wrap skirts. Still, my parents carried on, sharing with great feeling the complaints about the heat. Of course my father tried to eat a cracker full of shallots and burnt himself in an attempt to help Mr. Lardner turn the coals of the barbecue; but on the whole he seemed to be doing all right. Not nearly so well as my mother, though, who had accepted an entire cupful of Mrs. Lardner's magic punch, and seemed indeed to be under some spell. As Mona and Annie skirmished over whether some boy in their class inhaled when he smoked, I watched my mother take off her shoes, laughing and laughing as a man with a beard regaled her with navy stories by the pool. Apparently he had been stationed in the Orient and remembered a few words of Chinese, which made my mother laugh still more. My father excused himself to go to the men's room then drifted back and dropped anchor at the hors d'oeuvre table, while my mother sailed on to a group of women, who tinkled at length over the clarity of her complexion. I dug out a book I had brought.

Just when I'd cracked the spine, though, Mrs. Lardner came by to bewail 119 her shortage of servers. Her caterers were criminals, I agreed; and the next thing I knew I was handing out bits of marine life, making the rounds as amiably as I could.

"Here you go, Dad," I said when I got to the hors d'oeuvre table. 120

"Everything is fine," he said. 121

I hesitated to leave him alone; but then the man with the beard zeroed 122 in on him, and though he talked of nothing but my mother, I thought it would be okay to get back to work. Just that moment, though, Jeremy Brothers lurched our way, an empty, albeit corked, wine bottle in hand. He was a slim, well-proportioned man, with a Roman nose and small eyes and a nice manly jaw that he allowed to hang agape.

"Hello," he said drunkenly. "Pleased to meet you." 123

"Pleased to meeting you," said my father. 124

"Right," said Jeremy. "Right. Listen. I have this bottle here, this most 125 recalcitrant bottle. You see that it refuses to do my bidding. I bid it open sesame, please, and it does nothing." He pulled the cork out with his teeth, then turned the bottle upside down.

My father nodded. 126

"Would you have a word with it please?" said Jeremy. The man with 127 the beard excused himself. "Would you please have a goddamned word with it?"

My father laughed uncomfortably. 128

"Ah!" Jeremy bowed a little. "Excuse me, excuse me, excuse me. You 129 are not my man, not my man at all." He bowed again and started to leave, but then circled back. "Viticulture is not your forte, yes I can see that, see that plainly. But may I trouble you on another matter? Forget the damned bottle." He threw it into the pool, and winked at the people he splashed. "I have another matter. Do you speak Chinese?"

My father said he did not, but Jeremy pulled out a handkerchief with 130 some characters on it anyway, saying that his daughter had sent it from Hong Kong and that he thought the characters might be some secret message.

"Long life," said my father. 131

"But you haven't looked at it yet." 132

"I know what it says without looking." My father winked at me. 133

"You do?" 134

"Yes, I do." 135

"You're making fun of me, aren't you?" 136

"No, no, no," said my father, winking again. 137

"Who are you anyway?" said Jeremy. 138

His smile fading, my father shrugged. 139

"*Who are you?*" 140

My father shrugged again. 141

Jeremy began to roar. "This is my party, *my party*, and I've never seen 142
you before in my life." My father backed up as Jeremy came toward him.
"*Who are you? WHO ARE YOU?*"

Just as my father was going to step back into the pool, Mrs. Lardner 143
came running up. Jeremy informed her that there was a man crashing his
party.

"Nonsense," said Mrs. Lardner. "This is Ralph Chang, who I invited 144
extra especially so he could meet you." She straightened the collar of Jeremy's peach-colored polo shirt for him.

"Yes, well we've had a chance to chat," said Jeremy. 145

She whispered in his ear; he mumbled something; she whispered some- 146
thing more.

"I do apologize," he said finally. 147

My father didn't say anything. 148

"I do." Jeremy seemed genuinely contrite. "Doubtless you've seen drunks 149
before, haven't you? You must have them in China."

"Okay," said my father. 150

As Mrs. Lardner glided off, Jeremy clapped his arm over my father's 151
shoulders. "You know, I really am quite sorry, quite sorry."

My father nodded. 152

"What can I do, how can I make it up to you?" 153

"No thank you." 154

"No, tell me, tell me," wheedled Jeremy. "Tickets to casino night?" My 155
father shook his head. "You don't gamble. Dinner at Bartholomew's?" My
father shook his head again. "You don't eat." Jeremy scratched his chin.
"You know, my wife was like you. Old Annabelle could never let me make
things up—never, never, never, never, never."

My father wriggled out from under his arm. 156

"How about sport clothes? You are rather overdressed, you know, excuse 157
me for saying so. But here." He took off his polo shirt and folded it up. "You
can have this with my most profound apologies." He ruffled his chest hairs
with his free hand.

"No thank you," said my father. 158

"No, take it, take it. Accept my apologies," He thrust the shirt into my 159
father's arms. "I'm so very sorry, so very sorry. Please, try it on."

Helplessly holding the shirt, my father searched the crowd for my mother. 160

"Here, I'll help you off with your coat." 161

My father froze. 162

Jeremy reached over and took his jacket off. "Milton's, one hundred 163
twenty-five dollars reduced to one hundred twelve-fifty," he read. "What a
bargain, what a bargain!"

"Please give it back," pleaded my father. "Please." 164

"Now for your shirt," ordered Jeremy. 165

Heads began to turn. 166

"Take off your shirt." 167

"I do not take orders like a servant," announced my father. 168

"Take off your shirt, or I'm going to throw this jacket right into the 169
pool, just right into this little pool here." Jeremy held it over the water.

"Go ahead." 170

"One hundred twelve-fifty," taunted Jeremy. "One hundred twelve . . ." 171

My father flung the polo shirt into the water with such force that part 172
of it bounced back up into the air like a fluorescent fountain. Then it settled
into a soft heap on top of the water. My mother hurried up.

"You're a sport!" said Jeremy, suddenly breaking into a smile and slap- 173
ping my father on the back. "You're a sport! I like that. A man with spirit,
that's what you are. A man with panache. Allow me to return to you your
jacket." He handed it back to my father. "Good value you got on that, good
value."

My father hurled the coat into the pool too. "We're leaving," he said 174
grimly. "Leaving!"

"Now, Ralphie," said Mrs. Lardner, bustling up; but my father was 175
already stomping off.

"Get your sister," he told me. To my mother: "Get your shoes." 176

"That was *great*, Dad," said Mona as we walked down to the car. "You 177
were *stupendous.*"

"Way to show 'em," I said. 178

"What?" said my father offhandedly. 179

Although it was only just dusk, we were in a gulch, which made it hard 180
to see anything except the gleam of his white shirt moving up the hill ahead
of us.

"It was all my fault," began my mother. 181

"Forget it," said my father grandly. Then he said, "The only trouble is 182
I left those keys in my jacket pocket."

"Oh, *no*, said Mona. 183

"Oh no is right," said my mother. 184

"So we'll walk home," I said. 185

"But how're we going to get into the *house*," said Mona. 186

The noise of the party churned through the silence. 187

"Someone has to going back," said my father. 188

"Let's go to the pancake house first," suggested my mother. "We can 189
wait there until the party is finished, and then call Mrs. Lardner."

Having all agreed that that was a good plan, we started walking again. 190

"God, just think," said Mona. "We're going to have to *dive* for them." 191

My father stopped a moment. We waited. 192

"You girls are good swimmers," he said finally. "Not like me." 193

Then his shirt started moving again, and we trooped up the hill after it, 194
into the dark.

## STUDY QUESTIONS

1. Describe the father's essential CHARACTER* traits. What desires motivate him most strongly? What is the source of his values? How important to him are the opinions of others? How important is money? family? his own authority?

2. Under what conditions is the mother "licensed" to disagree with the father or trick him? In what ways do the mother's values differ from the father's?

3. How much do we learn, during the story, about the NARRATOR's values? Why does she remain an amused observer through most of the story? What are her attitudes toward the father? Which episodes demonstrate the narrator's attitudes toward the father most vividly?

4. What strategies does the author use to keep the father from seeming tyrannical and foolish? How is Jeremy Brothers characterized? What new aspects of the father's personality are revealed by his confrontation with Jeremy?

5. How can you tell what the narrator thinks of her father?

6. Why is the SETTING of the story's final episode especially appropriate? How does the mother's conduct at the party affirm aspects of her personality and character revealed earlier in the story? In what ways is the narrator like her father?

7. In what different ways are possessions and cultural "symbols" important to the PLOT of the story? Describe the effect of the final IMAGE of the daughters' diving for their father's keys in the Lardners' swimming pool. How does the previous image—the family waiting in the pancake house for the party to end—affect the final one?

8. Why does the story emphasize so strongly the father's imperfect understanding of English? What signs are there that the daughters are embarrassed by their parents' language skills? In what other ways do generational gaps stand for differences in cultural understanding?

# Nicholas Gerros

Born in a rural village in Macedonia, Greece, Nicholas Gerros came to the United States as a teenager in 1912, first settling with his father in Cincinnati.

The following oral account of his life was transcribed from an interview in 1975, when Gerros was in his mid-seventies. In this autobiographical sketch, Gerros expresses a strong sense of self-determination and powerfully defends the kinds of individual

---

*Words in small capitals are defined in the glossary.

self-assertion and hard work that led to success in the Horatio Alger novels, which helped to create the American myth of success and "self-made men."

# GREEK HORATIO ALGER

My mother died when I was nine years old. My aunt and my uncle took care of me. I had a brother who was three or four years younger, then still another brother when my mother died of childbirth. 1

My father was in the United States previously to my coming here. He moved to Cincinnati, Ohio. When I came to the United States, I came direct to Cincinnati. I came alone with other boys in a similar age bracket with me, from the same village—Menopilon in the Macedonian part of Greece, Kastoria province. 2

The way life in the village was the men always had to go out of their homes into other lands to make a living, come back, stay with the family a length of time till the money was gone. They used to have little farms around, that didn't produce enough to live on, so naturally they had to go to other countries. My father had been working in industry. They have some farming in Macedonia, but he was in lumber. When he came here he sent for me, sent me money and everything else. 3

I was at that time fourteen years old. Our village was 'way up in the mountains. We didn't use anything with wheels to carry things. We always loaded the backs of different animals. When I went to get my passport at this Kastoria place was the first time I saw a wagon with wheels. From there on we went south to Thessalia. We stopped in the city by the name of Trikkala. From there we left for Athens. 4

We were in Athens about three or four days. I was with some distant relatives, no brothers, but they were all the same age. They were all leaving Greece for the same purpose. There were about half a dozen or so of us. On the boat we stopped in Naples. We were there about a week [for] some reason or other. It was just like a big armory, just plain buildings, not much accommodations. I remember reading all kind of writings on the wall, how bad this place was, get away from it as soon as you can. Some were in Greek and some were in Yugoslavian, all kinds of languages. Then we got into an Italian boat by the name of *Saint Georgio*. It took us two weeks from Italy. We left the village March first; we left Greece March 15; then we arrived in New York April 15. It was a little rocky. Most were a little seasick. I was a little seasick, not too much. 5

We got to New York, a place they call in Greek *Castn Gare*; in English it's something called Castle Island. We used to unload there. From there we go for examination, for eyes, for sickness of all kinds so it would not get into the United States. We stayed there couple of days, I think. 6

The first thing shown to us was some [church] pamphlets written in English. We couldn't read them. Some man came along. He gave us a box containing food of some kind, a little bit of everything, and [a nurse] gave us the food and a Bible.

We had a ticket on us because we couldn't speak English. They look at you and tell you, you go there, or you go there. Traveling was easy because it was prearranged by the agents. We took a small boat from New York to Norfolk, Virginia. Some of us went somewhere else. I remember three or four of us was together, all young men and boys. We were waiting on the train and begun to look in the package to see what we had. Each of us had a banana to go with the rest of the food that was given him. We didn't know how to eat it. We'd never seen bananas. Finally somebody realizes that on the train and showed us.

When we went to Cincinnati, there were some people there waiting for us. They showed us [how] to go direct to the apartment. When we got into this apartment they treated us with ice cream. It was the first time we all had ice cream. These people before us organized a room for us. There were more than a half-dozen rooms and a big kitchen.

I stayed with my father for a while, for all the while he was there. He was working in something concerning furniture. Just before the Balkan War started, he went back to Greece.

Those years there were no Greek woman coming to the United States. Mostly all the Greeks were young, between twelve and thirty. They had to kinda stick together because none of them knew any more of the English language than they did themselves.

I remember how hard—this you can put with a line under the words because they mean so much. The young people in America, they've got it so easy and they don't know how easy it is. I was asked to go out to buy something. I think I was in this country for two months. It was late spring. It was still cold, and I had to go down from the second floor. There were stairs going right straight down to the door. There was a bunch of young fellows there talking to each other and having a lot of fun. I was their age, but I couldn't speak any English. I didn't want to get into any trouble with them so they're sitting down on the stairs and I tried to pass by to go do what I wanted to do. I didn't want to step on their clothes, so I was kind of careful and they realized that. One fellow, he wasn't sitting down, he was talking to a girl. I didn't know what he was saying. As far as I was concerned, any language was English to me. The only thing I could speak was Greek. I surmise now that he told me, "Let's have some fun with this fellow." So he came to me and talked, "Blah blah." The first thing I know he gives me one upper cut and down I went.

Right in front of there was a bakery shop. This man is selling bread as well as cakes. He came out and the kids run away. He took me in. He asked me if I was hurt. Well, I [looked] and there was no blood so I says I wasn't hurt.

Right there and then I made up my mind. I'm going to go to school 14
nights, learn the language, read, write, and spoken, and go to the YMCA to
prepare myself to defend myself.

Here the oldest boy is supposedly boss of the rest of us living in this 15
particular apartment. It is up to him, the rules and regulations and how to
behave. The boy was about ten, twelve years older than I was. The older
ones felt certain responsibility for the younger ones. They thought that they
should keep us as close to them as possible, possibly as ignorant of life in the
United States as possible. They thought that everything in the United States
was out of proportion, was too free. They thought that I was going to school
because there were girls. There *were* girls, from other countries because they
moved here, from Hungary, from Italy, from Austria. So when I announced
it to the crowd what I was gonna do was go to school and go to YMCA they
told me, "Look, you didn't have a YMCA in the village where you come
from. What do you want to go to YMCA for?"

"Exercise, take baths, and meet people." 16

"No, you can't go." 17

"Can I go to night school?" 18

He said, "No, you can't go to night school." He said, "You don't go 19
there for an education, you go there because girls are there."

I says, "No." I says, "I learned my lesson. I go there for an education." 20
And I remember, he tried to stop me.

He says, "You can't go. You have to be in bed at nine o'clock, the lat- 21
est."

I says, "I can't be [in] at nine o'clock because school doesn't end until 22
nine o'clock or quarter past. Then it takes me time to walk from there to
here. The earliest I can be is nine-thirty."

He says, "I don't care what time it takes. As far as I'm concerned, you 23
shouldn't go."

For the first night I went and I found the door closed. I made a lot of 24
noise and he opened up and we had a big verbal fight and he says, "Well, I'll
let you in this time, but tomorrow, nine o'clock."

I couldn't get back. I came late, same thing. I was the only rebel. He 25
told everyone not to say a word to anybody and to keep on pretending they
were asleep. I knocked on the door and nothing. I knocked and knocked. So
I looked around and there's an old broken-up chair in the hall and I says,
"There's an old broken-up chair here. I'm going to pick it up and break the
door down." After that he opened the door and gave me heck. Right there
and then I decided to move. Some of the boys came with me and we went to
another apartment.

In the meantime, we were working in the shoe shop. They all made a 26
small living in wages at that time. Like for instance, I worked from seven
o'clock till six o'clock, and one hour in between for lunch. We got work. We
used to take care of ourselves, no mother, no father, no uncles, no aunts, no
nothing. You have to earn a living, take care of your clothing. You could eat,

cook, and go to school. All this we did together, maybe six of us, but we were all over twelve then, fifteen, fourteen, and to twenty.

After a year or so I was going to school nights in a different school. At that time, TB was the biggest killer of all the diseases, and people were scared stiff no matter if they just coughed a bit. This teacher noticed that I was sweating. She says, "You should go to the doctor." I went to this dispensary. At the end of three weeks they told me there was nothing wrong with me. In the meantime, though, I was totally scared of all this business and lots of my young fellas, they afraid to be with me. 27

I was determined to get well. I quit my job. I had saved some money. The salaries those years were $4.75 to $7.50 a week. Imagine what you had to figure on to eat. I also shined shoes on Sundays to make some extra money. We applied ourselves to the necessity of times. 28

I left those boys. I left them because first of all they didn't want me anyway because they were afraid and then because they didn't contribute anything to my life. Then I went to the farm. I figured I would get well out in the open. I was going to get well in spite of anybody. I used to take trolley in Cincinnati, go to the end of the line and get out and walk out on a farm. I remember I used to go out on both sides of Cincinnati. Cross the Ohio River from Cincinnati and you are in Kentucky. I went there just at the beginning of World War I. I stayed there on [different] farms until April or May the following year. 29

I had a cousin in Manchester, New Hampshire. She knew I was there and she wrote to me and she says, "Come here." She says, "The climate is better in New England. You come here and you be better off." So I came to Manchester, New Hampshire, and I got a job in one of the shoe factories. 30

When I lived in Manchester I used to love the men's clothing business. Even in Cincinnati I used to admire the good clothing stores and look at the way they kept their merchandise. That was my idea—sometimes to have my own business. When I come to Manchester, I went to get a job in a store, part-time. They were hard to get, those jobs. I went to this place to a German. He said, "What can you do?" He says, "Well, I don't need you today." For four or six weeks I went every day for a job. He says to me, "Why do you want a job here?" 31

I says, " 'Cause I like your store." 32

He asked me more questions and he said, "All right. You can work Thursday evenings and Saturdays." I think it was $1.75 for a week. Three hours on Thursday and eight hours on Saturday. Then he went up to $2.25, then he went up again. He had me sell on the floor. 33

In this process I met some people and they told me there were a lot of shops in Haverhill. That was 1917, 1918. I went there and I got a job in the shoe factory and was doing pretty well. I was doing finishing, pressing the shoe all around, finishing the job so it will look nice for the customer. They were all small shoe companies; there were hundreds of them. The foreman 34 maybe Yankee and all that, but mostly Italians, Greeks, Irish, French, and all nationalities. The hours were not bad. Seven o'clock in the morning until twelve, then you go and come back at one, and then one till five. I made a lot of friends here in Haverhill. They were all in just three or four blocks around. We had a center and we felt at home. Lacking a home life, you have to be with people naturally, and so I stayed in Haverhill. I was in the shoe shop, then I was in the life-insurance business. In Haverhill, I was selling to anybody. I earned quite a lot.

A couple of fellows, one was in a shoe factory and the other had a small business, wasn't doing too well, and they wanted to go into the clothing business. They went in the clothing business and they found they didn't know a damn thing. In fact, they couldn't even speak English very well. I had a *little* experience, more than they had, so they convinced me to go with them. I was making about $75 a week at the insurance and I wanted to go in the clothing business for myself, so I went with them. I had $600 in invest. I put that in there with them. Later one didn't want any part of it any more. We paid him off with $300 and we kept the store between the two of us. 35

The younger man, he was my age, he didn't care much for the business either. In fact, he didn't know the difference between beautiful and terrible. This is my partner. I was about twenty-two, twenty-three. I told him that if he wanted to sell, to get somebody. So he finally got somebody and he sold his share to him. The new man spoke much better English. They are from one of the good families in Greece. 36

My dream was a store of some kind. I worked with this man for about three years and I gave him a proposition: "Either you get out of the factory and come with me," I says, "or I have to do it alone." He tried to convince me. He tried the hard way and the easy way. I told him, I says, "The only way we can do it together, we got to be within the family." In the course of talking back and forth for about two weeks, three weeks, in February I said, "Look, the time's late already for spring. We've got to get ready." He says, "All right, you buy me out." I bought him out with $6,750 for his share. From there the business grew up. 37

I borrowed the money from the bank and I put on a Dissolution of Partnership Sale, and I took in more money than I gave him. I went to the bank and paid 'em up. I had borrowed for five months, and I paid 'em up in five weeks. When I had the big sale on, people were coming in and out. He was across the street watching it and he felt that small, he wanted to buy the place back. Of course, I wouldn't sell. 38

*How did the Depression influence you?*

In 1931 [the building was sold and] I had to move to another place. When I moved it was three hundred percent better location. I was paying $150 a month rent and had two people working. The Depression did influence me and I'll tell you why. The prices went down, and I lost some money at that time, not too much. It didn't bother me too much because I was young 39 in the business and I also was young. My future wife, she had to wait quite a few years 'cause I couldn't make up my mind. I wasn't secure enough in my business.

She was from Haverhill. She was born in Greece and came here when 40 she was four years old. She was working for an office where they used to sell oil burners. She was the bookkeeper there. She was an orphan from her father. She came here to this country with her mother alone. She was very, very smart and a good bookkeeper, and had a very good personality. She meets people she makes friends.

Her mother used to come quite often to the store. She got friendly with 41 me and all that business. At that time you couldn't go out with a girl and not be engaged to her. In order to get to know her better, I had to get engaged to her. I used to go up to her office on my break quite often and talk to her. We decided to get married. I proposed to her and to her mother. This was the way it was. I got married in 1935. We had three children, all three girls. We lost the first one. That was also a girl. The years went by and we were associated in the business. She's got a very good business head. She's very easy and she's got the gift of gab. She can really move people and their friends.

Me and my wife, during the World War II we tried to help with Greek 42 relief. The poor people are suffering too much. After the war was over the people who were with the Nazis were put *back* in power. Why should you award the people who did wrong for the country? That's just what they were doing. The government destroyed the church, bombarded the village, my village where I was born.

In 1946 I went to Florida, St. Petersburg, around there. I was reading 43 the newspapers. I see where a Greek prince was visiting some port in the South and they give him a reception. I wrote a letter to the newspaper criticizing the United States, the government, especially the cities. Why do they do that when we don't believe in kings and princes? It was quite a nice letter.

Naturally I took part in supporting the leftists in Greece. I did all kinds 44 of support. This fellow from Athens was representing the leftist newspaper in Greece. He came to New York to Boston, Boston to Haverhill. I introduced him to the newspaper in Haverhill. The city accepted him for the *Gazette* to go to work for them.

Quite a few years later, they went over to my house, I don't know, FBI, 45 CIA. They said this, "We're going to ask you a few questions regarding the security of the United States. Why you have joined this particular organization?" It was some organization to help poor people when they die so they can be buried.

"Well," I said, "I see no reason why I shouldn't support that." 46

They said, "But you're not a member of that." 47

I said, "I know it. I'm not a member." [aside] Because they just didn't 48 know how to organize. "But I see no reason why I shouldn't do it. The United States Constitution doesn't bother me for that."

He says, "Well, you were in Florida such and such a year such and such a month and this is what you wrote in the paper. Why'd you do that?" And one of the men is a Greek. He asked me that question. 49

"I tell you," I said. "Democracy was instituted first in Greece, and I'm proud of it, and you should be. The United States is a democracy. We don't believe in kings or princes. Why should we give such an honor to them? My Constitution does not tell me anything like that at all." So he shut up. 50

We sent a lot of stuff to Greece. I had a Greek committee, and we sent four tons of clothing and $6,000 in money during the war. So they called me on that. I said, "Since when does the United States forbid charity?" I wasn't afraid. "I'll do this right over again," I said. "I see nothing to stop me from doing this." They run out of questions so I say, "If you people got anything else, out with it fast because I work all day long here and I want to go out to get my supper." They never bothered me again. 51

*What ever happened to your store?*

In 1936 we changed the name to my own name—Gerros' Mens' Shop Incorporated. 52

I don't have the business today. I work part-time now. I was in business with the other fellow, it was $12,000 dollars for the year. When I got out of the business, it was $300,000 dollars a year. Some difference. 53

*To what do you attribute your success?*

Just hard work—that's all. You gotta be young. When you're young you've got to have ambition with no limit, because otherwise you are satisfied with small aims. You've got to have a challenge, feel inside of you that really you *could* do it without anyone else discouraging you. Don't begin to ask too much advice from people that haven't got that problem in their hands. You've got to listen to them, but do your own decisions. Most of all, you gotta be fair with the people you do business with. Nobody can move you if you are right, and if you know you're right and if you stick to it and fight back. Nobody can move you, no matter how strong they are. 54

This maybe is the only thing that stopped me from being even better than I am or was, because my dreams were not big enough or long enough. I should have dreamed a bigger business, and I would have had a bigger business. I should have gone to school further when I was much younger. I should have gone to work for a big store, like Jordan's, for instance, for a little while. Go to school, to Harvard, if possible. First of all, you've got to get a goal. You have to have a dream of what you want to be. You can find it. It will take time, like everything else takes time, the sooner you dream the better. 55

*Many immigrants who came when you did didn't do well. Perhaps they had too much to overcome?*

No. Let me tell you something. Don't forget, everything in your life, 56 *you decide*, nobody else decides, unless they come with a gun at your head and say, "Look, decide my way or else." Even then you got a choice, either die or do what he says. [Laughs.] You see what I mean? But most of the time you're free to decide. Everything else we bring as alibis, that's all. They can't stop you from going on your own.

There was discrimination on account of different nationalities. They did discriminate, no doubt about it. There is a Greek organization in America called AHEPA, the American Hellenic Association. I was chairman of that, president in my city for about a year. At that time, as I told you before, there was too many Greek boys from twelve years old to thirty. Well, naturally they would be interested in girls. They couldn't speak English, and they certainly didn't meet the right kind of girls anyway, and they created a very ill name in the United States. With so much against 'em at that time they decided that they couldn't get justice anywhere, even if they were right. Certain people began to think what should we do? They organized this AHEPA. They did that to offset those impressions that the American people had. This same thing happened with all the nationalities at that time. Naturally, there were some obstacles, but listen, we have rainy days and we have sunny days and how we gonna know the difference if we didn't have them both?

You were born poor, so what? But it's all up to you. You're free to do what you want. You've got to gain it within the law. Not only political law, but natural law. You've got to know the truth. This is what I say to my daughters because they expect things to be easy; they don't want to sacrifice much. We spoiled 'em. There is actually nothing in life that you cannot do if you plan it, but it takes time.

## STUDY QUESTIONS

1. Compare Gerros's account of himself with those of Lee Ki Chuck (chapter 1) and James Seilsopour (chapter 7). What notions of American customs and values do the three accounts share? How do their attitudes toward America differ? To what extent does what happens to them in America derive from their preexisting ideas about America? What external events intervene to produce experiences different from what each had anticipated?

2. What seem to have been the most important formative influences on Gerros's habits and attitudes? To what extent are those influences derived from the culture from which he came? To what extent does the immigration experience itself lead to specific expectations, drives, and needs?

3. Of which of his successes does Gerros seem proudest? What aspects of negotiations seem to give him the most pleasure?

4. What values seem most powerfully to inform Gerros's actions? What sort of advice do you think he would give present-day immigrants? How helpful would that

advice be in today's contexts? What do you think are the basic differences between the problems faced by Gerros's generation and yours?

# Jimmy Santiago Baca

Born in New Mexico in 1952, Jimmy Santiago Baca wrote the poems in his collection *Immigrants in Our Own Land* (1979), from which this poem is taken, while he was in prison. His most recent volume, *Martin & Meditations on the South Valley* (1987), consists of two long narrative poems. He now lives on a small farm outside Albuquerque.

The following poem examines a popular cliché about immigrants from Mexico, literalizing it in order to ridicule it.

## SO MEXICANS ARE TAKING JOBS FROM AMERICANS

O Yes? Do they come on horses
with rifles, and say,
               Ese gringo, gimmee your job?
And do you, gringo, take off your ring,
drop your wallet into a blanket                      5
spread over the ground, and walk away?

I hear Mexicans are taking your jobs away.
Do they sneak into town at night,
and as you're walking home with a whore,
do they mug you, a knife at your throat,           10
saying, I want your job?

Even on TV, an asthmatic leader
crawls turtle heavy, leaning on an assistant,
and from a nest of wrinkles on his face,
a tongue paddles through flashing waves          15
of lightbulbs, of cameramen, rasping
"They're taking our jobs away."

Well, I've gone about trying to find them,
asking just where the hell are these fighters.

The rifles I hear sound in the night                                    20
are white farmers shooting blacks and browns
whose ribs I see jutting out
and starving children,
I see the poor marching for a little work,
I see small white farmers selling out                                   25
to clean-suited farmers living in New York,
who've never been on a farm,
don't know the look of a hoof or the smell
of a woman's body bending all day long in fields.

I see this, and I hear only a few people                                30
got all the money in this world, the rest
count their pennies to buy bread and butter.

Below that cool green sea of money,
millions and millions of people fight to live,
search for pearls in the darkest depths                                 35
of their dreams, hold their breath for years
trying to cross poverty to just having something.

The children are dead already. We are killing them,
that is what America should be saying;
on TV, in the streets, in offices, should be saying,
    "We aren't giving the children a chance to live."                   40

    Mexicans are taking our jobs, they say instead.
    What they really say is, let them die,
    and the children too.

## STUDY QUESTIONS

1. How many different ways does the poem literalize the notion that jobs are being
   "taken" from Americans? Which literalization seems to you the most effective?
   Why?

2. Describe the STRUCTURE of the poem. Where does the TONE change? At what point
   does the poem begin to concentrate on human needs? on the lives of the disadvantaged? How many different ways does the poem use the principle of contrast?

3. Which details in the poem are the most vivid? What strategies account for the
   vividness? Which IMAGES seem to you especially effective?

4. What value system does the poem accuse America of having? What value system does the poem itself support?

# Mari Evans

B orn in Toledo, Ohio, Mari Evans now lives in Indianapolis. She attended the University of Toledo, has taught at Indiana University, Purdue, Northwestern, Cornell, and Washington University in St.Louis, and has also worked as a television writer, producer, and director. She is the author of two plays, four books of poetry, and two children's books, and she is the editor of *Black Women Writers 1950–80: A Critical Perspective* (1984). She has won many awards for her writing, including a MacDowell Fellowship, a Copeland Fellowship, a John Hay Whitney Fellowship, a Yaddo Fellowship, and a National Endowment for the Arts Award.

The following poem describes the quiet desperation of the lives of women as they ritualistically wait for the weekly pay envelopes.

## THE FRIDAY LADIES OF THE PAY ENVELOPE

they take
stations
in the broken doorways
the narrow alcoves
and the flaking                                    5
gray paint
the rainandsoot paint
clings
to their limpworn
sweaters clings                                   10
hair and limpworn souls they
wait
for the sullen
triumph
for the crumpled lifeblood                        15
wet with reluctance
thrust

at them
in the direction
of them                                            20
        of their reaching
of their drydamp
        limpworn hands


## STUDY QUESTIONS

1. What details are we given about the SETTING? In what ways does the setting contribute to the MOOD of the poem? to its THEME? Why are the "ladies" described collectively rather than individually?

2. Describe the TONE of the poem. How do you account for the intensity of the poem? Why are certain words ("limpworn," for example) repeated?

3. Why does the arrival of the pay envelope involve "sullen / triumph" (lines 13–14)? Why are the envelopes "thrust / at them" (ll. 17–18)? Why are the envelopes "wet with reluctance" (l. 16)?

4. What ATTITUDE does the poem take toward the "ladies"? What strategies are used to produce in readers an attitude toward them? What attitude does the poem take toward the men who bring the envelopes? Why are the women said to "take / stations" (ll. 1–2)?


# Toni Cade Bambara


D ancer, teacher, critic, editor, activist, and writer, Toni Cade Bambara was born in New York and educated there (B.A. from Queens College, M.A. from City College of the City University of New York). She has published two collections of short stories—*Gorilla, My Love* (1972) and *The Sea Birds Are Still Alive* (1977)—and a novel, *The Salt Eaters* (1980).

This hilarious and radically serious, loving, and bitter story is masterfully told in uncondescending, witty, poetic Black English.

# THE LESSON

Back in the days when everyone was old and stupid or young and foolish and me and Sugar were the only ones just right, this lady moved on our block with nappy hair and proper speech and no makeup. And quite naturally we laughed at her, laughed the way we did at the junk man who went about his business like he was some big-time president and his sorry-ass horse his secretary. And we kinda hated her too, hated the way we did the winos who cluttered up our parks and pissed on our handball walls and stank up our hallways and stairs so you couldn't halfway play hide-and-seek without a goddamn gas mask. Miss Moore was her name. The only woman on the block with no first name. And she was black as hell, cept for her feet, which were fish-white and spooky. And she was always planning these boring-ass things for us to do, us being my cousin, mostly, who lived on the block cause we all moved North the same time and to the same apartment then spread out gradual to breathe. And our parents would yank our heads into some kinda shape and crisp up our clothes so we'd be presentable for travel with Miss Moore, who always looked like she was going to church, though she never did. Which is just one of things the grown-ups talked about when they talked behind her back like a dog. But when she came calling with some sachet she'd sewed up or some gingerbread she'd made or some book, why then they'd all be too embarrassed to turn her down and we'd get handed over all spruced up. She'd been to college and said it was only right that she should take responsibility for the young ones' education, and she not even related by marriage or blood. So they'd go for it. Specially Aunt Gretchen. She was the main gofer in the family. You got some ole dumb shit foolishness you want somebody to go for, you send for Aunt Gretchen. She been screwed into the go-along for so long, it's a blood-deep natural thing with her. Which is how she got saddled with me and Sugar and Junior in the first place while our mothers were in a la-de-da apartment up the block having a good ole time.

So this one day Miss Moore rounds us all up at the mailbox and it's puredee hot and she's knockin herself out about arithmetic. And school suppose to let up in summer I heard, but she don't never let up. And the starch in my pinafore scratching the shit outta me and I'm really hating this nappy-head bitch and her goddamn college degree. I'd much rather go to the pool or to the show where it's cool. So me and Sugar leaning on the mailbox being surly, which is a Miss Moore word. And Flyboy checking out what everybody brought for lunch. And Fat Butt already wasting his peanut-butter-and jelly sandwich like the pig he is. And Junebug punchin on Q.T.'s arm for potato chips. And Rosie Giraffe shifting from one hip to the other waiting for somebody to step on her foot or ask her if she from Georgia so she can kick ass, perferably Mercedes'. And Miss Moore asking us do we know what money is, like we a bunch of retards. I mean real money, she say, like it's only poker chips or monopoly papers we lay on the grocer. So right away I'm tired of this and say so. And would much rather snatch Sugar and go to the Sunset and terrorize the West Indian kids and take their hair ribbons and their money too. And Miss Moore files that remark away for next week's lesson on brotherhood, I can tell. And finally I say we oughta get to the subway cause it's cooler and besides we might meet some cute boys. Sugar done swiped her mama's lipstick, so we ready.

So we heading down the street and she's boring us silly about what things cost and what our parents make and how much goes for rent and how money ain't divided up right in this country. And then she gets to the part about we all poor and live in the slums, which I don't feature. And I'm ready to speak on that, but she steps out in the street and hails two cabs just like that. Then she hustles half the crew in with her and hands me a five-dollar bill and tells me to calculate 10 percent tip for the driver. And we're off. Me and Sugar and Junebug and Flyboy hangin out the window and hollering to everybody, putting lipstick on each other cause Flyboy a faggot anyway, and making farts with our sweaty armpits. But I'm mostly trying to figure how to spend this money. But they all fascinated with the meter ticking and June-bug starts laying bets as to how much it'll read when Flyboy can't hold his breath no more. Then Sugar lays bets as to how much it'll be when we get there. So I'm stuck. Don't nobody want to go for my plan, which is to jump out at the next light and run off to the first bar-b-que we can find. Then the driver tells us to get the hell out cause we there already. And the meter reads eighty-five cents. And I'm stalling to figure out the tip and Sugar say give him a dime. And I decide he don't need it bad as I do, so later for him. But then he tries to take off with Junebug foot still in the door so we talk about his mama something ferocious. Then we check out that we on Fifth Avenue and everybody dressed up in stockings. One lady in a fur coat, hot as it is. White folks crazy.

"This is the place," Miss Moore say, presenting it to us in the voice she   4
uses at the museum. "Let's look in the windows before we go in."

"Can we steal?" Sugar asks very serious like she's getting the ground   5
rules squared away before she plays. "I beg your pardon," say Miss Moore, and we fall out. So she leads us around the windows of the toy store and me and Sugar screamin, "This is mine, that's mine, I gotta have that, that was made for me, I was born for that," till Big Butt drowns us out.

"Hey, I'm goin to buy that there."   6

"That there? You don't even know what it is, stupid."   7

"I do so," he say punchin on Rosie Giraffe. "It's a microscope."   8

"Whatcha gonna do with a microscope, fool?"   9

"Look at things."   10

"Like what, Ronald?" ask Miss Moore. And Big Butt ain't got the first   11 notion. So here go Miss Moore gabbing about the thousands of bacteria in a drop of water and the somethinorother in a speck of blood and the million and one living things in the air around us is invisible to the naked eye. And what she say that for? Junebug go to town on that "naked" and we rolling. Then Miss Moore ask what it cost. So we all jam into the window smudgin it up and the price tag say $300. So then she ask how long'd take for Big Butt and Junebug to save up their allowances. "Too long," I say. "Yeh," adds Sugar, "outgrown it by that time." And Miss Moore say no, you never outgrow learning instruments. "Why, even medical students and interns and," blah, blah, blah. And we ready to choke Big Butt for bringing it up in the first damn place.

"This here costs four hundred eighty dollars," say Rosie Giraffe. So we pile up all over her to see what she pointin out. My eyes tell me it's a chunk of glass cracked with something heavy, and different-color inks dripped into the splits, then the whole thing put into a oven or something. But the $480 it don't make sense.

"That's a paperweight made of semi-precious stones fused together under tremendous pressure," she explains slowly, with her hands doing the mining and all the factory work.

"So what's a paperweight?" asks Rosie Giraffe.

"To weigh paper with, dumbbell," say Flyboy, the wise man from the East.

"Not exactly," say Miss Moore, which is what she say when you warm or way off too. "It's to weigh paper down so it won't scatter and make your desk untidy." So right away me and Sugar curtsy to each other and then to Mercedes who is more the tidy type.

"We don't keep paper on top of the desk in my class," say Junebug, figuring Miss Moore crazy or lyin one.

"At home, then," she say. "Don't you have a calendar and a pencil case and a blotter and a letter-opener on your desk at home where you do your homework?" And she know damn well what our homes look like cause she nosys around in them every chance she gets.

"I don't even have a desk," say Junebug. "Do we?"

"No. And I don't get no homework neither," say Big Butt.

"And I don't even have a home," say Flyboy like he do at school to keep the white folks off his back and sorry for him. Send this poor kid to camp posters, is his specialty.

"I do," says Mercedes. "I have a box of stationery on my desk and a picture of my cat. My godmother bought the stationery and the desk. There's a big rose on each sheet and the envelopes smell like roses."

"Who wants to know about your smelly-ass stationery," say Rosie Giraffe fore I can get my two cents in.

"It's important to have a work area all your own so that . . ."

"Will you look at this sailboat, please," say Flyboy, cuttin her off and pointin to the thing like it was his. So once again we tumble all over each other to gaze at this magnificent thing in the toy store which is just big enough to maybe sail two kittens across the pond if you strap them to the posts tight. We all start reciting the price tag like we in assembly. "Handcrafted sailboat of fiberglass at one thousand one hundred ninety-five dollars."

"Unbelievable," I hear myself say and am really stunned. I read it again 26 for myself just in case the group recitation put me in a trance. Same thing. For some reason this pisses me off. We look at Miss Moore and she lookin at us, waiting for I dunno what.

Who'd pay all that when you can buy a sailboat set for a quarter at 27 Pop's, a tube of blue for a dime, and a ball of string for eight cents? "It must have a motor and a whole lot else besides," I say. "My sailboat cost me about fifty cents."

"But will it take water?" say Mercedes with her smart ass. 28

"Took mine to Alley Pond Park once," say Flyboy. "String broke. Lost 29 it. Pity."

"Sailed mine in Central Park and it keeled over and sank. Had to ask 30 my father for another dollar."

"And you got the strap," laugh Big Butt. "The jerk didn't even have a 31 string on it. My old man wailed on his behind."

Little Q.T. was staring hard at the sailboat and you could see he wanted 32 it bad. But he too little and somebody'd just take it from him. So what the hell. "This boat for kids, Miss Moore?"

"Parents silly to buy something like that just to get all broke up," say 33 Rosie Giraffe.

"That much money it should last forever," I figure. 34

"My father'd buy it for me if I wanted it." 35

"Your father, my ass," say Rosie Giraffe getting a chance to finally push 36 Mercedes.

"Must be rich people shop here," say Q.T. 37

"You are a very bright boy," say Flyboy. "What was your first clue?" 38 And he rap him on the head with the back of his knuckles, since Q.T. the only one he could get away with. Though Q.T. liable to come up behind you years later and get his licks in when you half expect it.

"What I want to know," I says to Miss Moore though I never talk to 39 her, I wouldn't give the bitch that satisfaction, "is how much a real boat costs? I figure a thousand'd get you a yacht any day."

"Why don't you check that out," she says, "and report back to the group?" 40 Which really pains my ass. If you gonna mess up a perfectly good swim day least you could do is have some answers. "Let's go in," she say like she got something up her sleeve. Only she don't lead the way. So me and Sugar turn the corner to where the entrance is, but when we get there I kinda hang back. Not that I'm scared, what's there to be afraid of, just a toy store. But I feel funny, shame. But what I got to be shamed about? Got as much right to go in as anybody. But somehow I can't seem to get hold of the door, so I step away for Sugar to lead. But she hangs back too. And I look at her and she looks at me and this is ridiculous. I mean, damn, I have never ever been shy about doing nothing or going nowhere. But then Mercedes steps up and then Rosie Giraffe and Big Butt crowd in behind and shove, and next thing we all stuffed into the doorway with only Mercedes squeezing past us, smoothing out her jumper and walking right down the aisle. Then the rest of us tumble in like a glued-together jigsaw done all wrong. And people lookin at us. And it's like the time me and Sugar crashed into the Catholic church on a dare. But once we got in there and everything so hushed and holy and the candles and the bowin and the handkerchiefs on all the drooping heads, I just couldn't go through with the plan. Which was for me to run up to the altar and do a tap dance while Sugar played the nose flute and messed around in the holy water. And Sugar kept givin me the elbow. Then later teased me so bad I tied her up in the shower and turned it on and locked her in. And she'd be there till this day if Aunt Gretchen hadn't finally figured I was lyin about the boarder takin a shower.

Same thing in the store. We all walkin on tiptoe and hardly touchin the games and puzzles and things. And I watched Miss Moore who is steady watchin us like she waitin for a sign. Like Mama Drewery watches the sky and sniffs the air and takes note of just how much slant is in the bird formation. Then me and Sugar bump smack into each other, so busy gazing at the toys, 'specially the sailboat. But we don't laugh and go into our fat-lady bump-stomach routine. We just stare at that price tag. Then Sugar run a finger over the whole boat. And I'm jealous and want to hit her. Maybe not her, but I sure want to punch somebody in the mouth. 41

"Watcha bring us here for, Miss Moore?" 42

"You sound angry, Sylvia. Are you mad about something?" Givin me one of them grins like she tellin a grown-up joke that never turns out to be funny. And she's lookin very closely at me like maybe she plannin to do my portrait from memory. I'm mad, but I won't give her that satisfaction. So I slouch around the store bein very bored and say, "Let's go." 43

Me and Sugar at the back of the train watchin the tracks whizzin by large then small then gettin gobbled up in the dark. I'm thinkin about this tricky toy I saw in the store. A clown that somersaults on a bar then does chin-ups just cause you yank lightly at his leg. Cost $35. I could see me askin my mother for a $35 birthday clown. "You wanna who that costs what?" she'd say, cocking her head to the side to get a better view of the hole in my head. Thirty-five dollars could buy new bunk beds for Junior and Gretchen's boy. Thirty-five dollars and the whole household could visit Grandaddy Nelson in the country. Thirty-five dollars would pay for the rent and the piano bill too. Who are these people that spend that much for performing clowns and $1,000 for toy sailboats? What kinda work they do and how they live and how come we ain't in on it? Where we are is who we are, Miss Moore always pointin out. But it don't necessarily have to be that way, she always adds then waits for somebody to say that poor people have to wake up and demand their share of the pie and don't none of us know what kind of pie she talkin 44 about in the first damn place. But she ain't so smart cause I still got her four dollars from the taxi and she sure ain't gettin it. Messin up my day with this shit. Sugar nudges me in my pocket and winks.

Miss Moore lines us up in front of the mailbox where we started from, 45 seem like years ago, and I got a headache for thinkin so hard. And we lean all over each other so we can hold up under the draggy-ass lecture she always finishes us off with at the end before we thank her for borin us to tears. But she just looks at us like she readin tea leaves. Finally she say, "Well, what did you think of F.A.O. Schwarz?"

Rosie Giraffe mumbles, "White folks crazy." 46

"I'd like to go there again when I get my birthday money," says Mercedes, 47 and we shove her out the pack so she has to lean on the mailbox by herself.

"I'd like a shower. Tiring day," say Flyboy. 48

Then Sugar surprises me by sayin, "You know, Miss Moore, I don't 49 think all of us here put together eat in a year what that sailboat costs." And Miss Moore lights up like somebody goosed her. "And?" she say, urging Sugar on. Only I'm standin on her foot so she don't continue.

"Imagine for a minute what kind of society it is in which some people 50 can spend on a toy what it would cost to feed a family of six or seven. What do you think?"

"I think," say Sugar pushing me off her feet like she never done before, 51 cause I whip her ass in a minute, "that this is not much of a democracy if you ask me. Equal chance to pursue happiness means an equal crack at the dough, don't it?" Miss Moore is besides herself and I am disgusted with Sugar's treachery. So I stand on her foot one more time to see if she'll shove me. She shuts up, and Miss Moore looks at me, sorrowfully I'm thinkin. And somethin weird is goin on, I can feel it in my chest.

"Anybody else learn anything today?" lookin dead at me. I walk away 52 and Sugar has to run to catch up and don't even seem to notice when I shrug her arm off my shoulder.

"Well, we got four dollars anyway," she says. 53

"Uh hunh." 54

"We could go to Hascombs and get half a chocolate layer and then go to 55 the Sunset and still have plenty money for potato chips and ice-cream sodas."

"Uh hunh." 56

"Race you to Hascombs," she say. 57

We start down the block and she gets ahead which is O.K. by me cause 58 I'm going to the West End and then over to the Drive to think this day through. She can run if she want to and even run faster. But ain't nobody gonna beat me at nuthin.

## STUDY QUESTIONS

1. What does the opening sentence tell you about the ATTITUDE of the SPEAKER "back in [those] days" *and* the attitude of the speaker at the time of the writing or telling of the story? What else do you learn in the very first paragraph about "Miss Moore"? about the neighborhood? about the speaker's family? When do you know the speaker is a girl? that her name is Sylvia?

2. In paragraph 2, the speaker uses a "Miss Moore word": "surly." Can you find any other Miss Moore words in the story? What does this "double VOICE" suggest about what may have happened to the speaker since the time of the story? What effect does the double voice have (even if you did not notice the specific words and identify their "source" at the time you were first reading the story)?

3. How are the rest of the youngsters introduced into the story?

4. What strikes the speaker first about the "white folks" who are in the American society on Fifth Avenue?

5. Early in the story you may be amused by the youngsters' naïveté, and perhaps a little appalled at their amorality, but there seems to be a shift in the story's or the reader's relationship to the attitudes of the children when the $480 paperweight is introduced. Describe that shift. How long does it last? What is its effect? implication?

6. When the speaker reads for herself the price of the toy model sailboat, she says, "For some reason this pisses me off"; what's the reason? Then, "We look at Miss Moore and she lookin at us, waiting for I dunno what"; what is she waiting for?

7. Describe the speaker's hesitation in entering the store and her unarticulated reasons. What previous experience does she compare the children's behavior with when they first enter the store (par. 40)? Why does she feel like punching somebody in the mouth (par. 41)?

8. What is "the lesson"?

# Richard Dokey

A native of Stockton, California, and graduate of the University of California, Berkeley, Richard Dokey has worked as a laborer on a railroad, in a shipyard, for a soft drink bottling company, and for an ink factory, but he is now a teacher.

His works include *August Heat* (1982), *Funeral: A Play* (1982), and *Sánchez and Other Stories* (1981).

This "generation gap" story is seen from the point of view of the older generation.

# SÁNCHEZ

That summer the son of Juan Sánchez went to work for the Flotill Cannery in Stockton. Juan drove with him to the valley in the old Ford.

While they drove, the boy, whose name was Jesús, told him of the greatness of the cannery, of the great aluminum buildings, the marvelous machines, and the belts of cans that never stopped running. He told him of the building on one side of the road where the cans were made and how the cans ran in a metal tube across the road to the cannery. He described the food machines, the sanitary precautions. He laughed when he spoke of the labeling. His voice was serious about the money.

When they got to Stockton, Jesús directed him to the central district of town, the skid row where the boy was to live while he worked for the Flotill. It was a cheap hotel on Center Street. The room smelled. There was a table with one chair. The floor was stained like the floor of a public urinal and the bed was soiled, as were the walls. There were no drapes on the windows. A pall spread out from the single light bulb overhead that was worked with a length of grimy string.

"I will not stay much in the room," Jesús said, seeing his father's face. "It is only for sleep. I will be working overtime, too. There is also the entertainment."

Jesús led him from the room and they went out into the street. Next to the hotel there was a vacant lot where a building had stood. The hole which was left had that recent, peculiar look of uprootedness. There were the remains of the foundation, the broken flooring, and the cracked bricks of tired red to which the gray blotches of mortar clung like dried phlegm. But the ground had not yet taken on the opaqueness of wear that the air and sun give it. It gleamed dully in the light and held to itself where it had been torn, as earth does behind a plow. Juan studied the hole for a time; then they walked up Center Street to Main, passing other empty lots, and then moved east toward Hunter Street. At the corner of Hunter and Main a wrecking crew was at work. An iron ball was suspended from the end of a cable and a tall machine swung the ball up and back and then whipped it forward against the building. The ball was very thick-looking, and when it struck the wall the building trembled, spurted dust, and seemed to cringe inward. The vertical lines of the building had gone awry. Juan shook each time the iron struck the wall.

"They are tearing down the old buildings," Jesús explained. "Redevelopment," he pronounced. "Even my building is to go someday." 6

Juan looked at his son. "And what of the men?" he asked. "Where do the men go when there are no buildings?" 7

Jesús, who was a head taller than his father, looked down at him and then shrugged in that Mexican way, the head descending and cocking while the shoulders rise as though on puppet strings. *"Quien sabe?"*[1] 8

"And the large building there?" Juan said, looking across the rows of parked cars in Hunter Square. "The one whose roof rubs the sky. Of what significance?" 9

"That is the new courthouse," Jesús said. 10

"There are no curtains on the windows." 11

"They do not put curtains on such windows," Jesús explained. 12

"No," sighed Juan, "that is true." 13

They walked north on Hunter past the new Bank of America and entered an old building. They stood to one side of the entrance. Jesús smiled proudly and inhaled the stale air. 14

"This is the entertainment," he said. 15

Juan looked about. A bar was at his immediate left, and a bald man in a soiled apron stood behind it. Beyond the bar there were many thick-wooded tables covered with green material. Men crouched over them and cone-shaped lights hung low from the ceiling casting broad cones of light downward upon the men and tables. Smoke drifted and rolled in the light and pursued the men when they moved quickly. There was the breaking noise of balls striking together, the hard wooden rattle of the cues in the racks upon the wall, the humming slither of the scoring disks along the loose wires overhead, the explosive cursing of the men. The room was warm and dirty. Juan shook his head. 16

"I have become proficient at the game," Jesús said. 17

"This is the entertainment," Juan said, still moving his head. 18

Jesús turned and walked outside. Juan followed. The boy pointed across the parked cars past the courthouse to a marquee on Main Street. "There are also motion pictures," Jesús said. 19

Juan had seen a movie as a young man working in the fields near Fresno. He had understood no English then. He sat with his friends in the leather seats that had gum under the arms and watched the images move upon the white canvas. The images were dressed in expensive clothes. There was laughing and dancing. One of the men did kissing with two very beautiful women, taking turns with each when the other was absent. This had embarrassed Juan, the embracing and unhesitating submission of the women with so many unfamiliar people to watch. Juan loved his wife, was very tender and gentle with her before she died. He never went to another motion pic- 20

1. Who knows?

ture, even after he had learned English, and this kept him from the Spanish films as well.

"We will go to the cannery now," Jesús said, taking his father's arm. "I will show you the machines." 21

Juan permitted himself to be led away, and they moved back past the bank to where the men were destroying the building. A ragged hole, like a wound, had been opened in the wall. Juan stopped and watched. The iron ball came forward tearing at the hole, enlarging it, exposing the empty interior space that had once been a room. The floor of the room teetered at a precarious angle. The wood was splintered and very dry in the noon light. 22

"I do not think I will go to the cannery," Juan said. 23

The boy looked at his father like a child who has made a toy out of string and bottle caps only to have it ignored. 24

"But it is honorable work," Jesús said, suspecting his father. "And it pays well." 25

"Honor," Juan said. "Honor is a serious matter. It is not a question of honor. You are a man now. All that is needed is a room and a job at the Flotill. Your father is tired, that is all." 26

"You are disappointed," Jesús said, hanging his head. 27

"No," Juan said. "I am beyond disappointment. You are my son. Now you have a place in the world. You have the Flotill." 28

Nothing more was said, and they walked to the car. Juan got in behind the wheel. Jesús stood beside the door, his arms at his sides, the fingers spread. Juan looked up at him. The boy's eyes were big. 29

"You are my son," Juan said, "and I love you. Do not have disappointment. I am not of the Flotill. Seeing the machines would make it worse. You understand, *niño?*"[2] 30

"*Sí*, Papa," Jesús said. He put a hand on his father's shoulder. 31

"It is a strange world, *niñito*," Juan said. 32

"I will earn money. I will buy a red car and visit you. All in Twin Pines will be envious of the son of Sánchez, and they will say that Juan Sánchez has a son of purpose." 33

"Of course, Jesús *mío*," Juan said. He bent and placed his lips against the boy's hand. "I will look for the bright car. I will write regardless." He smiled, showing yellowed teeth. "Goodbye, *querido*," he said. He started the car, raced the engine once too high, and drove off up the street. 34

When Juan Sánchez returned to Twin Pines, he drove the old Ford to the top of Bear Mountain and pushed it over. He then proceeded systematically to burn all that was of importance to him, all that was of nostalgic value, and all else that meant nothing in itself, like the extra chest of drawers he had kept after his wife's death, the small table in the bedroom, and the faded mahogany stand in which he kept his pipe and tobacco and which sat next to the stuffed chair in the front room. He broke all the dishes, cups, plates, 35

2. Son. *Niñito:* dear son. *Querido:* dear one.

discarded all the cooking and eating utensils in the same way. The fire rose in the blue wind carrying dust wafers of ash in quick, breathless spirals and then released them in a panoply of diluted smoke, from which they drifted and spun and fell like burnt snow. The forks, knives, and spoons became very black with a flaky crust of oxidized metal. Then Juan burned his clothing, all that was unnecessary, and the smoke dampened and took on a thick smell. Finally he threw his wife's rosary into the flames. It was a cheap one, made of wood, and disappeared immediately. He went into his room then and lay down on the bed. He went to sleep.

When he woke, it was dark and cool. He stepped outside, urinated, and then returned, shutting the door. The darkness was like a mammoth held breath, and he felt very awake listening to the beating of his heart. He would not be able to sleep now, and so he lay awake thinking. 36

He thought of his village in Mexico, the baked white clay of the small houses spread like little forts against the stillness of the bare mountains, the men with their great wide hats, their wide, white pants, and their naked, brown-skinned feet, splayed against the fine dust of the road. He saw the village cistern and the women all so big and slow, always with child, enervated by the earth and the unbearable sun, the enervation passing into their very wombs like the acceptance, slow, silent blood. The men walked bent as though carrying the air or sky, slept against the buildings in the shade like old dogs, ate dry, hot food that dried them inside and seemed to bake the moisture from the flesh, so that the men and women while still young had faces like eroded fields and fingers like stringy, empty stream beds. It was a hard land. It took the life of his father and mother before he was twelve and the life of his aunt, with whom he then lived, before he was sixteen. 37

When he was seventeen he went to Mexicali because he had heard much of America and the money to be obtained there. They took him in a truck with other men to work in the fields around Bakersfield, then in the fields near Fresno. On his return to Mexicali he met La Belleza, as he came to call her: loveliness. He married her when he was nineteen and she only fifteen. The following year she had a baby girl. It was stillborn and the birth almost killed her, for the doctor said the passage was oversmall. The doctor cautioned him (warned him, really) La Belleza could not have children and live, and he went outside into the moonlight and wept. 38

He had heard much of the liveliness of the Sierra Nevada above what was called the Mother Lode, and because he feared the land, believed almost that it possessed the power to kill him—as it had killed his mother and father, his aunt, was, in fact, slow killing so many of his people—he wanted to run away from it to the high white cold of the California mountains, where he believed his heart would grow, his blood run and, perhaps, the passage of La Belleza might open. Two years later he was taken in the trucks to Stockton in the San Joaquin Valley to pick tomatoes, and he saw the Sierra Nevada above the Mother Lode. 39

It was from a distance, of course, and in the summer, so that there was no snow. But when he returned he told La Belleza about the blueness of the 40 mountains in the warm, still dawn, the extension of them, the aristocracy of their unmoving height, and that they were only fifty miles away from where he had stood.

He worked very hard now and saved his money. He took La Belleza 41 back to his village, where he owned the white clay house of his father. It was cheaper to live there while he waited, fearing the sun, the dust, and the dry, airless silence, for the money to accumulate. That fall La Belleza became pregnant again by an accident of passion and the pregnancy was very difficult. In the fifth month the doctor—who was an atheist—said that the baby would have to be taken or else the mother would die. The village priest, a very loud, dramatic man—an educated man who took pleasure in striking a pose—proclaimed the wrath of God in the face of such sacrilege. It was the child who must live, the priest cried. The pregnancy must go on. There was the immortal soul of the child to consider. But Juan decided for the atheist doctor, who did take the child. La Belleza lost much blood. At one point her heart had stopped beating. When the child was torn from its mother and Juan saw that it was a boy, he ran out of the clay house of his father and up the dusty road straight into a hideous red moon. He cursed the earth, the sky. He cursed his village, himself, the soulless indifference of the burnt mountains. He cursed God.

Juan was very afraid now, and though it cost more money, he had him- 42 self tied by the atheist doctor so that he could never again put the life of La Belleza in danger, for the next time, he knew with certainty, would kill her.

The following summer he went again on the trucks to the San Joaquin 43 Valley. The mountains were still there, high and blue in the quiet dawn, turned to a milky pastel by the heat swirls and haze of midday. Sometimes at night he stepped outside the shacks in which the men were housed and faced the darkness. It was tragic to be so close to what you wanted, he would think, and be unable to possess it. So strong was the feeling in him, particularly during the hot, windless evenings, that he sometimes went with the other men into Stockton, where he stood on the street corners of skid row and talked, though he did not get drunk on cheap wine or go to the whores, as did the other men. Nor did he fight.

They rode in old tilted trucks covered with canvas and sat on rude benches 44 staring out over the slats of the tail gate. The white glare of headlights crawled up and lay upon them, waiting to pass. They stared over the whiteness. When the lights swept out and by, the glass of the side windows shone. Behind the windows sometimes there would be the ghost flash of an upturned face, before the darkness clamped shut. Also, if one of the men had a relative who lived in the area, there was the opportunity to ride in a car.

He had done so once. He had watched the headlights of the car pale, 45 then whiten the back of one of the trucks. He saw the faces of the men turned outward and the looks on the faces that seemed to float upon the whiteness of the light. The men sat forward, arms on knees, and looked over the glare into the darkness. After that he always rode in the trucks.

When he returned to his village after that season's harvest, he knew they 46 could wait no longer. He purchased a dress of silk for La Belleza and in a secondhand store bought an American suit for himself. He had worked hard, sold his father's house, saved all his money, and on a bright day in early September they crossed the border at Mexicali and caught the Greyhound for Fresno.

Juan got up from his bed to go outside. He stood looking up at the stars.   47
The stars were pinned to the darkness, uttering little flickering cries of light, and as always he was moved by the nearness and profusion of their agony. His mother had told him the stars were a kind of purgatory in which souls burned in cold, silent repentance. He had wondered after her death if the earth too were not a star burning in loneliness, and he could never look at them later without thinking this and believing that the earth must be the brightest of all stars. He walked over to the remains of the fire. A dull heat came from the ashes and a column of limp smoke rose and then bent against the night wind. He studied the ashes for a time and then looked over the tall pine shapes to the southern sky. It was there all right. He could feel the dry char of its heat, that deeper, dryer burning. He imagined it, of course. But it was there nevertheless. He went back into the cabin and lay down, but now his thoughts were only of La Belleza and the beautiful Sierra Nevada.

From Fresno all the way up the long valley to Stockton they had been   48
full with pride and expectation. They had purchased oranges and chocolate bars and they ate them laughing. The other people on the bus looked at them, shook their heads, and slept or read magazines. He and La Belleza gazed out the window at the land.

In Stockton they were helped by a man named Eugenio Mendez. Juan   49
had met him while picking tomatoes in the delta. Eugenio had eight children and a very fat but very kind and tolerant wife named Anilla. He had helped them find a cheap room off Center Street, where they stayed while determining their next course of action. Eugenio had access to a car, and it was he who drove them finally to the mountains.

It was a day like no other day in his life: to be sitting in the car with La   50
Belleza, to be in this moving car with his Belleza heading straight toward the high, lovely mountains. The car traveled from the flatness of the valley into the rolling brown swells of the foothills, where hundreds of deciduous and evergreen oaks grew, their puffballs shapes like still pictures of exploding holiday rockets, only green, but spreading up and out and then around and down in nearly perfect canopies. At Jackson the road turned and began an immediate, constant climb upward.

It was as though his dream about it had materialized. He had never seen   51
so many trees, great with dignity: pines that had gray bark twisted and stringy like hemp; others whose bark resembled dry, flat ginger cookies fastened with black glue about a drum, and others whose bark pulled easily away; and those called redwoods, standing stiff and tall, amber-hued with straight rolls of bark as thick as his fist, flinging out high above great arms of green. And the earth, rich red, as though the blood of scores of Indians had just flowed

there and dried. Dark patches of shadow stunned with light, blue flowers, orange flowers, birds, even deer. They saw them all on that first day.

"*¿A dónde vamos?*" Eugenio had asked. "Where are we going?" 52

"*Bellísima*," Juan replied. "Into much loveliness." 53

They did not reach Twin Pines that day. But on their return a week 54 later they inquired in Jackson about the opportunity of buying land or a house in the mountains. The man, though surprised, told them of the saw-mill town of Twin Pines, where there were houses for sale.

Their continued luck on that day precipitated the feeling in Juan that it 55 was indeed the materialization of a dream. He had been able in all those years to save two thousand dollars, and a man had a small shack for sale at the far edge of town. He looked carefully at Juan, at La Belleza and Eugenio and said "One thousand dollars," believing they could never begin to possess such a sum. When Juan handed him the money, the man was so struck that he made out a bill of sale. Juan Sanchez and his wife had their home in the Sierra.

When Juan saw the cabin close up, he knew the man had stolen their 56 money. It was small, the roof slanted to one side, the door would not close evenly. The cabin was gradually falling downhill. But it was theirs and he could, with work, repair it. Hurriedly they drove back to Jackson, rented a truck, bought some cheap furniture and hauled it back to the cabin. When they had moved in, Juan brought forth a bottle of whiskey and for the first time in his life proceeded to get truly drunk.

Juan was very happy with La Belleza. She accepted his philosophy com- 57 pletely, understood his need, made it her own. In spite of the people of the town, they created a peculiar kind of joy. And anyway Juan had knowledge about the people.

Twin Pines had been founded, he learned, by one Benjamin Carter, 58 who lived with his daughter in a magnificent house on the hill overlooking town. This Benjamin Carter was a very wealthy man. He had come to the mountains thirty years before to save his marriage, for he had been poor once and loved when he was poor, but then he grew very rich because of oil discovered on his father's Ohio farm and he went away to the city and became incapable of love in the pursuit of money and power. When he at last married the woman whom he had loved, a barrier had grown between them, for Ben Carter had changed but the woman had not. Then the woman became ill and Ben Carter promised her he would take her West, all the way West away from the city so that it could be as it had been in the beginning of their love. But the woman was with child. And so Ben Carter rushed to the California mountains, bought a thousand acres of land, and hurried to build his house before the rain and snows came. He hired many men and the house was completed, except for the interior work and the furnishings. All that winter men he had hired worked in the snow to finish the house while Ben Carter waited with his wife in the city. When it was early spring they set out for California, Ben Carter, his wife, and the doctor, who strongly advised against the rough train trip and the still rougher climb by horse and wagon from Jackson to the house. But the woman wanted the child born properly, so they went. The baby came the evening of their arrival at the house, and the woman died all night having it. It was this Ben Carter who lived with that daughter now in the great house on the hill, possessing her to the point, it was said about his madness, that he had murdered a young man who had shown interest in her.

Juan learned all this from a Mexican servant who had worked at the great house from the beginning, and when he told the story to La Belleza she wept because of its sadness. It was a tragedy of love, she explained, and Juan—soaring to the heights of his imagination—believed that the town, all one hundred souls, had somehow been infected with the tragedy, as they were touched by the shadow of the house itself, which crept directly up the highway each night when the sun set. This was why they left dead chickens and fish on the porch of the cabin or dumped garbage into the yard. He believed he understood something profound and so did nothing about these incidents, which, after all, might have been the pranks of boys. He did not want the infection to touch him, nor the deeper infection of their prejudice because he was Mexican. He was not indifferent. He was simply too much in love with La Belleza and the Sierra Nevada. Finally the incidents stopped.

Now the life of Juan Sánchez entered its most beautiful time. When the first snows fell he became delirious, running through the pines, shouting, rolling on the ground, catching the flakes in his open mouth, bringing them in his cupped hands to rub in the hair of La Belleza, who stood in the doorway of their cabin laughing at him. He danced, made up a song about snowflakes falling on a desert and then a prayer which he addressed to the Virgin of Snowflakes. That night while the snow fluttered like wings against the bedroom window, he celebrated the coming of the whiteness with La Belleza.

He understood that first year in the mountains that love was an enlargement of himself, that it enabled him to be somehow more than he had ever been before, as though certain pores of his senses had only just been opened. Whereas before he had desired the Sierra Nevada for its beauty and contrast to his harsh fatherland, now he came to acquire a love for it, and he loved it as he loved La Belleza; he loved it as a woman. Also in that year he came to realize that there was a fear or dread about such love. It was more a feeling than anything else, something which reached thought now and then, particularly in those last moments before sleep. It was an absolutely minor thing. The primary knowledge was of the manner in which this love seemed to assimilate everything, rejecting all that would not yield. This love was a kind of blindness.

That summer Juan left La Belleza at times to pick the crops of the San Joaquin Valley. He had become good friends with the servant of the big house and this man had access to the owner's car, which he always drove down the mountain in a reckless but confident manner. After that summer

Juan planned also to buy a car, not out of material desire, but simply because he believed this man would one day kill himself, and also because he did not wish to be dependent.

He worked in the walnuts near the town of Linden and again in the tomatoes of the rich delta. He wanted very much to have La Belleza with him, but that would have meant more money and a hotel room in the skid row, and that was impossible because of the pimps and whores, the drunks and criminals and the general despair, which the police always tapped at periodic intervals, as one does a vat of fermenting wine. The skid row was a place his love could not assimilate, but he could not ignore it because so many of his people were lost there. He stayed in the labor camps, which were also bad because of what the men did with themselves, but they were tolerable. He worked hard and as often as he could and gazed at the mountains, which he could always see clearly in the morning light. When tomato season was over he returned to La Belleza.

Though the town would never accept them as equals, it came that summer to tolerate their presence. La Belleza made straw baskets which she sold to the townspeople and which were desired for their beauty and intricacy of design. Juan carved animals, a skill he had acquired from his father, and these were also sold. The activity succeeded so well that Juan took a box of these things to Jackson, where they were readily purchased. The following spring he was able to buy the Ford.

Juan acquired another understanding that second year in the mountains. It was, he believed, that love, his love, was the single greatness of which he was capable, the thing which ennobled him and gave him honor. Love, he became convinced, was his only ability, the one success he had accomplished in a world of insignificance. It was a simple thing, after all, made so painfully simple each time he went to the valley to work with his face toward the ground, every time he saw the men in the fields and listened to their talk and watched them drive off to the skid row at night. After he had acquired this knowledge, the nights he had to spend away from La Belleza were occupied by a new kind of loneliness, as though a part of his body had been separated from the whole. He began also to understand something more of the fear or dread that seemed to trail behind love.

It happened late in the sixth year of their marriage. It was impossible, of course, and he spent many hours at the fire in their cabin telling La Belleza of the impossibility, for the doctor had assured him that all had been well tied. He had conducted himself on the basis of that assumption. But doctors can be wrong. Doctors can make mistakes. La Belleza was with child.

For the first five months the pregnancy was not difficult, and he came almost to believe that indeed the passage of La Belleza would open. He prayed to God. He prayed to the earth and sky. He prayed to the soul of his mother. But after the fifth month the true sickness began and he discarded prayer completely in favor of blasphemy. There was no God and never could be God in the face of such sickness, such unbelievable human sickness. Even when he had her removed to the hospital in Stockton, the doctors could not stop it, but it continued so terribly that he believed that La Belleza carried sickness itself in her womb.

After seven months the doctors decided to take the child. They brought La Belleza into a room with lights and instruments. They worked on her for a long time and she died there under the lights with the doctors cursing and perspiring above the large wound of her pain. They did not tell him of the child, which they had cleaned and placed in an incubator, until the next day. That night he sat in the Ford and tried to see it all, but he could only remember the eyes of La Belleza in the vortex of pain. They were of an almost eerie calmness. They had possessed calmness, as one possesses the truth. Toward morning he slumped sideways on the seat and went to sleep. 68

So he put her body away in the red earth of the town cemetery beyond the cabin. The pines came together overhead and in the heat of midday a shadow sprinkled with spires of light lay upon the ground so that the earth was cool and clean to smell. He did not even think of taking her back to Mexico, since, from the very beginning she had always been part of that dream he had dreamed. Now she would be always in the Sierra Nevada, with the orange and blue flowers, the quiet, deep whiteness of winter, and all that he ever was or could be was with her. 69

But he did not think these last thoughts then, as he did now. He had simply performed them out of instinct for their necessity, as he had performed the years of labor while waiting for the infant Jesús to grow to manhood. Jesús. Why had he named the boy Jesús? That, perhaps, had been instinct too. He had stayed after La Belleza's death for the boy, to be with him until manhood, to show him the loveliness of the Sierra Nevada, to instruct him toward true manhood. But Jesús. Ah, Jesús. Jesús the American. Jesús of the Flotill. Jesús understood nothing. Jesús, he believed, was forever lost to knowledge. That day with Jesús had been his own liberation. 70

For a truth had come upon him after the years of waiting, the ultimate truth that he understood only because La Belleza had passed through his life. Love was beauty, La Belleza and the Sierra Nevada, a kind of created or made thing. But there was another kind of love, a very profound, embracing love that he had felt of late blowing across the mountains from the south and that, he knew now, had always been there from the beginning of his life, disguised in the sun and wind. In this love there was blood and earth and, yes, even God, some kind of god, at least the power of a god. This love wanted him for its own. He understood it, that it had permitted him to have La Belleza and that without it there could have been no Belleza. 71

Juan placed an arm over his eyes and turned to face the wall. The old bed sighed. An image went off in his head and he remembered vividly the lovely body of La Belleza. In that instant the sound that loving had produced with the bed was alive in him like a forgotten melody, and his body seemed to swell and press against the ceiling. It was particularly cruel because it was so sudden, so intense, and came from so deep within him that he knew it 72 must all still be alive somewhere, and that was the cruelest part of all. He wept softly and held the arm across his eyes.

In the dark morning the people of the town were awakened by the blaze ₇₃ of fire that was the house of Juan Sánchez. Believing that he had perished in the flames, several of the townspeople placed a marker next to the grave of his wife with his name on it. But, of course, on that score they were mistaken. Juan Sánchez had simply gone home.

## STUDY QUESTIONS

1. In two or three words each, describe the central district of Stockton and the "entertainment." How does it appear to Juan? to Jesús? to you?

2. Why does Juan refuse to visit the cannery? What does he mean by his being "beyond disappointment"?

3. Why did Juan, years earlier, want to leave his native village in Mexico? Why did he choose the Sierra Nevada above Stockton as his new home?

4. Why does the man offer to sell Juan a cabin for a thousand dollars? What does the clause "the man was so struck that he made out a bill of sale" (paragraph 55) imply about the man's ATTITUDE toward Juan?

5. What might be the reason—if there is one—for the brief history of Ben Carter in the middle of this story?

6. "Jesús. Why had he named the boy Jesús? That, perhaps, had been instinct too" (par. 70). Why *had* he named the boy Jesús? Is this blasphemy? What is meant here by his "instinct"?

7. Sánchez has been unable to instruct Jesús in "true manhood. . . . Jesús, he believed, was forever lost to knowledge. That day with Jesús had been his own liberation" (par. 70). Explain.

8. What is the "other kind of love" that Juan discovers?

9. "Believing that he had perished in the flames, several of the townspeople placed a marker next to the grave of his wife with his name on it. But, of course, on that score they were mistaken. Juan Sánchez had simply gone home" (par. 73). Explain.

# Bharati Mukherjee

Author of two novels, two volumes of short stories, and—with her husband, Clarke Blaise—two non-fiction books, Bharati Mukherjee has been awarded Guggenheim, National Endowment for the Arts, and Woodrow Wilson Fellowships. Born in Calcutta in 1940, she believes she and her writing have changed since she began to see herself not as an expatriate, an exile looking back to a lost home, but as an immigrant, a citizen of a new country finding her place in that country made up largely of other immigrants.

In the following story, the "new world" of America and the old world of India are dramatized in the consciousness of an Indian woman of high caste. The central character likes to think of herself as a thoroughly Westernized and sophisticated New Yorker but discovers that older habits and ways are still deeply set in her character.

# HINDUS

I ran into Pat at Sotheby's[1] on a Friday morning two years ago. Derek and I had gone to view the Fraser Collection of Islamic miniatures at the York Avenue galleries. It bothered Derek that I knew so little about my heritage. Islam is nothing more than a marauder's faith to me, but the Mogul emperors stayed a long time in the green delta of the Ganges, flattening and reflattening a fort in the village where I was born, and forcing my priestly ancestors to prove themselves brave. Evidence on that score is still inconclusive. That village is now in Bangladesh.    1

Derek was a filmmaker, lightly employed at that time. We had been married three hundred and thirty-one days.    2

"So," Pat said, in his flashy, plummy, drawn-out intonation, "you finally made it to the States!"    3

It was one of those early November mornings when the woodsy smell of overheated bodies in cloth coats clogged the public stairwells. Everywhere around me I detected the plaintive signs of over-preparedness.    4

"Whatever are you doing here?" He engulfed me in a swirl of Liberty[2] scarf and cashmere lapels.    5

"Trying to get the woman there to sell me the right catalog," I said.    6

The woman, a very young thing with slippery skin, ate a lusty Granny Smith apple and ignored the dark, hesitant miniature-lovers hanging about like bats in the daytime.    7

"They have more class in London," Pat said.    8

"I wouldn't know. I haven't been back since that unfortunate year at Roedean."[3]    9

"It was always New York you wanted," Pat laughed. "Don't say I didn't warn you. The world is full of empty promises."    10

I didn't remember his having warned me about life and the inevitability of grief. It was entirely possible that he had—he had always been given to    11

1. Famous auction house for rare manuscripts, books, and art objects.
2. Fashionable London store for fabrics.
3. Elite British boarding school for women.

clowning pronouncements—but I had not seen him in nine years and in Calcutta he had never really broken through the fortifications of my shyness.

"Come have a drink with me," Pat said. 12

It was my turn to laugh. "You must meet Derek," I said. 13

Derek had learned a great deal about India. He could reel off statistics 14 of Panchayati Raj[4] and the electrification of villages and the introduction of mass media, though he reserved his love for birds migrating through the wintry deserts of Jaisalmer. Knowledge of India made Derek more sympathetic than bitter, a common trait of decent outsiders. He was charmed by Pat's heedless, old-world insularity.

"Is this the lucky man?" he said to Derek. He did not hold out his hand. 15 He waved us outside; a taxi magically appeared. "Come have a drink with me tomorrow. At my place."

He gave Derek his card. It was big and would not fit into a wallet made 16 to hold Visa and American Express. Derek read it with his usual curiosity.

17

H.R.H. Maharajah Patwant Singh
of
Gotlah
Purveyor and Exporter

He tucked the card in the pocket of his raincoat. "I'll be shooting in 18 Toronto tomorrow," he said, "but I'm sure Leela would like to keep it."

There was, in the retention of those final "h's"—even Indian maps and 19 newspapers now referred to Gotla and to maharajas, and I had dropped the old "Leelah" in my first month in America—something of the reclusive mountebank. "I'm going to the Patels for dinner tomorrow," I said, afraid that Pat would misread the signs of healthy unpossessiveness in our marriage.

"Come for a drink before. What's the matter, Leela? Turning a prude 20 in your old age?" To Derek he explained, "I used to rock her on my knee when she was four. She was gorgeous then, but I am no lecher."

It is true that I was very pretty at four and that Pat spent a lot of time 21 in our house fondling us children. He brought us imported chocolates in beautiful tins and made a show of giving me the biggest. In my family, in every generation, one infant seems destined to be the repository of the family's comeliness. In my generation, I inherited the looks, like an heirloom, to keep in good condition and pass on to the next. Beauty teaches humility and responsibility in the culture I came from. By marrying well, I could have seen to the education of my poorer cousins.

Pat was in a third floor sublet in Gramercy Park South. A West Indian 22 doorman with pendulous cheeks and an unbuttoned jacket let me into the

---

4. Village rule by a council of five elders.

building. He didn't give me a chance to say where I was going as I moved toward the elevator.

"The maharaja is third floor, to the right. All the way down." 23

I had misunderstood the invitation. It was not to be an hour of wit and 24 nostalgia among exotic knick-knacks squirreled into New York from the Gotla Palace. I counted thirty guests in the first quarter hour of my short stay. Plump young men in tight-fitting suits scuttled from living room to kitchen, balancing overfull glasses of gin and tonic. The women were mostly blondes, with luridly mascaraed, brooding eyes, blonde the way South Americans are blonde, with deep residual shading. I tried to edge into a group of three women. One of them said, "I thought India was spellbinding. Naresh's partner managed to get us into the Lake Palace Hotel."

"I don't think I could take the poverty," said her friend, as I retreated. 25

The living room walls were hung with prints of British East India Com- 26 pany officials at work and play, the vestibule with mirror-images of Hindu gods and goddesses.

"Take my advice," a Gujarati man said to Pat in the dim and plantless 27 kitchen. "Get out of diamonds—emeralds *won't* bottom out. These days it *has* to be rubies and emeralds."

In my six years in Manhattan I had not entered a kitchen without plants. 28 There was not even a straggly avocado pushing its nervous way out of a shrivelling seed.

I moved back into the living room where the smell of stale turmeric hung 29 like yellow fog from the ceiling. A man rose from the brocade-covered cushions of a banquette near me and plumped them, smiling, to make room for me.

"You're Pat's niece, no?" The man was francophone, a Lebanese. "Pat 30 has such pretty nieces. You have just come from Bombay? I love Bombay. Personally, Bombay to me is like a jewel. Like Paris, like Beirut before, now like Bombay. You agree?"

I disclaimed all kinship to H.R.H. I was a Bengali Brahmin; mahara- 31 jas—not to put too sharp a point on it—were frankly beneath me, by at least one caste, though some of them, like Pat, would dispute it. Before my marriage to Derek no one in my family since our initial eruption from Vishnu's knee had broken caste etiquette. I disclaimed any recent connection with India. "I haven't been home in ages," I told the Lebanese. "I am an American citizen."

"I too am. I am American," he practically squealed. He rinsed his glass 32 with a bit of gin still left in the bottom, as though he were trying to dislodge lemon pulp stuck and drying on its sides. "You want to have dinner with me tonight, yes? I know Lebanese places, secret and intimate. Food and ambiance very romantic."

"She's going to the Patels." It was Pat. The Gujarati with advice on 33 emeralds was still lodged in the kitchen, huddling with a stocky blonde in a fuchsia silk sari.

"Oh, the Patels," said the Lebanese. "You did not say. Super guy, no? He's doing all right for himself. Not as well as me, of course. I own ten stores and he only has four."  34

Why, I often ask myself, was Derek never around to share these intimacies? Derek would have drawn out the suave, French-speaking, soulful side of this Seventh Avenue *shmattiste.*[5]  35

It shouldn't have surprised me that the Lebanese man in the ruffled shirt should have known Mohan and Motibehn Patel. For immigrants in similar trades, Manhattan is still a village. Mohan had been in the States for eighteen years and last year had become a citizen. They'd been fortunate in having only sons, now at Cal Tech and Cornell; with daughters there would have been pressure on them to return to India for a proper, arranged marriage.  36

"Is he still in Queens?"  37

"No," I told him. "They've moved to a biggish old place on Central Park West."  38

"Very foolish move," said the Lebanese. "They will only spend their money now." He seemed genuinely appalled.  39

Pat looked at me surprised. "I can't believe it," he exclaimed. "Leela Lahiri actually going crosstown at night by herself. I remember when your Daddy wouldn't let you walk the two blocks from school to the house without that armed Nepali, what was his name, dogging your steps."  40

"Gulseng," I said. "He was run over by a lorry three years ago. I think his name was really something-or-other-Rana, but he never corrected us."  41

"Short, nasty and brutal," said Pat. "They don't come that polite and loyal these days. Just as likely to slit your throat as anyone else, these days."  42

The Lebanese, sensing the end of brave New World overtures, the gathering of the darknesses we shared, drifted away.  43

"The country's changed totally, you know," Pat continued. "Crude rustic types have taken over. The *dhoti-wallahs*, you know what I mean, they would wrap themselves in loincloths if it got them more votes. No integrity, no finesse. The country's gone to the dogs, I tell you."  44

"That whole life's outmoded, Pat. Obsolete. All over the world."  45

"They tried to put me in jail," he said. His face was small with bitterness and alarm. "They didn't like my politics, I tell you. Those Communists back home arrested me and threw me in jail. Me. Like a common criminal."  46

"On what charges?"  47

"Smuggling. For selling family heirlooms to Americans who understand them. No one at home understands their value. Here, I can sell off a little Pahari painting for ten thousand dollars. Americans understand our things better than we do ourselves. India wants me to starve in my overgrown palace."  48

"Did you really spend a night in jail?" I couldn't believe that moderni-  49

5. A contrived word, joining a Yiddish root meaning "rag" with a French ending: a rag artist, or clothing manufacturer. Seventh Avenue is the main artery of New York's Garment District.

zation had finally come to India and that even there, no one was immune from consequences.

"Three nights!" he fumed. "Like a common *dacoit*. The country has no respect anymore. The country has nothing. It has driven us abroad with whatever assets we could salvage."

"You did well, I take it." I did not share his perspective; I did not feel my country owed me anything. Comfort, perhaps, when I was there; a different comfort when I left it. India teaches her children: you have seen the worst. Now go out and don't be afraid.

"I have nothing," he spat. "They've stripped me of everything. At night I hear the jackals singing in the courtyard of my palace."

But he had recovered by the time I left for the crosstown cab ride to the Patels. I saw him sitting on the banquette where not too long before the Lebanese had invited me to share an evening of unwholesomeness. On his knee he balanced a tall, silver-haired woman who looked like Candice Bergen. She wore a pink cashmere sweater which she must have put through the washing machine. Creases, like worms, curled around her sweatered bosom.

I didn't see Pat for another two years. In those two years I did see a man who claimed to have bounced the real Candice Bergen on his knee. He had been a juggler at one time, had worked with Edgar Bergen on some vaudeville act and could still pull off card tricks and walk on his hands up and down my dining table. I kept the dining table when Derek and I split last May. He went back to Canada which we both realized too late he should never have left and the table was too massive to move out of our West 11th Street place and into his downtown Toronto, chic renovated apartment. The ex-juggler is my boss at a publishing house. My job is menial but I have a soothing title. I am called an Administrative Assistant.

In the two years I have tried to treat the city not as an island of dark immigrants but as a vast sea in which new Americans like myself could disappear and resurface at will. I did not avoid Indians, but without Derek's urging for me to be proud of my heritage, I did not seek them out. The Patels did invite me to large dinners where all the guests seemed to know with the first flick of their eyes in my direction that I had married a white man and was now separated, and there our friendships hit rock. I was a curiosity, a novel and daring element in the community; everyone knew my name. After a while I began to say I was busy to Motibehn Patel.

Pat came to the office with my boss, Bill Haines, the other day. "I wanted you to meet one of our new authors, Leela," Bill said.

"Leela, *dar-ling!*" Pat cried. His voice was shrill with enthusiasm, and he pressed me histrionically against his Burberry raincoat. I could feel a button tap my collarbone. "It's been years! Where have you been hiding your gorgeous self?"

"I didn't realize you two knew each other," Bill said.

All Indians in America, I could have told him, constitute a village.   59

"Her father bailed me out when the Indian government sought to per-   60
secute me," he said with a pout. "If it hadn't been for courageous friends like
her daddy, I and my poor subjects might just as well have kicked the bucket."

"She's told me nothing about India," said Bill Haines. "No accent, Western   61
clothes—"

"Yes, a shame, that. By the way, Leela, I just found a picture of Lahiri-   62
*sahab* on an elephant when I was going through my official papers for Bill. If
you come over for drinks—after getting out of those ridiculous clothes, I
must insist—I can give it to you. Lahiri-*sahab* looks like Ernest Hemingway
in that photo. You tell him I said he looks like Hemingway."

"Daddy's in Ranikhet this month," I said. "He's been bedridden for a   63
while. Arthritis. He's just beginning to move around a bit again."

"I have hundreds of good anecdotes, Bill, about her daddy and me doing   64
*shikar* in the Sundarban forest. Absolutely *huge* Bengal tigers. I want to balance the politics—which as you rightly say are central—with some stirring
bits about what it was like in the good old days."

"What are you writing?" I asked.   65

"I thought you'd never ask, my dear. My memoirs. At night I leave a   66
Sony by my bed. Night is the best time for remembering. I hear the old
sounds and voices. You remember, Leela, how the palace ballroom used to
hum with dancing feet on my birthdays?"

"*Memoirs of a Modern Maharajah*," Bill Haines said.   67

"I seem to remember the singing of jackals," I said, not unkindly, though   68
he chose to ignore it.

"Writing is what keeps me from going through death's gate. There are   69
nights . . ." He didn't finish. His posture had stiffened with self-regard; he
communicated great oceans of anguish. He'd probably do well. It was what
people wanted to hear.

"The indignities," he said suddenly. "The atrocities." He stared straight   70
ahead, at a watercooler. "The nights in jail, the hyenas sniffing outside your
barred window. I will never forget their smell, never! It is the smell of death,
Leela. The new powers-that-be are peasants. Peasants! They cannot know,
they cannot suspect how they have made me suffer. The country is in the
hands of tyrannical peasants!"

"Look, Pat," Bill Haines said, leading the writer toward his office, "I   71
have to see Bob Savage, the sub-rights man one floor down. Make yourself
at home. Just pull down any book you want to read. I'll be back in a minute."

"Don't worry about me. I shall be all right, Bill. I have my Sony in my   72
pocket. I shall just sit in a corner beside the daughter of my oldest friend,
this child I used to bounce on my knee, and I shall let my mind skip into the
nooks and crannies of Gotlah Palace. Did I tell you, when I was a young lad
my mother kept pet crocs? Big, huge gents and ladies with ugly jaws full of
nasty teeth. They were her pets. She gave them names and fed them chickens every day. Come to me, Padma. Come to me, Prem."

"It'll be dynamite," Bill Haines said. "The whole project's dynamite." He pressed my hand as he eased his stubby, muscular body past the stack of dossiers on my desk. "And *you'll* be a godsend in developing this project." 73

"And what's with you?" Pat asked me. I could tell he already knew the essentials. 74

"Nothing much." But he wasn't listening anyway. 75

"You remember the thief my security men caught in the early days of your father's setting up a factory in my hills? You remember how the mob got excited and poured acid on his face?" 76

I remembered. Was the Sony recording it? Was the memory an illustration of swift and righteous justice in a collapsed Himalayan princely state, or was it the savage and disproportionate fury of a people resisting change? 77

"Yes, certainly I do. Can I get you a cup of coffee? Or tea?" That, of course, was an important part of my job. 78

"No thanks," he said with a flutter of his wrinkled hands. "I have given up all stimulants. I've even given up bed-tea. It interferes with my writing. Writing is everything to me nowadays. It has been my nirvana." 79

"The book sounds dynamite," I assured him. An Indian woman is brought up to please. No matter how passionately we link bodies with our new countries, we never escape the early days. 80

Pat dropped his voice, and, stooping conspiratorially, said to me in Hindi, "There's one big favor you can do for me, though. Bill has spoken of a chap I should be knowing. Who is this Edgar Bergen?" 81

"I think he was the father of a movie actress," I said. I, too, had gone through the same contortion of recognition with Bill Haines. Fortunately, like most Americans, he could not conceive of a world in which Edgar Bergen had no currency. Again in Hindi, Pat asked me for directions to the facilities, and this time I could give a full response. He left his rolled-slim umbrella propped against my desk and walked toward the fountain. 82

"Is he really a maharaja?" Lisa leaned over from her desk to ask me. She is from Rhode Island. Brown hasn't cured her of responding too enthusiastically to each call or visit from a literary personage. "He's terrific. So suave and distinguished! Have you known him from way back when?" 83

"Yes," I said, all the way from when. 84

"I had no idea you spoke Hindu. It's eerie to think you can speak such a hard language. I'm having trouble enough with French. I keep forgetting that you haven't lived here always." 85

I keep forgetting it too. I was about to correct her silly mistake—I'd learned from Derek to be easily incensed over ignorant confusions between Hindi and Hindu—but then I thought, why bother? Maybe she's right. That slight undetectable error, call it an accent, isn't part of language at all. I speak Hindu. No matter what language I speak it will come out slightly foreign, no matter how perfectly I mouth it. There's a whole world of us now, speaking Hindu. 86

The manuscript of *Memoirs* was not dynamite, but I stayed up all night  87
to finish it. In spite of the arch locutions and the aggrieved posture that Pat
had stubbornly clung to, I knew I was reading about myself, blind and groping conquistador who had come to the New World too late.

## STUDY QUESTIONS

1. Describe how Leela thinks of herself. What kinds of clothes does she wear? What
   kinds of social gatherings does she like? What characteristics of other people does
   she tend to emphasize? How does she talk about her own background in India?

2. What is the significance of her changing her name from Leelah to Leela?

3. In what ways is the New York SETTING important to the story? What different
   aspects of New York are detailed? What particular places are mentioned? In what
   kinds of New York social circles does the ACTION take place?

4. What function does Derek perform in Leela's life? in the story as she presents it?
   Why do Candice and Edgar Bergen keep coming up in the story?

5. In what ways is the maharaja important to Leela's sense of herself? What different
   kinds of Hindus does the story present? What does the title of the story mean?

# Linda Hogan

Linda Hogan, a Chickasaw, was born in Denver in 1947, grew up in Oklahoma,
and earned an M.A. in English and creative writing from the University of
Colorado. Now an associate professor of American studies and American Indian studies
at the University of Minnesota, she has published several books of poems, including
*Calling Myself Home; Daughters, I Love You; Eclipse; That House;* and *Seeing Through the
Sun* (which won the 1986 American Book Award from the Before Columbus Foundation). Her first novel, *Mean Spirit*, appeared in 1989.

In 1981, a group of Native Americans, ranchers, and environmentalists gathered
over several weeks to protest development in the Black Hills of South Dakota.

# BLACK HILLS SURVIVAL GATHERING,
## 1980

Bodies on fire
the monks in orange cloth
sing morning into light.

Men wake on the hill.
Dry grass blows from their hair.                        5
B52's blow over their heads
leaving a cross on the ground.
Air returns to itself and silence.

Rainclouds are disappearing
with fractures of light in the distance.              10
Fierce gases forming,
the sky bending
where people arrive
on dusty roads that change
matter to energy.                                                15

My husband wakes.
My daughter wakes.
Quiet morning, she stands
in a pail of water
naked, reflecting light                                        20
and this man I love,
with kind hands
he washes her slim hips,
narrow shoulders, splashes
the skin containing                                            25
wind and fragile fire,
the pulse in her wrist.

My other daughter wakes
to comb warm sun across her hair.
While I make coffee I tell her                             30
this is the land of her ancestors,
blood and heart.
Does her hair become a mane

blowing in the electric breeze,
her eyes dilate and darken?                                    35

The sun rises on all of them
in the center of light
hills that have no boundary,
the child named Thunder Horse,
the child named Dawn Protector                                 40
and the man
whose name would mean home in Navajo.

At ground zero
in the center of light we stand.
Bombs are buried beneath us,                                   45
destruction flies overhead.
We are waking
in the expanding light
the sulphur-colored grass.
A red horse standing on a distant ridge                        50
looks like one burned
over Hiroshima,
silent, head hanging in sickness.
But look
she raises her head                                            55
and surges toward the bluing sky.

Radiant morning.
The dark tunnels inside us carry life.
Red.
Blue.                                                          60
The children's dark hair against my breast.
On the burning hills
in flaring orange cloth
men are singing and drumming
Heartbeat.                                                     65

## STUDY QUESTIONS

1. What different kinds of survival is the poem about? How does the sense of family
   and the passing on of personal values relate to the threats posed by war machines?

2. What different ways is the sun reflected in people, animals, and landscape? In what
   sections of the poem does bright light suggest hope and possibility? Where does it
   suggest potential disaster?

3. Explain the effect of portraying simple family rituals in the middle of the poem. How are IMAGES from the beginning and the ending of the poem reflected in family scenes?

4. What different meanings does "cross" have in line 7? Explain how its SYMBOLISM relates to the THEMES of the poem.

5. How many different images of life and energy does the poem contain? What effect does each create? How are they differentiated? How are human bodies made to seem vessels of life and transmitters of tradition? In what ways is the SETTING of the poem significant?

# Clark Blaise

Born in North Dakota in 1941, Clark Blaise was educated at Denison and the University of Iowa. He has taught in Montreal and Toronto and at Skidmore College and the Iowa Writers' Workshop, and he has won several prizes and fellowships for his writing, including a John Simon Guggenheim Fellowship. His most recent novel is *Lusts*.

In the story that follows, a young university teacher in Montreal evaluates his own itinerant life and values against the lives of several immigrant students who regard Montreal as only a way station on their way to someplace more permanent.

## A CLASS OF NEW CANADIANS

Norman Dyer hurried down Sherbrooke Street, collar turned against the snow. "Superb!" he muttered, passing a basement gallery next to a French bookstore. Bleached and tanned women in furs dashed from hotel lobbies into waiting cabs. Even the neon clutter of the side streets and the honks of slithering taxis seemed remote tonight through the peaceful snow. *Superb*, he thought again, waiting for a light and backing from a slushy curb: a word reserved for wines, cigars, and delicate sauces; he was feeling superb this evening. After eighteen months in Montreal, he still found himself freshly impressed by everything he saw. He was proud of himself for having steered his life north, even for jobs that were menial by standards he could have demanded. Great just being here no matter what they paid, looking at these buildings, these faces, and hearing all the languages. He was learning to be insulted by simple bad taste, wherever he encountered it.

Since leaving graduate school and coming to Montreal, he had sampled every ethnic restaurant downtown and in the old city, plus a few Levantine places out in Outremont. He had worked on conversational French and mastered much of the local dialect, done reviews for local papers, translated French-Canadian poets for Toronto quarterlies, and tweaked his colleagues for not sympathizing enough with Quebec separatism. He attended French performances of plays he had ignored in English, and kept a small but elegant apartment near a colony of *émigré* Russians just off Park Avenue. Since coming to Montreal he'd witnessed a hold-up, watched a murder, and seen several riots. When stopped on the street for directions, he would answer in French or accented English. To live this well and travel each long academic summer, he held two jobs. He had no intention of returning to the States. In fact, he had begun to think of himself as a semi-permanent, semi-political exile.

Now, stopped again a few blocks farther, he studied the window of Holt-Renfrew's exclusive men's shop. Incredible, he thought, the authority of simple good taste. Double-breasted chalk-striped suits he would never dare to buy. Knitted sweaters, and fifty-dollar shoes. One tanned mannequin was decked out in a brash checkered sportscoat with a burgundy vest and dashing ascot. Not a price tag under three hundred dollars. Unlike food, drink, cinema, and literature, clothing had never really involved him. Someday, he now realized, it would. Dyer's clothes, thus far, had all been bought in a chain department store. He was a walking violation of American law, clad shoes to scarf in Egyptian cottons, Polish leathers, and woolens from the People's Republic of China.

He had no time for dinner tonight; this was Wednesday, a day of lectures at one university, and then an evening course in English as a Foreign Language at McGill, beginning at six. He would eat afterwards.

Besides the money, he had kept this second job because it flattered him. There was to Dyer something fiercely elemental, almost existential, about teaching both his language and his literature in a foreign country—like Joyce in Trieste, Isherwood and Nabokov in Berlin, Beckett in Paris. Also it was necessary for his students. It was the first time in his life that he had done something socially useful. What difference did it make that the job was beneath him, a recent Ph.D., while most of his colleagues in the evening school at McGill were idle housewives and bachelor civil servants? It didn't matter, even, that this job was a perversion of all the sentiments he held as a progressive young teacher. He was a god two evenings a week, sometimes suffering and fatigued, but nevertheless an omniscient, benevolent god. His students were silent, ignorant, and dedicated to learning English. No discussions, no demonstrations, no dialogue.

*I love them*, he thought. They need me.

He entered the room, pocketed his cap and ear muffs, and dropped his briefcase on the podium. Two girls smiled good evening.

*They love me*, he thought, taking off his boots and hanging up his coat; I'm not like their English-speaking bosses.

*I love myself,* he thought with amazement even while conducting a drill    9
on word order. I love myself for tramping down Sherbrooke Street in zero
weather just to help them with noun clauses. I love myself standing behind
this podium and showing Gilles Carrier and Claude Veilleux the difference
between the past continuous and the simple past; or the sultry Armenian girl
with the bewitching half-glasses that "put on" is not the same as "take on";
or telling the dashing Mr. Miguel Mayor, late of Madrid, that simple futurity
can be expressed in four different ways, at least.

This is what mastery is like, he thought. Being superb in one's chosen    10
field, not merely in one's mother tongue. A respected performer in the lecture halls of the major universities, equipped by twenty years' research in
the remotest libraries, and slowly giving it back to those who must have it.
Dishing it out suavely, even wittily. Being a legend. Being loved and a little
feared.

"Yes, Mrs. David?"    11

A *sabra:* freckled, reddish hair, looking like a British model, speaks with    12
a nifty British accent, and loves me.

"No," he smiled, *"I were* is not correct except in the present subjunctive,    13
which you haven't studied yet."

The first hour's bell rang. The students closed their books for the inter-    14
mission. Dyer put his away, then noticed a page of his Faulkner lecture from
the afternoon class. *Absalom, Absalom!* his favorite.

"Can anyone here tell me what the *impregnable citadel of his passive rectitude*    15
means?"

"What, sir?" asked Mr. Vassilopoulos, ready to copy.    16

"What about *the presbyterian and lugubrious effluvium of his passive vindic-*    17
*tiveness?"* A few girls giggled. "O.K.," said Dyer, "take your break."

In the halls of McGill they broke into the usual groups. French-Cana-    18
dians and South Americans into two large circles, then the Greeks, Germans, Spanish, and French into smaller groups. The patterns interested Dyer.
Madrid Spaniards and Parisian French always spoke English with their New
World co-linguals. The Middle Europeans spoke German together, not Russian, preferring one occupier to the other. Two Israeli men went off alone.
Dyer decided to join them for the break.

Not *sabras,* Dyer concluded, not like Mrs. David. The shorter one, dark    19
and wavy-haired, held his cigarette like a violin bow. The other, Mr. Weinrot, was tall and pot-bellied, with a ruddy face and thick stubby fingers.
Something about him suggested truck-driving, perhaps of beer, maybe in
Germany. Neither one, he decided, could supply the name of a good Israeli
restaurant.

"This is really hard, you know?" said Weinrot.    20

"Why?"    21

"I think it's because I'm not speaking much of English at my job."    22

"French?" asked Dyer.    23

"French? Pah! All the time Hebrew, sometimes German, sometimes little Polish. Crazy thing, eh? How long you think they let me speak Hebrew if I'm working in America?" 24

"Depends on where you're working," he said. 25

"Hell, I'm working for the Canadian government, what you think? Plant I work in—I'm engineer, see—makes boilers for the turbines going up North. Look. When I'm leaving Israel I go first to Italy. Right away—bamm I'm working in Italy I'm speaking Italian like a native. Passing for a native." 26

"A native Jew," said his dark-haired friend. 27

"Listen to him. So in Rome they think I'm from Tyrol—that's still native, eh? So I speak Russian and German and Italian like a Jew. My Hebrew is bad, I admit it, but it's a lousy language anyway. Nobody likes it. French I understand but English I'm talking like a bum. Arabic I know five dialects. Danish fluent. So what's the matter I can't learn English?" 28

"It'll come, don't worry," Dyer smiled. *Don't worry, my son;* he wanted to pat him on the arm. "Anyway, that's what makes Canada so appealing. Here they don't force you." 29

"What's this *appealing?* Means nice? Look, my friend, keep it, eh? Two years in a country I don't learn the language means it isn't a country." 30

"Come on," said Dyer. "Neither does forcing you." 31

"Let me tell you a story why I come to Canada. Then you tell me if I was wrong, O.K.?" 32

"Certainly," said Dyer, flattered. 33

In Italy, Weinrot told him, he had lost his job to a Communist union. He left Italy for Denmark and opened up an Israeli restaurant with five other friends. Then the six Israelis decided to rent a bigger apartment downtown near the restaurant. They found a perfect nine-room place for two thousand kroner a month, not bad shared six ways. Next day the landlord told them the deal was off. "You tell me why," Weinrot demanded. 34

*No Jews?* Dyer wondered. "He wanted more rent," he finally said. 35

"More—you kidding? More we expected. *Less* we didn't expect. A couple with eight kids is showing up after we're gone and the law in Denmark says a man has a right to a room for each kid plus a hundred kroner knocked off the rent for each kid. What you think of that? So a guy who comes in *after* us gets a nine-room place for a thousand kroner *less.* Law says no way a bachelor can get a place ahead of a family, and bachelors pay twice as much." 36

Dyer waited, then asked, "So?" 37

"So, I make up my mind the world is full of communisms, just like Israel. So I take out applications next day for Australia, South Africa, U.S.A., and Canada. Canada says come right away, so I go. Should have waited for South Africa." 38

"How could you?" Dyer cried. "What's wrong with you anyway? South Africa is fascist. Australia is racist." 39

The bell rang, and the Israelis, with Dyer, began walking to the room. 40

"What I was wondering, then," said Mr. Weinrot, ignoring Dyer's out- 41 burst, "was if my English is good enough to be working in the United States. You're American, aren't you?"

It was a question Dyer had often avoided in Europe, but had rarely been asked in Montreal. "Yes," he admitted, "your English is probably good enough for the States or South Africa, whichever one wants you first." 42

He hurried ahead to the room, feeling that he had let Montreal down. He wanted to turn and shout to Weinrot and to all the others that Montreal was the greatest city on the continent, if only they knew it as well as he did. If they'd just break out of their little ghettos. 43

At the door, the Armenian girl with the half-glasses caught his arm. She was standing with Mrs. David and Miss Parizeau, a jolly French-Canadian girl that Dyer had been thinking of asking out. 44

"Please, sir," she said, looking at him over the tops of her tiny glasses, "what I was asking earlier—*put on*—I heard on the television. A man said *You are putting me on* and everybody laughed. I think it was supposed to be funny but *put on* we learned means get dressed, no?" 45

"Ah—*don't put me on*," Dyer laughed. 46

"I yaven't erd it neither," said Miss Parizeau. 47

"To put some*body* on means to make a fool of him. To put some*thing* on is to wear it. O.K.?" He gave examples. 48

"Ah, now I know," said Miss Parizeau. "Like bullshitting somebody. Is it the same?" 49

"Ah, yes," he said, smiling. French-Canadians were like children learning the language. "Your example isn't considered polite. 'Put on' is very common now in the States." 50

"Then maybe," said Miss Parizeau, "we'll ave it ere in twenty years." The Armenian giggled. 51

"No—I've heard it here just as often," Dyer protested, but the girls had already entered the room. 52

He began the second hour with a smile which slowly soured as he thought of the Israelis. America's anticommunism was bad enough, but it was worse hearing it echoed by immigrants, by Jews, here in Montreal. Wasn't there a psychological type who chose Canada over South Africa? Or was it just a matter of visas and slow adjustment? Did Johannesburg lose its Greeks, and Melbourne its Italians, the way Dyer's students were always leaving Montreal? 53

And after class when Dyer was again feeling content and thinking of approaching one of the Israelis for a restaurant tip, there came the flood of small requests: should Mrs. Papadopoulos go into a more advanced course; could Mr. Perez miss a week for an interview in Toronto; could Mr. Giguère, who spoke English perfectly, have a harder book; Mr. Coté an easier one? 54

Then as he packed his briefcase in the empty room, Miguel Mayor, the vain and impeccable Spaniard, came forward from the hallway. 55

"Sir," he began, walking stiffly, ready to bow or salute. He wore a loud gray checkered sportscoat this evening, blue shirt, and matching ascot-hand- 56 kerchief, slightly mauve. He must have shaved just before class, Dyer noticed, for two fresh daubs of antiseptic cream stood out on his jaw, just under his earlobe.

"I have been wanting to ask *you* something, as a matter of fact," said Dyer. "Do you know any good Spanish restaurants I might try tonight?"  57

"There are not any good Spanish restaurants in Montreal," he said. He stepped closer. "Sir?"  58

"What's on your mind, then?"  59

"Please—have you the time to look on a letter for me?"  60

He laid the letter on the podium.  61

"Look *over* a letter," said Dyer. "What is it for?"  62

"I have applied," he began, stopping to emphasize the present perfect construction, "for a job in Cleveland, Ohio, and I want to know if my letter will be good. Will an American, I mean—"  63

"Why are you going there?"  64

"It is a good job."  65

"But Cleveland—"  66

"They have a blackman mayor, I have read. But the job is not in Cleveland."  67

"Let me see it."  68

*Most honourable Sir: I humbly beg consideration for a position in your grand company . . .*  69

"Who are you writing this to?"  70

"The president," said Miguel Mayor.  71

*I am once a student of Dr. Ramiro Gutierrez of the Hydraulic Institute of Sevilla, Spain . . .*  72

"Does the president know this Ramiro Gutierrez?"  73

"Oh, everybody is knowing him," Miguel Mayor assured, "he is the most famous expert in all Spain."  74

"Did he recommend this company to you?"  75

"No—I have said in my letter, if you look—"  76

*An ancient student of Dr. Gutierrez, Salvador del Este, is actually a boiler expert who is being employed like supervisor is formerly a friend of mine . . .*  77

"Is he still your friend?"  78

*Whenever you say come to my city Miguel Mayor for talking I will be coming. I am working in Montreal since two years and am now wanting more money than I am getting here now . . .*  79

"Well . . ." Dyer sighed.  80

"Sir—what I want from you is knowing in good English how to interview me by this man. The letters in Spanish are not the same to English ones, you know?"  81

*I remain humbly at your orders . . .*  82

"Why do you want to leave Montreal?"  83

"It's time for a change."  84

"Have you ever been to Cleveland?"  85

"I am one summer in California. Very beautiful there and hot like my country. Montreal is big port like Barcelona. Everybody mixed together and having no money. It is just a place to land, no?" 86

"Montreal? Don't be silly." 87

"I thought I come here and learn good English but where I work I get by in Spanish and French. It's hard, you know?" he smiled. Then he took a few steps back and gave his cuffs a gentle tug, exposing a set of jade cufflinks. 88

Dyer looked at the letter again and calculated how long he would be correcting it, then up at his student. How old is he? My age? Thirty? Is he married? Where do the Spanish live in Montreal? He looks so prosperous, so confident, like a male model off a page of *Playboy*. For an instant Dyer felt that his student was mocking him, somehow pitting his astounding confidence and wardrobe, sharp chin and matador's bearing against Dyer's command of English and mastery of the side streets, bistros, and ethnic restaurants. Mayor's letter was painful, yet he remained somehow competent. He would pass his interview, if he got one. What would he care about America, and the odiousness he'd soon be supporting? It was as though a superstructure of exploitation had been revealed, and Dyer felt himself abused by the very people he wanted so much to help. It had to end someplace. 89

He scratched out the second "humbly" from the letter, then folded the sheet of foolscap. "Get it typed right away," he said. "Good luck." 90

"Thank you, sir," said his student, with a bow. Dyer watched the letter disappear in the inner pocket of the checkered sportscoat. Then the folding of the cashmere scarf, the draping of the camel's hair coat about the shoulders, the easing of the fur hat down to the rims of his ears. The meticulous filling of the pigskin gloves. Mayor's patent leather galoshes glistened. 91

"Good evening, sir," he said. 92

"*Buenas noches*," Dyer replied. 93

He hurried now, back down Sherbrooke Street to his daytime office where he could deposit his books. Montreal on a winter night was still mysterious, still magical. Snow blurred the arc lights. The wind was dying. Every second car was now a taxi, crowned with an orange crescent. Slushy curbs had hardened. The window of Holt-Renfrew's was still attractive. The legless dummies invited a final stare. He stood longer than he had earlier, in front of the sporty mannequin with a burgundy waistcoat, the mauve and blue ensemble, the jade cufflinks. 94

*Good evening, sir,* he could almost hear. The ascot, the shirt, the complete outfit, had leaped off the back of Miguel Mayor. He pictured how he must have entered the store with three hundred dollars and a prepared speech, and walked out again with everything off the torso's back. 95

I want that. 96

What, sir? 97

*That*. 98

The coat, sir? 99

Yes. 100

Very well, sir. 101
And *that.* 102
Which, sir? 103
All that. 104

"Absurd man!" Dyer whispered. There had been a moment of fear, as 105
though the naked body would leap from the window, and legless, chase him
down Sherbrooke Street. But the moment was passing. Dyer realized now
that it was comic, even touching. Miguel Mayor had simply tried too hard,
too fast, and it would be good for him to stay in Montreal until he deserved
those clothes, that touching vanity and confidence. With one last look at the
window, he turned sharply, before the clothes could speak again.

## STUDY QUESTIONS

1. How much information are we given about the earlier life of Norman Dyer? Why is he happy to be away from the States? What, exactly, is he happy about in his life in Montreal? Why is he so offended that his students wish to leave Montreal?

2. What does Norman Dyer learn about himself in the course of the story? Do we gain insights into his motivations and behavior that he himself does not have? How does the story's choice of FOCUS help to distinguish between what we learn and what Dyer learns?

3. What differences are implied in the story between the cultures of Canada and the United States? What different views do various CHARACTERS have of these differences? What are Norman Dyer's views? What views does the author seem to have?

4. Describe Norman Dyer's way of life in Montreal. What pleasures does he find there that seem specific to Montreal? Why does he seem to be so attached to Montreal as a place?

5. Why is Norman Dyer so haunted by the IMAGE of expensive clothes? Explain the final scene of the story. In what ways is the conversation with Miguel Mayor important to Dyer? What functions does Mayor perform in the story?

6. How do the functions Norman Dyer performs for his students relate to his idea of himself?

# Norma Rosen

Born in New York City in 1925, Norma Rosen was educated at Mt. Holyoke and Columbia. She has taught writing at the New School for Social Research, Harvard, Lehman College, the University of Pennsylvania, and the College of New

Rochelle. Her novels include *Joy to Levine!* (1962) and *Touching Evil* (1969), but her collections of stories, *Green* (1967), from which the following story is taken, is perhaps her most celebrated and popular book.

In "A Thousand Tears," a woman who lives on the West Side of Manhattan in New York City comes to recognize the deep prejudices against Puerto Ricans in her neighborhood. The story is set in two places and two time frames: the main story takes place on the West Side (probably in the 1960s), but a long flashback to the woman's honeymoon in Puerto Rico ten years earlier provides perspective on later events.

# A THOUSAND TEARS

Twice in one day Sandra Loeb, who lives a careful life in New York City, hears a tale of murder close by. The day, as it happens, is one during a newspaper strike. People feel a need to tell what they hear, some revived obligation to pass on news of the world's woe. That, at least, is Sandra's explanation to herself, and afterward to her husband Ben when they get a chance to talk. On top of everything else, this day is Sandra and Ben's tenth wedding anniversary—a time of welled-up feelings that, in the rush of things, must be swallowed again, making a hot friction around the heart. One tale in the morning, one in the evening, form brackets around Sandra's well-ordered hours and squeeze from them drops of blood.

Ben never brings flowers. They are in the same category as tears, and to be avoided. Sandra understands this. All the same, to be sure there will be no gap into which hurt feelings might stumble, on her way home from work the evening before the anniversary she buys armfuls of fresh greens—rhododendron and magnolia leaves—and fills all the vases in the house. Then late at night she remembers that Lily, their day maid, has asked for extra cream to make the cake. So early in the morning, while Ben can still be home with their two preschool children and before Sandra herself must leave for work, she hurries out to buy some.

Now! How stupid! The moment Sandra is in the street she sees what she has done—quite automatically put on the new fur coat that she means to wear to work today. For a moment she hesitates, then decides, "No, I won't go in."

Sandra has lived all her life in or close to this part of New York's West Side, where great blocks of buildings line the avenues from park to park. "Democratic people" were her mother's words for those who preferred the West Side's rich population mix to the distilled elements of the East Side. The description holds good, Sandra feels, although she has added to it her own: "Hopeful people." Hopeful of education. Renewal. Good will. Above all, good will. "We're all idealists. . . ." Sandra frowns. Who was it who said that to her quite recently?

The store she does not enter is a small *bodega* where she often goes for    5
dairy items and bananas. The Puerto Rican woman who keeps the store has
pictures of her grandchildren taped to the counter. The woman is unquestionably better off, in money as well as English, than most of the Puerto
Ricans Sandra sees on the streets. No doubt the friendliness between them
would survive the interpolation of a fur coat. But it might not, Sandra thinks,
survive the effort they would have to make to convince each other that the
fur coat did not matter. She hurries on, annoyed with herself, to the specialty
grocer's, half a block farther on.

The store is cold. Along with the new coat, Sandra has hastily pulled a    6
scarf from the closet and tied it around her head. A black alligator shoulder
bag, which Ben calls "the survivor" because it is as old as their marriage,
hangs at her side like animal armor. All the same, an iciness creeps in at her
shoulder blades and travels down her back. A policeman—in Sandra's youth
a symbol of order as substantial as the West Side itself—is speaking.

"So the Puerto Ricans got up a little excitement around here last night."    7
He takes a quick check of the faces in the store. Then he goes on, telling the
grocer, "Some guy runs with a gun to an apartment on Eighty-first Street
and he shoots two bullets into a guy, and then he finds out he shot the wrong
guy so then he runs to an apartment on Eighty-fourth Street and shoots the
guy he thinks he wants. Meantime the first, *wrong* guy runs down into the
street and then runs up Amsterdam Avenue but in the middle of running he
drops dead."

The policeman stops for another quick look around. He then says his    8
last word: "Well, at least as long as they only kill each other . . ."

The grocer, whom Sandra knows for a simple man, looks bewildered.    9
"Why'd he do it? For what reason?"

Sandra by now has placed the policeman—a traffic cop from a Broad-    10
way corner in the Seventies. He is a serious-faced young man. His open-air
life has not yet given him the invulnerable look of ruddy-faced policemen.
He shakes his head in a quick movement that is almost a shudder. "How
much does it take in this town to send somebody nuts?" His words seem to
hold an angry sympathy that softens his earlier, callous remark.

Is the remark callous? Sandra hears it again and again: "As long as they    11
only kill each other . . ." It is the West Side's policy of containment. In this
the West Side is like the world, holding its skirts lest they brush against
intolerable dangers: the small war ("As long as it doesn't get big"), the cold
war ("As long as it doesn't get hot"), atomic stockpiles ("As long as some
maniac doesn't set one off"). But even "as long as they only kill each other,"
there is always the chance of the stray bullet, the miscalculated knife throw,
the splashing drop of acid, the warring gangs made up of "each other" who
may fall on a boy of no gang at all. It is infuriating to live, in the world, with
the fear of the bomb that some maniac may set off. And along with one's
hope one lives, on the West Side, in a state of anger as well, because of this
overflow of danger that cannot be contained.

Sandra's hope now, at this early hour, is to be spared any encounters as      12
she strides quickly home. But at the corner of Seventy-fifth Street she crosses
paths with a Puerto Rican boy of four or five. One hand holds his wedge of
breakfast pizza; the other is fisted against his chest as if to beat out the cold
there. He gives her a brief, brown stare as he passes and she, before she
knows what she is up to, turns her head after him to check. She learns nothing she didn't already know. There are no socks in his shoes, no jacket over
his shirt, and from the flapping around his skinny thighs, no underwear under
his dirty white shorts with a green stripe down the outer seam—a discard
from the camp outfit of some boy who lives in another world.

What will become of him? Sandra finds herself paying out the question      13
like a toll before she can pass along. *Mira! Mira!*[1] What will become . . .
Then her first thoughts repossess her and she hurries. Shooting in the street
not ten blocks from us! That is what, if there is time, she must tell Ben.

But as usual, there is no time. Lily arrives, Ben goes, and soon Sandra      14
is hurrying after, swinging her gloved hand in the street for a cab. She has a
picture of herself standing in this spot morning after morning, waving the
same hand, differently gloved with the seasons. Then she takes the short
ride, made dear by the waits at intersections, to her desk.

At lunchtime Sandra is again in a cab. This time she is going farther      15
downtown to meet a friend who particularly wants Sandra's advice because
the friend is about to vacation in Puerto Rico.

"I know you went there on your honeymoon," Elizabeth had said on the      16
phone the previous week when they made the date.

"Do you know what that Tuesday we're meeting will be? My tenth      17
anniversary," Sandra said.

"Congratulations. You must remember something about the place."      18

"As a matter of fact, I remember quite a bit. I've even got some folders      19
somewhere, and a journal—I kept a journal in those days."

"Oh, bring it! That's my idea of *lunch*." Then Elizabeth asked, "Was it      20
a good honeymoon?" and when Sandra stopped for a thoughtful moment,
added: "Aren't they all sort of sad?" Elizabeth is divorced, so there was nothing to say but yes.

At lunch Sandra warns Elizabeth, who lives singly and elegantly East,      21
"You're in for some heartbreaking sights. We see them every day in our
neighborhood, so things can't have changed that much in ten years."

Elizabeth raises mildly reproachful eyes. "I no longer travel as the shocked      22
American. Haven't for some time."

"Worst of all is when you *don't* see them. Sometimes they walk right by      23
and you don't see them."

Elizabeth nods and sips her drink.      24

1. Look! Look!

"I'm talking about my *own* neighborhood." Sandra gropes and shrugs    25
helplessly. "It's like—"

"Blindness," Elizabeth supplies. "I loathe that in me too. But it's indis-    26
pensable. I know it is."

Sandra then tells Elizabeth about the shooting.    27

"How horrible for you," Elizabeth says. "I *loathe* their being here."    28

Sandra wonders if it is possible to hate the sympathy of women—that    29
good trait with its own reverse image stamped to its back.

"Although I would hate to see you move . . ." Elizabeth says.    30

"No. No suburbs, thank you."    31

Because Sandra is engaged in the working woman's race to stand for    32
Home and Mother in the nick of time, she suggests to her last cab driver of
the day that he try the route through Central Park. Soon they are rounding
the curves of the road at a good speed. Sandra, watching the movement of
the snowy landscape, is suddenly aware that this evening looks more like
dusk than the pitch-black it was a few weeks before, around Christmas. A
thin purple lifts the sky above the filamented trees.

When the driver stops for the light near the Seventy-second Street exit    33
she sees a small parade of mounted police coming along the bridle path in
twos. They do not, as she expects they will, turn off at the cross-park highway. Instead they allow their horses to trot across the highway and take the
bridle path on the other side. The policemen chatter and gesture within their
pairs like pilgrims to Canterbury and their horses converse in steam.

"I didn't know," Sandra says to the back of her cab driver's head, "that    34
there were all these mounted police in the park at night. I'm so glad." She
feels a rising hope—because the evening sky is lifting—that this lovely, lost
park is to be reclaimed.

"Sure," says the driver. "Since what happened."    35

Sandra notices that the ear pieces of his glasses are taped with adhesive,    36
one white, one black.

"I guess you don't get the chance to know these things during the strike,"    37
says the cabbie. Stimulated by her silence, he half turns toward her while
his hands and feet, at the light change, work out the rhythm of shifting into
first. "They found some guy in pieces. Some Puerto Rican." He gestures at
a snowy hill. "Right around here someplace."

While she is still blocks from home Sandra estimates the fare, adds the    38
tip, readies her money and finds when they get to her door that she has
guessed close enough so that she needn't open her purse again, and she is
already swinging one leg to the curb when the driver's words catch her—one
foot in, one foot out and back absurdly bent. "At least," he says, "as long as
they only kill each other."

What in the world makes her wonder at this moment if they have can-    39
dles? Surely they have some left over from a birthday. But if they haven't?
Sandra is scrupulous about these ceremonies. She can't, as a mother who

gives her day to her children might do, fob them off with some story—
"Anniversary cakes don't *need* candles." They must have candles, and it's
simpler to get them now than go upstairs first and check. She heads again—
it's a day of repetitions—for the little grocery store.

Near the corner, in front of the doughnut shop, the nightly group is       40
forming. Henna-haired boys, with hips fined down to a sole suggestion, converse in clattering Spanish. Sandra gives them the barest side glance as she
passes. They are what they are—the oldest no more than seventeen, perhaps—as stoical and tough as a band of Elizabethan mummers. But on the
walk back, having bought her candles, she sees a new boy has been added,
with the face of a dark angel—beauty with no place to go but down. He
stands with his hands in his pockets, watching the charade to be learned.

What will become of him—the voice inside Sandra's head begins its         41
chant—when he's twenty? Then she stops in the street for a moment because
the obscene parody jumps with such force into her head: "At least as long as
they only seduce each other."

Sandra's clean, beautiful children, whom Lily has dressed in brother       42
and sister outfits of red velvet, race each other to her arms. Almost as soon
as Sandra is in, Lily is out—she has her own dinner to fix at home. But first,
quickly, information passes from Lily to Sandra: The children ate good lunches,
they were good about their rest times, and Lily kept them in the sunny part
of the playground where it wasn't too cold.

Sandra steps into the hall for a minute with Lily. "I heard about—an       43
accident in the park today," she says.

"Oh, my," Lily says. "Was it a car?"                                       44

"No." Sandra is whispering now. "Someone was murdered."                    45

Lily's eyebrows lift at the inner edges, making downcurves of pity. "It's  46
hard to raise children in the city," she says. A ring of grayish-white rims the
iris of each eye. How old is Lily? Her black face seems ageless, no gray in
her neatly bunned hair. Good Lily, lend us your protection for a few more
years. Why should you? But do it.

"I was thinking, Lily, perhaps you could keep the children out of the      47
park for a while. It must be awfully cold there, anyway. Just—go window-
shopping with them?"

"Yes, I'll do that, Mrs. Loeb."                                            48

Moments after Lily goes, Ben is home.                                      49

"Oh-oh!" Ben says when he sees the faces of the children, pale with        50
excitement above the red velvet.

They hang their arms around his neck and bow his head with their           51
weight. Content for now to let the children's greeting stand for their own,
Sandra and Ben exchange a look above the shouts and then Sandra slips back
to the kitchen to keep her eye on Lily's roast. Unexpectedly—the children
are busy in the hall dividing Ben's spoils of rubbers, muffler, and gloves—
Ben appears. Sandra intercepts the myriad possibilities of his greeting with
a thick whisper: "Two people were shot right around here last night. And

somebody else was chopped up in the park. Near where the children play!"

"All right," Ben says quietly. He takes a quick turn around the kitchen 52 and his loose arms bang against the dishwasher. Sandra wishes she had spoken differently. She had forgotten (how could she?) that Ben longs to protect them—against bullets, maniacs, bombs. But he can't, so his voice gets quiet and thin and his arms throw themselves uselessly about. "We'll leave. Let's go. Move."

"Well, we can't say it happens often." Sandra pays double dues now to 53 the tact she forgot. "There are *hundreds* of police out now." After a short wait she asks, "Do you ever think about Puerto Rico?" It sounds so coy, though she hadn't meant the honeymoon part, that she doesn't blame Ben for looking as if she'd rolled marbles under his feet.

"No," he says. "I've forgotten. Is that where we went?" 54

This is silly, Sandra says to herself. She supposes hurt feelings show in 55 her face. Now it is Ben's turn to weave and spin. To show how much he remembers—every moment, in fact—he begins to hum, in an appropriately dying voice. After a quick glance at her, he goes to change. The children follow him, asking in loud whispers to see the box with the present. Sandra takes up Ben's tune while she looks after Lily's dinner: *"Mil lágrimas, mil lágrimas de amor."*[2] She fishes in her apron pocket for a tissue. It is something, after all, to be able to blow your nose unobserved.

She knows what the trouble is. It's the research she did for Elizabeth. 56 Her memories of ten years ago have been freshened. Unless you were Proust there was little point in having memories come back so fresh. The blessing of passing time—that it could carry off foreground and dwindle it into background—was lost. If everything came back stark, staring and foregrounded again, like a primitive painting—well, there was little point to that either. All it led to was a lot of secret nose-blowing in the kitchen. Idiotic. She and Ben and everybody else live, as any moron could point out, in difficult times. It's time to get used to the times. But her memories have been freshened. . . .

Their room in the hotel had a balcony that overlooked the sea and the 57 mountains beyond the distant town. There was one wall of glass through which they could, while lying in bed, look out at the large, unbroken clouds. Below were the coconut palms and the pool. Next to that was the dining plaza, mosaic-floored, open on three sides to the trade winds and the view. At lunch the tables and the waiters wore white starched cloth, but the guests could sit like pampered children with dripping suits and bare feet. Next to this alfresco delight was the evening dining room—as enclosed, carpeted, and muffled as this one was open and fresh. The three guitarists and the girl who wore purple lipstick came to the dining room twice nightly to shed their thousand tears—*"Mil Lágrimas,"* the song with which they opened and closed their program. So twice each evening (their contempt made them tireless)

---

2. A thousand tears, a thousand tears of love.

Ben and Sandra clutched each other's hands and monkeyed up anguish into their faces. They did so well that one night the group came and sang at their table. Afterward Sandra was ashamed. But Ben said they deserved to be fooled.

"*Mil lágrimas*, for God's sake!" Ben said. "That's no way to talk about sorrow." 58

"What is, then?" Sandra had asked. She thought that Ben, who knew a great deal, would also know that. 59

But Ben only scowled and rummaged in his crew cut. "It's just no way!" 60

After that, *mil lágrimas* was shown its place. When the unfamiliar rum 61 drinks went to Ben's head in a night club and they had to leave before the dancers came on, Ben told her with mock gravity that he was suffering from *mil lágrimas*. And when Sandra got sick on the twisty ride up the mountain to El Yunque, the rain forest, it was the same thing.

The Sandra who stands in the kitchen over Lily's dinner now sees, with 62 idiotically pricking eyelids, the other Sandra and Ben. She no longer sees them tiny, through ten years' distance. But still they stumble and suffer like children. She sees the other Sandra and Ben signing up for the trip to the rain forest—their one and only venture into organized sight-seeing—with disdain, naturally. Then, half hoping they will miss it, they are late, the last ones to enter the shiny black limousine parked at the entrance to their hotel.

Their driver and guide is a tan-skinned man of athletic though portly 63 build. His hair is well brushed; he wears a natty sports shirt and slacks. Down here, until he speaks, he might be mistaken for an American business-man with a really good tan. But of course he is not. He is only the driver and guide, with much good will toward the United States.

In the back of the car are two young men close in age, possibly brothers, 64 the older no more than twenty. They sit tall and look clean, with long, clean fingers wearing gold college rings. Sandra sits beside the younger brother and Ben takes the well-padded jump seat ahead, turning halfway round to her. A plump, dark-haired woman, perhaps in her middle forties, sits up front and is quickly classified, by signs and looks, as one of the dreadful drawbacks of sight-seeing trips. She wears more jewelry than she ought with a cotton dress, and she rivals the guide for cheery chattiness in a situation that obviously, unless you are a guide, calls for aloof silence. Other than that it is not clear why Ben and Sandra make their uncompromising judgment of her, though they seem in perfect agreement on it.

Aproned Sandra now gives her nose another blow. Poor, talkative woman, 65 worried all during the trip about their being so young and possibly cold-hearted, and trying to rouse them. . . .

They drive through the open country that connects the towns. Words 66 flow from the driver as easily as miles from the wheels.

". . . Here was once coconut plantations. Now no more. Why? Pay very 67 little. Coconuts not so much any more in demand. What they get? A man who pick a thousand coconuts . . ."

Sandra and Ben crane necks upward, following the curving trunks, to the fruit high above. Then how many trees would he have to climb to pick . . . They calculate, are shocked by their own arithmetic. He must climb all day, monkey-fashion, with only the aid of a band of cloth tied ankle to ankle. ⁶⁸

". . . An' how much you think the man who chop the coconut get?" the guide goes on. "Chop off the husk with the machete?" ⁶⁹

Ben and Sandra listen, stricken again. He must chop all day, all day, never straightening his back. ⁷⁰

The woman in front gives her bracelets a jangle. "And let's hope," she says, "he doesn't lose a hand in the process." ⁷¹

More flatness. They begin to see at intervals some cement-block buildings. Stuck in the earth before each is a sign with a picture of a spoked wheel, like a party symbol. One of the brothers wants to know what that is. The plump woman in the front looks knowingly around to the back and then up at the guide. ⁷²

"That is *Fomento*," the guide says. "That is our government's effort to establish our own industry on the island. With the help, of course, of the United States. But is a wonderful effort to help the people by giving them industry here." ⁷³

The older brother wants to know if it is working out. He doesn't see much going on. ⁷⁴

"Is going on," the guide says. "Sometimes wait for machines from the United States, sometimes wait for people to show how to use machines, sometimes wait for material, but is going on. *Fomento* is the same in English— to rouse the people?" ⁷⁵

The woman up front moves restlessly and then twists to the back. "It is going on, you can take it from me," she says. ⁷⁶

The two brothers continue to gaze out their near window as if to show that no matter how baffled they may be, *her* reassurance is not wanted. ⁷⁷

Soon the car begins the slow climb up the mountain that leads to the rain forest. They see clumps of bamboo and ferns grown into trees—long, slender trunks leaping up, absurd as giraffe necks. Now and then they see wet in the road. Spatters of rain fall all the time, but never for very long, the guide tells them, as if he has arranged everything for their comfort. Suddenly, at a bend, there is a lovely waterfall, a flat cutout for cars, with a few people standing around and several little boys with wooden crates that serve as tables for bananas and flowers. The driver pulls over to the cutout and parks. ⁷⁸

"Only for a few minutes . . ." The driver is already out the door, pursing his lips in a very Latin, very deprecating manner. "To stretch, to look at the water, eat a banana, smell a flower . . ." ⁷⁹

The little boys chatter at the tourists. They lift up their wares—brown- ⁸⁰

skinned bananas, some so ripe their seams have burst, and the heavy-scented, white ginger flowers.

Nearby, a couple from the States are arguing. The man has heard the fruit is not safe to eat. He stands balky as a child while his wife stares at him with fury. Ben draws Sandra away. They are so newly married they feel that any quarrel between husband and wife diminishes their honor. *"Mil lágrimas,"* he whispers to her, his voice doleful with irony. *"Ay-ay-ay,"* Sandra whispers back. 81

The car resumes its twisting climb. The flower stalk Ben tosses onto Sandra's lap ("I just boomed the economy," he says, frowning) begins to ooze. Scent hangs in the humid air, bringing on a memory of the near-nauseating excitement of their wedding and translating itself into *mil lágrimas* in Sandra's stomach. Ben sees, then rolls down his window and leans forward so she can get the air. 82

At last they are at the top of the road. Of course it is disappointing. Of course there is nothing to be seen there that they have not already seen on the way up. The sole point of this forest on the mountain seems to be to draw more height from its plant stalks. Everything Sandra has seen at home, growing nicely as a plant in a pot, is here a tree. 83

In the silence of the descent the woman in the front seat grows restless again. She alters her position, gazes more than once at the guide, jangles her bracelets above her head and consults her watch. At last the guide clears his throat. "We are going to make an extra little sight-seeing today. At no extra cost. Something very interesting for you." 84

Ben, Sandra's protector against *mil lágrimas*, strengthens his shy voice to give it authority: "It's out if it means additional riding." 85

"No additional riding," the guide says, holding up his brown hand. "We go back to the hotel another way, that is all. Through some villages in the mountains. There we make one little stop. You will see our sad poor people and also what we do for them. Very interesting for you." 86

After the car twists down some more of the mountain, he parks at the side of a narrow road. They all sit in the car and stare. Sandra is not well traveled, but she is willing to accept as truth the guide's sad boast that "nobody has less than they do." The stilt village of crazily sloping walls and roofs (made of what—paper? tin cans?) is dark with the darkness of a forest and of the faces that seem to sleep with open eyes. The bodies to which the faces belong sit in the dirt, leaning against a tree trunk or, like last straws, against a hut whose side already leans halfway to the ground. Children peep from every corner, some wearing little filthy shirts, some naked. They are testimony to the fact that there is one activity that still goes on in the motionless village. The children, though they do not know it yet, are its thousand tears. 87

The plump woman in the front seat begins to instruct them, her voice breaking in like the voice in a documentary. "This is how they live. This is the meaning of *Fomento*. From this village and from others like it the workers will come." 88

They all look at her. She flushes, shakes her bracelets, rocks her head a    89
little in nervousness and pride.

"My husband has a factory," she says. "He gave up a thriving business    90
in New York to start again here. It isn't easy. He has to teach everything.
Machines are broken, cloth is ruined."

She puts her hands to her cheeks, mottled with excitement. "Americans    91
should see this. To know what's being done. . . ."

Sandra feels the young man next to her take a deep breath. "I suppose,"    92
he says coldly, "it has nothing to do with the fact that it's tax-free. Nothing
to do with cheap labor."

The woman looks stunned. Her eyes shine with tears of disappoint-    93
ment. "I resent that," she manages to say. "I resent that very much." Her
voice trembles under its weight of feeling. "These people will have an industry, these children will have a future. . . ." She twists to the back, reaches
out a bangle-jangling arm to the brothers. "I understand your feelings. You're
afraid a few will do something to disappoint you." The brothers' faces redden. No one looks at the plump woman and no one answers her. "We're all
of us idealistic. All Americans . . ."

To the guide's credit it must be said that he gets them home as fast as    94
he can—without chatter, without slowdowns and with nothing but a no-no
wave to a little brown boy who calls frantically to him from behind a pile of
ripe bananas. But it is hardly fast enough for Sandra. As soon as they are
back she flings herself on the bed.

"I think I'll sleep," she mutters to Ben. "Why don't you go down and    95
swim?"

"Good idea." He watches from a chair, his hands wrung together. "Maybe    96
I'll stay and just be quiet."

"No—go down, go down!"    97

Ben gets up slowly. It is as if she had depressed one side of a scale and    98
he were rising with the other side, to be weighted. Just before he leaves,
Sandra pats her belly and whispers, *"Mil lágrimas."* In a way it is true. The
dinners *en brochette*, the icy rum drinks, the dessert-heavy luncheons by the
pool, all curdle in her stomach. Beyond their honeymoon, surrounding it like
plague outside the walls, has been all the while, running like fire, this terrible
cycle of the people who have no luck.

She has already heard, in New York, stories about Puerto Ricans. But    99
now—what if some of these forgotten ones she has just seen are to become
the unknown ones about whom the tales in New York are told? What if,
when *Fomento* rolls on, some of these people, roused from their lethargy, go
north with their new trade? Or with no trade? Killed in brawls; killed when
the gas heaters fail or fire breaks out, overwhelming ten children at once;
killed with bullets or clubs. It is like terror in childhood. A giant hand covers
the universe. "I'll get you in your bed or I'll get you on the ship or I'll get
you . . ."

Next morning they take the plane home, where Sandra promptly devel-    100 ops flu. Watched by her mother, who had hoped to see her fatted and calmed by the mystery of consummation, Sandra hacks and sneezes and loses her tan. It is all very satisfying. When she recovers, everything is normal again. Ben is Ben and Puerto Rico is far away. The bits of it that have come to New York sink easily from her sight. . . .

The children shout, "Happy anniversary!" at her again. Her son stops to joggle on one foot as he follows his father into the kitchen.    101

"Why," Ben asks without warning, "were you thinking of Puerto Rico?" He pretends to grumble. "It wasn't that long ago."    102

Sandra isn't looking at Ben. She is peering into the oven at Lily's roast. But she is sure that Ben is smiling at the children to show them: "This is nothing serious. Your mother and I have this joke."    103

In the same way Sandra turns to smile at them when she answers, "I was thinking of the people we saw in the villages there. Remember how they looked?" And in the same way again she smiles at the children after the gifts are opened, because a queer feeling has taken hold of her. It seems to Sandra that as the children's eyes shift from one face to the other, doting on their parents' pleasure (Sandra's bangle, Ben's cuff links), they are foreshadowing their own far-off time as parents. Sandra's heart thuds once, as if it had run ahead of itself and collided with something. *Mira! Mira!* What will become . . .    104

When the children are in bed Ben pours brandy. He fits the glass into Sandra's lifted hand and kisses her. "Anyway, darling, happy anniversary. . . ."    105

"Happy anniversary anyway, darling," Sandra says.    106

Ben sits beside her on the sofa and stretches his legs. "Do you remember . . ." he begins. At the same time a hoarse wail pierces the room. It is the siren of a police van or an ambulance, racing along the freezing streets. "Do you remember . . ." Ben begins again. "We took a tour. And there was this woman . . ." The siren reaches full cry, as if at their door. Elsewhere at that moment—Sandra feels it with a resonant certainty—klaxons scream; bombers roar aloft. From the city and from the world, the clamor that goes up fills the house. Ben and Sandra sit in silence, waiting for it to recede.    107

## STUDY QUESTIONS

1. How much do we know about Sandra Loeb? about her husband Ben? about her children? How much of the story is about her marriage and family? about her life in a "mixed" neighborhood?

2. How important to the story is Sandra Loeb's own ethnic background? What bothers her most about the attitudes of others in her neighborhood? How defensive is she about her own relative affluence? How does she feel about specific people in her

neighborhood? about the presence there of Puerto Ricans? How do her opinions differ from those of others in the neighborhood?

3. What function does the newspaper strike perform for the story? How are people's responses to "news" different during the strike? How reliable does the "news" passed along orally seem to be? Do you believe the two accounts of death as they are presented? How reliable do the tellers of these stories seem to be?

4. How does Sandra Loeb respond to the phrase "as long as they only kill each other"? How do you respond? Describe the effect produced by using a "code" word like "they." How do you think the author expects us as readers to respond to people who use such a phrase?

5. What "characteristics" do Puerto Ricans possess, according to the policeman and the taxi driver? What evidence does the story present that such conclusions are not valid?

6. What does Sandra Loeb "learn" about Puerto Ricans from her honeymoon trip? Why does she remember the trip so vividly on this particular day? What relationship does she imply that the trip and the day's events have to each other? What is her husband's role in her memories? What is his role in the story?

7. Describe the effect of the repeated phrase "mil lágrimas." Where in the story does it begin to accumulate specific meaning for you? Explain the different meanings of the title of the story.

8. What function does the "plump, dark-haired woman" (paragraph 64) in the sightseeing limousine perform for the story? What function do the two young men in the back of the limousine perform? What function does Lily perform?

9. Describe the behavior of Americans in Puerto Rico. What aspects of their behavior does the story emphasize?

10. How much of the story's impact is produced by the SETTING in time? in place? How does the contrast between the urban settings of the West Side and the rural countryside in Puerto Rico affect the story's TONE? its THEME? How does it affect the total portrayal of Puerto Ricans in the story?

# Pat Mora

Born in El Paso, Pat Mora writes poems in which her Chicana heritage and Southwestern background are central. Her first book, *Chants* (which won the Southwest Book Award), is largely composed of what she calls "desert incantations." Her second, *Borders* (from which the following poem is taken), describes the two cultures that create her own "border" life.

This poem offers ironic advice to immigrants about how to make their children fit in.

# IMMIGRANTS

wrap their babies in the American flag,
feed them mashed hot dogs and apple pie,
name them Bill and Daisy,
buy them blonde dolls that blink blue
eyes or a football and tiny cleats                              5
before the baby can even walk,
speak to them in thick English,
        hallo, babee, hallo,
whisper in Spanish or Polish
when the babies sleep, whisper                                  10
in a dark parent bed, that dark
parent fear, "Will they like
our boy, our girl, our fine american
boy, our fine american girl?"

## STUDY QUESTIONS

1. What, according to the poem, does being an "American" consist of? What are "typical" Americans like? What do they do? What do they look like? What does the poem imply about American tolerance for difference or individuality?

2. Who is the "their" in line 1? the "they" in line 12?

3. Explain the implied differences between "speak" (l. 7) and "whisper" (ll. 9, 10). What is the source of the parents' "dark" fears?

4. What ATTITUDE does the poem ultimately take toward conformity? toward assimilation? How, exactly, does the IRONY of the poem work?

# Mitsuye Yamada

Born in Kyushu, Japan, Mitsuye Yamada now lives in California, where she teaches at Cypress College. She was reared in Seattle until, when World War II began, her family was removed to a concentration camp in Idaho. Her book of poems, *Camp*

*Notes and Other Poems* (1976), was in part written during her years in the concentration camp.

The following poem describes an experience of divided loyalty felt by someone asked to renounce all allegiance to her Japanese heritage.

# THE QUESTION OF LOYALTY

I met the deadline
for alien registration
once before
was numbered fingerprinted
and ordered not to travel                                           5
without permit.

But alien still they said I must
forswear allegiance to the emperor.
for me that was easy
I didn't even know him                                            10
but my mother who did cried out
    If I sign this
    What will I be?
    I am doubly loyal
    to my American children                                 15
    also to my own people.
    How can double mean nothing?
    I wish no one to lose this war.
    Everyone does.

I was poor                                                        20
at math.
I signed
my only ticket out.

## STUDY QUESTIONS

1. How much are we told about the SPEAKER? What do the earlier events in her life suggest about her background? her feelings? about the way she perceives her place in American society? What indications are there of her age? What suggestions are there that the "present" of the poem is long after the central event described in it?

2. Explain the different generational responses to the question of loyalty. How does each interpret what loyalty means? What is the speaker's motivation for her decision to sign? How does she feel about her decision?

3. How does the poem make use of contrasts between human feelings and routine, impersonal, and "numbered" outlooks on human life? How does the speaker respond to such choices? In what sense is her signature a "ticket" (line 23)?

4. What, exactly, does the final word of the poem mean?

# Martin Luther King, Jr.

Born in Atlanta, the son and grandson of ministers, Martin Luther King, Jr., attended Morehouse College, Crozier Theological Seminary, and Boston University, from which he received the doctorate. Eventually he became minister of the same congregation, Ebenezer Baptist Church in Atlanta, led by his father and founded by his maternal grandfather. His leadership of the Civil Rights movement through his position with the Southern Christian Leadership Conference is legendary. He died a martyr in 1968, the victim of an assassin's bullet in Memphis.

"I Have a Dream," perhaps the most famous words uttered by King, was a speech delivered in 1963 in front of the Lincoln Memorial in Washington, D.C.

# I HAVE A DREAM

I am happy to join with you today in what will go down in history as the greatest demonstration for freedom in the history of our nation. 1

Five score years ago, a great American, in whose symbolic shadow we stand today, signed the Emancipation Proclamation. This momentous decree came as a great beacon light of hope to millions of Negro slaves who had been seared in the flames of withering injustice. It came as a joyous daybreak to end the long night of their captivity. 2

But one hundred years later, the Negro still is not free; one hundred years later, the life of the Negro is still sadly crippled by the manacles of segregation and the chains of discrimination; one hundred years later, the Negro lives on a lonely island of poverty in the midst of a vast ocean of material prosperity; one hundred years later, the Negro is still languished in the corners of American society and finds himself in exile in his own land. 3

So we've come here today to dramatize a shameful condition. In a sense we've come to our nation's capital to cash a check. When the architects of our republic wrote the magnificent words of the Constitution and the Declaration of Independence, they were signing a promissory note to which every 4

American was to fall heir. This note was the promise that all men, yes, black men as well as white men, would be guaranteed the unalienable rights of life, liberty, and the pursuit of happiness.

It is obvious today that America has defaulted on this promissory note in so far as her citizens of color are concerned. Instead of honoring this sacred obligation, America has given the Negro people a bad check; a check which has come back marked "insufficient funds." But we refuse to believe that the bank of justice is bankrupt. We refuse to believe that there are insufficient funds in the great vaults of opportunity of this nation. And so we've come to cash this check, a check that will give us upon demand the riches of freedom and the security of justice.

We have also come to this hallowed spot to remind America of the fierce urgency of now. This is no time to engage in the luxury of cooling off or to take the tranquilizing drug of gradualism. Now is the time to make real the promises of democracy; now is the time to rise from the dark and desolate valley of segregation to the sunlit path of racial justice; now is the time to lift our nation from the quicksands of racial injustice to the solid rock of brotherhood; now is the time to make justice a reality for all of God's children. It would be fatal for the nation to overlook the urgency of the moment. This sweltering summer of the Negro's legitimate discontent will not pass until there is an invigorating autumn of freedom and equality.

Nineteen sixty-three is not an end, but a beginning. And those who hope that the Negro needed to blow off steam and will now be content, will have a rude awakening if the nation returns to business as usual. There will be neither rest nor tranquility in America until the Negro is granted his citizenship rights. The whirlwinds of revolt will continue to shake the foundations of our nation until the bright day of justice emerges.

But there is something that I must say to my people, who stand on the worn threshold which leads into the palace of justice. In the process of gaining our rightful place, we must not be guilty of wrongful deeds. Let us not seek to satisfy our thirst for freedom by drinking from the cup of bitterness and hatred. We must forever conduct our struggle on the high plain of dignity and discipline. We must not allow our creative protests to degenerate into physical violence. Again and again we must rise to the majestic heights of meeting physical force with soul force. The marvelous new militancy, which has engulfed the Negro community, must not lead us to a distrust of all white people. For many of our white brothers, as evidenced by their presence here today, have come to realize that their destiny is tied up with our destiny. And they have come to realize that their freedom is inextricably bound to our freedom. We cannot walk alone. And as we walk, we must make the pledge that we shall always march ahead. We cannot turn back.

There are those who are asking the devotees of Civil Rights, "When will you be satisfied?" We can never be satisfied as long as the Negro is the victim of the unspeakable horrors of police brutality; we can never be satisfied as long as our bodies, heavy with the fatigue of travel, cannot gain lodging in the motels of the highways and the hotels of the cities; we cannot be satisfied as long as the Negro's basic mobility is from a smaller ghetto to a larger one; we can never be satisfied as long as our children are stripped of their selfhood and robbed of their dignity by signs stating "For White Only"; we cannot be satisfied as long as the Negro in Mississippi cannot vote and a Negro in New York believes he has nothing for which to vote. No! No, we are not satisfied, and we will not be satisfied until "justice rolls down like waters and righteousness like a mighty stream."

I am not unmindful that some of you have come here out of great trials and tribulations. Some of you have come fresh from narrow jail cells. Some of you have come from areas where your quest for freedom left you battered by the storms of persecution and staggered by the winds of police brutality. You have been the veterans of creative suffering. Continue to work with the faith that unearned suffering is redemptive. Go back to Mississippi. Go back to Alabama. Go back to South Carolina. Go back to Georgia. Go back to Louisiana. Go back to the slums and ghettos of our Northern cities, knowing that somehow this situation can and will be changed. Let us not wallow in the valley of despair.

I say to you today, my friends, so even though we face the difficulties of today and tomorrow, I still have a dream. It is a dream deeply rooted in the American dream. I have a dream that one day this nation will rise up and live out the true meaning of its creed, "We hold these truths to be self-evident, that all men are created equal." I have a dream that one day on the red hills of Georgia, sons of former slaves and the sons of former slave owners will be able to sit down together at the table of brotherhood. I have a dream that one day even the state of Mississippi, a state sweltering with the heat of injustice, sweltering with the heat of oppression, will be transformed into an oasis of freedom and justice. I have a dream that my four little children will one day live in a nation where they will not be judged by the color of their skin, but by the content of their character.

I HAVE A DREAM TODAY!

I have a dream that one day down in Alabama—with its vicious racists, with its Governor having his lips dripping with the words of interposition and nullification—one day right there in Alabama, little black boys and black girls will be able to join hands with little white boys and white girls as sisters and brothers.

I HAVE A DREAM TODAY!

I have a dream that one day every valley shall be exalted, every hill and mountain shall be made low. The rough places will be plain and the crooked places will be made straight, "and the glory of the Lord shall be revealed, and all flesh shall see it together."

This is our hope. This is the faith that I go back to the South with. With this faith we will be able to hew out of the mountain of despair, a stone of hope. With this faith we will be able to transform the jangling discords of our nation into a beautiful symphony of brotherhood. With this faith we will be able to work together, to pray together, to struggle together, to go to jail together, to stand up for freedom together, knowing that we will be free one day. And this will be the day. This will be the day when all of God's children will be able to sing with new meaning, "My country 'tis of thee, sweet land of liberty, of thee I sing. Land where my father died, land of the pilgrim's pride, from every mountainside, let freedom ring." And if America is to be a great nation, this must become true.

So let freedom ring from the prodigious hilltops of New Hampshire; let 17 freedom ring from the mighty mountains of New York; let freedom ring from the heightening Alleghenies of Pennsylvania; let freedom ring from the snow-capped Rockies of Colorado; let freedom ring from the curvaceous slopes of California. But not only that. Let freedom ring from Stone Mountain of Georgia; let freedom ring from Lookout Mountain of Tennessee; let freedom ring from every hill and mole hill of Mississippi. "From every mountainside, let freedom ring."

And when this happens, and when we allow freedom to ring, when we 18 let it ring from every village and every hamlet, from every state and every city, we will be able to speed up that day when all of God's children, black men and white men, Jews and Gentiles, Protestants and Catholics, will be able to join hands and sing in the words of the old Negro spiritual: "Free at last. Free at last. Thank God Almighty, we are free at last."

## STUDY QUESTIONS

1. What, specifically, is accomplished by echoing, at the beginning, the words of Abraham Lincoln? What echoes of Lincoln do you find elsewhere in the speech?

2. What effects are produced by the frequent patterns of repetition? How is the device of repetition related to the way history is conceived in the speech? How is the repetition related to THEMES developed in the speech?

3. Explain the check / promissory note IMAGERY beginning in paragraph 4. In what different ways is the image developed? What other extended images does the speech present? Besides Lincoln, what other familiar sources are echoed or alluded to?

4. Why is it significant that the most forceful part of the speech is presented through the imagery of a dream?

# Luis Valdez

B orn in 1940 in Delano, California, Luis Valdez was educated at San Jose State University. Son of a migrant farm worker, Valdez himself became a union organizer and worked with Cesar Chavez, but he has also taught at the University of California, both at Santa Cruz and at Berkeley. He is founder and artistic director of El Teatro Campesino. He has written a number of plays, including *Zoot Suit* and *I Don't Have to Show You No Stinking Badges*. He also wrote and directed the hit movie *La Bamba*.

The Shrunken Head of Pancho Villa uses both realistic and surrealistic strategies to create symbolic effects and to achieve a strong political statement.

## THE SHRUNKEN HEAD OF PANCHO VILLA

*A Mi Padre,*[1] *Francisco "Pancho" Valdez*

### Personajes

PEDRO, the jefito,[2] an old Villista con huevos.
CRUZ, the madre, long-suffering but loving.
JOAQUIN, the youngest son, a vato loco[3] and a Chicano.
LUPE, the daughter.
MINGO, the son, a Mexican-American.
CHATO, Joaquin's camarada.[4]
BELARMINO, the oldest son.
LAJURA, a police officer.

---

1. To my father. [The editors wish to thank Philip Esparza of El Teatro Campesino for his help with these footnotes.]
2. Father. *Villista con huevos:* a gutsy follower of Pancho Villa.
3. Crazy guy.
4. Pal.

Scene

The interior of an old house: a large, imposing two-story building sagging into total dilapidation. The front room with tall cracked windows; doors to a stairwell and the kitchen; and an adjoining room with a curtained doorway, once a study now also a bedroom. This front room, which is the center of the play's action, has been repainted with a true Mexican folk taste. Bright reds, yellows and blues try to obscure the shabby, broken-down "chingado"[5] quality of it all.

Note on Style

The play is not intended as a "realistic" interpretation of Chicano life. The symbolism emerging from the character of Belarmino influences the style of acting, scene design, make-up, etc. The play therefore contains realistic and surrealistic elements working together to achieve a transcendental expression of the social condition of La Raza in los Estados Unidos.[6] The set, particularly, must be "real" for what it represents; but it must also contain a cartoon quality such as that found in the satirical sketches of Jose Clemente Orozco or the lithographs of Jose Guadalupe Posada. In short, it must reflect the psychological reality of the barrio.

Prologue

FRANCISCO VILLA, born 1878—died 1923[7]
    Campesino, bandit, guerrilla, martyr, general, head of Northern Division of the Revolutionary Army, and finally an undying legend.
    He is born and christened Doroteo Arango in the town of Rio Grande, state of Durango. In 1895, when he is 17, he is outlawed for killing an *hacendado*, a landowner—a member of the ruling class who had raped his sister. He is caught, but escapes and he takes the name of Francisco Villa. Thus, during the years between 1896 and 1909, the legend of Pancho Villa is born. The legend of the providential bandit: rob the rich to give to the poor. And the poor give him their faith.
    1910 brings the beginning of the Mexican Revolution. Pancho Villa enlists

5. Run-down.

6. The Mexican-American people.

7. As produced by El Teatro Campesino, this short biography formed the narrative of a slide show that opened the play, showing photographs from the life and career of Francisco Villa. [Author's note]

his band of men as a guerrilla force. Minor victories grow into major victories: San Andres, Camargo, Juarez, Torreon, Zacatecas, Irapuato, Queretaro. The bandit force becomes a Revolutionary Army with horses, trains, cavalry, artillery, and a mass of 50,000 men. The peasant outlaw evolves into one of the most brilliant military strategists of our century.

November 27, 1914: Pancho Villa and Emiliano Zapata meet in Mexico City. It is a triumph for the poor, the campesinos, the disinherited. Pancho Villa tries out the Presidential chair, yet neither he nor Zapata are compromising types. They are not politicians.

1915: Against the recommendations of his advisors, Woodrow Wilson, President of the United States, recognizes the rival Carranzista government, and permits Carranza to transport troops over American soil and thus outflank Villa's Division del Norte at Agua Prieta. Villa is defeated. It is the beginning of the end.

1916: Villa retaliates with a raid on Columbus, New Mexico. He is declared an outlaw by the Carranza government, and Wilson sends General John J. Pershing into Mexican Territory on a "punitive expedition" looking for Pancho Villa. Pershing fails, and Villa resumes his guerrilla warfare. His military strength, however, is flagging.

1919: Emiliano Zapata is murdered on April 10 in Chinameca.

1920: July 28. Francisco Villa surrenders the remains of his army to the government. He settles in Canutillo and lives peacefully.

July 23, 1923: Pancho Villa is ambushed and he dies in the streets of Parral, Chihuahua. His body is dumped into an unmarked grave. Three years later it is disinterred and the corpse is decapitated. The head is never found. This is the story of a people who followed him beyond borders, beyond death.

# ACT I

*A sharp-stringed guitar plays "La Cucaracha." It is afternoon.*

PEDRO, *the aged father of the family, is asleep on a broken-down couch. He is on his back—his paunch sagging—and snoring loudly. He has long, drooping white moustaches and tousled white hair.*

*The guitar concludes "La Cucaracha" with a sharp, final note.* PEDRO, *as if by cue, shouts violently.*

PEDRO: [*In his sleep.*] VIVA VILLAA!!

[BELARMINO *screams from the curtained bedroom. It is the cry of a full-grown man. He starts singing with vengeance.*]

BELARMINO: Aarrrrrrgh! [*Sings.*]

LA CUCARACHA! LA CUCARACHA
YA NO QUIERE CAMINAR
PORQUE LE FALTA, PORQUE NO TIENE
MARIJUANA QUE FUMAR![8]

CRUZ: [*Running from the kitchen.*] Dios mio, you see what you do, hombre? You have wake up your own son! [BELARMINO *repeats "La Cucaracha," getting louder and more viciously impatient.* CRUZ, *distraught, runs into the curtained bedroom. From off.*] Belarmino, Belarmino, my son, go to sleep. Go to sleep. A la rrurru, niño, duermete ya. [BELARMINO *dozes off singing and is finally silent.* CRUZ *emerges, sighing with relief.*] Gracios a dios! He's asleep! [*To* PEDRO, *a harsh whisper.*] Be quiet, you old loco! You know he always wakes up hungry. I got enough trouble catching your son's lices so they don' eat us alive! You are crawling with them already.
PEDRO: [*In his sleep.*] Señores, I am Francisco Villa! [*Scratches.*]
CRUZ: Sweet name of God.
PEDRO: Pancho Villa!
CRUZ: Pedro!
PEDRO: I am Pancho Villa!
CRUZ: Yes, with lices!
PEDRO: Viva Villa!
CRUZ: Que hombre. [*She goes to him.*]
PEDRO: VIVA PANCHO VEE-
CRUZ: [*Pulls his leg.*] PEDRO!
PEDRO: Yah! [*He wakes up.*] Uh!
CRUZ: Stop shouting, hombre.
PEDRO: Uh. [*He goes back to sleep, scratching his belly.*]
CRUZ: Viejo loco.[9] Pancho Villa. I don' know what goes through that head he gots. [JOAQUIN *rushes in and stops, panting against the door. His shirt is torn.*] Joaquin! What happen to you?
JOAQUIN: Nothing.
CRUZ: What did you do?
JOAQUIN: Nothing.
CRUZ: What happen to your shirt?
JOAQUIN: Nothing!
CRUZ: Don' you know nothing but nothing?
JOAQUIN: [*Pause.*] I beat up some vato.
CRUZ: Another fight, my son?
JOAQUIN: I never start it. Dumb gavacho.[1] He come up to me and says "Heh, Pancho!"

8. The cockroach! The cockroach! / does not want to go / because it is lacking, because it has no / marijuana to smoke.
9. Crazy old man.
1. Gringo; American.

PEDRO: [*In his sleep.*] Uh?

CRUZ: You hit him for that?

JOAQUIN: Well, how would you like it, man? I wasn' looking for no trouble. I even take Pancho at first, which was bad enough, but then he call me a lousy Pancho, and I hit the stupid vato in the mouth.

CRUZ: Dios mio! [*Pause.*] What is wrong with you hombre? Don' you think? You on patrol!

JOAQUIN: Parole.

CRUZ: Si. [*Sighs.*] And mañana it will be the jail again, no? How come you this way, hijo?[2] Your brother Mingo he never fight so much.

JOAQUIN: He was pus-pus.

CRUZ: [*Miserable.*] Don' you know nothing else? Your brother he's coming from the war today with muchos medals, Joaquin. That is not so pus-pus. If he fight, he do it in the right place. Only you turn out so lousy.

JOAQUIN: [*Fiercely.*] I ain' lousy, ma!

CRUZ: [*Pause.*] You goin' to hit me in the mouth too, my son? [JOAQUIN *starts to go.*] What you doin'?

JOAQUIN: Splittin'!

CRUZ: Joaquin!

JOAQUIN: [*He stops.*] Stop bugging me, jefita![3]

CRUZ: [*With deep concern.*] What trouble you so much, hijo?

JOAQUIN: The gavachos.

LUPE: [*Comes in from the kitchen.*] Mama, the beans are ready! You wan' me to bring 'em?

CRUZ: No, Lupe, Belarmino is asleep.

LUPE: What happen to our favorite jailbird?

JOAQUIN: Shut up!

LUPE: Been out duk'ing again, huh? Rotten pachuco.[4]

CRUZ: Guadalupe, don' say that.

LUPE: It's true. He barely got outa jail yesterday, and now look at him. He don' even care that Mingo's coming home from the war. I bet he's just jealous.

JOAQUIN: Of what?

LUPE: His medals.

JOAQUIN: Screw his medals!

CRUZ: Joaquin! Don' you even feel glad you brother's come home alive and safe?

JOAQUIN: Simon,[5] it make me feel real patriotic.

LUPE: Liar! Just wait till Mingo gets here. He'll cool your bird. Lousy hoodlum.

---

2. Son. *Mañana:* tomorrow.

3. Mother.

4. Hoodlum.

5. Yeah, sure.

JOAQUIN: Lousy, huh? Well, how about this? [*He grabs* LUPE *and pretends to set a louse loose in her hair.*] Ha! Who's lousy now, man?

LUPE: Ayy, Mama! Mama!

CRUZ: Haven' you do enough already, muchacho?[6]

JOAQUIN: I was only joking.

CRUZ: But Belarmino—

JOAQUIN: I was only joking, man! I don' got no piojos.[7]

LUPE: That's what you think.

JOAQUIN: Shut up!

LUPE: You lousy Mexican!

CRUZ: Stop it, señorita. Din't I tell you to go water the beans?

LUPE: No!

CRUZ: Go water the beans! [*Pause.*] Andale. Go, Guadalupe.

[LUPE *exits.*]

JOAQUIN: And stay out!

CRUZ: You stop too, Joaquin. Wha's wrong with you anyways? Are you as loco as your padre?

JOAQUIN: Loco?

CRUZ: Making noise! This morning your poor brother he eat 50 plates of beans and 100 tortillas. This afternoon I fine 30 lices on him—do you hear, hombre? 30! My poor Belarmino, some of this days if he don' eat us out of the house, his lices they will do it. [*She turns and notices* JOAQUIN *scratching his head.*] Joaquin, what you doing?

JOAQUIN: [*Stops.*] What? [*Lowers his hand.*]

CRUZ: You was scratching your head! Blessed be the Señor! Come here, sit down.

JOAQUIN: [*Guiltily.*] What?

CRUZ: [*Inspecting his head.*] Dios mio, this all we need.

JOAQUIN: [*Angry.*] What?

CRUZ: For you to catch the lices, muchacho.

JOAQUIN: [*Tries to rise.*] Lices!

CRUZ: Don' move. [JOAQUIN *remains still.*] Joaquin! I think I find one! No . . . si . . . si! It is one. It gots little legs!

JOAQUIN: [*Jumps up.*] Let's see.

CRUZ: Put him up to the light, my son. [*Pause.*] It is . . . one lice, no?

JOAQUIN: A louse.

CRUZ: What is that?

JOAQUIN: One lice.

CRUZ: May the Señor help us all! [BELARMINO *grunts.*] Ay. Now he's waking up again. I better fix his frijolitos. [*Exits to kitchen.*]

JOAQUIN: Me too, huh señora? My pipes are rumbling.

6. Boy, young man.

7. Lice.

PEDRO: Si, mi general. I hear the rumbling. The gringos got cannons y aeroplanos, pero no se apure . . . mi General! Que paso con su cabeza? Muchachos, abusados! Alguien se robo la cabeza de Pancho Villa![8] Ayyy.

JOAQUIN: [*Shaking him.*] Pa! 'apa!

PEDRO: [*Awaking.*] Uh? What?

JOAQUIN: You have a nightmare.

PEDRO: How you know?

JOAQUIN: You shout. Something about Pancho Villa and his head. I don' know. It was in Spanish.

PEDRO: Huh. [*Sits up.*] Where's your madre?

JOAQUIN: In the kitchen.

PEDRO: Frying beans no doubt, *eh?* Only I never get to try 'em. The loco in the room over theres always eat 'em first. Curse the day all my sons was born starving in the land of the gringos! [*He finds an empty wine bottle under the couch.*] Ay, here it is. No, hombre, my little bottle is dead. Oye, my son, you got enough maybe for one . . . bueno, you know, eh?

JOAQUIN: Nel,[9] I'm sorry, jefito.

PEDRO: No, don' start wis your "I'm sorrys." Don' you find work yet?

JOAQUIN: Work?

PEDRO: Field work.

JOAQUIN: You mean like farm labor?

PEDRO: Man's work!

JOAQUIN: Cool it, ese,[1] I just get here. They work me enough in the can. I pull off more than a year wisout pay.

PEDRO: Bueno, it's your own fault. For your itchy fingers . . . stealing tires.

JOAQUIN: What tires?

PEDRO: Pos[2] what ones? They din' catch you red-handed?

JOAQUIN: Simon, but it wasn' tires. They arrest me for a suspect together with nine other vatos. Then there at the station the placa[3] give us all matches, and the one wis the short one was guilty. They catch me red-handed! But I din't swipe no tires.

PEDRO: No, eh? Well, I hope maybe you learn something.

JOAQUIN: No sweat, jefito. I learn to play the guitar.

PEDRO: Tha's all?

JOAQUIN: Nel, I sing too. Honest. Loan me your guitar, I show you.

PEDRO: No, Joaquin, I don' like to loan that guitar. I have too many years

---

8. . . . but don't worry . . . my General! What happened to your head? Boys, watch out! Someone has stolen the head of Pancho Villa!

9. No.

1. Man.

2. Well.

3. Police.

with it, since the Revolucion! Que caray,[4] what happen if you break it.
Ees too old.

JOAQUIN: What about when I fix it that time?

PEDRO: When?

JOAQUIN: When you smash it on Mingo's head.

PEDRO: Oh si. But the babozo he talk back to me, tha's how come. Bueno,
que caray, go bring it pues[5]—I want to see if you really know how to
play it.

JOAQUIN: Orale.[6] [*He goes into the side room and comes out with an old guitar.*]

PEDRO: What you play? Corridos, rancheras?[7]

JOAQUIN: Rhythm and Blues.

PEDRO: [*Pause.*] What about "Siete Leguas"?

JOAQUIN: What about it?

PEDRO: You see, you don' know nothing.

JOAQUIN: What's "Siete Leguas"?

PEDRO: "Seven Leguas"! How you say leguas in—

JOAQUIN: Uh, leaguews.

PEDRO: What?

JOAQUIN: Lea-gews.

PEDRO: That's right. "Siete Leguas." The song of the horse of Pancho Villa.
The horse he mos' estimated. [*Solemnly.*] He ride that horse until the day
he die.

JOAQUIN: The general?

PEDRO: No, the horse. After that Pancho Villa buy a Chivi. Maybe it was a
Ford? No, it was a Chivi. 1923! That was the year they kill him, you
know. A revolutionary giant like he was.

JOAQUIN: Aaah, he wasn' a giant.

PEDRO: Oh, caray, you don' know, my son! Francisco Villa was a man to
respect. A man to fear! A man con muchos . . . ummmhhh [*Huevos.*] He
rob from the rich to give to the poor—like us. That's why the poor
follow him. Any time he could rise 50,000 men by snapping his fingers.
You should have see what he do to the gringos.

JOAQUIN: The gavachos?

PEDRO: No, the gringos. In them times they was only call gringos. Not gavachos. Pancho Villa have 'em running all over Mexico.

JOAQUIN: What was they doing in Mexico?

PEDRO: Chasing him! But they never catch him. He was too smart, eh? Too
much cabeza. He ride on Siete Leguas and stay in the mountains. Then
he ride his men around the back, and they kill gringos until they get

---

4. What the hell.
5. Then. *Babozo:* fool.
6. All right!
7. Ballads, cowboy songs.

tired! Sometimes they even get more tire' than picking potatoes, but they go back to the mountains to rest.

JOAQUIN: [*Impressed.*] Heh, man, tha's too much.

PEDRO: I myself ride with him, you know. See this scar? [*Points to his neck.*] From a bullet. And listen to this: VIVA VILLAAAA!

CRUZ: [*In the kitchen.*] Pedro, hombre! You wake your son!

PEDRO: [*Shouts back.*] Oh, you and that crazy loco! [*To* JOAQUIN] Huh, that stinking madre of yours! All she live for is to feed that bean belly! He has curse my life.

JOAQUIN: What about Pancho Villa? When he got the Chivi? I bet he run down a lotta gavachos, huh? Squashed 'em!

PEDRO: [*With exaggeration.*] Oh, si! He—[*Pause.*] The Chivi? No, hombre, when he get the Chivi then they get him. Right in Chihuahua too, in Parral. He was just driving down the street one day, not bothering nobody, when they shoot him down and kill him. [*Mournful pause.*] So . . . they bury him, and then in the night three years later, somebody come and—ZAS! They cut off his head.

JOAQUIN: His *head?*

PEDRO: Chattap! [*Whispering.*] You want Belarmino to hear?

JOAQUIN: How come they cut off his head? Who done it?

PEDRO: Pos who you think?

JOAQUIN: Los gavachos!

PEDRO: [*Nods.*] Maybe they still even got it too. To this day nobody has find it.

JOAQUIN: Hijola, how gacho,[8] man. [*Pause.*] How did that song goes?

PEDRO: "Siete Leguas"?

JOAQUIN: Simon.

PEDRO: [*Sings.*] "Siete Leguas, el caballo que Villa mas estimabaaa."[9]

BELARMINO: [*In his room.*] Ay! Yai! Yai! Yai!

PEDRO: Oh-oh, now we do it.

CRUZ: [*Entering.*] What have you do, hombre?

PEDRO: NOTHING.

[BELARMINO *yells and howls, sings* "La Cucaracha."]

CRUZ: No, eh? [*Shouting back.*] Lupe, bring the tortillas!

PEDRO: We eat now?

CRUZ: You wait!

PEDRO: I don' wan to wait!

[BELARMINO *yells.*]

CRUZ: Lupe, bring the beans too! [*She goes into the bedroom.*]

8. Aw, man, how gross.

9. The horse that Villa loved the most.

PEDRO: I don' got to wait! I wan' to eat—EAT! Quiero tragar![1]

[LUPE *comes out of the kitchen with beans and tortillas.* JOAQUIN *grabs a tortilla with a laugh.*]

LUPE: You pig!

PEDRO: [*Turns around.*] Pig?

LUPE: I meant Joaquin. [*She goes into the bedroom quickly.*]

PEDRO: Sinverguenzas![2] Who's the boss here pues? Who buys the eats!

CRUZ: [*Inside the room.*] El Welfare!

PEDRO: And before that?

CRUZ: Your son, Mingo.

PEDRO: Mingo? [*Throws his arms out in a helpless gesture.*] So this is what I get, eh? In 1927 I come here all the way from Zacatecas. For what? CHICK-ENSQUAT? Everybody talks back, that . . . that loco in there eats before his padre does, and Mingo . . . Mingo . . . Where's Mingo?

JOAQUIN: [*Eating the rolled up tortilla.*] Not home from the war yet.

[MINGO *walks into the room through the front door. He is in a soldier's uniform and carries a sack with his stuff in it.*]

MINGO: Somebody say war?

LUPE: [*Peeking out of* BELARMINO's *room.*] Mama, Mingo's home!

CRUZ: [*Coming out with the bowl of beans.*] My son! [*She embraces him and cries.*]

PEDRO: Bueno, bueno, lemme see him. He's my son too!

MINGO: Hello, Pa. [*Offers his hand.*]

PEDRO: Halo que?[3] Give me one abrazo, I'm your padre! [*He hugs him.*] Tha's it—strong like a man. Look, vieja, see how much medals he gots?

LUPE: Hi Mingo, remember me!

MINGO: Sure. Maria!

LUPE: Maria!

MINGO: [*Pause.*] Rosita?

LUPE: Lupe!

MINGO: Oh, yeah, Lupe.

PEDRO: And over heres you got your brother Joaquin.

MINGO: Hi, punk. Shake.

JOAQUIN: Orale. [*They shake hands.*]

CRUZ: Well, my son, sit down. Rest. You must be tired.

MINGO: Not at all, mom.

CRUZ: Tienes hambre?[4]

MINGO: What's for dinner?

1. I want to scarf up.
2. Scoundrels.
3. What do you mean hello? *Abrazo:* hug. *Vieja:* old lady, wife.
4. Are you hungry?

CRUZ: Papas con huevos.[5]

MINGO: What else?

LUPE: Huevos con papas.

MINGO: Is that all?

JOAQUIN: Papas a huevo.

MINGO: No thanks. I had a steak in town.

CRUZ: Oh. Well, thank God you have come home safe and sound. [*She takes him to the couch.*] Look, sit down over here. Tell us about . . . [*She sees the wine bottle.*] Pedro hombre, this dirty bottle!

MINGO: Still at it, huh pa?

PEDRO: No, only from time to time, hijo. For the cough. [*He coughs.*]

LUPE: Tell us of the war, Mingo.

CRUZ: What's wrong with you, women? Your brother he want to forget such things. It already pass, gracias a dios.

PEDRO: Huh, it pass. You mean we don' suppose to know where the muchacho was? War is war! If the sons fight today, we fight yesterday. Mira,[6] when I was with Pancho Villa, we kill more Americanos than—

MINGO: Americanos? Americans!

BELARMINO: [*In his room.*] ARRRRRGGGHHH!

MINGO: [*Alarmed.*] What the hell's that?

CRUZ: Belarmino! Lupe, please give him the beans that was left. I had forgot he didn't finish eating.

LUPE: He never finish eating. [*She exits.*]

MINGO: Mom, who's Belarmino?

CRUZ: [*Surprised.*] Pos . . . you know, hijo. You don' remember?

PEDRO: Of course, he remember! Caray, how he's going to forget that animal? Don' let him bother you, my son. Come here, tell me your plans. What you going to do now?

MINGO: Well, 'apa, I been thinking. [*Long pause.*]

PEDRO: He's been thinking, que bueno.[7] What you been thinking, hijo?

MINGO: I been thinking I wanna help the family!

CRUZ: Ay, mijito![8]

[*She embraces him.* PEDRO *shakes his hand.*]

MINGO: As a matter of fact, I gotta surprise for you. I bet you din't expect me till tonight, right? Well, you know how come I'm home early? I bought a new car!

JOAQUIN: A new car!

CRUZ: A new car!

LUPE: [*Reentering.*] A new car!

---

5. Potatoes with eggs; but *papas* and *huevos* are both slang for "balls."

6. Look.

7. How nice.

8. My dear son.

[BELARMINO *grunts three times, mimicking the sound of the words "A new car."*]

CRUZ: Dios mio!

LUPE: We din't even hear you drive up!

MINGO: Natch. She's as quiet as a fly in the beans. Mom, sis—hold on to your frijole bowl. There she is! [*Points out the window.*] A new Chevrolet!

LUPE: A Chevi! Mama, un Chevi!

CRUZ: Blessed by the name of the Señor. That one is ours, Mingo?

MINGO: All ours, only forty more payments to go. [*Everyone looks out the window except* PEDRO.] What's wrong, pa? Ain't you going to see?

PEDRO: For what? They going to come for it in two months.

MINGO: Not this baby. I'm gonna keep up all my payments.

PEDRO: Tha's what I used to say. I never make it.

MINGO: I know, but I ain't you. [*Pause.*] I mean it wasn' necessary, dad. Give me one good reason why you didn't keep good credit. Just one!

PEDRO: [BELARMINO *grunts hungrily in his room.*] There it is.

CRUZ: Guadalupe, go. [LUPE *exits to room.*]

MINGO: [*Pause. Everybody dejected.*] You know what's wrong with you people? You're all defeated! Just look at this place! Well, it ain't gonna get me down. I learned some skills in the Marines, and I'm gonna use 'em in the best place I know to get ahead!

PEDRO: Where?

MINGO: The fields.

JOAQUIN: A farm labor? [*Laughs*] You going to be a farm labor?

MINGO: Listen you cholo.[9]

CRUZ: Mingo, no!

PEDRO: Callate el hocico, babozo.[1]

MINGO: What's he ever done but land in jail, mom? What you ever done?

[JOAQUIN *blows a raspberry in his face.*]

CRUZ: Joaquin, es-stop it.

MINGO: You drop-out. You high school drop-out!

CRUZ: Mingo, please—

MINGO: You know what you're gonna end up like! Like the old man—a stinking *wino!*

PEDRO: WHAT?!

MINGO: [*Embarrassed pause.*] Aw, come on, dad. I din' mean nothing bad. Look, let's face it, okay? You're just a wino, right? Like I'm a Marine. What's wrong with that? There's a million of 'em. Today I was even going to buy you a bottle of Old Crow.

PEDRO: Whiskey?

MINGO: Damn rights. $6.50 a quart. It's better than that 35 cent stuff you

9. Young street tough.
1. Shut your mouth, you fool.

been drinking. From now on it's nothing but the best for us. Only we gotta be realistic. Plan everything. Okay, Tomahawk, you'll be working with me. You got a job now?

JOAQUIN: Chale.[2]

MINGO: You mean dad's the only one working?

PEDRO: [*Pause.*] Eh . . . no, I don' work neither, Mingo.

MINGO: Then how do you support yourselfs?

JOAQUIN: How come you don' tell him, pa? The jefitos are on welfare, ese.

MINGO: Welfare? WELFARE! [*He turns away, sick.*]

CRUZ: We always been poor, my son.

MINGO: [*Determined.*] That's true, mom. But now things are gonna be different. I'm here now, and we're going to be rich—middle class! I didn't come out the war without learning nothing.

JOAQUIN: Then how come you going back to the fields? Nobody get rich in that jale.[3]

MINGO: No, huh? [*He embraces* CRUZ *and* PEDRO.] Well, thanks to this old man and old lady, who were smart enough to cross the border, we live in the land of opportunity. The land I risk my life for. The land where you can start at the bottom, even in the fields, and become a rich man before you can say—

BELARMINO: ARRRGGGHHH!

[LUPE *comes running with her blouse torn on one side.*]

LUPE: AY! Mama! He eat all the beans then he try to bite me!

CRUZ: Por dios. The poor man.

LUPE: The poor man? He's a pig. Look at the hole he made.

CRUZ: All right pues, I see it.

LUPE: And he give me his piojos.

CRUZ: No matter. Go bring more tortillas!

MINGO: Wait a minute, *wait a minute!* Mom, for the last time, who's in there?

CRUZ: Your older brother, hijo. Belarmino.

MINGO: Brother? I don't remember no other brother. What's wrong with him, how come he shouts?

PEDRO: Hay, pos 'ta loco el babozo.[4]

CRUZ: [*Surprised.*] He's sick . . . but you should know. You used to play with him when you was little.

MINGO: Ma, don' lie to me. Are we so poor we gotta take in braceros? Or maybe it's a wetback you're hiding?

JOAQUIN: [*A whisper to* PEDRO] Or maybe he suffering from shellshock?

MINGO: I ain't suffering from nothing, man!

---

2. No.

3. Job, work.

4. Aah, because he's crazy, the fool.

JOAQUIN: Take it easy, carnal,[5] cool it.
MINGO: Well, ma, is that guy a wetback?
CRUZ: No, he's your brother.
MINGO: Brother, huh? We'll soon find out! [*He charges into the bedroom.*]
BELARMINO: [*After a pause.*] ARRRRRRGGGGHH.
MINGO: [*Running out.*] ARRRRGGGGHH! He ain't got a body. He's just a . . .
HEAD!

*Curtain.*

# ACT II

*Three months later. The walls of the house are moderately speckled with red cockroaches of various sizes.* LUPE *is standing behind* PEDRO, *who is asleep on a chair, delousing him. On an old sofa in the corner, a white lace veil covers* BELARMINO—*like a child. The radio is blaring out frantic mariachi music, "La Negra."[6]* LUPE *finds something in* PEDRO'*s hair.*

LUPE: [*Gasps.*] Lousy cucaracha!
CRUZ: [*Shouting from the kitchen.*]Negra, shut off the noises, diablo! [*Pause.*]
    Negra! Belarmino is sleeping!
LUPE: Mama, stop calling me negra.
CRUZ: Shut off the noises, sonavavichi!
LUPE: [*Shuts off radio.*] Okay pues, I did, man! [BELARMINO *grunts from under
    the veil*] What you want? [BELARMINO *grunts harder.*] No, no more radio.
    Din't you hear mi 'ama? Go to sleep! [BELARMINO *grunts again.*] Ay, that
    stupid cabeza!

    [*She removes the veil and* BELARMINO *is seen for the first time: he is the head of
    a man about 30–35 years old. That is all. He has no body. He has long hair and
    a large mustache. His black eyes are deep and expressive. The head is otherwise
    only distinguished by its tremendous size. A full eighteen inches in diameter.*]

BELARMINO: [*Singing.*] "La Cucarachaa!"
LUPE: Shut up! [BELARMINO *laughs idiotically.*] Idiot, because of you I'm like a
    slave in this house. Joaquin and Mingo and e'rybody goes to town but
    they never let me go. I gotta be here—ready to stuff you with frijoles.
    Like a maid, like a negra.
CHATO: [*At the front door.*] Hi, negra.
LUPE: [*Covering* BELARMINO.] What you call me?

5. Brother.
6. The Black Woman. *Diablo:* devil.

CHATO: N—othing.

BELARMINO: Callate el hocico!

CHATO: Why!

LUPE: Mi papa, he's asleep.

CHATO: Oh! Heh, tha's Belarmino behind there, huh?

LUPE: Where at?

CHATO: Under that velo. [*Points to veil.*]

LUPE: No! My brother's a man, how could he fit in there?

CHATO: You know. [*He laughs.*]

LUPE: Look, Chato, if you come to make fun of us you better cut it out, man. Belo's sick, he don'—[BELARMINO *grunts.*] Okay, okay hombre. In a minute. Here, have a cockroach. [*She takes a cockroach off the wall and gives it to him.*]

CHATO: [*Open mouthed.*] How come he eats cockaroaches?

LUPE: Because he's hungry, dumbbell.

CHATO: I'm not a dumb-bell!

LUPE: Oh no, *you're* real smart. Only you don't even know how to read or write. You think we din't go to the second grade together? Menso.[7]

CRUZ: [*In the kitchen.*] Guadalupe?

LUPE: Si, mama? [*She makes a sign to* CHATO *not to say anything.*]

CRUZ: Who you talking to?

LUPE: Belarmino, mama. I'm cleaning his cucarachas.

CRUZ: Okay pues, don' let him eat 'em.

CHATO: [*Looking under the veil.*] En la Madre,[8] what a big head.

LUPE: [*Turning, whispering furiously.*] What you doing? Let him alone! Nobody tell you to come in. Get out!

CHATO: How come?

LUPE: Because.

CHATO: Huy, huy que touchy. Come on, esa. Don' play hard-to-get.

LUPE: [*Menacing the fly-spray pump.*] Look stupid, I'll hit you.

CHATO: Okay, don't get mad. I come over to see Mingo. He don' pay me yet.

LUPE: Liar. He said he pay you two days ago.

CHATO: What days ago? I been searching for a week for him. He haven't pay me nothing. I go to the rancho, he ain't there. I come over here—same story. This whole thing is beginning to smell. [BELARMINO *farts loudly.*] Sacos! de potatoes. Heh, wha's wrong with this ruco?[9]

LUPE: None of your business. Pig!

CHATO: Din' he just learn to talk too?

LUPE: No!

CHATO: Joaquin says he sings "La Cucaracha."

LUPE: He's crazy, man.

7. Dummy.

8. By the Mother (the Virgin Mary).

9. Old guy.

BELARMINO: [*Singing.*] LA CUCARACHA, LA CUCARACHA!

CHATO: No que no?[1] That cat do okay.

LUPE: Oh, how you know? I'm sick and tired of this freak. Feeding him beans, taking out his louses. Listening to that stupid little song. That's all he knows. He don' talk. If he wants to eat he still shout or grunts like he's doing it all my life. I almost can't stand it no more!

CHATO: [*Putting his arms around her.*] Okay pues, mi honey. Don't cry. Some of these days I'm going to take you away from all this.

LUPE: What all this?

CHATO: This poverty, this cucarachas, this . . . this . . .

LUPE: This what?

CHATO: You know . . . Belarmino. I don' say nothing, but . . . well there's the Raza, no? El chisme.[2] People talk.

LUPE: [*Sobering.*] What they say?

CHATO: Well, you know . . . dicen que tu carnal es una cabeza.[3]

LUPE: Una what?

CHATO: Cabeza.

LUPE: Sorry, guy, I don' speak Spanish.

CHATO: Una HEAD! [PEDRO *wakes, goes back to sleep with a grunt.*] Tha's what they say. No arms, no legs, no nothing. Just a head. [*Laughs.*]

LUPE: You black negro! You dirty Mexican! [*She attacks* CHATO.]

CHATO: Orale, hold it there! [*He grabs her.*]

LUPE: Let me go, Chato.

CHATO: Who's a dirty Mexican!

LUPE: You, and ugly too. And more blacker than a Indian.

CHATO: Huy, huy, huy, and you like cream, uh. I'm dark because I work in the fields all day in the sun. I get burn! But look here. [*Shows her his armpit.*] See? Almost tan.

LUPE: You're loco.

CHATO: Chure, loco about you, mi vida.[4] Don' make me suffer. I don' care if Belarmino's a cabeza.

LUPE: Chato, mi papa'll wake up.

CHATO: So what? Te digo que te quiero, que te amo, que te adoro.[5]

LUPE: My mother's in the kitchen.

CHATO: Tu eres mi sol, mi lina, mi cielo . . .[6]

LUPE: Chatito, por favor.

CHATO: Mis tamales, mis tortillas, mis frijoles![7]

---

1. How about that.
2. The gossip.
3. They say that your brother is a head.
4. My life.
5. I tell you I want you, I love you, I adore you.
6. You are my sun, my moon, my sky.
7. My tamales, my tortillas, my beans!

CRUZ: [*Entering from the kitchen.*] GUADALUPE!
LUPE: [*Matter-of-factly.*] Mi mama.
CHATO: [*Turns.*] Buenas tardes.[8] [*He runs out.*]
CRUZ: Si, buenas tardes, you shameless goddammit! [*Turns.*] Pedro!
PEDRO: [*In his sleep.*] Si, mi General?
CRUZ: Pedro, hombre wake up!
PEDRO: Viva Villa.
CRUZ: You old loco.
PEDRO: Viva Pancho Vi—[CRUZ *pulls his leg.*] Yah! Uh? Que paso?[9]
CRUZ: Chato!
PEDRO: [*Jumps up.*] Chato? [*Pause.*] Chato who?
CRUZ: He was after Lupe, hombre!
PEDRO: [*Heads for kitchen.*] Where's he at?
CRUZ: [*Pulling him back.*] He went that way! Go, hombre. Serve for something!
PEDRO: Where's my rifle! WHERE'S MY GUN?
LUPE: [*Throws herself upon him.*] No, Papa!
PEDRO: You chattap! WHERE'S MY GUN, WOMEN!
CRUZ: [*Pause.*] You don' got a gun, Pedro. [*Silence.*]
LUPE: I din' do—
PEDRO: CHATTAP! Dios mio, how lousy. [*He grabs his wine bottle beside the chair.*] You see? This is what I get for coming to the land of the gringos. No respect! I should have stay in Zacatecas. [*He heads for the door.*]
CRUZ: Pedro, where you going?
PEDRO: Where I feel like it, sabes?[1] To look for work.
CRUZ: At sundown?
PEDRO: La night shift, mujer![2] Maybe I go back to Zacatecas.
CRUZ: O si, hitchi-hiking.
PEDRO: Callate si no quieres que te plante un guamaso! Vieja desgraciada![3]

[MINGO *enters dressed in new khaki work clothes, complete with new hat and boots. He carries a clipboard with papers and a money box.*]

MINGO: Home sweet home! E'erybody yelling as usual? What was Super-Mex running about?
CRUZ: Who?
MINGO: Chato. He come flying outa here like the immigration was after him.
CRUZ: He was after Lupe.
MINGO: [*To* PEDRO.] Where were you, man?
CRUZ: Your padre was asleep.

8. Good afternoon.
9. What happened?
1. You know?
2. Woman.
3. Shut up if you don't want me to plant you a good one! Stupid old woman!

MINGO: [*Deliberately.*] Oh.

PEDRO: [*Sensing disrespect.*] Oh, what?

MINGO: Oh, nothing—dad.

PEDRO: Some of this days, cabron,[4] you going to say "oh, something else." Then we see who's boss around here. [*To* LUPE.] I take care of you later, señorita. [*He exits.*]

CRUZ: Dios mio, that old loco. Now he won' be home until it is so late. Then he gots to cross the tracks in the dark. [*To* LUPE.] You see? You see what you do?

LUPE: I din' do nothing! Chato grab me!

MINGO: What you mean he grabbed you? Just took a little grab, huh?

LUPE: No, he was telling me about Belo. The whole neighborhood's talking about him! They say he don' got no arms or legs or nothing. That he's a—

CRUZ: What?

LUPE: You know what. [*Uncomfortable pause.*]

CRUZ: No, I don' know. My son is sick! How can they say such things?

MINGO: Forget 'em, ma. They do it from envy.

LUPE: Envy, of Belo?

MINGO: Of me! Since they always pass the time drunk or begging on welfare, they can't stand a man who betters himself. But they ain't seen nothing yet. Mom, sit down over here. I got something to tell you. You too, negra.

LUPE: Don' call me negra, Mingo.

MINGO: Can't you take a joke?

LUPE: No!

MINGO: Sit down. [*She sits.*] Okay now. Ma, remember that place where we picked prunes for so many years? On Merd Road? [CRUZ *nods.*] Well, it's called Merde[5] Boulevard now. They cut down the orchard and built new houses on the land. They got a big sign up: Prune Blossom Acres. And right under it: No Down Payment to Vets. You know what it means, ma? I'm a vet and we're gonna get a new house!

LUPE: A new house! Mama, a new house!

MINGO: [*Laughs.*] I thought that'd grab you. Well, mom, what do you say? Shall we move outa this dump? [CRUZ *is silent, she stands.*] Heh, what's wrong?

CRUZ: This ain't a dump, Mingo. It is the house of your padre.

MINGO: Padre, madre, so what? I'm talking about Prune Blossom Acres. America's at our doorstep. All we have to do is take one step.

CRUZ: What about Belarmino?

MINGO: Somebody can carry him, what else? Put him in a shoebox.

LUPE: He don't fit in a shoebox.

4. Bastard.
5. Shit.

MINGO: Not a real shoebox, stupid. A cardboard box. We can put holes in it so he can breathe. That ain't no problem.

CRUZ: I know, Mingo, but . . . it is not the same. In this barrio they don' care.

MINGO: I care!

CRUZ: And the gringos?

MINGO: Whatta you mean, gringos?

CRUZ: Who else lives in new houses?

MINGO: Americans, ma. American citizens like me and y— [*Pause.*] Aw, whatta you trying to do? Get me defeated too? You wanna spend the rest of your life in this stinking barrio? What about all the gossiping beanbellies? You know they're laughing at this head.

CRUZ: This what?

MINGO: [*Pause.*] Shorty.

LUPE: That's not what I heard.

MINGO: You shut up, sister.

CRUZ: His name ain't Chorti, Mingo.

MINGO: For pete's sake, Ma, I'm trying to help out here! He's my brother so I call him Shorty. What's wrong with that? He's short. The important thing's the lies people are telling about us, about Shorty, about me. I don't owe them peons nothing.

JOAQUIN: [*Standing in the doorway.*] Simon, just pay Chato what you owe him. Come on in, ese, don' be chicken.

MINGO: And what do I owe him?

JOAQUIN: His pay.

CHATO: Buenas tardes. [*He hides behind* JOAQUIN.]

CRUZ: You say that before, sinverguenza! [CHATO *runs out again.*] You dare to come in after he try to steal our respect?

CHATO: [*Reentering.*] Aw, I din't come to steal nothing. I come because you robbing me!

CRUZ: What?

CHATO: Well, maybe not you, but Mingo? Tell you right off the bat, Doña Cruz, this vato's nothing but a crooked contractor!

MINGO: Crooked?

LUPE: Mingo?

CRUZ: My son?

BELARMINO: AAARRRRGH!

CRUZ: [*To* BELARMINO.] Ay no, my son, not you. You ain't crooked.

MINGO: What the hell you trying to say, Chato?

JOAQUIN: What you think, you din't hear him? He says the big war hero's a thief just like e'rybody else! So you was going to get rich working in the fields, uh? Free country and all that chet! Simon, I believe it now. Anybody can get rich if he's a crooked farm labor contractor. Only this time it's no dice, ese. Chato's my friend. Pay him.

MINGO: I already paid him! If you don't believe me, look here in my paybook.

Here's everybody that receive their wages. See . . . what's signed here?
[*He shows* CHATO.]

CHATO: I don' know, ees in Spanish.

MINGO: Spanish? It's your name, stupid. Chato Reyes. You sign it yourself.

JOAQUIN: Nel, carnal, we got you there. Chato don' know how to read or
write.

MINGO: [*Pause.*] Of course he don't know—that's how come his "X" is here
instead of his name. See? [*He shows the* "X."] Okay, Chato, if you want
to prove that this ain' your "X" or that I haven't pay you, you got to
take me to court, right? But just to show you I ain't crooked, I'm gonna
pay you again. Sit down. [CHATO *and* MINGO *sit down.*] All right, how
many days do you work?

CHATO: Four.

MINGO: Four days, at ten hours each, is 40 hours. 40 hours at 85¢ an hour is
. . . $34, right?

CHATO: Si, muchas gracias.[6]

MINGO: One moment, social security.

CHATO: But I don't got a card.

MINGO: You an American citizen?

CHATO: Simon.

MINGO: Good. You can still pay. That's $15, plus a dollar fine for not having
a card. That leaves $18, right?

CHATO: Simon, gracias.

MINGO: Hold it, income tax. 50% of 18 is 9. That leaves you $9, correct?

CHATO: Orale, gra—

MINGO: The lunches. Five tacos at 40¢ each, one chili pepper at 15¢ and a
large-size coca cola at 35¢ . . . that's $2.50 a day. $2.50 for four days
are—

CHATO: Heh, cut it out!

MINGO: What's wrong, a mistake?

CHATO: Simon, that ain't right! I don't pay for mordidas.[7]

MINGO: [*Standing up.*] Mordidas! What you referring to?

CHATO: Pos what? The tacos. They have bites.

CRUZ: Bites?

CHATO: Mordidotas.

LUPE: Oh-oh, I know who done 'em.

CRUZ: You shut up, woman. [*To* MINGO, *smiling.*] I don't know who could
have do it, my son. I put 'em in new every day.

MINGO: Well, [*He sits.*] one cent discount for each taco for the bites are . . .
39¢ five times. $1.95, plus the chili pepper, the coke, etc . . . $2.45 a
day. For four days that's $9.80. You had 9 dollars; you owe me 80 cents.

CHATO: OWE?

6. Yes, thank you very much.
7. Bites.

MINGO: There's the proof. Pay me.

[CHATO *looks at the paper.*]

JOAQUIN: Lemme see that, ese. [*He takes the paper.*]

MINGO: [*Taking the paper from* JOAQUIN.] How about it, Chato? You pay me or what you gonna do?

BELARMINO: AARRRRRRRRGGGGGGHHHHHHH!

CRUZ: Ay mijo! [*She goes to quiet* BELARMINO.]

CHATO: Ay see you! [*He runs toward the door.*] And ees true what I say! You stupid, chet contractor! T'ief!

MINGO: Thief! You come here and say that you little—

CHATO: Ay! [*He runs out.*]

BELARMINO: AARRRRRRGGGGGGHHH!

CRUZ: Mingo, please, don' make so much fuss.

MINGO: Fuss? What you talking, señora? Din' you hear what—

CHATO: [*Peeking in again.*] I forget to say somet'ing. Stay wis you stinking head! [*He ducks out quickly.*]

CRUZ: Stinking head? Pos mira que jijo de—!⁸ [*At the door shouting.*] Arrastrado! Analfabeto! MUERTO DE HAMBRE!

MINGO: Mom!

CRUZ: YOU GODAMMIT!

MINGO: Okay, ma, that's enough! [*He pulls her back.*]

CRUZ: He call your brother a stinking head.

[BELARMINO *farts sonorously.* JOAQUIN *leaves.*]

LUPE: Ay! It's true! [*Everybody moves away from* BELARMINO *except* CRUZ.] It's true. He's disgusting.

CRUZ: And what you think you are, estupida? Don' think I forget what you do with Chato, eh? Go make tortillas.

LUPE: For what? Belarmino eat 'em all.

CRUZ: No matter, go do it.

LUPE: He eat all the lunches.

MINGO: Lunches?

CRUZ: Don' talk back, I tell you. Go make tortillas!

LUPE: Oh no! I'm not a tortilla factory.

CRUZ: Pos mira que— [CRUZ *starts to hit* LUPE.]

MINGO: Wait a minute, WAIT A MINUTE, ma! What's this about the lunches?

LUPE: It's Belarmino, Mingo. We make 200 tacos for the lunches tomorrow and he already eat 150! He never get full. That's why Chato's tacos have bites, because mi 'ama give 'em to Belo.

MINGO: You give 'em to him, ma? The tacos we sell to the men?

CRUZ: He was a little hungry, my son.

---

8. But look what a son of a—. *Arrastrado:* debased. *Analfabeto:* illiterate. *Muerto de hambre:* freeloader, tightwad.

MINGO: A little hungry! What about all the beans he's already eating? You seen the bills at the store lately? He's eating more and more every week.

LUPE: And that's not all, Mingo. He'a also crawling wis more and more lices! And he eats cucarachas, and he stinks! I can't stand him no more. He's just a stupid . . . HEAD!

CRUZ: [*Pause. She slaps* LUPE.] Your brother is not a head.

MINGO: I oughta knock your stupid lips off.

LUPE: [*Anger, disgust.*] Go to hell. I'll never use 'em. Give 'em to Belo so he can eat *more!* I rather get married so I can suffer in my own house, even if it's with the ugliest, most stupidest man in the world. It can't be worser than this. One of this days Belarmino's gonna grunt or yell for his frijoles, and I won't be here to stuff his throat. You going to *see!* [*She goes out crying.*]

JOAQUIN: [*Reenters.*] Ma? This a piojo?

MINGO: Piojo? A louse!

JOAQUIN: One lice.

CRUZ: This ain't a piojo, my son. Ees one little . . . cucaracha, que no?

BELARMINO: ARRRRGGGHHH!

CRUZ: Ay! [*She removes* BELARMINO'*s veil.*] Dios mio!

MINGO: What the hell's on his face?

JOAQUIN: Cucarachas! [BELARMINO'*s face is covered with cockroaches of various sizes.*]

> [BELARMINO *smiling, singing.*]
> LA CUCARACHA, LA CUCARACHA!
> YA NO PUEDE CAMINAR
> PORQUE LE FALTA, PORQUE NO TIENE
> MARIJUANA QUE FUMAR!

# ACT III

## Scene 1

*Later that same night.* BELARMINO *is on top of an old table, asleep.* JOAQUIN *staggers in drunk, singing, smoking a hand-rolled cigarette.*

> [JOAQUIN *singing.*]
> I'm gonna sing this corrido
> And I'm feeling very sad
> Cause the great Francisco Villa
> Some vato cut off his head.
>
> La Cucaracha, La Cucaracha
> She don' wanna go no more

> You give her pesos and marijuana
> Cuca open up her door!

[*Sees* BELARMINO, *moves toward him.*]

> When they murder Pancho Villa
> His body they lay to rest
> But his head somebody take it
> All the way to the U.S.

> La Cockaroacha, La Cockaroacha
> She don' wanna caminar
> Porque le falta, porque no tiene
> She's a dirty little whore!

[*Pause.*] Heh, Belo? You a wake, ese? Come on, man. Get your butt up! Oh yeah . . . you don't got one, huh? [*Laughs.*] So what? Get up! [*Pulls his hair.*]

BELARMINO: [*Roars.*] LA CUCARACHAAA!

JOAQUIN: Tha's all you know, huh stupid? [*Mocks him.*] "Cucaracha!" [*Pause.*] Oh, a real one, eh? They even coming outa your nose, ese. Look at her . . . she's a dirty little whore. A putita. [*Holds out the small cockroach with his fingers in front of* BELARMINO's *eyes.*] Puuu-teee-tita! [*Laughs, throws it down, squashes it.*] Well, what you looking so stupid about? It was only a stinking cockaroach. Dumb Mexican . . . not you, ese, this stupid cucaracha I squash. They love to be step on. [*Laughs.*] You know what happen tonight, man? I been all over the barrio running away from vatos. Simon, all my friends and camaradas. Like a big chingon[9] I get 'em at work with Mingo, and he chisle 'em. Now I'm the patsy and they wanna knife me. Even Chato. He's telling e'rybody you're a head, ese. [*Laughs.*] With no guts.

BELARMINO: [*As if disemboweled.*] ARRRGGGGGHHHH!

JOAQUIN: [*Whispering.*] Heh, MAN, CUT IT OUT! Shh, the jefita's gonna hear. Okay, you ask for it! [*He covers* BELARMINO *with his coat.*] Shhh. [BELARMINO *yells, muffled.* JOAQUIN *laughs.*] Come on, ese, be a sport. You wan' me to throw you out the window? [BELARMINO *stops shouting.* JOAQUIN *gives him a tug.*] Heh? [*No response.* JOAQUIN *peeks under the coat.*] You awright?

BELARMINO: Simon!

JOAQUIN: [*Covers him quickly.*] Dumb head. [*Pause.*] Heh, he say something. He's learning to talk! [*Uncovers him again.*]

BELARMINO: Cabron!

JOAQUIN: Spanish.

BELARMINO: [*Grunts.*] Uh, toque! Toque, cigarro!

9. Big shot.

JOAQUIN: What, you want a toke? [*He holds out the cigarette.* BELARMINO *puffs on it eagerly.*] No, man don't just puff on it. You gotta inhale it. See, like this. [JOAQUIN *inhales.*] Take in a little air wis it.

BELARMINO: [*Grunts.*] Uh-uh, toque!

[JOAQUIN *holds out the cigarette again.* BELARMINO *puffs noisely then sniffs vociferously.*]

JOAQUIN: How you like it, bueno?

BELARMINO: [*Holding his breath.*] Bueno.

JOAQUIN: [*Laughs.*] Chet, man, you just as bad as me. A lousy Mexican!

BELARMINO: ARRRGGGHHH! [JOAQUIN *covers him with his coat.*]

CRUZ: [*Runs in the front door.*] Joaquin!

JOAQUIN: Hi, Jefita.

CRUZ: What you doing? Where's Chorty?

JOAQUIN: [BELARMINO *grunts under the coat.*] He went out to take a piss.

CRUZ: Wha's that?

JOAQUIN: What? Oh, that—my coat. ˒

[BELARMINO *grunts.*]

CRUZ: Valgame dios,[1] do you got Belarmino in there, Joaquin?

JOAQUIN: Nel, there's nobody under here. [*Lifts coat.*] See? Nobody! [*He laughs.*]

CRUZ: Belarmino! [*She goes to him.* BELARMINO *grunts, moans, breathes hard.*] He shrink—

JOAQUIN: [*Moving away from* BELARMINO.] Don' let him fool you, jefita. Maybe you think the vato grunts and tha's it, but he talks. [CRUZ *looks at him.*] No chet, I mean no lie. He do it. And it's not only "La Cucaracha." He swing in pure words, huh, ese? Simon, he just barely talk to me. Go on, ask him something.

CRUZ: [*Emotionally.*] Mijito . . . my Chorti, ees true? You can talk at last? Ees me, your madre. Speak to me! [BELARMINO *grunts.*] Ay, dios, he can talk ingles.

JOAQUIN: That was a grunt. Come on, Belo. Talk right. [BELARMINO *laughs idiotically.*] Nel, ese, don' act stupid. This is the jefita. She want to hear you talk. [BELARMINO *grunts and makes idiotic noises.*] Come on, man!

BELARMINO: ARRRGGGH!

CRUZ: Tha's enough, Joaquin. You scare him. I don' know how you can make fun of your poor brother.

JOAQUIN: But he can talk, señora. He's faking.

CRUZ: Tha's enough! Din' I tell you not to bother him? I have enough to worry with your sister. She run out like crazy this afternoon, and haven' come back. Maybe she want to elope with Chato?

JOAQUIN: Pos so what? Chato's a good vato.

CRUZ: A good vato. An ignorant who let the contractors rob him!

---

1. God save me.

JOAQUIN: Simon, and who's the contractor? Mingo!

CRUZ: Shut up, liar! Thief!

JOAQUIN: T'ief?

CRUZ: Since you was born you have give me nothing but trouble. Going out in the streets at night, coming late, landing in jail. I don' got no more hope in you. Or in Lupe. The only one who haven' come out bad is my poor Chorti who's only hungry all the time. Why don' you rob something for your brother to eat, eh? Serve for something. [*Weeps.*] Valgame dios, nobody care about my poor sick Belarmino. Only his madre. [*She starts to go out.*]

BELARMINO: Mama.

CRUZ: [*Without turning.*] No, don' call me, Joaquin.

JOAQUIN: But I din'—

CRUZ: No, I tell you, comprende, sanavavichi! I got to be out in the street. Maybe with the help of the Virgen, your sister come back. [*Exits.*]

BELARMINO: Pobre viejita.[2]

JOAQUIN: Pobre nothing! If you care so much, how come you keep your mouth shut when it count?

BELARMINO: [*Brusquely, furiously.*] No seas torpe! Si todo el mundo se da cuenta que puedo habar, van ha saber quien soy. O mejor dicho, quien fui. Me vienen ha mochar la lengua o toda la maceta de una vez! Que no sabes que estamos en territorio enemigo?[3]

JOAQUIN: Orale pues, cool it, ese! You don't gotta make a speech. [*Pause.*] Man, what a trip! You know what? I think I been smoking too much. You din' really say all that, right? Simon, it's all in my head.

BELARMINO: Pos quien sabe lo que dices, vale.[4]

JOAQUIN: What?

BELARMINO: Que no hablo ingles. El totache. Hablame in espanish.[5]

JOAQUIN: Sorry, man, I don' speak it. No hablo español.[6]

BELARMINO: Mendigos pochos. [*Pause.*] Mira, chabo[7] . . . ah, you . . . Mexicano, no?

JOAQUIN: Who me? Nel, man, I'm Chicano.

BELARMINO: No seas pendejo.[8]

JOAQUIN: Who you calling a pendejo!

BELARMINO: You, tu, tu Mexican! Pendejo! Mira, esperate[9] . . . ahhh, you

---

2. Poor little woman.

3. Don't be stupid. If the whole world realizes that I can speak, they will know who I am. Or rather, who I was. They'll hack off my tongue or my whole head at once. Don't you know that we are in enemy territory?

4. What the hell are you saying, pal?

5. I don't speak English. Stay cool. Talk to me in Spanish.

6. I don't speak Spanish.

7. Americanized beggars. Look, kid.

8. Don't be stupid.

9. Look, wait a minute.

Mexican, me Mexican . . . ahhh, this one familia Mexican, eh? Mingo, no! Mingo es gringo. Comprendes?

JOAQUIN: Heh, yeah, now you talking my language!

BELARMINO: Mingo ees gavacho, eh?

JOAQUIN: Simon, and a t'ief.

BELARMINO: Okay maguey. Now . . . you don' puedes atinar quien soy?

JOAQUIN: Wait a minute man . . . Slower, I can't do what?

BELARMINO: Atinar.

JOAQUIN: Atinar . . . that's *guess*. I can't guess what?

BELARMINO: Quien soy.

JOAQUIN: Who you are. [*Pause.*] Who?

BELARMINO: Pos guess. You have hear . . . el Pueblo de Parral?

JOAQUIN: Parral?

BELARMINO: Chihuahua!

JOAQUIN: Oh, simon. Tha's the town where they kill Pancho Villa and they cut off his . . . [*Pause.*] HEAD.

BELARMINO: Exactamente.

JOAQUIN: Did you ever have a horse?

BELARMINO: Siete Leguas.

JOAQUIN: And a Chivi?

BELARMINO: One Dodge.

JOAQUIN: 1923?

BELARMINO: Simon—yes.

JOAQUIN: [*Pause.*] I don' believe it. You? The head of Pancho . . .

BELARMINO: Belarmino please! [*Secretively.*] Muchos carefuls. I only trust you. Ees one secret politico, comprendes?

JOAQUIN: [*Shocked.*] Simon, I don't tell nobody. [*Pause.*] Only the jefita. MAAA! [*He runs out the front door.*]

BELARMINO: OYE! [*Alone.*] Chi . . . huahua! Que feo no tener cuerpo, erdad de dios![1]

> PEDRO *is heard in the kitchen, yelling and singing drunkenly.* BELARMINO *feigns sleep.* PEDRO *enters with a wine bottle, and cartridge belts criss-crossed on his chest.*]

[PEDRO *sings.*]
"Adios torres de Chihuahua,
Adios torres de Canteraaa!
Ya vino Francisco Villaaa,
Pa' quitarles lo pantera.
Ya llego Francisco Villa
Ha de volver la fronteraaa!"[2]

---

1. How ugly not to have a body, mercy of God.

2. Farewell towers of Chihuahua / Farewell towers of Chihuahua! / Francisco Villa came / To get rid of the bully / Francisco Villa arrived / To return the frontier!

[*Shouts.*] Ay, yai, yai, YAI! I'm home, cabrones. Your padre is home, come out! come out from your holes! I am home!! [*Pause.*] Where's e'rybody at? [*He goes to* BELARMINO.] Oye, wake up, loco! [*He pulls* BELARMINO's *hair.*]

BELARMINO: [*Opening his eyes.*] ARRRRGGH! LA CUCARACHAA!

PEDRO: [*Furiously, in case of insult.*] What?

BELARMINO: Cucaracha.

PEDRO: [*Pause.*] You know "Siete Leguas"? [*Sings.*] "Siete Leguas el caballo que Villa mas—"

BELARMINO: AY, YAI, YAI!

PEDRO: Heh, you do that pretty good, cabron.

[CRUZ *runs in the front door.* JOAQUIN *follows her.*]

CRUZ: Pedro, what are you doing?

PEDRO: I am talking to my son.

CRUZ: Talking? [*She glances at* JOAQUIN.]

JOAQUIN: Din' I tell you? He can talk, huh pa? [BELARMINO *grunts and spits at* JOAQUIN.] Orale, carnal, take it easy. You can trust the jefitos . . . [BELARMINO *spits, hits* JOAQUIN's *shirt.*] Un pollo!³ [*He exits upstairs.*]

CRUZ: It ees true, Pedro, my son talks?

PEDRO: Who? This animal? No, wha's wrong wis you, not even with a gallon of vino. [BELARMINO *laughs idiotically.*] You see? How can this idiota talk? He don' know nothing.

CRUZ: He is still your son, Pedro.

PEDRO: Pos who knows, verdad?⁴ A man almost forty years old which he don' even know his own padre? That is no son. You got this one for you, woman.

CRUZ: Tha's not true, Pedro. He look like you.

PEDRO: Oh yes, the face!

CRUZ: And the hair, the eyes, the mustaches.

PEDRO: CHICKENSQUAT! Those are things a madre notice. A padre he wants a son with a strong back. And arms and legs to help him work! You cheat me, woman. Caray, I will never forget the day Belarmino was born. 1928 and my first son! They run to the field to get me, and when I arrive . . . there you was with the niño in your arms . . . his big eyes looking out, his mouth open . . . with ears, a nose, and mucho hair, everything his madre want. Then I open the blanket: NOTHING. *Nothing for his padre! Dios mio, what a lousy son!*

CRUZ: [*Hurt.*] Yes, lousy, but it hurt me to have him.

PEDRO: Pos I give him to you then. For your pains. I give 'em to you all. Joaquin, Mingo, Lupe, and the head for good measure. [JOAQUIN *enters*

3. Spit, trail of drool.
4. Right?

*with guitar.*] Anyway, I'm going to across the border. My carrilleras[5] and my 30–30 is all I take. Wis that I come, wis that I go.

JOAQUIN: And your guitar, jefito?

PEDRO: You keep it, hijo. Of all my sons I like you the most, because you're the only one who understand the Revolucion. Maybe this guitarrita serve to remind you of your padre . . . when he's dead.

CRUZ: You're crazy, viejo.

PEDRO: Well, you will see. I going back to Zacatecas, to my tierra,[6] to die.

CRUZ: [*Relieved.*] Okay pues, go die! I don' care. Right now I'm worry about my Lupe. [*She wraps her shawl around her neck.*]

PEDRO: Where you going, to the street again like a crazy loca?

CRUZ: I'm going over to Señora Reyes' house. Maybe Chato come back. I don' even know what to think, dios mio. [*Exits.*]

PEDRO: Stinking vieja.

JOAQUIN: Heh, pa, can I go to Mexico with you?

PEDRO: For what? You din' come from over theres, you was born over heres.

JOAQUIN: So what, maybe I gotta get outa town? I mean the U.S.

PEDRO: Can you ride a horse?

JOAQUIN: No, pero—

PEDRO: Or eat chili peppers?

JOAQUIN: No, but—

PEDRO: Ah! And tortillas, my son. How to know a good woman by her tortillas. You got to know. One don' buy burro just because she gots long eyelashes.

JOAQUIN: Okay pues, but you know what? I find the head of Pancho Villa!

PEDRO: [*Pause.*] When?

JOAQUIN: Today . . . tonight!

PEDRO: You crazy. How you going to find the head of the General? Pos mira . . . go say it up in the sierra, que! Where they believe you.

JOAQUIN: You wanna see it?

PEDRO: [*Pause.*] El General?

JOAQUIN: Pancho Villa himself.

PEDRO: You sure ees him? How you know? He don' be in bad shape?

JOAQUIN: He's like new.

PEDRO: [*Lowers his head emotionally.*] I don' believe it . . . after so many years? Just imagine, to rescue the General's head from the hands of the gringos, then to take it back to Mexico con honor! In a big train like the old days! Que caray, maybe even the Revolucion break out again! Maybe they give us a rancho—in Zacatecas. Ay, yai, yai! Think we better be careful, my son. [*Pause.*] Oye, you hide it good? If we lose that head again—!

5. Cartridge belts.
6. Land.

JOAQUIN: Nel, he's here in the house.

PEDRO: Who know about it?

JOAQUIN: Nobody, just me and you, and the General.

PEDRO: General? He's dead.

JOAQUIN: He ain' dead.

PEDRO: What you mean, hombre? They kill him.

JOAQUIN: Not all of him.

PEDRO: Yes, all of him!

JOAQUIN: Nel, he lives. Pancho Villa lives!

PEDRO: [*Pause.*] You chure?

JOAQUIN: Simon, and there he is! [*Points to* BELARMINO.]

PEDRO: [*Scandalized.*] Belarmino! Pos que jijos—! What you thinking, babozo? Laughing at your padre?

JOAQUIN: No, jefito! He prove it to you himself. Just give him a chance! [*Goes to* BELARMINO.] Heh, General? General Villa?

PEDRO: [*Pulls his hair.*] Wake up, bruto.

BELARMINO: AARRRAAGGHH!

JOAQUIN: Uh, General, here's one of your Villistas . . . my jefito. You know him already, tell him something, okay? Just a word or two.

BELARMINO: [*Smiles.*] UHHH.

JOAQUIN: He's warming up.

PEDRO: For what, more frijoles? No Joaquin, this go beyond a joke. I never going to forgive you this.

JOAQUIN: But he's Pancho Villa, 'apa. He tell me.

PEDRO: What I care what this animal tell you? How he's going to be the great Centauro del Norte? Pancho Villa was a giant, a legend, a big hombre!

JOAQUIN: Simon, and this a big hombre's head.

PEDRO: CHICKENSQUAT! Not in one thousand years can you compare this chompetita[7] to the head of my General! Men like Pancho Villa ain't born no more, just lousies like this one. And cowards! T'iefs! Useless cabrones! Tha's all I got for sons.

MINGO: [*Standing in the front.*] And we're only chips off the old block, no pa?

[PEDRO *turns toward* MINGO, *who is dressed in casual bowling clothes. He also carries a bowling bag.*]

PEDRO: Pos you tell me. What block you talking about?

MINGO: Skip it. What was the yelling about?

PEDRO: This pachuco . . . lying to his padre.

JOAQUIN: I din' lie, jefito.

PEDRO: Chatap! Pos this one . . . still at it, hombre? [*To* MINGO.] What you think he was saying, my son? That Belarmino is my General Villa! Mira . . . lousy godamit. [*To* JOAQUIN.] Why don' you be smart like your brother

7. Always eating big little head.

here. He don' go around wis stupid babozadas. He is a serious hombre con respeto y dinero.[8]

JOAQUIN: Orale, cool it pues.

PEDRO: Culo . . . a quien le dices culo![9] I still haven' die, cabron. I still the boss in this house.

JOAQUIN: Okay, okay. Keep your house. [*Gets the guitar and heads for the door.*]

PEDRO: Oye, oye, and my guitarra?

JOAQUIN: You give me it. Want it back?

PEDRO: No for what I want that junk?

JOAQUIN: Here. [*Gives him the guitar.*] I get a new one. Orale, carnal, hand over 75 bolas.

MINGO: Bolas?

JOAQUIN: Bones, maracas, bills, ese.

MINGO: Seventy-five dollars? What the hell for?

JOAQUIN: My cut, ese! I get the workers, you screw 'em, we split the take.

MINGO: You're crazy.

JOAQUIN: Simon, real loco. But I ain't stupid. All the vatos in the barrio go to work for you because I ask 'em!

MINGO: So what? I paid you 50¢ a head for that truckload you round up and that was it.

JOAQUIN: Nel, ese, you din' tell me you was going to burn 'em. Like Chato! Social security, income tax . . . that's a lotta chet, mano. You got itchy fingers too, que! You pocket them coins yourself.

MINGO: [*Calm.*] Can you prove it?

JOAQUIN: I see you do it!

MINGO: Then call the cops. Go on! Who you think the law's gonna believe, me or you?

JOAQUIN: [*Pause.*] Eh, jefe, you loan me your guitar?

PEDRO: Now you wan' it back, eh? Bueno, take it. [JOAQUIN *grabs the guitar and lifts it to smash it on* MINGO's *head.*] FOR YOU TO PLAY IT!!

[JOAQUIN *stops.*]

JOAQUIN: Don' you see he's cheating us?

PEDRO: I don' see nothing!

JOAQUIN: The General see it!

PEDRO: No que General ni nada![1] [JOAQUIN *leaves with the guitar.*] Useless! Huh, as if all people don' be crooked. No hombre, we all looking to see what we scratch up. [*Drinks from his bottle. It is empty.*] Chihuahua, it is finish. Bueno, no matter? Tha's how come we got money—for necessaries. Of all my sons I like you the most—porque tienes intelegencia, hijo

---

8. Man with respect and money.

9. Ass . . . who are you calling ass! ("Cool it" sounds like *culo,* Spanish for "ass.")

1. Not the General or nothing!

lo juro por los cielos. Andale,[2] my son, let loose one pesito to go for more. But this time we get a big one, eh?

MINGO: No, señor.

PEDRO: Bueno, a small one pues.

MINGO: No! Don' you understand? There's no money for booze.

PEDRO: Mira, mira, don't play the crooked contractor wis me, eh? I ain' Joaquin. All I ask is for 35 centavitos.

MINGO: I don't give a damn. That money ain't gonna support your habit. I want this family to be decent and that's how it's gonna be.

PEDRO: Oh si, eh? Well, who are you to decide everything? I'm your padre.

MINGO: You're nothing. If it wasn' for me, we'd still be in the gutter, like usual. Confess it. You could never handle Shorty's hunger. You had to drag us all to the fields together with mi 'ama. And for what? We still ended up owing the store just to feed the head! That head's a pushover for me. From now on, I'm in charge here and you can do what you damn well please.

PEDRO: [Pause.] Pos I think I damn well please to give you some chingasos[3] well-planted, sabes?

MINGO: If you can. Don' forget I was a Marine.

PEDRO: And I was a Villista!

MINGO: You want me to give you a judo chop?

PEDRO: [He runs to the door.] Joaquin! Joaquin! Bring me my guitarra!

MINGO: The guitar? You going to play or fight?

PEDRO: I going to smash it on your head, pendejo!

MINGO: What's the matter, old man? Not so good with your fists anymore? Been picking fruit too long? Come on, gimme a try! This hand only broke a Chink's red neck once. WHACK! Come on, wetback, get a taste of an American fighting man overseas! Come, farm laborer! Greaser! Spic! Nigger! [Pause.] GRINGO!

PEDRO: [The dam breaks.] VIVA VILLAAAAA!

[PEDRO leaps on MINGO and they wrestle. MINGO quickly subdues him giving him a couple of efficient judo chops. He pins him down and sits on him.]

MINGO: All right, green-carder, you give up?

PEDRO: Cabron.

MINGO: What?

PEDRO: Cabron!

MINGO: That's what I thought you said.

PEDRO: Joaquin!

MINGO: He ain't coming back man. You think he wants that guitar smashed? Besides you ran him out. You better give up. What you say? No hard feelings? Look, I'll even get up. [He rises.] Come on, Pete, be a sport.

2. Because you're intelligent, son, in heaven's name. Come on.
3. Punches . . . you know?

Don't be a bad loser. [*Nudges him with his foot.*] Come on, I don't like to see you sprawled out like that.

PEDRO: Get away, cabron! Get away!

MINGO: Okay, stay down. I don't give a damn. [*Exits.*]

PEDRO: Now I don't got any sons . . . except Belarmino. He was the first. I like him the most. Besides, he always remind me of Pancho Villa. [*He gets up and removes his cartridge belts.*] Eh, my son? You see this carrilleras? They're from the Revolucion. They don' got any bullets but I give 'em to you, eh? [*He places the belts around* BELARMINO.] Now you look like the General. You remember Pancho Villa? There was a man, a giant . . . he rob the rich to give to the poor. You should have see him when we take Zacatecas. [*He begins to walk around the room imagining the scene he describes.*] All the trains, the smoke, the people climbing all over like lices. [*Laughs.*] Caray, there was nothing like the trains. [*Train whistle in the distance.*] They would gather at the crossings. [*Under his voice: "Marcha de Zacatecas."*] Here comes Pancho Villa, they would say. Ahi viene Pancho Villa! And mi General he would come to the back of the car. VIVA VILLA! VIVA VILLA! Here come Pancho Villa! [*One final war cry.*] A ZACA-TECAAASS!

[*The music is like the sound of a train pulling in.* PEDRO *runs out in the direction of the train whistle. The sounds end abruptly and all that remains is the ringing of a small bell at a distant railroad crossing. This fades into the sound of a church bell. Light and sound fade.*

BELARMINO *is left illuminated by a single ray of light. He screams, a sorrowful cry of death. Darkness. Curtain.*]

Scene 2

*The front room. Morning. Church bells. A guitar plays "Siete Leguas." A procession in black enters,* CRUZ *in mourning,* MINGO *holding her. Then* LUPE *and* CHATO, *carrying* BELARMINO *wrapped in a sarape.*

LUPE: I'll put Belarmino away, mama. [*Goes into bedroom.*]

CRUZ: [*Sitting on the couch.*] The Señor knows what we shall do now, my sons.

MINGO: Pa was a good guy.

JOAQUIN: You liar!

MINGO: You insulting his memory already? [*Pause.*] I'll let that one go this time.

LUPE: [*Reentering.*] He's asleep.

CRUZ: He was tired, poor man.

MINGO: I don' think we shoulda take him.

CRUZ: It was his padre, my son.

MINGO: He sang "La Cucaracha," din't he? Pa was my pa too, ma. I wanted him to have a good quiet funeral. What was the name of that other "bit" you did?

JOAQUIN: "Siete Leguas."

MINGO: What?

JOAQUIN: Seven . . . leaguews. [*He chokes up with grief.*]

CHATO: That's okay, ese, e'rybody like what you did.

LUPE: It was so sad to see them let mi 'apa down into his grave and all the time Belarmino singing "La Cucaracha." E'rybody think you like it like that, mama.

CRUZ: We should have had a wake.

MINGO: You still on that, ma? The funeral parlor did the job.

CRUZ: They din' let me see him.

MINGO: There was nothing left to see. I mean, what you expect them to do? That train hit him. I'm not even sure it was him when I identified him. Maybe it wasn't. Maybe he went back to Mexico like he always wanted? That's possible.

JOAQUIN: Why don't you shut up!

CRUZ: We should have had a wake! [*She breaks down crying.*]

LUPE: Chato, help me.

[LUPE *and* CHATO *take* CRUZ *upstairs, crying.*]

MINGO: Everything's gonna be okay, ma. You'll see. I order him a stone with his name in Spanish, and a saying: "Here lies our Dad, By Angels Guarded—"

[CRUZ *has gone upstairs.*]

JOAQUIN: Tried to feel sad but only farted. [*Laughs until he cries.*]

MINGO: [*Going over to him, whispering.*] What the heck's the matter with you, tomahawk? Pa's dead. Don't you appreciate that? [*Pause.*] Heh, are you crying?

JOAQUIN: Lemme alone, ese.

MINGO: Listen, Joaquin, things ain't been the best between us but maybe we ought to sit down and talk, huh? Man to man? I'm your legal guardian now.

JOAQUIN: What you mean?

MINGO: I'm responsible for you. For the whole family. I wanna help you, Tomahawk.

JOAQUIN: Help me what?

MINGO: Help you. You wanna join the Marines? I'll sign for you. Sure, the service'll make a man outa you. Look what it did for me. How about it?

JOAQUIN: Nel, I awready tried. They don' like my record.

MINGO: That bad, huh? Well, how about night school? [JOAQUIN *makes a face.*] Okay then, come and work with me.

JOAQUIN: I awready worked with you.

MINGO: You still think I cheated your friends?

JOAQUIN: I know!

MINGO: Boy, that's rich. You know what's wrong with you? You can't imagine anybody making an honest buck. This is a free country, man. There's no law against making money.

JOAQUIN: How about being a Chicano?

MINGO: Is *that* what's eating you?

JOAQUIN: How come we're poor? How come mi jefito die like that?

MINGO: Not because he was a Mexican!

JOAQUIN: You ever have the placa work you over in jail, ese? Rubber hoses on the ribs? Calling you greaser! Mexican bastard!

MINGO: I've never been in jail remember?

JOAQUIN: You're still a greaser.

MINGO: Why you little punk, don't aim your inferiority complex at me. You're so twisted with hate you can't see straight.

JOAQUIN: Simon, I'm cross-eyed. But you wanna be a gavacho so bad, you can't see nothing. You hated mi 'apa. You hate all of us! You and your new clothes and bowling ball and shit. Well, take a good look, ese. We're greasy and lousy but we're your family!

MINGO: Damn rights, my family! But you don't have to be greasy and lousy!

JOAQUIN: You don't have to be a gavacho!

MINGO: Listen, man, there's only one thing I ever wanted in this life. That's not to be poor. I never got that until I become a Marine. Now I want it for the family. Is that so bad? You wanna go on this way, with that stupid head eating and stinking and farting?

JOAQUIN: He's the General!

MINGO: Come off it, buddy. Shorty ain't Pancho Villa. He's nothing but a mouth. I know, I have to feed it.

JOAQUIN: If you ever feed him nothing again, I'll kill you.

MINGO: Okay. But how are you going to feed it? On welfare, like the old man used to do it?

JOAQUIN: You don' even respect mi 'apa now! When he's dead!

MINGO: That's a damn lie! I loved that old wino.

JOAQUIN: Pinchi buey.[4]

MINGO: What did you call me!!!

JOAQUIN: Pinchi puto desgraciado![5]

MINGO: You talk to me in English!

JOAQUIN: [*Swings guitar at him.*] FUCK YOU! [*Runs out.*]

MINGO: [*Running to the door.*] You goddamned delinquent! I'd turn you in if pa wasn' dead today.

*Curtain.*

---

4. Fucking son of a bitch.

5. Fucking disgraceful queer.

# ACT IV

*Six months later. It is winter. The walls of the house are covered with red cockroaches of various sizes.* LUPE *is studying the walls, carrying a fly-swatter. She is pregnant, but is nevertheless knocking down cockroaches energetically and capturing them in her apron.* BELARMINO *is on top of an old, broken-down* TV *set. His eyes are wide open, following every move that* LUPE *makes. The door to the side bedroom is new and has "Private" painted on it in big black letters.*

LUPE: Cucarachas . . . big fat cucarachas. There's one! [*She knocks it down.*] Gee man, this is a big one!

BELARMINO: NARRH!

LUPE: No, you pig! This is mine and I'm gonna eat it by myself.

BELARMINO: NAAARRRRGGGH!

LUPE: Pediche![6] You ain' hungry. You just don' want me to have it, huh? Well now you going to have to eat it! And I hope you choke! [*She crams it into* BELARMINO'*s mouth.*]

CRUZ: [*In the kitchen.*] Guadalupe?

LUPE: Si, mama! [*She backs away from* BELARMINO.]

CRUZ: [*Enters.*] Did Belarmino shout? [BELARMINO *spits out the cockroach.*] Una cucaracha!

LUPE: It's not my fault, man. I can't watch him all the time.

CRUZ: Ay, little woman. Go bring the tortillas.

LUPE: There's no more.

CRUZ: And the dozen there was?

LUPE: I ate 'em. [*Pause.*] Well, what you want? I was hungry! Besides, there's plenty of food there—bread, steaks, milk, eggs, orange juice.

CRUZ: It all belong to Mingo.

LUPE: Sure, pure American food. Well, what about us? Are we suppose to eat cucarachas? [*Angry.*]

CRUZ: No! Now stop this foolishness and go make tortillas, andale.

LUPE: Tortillas . . . I should work in a taco bar. [*Exits, angry.*]

CRUZ: [*Loud voice.*] And don' touch Mingo's food! [BELARMINO *growls.*] Si, my son, I know. She coming with your frijolitos. You mus' be very hungry, no? You have eat nothing for days. [*Pause.*] Here. Eat one little cucaracha, eh? But don' spit out the shell. I don' want your sister to know. Here.

MINGO: [*In the kitchen.*] Aha, I caught you!

CRUZ: Mingo!

[*She turns, searching for him. Noises come from the kitchen. A chair falls, a glass breaks. We hear the voices of* MINGO *and* LUPE, *arguing.*]

6. Beggar!

MINGO: Drinking my orange juice, eh? What you eating?

LUPE: None of your business!

MINGO: What's that?

LUPE: Give 'em back!

MINGO: You crazy?

LUPE: Gimme 'em back!

MINGO: Oh no, sister, we're going to see ma.

LUPE: No, Mingo, please—ay!

MINGO: Shut up! [MINGO *comes in from the kitchen, pushing* LUPE *in front with her arm twisted behind her back.* MINGO *is dressed in fashionable casual clothing.*] Heh, ma, you know what this pig was eating?

CRUZ: [*Resigned.*] Cucarachas.

MINGO: How do you know?

CRUZ: What's wrong with you, woman? You want to kill that child you carry? You going to be a madre.

LUPE: I'm not either. I don' got no baby. Only a belly full of cocoaroaches! And I'm still hungry. We never have any meat in this house! [*Exits.*]

MINGO: [*Shouting after her.*] Meat? Well, tell your Chatito to get a goddamn job! How d'yuh like that? What's her husband for? Just to keep her pregnant? Tell the bum to go to work.

CRUZ: It is winter, Mingo. There's no work in the fields.

MINGO: Then to the breadlines, lady. The welfare department. Anyway that's all they know.

BELARMINO: [*With rage.*] ARRRRRGGGGGGH!

MINGO: Heh!

CRUZ: Belarmino, behave.

MINGO: [BELARMINO *stares at him with hate.*] Look at him, señora, look! He's enrage! Well now I seen everything. This freak getting insulted.

[BELARMINO *growls with rage.*]

CRUZ: My son, calm down!

MINGO: Let him blow his top. He can't do nothing anyway. Maybe he's been eating my food, too, no ma? You sure you ain't slip him one of my TV dinners?

CRUZ: No. Mingo, your poor brother he haven' eat nothing in four days.

MINGO: So what?

CRUZ: Look how skinny he is. He's shrinking on me, and he still don' wanna eat nothing.

MINGO: Maybe he knows something I know.

CRUZ: [*Suspiciously.*] What?

MINGO: [*Calmly, deliberately.*] That he ain't got no guts.

CRUZ: [*Alarmed.*] Don' say that!

MINGO: It's a fact.

CRUZ: No!

MINGO: Look at him!

CRUZ: He's sick.

MINGO: [*With meaning.*] He ain't got a body, señora. [CRUZ *stares at him unbelievingly.*] Let's face it, okay? He's a head. [CRUZ *turns away shaking her head.*] You gotta accept it, ma. Shorty's a head and that's it.

CRUZ: No!

MINGO: [*Angered.*] Then where's all the food going that he's eating? I become a contractor to make more money, but each week that I make more, he eat more. Last week it was $127. By himself! Beans and tortillas!! He blew my whole check. [BELARMINO *laughs.*] Shut up!

BELARMINO: ARRGGH!

MINGO: All these years we been poor and stinkin', working the fields, for what? To stuff his fat belly which he don't even got! What kinda stupid, useless life is that? I don't wanna end up like dad. I wanna get outa this slum!

CRUZ: Por favor, Mingo, no more.

MINGO: Look, ma, I wanna help you. I'll even let Lupe and Chato freeload on us for the winter, if you do one thing.

CRUZ: What?

MINGO: Stop wasting money on beans and tortillas. Admit Shorty's a head.

CRUZ: No!

MINGO: Ma, it's nothing but dumb pride. Be realistic. Be practical.

CRUZ: [*Determined.*] My son is not a head!

MINGO: [*Pause.*] Okay, suit yourself. Just don't expect me to pay the bills at the store no more. [*Adds quickly.*] But don't worry, I'm still gonna help the family—with my example. See that little red sports car in front of the house? It's mine.

CRUZ: Yours?

MINGO: I trade it in for my Chivi. I also took 200 bucks outa the bank and bought new clothes. See? Everything new. You should see how great it feels! Instead of the head, I'm spending money where it counts: on self-improvement. And with my credit, I can get anything else I want. Thirty dollar shoes, color TV, a Hi-Fi stereo, a new bowling ball, steak dinners, cocktails! I can even go to college. Sure, State College! The G.I. Bill will foot the bill. Heh, you get that? G.I. Bill foot the bill? I know it's below your mental intelligence to comprehend the simplicity . . . [*During this speech* MINGO's *voice changes from a Chicano accent to the nasal tones of an Anglo: he also begins to talk down his nose at his mother.*]

CRUZ: Mijo!

MINGO: [*Coming to his senses.*] Que?

CRUZ: What about us?

MINGO: Well . . . hustle! Din't Joaquin go to work?

CRUZ: He say he have little jobs to do.

MINGO: What little jobs?

CRUZ: I don't know.

MINGO: What about mi 'apa? He can still work. Where is he, boozing again?

CRUZ: [*With fearful surprise.*] Tu padre esta muerto!<sup>7</sup>

MINGO: Muerto? Dead? [*Laughs*] You're kidding.

CRUZ: For six months. That train kill him. [*She crosses herself.*] But . . . how did you forgot? Wha's happen to you, Mingo?

MINGO: Six months?

JOAQUIN: [*Outside the house.*] Viva mi jefito! [*Shouts of "Viva."*] Viva Pancho Villa! [*More "Vivas."*]

BELARMINO: AY, YAI, YAI, YAI, YAI!

[*Outside the house we hear the music of a band. Drums and trumpets sound with revolutionary enthusiasm.*]

MINGO: What the hell's that? [*Goes to the front door.*]

CRUZ: Mariachis.

MINGO: The hell, it's a pachuco band.

CRUZ: No, ees a Charro.<sup>8</sup> It's . . . Joaquin!! And Chato!

[*A police siren sounds in the distance. There is immediate confusion outside. "En la madre, the fuss!" "Le's go!" "No, don' run!" etc. Various voices, besides the voices of* JOAQUIN *and* CHATO, *indicate there is a small group of young men outside, which now breaks out running in all directions.* CHATO *runs in, frightened, dressed in huarache sandals and white Mexican peasant clothing. He wears a straw hat, and carries a drum and a trumpet. He enters tripping over his feet, making noise, trying to hide.*]

CRUZ: Chato, hombre, wha's happen?

CHATO: The placa!

MINGO: The police? What did you do?

CHATO: I din' do nothing!

JOAQUIN: [*Outside.*] Open the door, sergeant!

CRUZ: Joaquin!

JOAQUIN: [*Still outside.*] Sergeant, the door!

MINGO: How come you're dressed like that? You look like a peon.

JOAQUIN: [*Still outside.*] CHATO!

CHATO: Yes, my General! [*He opens the door.*]

JOAQUIN: It's about time, *corporal!* [JOAQUIN *enters dressed in the traditional costume of the Mexican charro, complete with a pair of cartridge belts crisscrossed on his chest. Hanging from one shoulder on a strap, he carries a 30–30 carbine. On his shoulders he carries two big sacks, one on each side.*] Here you are, jefita. [*He lowers the sacks.*] One hundred pounds of flour . . . and a hundred pounds of beans, like I promised you.

MINGO: Where did you get this?

JOAQUIN: I'm sorry, I don' speak gavacho.

7. Your father is dead.

8. Mexican cowboy.

MINGO: Don't act stupid. Where did you get these sacks? You swipe 'em, huh?

JOAQUIN: [*Ignores him.*] And this is for you, jefita. [*From his jacket he pulls out a beautiful white rebozo—a shawl.*]

CRUZ: Where did you got this, hijo?

MINGO: He swipe 'em, don' I tell you, señora? [*He grabs* JOAQUIN *by one arm.*] You going to have to return them!

JOAQUIN: 'tas lucas,[9] Gringo.

MINGO: Gringo?

JOAQUIN: Mingo el gringo.

BELARMINO: [*Joyfully.*] AY, YAI, YAI, YAI!

JOAQUIN: VIVA VILLAA! [*To* BELARMINO.] And this is for you, mi General. A box of cigars. [*He offers him one.*] You wan' one! [BELARMINO *smiles, grunts affirmatively.*] Orale, pues.

CRUZ: No, Joaquin, your brother don' smoke.

BELARMINO: [*Growling.*] ARRGH!

CRUZ: [*Backs up.*] Ay dios.

JOAQUIN: At your orders, mi General. [*Gives him a cigar.*] Que le haga buen provecho y que—[1] [*Pause.*] Corporal, a match! [*Chato comes forward with a match.*] Que Viva la Revolucion. [BELARMINO *smokes contentedly, making a lot of smoke.*]

MINGO: I don't believe it. [*Laughs.*] So this is the General, eh? Who the hell do you guys think you are? The Cisco Kid and Pancho?

CHATO: No, he's Pancho. [*Points to* BELARMINO.]

MINGO: You lousy clown! I oughta call the cops right now.

CRUZ: No, Mingo.

MINGO: Don't worry señora. The cops are already after 'em. I bet they even end up in jail tonight. For thiefs!

JOAQUIN: And you? You're the one that oughta be in jail for cheating the jefitos, the family, La Raza! You pinchi sell-out traitor!

CRUZ: Joaquin!

MINGO: No, no, señora. Let him spill the beans.

JOAQUIN: We rob the rich to give the poor, like Pancho Villa! But you . . .

MINGO: I worked to fill all of your stinking bellies! Especially your beloved General there. I got tired of stuffing his guts with . . .

JOAQUIN: What guts?

MINGO: [*Pause.*] I won't argue that.

JOAQUIN: Simon, because he don' got any. He's a head and tha's all.

CRUZ: No, head, no!

JOAQUIN: The head of Francisco Villa! No, my General?

BELARMINO: [*Triumphantly.*] AY, YAI, YAI!

LUPE: [*Entering.*] Ay! [*She doubles up with pain.*] Ay, mama!

---

9. You're crazy.

1. May we meet with success—

CHATO: Mi honey! [*He goes to her side.*]

CRUZ: Lupe, wha's wrong?

MINGO: It's the cockaroaches she ate.

LUPE: Ay! Ay, mama, help me.

CRUZ: Si, mijita. Diosito santo,[2] maybe she's going to have the baby?

CHATO: Baby?

CRUZ: Si, hombre, your son. Help me with her.

CHATO: Heh, ese, I going to have a son.

CRUZ: Joaquin, no you—Mingo! Go call the doctor!

JOAQUIN: Nel, jefita. I'll go!

MINGO: Not dressed like that! I'll go!

JOAQUIN: Dressed like what?!

MINGO: Like a stinking Mexican!

JOAQUIN: You dirty cabron, I'm proud to be a stinking Mexican! You're dress like a gavacho! Through and through!

MINGO: You're the one that's through, Mex! You can't even bring a sack of beans home without stealing it!

JOAQUIN: Simon, but I swipe from the supermarket not the poor! It's no crime to be a thief if you steal from thiefs!

MINGO: Who told you that?

CRUZ: [*Entering.*] Mingo, pronto! Go bring the doctor! Your sister . . .

JOAQUIN: Who you think? The one and only who knows. And that ain't all! He also tell me that he wasn't hungry for food all this time. He was hungry for justice!

MINGO: [*Laughs.*] Justice?

JOAQUIN: Social justice!

CRUZ: Mijos!

MINGO: What social, stupid? You don't even know what the word means!

JOAQUIN: That's what you think but we've had it wis your bones, ese! We're going to get rid of all the gavacho blood-suckers like you. The contractors, the judges, the cops, the stores!

MINGO: Bandit!

JOAQUIN: Simon, like Pancho Villa!

MINGO: You want me to give you a judo chop?

JOAQUIN: Pos ponte, ese![3]

CRUZ: Hijos, por favor . . .

MINGO: Greasy, low, ignorant, lousy . . .

JOAQUIN: Viva La Raza! [*They start to fight.*]

CRUZ: HIJOS DE SU CHINGADA MADRE![4] [CRUZ *is holding the 30–30 carbine.*]

MINGO: Ma!

2. Sacred dear God.

3. Go for it, man!

4. Sons of the damned Mother!

CRUZ: Shut up! Now you going to calm down and sit down like hombrecitos[5] or I pump holes in you! [*Ferociously.*] Okay, MARCH! [*She pushes them toward the sofa, with the carbine.*] Caramba, if you want to fight like dogs tha's how they going to treat you.

MINGO: But I din't.

JOAQUIN: Yo no hice . . .

CRUZ: Silencio! [JOAQUIN *and* MINGO *sit on the sofa.*] Now you, Mingo you goin' for the doctor, and bring him here, understand? Don' make me beg you again. And you, Joaquin. You goin' to take off that crazy clothes and you going to return everything you steal.

JOAQUIN: For what? So the fuzz can get me? Nel, jefita, I'm sorry. I rather go to the mountains and take the General with me. My jefito rode with Pancho Villa, now it's my turn!

CRUZ: NO!

JOAQUIN: Simon, Viva La Revolucion!

CRUZ: No, I tell you! Ees time you know . . . your padre never was in the Revolucion.

JOAQUIN: Chale.[6]

CRUZ: He was in Arizona all those years, working in the mines. For the gringos.

JOAQUIN: Aaah, tha's a lotta chet. And the scar he have here in the neck, from the bullet?

CRUZ: Belarmino bite him there before you was born.

JOAQUIN: [*Desperate.*] And this cartridge belts? And this 30–30? You going to tell me they're not from the Revolucion?

CRUZ: No, because they are.

JOAQUIN: Okay, then, mi 'apa use them. Who else could have use them?

CRUZ: [*Pause.*] I use them, Joaquin! [JOAQUIN *and* MINGO *are shocked.*] Si, mis hijos, your madre rode with Pancho Villa! And tha's how I'm certain Belarmino ees not the General.

[*Someone knocks at the door rudely. Silence, another knock.*]

POLICE: [*Outside.*] Okay, I know you're in there! Open up!

JOAQUIN: [*Runs to the window.*] La jura!

MINGO: The cops! Din't I tell you, señora? They're looking for him!

CRUZ: Ay dios! My son, pronto, hide. [*She puts the sombrero over* BELARMINO.]

MINGO: No, Ma! How can you tell him to hide? It's the law! [*He peeks out the window.*] For Pete's sake, this is embarrassing. All the neighbors are watching.

POLICE: [*Knocking furiously.*] OPEN UP IN THE NAME OF THE LAW, GODDAMMIT!

CRUZ: Mingo, do something.

5. Good little men.

6. No.

JOAQUIN: Don' ask nothing from that sonavavichi, jefita. (*More knocks.*) Open the door!

CRUZ: No, Joaquin, they get you. [*More strong knocks then the sound of glass and wood breaking.*] Ay dios!

POLICE: [*Entering with his club.*] What the hell's going on here? [*The* POLICEMAN is dressed in a uniform that half resembles a highway patrolman's and half a soldier's. He wears a helmet with the letters "M-P" printed in black. As soon as he barges in, JOAQUIN *takes the carbine from* CRUZ.]

JOAQUIN: [*Lifting the rifle.*] Put your stinking gavacho hands up!

CRUZ: Joaquin!

JOAQUIN: [*The* POLICEMAN *goes for his gun.*] Ah! Don't try it, man! I fill you full of holes!

POLICE: You're gonna regret this, boy.

JOAQUIN: Tha's what you think, man. [*He takes the officer's gun.*] Heh, wait a minute. Wha's that on your hat—M-P? Ain't you a city cop?

POLICE: What's the difference? You pachucos no le gusta mucho los cops[7] right? Maybe it's Military Police—maybe it's Mexican Patrol. We're looking for a couple of suspects. Supermarket thiefs. "El Ladron de los Supermercados."

CRUZ: Ladron? Ay no, forgive him, señor! He's a good boy. Him and Chato din' do nothing.

POLICE: Who's Chato?

CHATO: [*Entering the room.*] Heh, Doña Cruz, my wife is very—[*Sees the officer.*] Lonely! [*He exits.*]

POLICE: Heh!

JOAQUIN: Ah, ah! Cool it, gringo!

POLICE: You cholos are in mucho hot water, you savvy that? When did you swipe the car outside?

JOAQUIN: What car?

POLICE: The red sports car!

MINGO: [*Entering from his room.*] Sports car? Oh no, officer, that's my car!

POLICE: Who the hell are you?

MINGO: [*Pause.*] NOBODY! I don't have nothing to do with these people. I just room here. I'm a college student.

CRUZ: Tell him, Mingo, explain—you got the words.

MINGO: What my landlady here means, officer, is that the punk you want is right there. He's the Supermarket Thief.

JOAQUIN: Simon, ees me! But so what, you can't do nothing! Maybe the Revolucion break out right now. What you say, General? We go to the mountains?

BELARMINO: AY, YAI, YAI, YAI!

POLICE: Now what?

JOAQUIN: Pancho Villa!

7. You jerks don't much like the cops.

POLICE: What the hell's going on in this place?

JOAQUIN: I'm going to blow you to pieces, that's what. One side, jefita!

CRUZ: Oh, Joaquin, that carabina don' shoot. It don' got bullets.

MINGO: It's not loaded.

POLICE: Not loaded?! [*He tries to jump* JOAQUIN.]

CRUZ: NO! [*She steps in front of the officer.*] Por favor, señor, don' take him.

POLICE: Get outa my way, lady!

MINGO: Get away, landlady!

JOAQUIN: Hold 'em there, jefita! [JOAQUIN *pulls gun. He runs to* BELARMINO.]

CRUZ: Joaquin, what you doing?

JOAQUIN: I'm going to the mountains with my General!

CRUZ: No, hijo, you drop him!

> [MINGO *knocks down* JOAQUIN's *gun.*]

JOAQUIN: VIVA LA REVOLUCION!

POLICE: Why you little son of a—

CRUZ: JOAQUIN!

MINGO: I'll help you get him, officer!

POLICE: [*Chasing* JOAQUIN.] I warn you, punk! It'll go worse for you resisting arrest!

> [*Everyone chases* JOAQUIN *around the room, trying to catch him and* BELARMINO. CHATO *peeks in.*]

CHATO: Heh, ese, throw it over here! Over here!

> [JOAQUIN *throws* BELARMINO *like a ball.*]

MINGO: Stay out of this, Chato!

CHATO: [*To* JOAQUIN.] Run, ese, run!

JOAQUIN: Not wisout the General!

CRUZ: Gimme him, Chato!

JOAQUIN: Throw it back, ese!

> [CHATO *throws* BELARMINO *back to* JOAQUIN, *but* CRUZ *catches him. The police officer nabs* JOAQUIN. CRUZ *takes* BELARMINO *back to the* TV *set and examines him. In a corner of the room, the officer beats* JOAQUIN.]

CHATO: Orale, watcha eso!

> [*The officer pulls out handcuffs.*]

CRUZ: No! Not those, señor! [*She goes to* JOAQUIN, *leaving* BELARMINO *on top of the* TV *set.*] Por favor, he's my son, señor! Mijo!

POLICE: Sorry, lady, I'm only doing my job. [JOAQUIN *resists and the officer beats the sadistic hell out of him.*] It's only my job.

CRUZ: [*Embracing* JOAQUIN.] Hijo, mijo!

POLICE: Lady, I—[*Tries to pull her away.*]

JOAQUIN: Leave her alone!

POLICE: Shut your mouth, boy! [*He pulls* CRUZ *away.*] All right, señora.

CRUZ: Joaquin!

JOAQUIN: [*Blood on his nose.*] Don' worry, jefita. I ain' scared of 'em. You'll see. I going to return with 50,000 vatos on horses and Chivis! Lemme go, huh? [CRUZ *silently makes the sign of the cross on* JOAQUIN's *forehead with her thumb.*]

POLICE: Okay, boy, let's go!

MINGO: Here's your gun, officer.

POLICE: That's okay, boy. Just put it in my holster.

JOAQUIN: I'm coming back, jefita! I'm coming back! VIVA VILLAAAAAA!

[*The officer takes him out.*]

CRUZ: Joaquin! Joaquin, my son!! [*She weeps at the front door. Silence.* MINGO *approaches* CRUZ.]

MINGO: [*Pointing to* BELARMINO] Look, señora, there's your son.

CHATO: Hijo? Hijo de su! Lupe's gonna have my son! We need a doctor! Orale, brother-in-law, loan me your sports car to go fast. Ees for your carnala.

MINGO: What are you talking about?

CHATO: Tu sister, Lupe!

MINGO: I don't have a sister.

CHATO: La Negra!

MINGO: Negra? Not my sister, boy. You trying to be funny? I just room here.

BELARMINO: DESGRACIADO!

MINGO: Who said that?

CHATO: Not me.

BELARMINO: TRAIDOR A TU RAZA![8]

CRUZ: Ees Belarmino. He's talking!

MINGO: What did he say?

BELARMINO: LAMBISCON![9]

MINGO: Obscenity, obscenity.

BELARMINO: CABRON!

CRUZ: Ay dios! [*Crosses herself.*] Belarmino, don' say that!

BELARMINO: PENDEJO!

CRUZ: Ay dios! [*Crosses herself.*]

MINGO: I'll shut him up! [*He approaches* BELARMINO.]

BELARMINO: BEBOZO!

CRUZ: Ay dios, mi Chorti! [*She approaches* BELARMINO.]

BELARMINO: SINVERGUENZA!

CRUZ: Ees the devil!

CHATO: Nel, ees the General!

8. Traitor to your people.

9. Kiss ass.

MINGO: I'll fix this General!

BELARMINO: AARRRGGHH! [*He bites* MINGO.]

CRUZ: Dios. [*Crosses herself.*]

BELARMINO: [*Getting up steam.*] AMERICANIZADO, DESHECHADO, DESARRAIGADO, DESVERGONZADO, INTERESADO, TAPADO—[1]

CHATO: Go, go, General!

BELARMINO: AGARRADO, EMPAPADO, FIJADO, MALHABLADO, TROMPESADO, AHOGADO, CHIFLADO![2]

MINGO: Shut up! Shut up! Speak English!

[CHATO *whistles.*]

CRUZ: Chato, don' do that, por dios! Go bring the doctor! And a priest!

CHATO: Priest?

CRUZ: Tell him to bring Holy Water! Andale, run!

[CHATO *exits.*]

BELARMINO: NI SABES QUIEN SOY! NI SABES QUIEN SOY![3]

MINGO: Speak English! Speak English!

BELARMINO: PANCHO VILLA!

MINGO: SPEAK ENGLISH! [*Goes on repeating.*] SPEAK ENGLISH! SPEAK ENGLISH! SPEAK ENGLISH! SPEAK ENGLISH! SPEAK ENGLISH!

BELARMINO: [*Simultaneously with* MINGO.] PANCHO VILLA, PANCHO VILLA, PANCHO VILLA, PANCHO VILLA!

CRUZ: [*Simultaneously, kneeling, crossing herself hysterically.*] DIOS, DIOS, DIOS, DIOS, DIOS, DIOS, DIOS, DIOS, DIOS, DIOS, DIOS!!

*Curtain*

# ACT V

*Two years later. A winter night. The walls of the house are still covered with cockroaches. Some of them have grown to a tremendous size.* CRUZ *is sitting on the sofa, with* BELARMINO *to her side. A kerosene heater is nearby flickering with a weak, useless flame and heating absolutely nothing. Everything looks more run down than ever.*

[CRUZ *singing sadly.*]
Adios torres de Chihuahua
Adios torres de Cantera
Ya vino Francisco Villa
Pa' quitarles lo pantera

---

1. Americanized, broken down, rootless, shameless, self-centered, useless.

2. Stingy, softheaded, stubborn, foul-mouthed, amoral, drowned, insane!

3. You don't even know who I am!

Ya llego Francisco Villa
Ha de volver la Frontera.

[BELARMINO *esta roncando.*[4]]

CRUZ: Ay, my little Chorti. What a good hombre you are. I would not be sorprise if some of these days the Señor he give you a big body for being so good, no? Not a little body but a great big body with arms and legs strong like a macho. Tha's how Pedro always want you to be. May God keep him in peace. [*Crosses herself. We hear a terrible cry more animal than human coming from the kitchen.* CRUZ *rises and calls.*] Guadalupe, what you doing to the niña? [*More cries.*] Lupe! [*The cries stop.*] Don' you know how to feed her yet?

[*Lupe enters with a small bundle. She looks like* CRUZ *in hair style and dress, having taken on the role of a mother.*]

LUPE: How can I feed him? He bit the nipple on the bottle and eat it. Look he's all cover with bean soup.
CRUZ: What is she shewing?
LUPE: A cucaracha. [*Pause.*] Oh, don' look at me like that, man. He like 'em. At least I peel off the shell first.
CRUZ: Que muchacha, What kind of little mother you be, eh? You want to kill her?
LUPE: He's not a her, mama!
CRUZ: How you know? He don' get mustaches. His uncle Chorti was born wis mustaches.
LUPE: I don' care, I know. I'm his madre.
BELARMINO: [*In his sleep.*] La tuya.[5]
LUPE: There he goes again, man.
CRUZ: He's sleeping.
BELARMINO: [*Dreaming.*] Señores, I am Francisco Villa.
LUPE: See? He's dreaming just like mi 'apa used to do it.
BELARMINO: Pancho Villa!
CRUZ: My son?
LUPE: Why don' you pull his leg. [*Laughs.*]
CRUZ: You chattap. You think your son gots so much?
BELARMINO: I am Pancho Villa.
CRUZ: No, my son, you're Belarmino.
BELARMINO: VIVA VILLA!
LUPE: Shut him up, man! He's scaring my baby. Pull his ear!
BELARMINO: VIVA PANCHO VI—[CRUZ *pulls his ear.*] YAH-aay jijos! Who pull my ear?
CRUZ: I do it, my son. You was having a bad dream.

4. Belarmino is snoring.
5. Yours.

LUPE: And it gets worser every day. Look like that's all you learn to talk for. I'm Pancho Villa! Pancho Villa!

BELARMINO: I also talk something else, baboza jija de la—

LUPE: Ah ah. Speak English. Without English there's no welfare.

BELARMINO: How I'd like to keek your butt.

LUPE: Well, try it . . . Shorty! [*Laughs.*]

CRUZ: Stop it, Negra. You should have more respect for your older brother. Since Mingo leave and Joaquin's in jail, he's the man of the house.

LUPE: The head of the house.

BELARMINO: Chattap! Your madre's right. I'm in charge.

LUPE: Of what, our starvation?

CRUZ: [*Sighs.*] If Mingo was here, we wouldn't have to worry about nothing. He always work so hard.

BELARMINO: Chure, on us! Forget Mingo, señora. Mingo go away forever. I'm here and I take care of you now. Just wait till the Revolucion.

LUPE: What Revolucion? What we need is welfare so we can eat.

CRUZ: I only pray to Dios Nuestro Señor[6] that Joaquin come back from jail serious. Ready to marry and settle down and support a family.

BELARMINO: Si, like *our* family, for one ejemplo,[7] no? Huevonas! I know what you up to. You itching for Joaquin to come so he can support you! Well, what happen to all that pedo about welfare? We got a right to it. I'm disable.

CRUZ: They want to come to investigate first.

BELARMINO: To investigate? Wha's that?

LUPE: They wanna see how come you don' get a job.

BELARMINO: Huy, pos let 'em come. I don' hide nothing.

LUPE: You got nothing to hide.

BELARMINO: [*An angry burst.*] Tu ya me estas caendo gorda, sabes? Vale mas que te calles el hocico! Yo mando en esta casa y me tienes que guardar respeto? *Malcriada, Pendeja. Malhablada!!!*[8] [*Pause.*] Chihuahua, what a relief. There's nothing like saying what you got to say in Spanish. Like chili in the beans. But I say the same thing in English if you push me, eh? You goddamit!

LUPE: Ay, okay pues. Don' bite me.

BELARMINO: Well, don' come too close. Ma? What time is Joaquin coming from the jail?

CRUZ: I don' know, my son. I'm worry already. Chato go to get him this morning and ees already night. [*There is a knock at the door.*] Ay! Maybe tha's him?

LUPE: No, I bet it's the welfare man.

6. Our Lord God.

7. Example. *Huevonas:* lazybones. *Pedo:* bunk.

8. You're pissing me off, you know? You better shut your trap. I'm in charge in this house and you have to show me respect. Misbegotten, stupid, foul-mouthed.

CRUZ: No, ees my son. I feel it's Joaquin.

LUPE: No, señora, why should Joaquin knock? He lives here.

CRUZ: But maybe he's . . .

BELARMINO: Bueno pues, don' just argue. Open the door!

CRUZ: [*Hesitant.*] Ay dios. You open it, Lupe . . . I can't do it.

LUPE: [*Opens the door.*] There's nobody.

CRUZ: Nobody? [*She goes to the door.*]

BELARMINO: Look outside, maybe he's outside! Stinking viejas! If I had your legs I would have already run around the house. You don' see nobody?

CRUZ: Nothing. I wonder who it is?

[LUPE *crosses the door.*]

CHATO: [*Outside.*] Orale, don' close it! I'm coming!

LUPE: It's Chato! [CHATO *enters, dressed in* PEDRO'*s old clothes. He has a mustache now, and in appearance and behavior he has begun to resemble* PEDRO.] What a joke you trying to pull, hombre? Knocking at the door.

CHATO: What door? Vieja sonsa!⁹ I din' knock.

BELARMINO: Where's Joaquin?

CRUZ: Yes, Chato. Where's my son?

[CHATO *says nothing.*]

BELARMINO: Well talk, hombre!

CHATO: I din' find him.

CRUZ: What?

CHATO: I went to the prison door and wait, but he din' come out.

CRUZ: Ay no, my poor son! They din' let him come out!

LUPE: Din' I tell you? He haven' change. He do something and they take away his parole.

CHATO: They din' neither! I ask 'em. They let him out today.

BELARMINO: Then where's he at? Babozo, maybe you miss him.

CHATO: Nel, I notice good all the vatos that come out. Joaquin wasn' nobody of 'em. I mean . . . nobody look like Joaquin.

BELARMINO: Me lleva la . . . !¹ What you think Joaquin look like? Like Joaquin! A muchacho wis arms and legs! Did you look good by the road? Maybe he come walking?

CHATO: Nel, I look up and down. I even run outa gas and have to leave my carucha² by the road. I din' have even enough to buy a gallon of gas. [*Pause.*] Don' worry, Doña Cruz. Maybe Joaquin come in the bus or something. He'll come today. [*Pause.*] What about here? Did the welfare vato come?

[*There is another knock at the door.*]

9. Stupid old woman!

1. What the hell . . . !

2. Car.

CRUZ: Ees my son! [*She goes to the door and opens it.*]

BELARMINO: Ees him? [*Pause.*] How do he look? No la jodan pues![3] Tell me who is it?

CRUZ: Ees nobody.

[*She closes the door. There is another knock at the door. Stronger this time.*]

BELARMINO: Epale![4] They knocking over here, señora!

[CHATO *opens the door to the side room,* "MINGO's *room."* MINGO *is standing in the doorway. He is dressed in a professional gray suit and is carrying a briefcase. He wears a smart hat and glasses, shoes shined, etc. His face is unusually pale; in fact, it almost looks bleached.*]

MINGO: Good evening, is this the home of Mr. Belarmine?

LUPE: Who?

MINGO: Belarmine, I believe it is?

LUPE: Oh. You mean Belarmino!

BELARMINO: Abusados, raza, es el vato de la welfare.

LUPE: Yes, this is the home of Mr. Belarmino. Come in please.

MINGO: [*With an Anglo accent.*] Muchas gracias. [*Enters, takes off his hat.*]

CRUZ: [*Approaching* MINGO, *awed.*] Mingo? My son, my Domingo! [*She leaps at him and hugs him.*] You come home!

MINGO: I beg your pardon!

LUPE: [*Trying to pull* CRUZ *away.*] Mama! Please! This gentleman isn' Mingo! Mingo's gone! [CRUZ *backs up.*] This is my mother, please excuse her. She thinks you're my brother who went away.

CRUZ: [*Touching* MINGO's *face.*] Como te llamas?[5]

MINGO: [*Pause.*] Mi nombre is Sunday, señora.

LUPE: You speak Spanish?

MINGO: Un poquito.[6] It's part of my job.

LUPE: You see, ma? He's call Sunday, not Domingo.[7] Let him talk with Belarmino.

MINGO: Gracias, let me see . . . Usted es[8] Mr. Belarmine?

CHATO: No. him.

MINGO: Him?

BELARMINO: Quihubole, chabo.[9]

MINGO: Mucho gusto.[1] I have here your application to receive county welfare aid, and oh, do you speak English?

---

3. Don't annoy her already.

4. Listen to me.

5. What is your name?

6. A little bit.

7. Sunday.

8. You are.

9. How you doing, young man.

1. My pleasure.

BELARMINO: Oh yes, more better than a gringo.

LUPE: Belo!

MINGO: Ha ha. It's okay, I don't mind. It may surprise you to know that I'm Mexican-American and fully aware of the sympathies of the culturally deprived. Now Mr. Belarmine, all we want and need before your case goes through is a few personal facts about yourself for our records. Me entiende?[2]

BELARMINO: [Nods.] Picale a la burra.[3]

MINGO: Well, for example. You've applied for our disability coverage, so we need to know who you sleep with.

BELARMINO: Que?

MINGO: Do you sleep alone?

BELARMINO: None of you bis'ness! Pos mira . . . sonavavichi!

LUPE: Belo!

MINGO: I'm sorry, but we need to know.

CRUZ: He sleep with me.

MINGO: Oh yeah? And where's your husband, señora?

BELARMINO: Esta muerto!

MINGO: Let her answer please!

CRUZ: He is dead.

MINGO: Well, I don't mean to question your traditional moral values, but don't you think it's wrong just to shack up with this fellow? You're both old enough to know better. Why don't you get married?

CRUZ: Because he's my son!

MINGO: Oh. Oh!

BELARMINO: Cochino.[4]

MINGO: Well, what kind of disability do you have?

BELARMINO: Pos take a good look.

MINGO: [He looks.] Hmm. You did have a rather serious accident, didn't you? Have you tried to find any work at all?

BELARMINO: Doing what, being a futbol?

MINGO: Do you have any stocks or bonds or private property?

BELARMINO: Huuuy.

MINGO: Well?

BELARMINO: Nothing, nada, ni madre!

MINGO: Good. I guess that does it. We have your application with all other facts and with this, we'll be able to push your case through. But there's just one more thing.

BELARMINO: Pues si, there's always just one more thing.

MINGO: I would suggest you get a haircut.

BELARMINO: Haircut?

2. Do you understand me?

3. Scratch your itch (go for it).

4. Sleazeball.

MINGO: A crewcut.

CRUZ: No! No, señor, please. Not his hair! When he was born like he is, I promise the Virgin never to cut his hair if she let him live.

MINGO: Oh, I see. An old supersti—religion, huh? Well, I was only thinking of your health. I know it's hard in these barrios to keep the city clean, but we gotta give it that old 100% try, know what I mean? I'm going to let you in on a little secret, maybe you'll feel better. Once a long time ago . . . I was poor too. That's right. I also used to live in a lousy dump with cockroaches a lot like this one. Everything was almost exactly like this . . . but that was a lotta years back . . . in another barrio . . . another town . . . another time. [*Snapping out of it.*] Now I'm middle class! I got out of the poverty I lived in because I cared about myself. Because I did something to help myself. I went to college. So now I'm a social worker helping out the poor! Which means that I want to help you to take full advantage of what our society has to offer. There's nothing to lose and everything to gain, believe me!

BELARMINO: I believe you. When do the checks come?

MINGO: Oh, I figure in about thirty days.

BELARMINO: Thirty days!

LUPE: But we don' got nothing to eat.

MINGO: I'm sorry but that's the best we can do.

LUPE: What about Aid to Needy Children?

MINGO: What needy children?

LUPE: My baby. [*She shows him the baby.*]

MINGO: Cute. But what does he need?

LUPE: Look. [ *She opens the blanket.*]

MINGO: [*Double takes at* BELARMINO *then down at the baby again.*] Another one! What happen?

LUPE: He's sick. Like his uncle.

MINGO: Runs in the family, huh? Well, I'll tell you. There's a good chance you might be able to get some kind of help, but nothing before 30 days at least.

BELARMINO: Okay, that do it! Señora, fry me some cucarachas! I hungry.

CHATO: Don' worry, Doña Cruz. I bet Joaquin gets some coins.

MINGO: Joaquin who? Another man in the family?

BELARMINO: Simon limon, more man than you think! Es mas hombre que la ching—[5]

CRUZ: Mingo! Oh, Joaquin, no-Lupe, ah, tu—Chorti!

MINGO: Joaquin . . . ? Oh yeah! I forget! Where is this Joaquin? [*No one says anything.*] Okay, let me put it different. Where was this Joaquin? In prison?

CHATO: How you know?

MINGO: And he was just released today?

---

5. He is more of a man than the goddamn—.

CRUZ: Yes, on patrol.

BELARMINO: Parole.

MINGO: What's he like? Tall, short, light, dark?

CRUZ: Yes, tha's him! Why?

MINGO: Because tonight when I was coming across town I passed by this good-looking Mexican walking along the road. It was pretty cold, so I gave him a lift. He'd just gotten out on parole this morning.

CRUZ: Joaquin, ees my Joaquin!

CHATO: Where's he at?

MINGO: Outside in my car. I forgot he came with me. I'll go get him.

CRUZ: Ay dios! My son is outside!

MINGO: Oh, another thing. It looks like the prison term helped him a lot. He seems very reformed, rehabilitated. Lots of spunk. A clean-cut American boy! Be right back. [*He exits.*]

BELARMINO: AY, YAI, YAI! Now you going to see the Revolucion burst out! Joaquin is back!

CRUZ: [*Overexcited.*] Viva la Revolucion!! [*Pause.*] I mean gracias a dios, my son is back.

LUPE: I bet you pass up Joaquin when he was walking, huh? Menso!

CHATO: Como que menso? Quieres que te meta un guamazo en el hocico?[6] Huh, pos mira? Who's the boss around heres pues? [*He goes to door.*]

CRUZ: You hear what the social worker says, Lupe? My Joaquin is change, he's serious and reform.

BELARMINO: He don't say that. He say he got lots of spunk. He's revolutionary!!

CHATO: [*At the window.*] Here they come! [*Pause.*] Que caray! Tha's not Joaquin!

CRUZ: What?

LUPE: [*At the window.*] Oh no, Joaquin!

BELARMINO: Que, what you see?

MINGO: [*Opening the door.*] Okay, folks, here he is! [MINGO *comes in.*] Well, Jack, come in. This is where you live.

CRUZ: [*Standing in the doorway.*] Dios mio, my son. [*She weeps.*]

[JOAQUIN *comes into the house. He is well dressed.* BUT HE HAS NO HEAD.]

BELARMINO: Chingado, they got him.

MINGO: You see? Rehabilitated. He even grew a little. Congratulations, Jack, I know now you'll make it. Well, I guess I better be on my way. Don't forget the crewcut and general cleanliness, okay? Buenas noches. (*Exits.*)

LUPE: I don' think he looks so bad, mama. He look cleaner.

CHATO: Quihubole, ese. [*Shakes* JOAQUIN'S *hand.*] No wonder I din' reco'nize him on the road.

LUPE: You shut up. I think Joaq—Jack's gonna be okay, ma. He can still find

6. Who's a dumbbell? Do you want me to kick your teeth in?

a job in the fields. Now we can all plan together for the future. Like my son he's not going to have a poor life like us. I'm going to make sure he study so he can go to college someday like Mr. Sunday. With the help of God, my son will grow to be a decent man. Maybe someday he even find a body he can . . . [*Pause.*]

BELARMINO: [*Quickly.*] Heh, señora, bring Joaquin over here! I want to see him. Pos what you know? Look at the big arms he gots . . . and the big body! Oye, Ma, I got an idea.

LUPE: No you don't! I see him first!

BELARMINO: What firs'? I got years waiting for him! Anyway he don' even fit that little head you got.

CRUZ: What you two arguing?

BELARMINO: Pos what? There's the body and here's the head. Le's get together! Pick up me!

CRUZ: But how, hombre? Joaquin is your brother.

BELARMINO: Pos there you are. We keep it in the family. Pick me up somebody!

CRUZ: No, Belarmino.

BELARMINO: Orale, Chato, gimme a lift!

CRUZ: No, I say!

LUPE: See? He's mine, huh mama?

CRUZ: Neither his or yours or nobody but me. Joaquin is mine. Buenas noches. Come on, my son. [*Exits with* JOAQUIN.]

BELARMINO: Heh! Wait, señora! Wait one minute!

CRUZ: Callate tu, cabezon![7]

LUPE: You see, stupid? We both lose! Come on, Chato. (*Exits.*)

BELARMINO: [*Shouting after* LUPE.] Both lose, eh? Bueno, we see who have more pull wis the old lady! Stinking woman! They don' understand Revolucion for nothing. We men must carry on the fight. We machos! No, Chato?

CHATO: Simon, we machos!

LUPE: [*Shouting.*] Chato, come to bed!

CHATO: Oh, that vieja apestosa![8] Buenas noches, ese.

BELARMINO: Buenas noches. [CHATO *exits.*] Well, here I sit . . . broken hearted. But tha's okay cause I still got time to wait. Sooner or later, the jefita gots to come across wis Joaquin's body. All I need is to talk sweet when she give me my beans eh? In other words, organize her. Those people don' even believe who I am. Tha's how I wan' it. To catch 'em by surprise. So don' worry, my people, because one of this days Pancho Villa will pass among you again. Look to your mountains, your pueblos, your barrios. He will be there. Buenas noches.

*Curtain*

7. Shut up, you big head.
8. Stinky old woman. *Buenas noches, ese:* Good night, man.

# STUDY QUESTIONS

1. What different devices does Valdez use to establish each of the CHARACTERS' individuality when he or she first appears onstage? How important is the language he or she speaks to the individualization of each character? Which linguistic habits are particularly useful for establishing each character? How important are clothes to characterization?

2. What patterns are there in the way characters move in and out of Spanish when they speak? Analyze the various times when individual characters speak Spanish and the characters to whom they are speaking. At the end of Act IV, why does Mingo shout at Belarmino, "Speak English! Speak English!"?

3. When characters speak English that is ungrammatical, is the explanation for their behavior purely "realistic"—that is, are they made to do it to make them seem more "believable"? What other explanations might there be for their "lapses"? How does the portrayal of the characters' language relate to the different modes—realistic, surrealistic, symbolic—that the play deliberately mixes?

4. What strategies does Valdez use to make the audience like or dislike characters? to make us trust or distrust them? Which characters do you like least? most? How is Belarmino, in spite of his appearance and the gross behavior associated with him (eating cockroaches, grunting and screaming, farting), made finally to seem attractive? Why does the playwright deliberately make his appearance and his character so contrasting?

5. What staging problems are especially difficult to solve for the character of Belarmino? If you were producing or directing this play for the stage, how would you solve each of them?

6. Why is Mingo's "character" revealed gradually instead of being fully clear at the beginning? Explain how his change of voice and manner in Act IV (p. 1022) works in the total play. How does his modification of manner—a "change" of character—relate to cultural themes in the play? How does it relate to the shifting terms of praise and abuse, for Anglos and for Chicanos and for Mexican-Americans, in the play?

7. How much history do you have to know to understand the attitudes of the play? How much Spanish do you have to speak to follow the dialogue? What strategies does the playwright use to clarify both these matters for those who do not know Mexican history or the Spanish language? How many times are words specifically explained shortly after they are used? How much history is specifically explained in the play?

8. Why is Belarmino said to "talk ingles" (Act III, p. 1009) when he grunts? What other instances of anger against the English language does the play dramatize?

9. What attitude does the play ultimately take toward Anglo culture? toward Anglo values? toward those of Mexican heritage who adopt those values? How, specifi-

cally, does the play demonstrate its attitudes on these issues? What dramatic strategies does it use to influence audience attitudes? Which characters seem to you most effective in raising admiration for particular attitudes or values? in undercutting particular attitudes or values?

# CONTEXTS

J ust as no person is an island, so is no text. All texts are connected to
something else beyond themselves, usually to several things at once.
Texts are connected to the events they describe or reflect, and individuals
often need to know facts from outside the text to understand what is going
on. Texts are connected to the languages in which they are written, and the
habits and conventions of those languages—as well as the vocabulary, grammar, and syntax—determine what the texts can do and how they can do it.
Texts are connected to the cultures and value systems from which they
derive, and they are connected to concepts and larger patterns of thought,
so that a reader's understanding and appreciation of the text will often be
enhanced by a recognition of the idea. Texts come from specific authors
and are read by specific readers. No text, however "complete" and "formal"
in itself, exists alone as a totally separate world. Those things beyond the
text that may be relevant to reading the text itself are called CONTEXTS, literally things that go with texts. Often it is important to think about the various contexts that relate to a text. And sometimes it is crucial.

What a reader needs to know to read pleasurably and usefully varies
considerably from text to text. Some texts are very demanding in what they
expect readers to bring to them; others are "user friendly" to virtually any
reader. One thing that every text requires its reader to bring to it is some
knowledge of the language (or languages) in which it is written. Selections
in this book were chosen specifically for readers who know the English lan-

guage, and they draw on the reader's knowledge of how English works in a variety of ways. But many of them draw on other languages as well. *The Shrunken Head of Pancho Villa* has extensive dialogue in Spanish, but the reader who does not know Spanish well will be able to follow the drift of the conversation (even without consulting footnotes); for the play, conscious that its primary language is English, repeats its key terms often enough (and has characters respond directly enough in English) that a reader with no Spanish will not miss much. Many of the selections included here contain some words or phrases in a language other than English (French, Japanese, Yiddish, and several Indian languages, for example), primarily because they deal with situations in which one culture confronts another or people from one kind of national or linguistic background meet people with other traditions and knowledge.

Generally speaking, the more you know as a reader, about language or anything else, the better a reader you have the potential to be, although you still have to figure out how to apply your knowledge and just what parts of it are actually related to a particular text. Some texts use language in surprising and even confusing ways in order to disorient readers or make them adjust to very special uses of language; many of the selections in chapter 5 subvert reader expectations in that way. More often, texts explore the complex possibilities readers know in the vocabulary or syntax of language used in a conventional way. And sometimes—though rarely—writings try to "educate" a reader in a particular language from a dead stop: that is, they assume no reading ability at all in a particular language. Nora Dauenhauer's "Tlingit Concrete Poem" tells us in an authorial footnote what the three words of the poem mean, and then asks us to savor their sounds and "look" by arranging them in strange ways on the page.

*Historical contexts* or *cultural contexts* are often the most demanding in a text, and they can be the most difficult for a reader to discover and apply. Many texts are specifically *referential*, that is, they refer to specific events, people, or things in the "real" world, and references to these things (to Iran's holding of American hostages, for example, in James Seilsopour's "I Forgot the Words to the National Anthem") assume that a reader will know, or be willing to find out, the facts involved in a specific situation. A reader has to know, or find out, something about Pancho Villa as a historical figure to get much out of *The Shrunken Head of Pancho Villa*; and beyond such factual knowledge, it is important as well for the reader to have some sense of just how honorific a figure Villa is to people of Mexican background—what a culture hero he has become, what a MYTHIC status he holds, what a SYMBOL he is to millions of people.

Getting beyond factual references to the more subtle attitudes toward facts, people, and events is often far more difficult, for readers never quite know when they know enough, and sometimes no single reference in the text, or no single errand in the library, produces just the right key. To understand Ralph Ellison's "Battle Royal," it is not necessary to know about any particular historical incident, but it is important to have some sense of how blacks were treated at the time of the story—what barriers they faced, what attitudes were like, what cultural expectations there were among blacks and whites—in order to participate intellectually and emotionally in the story. The *cultural context* of a particular text may ask us not only to know but to empathize with a whole set of circumstances and traditions of a particular people in a particular place, and the text does not always give us a specific signal—the name of a person, place, or thing—that we have to look up in order to understand.

Another kind of context is the *generic context*. The kind of writing that the writer chooses—a poem, a play, or a story, for example—brings with it some quite specific expectations, for every *literary form* (or GENRE or *literary mode*) has a tradition of use, and this involves specific habits and expectations. A play, for example, involves the assumption that it can be produced on a stage, and one expects it to include CHARACTERS (who are going to be "played by" actors, thus adding an additional dimension of interpretation), and physical SETTING (another interpretive dimension determined beyond the text), and ACTION that can be successfully represented on a stage of a certain size and with specific physical limitations. Stories, poems, autobiographies, essays—all forms of literature—have CONVENTIONS of their own. Poems, for example, depend for some of their effects on rhythms and the sound of a voice reading them, stories move in a more or less chronological direction, etc. Of course, there are many different varieties within any genre—there are lyric poems, narrative poems, satirical poems, and many others, each with specific conventions that lead a reader to have specific EXPECTATIONS—and knowledge about kinds and subkinds can often lead a reader more deeply or more meaningfully into a particular text.

There are all kinds of other contexts as well. *Authorial contexts*, for example, involve a reader's potential knowledge of other works by the same writer or knowledge of biographical information that may or may not be relevant to interpretation. Anything that has a tradition behind it, or that develops specific, expectable habits and conventions, offers some kind of context. Setting, for example, often participates in general expectations about mood, and characterization in a particular text often participates in characterization that has gone before, drawing on particular STEREOTYPES in order to get a "quick fix" on a character before developing more individualistic traits through additional details and further action.

There is no simple rule of thumb to bring to bear on context. The more one knows the better, but skill, experience, and good personal judgment are necessary for the reader in figuring out just what he or she needs to know and how to apply it. Texts often give signals, referring to events or people that one has to look up, but not always. The best thing a reader can do is to be flexible and a bit humble in the face of a new text, for it will often ask more than it appears to ask of readers—sensitivity to the traditions of others, curiosity about the larger world, human wisdom as well as factual knowledge.

# WRITING
# ABOUT THE READING

## PERSONAL ESSAYS AND NARRATIVES

1. Write a short personal account in which you describe the most important compromise you have made in order to feel as if you belonged in some community, club, or group. How were you changed by the experience? Do you regret the compromise? Do you feel as if understanding the needs and expectations of others helped you grow? made you feel cheap? Do you feel that you were permanently affected by the experience? Be sure to organize your account of the experience so that you make clear what the personal and moral issues were for you at the time you entered into the compromise, and indicate clearly whether your feelings changed after the fact.

2. Make a list of the "typical" qualities shared by people of your age group in your neighborhood. Make another list of qualities that are devalued or distrusted. Then create an "inside" character and an "outside" character, and construct a dialogue in which the two characters argue about the appropriateness of peer values in your community.

3. Who is the person you have known who seems to have had the most trouble "fitting in" to a particular group? Write a story in which that person is the main character; construct a situation in which the person's inability to fulfill the expectations of others causes him or her pain. Construct the story and characterize the person in such a way that the reader is made to sympathize with his or her problem.

## IMITATIONS AND PARODIES

1. Using Pat Mora's "Immigrants" as a model, write a poem in which you give advice to an outsider about fitting in.

2. Using Martin Luther King, Jr.'s "I Have a Dream," prepare a speech to be delivered to your classmates in which you outline your ideals for American society.

## ANALYTIC PAPER

Write a critical essay analyzing the father's values in "In the American Society." (Alternative: Analyze the mother's values.)

# ARGUMENTATIVE PAPERS

1. Analyze carefully the motivations of Dyer in "A Class of New Canadians," and write an essay in which you defend his values against those of his various students.

2. Analyze the values expressed in "Greek Horatio Alger," and write an essay in which you attack those values as materialistic, superficial, and unsatisfying. (Alternative: Defend the values as character-building and socially constructive.)

3. Think carefully about the portrayal of the shrunken head in *The Shrunken Head of Pancho Villa*, and write an essay in which you either (a) explain the effectiveness of the stage strategy of presenting political values through this shocking visual device, or (b) attack the visual metaphor on aesthetic or moral grounds.

# RESEARCH PAPER

Go to the library and look up several (at least three) personal accounts of the Civil Rights March on Washington during which Martin Luther King, Jr., delivered his "I Have a Dream" speech. Find accounts that mention the speech specifically, and compare the reactions expressed by different hearers. Then, using periodical indexes (and getting help from a reference librarian if you need it), look up later articles commenting on and evaluating the speech. Write a paper comparing immediate and long-term responses to the speech, and try to account for the differences by looking carefully at the rhetoric of the speech itself.

# 10

# DOMINION

As we have seen, the individual, the self, is situated in widening gyres of time and space. Each of us is part of a family, of a culture both present and past, and of a larger society that also has its own traditions and culture. We are related as well to the human race and human history. But even then we have not necessarily reached the widest, deepest, or highest sphere in which we are located: we play our part within the animal kingdom, the planet earth, the cosmos. And many of us see ourselves in relation to some Higher Being, a spiritual entity or concept that has dominion over our world and ourselves.

Often our spiritual relationship to the universe is situated within our cultural heritage; our religion is that of our parents, or sometimes—especially when our parents have taken a different spiritual route from that of their own parents—that of our more remote forebears. Sometimes, however, as we cross over into another culture, we adopt the spiritual or cosmological orientation of that culture, or we are caught between two cultures, two ways of looking at the world and the universe.

Over the past several centuries, there has been an increasing, though not uniform, secularization of Western society. Some of us are a generation or two removed from any real spiritual or religious roots, though there may be residual cultural identities that have religious connections and can, in time, exert a pull back toward our religious heritage.

The search for a cosmological vision does not necessarily stop at the boundary lines of our own heritage. Those of us who no longer have traditional roots may search elsewhere, may "shop around" for a worldview that satisfies our needs and perspectives. This search is no longer confined to the major Western religions—Catholicism, Protestantism, Judaism. With the increased communication between the Western and Eastern and Southern worlds, with increasing numbers of immigrants from Asia, the Middle East, and other Third World countries, there are cosmologies and religious orientations that not only have their own traditional followers in America but also offer options to others seeking a way of looking at the world and the cosmos. Moslems, Hindus, and Buddhists, and the various sects related to those major religions, abound. Those who find one or another of these sects—the Hare Krishna, for example—somehow too strange, and therefore unacceptable, call these sects "cults," just as we sometimes call our beliefs "religion" and others' beliefs "myths."

Since the end of World War II especially, there seems to have been a revival of religious yearning, not only among the young. This spiritual quest may have something to do with the threat of a nuclear holocaust and the consequent loss of faith in science as the infallible guide to the good life and a better world. The vast movements of peoples, the stirring of dormant societies by the last war, the Holocaust and other religious persecutions of various kinds, have also contributed to the revival of religion, particularly the more fundamentalist sects within the major religions: Chasidic Judaism, Shiite Mohammedanism, evangelical, charismatic, and other fundamentalist forms of Christianity. Sometimes this revival is associated with the revival of cultural or nationalist feeling, as with Iranian fundamentalists, Black Muslims, Native American totemists.

Regardless of cause or even of form, there is undeniably a spiritual "revival" or search in progress, taking us back to our roots here or in our native European, Asian, African, or other heritage, to ancient but hitherto strange or foreign creeds and practices.

The works in this chapter are samples of the kinds of relationships in literature and life of our contemporaries to the cosmic, the universal, the eternal, the supernatural. They are far from exhaustive and may not be entirely representative, but they may give some notion of the kinds of search, within and without, that are going on, and the kinds of resting places or "homes" that some have found. This volume ends, then, as it began, with home and family devotion, but with the emphasis in this final chapter on *devotion*.

# Helena Maria Viramontes

B orn in East Los Angeles in 1954, Helena Maria Viramontes has published widely
and has been frequently anthologized, chiefly in Chicano/Chicana publications. Some of the stories have been collected in her 1985 volume *The Moths and Other
Stories*. She has recently co-edited, with Maria Herrera Sobek, *Chicana Creativity and
Criticism: Charting New Frontiers in American Literature* (1988).

In "The Moths," a young girl pays her last respects to her grandmother, whose
soul flutters away.

## THE MOTHS

I was fourteen years old when Abuelita requested my help. And it seemed       1
only fair. Abuelita had pulled me through the rages of scarlet fever by placing, removing and replacing potato slices on the temples of my forehead; she
had seen me through several whippings, an arm broken by a dare jump off
Tío Enrique's toolshed, puberty, and my first lie. Really, I told Amá, it was
only fair.

Not that I was her favorite granddaughter or anything special. I wasn't       2
even pretty or nice like my older sisters and I just couldn't do the girl things
they could do. My hands were too big to handle the fineries of crocheting or
embroidery and I always pricked my fingers or knotted my colored threads
time and time again while my sisters laughed and called me bull hands with
their cute waterlike voices. So I began keeping a piece of jagged brick in my
sock to bash my sisters or anyone who called me bull hands. Once, while we
all sat in the bedroom, I hit Teresa on the forehead, right above her eyebrow
and she ran to Amá with her mouth open, her hand over her eye while blood
seeped between her fingers. I was used to the whippings by then.

I wasn't respectful either. I even went so far as to doubt the power of       3
Abuelita's slices, the slices she said absorbed my fever. "You're still alive,
aren't you?" Abuelita snapped back, her pasty gray eye beaming at me and
burning holes in my suspicions. Regretful that I had let secret questions drop
out of my mouth, I couldn't look into her eyes. My hands began to fan out,
grow like a liar's nose until they hung by my side like low weights. Abuelita
made a balm out of dried moth wings and Vicks and rubbed my hands,
shaped them back to size and it was the strangest feeling. Like bones melting.

Like sun shining through the darkness of your eyelids. I didn't mind helping Abuelita after that, so Amá would always send me over to her.

In the early afternoon Amá would push her hair back, hand me my sweater and shoes, and tell me to go to Mama Luna's. This was to avoid another fight and another whipping, I knew. I would deliver one last direct shot on Marisela's arm and jump out of our house, the slam of the screen door burying her cries of anger, and I'd gladly go help Abuelita plant her wild lilies or jasmine or heliotrope or cilantro or hierbabuena in red Hills Brothers coffee cans. Abuelita would wait for me at the top step of her porch holding a hammer and nail and empty coffee cans. And although we hardly spoke, hardly looked at each other as we worked over root transplants, I always felt her gray eye on me. It made me feel, in a strange sort of way, safe and guarded and not alone. Like God was supposed to make you feel.

On Abuelita's porch, I would puncture holes in the bottom of the coffee cans with a nail and a precise hit of a hammer. This completed, my job was to fill them with red clay mud from beneath her rose bushes, packing it softly, then making a perfect hole, four fingers round, to nest a sprouting avocado pit, or the spidery sweet potatoes that Abuelita rooted in mayonnaise jars with toothpicks and daily water, or prickly chayotes that produced vines that twisted and wound all over her porch pillars, crawling to the roof, up and over the roof, and down the other side, making her small brick house look like it was cradled within the vines that grew pear-shaped squashes ready for the pick, ready to be steamed with onions and cheese and butter. The roots would burst out of the rusted coffee cans and search for a place to connect. I would then feed the seedlings with water.

But this was a different kind of help, Amá said, because Abuelita was dying. Looking into her gray eye, then into her brown one, the doctor said it was just a matter of days. And so it seemed only fair that these hands she had melted and formed found use in rubbing her caving body with alcohol and marihuana, rubbing her arms and legs, turning her face to the window so that she could watch the Bird of Paradise blooming or smell the scent of clove in the air. I toweled her face frequently and held her hand for hours. Her gray wiry hair hung over the mattress. Since I could remember, she'd kept her long hair in braids. Her mouth was vacant and when she slept, her eyelids never closed all the way. Up close, you could see her gray eye beaming out the window, staring hard as if to remember everything. I never kissed her. I left the window open when I went to the market.

Across the street from Jay's Market there was a chapel. I never knew its denomination, but I went in just the same to search for candles. I sat down on one of the pews because there were none. After I cleaned my fingernails, I looked up at the high ceiling. I had forgotten the vastness of these places, the coolness of the marble pillars and the frozen statues with blank eyes. I was alone. I knew why I had never returned.

That was one of Apá's biggest complaints. He would pound his hands on the table, rocking the sugar dish or spilling a cup of coffee and scream that if I didn't go to mass every Sunday to save my goddamn sinning soul, then I had no reason to go out of the house, period. Punto final. He would grab my arm and dig his nails into me to make sure I understood the importance of catechism. Did he make himself clear? Then he strategically directed his anger at Amá for her lousy ways of bringing up daughters, being disrespectful and unbelieving, and my older sisters would pull me aside and tell me if I didn't get to mass right this minute, they were all going to kick the holy shit out of me. Why am I so selfish? Can't you see what it's doing to Amá, you idiot? So I would wash my feet and stuff them in my black Easter shoes that shone with Vaseline, grab a missal and veil, and wave good-bye to Amá.

I would walk slowly down Lorena to First to Evergreen, counting the cracks on the cement. On Evergreen I would turn left and walk to Abuelita's. I liked her porch because it was shielded by the vines of the chayotes and I could get a good look at the people and car traffic on Evergreen without them knowing. I would jump up the porch steps, knock on the screen door as I wiped my feet and call Abuelita? mi Abuelita? As I opened the door and stuck my head in, I would catch the gagging scent of toasting chile on the placa. When I entered the sala,[1] she would greet me from the kitchen, wringing her hands in her apron. I'd sit at the corner of the table to keep from being in her way. The chiles made my eyes water. Am I crying? No, Mama Luna, I'm sure not crying. I don't like going to mass, but my eyes watered anyway, the tears dropping on the tablecloth like candle wax. Abuelita lifted the burnt chiles from the fire and sprinkled water on them until the skins began to separate. Placing them in front of me, she turned to check the menudo.[2] I peeled the skins off and put the flimsy, limp looking green and yellow chiles in the molcajete and began to crush and crush and twist and crush the heart out of the tomato, the clove of garlic, the stupid chiles that made me cry, crushed them until they turned into liquid under my bull hand. With a wooden spoon, I scraped hard to destroy the guilt, and my tears were gone. I put the bowl of chile next to a vase filled with freshly cut roses. Abuelita touched my hand and pointed to the bowl of menudo that steamed in front of me. I spooned some chile into the menudo and rolled a corn tortilla thin with the palms of my hands. As I ate, a fine Sunday breeze entered the kitchen and a rose petal calmly feathered down to the table.

I left the chapel without blessing myself and walked to Jay's. Most of the time Jay didn't have much of anything. The tomatoes were always soft and the cans of Campbell soups had rusted spots on them. There was dust on the tops of cereal boxes. I picked up what I needed: rubbing alcohol, five cans of chicken broth, a big bottle of Pine Sol. At first Jay got mad because I thought I had forgotten the money. But it was there all the time, in my back pocket.

1. Living room. *Placa:* griddle.
2. Tripe soup. *Molcajete:* Mexican mortar.

When I returned from the market, I heard Amá crying in Abuelita's   11
kitchen. She looked up at me with puffy eyes. I placed the bags of groceries
on the table and began putting the cans of soup away. Amá sobbed quietly.
I never kissed her. After a while, I patted her on the back for comfort. Finally:
"¿Y mi Amá?"[3] she asked in a whisper, then choked again and cried into her
apron.

Abuelita fell off the bed twice yesterday, I said, knowing that I shouldn't   12
have said it and wondering why I wanted to say it because it only made Amá
cry harder. I guess I became angry and just so tired of the quarrels and
beatings and unanswered prayers and my hands just there hanging helplessly
by my side. Amá looked at me again, confused, angry, and her eyes were
filled with sorrow. I went outside and sat on the porch swing and watched
the people pass. I sat there until she left. I dozed off repeating the words to
myself like rosary prayers: when do you stop giving when do you start giving
when do you . . . and when my hands fell from my lap, I awoke to catch
them. The sun was setting, an orange glow, and I knew Abuelita was hungry.

There comes a time when the sun is defiant. Just about the time when   13
moods change, inevitable seasons of a day, transitions from one color to another,
that hour or minute or second when the sun is finally defeated, finally sinks
into the realization that it cannot with all its power to heal or burn, exist
forever, there comes an illumination where the sun and earth meet, a final
burst of burning red orange fury reminding us that although endings are
inevitable, they are necessary for rebirths, and when that time came, just
when I switched on the light in the kitchen to open Abuelita's can of soup,
it was probably then that she died.

The room smelled of Pine Sol and vomit and Abuelita had defecated the   14
remains of her cancerous stomach. She had turned to the window and tried
to speak, but her mouth remained open and speechless. I heard you, Abuelita, I said, stroking her cheek, I heard you. I opened the windows of the
house and let the soup simmer and overboil on the stove. I turned the stove
off and poured the soup down the sink. From the cabinet I got a tin basin,
filled it with lukewarm water and carried it carefully to the room. I went to
the linen closet and took out some modest bleached white towels. With the
sacredness of a priest preparing his vestments, I unfolded the towels one by
one on my shoulders. I removed the sheets and blankets from her bed and
peeled off her thick flannel nightgown. I toweled her puzzled face, stretching
out the wrinkles, removing the coils of her neck, toweled her shoulders and
breasts. Then I changed the water. I returned to towel the creases of her
stretch-marked stomach, her sporadic vaginal hairs, and her sagging thighs.
I removed the lint from between her toes and noticed a mapped birthmark
on the fold of her buttock. The scars on her back which were as thin as the
life lines on the palms of her hands made me realize how little I really knew

3. And my mother?

of Abuelita. I covered her with a thin blanket and went into the bathroom. I washed my hands, and turned on the tub faucets and watched the water pour into the tub with vitality and steam. When it was full, I turned off the water and undressed. Then, I went to get Abuelita.

She was not as heavy as I thought and when I carried her in my arms, 15 her body fell into a V, and yet my legs were tired, shaky, and I felt as if the distance between the bedroom and bathroom was miles and years away. Amá, where are you?

I stepped into the bathtub one leg first, then the other. I bent my knees 16 slowly to descend into the water slowly so I wouldn't scald her skin. There, there, Abuelita, I said, cradling her, smoothing her as we descended, I heard you. Her hair fell back and spread across the water like eagle's wings. The water in the tub overflowed and poured onto the tile of the floor. Then the moths came. Small, gray ones that came from her soul and out through her mouth fluttering to light, circling the single dull light bulb of the bathroom. Dying is lonely and I wanted to go to where the moths were, stay with her and plant chayotes whose vines would crawl up her fingers and into the clouds; I wanted to rest my head on her chest with her stroking my hair, telling me about the moths that lay within the soul and slowly eat the spirit up; I wanted to return to the waters of the womb with her so that we would never be alone again. I wanted. I wanted my Amá. I removed a few strands of hair from Abuelita's face and held her small light head within the hollow of my neck. The bathroom was filled with moths, and for the first time in a long time I cried, rocking us, crying for her, for me, for Amá, the sobs emerging from the depths of anguish, the misery of feeling half born, sob-bing until finally the sobs rippled into circles and circles of sadness and relief. There, there, I said to Abuelita, rocking us gently, there, there.

## STUDY QUESTIONS

1. How does the first paragraph prepare the reader for the last one?

2. How would you describe the NARRATOR?* her CHARACTER?

3. How are the narrator's "bull hands" (par. 2) made normal?

4. Why does the narrator's grandmother make her feel "like God was supposed to make you feel" (par. 4)?

5. How does the detailed description of the transplanting of roots (par. 5) prepare for the final episode in the story? How does it relate to the "supernatural" or fantastic elements in the story?

6. Why doesn't the narrator go to Mass? Where does she go instead?

---

*Words in small capitals are defined in the glossary.

# Toshio Mori

Born in California of Japanese ancestry in 1910, Toshio Mori is the author of the novel *Woman from Hiroshima* (1979). He is, however, best known for his short stories, which have been collected in the volumes *Yokahama, California* (1949) and *The Chauvinist and Other Stories* (1979).

This very short, very pure little story has the Oriental beauty and charm of a Japanese poem or watercolor or of the inside of an abalone shell.

## ABALONE, ABALONE, ABALONE

Before Mr. Abe went away I used to see him quite often at his nursery. He was a carnation grower just as I am one today. At noontime I used to go to his front porch and look at his collection of abalone shells.

They were lined up side by side against the side of his house on the front porch. I was curious as to why he bothered to collect them. It was a lot of bother polishing them. I had often seen him sit for hours on Sundays and noon hours polishing each one of the shells with the greatest of care. Of course I knew these abalone shells were pretty. When the sun strikes the insides of these shells it is something beautiful to behold. But I could not understand why he continued collecting them when the front porch was practically full.

He used to watch for me every noon hour. When I appeared he would look out of his room and bellow, "Hello, young man!"

"Hello, Abe-*san*," I said. "I came to see the abalone shells."

Then he came out of the house and we sat on the front porch. But he did not tell me why he collected these shells. I think I have asked him dozens of times but each time he closed his mouth and refused to answer.

"Are you going to pass this collection of abalone shells on to your children?" I said.

"No," he said. "I want my children to collect for themselves. I wouldn't give it to them."

"Why?" I said. "When you die?"

Mr. Abe shook his head. "No. Not even when I die," he said. "I couldn't give the children what I see in these shells. The children must go out for themselves and find their own shells."

"Why, I thought this collecting hobby of abalone shells was a simple affair," I said.

"It is simple. Very simple," he said. But he would not tell me further.

For several years I went steadily to his front porch and looked at the beautiful shells. His collection was getting larger and larger. Mr. Abe sat and talked to me and on each occasion his hands were busy polishing shells.

"So you are still curious?" he said.

"Yes," I said.

One day while I was hauling the old soil from the benches and replacing it with new soil I found an abalone shell half buried in the dust between the benches. So I stopped working. I dropped my wheelbarrow and went to the faucet and washed the abalone shell with soap and water. I had a hard time taking the grime off the surface.

After forty minutes of cleaning and polishing the old shell it became interesting. I began polishing both the outside and the inside of the shell. I found after many minutes of polishing I could not do very much with the exterior side. It had scabs of the sea which would not come off by scrubbing and the surface itself was rough and hard. And in the crevices the grime stuck so that even with a needle it did not become clean.

But on the other side, the inside of the shell, the more I polished the more lustre I found. It had me going. There were colors which I had not seen in the abalone shells before or anywhere else. The different hues, running berserk in all directions, coming together in harmony. I guess I could say they were not unlike a rainbow which men once symbolized. As soon as I thought of this I thought of Mr. Abe.

I remember running to his place, looking for him. "Abe-*san!*" I said when I found him. "I know why you are collecting the abalone shells!"

He was watering the carnation plants in the greenhouse. He stopped watering and came over to where I stood. He looked me over closely for awhile and then his face beamed.

"All right," he said. "Do not say anything. Nothing, mind you. When you have found the reason why you must collect and preserve them, you do not have to say anything more."

"I want you to see it, Abe-*san*," I said.

"All right. Tonight," he said. "Where did you find it?"

"In my old greenhouse, half buried in the dust," I said.

He chuckled. "That is pretty far from the ocean," he said, "but pretty close to you."

At each noon hour I carried my abalone shell and went over to Mr. Abe's front porch. While I waited for his appearance I kept myself busy polishing the inside of the shell with a rag.

One day I said, "Abe-*san*, now I have three shells."

"Good!" he said. "Keep it up!"

"I have to keep them all," I said. "They are very much alike and very much different."

"Well! Well!" he said and smiled. 29

That was the last I saw of Abe-*san*. Before the month was over he sold 30
his nursery and went back to Japan. He brought his collection along and
thereafter I had no one to talk to at the noon hour. This was before I discovered the fourth abalone shell, and I should like to see Abe-*san* someday and
watch his eyes roll as he studies me whose face is now akin to the collectors
of shells or otherwise.

## STUDY QUESTIONS

1. Why doesn't Mr. Abe tell the NARRATOR why he collects abalone shells? Why will
   he not leave them to his children?

2. Mr. Abe says that collecting abalone shells is a very simple affair, yet it seems
   puzzling at first to the narrator. What is the explanation?

3. What is the TURNING POINT in the story?

4. The colors of the polished abalone shell, the narrator says, "were not unlike a
   rainbow which men once symbolized" (paragraph 17). What does he mean that
   men "once symbolized" the rainbow?

5. Explain the repetitions in the title of the story.

6. Does this story not appear to have more meaning than its simple narrative? What
   elements make it seem to have larger implications or wider applications?

# Walter Lew

B oth of his parents are doctors who left Korea not long before Walter Lew was
born—in Baltimore, in 1955—and Lew seemed headed for medical school, too.
He had the grades but chose poetry, his first love, instead. He is poetry editor of
*Bridge* and assistant editor of *Nuclear Times*, and he is interested in mixing poetry with
film, videos—and baseball.

# LEAVING SEOUL: 1953

We have to bury the urns,
Mother and I. We tried to leave them in a back room,
Decoyed by a gas lamp, and run out

But they landed behind us here, at the front gate.
It is 6th hour, early winter, black cold:                            5
Only, on the other side of the rice-paper doors

The yellow *ondol*[1] stone-heated floors
Are still warm. I look out to the blue
Lanterns along the runway, the bright airplane.

Off the back step, Mother, disorganized                             10
As usual, has devised a clumsy rope and pulley
To bury the urns. I wonder out loud

How she ever became a doctor.
*Get out*, she says    *Go to your father: he too*
*Does not realize what is happening.* You see,                      15

Father is waiting at the airfield in a discarded U.S. Army
Overcoat. He has lost his hat, lost
His father, and is smoking Lucky's like crazy . . .

We grab through the tall weeds and wind
That begin to shoot under us like river ice.                        20
It is snowing. We are crying, from the cold

Or what? It is only decades
Later that, tapping the tall glowing jars,
I find they contain all that has made
The father have dominion over hers.                                 25


# STUDY QUESTIONS

1. Line 1 suggests there is some sort of obligation to bury the urns; what sort of obligation do you imagine there is? In line 2, the SPEAKER and his mother, despite the obligation, try to leave the urns behind. Why? What does the phrase "Decoyed by a gas lamp" (l. 3) suggest is happening?

2. The poem does not say how it was that the urns arrived at the front gate. How do you think they did?

3. The father is waiting at the airfield, but the mother, somewhat disorganized herself, says he does not know what is happening (ll. 14–15). What *is* happening?

4. The first twenty-one and a half lines are written in the present tense, yet the last lines suggest that the event described occurred "decades" before. What is the effect

---

1. Korean under-floor heating system.

of the present tense in the first part of the poem? What is the effect when you realize that it all happened some time ago?

5. Were the urns buried?

6. Explain the last two lines.

# N. Scott Momaday

Poet, editor, novelist, and adapter of Indian tales, N. Scott Momaday was born in Lawton, Oklahoma, in 1934 of Kiowa parents. He earned a B.A. at the University of New Mexico, the state in which he grew up, and an M.A. and Ph.D. from Stanford University, where he is professor of English and comparative literature. In 1969, he published both *The Way to Rainy Mountain*, which contained personal memories, Kiowa myth, and expository prose, and his first novel, *House Made of Dawn*, which won the Pulitzer Prize for fiction. Again, in 1976, he struck twice—with a volume of poems, *The Gourd Dancer*, and *The Names: A Memoir*.

"The Eagle-Feather Fan" merges man, bird, and artifact in an incantatory rhythm that creates a dreamlike atmosphere in which the metamorphosis seems natural and convincing.

## THE EAGLE-FEATHER FAN

The eagle is my power,
And my fan is an eagle.
It is strong and beautiful
In my hand. And it is real.
My fingers hold upon it                              5
As if the beaded handle
Were the twist of bristlecone.
The bones of my hand are fine
And hollow; the fan bears them.
My hand veers in the thin air                        10
Of the summits. All morning
It scuds on the cold currents;
All afternoon it circles
To the singing, to the drums.

# STUDY QUESTIONS

1. What does "it" in line 4 refer to? What does the SPEAKER mean when he says that "it" is "real"?

2. In lines 8 and 9 the speaker says the bones of his hands are hollow. How do you read that statement? In the last five lines, the speaker's hand seems to fly away like an eagle but is responsive to the songs and drums. Is there a way of reading the description in these lines that gives a more "realistic" or secular sense to the lines? Must you choose one reading or the other? Must you believe in the literalness of the ritual in order to appreciate the poem?

# Garrison Keillor

B orn in Anoka, Minnesota, in 1942, Garrison Keillor, largely through his weekly radio program, "The Prairie Home Companion," has made Lake Wobegon the heart of America's heartland, located not far from the funny bone.

The following selection, from *Lake Wobegon Days* (1985), captures his unique mixture of nostalgia and sentiment with a dash of acerbic satire, baked till tender in a deadpan that makes his recipe for humor and memory unique.

# PROTESTANT

Our family was dirt poor, which I figured out as a child from the fact we had such a bad vacuum. When you vacuumed the living room, it would groan and stop and you had to sit and wait for it to groan and start up, then vacuum like mad before it quit again, but it didn't have good suction either. You had to stuff the hairballs into it. I also knew it because Donald Hoglund told me. He asked me how much my dad earned, and I said a thousand dollars, the most money I could imagine, and he shrieked, "You're poor! You're poor!" So we were. And, in a town where everyone was either Lutheran or Catholic, we were neither one. We were Sanctified Brethren, a sect so tiny that nobody but us and God knew about it, so when kids asked what I was, I just said Protestant. It was too much to explain, like having six toes. You would rather keep your shoes on.

Grandpa Cotten was once tempted toward Lutheranism by a preacher    2
who gave a rousing sermon on grace that Grandpa heard as a young man
while taking Aunt Esther's dog home who had chased a Model T across
town. He sat down on the church steps and listened to the voice boom out
the open windows until he made up his mind to go in and unite with the
truth, but he took one look from the vestibule and left. "He was dressed up
like the pope of Rome," said Grandpa, "and the altar and the paintings and
the gold candlesticks—my gosh, it was just a big show. And he was reading
the whole darn thing off a page, like an actor."

Jesus said, "Where two or three are gathered together in my name, there    3
am I in the midst of them," and the Brethren believed that was enough. We
met in Uncle Al's and Aunt Flo's bare living room with plain folding chairs
arranged facing in toward the middle. No clergyman in a black smock. No
organ or piano, for that would make one person too prominent. No upholstery, it would lead to complacency. No picture of Jesus, He was in our
hearts. The faithful sat down at the appointed hour and waited for the Spirit
to move one of them to speak or to pray or to give out a hymn from our Little
Flock hymnal. No musical notation, for music must come from the heart and
not off a page. We sang the texts to a tune that fit the meter, of the many
tunes we all knew. The idea of reading a prayer was sacrilege to us—"If a
man can't remember what he wants to say to God, let him sit down and
think a little harder," Grandpa said.

"There's the Lord's Prayer," said Aunt Esther meekly. We were sitting    4
on the porch after Sunday dinner. Esther and Harvey were visiting from
Minneapolis and had attended Lake Wobegon Lutheran, she having turned
Lutheran when she married him, a subject that was never brought up in our
family.

"You call that prayer? Sitting and reciting like a bunch of schoolchil-    5
dren?"

Harvey cleared his throat and turned to me with a weak smile. "Speak-    6
ing of school, how are you doing?" he asked.

There was a lovely silence in the Brethren assembled on Sunday morn-    7
ing as we waited for the Spirit. Either the Spirit was moving someone to
speak who was taking his sweet time or else the Spirit was playing a wonderful joke on us and letting us sit, or perhaps silence was the point of it. We sat
listening to rain on the roof, distant traffic, a radio playing from across the
street, kids whizzing by on bikes, dogs barking, as we waited for the Spirit
to inspire us. It was like sitting on the porch with your family, when nobody
feels that they have to make talk. So quiet in church. Minutes drifted by in
silence that was sweet to us. The old Regulator clock ticked, the rain stopped
and the room changed light as the sun broke through—shafts of brilliant sun
through the windows and motes of dust falling through it—the smell of clean
clothes and floor wax and wine and the fresh bread of Aunt Flo which was
Christ's body given for us. Jesus in our midst, who loved us. So peaceful,
and we loved each other too. I thought perhaps the Spirit was leading me to

say that, but I was just a boy, and children were supposed to keep still. And my affections were not pure. They were tainted with a sneaking admiration of Catholics—Catholic Christmas, Easter, the Living Rosary, and the Blessing of the Animals, all magnificent. Everything we did was plain, but they were regal and gorgeous—especially the Feast Day of St. Francis, which they did right out in the open, a feast for the eyes. Cows, horses, some pigs, right on the church lawn. The turmoil, animals bellowing and barking and clucking and cats scheming how to escape and suddenly leaping out of the girl's arms who was holding on tight, the cat dashing through the crowd, dogs straining at the leash, and the ocarina band of third-graders playing Catholic dirges, and the great calm of the sisters, and the flags, and the Knights of Columbus decked out in their handsome black suits—I stared at it until my eyes almost fell out, and then I wished it would go on much longer.

"Christians," my uncle Al used to say, "do not go in for show," referring    8
to the Catholics. We were sanctified by the blood of the Lord, therefore we were saints, like St. Francis, but we didn't go in for feasts or ceremonies, involving animals or not. We went in for sitting, all nineteen of us, in Uncle Al's and Aunt Flo's living room on Sunday morning and having a plain meeting and singing hymns in our poor thin voices while not far away the Catholics were whopping it up. I wasn't allowed inside Our Lady, of course, but if the Blessing of the Animals on the Feast Day of St. Francis was any indication, Lord, I didn't know but what they had elephants in there and acrobats. I sat in our little group and envied them for the splendor and gorgeousness, as we tried to sing without even a harmonica to give us the pitch. Hymns, Uncle Al said, didn't have to be sung perfect, because God looks on the heart, and if you are In The Spirit, then all praise is good.

The Brethren, also known as the Saints Gathered in the Name of Christ    9
Jesus, who met in the living room were all related to each other and raised in the Faith from infancy except Brother Mel who was rescued from a life of drunkenness, saved as a brand from the burning, a drowning sailor, a sheep on the hillside, whose immense red nose testified to his previous condition. I envied his amazing story of how he came to be with us. Born to godly parents, Mel left home at fifteen and joined the Navy. He sailed to distant lands in a submarine and had exciting experiences while traveling the downward path, which led him finally to the Union Gospel Mission in Minneapolis where he heard God's voice "as clear as my voice speaking to you." He was twenty-six, he slept under bridges and in abandoned buildings, he drank two quarts of white muscatel every day, and then God told him that he must be born again, and so he was, and became the new Mel, except for his nose.

Except for his nose, Mel Burgess looked like any forty-year-old Brethren    10
man: sober, preferring dark suits, soft-spoken, tending toward girth. His nose was what made you look twice: battered, swollen, very red with tiny purplish lines, it looked ancient and very dead on his otherwise fairly handsome face, the souvenir of what he had been saved from, the "Before" of his "Before . . . and After" advertisement for being born again.

For me, there was nothing before. I was born among the born-again. 11
This living room so hushed, the Brethren in their customary places on folding chairs (the comfortable ones were put away on Sunday morning) around
the end-table draped with a white cloth and the glass of wine and loaf of
bread (unsliced) was as familiar to me as my mother and father, the founders
of my life. I had always been here.

Our family sat in one row against the picture window. Al and Florence 12
and their three, Janet and Paul and Johnny, sat opposite us, I saw the sky
and the maple tree reflected in my uncle's glasses. To our left, Great-Aunt
Mary sat next to Aunt Becky and Uncle Louie, and to our right were Grandma
and Grandpa and Aunt Faith, and behind them was Mel, sitting on the piano
bench. His wife, Rita, was a Lutheran. She only came occasionally and when
she did, she stood out like a brass band. She used lipstick and had plucked
eyebrows and wore bright hats. Brethren women showed only a faint smudge
of powder on their cheeks and their hats were small and either black or navy
blue. Once Rita spoke up in the meeting—Al had stood up to read from the
Lord's Word, and she said, "Pardon me, which chapter did you say?"—and
we all shuddered as if she had dropped a plate on the floor: *women did not
speak in meeting*. Another time, Sunday morning, she made as if to partake of
the bread as it was passed, and Grandpa snatched it away from her. It had
to be explained to Rita later that she could not join in the Lord's Supper with
us because she was not in fellowship.

We were "exclusive" Brethren, a branch that believed in keeping itself 13
pure of false doctrine by avoiding association with the impure. Some Brethren assemblies, mostly in larger cities, were not so strict and broke bread
with strangers—we referred to them as "the so-called Open Brethren," the
"so-called" implying the shakiness of their position—whereas we made sure
that any who fellowshiped with us were straight on all the details of the
Faith, as set forth by the first Brethren who left the Anglican Church in 1865
to worship on the basis of correct principles. In the same year, they posed
for a photograph: twenty-one bearded gentlemen in black frock coats, twelve
sitting on a stone wall, nine standing behind, gazing solemnly into a sunny
day in Plymouth, England, united in their opposition to the pomp and cor-
ruption of the Christian aristocracy.

Unfortunately, once free of the worldly Anglicans, these firebrands were 14
not content to worship in peace but turned their guns on each other. Schol-
arly to the core and perfect literalists every one, they set to arguing over
points that, to any outsider, would have seemed very minor indeed but which
to them were crucial to the Faith, including the question: if Believer $A$ is
associated with Believer $B$ who has somehow associated himself with $C$ who
holds a False Doctrine, must $D$ break off association with $A$, even though $A$
does not hold the Doctrine, to avoid the taint?

The correct answer is: Yes. Some Brethren, however, felt that $D$ should 15
only speak with $A$ and urge him to break off with $B$. The Brethren who felt
otherwise promptly broke off with them. This was the Bedford Question,

one of several controversies that, inside of two years, split the Brethren into three branches.

Once having tasted the pleasure of being Correct and defending True Doctrine, they kept right on and broke up at every opportunity, until, by the time I came along, there were dozens of tiny Brethren groups, none of which were speaking to any of the others.

Our Lake Wobegon bunch was part of a Sanctified Brethren branch known as the Cox Brethren, which was one of a number of "exclusive" Brethren branches—that is, to *non*-Coxians, we were known as "Cox Brethren"; to ourselves, we were simply *The* Brethren, the last remnant of the true Church. Our name came from Brother Cox in South Dakota who was kicked out of the Johnson Brethren in 1932—for preaching the truth! So naturally my grandpa and most of our family went with Mr. Cox and formed the new fellowship.

The split with the Johnsons was triggered by Mr. Johnson's belief that what was abominable to God in the Old Testament must be abominable still, which he put forward at the Grace & Truth Bible Conference in Rapid City in 1932. Mr. Cox stood up and walked out, followed by others. The abomination doctrine not only went against the New Covenant of Grace principle, it opened up rich new areas of controversy in the vast annals of Jewish law. Should Brethren then refrain from pork, meat that God had labeled "Unclean"? Were we to be thrown into the maze of commandments laid out in Leviticus and Deuteronomy, where we are told to smite our enemies with the sword and stone to death rebellious children?

Mr. Johnson's sermon was against women's slacks, and he had quoted Deuteronomy 22:5, "The woman shall not wear that which pertaineth unto a man, neither shall a man put on a woman's garment: for all that do so are abomination unto the Lord thy God," but Mr. Cox, though he was hardly pro-slacks, felt Mr. Johnson failed to emphasize grace as having superseded the law, and when Mr. Johnson said, "An abomination to God under the law is still an abomination to God under grace," Mr. Cox smelled the burning rubber of Error and stood up and marched. He and the other walkouts proceeded to a grove of trees and prayed for Mr. Johnson's soul, and Mr. Johnson and those seated inside did the same for them. The split was never repaired, though as a result of being thought in favor of slacks, the Cox Brethren became death on the subject. My mother never wore slacks, though she did dress my sister in winter leggings, which troubled Grandpa. "It's not the leggings so much as what they represent and what they could lead to," he told her. He thought that baby boys should not wear sleepers unless they were the kind with snaps up the legs. Mother pointed out that the infant Jesus was wrapped in swaddling clothes. "That doesn't mean he wore a dress," Grandpa said. "They probably wrapped his legs separately."[1]

---

1. Brethren history is confusing, even to those of us who heard a lot on the subject at a young age—the Dennis Brethren, for example: I have no idea whether they left us or we left them. Ditto the Reformed

Intense scholarship was the heart of the problem. We had no ordained 20 clergy, believing in the priesthood of all believers, and all were exhorted to devote themselves to Bible study. Some did, Brother Louie and Brother Mel in particular. In Wednesday-night Bible reading, they carried the ball, and some nights you could see that the Coxes of Lake Wobegon might soon divide into the Louies and Mels.

One summer night, they set to over the issue of speaking in tongues, 21 Louie arguing that the manifestation of the Spirit was to be sought earnestly, Mel holding that it was a miraculous gift given to the early Church but not given by God today. I forget the Scripture verses each of them brought forward to defend his position, but I remember the pale faces, the throat-clearing, the anguished looks, as those two voices went back and forth, straining at the bit, giving no ground—the poisoned courtesy ("I think my brother is overlooking Paul's very *clear* message to the Corinthians . . . ," "Perhaps my brother needs to take a closer look, a *prayerful* look, at this verse in Hebrews . . .") as the sun went down, neighbor children were called indoors, the neighbors turned out their lights, eleven o'clock came—they wouldn't stop!

"Perhaps," Grandpa offered, "it would be meet for us to pray for the 22 Spirit to lead us," hoping to adjourn, but both Louie and Mel felt that the Spirit *had* led, that the Spirit had written the truth in big black letters—if only some people could see it.

The thought of Uncle Louie speaking in tongues was fascinating to me. 23 Uncle Louie worked at the bank, he spoke to me mostly about thrift and hard work. What tongue would he speak? Spanish? French? Or would it sound like gibberish? Louie said that speaking in tongues was the true sign, that those who believed *heard* and to those who didn't it was only gabble— what if he stood up and said, "Feemalator, jasperator, hoo ha ha, Wamalamagamanama, zis boom bah!" and everyone else said, "Amen! That's right, brother! Praise God!" and *I was the only one who said, "Huh?"*

Bible reading finally ended when Flo went up to bed. We heard her 24 crying in the bathroom. Al went up to comfort her. Grandpa took Louie aside in the kitchen. Mel went straight home. We all felt shaky.

It was soon after the tongues controversy that the Lake Wobegon Breth- 25 ren folded their tent and merged into another Cox Assembly in St. Cloud, thirty-two miles away. Twenty-eight Brethren worshiped there, in a large bare rented room on the second floor of the bus depot. We had often gone

Sanctified, and the Bird Brethren, though I think that Sabbath observance was involved in our (i.e., the *Beale* Brethren, what we were called before 1932 when we Coxes left the Johnson wing) dispute with the Birds, who tended to be lax about such things as listening to the radio on Sunday and who went in for hot baths to an extent the Beales considered sensual. The Beale, or Cold Water, Brethren felt that the body was a shell or a husk that the spirit rode around in and that it needed to be kept in line with cold baths. But by the time I came along, we listened to the radio on Sunday and ran the bath hot, and yet we never went back and patched things up with the Birds. Patching up was not a Brethren talent. As my grandpa once said of the Johnson Brethren, "Anytime they want to come to us and admit their mistake, we're perfectly happy to sit and listen to them and then come to a decision about accepting them back." [Author's note] there for special meetings, revivals, and now we made the long drive every Sunday and every Wednesday night. Grandpa fought for this. "It is right for Brethren to join together," he said. Louie agreed. Mel didn't. He felt God had put us in Lake Wobegon to be a witness. But finally he gave in. "Think of the children," Grandpa said. One fear of Grandpa's was that we children would grow up and marry outside the Faith if only because we knew nobody in the Faith except for relatives. Faced with the lonely alternative, we'd marry a Lutheran, and then, dazzled by the splendid music and vestments and stained glass, we'd forsake the truth for that carnival down the street. Grandpa knew us pretty well. He could see us perk up on Sunday morning when the Lutheran organ pealed out at ten-thirty. The contrast between the church of Aunt Flo's living room and the power and glory of Lutheranism was not lost on him. Among other Brethren boys and girls, nature would take its course, and in due time, we'd find someone and make a Brethren family. Grandpa was looking to the future.

The shift to St. Cloud changed things, all right, and not all for the better. 26

My mother hated the move from the start. She had no Scripture to quote, only a feeling that we had taken a step away from the family, from ourselves. We had walked to Flo's house, we had sat in Sunday school class in her kitchen and celebrated the Lord's death in the living room. The bread we broke was bread Flo baked, and she also made the wine, in a pickle crock in the basement. Flo's two cats, Ralph and Pumpkin, walked in and out of the service, and along toward the end, having confessed our unworthiness and accepted our redemption by Christ, the smell of Flo's pot roast, baking at low heat, arose to greet us. Before it was Flo's and Al's, the house had been Grandpa's and Grandma's—Mother had known this room since she was tiny, and though she bowed to Grandpa's wishes, she felt in her heart that she was leaving home. Sunday in St. Cloud meant a long drive, and Mother was a nervous rider who saw death at every turn. She arrived at the St. Cloud Assembly in a frazzled state. The second-floor room was huge and bare and held no associations for her. The long silences were often broken by the roar of bus engines and rumble of bus announcements downstairs. Waiting for the Spirit to guide us to a hymn, a prayer, a passage from Scripture, we heard, *"Now boarding at Gate One . . . Greyhound Bus service to Waite Park . . . St. Joseph . . . Collegeville . . . Avon . . . Albany . . . Freeport . . . Melrose . . . and Sauk Center. All aboard, please!"* 27

Whenever a special Bible study meeting was scheduled for Sunday afternoon at three, we couldn't drive home after morning meeting, have dinner, and get back to St. Cloud in time, so one Sunday our family traipsed over to a restaurant that a friend of Dad's had recommended, Phil's House of Good Food. The waitress pushed two tables together and we sat down and studied the menus. My mother blanched at the prices. A chicken dinner went for $2.50, the roast beef for $2.75. "It's a nice place," Dad said, multiplying the five of us times $2.50. "I'm not so hungry, I guess," he said, 28 "maybe I'll just have soup." We weren't restaurantgoers—"Why pay good money for food you could make better at home?" was Mother's philosophy—so we weren't at all sure about restaurant custom: could, for example, a person who had been seated in a restaurant simply get up and walk out? Would it be proper? Would it be *legal?*

The waitress came and stood by Dad. "Can I get you something from the bar?" she said. Dad blushed a deep red. The question seemed to imply that he looked like a drinker. "No," he whispered, as if she had offered to take off her clothes and dance on the table. Then another waitress brought a tray of glasses to a table of four couples next to us. "Martini," she said, setting the drinks down, "whiskey sour, whiskey sour, Manhattan, whiskey sour, gin and tonic, martini, whiskey sour." 29

"Ma'am? Something from the bar?" Mother looked at her in disbelief. 30

Suddenly the room changed for us. Our waitress looked hardened, rough, cheap—across the room, a woman laughed obscenely, "Haw, haw, haw"—the man with her lit a cigarette and blew a cloud of smoke—a swear word drifted out from the kitchen like a whiff of urine—even the soft lighting seemed suggestive, diabolical. To be seen in such a place on the Lord's Day—*what had we done?* 31

My mother rose from her chair. "We can't stay. I'm sorry," Dad told the waitress. We all got up and put on our coats. Everyone in the restaurant had a good long look at us. A bald little man in a filthy white shirt emerged from the kitchen, wiping his hands. "Folks? Something wrong?" he said. "We're in the wrong place," Mother told him. Mother always told the truth, or something close to it. 32

"This is *humiliating,*" I said out on the sidewalk. "I feel like a *leper* or something. Why do we always have to make such a big production out of everything? Why can't we be like regular people?" 33

She put her hand on my shoulder. "Be not conformed to this world," she said. I knew the rest by heart: ". . . but be ye transformed by the renewing of your mind, that ye may prove what is that good and acceptable and perfect will of God. 34

"Where we gonna eat?" Phyllis asked. "We'll find someplace reasonable," said Mother, and we walked six blocks across the river and found a lunch counter and ate sloppy joes (called Maid-Rites) for fifteen cents apiece. They did not agree with us, and we were aware of them all afternoon through prayer meeting and Young People's. 35

The Cox Brethren of St. Cloud held to the same doctrines as we did but they were not so exclusive, more trusting of the world—for example, several families owned television sets. They kept them in their living rooms, out in the open, and on Sunday, after meeting and before dinner, the dad might say, "Well, I wonder what's on," knowing perfectly well what was on, and turn it on—a Green Bay Packers game—and watch it. On Sunday. 36

I ate a few Sunday dinners at their houses, and the first time I saw a 37 television set in a Brethren house, I was dumbfounded. None of the Wobegonian Brethren had one; we were told that watching television was the same as going to the movies—*no*, in other words. I wondered why the St. Cloud people were unaware of the danger. You start getting entangled in the things of the world, and one thing leads to another. First it's television, then it's worldly books, and the next thing you know, God's people are sitting around drinking whiskey sours in dim smoky bars with waitresses in skimpy black outfits and their bosoms displayed like grapefruit.[2]

That was not my view but my parents'. "Beer is the drunkard's kindergarten," said Dad. Small things led to bigger ones. One road leads up, the other down. A man cannot serve two masters. Dancing was out, even the Virginia reel: it led to carnal desires. Card-playing was out, which led to gambling, though we did have Rook and Flinch—why those and not pinochle? "Because. They're different." No novels, which tended to glamorize iniquity. "How do you know if you don't read them?" I asked, but they *knew*. "You only have to touch a stove once to know it's hot," Mother said. (Which novel had she read? She wasn't saying.) Rock 'n' roll, jazz, swing, dance music, nightclub singing: all worldly. "How about Beethoven?" I asked, having heard something of his in school. "That depends," she said. "Was he a Christian?" I wasn't sure. I doubted he was.    38

On the long Sunday-night drive home, leaning forward from the back    39
seat, I pressed them on inconsistencies like a little prosecutor: if dancing leads to carnal desire, how about holding hands? Is it wrong to put your arm around a girl? People gamble on football: is football wrong? Can you say "darn"? What if your teacher told you to read a novel? Or a short story? What if you were hitchhiking in a blizzard and were picked up by a guy who was listening to rock 'n' roll on the radio, should you get out of the car even though you would freeze to death? "I guess the smart thing would be to dress warmly in the first place," offered Dad. "And wait until a Ford comes along." All Brethren drove Fords.

## STUDY QUESTIONS

1. How does Keillor turn the cliché "dirt poor" (paragraph 1) into a source of humor?

2. Among Keillor's other devices for achieving his tone of gentle humor and everyday flat-as-a-prairie realism are his analogies—as when he suggests that he identified

2. Clarence Bunsen: "Most Brethren I knew were death on card-playing, beer-drinking, and frowned on hand-holding, and of course they wouldn't go near a dance. They thought it brought out carnal desires. Well, maybe theirs lay closer to the surface, I don't know. Some were not only opposed to dancing but also felt that marching in formation was wrong, so we called them the Left-Footed Brethren. Some others were more liberal, Mr. Bell for example, he thought cards were okay so long as you didn't play with a full deck. The Bijou used to show good movies but the Brethren and some Lutherans ganged up on Art and made him stop, so now you have to drive to St. Cloud if you want to see unmarried people together in one room with the door closed. It's a shame. I think if the church put in half the time on covetousness that it does on lust, this would be a better world for all of us." [Author's note]

himself as a Protestant chiefly because belonging to the Sanctified Brethren "was too much to explain, like having six toes. You would rather keep your shoes on" (par. 1). Another device is his use of "irrelevant" but realistic detail: "Grandpa Cotten was once tempted toward Lutheranism by a preacher who gave a rousing sermon on grace that Grandpa heard as a young man while taking Aunt Esther's dog home who had chased a Model T across town" (par. 2). (What does Aunt Esther's dog have to do with Lutheranism, religion, or anything Keillor is talking about?) Find several instances of these devices. What other devices does Keillor use to create humor or a sense of everyday reality?

3. Religion is a difficult and delicate subject, especially when the tone is somewhat humorous. Do you find anything in this selection blasphemous? offensive? Does the selection seem antifundamentalist? anti-Lutheran? anti-Catholic? anti-Christian? If you were one of the Brethren, how would you feel about this selection? Do you get any sense of what Keillor's own present religious position might be? Do you read this selection as fact or fiction (or fact slightly fictionalized)? What evidence is there for your decision? Does the factuality or fictionality of this (or any other selection) make a difference in how you read it, how you respond to it? Explain.

4. What seems to be Keillor's attitude toward the people in his family? Which relatives might have some reason to resent their portrait or Keillor's attitude toward them?

# Durango Mendoza

Born in 1945 of a Mexican-American father and a Creek mother, Durango Mendoza felt an outsider to Chicano, Native American, and white cultures. His stories, he says, are "about human beings who happen to be brown, and being brown in a white culture, or Chicano in an Indian culture," but with the emphasis on *human* beings.

In this selection, Shirley is the center of the action, but it is her unnamed brother through whose eyes and consciousness we see the events in this strange and moving story.

## SUMMER WATER AND SHIRLEY

It was in the summer that had burned every stalk of corn and every blade of grass and dried up the creek until it only flowed in trickles across the ford below the house where in the pools the boy could scoop up fish in a dishpan.

The boy lived with his mother and his sister, Shirley, and the three    2
smaller children eleven miles from Weleetka, and near Lthwathlee Indian
church where it was Eighth Sunday meeting and everyone was there. The
boy and his family stayed at the camp house of his dead father's people.

Shirley and her brother, who was two years older and twelve, had just    3
escaped the deacon and were lying on the brown, sun-scorched grass behind
the last camp house. They were out of breath and giggled as they peeped
above the slope and saw the figure of the deacon, Hardy Eagle, walking
slowly toward the church house.

"Boy, we sure out-fooled him, huh?" Shirley laughed lightly and jabbed    4
her elbow in her brother's shaking side. "Whew!" She ran her slim hand over
her eyes and squinted at the sky. They both lay back and watched the cloud-
less sky until the heat in their blood went down and their breath slowed to
normal. They lay there on the hot grass until the sun became too much for
them.

"Hey, let's go down to the branch and find a pool to wade in, okay?"    5
She had rolled over suddenly and spoke directly into the boy's ear.

"I don't think we better. Mama said to stay around the church grounds."    6

"Aw, you're just afraid."    7

"No, it's just that—"    8

" 'Mama said to stay around the church grounds!' Fraidy-cat, I'll go by    9
myself then." She sat up and looked at him. He didn't move and she sighed.
Then she nudged him. "Hey." She nudged him again and assumed a stage
whisper. "Looky there! See that old man coming out of the woods?"

The boy looked and saw the old man shuffling slowly through the high    10
Johnson grass between the woods and the clearing for the church grounds.
He was very old and still wore his hair in the old way.

"Who is he?" Shirley whispered. "Who is he?"    11

"I can't tell yet. The heat makes everything blurry." The boy was look-    12
ing intently at the old man who was moving slowly in the weltering heat
through the swaying grass that moved with the sound of light tinsel in the
dry wind.

"Let's go sneak through the grass and scare him," Shirley suggested. "I    13
bet that'd make him even run." She moved her arms as if she were galloping
and broke down into giggles. "Come on," she said, getting to one knee.

"Wait!" He pulled her back.    14

"What do you mean, 'wait'? He'll be out of the grass pretty soon and we    15
won't—" She broke off. "What's the matter? What're you doing?"

The boy had started to crawl away on his hands and knees and was    16
motioning for her to follow. "Come on, Shirley," he whispered. "That's old
Ansul Middlecreek!"

"Who's *he*?"    17

"Don't you remember? Mama said he's the one that killed Haskell Day—    18
with witchcraft. He's a *stiginnee!*"

"A *stiginnee*? Aw, you don't believe that, do you? Mama says you can    19 tell them by the way they never have to go to the toilet, and that's where he's been. Look down there." She pointed to the little unpainted house that stood among the trees.

"I don't care *where* he's been! Come on, Shirley! Look! Oh my gosh! He saw you pointing!" 20

"I'm coming," she said and followed him quickly around the corner of the camp house. 21

They sat on the porch. Almost everyone was in for the afternoon service and they felt alone. The wind was hot and it blew from the southwest. It blew past them across the dry fields of yellow weeds that spread before them up to the low hills that wavered in the heat and distance. They could smell the dry harshness of the grass and they felt the porch boards hot underneath them. Shirley bent over and wiped her face with the skirt of her dress. 22

"Come on," she said. "Let's go down to the creek branch before that deacon comes back." She pulled at his sleeve and they stood up. 23

"Okay," he said and they skirted the outer camp houses and followed the dusty road to the bridge, stepping from tuft to tuft of scorched grass. 24

Toward evening and suppertime they climbed out of the dry bed of the branch, over the huge boulders to the road and started for the camp grounds. The sun was in their eyes as they trudged up the steep road from the bridge. They had found no water in the branch so they had gone on down to the creek. For the most part it too was dry. 25

Suddenly they saw a shadow move into the dust before them. They looked up and saw old Ansul Middlecreek shuffling toward them. His cracked shoes raised little clouds of dust that rose around his ankles and made whispering sounds as he moved along. 26

"Don't look when you go by," the boy whispered intently, and he pushed her behind him. But as they passed by, Shirley looked up. 27

"Hey, Ansul Middlecreek," she said cheerfully. "*Henkschay!*"[1] Then with a swish of her skirt she grabbed her brother and they ran. The old man stopped and the puffs of dust around his feet moved ahead as he grumbled, his face still in shadow because he did not turn around. The two didn't stop until they had reached the first gate. Then they slowed down and the boy scolded his sister all the way to their camp. And all through supper he looked at the dark opening of the door and then at Shirley who sat beside him, helping herself with childish appetite to the heavy, greasy food that was set before her. 28

"You better eat some," she told her brother. "Next meetin's not 'til next month." 29

Soon after they had left the table she began to complain that her head hurt and their mother got them ready to go home. They took the two little girls and the baby boy from where they were playing under the arbor and 30

---

1. Hey, hello. A greeting.

cleaned them up before they started out. Their uncle, George Hulegy, would go with them and carry the biggest girl. The mother carried the other one while the boy struggled in the rear with the baby. Shirley followed morosely behind them all as they started down the road that lay white and pale under the rising moon.

She began to fall further behind and shuffled her bare feet into the warm underlayer of dust. The boy gave to his uncle the sleeping child he carried and took Shirley by the hand, surprised that it was so hot and limp.

"Come on, Shirley, come on. Mama, Shirley's got a fever. Don't walk so fast—we can't keep up. Come on, Shirley," he coaxed. "Hurry."

They turned into their lane and followed it until they were on the little hill above the last stretch of road and started down its rocky slope to the sandy road below. Ahead, the house sat wanly under the stars, and Rey, the dog, came out to greet them, sniffing and wriggling his black body and tail.

George Hulegy and the mother were already on the porch as the boy led his sister into the yard. As they reached the porch they saw the lamp begin to glow orange in the window. Then Shirley took hold of the boy's arm and pointed weakly toward the back yard and the form of the storehouse.

"Look, Sonny! Over there, by the storehouse." The boy froze with fear but he saw nothing. "They were three little men," she said vaguely and then she collapsed.

"Mama!" But as he screamed he saw a great yellow dog with large brown spots jump off the other end of the porch with a click of its heavy nails and disappear into the shadows that led to the creek. The boy could hear the brush rustle and a few pebbles scatter as it went. Rey only whined uneasily and did not even look to where the creature had gone.

"What is it? What's wrong?" The two older persons had come quickly onto the porch and the mother bent immediately to help her daughter.

"Oh, Shirley! George! Help me. Oh gosh! She's burning up. Sonny, put back the covers of the big bed. Quick now!"

They were inside now and the boy spoke.

"She saw dwarfs," he said solemnly and the mother looked at George Hulegy. "And there was a big yellow dog that Rey didn't even see."

"Oh, no, no," the mother wailed and leaned over Shirley who had begun to writhe and moan. "Hush, baby, hush. Mama's here. Hush, baby, your Mama's here." She began to sing softly a very old song while George Hulegy took a lantern from behind the stove.

"I'm going to the creek and get some pebbles where the water still runs," he said. "I have to hurry." He closed the screen quietly behind him and the boy watched him as he disappeared with the swinging lantern through the brush and trees, down into the darkness to the ford. Behind him the mother still sang softly as Shirley's voice began to rise, high and thin like a very small child's. The boy shivered in the heat and sat down in the corner to wait helplessly as he tried not to look at the dark space of the window. He grew stiff and tired trying to control his trembling muscles as they began to jump.

Then George Hulegy came in with some pebbles that still were dripping 43 and they left little wet spots of dark on the floor as he placed them above all the doors and windows throughout the house. Finally he placed three round ones at the foot of the bed where Shirley lay twisting and crying with pain and fever.

The mother had managed to start a small fire in the kitchen stove and 44 told the boy to go out and bring in a few pieces of cook wood from the woodpile. He looked at her and couldn't move. He stood stiff and alert and heard George Hulegy, who was bending close over Shirley, muttering some words that he could not understand. He looked at the door but the sagging screen only reflected the yellow lamplight so that he couldn't see through into the darkness; he froze even tighter.

"Hurry, son!" 45

He looked at Shirley lying on the bed and moving from side to side. 46

"Sonny, I have to make Shirley some medicine!" His body shook from 47 a spasm. The mother saw and turned to the door.

"I'll get them," she said. 48

"Mama!" 49

She stopped and he barged through the door and found the darkness 50 envelop him. As he fixed his wide-open gaze on the woodpile that faintly reflected the starlight and that of the moon which had risen above the trees, he couldn't look to either side nor could he run. When he reached for the first piece of wood, the hysteria that was building inside him hardened into an aching bitter core. He squeezed the rough cool wood to his chest and felt the fibers press into his bare arms as he staggered toward the house and the two rectangles of light. The closer he came the higher the tension inside him stretched until he could scarcely breathe. Then he was inside again and he sat limply in the corner, light and drained of any support. He could feel nothing except that Shirley was lying in the big feather bed across the room, wailing with hurt and a scalding fever.

His mother was hurrying from the kitchen with a tin cup of grass tea 51 when Shirley began to scream, louder and louder until the boy thought that he would never hear another sound as he stood straight and hard, not leaning at all.

She stopped. 52

In the silence he saw his mother standing above and behind the lamp, 53 casting a shadow on the ceiling, stopped with fear as they heard the other sound. The little girls had come into the room from their bedroom and were standing whimpering in their nightgowns by the door. The mother signaled and they became still and quiet, their mouths slightly open and their eyes wide. They heard nothing.

Then like a great, beating heart the sound rose steadily until they could 54

smell the heat of a monstrous flesh, raw and hot. Steadily it grew to a gagging, stifling crescendo—then stopped. They heard the click of dog's nails
on the porch's wooden planks, and afterwards, nothing. In the complete silence
the air became cold for an instant and Shirley was quiet.

It was three days now since Shirley had begun to die and everyone knew    55
now and had given up any hope. Even the white doctor could find nothing
wrong and all the old Indians nodded their solemn heads when he went away
saying that Shirley would be up in a few days, for now, to them, her manner
of death was confirmed. He said to send for him if there was any "real"
change. No need to move her—there was nothing wrong—nothing physically wrong, he had said. He could not even feel her raging fever. To him
Shirley was only sleeping.

Everyone had accepted that Shirley was going to die and they were all    56
afraid to go near her. "There is evil around her," they said. They even convinced the mother to put her in the back room and close off all light and only
open it after three days. She would not die until the third day's night, nor
would she live to see the fourth day's dawn. This they could know. A very
old woman spoke these words to the mother and she could not disbelieve.

On this third day the boy sat and watched the flies as they crawled over    57
the dirty floor, over the specks and splotches, the dust and crumbs. They
buzzed and droned about some drops of water, rubbing their legs against
themselves, nibbling, strutting, until the drops dried into meaningless little
rings while the hot wind blew softly through the open window, stirring par-
ticles of dust from the torn screen. A droplet of sweat broke away from above
his eyebrow and ran a crooked rivulet down his temple until he wiped it
away. In his emptiness the boy did not want his sister to die.

"Mama?"    58
"What is it, son?"    59
"Is Shirley going to die?"    60
"Yes, son."    61

He watched her as she stood with her back to him. She moved the heavy    62
skillet away from the direct heat and turned the damper so that the flames
would begin to die. She moved automatically, as if faster movement would
cause her to breathe in too much of the stifling heat. And as she moved the
floor groaned under the shift in weight and her feet made whispering sounds
against the sagging boards. The flies still flitted about, mindless and nasty,
as the boy looked away from them to his mother.

"Does she have to, Mama?"    63
"Shirley is dying, son."    64

Again he saw how the flies went about, unaware of the heat, himself,    65
his mother across the room or that Shirley lay in her silence in the back room.
He splashed some more water from his glass and they knew he was there but
immediately forgot and settled back to their patternless walking about. And

even though the table was clean they walked jerkily among the dishes and inspected his tableware. The boy had lived all his life among these creatures, but now he could not stand their nature.

"Darn flies!"    66

"Well, we won't have to worry when cold weather gets here," she said.    67
"Now go call the kids and eat. I want to get some sewing done this afternoon."

He said nothing and watched her as she went into the other room. He    68
went to the door and leaned out to call the small children. Then he slipped quietly into the back room and closed the door behind him, fastening the latch in the dark. The heat was almost choking and he blinked away the saltiness that stung his eyes. He stood by the door until he could see a little better. High above his head a crack in the shingles filtered down a star of daylight and he stepped to the bed that stood low against the rough planks of the wall. There were no flies in this room and there was no sound.

The boy sat down on a crate and watched the face of his sister emerge    69
from the gloom where she lay. Straining his eyes, he finally saw the rough army blanket rise and fall, but so slight was the movement that when his eyes lost their focus he could not see it and he quickly put out his hand, but stopped. Air caught in his throat and he stifled a cough, still letting his hand hover over the motionless face. Then he touched the smooth forehead and jerked his hand away as if he had been burned.

He sat and watched his sister's well-formed profile and saw how the    70
skin of the nose and forehead had become taut and dry and now gleamed pale and smooth like old ivory in the semi-darkness. A smell like that of hot wood filled the room, but underneath it the boy could smell the odor of something raw, something evil—something that was making Shirley die.

The boy sat on the empty crate in the darkness through the late after-    71
noon and did not answer when his mother called him. He knew that she would not even try the door to this room. He waited patiently for his thoughts to come together, not moving in the lifeless heat, and let the sweat flow from his body. He smelled the raw smell, and when it became too strong he touched the smooth, round pebbles that had come from the creek where it still flowed, and the smell receded.

For many hours he sat, and then he got up and took down the heavy    72
blanket that had covered the single window and let the moonlight fall across the face of his sister through the opening. He began to force his thoughts to remember, to relive every living moment of his life and every part that Shirley had lived in it with him. And then he spoke softly, saying what they had done, and how they would do again what they had done because he had not given up, for he was alive, and she was alive, and they had lived and would *still* live. And so he prayed to his will and forced his will out through his thoughts and spoke softly his words and was not afraid to look out through the window into the darkness through which came the coolness of the summer night. He smelled its scents and let them touch his flesh and come to

rest around the "only sleeping" face of his sister. He stood, watching, listening, living.

Then they came, silently, dark-bellied clouds drifting up from the south, 73 and the wind, increasing, swept in the heavy scent of the approaching storm. Lightning flashed over the low, distant hills and the clouds closed quietly around the moon as the thunder rumbled and the heavy drops began to fall, slowly at first, then irregularly, then increasing to a rhythmic rush of noise as the gusts of wind forced the rain in vertical waves across the shingled roof.

Much later, when the rain had moved ahead and the room became chilly 74 when the water began to drip from the roof and the countless leaves, the boy slipped out of his worn denim pants and took off his shirt and lay down beside his sister. She felt him and woke up.

"You just now gettin' to bed?" she asked. "It's pretty late for that, ain't 75 it?"

"No, Shirley," he said. "Go on back to sleep. It'll be morning pretty 76 soon, and when it gets light again we'll go see how high the water's risen in the creek."

He pulled the cover over him and drew his bare arms beneath the blan- 77 ket and pulled it over their shoulders as he turned onto his side. Lying thus, he could see in the darkness the even darker shapes of the trees and the storehouse his father had built.

## STUDY QUESTIONS

1. In the opening paragraphs of the story, who seems the more adventurous, the brother or Shirley?

2. Who is Ansul Middlecreek? Why does the boy begin crawling away when he sees him? Why doesn't Shirley believe he is a wizard *(stiginnee)?* What happens when they see him again?

3. What does Shirley see by the storehouse? What does the boy see leap off the porch? Why doesn't Rey, the dog, growl or bark or seem to notice?

4. Why does George Hulegy, the children's uncle, rush to the ford?

5. What happens when Shirley stops screaming?

6. What is the white doctor's diagnosis? What do the Indians believe—or know— about her condition? Why is Shirley put in the back room and kept in the dark?

7. Why can the boy now, suddenly, not stand the "nature" of the flies (par. 65)? When he goes into the dark room where Shirley lies, what does he smell? How does he make the smell recede?

8. How does the boy try to combat his sister's illness? Why is it that he believes she can be saved? Will Shirley live? What evidence is there about what will happen? How does the story end?

9. Explain the title.

# Rafael Jesús González

Born in El Paso in 1935 and educated in Texas, Mexico, and Oregon, Rafael Jesús González teaches creative writing and literature at Laney College. He is the author of a collection of poems, *El Hacedor de Juegos*, and the recipient of National Endowment for the Arts and Woodrow Wilson fellowships.

## SESTINA: SANTA PRISCA

One would think that these
Dry standards of pink stone
Would whip the wind with iron
Tongues and speak the word
Kept by their chiseled, gesticulating saints          5
Weeping dust tears upon the courtyard floor.

From the chequered, knee-rubbed floor
Rise supplications cast with wings of iron
To perch with gentle claws upon the word
"God" carved with gold upon the pimpled stone.          10
Futile as this chasuble of rock, these
Prayers can never tame the gestures of the saints.

Now the sun strikes with glory the cold saints
Forcing their lips to simulate a word
Voiced in silver by the bells of iron.          15
Each note a silver globule floats to crack these
Shallow crystals of the morning hours lying on the floor
And scatter their potions of tranquility on the stone.

It is not time for winds to ruffle the starched stone
Which clothes the rock-ribbed bosoms of the saints          20
And checks the pulses of the word.
It will never be time to resuscitate these
Dead theologies groveling on the vestry floor
Rehearsing one-time truths from vellums bound in iron.

The lace work of the sun-forged iron                               25
Is not wide enough to let the saints
Escape wearing their still phylacteries of stone.
The bougainvillaea climbs its progress from the floor
To leave its purple knees on the saints' lips; these
Let the bits of passion drop, but keep the precious word.          30

But it is there, the tongue-tied word
Encapsuled in its throats of iron,
To shake to truth the rock hinged saints
Hanging like dead murmurs above the ocean floor.
The matutinal orations will rise on plumes of stone                35
And the loud tongues of candles whisper: "Listen to these."

The bells of iron will testify their love and these
Flowers on the floor become testaments from which the saints
Will preach the golden word and the green life-stone.

## STUDY QUESTIONS

1. The sestina is a very elaborate form. It contains six six-line STANZAS, in which the words ending each line of the first stanza are repeated in changed order in the following stanzas, and a final three-line stanza, with three of the end words at the ends of the lines and the other three within the lines. In what ways is the elaborateness of the poetic form justified by the SUBJECT MATTER? by the ideas of the poem?

2. Describe the church as precisely as you can, citing lines or passages to support your description.

3. How do the carved saints "[weep] dust tears" (line 6)? The prayers, the poem says, "can never tame the gestures of the saints" (l.12). What do you imagine those gestures to be? Why do they need to be tamed?

4. The poem begins with "One would think" that the saints would speak. Why have they not done so? What, does the poem say at the end, will make them finally speak?

# Audre Lorde

Author of nine books (mostly collections of poetry, such as *Coal* [1976] and *The Black Unicorn* [1978], but also a fictionalized memoir she calls a "biomythography," *Zami: A New Spelling of My Name* [1982]), Audre Lorde lives on Staten Island in New York City. She has taught at the John Jay College of Criminal Justice and, since 1981, at Hunter College. She was born in New York in 1934, but her family comes from the West Indies.

This poem seems to be a recitation of advice to the expectant mother, sort of a folk Dr. Spock.

# REINS

Refuse the meat of a female animal
when you are bearing
or her spirit may turn against you
and your child    fall in the blood.

Do not cook fish with bulging eyes                          5
nor step over running water
the spirits of streams are restless
and can pull your child    down and away.

Do not joke with your grandfather
if you wish many strong children                            10
nor hunt rabbits    in the afternoon

From the eighth day
when the child is named
to keep your milk flowing
do not eat coconut                                          15
after the sun goes down.

## STUDY QUESTIONS

1. Reins can be either "a means of guiding, controlling, checking, or restraining," or "the loins, thought of as the seat of the emotions and affections" (or simply "the emotions and affections"), or both. Which meaning(s) seems to apply here? How?

2. Who do you think is or might be the SPEAKER?

3. From the details in the poem, try to reconstruct the society and the country or territory from which this advice comes.

# Ishmael Reed

Ishmael Reed was born in Chattanooga, Tennessee, in 1938 and was educated at the University of Buffalo. One of the most outrageous—and humorous—of the writers of the counterculture that flourished in the 1960s and early 1970s, he is perhaps best known for his novels, such as *The Freelance Pallbearers*, *Mumbo Jumbo*, and *Yellow Back Radio Broke-Down*, though his poetry shows the same bite, the same mixture of real and surreal, present and past, the same brilliant wordplay.

"I Am a Cowboy in the Boat of Ra" is an almost typical example of Reed's work.

## I AM A COWBOY IN THE BOAT OF RA

"The devil must be forced to reveal any such physical evil (potions, charms, fetishes, etc.) still outside the body and these must be burned."—RITUALE ROMANUM, *published 1947, endorsed by the coat of arms and introduction letter from Francis Cardinal Spellman*

I am a cowboy in the boat of Ra,[1]
sidewinders in the saloons of fools
bit my forehead   like       O
the untrustworthiness of Egyptologists
Who do not know their trips. Who was that          5
dog-faced man?[2] they asked, the day I rode
from town.

School marms with halitosis cannot see
the Nefertiti[3] fake chipped on the run by slick
germans, the hawk behind Sonny Rollins' head or          10
the ritual beard of his axe,[4] a longhorn winding
its bells thru the Field of Reeds.

1. Chief of the ancient Egyptian gods, creator and protector of humans and vanquisher of Evil.

2. The Egyptian god of the dead Anubis was usually depicted as a man with the head of a dog or jackal.

3. Fourteenth-century B.C. Egyptian queen; elsewhere Reed says that German scholars are responsible for the notion that her dynasty was white.

4. Musical instrument. *Sonny Rollins:* jazz great of the late 1950s and early 1960s.

I am a cowboy in the boat of Ra. I bedded
down with Isis,[5] Lady of the Boogaloo, dove
down deep in her horny, stuck up her Wells-Far-ago          15
in daring midday get away. "Start grabbing the
blue," i said from top of my double crown.

I am a cowboy in the boat of Ra. Ezzard Charles[6]
of the Chisholm Trail. Took up the bass but they
blew off my thumb. Alchemist in ringmanship but a          20
sucker for the right cross.

I am a cowboy in the boat of Ra. Vamoosed from
the temple i bide my time. The price on the wanted
poster was a-going down, outlaw alias copped my stance
and moody greenhorns were making me dance; while my mouth's   25
shooting iron got its chambers jammed.

I am a cowboy in the boat of Ra. Boning-up in
the ol West i bide my time. You should see
me pick off these tin cans whippersnappers. I
write the motown long plays for the comeback of          30
Osiris.[7] Make them up when stars stare at sleeping
steer out here near the campfire. Women arrive
on the backs of goats and throw themselves on
my Bowie.[8]

I am a cowboy in the boat of Ra. Lord of the lash,          35
the Loup Garou[9] Kid. Half breed son of Pisces and
Aquarius. I hold the souls of men in my pot. I do
the dirty boogie with scorpions. I make the bulls
keep still and was the first swinger to grape the taste.

I am a cowboy in his boat. Pope Joan[1] of the          40
Ptah Ra. C/mere a minute willya doll?
Be a good girl and
Bring me my Buffalo horn of black powder
Bring me my headdress of black feathers

5. Principal goddess of ancient Egypt.

6. World heavyweight boxing champion, 1949–51.

7. Husband of Isis and constant foe of his brother Set (line 48). Tricked by Set, he died violently but later
rose from the dead.

8. Large hunting knife.

9. French for werewolf; in voodoo, a priest who has run amok or gone mad.

1. Mythical female pope, supposed to have succeeded to the papacy in 855. *Ptah Ra:* chief god of Memphis,
capital of ancient Egypt.

Bring me my bones of Ju-Ju snake                                    45
Go get my eyelids of red paint.
Hand me my shadow
I'm going into town after Set

I am a cowboy in the boat of Ra
look out Set      here i come Set                                   50
to get Set      to sunset Set
to unseat Set        to Set down Set
                    usurper of the Royal couch
                    imposter RAdio of Moses' bush[2]
                    party pooper O hater of dance                   55
                    vampire outlaw of the milky way

## STUDY QUESTIONS

1. In lines 11–12, there are, among other puns, references to musical instruments (once Sonny Rollins is mentioned) in "longhorn," "bells," "Reeds" (the last with a bow in the direction of the poet himself, no doubt). What other wordplay do you find in the poem? What is its effect on the TONE? In what ways is it appropriate to the strange juxtaposition of cowboy and Ra, the old Far West and the old (Middle) East?

2. In lines 31–32, there is some sound-play to reinforce the wordplay—"stars stare at sleeping / steer out here near the campfire." What other examples can you find? What is the effect of such devices?

3. Reed, as one footnote suggests, believes European Egyptologists misleadingly identify the Egyptian rulers as white. What elements in the poem celebrate blackness and the identification of the Egyptian culture with that of the rest of Africa and Africans?

# Cynthia Ozick

B orn in the Bronx in 1928 and educated at New York University and Ohio State University, Cynthia Ozick is the author of two novels—*Trust* (1966) and *The Cannibal Galaxy* (1983)—a separately published novella, *The Messiah of Stockholm* (1987),

---

2. Which, according to Exodus 3:2, burned but was not consumed and from which Moses heard the voice of God telling him to lead the Israelites out of Egypt.

and two collections of short fiction—*The Pagan Rabbi and Other Stories* (1971) and *Bloodshed and Three Novellas* (1976).

"Bloodshed," like many of her other stories, deals with modern American Jews and the psychological, moral, and religious legacy of the Holocaust.

# BLOODSHED

Bleilip took a Greyhound bus out of New York and rode through icy scenes half-urban and half-countrified until he arrived at the town of the hasidim. He had intended to walk, but his coat pockets were heavy, so he entered a loitering taxi. Though it was early on Sunday afternoon he saw no children at all. Then he remembered that they would be in the yeshivas until the darker slant of the day. Yeshivas not yeshiva: small as the community was, it had three or four schools, and still others, separate, for the little girls. Toby and Yussel were waiting for him and waved his taxi down the lumpy road above their half-built house—it was a new town, and everything in it was new or promised: pavements, trash cans, septic tanks, newspaper stores. But just because everything was unfinished, you could sniff rawness, the opened earth meaty and scratched up as if by big animal claws, the frozen puddles in the basins of ditches fresh-smelling, mossy. 1

Toby he regarded as a convert. She was just barely a relative, a third or fourth cousin, depending on how you counted, whether from his mother or from his father, who were also cousins to each other. She came from an ordinary family, not especially known for its venturesomeness, but now she looked to him altogether uncommon, freakish: her bun was a hairpiece pinned on, over it she wore a bandanna (a *tcheptichke*, she called it), her sleeves stopped below her wrists, her dress was outlandishly long. With her large red face over this costume she almost passed for some sort of peasant. Though still self-reliant, she had become like all their women. 2

She served him orange juice. Bleilip, feeling his bare bald head, wondered whether he was expected to say the blessing, whether they would thrust a headcovering on him: he was baffled, confused, but Yussel said, "You live your life and I'll live mine, do what you like," so he drank it all down quickly. Relief made him thirsty, and he drank more and more from a big can with pictures of sweating oranges on it—some things they bought at a supermarket like all mortals. 3

"So," he said to Toby, "how do you like your *shtetl?*" 4

She laughed and circled a finger around at the new refrigerator, vast-shouldered, gleaming, a presence. "What a village we are! A backwater!" 5

"State of mind," he said, "that's what I meant." 6

"Oh, state of mind. What's that?" 7

"Everything here feels different," was all he could say. 8

"We're in pieces, that's why. When the back rooms are put together    9
we'll seem more like a regular house."

"The carpenter," Yussel said, "works only six months a year—we got    10
started with him a month before he stopped. So we have to wait."

"What does he do the rest of the year?"    11

"He teaches."    12

"He teaches?"    13

"He trades with Shmulka Gershons. The other half of the year Shmulka    14
Gershons lays pipes. Six months *Gemara* with the boys, six months on the
job. Mr. Horowitz the carpenter also."

Bleilip said uncertainly, meaning to flatter, "It sounds like a wonderful    15
system."

"It's not a *system*," Yussel said.    16

"Yussel goes everywhere, a commuter," Toby said: Yussel was a sales-    17
man for a paper-box manufacturer. He wore a small trimmed beard, very
black, black-rimmed eyeglasses, and a vest over a rounding belly. Bleilip saw
that Yussel liked him—he led him away from Toby and showed him the new
hot air furnace in the cellar, the gas-fired hot water tank, the cinder blocks
piled in the yard, the deep cuts above the road where the sewer pipes would
go. He pointed over a little wooded crest—they could just see a bit of unpainted
roof. "That's our yeshiva, the one our boys go to. It's not the toughest, they're
not up to it. They weren't good enough. In the other yeshiva in the city they
didn't give them enough work. Here," he said proudly, "they go from seven
till half-past six."

They went back into the house by the rear door. Bleilip believed in    18
instant rapport and yearned for closeness—he wanted to be close, close. But
Yussel was impersonal, a guide, he froze Bleilip's vision. They passed through
the bedrooms and again it seemed to Bleilip that Yussel was a real estate
agent, a bureaucrat, a tourist office. There were a few shelves of books—
holy books, nothing frivolous—but no pictures on the walls, no radio anywhere, no television set. Bleilip had brought with him, half-furtively, a snapshot of Toby taken eight or nine years before: Toby squatting on the grass
at Brooklyn College, short curly hair with a barrette glinting in it, high socks
and loafers, glimpse of panties, wispy blouse blurred by wind, a book with
its title clear to the camera: Political Science. He offered this to Yussel: "A
classmate." Yussel looked at the wall. "Why do I need an image? I have my
wife right in front of me every morning." Toby held the wallet, saw, smiled,
gave it back. "Another life," she said.

Bleilip reminded her, "The joke was which would be the bigger break-    19
through, the woman or the Jew—" To Yussel he explained, "She used to say
she would be the first lady Jewish President."

"Another life, other jokes," Toby said.    20

"And this life? Do you like it so much?"    21

"Why do you keep asking? Don't you like your own life?"    22

Bleilip liked his life, he liked it excessively. He felt he was part of soci-    23 ety-at-large. He told her, without understanding why he was saying such a thing, "Here there's nothing to mock at, no jokes."

"You said we're a village," she contradicted. 24

"That wasn't mockery." 25

"It wasn't, you meant it. You think we're fanatics, primitives." 26

"Leave the man be," Yussel said. He had a cashier's tone, guide count- 27 ing up the day's take, and Bleilip was grieved, because Yussel was a survivor, everyone in the new town, except one or two oddities like Toby, was a survivor of the deathcamps or the child of a survivor. "He's looking for something. He wants to find. He's not the first and he won't be the last." The rigid truth of this—Bleilip had thought his purposes darkly hidden—shocked him. He hated accuracy in a survivor. It was an affront. He wanted some kind of haze, a nostalgia for suffering perhaps. He resented the orange juice can, the appliances, the furnace, the sewer pipes. "He's been led to expect saints," Yussel said. "Listen, Jules," he said, "I'm not a saint and Toby's not a saint and we don't have miracles and we don't have a rebbe who works miracles."

"You have a rebbe," Bleilip said; instantly a wash of blood filled his 28 head.

"He can't fly. What we came here for was to live a life of study. Our 29 own way, and not to be interrupted in it."

"For the man, not the woman. You, not Toby. Toby used to be smart. 30 Achievement goals and so forth."

"Give the mother of four sons a little credit too, it's not only college girls 31 who build the world," Yussel said in a voice so fair-minded and humorous and obtuse that Bleilip wanted to knock him down—the first lady Jewish President of the United States had succumbed in her junior year to the zealot's private pieties, rites, idiosyncrasies. Toby was less than lucid, she was crazy to follow deviants, not in the mainstream even of their own tradition. Bleilip, who had read a little, considered these hasidim actually christologized: everything had to go through a mediator. Of their popular romantic literature he knew the usual bits and pieces, legends, occult passions, quirks, histories—he had heard, for instance, about the holiday the Lubavitcher hasidim celebrate on the anniversary of their master's release from prison: pretty stories in the telling, even more touching in the reading—poetry. Bleilip, a lawyer though not in practice, an ex-labor consultant, a fund-raiser by profession, a rationalist, a *mitnagid*[1] (he scarcely knew the word), purist, skeptic, enemy of fresh revelation, enemy of the hasidim!—repelled by the sects themselves, he was nevertheless lured by their constituents. Refugees, survivors. He supposed they had a certain knowledge the unscathed could not guess at.

He said: "Toby makes her bed, she lies in it. I didn't come expecting 32 women's rights and God knows I didn't come expecting saints."

1. Naysayer, one who always opposes.

"If not saints then martyrs," Yussel said. 33

Bleilip said nothing. This was not the sort of closeness he coveted—he 34
shunned being seen into. His intention was to be a benefactor of the feelings.
He glimpsed Yussel's tattoo-number[2] (it almost seemed as if Yussel just then
lifted his wrist to display it) without the compassion he had schemed for it.
He had come to see a town of dead men. It spoiled Bleilip's mood that Yussel
understood this.

At dusk the three of them went up to the road to watch the boys slide 35
down the hill from the yeshiva. There was no danger: not a single car, except
Bleilip's taxi, had passed through all day. The snow was a week old, it was
coming on to March, the air struck like a bell-clapper, but Bleilip could smell
through the cold something different from the smell of winter. Smoke of
woodfire seeped into his throat from somewhere with a deep pineyness that
moved him: he had a sense of farness, clarity, other lands, displaced seasons,
the brooks of a village, a foreign bird piercing. The yeshiva boys came down
on their shoe-soles, one foot in front of the other, lurching, falling, rolling.
A pair of them tobogganed past on a garbage-can lid. The rest jostled, tumbled, squawked, their yarmulkas dropping from their heads into the snow
like gumdrops, coins, black inkwells. Bleilip saw hoops of halos wheeling
everywhere, and he saw their ear-curls leaping over their cheeks, and all at
once he penetrated into what he took to be the truth of this place—the children whirling on the hillside were false children, made of no flesh, it was a
crowd of ghosts coming down, a clamor of white smoke beat on the road.
Yussel said, "I'm on my way to *mincha*,[3] want to come?" Bleilip's grandfather, still a child but with an old man's pitted nose, appeared to be flying
toward him on the lid. The last light of day split into blue rays all around
them; the idea of going for evening prayer seemed natural to him now, but
Bleilip, privately elated, self-proud, asked, "Why, do you need someone?"—
because he was remembering what he had forgotten he knew. Ten men. He
congratulated his memory, also of his grandfather's nose, thin as an arrow—
the nose, the face, the body, all gone into the earth—and he went on piecing
together his grandfather's face, tan teeth that gave out small clicks and radiated
stale farina, shapely gray half-moon eyes with fleshy lids, eyebrows sparse
as a woman's, a prickly whiskbroom of a mustache whiter than cream. Yussel
took him by the arm: "Pessimist, joker, here we never run short, a *minyan*
always without fail, but come, anyhow you'll hear the rebbe, it's our turn
for him." Briefly behind them Bleilip saw Toby moving into the dark of the
door, trailed by two pairs of boys with golden earlocks: he felt the shock of
that sight, as if a beam of divinity had fixed on her head, her house. But in
an instant he was again humiliated by the sting of Yussel's eye—"She'll give
them supper," he said merely, "then they have homework." "You people
make them work." "Honey on the page is only for the beginning," Yussel
said, "afterward comes hard learning."

2. Prisoners in Nazi concentration camps had numbers tattooed on the inside of their wrists.
3. Evening prayers. A quorum for prayers is ten men, or *minyan*.

Bleilip accepted a cap for his cold-needled skull and they toiled on the        36
ice upward toward the schoolhouse: the rebbe gave himself each week to a
different *minyan*. When Bleilip reached for a prayer-shawl inside a cardboard
box Yussel thumbed a No at him, so he dropped it in again. No one else paid
him any attention. Through the window the sky deepened; the shouts were
gone from the hill. Yussel handed him a *sidur*,[4] but the alphabet was jumpy
and strange to him: it needed piecing together, like his grandfather's visage.
He stood up when the others did. Then he sat down again, fitting his haunches
into a boy's chair. It did not seem to him that they sang out with any special
fervor, as he had read the hasidim did, but the sounds were loud, cadenced,
earnest. The leader, unlike the others a mutterer, was the single one wearing
the fringed shawl—it made a cave for him, he looked out of it without mobility of heart. Bleilip turned his stare here and there into the tedium—which
was the rebbe? He went after a politician's face: his analogy was to the mayor
of a town. Or a patriarch's face—the father of a large family. They finished
*mincha* and herded themselves into a corner of the room—a long table (three
planks nailed together, two sawhorses) covered by a cloth. The cloth was
grimy: print lay on it, the backs of old *sidurim*, rubbing, shredding, the backs
of the open hands of the men. Bleilip drew himself in; he found a wooden
folding chair and wound his legs into the rungs, away from the men. It
stunned him that they were not old, but instead mainly in the forties, plump
and in their prime. Their cheeks were blooming hillocks above their beards;
some wore yarmulkas, some tall black hats, some black hats edged with fur,
some ordinary fedoras pushed back, one a workman's cap. Their mouths
especially struck him as extraordinary—vigorous, tender, blessed. He marveled at their mouths until it came to him that they were speaking another
language and that he could follow only a little of it: now and then it was
almost as if their words were visibly springing out of their mouths, like flags
or streamers. Whenever he understood the words the flags whipped at him,
otherwise they collapsed and vanished with a sort of hum. Bleilip himself
was a month short of forty-two, but next to these pious men he felt like a
boy; even his shoulder-blades weakened and thinned. He made himself concentrate: he heard *azazel*, and he heard *kohen gadol*, they were knitting something up, mixing strands of holy tongue with Yiddish. The noise of Yiddish
in his ear enfeebled him still more, like Titus's fly[5]—it was not an everyday
language with him, except to make cracks with, jokes, gags. . . . His dead
grandfather hung from the ceiling on a rope. Wrong, mistaken, impossible,
uncharacteristic of his grandfather!—who died old and safe in a Bronx bed,
mischief-maker, eager aged imp. The imp came to life and swung over Bleilip's black corner. Here ghosts sat as if already in the World-to-Come, expli-

---

4. Prayer book; plural, *sidurim*.

5. Roman general (later emperor) who in A.D. 70 destroyed the second Temple in Jerusalem. In rabbinical
   lore, he is said to have had a gnat fly up his nose and into his brain where it fed for seven years until Titus
   died, and physicians opening his skull found a large bird with brass beak and iron claws.

cating Scripture. Or whatever. Who knew? In his grandfather's garble the hasidim (refugees, dead men) were crying out Temple, were crying out High Priest, and the more Bleilip squeezed his brain toward them, the more he comprehended. Five times on the tenth day of the seventh month, the Day of Atonement, the High Priest changes his vestments, five times he lowers his body into the ritual bath. After the first immersion garments of gold, after the second immersion white linen, and wearing the white linen he confesses his sins and the sins of his household while holding on to the horns of a bullock. Walking eastward, he goes from the west of the altar to the north of the altar, where two goats stand, and he casts lots for the goats: one for the Lord, one for Azazel, and the one for the Lord is given a necklace of red wool and will be slaughtered and its blood caught in a bowl, but first the bullock will be slaughtered and its blood caught in a bowl; and once more he confesses his sins and the sins of his household, and now also the sins of the children of Aaron, this holy people. The blood of the bullock is sprinkled eight times, both upward and downward, the blood of the goat is sprinkled eight times, then the High Priest comes to the goat who was not slaughtered, the one for Azazel, and now he touches it and confesses the sins of the whole house of Israel, and utters the name of God, and pronounces the people cleansed of sin. And Bleilip, hearing all this through the web of a language gone stale in his marrow, was scraped to the edge of pity and belief, he pitied the hapless goats, the unlucky bullock, but more than this he pitied the God of Israel, whom he saw as an imp with a pitted nose dangling on a cord from the high beams of the Temple in Jerusalem, winking down at His tiny High Priest—now he leaps in and out of a box of water, now he hurries in and out of new clothes like a quick-change vaudevillian, now he sprinkles red drops up and red drops down, and all the while Bleilip, together with the God of the Jews, pities these toy children of Israel in the Temple long ago. Pity upon pity. What God could take the Temple rites seriously? What use does the King of the Universe have for goats? What, leaning on their dirty table-cloth—no vestments, altars, sacrifices—what do these survivors, exemptions, expect of God now?

All at once Bleilip knew which was the rebbe. The man in the work-cap, with a funny flat nose, black-haired and red-bearded, fist on mouth, elbows sunk into his lap—a self-stabber: in all that recitation, those calls and streamers of discourse, this blunt-nosed man had no word: but now he stood up, scratched his chair backward, and fell into an ordinary voice. Bleilip examined him: he looked fifty, his hands were brutish, two fingers missing, the nails on the others absent. A pair of muscles bunched in his neck like chains. The company did not breathe and gave him something more than attentiveness. Bleilip reversed his view and saw that the rebbe was their child, they gazed at him with the possessiveness of faces seized by a crib, and he too spoke in that mode, as if he were addressing parents, old fathers, deferential, awed, guilty. And still he was their child, and still he owed them his guilt. He said: "And what comes next? Next we read that the *kohen gadol* gives the goat fated for Azazel to one of the *kohanim*, and the *kohen* takes it out into a place all bare and wild, with a big cliff in the middle of it all, and he cuts off a bit of the red wool they had put on it, and ties it onto a piece of rock to mark the place, and then he drives the goat over the edge and it spins down, down, down, and is destroyed. But in the Temple the worship may not continue, not until it is known that the goat is already given over to the wilderness. How can they know this miles away in the far city? All along the way from the wilderness to Jerusalem, poles stand up out of the ground, and on top of every pole a man, and in the hand of every man a great shawl to shake out, so that pole flies out a wing to pole, wing after wing, until it comes to the notice of the *kohen gadol* in the Temple that the goat has been dashed into the ravine. And only then can the *kohen gadol* finish his readings, his invocations, his blessings, his beseechings. In the neighborhood of Sharon often there are earthquakes: the *kohen gadol* says: let their homes not become their graves. And after all this a procession, no, a parade, a celebration, all the people follow the *kohen gadol* to his own house, he is safe out of the Holy of Holies, their sins are atoned for, they are cleansed and healed, and they sing how like a flower he is, a lily, like the moon, the morning star among clouds, a dish of gold, an olive tree. . . . That, gentlemen, is how it was in the Temple, and how it will be again after the coming of Messiah. We learn it"—he tapped his book—"in *Mishna Yoma, Yoma*—Targum for Day, *yom hakipurim,*[6] but whose is the atonement, whose is the cleansing? Does the goat for Azazel atone, does the *kohen gadol* cleanse and hallow us? No, only the Most High can cleanse, only we ourselves can atone. Rabbi Akiva reminds us: 'Who is it that makes you clean? Our Father in Heaven.' So why, gentlemen, do you suppose the Temple was even then necessary, why the goats, the bullock, the blood? Why is it necessary for all of this to be restored by Messiah? These are questions we must torment ourselves with. Which of us would slaughter an animal, not for sustenance, but for an idea? Which of us would dash an animal to its death? Which of us would not feel himself to be a sinner in doing so? Or feel the shame of Esau? You may say that those were other days, the rituals are obsolete, we are purer now, better, we do not sprinkle blood so readily. But in truth you would not say so, you would not lie. For animals we in our day substitute men. What the word Azazel means exactly is not known—we call it wilderness, some say it is hell itself, demons live there. But whatever we mean by 'wilderness,' whatever we mean by 'hell,' surely the plainest meaning is *instead of*. Wilderness instead of easeful places, hell and devils instead of plenitude, life, peace. Goat instead of man. Was there no one present in the Temple who, seeing the animals in all their majesty of health, shining hair, glinting hooves, timid nostrils, muscled like ourselves, gifted with tender eyes no different from our own, the whole fine creature trembling—was there no one there when the knife slit the fur and

---

6. Day of atonement. The *Mishna* is the text section of the Talmud (the *Gemara* the interpretation). *Yoma:* days.

skin and the blood fled upward who did not feel the splendor of the living beast? Who was not in awe of the miracle of life turned to carcass? Who did not think: *how like that goat I am! The goat goes, I stay, the goat instead of me.* Who did not see in the goat led to Azazel his own destiny? Death takes us too at random, some at the altar, some over the cliff. . . . Gentlemen, we are this moment so to speak in the Temple, the Temple devoid of the Holy of Holies—when the Temple was destroyed it forsook the world, so the world itself had no recourse but to pretend to be the Temple by mockery. In the absence of Messiah there can be no *kohen gadol*, we have no authority to bless multitudes, we are not empowered, we cannot appeal except for ourselves, ourselves alone, in isolation, in futility, instead we are like the little goats, we are assigned our lot, we are designated for the altar or for Azazel, in either case we are meant to be cut down. . . . O little fathers, we cannot choose, we are driven, we are not free, we are only *instead of:* we stand *instead of*, instead of choice we have the yoke, instead of looseness we are pointed the way to go, instead of freedom we have the red cord around our throats, we were in villages, they drove us into camps, we were in trains, they drove us into showers of poison, in the absence of Messiah the secular ones made a nation, enemies bite at it. All that we do without Messiah is in vain. When the Temple forsook the world, and the world presumed to mock the Temple, everyone on earth became a goat or a bullock, he-animal or she-animal, all our prayers are bleats and neighs on the way to a forsaken altar, a teeming Azazel. Little fathers! How is it possible to live? When will Messiah come? You! You! Visitor! You're looking somewhere else, who are you not to look?"

He was addressing Bleilip—he pointed a finger without a nail.    38

"Who are you? Talk and look! Who!"    39

Bleilip spoke his own name and shook: a schoolboy in a schoolroom.    40
"I'm here with the deepest respect, Rabbi. I came out of interest for your community."

"We are not South Sea islanders, sir, our practices are well known since    41
Sinai. You don't have to turn your glance. We are not something new in the world."

"Excuse me, Rabbi, not new—unfamiliar."    42

"To you."    43

"To me," Bleilip admitted.    44

"Exactly my question! Who are you, what do you represent, what are    45
you to us?"

"A Jew. Like yourselves. One of you."    46

"Presumption! Atheist, devourer! For us there is the Most High, joy,    47
life. For us trust! But you! A moment ago I spoke your own heart for you, *emes?*"

Bleilip knew this word: truth, true, but he was only a visitor and did    48
not want so much: he wanted only what he needed, a certain piece of truth, not too big to swallow. He was afraid of choking on more. The rebbe said, "You believe the world is in vain, *emes?*"

"I don't follow any of that, I'm not looking for theology—"                    49

"Little fathers," said the rebbe, "everything you heard me say, every-        50
thing you heard me say in a voice of despair, emanates from the liver of this
man. My mouth made itself his parrot. My teeth became his beak. He fills
the study-house with a black light, as if he keeps a lump of radium inside his
belly. He would eat us up. Man he equates with the goats. The Temple, in
memory and anticipation, he considers an abattoir. The world he regards as
a graveyard. You are shocked, Mister Bleilip, that I know your kidneys, your
heart? Canker! Onset of cholera! You say you don't come for 'theology,'
Mister Bleilip, and yet you have a particular conception of us, *emes?* A certain
idea."

Bleilip wished himself mute. He looked at Yussel, but Yussel had his       51
eyes on his sleeve-button.

"Speak in your own language, please"—Bleilip was unable to do any-        52
thing else—"and I will understand you very well. Your idea about us, please.
Stand up!"

Bleilip obeyed. That he obeyed bewildered him. The crescents of faces       53
in profile on either side of him seemed sharp as scythes. His yarmulka fell
off his head but, rising, he failed to notice it—one of the men quickly clapped
it back on. The stranger's palm came like a blow.

"Your idea," the rebbe insisted.                                            54

"Things I've heard," Bleilip croaked. "That in the Zohar[7] it's written    55
how Moses coupled with the Shekhina on Mount Sinai. That there are books
to cast lots by, to tell fortunes, futures. That some Rabbis achieved levita-
tion, hung in air without end, made babies come in barren women, healed
miraculously. That there was once a Rabbi who snuffed out the Sabbath
light. Things," Bleilip said, "I suppose legends."

"Did you hope to witness any of these things?"                             56

Bleilip was silent.                                                        57

"Then let me again ask. Do you credit any of these things?"               58

"Do you?" asked Bleilip.                                                    59

Yussel intervened: "Forbidden to mock the rebbe!"                          60

But the rebbe replied, "I do not believe in magic. That there are influ-   61
ences I do believe."

Bleilip felt braver. "Influences?"                                         62

"Turnings. That a man can be turned from folly, error, wrong choices.      63
From misery, evil, private rage. From a mistaken life."

Now Bleilip viewed the rebbe; he was suspicious of such hands. The         64
hands a horror: deformity, mutilation: caught in what machine?—and above
them the worker's cap. But otherwise the man seemed simple, reasoned,
balanced, after certain harmonies, sanities, the ordinary article, no mystic, a
bit bossy, pedagogue, noisy preacher. Bleilip, himself a man with a profession and no schoolboy after all, again took heart. A commonplace figure.

---

7. Book of mystical teachings. *Shekhina:* female essence of God.

People did what he asked, nothing more complicated than this—but he had to ask. Or tell, or direct. A monarch perhaps. A community needs to be governed. A human relationship: of all words Bleilip, whose vocabulary was habitually sociological, best of all liked "relationship."

He said, "I don't have a mistaken life."                                      65

"Empty your pockets."                                                         66

Bleilip stood without moving.                                                 67

"Empty your pockets!"                                                         68

"Rabbi, I'm not an exercise, I'm not a demonstration—"                        69

"Despair must be earned."                                                     70

"I'm not in despair," Bleilip objected.                                       71

"To be an atheist is to be in despair."                                       72

"I'm not an atheist, I'm a secularist," but even Bleilip did not know what     73
he meant by this.

"Esau! For the third time: empty your pockets!"                               74

Bleilip pulled the black plastic thing out and threw it on the table. Instantly   75
all the men bent away from it.

"A certain rebbe," said the rebbe very quietly, "believed every man           76
should carry two slips of paper in his pockets. In one pocket should be written: 'I am but dust and ashes.' In the other: 'For my sake was the world
created.' This canker fills only one pocket, and with ashes." He picked up
Bleilip's five-and-ten gun and said "Esau! Beast! Lion! To whom did you
intend to do harm?"

"Nobody," said Bleilip out of his shame. "It isn't real. I keep it to get      77
used to. The feel of the thing. Listen," he said, "do you think it's easy for
me to carry that thing around and keep on thinking about it?"

The rebbe tried the trigger. It gave out a tin click. Then he wrapped it       78
in his handkerchief and put it in his pocket. "We will now proceed with
*ma'ariv*,"[8] he said. "The study hour is finished. Let us not learn more of this
matter. This is Jacob's tent."

The men left the study table and took up their old places, reciting. Blei-     79
lip, humiliated (the analogy to a teacher confiscating a forbidden toy was too
exact), still excited, the tremor in his groin worse, was in awe before this
incident. Was it amazing chance that the rebbe had challenged the contents
of his pockets, or was he a seer? At the conclusion of *ma'ariv* the men dispersed quickly; Bleilip recognized from Yussel's white stare that this was not
the usual way. He felt like an animal they were running from. He intended
to run himself—all the way to the Greyhound station—but the rebbe came
to him. "You," he said (*du*, as if to an animal, or to a child, or to God), "the
other pocket. The second one. The other side of your coat."

"What?"                                                                       80

"Disgorge."                                                                   81

So Bleilip took it out. And just as the toy gun could instantly be seen to     82

8. Evening service.

be a toy, all tin glint, so could this one be seen for what it was: monstrous, clumsy and hard, heavy, with a scarred trigger and a barrel that smelled. Dark, no gleam. An actuality, a thing for use. Yussel moaned, dipping his head up and down. "In my house! Stood in front of my wife with it! With two!"

"With one," said the rebbe. "One is a toy and one not, so only one need be feared. It is the toy we have to fear: the incapable—" 83

Yussel broke in, "We should call the police, rebbe." 84

"Because of a toy? How they will laugh." 85

"But the other! This!" 86

"Is it capable?" the rebbe asked Bleilip. 87

"Loaded, you mean? Sure it's loaded." 88

"Loaded, you hear him?" Yussel said. "He came as a curiosity-seeker, rebbe, my wife's cousin, I had no suspicion of this—" 89

The rebbe said, "Go home, Yussel. Go home, little father." 90

"Rebbe, he can shoot—" 91

"How can he shoot? The instrument is in my hand." 92

It was. The rebbe held the gun—the real one. Again Bleilip was drawn to those hands. This time the rebbe saw. "Buchenwald," he said. "Blocks of ice, a freezing experiment. In my case only to the elbow, but others were immersed wholly and perished. The fingers left are toy fingers. That is why you have been afraid of them and have looked away." 93

He said all this very clearly, in a voice without an opinion. 94

"Don't talk to him, rebbe!" 95

"Little father, go home." 96

"And if he shoots?" 97

"He will not shoot." 98

Alone in the schoolhouse with the rebbe—how dim the bulbs, dangling on cords—Bleilip regretted that because of the dishonor of the guns. He was pleased that the rebbe had dismissed Yussel. The day (but now it was night) felt full of miracles and lucky chances. Thanks to Yussel he had gotten to the rebbe. He never supposed he would get to the rebbe himself—all his hope was only for a glimpse of the effect of the rebbe. Of influences. With these he was satisfied. He said again, "I don't have a mistaken life." 99

The rebbe enclosed the second gun in his handkerchief. "This one has a bad odor." 100

"Once I killed a pigeon with it." 101

"A live bird?" 102

"You believers," Bleilip threw out, "you'd cut up those goats all over again if you got the Temple back!" 103

"Sometimes," the rebbe said, "even the rebbe does not believe. My father when he was the rebbe also sometimes did not believe. It is characteristic of believers sometimes not to believe. And it is characteristic of unbelievers sometimes to believe. Even you, Mister Bleilip—even you now and then 104 believe in the Holy One, Blessed Be He? Even you now and then apprehend the Most High?"

"No," Bleilip said; and then: "Yes." 105

"Then you are as bloody as anyone," the rebbe said (it was his first real 106 opinion), and with his terrible hands put the bulging white handkerchief on the table for Bleilip to take home with him, for whatever purpose he thought he needed it.

# STUDY QUESTIONS

1. In the second sentence, we are told that Bleilip's coat pockets are heavy, so he takes a taxi rather than walk. Did you notice that detail at all in reading the story? By the end of the story, what significance does it have?

2. How is Toby different from most of the inhabitants of the town?

3. Until Yussel tells him it is all right to do what he likes (paragraph 3), Bleilip is confused about how to behave in this fundamentalist religious community. In paragraph 18, he is described as wanting "to be close, close" to Yussel. In paragraph 34, however, we are told he "shunned being seen into." What picture of Bleilip is emerging? What does it mean that he wanted to be "a benefactor of the feelings" (par. 34)?

4. What seems to be Bleilip's purpose in coming to the community? Yussel tells Toby Bleilip is "looking for something," and Bleilip believes this a "rigid truth" (par. 27). What do you imagine at this point he is looking for? Later (pars. 55–63), Bleilip speaks of legends and cabalistic lore (from the Zohar) and is asked whether he had hoped to learn about or witness such things. What do you conclude from his dialogue with the rebbe about his expectations? the rebbe's beliefs?

5. What do you think of this community with no radio, television, pictures on the walls, no books other than holy books? Do you think, as Toby believes Bleilip does, that they are "fanatics, primitives" (par. 26)? Why does Bleilip "resent" the orange juice can, appliances, and so on (par. 27)? He is repelled by the sect, we are told in paragraph 31, but attracted to the congregation—why?

6. The men mix "strands of holy tongue with Yiddish" (par. 36); what is "holy tongue"? Why is Bleilip reminded of his grandfather?

7. Describe the procedures and purposes of the ritual involving the goats. The rebbe says (par. 50) that what he has said to them about the sacrifice and the issues it raises was really the inner thoughts of Bleilip. Explain.

8. Now you know why Bleilip's pockets were heavy. Why is it that the rebbe says that only the toy pistol need be feared (par. 83)? How is this related to the rebbe's mutilated fingers?

9. Bleilip says that the rebbe as a believer would cut up the goats all over again if the Temple were rebuilt; the rebbe's response is that sometimes believers do not

believe, just as sometimes nonbelievers believe. When Bleilip admits that sometimes he does believe, the rebbe responds, "Then you are as bloody as anyone"
(par. 106). Explain the logic of that retort.

10. Bleilip's gun is returned to him "for whatever purpose he thought he needed it"
(final sentence). What purpose or purposes seem to be implied? How is this the
fitting conclusion of the story?

11. Explain the title.

# Barry Targan

Barry Targan was born in Atlantic City, New Jersey, and educated at Rutgers
University, the University of Chicago, and Brandeis University. He currently
teaches creative writing at the State University of New York at Binghamton. He is
the author of two collections of short stories—*Harry Belten and the Mendelssohn Violin
Concerto* (winner of the Iowa School of Letters Award in short fiction) and *Surviving
Adverse Seasons* (winner of the Saxifrage Award from the University of North Carolina); two collections of poetry—*Thoreau Stalks the Land Disguised as a Father* and *Let the
Wild Rumpus Start*; and a novel—*Kingdoms* (winner of the Associated Writing Programs Award in the novel).

In "Dominion," a hard-sell salesman sells himself for his son and sells his son on
himself.

## DOMINION

> In a moment, in the twinkling of an eye, at the last trump: for the
> trumpet shall sound, and the dead shall be raised incorruptible, and
> we shall be changed.
>
> *I Corinthians* 15:52

He played absently with the tiny party hat in his hand, a hat such as a
leprechaun in a movie cartoon might wear, a truncated cone of metallic green
paper board with a flat silver brim and a black paper buckle. He pulled at
the thin rubber band that would hold the hat in place and listened carefully
to what the men were explaining. Sometimes he would nod in comprehen-
sion. Last night he and Sandra had gone to the Balmuths' New Year's Eve
party. And now, January the first, suddenly a lifetime later, he listened to

the two men, the accountant and the lawyer, explain what had happened.

What had happened was that Poverman and Charney, a small manufacturer of lightweight women's clothing, was ruined, embezzled into insolvency by Charney, who even now sat in Florida in the noonday sun. Morton Poverman sat here, at his chilling dining room table cloaked with the fabric of his loss, the neat stacks of paper—bills, letters, invoices, bank statements, memoranda, and packets of canceled checks—that chronicled Charney's wretched course, his wicked testament.

Poverman said, "And all this could have happened without my knowing? Amazing."

In a corner off from the table, Poverman's wife, Sandra, sat in a stuffed chair with her right leg raised up on an ottoman. Her leg, up to the middle of the calf, was in a cast, her ankle broken. "Oh," she said like a moan, a curse, a threat. "Oh God." It was all she could say now, though later, Poverman knew, she would say more, her vehemence strident, hot, and deep. For twenty years she had disliked Phil Charney, distrusted him always, his flamboyance, his fancy women and his fancy ways, the frivolous instability of his unmarried state. And now to be right! To be helplessly confirmed! She put her head back against the chair and closed her eyes as she clogged with rage nearly to fainting. "Oh God."

"Not so amazing," Friedsen, the accountant, snapped. "You never looked at the books. You never asked a question." He slapped at some figures on a pad before him. "Five thousand dollars for the material for the chemises? When is the last time you made a chemise? Who buys chemises any more? And this?" He looked down at the pad. "The bias tape? Forty cases? and here," he jabbed at the entry with his finger, his nail piercing at the numbers like the beak of a ravening bird. "The printing bill on the new boxes? You weren't suspicious of that?" Friedsen was angry. He had done their books from the start, had managed them well. And now he held them in his hands like smudged ashes. Like dirt. Like an affront. If one was a thief, then the other was a fool.

"I never looked at the books," Poverman told him, though Friedsen knew that already, knew everything. "If I had looked, so what would I have known? I did the selling, Philly did the rest. For twenty-five years it worked okay."

"The bastard," Friedsen said.

Poverman could not find his own anger. Perhaps he was still too startled. What Phil Charney had done, he had done quickly, in less than a year altogether, but conclusively in the last quarter before the Christmas season, when their money moved about most rapidly and in the largest amounts. Friedsen, for his own orderly reasons, liked to see his client's fiscal shape at the end of the calendar year. He had gotten to Poverman and Charney two days ago and, hour by hour, he had tumbled ever more quickly through the shreds that Charney had made of the once solid company. Friedsen had gone to no New Year's Eve party. And this morning he had pulled the lawyer, Kuhn, to this dreadful meeting. It had not taken him long to explain and demonstrate the bankruptcy and its cause. Now Kuhn explained the rest, the mechanism of foreclosure and collection, the actual bankruptcy petition to the courts, the appointment of the referee, the slim possibility of criminal action against Charney. He went on, but to Poverman, the intricacies of his disaster like the details of his success were equally abstractions. He could not contain them. He could understand the results, of course. He could understand purposes and conclusions. Consequences. But he had always been the man in front, the one to whom you spoke when you called Poverman and Charney. Morton Poverman, a man of good will and even humor who had put in his working years directly, flesh on flesh, voice against voice, eye to eye. Let Friedsen and Kuhn do what must be done in their rigorous and judicial way. But let him do what he could do in his.

"So what's left?" he asked, first to one then the other. "Anything?"          9

Of the business there was not much. He would lose the factory and          10
everything in it and connected to it, including the dresses, housecoats, and nightgowns already on the racks. There were two outlet stores, the largest, the newer store in Fairlawn Shopping Mall he would have to close. The older store in the business strip just off of North Broadway, he could probably keep. Where he and Phil had begun.

Personally, there was the paid-up life insurance, fifty-thousand. That          11
was safe. There was also about twenty thousand in cash. There were things like the cars and all that was in the house. The house itself might be a question. Kuhn said the house would depend on too many variables to discuss now. And there was the trust fund for Robert's education. Twenty-five thousand dollars. Nothing could touch that. There were some small investments, mostly stocks. Those would probably have to be called in, for one reason or another. For one bill or another, like Friedsen's perhaps, or Kuhn's. Or merchandise for the store. At this point who could say?

"So? That's it?"          12

"That's about it," Kuhn said.          13

"Well, it's not nothing, is it?" Poverman said.          14

"No," Kuhn said. "It's not nothing."          15

Sandra Poverman sobbed high and quietly at the top of her voice, still          16
unable to open her eyes to what she would have to look at forever after.

When the men left he did some small figuring of his own. Immediately          17
there would be no Florida vacation this winter. Perhaps he would sell one car. The membership in the country club? What did he need that for, he didn't even play golf. He started to write down numbers—mortgage payment, property tax, homeowner's insurance, the car payments, but after these he could not say. He did not know what his heating bill was, his electricity, food, clothing. And the rest. Did Sandra? Did anyone in this house know such things? Probably not. He had earned, each year a little more, and in the last five years nearly, though not quite, a lot. Yesterday the future was all before him various with pleasures just about to come within his grasp, the long-planned trips to Europe, to South America the year after that, Hawaii.

The house in the semi-retirement village at Seadale, a hundred miles north of Miami. Gone. Today only the future itself was waiting, empty and dangerous. The little store on North Broadway with the old lighting fixtures and the cracked linoleum flooring from twenty-five years ago. That was waiting.

He had earned and they all had spent what they needed, and each year <sub></sub> 18 they had needed a little more. So now they would need less. They would make an accommodation. Tomorrow he would go to the outlet store and take stock and make arrangements. Begin. He was fifty-three.

The phone rang. It was Phil Charney calling from Miami. He knew that 19 Friedsen would find him in the year-end audit.

"Morty, this is Phil. You know why I'm calling?" 20

"Friedsen was here. Just now. And Kuhn. They just left." 21

"Morty, this is so terrible, I can't say how terrible." 22

Sandra stiffened. "That's him?" she hissed. He nodded. "Give me." She 23 motioned the phone to her. "Give me. I'll tell him something. I'll tell that filth something. Give me. Give me." She waved for the phone, her voice rising. He covered the mouthpiece. She tried to stand up.

"Morty, I'm sitting here weeping. I didn't sleep all night. Not for two 24 nights. Not for three nights. I couldn't help it. I still can't. She wants and wants and I must give. *Must!* Who knows where it ends. There's not so much money I can go on like this. Then what? But what can I do? *Morty*, what can I do, kill myself?"

"No, no, of course not." 25

He scrambled for his outrage like a weapon, but a weapon with which 26 to defend himself and not attack. He was embarrassed for the man sobbing at the other end of the line, his agony. He summoned his hatred for protection, but it would not come. But he had always lacked sufficient imagination, and what he felt now was more the loss of his life-long friend, the swoop and gaiety of his presence as he would click about the factory, kidding the women on the machines, hassling in mocking fights the blacks on the loading platforms. He had even picked up enough Spanish to jabber back at the volatile Puerto Ricans. Even the Puerto Ricans Phil could make laugh and work.

That would be gone. And the flitting elegance, the Cadillacs and the 27 women. The clothing and the jewelry. The flights to anywhere, to Timbuktu. He would miss the women. They were an excitement, these strenuous pursuits of Phil Charney's, these expensive pursuits. He was a tone, an exuberant vibrato that pushed into and fluttered the lives of anyone near him. Battered floozies or sometimes women much younger, but often enough recently divorced or widowed women ready at last for madder music, headier wine. Sandra Poverman condemned it, but her husband could afford his own small envy, safe enough within his wife's slowly thickening arms to tease her with his short-reined lust. That would be gone. Tomorrow he would go to work as he had known he would even before Friedsen, but now in silence with no edge of scandal or tightly-fleshed surprise.

"Filth. Murderer," Sandra shouted into the phone. She had gotten up 28 and hobbled over to him. "Liar. Dog."

"She's right, Morty. She's right. I'm no better than a murderer." 29

"No. Stop this, Phil. Get a hold." 30

"Die," Sandra screamed. "Die in hell. Bastard. Scum." She pulled at 31
the phone in his hand but he forced it back.

"Oh Morty, Morty, what I've done to you! Oh Morty, forgive me." 32

"Yes, Phil. OK. I do." He hung up before either could say more. 33

What more? That time had come to take away their life together, aban- 34
doning Phil Charney more severely than himself? But if he had said that,
would he be certain enough himself what he meant? That only the sorrow
was left, enough of that to go around for them all, so what did the rest of
anything else matter?

"What?" Sandra demanded. "What did he want? 'I do' you said. You 35
'do' what?" He told her. And then she screamed, raised her fists to her ears
to block his words, but too late. She fell against him, staggered by the shaking that was bringing down upon her the castles they had built. And now he
had even taken from her the solid and pure energy of revenge.

The large, good, sustaining thing that happened in January was that his 36
son, Robert, received the report of his Scholastic Aptitude Tests: 690 in
Verbal, 710 in Math. In the achievement tests he did comparably well. The
rest of the month, however, was not unexpected as what he had come to do
grew clearer. The store had made economic sense as an outlet for the factory,
a nice way of taking some retail profit right off the top. But without the
factory as the primary supplier, the store was just another women's clothing
store, in competition everywhere. That situation would be impossible. But
Morton Poverman had his accrued advantages from twenty-five years in both
ends of the business. He knew enough to know where he could get over-
runs, returns, seconds from other manufacturers, small producers such as he
had been. What credit he needed, at least with some cash down, he could
still get from them.

By the end of January he could at least begin to think seriously about 37
his spring line; various enough and inexpensive as it was, he had a chance to
exist. Not much more. But already the stock was coming into the storeroom
in the back faster than he could handle it. Still, that was not so bad. Better
more than not enough. He would put in the time to inventory and price and
mark it all.

In January he had let go all the workers in the store, three of them, and 38
handled the front himself. Only on Saturday, dashing back and forth from
customer to cash register, was it too difficult. The stock he worked on at
night. At first until nine o'clock and now until midnight. But it was coming
together, the store brightening with variety and loading up with goods. And
people were still shopping downtown, he could tell. He would get by on his
low pricing and his long hours. And now he was bringing in a whole line of
Playtex girdles and bras, all kinds of pantyhose and lingerie. In a year maybe
he would bring in sewing articles, fabrics, patterns. In a year. Or two.

It was easier to say that twenty-five years ago when there was still a year 39
or two or three or five to invest. And two of them to do it. But he could say
it now, nonetheless, again and alone. His flame burned, steadily if low, even
by the end of January when, like fuel for the flame, Bobby's SAT's had
arrived. 690 / 710. Fuel enough. Then Morton Poverman would crush back
in the large cardboard boxes under the dim, bare-bulbed lighting of the storeroom with his supper sandwich and the last of his thermos of coffee and think
that though he was bone-weary and hard-pressed, he was not without intelligent purpose and a decent man's hope. More he did not ask. Or need.

February, March—a time for clinging to the steep, roughly-grained rock 40
face of his endeavor, seeking the small, icy handholds, the cracks and fissures
of little victories to gain a purchase on, by which to lever himself up an inch:
he picked up one hundred assorted dusters for nearly nothing, garbage from
South Korea with half their buttons gone. He would replace the buttons.
Kurtlanger's, the largest women's clothing store in the area, was dropping its
entire line of womens' nylons. It was not worth the bother to Kurtlanger's to
supply the relatively few women who still wore separate stockings. It was all
pantyhose now. For Poverman the bother could become his business. He
stocked the nylons and put an ad in the newspaper saying so. Seeds for
springtime. He put money into a new floor, found bags in Waltham, Massachusetts, at a ten percent saving, joined the Downtown Merchants Association protesting for increased side-street lighting and greater police
surveillance. He checked three times a day the long-range weather reports.
Would winter freeze him shut, March blow his straw house down?

At first Sandra had gone mad with anger calling everyone to behold her 41
suffering. She called her friends and relatives, *Charney's* friends and relatives,
the police. Worse than the stunning death of a loved one in a car crash or by
the quick, violent blooming of a cancer in the lymph, where you could curse
God and be done with it, this that Charney had done to her was an unshared
burden, separate from life and others' fate, and unsupportable for being so.
If we all owe life a death and perhaps even pain, certainly we do not owe it
bankruptcy and humiliation. She cried out, howled, keening in the ancient
way of grief and lamentation.

And then she dropped into silence like a stone. 42

She would hardly speak to him, as if his failure to share her intensity of 43
anger had separated them. Or to speak to anyone. She grew hard and dense
with her misery, imploded beneath the gravity of her fury and chagrin. At
first she had fought with her simple terrifying questions: Who could she face?
What was the rest of her life to be like? But then, far beyond her questions,
she grew smaller yet until at the last she atomized into the vast unspecific sea
of justice and worth, and there she floated like zero.

Late at night Poverman would come home and get into bed beside her 44
and chafe her arms and rub her back. Sometimes he would kiss her gently
on the neck as she had always liked. But she was wood. Still, he would talk
to her, tell her the good things that were happening, his incremental prog-

ress, prepare her for the future. But she would not go with him. The future, like her past, had betrayed her, had disintegrated. She would trust in no future again.

Robert Poverman said to his father, "I'll come in after school. You'll show me how to mark the clothing, and that will be a help." 45

"No," his father said. "By the time you come in after school, get downtown, it would already be late. What could you do in an hour?" 46

"What do you mean, 'an hour'? I'd work with you at night. I'd come home with you. If I helped, then we'd both get home earlier." 47

"No. Absolutely not. You're in school. You do the school, I'll do the business. In the summer, we'll see. Not now, Sonny. Not now." 48

"Are you kidding, Dad? School's over. I'm a second semester senior. It's all fun and games, messing around. It's nothing." 49

"So do fun and games. Mess around. That's part of school, too. Next year you'll be in college, with no messing around. And what about your activities, the Photography Club, the Chess Club, Current Events Club, Student Council, French Club, the math team. Your guitar. And soon it's track season. So what about track?" Poverman knew it all, remembered everything. 50

"Dad, listen. I'm a third-string miler. Sometimes they don't even run me. I struggle to break six minutes. And the clubs are strictly baloney. Nothing. Believe me, *nothing*. Let me help you, please. Let me *do* something." 51

"No. NO. If you want to do something, Sonny, do school, *all* of it just the way you always did. Do it the way you would have before . . . *this*." He smeared his hand in the air. 52

His son took his hand out of the air and kissed it. "OK, Daddy," he said softly. "OK. And I'll pray for you, too." 53

That night, turning the handle of the machine that ground out the gummed pricing tags, Poverman recalled what his son had said, that he would pray for him. The machine clicked on: size, stock number, price. What could that mean? But Poverman had enough to think about without adding prayer. He had ten crates of L'Eggs to unpack by morning, two dozen bathrobes that had arrived that day without belts, and all the leather accessories that he still had to stick these tags on. He turned the crank faster. 54

February, March, and now, somehow, April. Already the first wavelets of Easter buying had lapped at his shore, eroded slightly the cloth of his island. Good. Let it all be washed away in a flood of gold. Poverman walked about. He was working harder than ever, but accomplishing more. The hard, heaving work was mostly done, and there was a shape to everything now, his possibilities limited but definite, and definite perhaps because they were limited. So be it. He had started in quicksand and had built this island. The rest now was mostly up to the weather and the caprice of the economy. At least it was out of the hands of men like Phil Charney. 55

Poverman seldom thought of him even though he had to meet often enough with Friedsen and Kuhn. He had even made a joke once that he had 56 to work for Charney twice, before and after. Friedsen had not laughed. But what did it matter? What mattered was what *could* matter.

It was six o'clock. He walked about in the crisp store, straightening a few boxes, clothes loosely strewn in bins, the merchandise hanging on the racks. Tonight, for the first time in months, he was closing now. Tonight he was going home early. To celebrate. Let the three hundred pairs of slaps from the Philippines wait. Let the gross of white gloves wait. Tonight he was going home to celebrate. Today, all on the same day, Robert Poverman had been accepted at Yale, Cornell, and the State University of New York at Binghamton, a university center. He had until May fifteenth to make his decision and send in his deposit. They would talk about it tonight. And everything.

Poverman turned out all the lights after checking the locks on the back door. He walked out of the store pulling the door to and double locking it. He looked up at the sign recently painted on the door, the new name he had decided upon: The Fashion Center. Nothing too fancy. Nothing too smart. But what did he need with fancy or smart? He had Robert Poverman of Yale or Cornell. *That* was fancy. *That* was smart.

After supper Poverman spread out on the diningroom table the various catalogues and forms and descriptive literature from the three colleges. He had also added to that, clippings from magazines and newspapers. They had seen most of it all before, when Robert had applied, but now it was to be examined differently as one seriously considered the tangibilities of life in Harkness Memorial Hall or Mary Donlon Hall. Here, this material, was what they had from which to read the auguries of Robert Poverman's future. Even Sandra leavened as they discussed (As always. Again.) what he would study. Which school might be best for what. Neither Poverman nor his wife knew how to make their comparisons. It would, now as before, be their son's choice. But who could refrain from the talking? The saying of such things as law or medicine or physics or international relations? Poverman again looked up the size of the libraries. Yale: 6,518,848. Cornell: 4,272,959. SUNY at Binghamton: 729,000. 6,518,848 books. How could he imagine that? Still, it was one measure. But what did Robert Poverman want? His interests were so wide, his accomplishments so great, what could he *not* decide for? What could he not illimitably cast for and catch?

They drank tea and talked. In two days Sandra would go for a small operation on the ankle to adjust a bone that had drifted slightly. Even with his medical coverage it would cost him a thousand dollars. But okay. Of course. Let her walk straight. Let her life go on. He had hoped that she would be able to help him in the store now that the Easter push was happening, but instead he had hired someone part time.

He looked at the pictures in the college catalogues, the jungle of glass tubes in the laboratories, the pretty girls intensely painting things on large canvases, the professor standing at the blackboard filled with lines and numbers and signs like a magical incantation, smiling young men like Robert flinging frisbees across the wide Commons, the view of Cayuga Lake, the wondrous glowing cube of the Beinecke Library at Yale (*another* library, a *special* library for the rare books alone). Yale. Yale began to creep into Morton Poverman's heart. He would say nothing. What did he know? It was up to Robert. But he hoped for Yale. 6,518,848 books.

"I don't know," Robert said. "What's the rush?" He turned to Sandra.   62

"This is an important decision, right? And he's got a month. Think   63
about it, that's the smart thing," he said to his son. "Sure. Don't jump before you look." He gathered up the evidence of what was to come, the scattered materials about one of Robert Poverman's schools, and put it all back into the reddish brown paper portfolio. He took the letters of acceptance and the letters to be returned with the deposit and put them elsewhere. He wished that he could have sent one back in the morning with a check enclosed, a down payment on his son's happiness, a bond, a covenant.

That night in bed he held his wife's hand.   64

"Which do you like?" he asked.   65

"Cornell, I think."   66

"Not Yale? Why not Yale?"   67

"The bulldog," she said. "It's so ugly. What kind of animal is that for a   68
school?"

The weather was warm and balmy. Good for light cotton prints. Easter   69
did well by him and spring, too. Business was beating through the veins of the store. Sandra's ankle was fixed for good now, mending correctly, though she would still need more weeks of resting it. This Sunday he had asked Robert to come to the store with him to help him catch up on some stock work. Also he wanted to describe what Robert would do in the store that summer, his job. Robert would work in the store and his pay, except for some spending money, would be put into a bank account for his use in college. And today Poverman would push his son, slightly, toward his decision. Time was now growing short. Ten days till the deadline. He would like to have this settled.

At three o'clock they sat down to some sandwiches that Sandra had   70
packed for them.

"So? What do you think?" he asked his son. "Do you think you can last   71
the summer? Listen, this is the easy part. The stock don't talk back. The stock don't complain. You think you can explain to a size twelve lady why she don't fit into a size ten dress? Hah? Let me tell you sweetheart, everything to know is not in books." Then he reached across and stroked his son's softly stubbled cheek. His oldest gesture. "But Sonny, all of this is nothing to know. What you're going to learn, compared to this, you could put all this into a little nut shell." Then, "Did you choose a college yet?"

Robert Poverman said, "I don't know."   72

"There's only ten days," his father said. "What can you know in ten   73
more days that you don't know already? What do you want to know? Who

can you ask? Sonny, maybe you think you have to be certain. Well let me tell you, you can't be certain of nothing. And with any one of these schools, you can't go so far wrong. You can't lose anyway."

"It's about college," Robert Poverman said. "I'm not so sure about that." 74

His father did not understand. 75

"Maybe college isn't for me. Just yet, anyway. I don't know." 76

"Know?" his father said. "Know what? What is there to know? You 77 think you want *this?*" he indicated the store around them. "Maybe you want to go into the Army? Shoot guns? Maybe you want to be a fireman and ride on a red truck?" He was filling out.

"Don't be angry, Dad. Please." But it wasn't anger ballooning in Morton 78 Poverman now, it was panic.

"Then what are you talking about? *What* don't you know? You go to 79 college to find out what you don't know. Ah," it occurred to him, "it's the money. Is that it? You're worried about the money, about me and your mother. But I told you, the money is already there. Twenty-five thousand and that will make interest. Plus a little more I've got. Plus what you'll earn. Don't worry about the money, Bobby, please. I swear to you, your mother and I are going to be okay that way. Look, look. The store is working out, Sonny."

"Daddy, it's not that. Maybe there's another way." They were silent. 80

"So?" Poverman finally asked. "What other way?" 81

"I've been thinking about religion." He looked at his father evenly. 82 "There's a religious retreat down at this place in Nyack this summer, from the middle of July to the middle of August. I think maybe I should go there." He looked down away from his reflection in his father's brightening eyes.

"Why?" 83

"Yes, *why*. I need to find out the meaning of things. Not *what* I want to 84 do or where I want to go to college, but *why*. Is that unreasonable?"

But what did Morton Poverman know about reasonableness? What he 85 knew about was hanging on, like a boxer after he has been hit very hard.

"So what has this to do with college? Why can't I send in the deposit?" 86

"I might not go to college right away. I can't honestly say now. Or I 87 might not want to go to one of those colleges. Where I was accepted. I might find out that I want to go to a . . . a religious type of college. I just don't know. I've got to think about it. I don't want you wasting the money. If I change my mind, I can probably still get into a good college somewhere."

"Money again," Poverman roared. He stood. "I'm telling you, money is 88 shit. I know. I've lost money before. That's nothing."

Driving home from the store Robert told his father that for the past six 89 months he had been attending weekly meetings organized by the Society of the Holy Word for high school age people. Driving down Pearl Street, he pointed to a store with many books in the window and the name of the organization neatly lettered on the panes of glass.

"So everybody's in business," Poverman said as he drove by. "Do they 90 belong to the Downtown Businessmen's Association?"

"They're not selling," his son said. 91

"Oh no? Aren't they? So what's that, a church?" 92

"No, Dad. It isn't a business and it isn't a church. It's a place for people 93
to meet to discuss things."

"Yeah? Like what?" 94

"Religion, meaning of life, ethical conduct. The Bible, mostly. The Bible 95
as the word of God."

"Is that right? The Bible tells you what college to go to? Yale or Cornell? 96
Amazing. I never knew. But then, there's so much I don't know."

"Daddy, please don't be angry. Don't be bitter." 97

"No? So what should I be, happy? For eighteen years I'm thinking Chief 98
Justice of the Supreme Court and now my son tells me he's thinking of
becoming a monk. Wonderful. Terrific." He drove faster.

"Ah Daddy, come on. It's not that way at all. We sit and talk about how 99
religion can give a full and wonderful meaning to our lives. It's raised some
important questions for me about my future. And it's offered some possible
answers and solutions."

"Solutions? Why? You've got problems?" 100

"We've all got problems, Daddy." 101

"Like?" 102

"Like our souls," Robert Poverman said. "Like the fate of our immortal 103
souls."

"Souls? *Souls?* You're eighteen and you're worried about your soul? What 104
about your body?"

But his son closed down then, as did he, each caught in the other's orbit 105
as they would ever be, but as silent now and awesomely distant as Venus to
Pluto. And what could the earthbound Morton Poverman breathe in such
empty space?

"Yes? Can I help you?" the tall man asked. He was very clean, scrubbed 106
so that he was pink and white. He did not seem to need to shave, his skin as
smooth as thin polished stone, nearly translucent. His steel gray hair was
combed straight back over his head. He wore small octagonal rimless glasses.

"Just looking," Poverman said. He walked about in the converted store. 107
Converted to what? All he saw were arrangements of books with such titles
as *Satan in the Sanctuary* and *Which Will You Believe.* There were piles of small
folded tracts and pamphlets on different color paper, pink, green, blue.
Newspapers called the *New Word Times* and *Revelation Tribune.* On the walls
were large, poster-sized photographs of people, mostly healthy young people, working at good deeds in foreign countries, in ghettos, in hospitals, in
old folks' homes. Even Poverman could quickly see that the young people in
the photographs were shining with pleasure in the midst of the misery and
needs they were serving, gleaming and casting light so that, behold, their
light warmed and illuminated the rheumy-eyed old woman in the wheelchair
smiling toothlessly; the bloated-bellied eczema-scabbed children in the jungle

clearing; the slit-eyed hoodlum sucking deeply on his joint of dope. All down the wall—growing, building, feeding, helping. Hallelujah.

Past the main room, behind a partition, was another room. He turned   108
and walked back to the pink and white man.

"I'm Morton Poverman," he said, and put out his hand.   109

"I'm George Fetler," the pink and white man said, and took the hand.   110

"I've got a son, Robert Poverman. He comes here."   111

"Oh yes. Robert. A wonderful boy. Brilliant. Absolutely brilliant. I'm   112
very pleased to meet you. You must be very proud of such a son."

But Poverman did not have time for this playing. Even now, four blocks   113
away in his own store, United Parcel trucks would be arriving with goods he
must pay for and he had not yet made the deposit in the bank that would
cover them, and Francine Feynman (now working full time) would be on
two customers at once (or worse, none), and the phone would ring with the
call from Philadelphia about the slightly faded orlon sweaters. And what had
he come here for, this man's opinions?

"Yes," Poverman said. "Proud." But he did not know what to say, nor   114
what to do. What he *wanted* to do was dump five gallons of gasoline over
everything—the books, the newspapers, the green pamphlets—and put a match
to it. But there were too many other empty store fronts downtown for that
to matter. So he was stuck.

George Fetler said, "You're probably here because you're worried about   115
Robert."

"Yes. That's right. Exactly." Poverman beat down the small loop of   116
gratitude.

"Robert's such a thoughtful fellow. He's quite uncertain about college   117
now, about his future. I suppose you and Mrs. Poverman must be concerned."

"Yes," Poverman said again, eagerly, even before he could stop himself.   118
Oh this guy was smooth. He was a salesman, all right, as soft as Poverman
was hard.

"You're probably upset with the Society of the Holy Word, too."   119

Poverman clamped his lips but nodded.   120

"You must think that we've probably poisoned your son's mind."   121

Poverman nodded again. What else?   122

"Let's sit down, Mr. Poverman, and let me tell you about us. Briefly.   123
You're probably anxious to get back to your business.

Oh good, good. Oh terrific. All his life Morton Poverman wished he   124
could have been so smooth with customers—buying, selling, complaints, but
with him it had always been a frontal attack. A joke, a little screaming or a
quick retreat into a deal for twenty percent off. But never like this, quiet,
slick as oil, full of probabilities, the ways so easily greased. Yes yes yes where
do I sign?

He took Poverman into the back room. Half the room was set up like a   125
small class, rows of metal chairs facing a small table and blackboard. The

other half of the room was soft chairs drawn around in a circle. They sat there.

George Fetler described simply and directly what the Society of the    126
Holy Word did as far as Robert Poverman was concerned. On Thursday evening it conducted, right here, right in these soft chairs, discussions about religion generally, Christianity specifically, and most of all the idea that the Bible was the exact word of God.

"That's it?" Poverman asked.    127

"Let's be frank. Let *me* be frank. If you believe that the Bible is the exact    128
word of God, then that can certainly raise some important questions about how you lead your life henceforth. I think this is what has happened to Robert. He came to us six months ago with two friends. I'm sure he came because his two friends, already Christians, wanted him to come. Like many before him, he came more as a lark, skeptical and doubting. But he read the Bible and he discussed what he read and the questions arose, Mr. Poverman, they just arose. And Mr. Poverman, I just wish you could see him, his openness, his honesty, his intelligence. It is very gratifying. Very." Fetler sat back and locked his hands together in front of him.

"You'll pardon me for asking," Poverman asked anyway, "but how does    129
this all get paid for?"

George Fetler smiled, unlocked his hands, and stood up. "Here. This    130
will explain it in detail." He went out to the tables in the front and returned with a booklet. "This will tell you what you probably want to know, including a financial statement. The Society of the Holy Word is but one arm of the Church of the Resurrection, Incorporated. We're based in Chicago. We've got our printing operation there and headquarters for our evangelical units. The Church also has two colleges, one in San Diego, the other . . ."

"In Nyack?"    131

"Yes. Has Robert mentioned that? He's thinking of going on our sum-    132
mer retreat there."

"But sooner or later, it all comes down to them—what do you call it?—    133
coming out for Jesus? Right?"

"One need not declare for Christ, but that is what we hope will hap-    134
pen." George Fetler and Morton Poverman were coming closer now to what they thought of the other. "Yes. That is what we hope and pray for."

"Why?"    135

"It is," George Fetler said, not such a soft guy anymore (no sale here),    136
"the only way to avoid the everlasting torments of Hell."

Morton Poverman had never been able to handle the Christian's Hell. It    137
looked to him like the answer to everything and to nothing. And what did they need it for, this endless knife at the throat? Besides, about Hell—here, now, right away—he had his own ideas. No. Not ideas. Necessities.

His week went on, all his life became a tactical adventure now, no crease    138
in it without its further unexpected bend, no crack that might not open up

suddenly into an abyss from which he could not scramble back. This is what he slept with now. Battle. War.

On Thursday evening at seven o'clock he went to the discussion meeting 139 at 183 Pearl Street, to the Society of the Holy Word. And he had studied. From the array of pamphlets and tracts on the tables in the Society's store he had taken copiously. And he had read them, late at night in the back of the store, later than ever, he had read slowly in the bad light, bent to this new labor as the unopened cartons piled up on each other and each morning Francine Feynman would complain of empty this and replaced that.

THE BIBLE SAYS YOU HAVE SINNED! 140

For all have sinned, and come short of the glory of God *(Rom. 3:23)* 141

THE BIBLE SAYS YOU DESERVE HELL! 142

For the wages of sin is death: but the gift of God is eternal life through 143 Jesus Christ our Lord *(Rom. 6:23)*

THE BIBLE SAYS YOU HAVE A CHOICE! 144

And if it seem evil unto you to serve the Lord, choose you this day 145 whom ye will serve . . . *(Joshua 24:15)*

THE BIBLE SAYS JESUS DIED FOR YOU! 146

But God commendeth his love toward us, in that while we were yet 147 sinners, Christ died for us *(Rom. 5:8)*

THE BIBLE SAYS YOU MUST BELIEVE JESUS! 148

For whosoever shall call upon the name of the Lord shall be saved *(Rom.* 149 *10:13)*

THE BIBLE SAYS YOU HAVE ETERNAL LIFE! 150

And this is the record, that God hath given to us eternal life, and this 151 life is in his Son. He that hath the Son hath life. *(I John 5:11)* Poverman got himself a Bible and checked it out. It was all there.

There were ten people at the Thursday night meeting, all as young as 152 Robert or a little older, all regulars, except for the new member, Morton Poverman, who was introduced all around. Also attending were George Fetler and the Reverend Julius Meadly, who more or less conducted things.

It went well enough. After Poverman explained to them that he had 153 come out of interest in his son's interest and his talk with Mr. Fetler, the discussion picked up where, apparently, it had left off last week.

The point of concern, always a tough one, Reverend Meadly told them, 154 was whether those born before Christ, before, that is, the opportunity to receive Christ, would go to Hell. The Reverend drew the distinction between Pagans, who had not had the chance to embrace Christ, and the Heathens, those born since Christ who did and do have the opportunity but reject it. Heathens were unquestionably doomed to Hell, but about Pagans there was still some serious debate, for surely Abraham and the Prophets were in Heaven already, and Moses as well as Adam.

They all discussed at length the fairness of this, that those who had had 155 no choice should be so grievously punished. The Reverend said that indeed the ways of the Lord were not always apparent to Man, and they were certainly unfathomable, but it did no good to question what was *not* going to happen to the Pagans, and one should concentrate instead on the glory of what *was* going to happen to the Saved. And he concluded, "You know, sometimes I think that the last chapter and verse isn't completed. That on Judgment Day, God in his infinite wisdom and mercy will raise up even the unfortunate Pagans." They closed on that high note. Through the evening Robert Poverman had said nothing.

Driving home he said, "What are you doing?"  156

"What do you mean?" his father said.  157

"You know what I mean. Why did you come tonight?"  158

"What's the matter, suddenly it's not a free country? A man can't worship how he wants anymore?"  159

"Cut it out, Dad. You know what I mean."  160

"You go to this place because you've got questions, right?" Poverman said. "Well, I've got questions too."  161

"Like what?"  162

"Like have you declared for Jesus, or whatever you call it?"  163

"No."  164

"Are you going to?"  165

"I don't know. I can't say."  166

"Do you believe in all that . . . stuff?"  167

"I think about it." They drove on in silence. "Are you going back? To another meeting?" Robert asked.  168

"Yeah. Sure. I still got my questions. What about you? Are you going back?"  169

Robert did not answer that. "You're not sincere," he said.  170

But there, Morton Poverman knew, without any doubt at all, his son was wrong.  171

He hacked at his store and grew bleary with fatigue. What he sold in front he brought in through the back and touched everything once, twice, thrice in its passage. Slips, underwear, dresses, bandanas, now bathing suits and beach or pool ensembles. From passing over all that plastic, his fingertips were sanded as smooth as a safecracker's. And doggedly he studied the Word of the Lord. Bore up his wife. Bore his son.  172

At the second meeting that Poverman attended, Fetler understood. Robert Poverman, once so animated and involved, would not participate, not in the presence of his father. And the blunt intensity of his father's questions caused the Reverend Meadly to veer about, put his helm over frequently to avoid the jutting rocks of Morton Poverman's intent, not that he was making an argument. He was polite enough, whatever that cost him. But his questions, they were so fundamental.  173

Almost all of the group had been together for months and had already covered the ecclesiastical ground that was new to him. It was not fair to the group to have to pause so often while the Reverend Meadly (the soul of  174

patience) answered in detail what they all had heard and discussed before.
This is what Fetler explained to Poverman after the meeting.

"You're throwing me out?" Poverman said. "You're telling me to go    175
elsewhere with my soul in danger of eternal perdition?" He had studied well.
He had the lingo, like in every line of work.

"No no no," Fetler said, growing more pink than ever. Close to him,    176
Poverman could see the blue fretwork of his veining. His whole face was like
a stained-glass window. "That would be unthinkable, of course. What I had
in mind was our Sunday afternoon group for older people." Poverman shook
his head at Sunday afternoon. "Or private instruction," Fetler followed up.
"Perhaps you could come to us, the Reverend Meadly or me, on another
evening? Then we could give you a 'cram course,' so to speak?"

"OK," Poverman said. They agreed on Tuesday night.    177

On Tuesday night Poverman met with Reverend Meadly and after two    178
hours of explaining—starting with Genesis (oh it would be a long time before
he would be able to rejoin the young group already well into Corinthians),
Poverman leaned back and said.

"But it's all faith, isn't it? All this reasoning, all this explaining, if you've    179
got the faith that's all that matters."

"Yes," the Reverend said. "Faith more than anything else."    180

"And if you get the faith, then what?"    181

"You must declare it. You must stand forth and join God through His    182
Son, Jesus Christ."

"Yes, but how? I mean could I just say it to you now? Is that enough?    183
Would God know?"

"If you declare yourself through us, the Church of the Resurrection,    184
there are certain formalities."

"A ceremony?"    185

"Yes, that's right. You must answer certain questions, take certain vows    186
before a congregation."

"What about this?" Poverman produced one of the pamphlets that the    187
Society of the Holy Word published. "Wherever I look, I'm always on trial.
Some trial. Listen." He read the fiery, imprescriptible indictment through
to the end. " 'Verdict: Guilty as charged. Appeal: None. Sentence: Immediately eternal, conscious, tormenting, separational death in a burning lake
of fire and brimstone.' "

"Well?" Reverend Meadly asked. Nothing else.    188

"So that's it for me? For Robert?"    189

"Unless you embrace the Lord Jesus as your Savior, that is your fate    190
and Robert's fate, yes."

"No either / or huh?"    191

"Either Love or Damnation," Reverend Meadly said. Kindly.    192

On Thursday Poverman showed up at the meeting. Fetler called him    193
aside. "I thought we agreed that you would work privately?"

"I wouldn't say a single word," Poverman promised. "I'll listen. I'll watch.    194
I can learn a lot that way, and I won't interrupt. Not one word."

But there were no longer any words to say, for Morton Poverman had    195
decided that at long last the time and event had come for God to stand forth
and defend Himself, make good his terrible threat and vaunt or scram. He
had paid enough with good faith and would not bargain now. He had reached
his sticking price. Take it or leave it. What was his, was his, and what belonged
to his son, the legacy of his life, for all his—Poverman's—own clumsiness on
this earth, *that* he would not let be stolen easily. And whatsoever should raise
his hand or voice against his son must answer for that to him.

Thus girded, midway through the meeting Poverman suddenly stood    196
up. The Reverend Meadly had just finished an intricate restatement of Paul's
words:

> In a moment, in the twinkling of an eye, at the last trump: for the trumpet
> shall sound, and the dead shall be raised incorruptible, and we shall be
> changed.

Poverman stood up and said:

"Me too. I have seen the way and the light. I want to declare for Jesus."    197
There was commotion.

"Mr. Poverman!" George Fetler said, standing too, quickly in his alarm.    198

"Now," Poverman said. "Right now. The spirit is in me." He stepped    199
away from the group of seated young people and then turned to them. "Be
ye followers of me, even as I also am of Christ," he intoned, trying to get it
right. One of the group clapped. "I've been thinking and so this is what I
want to do, thanks to Reverend Meadly." Reverend Meadly smiled, but Fetler
curdled, his pink now blotched redness.

"So what's next?" Poverman asked. "What do I got to do?"    200

There was a happy excitement in the young people at this immanence    201
of spirit, all the thick words of the past months came true like a miracle.
Fetler urged a later time, a more appropriate time for the declaration, but
"Now," Poverman insisted. "Betweeen now and later, who knows what could
happen? And *then* what about my soul?" He looked at Fetler. "Now."

Robert Poverman, stiff and frozen, watched his father don white robes    202
(cotton / polyester—60 / 40, not silk) that drooped to the floor and take in
either hand a large Bible and a heavy brass crucifix. The classroom was turned
into a chapel, the lights dimmed. The Reverend Meadly took his place behind
the table. From a drawer in the table he took out a paper.

"Wait," Poverman said. "I want my son Robert to stand next to me. He    203
should see this up close." He motioned Robert to him.

The Reverend said, "You must be delivered to Christ by one who has    204
already received Him. Robert has not yet."

"That's okay," Poverman said. "Let Mr. Fetler deliver me. I just want    205
my son to stand by. This is a big thing for me." And so it was arranged,

George Fetler, crimson and his eyes like thin slivers, on Poverman's right, Robert Poverman, cast into numb darkness, on his father's left. "Okay," Poverman said. "Let's go."

It was simple enough. The Reverend would read statements that Poverman would repeat. After a brief preamble in which Reverend Meadly explained the beauty and importance of this glorious step toward Salvation, the ceremony began. 206

"Oh Lord I have offended thee mightily," Poverman echoed the Reverend Meadly flatly. 207

"Oh Lord I am an infection of evil that I ask you to heal and make clean," he went on. 208

"Oh Lord I ask you to break open my hard and selfish heart to allow your mercy into it that I might learn love." 209

"Oh Lord I have made the world foul with my pride." 210

"Oh Lord I am a bad man and stained with sin." 211

"No," Robert Poverman said out of his darkness. 212

"Sha,"[1] his father said. He motioned for the Reverend Meadly with his cross to go on. 213

"Daddy, please. Stop this. Don't." He wept. 214

"I am an abomination in Your eyes," the Reverend read from his paper. 215

"NO!" Robert Poverman shouted. Demanded. "NO!" He stepped forward, but his father held out his Bible-loaded hand like a rod. 216

"Don't you be afraid," he said to his son. "Don't you worry *now*, Sonny," he said. "I'm here." And unsheathing the great sword of his love, he waved it about his balding, sweaty head and advanced upon his Hosts in dubious battle. And fought. 217

Not without glory. 218

## STUDY QUESTIONS

1. How is the word "testament" being used at the end of the second paragraph? What other meanings does the word suggest? What other words could have been used instead of "testament"? Why does this word seem the best possible choice in this passage?

2. After the first five paragraphs, what image of Poverman's character do you have? How is that confirmed or modulated by the telephone conversation with Charney in paragraphs 20–25? How is your image of Poverman changed later in the story?

3. The first part of the story centers on Poverman's bankruptcy and his attempt to make a new start. Why does Targan begin the story this way? What new complication and focus of attention is introduced in the midst of the details of Poverman's beginning again?

1. Be quiet (Yiddish).

4. Why are Bobby's SAT scores described as fuel for Poverman's flame (par. 39)?

5. Paragraph 40 goes into considerable detail about Poverman's business dealings in the store; what does that contribute to your view of him? What image is used to describe his actions in this paragraph? Does the image seem too dramatic? What does it lend to your view of Poverman? How does it contribute to your expectations?

6. Why does Poverman not want his son Robert to help him in the store at night? What does Robert mean when he says he will pray for his father (par. 53)? What is Poverman's reaction?

7. ". . . what did he [Mr. Poverman] need with fancy or smart? He had Robert Poverman of Yale or Cornell. *That* was fancy. *That* was smart" (par. 58). Is this selfish of Poverman? Is he trying to live through or succeed through his son? Why does he "hope for Yale" (par. 61)? Why does Mrs. Poverman prefer Cornell?

8. Do you recognize the descriptions of the college catalogue in paragraph 61? Do you remember looking at such catalogues? What is the effect of having had emotional experiences similar to the one you are reading about? How does it influence your reading or judgment of the story?

9. What sudden turn does the story take around paragraphs 72–82?

10. Poverman is not "reasonable," paragraph 85 suggests; he just knows how to hang on. Which seems the greater virtue? Where are your sympathies and loyalties at this point, with the father or son?

11. What does Poverman think about George Fetler during their first conversation? What do you think of him? What did you expect would happen from this point on?

12. Why is Poverman's life now described as a battle, a war (par. 138)? A battle or war for or against what?

13. Coming home from the meeting of the Society of the Holy Word, Robert accuses his father of not being sincere. "But there, Morton Poverman knew, without any doubt at all, his son was wrong" (par. 171). Why is Robert wrong?

14. "At the second meeting that Poverman attended, Fetler understood" (par. 173). What did he understand?

15. Poverman decides (par. 195) "that at long last the time and event had come for God to stand forth and defend Himself, make good his terrible threat and vaunt or scram." What "threat"? What "vaunt"? Is this blasphemous? What, if anything, justifies the vehemence or daring of Poverman's decision?

16. Why does Fetler "curdle" (par. 199) when Poverman declares for Jesus?

17. Why does Poverman want Robert to stand next to him during the ceremony?

18. Why does Robert say "No," ask his father to stop, and weep (pars. 212–14)?

19. Explain the last two paragraphs of the story, especially the sword, the Hosts, the glory.

# Estela Portillo

D irector of the arts at El Paso Community College in the city in which she was born (1936) and where she has taught in high school, conducted a television talk show, and helped found a bilingual theater, Estela Portillo is best known for her play *The Day of the Swallows* (1972), though her work also includes *Sor Juana and Other Plays* (1983), *Rain of Scorpions* (short stories, 1975), and *Trini* (novel, 1986).

# THE DAY OF THE SWALLOWS

## THE CHARACTERS
### IN ORDER OF APPEARANCE

| | |
|---|---|
| ALYSEA | EDUARDO |
| CLEMENCIA | CLARA |
| JOSEFA | DON ESQUINAS |
| TOMÁS | FATHER PRADO |

*The tierra of Lago de San Lorenzo is within memory of mountain sweet pine. Then the maguey thickens with the ferocity of chaotic existence; here the desert yawns. Here it drinks the sun in madness.*

*The village of Lago de San Lorenzo is a stepchild; it is a stepchild to the Esquinas hacienda, for the hacienda has been a frugal mother and a demanding father. Its name comes from the yearly ritual of the saint-day of San Lorenzo when all the young women gather around the lake to wash their hair and bathe in promise of a future husband. The tempo of life, unbroken, conditioned, flavors its heartbeat with dreams and myths. The hacienda is the fiber upon which existence hangs. The church, the fluid rose, assures the future promise of Elysium fields. No one dares ask for life.*

*What is this footfall beyond ritual, beyond livelihood? What is this faint unknown ache in the heart? It's more than just the rasp of hope. . . . The young know this; and they go to the spring with lyrical intimacy. By the lake, eyes burn and feet dig the mud of the spring; someone traces mountain against sky and gulf expands drowning, drowning. The obligation is remembered back in the village; the toll of the church bell offering sanctuary is a relief; the lake becomes too much for them.*

*At daybreak the fiesta day is sanctified with a misa[1] at sunrise; the choir rejoices the promise of day. A holy procession is led by the priest and an "honored member" of the church. Offerings to the patron saint are generous amidst frugality. The animals are blessed; the people are blessed; all is washed clean.*

*Perhaps secretly each villager senses the werewolf moon inside him; the bite into passions will be hard and fierce after sunset.*

*On the day of San Lorenzo, in the heat of July, everybody goes to the lake; this day the lake is invaded by village life. When the church bells toll eleven in the sun, the late morning is the sole witness to the bathing of the virgins. The lake becomes a sacred temple. The high priestesses talk of hopes, lovers, and promises. In earnest belief, they wash their hair in spring water to insure future marriages in heaven. It is true, no one has seen a marriage made in heaven, but each girl hugs the private truth that hers will be the one.*

*Two hundred years before the Esquinas family had settled in Lago de San Lorenzo on a Spanish grant of fifty thousand acres, the Indians were pushed out further into the desert. This was the way of the bearded gachupín,[2] with his hot grasp and his hot looks. Their greedy vitality was a wonder to the Indian. It was also death.*

*But now the barrio clustered itself around the hacienda. The conquered conquered the conquerors.*

*There is a house, the only house close to the edge of the lake. Here our story begins. . . .*


# ACT I


## Scene 1

JOSEFA's *sitting room; it is an unusually beautiful room, thoroughly feminine and in good taste; the profusion of lace everywhere gives the room a safe, homey look. The lace pieces are lovely, needlepoint, hairpin, limerick, the work of patience and love. Upstage left is a large French window; from it one can view a large tree. On the tree is a freshly painted tree house of unusual size and shape. It is an orb that accommodates a great number of birds. The room faces south, so it is flooded with light; the light, the lace, the open window all add to the beauty of the room, a storybook beauty of serenity. To the right is a door leading to the kitchen; there is another door leading to a bedroom; downstage left there is a door leading to the outside.*

ALYSEA *is sitting on the floor when the curtain rises. It is before dawn; but a few*

---

1. Mass.
2. Spaniard who settled in Spanish America.

*minutes after the curtain rises, light begins to fill the room.* ALYSEA *is cleaning the sitting room carpet, an unusual task for this hour. Next to her is a pail; she uses a piece of cloth with quick frantic movements, rinses, and continues the scrubbing. After a while she looks at the cloth in her hand intently, as in realization of what she is doing. Suddenly she drops it seemingly in horror. She looks helpless and lost. Still sitting on the floor she leans her head against a chair and cries silently staring up into the now streaming light from the window. There is the sound of the milk bell. It is* CLEMENCIA *delivering. When she hears it,* ALYSEA *jumps up, wipes away traces of tears with her apron, then opens the French window and looks out.*

ALYSEA: She'll come right in if I'm not at the door to pay her.

> [*She looks around the room. Her eyes fall on a small side table next to the couch. She goes to the table and stares at a long kitchen knife with traces of blood on it. Hurriedly, she picks up the cleaning cloth, and uses it to pick up the knife gingerly. She wraps the cloth around the knife and places it in a side table drawer. During this interval,* CLEMENCIA's *noisy arrival is heard. The kitchen door is opened; there is a tug of milk can, then a pouring of milk. Several sighs and ejaculations about hard work are heard.* ALYSEA *looks around the room one last time as* CLEMENCIA *walks in.*]

CLEMENCIA: Josefa! Alysea! My centavos for the week are not on the kitchen table. Hombre . . . do I have to beg for my money? Oye. . . ¿dónde están?[3]

ALYSEA: Buenos días, Clemencia . . . early?

CLEMENCIA: [*Staring at* ALYSEA.] Que horror! What is the matter? You look terrible. Have you been up all night?

ALYSEA: [*Smooths her hair; looks at her hands guiltily.*] Yes . . . I stayed up late. A new pattern in lace.

CLEMENCIA: You work hard to please Josefa, don't you? [*She notices* ALYSEA *looking at her hands.*] What's the matter with your hands? Not rheumatism . . . you're just a girl . . . Look at mine! Life has eaten them up . . . I feel pain . . . ay! . . . it is my destiny to suffer . . . You owe me seven pesos.

ALYSEA: Yes, of course. [*She goes to the household money box, takes a set of keys from her apron pocket and opens it. She counts out the money.*] Cinco . . . seis . . . siete.[4]

CLEMENCIA: Gracias . . . [*Looks at* ALYSEA *again and shakes her head.*] Rest in the afternoon . . . you look all in. You can in this house. There is beautiful peace here.

ALYSEA: Yes . . . here it stretches itself out to breathe. . . .

CLEMENCIA: You begin to talk like Josefa now . . . you like her . . . eh? She doesn't want you to work yourself to death . . . she is too kind.

3. Where are they?

4. Five . . . six . . . seven.

ALYSEA: The most considerate of persons . . . but there is so much to do.

CLEMENCIA: Of course, San Lorenzo . . . mañana . . . Josefa will be so grand leading the procession with the Father to the church . . . a happy day for the barrio . . . we all share Josefa's honor like we have shared her goodness . . . a great lady.

ALYSEA: I had forgotten . . . the procession tomorrow.

CLEMENCIA: What's the matter with you? Forgotten?

ALYSEA: Don't mind me . . . I'm not myself today . . . Clemencia.

CLEMENCIA: Doña Josefa is an angel. All her life, she goes around . . . with that walking stick of hers . . . always she goes . . . like an avenging angel . . . helping . . . what a sight she must be . . . pounding with her stick on those evil people . . . One, two . . . that's for wickedness! [*She makes motions of one pounding away.*] She takes care of the devil all right . . . eh? Yes . . . she saved you from the sickness. . . .

ALYSEA: Saved me . . . from the sickness . . . what is shadow? What is sickness?

CLEMENCIA: Talk sense, child! . . . you need rest. [*She looks at lace work on table.*] My . . . you are making lace as beautiful as Josefa's! You are lucky.

ALYSEA: Lucky? [*She goes to the window.*] This room is beautiful . . . isn't it? I'm lucky to be here . . . aren't I? [*Pause.*] Appearances . . . they are very funny! Tomorrow the church will honor Josefa . . . how very funny! [*She begins to laugh; then, the laugh is eventually lost in sobbing.*] Oh, God!

CLEMENCIA: What is the matter? [*She looks around.*] Where is Josefa. . . . Josefa! [*She goes to* ALYSEA *and feels her forehead.*] Are you feverish?

[*At this point,* JOSEFA *enters. She is a tall regal woman about thirty-five. Her bones are Indian's; her coloring is Aryan. She wears her hair back severely. Her movements are graceful and quiet. The cuffs and collar of her dress are of exquisite lace. She walks up to* ALYSEA *and puts her arm around her.*]

JOSEFA: Alysea, quiet! [*She turns to* CLEMENCIA.] She's not feeling well, I suppose.

CLEMENCIA: She worked all night.

JOSEFA: Oh?

CLEMENCIA: You must make her rest.

JOSEFA: You're right, of course. . . .

CLEMENCIA: Well . . . I must be going . . . I'm late on my rounds . . . [*She sighs.*] I wish I could stay here. [*She looks around.*] What heavenly peace . . .

JOSEFA: [*Smiling.*] You are welcome . . . this is your home . . .

CLEMENCIA: Doña Josefa . . . you are an angel!

JOSEFA: No . . . just happy! . . . Did you get your money?

[JOSEFA *escorts* CLEMENCIA *to the door.* CLEMENCIA *gives a last anxious look at* ALYSEA.]

CLEMENCIA: She'll be all right in your hands, Josefa.

JOSEFA: I'll see that she rests.

[CLEMENCIA *leaves through the kitchen door.* JOSEFA *remains silent as the sounds of departure from the kitchen are heard.*]

JOSEFA: You should rest . . . Clemencia's right.

[ALYSEA *shakes her head.*]

JOSEFA: Do you think it's wise. . . .

ALYSEA: Wise! the way you word it . . . wise!

JOSEFA: Very well, I'll put it another way . . . is this the time to break down? Beautiful days demand our strength . . . We must be faithful to loveliness.

ALYSEA: [*Incredulously.*] You believe that? [*She walks up to* JOSEFA *almost menacingly.*] How can you justify in that way? You!

JOSEFA: [*Softly.*] There are things we must do . . . to keep a sanity . . . to make the moment clear. [*Pause.*] Any signs of the swallows? Isn't the tree lovely?

ALYSEA: Have you forgotten? . . . how can you! . . . Josefa, last night . . .

[ALYSEA *is overwhelmed with the memory; she runs out of the room.* JOSEFA *looks for a moment after her; then she touches the lace curtains on the window.*]

JOSEFA: We pattern our lives for one beautiful moment . . . like this lace . . . little bits and pieces come together . . . to make all this . . . my world . . . a crystal thing of light; Alysea must understand . . . she must!

[*There is a knock to the door leading outside.* JOSEFA *goes to the door; she opens it; it is* TOMÁS, *her shiftless uncle.*]

TOMÁS: Oh . . . it is you, Josefa! You're not at the hacienda this morning.

JOSEFA: What are you doing here?

TOMÁS: The pump. . . .

JOSEFA: You fixed that already . . . I've told you not to come around here at this time of day. . . .

TOMÁS: You do not appreciate . . . always suspicious. . . .

JOSEFA: I don't want you bothering Alysea . . . ever. . . .

TOMÁS: It is like you . . . to think the worse of me.

JOSEFA: [*With resignation.*] How are the children? Your wife Anita?

TOMÁS: They manage better than me . . . thanks to you . . . there is little steady work . . . I need a few centavos . . . Josefa . . . you're rich!

JOSEFA: What for . . . Tequila?

TOMÁS: Just a little money . . . look, my hands . . . they shake . . . I need it, Josefa . . . please!

JOSEFA: Don't beg!

TOMÁS: You let Clara have all she wants. . . .

JOSEFA: That is none of your business.

TOMÁS: [*Noticing the pail.*] Eh . . . what's this? Looks like blood!

JOSEFA: Go to the kitchen . . . help yourself to meal and beans . . . for the family.

[TOMÁS *is still staring at the pail.*]

JOSEFA: Did you hear me?

TOMÁS: Yes . . . yes, Doña Perfecta . . . Doña Perfecta . . . so charitable . . . ha! ha!

JOSEFA: I'm not in the mood for your sarcasm.

TOMÁS: You will lead the procession tomorrow like the queen of the world . . . eh? You can spare a few centavos? a bottle? Do you keep some in the house when you get it for Clara?

JOSEFA: You're not getting any money.

TOMÁS: [*Starting to leave.*] What's in that pail?

JOSEFA: [*Indignant.*] I don't have to satisfy your curiosity.

TOMÁS: Cálmate[5] . . . I was just asking. . . .

[JOSEFA *turns her back to him; he leaves through the kitchen door; his grumbling is heard as he helps himself to the food offered by* JOSEFA. JOSEFA *stares at the contents of the pail; she looks away and touches her temples with her fingertips. She sits in a rocking chair; leans back, closes her eyes, and grips the arms of the chair; she rocks back and forth.*]

JOSEFA: There is no desert here . . . only light . . . to live each day with nothing . . . to sink . . . [*She closes her eyes and rocks.*] The lonely, lonely struggle . . . then to emerge . . . to find the light . . . I have so much now . . . I want to give so much now . . . Alysea must understand! We must keep this world of light at all costs. . . . [*She rises and walks to the window and stands absorbing the light; one can sense an obvious union between the light and* JOSEFA.]

JOSEFA: [*Softly.*] How moist your lips, my light . . . Through me . . . through me . . . you live. [*She comes back from her intimate world and looks at the bird house with pleasure.*] The long flight . . . how tired they will be; how thirsty after the desert . . . here my swallows will find peace . . . home.

[*As she looks at the tree,* TOMÁS *comes through the patio outside the window. He has a sack over his shoulder.* JOSEFA *does not seem to be mindful of him.* TOMÁS *calls.*]

TOMÁS: Hey, Josefa! Are you casting a spell . . . so early? You don't scare me . . . I know you, querida[6] . . . I know many things . . . you burn inside. . . .

[JOSEFA *stares at him unbelievingly, as if he has destroyed a beauty; then she turns away from the window.*]

5. Calm down.
6. Dear.

TOMÁS: Hey, Josefa . . . don't run away . . . great Doña Perfecta runs away from her good-for-nothing uncle . . . that's funny . . . ha, ha!

JOSEFA: [*Firmly, but in an ominous tone.*] Go home, Tomás, go home.

[*She closes the window and walks to an unfinished damask close to the window. She sits down, unhooks the needle, and begins to work on it. Her concentration is a fiery intensity; this is obvious in her finger movements.* ALYSEA *comes back into the room; she is now composed and refreshed; she has put on a pretty dress. She sees the pail and removes it; taking it into the kitchen; all this time* JOSEFA *remains absorbed in the damask.* ALYSEA *comes back.* JOSEFA *looks up.*]

JOSEFA: You look so nice! Every morning now . . . you look like the garden. . . .

ALYSEA: Nothing is as beautiful as your garden . . . paradise must look like that.

JOSEFA: A garden of light . . . perhaps it has a sense of paradise. . . .

ALYSEA: Tomás was here?

JOSEFA: Sneaking around as usual. [*Pause.*] The pretty dress . . . for Eduardo again?

ALYSEA: Yes . . . I'll bring in the morning coffee . . . scones?

JOSEFA: Fine . . . and honey . . . suddenly I'm hungry . . . [*She leaves the damask, and begins to clear the coffee table.*] By the way . . . ask Eduardo to have some morning coffee with us today . . . don't run off for your usual morning walk.

ALYSEA: May I? Thank you . . . he's been coaxing me . . . he's absolutely fascinated by you.

JOSEFA: Do invite him.

[ALYSEA *seems to be holding back tears, although she has pretended calm through the conversation.*]

JOSEFA: What's the matter?

[ALYSEA *is not able to answer; she just shakes her head.* JOSEFA *walks up to her.* ALYSEA *stands still and helpless.* JOSEFA *takes* ALYSEA's *face in her hands.*]

JOSEFA: You are so dear to me . . . I don't like to see you like this . . . Alysea, don't dwell on what happened . . . things will be all right. Haven't I always made things all right?

[ALYSEA *still doesn't answer.*]

JOSEFA: The tragic things in my life taught me one thing . . . calm. The waiting . . . that is harder than struggle . . . Alysea, learn how . . . to find a strength . . . this loveliness here . . . our world . . . isn't it worth it?

[ALYSEA *begins to cry gently.* JOSEFA *comforts her.* ALYSEA *becomes limp; she places her head on* JOSEFA's *shoulder like a child.* JOSEFA *strokes her hair.*]

JOSEFA: Your hair . . . your beautiful hair . . . here, let me comb it. . . .

[*Suddenly* ALYSEA *breaks away. She seems at a loss, then remembers the coffee.*]

ALYSEA: I'll get things started in the kitchen . . . Eduardo will be here any moment now.
JOSEFA: About last night, Alysea . . . we must have a story.
ALYSEA: [*She seems to shiver.*] Story?
JOSEFA: When I took David to the hospital . . . the doctors . . . everyone was sympathetic . . . I told them someone had broken in. . . .
ALYSEA: And David?
JOSEFA: He will be all right.
ALYSEA: I can never believe that. . . .
JOSEFA: I will take care of him always. . . .
ALYSEA: You killed him!
JOSEFA: Don't! He'll be back with us in a few weeks . . . I will make a fine life for him always. . . .
ALYSEA: He'll never . . . he'll never. . . .

[*She is overcome by emotion; she walks out of the room into the kitchen.* JOSEFA *looks after her. She remains standing for a moment; then she picks up a book of poetry from the lamp table.*]

JOSEFA: Santa Teresita . . .

> "El hombre toma . . . toma y hiere,
> La flor desnuda . . . temblorosa . . ."[7]

In her world of God . . . she saw what I see . . . she knew the light . . . beauty . . . truth . . . yes . . . in a cloister. [*She looks around the room. Then she walks up to a workbasket and picks up a piece of lace. She holds it to the light and intently traces the pattern.*] The web . . . the beautiful web we weave! Anything . . . anything is worth this!

## Scene 2

*A few minutes later;* ALYSEA *comes from the kitchen with a morning tray; coffee, scones, juice. She places the tray on the coffee table. There is a knock.* ALYSEA *goes to the door. It is* EDUARDO, *a young man of mixed heritage.*

EDUARDO: I came through the path. . . .
ALYSEA: [*Drawing him in.*] I'm glad. Josefa wants you to have morning coffee . . . in here . . . with her. You always come for me in such a hurry . . . you hadn't seen this room . . . had you?

---

7. From a poem by Saint Theresa of Ávila (1515–82): "Man takes . . . . takes and wounds/The stripped flower . . . shivering . . ."

EDUARDO: No . . . never! [*Looking around.*] Well . . . you were right . . . what a room! . . . for women.

ALYSEA: What do you mean?

EDUARDO: It is a dream of gentleness . . . peace; it is not a man's room . . . but it is beautiful.

ALYSEA: You're right . . . Josefa made this haven . . . away from the world of men.

EDUARDO: [*Looking at her quizzically.*] You like that?

ALYSEA: After what I've lived through . . . yes; this was heaven . . . when she brought me here. Sit down . . . she'll be here any moment.

[EDUARDO *watches* ALYSEA *as she arranges napkins, spoons.*]

EDUARDO: Have you told her . . . about our plans?

ALYSEA: No . . . she suspects something between us.

EDUARDO: And?

ALYSEA: It is hard to understand her feelings . . . there is a stillness in her.

EDUARDO: She dotes on you . . . I don't think she will be pleased . . . after all, I'm taking you away to a wilderness . . . mountain, pines. My squaw . . . living and loving in the open.

[*He goes to her, gathers her in his arms; they kiss;* ALYSEA *clings to him.*]

EDUARDO: It won't be like this . . . you know!

ALYSEA: I'll be with you . . . isn't that everything?

EDUARDO: And the gentle life you love?

ALYSEA: What you will share with me . . . will be so much more.

[*They embrace again.*]

EDUARDO: Say! Have you seen the morning? It is a conspiracy . . . sun, clouds, green fields . . . and the pines from the distance . . . I can hardly wait. Let's leave right now . . . pack the horses . . . take the mountain trail past the lake . . . the way of my people.

ALYSEA: Not now . . . you crazy Indian!

EDUARDO: We'll find a clearing . . . plow . . . build a cabin . . . have babies. . . .

ALYSEA: Sometimes I think you have to be out in the open . . . no matter what. . . .

EDUARDO: That's where my God is.

[EDUARDO *sits down.* ALYSEA *stands behind his chair and gently traces his cheek.*]

ALYSEA: Your world! A beautiful God exists . . . in your world . . . when you talk . . . He is free . . . green . . . open. You know something?

EDUARDO: [*Catching her hand and kissing it.*] What?

ALYSEA: Father Prado understands your God too. At confession . . . I told him about not attending Mass because we go exploring . . . to find the tallest pines . . . I told him about your God . . . he smiled and told me I had found a holier temple.

EDUARDO: Let's take him with us.

ALYSEA: [*Laughing.*] You know better . . . his life is the barrio . . . the people.

EDUARDO: He will marry us . . . before we leave. . . .

ALYSEA: [*Pulling away.*] No . . . we must wait. . . .

EDUARDO: Why? Listen, woman . . . no one in her right mind turns down a marriage proposal. . . .

ALYSEA: I want you to be sure . . . after a while . . . after we have shared. . . .

EDUARDO: [*In jest.*] You shameless hussy . . . you wish to live in sin, eh?

ALYSEA: Don't jest . . . there was so much ugliness . . . before Josefa brought me here . . . I remember . . . they brought a bunch of us from the country . . . they promised jobs as seamstresses; my barrio was poor . . . we went hungry . . . so I came . . . the city was a nightmare . . . they locked us up in an old house . . . they gave us disgusting soiled dresses to wear . . . then we found out.

EDUARDO: Stop torturing yourself.

ALYSEA: No . . . let me finish . . . I've never told you . . . I hid in the closet of the room; an ugly man with fat hands asked the girls where I was . . . they didn't know . . . he cursed; I was trembling underneath a pile of dirty dresses suffering with the sweat of lust . . . I closed my eyes. Then, I decided to run . . . I simply got up . . . and ran . . . down the stairs . . . into an open hall . . . where men . . . men with hard dead looks stared . . . no one expected me to try and escape through the front door . . . but I did . . . I got as far as the street . . . then he caught up with me; his hands were at my throat. . . .

EDUARDO: That's enough. . . .

ALYSEA: All of a sudden . . . Josefa appeared . . . with her walking stick. She raised it over her head and beat the man . . . he cried out in pain . . . she never faltered . . . then, she brought me to this world of light. . . .

EDUARDO: We shall marry tomorrow night . . . that's it!

ALYSEA: No . . . no . . . there's something else . . . [*She becomes very agitated.*] Eduardo . . . last night . . .

[JOSEFA *enters.*]

JOSEFA: Good morning . . . am I late? Is the coffee cold?

ALYSEA: No . . . no . . . you are just in time.

EDUARDO: [*Drawing out a chair for her.*] Our great lady!

[ALYSEA *becomes busy with the food.*]

ALYSEA: [*To* JOSEFA.] Juice?

JOSEFA: Yes . . . thank you. Eduardo, what are you up to . . . charming the women so early in the morning?

EDUARDO: What better time?

JOSEFA: You are different! Alysea . . . give Eduardo . . . some of this orange . . . it's delicious. . . .

EDUARDO: No! No! just coffee . . . and what's this? [*He picks up a scone, tastes it.*] Wonderful! I had heard about all your wonders . . . but . . . cooking too!

JOSEFA: Alysea baked them . . . from an old recipe of mine. . . .

[ALYSEA *hands* EDUARDO *some coffee.*]

EDUARDO: Thank you, Linda. . . .

[ALYSEA *serves herself.* JOSEFA *looks intently from one to the other.*]

JOSEFA: All these walks you two take . . . into forbidden country. . . .

EDUARDO: How can beauty be forbidden. . . .

JOSEFA: I feel the same way . . . but the desert mind forbids it . . . many times.

ALYSEA: It won't be forbidden tomorrow . . . all the young girls will bathe in the lake at noontime . . . the promise of a perfect love. . . .

EDUARDO: I hear it is your year. Josefa . . . you will lead the church procession. . . .

JOSEFA: My people enjoy planning for it. . . .

ALYSEA: Josefa is as bad as Father Prado about the barrio people . . . all is to please them. . . .

EDUARDO: And what pleases you, Josefa?

JOSEFA: To make them happy!

EDUARDO: I can see why they talk of you with awe. . . .

JOSEFA: I am Indian you know . . . yet not of desert, not of them, in a way. Yet . . . totally theirs.

ALYSEA: [*Rising.*] Well . . . I shall leave you for a few moments; Josefa . . . the lace for the capitol . . . must make the morning express . . . excuse me.

[ALYSEA *leaves.* EDUARDO *finishes his coffee.*]

JOSEFA: She's falling in love with you. . . .

EDUARDO: It's mutual. . . .

JOSEFA: For how long, Eduardo?

EDUARDO: [*Stands, hands in pocket, somewhat ill at ease.*] Love is not timed.

JOSEFA: Isn't it?

EDUARDO: What do you mean?

JOSEFA: Clara.

EDUARDO: You know?

JOSEFA: She has described to me . . . your every mood . . . your every gesture . . . in love. . . .

EDUARDO: I don't know what to say!

JOSEFA: Guilt?

EDUARDO: Ridiculous . . . there's no guilt in love!

JOSEFA: [*Laughing as if to herself.*] The way you men justify . . . the word "love" doesn't it really mean . . . take? . . . destroy?

EDUARDO: It isn't that. . . .

JOSEFA: Of course not! Disguised in a man's words . . . in a man's promises . . . oh, I know, you make a dream of your deadly game.

EDUARDO: Alysea's happy.

JOSEFA: Is she? For how long . . . until you find another fancy?

EDUARDO: What I feel for her is different. . . .

JOSEFA: I remember Clara telling me the same things about you and her . . . how easily you put her out of your life.

EDUARDO: Clara understands.

JOSEFA: No, Eduardo . . . she just accepts . . . she knows nothing else.

EDUARDO: You make me feel guilty . . . why?

JOSEFA: I'll tell you why . . . Alysea has love here; she is happy . . . she has found her place in the world . . . safe with me . . . there is a constancy here. . . .

EDUARDO: All right! I don't think one should have Conditions . . . I know I love her now . . . I want to love her forever . . . but it is not for me to know. . . .

JOSEFA: She belongs here . . . with me . . . You men explain away all your indiscretions, so easily . . . after all, you make the rules and enjoy the abuses!

EDUARDO: That's not fair. . . .

JOSEFA: That's funny . . . When has a man been fair to . . . women?

EDUARDO: You are distorting. . . .

JOSEFA: What I offer her is not a violence . . . Man's love is always a violence.

EDUARDO: I'm sorry.

JOSEFA: For what . . . the evil in the world?

EDUARDO: I love Alysea.

JOSEFA: Oh, yes . . . you love, he loves, they love . . . how convenient the word "love"!

[EDUARDO *remains silent.* JOSEFA *suddenly realizes he is a guest.*]

JOSEFA: [*In an even pleasant voice.*] Come, Eduardo, you must forgive me for such an outburst . . . What a terrible hostess I am! Don't mind me, when there is concern for the people you love . . . Here let me refill your cup! [*She pours him some coffee and hands it to him.*] There is a special happiness in this house, you know. . . .

EDUARDO: [*Reassured.*] I know . . . it is the soaring sea in you.

JOSEFA: What?

EDUARDO: You carry things, people with you . . . when your strength is washed away . . . you leave beauty behind.

JOSEFA: How lovely . . . you are easy to fall in love with. . . .

EDUARDO: So are you . . . if a man is brave enough.

JOSEFA: Brave?

EDUARDO: You are a whirlwind. . . .

JOSEFA: I have always sought the calm. . . .

EDUARDO: Ah . . . but your depths! Josefa, I sense them . . . you are not in the barrio.

JOSEFA: [*Amused.*] Such discernment! . . . but then, you are right . . . I am of the lake.

EDUARDO: I've heard . . . I hear you dare the lake alone . . . in solitude. . . .

JOSEFA: The barrio stories are myth . . . primitive fears . . . what most of the people fear is instinctive. . . .

EDUARDO: In what way?

JOSEFA: Out in the lake . . . out in the pines . . . they see themselves too well . . . they have become the desert . . . it is too much to accept . . . so monsters are created. . . . but for me . . . ah . . . for me!

EDUARDO: Tell me. . . .

JOSEFA: When I was young . . . when I refused to go bathe on San Lorenzo's day, when I chose the moonlight in any season . . . it was defiance. . . .

EDUARDO: What did you defy?

JOSEFA: What defied me . . . the world! Yes, I would go . . . to defy . . . then . . . but it became something else.

EDUARDO: [*Looking at her intently.*] Why didn't you ever marry? No one good enough?

JOSEFA: [*Shrugs it off.*] I never saw the dream . . . I never felt the hope . . . there was always too much clarity for me . . . [*Pause.*] . . . Do you think me beautiful?

EDUARDO: Yes . . . very . . . mixed in with a dangerous excitement. . . .

JOSEFA: You are making love to me. . . .

EDUARDO: I make love to all things beautiful . . . don't you?

JOSEFA: [*In a whisper.*] Yes . . . oh, yes. . . .

[ALYSEA *comes in breathless.*]

ALYSEA: Well . . . you two . . . that wasn't long was it? [*Looks at both of them.*] You two must have found marvelous things to talk about . . . it shows!

JOSEFA: I tell you Eduardo . . . this girl has possibilities. . . .

EDUARDO: I know. . . .

ALYSEA: Did she tell you about her magicians?

EDUARDO: She was about to . . . when you came.

JOSEFA: [*Looking at him intently.*] How did you know . . . I was about to?

EDUARDO: The light in your eyes . . . the sudden magic in you. . . .

ALYSEA: I know what you mean, Eduardo . . . such a mystical thing. . . .

JOSEFA: You have laid the setting . . . so kindly. [*She walks to the window and looks out with her eyes closed as she speaks.*]

JOSEFA: The magicians are real, you know! I found them . . . long ago . . . the night of the Festival of San Lorenzo. The virgins had bathed by the noon day sun . . . I . . . I went after the Rosary bell . . . I went when they were all celebrating; the silence was perfumed . . . desire was heavy . . . painful. Does it surprise you that I speak of desire? Oh, yes . . . I felt it . . . to my fingertips . . . it was so real, the beautiful need . . . the lights of the barrio were far off in another world . . . this always affected me . . . I became another being far from my kind . . . even my desire was a special suffering. . . .

EDUARDO: You still did not marry.

JOSEFA: What does that have to do with desire? My desire . . . like my being . . . became a purer grain. It was more than someone to see or touch . . . or embrace . . . it was a need for a pouring of self . . . a gentleness . . . a faith. I did not want the callous Indian youth . . . with hot breath and awkward hands . . . a taking without feeling . . . no, not that! I wanted so much more. . . . [*She turns to look at* ALYSEA *and* EDUARDO *caught in her spell.*] Look at you . . . children . . . listening to fairy tales. . . .

EDUARDO: Children believe. . . .

JOSEFA: So do I! . . . isn't it funny?

EDUARDO: No . . . it is like that with some people.

JOSEFA: For me . . . it came true! . . . the wonder was my magicians. That night at the lake there was a different music . . . the stillness sung inside me . . . the moonlight grew in me . . . it became my lover . . . There by the lake, I felt the light finding its way among the pines . . . to me . . . It took me . . . then . . . perhaps it was my imagination . . . it said to me . . . "We are one . . . make your beauty . . . make your truth." Deep, I felt a burning spiral . . . it roared in my ears . . . my heart . . . [*Pause.*] It was too much to bear . . . so I ran, and ran and ran until I fell . . . not knowing where; I lay there in utter quiet . . . then I opened my eyes and found myself calmly looking up at the stars . . . sisters of my love! The moon had followed me; it lay a lake around me, on the grass. . . .

EDUARDO: Were you afraid?

JOSEFA: Afraid! There was no room . . . the joy was too great. I had the secret of the magicians . . . the wine of love . . . the light was me; I knew that I would bear the children of light . . . the moon . . . the burning lake.

ALYSEA: [*In a whisper.*] I believe her . . . look around you, the children of light . . . her garden . . . the lace . . . her love for the barrio people . . . her bright, bright calm. . . .

EDUARDO: [*Taking up the pace.*] Her person. . . .

JOSEFA: Hush . . . you two . . . don't go on so!

[*The voice of* TOMÁS *from the outside window breaks the spell.*]

TOMÁS: Josefa! . . . David's horse! . . . I found it out in the pasture . . . without a bridle . . . Josefa!

JOSEFA: [*Goes to the window.*] David's horse?

EDUARDO: [*Going to the window.*] Need any help?

JOSEFA: He didn't hear you . . . he's coming in. . . .

[ALYSEA *all of a sudden loses all her brightness; she seems frightened and lost. She looks at* JOSEFA's *every move;* JOSEFA *shows no reaction; she calmly begins to pick up cups, napkins.*]

JOSEFA: It is getting late . . . my! The morning has flown . . . such wonderful time . . . I hope it isn't too late for you two to go for your walk.

EDUARDO: No . . . no . . . there's plenty of time.

[TOMÁS *comes in through the kitchen door.*]

TOMÁS: He must have broken out from the stable . . . I thought I would tell you before I took him back to the hacienda. . . .

JOSEFA: Yes . . . take him back . . . horses will do that.

[EDUARDO *takes* ALYSEA *by the hands. He looks at her intently.*]

EDUARDO: What on earth is the matter? You need some morning air . . . I'll tell you what . . . I'll take you to a place where I can trace the path of the swallows any day now. . . .

[ALYSEA *doesn't seem to be listening to him;* JOSEFA *notices this and promptly suggests.*]

JOSEFA: Yes . . . I insist on it . . . take her; right now . . . enjoy this lovely day. . . .

[EDUARDO *takes* ALYSEA *by the shoulder.*]

EDUARDO: Come on. . . .

[*He stirs her to the door;* ALYSEA *does not resist. They exit.*]

TOMÁS: [*Shyly.*] I guess she feels bad about David . . . what happened last night. . . .

JOSEFA: What?

TOMÁS: I heard the talk in the barrio . . . someone broke into the house . . . that is . . . that is what you claim.

JOSEFA: What do you mean?

TOMÁS: You didn't tell me earlier. . . .

JOSEFA: Tell you? Why should I tell you anything.

TOMÁS: The blood in the pail . . . you didn't tell me anything about that either. . . .

JOSEFA: So?

TOMÁS: Well . . . I remember . . . all those times . . . you save the poor; innocent, helpless ones . . . you never say anything . . . it's always the barrio who puts the story together . . . you are clever. . . .

JOSEFA: Don't be ridiculous. . . .

TOMÁS: Yes . . . people have no idea how clever you really are . . . la doña Perfecta! You saved Alysea from the evil man . . . you saved David from a drunken father, the barrio tells the story of an angel . . . but it's funny . . . somehow . . . they never remember to tell that you crippled one man and the other died on the road where you left him. . . .

JOSEFA: You are pitiful . . . like those two men . . . destructive and pitiful. . . .

TOMÁS: Perhaps you'll get your hands on me too.

JOSEFA: [*Calmly, with disdain.*] Hadn't you better see about that horse?

TOMÁS: Now the town is busy making you out a heroine . . . an intruder? That's hard to believe . . . the girl looked too guilty a while ago . . . [*He studies* JOSEFA *who is straightening up.*] But you . . . it's amazing! . . . such grace . . . such pious silence . . . yes . . . you are a dangerous one, all right!

JOSEFA: All this . . . this foolishness, I know, is leading up to some sort of blackmail . . . you want money . . . don't you?

TOMÁS: You know me so well! . . . after all, I'm on your side . . . we are of the same blood. . . .

JOSEFA: Get out of here . . . and be careful about what you say . . . you clown! . . . who's going to believe anything you say? Be careful . . . or I may let you starve.

TOMÁS: Didn't work . . . eh? No money?

JOSEFA: You've tried my patience long enough . . . I have better things to do with my time . . . go and see about that horse. . . . [*She picks up the tray and starts toward the kitchen.*]

TOMÁS: Not even a few pesos?

[JOSEFA *looks at him contemptuously and walks out into the kitchen without a word.*]

TOMÁS: She'll break! She'll break . . . once I lay all my cards on the table. . . . stupid women! . . . (*He looks around the room.*) I know they keep the household money somewhere around here . . . yes.

[*He begins to look in the drawers.*]

## Scene 3

*Later the same morning. The room is empty, full of light, when* CLARA *enters. She is the wife of* DON ESQUINAS, *owner of the hacienda. She has the grace and elegance of good living. But, at closer scrutiny, one can see that this once beautiful woman is dissipated. Her blond beauty, although meticulously enhanced by great care, has the flavor of fading youth. She carries a knitting bag. Although she has been in this room many times, she is each time overwhelmed by the unusual light. She walks up to the table, lays her bag on it, opens it, searches for a cigarette; she finds one, lights it, and draws its flavor leisurely. She catches sight of* JOSEFA's *workbasket; she also sees the damask; she traces the design; then she picks up a piece of lace from the workbasket and examines it admiringly.*

CLARA: Angel filigree . . . how lovely . . . it's unearthly. . . .

[*As she examines the lace,* ALYSEA *walks into the room breathlessly. Her arms are full of freshly cut flowers. She glances at Doña Clara apologetically.*]

ALYSEA: Doña Clara . . . am I late?

CLARA: No, no . . . I just got here.

ALYSEA: [*Going to the vase and setting the flowers next to it.*] I always linger too long in the garden. . . .

CLARA: What a garden . . . what incantations does Josefa use?

ALYSEA: It's marvelous, the way she does it. . . .

CLARA: She talks to the flowers. . . .

ALYSEA: She talks to all living things. . . .

CLARA: [*Looking at* ALYSEA *as she arranges the flowers on the vase.*] You too . . . how you have blossomed in this house.

ALYSEA: Me?

CLARA: [*In a deliberately contained voice.*] Of course, this time it could be Eduardo . . . I hear he loves you.

ALYSEA: Love does that . . . doesn't it?

CLARA: It's true then! . . . and you love him too?

ALYSEA: Yes.

CLARA: Well . . . [*She puts out her cigarette.*] That's that! . . . where is my dress?

ALYSEA: [*Coming out of her reverie.*] Oh, I'm sorry . . . of course, your fitting.

[ALYSEA *goes to a wardrobe and takes out a simple gown. She hands it to* CLARA. CLARA *goes behind the screen.*]

CLARA: I suppose you'll go away with him?

ALYSEA: He wants me to . . . I haven't quite decided. . . .

CLARA: About love?

ALYSEA: Am I good enough for him? I have to use reason. . . .

CLARA: [*Almost impatiently.*] You don't have to reason love . . . my God!

ALYSEA: Will it be fair to him!

CLARA: What love there is . . . you take . . . don't reason it away . . . take it!

[*She comes from around the screen and gives her back to* ALYSEA *so* ALYSEA *will fasten the dress. Both are facing the mirror.* CLARA *looks* ALYSEA *directly in the eyes.*]

CLARA: Love is always fair just because it is. [*She can't look in the mirror any longer.*] What's the matter with me . . . look at me . . . an expert on love . . . ha! [*She bites her lip.*]

ALYSEA: You are beautiful and wise.

[CLARA *doesn't answer; she deliberately becomes absorbed with the gown. She surveys herself in the mirror.*]

CLARA: It seems to lack something . . . Alysea . . . what do you think?

ALYSEA: Of course . . . Josefa made something very special for it . . . [*She looks around.*] Where is it? Oh, yes . . . I'll be back in a minute.

[ALYSEA *goes through the bedroom door.* CLARA *goes to the mirror and traces the lines on her face. She then walks up to her knitting bag; takes a flask, opens it.*]

CLARA: [*Bitterly.*] Here's to youth! [*She drinks long draughts. She does it three times; then, she puts the flask away. She walks up to the mirror again.*]

CLARA: Well, my girl . . . what's in store for you? He's left you . . . you always knew he would leave you . . . what is there now, my girl . . . except time? . . . [*She covers her face with her hands.*]

[ALYSEA *comes in from the bedroom with a beautiful lace shawl.* CLARA *quickly recovers and looks at the shawl.*]

ALYSEA: Look . . . isn't it beautiful . . . a duende[8] design.

CLARA: Andalucian?

ALYSEA: Yes . . . Josefa copied it!

CLARA: Superb!

[ALYSEA *drapes it over one shoulder and claps it on* CLARA'*s waist.*]

CLARA: Oh, thank you . . . but . . . these days I need the right lights . . . not all things are kind to me anymore . . . Yes, it is beautiful. . . . [*She turns and contemplates* ALYSEA.] Look at you . . . you are so young . . . your beauty so sharp . . . only yesterday, my dear, only yesterday, I was young like you . . . mark that well!

[JOSEFA *comes in through the outside door.* CLARA *sees her. She goes to* JOSEFA *and kisses her cheek.*]

CLARA: I missed you this morning . . . you didn't come.

JOSEFA: Didn't I tell you? . . . there's a million things to do before tomorrow.

CLARA: The shawl . . . it's beautiful . . . only Josefa!

JOSEFA: [*Surveying her handiwork.*] The design . . . the delicacy against the dark dress . . . it is impressive . . . you wear it well. [*She notices that* CLARA *is somewhat too gay; a little bit unsteady.*]

ALYSEA: Shall I get the combs?

CLARA: Combs?

JOSEFA: Mantilla combs . . . made by the gypsies. . . .

CLARA: To go with the gown.

ALYSEA: I'll get them. [*She walks back to the bedroom.* JOSEFA *looks at* CLARA, *realizing what the matter is.*]

JOSEFA: You must have started early. . . .

CLARA: What? [*She busies herself at the mirror.*] You worry too much . . . just a little courage . . . I needed a little courage. . . .

8. Elf.

JOSEFA: Eduardo?

CLARA: [*Turns and faces* JOSEFA; *pain in her eyes.*] He loves her.

JOSEFA: I know. . . .

CLARA: You see . . . I needed a little courage this morning.

JOSEFA: If you start again . . . promise me you won't!

CLARA: [*With false gaiety.*] I promise! [*She closes her eyes.*] I wish . . . I wish I were young for one day . . . just one day . . . so he would love me the way I love him.

JOSEFA: Men don't love . . . they take . . . haven't you learned that by now?

CLARA: Oh, Josefa . . . you are wrong . . . you are wrong . . . a woman was made to love a man . . . to love is enough for a woman . . . if only they would let us love them without negating, without negating. . . .

JOSEFA: Why, Clara? Why must you give . . . so easily? Not to them . . . Clara . . . not to men!

CLARA: [*Shrugs.*] My downfall? [*In a whisper.*] My life?

JOSEFA: Here . . . enough of that . . . there are beautiful things to love. . . .

[ALYSEA *returns with the combs. She hands them to* JOSEFA, *who goes to* CLARA *and expertly places them in her hair.*]

CLARA: Without mantilla?

JOSEFA: It would be too much with the shawl. . . .

CLARA: Yes . . . of course . . . you're right . . . a gypsy with majesty!

ALYSEA: Yes . . . That's what you look like . . . a gypsy queen.

JOSEFA: El espíritu duende. . . .

CLARA: Like your magicians?

JOSEFA: Perhaps. . . .

[*The church bell rings midday; suddenly two swallows are seen outside the window.*]

ALYSEA: Look!

JOSEFA: They're coming . . . the advance guard . . . every year.

CLARA: You love them . . . don't you? . . . your magicians let you find so many things to love . . . lucky . . . lucky Josefa.

JOSEFA: The swallows are safe here . . . after the long, long, lonely flight. . . .

CLARA: Lonely? . . . they come in droves. . . .

[*The three look outside the window for a minute. Choir practice begins.*]

JOSEFA: Look at the lake . . . it shimmers with love . . . [*Turns to Clara.*] I said lonely, Clara, because finding direction . . . is lonely . . . it is too personal a thing. . . .

CLARA: I see what you mean . . . Josefa [*Looks out the window pensively.*] why don't I see the love shimmering in your lake?

[JOSEFA *smiles.*]

ALYSEA: Her magicians . . . isn't it, Josefa?

JOSEFA: Yes . . . my magicians.

## ACT II

*It is early afternoon of the same day.* JOSEFA *comes through the outside door. There is a small injured bird in her hands. She cradles it gently and examines it.*

JOSEFA: You poor little thing . . . a broken wing . . . don't worry, you'll be fine in a little while . . . [*She puts the soft piece of life against her cheek.*] There will be no second pain . . . Alysea!

ALYSEA: [*Comes in through the kitchen door.*] Yes?

JOSEFA: Look . . . I found it in the garden . . . it lay there . . . small, helpless . . . look, he's thirsty . . . quick get some water and an eye-dropper.

[ALYSEA *goes into the bedroom.* JOSEFA *sits in her rocking chair and places the bird gently on her lap. . . .* ALYSEA *comes back with a cup and an eye-dropper.* JOSEFA *picks up the bird, fills the eye-dropper and patiently feeds the bird water. The bird drinks.*]

JOSEFA: See . . . oh, he has life . . . this one!

ALYSEA: Just a baby . . . let us set the wing . . . I'll get some small twigs and a bandage. . . .

[*She leaves again;* JOSEFA *continues feeding the bird.*]

JOSEFA: How did you find the bird-house . . . eh? My magicians must have led you here . . . before the others . . . every year . . . the sky is black with their wings . . . here they rest . . . and eat . . . you will be safe . . . until you join your brothers and sisters . . . yes. . . .

[ALYSEA *comes back; together they carefully set the small wing.*]

JOSEFA: There!

ALYSEA: Let's put him in the bird-house . . . he's tired. . . .

[JOSEFA *kisses the bird; then both of them go to the window, lean out to the tree, and place the bird in the tree house. Satisfied,* JOSEFA *and* ALYSEA *look at each other.* JOSEFA *reaches out and begins to stroke* ALYSEA's *hair.*]

JOSEFA: [*Softly.*] We share so much . . . just wait . . . the magicians will come to you . . . I know. . . .

ALYSEA: What?

JOSEFA: Remember how much you wished for the magicians?

ALYSEA: No . . . no . . . I don't want them anymore. . . .

JOSEFA: But. . . .

ALYSEA: When you brought me here . . . all that's happened . . . it is so unreal . . . a year of mists and deep sinking dreams . . . but not any more!

JOSEFA: Hush . . . you're just upset . . . that's all. . . .

ALYSEA: No . . . last night . . . no . . . never again. . . .

JOSEFA: Poor little girl . . . you've tired yourself out all morning . . . I forgot . . . I don't know why . . . but I just forgot about . . . about last night.

ALYSEA: [*Looking at her with horror.*] Josefa . . . no! Forgot? How could you.

JOSEFA: [*Becoming slightly agitated.*] Habit . . . to keep strong . . . since I was little . . . to keep strong . . . I put ugliness away.

ALYSEA: Where? Where?

JOSEFA: What do you mean?

ALYSEA: If you have a conscience . . . where could you put it away?

JOSEFA: There will be atonement. . . .

ALYSEA: No. . . . that's impossible . . . you think . . . it will . . . disappear? The blood . . . the knife . . . [*She runs to the table where she had placed the knife.*] Look . . . I'll show you . . . you make it disappear! [*She opens the drawer and stares unbelievingly.*] The knife . . . it's gone! [*She begins to look frantically everywhere.*] Did you hear me?

[JOSEFA *seems almost unaware of* ALYSEA's *frenzy.*]

JOSEFA: Yes . . . of course. . . .

[ALYSEA *begins to look again and this time finds the money box gone.*]

ALYSEA: The money box . . . it's gone too.

JOSEFA: Tomás . . . of course . . . he took the money and the knife.

[ALYSEA *collapses into a chair and covers her face with her hands.* TOMÁS's *voice is heard singing a barrio love song;* ALYSEA *looks up in fright.* JOSEFA *goes to the door of the kitchen and calls out into the patio behind the kitchen.*]

JOSEFA: Tomás! Come in here. . . .

[TOMÁS *comes into the kitchen still singing. He walks into the room.* JOSEFA *watches him warily.* ALYSEA *in terror.*]

TOMÁS: Well . . . well . . . Did you call me, querida? [*He strokes* JOSEFA's *arm intimately. She breaks away.*]

JOSEFA: Don't you ever put your hands on me!

TOMÁS: Ha! ha! ha! . . . Doña Perfecta . . . [*He looks around the room.*] You know . . . I think I'll move over here . . . I like this house . . . ah! . . . it is time I had a little elegance in my life . . . yes. [*He sprawls out in a chair.*]

JOSEFA: You've been drinking. . . .

TOMÁS: Yes . . . I have been drinking . . . and I shall drink some more . . . you can afford it. . . .

[ALYSEA *begins to cry.*]

TOMÁS: What's the matter with her?

JOSEFA: She is tired . . . and I . . . have had enough of your insolence. . . .

TOMÁS: Que maravilla[9] . . . How long . . . Josefa . . . how long . . . can you keep it up? [*He paces in front of her; she remains calm.*]

9. Amazing.

TOMÁS: [*Practically shouting in her face.*] I took the knife! Do you understand . . . I took the knife! . . . aren't you afraid, Josefa?

[ALYSEA *begins to cry desperately.* JOSEFA *goes to her. She tries to comfort her.*]

JOSEFA: Don't, Alysea . . . remember . . . it's late . . . we have to pack for David . . . he'll need his things in the hospital . . . compose yourself . . . Why don't you go and start packing . . . I'll talk to Tomás.

[ALYSEA *nods her head in agreement; she rises and leaves as if she wanted escape.*]

JOSEFA: [*Turns and faces* TOMÁS.] Have you ever . . . have you ever . . . done anything kind for anybody?
TOMÁS: [*Sarcastically.*] No . . . just you . . . querida . . . you are the angel. . . .
JOSEFA: All right . . . what do you intend to do?
TOMÁS: Nothing . . . you see . . . we . . . you and I . . . must have a clearer understanding . . . I know much more than you think . . . about you and [*Nods towards bedroom.*] her!
JOSEFA: [*Stiffens.*] All right . . . you win . . . I'll give you money. . . .
TOMÁS: No more crumbs . . . dear niece . . . I call the play . . . from now on.
JOSEFA: You're bluffing . . . lying . . . as usual.
TOMÁS: Am I?

[*There is a knock at the door; with alacrity* TOMÁS *springs up and goes to the door and opens it. It is* DON ESQUINAS, CLARA's *husband.*]

TOMÁS: Ah . . . Don Esquinas, won't you come in?

[DON ESQUINAS *brushes past* TOMÁS, *totally ignoring him.* TOMÁS *makes a mock gesture of humility.*]

DON ESQUINAS: Josefa . . . the worst has happened . . . I warned you!
JOSEFA: [*Placing her hands on her heart.*] Clara . . . let me go to her. [*She starts to go;* DON ESQUINAS *stops her.*]
DON ESQUINAS: It's too late. . . .
JOSEFA: [*Savagely.*] It isn't . . . I can take care of her.
DON ESQUINAS: How? By giving her more drink . . . you've done enough harm. . . .
JOSEFA: Harm? I have been her sole companion for years . . . I have suffered with her . . . nursed her . . . Harm?
DON ESQUINAS: Do you know how I found my wife this afternoon when I got home? She was lying in bed . . . stark naked . . . screaming about crawling . . . crawling, dark . . . she slashed everything in sight . . . broke the mirror . . . there were bottles . . . everywhere. . . .
JOSEFA: My poor, poor darling. . . .
DON ESQUINAS: I . . . the servants . . . we were helpless . . . it was dreadful . . . she kept screaming and sobbing that your magicians had . . . had no faces. . . .

JOSEFA: She's so alone. . . .

DON ESQUINAS: Your lies . . . the liquor and your lies . . . both supplied by you! I'm taking her to the sanitorium . . . this time for good.

JOSEFA: She is so alone. . . .

DON ESQUINAS: Stop saying that! You . . . you supplied her with liquor. . . .

JOSEFA: All that unhappiness . . . she is so lost . . . there was nothing else . . . She promised me this afternoon.

DON ESQUINAS: Promised? You stupid woman . . . you know she wouldn't keep the promise. . . .

JOSEFA: [*Suddenly in anger.*] I tell you . . . you won't listen . . . you men never listen . . . all she had was hopelessness. . . .

DON ESQUINAS: You don't know what you are talking about . . . she always had everything . . . since the day she was born . . . never, never did she have to lift a finger . . . anything she desires. . . .

JOSEFA: Except her husband!

DON ESQUINAS: What in damnation?

JOSEFA: She wanted you to love her. . . .

DON ESQUINAS: Love her? You women are insane! I married her . . . didn't I?

JOSEFA: She knew all about your . . . your women. . . .

DON ESQUINAS: That is a man's way! You have no right to question . . . Tell me, how much liquor did you give her? When did you give it to her?

[JOSEFA *remains silent.*]

DON ESQUINAS: Well?

JOSEFA: She wanted a baby. . . .

DON ESQUINAS: Nonsense! We settled that long ago . . . that was past and forgotten. . . .

JOSEFA: No . . . it was never forgotten . . . she cried every night. . . .

DON ESQUINAS: Silly tears of a drunken woman . . . adopt a baby . . . a baby not of the Esquinas blood? For my heir? Absurd!

JOSEFA: [*Bitterly.*] Which of your bastards are you going to choose as your heir?

DON ESQUINAS: You ungrateful peasant . . . let me tell you . . . you influenced her too much . . . this is probably all your fault . . . I don't want you around the hacienda now that she is gone . . . do you hear?

[JOSEFA *turns her back on him;* DON ESQUINAS *is somewhat at a loss. Her calm toward his anger is disconcerting. He stands for a moment, then, he walks out of the room. On his way out,* TOMÁS *follows him, still assuming a pose of mock humility.*]

TOMÁS: It is terrible, Don Esquinas, what my niece has done . . . if I can make up for it in any way . . . please call on me. . . .

[DON ESQUINAS *ignores him and leaves.* TOMÁS *turns to* JOSEFA.]

TOMÁS: See what you have done to your friend . . . the wife of our Don?

[JOSEFA *too ignores him.* TOMÁS's *attitude of humility is now gone. His attitude is again cunning and sly. He walks up to* JOSEFA.]

TOMÁS: Tch, tch, tch . . . Doña Perfecta is not perfecta . . . eh?

JOSEFA: [*Not listening to him.*] She's gone . . . the light of my magicians never came to her . . . poor, poor lost child.

TOMÁS: You are insane about those magicians. [JOSEFA *walks away from him;* TOMÁS *grabs her arm angrily.*] I'm sick and tired of you ignoring me! You think I'm scum? I don't matter . . . do I? Well, you listen. Doña Perfecta, you listen to me!

JOSEFA: [*Waits silently for him to let go of her arm. When he does, she touches her temples with her fingertips.*] I have a headache. . . .

TOMÁS: None of your tricks . . . listen to me! I saw you . . . do you hear . . . I saw you. Last San Lorenzo's Day, I remember. I left the fiesta . . . I was too drunk; I walked toward the lake . . . I remember, it was a clear, clear night; the moon lighted everything . . . as I came near the lake past the back of this house . . . I saw two figures come from the water's edge . . . they ran . . . one caught up with the other! [*He watches her maliciously and intently wishing to get a reaction; her surface is still calm as he scrutinizes her face.*]

JOSEFA: What are you trying to do?

TOMÁS: [*Laughing slyly and triumphantly.*] It was you and the girl . . . you and the girl . . . wasn't it? Now . . . I begin to put things together . . . it all fits!

JOSEFA: Your drunken hallucinations. . . .

TOMÁS: I know better, reina del barrio[1] . . . you are a. . . .

JOSEFA: If you have nothing else to threaten me with. . . . [*She walks away from him with disdain.*]

TOMÁS: [*Practically screaming with exasperation.*] You think you can always win, with your calm; you're not made of stone . . . you'll break, milady . . . I'll be back. Inside you're trembling with fear. . . .

[*She turns abruptly and faces him haughtily.* TOMÁS *falters first; he turns and leaves. As* JOSEFA *looks after him,* ALYSEA *comes from the bedroom wearing street clothes.*]

JOSEFA: [*Turns and sees her.*] Finished?

ALYSEA: Yes, I'm ready.

JOSEFA: [*Walks up to her and puts her arm around her.*] The ride will do you good; after you come back from the hospital . . . after you see my little David, we'll have supper here . . . then, we can have one of our little chats.

ALYSEA: [*Gently breaks away from Josefa.*] I'm not coming back.

---

1. Queen of the barrio.

JOSEFA: Not coming back?

ALYSEA: I meant to tell you earlier . . . I'm going away with Eduardo.

JOSEFA: Because of what happened last night?

ALYSEA: Many reasons, but mostly because I want to be with him.

JOSEFA: You are like all the rest . . . you insist on being a useless, empty sacrifice!

ALYSEA: I love him.

JOSEFA: Love him? Tell me, how long will your precious Eduardo love you? [*Pause.*] You know who was here? Don Esquinas! Clara drank herself insane because your Eduardo left her. What do you think he'll do to you?

ALYSEA: I can't believe that . . . there's more to love.

JOSEFA: [*Ironically and bitterly.*] Love! Remember the brothel? No different . . . you choose darkness . . . all your pains are still to come! Haven't I taught you anything?

ALYSEA: It all fell apart . . . last night. All I can remember are David's eyes. [*She breaks down sobbing.*]

JOSEFA: He'll be all right . . . I'll take care of my little love . . . as long as he lives. . . .

ALYSEA: His eyes told me. You and I were all the terror in the world.

JOSEFA: No . . . the terror is in the world out there . . . don't say that!

ALYSEA: The violence . . . the useless violence. . . .

JOSEFA: I forbid you to go on like this. [*She walks to the window and reaches into the bird house until she finds the crippled bird. She picks it up; fondles him and holds him against her cheek.*]

JOSEFA: [*With eyes closed.*] Remember how he came . . . crippled, starved, half dead?

ALYSEA: The way I came?

JOSEFA: It will be safe here and happy; you have always been safe and happy! We have so much, Alysea.

[ALYSEA *remains silent.*]

JOSEFA: You know why I built the bird-house? [*She seems to be remembering something painful; she goes to the rocking chair; places the bird on her lap and strokes it gently.*] When I was seven . . . the swallows came . . . they came one hot dry dawn . . . and continued all day . . . on the edge of the desert that still hotter afternoon . . . I saw noisy boys with desert time on their hands . . . playing . . . I watched the playing become a violence . . . they were catching birds . . . now it became a killing . . . they stoned them . . . plucked them . . . laughing with a fearful joy . . . the sand was a sea of dead birds . . . I . . . I . . . couldn't stand it . . . I ran . . . I hit them . . . I said, "Stop! Stop!" [*Pause.*] They laughed; then for a joke . . . for a joke they said . . . they held me down, the burning sand against my back . . . In spite of all my terror, I opened my eyes . . . a boy . . . a big boy . . . held a swallow over me; he took a knife

. . . cut the bird . . . Oh, God! so much blood . . . all that blood. [JOSEFA *strokes the bird gently and shakes her head, closes her eyes.*] It spilled . . . spilled into my face . . . ran into my mouth . . . warm . . . warm . . . salt warm . . . was it my tears? the blood? [*She stands and goes to the window still with the bird; she caresses the bird with her cheek and places it gently in the bird house. The rosary bell begins to toll. It is sunset. JOSEFA looks out in silence.*] Alysea . . . look, the lake is screaming with life . . . look . . . the colors of love . . . then . . . the day went . . . [*She turns to ALYSEA.*] Out there . . . the beauty is lost in fears . . . what do you expect out there? Stay with the radiance . . . Alysea, stay with me?

ALYSEA: I won't be coming back.

[ALYSEA *turns and leaves, going into the bedroom; JOSEFA looks after her for a moment; seems to start after ALYSEA, then changes her mind. She turns to the unfinished damask; she unhooks the needle and begins to work on it in deep concentration. ALYSEA returns with a suitcase. JOSEFA does not look up although she is aware of ALYSEA. ALYSEA comes close to JOSEFA rather hesitantly. JOSEFA looks up and smiles.*]

JOSEFA: [*In a casual tone.*] Look . . . do you think I ought to give the design a name? I saw it in a dream the other night . . . so vivid! Perhaps I should call it "Swallow Song." What do you think?

ALYSEA: [*Looking intently at the design over JOSEFA's shoulder.*] It looks like flowing grain . . . with . . . with a streak of lightning . . . so well intermingled . . . how strange! . . . beauty and terror as one . . . see? [*She traces the pattern with her finger.*]

JOSEFA: How foolish of you . . . that is not lightning . . . it is . . . it is sweet rain.

[ALYSEA *looks intently at the pattern, then at JOSEFA.*]

ALYSEA: [*Softly.*] Lovely Josefa . . . no, no . . . you could never see the lightning . . . only your gentle lights. [*She picks up her suitcase and starts to leave.*] Goodbye, sweet lady of light!

[JOSEFA *looks up but does not answer. ALYSEA moves toward the outside door.*]

JOSEFA: [*As if in afterthought.*] Alysea?
ALYSEA: Yes?
JOSEFA: On the way . . . please stop by the rectory . . . will you? Tell Father Prado I cannot make rosary tonight. Tell him . . . if he would be so kind . . . to come later this evening. . . .
ALYSEA: Of course.

[*She hesitates for a moment, as if at a loss for words. Then with one last look of love for JOSEFA and the room, she departs. After ALYSEA leaves, JOSEFA continues putting the final stitches on the damask.*]

JOSEFA: There! finished . . . another birth of light! [*She stands and stretches as if very tired. She rubs the back of her neck and breathes deep. She goes to the window again. It is now dark.*] My lover! You look morning crystal in the water . . . so still . . . so deep . . . I ache for you so! You beckon me shamelessly. . . . [*She stands at the window as the curtain drops for Act II.*]

## ACT III

*Late the same evening. The church bells are announcing the end of rosary.* JOSEFA *is sitting in her rocking chair saying her prayer beads. Every so often she pauses in thought. There is a knock at the door.* JOSEFA *rises and goes to the door.* FATHER PRADO *enters.*

FATHER PRADO: [*Kissing her on the cheek.*] My dear . . . how are you this evening? We missed you at rosary . . . you always lead prayer with the confidence of an angel . . . a hundred things to do before tomorrow . . . eh?

JOSEFA: It's good to see you! [*She leads him by the arm to a settee.*]

FATHER PRADO: Tell me . . . can I help with anything?

JOSEFA: You are here . . . that is more than enough.

FATHER PRADO: You must give me a chance . . . you do so much for the church, for me . . . now let me do something for you.

JOSEFA: Father . . . you are my kindred spirit . . . the oasis in the middle of the desert.

FATHER PRADO: You spoil me. . . .

JOSEFA: I finished the boys' surplices for tomorrow. . . .

FATHER PRADO: See what I mean? Your lovely little hands [*Kisses them.*] produce such lovely wondrous things for us . . . [*Looks around.*] And this place! A sanctuary . . . who would think? To find such a place as this in our desert barrio? Ah . . . all things and all people here are too mindful of the desert . . . except you.

JOSEFA: My magicians, Father!

FATHER PRADO: [*In jest.*] Of course, your magicians!

JOSEFA: I wonder if you take me seriously? Come . . . would you like some coffee? tea?

FATHER PRADO: No . . . no, it is late; I ate too much at supper . . . I tell myself every night it seems . . . but I go on eating just the same.

JOSEFA: The way you work for the barrio people! Every church festival is such a chore for you . . . you work yourself to death. . . .

FATHER PRADO: So do you!

JOSEFA: We can't help it . . . can we, Father? You love the people as much as I do.

FATHER PRADO: It means so much to them . . . these festivals . . . they are just ritual to you . . . aren't they?

JOSEFA: Maybe . . . but what blossoms from the barrio people because of the festival . . . that is not ritual . . . there is a rebirth . . . they come to life for a little while.

FATHER PRADO: Tomorrow will be very special for them . . . a day to honor their Josefa. Such a legend you are!

JOSEFA: If it makes them happy.

FATHER PRADO: [*Looks at her intently.*] Are you feeling all right? You look a little pale . . . of course! How stupid of me . . . so many things have been happening today . . . even in the rectory life seeps in. . . .

JOSEFA: You know about Clara?

FATHER PRADO: Unfortunate . . . pobrecita[2] . . . such a beautiful child.

JOSEFA: She won't be coming back this time. [*She begins to cry softly. She brushes a tear from her cheek.*]

FATHER PRADO: There . . . there, don't cry! [*Comforts her.*] I know how you feel . . . you two were so close . . . she depended on you so!

JOSEFA: When life is a farce. . . .

FATHER PRADO: In her own way . . . there was so much meaning . . . Alysea has found something special too . . . she and Eduardo stopped by the rectory.

JOSEFA: One by one . . . like leaves from a tree. . . .

FATHER PRADO: I know! Then . . . the terrible thing . . . I heard in the village . . . the terrible thing that happened to David . . . I hope they catch. . . .

JOSEFA: [*Interrupts violently.*] Father!

FATHER PRADO: What is it, child?

JOSEFA: May I have confession now?

FATHER PRADO: [*Puzzled.*] Here?

JOSEFA: Please, Father!

FATHER PRADO: Of course, if that's what you want. . . . [*He comes near her; as he does, she falls to her knees and leans her head against his body.*] What is wrong?

JOSEFA: Forgive me, Father, for I have sinned. . . . [FATHER *remains silent.*] I have sinned . . . I have sinned. . . .

FATHER PRADO: God forgives. . . .

JOSEFA: Oh, Father . . . I'm lost! I'm lost. . . .

FATHER PRADO: All of us . . . at one time. . . .

JOSEFA: I am guilty of grievous sins . . . they are beyond forgiveness . . . people will judge them so! Father . . . before I tell you . . . you must know . . . I do not feel sorry . . . I want . . . I need . . . the calm . . . to keep things as they are.

[FATHER *simply nods his head.*]

JOSEFA: David was hurt last night . . . I lied about the intruder. There was no intruder . . . I was the one.

2. Poor little one.

FATHER PRADO: [*Incredulously.*] You . . . did that to David?

JOSEFA: Yes . . . [*She braces herself as if to accept the fact.*] I did that to David.

FATHER PRADO: I can't believe it . . . you! Not you!

JOSEFA: Me, Father, Me!

FATHER PRADO: It was inhuman. . . .

JOSEFA: Oh, Father! I . . . I don't know . . . why? why?

FATHER PRADO: Tell me, my child, there must have been a reason. . . .

JOSEFA: Last night . . . last night . . . after supper . . . David helped Alysea and me put the last touches on the bird house. David was so excited . . . [*Pause.*] The moon . . . the reflection of diamonds on the lake . . . life . . . all were too much for me . . . I was overflowing . . . I felt the sweetness of the night with every fiber . . . every fiber . . . [*Lost in memory; then she resumes her story.*] David didn't want to go to bed . . . he insisted on staying up all night to wait for the swallows . . . Of course I said, "No!" He left for bed reluctantly . . . [*Pause.*] Father?

FATHER PRADO: Yes?

JOSEFA: Have you ever felt as if you were one total yearning . . . it roars and spills. . . .

[FATHER PRADO *remains silent.*]

JOSEFA: Alysea and I are lovers.

FATHER PRADO: What?

JOSEFA: A year ago tonight we became lovers . . . if you remember she had been with me for some months before San Lorenzo's Day . . . she was something new in my life . . . she felt and responded to my every mood . . . my every act . . . Oh! To have someone in your life! I had repulsed all the men in the barrio . . . the coarseness! The taking! No . . . no . . . I could never surrender to that . . . but when she came, she filled my life in so many ways . . . so many ways . . . it was natural that the yearning grow for more . . . the body too is master . . . .

FATHER PRADO: Yes, my child, of course it is!

JOSEFA: A year ago I took Alysea to the lake on the eve of San Lorenzo . . . She had heard about the Bathing of the Virgins at noon the next day . . . Could she go . . . she asked! I was angry . . . I knew all the hope . . . all the dreams of those girls would turn to jagged violence . . . it was a lie . . . The whole ritual is a lie!

FATHER PRADO: No . . . no, Josefa . . . to those girls the dream of a perfect love is true as long as it gives meaning to their lives. . . .

JOSEFA: I know what men are!

[FATHER PRADO *remains silent.*]

JOSEFA: I told her . . . go with me when the moon comes out . . . when the lake waits for just me . . . it is my lover! [*Pause.*] She believed me . . . It is true, Father . . . the lake is my lover. . . .

FATHER PRADO: Oh, my child!

JOSEFA: We bathed . . . and then . . . it happened . . . [*Pause.*] Last night after David went to bed . . . I felt the nymph magic . . . I took Alysea . . . Suddenly . . . there was David . . . in the middle of the room. The horror in his eyes . . . Why? Why? There was horror in his eyes. . . .

FATHER PRADO: He did not understand. . . .

JOSEFA: Oh, Father! Now . . . I can see why . . . now! But . . . last night . . . it was not the Josefa he loved that David saw . . . I could not stand what he saw! I could not!

FATHER PRADO: God forgive you!

JOSEFA: Something happened in me . . . I don't know what it was . . . I ran . . . I ran into the kitchen and found a kitchen knife . . . Somehow . . . somehow I knew David would tell . . . the barrio people would look at me that way too. . . .

FATHER PRADO: I never thought you would care about what people. . . .

JOSEFA: Oh, Father . . . until last night I never knew my fears . . . I went back to where Alysea was holding the frightened child . . . then . . . then I made Alysea hold him tight . . . Father, it was not her fault! There have been so many furies in her life . . . she drowned in my agony . . . she trusted me . . . what else could she do? [*She goes to the window, looks out at the lake for a moment.*] Father . . . look . . . come look at the lake . . . maybe you can understand the power it has over me . . . Look. . . .

[FATHER PRADO *goes somewhat reluctantly to the window. He also looks out, but remains silent.*]

JOSEFA: I took the knife and cut David's tongue. . . .

FATHER PRADO: Jesucristo, perdona a tu hija. . . .[3]

JOSEFA: I was silencing the world from reprimand . . . I knew I had to silence the world from reprimand . . . I felt no guilt . . . all I knew . . . the life I had . . . the faith of the barrio people . . . this house of light . . . must be preserved . . . I silenced all reprimand with my terrible deed . . . [*She covers her face for a moment. Then, she gathers strength and continues talking.*] With the light of day . . . I knew better . . . others had not my eyes . . . others had not my eyes . . . others had not my reasons . . . or my magicians . . . [*She looks at* FATHER PRADO *intently.*] Can you ever understand?

FATHER PRADO: [*As if talking to himself.*] I don't understand . . . I don't understand why I didn't see . . . detect what was happening to you. . . .

JOSEFA: [*Puzzled.*] Happening to me?

FATHER PRADO: All your beauty . . . your calm . . . your giving was . . . your talent . . . what a splended canopy for the twisted fears of so many years . . . so many years . . . I'm an old fool . . . forgive me, my daughter, I

3. (Praying) Jesus Christ, forgive your daughter.

have never really seen you . . . I pride myself in knowing you so well
. . . I claimed I loved you . . . how blind . . . how blind. . . .

JOSEFA: Don't blame yourself, Father . . . I am what you see . . . that is
really what I am . . . Not what you discovered this moment. . . .

FATHER PRADO: My poor, poor child. . . .

JOSEFA: No . . . Father . . . don't pity me . . . anything but that! That is one
thing I shall never suffer. . . .

FATHER PRADO: I have never seen you cry . . . Josefa . . . until tonight. . . .

JOSEFA: The past . . . the dark gnawing . . . such hungers! I must not be a
desert . . . now they are harmless ghosts. . . .

FATHER PRADO: Are they?

JOSEFA: You don't understand . . . do you?

FATHER PRADO: I want to. . . .

JOSEFA: The magicians created "me!" . . . the blight of meniality never touched
me . . . The magicians gave me the purity of light . . . and the wisp of
beauties at my fingertips . . . so . . . I really am . . . what you always
thought I was. . . .

FATHER PRADO: There is so much God in you! . . .

JOSEFA: God in me? . . . no, Father, . . . no . . . I failed goodness . . . I
wanted, I prayed . . . to save my soul as the church instructed . . . as
your faith believed. . . .

FATHER PRADO: [*Somewhat taken aback.*] But . . . you are the most pious . . .
the most constant . . . in the barrio . . . Faith shines in you . . . all the
beauty you create. . . .

JOSEFA: Faith? Oh, no, Father . . . no . . . It was not faith, it was the light
of my magicians . . . I bear the children of light! I am its high priest-
ess. . . .

FATHER PRADO: I . . . I . . .

[*He can't go on; he sits down and places his head in his hands.* JOSEFA *looks at
him and is full of concern. She goes to comfort him.*]

JOSEFA: [*She says this as if she does not believe it herself.*] Don't grieve for me,
Father . . . for what I have done, I am willing to atone . . . David will
be my whole life . . . I will create beauty for him . . . for you . . . for
the barrio people . . . longings will fade away with commitment . . .
Father . . . Father. [*She kneels in front of him.*] Forgive me, Father, for I
have sinned . . . I have grievously sinned.

FATHER PRADO: [*With tears in his eyes . . . He strokes her hair in silence.*]


## Final Scene

*Dawn the next morning; the sitting room is a pastel paradise; there is life in the bird
house, a roar of bird sounds;* JOSEFA *comes from the bedroom with a white gown over
her arm. It is the gown to be worn at the procession. She goes to the window and looks
at the tree with great happiness.*

JOSEFA: I waited for you . . . before dawn I heard the flurry of the sea . . .
oh, what a sight you were over my burning lake . . . straight . . . straight
. . . you came to me . . . to this temple of peace . . . no more songs of
pain for you. . . .

[*Church bells sound morning vigil. The procession will follow in the freshness of
the early morning.* JOSEFA *remembers the barrio world.*]

JOSEFA: My day . . . my day . . . but, oh my people! . . . it was not meant
to be shared with you . . . my day was planned by my magicians . . .
long before you planned this one for me . . . I must get ready. . . . [*She
goes behind the screen; puts on her gown, comes back and looks in the mirror. Her
dress is white. She looks unusually young and beautiful. All of a sudden she
touches her rather severe hair-do. Then she lets down her hair.*]

JOSEFA: [*Looking at herself intently in the mirror.*] Yes . . . yes . . . this way . . .
there is a wildness in me . . . [*She laughs in joyous delirium. Then she becomes
the usual* JOSEFA *for a moment. She remembers the boys' surplices. She goes to the
wardrobe and takes them out. She lays them carefully over a chair.*] There . . .
something of me will be at the procession . . . yes, even that . . . the
boys will find them here . . . . [*She takes a final look in the mirror, then she
goes to the window and looks out to the lake.*] So still your water . . . but I
know your passions underneath . . . deep . . . deep . . . for all time . . .
Hush! I'm coming. . . . [*As she turns to leave, she touches the lace, the damask
now finished, the fresh flowers on the table . . . with love . . . with a tender
regret . . . but a secret within her. . . .*] My magicians will let me come
back as light . . . yes, yes! [*She goes to the door and gives the room one final
glance.*]

JOSEFA: [*In a whisper.*] Wait for me. . . .

[*Church bells begin to toll for the gathering of the procession. Voices are heard
outside the window.*]

VOICES: "Here! the starting will be here . . . in front of Josefa's garden." "Has
anyone seen Josefa this morning?"

[*The sitting room seems alive even without people; then, two boys enter. They
have come for the surplices.*]

1ST BOY: Hey . . . look . . . they're over there. [*Each of the boys takes one. . . .*]
2ND BOY: Aren't they something . . . grand . . . like at the cathedral. . . .
1ST BOY: That's what he said. . . .
2ND BOY: Who said?
1ST BOY: Father Prado . . . he said Josefa was like a Cathedral. . . .
2ND BOY: 'Cause she makes all this grand stuff?
1ST BOY: I guess so . . . 'cause she's different . . . don't you think?
2ND BOY: Ah . . . ha! She made all the altar linen. . . .
1ST BOY: Yeah . . . Father Prado said she was like the silence of the cathedral
. . . and you know those glass-stained windows?

2ND BOY: Yeah. . . .

1ST BOY: That's her soul. . . .

2ND BOY: You think something is wrong with Father Prado?

[*They laugh in jest; shove each other around in horse play, then stop when the church bells ring again.*]

1ST BOY: Hey, come on . . . the procession is going to start. . . .

[*The room is empty again; this time the voices of the choir beginning the procession hymns are heard . . . They are as ethereal as the room. Combined, the room and the voices have a cathedral-like awesomeness.* CLEMENCIA *breaks the atmosphere. She is in her Sunday best.*]

CLEMENCIA: Josefa! . . . Where are you? [*She looks in the bedroom; then, she peeks through the kitchen door.*] Mnnnn . . . where could she be? Everybody's waiting. Josefa! Oh, dear, oh, dear! They've started without her. . . . [*She goes to the window.*] Look at those birds! Every year! . . . they come straight to this tree. Ah . . . God's morning . . . the lake . . . the green pines . . . [*Suddenly something out in the lake catches her eye.*] What is that . . . floating in the lake? Mmmmmmmm . . . looks like a girl dressed in white . . . That's foolish! It is too early for the Bathing of the Virgins, yet . . . yes, wearing clothes? [*As she hears the choir, she loses interest and goes to the mirror and straightens her hat.*]

CLEMENCIA: [*With a sigh.*] Why do we all end up looking like scarecrows? [*She turns to leave and catches sight of the open window.*] I better close the window . . . the room will be covered with birds! [*She goes to the window again; as she starts to close it, she gazes out into the lake again fascinated by what she saw before.*] Yes . . . it is a body! A body floating in the lake . . . I'm sure of it! [*She gasps, but at this moment the church bells ring again. Out of habit, she starts to hurry off, shrugging off what she has seen.*] The sun is too bright . . . it is my imagination! I better hurry . . . what a day this will be. . . .

[*She leaves the room. The voices of the choir, the church bells, the birds on the tree in full life, and the almost unearthly light streaming through the windows give the essence of a presence in the room . . . of something beautiful.*]

## STUDY QUESTIONS

1. What is the annual ritual in the village of Lago de San Lorenzo on their saint's day?

### ACT I

1. Why does Alysea, while she is cleaning the sitting room carpet in scene 1, "[look] at the cloth in her hand intently"?

2. What does the conversation with Clemencia add to your expectations? How does it characterize Josefa? What questions about Alysea's attitude toward Josefa does

it leave in your mind? What contradictory information or feelings do you have about Josefa? Are these clarified or intensified by the first scene between Alysea and Josefa? Can you recall what possibilities ran through your mind about what had happened on the night before the opening scene?

3. What do you make of Josefa's references in this scene to the swallows? to light?

4. Summarize what you know of the CHARACTERS and the situation at the end of this first scene.

5. Explain Josefa's final line (curtain speech) in this scene. What images have been planted in your mind during this scene?

6. Since neither the place nor, except for a few moments, the time has changed since the ending of the first scene, why is scene 2 a separate scene?

7. Eduardo is described as of "mixed heritage"; what does that mean to you? How was Josefa described in the stage directions in scene 1? How does ethnic heritage condition your view of and expectations about the characters? What does Eduardo mean when he describes the room as a room "for women"? What gender STEREOTYPES are suggested? To what extent does the play seem to endorse his stereotypical view? to criticize it? How are the ethnic and sexual stereotypes related?

8. Eduardo says his "God" is in the open, Alysea adds that Eduardo's God is beautiful, "free . . . green," and that Father Prado approves of that God. How is this a commentary on Josefa's room? on gender?

9. Describe how it was that Alysea came to live with Josefa.

10. Josefa has been described as an angel, and Alysea here compares her with Father Prado in her concern for the poor, yet Alysea has, at the end of scene 1, accused her of killing someone named David. There has been talk of gods and rooms for women and the open air. What kind of moral struggles and themes do you see beginning to form in this first act?

11. Who is Clara? What do we learn about her in the conversation between Josefa and Eduardo when they are alone? Has your opinion of Eduardo been changed by this conversation?

12. Josefa says to Eduardo that people out in the lake or among the pines see themselves too well, cannot accept what they see, and "so monsters are created." Explain.

13. How would you play Eduardo in the tête-à-tête with Josefa? Is he flirting with her? trying to impress her? trying to seduce her? simply trying to get her approval of his courting Alysea? To what degree is the decision about how to play his scene here an interpretation of this character?

14. How would you play Josefa in her conversation with Eduardo? Is she defying him and his "male" ways as a feminist? Is she impressed with him despite herself? Is she trying to taunt him? tease him?

15. How does Josefa define what she means by "desire"? Describe her experience out in the lake on the night of the Festival of San Lorenzo.

16. In what way has Josefa given birth to "the children of light"?

17. When, in response to Doña Clara's questions in scene 3, Alysea admits that she loves Eduardo and he her, Doña Clara puts out a cigarette and says, "Well . . . That's that!" What does she mean by the remark?

18. When Alysea leaves them alone, Josefa says to Clara, "You must have started early." What does she mean?

19. What is Clara's view of love? Josefa's?

20. Who or what are Josefa's "magicians"?

21. What does she mean when she says the swallows, even though they are in flocks, are "lonely"?

## ACT II

1. What does Doña Clara mean when she says that Josefa's magicians have no faces?

2. How does Don Esquinas "justify" his philandering?

3. What does Tomás say he saw the night of the previous San Lorenzo Festival?

4. David's eyes, Alysea says, told her that she and Josefa were "all the terror in the world"? What did he—or she—mean by this?

5. Describe Josefa's childhood experience with a bird. Why does she tell Alysea the story at this point?

6. Whom does Josefa address as her lover at the end of the act?

7. What action ends this act?

## ACT III

1. What does Father Prado mean when he says the festival is "just ritual" to Josefa?

2. Why does Josefa confess to Father Prado? What does she confess?

3. What reason does Josefa give for her violence toward David?

4. Why does Father Prado ask Josefa to forgive him?

5. It was not faith that made her create beauty and do good, Josefa says, but "the light of my magicians." But at the end of the act, she asks forgiveness, "for . . . I have grievously sinned." Does this suggest that she has been reunited with her religious faith? What is meant by the stage directions that say what she says here is said "as if she does not believe it herself"? Does she or doesn't she?

## FINAL SCENE

1. What does Josefa mean when she says that her magicians will let her come back as light? that they planned this day for her long before the people did?

2. What does Clemencia see on the lake?

3. Explain the implications of Clemencia's last words; of the final stage direction.

## GENERAL QUESTIONS

1. Is this a feminist play?

2. Is this play "religious"? If so, does it support the Catholic religion? an ancient, "pagan," perhaps Native American religion? both? neither?

3. How do such IMAGES or SYMBOLS as the lake, the swallows, light, function in the play?

# MYTH AND SYMBOL

A MYTH is a communal narrative about the unknown or unknowable, the remote in time or space, the spiritual universe, or our place in that universe. For some, a myth is a fiction: *their* view of the universe is myth; *ours* is a religious truth. For the past century or more, however, many have seen in myths of highly diverse and far-flung cultures an underlying unity. They therefore consider myths each culture's attempt to understand and articulate the same underlying, universal truths. All such attempts, then, are valuable and "true" in one way or another. If nothing else, many believe, myth reveals the way the human mind universally confronts and interprets the mysterious aspects of its surroundings.

A RITUAL—a rite or ceremony in which an act or series of acts is exactly repeated on specific occasions—is, like a myth, communal. It is, indeed, usually part of the communal religion. Sometimes its purpose is to seek some sort of blessing or gift from a Higher Power. In *The Day of the Swallows*, for example, each year on the saint day of San Lorenzo at eleven in the morning, the young women of the village "gather around the lake to wash their hair and bathe in promise of a future husband." Other rituals may involve a confession of sin, often accompanied by a gift or sacrifice to the deity and a plea for forgiveness. In "Bloodshed," for example, there is a lengthy description of the Hebrew ritual of the sacrifice of the goat on the Day of Atonement. As in most rituals, the acts are precisely repeated at precise times and in a precise manner—"Five times on the tenth day of the seventh month, the Day of Atonement, the High Priest changes his vestments, five times he lowers his body into the ritual bath. After the first immersion garments of gold, after the second immersion white linen . . ." and so on.

Ritual is a symbolic representation in action—often including music and words. A SYMBOL at its simplest is something (often something concrete) that stands for something else (often abstract, indefinite, religious). We all know what the Stars and Stripes stand for. Usually symbols, even well-understood ones, are a bit more complex: most of us believe we know what, in a religious context, the cross represents, but in putting its MEANING in words we are likely to get into the area of INTERPRETATION, emphasizing different aspects or using words with slightly different meanings or connotations. The rebbe, in "Bloodshed," admits that there are differences in interpretation of the meaning of certain elements in the ritual of atonement, of the term Azazel, for example: "What the word Azazel means exactly is not known—we call it wilderness, some say it is hell itself, demons live there. But . . . surely the plainest meaning is *instead of*. Wilderness instead of easeful places, hell and devils instead of plenitude, life, peace. Goat instead of man" (paragraph 37).

It is sometimes difficult, especially in a ritual with which we are not familiar, to distinguish when an act, a word, a belief, is meant to be literal and when it is symbolic, something "instead of" something else, a figure of speech or metaphor. The SPEAKER in "The Eagle-Feather Fan" first says, "The eagle is my power," which many will interpret as symbolic (after all, the bald eagle is a symbol of America); then he says, "my fan is an eagle," which secular readers surely interpret to mean that the fan made of eagle feathers represents, symbolizes, stands for, is "instead of," the eagle. But later he says of the fan, "it is real," and the poem/ritual metamorphosizes the speaker's hand with the fan into the eagle itself: "The bones of my hand are fine / And hollow . . . / My hand veers in the thin air / Of the summits." The speaker's hands and fan *actually* turn into an eagle and soar above the mountains, or does he only *believe* he is soaring? Or does he not *really* believe he is, but is representing the flight of the eagle with his hands and fan, they being there "instead of" the eagle itself? Before you answer too readily, think of a ritual or a mystery in your own religion, and ask yourself similar questions; you may find the line between the real and the symbolic or mythic becoming a little shadowy and uncertain.

Though myth and ritual are communal—not the invention or property of the individual, priest or poet—and traditional, even absolutely literal, nonsymbolic beliefs or religious texts seem to require interpretation so that in order to maintain the sense of community, a certain amount of latitude must be allowed. Among Garrison Keillor's Brethren, however, "perfect literalists every one," who therefore believe in reading the Bible in absolutely literal, nonsymbolic terms, schism, or splitting into smaller and smaller groups, is rampant. Keillor tells us that the Cox Brethren split with the Johnson Brethren because the Johnsons believed "that what was abominable to God in the Old Testament must be abominable still" (par. 18), but Mr. Cox held to "the New Covenant of Grace." Keillor wryly reduces the principles to near-absurdity when he recounts the actual issue over which the Brethren split, Johnson's application of the controversial principle to a modern instance: "Mr. Johnson's sermon was against women's slacks, and he had quoted Deuteronomy 22:5, 'The woman shall not wear that which pertaineth unto a man . . .'" (par. 19). His people, the Cox Brethren, walk out. Perhaps it is a function of myth, ritual, and symbol to offer not unyielding principles, but flexible, affective, sensory images and meaning that bind rather than separate.

Though myths and rituals are most often used in a more or less religious and communal context, symbols, though they can be part of ritual or myth and certainly may be religious, may also be literary rather than religious. The literary symbols may be traditional—a rose has often been used by poets to suggest beauty and romance—or it may be invented by the writer. The abalone shell in Mori's story, for example, takes on symbolic meaning though it is not part of a mythic or ritualistic or even literary tradition.

Because it is not part of a preexistent tradition, and because it is complex and particular, the precise meaning of the symbol of the abalone shell may be difficult to paraphrase. That it does, however, have meaning—that it is symbolic—is created and insisted upon by context: something that has such value it controls one's life, something that has indescribable beauty, every example of which is equally beautiful and valuable but different, surely means *something*, either in itself or in the way it is invested with meaning by the mind of the collector of the shells. Here the individual symbol—the shell—seems to be part of a ritual that is not specifically communal (though it was passed on from one man to another) and is certainly not traditional, and, since it suggests something almost religious in its beauty and value, it seems almost to create its own myth. It is because of works like "Abalone, Abalone, Abalone" that "myth" and "ritual" have come to be used as literary terms.

# WRITING
# ABOUT THE READING

## PERSONAL ESSAYS AND NARRATIVES

1. Tell about your experience(s) or your family's in your place of worship.

2. Recount an experience of a ceremony or ritual in a place of worship other than your own.

3. Write about an event or experience that seems to have been or that you believe to have been supernatural.

4. Recount a conflict between you and one or more members of your family involving religion.

## IMITATIONS AND PARODIES

1. Write a parody of "Reins," perhaps as instructions for a young man courting or an expectant father.

2. Write an important scene in "Dominion" from Robert's or Mrs. Poverman's point of view.

3. Parody "Abalone, Abalone, Abalone," perhaps by adding a "y" to each word of the title, perhaps by making the object collected baseball cards or Barbie dolls.

4. Write a final scene for *The Day of the Swallows* or for "Bloodshed" in which the outcome is quite different. Make sure, however, that your ending is true to the earlier part of the work.

## DESCRIPTIVE PAPERS

1. In prose or poetry, describe your place of worship as Rafael Jesús González does.

2. Describe a religious ritual in which you have participated or that you have witnessed; try to do so in such a way that the reader will understand and sympathize with the meaning and emotions involved in the ritual.

## COMPARISON-CONTRAST PAPER

Compare a ritual or service in your religion with another that you have witnessed or with which you are familiar.

## ANALYTICAL PAPERS

1. Analyze the imagery—the swallows, the lake, the light, and so on—in *The Day of the Swallows*.

2. Analyze the use of the supernatural or the apparently supernatural in at least three of the pieces in the chapter—for example, "The Moths," "Summer Water and Shirley," "Reins"—with particular (but not necessarily exclusive) emphasis on to what degree the reader must accept (or deny) the irrational or supernatural in the work.

## ARGUMENTATIVE PAPER

Construct both sides of a debate on one of the following topics: Resolved, that Garrison Keillor is blasphemous and makes fun of his friends and family (or his characters) in "Protestant." Or *The Day of the Swallows* is a feminist (or antifeminist) play.

# ACKNOWLEDGMENTS

Agha Shahid Ali: "Postcard from Kashmir" and "Snowmen." Copyright © 1987 by Shahid Ali Agha. Reprinted from *The Half-Inch Himalayas* by permission of Wesleyan University Press.

Paula Gunn Allen: "Powwow 79, Durango." Published by the American Indian Studies Center, University of California, Los Angeles, copyright © 1984. Reprinted by permission. "Grandmother" from *Coyote's Daylight Trip* (La Confluencia Press: Albuquerque, 1978) by Paula Gunn Allen. Reprinted by permission of author. "Pocahontas to Her English Husband, John Rolfe." Reprinted by permission of author.

Maya Angelou: "My Brother Bailey and Kay Francis" (editors' title) reprinted from *I Know Why the Caged Bird Sings*. Copyright © 1969 by Maya Angelou. Reprinted by permission of Random House, Inc. "The Languages of Home" (editors' title) reprinted from *Gather Together in My Name*. Copyright © 1974 by Maya Angelou. Reprinted by permission of Random House, Inc.

Michael Anthony: "Sandra Street" reprinted from *Cricket in the Road* by Michael Anthony. Reprinted by permission of Andre Deutsch Ltd.

Tony Ardizzone: "My Mother's Stories" reprinted from *The Evening News* by Tony Ardizzone. Copyright © 1986 by the University of Georgia Press. Reprinted by permission of the University of Georgia Press.

Margaret Atwood: "The Man from Mars" from *Dancing Girls* by Margaret Atwood. Copyright © 1977, 1982 by O.W. Toad, Ltd. Reprinted by permission of Simon & Schuster, Inc., and the Canadian Publishers, McClelland and Stewart, Toronto.

Jimmy Santiago Baca: "Ancestor" and "So Mexicans Are Taking Jobs from Americans" reprinted by permission of Louisiana State University Press from *Immigrants in Our Own Land* by Jimmy Santiago Baca. Copyright © 1979 by Jimmy Santiago Baca.

Toni Cade Bambara: "The Lesson" from *Gorilla, My Love* by Toni Cade Bambara. Copyright © 1972 by Toni Cade Bambara. Reprinted by permission of Random House, Inc.

Saul Bellow: "A Silver Dish" from *Him with His Foot in His Mouth and Other Stories* by Saul Bellow. Copyright © 1974, 1978, 1982, 1984 by Saul Bellow Ltd. Reprinted by permission of Harper & Row, Publishers, Inc.

Salli Benedict: "Tahotahontanekentseratkerontakwenhakie." Reprinted by permission of Salli M. K. Benedict, Akwesasne Mohawk.

Neil Bissoondath: "There Are a Lot of Ways to Die" from *Digging Up the Mountains* by Neil Bissoondath. Copyright © 1986 by Neil Bissoondath. All rights reserved. Reprinted by permission of Viking Penguin, Inc.

Clark Blaise: "A Class of New Canadians" from *A North American Education* by Clark Blaise. Copyright © 1973 by Clark Blaise. Reprinted by permission of author.

Peter Blue Cloud: "To-ta Ti-om (for an aunt)." Reprinted by permission from Akwesasne Notes, Mohawk Nation, Roosevelt, NY, 13683.

Michael Blumenthal: "Washington Heights, 1959." Copyright 1980 by Michael Blumenthal. Reprinted by permission of author.

Joseph Bruchac: "Ellis Island." Reprinted by permission of author.

Diane Burns: "Sure You Can Ask Me a Personal Question." Reprinted by permission of author.

Luis Cabalquinto: "Hometown." First appeared in *Breaking Silence*, The Greenfield Review Press. Reprinted by permission of Luis Cabalquinto.

Barbara Cameron: "Gee, You Don't Seem Like an Indian from the Reservation" first appeared in *This Bridge Called My Back, Writings by Radical Women of Color*, Kitchen Table: Women of Color Press. Reprinted by permission of Kitchen Table Press, P.O. Box 908, Latham, NY 12110.

Ana Castillo: "Our Tongue Was Nahuatl." Reprinted by permission of Arte Publico Press.

Virginia Cerenio: "[we who carry the endless seasons]." First appeared in *Breaking Silence*, The Greenfield Review Press. Reprinted by permission of The Greenfield Review Press.

Lorna Dee Cervantes: "Freeway 280." First appeared in *Latin American Literary Review* (Spring–Summer 1977), vol. 5, no. 10. Reprinted by permission of Latin American Literary Review Press. "Heritage." First appeared in *The Americas Review* (1982), vol. 10, no 1–2. University of Houston. Reprinted by permission of Arte Publico Press. "Refugee Ship." Reprinted by permission of Arte Publico Press.

Jeffery Paul Chan: "The Chinese in Haifa." Reprinted by permission of author.

Alice Childress: *Wedding Band*. Copyright © 1973 by Alice Childress. Used by permission of Flora Roberts, Inc.

Michelle Cliff: "If I Could Write This in Fire I Would Write This in Fire" from *The Land of Look Behind* by Michelle Cliff. Copyright © 1985 by Michelle Cliff. Reprinted by permission of author.

Edward Corsi: "I Behold America." From *In the Shadow of Liberty* by Edward Corsi, 1935, reprinted 1969, courtesy of Ayer Company Publishers, P.O. Box 958, Salem, NH 03079.

Countee Cullen: "Heritage" and "Incident." Reprinted by permission of GRM Associates, Inc., agents for the Estate of Ida M. Cullen. From the book *On These I Stand* by Countee Cullen. Copyright © 1947 by Harper & Brothers; copyright renewed 1975 by Ida M. Cullen.

Nora Dauenhauer: "Tlingit Concrete Poem." Copyright © by Nora Dauenhauer. Reprinted by permission of author.

Richard Dokey: "Sánchez." Copyright © 1967 by Richard Dokey. This story first appeared in the *Southwest Review*. Reprinted by permission.

Rita Dove: "Parsley." Reprinted from *Museum* by permission of Carnegie-Mellon University Press. Copyright © 1983 by Rita Dove.

Pam Durban: "All Set About with Fever Trees" from *All Set About with Fever Trees* by Pam Durban. Copyright © 1985 by Pam Durban. Reprinted by permission of David R. Godine, Publisher.

Ralph Ellison: "Battle Royal" from *Invisible Man* by Ralph Ellison. Copyright 1948 by Ralph Ellison. Reprinted by permission of Random House, Inc.

Louise Erdrich: "Jacklight" and "Indian Boarding School: The Runaways" from *Jacklight* by Louise Erdrich. Copyright © 1984 by Louise Erdrich. Reprinted by permission of Henry Holt and Company, Inc.

Mari Evans: "The Friday Ladies of the Pay Envelope." Reprinted by permission of author.

James Fallows: "The Japanese Are Different from You and Me" from *The Atlantic Monthly*, September 1986. Reprinted by permission of author.

John Fante: "The Odyssey of a Wop." Copyright © 1933 by John Fante, copyright renewed. Reprinted by permission of McIntosh and Otis, Inc.

Nicholas Gerros: "Greek Horatio Alger" reprinted from *First Generation: In the Words of Twentieth-Century American Immigrants*, edited by June Namias (Beacon Press, 1978). Reprinted by permission of June Namias.

Ellen Gilchrist: "Traveler" from *In the Land of the Dreamy Dreams* by Ellen Gilchrist. Copyright © 1981 by Ellen Gilchrist. Reprinted by permission of Little, Brown and Company.

Gogisgi/Carroll Arnett: "Song of the Breed." Copyright © 1982 by Gogisgi/Carroll Arnett, from *Rounds* (Cross-Cultural Communications Press, 1982). Reprinted by permission.

Rafael Jesús González: "Sestina: Santa Prisca." Reprinted by permission of author.

Francine du Plessix Gray: "Tribe" from *Lovers and Tyrants* by Francine du Plessix Gray. Copyright © 1976 by Francine du Plessix Gray. Reprinted by permission of Georges Borchardt, Inc. for the author. First appeared in *The New Yorker*.

Michael Harper: "Grandfather" from *Images of Kin: New and Selected Poems* by Michael Harper. Reprinted by permission of the University of Illinois Press.

Lance Henson: "poem near midway truck stop" from *Selected Poems, 1970–1983* by Lance Henson, The Greenfield Review Press, 1986. Reprinted by permission of The Greenfield Review Press.

Edward Hirsch: "In a Polish Home for the Aged (Chicago, 1983)" from *Wild Gratitude* by Edward Hirsch. Copyright © 1985 by Edward Hirsch. First appeared in *Grand Street*. Reprinted by permission of Alfred A. Knopf, Inc.

Linda Hogan: "Black Hills Survival Gathering, 1980," "Heritage," and "Song for My Name" from *Calling Myself Home;* first published by The Greenfield Review Press. Reprinted by permission of author.

Israel Horovitz: *The Indian Wants the Bronx* from *First Season* by Israel Horovitz. Copyright © 1967, 1968 by Israel Horovitz. Reprinted by permission of author. Any inquiries for performing rights should be addressed to Writers & Artists Agency, attention William Craven, 70 West 36th St., Suite 501, New York, NY 10018.

Vanessa Howard: "Escape the Ghettos of New York." We have made diligent efforts to contact the copyright holder to obtain permission to reprint this selection. If you have information that would help us, please write W. W. Norton & Co., 500 Fifth Avenue, New York, NY 10110.

David Henry Hwang: *Family Devotions.* Copyright © 1983 by David Henry Hwang. CAUTION: Professionals and amateurs are hereby warned that *Family Devotions* is subject to a royalty. It is fully protected under the copyright laws of the United States of America, and of all countries covered by the International Copyright Union (including the Dominion of Canada and the rest of the British Commonwealth), and of all countries covered by the Pan-American Copyright Convention and the Universal Copyright Convention, and of all countries with which the United States has reciprocal copyright relations. All rights, including professional, amateur, motion picture, recitation, lecturing, public reading, radio broadcasting, television, video or sound taping, all other forms of mechanical or electronic reproduction, such as information storage and retrieval systems and photocopying, and the rights of translation into foreign languages, are strictly reserved. Particular emphasis is laid upon the question of readings, permission for which must be secured from the author's agent in writing. All inquiries concerning rights (other than stock and amateur rights) should be addressed to Helen Merrill, Ltd., 435 West 23rd Street, #1A, New York, NY 10011. The stock and amateur production rights in *Family Devotions* are controlled exclusively by the Dramatists Play Service, Inc., 440 Park Avenue South, New York, NY 10016. No stock or amateur performance of the play may be given without obtaining in advance the written permission of the Dramatists Play Service, Inc., and paying the requisite fee.

Gish Jen: "In the American Society." Copyright © 1987 by Gish Jen. Originally appeared in *The Southern Review*. Reprinted by permission of author.

Cynthia Kadohata: "Charlie-O." Reprinted by permission. Copyright © 1986 by Cynthia Kadohata. Originally appeared in *The New Yorker*.

Garrison Keillor: "Protestant" from *Lake Wobegon Days* by Garrison Keillor. Copyright © 1985 by Garrison Keillor. All rights reserved. Reprinted by permission of Viking Penguin, Inc.

Maurice Kenny: "Going Home" from *Between Two Rivers: Selected Poems* by Maurice Kenny. Reprinted by permission of White Pine Press.

Jamaica Kincaid: "Girl" from *At the Bottom of the River* by Jamaica Kincaid. Copyright © 1978, 1979, 1981, 1982, 1983 by Jamaica Kincaid. Originally appeared in *The New Yorker*. Reprinted by permission of Farrar, Straus and Giroux, Inc.

Martin Luther King, Jr.: "I Have a Dream." Copyright © 1963 by Martin Luther King, Jr. Reprinted by permission of Joan Daves.

Maxine Hong Kingston: "No Name Woman" from *The Woman Warrior: Memoirs of a Girlhood Among Ghosts* by Maxine Hong Kingston. Copyright © 1975, 1976 by Maxine Hong Kingston. Reprinted by permission of Alfred A. Knopf, Inc. "The Wild Man of the Green Swamp" from *China Men* by Maxine Hong Kingston. Copyright © 1977, 1978, 1979, 1980 by Maxine Hong Kingston. Reprinted by permission of Alfred A. Knopf, Inc.

Arthur Laurents: *West Side Story* by Arthur Laurents. Copyright © 1956, 1958 by Arthur Laurents, Leonard Bernstein, Stephen Sondheim, Jerome Robbins. Reprinted by permission of Random House, Inc.

Irving Layton: "Keine Lazarovitch, 1870–1959" from *Selected Poems* by Irving Layton. Used by permission of the Canadian Publishers McClelland and Stewart, Toronto.

Lee Ki Chuck: "From Korea to Heaven Country" from *First Generation: In the Words of Twentieth-Century American Immigrants*, edited by June Namias (Beacon Press, 1978). Reprinted by permission of June Namias.

Li-Young Lee: "Persimmons," "The Gift," and "Eating Together." Copyright © 1986 by Li-Young Lee. Reprinted from *Rose* with the permission of BOA Editions, Ltd.

Walter Lew: "Leaving Seoul: 1953." First appeared in *Breaking Silence*, The Greenfield Review Press. Reprinted by permission of The Greenfield Review Press.

Stephen Shu Ning Liu: "My Father's Martial Art." Copyright © 1981 by The Antioch Review, Inc. First appeared in the *Antioch Review*, vol. 39, no. 3 (Summer 1981).

Audre Lorde: "Home" and "Reins" from *Our Dead Behind Us* by Audre Lorde. Copyright © 1986 by Audre Lorde. Reprinted by permission of W.W. Norton & Co., Inc.

Marcela Christine Lucero-Trujillo: "Roseville, Minn., U.S.A." and "The Musicos from Capulín." Reprinted by permission of Patricia Villalobos, for the estate of Marcela Lucero-Trujillo.

Naomi Long Madgett: "Offspring" from *Pink Ladies in the Afternoon* (Detroit: Lotus Press, 1972) by Naomi Long Madgett. Reprinted by permission of author.

James Alan McPherson: "I Am an American" from *Elbow Room* by James Alan McPherson. Copyright © 1974 by James Alan McPherson. First appeared in *Ploughshares*. Reprinted by permission of Little, Brown and Company.

Durango Mendoza: "Summer Water and Shirley." Reprinted from *Prairie Schooner*, by permission of University of Nebraska Press. Copyright © 1966 by the University of Nebraska Press.

Gail Y. Miyasaki: "Obāchan." We have made diligent efforts to contact the copyright holder to obtain permission to reprint this selection. If you have information that would help us, please write W. W. Norton & Co., 500 Fifth Avenue, New York, NY 10110.

N. Scott Momaday: "The Eagle-Feather Fan" from *The Gourd Dancer* by N. Scott Momaday. Reprinted by permission of author.

Pat Mora: "Borders," "Immigrants," and "Sonrisas." First printed in *Borders* by Pat Mora (Houston: Arte Publico Press of the University of Houston, 1986). Reprinted by permission of Arte Publico Press.

Toshio Mori: "Abalone, Abalone, Abalone" and "Japanese Hamlet" from *The Chauvinist and Other Stories* by Toshio Mori. Reprinted by permission of the Asian American Studies Center, University of California, Los Angeles. Copyright © 1979 by the Regents of the University of California.

Toni Morrison: "1920" from *Sula* by Toni Morrison. Copyright © 1973 by Toni Morrison. Reprinted by permission of Alfred A. Knopf, Inc.

Bharati Mukherjee: "Hindus" from *Darkness* by Bharati Mukherjee. Copyright © 1985 by Bharati Mukherjee. Reprinted by permission of Penguin Books Canada Limited.

Gloria Naylor: "Mommy, What Does 'Nigger' Mean?" Copyright © 1986 by The New York Times Company. Reprinted by permission of The New York Times Company and Sterling Lord Literistic, Inc.

nila northSun: "up & out" and "what gramma said about her grandpa." Reprinted by permission of The Greenfield Review Press.

Dwight Okita: "In Response to Executive Order 9066: ALL AMERICANS OF JAPANESE DESCENT MUST REPORT TO RELOCATION CENTERS." Reprinted by permission of The Greenfield Review Press.

Sharon Olds: "On the Subway" from *The Gold Cell* by Sharon Olds. Copyright © 1987 by Sharon Olds. Reprinted by permission of Alfred A. Knopf, Inc.

Richard Olivas: "[I'm sitting in my history class]." We have made diligent efforts to contact the copyright holder to obtain permission to reprint this selection. If you have information that would help us, please write W. W. Norton & Co., 500 Fifth Avenue, New York, NY 10110.

Michael Ondaatje: "Light" from *There's a Trick with a Knife I'm Learning to Do, Poems 1963–1978* by Michael Ondaatje. Copyright © 1979 by Michael Ondaatje. Reprinted by permission of W.W. Norton & Co., Inc., and the author.

Simon J. Ortiz: "Speaking" and "My Father's Song." Reprinted by permission of author, Simon J. Ortiz.

Cynthia Ozick: "Bloodshed" from *Bloodshed and Three Novellas* by Cynthia Ozick. Copyright © 1976 by Cynthia Ozick. Reprinted by permission of Alfred A. Knopf, Inc.

Elena Padilla: "Migrants: Transients or Settlers?" pp. 301–308, from *Up from Puerto Rico*. Copyright © 1986 by Elena Padilla. Reprinted by permission of Columbia University Press.

Linda Pastan: "Grudnow" from *The Imperfect Paradise* by Linda Pastan. Copyright © 1988 by Linda Pastan. Reprinted by permission of W.W. Norton & Co., Inc.

Noel Perrin: "Old MacBerlitz Had a Farm" from *First Person Rural* by Noel Perrin. Copyright © 1978 by Noel Perrin. Reprinted by permission of David R. Godine, Publisher, Boston.

Katherine Anne Porter: "Holiday" from *The Collected Stories of Katherine Anne Porter*. Reprinted by permission of Isabel Bayley, Literary Trustee for the Estate of Katherine Anne Porter. Copyright © 1960 by Katherine Anne Porter.

Estela Portillo: *The Day of the Swallows* by Estela Portillo. Reprinted by permission of the University of Notre Dame Press. First appeared in *Contemporary Chicano Theatre*

Ishmael Reed: "I Am a Cowboy in the Boat of Ra" by Ishmael Reed. Copyright © 1972 by Ishmael Reed. Reprinted by permission of author.

Carter Revard: "Discovery of the New World" and "Driving in Oklahoma." Reprinted by permission of author.

Alberto Ríos: "Mi Abuelo." Copyright © 1980, from *Selections, University & College Poetry Prizes, 1973–78*, reprinted with permission from the Academy of American Poets, Inc.

Richard Rodriguez: "Aria: A Memoir of a Bilingual Childhood." Reprinted by permission of author. Copyright © 1980 by Richard Rodriguez. First published in *The American Scholar*.

Leo Romero: "What the Gossips Saw." Copyright © 1981 by Leo Romero. Reprinted from *Agua Negra* by permission of Ahsahta Press at Boise State University.

Wendy Rose: "Julia." Reprinted by permission of West End Press. "To Some Few Hopi Ancestors." Reprinted by permission of author.

Norma Rosen: "A Thousand Tears." Reprinted by permission of Watkins/Loomis Agency, Inc.,

Leo Rosten: "Danger: Foreign Tongue" from *Passions and Prejudice* by Leo Rosten. Reprinted by permission of McGraw-Hill Book Company.

Gabrielle Roy: "Wilhelm" from *Street of Riches* by Gabrielle Roy. Copyright © by Fonds Gabrielle Roy. Reprinted by permission of Fonds Gabrielle Roy.

Muriel Rukeyser: "To Be a Jew in the Twentieth Century" from *Beast in View* by Muriel Rukeyser. Reprinted by permission of International Creative Management, Inc. Copyright © 1944 and 1972 by Muriel Rukeyser.

Donna Kate Rushin: "The Bridge Poem." First appeared in *This Bridge Called My Back: Writings by Radical Women of Color*, Kitchen Table: Women of Color Press. Copyright 1983. Reprinted by permission of Kitchen Table Press, P.O. Box 908, Latham, NY 12110.

Mark Salzman: "Teacher Wei" from *Iron and Silk* by Mark Salzman. Copyright © 1986 by Mark Salzman. Reprinted by permission of Random House, Inc.

Yvonne Sapia: "Defining the Grateful Gesture" and "Grandmother, a Caribbean Indian, Described by My Father" from *Valentino's Hair* by Yvonne Sapia. Copyright © 1987 by Yvonne Sapia. Reprinted by permission of Northeastern University Press.

William Saroyan: "Najari Levon's Old Country Advice to the Young Americans on How to Live with a Snake" from *Madness in the Family* by William Saroyan. Copyright © 1988 by The Saroyan Foundation. Reprinted by permission of New Directions Publishing Corporation.

Rhoda Schwartz: "Old Photographs." Copyright © 1974 by Rhoda Schwartz. Originally appeared in *Jewish-American Literature: An Anthology*, edited by Abraham Chapman, a Mentor Book. Reprinted from manuscript by permission of the author.

James Seilsopour: "I Forgot the Words to the National Anthem." From *Student Writers at Work*, edited by Nancy Sommers and Donald McQuade. Copyright © St. Martin's Press, 1984, and used with permission of the publisher.

Jack G. Shaheen: "The Media's Image of Arabs." From *Newsweek*, February 29, 1988. Copyright © 1988 by Newsweek, Inc. All rights reserved. Reprinted by permission.

Leslie Marmon Silko: "Private Property" and "Long Time Ago." Reprinted by permission of author.

Mark Singer: "Typical." Reprinted by permission. Copyright © 1987 by The New Yorker Magazine, Inc.

Tess Slesinger: "White on Black" from *On Being Told That Her Second Husband Has Taken His First Lover* by Tess Slesinger. Copyright © 1935 by Tess Slesinger, renewal copyright © 1963 by Frank Davis. Reprinted by permission of Times Books, a division of Random House, Inc.

R. T. Smith: "Red Anger" and "Yonosa House." Copyright © by R. T. Smith. Reprinted by permission of author.

Cathy Song: "Lost Sister" from *Picture Bride* by Cathy Song. Reprinted by permission of Yale University Press. "Heaven." Reprinted by permission of W.W. Norton & Co., Inc.

Gary Soto: "Like Mexicans." First printed in *Small Faces* (Houston: Arte Publico Press of the University of Houston) by Gary Soto. Copyright © 1986 by Gary Soto. Reprinted by permission of Arte Publico Press.

Mary TallMountain: "There Is No Word for Goodbye" from *The Blue Cloud Quarterly*, vol. 27, no. 1. Copyright © 1981 by Mary TallMountain. Reprinted by permission.

Barry Targan: "Dominion." First appeared in *The Iowa Review* (Spring 1979), vol. 10, no. 2. Reprinted by permission of author.

Barbara Thompson: "Crossing." Copyright © 1982 by Washington and Lee University, reprinted from *Shenandoah: The Washington and Lee University Review* with the permission of the editor.

Luis Valdez: *The Shrunken Head of Pancho Villa*. Copyright © 1982 by Luis Valdez. CAUTION: All rights strictly reserved. Professionals and amateurs are hereby warned that *The Shrunken Head of Pancho Villa* is subject to a royalty. It is protected under copyright laws of all countries covered by the International Copyright Union, Pan American Convention, and/or the Universal Copyright Convention. Permission in writing must be secured before any kind of performance is given. All inquiries should be addressed to the author, Luis Valdez, El Teatro Campesino, P.O. Box 1240, San Juan Bautista, CA 95045.

Helena Maria Viramontes: "The Moths" from *The Moths and Other Stories* by Helena Maria Viramontes (Houston: Arte Publico Press of the University of Houston, 1985). Reprinted by permission of Arte Publico Press of the University of Houston.

Alice Walker: "Everyday Use" from *In Love and Trouble* by Alice Walker. Copyright © 1973 by Alice Walker. Reprinted by permission of Harcourt Brace Jovanovich, Inc.

Barbara Watkins: "Josefa Kankovska." We have made diligent efforts to contact the copyright holder to obtain permission to reprint this selection. If you have any information that would help us, please write W. W. Norton & Co., 500 Fifth Avenue, New York, NY 10110.

Sherley Williams: "The Collateral Adjective" and "Say Hello to John." Copyright © 1975 by Sherley Williams. Reprinted from *The Peacock Poems* by permission of Wesleyan University Press.

August Wilson: *Fences*. Copyright © 1986 August Wilson. Reprinted by arrangement with NAL Penguin, Inc., New York, NY.

Merle Woo: "Letter to Ma." First appeared in *This Bridge Called My Back: Writings by Radical Women of Color*, Kitchen Table : Women of Color Press. Copyright © 1983. Reprinted by permission of Kitchen Table Press, P.O. Box 908, Latham, NY 12110.

Mitsuye Yamada: "Looking Out" and "The Question of Loyalty" from *Camp Notes and Other Poems* (Shameless Hussy Press) by Mitsuye Yamada. Copyright © 1976, 1980, 1986 by Mitsuye Yamada. Reprinted by permission of author.

Wakako Yamauchi: *And the Soul Shall Dance*. Reprinted by permission of author.

Ray A. Young Bear: "In the first place of my life." Reprinted by permission of author.

Cyn. Zarco: "Flipochinos" from *Cir'cum-nav'i-ga'tion* by Cyn. Zarco. Reprinted by permission of author. Copyright © 1986 by Cyn. Zarco.

# GLOSSARY

ACTION. What happens in a narrative, play, or other piece of writing. Action usually involves CONFLICT. In a play, action usually refers to what happens onstage (as distinguished from what has happened before the play begins or what happens offstage); in a narrative, it refers to what happens as the story unfolds (as distinguished from events that have occurred earlier or ones that are simply mentioned). PLOT is a more comprehensive term that includes events that have occurred earlier, the situation that brings about the events, the motivations that lead to the conflict, and the arrangement of the action.

ALLEGORY. In an allegory, the events usually make sense on a literal level, but a second and more complex level of meaning is also available to the reader. That special meaning is usually moral, religious, or political. An allegory is an extended form of METAPHOR and is more systematic and its meaning more paraphrasable than a SYMBOL.

ALLUSION. A brief reference to a person, place, thing, or passage in another literary work, usually for the purpose of associating the meaning or tone of one work with another. Sometimes the term *allusion* is used as the general equivalent of "reference"—to indicate any glance in a literary work at something outside itself, to an event or person or idea, as well as to another piece of writing.

ATTITUDE. The position—emotional or intellectual—assumed toward an idea, event, or person by an author or a literary work. Attitude is closely related to TONE. The tone of a work—the way its words are spoken by a human voice—derives from the attitude of the author and work and is the key device for expressing attitude, but tone of voice may express the attitude indirectly or ironically, through such devices as UNDERSTATEMENT, HYPERBOLE, or SARCASM.

CATASTROPHE. See CONCLUSION.

CHARACTER, CHARACTERIZATION. The particular traits (or characteristics) of a person suggest that person's character—what it is that makes that person distinctive from other people. Individuals portrayed in literature are often referred to as characters. Characterization is the way in which an author describes and defines characters.

CLIMAX, or TURNING POINT. During the RISING ACTION of a play, the flow or movement is in one direction; the climax is the crucial moment at which the direction of the action changes and the FALLING ACTION begins. The term *climax* is also used to suggest the moment in a narrative in which the flow of the action changes direction.

CONCLUSION, or CATASTROPHE or DENOUEMENT. The moment in a play (or a narrative) at which a stable situation is reestablished so that the drama (or story) may end.

CONCRETE POEM. A poem in which the words are arranged on a page so as to imitate the shape of a "concrete" or material object.

CONFLICT. The struggle between opposing forces—characters, families, nations, ideas, or ideological systems—that provides the central ACTION and interest in any literary PLOT.

CONTEXT. Anything beyond the text that may be relevant to reading the text itself. Contexts may be historical or literary or authorial or of several other kinds. Sometimes relevant contexts have to do with when a piece of writing was written or what times or events it refers to, sometimes to the wider climate of ideas a piece of writing may engage.

CONVENTION. Within traditions of rhetoric and within literary history, certain standard literary features develop over a period of time, and when such features become commonly accepted and frequently reused, they are called conventions. When such features come to seem tired, they become clichés and are useless as ways of calling up expected responses. But often conventions provide shortcuts to meaning or feeling because they rely on ways of thinking that have become established enough in the public mind to generate a specific reaction in readers. See EXPECTATION.

DENOUEMENT. See CONCLUSION.

EPIGRAPH. An inscription at the beginning of a piece of writing, usually a quotation from another literary work. An epigraph ordinarily suggests the THEME of the writing or otherwise suggests what is to be expected in what follows, or serves as an ALLUSION.

EXPECTATION. What readers think they will find in a piece of writing. Most frequently used in fiction or drama to refer to "what will happen next," it can also refer to anticipation of rhymes (in poetry), structure, character development, or development of ideas. Expectations are suggested by a variety of literary devices and strategies, including the title, epigraph, choice of literary kind, allusion, and other literary conventions.

EXPOSITION. The structural element in a play in which the situation is explained, the characters introduced, and the basis of the conflict set up. Exposition in narrative performs similar functions in order to set the plot in motion. The term *exposition* is also used to distinguish discourse that explains the nature of something—a thing, a person, an idea—from other kinds of discourse: argumentation, description, narration.

FABLE. A brief tale, told in order to illustrate a moral. See PARABLE.

FALLING ACTION. The term used to describe the structural element just after the CLIMAX in a play, when the complications begin to unwind. Sometimes the term is also used to describe the corresponding structural part of a narrative.

FOCUS. The angle of vision from which a narrative is presented, the point from which people, events, and other details are viewed. Compare POINT OF VIEW and VOICE.

GENRE. See LITERARY KIND.

HYPERBOLE, or OVERSTATEMENT. Exaggeration used for rhetorical purposes.

IMAGE, IMAGERY. Imagery visualizes something that is being described by comparing it to something else that is more familiar, through either a *simile* (in which something is compared directly and explicitly to something else) or a METAPHOR (in which something is described in terms that pretend it *is* something else). Though the term *image* literally refers to the visual, images may involve the other senses. Sometimes, however, the term *imagery* is extended to include any strategy of visualization, including straightforward description. An image is a specific visualization.

INTERPRETATION. The explanation of a piece of writing, how it works and what it means. When readers interpret a literary work, they provide what is sometimes called a *reading* of the work, that is, a specific explanation of its THEME, TONE, and MEANING.

IRONIC, IRONY. The calculated discrepancy between what something appears to mean and what it really means. *Verbal irony* is the use of words to say, deliberately, something other than what one really means. Irony is usually thought of as a tone that suggests that a word or phrase "really" means the opposite of what it seems to say, but irony does not necessarily imply the exact opposite: it can be oblique, deviating indirectly from what is apparently said rather than directly reversing meaning. Sometimes, too, an event is said to be *ironic* (in a colloquial sense) when it is surprising compared with the expected outcome, especially when there is a discrepancy between what might be expected from the way events have gone so far and what the characters seem to deserve.

LITERARY KIND, or GENRE. A traditional literary way of organizing experience. The division of literature into different *kinds* or *forms* is, in part, a convenience for purposes of description, but every literary kind develops habits, traditions, and CONVENTIONS that distinguish it from other literary ways of organizing and presenting human experience. Often writers choose to write in a particular literary kind—the short story, for example, or the lyric poem—as a way of indicating to readers what sorts of expectations to bring to the work; in that sense, the literary kind that an author chooses represents a contract with the reader, a contract that involves what the author is most likely to do because of the conventions of the *kind*. Writers often build surprise into what they do, however, using a reader's expectations to create quite unexpected effects, thus modifying a kind even as they employ it.

MEANING. The whole complex of effects produced by a work on readers. The full meaning of a work involves both its intellectual and emotional implications, a recognition of its THEME and TONE. The meaning of a work depends not only on the statements that the work makes about a particular subject or theme, but also the tone in which it makes those statements. Most works have more than a single meaning, having different effects upon different readers and sometimes several distinctive effects on a single reader; but there is usually a core or range of meaning or meanings upon which different readers can agree.

METAPHOR. A figure of speech in which something is described in terms more appropriate for something else, as if the thing really were something else. Sometimes *metaphor* is used to include all figures of speech, especially those, like *simile*, that involve comparison. See IMAGE.

MONOLOGUE. A speech, often a length one, by one person. Poems are sometimes presented as monologues, often involving IRONY, because the person does not fully understand what he or she is saying. Short stories are sometimes monologues, too, but in plays, monologues have a special and specific function—to let the audience know (confidentially) something that is on the mind of a particular CHARACTER.

MOOD. The atmosphere that pervades a work and gives the reader or audience a sense of what to expect. In drama, it involves the set and music as well as the words; in a poem or story, it can involve the reader's inferences beyond the VOICE or NARRATOR.

MYTH. A communal narrative about the unknown or unknowable, the remote in time or space, the spiritual universe, or humankind's place in that universe. A narrative takes on *mythic* dimensions when it comes to speak for a common perception experienced by a coherent group—a nation, a people, or a community. Communal representation is crucial to the attainment of mythic status.

NARRATION, NARRATOR. Unlike drama, narrative is mediated: someone "tells" the story and therefore stands between the reader and the ACTION, CHARACTERS, and other elements of the story. The narrator—roughly the equivalent of the SPEAKER in a poem—is an integral part of the story, its effect, and its meaning. Words are the only means we have of visualizing, and what we visualize depends completely on what someone tells us to see.

OVERSTATEMENT. See HYPERBOLE.

PARABLE. A short, usually familiar story that has as its major aim to teach a moral or religious message. Unlike a FABLE, a parable makes its point by directly comparing things or events in its narrative with actual things or events.

PARODY. Imitation of the style or prominent characteristics of a particular piece of writing, often for comic purposes. Ordinarily, HYPERBOLE (or overstatement) is used in parody to mock a subject or a work by treating common or "low" things in language that is exaggeratedly formal or high-flown.

PERSONA. The mask or representation through which an author speaks when he or she is not necessarily expressing his or her own opinion, often halfway between the personal voice of the author and the self-presentation of a named and fully developed character in a play or narrative.

PLOT. *What* happens (ACTION) and *why* in a narrative, play, or (sometimes) poem. Plot, or *plot structure*, also includes the *how*: the arrangement of events and the way the action is presented to readers or an audience.

POINT OF VIEW. The perspective from which a narrative is presented, including both the angle of vision (FOCUS) and the words in which it is communicated (VOICE). While *point of view* is usually an adequate term, in some works the focus and voice are distinct: what we are seeing from a particular vantage point may be more limited than how it is being described; the language may be more sophisticated and knowledgeable.

RHETORIC, RHETORICAL DEVICES. The formal study of how words work is called *rhetoric*. One can speak of the rhetoric of a given narrative or poem or play—what effects it is calculated to produce—or more generally of the rhetoric of an author (what particular strategies of persuasion he or she uses), or the rhetoric of fiction or of poetry (the way a particular literary mode uses language to accomplish its particular ends).

RISING ACTION. The second stage in formal dramatic structure, the period between EXPOSITION and CLIMAX. During the rising action, a series of events occur to complicate the original situation and create CONFLICT among the characters.

RITUAL. A rite or ceremony in which an act or series of acts is exactly repeated on specific occasions in order to recall or celebrate an event or an idea. In ritual, the communal sharing of action or behavior stands for some common agreement about meaning or value in the society or group.

SARCASM. IRONY of a simple, snide, and derogatory kind. Sarcasm, unlike most forms of irony, is specifically directed at someone and is usually intended to wound.

SETTING. The location and context in which the ACTION of a literary work takes place. It involves both time and place; it establishes MOOD, gives particularity to the action, and often makes the action possible, believable, or meaningful.

SIMILE. See IMAGERY.

SPEAKER. The person who speaks the words of a poem. The speaker in a poem is similar to the NARRATOR in a story. See also PERSONA.

STANZA. Identifiable on a page by the spaces used to set them apart from one another, stanzas are the structural units into which many poems are divided. They suggest the rhythmic patterns of a poem, indicate the pacing, and may or may not reflect the divisions of meaning in a poem.

STEREOTYPE. A CHARACTER based upon conscious or unconscious generalizations about age, sex, national or ethnic identification, occupation, marital status, etc. Often even complex characters in a story or play have some stereotypical features. Writers sometimes build a character upon the base of a stereotype and then complicate the expectations as the plot develops. Stereotypes, though often offensive to the group on whom the stereotype is based, do not necessarily represent prejudice on the part of an author, but sometimes are used to set up some larger conclusion about easy generalizations and biases.

STRUCTURE. The framework of a piece of writing, the way it is put together, its organization. It is common to distinguish between the *structure* of a work and its *form:* the form, like the form of a physical object such as a house, has to do with external appearance and visible shape; the structure, with the principles involved in putting it together.

SUBJECT. See THEME.

SYMBOL, SYMBOLISM. A symbol in general usage is something that stands for, or signifies, something else. Often a material object, such as a cross or a flag, symbolizes something abstract, something that has been communally agreed upon over a long period of time (a *traditional symbol*). Works of literature, however, sometimes create symbols having a significance solely within the limits of the work itself, just as individuals can create symbols in their own minds. These symbols are usually not paraphrasable, not because they have no meaning, but because their meanings are complex or multiple. Owning a home, for example, may symbolize freedom, independence, stability, security, or financial worries. When symbols are used densely throughout a work to establish a frame of reference different from that of ordinary reality, the work itself is said to be symbolic. When a series of symbols is agreed upon within a culture over a long period of time so that they become established as a belief system commonly available to all members of the group, the combination of symbols is often called a MYTH.

THEME. *Theme* is closely related to *subject*, but the two terms should be distinguished for precision in specifying how writings embody ideas. Literary works—in fact, all pieces of writing, however simple or informal—are about something. A work is always "about" something concrete—a particular action, a specific event, what happens to someone, what something feels like. But literature is also about things other than specific events and details—it is about concepts, ideas, and institutions, relationships, problems. The *specific subject* of a poem might be how it feels to shoot a deer or meet a stranger; its *general subject* might involve pursuit or ritualistic killing or the question of human and animal relationships, or cultural biases against people from outside one's own group or the love or fear of the alien and exotic.

Most works of literature not only imply that individual actions and events reflect more general human patterns, they often also take stances and attitudes and express opinions. That is, they express—or, more often, imply—a position, a value judgment about behavior, relationships, institutions, about what people do and how they do it. The stance that a work takes toward something is its *theme*. Most works may be said to have more than a single theme, just as a symbol may be said to have more than one meaning. The role of the individual reader is very great in determining the theme of a work, but the general subject, TONE, and other elements in the work set limits to the reader's freedom to interpret.

TONE. The attitude of a literary work toward its subject (see THEME). To describe tone, it is customary to use words that would ordinarily be used to describe the modulations of a human voice; thus the tone of a literary work might be described as "somber," "gloomy," "sarcastic," "resigned," "celebratory," or "angry." Tone may be used to describe individual sentences, phrases, or even words as well as whole works.

TURNING POINT. See CLIMAX.

UNDERSTATEMENT. A rhetorical figure of speech in which something is represented as less important than it really is or in which something is stated less forcibly than it would be if the writer's actual feelings were expressed. Understatement (its technical name in classical rhetoric is *meiosis*) is often used when a writer wishes readers to find and state for themselves the true importance of a particular thought or value, rather than forcing upon them some strong opinion or feeling that they might resist.

VOICE. The verbal aspect of the perspective or point of view in a narrative. See FOCUS and POINT OF VIEW.

# INDEX OF AUTHORS
# AND TITLES